MARK

Baker Exegetical Commentary on the New Testament

ROBERT W. YARBROUGH
AND ROBERT H. STEIN, EDITORS

Volumes now available:

Matthew *David L. Turner*
Mark *Robert H. Stein*
Luke *Darrell L. Bock*
John *Andreas J. Köstenberger*
Acts *Darrell L. Bock*
Romans *Thomas R. Schreiner*
1 Corinthians *David E. Garland*
Philippians *Moisés Silva*
1 Peter *Karen H. Jobes*
1–3 John *Robert W. Yarbrough*
Jude and 2 Peter *Gene L. Green*
Revelation *Grant R. Osborne*

Robert H. Stein (PhD, Princeton Theological Seminary) taught New Testament studies for many years at both Bethel Seminary and the Southern Baptist Theological Seminary. Specializing in Gospel interpretation and hermeneutics, he has written *A Basic Guide to Interpreting the Bible, Studying the Synoptic Gospels, The Method and Message of Jesus' Teachings, Jesus the Messiah*, and a commentary on the Gospel of Luke.

MARK

ROBERT H. STEIN

Baker Exegetical Commentary on the New Testament

Baker Academic
a division of Baker Publishing Group
Grand Rapids, Michigan

© 2008 by Robert H. Stein

Published by Baker Academic
a division of Baker Publishing Group
P.O. Box 6287, Grand Rapids, MI 49516-6287
www.bakeracademic.com

Printed in the United States of America

Library of Congress Cataloging-in-Publication Data
Stein, Robert H., 1935–
    Mark / Robert H. Stein.
        p. cm. — (Baker exegetical commentary on the New Testament)
    Includes bibliographical references and indexes.
    ISBN 978-0-8010-2682-9 (cloth)
    1. Bible. N.T. Mark—Commentaries. I. Title.
    BS2585.53.S74 2008
    226.3'07—dc22   2008020734

16   17   18   19   20   21   22   10   9   8   7   6   5   4

To my grandchildren: Samuel, Matthew, Daniel, Jacob, and Julia

With the prayer that they will love and serve
"Jesus Christ, the Son of God" (Mark 1:1)

Contents

Series Preface

The chief concern of the Baker Exegetical Commentary on the New Testament (BECNT) is to provide, within the framework of informed evangelical thought, commentaries that blend scholarly depth with readability, exegetical detail with sensitivity to the whole, and attention to critical problems with theological awareness. We hope thereby to attract the interest of a fairly wide audience, from the scholar who is looking for a thoughtful and independent examination of the text to the motivated lay Christian who craves a solid but accessible exposition.

Nevertheless, a major purpose is to address the needs of pastors and others involved in the preaching and exposition of the Scriptures as the uniquely inspired Word of God. This consideration affects directly the parameters of the series. For example, serious biblical expositors cannot afford to depend on a superficial treatment that avoids the difficult questions, but neither are they interested in encyclopedic commentaries that seek to cover every conceivable issue that may arise. Our aim therefore is to focus on problems that have a direct bearing on the meaning of the text (although selected technical details are treated in the additional notes).

Similarly, a special effort is made to avoid treating exegetical questions for their own sake, that is, in relative isolation from the thrust of the argument as a whole. This effort may involve (at the discretion of the individual contributors) abandoning the verse-by-verse approach in favor of an exposition that focuses on the paragraph as the main unit of thought. In all cases, however, the commentaries will stress the development of the argument and explicitly relate each passage to what precedes and follows it so as to identify its function in context as clearly as possible.

We believe, moreover, that a responsible exegetical commentary must take fully into account the latest scholarly research, regardless of its source. The attempt to do this in the context of a conservative theological tradition presents certain challenges, and in the past the results have not always been commendable. In some cases, evangelicals appear to make use of critical scholarship not for the purpose of genuine interaction but only to dismiss it. In other cases, the interaction glides over into assimilation, theological distinctives are ignored or suppressed, and the end product cannot be differentiated from works that arise from a fundamentally different starting point.

The contributors to this series attempt to avoid these pitfalls. On the one hand, they do not consider traditional opinions to be sacrosanct, and they are certainly committed to do justice to the biblical text whether or not it supports such opinions. On the other hand, they will not quickly abandon a long-standing view, if there is persuasive evidence in its favor, for the sake of fashionable theories. What is more important, the contributors share a belief in the trustworthiness and essential unity of Scripture. They also consider that the historic formulations of Christian doctrine, such as the ecumenical creeds and many of the documents originating in the sixteenth-century Reformation, arose from a legitimate reading of Scripture, thus providing a proper framework for its further interpretation. No doubt, the use of such a starting point sometimes results in the imposition of a foreign construct on the text, but we deny that it must necessarily do so or that the writers who claim to approach the text without prejudices are invulnerable to the same danger.

Accordingly, we do not consider theological assumptions—from which, in any case, no commentator is free—to be obstacles to biblical interpretation. On the contrary, an exegete who hopes to understand the apostle Paul in a theological vacuum might just as easily try to interpret Aristotle without regard for the philosophical framework of his whole work or without having recourse to the subsequent philosophical categories that make possible a meaningful contextualization of his thought. It must be emphasized, however, that the contributors to the present series come from a variety of theological traditions and that they do not all have identical views with regard to the proper implementation of these general principles. In the end, all that really matters is whether the series succeeds in representing the original text accurately, clearly, and meaningfully to the contemporary reader.

Shading has been used to assist the reader in locating salient sections of the treatment of each passage: introductory comments and concluding summaries. Textual variants in the Greek text are signaled in the author's translation by means of half-brackets around the relevant word or phrase (e.g., ⌜Gerasenes⌝), thereby alerting the reader to turn to the additional notes at the end of each exegetical unit for a discussion of the textual problem. The documentation uses the author-date method, in which the basic reference consists of author's surname + year + page number(s): Fitzmyer 1992: 58. The only exceptions to this system are well-known reference works (e.g., BDAG, LSJ, *TDNT*). Full publication data and a complete set of indexes can be found at the end of the volume.

Robert Yarbrough
Robert H. Stein

Author's Preface

The format followed in this commentary divides each section being discussed into four parts to assist the reader: (1) First, in gray shading, is a discussion of the context in which the section is found, both the immediate context and the extended context. This context, given by Mark, provides the means for understanding the present passage and how it fits the message of the entire Gospel. The larger sections of Mark (1:1–13; 1:14–3:6; 3:7–6:6a; 6:6b–8:21; 8:22–10:52; 11:1–13:37; and 14:1–16:8) are also discussed at the beginning of each of these sections. (2) Second, a literal translation is given, at the expense of fluidity, in order to better assist in the discussion of words and phrases in the comment section. Italics are used to indicate emphasis in the original. (3) Within the comment section, the discussion is further divided into logical subsections. Several verses are frequently included together as a subsection, but at times a subsection contains only a single verse. Here in the commentary proper are discussed the words, phrases, sentences, and information that make up the passage. Occasionally, in the comment section, an important theme of Mark is discussed at length, and later in the commentary, when this theme comes up again, the reader will be referred to the original discussion by "see" followed by the passage (for example, "see 1:45"). (4) The fourth part of the discussion of each section, titled "Summary" and also in gray shading, summarizes the Markan message. Here I delineate Mark's main emphases in the section. Here, more than anywhere else, I seek to complete the sentence "I, Mark, have told you this account/saying of Jesus because. . . ." The focus here is not on the information found in the passage (whether about Jesus, John the Baptist, the Pharisees, first-century Judaism, the geography of Judea and Galilee, etc.) but rather on what Mark is seeking to teach his readers through the information he has provided in the passage. Consequently, the primary goal of this commentary is not to construct a life of Jesus of Nazareth but to ascertain the meaning of Mark, that is, what the second evangelist sought to teach by his Gospel. In his inspired inscripturation of this meaning by the words and content he chose, Mark's original audience and readers ever since have found a word from God.

This commentary was not written in a vacuum but owes a great debt to the many scholars who over the centuries have contributed to the advancement of our understanding of the Gospel according to Mark. It is hoped that the present work will serve in some way to add to this understanding. I wish to thank the many people who have assisted in the writing of this commentary. These include Gloria Metz, faculty secretary at Bethel Seminary, who for twenty years has been a God-given gift to me and has saved me from the many demons lurking within my computer; James M. Hamilton Jr., who as a graduate student carefully read various parts of the manuscript and laboriously checked their references; my students who through the years have challenged and sharpened my thinking as we worked our way through the study of Mark; Bethel University, Bethel Seminary, and The Southern Baptist Theological Seminary, where it has been my privilege to teach for over thirty-five years; Robert W. Yarbrough, my coeditor of the BECNT series, whose suggestions have made this a better work than it would have been otherwise; Baker Academic for the many years in which we have collaborated in the publishing of some nine works; and above all to my wife, Joan, who has patiently encouraged me and willingly put off various plans over the years so this work could be finished. My gratitude for her partnership in this and my other works can never be overstated. She has always been and will always be the love of my life and my partner in ministry.

Abbreviations

Bibliographic and General

ABD	*The Anchor Bible Dictionary*, edited by D. N. Freedman et al., 6 vols. (New York: Doubleday, 1992)
ANF	*Ante-Nicene Fathers*
b.	Babylonian Talmud
BDAG	*A Greek-English Lexicon of the New Testament and Other Early Christian Literature*, by W. Bauer, F. W. Danker, W. F. Arndt, and F. W. Gingrich, 4th ed. (Chicago: University of Chicago Press, 2000)
BDF	*A Greek Grammar of the New Testament and Other Early Christian Literature*, by F. Blass, A. Debrunner, and R. W. Funk (Chicago: University of Chicago Press, 1961)
DJG	*Dictionary of Jesus and the Gospels*, edited by J. B. Green and S. McKnight (Downers Grove, IL: InterVarsity, 1992)
DNTB	*Dictionary of New Testament Background*, edited by C. A. Evans and S. E. Porter (Downers Grove, IL: InterVarsity, 2000)
Eng.	English (versions)
ESV	English Standard Version
ET	English translation
IDB	*Interpreter's Dictionary of the Bible*, edited by G. A. Buttrick, 4 vols. (Nashville: Abingdon, 1962)
JB	Jerusalem Bible
KJV	King James Version
LCL	Loeb Classical Library
LXX	Septuagint
m.	Mishnah
MS(S)	manuscript(s)
MT	Masoretic Text
NA^{27}	*Novum Testamentum Graece*, edited by B. Aland et al., 27th ed. (Stuttgart: Deutsche Bibelgesellschaft, 1993)
NAB	New American Bible
NASB	New American Standard Bible
NEB	New English Bible
NIV	New International Version

NJB	New Jerusalem Bible
NLB	New Living Bible
NLT	New Living Translation
NRSV	New Revised Standard Version
NT	New Testament
OT	Old Testament
Q	*Quelle* (German for "source"), common material in Matthew and Luke not found in Mark
Rab.	Rabbah
REB	Revised English Bible
RSV	Revised Standard Version
t.	Tosefta
TDNT	*Theological Dictionary of the New Testament*, edited by G. Kittel and G. Friedrich, translated and edited by G. W. Bromiley, 10 vols. (Grand Rapids: Eerdmans, 1964–76)
TNIV	Today's New International Version
TR	Textus Receptus
UBS⁴	*The Greek New Testament*, edited by B. Aland et al., 4th rev. ed. (Stuttgart: Deutsche Bibelgesellschaft and United Bible Societies, 1994)
y.	Jerusalem/Palestinian Talmud

Hebrew Bible

Gen.	Genesis	2 Chron.	2 Chronicles	Dan.	Daniel
Exod.	Exodus	Ezra	Ezra	Hos.	Hosea
Lev.	Leviticus	Neh.	Nehemiah	Joel	Joel
Num.	Numbers	Esth.	Esther	Amos	Amos
Deut.	Deuteronomy	Job	Job	Obad.	Obadiah
Josh.	Joshua	Ps(s).	Psalms	Jon.	Jonah
Judg.	Judges	Prov.	Proverbs	Mic.	Micah
Ruth	Ruth	Eccles.	Ecclesiastes	Nah.	Nahum
1 Sam.	1 Samuel	Song	Song of Songs	Hab.	Habbakuk
2 Sam.	2 Samuel	Isa.	Isaiah	Zeph.	Zephaniah
1 Kings	1 Kings	Jer.	Jeremiah	Hag.	Haggai
2 Kings	2 Kings	Lam.	Lamentations	Zech.	Zechariah
1 Chron.	1 Chronicles	Ezek.	Ezekiel	Mal.	Malachi

Greek Testament

Matt.	Matthew	Eph.	Ephesians	Heb.	Hebrews
Mark	Mark	Phil.	Philippians	James	James
Luke	Luke	Col.	Colossians	1 Pet.	1 Peter
John	John	1 Thess.	1 Thessalonians	2 Pet.	2 Peter
Acts	Acts	2 Thess.	2 Thessalonians	1 John	1 John
Rom.	Romans	1 Tim.	1 Timothy	2 John	2 John
1 Cor.	1 Corinthians	2 Tim.	2 Timothy	3 John	3 John
2 Cor.	2 Corinthians	Titus	Titus	Jude	Jude
Gal.	Galatians	Philem.	Philemon	Rev.	Revelation

Other Jewish and Christian Writings

Apoc. Ab.	Apocalypse of Abraham	Let. Aris.	Letter of Aristeas
1 Apol.	Justin Martyr, *First Apology*	1–4 Macc.	1–4 Maccabees
As. Mos.	Assumption of Moses	Mart. Isa.	Martyrdom and Ascension of Isaiah
Bar.	Baruch	Mart. Pol.	Martyrdom of Polycarp
2 Bar.	2 (Syrian Apocalypse of) Baruch	Mek.	Mekilta de Rabbi Ishmael
		Midr.	Midrash
3 Bar.	3 (Greek Apocalypse of) Baruch	Ps. Sol.	Psalms of Solomon
		Sib. Or.	Sibylline Oracles
Barn.	Barnabas	Sir.	Sirach
Cels.	Origen, *Contra Celsum* (*Against Celsus*)	Sus.	Susanna
		T. Ab.	Testament of Abraham
1–2 Clem.	1–2 Clement	T. Ash.	Testament of Asher
Dial.	Justin Martyr, *Dialogue with Trypho*	T. Benj.	Testament of Benjamin
		T. Dan	Testament of Dan
Did.	Didache	T. Iss.	Testament of Issachar
Eccl. Hist.	Eusebius, *Ecclesiastical History*	T. Job	Testament of Job
		T. Jud.	Testament of Judah
1 En.	1 (Ethiopic) Enoch	T. Levi	Testament of Levi
2 En.	2 (Slavonic) Enoch	T. Mos.	Testament of Moses
2 Esd.	2 Esdras (or 4 Ezra)	T. Naph.	Testament of Naphtali
Gos. Thom.	Gospel of Thomas	T. Sol.	Testament of Solomon
Haer.	Irenaeus, *Adversus haereses* (*Against Heresies*)	Tob.	Tobit
		Vis.	Shepherd of Hermas, *Visions*
Inf. Gos. Thom.	Infancy Gospel of Thomas		
Jdt.	Judith	Wis.	Wisdom of Solomon
Jos. Asen.	Joseph and Aseneth		
Jub.	Jubilees		

Josephus and Philo

Ag. Ap.	*Against Apion*
Ant.	*Jewish Antiquities*
Dec.	*On the Decalogue*
Embassy	*On the Embassy to Gaius*
Flaccus	*Against Flaccus*
J.W.	*Jewish War*
Moses	*On the Life of Moses*
Posterity	*On the Posterity of Cain*
Spec. Laws	*On the Special Laws*

Rabbinic Tractates

The abbreviations below are used for the names of the tractates in the Mishnah (indicated by a prefixed *m.*), Tosefta (*t.*), Babylonian Talmud (*b.*), and Jerusalem/Palestinian Talmud (*y.*).

ʿAbod. Zar.	*ʿAbodah Zarah*	*B. Meṣiʿa*	*Baba Meṣiʿa*
ʾAbot	*ʾAbot*	*B. Qam.*	*Baba Qamma*
ʿArak.	*ʿArakin*	*Ber.*	*Berakot*
B. Bat.	*Baba Batra*	*ʿEd.*	*ʿEduyyot*

'Erub.	'Erubin	Pesaḥ.	Pesahim
Giṭ.	Giṭṭin	Qidd.	Qiddušin
Ḥag.	Ḥagigah	Šabb.	Šabbat
Ker.	Kerithot	Sanh.	Sanhedrin
Ketub.	Ketubbot	Šeb.	Šebi'it
Kil.	Kil'ayim	Šebu.	Šebu'ot
Mak.	Makkot	Šeqal.	Šeqalim
Meg.	Megillah	Soṭah	Soṭah
Me'il.	Me'ilah	Suk.	Sukkah
Menaḥ.	Menaḥot	Ta'an.	Ta'anit
Mid.	Middot	Tamid	Tamid
Ned.	Nedarim	Ṭohar.	Ṭoharot
Neg.	Nega'im	Yad.	Yadayim
Nid.	Niddah	Yebam.	Yebamot
Pe'ah	Pe'ah	Yoma	Yoma

Targums

Tg. Hos.	Targum of Hosea
Tg. Isa.	Targum of Isaiah
Tg. Mic.	Targum of Micah
Tg. Neof.	Targum Neofiti
Tg. Qoh.	Targum of Ecclesiastes
Tg. Song	Targum of Song of Songs

Qumran/Dead Sea Scrolls

1QapGen	Genesis Apocryphon
1QH	Thanksgiving Hymns
1QpHab	Commentary on Habakkuk
1QM	War Scroll
1QS	Manual of Discipline
1QSa	Rule of the Congregation
1QSb	Rule of the Blessings
4Q172	Unidentified Pesher Fragments
4Q174	Florilegium (also 4QFlor)
4Q242	Prayer of Nabonidus
4Q246	(formerly 4QpsDan ar^a)
4Q372	Apocryphon of Joseph
4Q385	Pseudo-Ezekiel
4Q460	Pseudepigraphic Work
4Q500	Benediction
4Q521	Messianic Apocalypse
11QTemple	Temple Scroll
CD	Damascus Document

Greek Papyri

P.Oxy.	Oxyrhynchus Papyrus
PGM	Greek Magical Papyri

Classical Writers

Ep.	*Epistle(s)* (various writers)
Hist.	*History/Histories* (various writers)
Nat. Hist.	Pliny the Elder, *Natural History*

Transliteration

Greek

α	*a*	ζ	*z*	λ	*l*	π	*p*	φ	*ph*
β	*b*	η	*ē*	μ	*m*	ρ	*r*	χ	*ch*
γ	*g/n*	θ	*th*	ν	*n*	σ/ς	*s*	ψ	*ps*
δ	*d*	ι	*i*	ξ	*x*	τ	*t*	ω	*ō*
ε	*e*	κ	*k*	ο	*o*	υ	*y/u*	'	*h*

Notes on the Transliteration of Greek

1. Accents, lenis (smooth breathing), and *iota* subscript are not shown in transliteration.
2. The transliteration of asper (rough breathing) precedes a vowel or diphthong (e.g., ἁ = *ha*; αἱ = *hai*) and follows ρ (i.e., ῥ = *rh*).
3. *Gamma* is transliterated *n* only when it precedes γ, κ, ξ, or χ.
4. *Upsilon* is transliterated *u* only when it is part of a diphthong (i.e., αυ, ευ, ου, υι).

Hebrew

א	'	ע	ʿ	
בּ	*b*	פּ/ף	*p*	
ג	*g*	צ/ץ	*ṣ*	
ד	*d*	ק	*q*	
ה	*h*	ר	*r*	
ו	*w*	שׂ	*ś*	
ז	*z*	שׁ	*š*	
ח	*ḥ*	ת	*t*	
ט	*ṭ*			
י	*y*	בָ	*ā*	*qāmeṣ*
כּ/ך	*k*	בַ	*a*	*pataḥ*
ל	*l*	הַ	*a*	furtive *pataḥ*
מ/ם	*m*	בֶ	*e*	*sĕgôl*
נ/ן	*n*	בֵ	*ē*	*ṣērê*
ס	*s*	בִ	*i*	short *ḥîreq*

בִ	ī	long *ḥîreq* written defectively	בֶּי	ê	*sĕgôl yôd* (בֶּי = êy)
בָ	o	*qāmeṣ ḥāṭûp*	בֵי	ê	*ṣērê yôd* (בֵי = êy)
בוֹ	ô	*ḥôlem* written fully	בִי	î	*ḥîreq yôd* (בִי = îy)
בֹ	ō	*ḥôlem* written defectively	בֲ	ă	*ḥāṭēp pataḥ*
בוּ	û	*šûreq*	בֱ	ĕ	*ḥāṭēp sĕgôl*
בֻ	u	short *qibbûṣ*	בֳ	ŏ	*ḥāṭēp qāmeṣ*
בֻ	ū	long *qibbûṣ* written defectively	בְ	ĕ	vocal *šĕwā'*
בָה	â	final *qāmeṣ hē'* (בָה = āh)			

Notes on the Transliteration of Hebrew

1. Accents are not shown in transliteration.
2. Silent *šĕwā'* is not indicated in transliteration.
3. The spirant forms ב ג ד כ פ ת are usually not specially indicated in transliteration.
4. *Dāgeš forte* is indicated by doubling the consonant. Euphonic *dāgeš* and *dāgeš lene* are not indicated in transliteration.
5. *Maqqēp* is represented by a hyphen.

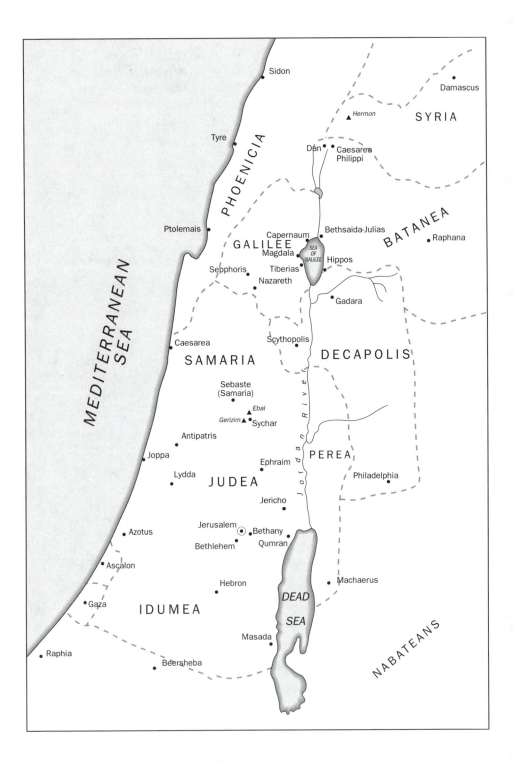

Introduction to the Gospel of Mark

Authorship

Like the other canonical Gospels, the author Mark does not identify himself[1] and makes no claim to be an eyewitness (cf. Luke 1:2; contrast John 21:24). The present titles associated with the four Gospels are not original but were added later (see below). Why the Gospels are anonymous is uncertain. Some have suggested that this may have been due to fear of persecution, but this can be neither proven nor disproven. What is reasonably certain is that this indicates there was no need for the authors to identify themselves. In the case of the second Gospel, which for the sake of convenience I will simply call "Mark," the author was well known to his original readers and part of the same Christian community (Marcus 2000: 17). The lack of identification may also be due to the fact that Mark and the other Gospel writers did not think that what they wrote was "their Gospel." Mark is not the Gospel of the "Good News of Mark" but the "Good News of Jesus Christ, the Son of God" (1:1). The later titles associated with the canonical Gospels recognize this, for they do not describe the four Gospels as "The Gospel *of* Matthew," ". . . *of* Mark," ". . . *of* Luke," and ". . . *of* John," but rather as "The Gospel *according to* Matthew," ". . . *according to* Mark," ". . . *according to* Luke," and ". . . *according to* John" (Hengel 2000: 48–53).

Evidence for the Markan authorship of the Second Gospel can be divided into two types, external evidence (tradition) and internal evidence (what we can learn about the author from the text of Mark itself). The evidence of the tradition supporting Markan authorship can be described in general as early, universal, and extensive. The earliest and most important involves the testimony of Papias found in Eusebius (*Eccl. Hist.* 3.39.1–17). Eusebius, the foremost early church historian, writing in the early fourth century, quotes from Papias's now lost *Interpretation of the Oracles of the Lord*.

> Mark became Peter's interpreter [ἑρμηνευτής, *hermēneutēs*] and wrote accurately all that he remembered, not, indeed, in order, of the things said or done by the Lord. For he had not heard the Lord, nor had he followed him, but later on, as I said, followed Peter, who used to give teaching as necessity demanded but not making, as it were, an arrangement of the Lord's oracles, so that Mark did nothing wrong in thus writing down single points as he remembered them.

1. The identity of the author of the Fourth Gospel as the "beloved disciple" in John 21:20–24 is not made by the author but by his followers, as "*we* know that *his* testimony is true" (21:24c, italics added) indicates.

> For to one thing he gave attention, to leave out nothing of what he had heard and to make no false statements in them. (*Eccl. Hist.* 3.39.15)[2]

According to Eusebius, Papias received this information from John the Elder and Aristion (*Eccl. Hist.* 3.39.4). Since John the Elder died shortly after AD 100 (Hengel 2000: 65–66), the tradition Papias is quoting must date back to the last decades of the first century and near to the time when Mark was written (65–70).[3] This is supported by Eusebius's statement that Papias became famous during the time of Polycarp (d. ca. 155) and Ignatius (d. ca. 107; *Eccl. Hist.* 3.36.1–2; cf. also 3.39.1), as well as Papias's association with Clement of Rome (d. ca. 100; *Eccl. Hist.* 3.39.1). That Eusebius's discussion of Papias comes before his discussion of the persecution under Trajan (ca. 110) in *Eccl. Hist.* 4 also supports a late-first-century date (Yarbrough 1983: 186–90; Orchard 1984: 393–403; Gundry 1993: 1027). Finally, if we acknowledge Papias's acquaintance with the daughters of "Philip the apostle" (*Eccl. Hist.* 3.39.9; cf. Acts 21:8–9), this also supports a late-first-century date. Thus the testimony of Papias is early (within thirty years of the writing of the Gospel of Mark) and at most only one generation removed from eyewitness tradition (the apostles—John the Elder and Aristion—Papias)[4] and was probably written down by him in the first decade of the second century.[5]

Other traditions concerning the authorship of Mark include the following:

The Titles of Mark (70–100). The titles of this Gospel found in most Greek MSS involve a longer form (The Gospel according to Mark, εὐαγγέλιον κατὰ Μᾶρκον, *euangelion kata Markon*; A D L W Θ f¹³) and a shorter

---

2. The Greek and Latin texts of Eusebius and the following quotations can be found at the back of Aland 2001. English translations of these and other early church references to Mark as the author of the Second Gospel can be found in C. Black 1994: 80–182.

3. *"There is wide scholarly agreement that Mark was written in the late 60s or just after 70"* (R. Brown 1997: 164, italics his).

4. A statement of Papias found in Eusebius suggests that he may have had direct access to eyewitness testimony: "For unlike most I did not rejoice in them who say much, but in them who teach the truth, nor in them who recount the commandments of others, but in them who repeated those given to the faith by the Lord and derived from truth itself; but if ever anyone came who had followed the presbyters [i.e., 'elders'], I inquired into the words of the presbyters, what Andrew or Peter or Philip or Thomas or James or John or Matthew, or any other of the Lord's disciples, had said, and what Aristion and the presbyter John, the Lord's disciples, were saying. For I did not suppose that information from books would help me so much as the word of a living and surviving voice" (Eusebius, *Eccl. Hist.* 3.39.3–4). It is possible to interpret the quotation of Eusebius to mean that "Papias was auditor of the apostle John, the Lord's disciple" (C. Black 1994: 87), but Eusebius himself seems to place Aristion and the presbyter John after the apostolic eyewitnesses and states that Papias did not have direct access to the apostles but received their words via Aristion and the presbyter John (*Eccl. Hist.* 3.39.2, 6). For the view that Aristion and the presbyter John were the last of the eyewitnesses, see Bauckham 2006: 15–21.

5. The only real evidence in the tradition that would date the testimony of Papias later comes from Philip of Side, who wrote a century after Eusebius (ca. 430 versus ca. 324) and was "notoriously unreliable" (Gundry 1993: 1028). Despite various attempts to read a later anti-gnostic tendenz in Papias's writings, there is no clear anti-gnostic polemic in Papias (Yarbrough 1983: 182–83; Hengel 1985: 48).

form (According to Mark, κατὰ Μᾶρκον, *kata Markon*; ℵ B). Both these unusual forms consciously avoid the genitive of authorship ("*of* Mark" [Μᾶρκου, *Markou*]) to emphasize that what follows is not the Gospel *of* Mark but the (one and only) Gospel accordïng to Mark's account (Hengel 1985: 65–66). The unanimity of the κατὰ Μᾶρκον superscription in one form or another argues against a mid-second-century origin, and the Papias quotation (see above) seems to presuppose its existence both for Mark and for Matthew (von Campenhausen 1972: 173n123; Hengel 1985: 69), so that the association of κατὰ Μᾶρκον with the Second Gospel already existed in the late first century. The antiquity of this inscription is also confirmed by its naming a nonapostle, Mark, as its author, for, as the apocryphal Gospels indicate, by the mid-second century it was popular to ascribe apostolic authorship to Gospel-like works. It is furthermore quite unlikely that the original Gospel of Mark simply fell anonymously and unannounced into the hands of its first readers. Therefore some sort of title was probably associated with Mark from the very beginning (Hengel 1985: 74–84; 2000: 50–56; contra Marcus 2000: 17–18).[6]

The Anti-Marcionite Prologue (ca. 150–180). "Mark related, who was called 'Stumpfinger' because for the size of the rest of his body he had fingers that were too short. He was the interpreter of Peter. After Peter's death the same man wrote this gospel in the regions of Italy" (Grant 1946: 92). The negative comment about Mark's "stumpfingers" has every appearance of being a historically reliable tradition.[7] It is most unlikely that secondary tradition would demean Mark by such a description. Rather, it is more likely that it would have sought to extol the Gospel writer by adding something like "who was called 'Beautiful Hands,' for with them he would write 'the Gospel of Jesus Christ, the Son of God.'"

Justin Martyr (ca. 150). Justin quotes Mark 3:17 ("the sons of Zebedee, to that of Boanerges, which means 'sons of thunder'") and refers to this being found in the Memoirs of Peter (*Dial.* 106.3).

Irenaeus (ca. 170). "But after their departure [ἔξοδον, *exodon*] Mark, the disciple and interpreter [ἑρμηνευτής, *hermēneutēs*] of Peter, himself also handed over to us, in writing, the things preached by Peter" (*Haer.* 3.1.1; C. Black 1994: 99–100).

Clement of Alexandria (ca. 180). "When Peter had publicly preached the word at Rome, and by the Spirit had proclaimed the Gospel, that those present, who were many, exhorted Mark, as one who had followed him for a long time and remembered what had been spoken, to make a re-cord of what was said; and that he did this, and distributed the Gospel

---

6. Hengel (1985: 81) points out that as soon as a church community possessed two different Gospels in their church library, there would have been a need of titles to distinguish them.

7. Mark is also referred to as "Stumpfinger" in Hippolytus, *Refutation of All Heresies* 7.30.1 (C. Black 1994: 116; the reference is found in *ANF* 5:112 [7.18.1]).

among those that asked him. And that when the matter came to Peter's knowledge he neither strongly forbade it nor urged it forward" (Eusebius, *Eccl. Hist.* 6.14.6–7 LCL).[8] Although Clement of Alexandria refers to Mark writing his Gospel while Peter was still alive, the great majority of early witnesses claim that he wrote it after Peter's death.

Origen (ca. 200). "Secondly, that according to Mark, who wrote it in accordance with Peter's instructions, whom also Peter acknowledged as his son in the catholic epistle, speaking in these terms: 'She that is in Babylon, elect together with you, saluteth you; and so doth Mark my son'" (Eusebius, *Eccl. Hist.* 6.25.5 LCL).

Tertullian (ca. 200). "That gospel which Mark edited may be affirmed to be of Peter, whose interpreter Mark was" (*Against Marcion* 4.5; Barclay 1976: 121).

Eusebius (ca. 324). "They say that this Mark was the first to be sent to preach in Egypt the Gospel which he had also put into writing, and was the first to establish churches in Alexandria itself. The number of men and women who were there converted at the first attempt was so great, and their asceticism was so extraordinary philosophic, that Philo thought it right to describe their conduct and assemblies and meals and all the rest of their manner of life. Tradition says that he came to Rome in the time of Claudius to speak to Peter, who was at that time preaching to those there" (*Eccl. Hist.* 2.16–17.1 LCL).

Jerome (ca. 400). "Mark, the interpreter of the apostle Peter, and the first bishop of the church of Alexandria, who himself had not seen the Lord, the very Saviour, is the second who published a gospel; but he narrated those things he had heard his master preaching more in accordance with the trustworthiness of the things performed than in order" (*Commentary on Matthew*, prologue 6; Barclay 1976: 121).

From the above it is evident that the attribution of the authorship of the Second Gospel to John Mark is early and widespread. As for the internal evidence found in the Gospel itself, although it is not able to demonstrate that its author was John Mark, it lends indirect support to the tradition that he was its author and that it was written for the Christian community in Rome. That the author knew Greek (cf. Acts 12:25–13:13; 15:36–39) does not, of course, narrow the field of possible authors a great deal, but that he also knew Hebrew/Aramaic (Mark 3:17, 22; 5:41; 7:11, 34; 9:43; 10:46; 14:36; 15:22, 34) fits well the John Mark of the tradition, whose home was in Jerusalem (Acts 12:12). That he knew Jewish customs and religious groups, though his audience did not (Mark 7:1–4; 14:12; 15:42), also supports the tradition, as does his explanation of all the Semitic expressions,[9] and his knowledge of various Jewish parties and

---

8. In *Eccl. Hist.* 2.15.1–2 Peter is said to have "authorized Mark's work."

9. Contra Koester (1990: 289) and Schnelle (1998: 200), who argue that the author of Mark was not a Jewish Christian. Cf., however, Hengel 1985: 46, "I do not know any other work in

groups (Pharisees, Sadducees, Herodians, scribes, priests, chief priests, high priests, etc.). The presence of various "Latinisms" (see below, "Audience") also supports the tradition that Mark was the author of the Second Gospel and that he wrote it for the Christian community in Rome (Gundry 1993: 1043–44). In summarizing the internal evidence concerning the authorship of the second Gospel, we can conclude that it fits well the tradition of the early church that it was written by John Mark to the church in Rome.[10]

Critical scholars have raised a number of objections to the above arguments. One involves the reliability of the Papias tradition in claiming that Mark was the "interpreter" of Peter and wrote down in his Gospel what he had heard Peter say. There is no clear evidence that Mark recorded autobiographical stories spoken by the apostle. Yet this argument, which assumes that the well-rounded form of the traditions in Mark could not come from an eyewitness, loses sight of the fact that repeated storytelling even by an eyewitness would become more polished and smooth over time. If the stories spoken by Peter in the 60s had been reported by him for over thirty years (cf. Luke 1:2; Acts 1:21–22; 2:42; 4:2, 13, 19–20; 5:29–32; 6:4; 8:25; 10:22, 33, 39–43; etc.) and he had repeated them once a month, this would mean that he had repeated the same stories over 360 times by the time Mark heard them in the 60s. If he had repeated them only once every six months, he would have repeated them over sixty times. Surely by then they would have become more "rounded" and stereotyped! In addition, if the author of the Second Gospel is the John Mark of Acts 12:12, he would have heard these traditions thirty years earlier and been involved in passing them on in his own ministry (cf. Acts 12:25–13:13; 15:36–39; Col. 4:10; 2 Tim. 4:11; Philem. 24; 1 Pet. 5:13). We should also note that Papias refers to Mark as Peter's ἑρμηνευτής, or "interpreter," not as his amanuensis or "secretary" (cf. C. Black 1994: 89–91). Thus it is incorrect to assume that if the Second Gospel stems from "personal reminiscence, we would expect more detail" (Marcus 2000: 23). On the other hand, the amount of material found in Mark concerning Peter (1:16–18, 29–31, 36; 3:16; 5:37–43; 8:29, 31–33; 9:2–8; 10:28–31; 11:21; 13:3–37; 14:27–31, 32–42, 54, 66–72; 16:7) fits well with a tie between the author of the Second Gospel and Petrine testimony.

Another argument raised against Markan authorship involves supposed errors in geography found in the Gospel (Niederwimmer 1967: 178–83; P. Parker 1983: 68–70). The most frequently cited is 7:31, "And having departed from

---

Greek which has as many Aramaic or Hebrew words and formulae in so narrow a space as does the second Gospel."

10. The most vigorous attempt to associate Peter with the Gospel of Mark involving internal evidence from the Gospel itself is that of C. Turner (1925; 1926; 1928). He argues that "in all these passages [1:21, 29; 5:1, 38; 6:53, 54; 8:22; 9:14, 30, 33; 10:32, 46; 11:1, 12, 15, 20, 27; 14:18, 22, 26, 32] Mark's third person plural may be reasonably understood as representing a first person plural of Peter's discourses" (C. Turner 1928: 54). Cf. Manson (1962: 42), who, following C. Turner, sees Peter as the source for 1:16–39; 2:1–14; 3:13–19; 4:35–5:43; 6:7–13, 30–56; 8:14–9:48; 10:32–35; 11:1–33; 13:3–4, 32–37; 14:17–50, 53–54, 66–72. Cf. also Bauckham 2006: 155–82.

the regions of Tyre, he again came to the Sea of Galilee by way of Sidon and through the middle of the Decapolis." If one draws a line from Tyre to Sidon to the Sea of Galilee to the Decapolis, this involves a strange journey indeed. A comparable trip (in direction, not distance) would be to travel from Portland to Denver via Seattle and the Great Plains (Marcus 2000: 472). Such a trip envisions leaving Tyre and proceeding 22 miles north to Sidon, then southeast from Sidon to the Decapolis, and then northwest to the Sea of Galilee. This supposedly reveals that the author of Mark was ignorant of Palestinian geography and could not have been the John Mark of Acts 12:12, whose home was Jerusalem and who journeyed with Paul and Barnabas from Jerusalem to Antioch (Acts 12:25–13:4). A similar alleged error in geography is found in Mark 11:1. Here the journey from Jericho (10:46–52) to Jerusalem, Bethphage, and Bethany, if understood as occurring in that order, would be strange indeed, for if one proceeds from Jericho, the order of progression is Bethany (the eastern side of the Mount of Olives), Bethphage (the summit of the Mount of Olives), and Jerusalem (west of the Mount of Olives). The order in both these instances, however, reflects not an ignorance of Palestinian or Judean geography, as some suggest, but rather Mark's desire to list the ultimate goal of the journey from Tyre (i.e., the Sea of Galilee) and Jericho (i.e., Jerusalem) first and the intervening places next (Sidon and the Decapolis; Bethpage[11] and Bethany; see 7:31 and 11:1).[12] Consequently, these alleged geographical errors found in the Second Gospel are not evidence of Mark's ignorance of Palestinian geography but rather reflect various critics' misunderstanding of the Markan style used to describe such journeys.

Still another alleged error on the part of the author of Mark that supposedly prevents him from being the John Mark of Acts 12:12 is his ignorance of Jewish laws and customs (P. Parker 1983: 73–75).[13] In 7:3–4 Mark comments parenthetically, "(For the Pharisees and all the Jews, unless they wash their hands with the fist, do not eat because of holding to the tradition of the elders, and [when they come] from the marketplace unless they wash themselves, they do not eat, and there are many other traditions they have received and observe [lit. 'received to hold'] [such as] the washings of cups and pitchers and bronze vessels)." This is not literally true, for such washing rites were not universally practiced by all Jews. Consequently, 7:3–4 is not technically correct

11. Bethphage is probably mentioned before Bethany because it is closer to Jerusalem and may reflect the order of the journey from Jerusalem through Bethphage to Bethany in 11:11. Cf., however, J. Edwards (2002: 334), who argues that the ancient road from Jericho to Jerusalem passed through Bethphage before Bethany.

12. Another supposed geographical error in Mark is found in 10:1. Here again, however, we have the place of departure mentioned first ("there," i.e., Capernaum [9:33]), the ultimate goal second ("the regions of Judea"), and the intervening route last ("across the Jordan"). See 10:1.

13. Contrast Hengel (1985: 9), who states that Mark knows "the 'historical contours' of Palestinian Judaism before the destruction of the second temple more accurately than the later Evangelists" and uses as an example his distinguishing among the scribes, Pharisees, and Sadducees.

(Niederwimmer 1967: 183–85). The term "all," however, is frequently used as an exaggerated adjective for emphasis (Stein 1994a: 134). For the gentile readers of Mark, one of the most distinctive features of the Jewish people was the kosher regulations that pervaded their lives, and no clear distinction would have been made by them between OT regulations and Pharisaic oral traditions (cf. Let. Aris. 305). As a broad generalization, what Mark states in 7:3–4 is correct, and one should not expect from him a statistical analysis of the percentage of Jews who followed the Pharisaic rules of washing. See 7:3–4.[14]

The debate about the authorship of the Second Gospel does not involve the "meaning" of the Gospel (Guelich 1989: xxix). The meaning of the Gospel of Mark involves what its author meant by the words that make up the Gospel. This is true regardless of whether the author's name was John Mark. The reason why there is vigorous debate about Markan authorship lies elsewhere, and it does not involve a simple, objective pursuit of knowledge. Various presuppositions are often involved that are seldom discussed and at times may not even be consciously recognized but predispose scholars to a particular viewpoint. What is involved in the issue of authorship concerns primarily the "significance" that a person attributes to Mark (Stein 1994a: 43–46). If one brings to the study of Mark naturalistic presuppositions and denies the historicity of much or all of the miracles recorded in Mark, then how can one attribute the authorship of Mark to the John Mark of Acts 12:12 and 1 Pet. 5:13, whose main source for this information was the apostle Peter, an eyewitness of the events? One must conclude either that the author was not John Mark but an anonymous author who believed the fictional accounts created by the anonymous community and incorporated them into his Gospel or that John Mark was an unabashed deceiver who created fictional accounts to deceive or to edify the church. The latter "accommodationist" view had a brief period of popularity during the late eighteenth and early nineteenth centuries but is generally discredited because it is clear that the Gospel writers believed what they were writing (cf. Luke 1:3–4; John 21:24).

On the other hand, those who believe in the historicity of the miracle accounts in the Second Gospel and/or believe that it was in some way divinely inspired see support for this in the view that the Gospel was written by Mark and that he obtained his information from an eyewitness, the apostle Peter. Thus, just as the former view seeks to discredit the arguments in favor of Markan authorship and supports the various objections raised against it, this view seeks to support the arguments in favor of Markan authorship and attempts to refute the objections raised against it. As a result, although the meaning of the Second Gospel is unaffected by the issue of who wrote it, the issue of authorship is a critical one with respect to the significance or value

14. Technically, Mark's statement "on the first day of [the Feast of] Unleavened Bread, when they were sacrificing the Passover lamb" (14:12) is also incorrect, for the sacrificing of the Passover lamb took place on the fourteenth of Nisan, and the first day of the Feast of Unleavened Bread was the fifteenth of Nisan. But it was common to describe the sacrificing of the Passover lamb as taking place on the fifteenth of Nisan (see 14:12).

one attributes to the Gospel. It would seem, however, that the presuppositions of critical scholarship play a more dominant and decisive role with respect to the question of authorship than those of evangelical scholarship. For critical scholarship, the antisupernaturalist presupposition usually associated with this position requires a non–John Mark authorship and a denial that behind the accounts found in Mark stands the eyewitness testimony of the apostle Peter. For evangelical scholarship, Markan authorship in association with the eyewitness testimony of Peter would be nice but is not necessary, for the truthfulness of the miracle accounts in Mark does not require Markan authorship.

For me, the case for Markan[15] authorship is strong and involves the following:

1. The universal and early tradition ascribing Markan authorship to the Second Gospel. It is highly unlikely that a purely fictional ascription would have named a nonapostle as the author, and especially one with a less-than-exemplary history (Acts 13:13; 15:36–41). One need only compare the attribution of apostolic authorship to the apocryphal Gospels (the Gospels of Philip, Thomas, Bartholomew, Peter, etc.) to see that a fictional attribution of the Second Gospel to a nonapostle is contrary to what one would expect. Furthermore, if we assume that the tie to the apostle Peter was intended to give apostolic sanction to a nonapostolic work, then the tradition from the beginning associated the Second Gospel with Mark.
2. The negative comment in the Anti-Marcionite Prologue and Hippolytus that attributes authorship of the Second Gospel to John Mark, who is called "Stumpfinger," has every appearance of being reliable tradition. Why would a completely fictional tradition attribute such a negative comment to the author of one of the sacred Gospels?
3. It is quite unlikely that the Second Gospel simply fell anonymously, without any knowledge of its origin, into the hands of its first readers. The comment in Mark 15:21 that Simon of Cyrene was "the father of Alexander and Rufus" indicates that the Gospel was written to a church that the author knew and that no doubt knew him. Thus the authorship of the Second Gospel was never unknown to its first hearers.
4. While internal evidence cannot prove Markan authorship, various aspects of the Gospel support Markan authorship (knowledge of Aramaic; the presence of numerous Latinisms; knowledge of Jewish customs; a more accurate knowledge of "the 'historical contours' of Palestinian Judaism before the destruction of the second temple . . . than the later evangelists"

---

15. Since the only "Mark" referred to in the NT is the John Mark of Acts 12:12; 13:5, 13; 15:36–40; Philem. 24; Col. 4:10; 2 Tim. 4:11; and 1 Pet. 5:13, the tradition concerning the Markan authorship of the Second Gospel assumes that "Mark" is the John Mark of the NT (contra Marcus 2000: 24). If the tradition were referring to a different "Mark," it would have had to make a clear distinction between the two.

[Hengel 1985: 9]; the distinguishing of various Jewish groups such as the scribes, Pharisees, and Sadducees; etc.).

5. The negative arguments raised against Markan authorship (lack of knowledge of Palestinian geography and Jewish customs) misunderstand Mark's style in describing the geography of Jesus's journeys and his general way of describing Jewish customs for his gentile readers.

Audience

From within Mark we learn a great deal about the audience for whom it was written. We know it was a Greek-speaking audience that did not know Aramaic, as Mark's explanations of Aramaic expressions indicate (3:17–22; 5:41; 7:11, 34; 9:43; 10:46; 14:36; 15:22, 34). We also know that it was a Christian audience familiar with the gospel traditions. Evidence for this is as follows:

1. The various titles used to describe Jesus (Christ, Son of God, Son of David, Lord, and especially the enigmatic title "Son of Man") are not explained; it is assumed that the readers understand them.
2. The expression "the word" (1:45; 2:2; 4:33; 8:32; cf. Acts 2:41; 4:4, 29, 31; etc.) is not defined but understood as a synonym for "the gospel."
3. The expression "his disciples" is never explained but assumed to be understood.
4. The meaning of John the Baptist's "*I* baptized you with water, but *he* will baptize you with the Holy Spirit" (1:8) is nowhere explained but assumes that what it refers to (the coming of the Spirit into the life of the believer at conversion) is understood by the readers.
5. It is a church in whose membership were apparently two sons of a Gospel eyewitness, Simon of Cyrene (15:21).
6. The readers knew the main characters and places of the Gospel story, so that when they are mentioned, no explanation is needed. The former include John the Baptist, simply introduced as "John" (1:4), whose unique clothing is described and not explained but whose significance the readers are expected to understand (cf. 1:6 and 9:11–13 with 2 Kings 1:8) and whose martyrdom by King Herod was apparently known to the readers (Mark 6:14–29). Pilate is simply introduced to the readers as "Pilate" without any explanatory title (contrast Matt. 27:2, "Pilate, the governor"; and Luke 3:1, "Pontius Pilate, being governor of Judea"). The area ruled by King Herod (Mark 5:14, 29; 8:15) is not delineated, and "James the younger and Joses" (15:40; 16:1) were apparently known to the readers, as was Jesus's hometown, whose name "Nazareth" is not mentioned.[16]
7. Mark assumes that various cities (Capernaum: 1:21; 2:1; 9:3; Tyre: 3:8; 7:24, 31; Sidon: 3:8; 7:31; Jerusalem: 3:8, 22; 7:1; 10:32–33; Bethsaida: 6:45; 8:22; Caesarea Philippi: 8:27; Jericho: 10:46; Bethany: 11:1, 11–12;

---

16. It is possible that Mark assumed that his readers would arrive at this conclusion due to such references as 1:9, 24 (cf. also 14:67).

14:3; and Bethphage: 11:1) do not have to be explained to his readers. Similarly, various places are not explained (the Jordan River: 1:5, 9; 3:8; 10:1; Judea: 1:5; 3:7; 10:1; 13:14; Galilee: 1:9, 14, 28, 39; 3:7; 6:21; 9:30; 14:28; 15:41; 16:7; the Sea of Galilee: 1:16; 7:31 [cf. also 2:13; 3:7; 4:1, 39, 41; 5:1, 13, 21; 6:47–49]; 11:1, 11, 15, 27; 15:41; the Decapolis: 5:20; 7:31; Gennesaret: 6:53; the Mount of Olives: 11:1; 13:3; 14:26; etc.). Though one can grant that a non-Christian could know a number of these places, some were insignificant to the Roman world of the first century. For Christians, however, they were known because they were part of "the greatest story ever told."

It is also apparent Mark's readers were familiar with various OT characters and possessed considerable knowledge of the Jewish religion. This is seen in references to Isaiah, mentioned without explanation in 1:2; 7:6–7; Moses, 1:44; 7:10; 9:4–5; 10:3–4; 12:19, 26; David, 2:25; 10:47–48; 11:10; 12:35–37; Elijah, 6:15; 8:28; 9:11–13 (cf. 1:6); 15:35–36; Elijah and Moses, 9:4–5; and Abraham, Isaac, and Jacob, 12:26. There is frequent mention of the OT "Scriptures" (12:10, 24; 14:49; cf. also 1:2; 7:6; 9:12–13; 10:4–5; 11:17; 12:19; 14:21, 27). They knew that the ruling body of Israel was called the Sanhedrin (14:55; 15:21). They were expected to understand the symbolism, and probably the significance, of Jesus's choosing "twelve" disciples (see 3:14–15). They were furthermore familiar with certain Jewish festivals (14:1, 12a; 15:42), the importance of the Sabbath in the life of Israel (1:21; 2:23–28; 3:2, 4; 6:2; 16:1–2), various Jewish groups that are introduced without explanation (the Pharisees and scribes, 2:16, 18, 24), and various Jewish traditions and their importance to the people of Israel (7:6–7, 9–13). Certain oral traditions on ritual purity nevertheless needed to be explained (7:3–5). All this suggests that the original audience of Mark consisted primarily of gentile Christians, familiar with both the gospel traditions and the Judaism of the first century. It is possible that many of them were originally "God-fearers" (Acts 10:2, 22; 13:16, 26), but this cannot be proven.

With respect to the geographical location of Mark's intended readers, the tradition states that Mark wrote his Gospel for the church at Rome.[17] This was the general consensus until the second half of the twentieth century. Since then several other locations have been suggested as the Gospel's intended audience. Some of them, such as Galilee (Marxsen 1968: 143; 1969: 54–95) and the Decapolis (the alleged flight of the Judean church to Pella), have received little

17. See the Anti-Marcionite Prologue, Clement of Alexandria, and Eusebius quotations in the discussion of authorship above and the association of Mark with Peter and Rome in 1 Pet. 5:13. The much debated and previously unknown Epistle of Clement discovered by Morton Smith in 1958 in the monastery library of Mar Saba states that whereas Mark wrote his Gospel in Rome, after Peter's death he went to Alexandria and wrote a revised and more spiritual Gospel. This more spiritual Gospel had been called Mark's Secret Gospel (C. Black 1994: 139–45). Cf. John Chrysostom (*Homily on Matthew* 1.7), who states that Mark wrote his Gospel in Alexandria.

endorsement. The only other suggested audience that has received substantial support is the Christian community in Syria (Kümmel 1975: 98; Theissen 1991: 236–58; Marcus 2000: 33–37). Several reasons are given for this. One is the close agreement between the descriptions found in Mark 13 and the general course of events of the Jewish War in AD 66–70. This is supposedly better explained and understood in a Syrian context than a Roman one. Second, if the "abomination of desolation" of 13:14 is understood as an event associated with the Jewish War and the need to flee Jerusalem before its encirclement by the Roman army, one can argue that this would be more applicable in a Syrian context than a Roman one (Marcus 2000: 34). There is no evidence, however, of Christians being persecuted by the Romans during the Jewish War. Some also argue that the depiction of agriculture (4:2–8, 26ff.), housing (2:4; 4:21), employment, landownership, taxation (12:1–9, 13–17), and land (Kee 1977: 102) accurately reflects and favors a Syrian-Palestinian provenance and audience for the Gospel. But much of this material in Mark is also found in Matthew and Luke, and it is far more likely that its presence is due not to Mark having reworked the gospel materials for a Syrian-Palestinian audience but rather to the fact that this material reflects its origin in the Palestinian environment of the historical Jesus.

The association of the Gospel of Mark with Rome found in the early church tradition is quite weighty and receives support from several quarters. If the warnings of Mark 13:9–13 and elsewhere are directed to the readers of the Gospel and meant to prepare them for persecution from both the synagogue (13:9a–b) and the state (13:9c), the latter fits the time of Nero far better than the supposed persecution of the Palestinian church during the Jewish War (see, however, the discussion of 13:9–13 below). We know of no clear example of Roman persecution of the Christian church in the first century other than that experienced by the Roman church during the time of Nero in the mid-60s (Hengel 2000: 79). In addition, the description of the Greek woman in 7:26 as "Syrophoenician by birth" makes far better sense if addressed to a Roman audience than a Syrian one. For the latter, "Phoenician" would have been sufficient, whereas "Syrophoenician" would seem "nonsensical" (Hengel 1985: 29). The application of Jesus's teaching on divorce to women divorcing their husbands in 10:12 would be especially meaningful for a gentile and Roman audience.

An additional argument in support of the traditional view that Rome was the Gospel's intended audience is the presence of numerous "Latinisms" in Mark. These include the following:

to make their way (ὁδὸν ποιεῖν, *hodon poiein*; Lat. *iter facere*)—2:23

mat (κράβαττος, *krabattos*; Lat. *grabatus*)—2:4, 9, 11, 12; 6:55

basket (μόδιος, *modios*; Lat. *modius*)—4:21

legion (λεγιών, *legiōn*; Lat. *legio*)—5:9, 15

soldier of the guard (σπεκουλάτωρ, *spekoulatōr*; Lat. *speculator*)—6:27

denarius (δηνάριον, *dēnarion*; Lat. *denarius*)—6:37; 12:15; 14:5

fist (πυγμή, *pygmē*; Lat. *pugnus*)—7:3

pitcher (ξέστης, *xestēs*; Lat. *sextarius*)—7:4

tax (κῆνσος, *kēnsos*; Lat. *census*)—12:14

penny (κοδράντης, *kodrantēs*; Lat. *quadrans*)—12:42

centurion (κεντυρίων, *kentyriōn*; Lat. *centurio*)—15:39, 44, 45

to satisfy (τὸ ἱκανὸν ποιῆσαι, *to hikanon poiēsai*; Lat. *satis facere*)—15:15

scourge (φραγελλόω, *phragelloō*; Lat. *flagello*)—15:15

praetorium (πραιτώριον, *praitōrion*; Lat. *praetorium*)—15:16[18]

Although the presence of these Latinisms does not prove a Roman provenance for the Gospel of Mark (some of these same Latinisms are also found in the Gospels of Matthew and Luke, although "soldier of the guard," "fist," "pitcher," and "centurion" are found only in Mark, and "penny" is a Roman coin that fits a Roman audience extremely well),[19] the number of them in Mark is significant and suggests a Roman audience. V. Taylor's comment (1952: 45) seems judicious, "The presence of almost all these words in the papyri shows that they belonged to the Koine, but their frequency in Mark suggests that the Evangelist wrote in a Roman environment."[20]

Date

Although there is a wide consensus that Mark was written around AD 70, there have been several attempts to date Mark earlier. One involves the generally accepted assumption that Luke made use of Mark in writing his Gospel (Stein 2001: 29–169) and the ending of Acts. If Luke ended Acts with the most recent information available concerning the situation of Paul (in Rome awaiting trial), then Luke–Acts could not have been written after AD 62. Consequently, Mark must date earlier, and this would suggest a date in the late 50s (Carson and Moo 2005: 179–82). Yet did Luke write all that he knew about Paul and his fate in Rome? His reporting of Peter's activities in Acts provides insight for answering this question. We read of Peter in Acts 1–15 but not at all in 16–28. This reveals that Acts is not a biography of the life of Peter and/or Paul. Luke refers to Peter in Acts only to the extent that Peter assists in the fulfillment of the theme of Acts—"But you will receive power when the Holy Spirit has come upon you; and you will be my witnesses in Jerusalem, in all Judea and Samaria, and to the end of the earth" (1:8). Thus Peter is on

18. Cf. also "fourth watch" (τετάρτη φυλακή, *tetartē phylakē*)—6:48, which reflects a Roman reckoning of time. According to the Jewish reckoning of time, there were three watches of the night, but according to the Roman reckoning, there were four (cf. 13:35). See BDAG 1067–68.

19. Cf. how the explanation of an American sum of money in dollars by "pounds," "lira," "yen," "pesos," "rubles," "francs," and so on suggests a specific audience.

20. For additional discussion of the Latinisms found in Mark, see BDF §§4–6; Dschulnigg 1986: 276–78; and Gundry 1993: 1043–44.

center stage in the spread of the gospel in Jerusalem (2:1–8:1b), Judea and Samaria (9:1c–12:19), and to both Jews (2:1–9:43) and gentiles (10:1–15:11). After this, Luke has no further interest in Peter. This is not because Luke has brought his readers up-to-date on the life of Peter or because he possessed no further information about him (cf. the "we" sections in Acts that take place in Jerusalem and Judea, where all sorts of information about Peter would have been available for Luke—21:3–18; 27:1). It is rather because Peter's role in the spread of the gospel to Jerusalem-Judea-Samaria in fulfillment of Acts 1:8 has been completed. Similarly, Acts is not a biography about the life of Paul, and when Paul has fulfilled his mission in bringing the gospel to the end of the earth (9:1–28:31) by preaching it in Rome to Caesar himself, Luke ends Acts. Acts 1:8 is fulfilled! Thus Acts 28:31 may be an unsatisfying ending to a biography of Paul, but it is a quite satisfying ending for Acts. The gospel has spread from Jerusalem to Judea to Samaria and to the end of the earth (1:8), and the emperor of the whole Roman Empire is hearing it. If this is true, then the ending of Acts does not necessarily serve as a *terminus ad quem*, or the latest possible date, at which Mark could have been written. It could have been written after AD 62.

Another attempt to ascribe an early date to Mark that received a spectacular amount of publicity came in 1972 when José O'Callaghan argued that two Greek papyrus scraps found at Qumran (7Q5 and 7Q6) were fragments of Mark 6:52–53 and 4:28. If correct, this would require a date for Mark before AD 68–69, when Qumran was destroyed by the Romans. Paleographically 7Q5 and 7Q6 date around AD 50 (plus or minus twenty-five years). The larger fragment (7Q5) consists of twenty letters found in five lines. O'Callaghan's delineation of the letters required for his identification of this as part of Mark 6:52–53 involves several emendations (only ten letters are really clear) and is highly dubious (Gundry 1999). Furthermore, his reconstruction of the lines is unlikely as well (W. Lane 1974: 18–21). Now that the excitement created by the original claim has died down, scholars agree that these two scraps are not fragments from the Gospel of Mark. In reality 7Q5 is more likely a part of the Greek text of 1 Enoch.

The strongest external evidence for dating Mark comes from tradition, and this associates the origin of the Gospel with the death of Peter. The Anti-Marcionite Prologue and Irenaeus (*Haer.* 3.1.1) make the connection quite explicit (cf. also Papias [Eusebius, *Eccl. Hist.* 3.39.15] and Justin Martyr [*Dial.* 106.3], who seem to presume this). Since Peter is assumed to have died during the latter part of Nero's reign in AD 64/65 (cf. 1 Clem. 5.2–4), this suggests that Mark was written in the late 60s. This scenario appears far more likely than that suggested by Clement of Alexandria (Eusebius, *Eccl. Hist.* 6.14.6–7) and Origen (ibid., 6.25.5), who state that Mark was written before Peter's death. The dating of Mark before Peter's death would have been more advantageous for apologetic purposes, so that the dating of Mark after Peter's death appears to be a more reliable tradition. The tie between Mark, Peter, and Rome found in 1 Pet. 5:13 ("She who is at Babylon, who is likewise chosen, sends you greetings, and so does Mark, my son") also supports a dating in the late 60s.

Numerous scholars have sought by means of internal evidence to date the Gospel. Some see the emphasis on the suffering of Jesus (8:31–10:45; 14:1ff.) and the warning to the church to prepare for persecution (8:31–38; 13:3–13) as indicating that Mark was seeking to encourage his readers during their time of persecution and that this reflects the Neronian persecution of Christians in Rome in the mid-60s. Yet Acts reveals that from the beginning the church experienced persecution, and most of Paul's warnings concerning Christian persecution were written before AD 64/65 (2 Thess. 1:4–7; Rom. 8:35; 12:14; 1 Cor. 4:12; Phil. 1:29–30; etc.). Thus a mirror reading of the passages in Mark to reflect the persecution under Nero is questionable. The origin of most of these warnings to prepare for persecution and suffering almost certainly goes back to the ministry and teachings of Jesus himself.

The second main area of internal evidence scholars tend to use for dating Mark involves supposed allusions to the Jewish War in Mark 13. These include the reference to the "abomination of desolation" in 13:14. The editorial aside in 13:14b calling upon the readers to note this reference is seen as being especially relevant for the dating of Mark. The event is associated with the forthcoming destruction of Jerusalem and serves as a warning for people in Judea and Jerusalem to flee from the city before its encirclement by the Romans (13:14c). The value of this passage for dating Mark must be questioned, however. The exhortation to flee Jerusalem is not addressed to Mark's readers, who probably reside in either Rome or Syria but certainly not Judea(!), as his explanation of Aramaic terms (5:41; 7:34; 14:36; 15:34; etc.) and Jewish traditions (7:3–5) clearly indicates. Thus the warning of the historical Jesus, which would have benefited Jewish believers in Judea and Jerusalem in the late 60s and led them to flee from (not into!) Jerusalem, had great relevance for believers living in Judea, but it is not addressed to Mark's audience as an exhortation that serves to date the Gospel. See 13:14.[21]

Another allusion in Mark 13 that some see as evidence for dating Mark is found in 13:7, which refers to "wars and reports of wars." It is argued that this refers to a specific time, AD 68–69, when after Nero's death the Roman Empire experienced a unique period of war and turmoil. This involved not only the Jewish War but also the bloody civil wars involving the emperors Galba, Otho, and Vitellius, who all died within one year, and rebellions in Germany, Gaul, Britain, Africa, the lower Danube, and Pontus (Hengel 1985: 22; cf. Tacitus, *Hist.* 1.2.1). Yet "wars and reports of wars" is a common apocalyptic idea found in judgment prophecies and descriptions of the end times and the "birth pangs" of the messianic age (Isa. 19:2; Jer. 51:46; Ezek. 5:12; Rev. 6:8;

---

21. Crossley (2004) has argued that the portrayal of Jesus as a Torah-observing Jew in Mark betrays a period before the mid-40s when both Jewish and gentile Christians no longer felt bound to observe certain parts of the Torah. It is far more likely, however, that the Torah-observing Jesus in Mark reflects the practice of the historical Jesus and that Mark (and Matthew, who clearly writes after the mid-40s) did not feel compelled to re-create Jesus to fit their own situations.

2 Esd. 13:31; 1 En. 99.4–6; Sib. Or. 3.635–36; 2 Bar. 27.3–9; 70.3–8; Josephus, *J.W.* 2.10.1 §187; etc.). In actuality nothing in the description of the destruction of Jerusalem in Mark 13 is not already found in the imagery of various prophecies of judgment found in the OT and the apocryphal literature of the intertestamental period. Thus the reference to "wars and reports of wars" cannot be used to determine the date of Mark any more than the exact same phrase in Matt. 24:6 and the parallel expression in Luke 21:9, written after Mark wrote his Gospel, can date the origin of their Gospels to AD 68–69. The use of Mark 13 to date Mark is highly questionable. There is no doubt that Jesus prophesied the destruction of the temple (see 14:55–59), and the imagery found in Mark 13 could very well have been spoken by Jesus himself and written down anytime between the mid-30s and the early 70s.

Some scholars have attempted to date Mark after AD 70 and the fall of Jerusalem by claiming that the description of the destruction of Jerusalem in Mark 13 is so precise that it requires a post–AD 70 date for the composition of the Gospel. However, whereas this may be valid with respect to the Lukan material (cf. Luke 19:41–44; 21:20–21, 24), the very opposite appears to be true with respect to Mark. If Mark were written after the destruction of Jerusalem and reflects the events surrounding this horrific event, it is difficult to understand why no reference is made to the catastrophic fire that destroyed the temple (Josephus, *J.W.* 6.2.9–6.9.4 §§164–434). Matthew and Luke also do not mention the great fire, and this may suggest that the Gospel writers were quite faithful to what Jesus said on the subject and were far less creative and free in describing Jesus's teaching on this subject than is often thought. "The lack of precision in the prophetic description of the fate of Jerusalem in Mark 13 . . . points to its having been written prior to the events which it depicts" (Kee 1977: 100–101).

The Emergence of Mark in Gospel Studies

During the first seventeen centuries of church history the Gospel of Mark was for the most part the forgotten Gospel. Matthew proved far more useful for catechetical purposes than Mark (or Luke) because of its careful arrangement of Jesus's teachings into five sections (chs. 5–7, 10, 13, 18, 23–25) that all end similarly ("And when Jesus finished these sayings" [7:28]; "And when Jesus had finished instructing his twelve disciples" [11:1]; "And when Jesus had finished these parables" [13:53]; "Now when Jesus had finished these sayings" [19:1]; and "When Jesus had finished *all* these sayings" [26:1 italics added]) and are placed alternately between six sections of narrative (chs. 1–4, 8–9, 11–12, 14–17, 19–22, and 26–28). Consequently, Mark received little attention during this period.[22] That almost all the material in Mark, except

---

22. Hengel (1985: 67) points out that among the twenty papyri of the Gospels found in Egypt dating before Constantine, eleven contain John, nine contain Matthew, four contain Luke, but only one contains Mark. The earliest known commentary on Mark, once thought to have been written by Jerome but now recognized as having been written by an unknown author, did not

1:1; 3:20–21; 4:21–25; 6:30–31; 8:22–26; 9:38–40; 12:32–34; and 14:51–52 (23 of the 666 verses in Mark), is contained in some form in Matthew,[23] along with much additional material (the "Q" material [common material found in Matthew and Luke but not in Mark] and "M" material [material found only in Matthew]), gave additional importance and prominence to Matthew. In addition, Augustine's statement also contributed to the relative insignificance of Mark during this period:

> Mark follows him [Matthew] closely, and looks like his attendant and epitomizer. For in his narrative he gives nothing in concert with John apart from the others; by himself separately, he has little to record; in conjunction with Luke, as distinguished from the rest, he has still less; but in concord with Matthew, he has a very large number of passages. Much, too, he narrates in words almost numerically and identically the same as those used by Matthew, where the agreement is either with that evangelist alone, or with him in connection with the rest. (*De consensu evangelistarum* 1.2.4)

This changed radically in the eighteenth century, when the search for the earliest sources available for "the quest of the historical Jesus" came to recognize that Mark was not the abbreviator of Matthew but rather his predecessor and source. The view that Mark was the first canonical Gospel written and served as a source for both Matthew and Luke came to be the prevailing view of nineteenth-century NT scholarship and continues to be the dominant view today.[24] The impetus to discover the Jesus of history led to an intense study of the oldest written source available for such an investigation—the Gospel of Mark. From its place of obscurity in Gospel studies for over seventeen hundred years, Mark now gained the place of prominence, and its arrangement of the Jesus traditions was seen as providing a chronological framework for understanding the life of Jesus.

---

appear until the early seventh century, and its author was aware that he was doing something fresh and new in producing this commentary (Cahill 1998: 4–6).

23. From this, Hengel (1985: 52) argues, "The best explanation of the fact that the Second Gospel lived on in the church, although Matthew had taken over about ninety per cent of the material in it, is that the work of Mark was from the beginning bound up with the authority of the name of Peter." See, however, Yarbrough 1998: 158–84, esp. 177–79.

24. Some of the main reasons for the priority of Mark (i.e., that Mark was the first Gospel written) are that it is easier to understand (1) Matthew and Luke adding material to their Gospels (the Lord's Prayer, the Beatitudes, the birth narratives, etc.) than Mark omitting this material from Matthew and/or Luke, and at the same time often making the accounts he shares with Matthew and Luke longer; (2) Matthew and Luke improving on Mark's grammar and style than Mark choosing to "worsen" the better grammar and style that he found in Matthew and/or Luke; (3) Matthew and Luke seeking to eliminate some of the harder readings in Mark that cause theological difficulties and problems than Mark choosing to add them to Matthew and/or Luke; (4) Matthew and Luke wanting to omit various Aramaic expressions found in Mark (3:17; 5:41; 7:11, 34; 14:36; 15:22, 34) than Mark choosing to add them to Matthew and/or Luke and then explain them to his readers; and (5) Matthew and Luke adding to Mark their theological emphases (the "fulfillment quotations" and the emphasis on Jesus as the Son of David in Matthew; the role of the Holy Spirit and the importance of prayer in Luke) than Mark choosing to eliminate them. See Stein 2001: 49–96.

By the end of the nineteenth century and early in the twentieth century, NT scholars saw in Mark the earliest written account of the life of Jesus dating in the late 60s,[25] but a new question came to the forefront: "What was the shape of the gospel traditions found in Mark (and also Matthew and Luke) before being written down?" After World War I, the discipline of form criticism, led by a triumvirate of German scholars (K. L. Schmidt, 1919; M. Dibelius, 1919; and R. Bultmann, 1921) and already applied to the study of the OT, now began to dominate Gospel studies. The focus now shifted from the study of the Gospels as wholes to the study of the individual units and building blocks that make up the Gospels (Stein 2001: 173–233). These blocks were investigated to learn about the Christian community during the "oral period" between the resurrection of Jesus and the writing of the Gospels. For some, this new discipline also served as a tool for studying the life and teachings of Jesus.[26] The form critics lost interest in a holistic approach to the Gospels and now considered the Gospel writers as simply collectors of tradition and editors who patched together tradition collections using scissors and paste.

It was not until the second half of the twentieth century that interest in the Gospel writers surfaced again in the rise of a new discipline—redaction criticism. Most responsible for this was again a triumvirate of German scholars (Bornkamm, 1948; Conzelmann, 1954; and W. Marxsen, 1956). This new discipline demonstrated that the Gospel writers were not bland, disinterested editors who simply collected various gospel traditions and pasted them together. They were rather evangelists who collected, arranged, edited, and shaped these traditions with specific theological purposes in mind. As a result, a great interest arose in the study of the specific theological contributions given to the gospel traditions by the individual evangelists. This was most

25. The evaluation of the historicity of the Gospel of Mark during this period depended essentially on one's presupposition as to whether history was "open" or "closed": Is history a closed continuum of time and space in which God cannot, or chooses not to, intervene and thus is closed to the supernatural? Or is God sovereign over history and not bound by the "laws of nature"?

26. In general the quest for the historical Jesus had by then been dealt several deadly blows that caused almost as much disinterest in the study of the life of Jesus in the first half of the twentieth century as there was interest in the nineteenth. There were several reasons for this: (1) A. Schweitzer's *Quest of the Historical Jesus* (1910; original German, 1906) demonstrated that the liberal Jesus of the "old quest" was a creation by liberal scholars of a Jesus made in their own image and that the real Jesus was an enigma and offense for them; (2) W. Wrede's *Messianic Secret* (1971; original German, 1901) indicated that Mark was not a simple objective, historical biography of the life of Jesus that could be used simplistically as a historical source; (3) M. Kähler's *So-Called Historical Jesus and the Historic, Biblical Christ* (1964; original German, 1892) showed that the Jesus who evoked faith and commitment over the nineteen centuries of church history was not the liberal Jesus of the "quest" but rather the Christ of faith described and proclaimed in the Gospel accounts. Additional influences that helped bring about the end of the "old quest" included W. Dilthey (1957: 5.317–38), who revealed that there was no such thing as objective, presuppositionless historiography and form criticism, which demonstrated that the gospel traditions circulated during the oral period as independent units shaped by the faith of the church did not allow the reconstruction of a chronological biography of the life of Jesus.

easily carried out with Matthew and Luke by comparing how they used their Markan source and by comparing their use of the Q material. By comparing them to Mark in a synopsis, various emphases of Matthew and Luke became quite clear, and their individual editorial contributions were then investigated throughout each Gospel. Thus a more holistic approach to Gospel studies developed that viewed the Gospels not as collections of isolated fragments of gospel traditions but rather as "the Gospel *according to* Matthew" and "the Gospel *according to* Luke."

The application of redaction criticism to the study of Mark, however, is far more complicated, for whereas we possess the main source of Matthew and Luke (the Gospel of Mark) and can reconstruct to a reasonable extent the content of their Q source, we do not possess the source(s) of Mark, and the reconstruction of their shape and form is much more hypothetical (Stein 1970; 1971; 2001: 262–72). Nevertheless, a cautious use of redaction criticism in Mark is both possible and profitable, and throughout this commentary examples of this can be found in the introductory and summary sections. Traditional redaction criticism is nevertheless not as holistic a discipline as it first seems, for it is primarily concerned not with the evangelist's theology as a whole but rather with his unique theological contribution (Stein 1969: 54). Thus the main emphases shared by Matthew, Mark, and Luke are essentially ignored.

A recent attempt to address this is found in literary and narrative criticism, where the total Gospel narrative is the focus of attention. Here great attention is given to the plot of the entire narrative, and we are introduced to such concepts as characterization, point of view, plot, setting, viewpoint, narrator, real author, implied author, real reader, implied reader, and so on. Whereas the holistic approach taken by narrative criticism to the entire narrative is commendable, its practice is often associated with assumptions that when applied to the Gospels are highly questionable. One involves the fact that the principles of narrative criticism have been obtained primarily from the study of fictional literature. Consequently, the approach often assumes that "Mark is a self-consciously crafted narrative, a fiction, resulting from literary imagination, not photographic recall" (Tolbert 1989: 30). It emphasizes far more the freedom of the author in composing the narrative than the restrictions placed upon him by history and tradition. In fiction such questions as the following are legitimate: Why does the author choose to have the main character crucified? Why does the main character rise from the dead? Why does the story choose to have a particular character (King Herod, Pilate, Caiaphas, etc.) act in a particular way? Why is a particular group portrayed in this manner? Yet in the study of Mark such questions are often out of place. It makes no sense to ask: Why does Mark have Jesus crucified at the end? Why does he have the high priests and chief priest involved in the death of Jesus? Why does he have a disciple, Judas Iscariot, betray Jesus? Why does he have Jesus rise from the dead? Such questions are illegitimate in that Mark is a "historical narrative," and Mark did not have the freedom to construct his plot and characterizations in the same way that a writer of fiction does. The historical events surrounding the life of Jesus controlled what Mark could or could not do. Even if one denies the historicity of much or all of the Gospel accounts, the fact remains that Mark was constrained by the gospel traditions he inherited and with which his readers were familiar. Thus some of the questions that one can ask about the narrative of a fictional account created by an author de novo are inappropriate when asked concerning historical narrative (Horsley 2001: 7).

A second weakness of much narrative criticism is its close association with reader-response criticism. The lasting quality of a good commentary on Mark (or on any biblical book) lies not in the meaning that a commentator chooses to read into it but in how well it enables the reader to understand the meaning of the evangelist contained in the written text he has provided. The great majority of readers seek help in a commentary on Mark for understanding the word from God that he has spoken through his servant Mark. Consequently, the present commentary is not a "reader-response" commentary revealing how I choose to read Mark. Such an approach (in the past often called "eisegesis") is rejected in favor of seeking to describe for the reader what Mark sought to convey by the words of the text he has written. The purpose of this commentary is also not primarily to investigate the life of Jesus of Nazareth, although historical issues relevant to this topic are frequently discussed in the introduction to the exegetical unit and in the comments on specific verses. The dominating purpose in each section of the Gospel is to answer the following: *I, Mark, have told you* [the unit under discussion] *because. . . .* Thus the primary purpose of this commentary is to explain not what happened in the life of Jesus or exactly what he said, but rather what Mark is seeking to teach by this event/saying that he shares with his readers (cf. Donahue and Harrington 2002: 2–3).

Since the latter part of the twentieth century, there has been a lengthy and extensive debate over the exact genre of the Gospel of Mark. Some have suggested that Mark's "Gospel" created an essentially new genre, a genre *sui generis* (Guelich 1991: 173–208). This has generally been rejected (Bryan 1993: 22–23). Others have suggested that it follows the genre of a Greek drama, in particular a Greek tragedy (Bilezikian 1977; cf. France 2002: 10–15, who describes Mark as a "Drama in Three Acts"). Yet Mark does not end as a tragedy but with the triumphant angelic message, "He has been raised, he is not here" (16:6), and it probably ended with a resurrection appearance to the disciples in Galilee (14:28; 16:7; see 16:1–8, "The Ending of Mark"). As for it being read as a drama, there are several reasons why this is unlikely. For one, the nearest analogy to reading sacred texts for the readers of Mark as Jews and God-fearers came from their experience of hearing the OT Scriptures in the synagogue services; readings of the OT in Hebrew and then Aramaic in Palestine and of the Greek Septuagint in the Diaspora were not "performances."[27] They were

---

27. "Mark's 'pre-texts' are the Jewish Scriptures" (Donahue and Harrington 2002: 16; cf. also Vines [2002: 144–64], who compares Mark with Daniel, Tobit, Judith, Susanna, etc.).

not read as dramas. Major parts of the OT were simply not appropriate for this (namely, most of the Prophets [Joshua—Kings and Isaiah—Malachi] and most of the Writings [Psalms, Job, Proverbs, Ruth, Song of Songs, Ecclesiastes, Lamentations, Esther, Daniel, Ezra, Nehemiah, Chronicles]). The reverential reading of the Scriptures in the synagogue no doubt carried over to the house church, where the letters of Paul and the Jesus traditions were also read or told with great reverence. Although Mark makes for "dramatic" reading, this is not because it is written in the genre of a Greek tragedy but because it tells the story of the most important person who ever lived—Jesus Christ, the Son of God! And it ends not in tragedy and death but in victory and resurrection. The second reason why it is improbable that Mark consciously wrote his Gospel in the form of a Greek drama or tragedy is because of the general revulsion of Jews and Christians toward the idolatry and immorality so often associated with the Greek theater.[28] It is extremely unlikely that the genre of drama, whose content was often repugnant to Christians, would have served as the model according to which Mark chose to pattern his Gospel.

The two main genre possibilities that best describe Mark are that of a biography (sometimes described as "Greco-Roman biography"; Talbert 1977; Burridge 1992; Bryan 1993: 9–64; Witherington 2001: 1–9) or as a historical narrative (A. Collins 1992: 1–38). "Ancient biography is prose narration about a person's life, presenting supposedly historical facts which are selected to reveal the character or essence of the individual, often with the purpose of affecting the behavior of the reader" (Talbert 1977: 17). Whereas historical narrative tends to focus on the actions of an individual, biography is more concerned with a person's character or essence. The earliest readers of Mark would not have concluded that this Gospel was something quite unique, a new genre. They would have seen similarities with OT accounts concerning the patriarchs, Moses,[29] Joshua, David, and so on, and they would already have been familiar with much of the content of Mark from the oral traditions that they had been taught about Jesus. What was unique about Mark was not the "form" of the Gospel but its contents concerning the unique person, teachings, and deeds of Jesus Christ, the Son of God. While not fitting the modern-day genre of biography in that it omits the first thirty-plus years of Jesus's life, it fits the general form of Greco-Roman biography of his day. It is quite clear from 1:1 that Mark involves the "good news about Jesus Christ, the Son of

28. A distinction should be made between the use of "the Greek theater" to describe an ancient architectural edifice and to describe the plays and performances that took place there. As a building the Greek theater served as a meeting place for many civil functions and public meetings (cf. Acts 19:29ff.). (The inscription on the seats of the theater at Miletus describing a certain location as the "Place of the Jews and God-fearers" may have involved their presence at various public meetings [see Ferguson 1993: 516 for an example].) It was not the building but the drama and games performed there that brought revulsion to Jews and Christians and pious pagans.

29. Cf. Kline (1975: 1–27), who refers to Exodus as the "Gospel of Moses" and argues that its influence on Mark would have been considerably greater than that of Greco-Roman biographies.

God," and that the evangelist wants his readers to wrestle with the question "Who then is this man that even the wind and the sea obey him?" (4:41). On the other hand, various accounts (the account of John the Baptist's death [6:14–29]; the arrest, trial, crucifixion, and burial of Jesus [14:43–15:47]) are in the form of a historical narrative. There is clearly an overlapping of these genres in Mark. Attempts to describe Mark as one or the other stumble over the fact that elements of both are present and intermingled without embarrassment, for the biography of Jesus is intimately interwoven in a historical narrative. As a result, it may be best to describe the genre of Mark as "a historical biography."[30]

Theological Emphases

Within Mark we encounter several theological emphases. Some of them are more important than others. What is clear from the beginning, however, is that the central and dominating theme of Mark is christological in nature. This is made clear from the start. Mark is about "the gospel concerning Jesus Christ, the Son of God" (1:1). Every account in Mark focuses the reader's attention in some way on Jesus. Even those dealing with the ministry (1:2–8) and death (6:14–29) of John the Baptist serve to help the reader understand who Jesus of Nazareth is. The account of John's ministry reveals that Jesus is greater than John the Baptist (1:7–8) and is the "Lord" (1:3) whose path this greatest of the prophets (cf. Matt. 11:7–15) came to prepare. The account of John's death serves not only as a literary time gap for the mission of the disciples (6:7–13) and their return (6:30) but also as a foreshadowing of the death of Jesus (cf. 9:13, "and they did to him whatever they wanted, just as it has been written [καθὼς γέγραπται, kathōs gegraptai] concerning him [John the Baptist]," and 14:21, "For the Son of Man goes just as it has been written [καθὼς γέγραπται, kathōs gegraptai] concerning him").

Christology

Mark's portrayal of Jesus Christ, the Son of God, is multifaceted. The following are ways in which he seeks to help his readers to understand who Jesus is:

1. *The Miracles of Jesus.* Within Mark we encounter eight healing miracles (1:29–31, 40–45; 2:1–12; 3:1–6; 5:25–34; 7:31–37; 8:22–26; 10:46–52) and a resurrection from the dead (5:21–24, 35–43). In addition we encounter several Markan summaries that refer to Jesus's healing ministry (1:34; 3:10; 6:5, 13, 54–56). Jesus's healings include fever, leprosy, paralysis, a withered hand, hemorrhage, deafness and muteness, and blindness. There are also four examples of exorcism (1:21–28; 5:1–13; 7:24–30; 9:14–29), and several references to Jesus's ministry of exorcism in various summaries and accounts (1:34, 39; 3:11, 22–30; 6:7, 13; cf. 9:38). In addition,

30. The term "historical" here is not used as a value judgment concerning the truthfulness of the Markan narrative, but simply as a shorthand term for "historical narrative biography."

we encounter five nature miracles: 4:35–41 (the stilling of a storm); 6:35–44 (the feeding of the five thousand); 6:45–52 (the walking on the sea); 8:1–9 (the feeding of the four thousand); and 11:12–14, 20–25 (the cursing of the fig tree).

2. *The Words and Actions of Jesus.* Within Jesus's teachings we encounter numerous examples of his claim to a unique authority. He claims the divine prerogative of forgiving sins (2:5–12; cf. Luke 7:36–50), that one's eternal destiny depends on following him (Mark 8:34–38; 9:37–42; 10:28–31; 12:6–12; 13:9–13), that he has authority over the Sabbath (2:23–28; 3:1–6), that he has authority to cleanse the temple (11:27–33; cf. 11:15–19; cf. also the connection of the question of Jesus's authority and the cleansing of the temple in John 2:13–22). He claims that with his coming the kingdom of God has arrived (Mark 1:14–15; 2:18–20, 21–22; 14:22–24; cf. 3:23–27) and provides a symbolic act illustrating this by appointing twelve disciples (3:13–19) to indicate that in his ministry God is bringing about the restoration of the twelve tribes of Israel. His teaching possesses a unique authority unlike that of the scribes (cf. 1:21–28); he needs no authority to support his teachings—a simple "Truly" (Ἀμήν, *Amēn*) suffices (3:28; 8:12; 9:1, 41; 10:15, 29; 11:23; 12:43; 13:30; 14:9, 18, 25, 30).

3. *The Titles of Jesus in Mark.* Within Mark numerous titles are used to describe Jesus of Nazareth (1:24; 10:47; 14:67). Those that occur most frequently are "Teacher" (4:38; 5:35; 9:17, 38; 10:17, 20, 35; 12:14, 19, 32; 13:1; 14:14)[31] and "Son of Man" (2:10, 20, 35; 8:31, 38; 9:9, 12, 31; 10:33, 45; 13:26; 14:21 [2×], 41, 62). The first title is used in Mark to describe Jesus not simply as one teacher among many but rather as the supreme and definitive teacher sent from God (1:22, 27; 6:2), the one who provides the authoritative interpretation of the Scriptures (7:6–13; 10:2–12; 12:18–27, 28–34, 35–37; 13:31). "Son of Man" serves clearly as a title in Mark and refers to Jesus in his present ministry (2:10, 28), his forthcoming passion and resurrection (8:31; 9:9, 12, 31; 10:33, 45; 14:21 [2×], 41), and his parousia, when he will come to judge the world (8:38; 13:26; 14:62). The latter role of the Son of Man clearly has Dan. 7:13 in mind. Other titles that are used in Mark to describe Jesus are "Christ" (1:1; 8:29; 9:41; 14:61; 15:32), the synonymous expressions "Son of David" (10:47, 48) and "King of the Jews" (15:2, 9, 12, 18, 26), "Prophet" (6:4, 15; 8:28), and "Lord" (1:3; 2:28; 5:19 [cf. v. 20]; 7:28; 11:3). Yet the most important christological term for Mark to describe Jesus is "Son" (13:32) and its related expressions: "Son of God" (1:1; 3:11; 15:39), "my beloved Son" (1:11), "Son of the Most High God" (5:7), "Son of the Blessed" (14:61), and "Holy One of God" (1:24). Although other titles for Jesus may be

---

31. Cf. also the Markan use of the verb "teach" to describe Jesus in 1:21–22; 2:13; 4:1–2; 6:2, 34; 8:31–32; 9:31; 12:38; cf. also 7:14–23; and the use of the titles "Rabbi" and "Rabbouni" in 9:5; 10:51; 11:21; 14:45.

used more frequently than "Son," the importance of this title is seen in how it is used in Mark. First, it is the first clear title used to describe Jesus in Mark. In the opening verse, which serves as an introduction for 1:1–13 and also for the whole book, Mark states that the gospel is about Jesus Christ (in 1:1 "Christ" serves primarily as a name rather than a title), who is the "Son of God."[32] Second, it is the way God describes Jesus at his baptism (1:11, "You are my beloved Son") and at his transfiguration (9:7, "This is my beloved Son"). Third, it is the way the demons describe Jesus in his exorcisms (1:24, "the Holy One of God"; and 5:7, "Son of the Most High God") and in the Markan summary in 3:11 ("And whenever the unclean spirits saw him, they would fall down before him and cry out, saying, 'You are the Son of God'"). The importance of the demonic confession of Jesus as the Son of God is made clear by Mark, who states in 1:34, "and he [Jesus] would not permit the demons to speak because they knew him." This indicates that the demons serve as authoritative "spokesmen" for the Markan Christology.

From the above it is clear that the Gospel of Mark is essentially a historical biography/narrative of Jesus Christ, the Son of God, that focuses on his ministry, passion, and resurrection.[33] Mark reveals this implicitly through his description of Jesus's words and deeds (cf. Luke 24:19). His words assume that he has the authority to do things no other human being can do, for he assumes even divine prerogatives (2:5–12). By his deeds he demonstrates that he is Lord and master of nature (4:35–43), the demonic world (5:1–20), disease (5:25–34), and even death (5:21–24, 35–43). Explicitly, the titles used to describe Jesus not only reveal that he is the one whom Israel has long awaited, the promised Christ/Son of David/King of the Jews, but also demonstrate his unique relationship with God. He is not just greater than Moses or Elijah (9:4–6), but he possesses a uniqueness in essence (1:11; 9:7; 12:6; 13:32; 14:61–62)—he is the Son of God! Although it would be anachronistic to read into the Gospel of Mark the later Nicene Christology and its discussions of the "substance" (*ousias*) or "nature" (*homoousion*) of Jesus, it nevertheless teaches a "more-than-human status," "a near-divinity," a Messiah "who bears the marks of divinity" (Marcus 2000: 222, 340).

The "Messianic Secret"

Several times within the Gospel of Mark, Jesus commands that knowledge of who he is, what he has done, and where he can be found be kept secret. Since Wrede (1971; German original 1901) this has been described as "the messianic secret." The clearest examples of this involve Jesus's command to his disciples

32. For a discussion of the textual problem associated with this title in 1:1, see comments on 1:1.

33. Contra Peace 1999: 110–25, who argues that "*the theme which plays the controlling part in the unfolding of the Gospel of Mark is the conversion of the Twelve*" (112, his italics).

not to reveal his messianic identity (8:29–30) and not to tell anyone concerning his transfiguration and the divine affirmation that he is God's beloved Son until after his resurrection (9:9).[34] Similarly, the demons who recognize full well that Jesus is the Son of God (1:34) are forbidden to reveal this to others (1:25; 3:11–12; cf. 5:6–7, where it is supposed that since this demonic confession takes place outside Israel, such a command is unnecessary or that, because of 1:25 and 3:11–12, Jesus's unique status is to be assumed). In numerous healing miracles we find similar commands by Jesus to tell no one (1:43–44; 5:43; 7:36; 8:26 [this seems to be implied]). During his ministry, Jesus at times also sought to conceal his presence from the public (7:24; 9:30). Often he taught his disciples privately (4:13, 34; 7:17; 9:28–29, 30–31; 10:10–11; 13:3) and concealed his teaching from others (4:10–12, 33–34).

The most famous interpretation of these materials in Mark was by Wrede. According to him, whereas some of the secrecy material found in Mark is traditional, the majority of it was created by Mark in order to explain to his readers why the life of Jesus was so "unmessianic" and that Jesus became the Messiah only after his resurrection (9:9; cf. Acts 2:36; Rom. 1:3–4; cf. Bultmann 1968: 346–47). It is evident, however, that one cannot eliminate all the messianic claims and actions found in the Gospels from the life of Jesus of Nazareth. One cannot simply deny the history of all such passages as Peter's messianic confession (8:27–29), the events of Palm Sunday (11:1–10), the cleansing of the temple (11:15–19), Jesus's trial and condemnation by the Sanhedrin (14:43–65), Jesus's condemnation to death by Pilate (15:1–39), and the superscription on the cross (15:26).[35] It is unclear how even faith in Jesus's resurrection could have created the belief that one who never made such claims now became the Messiah, for messianic belief at the time did not associate a resurrection with the Messiah's death (cf. 2 Esd. 7:28–29). (There was never any thought in the tradition that the resurrection of Lazarus made or proved that he was the Messiah.) It is furthermore evident that by the time Mark wrote his Gospel in the late 60s, the gospel traditions were and had been for a long time fully messianic in nature (Strecker 1983: 54). Consequently, there was no need for Mark to explain why the Jesus Christ of faith was so unmessianic in the gospel traditions, because the pre-Markan traditions were thoroughly messianic.

The attempt by Wrede and others to find a single, overarching theme in Mark to explain all the secrecy materials is likewise unconvincing because of the disparate nature of these materials. Whereas much of the emphasis on the messianic secret comes from the hand of Mark (1:34; 7:36a), the emphasis was already present in the pre-Markan tradition (1:44; 5:43; 8:26; cf. Räisänen 1990: 145–49, 162–66; Theissen 1991: 140–52) and stemmed from the historical

---

34. The command to silence directed to Bartimaeus, who calls Jesus "Son of David" (10:47–48), is not part of Jesus's "messianic secret," because it comes from the crowd.

35. The crucifixion of Jesus and the titulus on the cross saying "The King of the Jews" is completely unintelligible if the life of Jesus of Nazareth was entirely unmessianic.

Jesus. This refutes Wrede's explanation of why Mark emphasized the motif of the messianic secret in his Gospel. The responses to the injunction to secrecy are also quite different. The "messianic secret" (8:29–30; 9:9) is kept until the trial (14:61–64; 15:2, 9, 12, 18) and crucifixion (15:26, 32, 39), but the "miracle secret" is continually disobeyed (1:45; 7:36b). As for the demons, although commanded to be silent (1:25; 3:12), they continually confess that Jesus is the Son of God (1:24; 3:11; 5:7).

In the life of the historical Jesus, the command to secrecy makes perfectly good sense in numerous instances. The avoidance of an open proclamation of Jesus's messiahship averted an immediate confrontation with Rome, for Pilate would not tolerate a popular, charismatic teacher who drew thousands of enthusiastic followers and referred to himself as the Christ/Messiah, the Son of David, the long-awaited King of the Jews. For the masses and Rome, this would have been interpreted to mean that Jesus came to deliver the Jewish people by force from the rule and bondage of Rome. (Note that the command to keep the messianic secret in 8:30 is also found in Matt. 16:20 and Luke 9:21.) Furthermore, since Jesus's own understanding of his messiahship was so radically different from that of his audience, it was expedient to avoid the public use of such titles. The more enigmatic "Son of Man" served as a better designation, and through it he was able to teach that his ministry involved not political revolution but giving his life as a ransom for many (10:45; 14:24). The public proclamation of his miracles could also be a hindrance to his ministry, for, as 1:45 indicates, this often resulted in his having little time to teach his disciples (7:24; 9:30). Even Jesus's teaching concerning the arrival of the kingdom of God had the potential of inflaming the passion for rebellion that later erupted in the Jewish War of AD 66–70. The arrival of the kingdom of God and the call to receive it (1:15) could, in the revolutionary atmosphere of first-century Palestine, be easily misunderstood as a call to arms. Thus it was wise to teach the crowds concerning its arrival in parables (4:10–12, 33–34).

With respect to Mark, the secrecy material serves at least two important purposes. For one, it demonstrates that Jesus was not put to death because he was a political revolutionary. In his ministry, Jesus avoided the open use of politically volatile self-designations such as Christ/Messiah, Son of David, King of the Jews. Along with the emphasis on the religious leadership's desire to kill Jesus (3:6; 8:31; 9:31; 10:33–34; 12:12; 14:1–2, 10–11; etc.), this indicates that Jesus's death was due not to his having been a revolutionary but rather to the hostility of the religious leadership and above all to the will of God (8:31; 10:45; 14:12, 27, 32–42, 49). Second, the command to secrecy with respect to Jesus's miracles and exorcisms serves as a literary device to highlight the greatness and glory of Jesus and his identity. Jesus is too great to be hidden. The demons, whom Mark wants his readers to understand as authoritative "spokesmen" for his (and God's) point of view, are to be silent as to who Jesus is. But they are so commanded (1:25; 3:12) *after* they have already confessed that Jesus is the Son of God (1:24; 3:11). Those who are healed may be told not to proclaim that Jesus healed them (1:44; 6:36a), but they cannot help but do so (1:45; 7:36b). Like a city set on a hill (Matt. 5:14), the person and work of Jesus Christ, the Son of God, cannot be hidden. See 1:45.

The Disciples

With the rise of redaction criticism, there arose a view of Mark's portrayal of the disciples[36] that was both new and unique. According to this view, Mark deliberately sought in his Gospel to portray the twelve disciples in a negative light and to attack the Christology they represented (Weeden 1971; Kelber 1979; Tolbert 1989). Evidence for this was seen in the misunderstandings of the disciples (6:52; 7:18; 8:4, 17–21, 32–33; 9:5–7, 10, 32) and their failures (9:14–29, 33–34; 10:35–41; 14:32–41, 50, 66–72). (The character of Judas Iscariot [3:19; 14:10–11, 43–46] cannot be used to support a negative portrayal of the disciples because he is set in sharp contrast to the other disciples in 3:13–19.) That Jesus had twelve disciples was already known to Mark's readers, who were also aware that the disciples held a unique place in Jesus's ministry and possessed the leading position of authority in the early church. In 1 Cor. 15:3–8 Paul repeats a confessional formula that he had taught the church during his first visit (ca. AD 49–50). This formula, which he himself had received much earlier, refers to the "Twelve" and Peter having seen the risen Christ (1 Cor. 15:4). Despite the betrayal of Judas, the need to maintain the symbolism of the "Twelve" was so important that Luke portrays the replacement of Judas with Matthias as the first act of the early church (Acts 1:15–26). In addition, the acknowledgment that it was one of the twelve disciples whom Jesus personally chose that betrayed him is certainly not something the early church would have created. That Mark's readers knew of the twelve disciples and had a positive perception of them is clear (Tannehill 1977: 393; even Weeden 1971 acknowledges this). In light of this, if Mark had wanted his readers to change from a positive to a negative attitude

---

36. In Mark, "his disciples" (2:15, 16, 23; 3:7, 9; 5:31; 6:1, 29, 35, 41, 45; 7:2, 17; 8:4, 6, 10, 27 [2×], 33, 34; 9:28, 31; 10:23, 46; 11:1, 14; 12:43; 13:1; 14:12, 13, 32; 16:7), "your disciples" (2:18; 7:5; 9:18), "his own disciples" (4:34), "my disciples" (14:14), "the disciples" (8:1; 9:14; 10:10, 13, 24; 14:16), "the Twelve" (3:14, 16; 4:10; 6:7; 9:35; 10:32; 11:11; 14:10, 17, 20, 43), and "the apostles" (3:14; 6:30) are used interchangeably and refer to the same group of Jesus's followers (Meye 1968: 97–99; 173–91; contra Best 1978: 32–35). Cf. how in 6:7 "the Twelve" are sent out to preach, heal, and cast out demons in fulfillment of Jesus's calling in 3:14; and they are called "apostles" in 3:14 (there is a textual problem here) and in their return in 6:30. Shortly after their return, they are then referred to as "his disciples" in 6:35. In 9:35 "his disciples" of 9:31–34 are referred to as "the Twelve," and in 10:32 "his disciples" of 10:23–31 are again referred to as "the Twelve." Mark makes no attempt to differentiate these groups. In 14:14 the Passover/Last Supper is said to be for Jesus and "his [lit. 'my'] disciples," but in 14:17 and 20 it is "the Twelve" who participate in the meal with Jesus. After Jesus and "the Twelve" leave the upper room (14:17, 20, 26–32), he and "his disciples" arrive at Gethsemane (14:32). Cf. also how Matthew refers to the "twelve disciples" (10:1; 11:1; 20:17; cf. also 26:20; 19:23 and 28, which refer to the "disciples" judging the "twelve" tribes of Israel) and to the "twelve apostles" (10:2; cf. J. Brown 2002: 39–43). Jesus, of course, had other followers as well (cf. Mark 1:45; 2:13–14; 3:7, 34–35; 4:10, 33–34; 5:18–20, 34; 8:34–38; 9:38–41, 42; 10:29–31, 32, 46–52; 14:3–9; 15:40–41, 42–47; 16:1–8), but they are not called "disciples" in Mark.

toward the disciples, he would have had to argue forcefully and powerfully from the very beginning of his Gospel to change their present viewpoint. One would certainly expect Mark to minimize or omit such positive descriptions of the disciples as found in 1:16–20; 3:13–19; and 6:7–13, but he does not (Tannehill 1977: 394).

The earliest portrayal of the disciples in Mark, however, clearly paints them in a positive light. Jesus calls Peter and Andrew (1:16–18) and James and John (1:19–20) to follow him, and they leave their nets and family to follow him. In so describing their response, Mark sharply contrasts their actions with those of the rich young ruler, who, because of his possessions, does not follow Jesus (10:21–22). The first description of the disciples therefore reinforces the positive view of them that his readers held. The second mention of the four disciples involves the healing of Peter's mother-in-law (1:29–31). There is nothing negative about the disciples here. The third reference (1:36–38) involves Peter, as a good disciple,[37] telling Jesus of the crowds seeking him and being invited to follow Jesus as he preaches and exorcises demons throughout Galilee. All this reinforces the preunderstanding of Mark's readers that the disciples were chosen by Jesus, followed him, and were witnesses of Jesus's preaching and healing ministry. In 2:16 the disciples are again portrayed as present with Jesus and acting in 2:18–22 and 23–28 in accordance with Jesus's teachings. In 3:7 and 9 they are present with Jesus and obey his command to have a boat ready for him (cf. 4:1). In 3:13–19 the disciples are called apostles[38] and are uniquely appointed by Jesus to be his companions, recipients of his teachings, and partners in his ministry of preaching and exorcising demons. They furthermore are sharply contrasted with Judas Iscariot in 3:19. In all of this so far, Mark gives a highly positive portrayal of the disciples, confirming and supporting his readers' preunderstanding of the disciples. It is most unlikely that Mark would describe the disciples so positively at the beginning of his Gospel if he were on a vendetta against them and their views and sought to portray them as heretics and reprobates.

The first negative description of the disciples is generally seen as occurring in 4:10–13. Yet 4:10 seems to be a natural question by the disciples concerning the meaning of Jesus's parable(s). There is no stinging rebuke of the disciples by Jesus but rather an explanation that indicates their privileged position (4:11–12 and 34b; cf. 7:17; 10:10). Even 4:13b ("Do you not understand this parable? Then how will you understand all [of the other] parables?") functions less as a castigation of the disciples than as an emphasis on the importance of understanding the parable of the four soils. The second supposedly negative description of the disciples is found in 4:38–40 and functions less as a rebuke of the disciples than as a foil for the greatness of Jesus and the disciples' rightful

---

37. There is no need to interpret "pursued" (κατεδίωξεν, katediōxen; 1:36) negatively (see 1:36–37). In the present context it serves primarily to emphasize that all the people are seeking Jesus (1:37), an example of Jesus's great popularity.

38. See additional note on 3:16 concerning the textual problem involved here.

awe of "this man," who is Lord of nature. That these verses are also found in the parallels in Matt. 8:25–26 and Luke 8:26 indicates that these evangelists did not see this statement as indicating that the disciples were heretical and disqualified from any leadership role in the church. The next reference to the disciples comes in Mark 5:37–43, where, in contrast to the ridiculing crowd, Peter, James, and John are invited to witness the raising of Jairus's daughter. In 6:1 the disciples continue to follow Jesus, and in 6:7–13 they are sent out as extensions of Jesus's ministry to preach, heal, and cast out demons. Their successful mission is summarized in 6:30. In 6:37 the response of the disciples to Jesus's command to feed the five thousand would probably have been seen as natural by Mark's readers, for they knew that, unlike Jesus, the disciples could not miraculously feed five thousand people. Consequently, they would probably not have understood 6:37 as a failure of the disciples, for no rebuke of the disciples is present. The disciples' response serves rather to heighten Jesus's miracle-working power. He could do things that the disciples could not even dream of doing.

The clearest negative description of the disciples so far comes in Mark's editorial comment in 6:52: "they did not understand about the loaves, but [on the contrary] their heart had been hardened." Here the disciples are described not only as lacking understanding but also as having a hardened heart. Matthew and Luke omit this verse, but Matthew adds the following words in Matt. 14:21: "You of little faith, why did you doubt?" The disciples' hardness of heart is mentioned again in Mark 8:17 and recalls the use of this expression to describe Jesus's critics who seek to kill him (3:5–6). In 7:17 the disciples are again portrayed as seeking further instruction concerning Jesus's teachings (cf. also 10:10), and Jesus is surprised at their lack of understanding (7:18). The latter statement is also found in the parallel in Matt. 15:17, which indicates that for Matthew this was not understood as an attack on the character of the disciples that disqualified them as leaders of the church. Although Mark 8:4 is often given as another example of the disciples' lack of understanding, it functions in Mark not to portray a failure of the disciples but rather to demonstrate the greatness of Jesus in feeding the four thousand. Its presence in the parallel account in Matt. 15:33 and the lack of any rebuke of the disciples or a reference to their dullness indicate this point. On the other hand, in 8:17–21 we have a clear example of the disciples' lack of understanding, and reference is made for the second time to the disciples' hardened hearts (8:17). Although Matthew omits the reference to their hardened hearts, he retains the rest of the account portraying the failure of the disciples (16:5–12).

In the first passion prediction in Mark, we find a harsh rebuke of Peter by Jesus. After Peter's confession in 8:29 that Jesus is the Christ and Jesus's command to secrecy in 8:30, we find Jesus's first passion prediction (8:31; Matt. 16:21; Luke 9:22). In both Mark 8:32 and Matt. 16:23 we find a rejection of Jesus's teaching by Peter followed by a stern rebuke of Peter ("Get behind me, Satan . . ."). The presence of the rebuke in Mark is not due to Mark's attempt to portray Peter negatively but because it was part of the tradition. This is evident in that the rebuke of Peter in Matthew is made even more severe by the addition of "You are a stumbling block to me," and yet in Matt. 16:17–19 Jesus praises Peter's christological confession and attributes to him the leadership role in the early church. Clearly, Matthew had no desire to denigrate Peter in his Gospel, as his omission of various negative statements in Mark indicates. (Cf. his parallels to Mark 6:52; 8:17; 9:32 [note, however, how Luke, who clearly does not seek to demean the disciples, retains and heightens the disciples' lack of understanding in his parallel in 9:45], 34; and 10:35.) The disciples' lack of understanding in the transfiguration account (Mark 9:5–7) is not uniquely Markan but is traditional, as the parallels in Matt. 17:4–5 and Luke 9:33–34 indicate. Indeed, the Markan comment in 9:6 seeks to explain Peter's error in equating Jesus with Moses and Elijah in a more sympathetic way than Luke (9:33) and Matthew (17:4) do. The failure of the disciples in 9:34, while ameliorated in Matt. 18:1, is reported with a clarification in Luke 9:46 that the disciples were debating which one of them was the greatest. The reference to the disciples asking Jesus concerning his teaching on divorce (Mark 10:10; cf. Matthew's addition of a similar question in 13:36) should not be interpreted negatively but is an example of their unique and privileged position of having access to Jesus's private explanations (Mark 4:34). (Is it out of place to point out that teachers in general like to have their students interact with their teachings and ask questions?) Similarly, the amazement of the disciples in 10:24 over Jesus's teaching concerning the difficulty of a rich man entering the kingdom of God functions in Mark to emphasize the cost of discipleship and the reversal of the common belief that wealth and piety were assured signs of God's favor and blessing.

The clear misunderstanding and failure of the disciples to understand what greatness in the kingdom of God involves (10:35–41) is also found in Matt. 20:20–24. Matthew attempts to ameliorate the error by having the self-ish request come from their mother rather than from the sons of Zebedee. Nevertheless, Matthew in 20:22–24 portrays Jesus's rebuke in Mark 10:28–41 as directed at James and John. The failure of the disciples at Gethsemane is recorded in all three Synoptic Gospels, and all three rebukes of the disciples in Mark (14:37, 40, 41) are found in Matthew (26:40, 43, 45). Luke in his very abbreviated account of the incident records only the first rebuke (22:46) and in condensed form.[39] After Jesus is seized at Gethsemane, Mark mentions the disciples' flight (14:50). This is also mentioned in Matthew (26:56) but not in Luke. The last major failure of the disciples recorded in Mark involves the denial of Peter. All three denials of Peter in Mark (14:68, 70, 71) are found in Matthew (26:70, 72, 74) and Luke (22:57, 58, 60). This indicates that their presence in Mark is due less to a desire to vilify the disciples, for certainly Matthew and Luke do not seek to do so, than to the fact that the incident was part of the tradition of Jesus's passion.

39. In Greek, Luke's account contains only 88 words in comparison to Mark's 181 and Matthew's 194.

As we reflect upon the Markan portrayal of the disciples, we observe the following:

1. The preunderstanding of Mark's readers with regard to the disciples was positive, even though they knew of such things as Judas's betrayal, Peter's denial, the disciples' failure at Gethsemane, their desertion at Jesus's arrest, and so on. The portrayal of the disciples in the Jesus traditions was not a brittle, overly romantic fiction of twelve perfect disciples that could easily be shattered. On the contrary, they were well aware not only of their unique role as Jesus's twelve disciples and the leaders of the early church, but also of their failures.

2. Mark begins his Gospel with a highly positive portrayal of the disciples. This includes the calling of Peter, Andrew, James, and John, which provides a paradigm of what it means to follow Jesus (1:16–20). Their unique calling by Jesus to carry on his mission (3:13–19) and their successful carrying out of that mission (6:7–13, 30) would reinforce Mark's readers' positive preunderstanding of them. Other material in the early chapters (1:29–31; 2:16, 18–22, 23–26; 3:7–9; 4:10–12, 33–34; 5:1–43; etc.) reveals their presence with Jesus and, lacking any clear negative features, would tend to be interpreted positively by his readers. The supposed exceptions to this found in 4:13 and 38–40 (the latter of which is found in both the Matthean and Lukan parallels) are insufficient to change the positive understanding of Mark's readers into thinking that the disciples were heretics and reprobates. If Mark intended to do this, he "surely failed" (Tannehill 1977: 394).

3. Many of the passages in Mark where a severely negative portrayal is found occur in the parallels in Matthew and Luke: Mark 7:18 (cf. Matt. 15:17); 8:4 (cf. Matt. 15:33); 9:5–7 (cf. Matt. 17:4–5; Luke 9:33–34); 9:18 (cf. Matt. 17:16; Luke 9:40); 9:32 (cf. Luke 9:45); 9:33–34 (cf. Luke 9:46); 14:32–42 (cf. Matt. 26:36–46; Luke 22:39–46); 14:50 (cf. Matt. 26:46); 14:66–72 (cf. Matt. 26:69–75; Luke 22:56–62). These passages in Mark do not require us to interpret them as attempts to vilify the disciples any more than their presence in Matthew and Luke and in the gospel traditions require that they be seen in this light.

4. Whereas at times Matthew downplays the negative portrayals of the disciples found in Mark (cf. the Matthean parallels to Mark 6:52; 8:17; 9:32, 34; 10:35), at times he intensifies them (cf. Mark 4:38–40/Matt. 8:25–27; Mark 8:32–33/Matt. 16:23; Mark 9:28–29/Matt. 17:19–20; Mark 14:4/Matt. 26:8), and yet scholars agree that Matthew is not seeking in his Gospel to vilify the disciples and portray them as heretics.

5. The clearest examples of Mark's intensifying the disciples' lack of understanding are found in 6:52 (omitted by both Matthew, who adds a reference to Peter's failure in his attempt to walk on the sea, and Luke) and 8:17 (Matthew includes this in 16:9), where in addition to their lack of understanding the disciples are described as having a "hardened heart."

The latter expression is especially harsh in that it is used only one other time in Mark: to describe the hardness of heart of Jesus's opponents who seek to kill him (3:5). That 8:17 is in the form of a question and not a statement, however, tends to lessen its harshness somewhat (see 8:17–20).

6. Just as the beginning of the Gospel portrays the disciples positively, so does the present ending in 16:1–8. The angelic message in 16:7 that the disciples and Peter should go to Galilee, where they will meet the risen Christ, reinforces the prophecy that Jesus had made in 14:28, and this must be understood positively as a regathering of his scattered sheep (14:27) by the risen Christ. I will argue (see Mark 16:1–8, "The Ending of Mark") that the original ending of Mark has been lost, and that it concluded with a resurrection account in which Jesus met the disciples in Galilee. Perhaps Matt. 28:16–20 and John 21 (esp. vv. 15–19) reflect aspects of this missing account. That Mark 14:28 and 16:7 are heavily redactional in nature argues strongly that the evangelist did not want to leave his readers with a negative understanding of the disciples but sought to show how these twelve chosen men, although flawed and imperfect, were reaffirmed as Jesus's disciples and leaders of the church after the resurrection.

For the historian, the question of how the disciples could be so obtuse and dull often loses sight of the pre-Pentecost situation of the disciples. Before Easter and Pentecost, it is easy to see how the passion of Jesus would have been hard to accept. The idea that the Messiah/Christ/Lord's Anointed/Son of David would die by crucifixion was totally foreign to the messianic understanding and hopes of first-century Judaism. For the disciples, it would take the resurrection to change this and put the divine seal of approval on this and other difficult teachings of Jesus. It is therefore not at all inconceivable that the disciples could have responded and reacted in the way portrayed in Mark (France 2002: 29). That Mark at times purposely portrays the disciples in a negative light cannot be denied. Why he chose to do this is unclear. Various suggestions have been made, but none of them is convincing.[40] That the pre-Markan gospel traditions contained such material is evident from the fact that Matthew (and Luke) not only includes such material from his Markan source, but he also adds material from outside Mark that portrays a negative picture of the disciples (cf. Matt. 13:36; 14:28–31; 18:19–20; 28:7). Mark's portrayal of the disciples is in places negative. Yet it is clear that Mark portrays the disciples as chosen by Jesus, and despite their failures they are reunited with Jesus

---

40. Among the suggestions are the following: Mark sought to portray the paradoxical character of true discipleship, to encourage his readers that their failures can be forgiven and they can be restored, to indicate that discipleship involves both failure and reconciliation, to use the failure of the disciples as a foil for his readers in order to have them follow Jesus more closely, for readers to derive hope from Jesus's gracious attitude toward them despite their failures, to refute a *theios anēr* (divine man) Christology of glory or an overly realized eschatology by demonstrating that the disciples were heretics.

after the resurrection (14:28; 16:7; cf. 1 Cor. 15:3–8) to serve as his apostles. That Christians throughout the centuries have found encouragement in this is obvious, but unfortunately the reason for Mark's emphasis of this is not.

Discipleship

Mark teaches his readers about discipleship in two ways. One is by recounting Jesus's general teaching on the subject, and the other is by narrating different accounts in which Jesus invites various individuals to follow him. The clearest example of the former is found in 8:34–38. Here the general invitation to follow Jesus is extended to "anyone" (note the reference to the crowd in 8:34a) and involves three requirements: denying oneself, taking up one's cross, and following Jesus. The first involves not just denying oneself of things, such as giving up something for Lent, but denying oneself as the determiner of one's goals and purposes in life. It is to deny mastery over one's life and ambitions and place oneself under the lordship of Jesus. That this involves denying various things is evident from the examples of Jesus and of those who chose or chose not to follow him (see below), but these "things" are simply the consequences of denying oneself. Denying oneself refers to an initial act of commitment (an aorist imperative; Best 1981: 32–33). It is a negative command involving an inner decision, and it functions much like the command to repent (1:4, 15; 6:12).

Like the first command, the second, "to take up one's cross," refers to the act of becoming a Christian. Mark understands this as standing in parallel to the first command and giving a specific example of what "denying oneself" might entail. To "take up one's cross" recalls Jesus denying himself (14:36–39) and committing himself to fulfill God's will even to death (8:35; 13:12–13). For Jesus's hearers, Mark's readers, and present-day readers, the figurative nature of this expression was/is self-evident. The command does not require actual martyrdom or a particular form of martyrdom—crucifixion—for all who choose to follow Jesus. Luke makes this clear by adding "daily" to this command (9:23). The expression refers rather to a total commitment to follow Jesus that accepts even the possibility of martyrdom.

In contrast to the first and second requirements, the command "to follow Jesus" is a present imperative and refers to a continuing action. This expression is a popular one in Mark to describe being a Christian, or "follower" of Jesus (1:18; 2:14–15; 9:38; 10:21, 28, 52; 15:41; cf. also the use of a verb followed by "after me" in 1:17 and 20). It emphasizes outward, continual actions and refers to the living out of Jesus's teachings and example, such as loving God with one's entire being and loving one's neighbor as one loves oneself (12:29–31), becoming a servant/slave of others (9:35; 10:43–44), keeping the commandments (10:19), following Jesus above even one's love and commitment to family (9:29; cf. Matt. 10:37–38/Luke 14:26–27 and note that loving Jesus more than one's family is followed immediately by a reference to taking up one's cross), having faith (Mark 1:15; 2:5; 4:40; 5:36; 9:42; 11:22), praying (11:24; 14:38), confessing Jesus and not denying or being ashamed of him (8:38), and removing any stumbling block from one's life (9:43–47).

Mark also reveals what discipleship consists of through various examples. The greatest example is Jesus. What discipleship demands, Jesus himself lived out. From the beginning he was aware of his forthcoming passion (see below "The Death of Jesus Christ") and denied himself in order to fulfill God's will (14:36, 39). He modeled a life of prayer (1:35; 6:46; 14:32–39) and served as the supreme example of what it means to be a servant of all (10:43–44) by giving his life as a ransom for many (10:45). The disciples also modeled what discipleship involves by denying themselves, as witnessed by their leaving their "nets" or livelihood (1:18) and family (1:20; 10:28–30). Despite their failures, through the grace of forgiveness (14:28; 16:7), they demonstrated what it means to follow Jesus. Positive examples of the importance of faith are found throughout Mark (2:5; 5:28–34; 7:24–30; 10:52; etc.), along with negative examples (see above "The Disciples"). The story of the rich man provides an important example of what it means to deny oneself. Here Jesus points out that entering the kingdom of God involves denying oneself and that, for the rich man, this requires that he sell whatever he has, give it to the poor, and follow Jesus (10:21). Unwilling to do this, he provides a negative example of what not denying oneself involves (10:22) and its consequences (10:22–25; cf. 8:36–37).

The Death of Jesus Christ

Mark has been described as "a Passion Narrative with an extended introduction." Although this is somewhat exaggerated (chs. 1–13 are more than an "introduction"), this correctly recognizes the central role that the death of Jesus plays in the "gospel of Jesus Christ, the Son of God" (1:1). Already in the second chapter of the Gospel, the Markan Jesus is aware of his future death and refers to it in cryptic terms: "But days will come when the bridegroom will be taken away from them" (2:19–20). Mark's readers at this point know far better than the disciples that this is a reference to Jesus's crucifixion.[41] In chapter 3, after a controversy story involving Jesus healing on the Sabbath (3:1–5), Mark adds the comment that the Pharisees and Herodians took counsel to destroy Jesus (3:6); and after the selection of Judas Iscariot as one of the Twelve, Mark adds the comment, "who also betrayed him" (3:19), thus reminding and preparing his readers for Judas's role in the crucifixion of Jesus.

It is, however, after Peter's confession of Jesus as the Christ at Caesarea Philippi that Mark systematically tells his readers how Jesus at this point begins to teach the disciples of his coming death (cf. 8:31 and Matt. 16:21). Although the death of John the Baptist foreshadows the death of Jesus (Mark 6:14–29), it is at 8:31 that Jesus begins to teach the disciples of the divine necessity (note the "it is necessary" [δεῖ, *dei*] that parallels "it is written" in 9:12; 14:12, 27, 49). Jesus teaches, and Mark emphasizes, that his death is not a tragedy due to fate but is God's plan for Jesus. God is the ultimate cause of

---

41. This would be especially true if Mark was written to the Roman church, which was familiar with the Pauline message of "Christ crucified" (1 Cor. 1:23; cf. Rom. 6:6).

Jesus's death. He will smite him (14:27), and Jesus's coming is for this very purpose (10:45). Beginning with 8:31 we find Jesus repeatedly teaching the disciples about his coming death. An allusion to Jesus's crucifixion is found in 8:34, and mention of his death is made after the transfiguration in 9:9–10, but in 9:31 and 10:33–34 we find Jesus explicitly repeating a second and third time that he will soon be killed. The third reference is the most explicit of the three. In 10:45 Jesus teaches that he has been sent by God to give his life as a ransom for many. In 11:18 we find another reference to the religious leadership seeking to kill Jesus. Then, in the parable of the vineyard, Jesus talks about how the religious leadership (the tenants in charge of the vineyard) not only killed the prophets sent to them (the servants of the vineyard owner) but also would kill the owner's "beloved son" (12:6–8), and after the parable Mark adds the comment that the leaders sought to seize Jesus but could not because of the crowd (12:12).

In 14:1–2 we read of the desire of the chief priests and scribes to kill Jesus and how the presence of the people thwarted their desire. Sandwiched between this and how Judas provided the opportunity for the chief priests to do this (14:10–11) is the account of an unnamed woman in Bethany anointing Jesus (14:3–9). Jesus interprets this generous act of love as preparing him for his coming death (14:8). The account of the Last Supper not only refers to the betrayal of Jesus (14:18–21) and his death (14:22–25) but also explains that his death is sacrificial in nature, sealing a new covenant (14:24). Jesus will be smitten by God himself, for the Scripture states that this is the divine purpose of his life (14:27). At Gethsemane Jesus struggles with this divine purpose, which is described as a "cup" that he must drink (14:36a–b, 39; cf. 10:38–39). Yet he submits, for his death is the will of God (14:36c). At this point the death of Jesus is described by various narratives. The first involves his betrayal and seizure (14:43–50), and what is taking place is described as the will of God as revealed in the Scriptures (14:49). This is followed by Jesus's trial before the Sanhedrin (14:53–65) and his condemnation to death (14:64). After the account of Peter's denial (14:66–72), we read of Jesus's trial before Pilate (15:1–15), in which Jesus is sentenced to be crucified, and then of the crucifixion (15:16–41), burial (15:42–47), and resurrection (16:1–8).

It is obvious that Mark seeks to emphasize that Jesus's death is part of the divine plan for his life. It is not a tragedy, an example of how things can take an unfortunate turn or how the best laid plans can go awry. On the contrary, in the death of Jesus all things go exactly according to the divine plan. It is God's plan, foretold centuries earlier in the Scriptures, that Jesus should die in order to be a ransom for many (10:45) and by his sacrificial death seal a new covenant that God is making with his people (14:24). Thus Jesus willingly accepts the cup given to him. There is nothing new or unique in Mark's portrayal of the death of Jesus. It is traditional. That he emphasizes this in his Gospel is clear, but *why* he does so is unclear. Attempts to reconstruct the specific situation or concern that Mark sought to address is debated. There have been numerous suggestions: to combat a *theios anēr* (divine man) Christology that emphasized the glory and majesty of the earthly Son of God; to explain why Jesus Christ, the Son of God, died such a shameful death; to encourage his readers who were facing persecution and death and help them accept their situation and face it with courage by showing how Jesus faced persecution and death; to emphasize that Jesus did not die as a revolutionary but that the human cause of his death was the jealousy and animosity of the Jewish leadership; to emphasize that God's will and purpose was the ultimate cause of Jesus's death; and so on. Some of these explanations are less likely than others, but all are speculative and none can be demonstrated from the text of Mark. Fortunately, however, we can know *what* Mark is emphasizing in his Gospel, even if the exact understanding of the *why* eludes us.

An Outline of the Gospel of Mark

The following outline of the Gospel of Mark is intentionally worded to remind the reader that, according to Mark 1:1, this Gospel is about "Jesus Christ, the Son of God."

   I. Prologue: The beginning of the good news about Jesus Christ, the Son of God (1:1–13)
- A. The witness of John the Baptist to Jesus (1:1–8)
- B. The baptism of Jesus (1:9–11)
- C. The temptation of Jesus (1:12–13)

  II. Who is this Jesus? Part 1 (1:14–3:6)
- A. A summary of Jesus's message (1:14–15)
- B. Jesus calls the first disciples (1:16–20)
- C. Jesus's healing ministry in Capernaum and Galilee (1:21–45)
  1. Jesus's authority as a teacher (1:21–28)
  2. An evening in Capernaum (1:29–34)
  3. Jesus's ever-increasing fame (1:35–39)
  4. Jesus heals a leper (1:40–45)
- D. Jesus's mighty acts in Capernaum and Galilee (2:1–3:6)
  1. Jesus forgives the sins of a paralytic (2:1–12)
  2. Jesus dines with toll collectors and sinners (2:13–17)
  3. Jesus and fasting do not mix (2:18–22)
  4. Jesus and the Sabbath, part 1 (2:23–28)
  5. Jesus and the Sabbath, part 2 (3:1–6)

 III. Who is this Jesus? Part 2 (3:7–6:6a)
- A. A summary of Jesus's ministry (3:7–12)
- B. Jesus calls the twelve apostles (3:13–19)
- C. Jesus, his family, and Beelzebul (3:20–35)
- D. Jesus teaches in parables (4:1–34)
  1. Jesus's parable of the sower, seed, and soils (4:1–9)
  2. Jesus's purpose for teaching in parables (4:10–12)
  3. Jesus's interpretation of the parable of the soils (4:13–20)

I. Prologue: The Beginning of the Good News about Jesus Christ, the Son of God (1:1–13)

In the opening prologue, Mark informs his readers that the content of his Gospel is Jesus Christ, the Son of God (1:1), and 1:1–13 serves as the beginning of the good news concerning him (Matera 1988; Hooker 1991: 31–52; France 2002: 54–87; J. Edwards 2002: 23–42; Donahue and Harrington 2002: 59–70;[1] contra Keck 1965: 352–70; Guelich 1989: 3–46; Boring 1991: 53–59; Marcus 2000: 137–76). These verses serve as the lens through which all of Mark is to be viewed and prepare the reader for the story of Jesus of Nazareth found in 1:14–16:8. They provide the key for understanding this by their heavy concentration of christological materials in 1:1, 2–3, 7–8, 9–11, and 12–13.

The beginning of this good news starts with John the Baptist, who in fulfillment of the OT (1:2–3) ministered in the wilderness to prepare the people for the Coming One (1:4–8). In calling people to repent and be baptized to receive the forgiveness of their sins, he prepared them for the one greater than he who was coming and would baptize with the Holy Spirit. Mark then tells of Jesus's arrival on the scene and his baptism (1:9–11). At his baptism God bears witness that Jesus of Nazareth is the Son of God by splitting the heavens, having his Spirit descend upon him, and affirming this by a voice from heaven. Mark then concludes the "beginning" of the good news by telling of Jesus's successful resistance to the temptation of Satan (1:12–13).[2]

---

1. Kingsbury (1990: 43) argues that Jesus is pictured throughout 1:1–13 as passive rather than active. Only in 1:14ff. does he become the initiator of the action, so that 1:14–15 begins a new section.

2. For a discussion of the possible sources used by Mark in 1:1–13(15), see Lambrecht 1992.

A. The Witness of John the Baptist to Jesus (1:1–8)

Mark's opening statement in 1:1 is not a title for the entire book (contra Boring 1991: 47–53; Marcus 2000: 143, 145; Donahue and Harrington 2002: 59–60), but introduces the reader directly to the first section of his work (1:1–13; V. Taylor 1952: 151–64; W. Lane 1974: 39–62; Kuthirakkattel 1990: 4–11; Hooker 1991: 31–52; J. Edwards 2002: 23–42).[1] Indirectly, however, it also introduces the reader to the entire work as well (1:1–16:8), for by telling his readers that what follows in 1:1–13 is the "beginning" of the good news about Jesus Christ, the Son of God, he also informs them that the entire work is to be understood as the good news about Jesus Christ, the Son of God. He then points out that this good news is the fulfillment of the OT promises (1:2–3), which spoke of one who would prepare the way for the Coming One. Thereupon Mark recites the church tradition about John the Baptist (1:4–8). The lack of any explanatory notes with respect to the Baptist indicates that the intended readers of the Gospel were Christians familiar with his ministry and role. Mark tells his readers that John was divinely called to fill the role of Elijah (9:11–13) and to prepare the way for his successor and superior.

The clearest example of Mark's editorial work in this section is found in 1:1. The theology (Jesus as the "Son of God") and the vocabulary ("gospel") are clearly Markan (see 1:1), and it is difficult to imagine this verse ever existing as an independent tradition during the oral period. There is no textual evidence to support the view that 1:1 was a later scribal addition (contra Schmithals 1979: 1.73),[2] and its heavily Markan character refutes this. The association of Exod. 23:20 and Mal. 3:1 in Mark 1:2 with Isa. 40:3 in Mark 1:3 may be due to Mark, since the former two references were associated together apart from Isa. 40:3 in the Q material (Matt. 11:20/Luke 7:27), but it is possible that all three OT passages were already associated together in a pre-Markan collection of scriptural "testimonia" (Fitzmyer 1971: 62–63). The replacement of "highway of our God" (MT) and "paths of our God" (LXX) in Isa. 40:3 by "*his* paths" in 1:3 looks Markan (Gnilka 1978: 41), as does "preaching" in 1:4 and 7, for the latter is a favorite Markan term frequently found in editorial summaries and insertions (1:14, 39, 45; 3:14;

---

1. Some advocates for the view that the first section of Mark consists of 1:1–15 are Pesch 1980a: 71–73; Gnilka 1978: 39–71; Guelich 1989: 3–48; Marcus 2000: 137–76; Witherington 2001: 67–81.

2. Croy (2001) seeks to argue that the original beginning of Mark (before 1:2) was lost and that 1:1 was added later.

5:20; 6:12; 7:36; 13:10; 14:9). For the most part 1:4–8 appears to be made up of traditional material, and Mark's editorial work appears to be minimal and more stylistic in nature than theological, although it is quite possible that Mark was the first one to bring together various isolated traditions concerning John the Baptist (1:4–5, 6, and 7–8; Guelich 1989: 16–17; Marcus 1992a: 15–17). It is speculative, as all arguments from silence tend to be, to conclude that Mark deliberately omitted the material about John the Baptist found in Matt. 3:7–12/Luke 3:7–9, 15–18. There is simply no way of determining whether Mark knew this material.

Exegesis and Exposition

[1]The beginning of the gospel concerning Jesus Christ, ⌜the Son of God⌝—[2]as it is written [in the book of] Isaiah the prophet, "Behold, ⌜I shall send⌝ my messenger before you, who will prepare your way. [3]The voice of one calling out in the wilderness, 'Prepare the way of the Lord, make straight his paths.'" [4]John came ⌜baptizing⌝ in the wilderness and preaching a baptism of repentance for the forgiveness of sins. [5]And the whole Judean countryside and all the people of Jerusalem were going out to him and were being baptized by him in the Jordan River, confessing their sins. [6]And John was clothed with camel's hair and a leather belt around his waist, and was eating locusts and wild honey. [7]And he was preaching, saying, "The one stronger than me is coming after me. I am not worthy to stoop down and untie the thongs of his sandals. [8]I baptized you ⌜with⌝ water, but *he* will baptize you with the Holy Spirit."

1:1   The term "beginning" (ἀρχή, *archē*) can refer to the temporal beginning of the Gospel's appearance, to the beginning of a description of its content, or both. The temporal understanding of the term is supported by the fact that in its other instances in Mark (10:6; 13:8, 19), it has a clear, temporal meaning (cf. also its temporal quality in Luke 1:2; 1 John 1:1; Phil. 4:15). Although this verse serves as the theme verse (not the title) for the entire book—that is, this book is about the good news of Jesus Christ, the Son of God—the use of "beginning" in 1:1 signals the temporal introduction of this good news in history. The lack of the article before "beginning" does not mean that Mark is referring to "a" or "one of several" beginnings of the Gospel. In the context of Mark, the evangelist is referring to "the" beginning. For similar anarthrous introductions, compare Rev. 1:1; and in the LXX, see Isa. 1:1; Hos. 1:1, 2; Joel 1:1; Amos 1:1; Obad. 1; Nah. 1:1; Zeph. 1:1; Zech. 1:1; Mal. 1:1.

In the NT the term "gospel" (εὐαγγέλιον, *euangelion*) usually refers to the "good news" about Jesus Christ. The first recorded instance of its use as a technical term for our written "Gospels" is with Marcion in the mid-second century (Koester 1989; Gundry 1996: 321–25). The pre-Markan association of this term with the gospel message is clearly seen in Paul, who uses the noun sixty times and the verb twenty-one times in his letters (cf. 1 Cor. 15:3–8). In Mark this term is associated with the life and ministry of Jesus, and most of its occurrences, if not all, appear to be editorial insertions of the evangelist into the tradition (1:1, 14–15; 8:35; 10:29; 13:10; 14:9). Mark is furthermore the only Gospel in which "gospel" is used "absolutely," without qualification. In 1:1 the "gospel" is described as the gospel "of Jesus Christ." Although this can be understood as a subjective genitive—"the gospel that Jesus Christ preached," it is best interpreted as an objective genitive—"the gospel concerning/about Jesus Christ" (Guelich 1989: 9; Boring 1991: 51–52; France 2002: 53). This is because Mark is not primarily a collection of Jesus's teachings, such as one finds in the Q material and the Gospel of Thomas. It is rather a Gospel concerning the person, deeds, and acts of Jesus. The additional description, "Son of God," which stands in apposition to "Jesus Christ," also argues in favor of its being an objective genitive, for Mark is clearly about the Son of God. Mark is certainly not devoid of information concerning what Jesus taught (cf. 1:15; 4:1–32; 13:2–37), but it concentrates primarily on who Jesus is and what he did. That Jesus does not begin to preach until after the arrest of John the Baptist (1:14–15) indicates that the good news of 1:1, which introduces 1:2–8, must be understood as the good news concerning/about Jesus Christ found in these opening verses.

Although "Christ" (Χριστός, *Christos* [Hebrew מָשִׁיחַ, *māšîaḥ*, messiah], meaning "the anointed one") can function as a title when used with "Jesus" (cf. Acts 3:20; 5:42; 17:3), by the time Mark was written its titular nature, while never completely missing, had given way to its use as a name. Elsewhere in Mark, "Christ" is used as a title (8:29; 9:41; 12:35; 13:21; 14:61; 15:32), but in these instances it is not joined to the name "Jesus." Thus the term "Christ" in 1:1 functions primarily as a name (V. Taylor 1952: 152; Pesch 1980a: 76; contra W. Lane 1974: 44; Gundry 1993: 34) that identifies, rather than as a title that describes, as in Matt. 1:1, 18; John 1:17; 17:3. Yet even as a name, for the first-century reader its titular sense would have been more recognized than today. In Mark the title "Son of God" reveals Jesus's unique and unparalleled relationship with God. It is the favorite title of Mark for identifying Jesus (1:11, 24; 3:11 [cf. 1:34]; 5:7; 9:7; 12:6; 13:32; 14:61–62; 15:39), and when Mark was written, it conveyed to the Christian community the idea of both preexistence and deity (cf. Phil. 2:6–8; Col. 1:15–20).

The question of how 1:1 functions in Mark is debated. Does it function as a title for the entire book (cf. Hos. 1:2)? That the term "beginning" and the prophecy in 1:2–3 are associated with 1:4–8 rather than 1:4–16:8 (see 1:2–3) argues against this, however. It is best to understand 1:1 as an introduction to 1:2–8. Nevertheless, 1:1 does provide the key for understanding the whole book. This Gospel is about Jesus Christ, the Son of God. By this verse, Mark wants his readers to understand that the "good news of God" (1:14) is in reality the "good news about Jesus Christ, the Son of God."

The "gospel," beginning with the coming of John the Baptist, is the fulfill- **1:2–3** ment of the divine plan recorded in Scripture. This is also true for John, who in his prologue locates the coming of John the Baptist (1:6ff.) immediately after the cosmological setting of 1:1–5. Luke, even though he does not speak of John's mission and Jesus's baptism until 3:1ff., nevertheless understood that the beginning of the good news of Jesus begins with John. This is seen by the fact that the birth of John is foretold immediately after the Lukan prologue (1:5ff.) and that the gospel message of the early church also "begins" (ἀρξάμενος, arxamenos) with John the Baptist (Acts 1:22; 10:36–37; 13:24). To the extent that Luke is sharing with Theophilus the early Christian preaching (cf. Luke 1:1–4), the beginning of the gospel is seen as inaugurated with the coming of John the Baptist. This was probably the view of Jesus as well (cf. Matt. 11:11–15/Luke 7:24–35; 16:16).

The conjunction "as" (καθώς, kathōs) can be understood as connecting 1:2–3 with what precedes (1:1) or what follows (1:4ff.). If it goes with the latter, we should translate these verses: "John came, just as it is written in Isaiah the prophet . . . , baptizing in the wilderness and . . ." (1:4ff.). In support of this is that the Isaiah quotation was associated with the Baptist tradition before Mark wrote his Gospel (cf. Matt. 11:10/Luke 7:27), so that in the pre-Markan tradition the prophecy of 1:3 went with 1:4ff. The prophecies in 1:2 also go better with what follows than with 1:1. On the other hand, in every other instance in Mark, "as" (καθώς) does not introduce a new sentence or thought but serves rather to support what has preceded (cf. 9:13 and 14:21, where it introduces "it is written"; and 4:33; 11:6; 14:16; 15:8; 16:7). Also the "you" (lit. "your face") and "your" of 1:2 refer back to "Jesus Christ, the Son of God," in 1:1. As a result it is best to interpret Mark's use of "as" here in the same way that he uses it elsewhere, as tying 1:2–3 with what precedes in 1:1 (Guelich 1982: 6; Marcus 1992a: 17–18; Watts 2000: 55–56). To show this connection, I have joined 1:1 and 2 with a dash in the translation. This indicates that 1:1 is not to be understood as a title to the entire book (France 2002: 50–51) and that the key figure in the following OT quotations (1:2–3) is not John the Baptist (contra France 2002: 61) but Jesus (Tolbert 1989: 239–48). This is evident from the fact that after 1:10, John the Baptist does not appear elsewhere in Mark outside of 6:14–29 and in brief reminiscences in 1:14; 9:13; and 11:30 (Marcus 2000: 137).

The tradition about John the Baptist is introduced by a combination of OT quotations ("it is written") from Exod. 23:20 ("Behold, I shall send my messenger before you"), Mal. 3:1 ("who will prepare your way"), and Isa. 40:3 ("The voice of one calling out in the wilderness, 'Prepare the way of the Lord; make straight his paths'"). These quotations occupy a prominent position by their location immediately after the introductory statement in 1:1. This is the only occasion where Mark himself in his redactional work refers to the fulfillment of Scripture. Elsewhere in Mark this is found in the traditions he uses (7:6; 9:12–13; 10:4–5; 11:17; 14:21, 27). The verb "it is written" (γέγραπται, gegraptai) is an intensive perfect, emphasizing the abiding value of the divine message contained in these prophetic passages. Rather than mention all the sources from which this composite quotation comes, Mark follows the Jewish practice of naming only the most important source—Isaiah (Gundry 1967: 125;

cf. Marcus 2000: 147). The Isaiah quotation (1:3) is associated with John in all four Gospel accounts (Matt. 3:3; Luke 3:4; John 1:23), and there is no reason to deny that this came from John's own understanding of his ministry, as John 1:23 claims (cf. Luke 1:76). Exodus 23:30 and Mal. 3:1 were already associated in the Baptist traditions (the Q material—Matt. 11:7–19/Luke 7:24–35; cf. also Luke 1:17), and here Jesus himself bears witness to John. The association of Exod. 23:20 and Mal. 3:1 with Isa. 40:3 in the present account may, however, be due to the editorial work of Mark (see the introduction to this unit).

John's ministry in the wilderness is best understood as due to his desire to fulfill Isa. 40:3, even as the location of the Qumran community in the wilderness was due to their desire to fulfill this same passage (Isa. 40:3 served as their theme verse as well [1QS 8.14; cf. also 9.19–21]). A great deal of speculation has arisen over the fact that both John and the Qumran community perceived their mission as involving the fulfillment of Isa. 40:3. Was John originally a member of the Qumran community? Did his elderly parents bring him to Qumran because they were too old to raise him themselves? Did John later break with the Qumran community over how best to fulfill Isa. 40:3? Novelists spin lengthy romances from this coincidence and the fact that both were identified with "the wilderness," but we simply do not know what, if any, relationship existed between John and Qumran.[3]

Though in Exod. 23:30 "your face" refers to the people of Israel, here it refers to Jesus. Similarly, whereas in Mal. 3:1 "the way before me" (MT) or "the way before my face" (LXX) refers to God, here it refers to Jesus and his ministry—"your way." For Mark, Jesus's mission involves the fulfillment of the divine plan for history. The quotation from Mal. 3:1 does not follow exactly either the MT or the LXX. The same is true also in the other places where this quotation is found (Matt. 11:10; Luke 7:27; cf. also 1:17). This suggests that this prophecy had already taken on its own unique form and shape during the oral period. Since Mark 1:2 is to be interpreted in light of 1:1, the emphasis does not fall on "my messenger . . . , who will prepare your way," that is, on John the Baptist. Rather, the emphasis falls on "before you" (lit. "your face") and "your way," that is, on Jesus Christ, the Son of God, and what John says about him. "You" and "your" are not to be understood as examples of substitution for the divine name (contra Snodgrass 1980: 34). The Lord's coming in these OT prophecies is seen by Mark as the coming of the Lord Jesus Christ, the Son of God. This is also evident from the fact that whereas Isa. 40:3 in the MT reads "highway for our God" and the LXX reads "the paths of our God," the tradition (or Mark) changed this to "*his* paths," because these passages were understood as referring to Jesus. John was calling the people to "Prepare ['*you*'—plural] the way of the Lord, make straight ['*you*'—plural] his paths," as the two plural verbs indicate. In Isaiah "the way of the Lord" refers to "the way of the Lord," that is, "YHWH," but in Mark it refers to

---

3. For a succinct and judicious discussion, see VanderKam 1994: 168–70; for a more detailed one, see Badia 1980.

the "Lord" Jesus (cf. 2:28; 5:19–20; 7:28; 11:3; 13:35; and esp. 12:35–37). The Isaiah quotation is used by Mark not primarily to describe John the Baptist but rather to describe Jesus. John, this famous prophet as foretold in the OT, was a preparatory agent for the coming of the Lord Jesus Christ. Thus the emphasis in the quotation falls not on "the *voice* of one crying in the wilderness" or the *people* who are to prepare and make the way ready but on "the *Lord*" and "*his* way" and "*his* paths." It is not surprising, therefore, that the followers of Jesus became known as the followers of "the way" (Acts 9:2; 19:9, 23; 22:4; 24:14, 22; cf. also 13:10; 16:17; 18:25–26).

1:4–6 The verb ἐγένετο (*egeneto*), which I here translate "came," is frequently used to introduce a narrative in Mark (cf. 1:9; 2:23; 4:10; 11:19; 15:23; cf. also 1:11; 2:27; 4:4, 22, 39; 6:14; 9:3, 7 [2×], 26.) The matter-of-fact way in which John the Baptist is introduced assumes that Mark's readers already knew who he was. If the reader had never heard of him, one might expect something like "There was a man sent from God, whose name was John" (John 1:6). The importance of John for Mark does not lie in what he did in the history of first-century Judaism but that he points to Jesus and sheds light on who he is. Mark starts his Gospel with the story of John because he proclaimed the Coming One to whom the prophets pointed.

That the tradition refers to John as "baptizing" (βαπτίζων, *baptizōn*) indicates that his ministry was intimately associated with this rite and with explaining why his hearers should be baptized. If the omission of the definite article (ὁ, *ho*) is to be followed (see the additional note on 1:4), Mark ties these two activities closely together—John was baptizing and preaching (κηρύσσων, *kēryssōn*). With the discovery of the Dead Sea Scrolls, the question of precedents for John's baptism came once again to the forefront of discussion. Lustrations, or ceremonial washings, are found in Judaism (Lev. 13–17; Num. 19), the mystery religions, and numerous other religions. The most likely "source" for John's baptism, however, is either Jewish proselyte baptism or the "baptism" of the Qumran community. With respect to the former, gentile proselytes to Judaism experienced, along with circumcision and a ritual sacrifice, a baptism as well. Unfortunately, it is impossible to date Jewish proselyte baptism with certainty (see McKnight 1991: 78–89; Hooker 1991: 39–43), and such baptisms were apparently self-administered (Hartman 1997: 5–8, 12n8, 31–32). Furthermore, Jewish proselyte baptism involved only gentiles, whereas John's baptism involved primarily Jews. As for the "baptisms" of Qumran, although intimately associated with repentance (1QS 3.4–5, 9; 5.13–14), the Qumran ritual involved repeated lustrations rather than a once-for-all initiation rite as was John's (and Christian) baptism. As a result the origin of John's baptism remains uncertain.

The uniqueness of John's baptism does not lie in it being an initiatory rite. Almost every religion has some sort of an initiation rite. Nor does its uniqueness lie in its form: immersion in water. It does not lie in its being administered by someone else (cf. 1:5). In Mark's understanding, the uniqueness of John's baptism did not lie in the fact that, accompanied with repentance, it resulted in the forgiveness of sins. Its uniqueness was seen in its purpose—to "prepare the way of the Lord." John's ministry was not simply a revival movement in Israel turning people back to God with forgiveness as its goal. Rather, it was to prepare an eschatological community for the Coming One and the arrival of the kingdom of God. (For examples of how John prepared the way, see Luke 7:29–30 and John 1:29–51.)

The expression "in the wilderness" (ἐν τῇ ἐρήμῳ, *en tē erēmō*) appears to have been part of the tradition that Mark inherited concerning John the Baptist (cf. John 1:23; Luke 1:80; 7:24–28). It was associated with John, in part at least, because he preached and baptized in the wilderness or desert of Judea. The presence of the expression in Mark 1:4, however, is not for the purpose of tying John with "the eschatological role of the 'wilderness' for the prophets" or to express "the eschatological hope of the Exodus typology" or to recount that the wilderness was "the place where God would once again act to deliver the people" (Guelich 1989: 18; cf. Mauser 1963: 46–52; J. Edwards 2002: 29). For Mark's readers, the "wilderness" of 1:4 would bring to mind not the OT themes of hope and new beginnings (France 2002: 57) but the "wilderness" just referred to in 1:3, the wilderness of Isa. 40:3 (Marxsen 1969: 37). As a result the expression functions not so much as a designation of a specific geographical location but as a means of identifying John the Baptist. It indicates that John the Baptist was the OT "wilderness" messenger referred to in 1:2–3, the prophet who Isaiah said would come and prepare the way for the Coming One. The reader therefore should pay special attention to what John says in 1:7–8 about Jesus. Unlike Matt. 3:1 ("the wilderness of Judea") and Luke 3:2 ("in the wilderness . . . [and] all the region around the Jordan"), where this expression is qualified and functions as a geographical designation, Mark does not qualify the expression. Its appearance after the Isaiah prophecy, rather than before it as in Matthew and Luke, reveals that Mark wants his readers to associate the wilderness of 1:4 with that of Isaiah's prophecy in 1:3. John is the prophet who Isaiah said would appear in the wilderness, wherever that wilderness might be located.

The content of John's "preaching" is described in 1:4 as "a repentance baptism for the forgiveness of sins," but in 1:7–8 its content is christological in nature. Rather than seeing these as two unrelated or contradictory messages, we should understand John as preaching a repentance baptism for the forgiveness of sins (1:4) to prepare people for the "Stronger One" who was about to come (1:7–8). Thus repentance and its consequences are urged by John not because this is what God has always demanded but because of the christological and eschatological events that are taking place. Because "he is coming" (1:7) and brings with him the kingdom of God (1:15), people need to repent. The genitive "of" in the expression "baptism of repentance" (βάπτισμα μετανοίας, *baptisma metanoias*) is best understood as a genitive of description and translated "repentance baptism" (Donahue and Harrington 2002: 62). It is not an objective genitive ("a baptism for repentance") or a genitive of source ("a baptism arising out of repentance").

The etymological meaning of the Greek word for "repentance" involves a change of mind and refers to the human dimension of conversion. This human dimension involves repentance and faith (1:15), whereas the divine dimension involves regeneration by the Holy Spirit. Mark would no doubt have agreed with Josephus that John's message of repentance was to result in righteous living, practicing justice toward one's neighbor, and a life of true piety before God (Josephus, *Ant.* 18.5.2 §117). The intimate connection of baptism with repentance (cf. their association in 1QS 3.4–5, 9; 5.13–14) indicates that this baptism was not perceived as an isolated ritual. For John, and for the later Christian community, repentance and baptism were integrally related. One was inconceivable without the other. True repentance required being baptized, but a baptism apart from repentance was worthless. Without repentance, baptism was a futile immersing with water (cf. 1QS 3.14–15). On the other hand, repentance apart from baptism was unthinkable, for John did not allow such a possibility. The two were indivisible.[4] John's baptism was not sacramental in the sense that by itself (*ex opere operato*) it brought about the forgiveness of sins. However, in association with repentance and, by implication, faith, the experience of John's baptism resulted in the forgiveness of sins.[5] Although the mode of John's baptism is not specified, the terms used to describe Jesus's baptism (1:9–10)—"into [εἰς, *eis*] the Jordan" and "coming out [ἀναβαίνων, *anabainōn*] of the water" and the root meaning of "baptize" (βαπτίζω, *baptizō*) being to dip or immerse—strongly suggest immersion.[6]

Mark describes "the whole Judean countryside and all the people of Jerusalem" going out to hear John and being baptized by him (1:5). The verb "were going out" (ἐξεπορεύετο, *exeporeueto*) is singular even though it is followed by a compound subject, because in Greek a verb followed by a compound subject usually takes the number of the first of the two subjects, and "countryside" is singular (see 1:36–37). The compound subject appears in the Greek text as a chiasmus:

A all (πᾶσα, *pasa*)
   B the Judean countryside
   B′ and the people of Jerusalem
A′ all (πάντες, *pantes*)

4. Marcus (2000: 156) argues that the forgiveness of sins associated with John's baptism refers to the forgiveness of sins in the future eschaton. However, Jesus's followers were taught to pray, "Forgive us our sins, for we ourselves forgive everyone" (Luke 11:4), and the early church taught that baptism was associated with repentance and faith and resulted in both the forgiveness of sins and the reception of the gift of the Holy Spirit (Acts 2:38; cf. 11:16–18). Such prayers as found in Ps. 51:1–14 and promises as found in 1 John 1:9 were understood to bring immediate forgiveness and cleansing.

5. For the association of repentance and the forgiveness of sins, see Luke 24:47; Acts 2:38; 5:31; cf. also 10:43 and 11:18. For additional references to baptism and the forgiveness of sins, cf. Matt. 26:28; Acts 2:38; 13:38; 26:14; Col. 1:14; Stein 2006.

6. For Christian baptism, the symbolism of being buried and raised, associated with baptism in Rom. 6:3–5, also suggests immersion.

This verse is an example of overstatement, but it effectively indicates the great impact that John had on the people of Israel. The greatness of John, witnessed to independently by Josephus (*Ant.* 18.5.2 §§116–19), has christological significance, for although John is the greatest of the prophets (cf. Matt. 11:7–15), Jesus is greater still. Although all the people of Jerusalem and Judea come out to see John, a greater multitude comes out to see Jesus, not only from Judea and Jerusalem, but also from Galilee, from Idumea, from the other side of the Jordan, and even from Tyre and Sidon (3:7–8). (Cf. how in 5:3–5 Mark heightens the power of the demon for the same purpose. If this demon was great and powerful, how much greater and more powerful must Jesus be in exercising authority over him!)

"By him" indicates that John's baptism was not self-administered as in Jewish proselyte baptism but that John was the baptizer (1:4). The passive "were baptized" supports this understanding, as does John's name—the Baptist. While baptism functioned as a visible indication of the inward act of repentance, "confessing their sins" (1:5) functioned as a verbal one (cf. Acts 19:18; 1 John 1:9; Matt. 10:32/Luke 12:8; Rom. 10:9–10). The site for John's ministry was "the Jordan River." Since this is part of the "wilderness" (Mark 1:4; cf. Josephus, *J.W.* 3.10.7 §515) and since water was necessary for baptism, the area around the lower part of the Jordan River is a likely location for John's baptism. The traditional site, Wadi el-Kilt, is situated just south of Jericho. It would be incorrect to limit John's baptismal activity to any one location, however, for the Gospel writers claim a much larger area: "all the region around the Jordan" (Luke 3:3); "in Bethany beyond the Jordan" (John 1:28); "at Aenon near Salim" (John 3:23). Reference to the Judean countryside and the people of Jerusalem coming to John's baptism suggests that the main location of John's ministry was probably the southern part of the Jordan River valley near the Dead Sea (France 2002: 65; contra Riesner 1987: 29–63, who locates it further north at Batanea [the Bethany of John 1:28], east of the Sea of Galilee). Mark, however, has little interest in the exact geographical location(s) of John's ministry. For him, it was what John did and represented that was important, not where. (Cf. the inexact location he gives for the place of the transfiguration in 9:2.)

In 1:6 Mark describes the dress of John the Baptist because of its symbolism—"John was clothed with camel's hair and a leather belt around his waist." This description of John's mode of dress (cf. Matt. 3:4) was part of the pre-Markan tradition (cf. Matt. 11:8/Luke 7:25). The lack of any special explanation about John's dress indicates that Mark (and Matthew) assumed their readers would have understood its significance. The reference to "camel's hair" might have caused Mark's readers to identify John as a prophet (Zech. 13:4), but the reference to his wearing a leather belt around his waist implied far more. This description of John in Mark 1:6b is almost identical with that of Elijah in 2 Kings 1:8. In light of Malachi's prophecy concerning the future return of Elijah (4:5), readers would have seen a connection between John's coming and the prophecy concerning the return of

Elijah (cf. Luke 1:17; John 1:21, 25). Later Mark makes this connection even more explicit (9:11–13).

At this point several questions arise concerning this description that are historical and interpretive in nature. One involves whether John actually wore such clothing or whether this was a later creation of the church read back into the life of John to have him fulfill the Malachi prophecy. There is no evidence, however, that first-century Judaism believed that Elijah would serve as a precursor for the Messiah. The first clear reference to this belief in Judaism is apparently found in Justin Martyr, *Dial.* 8.4 and 49.1. Since this tradition concerning John's clothing is found not just in the present passage but in the Q material as well (Matt. 11:8/Luke 7:25; cf. also Mark 6:15 and John 1:21, where John is associated with Elijah), there is no reason to doubt the accuracy of this description of John's attire. Another question is whether John consciously dressed in this manner because he believed that he was called to fulfill Mal. 4:5. It would have been most unusual for John to dress this way and not to realize how his audience would have interpreted this. Camel's hair and a leather belt were not normal wilderness wear or standard nomadic attire. Mark and the tradition would have had little interest in pointing out that John wore normal wilderness attire during his ministry. Nor was this the daily attire prophets always wore (despite Zech. 13:4), for there was no standard prophetic dress code. What John's clothing represented was clear: John came dressed like the prophet Elijah (cf. 2 Kings 1:8). Thus it appears reasonably certain that John purposely dressed in this unique manner, and it is probable that he consciously did so to fulfill Mal. 4:5 (Öhler 1999: 470–73). If the Qumran community saw itself as fulfilling the role of the servant of Isa. 40:3, there is no reason why John could not have seen himself as called to fulfill the same prophecy as well as the prophecy of Mal. 4:5. Still another question that can be raised is whether Jesus saw John as fulfilling this role. The evidence found in Mark 9:11–13 (cf. the parallel in Matt. 17:10–13 and Luke 7:24–30/Matt. 11:7–15) assumes that he did. That several of Jesus's disciples were originally disciples of John (John 1:35–51) and had a major role in passing down the Christian tradition (Luke 1:2) favors its historicity.

How Mark understood 1:6 is clear. In light of 9:11–13, this verse can only be understood as teaching that John the Baptist was the fulfillment of Mal. 4:5 and that he taught that Jesus was the Coming One, the Christ, the Son of God. The other Gospel writers also wanted their readers to understand the ministry of John this way. Although John may personally have had doubts at one time as to whether Jesus was indeed the Coming One (Matt. 11:2–6/Luke 7:18–23), the Gospel writers saw this as temporary and that he was satisfied by Jesus's reply to his question. Whatever conclusions one arrives at with respect to John's personal view of Jesus of Nazareth, Matthew and Luke did not see this passage as conflicting with the present text in which John points to Jesus as the Christ. If they thought that Matt. 11:2–6/Luke 7:18–23 conflicted with our text, they would simply have omitted it from their Gospels.

John is also described as feeding on "locusts" (ἀκρίδας, *akridas*) and "wild honey" (μέλι ἄγριον, *meli agrion*). Locusts (the only insect permitted as food, Lev. 11:20–23; CD 12.14–15) and honey from wild bees were typical of the food found in the wilderness (cf. Lev. 11:21–23; 2 Macc. 5:27). This was not all that John ate, but it was what the tradition and Mark wanted to emphasize. John's eating habits are referred to in several places in the tradition. Like a nazirite (Num. 6:2–21; Judg. 13:2–7), he drank no wine (Luke 1:15; 7:33), for he was set aside by God for a holy task, and his ascetic eating habits were well known (Luke 7:33/Matt. 11:18). The nature of his eating is emphasized by Mark to show that John ministered in the "wilderness," where he preached in fulfillment of Isa. 40:3.[7]

1:7–8

John's preaching has already been referred to in 1:4, but now the reason for John's repentance baptism for the forgiveness of sins is described. Whether Mark was aware of John's ethical teachings found in Luke 3:7–9/Matt. 3:7–10 is uncertain, but Mark wanted his readers to know that the essence of John's preaching was the announcement of the coming of Jesus Christ, the Son of God. To record at this point the content of John's ethical teaching would have detracted from the christological focus and purpose of Mark's message. The heart of his preaching was, "He is coming." The emphatic position of this futuristic present (ἔρχεται, *erchetai*) should be noted. Placed first in the sentence, it underscores the urgency of John's message. "He is coming. . . . Therefore repent and be baptized!"

The first description of the Coming One is that he is "stronger" than John the Baptist. The term "Stronger One" (ὁ ἰσχυρότερος, *ho ischyroteros*) does not appear to have been a technical term for the Messiah, but in the context of 1:1–8 it is clear to whom John was referring. The Stronger One is Jesus Christ, the Son of God (1:1), the Lord (1:2), for whom John was preparing the way (1:3; cf. 3:27). On the historical level the question can be raised, however, as to whom John expected the Stronger One to be. Several suggestions have been made: (1) God,[8] (2) an/the eschatological prophet (Deut. 18:15), (3) the Messiah, (4) the Son of Man, (5) some unknown prophet. The first suggestion encounters the problem that to describe God as one "stronger" than John is meaningless, and untying "God's" sandal would be a most unusual metaphor for describing this relationship (Donahue and Harrington 2002: 63). Furthermore, John's later question to Jesus, "Are you the Coming One or are we awaiting another?" (cf. Matt. 11:3/Luke 7:19), indicates that he had in mind a human rather than a divine figure as filling this role. The title "Son of Man" was almost certainly not a popular "messianic" title in first-century Judaism

---

7. Cf. Kelhoffer (2005: 121–23, 132–33), who sees 1:6 as "confirm[ing] the citation of 'Isaiah' in Mark 1:2–3."

8. So Tolbert (1989: 239–48), who, however, is forced to argue that the messenger sent to proclaim the way of the Lord, i.e., God, is Jesus and not John the Baptist. Clearly the present state of the tradition does not support such a view. The understanding of Mark (and the other Gospel writers) is clear: the Stronger One is Jesus.

(Stein 1994b: 136–46), so that it seems unlikely that John was referring to this enigmatic figure. Finally, the idea that John was referring to the ambiguous eschatological prophet of Deut. 18:15 or some even more nebulous prophet also seems unlikely. If John did refer to a Stronger One coming, his hearers would have understood this as a reference to the coming of the Messiah. For Mark and the Christian community, there would have been no question that John was referring to Jesus (the) Christ. As to the "stronger" nature of the Coming One, for Mark this lay not in his possessing greater political, economic, or military authority or power but in his having a greater divine authority, as manifested in his exorcisms (3:22–27; 9:14–29), healings (6:53–56), and miracles (4:35–5:43; 6:45–52; cf. John 10:41) and in the greater role he would play in God's plan of redemption for the world (Mark 10:45; 14:22–24). A number of scholars have attempted to interpret "after me" (ὀπίσω μου, opisō mou) in 1:7 as a technical term for being a disciple (cf. 1:17, 20; 8:33, 34; 13:16), hence that John was saying that the Stronger One was a disciple of his. This, however, confuses the present meaning, which for Mark is clearly temporal ("in time after me"), with what John himself supposedly meant by the phrase. For Mark, Jesus clearly comes after John in time ("After John was arrested, Jesus came into Galilee preaching . . ."; 1:14; France 2002: 70–71). Furthermore, there is no concrete historical evidence that Jesus of Nazareth was ever a disciple of John (contra Meier 1994: 1.116–30), and "the Marcan story line is constructed precisely to exclude any time when Jesus might have stayed in John's circle of disciples" (Meier 1994: 1.118).

The second description of the Coming One found in John's preaching is that John was not worthy to untie "the straps of his sandals." Such a task was seen as extremely demeaning (b. Ketub. 96a: "All manner of service that a slave must render to his master a student must render to his teacher, except that of taking off [lit. 'loosing'] his shoe"; cf. also b. Qidd. 22b; Sifre on Num. 21:41). Even though John saw himself as the prophet sent by God to prepare the way, he was not worthy to perform this menial act, which even a Hebrew slave was at times exempt from doing (Mek. on Exod. 21:2). In Mark 1:8 John describes his mission as follows: "I baptized you with water, but he will baptize you with the Holy Spirit." The third description of the Coming One involves the greater baptism that he would bring. The emphatic nature of this comparison is seen in the unnecessary use of the Greek pronouns ἐγώ (egō, I) and αὐτός (autos, he). Since John, Jesus (John 3:22; 4:1–2), and the early church all practiced a water baptism, it would be an error to think that Mark intended his readers to interpret the verb "baptize" in two very different ways—the first literally (for John's baptism) and the second figuratively (for Jesus's baptism). No doubt Mark intended that his readers should interpret John's words in light of their Christian baptism. The difference between the baptism of Jesus and that of John did not involve the form of baptism (immersion) or the medium of baptism (water), but the benefit associated with it. Both practiced an immersion in water associated with repentance (1:4, 15). Both associated baptism with the forgiveness of sins (Acts 2:38; 10:43, 47).

John, however, was pointing forward to the day when the Stronger One would bring with him the arrival of the new age and the Spirit as the guarantee of the kingdom of God (2 Cor. 1:22; 5:5; Eph. 1:14). The chiastic form of 1:7–8 should be noticed:

A he, the one stronger (1:7)
  B I (1:7)
  B′ I (1:8)
A′ he (1:8)

Mark portrays John the Baptist as being part of the old age and covenant. Like Moses, he prepared the people for the coming of the kingdom of God but was not himself able to enter the "promised land" (Deut. 34). The Stronger One, coming after John, would bring the kingdom of God (Mark 1:14–15) and the gift of the Spirit (Luke 24:49; Acts 1:4–5, 8; 2:1ff.; John 7:39; 14:16–17, 25–26; 16:13–14). Mark's readers were undoubtedly familiar with the promise of the Spirit's coming since this was *the* mark of being a Christian (Acts 11:15–18; 15:7–11; 19:2; Gal. 3:2–5). The expression "the baptism of the Spirit" occurs seven times in the NT (Matt. 3:11; Mark 1:8; Luke 3:16; John 1:33; Acts 1:5; 11:16; 1 Cor. 12:13). In all but the last instance, there is an explicit comparison between what the baptism of John accomplished and what the baptism of Jesus (i.e., Christian baptism) would accomplish. The universality of this experience for each Christian is seen clearly in the comparison—"I, John, do this [a baptism of repentance] for all my disciples; he, the Stronger One, will do that [a baptism of the Holy Spirit] for all [not some] of his disciples"; and Paul in 1 Cor. 12:13 explicitly states that all Christians have been "baptized by the Spirit." The unique blessing of the Spirit, promised by the prophets (Isa. 32:15; 44:3; Ezek. 36:26–27; 39:29; Joel 2:28–32; cf. Acts 2:17–21) as the mark of the new age, would be brought by the Stronger One to all his followers. The "baptism of the Spirit" therefore cannot be interpreted as referring to a second stage in the Christian life experienced by a minority of Jesus's followers.

Mark does not record the arrival of the Spirit in fulfillment of 1:8, for this took place after the events recorded in his Gospel. Whether he knew of the events surrounding the day of Pentecost depends on several factors: (1) the historicity of the event recorded in Acts 2; (2) whether the author of this Gospel was the John Mark of Acts 12:12; and related to this, (3) whether this Mark was associated with the missions of Paul, Barnabas, and later Peter. If any of these is likely, then Mark and his readers would have known how the prophecy recorded in this verse was fulfilled.

Summary

The opening eight verses in Mark provide parameters by which Mark intends his readers to interpret his work. Everything in this section is meant to describe the beginning of the good news about Jesus Christ, the Son of God. These verses are therefore not about John the Baptist. He is not the focal point of this section of Mark. These verses are rather about Jesus Christ, the Son of God, and how the ministry of John the Baptist sheds light on Jesus. As the story unfolds, this will be demonstrated by various confessions from God (1:11; 9:7), the demons (1:24; 3:11; 5:7), the disciples (8:27), Jesus himself (12:6; 13:32; 14:62), and a Roman centurion (15:39), and by the reaction of the multitudes who witness his healings and exorcisms, his miracles and wonders.

This passage also reveals that what Jesus did and what happened to him all took place "as it is written" (1:2). The emphasis on the fulfillment of Scripture in the coming of Jesus underscores that the new covenant (14:24) is not a rejection of the old covenant but its culmination. While the immediate fulfillment of this prophecy involves how John the Baptist's coming and announcement concerning Jesus fulfill the Scriptures in 1:2–3 (and thus God's plan), so also the rest of what Jesus does and what happens to him must be understood as occurring in accordance with the divine plan. This includes the necessity of his death and resurrection (8:31; 9:31; 10:31, 45; 14:21, 49; cf. Acts 2:23).

Additional Notes

1:1. "Son of God" is not found in ℵ* Θ Origen and several lesser witnesses. The strong support of such witnesses as ℵ¹ B D W f¹ f¹³ and the early church fathers argues for its authenticity. The portrayal of Jesus as the Son of God is a strong Markan theological emphasis (1:11; cf. 1:34 with 3:11; 5:7; 9:7; 14:61; 15:39; cf. also 12:6 and 13:32) and argues for its authenticity. It appears less likely that a scribe added "Son of God" to the end of 1:1 because he knew that this was a strong Markan redactional emphasis (contra Head 1991: 621–29; Marcus 2000: 146–47).

1:2. The present tense ἀποστέλλω (I am sending) functions as a futuristic present.

1:4. Several important MSS have the article before this participle (ℵ and B being the most weighty witnesses). If the article is read, then the participle "baptizing" (βαπτίζων) functions as a title—John the Baptizer. Although this would be somewhat unusual since the Synoptic Gospels tend to use the name "Baptist" (Βαπτιστής) for this purpose (6:25; 8:28; Matt. 3:1; 11:11, 12; 14:2, 8; 16:14; 17:13; Luke 7:20, 33; 9:19), Mark does use the participle in this manner in 6:14 and 24. (There are variants in the textual tradition of these verses in which the noun rather than the participle appears.) There are two internal arguments against seeing the article as part of the original text. First, it appears less likely that a scribe would have omitted the article than that he would have added it. Second, the presence in the sentence of "and" (καί), which has strong textual support, argues that the participles "baptizing" and "preaching" stand in parallel (Metzger 1971: 73). To make the first a nominal participle or name and the second a verbal participle connected by "and" would be most confusing. They are best understood in the following manner: ". . . baptizing . . . and preaching. . . ." Without the article the participles "baptizing" and "preaching" function as a periphrasis with the verb ἐγένετο. (Cf. the periphrasis using ἐγένετο in 9:7 and the double periphrasis ["clothed" and "eating"] with the verb "to be" in 1:6; cf. also 2:6; 5:5; and 14:54. For further examples of this construction, see BDF §180; cf. also V. Taylor 1952: 154; Pryke 1978: 103–5.) Other examples of periphrasis in Mark are found in 1:6, 13, 22, 33; 2:6, 18; 4:38; 5:5, 11,

41; 6:52; 9:4; 10:22, 32 (2×); 14:4, 40, 49; 15:7, 22, 26, 34, 40, 43, 46. It seems best, therefore, to view the article as a scribal addition (Marcus 2000: 150; contra V. Taylor 1952: 154; Guelich 1989: 16; Hooker 1991: 36–37).

1:8. Numerous MSS (A D W f¹ f¹³ it) add "in" (ἐν), but it is best to follow its omission, as in ℵ B Δ vg, since it is more likely that a scribe would have added ἐν to balance the ἐν before the "Holy Spirit."

B. The Baptism of Jesus (1:9–11)

Having introduced the forerunner of the Coming One, Mark now directs his readers' attention to the one John proclaimed. It is therefore not surprising that "after John" (1:7, lit. "after me") we read that "in those days Jesus came" (1:9). After telling how John spoke of the Stronger One "coming" and who would bring the Spirit, Mark now tells of the coming of Jesus of Nazareth (1:9) and his baptism at which the Anointed One (the Christ/Messiah) is anointed by the Spirit (1:10). It is likely that the tradition of the coming of John was closely associated with the tradition of Jesus's baptism, so that it was natural for Mark to place them next to each other. Unlike Matthew (1–2) and Luke (1–2), where we first encounter Jesus in the birth narratives, Mark contains no birth narrative. Whether he knew of such birth accounts and chose to omit them is impossible to determine. What we do know is that in Mark the traditions of John the Baptist and Jesus's baptism by John are combined in a way that helps introduce the good news of Jesus Christ, the Son of God (1:1–13), and that in the present account we have the crowning piece of Mark's "beginning" of the good news.

The material found in 1:9–11 is traditional. Although the wording (esp. in 1:9) is Markan, its content was part of the Jesus traditions inherited by the evangelist. Along with Jesus's baptism, the descent of the Spirit and the voice from heaven were also part of the pre-Markan material (cf. Matt. 3:17; Luke 3:22; and John 1:33–34). Whether 1:9–11 was associated with 1:2–8 before Mark's Gospel or whether Mark joined two separate traditions (Pesch 1980a: 89; Guelich 1989: 30) is uncertain. The present account consists of two parts: an introductory summary (1:9) and a twofold identification of Jesus as the Coming One anointed by the Spirit as the "Christ/ Messiah" (1:10) and acknowledged as the Son of God by the divine voice from heaven (1:11).

Exegesis and Exposition

⁹And it came to pass in those days [that] Jesus came from Nazareth in Galilee and was baptized ⌜in⌝ the Jordan by John. ¹⁰And immediately, as he was coming out of the water, he saw the heavens being torn apart and the Spirit, like a dove, descending ⌜upon⌝ him. ¹¹And a voice ⌜came out⌝ of heaven, "*You* are my beloved Son; with you I am well pleased."

1:9   Having spoken of the forerunner, who prepared the way for the greater one coming after him, Mark now proceeds to tell his readers about this greater one—Jesus Christ, the Son of God. The account is introduced by a common connective indicating the start of a new unit (Lambrecht 1992: 360): "And it came to pass" (Καὶ ἐγένετο, *Kai egeneto*; cf. 2:15, 23; 4:4, 10; cf. also Judg. 19:1; 1 Sam. 28:1; Luke 1:5; 2:1; etc.). Mark uses the same verb in the form of a genitive absolute to serve as a connective in 1:32; 4:35; 6:2, 21, 47; 14:17; 15:33, 42. Whereas "in those days" (ἐν ἐκείναις ταῖς ἡμέραις, *en ekeinais tais hēmerais*) can refer to the end of history when the Son of Man returns (13:24), here and in 8:1 it refers to the days of Jesus's ministry, and in 13:17 (cf. also 13:19) it refers to the fall of Jerusalem in AD 70. The singular "in that day" (ἐν ἐκείνῃ τῇ ἡμέρᾳ, *en ekeinē tē hēmera*) is used in 2:20 to refer to the death of Jesus, in 4:35 to the ministry of Jesus, and in 13:32 to the return of the Son of Man. That Jesus is not introduced to the reader indicates that Mark assumed his readers were familiar with Jesus's identity due to 1:1 and their knowledge of the Jesus traditions (Guelich 1989: 31). That Jesus "came" picks up the "he is coming" of 1:7 and is the main focus of the verse. "From Nazareth" functions adverbially, not adjectivally, and modifies the verb "came." The latter would require the article, "Jesus *the one* from Nazareth" (τὸν ἀπὸ Ναζαρέτ, *ton apo Nazaret*), as in John 1:45 and Acts 10:38 (cf. also Matt. 21:11; Mark 15:43). The description of Nazareth as being in Galilee (a region bounded by Phoenicia in the west, the Sea of Galilee and the Jordan River in the east, Syria in the north, and Samaria in the south) also indicates that "from Nazareth" functions adverbially. Nevertheless "from Nazareth" also prepares for the designation "Jesus of Nazareth" in 1:24; 10:47; 14:67; 16:6. For the negative view some Judean Jews had toward Jews in Galilee, see 14:70; John 1:46; 7:40–52.

Some have suggested that "Nazareth" and "Galilee" were intentionally inserted into the text by Mark to balance "all the country of Judea" and "all the Jerusalemites" in 1:5 (Mauser 1963: 93–95; W. Lane 1974: 54–55). That Nazareth and Galilee are in the genitive case, whereas the former designations are in the nominative, argues somewhat against this. It is doubtful that Mark intended to point out that Jesus was from Galilee to indicate that he was the only Galilean baptized by John. Since "Galilee" receives a much more favorable status in Mark than Jerusalem or Judea and since receiving John's baptism is viewed positively, it would be strange for the evangelist to portray that a far greater number of Jerusalemites and Judeans responded to John's baptism than Galileans. Because Mark does not comment on "Galilee" as he does with respect to the "wilderness" in 1:2–3, we should not read into this geographical reference any great theological significance (Pesch 1980a: 104; contra Lohmeyer 1936; Marxsen 1969: 54–116). His purpose in mentioning Galilee is to help his readers locate Nazareth, for Nazareth was a small, insignificant village, unmentioned in the OT, the Talmud, or Josephus and numbering less than five hundred residents (J. F. Strange, *ABD* 4:1050–51; Donahue and Harrington 2002: 64).

Jesus's baptism by John is one of the most certain historical facts we possess concerning the life of Jesus (Schmithals 1979: 1.82). The difficulty of Jesus experiencing John's "baptism of repentance for the forgiveness of sins" (1:4) is apparent from the various attempts to explain why Jesus underwent such a baptism (cf. Matt. 3:14–15; cf. also the Gospel of the Nazareans).[1] No one in the early church would have created an account in which the sinless Son of God experienced John's baptism of repentance. The theological difficulty created by this account guarantees its historicity. The presence of some of John's disciples among the Twelve (John 1:35–51) also argues in favor of the historicity of this tradition. The uniqueness of Jesus's baptism is such that nowhere in the NT is it used as an example for Christians to follow (contra Marcus 1995: 513). As in 1:5, autobaptism is ruled out. The role of John in Jesus's baptism is minimal, and with the baptism of Jesus, John's time and role now come to an end. The Coming One has arrived, and for Mark "[Jesus] must increase, and [John] must decrease" (cf. John 3:30). As a result, "by John" (ὑπὸ Ἰωάννου, hypo Iōannou) are the last words in this sentence.[2]

1:10–11   The first acknowledgment that Jesus is the Coming One proclaimed by John involves the heavens being torn apart and the Spirit coming upon Jesus (1:10). Mark introduces the second part of the baptismal account with a favorite conjunctive expression, "and immediately" (καὶ εὐθύς, kai euthys; e.g., 1:12, 18, 20, 21, 23, 29, 30, 42, 43; 2:8, 12; 4:5; 5:29, 30, 42; 6:27, 45; 8:10; 9:15; 10:52; 11:2, 3; 14:43, 72; 15:1). Of the fifty-one times "immediately" (εὐθύς) is used in the NT, forty-one are in Mark. Frequently, especially when beginning an account, the expression is little more than a mild conjunctive, meaning "and then." In such instances it is unwise to associate a strong temporal meaning with the expression. Here, because it is found in the middle of the account, the temporal dimension is more significant. It is unclear, however, whether "immediately" modifies the participle "coming up" (cf. Matt. 3:16) or the verb "he saw" (Marcus 2000: 159). Jesus "coming up out of the water" is balanced later in the sentence by the Spirit "coming down." The present participle "coming up" indicates that the anointing of Jesus by the Spirit is intimately associated with his baptism. Yet Jesus's baptism is not so much the cause of his being anointed as the occasion, for the mission of John and the baptism are the temporal "beginning" of the good news about Jesus, not the causal beginning.

     The only other instance in Mark where we find the verb "being torn apart" (σχιζομένους, schizomenous) or "splitting" is in 15:38, where the curtain of the temple is "torn apart" from top to bottom. The use of this term is sufficiently strange that both Matthew and Luke changed it to forms of the more common

---

1. The account in the Gospel of the Nazareans reads, "Behold, the mother of the Lord and his brothers said to him, 'John the Baptist baptizes for the remission of sins; let us go and be baptized by him.' But he said, 'What have I committed, that I should be baptized by him, unless it be that in saying this I am in ignorance?'" (Elliott 1993: 13).

2. We have something of a parallel in the book of Acts with Peter and Paul. In telling of how the disciples became Jesus's witnesses in Jerusalem, Judea, Samaria, and to the end of the earth, Luke begins with Peter, who brings the witness concerning Jesus to Jerusalem, Judea, and Samaria. He is even involved in the first conversion of a gentile, Cornelius. But when Luke switches to Paul, who will bring the gospel to the end of the earth (1:8), Peter is essentially forgotten.

"open" (ἀνοίγω, *anoigō*). This agreement against Mark may be due to their familiarity with a pre-Markan form of the oral tradition containing "opened" rather than "torn apart" or by their common use of the account of Jesus's baptism found in the Q tradition. A number of OT parallels, such as Isa. 64:1 (in the MT), have been suggested as providing the key for understanding the significance of the heavens splitting, but none is convincing. The "splitting" here and in 15:38 indicates that these are eschatological events. It does not serve as a means for the Spirit descending from heaven, for the closest parallel of 1:10 is 15:38, not Acts 10:22; Rev. 19:11; Gen. 7:11; or Ps. 78:23–24; and in Mark 15:38 there is no descending entity. See 15:38.

The absolute use of the expression "the Spirit" (τὸ πνεῦμα, *to pneuma*) without qualification is due to its referring back to the Holy Spirit in 1:8. Earlier suggestions that this reflected a Hellenistic origin of this tradition have been refuted by the absolute use of "the Spirit" at Qumran (cf. 1QS 4.6; 1QH 12.11–12; 13.18–19; 16.11). The coming of the Spirit upon Jesus (and the early church) should be understood not in the framework of a "Hellenistic divine man theology" (Kingsbury 1983: 61–63; J. Edwards 2002: 105–9), but in light of such OT passages as Isa. 11:2; 42:1; 61:1 (cf. Luke 4:16ff.); Isa. 63:11; cf. also Ps. Sol. 17.37. Because of its placement, the simile "as a dove" (ὡς περιστεράν, *hōs peristeran*) is best understood adjectivally as describing "the Spirit" (cf. Luke 3:22; Marcus 2000: 159), rather than adverbially as describing the participle "descending." Although this simile is found in all four Gospels (Matt. 3:3; Luke 3:22; John 1:32), its meaning is far from clear. Since this was part of the tradition, it may be that Mark did not associate any particular meaning with it but simply included it because it was part of the tradition. References to the innocence of a dove (Matt. 10:16) or to a dove being one of the few sacrificial birds permitted by Jewish law (Lev. 1:14), while interesting, shed no real light on our passage. Also, rabbinic references such as Tg. Song 2:12 and *b. Ḥag.* 15a, where the Spirit in Gen. 1:2 hovers over creation like a dove, though appearing helpful, are too late to be useful. Some suggest that the dove serves to visualize the coming of the Spirit. Such an explanation might be useful to explain the "event" for Jesus, but for Mark and his audience, this would have been unnecessary. The OT does not require such a visible sign for its readers to understand the coming of the Spirit upon individuals, for the texts explain this sufficiently without such imagery (cf. Exod. 31:3; 35:31; Judg. 3:10; 6:34; cf. also Acts 10:44; 11:16; 19:6; etc.). Thus it is best to acknowledge that no clear parallel exists that provides a clear, interpretive clue for understanding this simile. Whereas the coming of the Spirit upon individuals is witnessed to by what occurs as a result of receiving the Spirit, no visible symbol is given to show the Spirit entering them. As a result there is no reason to assume that the dove functions this way in our present account.[3]

---

3. Cf. Guelich (1989: 33), who states, "The absence of clear precedent for identifying the dove symbolically with the Spirit . . . makes any symbolic explanation of the dove's role in this pericope . . . tenuous at best." And France (2002: 79) says: "We are not aware of any ready-made dove symbolism at the time of Mark, and it seems futile to try to provide one."

Along with the visual acknowledgment of Jesus's sonship in 1:10, there is a second that is oral in nature. In 1:1–13 both John the Baptist and Jesus receive a divine affirmation. The former receives it via the written word of God (1:2–3), the latter by an oral word from God. Mark does not give any indication that these two witnesses are to be contrasted (contra Guelich 1989: 33). The emphasis on seeing (1:10) and hearing (1:11) attests to the empirical objectivity of the event (J. Edwards 2002: 37; cf. Bultmann 1968: 248). The voice functions in conjunction with 1:1 as an authoritative spokesman for what Mark's readers should think about Jesus of Nazareth. Though numerous OT texts are suggestive as to the meaning of the divine affirmation (Gen. 22:2, 12, 16; Exod. 4:22–23; Ps. 2:7; Isa. 42:1),[4] the meaning of the voice should be understood within the context Mark provides in 1:1; 3:11; 5:7; 9:7; 13:32; 14:61; 15:39; cf. also 12:6. In light of these references, Jesus is presented in this verse as the beloved and only Son of God (12:6), who possesses a unique relationship with God that distinguishes him from all others (13:32). This is not a "functional" sonship, for up to this point Jesus has done nothing to earn such an affirmation. He is not the Son of God because he does certain things; he does certain things because he is the Son of God. Who he *is* determines what he does, not vice versa.

The pronoun "you" (σύ, *sy*) is emphatic, because it is unnecessary and located at the beginning of the sentence. Being the first word in the sentence indicates that the focus of the saying involves the identification of Jesus rather than God's supposed adoption of Jesus as the Son of God or of his being enthroned as the Son of God à la Ps. 2:7 (France 2002: 82–83). Just as the voice in 9:7 does not imply a *second* adoption of Jesus as the Son of God, so the voice here should not be interpreted as implying Jesus's adoption as the Son of God. In both Matt. 2:4 and 15 and Luke 1:32–35; 2:11, 26, the titles "Christ" and "Son of God" are used of the infant Jesus long before his baptism. Also, the parallel voice in Mark 9:7 is a declaration addressed to the disciples ("This is my beloved Son. You listen to him") and clearly shows that "*You* are my beloved Son; with you I am well pleased" must be understood as an identifying declaration, not an act of adoption (Hooker 1991: 48).[5] Added emphasis is placed on "you" by the "with you" (ἐν σοί, *en soi*) in the latter part of the saying. The tense of the verb "are" should not be interpreted, "You are *now*, due to the gift of the Spirit, my beloved Son." Unlike Ps. 2:7, there is no "Today I have begotten you" in

4. Comparisons of the voice with the *bat qôl* (lit. "daughter of a voice") are of questionable value, for the *bat qôl* was understood as being merely a weak echo of the heavenly voice. The voice in 1:11 and 9:7, on the other hand, is no weak echo (Hooker 1991: 46–47)!

5. Kingsbury (1983: 67) points out, "In presenting John, the focus of Mark's attention is not on his 'becoming' Jesus' forerunner but on his 'being' Jesus' forerunner. If this can be taken as guide, then with Jesus, too, the focus of Mark's attention is on who he is. Hence, at the level of Mark's story, the purpose of 1:11 is that God himself, at that juncture where Jesus is about to embark upon his public ministry, should solemnly affirm both his station and call."

the words of the heavenly voice.[6] (In the parallel in Matt. 3:17, the voice is reported from the perspective of Matthew's readers as "This is my Son, the Beloved, in whom I am pleased.") The term "beloved" (ὁ ἀγαπητός, *ho agapētos*) can mean "only," as in 12:6, where the "beloved" son must be an only son since he is the heir. This is also the way the term is understood in Gen. 22:2, 12, 16, where the LXX translates Hebrew יָחִיד (*yāḥîd*, only) as ἀγαπητός (C. Turner 1926). In Mark 1:11 "beloved" functions much as "one and only" (μονογενής, *monogenēs*) in John 1:14, 18; 3:16, 18 (Guelich 1989: 34; France 2002: 82).

The question of whether "Son" was understood as a messianic title must be raised at this point. For Mark and his readers the answer was obvious, for the entire Gospel is about "Jesus Christ, the Son of God" (1:1; cf. 14:61). Whether Jesus's audience understood "Son" as a messianic title is less certain. The idea of an individual being God's Son was not common in Judaism. The use of it as a title in 2 Esd. 7:28; 13:32, 37, 52; 14:9; and 1 En. 105.2 all appear to be post-Christian. In the Dead Sea Scrolls, "Son" is used messianically when discussing such biblical passages as Ps. 2:7 or 2 Sam. 7:14, and some scholars have argued that in 4Q246 the term is used as a title for the messiah. It is unclear, however, whether the term is positively attributed to a messianic figure or is being claimed by an evil ruler who is clearly not the Son of God (Fitzmyer 1993; J. Collins 1995: 154–69). In 4Q172 "Son" is more clearly attributed to the messianic king (France 2002: 80).

Some have argued that "with you I am well pleased" should be interpreted, "You are my beloved Son, therefore I am well pleased in (with) you" (Gundry 1993: 49). In the present context it appears best to see 1:11 as making two independent statements whose relationship is uncertain—"You are my beloved Son. I am well pleased in (with) you." There is no causal relationship between the second statement and the first. The closest OT parallel to this saying is in Isa. 42:1, in which God refers to "my chosen, in whom my soul delights." It is precarious, however, to see in these words a "suffering servant" motif, because of the paucity of this theme elsewhere in Mark[7] and because the Isaiah quotation refers to the "suffering servant" (παῖς, *pais*), whereas the title used by the voice is the "Son" (υἱός, *huios*) of God (I. Marshall 1968: 326–36; J. Edwards 1991: 50–51). For Mark's readers, this divine affirmation would probably have been understood as a commendation of Jesus's life, even though no incidents are reported concerning this period. It would also have been understood as implying that his future activities were also pleasing to God. As a result, even Jesus's crucifixion should be understood as pleasing to God (14:21, 27, 36, 49c).

6. Contrast D and it, which add to the parallel text in Luke 3:22, "This day I have begotten you."

7. Hooker 1959 is still a critical text on the subject of how influential the image of the "suffering servant" of Isaiah was for Jesus and the early church.

Summary

Historical questions concerning this passage abound. Did Jesus's baptism give birth to his messianic consciousness and result in his "call"? Did it clarify and/or confirm his calling? Did it provide a sign for him to begin his mission? These questions all assume the historicity of the tradition in one form or another. If one denies the historicity of the tradition (or at least a substantial part of it), another set of questions arises. Did the church create the entire scene or radically modify the tradition to have it serve as a prototype for Christian baptism? (The lack of any appeal in the NT to Jesus's baptism as a model of Christian baptism argues strongly against this.) Did the church seek to mollify Jesus's baptism of repentance by John the Baptist with his being anointed by the Spirit and being affirmed by a voice from heaven to make it more palatable to its view that Jesus was the sinless Son of God? Was the account modified or created in order to fulfill such OT passages as Ps. 2:7 and Isa. 42:1?

Although the first set of questions allows room for the supernatural and takes the tradition seriously, it nevertheless errs in seeking to psychoanalyze someone who lived two thousand years ago without the benefit of any biographical and historical data necessary for such an analysis. Mark and the other Gospel writers concentrate their attention on what Jesus did and who they believed he was, not on his inner feelings and thoughts. They seek to present a christological statement concerning Jesus, not to write a spiritual biography about him.[8] The "old quest" for the historical Jesus fell into the error of concentrating on Jesus's psychological development, and the result was a Jesus who reflected the values and experiences of the investigator. Those who deny the supernatural elements in the tradition generally do so on the basis of presuppositions that allow no room for the miraculous. That Jesus of Nazareth was baptized by John the Baptist is as certain a fact in the life of Jesus as we possess. To those with a positive attitude toward the gospel traditions, the baptism of Jesus is viewed as an experience that Jesus shared with his disciples. It is difficult, if not impossible, to separate from the present account what belongs to the pre-Markan tradition and what Mark himself added or modified.

For a commentary on Mark, however, the key exegetical question is, What was Mark seeking to teach his readers by this tradition? In light of 1:1 we may sharpen this question and ask, What does Mark in 1:9–11 tell us about Jesus Christ, the Son of God? Two divine acts are related in the account that are intended to affirm what Mark has said in 1:1–8 about the identity of Jesus of Nazareth. The heavens are torn apart and the Spirit descends upon Jesus, and God states that Jesus is his beloved Son. As a

---

8. Cf. Hooker (1991: 44), "Mark's purpose is not to write a spiritual biography, but to present a Christological statement. Even though the story may well go back to Jesus himself, it is told now from the viewpoint of one who sees Jesus through the eyes of faith and knows him to be the Son of God."

result, this passage serves as the centerpiece of 1:1–13 (Kingsbury 1983: 66). What Mark has said about Jesus in his introduction (1:1) is now confirmed by God himself (1:11). John the Baptist now passes from the scene. (He is later recalled in 6:14–29 to provide a temporal pause for the mission of the disciples in 6:7–13 and 30ff.) With the baptism of Jesus and his temptation, which the tradition associated together (cf. Matt. 3:13–4:11; Luke 3:21–22 and 4:1–13 [Luke inserts his genealogy of Jesus between these traditions]), the "beginning of the good news" now comes to an end. What follows in Mark 1:14–16:8 is the good news about Jesus.

Within 1:9–11 (and the entire prologue as well) there is present both an eschatological and christological emphasis. With respect to the former, this involves the coming of the long-awaited Spirit (1:8, 10) and the return of the prophetic voice in John the Baptist, the returning Elijah (1:2–8; cf. 9:11–13). This indicates that the messianic age is now beginning. The kingdom has now arrived (1:15). The christological emphasis is present because the Christ, the Son of God, has arrived (1:1). The "Lord" (1:2–3) has come, and God himself bears witness to Jesus being his Son (1:11)! The eschatological reality of the kingdom's arrival and the christological reality of the arrival of the Christ, the Son of God, are not simply coincidental realities that occurred at the same time. They are intimately related and inseparable. For Mark, however, the christological reality brings the eschatological arrival of the kingdom, not vice versa, as 1:1 indicates.

Additional Notes

1:9. For a similar use of εἰς to mean "in," cf. 6:8; 10:10; 13:3 (BDF §§110–11; contra O'Rourke 1966).

1:10. The preposition εἰς is usually translated "into," as in 1:12, 14, 21, etc. It can, however, be used to mean "in" (ἐν; see 1:9), "for," or "unto the goal of," as in 1:4. Here it serves as a substitute for "upon" (ἐπί). This is clear in that the parallels in Matt. 3:16; Luke 3:22; and John 1:33 all have ἐπ᾽ αὐτόν rather than εἰς αὐτόν. For other examples of εἰς meaning "upon," cf. 4:5, 8; 11:8; 12:14; 13:3 (Moulton and Turner 1963: 256–57; France 2002: 78).

1:11. A number of important MSS (e.g., ℵ* D) omit the verb, but this is probably accidental.

C. The Temptation of Jesus (1:12–13)

The brief account of the temptation in Mark differs considerably from that found in Matt. 4:1–11 and Luke 4:1–13. (Mark does not mention Jesus's fasting, which is singled out in Matthew and Luke, and Matthew and Luke make no mention of the wild beasts in Mark.) Questions such as whether Mark knew the longer Q version and chose to abbreviate it or whether he was unaware of it and used a different tradition are ultimately unanswerable. It is probable that the tradition of the temptation was associated with the baptism of Jesus before Mark wrote his Gospel (Gnilka 1978: 56). Its placement at this point is therefore due not so much to his editorial work as to the tradition, and although the wording of 1:12 is Markan, it and 1:13 were part of the pre-Markan tradition that the evangelist inherited. The account consists of four statements about Jesus connected by "and": (1) after his baptism the Spirit drove Jesus into the wilderness; (2) he was in the wilderness forty days, tempted by Satan; (3) he was with the wild beasts; and (4) the angels were ministering to him.

Exegesis and Exposition

¹²And immediately the Spirit drives him into the wilderness. ¹³And he was being tempted in the wilderness for forty days by Satan, and he was with the wild beasts, and the angels were ministering to him.

1:12   Mark begins the present account with "And immediately" (Καὶ εὐθύς, *Kai euthys*; see 1:10). Although some see this as creating a close chronological tie with the baptism (Gibson 1994: 8; contra Gnilka 1978: 56), Matthew (4:1, "Then" [τότε, *tote*]) and Luke (4:1, "And") do not appear to have understood it this way. The reference to the "Spirit" is the third time he is mentioned in the prologue (Mark 1:8, 10) and indicates that after being anointed by the Spirit at his baptism, Jesus is now led by the Spirit to the final preparation for his ministry—the temptation. Luke heightens this in his parallel (4:1) by a double reference to the Spirit ("Jesus, full of the Holy Spirit, returned from the Jordan and was led by the Spirit in the wilderness"). Mark describes the Spirit as "casting [Jesus] out" (ἐκβάλλει, *ekballei*) into the wilderness. This is the first occurrence of the "historical present" in Mark. This use of the present tense to describe historical actions that occurred in the past is typically Markan and occurs 151 times in the Gospel. In contrast, Matthew and Luke use the historical present only 78 and 6 times, respectively, even though each is approximately 70 percent larger than Mark.[1] The verb "casts" is somewhat strange. Although it is used elsewhere without the connotation of force (1:43; cf. Matt. 9:38/Luke 10:2; John 10:4; James 2:25; cf. also Acts 16:37), it is not surprising that both Matt. 4:1 and Luke 4:1 change it to "led" (ἤγετο, ēgeto) or a related root of "led" (ἀνήχθη, anēchthē).

Mark gives no explanation why the Spirit drove Jesus "into the wilderness" (εἰς τὴν ἔρημον, eis tēn erēmon). This location is probably part of the tradition that Mark inherited, and its meaning here is quite different from 1:3 and 4. There it functions as a prophetic identification mark associating John the Baptist with the voice of Isa. 40:3. Here there is no logical connection with the wilderness of 1:3 and 4, for Jesus being baptized by John (a "voice crying in the wilderness") is already in the "wilderness." In the tradition that Mark inherited, however, the "wilderness" serves as a geographical location for "the wilderness of Judea" (cf. Matt. 3:1; Pesch 1978: 94). Although "in the wilderness" (ἐν τῇ ἐρήμῳ, en tē erēmō) is repeated in 1:13, Mark gives no theological freight to the expression here, unlike 1:3–4, and it is doubtful that his readers would have assumed that it was not a geographical location but a theological concept. It functions primarily as a geographical location as in 1:35, 45; 6:31, 32, 35 (cf. Matt. 3:1; 7:24; 15:4; John 11:54; Acts 8:26; 21:38). Along with the "wild beasts" (τῶν θηρίων, tōn thēriōn) in 1:13, the "wilderness" should be understood negatively as the evil abode of Satan and the desolate domain of wild animals (Isa. 13:19–22; 34:13–14; Ezek. 34:5, 25; T. Naph. 8.4; T. Iss. 7.7; T. Benj. 5.2; Best 1965: 7–9; J. Edwards 2002: 40–41; France 2002: 83, 86; Heil 2006),[2] not as a place of divine visitation and deliverance (Isa. 11:6–9; 32:14–20; 40:3; 65:25; Hos. 2:18; 2 Bar. 73.6; contra Guelich 1989: 38–39; Bauckham 1994b).

The repetition of the phrase "in the wilderness" gives additional emphasis to the location of the temptation. The purpose of Jesus being led into the wilderness is "to be tempted" (cf. Matt. 4:1).[3] The temporal duration of "forty days" is encountered frequently in the Bible (Gen. 7:12; Exod. 24:18; 34:28; Num. 14:34; Deut. 9:9, 18; 1 Kings 19:8; Jon. 3:4; Acts 1:3; cf. also "forty years" in Deut. 2:7; Judg. 13:1; Ps. 95:10; Acts 7:23, 30). It appears that this temporal designation was part of the tradition that Mark received (cf. Matt. 4:2; Luke 4:2). If traditional, the question remains whether Mark attributed any specific theological significance to it. If he did, he unfortunately did not provide his readers with any clear editorial markers. Nowhere else in Mark do we find "forty." We should therefore not give it any theological significance. It probably functions simply as a temporal designation for a "conventional biblical round number, indicating a long period of time" (Hooker 1991: 50).

1:13

1. Mark contains 11,025 words, whereas Matthew contains 18,293 and Luke 19,376.
2. Best (1965: 8–9) and J. Edwards (2002: 41–42) suggest that this imagery would remind Mark's Roman readers, some of whom were being thrown to the wild beasts in the arena, that Jesus was also "thrown" to the wild beasts.
3. Stegner (1967) argues that a strong correlation exists between testing and the wilderness in the Qumran literature and in parts of the NT.

The participle "being tempted" (πειραζόμενος, *peirazomenos*) functions as a periphrasis (contra Gundry 1993: 54) with the verb "was" (ἦν, *ēn*). The separation of the participle by two elements ("in the wilderness" and "forty days") is no greater than in the examples of periphrasis in 2:6, 18; 4:38; 14:49; 15:25, 40, and less than in 5:11; 15:7. Although "tempted" can refer positively to being tested (John 6:6; 1 Cor. 10:13; 2 Cor. 13:5; Heb. 2:18; 4:15; 11:17; Rev. 2:2) or negatively (Mark 8:11; 10:2; 12:15), it must be understood negatively here as "tempted" since the agent is Satan. How Jesus is tempted is not mentioned. He is tempted by Satan, but nothing more is said. Whether Mark assumed his readers knew the larger temptation account in Matthew and/or Luke and would fill in what he omitted is impossible to say. Mark gives no hint in the rest of his Gospel that he knew of the larger temptation account in Q. What is clear is that apart from revealing that Jesus was tempted by Satan, Mark is not concerned with sharing the content of that temptation (contra Gibson 1994). A victorious outcome of Jesus's temptation is assumed (Gibson 1994: 30–32), but Mark makes no explicit mention of this. It is simply implied from the Christology of Mark's Gospel and the larger temptation tradition found in Q (Matt. 4:1–11; Luke 4:1–13). In 1:11, God is "well pleased" with Jesus. Such a comment would be strange if immediately after this divine benediction Jesus succumbed to temptation. The triumphant pronouncement of the arrival of the kingdom of God in 1:15 assumes this also (Marcus 2000: 170). No emphasis is placed, however, on his victory over Satan's temptation. Thus theories that see the temptation as Jesus's once-and-for-all defeat of Satan (Robinson 1957: 26–27; Best 1965: 3–60) read this into the account. The Semitic term שָׂטָן (*śāṭān*) originally referred to an "adversary" (1 Kings 11:14) but later began to be used of "the Adversary." By the time of Mark, the former sense had pretty much been lost, and the term had become a name, "Satan" or "the devil." Mark favored the use of the Semitic term for *Satan* (Greek σατανᾶς, *satanas*; 3:23 [2×], 26; 4:15; 8:33) rather than the Greek term for the *devil* (διάβολος, *diabolos*). Matthew 4:1 and Luke 4:2 preferred the latter term.

Since the scene is the wilderness, the presence of wild beasts is not surprising. As mentioned in the discussion of "wilderness," it is best to understand their presence negatively. Jesus is portrayed as in a hostile and evil environment, the realm of the wild beasts (Mauser 1963: 100–101), and this intensifies the double references to his being "in the wilderness." There is no suggestion here of a paradisal renewal in which Jesus is replacing a cursed creation with a renewed heaven and earth (contra Marcus 2000: 168, 170), for Jesus is with the wild beasts, in their evil locale. The wild beasts are not with Jesus in a renewed creation. It is who accompanies Jesus that determines the way the scene should be interpreted. In 8:38 Jesus is described as being "with the holy angels," and this reveals where Jesus is, not where the angels are. (Cf. also Luke 22:37, where "with transgressors" determines where Jesus is rather than where the transgressors are.) Still another reason it is incorrect to see 1:13 as a paradisal scene in which Jesus dwells peaceably with the wild animals (cf. Isa. 11:6–9; 65:17–25; Hos. 2:18) is that the "wild beasts" stand over against and in contrast to the angels (Gibson 1994: 19–23). We should not interpret 1:12–13 as an Adam-Christ typology where Jesus is undoing Adam's temptation and fall (contra Guelich 1989: 39; Marcus 2000: 168). Such a typology plays no real part in Mark's Christology elsewhere in his Gospel. The closest biblical analogy to 1:12–13 is Elijah's forty-day experience in the wilderness, where he is fed by an angel (1 Kings 19:4–8; Marcus 2000: 169), but neither he nor Moses (Exod. 34:28) went into the wilderness to be tempted forty days by Satan. Israel's forty-year experience in the wilderness appears to be an even less applicable parallel (contra France 2002: 85).

The christological significance of the angels serving Jesus should be noted. It is the angels of God, not simply ravens as with Elijah in 1 Kings 17:6 (cf., however, 1 Kings 19:5–8), who serve Jesus in the wilderness. Unlike Matt. 4:2 and Luke 4:2, Mark makes no mention of Jesus's fasting and being hungry. Although Mark does not specify how the angels were "ministering to" (διηκόνουν, *diēkonoun*) Jesus, the verb is frequently associated with serving food (cf. 1:32; Luke 12:37; 17:8; Acts 6:2; and esp. Matt. 4:11, where, after Jesus has fasted, he is hungry and is tempted to turn stone to bread, and the angels "minister" to him [4:11], i.e., serve him food). It seems plausible therefore to interpret this as indicating that at the end of forty days, the angels serve Jesus food.

Summary

It is strange that this short passage has received so many varied interpretations. The very brevity of the passage and its enigmatic nature may be the reason for this. Some of the more common interpretations of the meaning of the Markan temptation narrative are (Gundry 1993: 55–60): (1) It serves as an example and encouragement for Christians in their temptations. Yet we do not read of any struggle of Jesus with temptation in the account, and no explicit mention is made of Jesus's victory over such temptations. This is only implied. If it were the point of the account, however, we would expect an explicit reference to this (Hooker 1991: 49). Furthermore, if this was meant to serve as an example for Christians undergoing persecution, would not the crucifixion of Jesus have served as a better example? In the temptation no harm comes to Jesus. On the contrary, the angels come and care for him. (2) The account contrasts Jesus's success in overcoming temptation with Israel's failure during its time in the wilderness. But again the victory of Jesus over temptation receives less emphasis than one would expect if this interpretation were correct. No explicit comparison of Israel's failure and Jesus's success in encountering temptation is found in the passage, and the analogy between the forty days of Jesus in the wilderness and the forty years of wandering by Israel encounters the problem of forty years versus forty days. It is at least questionable whether Mark's readers would have made such a connection merely by the term "forty." Mark's readers (and the modern-day reader as well) have no clear markers for understanding the account in this manner. (3) The temptation should be understood as the apocalyptic restoration of the pre-fall paradisal bliss through Jesus's undoing of Adam's failure. Yet again explicit pointers to an Adam-Christ comparison are lacking. Attempts to see them in the term "casts" (1:12 and Gen. 3:24) lose sight of the fact that the actions are quite different. In the former, the Spirit casts Jesus into the evil wilderness; in the latter, God casts Adam and Eve out of the blessed garden. We furthermore find nothing in the Genesis account involving forty days. Once again, the lack of any explicit statement of Jesus being victorious over the temptation should be noted, for it weakens considerably such a comparison. (4) The account teaches the once-for-all defeat of Satan by Jesus. After this, Jesus's encounters with Satan are little more than mopping-up operations. Yet we find no clear statement to this effect in Mark, and we find nothing in Mark like "I saw Satan fall like lightning from heaven" (Luke 10:18) to support such a view. There is no suggestion that the reference to the binding of Satan in 3:27 was interpreted by Mark as occurring at the temptation. On the contrary, this verse is best understood as indicating that in Jesus's exorcisms the kingdom of God had arrived, and this meant the defeat of Satan. There is no clear statement or allusion here that would lead the reader to see Jesus as having defeated Satan once and for all in the temptation.

The point that Mark is making in 1:12–13 is christological in nature. The temptation shows that the Spirit-led Jesus is the Son of God. This is seen in his facing a great temptation by Satan himself, which lasted for forty days. But Jesus is stronger than Satan! He goes out into the wilderness—a place of wild beasts and the realm of Satan—and returns victorious, for he is stronger than the evil one. He is ministered to by angels—the lesser (the angels of God) serving the greater (the Stronger One—Jesus Christ, the Son of God).[4] Along with 1:1–11 the present account portrays Jesus Christ, the Son of God as *announced* by John the Baptist (1:2–8), *anointed* by the Spirit (1:10), *acknowledged* by the divine voice from heaven (1:11), *approved* by testing in the wilderness (1:12–13), and now prepared for his ministry and mission (1:14–16:8).

---

4. Gundry (1993: 60) deserves to be quoted here, "All that we have [in this account] is a dignifying of Jesus, a series of acknowledgments—a backhanded acknowledgment by Satan, a pacifistic acknowledgment by the wild beasts, and a ministerial acknowledgment by the angels—in recognition of the status of Jesus as God's beloved Son. Mark 1:12–13 is neither exemplary nor proclamatory nor promissory, but Christological."

II. Who Is This Jesus? Part 1 (1:14–3:6)

After the prologue (1:1–13) the first three sections of Mark (1:14–3:6; 3:7–6:6a; 6:6b–8:21) all begin with the same pattern. This involves an introductory summary (1:14–15; 3:7–12; and 6:6b; France 2002: 59–60; contra Guelich 1989: 41–42) followed by a pericope concerning the disciples (1:16–20; 3:13–19; 6:7–13; Lambrecht 1992: 360–61). Each section ends with a negative concluding summary (3:6; 6:6a) or question (8:21). The present section consists of two major collections of traditions. The first (1:21–39 or 1:21–45) involves a series of healings (1:21–28, 29–31, 32–34, 35–39, and 40–45) centering on a day (1:29, 32, 35) in Capernaum (1:21). The second (2:1–3:6) also centers on Capernaum and involves a series of conflict stories (2:1–12, 15–17, 18–22, 23–28; 3:1–6).[1] Mark begins this section with a summary abstract of Jesus's teachings (1:15) that informs his readers concerning the content of that teaching in 1:21–22, 27, 38, 39; 2:2, 13. Since Jesus is portrayed as accompanied by his disciples in the stories found in this section (1:29–31, 36; 2:15, 18–22, 23–28; note also the plural verbs in 1:21–22, 37, 38), Mark follows his introductory summary with an account of the call of Peter, Andrew, James, and John (1:16–20).

There has been a great deal of discussion as to whether these two collections (1:21–39 or 1:21–45 and 2:1–3:6) existed as "pre-Markan complexes" before the Gospel was written.[2] The issue of whether the material in 1:21–39 (or 1:21–45) and 2:1–3:6 existed together before Mark was written is made even more confusing by the suggestion that Mark himself composed the present two complexes before he wrote his Gospel. It would be impossible to determine if the complexes were composed by Mark before he wrote his Gospel, however, for we lack the tools to make so precise a distinction in a work written two thousand years ago. The issue of whether these are non-Markan complexes that existed together before Mark wrote his Gospel is best answered by observing how the stories in these collections are joined together. In investigating the seams of the individual stories, it is evident that they betray a strongly Markan content and style. The seams in 1:21–22, 29, 32, 35, 40; 2:1–2, 13, 15, 18, 23, and the concluding summaries in 1:28, 34, 39, and 45 are so typically

---

1. The literary categories "healing stories" and "conflict stories" are not rigid. History and the art of storytelling know no rules prohibiting a healing story from involving a conflict or teaching, or a conflict story from containing a healing or teaching. As a result, it is not surprising that the healing story in 1:21–28 also focuses on Jesus's teaching (1:21–22, 27) or that the conflict stories in 2:1–12 and 3:1–6 involve healings.

2. Other possible pre-Markan complexes are sometimes seen in 4:1–34; 4:35–5:43; 7:1–23; 10:1–31; 13:3–37, and the Passion Narrative. For a discussion, see Kuhn 1971.

Markan in style and content that it appears reasonably certain that he has composed them (probably from traditional materials) and that he is responsible for bringing together the materials found in 1:21–39 or 1:21–45 and 2:1–3:6. It is best, therefore, to see these collections as having been arranged and created by Mark from traditional material.

A. A Summary of Jesus's Message (1:14–15)

This summary introduces a new section (1:14–3:6) in Mark. This is indicated by the radical shift in both scene and perspective. John the Baptist and the wilderness are left behind, and the focus of attention now centers on the preaching ministry of Jesus. Grammatically this is indicated by the switch from "and" (καί, *kai*) in 1:7, 9, 12 (cf. also 1:6) to "Now after" (Μετὰ δέ, *Meta de*) in 1:14. Even as 1:1 introduces 1:1–13 (Kuthirakkattel 1990: 4–12), so 1:14–15 introduces 1:14–3:6. Mark often introduces a new section in his Gospel with a summary statement (cf. 3:7–12 and 6:6b; Perrin and Duling 1982: 239–40; contra Hedrick 1984). Numerous summary-like statements appear in Mark.[1] The present summary is not a conclusion of what has preceded but a transitional summary of the content of Jesus's preaching in 1:16–3:6 (1:21–22, 27, 38–39; 2:2, 13) and also of the rest of Mark (3:14, 23a; 4:1–2, 33–34; 6:2, 6b, 34; 7:14; 8:31; 9:31; 10:1; 11:17–18; 12:35, 38; 14:49).[2]

Although some see 1:14–15 as a pre-Markan tradition (Lohmeyer 1957: 29–30; Pesch 1980a: 100) and others as a completely Markan creation (Marxsen 1969: 132–35; Egger 1976: 61–62; Pryke 1978: 10, 139, 151–52; Schmithals 1979: 1.95), it is more likely that 1:15 is a Markan rewording of a pre-Markan tradition concerning Jesus's message and that 1:14 is a transitional seam from the hand of Mark based upon general information about the life of Jesus. The Markan nature of 1:14 is seen by various Markan terms and themes: "arrested/deliver over" (παραδοθῆναι, *paradothēnai*; cf. the same passive form of the verb in 9:31; 10:33 [2×]; 14:21, 41; cf. also 3:19; 14:1, 11, 18; etc.); "Jesus came" (ἦλθεν ὁ Ἰησοῦς, *ēlthen ho Iēsous*; 1:9, 39; 2:17; 8:10; 10:45; etc.); "Galilee" (1:9, 16, 28, 39; 3:7; etc.); "preaching" (κηρύσσων, *kēryssōn*; 1:4, 7, 38, 39, 45; 3:14; etc.); "gospel" (εὐαγγέλιον, *euangelion*; 1:1; 8:35; 10:29; 13:10; 14:9 [Marcus 2000: 174]). Though the wording of 1:15 also betrays the hand of Mark, the content of 1:15 is understood by most as being traditional (Beasley-Murray 1986: 71–72; Marcus 2000: 174; Donahue and Harrington 2002: 72; contra Bultmann 1968: 118; Ambrozic 1972: 4–6).

---

1. Cf. 1:1, 5, 14–15, 21–22, 28, 32–34, 39, 45; 2:1–2, 13, 15; 3:6, 7–12; 4:1–2, 33–34; 5:21; 6:1, 6b, 7, 12–13, 30–33, 53–56; 7:1–2, 24, 31; 8:1, 10, 27, 31; 9:2, 30–32; 10:1, 32–34; 11:1, 11, 12, 15, 19, 20, 27; 12:1; 13:3; 14:1, 3, 12, 16, 32; 15:1 (cf. Donahue and Harrington 2002: 71–72).

2. For additional content in Jesus's teaching/preaching, cf. 2:17, 19–22, 25–28; 3:23b–29; 4:3–32; 7:6–23; 8:34b–9:1; 9:12–13, 31, 35, 37, 39–50; 10:5–12, 14–15, 18–19, 21, 23–31, 33–34, 42–45; 11:22b–25; 12:1–11, 17, 24–27, 29–31, 35–37, 38–40, 43b–44; 13:2, 5–37; 14:17–21, 22–25, 27–28, 30, 48, 62.

Jesus surely taught a great deal more than the fifteen words making up his message in 1:15, but Mark wants his readers to see Jesus's announcement of the kingdom's coming and the necessity of repentance and faith as the heart of Jesus's preaching. The present summary comes from the traditions Mark inherited and serves as an abstract of Jesus's preaching. Whereas 1:14 serves as an introduction to Jesus's preaching ministry, 1:15 reveals the content of the gospel he preached. That content comes in the form of two synonymous or synthetic parallel statements. The first is, "The time is fulfilled, and the kingdom of God has come," in which both verbs are in the perfect tense. The second involves two imperatives in the present tense: "Repent and believe in the gospel." The two imperatives correspond with the two statements as follows: "The time is fulfilled—[therefore] repent" and "The kingdom of God has come—[therefore] believe in the gospel."

Exegesis and Exposition

¹⁴Now ⌜after⌝ John was arrested, Jesus came into Galilee preaching the gospel ⌜from⌝ God ¹⁵and saying, "The time is fulfilled, and the kingdom of God has come; repent and believe in the gospel."

1:14   The disjunctive phrase "Now after" (Μετὰ δέ, *Meta de*) indicates a turning point in the story and separates 1:14ff. from what has preceded (V. Taylor 1952: 165; Donahue and Harrington 2002: 70). It is introduced by a "now" (δέ) rather than the typically Markan "and" (καί, *kai*) found in 1:5, 6, 7, 9, 10, 11, 12, 13. Even though the word "after" is different (μετά vs. ὀπίσω, *opisō*), it recalls the words of John the Baptist in 1:7, "The one stronger than me is coming after me." Thus the temporal designation "after" is not simply a chronological designation of time (cf. Matt. 4:12) but an eschatological one as well. The lack of specificity, as to how soon Jesus began his ministry after John was arrested, emphasizes the eschatological nature of "after." For Mark, John the Baptist belonged to the old era (2:21; cf. also Luke 16:16; Acts 10:36–37), and with him the "old covenant" came to an end, whereas with Jesus the "new covenant" begins. According to John 3:22–4:2 there existed a period of overlap in the ministries of John the Baptist and Jesus. If Mark were writing a biography of the life of Jesus, the present statement would be a serious problem. Already in the early part of the second century, however, Papias (d. 130) recognized that Mark did not write his Gospel "in order" (Eusebius, *Eccl. Hist.* 3.39.15–16). Once we realize that Mark did not seek to provide a chronological log of Jesus's ministry, and this is evident by his geographical grouping of material (Jesus in and around Galilee—1:14–9:50; Jesus's journey to Jerusalem—10:1–52; Jesus in Jerusalem—11:1–16:8), then the alleged problem disappears. Mark does not mention how soon after Jesus's baptism John was arrested or how long their ministries overlapped. In this way, he emphasizes that the old covenant ends with the ministry of John the

Baptist, and the new covenant/kingdom of God arrives with the ministry of Jesus (Hooker 1991: 53; Marcus 2000: 175).

John's arrest is described in the passive voice. The term παραδοθῆναι (*paradothēnai*; lit. "was delivered over") is a technical term in police and lawcourt jargon for delivering up a prisoner. Here, however, it functions as a divine passive for "God delivered John over" (Marxsen 1969: 38–40; Pesch 1980a: 101; Guelich 1989: 42; contra Gundry 1993: 63–64). This emphasizes God's control of John's life and ministry. The same term is used in the passive with respect to Jesus in 9:31; 10:33; 14:21, 41, where it also serves as a divine passive, and of Christians in 13:9–12. Compare how "deliver over" (παραδίδωμι, *paradidōmi*) is used of God delivering his Son over to death in Rom. 4:25; 8:32; 1 Cor. 11:23; cf. also Gal. 2:20. The lack of any explanation for John's arrest probably indicates that Mark's readers were familiar with the story. Although in 6:14–29 Mark will pick up the story of John the Baptist and tell of his arrest and death, it does not serve primarily to provide information about John but rather to provide a temporal interlude for the mission of the disciples (6:7–13 and 30ff.).

In 1:9 Jesus leaves Galilee to be baptized by John. After being anointed as the Messiah by the Spirit (1:9–11) and successfully completing his testing (1:12–13), Jesus returns to Galilee to begin his ministry. The location of the early part of Jesus's ministry in Galilee has its roots in the historical circumstances of his life. It is not primarily due to a Markan redactional interest in Galilee as a theological concept (contra Lohmeyer 1936; Marxsen 1969: 54–116, esp. 58–60).[3] Mark simply has Jesus return from the wilderness of 1:12–13 to the place of his early ministry (Stemberger 1974). In contrast to the Gospel of John, where Jesus moves back and forth from Galilee to Judea/Jerusalem (cf. 2:13–4:43; 5:1–47; 7:10ff.), Mark structures his Gospel around the geographical scheme of Jesus's ministry in (1:14–7:23) and around Galilee (7:24–9:50), and in Judea (10:1–16:8). Whether he was aware that Jesus had ministered in Judea/Jerusalem before 11:1 is uncertain. Some of the material in Mark, however, suggests that Jesus had ministered there before 11:1 (cf. 10:46–52; 11:2–6; 14:3–9, 13–16, 49; cf. also Luke 13:34).

The expression "from God" (τοῦ θεοῦ, *tou theou*) is best understood as an ablative of source, that is, the gospel whose source is God (Guelich 1989: 43; J. Edwards 2002: 45).[4] Attempts to contrast the preaching of Jesus and that of John the Baptist in 1:4 and 1:7–8 are misguided, for Mark emphasizes not the discontinuity of Jesus's preaching with John's but its continuity. This can be seen in the parallel between Jesus's *preaching of repentance* in light of the arrival of the kingdom of God (1:14–15) and John's *preaching of repentance* (1:4) in light of the arrival of the Coming One, who brings the kingdom (1:7–8).

---

3. In Matt. 4:14–16 the evangelist associates certain theological implications with Jesus's return into Galilee by means of an OT quotation. Mark, however, provides no such comment here that might suggest that Jesus's return to Galilee possesses theological implications.

4. Some understand "the gospel of God" as "the gospel about God" (an objective genitive; Marcus 2000: 172), but "of" is best understood as an ablative of source.

(Note also the continuity with the *preaching of repentance* by Jesus's disciples in 6:12.) This continuity is also seen in Matt. 3:2 and 4:17, where both John and Jesus proclaim the identical message—"Repent, for the kingdom of heaven has come near." The message of the disciples is also the same (Matt. 10:7; cf. also Luke 10:9, 11). In Mark, John the Baptist serves as the forerunner of Jesus with respect to both his message and his fate.

1:15   By this summary, Mark reveals that the central theme of Jesus's preaching involves the coming of the kingdom of God. Matthew shows his agreement by his inclusion of this summary in 4:17, and Luke 4:42–43 also summarizes Jesus's message in this manner. The expression "kingdom of God" occurs thirteen other times in Mark (4:11, 26, 30; 9:1, 47; 10:14, 15, 23, 24, 25; 12:34; 14:25; 15:43) and together with the Matthean parallel "kingdom of heaven" in sixty-one separate sayings in the Synoptic Gospels (Stein 1994b: 60). The expression is found in such critical sayings as the Lord's Prayer (Matt. 6:10), the Beatitudes (Matt. 5:3), the Last Supper (Mark 14:25), and numerous parables (Mark 4:26, 30; Matt. 13:24, 33, 44, 45, 47; Luke 19:11; etc.). The most common interpretations of what Jesus meant by the coming/nearing of the kingdom of God are that it refers to (1) a Davidic-like kingdom about to be established in Jerusalem (the political view); (2) a new, spiritual rule of God being established in the human heart (the noneschatological view); (3) the end of history soon occurring and the final judgment taking place (the consistent eschatological view); (4) the promised rule of God now having arrived in its entirety (the realized eschatological view); and (5) the reign of God now beginning, in that the OT promises are being fulfilled, the promised Spirit is once again being active and soon dwelling in every believer, but the final consummation still lying in the future (the "already but not yet" view).

The first of these views is refuted by such teachings of Jesus as found in Matt. 5:39–42, 44–47; 26:52; Mark 12:13–17, which clearly indicate that Jesus was not a revolutionary seeking to establish a substitute political government that would replace Roman rule. The second is refuted by the fact that Jesus never spoke of the kingdom of God as a subjective principle within the human heart involving such things as the fatherhood of God, the interconnection of all humans, and the infinite value of the human soul. The lack of taking seriously the eschatological nature of Jesus's teaching on the kingdom of God is a critical problem for this view. It is not the kingdom that enters into the believer but rather the believer who enters into the kingdom! The third view finds supports in such passages as Mark 9:1; 14:25; Luke 11:2; 13:22–30; Matt. 7:21–23; 8:11–12; 25:31–46. The fourth view finds support in passages such as Mark 2:21–22; Luke 11:20; 16:16; 17:20–21; Matt. 11:4–6; 13:16–17. It is best to understand the expression "kingdom of God" in the context of the OT's dynamic use of the term "kingdom" (מַלְכוּת, *malkût*) as referring to the reign of a king rather than statically as referring to the territory or realm over which a king rules. The Greek equivalent βασιλεία (*basileia*) is likewise best understood in the NT dynamically as referring to the "reign" of God (cf.

Luke 19:12, 15; 23:42; Matt. 6:33; 20:20–21). In Mark 1:15 it must be interpreted dynamically, for it is not the "territory," a geographical place, that has arrived but the "rule" of God (Marcus 2000: 172). Understood in this manner, the references emphasizing the arrival of the kingdom of God can be seen as indicating that in fulfillment of the OT promises, the kingdom of God has arrived in the ministry of Jesus. The reign of God has come; the Spirit is coming soon (after Pentecost) upon all believers.[5] Yet the ultimate consummation of all things awaits the return of the Son of Man, so that believers continue to pray, "Your kingdom come" (Luke 11:2). Thus the kingdom of God is both "already but not yet" (Stein 1994b: 60–81).

The term "time" (καιρός, *kairos*) refers to the decisive point in history having now occurred, to a particular point of time now having arrived (Guelich 1989: 43; Hooker 1991: 54; France 2002: 91), rather than to a span or period of time now taking place (Marcus 1989b: 50–53). This time being "fulfilled" (πεπλήρωται, *peplērōtai*; lit. "has been fulfilled") emphasizes not so much the ending of the old covenantal period as the present arrival of what the OT predicted would one day occur. The focus is not on the end of the old age, although it is certainly implied, but the beginning of the new. The passive voice of the verb functions as a divine passive, for "God has brought to fulfillment the decisive time [spoken of in the OT]" (cf. Gal. 4:4; Eph. 1:10). The perfect tense of the verb "is fulfilled" indicates that the time of the coming of the kingdom of God has now arrived. It stands in synonymous or synthetic parallelism with the second statement: "The kingdom of God has come." The meaning of "has come" (ἤγγικεν, *ēngiken*) has been much debated. Whatever the meaning of the original term Jesus used, the Markan meaning is clear. For him the kingdom was not simply "nearer" but had come (cf. 14:41; Luke 11:20). It was already "near" with the coming of John, who fulfilled the role of the promised Elijah (Mark 9:11–13; cf. Mal. 4:5) and the prophetic promises (Mark 1:2–3). Although the question of whether Jesus thought that the kingdom of God had arrived in his ministry can be debated, the question of whether Mark in AD 65–70 thought that Jesus had initiated the kingdom of God cannot be. Jesus's resurrection clearly meant that the new covenant/kingdom of God had come. Because of the fulfillment of the Scriptures (1:2–3) and the time having been fulfilled (note the tense of the verb), the kingdom of God "has come" (France 2002: 92–94). The parallel statements, "The time is fulfilled" and "The kingdom of God has come," require this (Ambrozic 1972: 21–22; Beasley-Murray 1986: 73; C. Marshall 1989: 35), and Jesus's saying in 2:21–22 makes sense only if the kingdom had in some way arrived in his ministry. It is the arrival of the kingdom that explains why one cannot mix the old garment and wineskin with the new patch and wine.

The two imperatives "repent and believe" correspond to the two statements concerning the fulfillment of time and the arrival of the kingdom of

5. See Stein (1994b: 167n50) for examples of how the arrival of the kingdom is manifested in the present time.

God. "Repent" (μετανοεῖτε, *metanoeite*) is the appropriate response to the eschatological crisis created by the fulfillment of time (cf. 6:12); "believe" is the appropriate response to the good news of the gospel. What this entails will be spelled out in more detail in the following chapters. For the combination of the terms "repent/repentance" and "believe/faith," see Acts 11:17–18; 19:4; 20:21; Heb. 6:1; cf. also Acts 26:20. For the comparison of two similar statements followed by two imperatives, see Rom. 13:12; 1 Thess. 5:5–6 (Marcus 2000: 174–75). In the NT, even when not mentioned, the presence of one of these terms assumes the accompaniment of the other. To "repent and be baptized" (Acts 2:38) is inconceivable apart from the command to "believe." Similarly, to "believe in the Lord Jesus" (Acts 16:31) is likewise inconceivable apart from the command to "repent." Because of the arrival of the kingdom of God, it is imperative to repent and believe the gospel in order to enter the kingdom. Even as the preaching of John the Baptist was twofold in nature, possessing both a soteriological (1:4) and a christological dimension (1:7–8), so Jesus's preaching is twofold as well. Here the soteriological dimension is given (cf. also 10:45; 14:22–25). To this we must also add the christological (cf. 1:1, 11, 24; 3:11; 8:31; 9:7, 31; 10:33–34, 45).

Just as the opening verse of Mark refers to the "gospel," so here the opening summary of the first section in Mark begins with a similar reference. There is little doubt that for Mark and his readers the "gospel" had a more pregnant meaning than for Jesus's original audience. As believers they were privy to a great deal more christological and soteriological information as to both who Jesus was and how his death and resurrection brought the kingdom of God. For Mark, to believe the gospel is another way of saying to believe in Jesus (8:35; 10:29).

Summary

Mark in this summary places Jesus's teaching within an eschatological framework. After John, the last of the prophets, has been arrested (cf. Luke 16:16), Jesus returns to Galilee and proclaims the beginning of a new age and the arrival of the kingdom of God. Jesus's appearance on the scene and the coming of the kingdom are not simply coincidental. They are not two unrelated events that simply occur simultaneously in time. Jesus is not merely a prophet announcing the arrival of the kingdom but its "effector." He brings the kingdom with him. It is because the King (15:2, 9, 12, 18, 26, 32) has come that the kingdom is present. Thus the kingdom of God is not only theocentric in nature but christocentric as well, for the kingdom of God has come precisely because Jesus Christ, the Son of God, has come. In light of the kingdom's arrival, it is imperative that one repent and believe. In the Markan setting this means to repent, believe in Jesus Christ (the Son of God), be baptized (1:4, 8; cf. John 4:1–2; Acts 2:38), and "follow" Jesus (see 8:34). For Mark's Christian readers, this gospel summary was intended to remind them of the commitment they had made to God and of God's commitment to them. For non-Christians who might be present and hearing the reading of this Gospel, it would challenge them to "repent and believe the good news from God about Jesus Christ."

Additional Notes

1:14. Codices B and D have "And after," but this is obviously a scribal attempt to maintain Mark's paratactic style of "and. . . ."

1:14. The MSS A D W lat read τῆς βασιλείας, "of the kingdom," which appears to be a scribal attempt to make the unusual and more difficult statement εὐαγγέλιον τοῦ θεοῦ, "gospel of God," conform to the βασιλεία τοῦ θεοῦ, "kingdom of God," in 1:15 (Metzger 1994: 64).

B. Jesus Calls the First Disciples (1:16–20)

At the beginning of this section and the next two sections of Mark (1:14–3:6; 3:7–6:6a; 6:6b–8:21), after an introductory summary we find a pericope involving the Twelve dealing with discipleship (1:16–20; 3:13–19; 6:7–13). The present pericope consists of two parallel accounts involving the calls of Peter and Andrew (1:16–18) and James and John (1:19–20). The source for these accounts was probably the disciples themselves, who later shared with others the circumstances surrounding their call. There is no reason to doubt the historicity of the incident and that these four disciples accompanied Jesus from the beginning of his ministry (contra Bultmann 1968: 28).[1] The issue of whether to classify this pericope as a biographical apothegm or as an epiphany story does not affect the historicity of the tradition or the meaning Mark seeks to convey. It is often difficult to place historical traditions such as the call of the first disciples into neat categories. Although there are a few parallels between the present pericope and the call of Elisha in 1 Kings 19:19–21,[2] the present account does not appear to have been shaped according to the OT account (Best 1981: 168–69; Gundry 1993: 70; Donahue and Harrington 2002: 77).

The Markan editorial work is seen most clearly in the "for" (γάρ, *gar*) explanatory clause in 1:16c (see 1:16–18), "and immediately" (καὶ εὐθύς, *kai euthys*) in 1:18 and 20 (see 1:10–11), the choice of the verb "followed" (ἠκολούθησαν, *ēkolouthēsan*) in 1:18 (see 3:7–8), and the location of the double call narratives (Pryke 1978: 10, 139, 152; Marcus 2000: 182). The literary construction of these verses also appears to be Markan in that we have a similar construction in the call of Levi in 2:14: (1) a participle followed by the verb "saw" (εἶδεν, *eiden*; 1:16a–b, 19a; 2:14a); (2) a second participle describing the activity of the persons seen (1:16c, 9b; 2:14b); (3) Jesus's call to follow (1:17, 20a; 2:14c); and (4) the abandonment of their occupation to follow Jesus (1:18, 20b; 2:14d; Best 1981: 166; Shiner 1995: 172–75; Marcus 2000: 182).

1. The role of the disciples as eyewitnesses of Jesus's life and teaching is especially important for Luke (cf. 1:1–2; Acts 1:21–22; 10:37–39), but Mark does not emphasize this as strongly.

2. These consist mainly of the terms "after me" and "follow." The expression "follow after you" (ἀκολουθήσω ὀπίσω σου, *akolouthēsō opisō sou*) in 1 Kings 19:20 LXX, however, is not what we find in Mark 1:17. It would be strange if Mark (or those before him) had consciously shaped the present account after 1 Kings 19:19–21 but did not have Jesus use these words in Mark 1:17.

Exegesis and Exposition

¹⁶And as he was walking along the shore of the Sea of Galilee, he saw Simon and Andrew, the brother of Simon, casting [their] net(s) into the sea, for they were fishermen. ¹⁷And Jesus said to them, "Come after me, and I will make you to become fishers of men." ¹⁸And immediately they left their nets [and] followed him. ¹⁹And after proceeding a little further, he saw James, the son of Zebedee, and John his brother who were preparing the nets in the boat, ²⁰and immediately he called them. And leaving their father Zebedee in the boat with the hired men, they followed him.

"The sea" (θάλασσα, *thalassa*; 2:13; 3:7; 4:1, 39; 5:1, 13 [2×], 21; 6:47, 48, 49) is **1:16–18** Mark's favorite way of referring to the "Sea of Galilee" (1:16; 7:31). Elsewhere it is also referred to as the Sea of Tiberias (John 6:1; 21:1), the Lake of Gennesaret (Luke 5:1; Josephus, *J.W.* 2.20.6 §573), the Sea of Chinnereth (Num. 34:11; Josh. 12:3; 13:27), or the Sea of Gennesaret (Josephus, *J.W.* 3.10.1 §463; 3.10.7 §506). Supplied by the melting snows of Mount Hermon in the north, it is better described as a "lake" (λίμνη, *limnē*; Luke 5:1; 8:22, 33) due to its size (12.5 miles long and 7 miles wide at its widest point) and its geography (it is inland). Located in the Jordan Rift Valley, it lies about 700 feet below sea level. In the NT it is generally referred to as a "sea." The location of this event, even if redactional in its wording, comes from the tradition, since the present account takes place by the sea ("shore" [lit. "passing by"], "casting a net into the sea," "fishermen," "in a boat preparing their nets"). Ancient writers (Strabo, *Geography* 16.2.45; Pliny, *Nat. Hist.* 5.15.71–72; Josephus, *J.W.* 3.10.7 §§506–15) refer to the fertility of the lake and its extensive fishing industry.

Simon and Andrew are one of two sets of brothers among the twelve disciples. "Simon" (Σίμων, *Simōn*) is used to describe the apostle seven times in Mark (1:16 [2×], 29, 30, 36; 3:16; 14:37), but after 3:19 he is referred to by his Greek nickname "Peter" (Πέτρος, *Petros*) nineteen times. The only exception is 14:37. According to John 1:44 Peter and Andrew were from Bethsaida, and Andrew was a disciple of John the Baptist (1:35, 40–42). The dominant position of Peter among the two brothers is indicated by Mark's explanation that Andrew was Peter's brother. Peter also receives pride of place in the list of the twelve disciples (3:16–19) and in the places where he is mentioned along with James and John (5:37; 9:2; 14:33; cf. also 13:3). This indicates his leadership role among the disciples both "by folly as well as by insight" (see Marcus 2000: 180; Mark 8:32–33; 9:5–6; 14:29–31, 66–72). In their encounter with Jesus, the two brothers are portrayed as casting a net or nets (ἀμφιβάλλοντας, *amphiballontas*) into the sea. A casting net was a circular net up to twenty feet in diameter with stone weights attached to the ends. An attached rope, when pulled, drew the net together and enclosed the fish. The net was thrown and drawn together by a single individual (Wuellner 1967: 39) and could be thrown from a boat or while wading along the shore. The latter appears to be the case here. There is no reason to suggest that Peter and Andrew, in contrast to James and John, did not own a boat (contra Waetjen 1989: 10, 79) and to doubt the assertion of Luke 5:3 (cf. 5:10 with 5:2).

"For they were fishermen" (ἦσαν γὰρ ἁλιεῖς, ēsan gar halieis) is the first occurrence in the Gospel of an explanatory comment introduced by "for." Additional examples of this are found in 1:22; 2:15; 3:10; 5:8, 28, 42; 6:14, 17, 18, 20, 31, 48, 52; 7:3; 9:6 (2×), 31; 11:13, 18 (2×), 37; 12:12; 14:2, 56; 15:10; 16:4, 8 (2×). Most, if not all, of these are Markan in origin and provide a rich source for observing his redactional concerns and interests. The explanation is somewhat superfluous but is in keeping with Mark's love of dual expressions and repetition (Neirynck 1988: 114; Donahue 1973: 241–43).

The expressions "Come after me" (Δεῦτε ὀπίσω μου, Deute opisō mou) in 1:17 and "followed" in 1:18 are two Markan ways of describing what it means to be a "follower" of Jesus (cf. also 1:20; 2:14, 15; 3:7; 5:24; 6:1; 8:34; 9:38; 10:21, 28, 32, 52; 15:41). The terms are not used simply to describe what one must do to become a member of the Twelve but rather what any person must do to become a follower of Jesus, as 8:34 and 10:28–29 indicate (contra Hengel 1981: 61–63). The expression "after me" indicates that Jesus was not calling Peter, Andrew, James, and John into a partnership of equals but to be his followers and servants. Unlike the rabbis, Jesus is the one who initiates the invitation to follow him, not the disciples; and unlike rabbinic disciples, Jesus's followers are not called to follow the study of the law but to follow "him" (J. Edwards 2002: 49–50). As a result, Jesus's followers were soon called "Christians" (Acts 11:26) because they were not so much followers of a particular teaching, sacrament, hermeneutical theory, or ethic but of a person—Jesus Christ. The object of their faith and hope was Jesus Christ, the Son of God (1:1). The call of Jesus also differed from that of the OT prophets, for whereas they called people to follow God, Jesus called people to follow him (Gundry 1993: 70–71; Hengel 1981: 16–83).

The fulfillment of Jesus's prediction, "I will make you to become fishers of men," is described in 3:14–15; 6:7–13, 30, and the readers of Mark were fully aware that after the resurrection the ministry of the twelve apostles reached even to them (Acts 1:8; Eph. 2:19–20; Rev. 21:14). The call of Jesus was not to find fulfillment in what they were already doing but to a radically new purpose in life. From henceforth they would serve not their own interests and desires but those of Jesus who called them. There does not appear to be any OT precedent for the expression "fishers of men."[3] Indeed, the images in the OT involving fishing/fishers are quite negative (cf. Jer. 16:16; Ezek. 29:4–5; 38:4; Amos 4:2; Hab. 1:14–17; cf. Matt. 13:47–50; 1QH 3.26; 5.7–8). Here, however, the metaphor is positive, as their "fishing" ministry reveals (3:14–15; 6:7–13, 30; Donahue and Harrington 2002: 74).

Although the phrase "And immediately" is usually a simple connective lacking any serious temporal dimension (see 1:10), here it appears that Mark

---

3. For a discussion of the use of fishing imagery in the non-Christian world of Jesus's day, see Wuellner 1967: 64–133.

gives it a full temporal significance (Cranfield 1959: 70). In so doing, Mark emphasizes the importance of responding speedily to Jesus's call to discipleship (note ἀφέντες, *aphentes*, lit. "leaving"). The kingdom of God has come. One must drop everything, because entering the kingdom is more important than even life itself (8:36). Peter and Andrew therefore did not even gather in the net but left it in the sea (10:28–29; cf. Luke 9:57–62; cf. 1 Kings 19:19–21). They left their occupation and livelihood, for one cannot serve God and things (Matt. 6:24). In leaving everything to follow Jesus, Peter and Andrew serve as examples for prospective followers of Christ (Mark 8:34). This scene is more historically understandable if, as John 1:35–42 claims, Peter and Andrew had earlier met Jesus and formed an opinion concerning who he was (John 1:41). Geographically, the call to follow Jesus was not as drastic as might at first appear, for Jesus continued his mission in Galilee for some time (Stein 1996: 112–14). The availability of a boat in Jesus's ministry (Mark 3:9; 4:1, 35; 5:21; 6:32, 45, 54; 8:13) suggests that Peter and Andrew (and James and John) used their possessions in these instances in the service of Jesus.

The literary connections found in 1:16–20 are typically Markan: "and" (1:16),   **1:19–20**
"and" (1:17), "and immediately" (1:18), "and" (1:19), "and immediately" (1:20a), "and" (1:20b). James[4] and John his brother are the second set of brothers among the disciples. They are described as son(s) of Zebedee to distinguish them from others with similar names: John the Baptist (the only other "John" in Mark); the apostle James (the son of Alphaeus, 3:18); James the brother of Jesus (James the Just), who became the leader of the church in Jerusalem (6:3; Gal. 1:19; 2:9, 12; Acts 12:17; 15:13–21); and James the Less, the son of Mary (15:40; 16:1). According to Luke 5:10, the two sets of brothers were "partners" in the fishing business. James the brother of John was killed by Herod Agrippa I in AD 44 (Acts 12:2), and James the brother of Jesus was martyred in AD 62 (Josephus, *Ant.* 20.9.1 §§197–203). Peter, James, and John appear to have made up an inner circle of the disciples and were the only disciples present with Jesus on several important occasions (Mark 5:37; 9:2; 14:33; cf. 13:3, where Andrew was also present).

James and John are described as "preparing the nets." The term "preparing/ mending" (καταρτίζοντας, *katartizontas*) can refer to taking care of the nets in ways such as mending them, folding them for storage, or preparing them in various ways for immediate or future use. These nets were probably dragnets, which were much larger than the one-man net(s) mentioned in 1:16 and would involve several people (cf. John 21:6, 8, 11). "Preparing" or "getting ready" is a better translation than "mending," for the latter took place *after* fishing, and James and John were probably getting ready to fish, even as Peter and Andrew were already fishing. Most scholars interpret καὶ αὐτούς (*kai autous*, lit. "and them"; translated above as "who were") as a circumstantial clause

4. For a discussion of how "Jacob" in the OT and NT became "James" in English, see Marcus 2000: 180–81.

referring to James and John ("them") introduced by "and." As a result the pronoun αὐτούς is left untranslated.[5]

"And immediately" in 1:20 appears to function primarily as a conjunction with little or no chronological significance (see 1:10), and as a result Matt. 4:20 places "immediately" with the participle "leaving" (ἀφέντες, *aphentes*). Whereas in 1:18 the immediate quality of Peter's and Andrew's response makes a theological point, here "immediately he called" appears to carry no real theological or temporal significance. "Leaving their father" (ἀφέντες τὸν πατέρα αὐτῶν, *aphentes ton patera autōn*) emphasizes another aspect of what is involved in following Jesus. One must leave everything to follow Jesus (10:28). This involves possessions (1:18) and home (10:29; cf. Luke 14:26; 18:29). Not even the most intimate of family ties can stand between the believer and Jesus. Viewed in light of such teachings as Exod. 20:12; Deut. 5:16; Prov. 23:22–25 (cf. also Tob. 5:1; Sir. 3:1–16, esp. v. 16, "Whoever forsakes a father is like a blasphemer"), the response of James and John (cf. Mark 10:28–29) would have appeared blasphemous. Such a "totalitarian" demand contains a powerful and undeniable christological claim (Balla 2005: 155–56, 230). The reference to "the hired men" (τῶν μισθωτῶν, *tōn misthōtōn*) appears to be a historical remembrance associated with the call of James and John. It suggests that they were not economically poor but reasonably prosperous (cf. 10:28), belonging to the middle class and thus not a "dominated class" (contra Belo 1981: 102). "They followed him" (ἀπῆλθον ὀπίσω αὐτοῦ, *apēlthon opisō autou*; lit. "they followed after him") recalls "Come after me" in 1:17.

Summary

Mark's theological purpose in this pericope is seen both in his placement of the account and in its emphasis on what it means to be a follower of Jesus. The placement of the pericope serves both a literary and a theological function. The literary function is to prepare the readers for the disciples' presence in 1:29–31, 36; 2:15, 18–22, and 23–38 (note also the plural verbs in 1:21–22, 37, 38). The theological function is seen in that after a preliminary summary, Mark introduces each of the next three sections of Jesus's traditions with teachings concerning discipleship: 1:16–20; 3:13–19; 6:7–13. What it means to follow Jesus lies in the forefront of Mark's mind. The call to discipleship addressed to the four disciples is a pattern for every potential believer (8:34). As 1:15 demonstrates, it involves both a positive and a negative aspect. The negative involves repentance and leaving anything that might come between the believer and God (possessions and family), and the positive involves faith or following Jesus and becoming fishers of people. Within this passage there is present an escalating demand: (1) Peter and Andrew leave their nets (possessions), and (2) James and John leave

5. So Moulton and Howard 1929: 423; M. Black 1967: 81–82; Gundry 1993: 72–73; RSV, NRSV, NIV, NEB, REB, NAB, JB.

not only their nets and boat (possessions) but their father (family) as well (Marcus 2000: 185).

The call to discipleship contains within it a sovereign christological claim (Schmithals 1979: 1.105). The present pericope is dominated by Jesus's call to absolute obedience and surrender. From the lips of anyone else, such a totalitarian call is appalling and outrageous, but the one who calls here is not just anyone. He is Jesus Christ, the Son of God (1:1), and the reader knows that this Jesus asks less from his followers than he gives. When he "who gave his life as a ransom for many" (10:45) and by his sacrificial death brought redemption and the new covenant (14:22–25) calls, believers gladly respond with loving and grateful hearts and follow him.

C. Jesus's Healing Ministry in Capernaum and Galilee (1:21–45)

It is unlikely that 1:21–39 (or 1:21–45) existed as a pre-Markan complex (see 1:14–3:6). Although this material is sometimes described as "a day in the life of Jesus," only 1:21–31 actually takes place on the same day. The next two accounts (1:32–34 and 1:35–38) take place on the following day, according to the Jewish understanding of time, since evening (see 1:32) marks the end of the Sabbath referred to in 1:21. The final two incidents (1:39 and 1:40–45) have no temporal connection with what has preceded. Even if we were to reckon time by the Roman legal day, 1:35–38 would not fit within the same day as 1:21–34. How the events of 1:21–31 and 1:32–38 were related in the pre-Markan tradition is impossible to determine.

1. Jesus's Authority as a Teacher (1:21–28)

The first miracle of Jesus recorded in Mark involves an exorcism performed in the synagogue of Capernaum. Three other exorcisms are reported in 5:1–20; 7:24–30; and 9:14–29, and there are references to others in various summaries and traditions (1:32–34, 39; 3:11, 22–30; 6:7, 13; cf. 9:38). Mark also records nine healing miracles (1:29–31, 40–45; 2:1–12; 3:1–6; 5:21–43 [two]; 7:31–37; 8:22–26; 10:46–52) and five nature miracles (4:35–41; 6:35–44, 45–52; 8:1–9; 11:12–14, 20–25). Whether Mark knew more exorcism stories and chose not to include them (or whether he knew more healing and nature miracles and chose not to include them) is impossible to determine (Stein 1971: 190–91).

Mark introduces the story of this exorcism with a summary of Jesus's authority as a teacher (1:21–22). In so doing, he ties the present account with his introductory summary of Jesus's teaching in 1:14–15. For Mark, Jesus's preaching/teaching, healing, and casting out demons are all part of Jesus's teaching ministry. We should note the unity in all this. The content of Jesus's teaching ministry in 1:14–15, involving the arrival of the kingdom of God, includes the manifestation of the kingdom's arrival in his healing miracles and exorcisms. Thus the summary of Jesus's authoritative teaching in 1:21–22 is followed by an account of an exorcism containing an additional statement about his authoritative teaching (1:27). The account of the exorcism follows the normal pattern. After the introductory summary (1:21–22) we have an encounter with a demoniac (1:23), the demon's reaction (1:24), Jesus's exorcism of the demon (1:25), the departure of the demon (1:26), a description of the people's response (1:27), and a concluding summary (1:28). This order and arrangement is due less to the "form" of an exorcism story than to the necessity of these elements in telling such a story. Mark's own editorial work is seen most clearly in the introductory summary and "for" (γάρ, *gar*) clause (1:21–22), the comment by the onlookers in 1:27 concerning Jesus's "new teaching with authority," the concluding summary (1:28), such terms as "and" and "immediately," and the references to Jesus's "teaching" and "authority" and the "amazement" that his actions produce (Stein 1970: 84–85; Pryke 1978: 10, 139, 152; Guelich 1989: 55; Marcus 2000: 190–91). In this account, Mark has taken a traditional story of an exorcism by Jesus, placed it at the beginning of his ministry, and edited it to emphasize the authoritative teaching ministry of Jesus (Donahue and Harrington 2002: 83).

Exegesis and Exposition

[21]And they proceed into Capernaum. And immediately on the ⌜sabbath⌝, after ⌜entering⌝ into the synagogue, he began to teach. [22]And they were astonished at his teaching, for he was teaching them as having authority and not as the scribes. [23]And immediately there was in their synagogue a man with an unclean spirit, and he cried out, [24]saying, "What have you to do with us, Jesus of Nazareth? Have you come to destroy us? I know who you are—the Holy One of God." [25]And Jesus rebuked him, saying, "Be silent and come out of him."[26]And the unclean spirit, having convulsed him and having cried out with a loud cry, came out of him. [27]And all were amazed, so that ⌜[they] were discussing⌝ among themselves, saying, "What is this? A ⌜new⌝ teaching with authority! He even commands the unclean spirits, and they obey him." [28]And immediately his fame went out everywhere into all the countryside of Galilee.

1:21–22   The hand of Mark is seen throughout these verses: the "and" followed by the historical present tense of the verb "they proceed into" (εἰσπορεύονται, *eisporeuontai*) are Markan literary characteristics (V. Taylor 1952: 46–49); the verb "enter" (εἰσέρχομαι, *eiserchomai*) and its compounds are found seventeen times in 1:21–45 (1:21, 24, 25, 26, 28 [2×], 29, 31, 35 [2×], 38, 39, 40, 42, 45 [3×]); "and immediately" is typically Markan (see 1:10); the redundancy and emphasis on Jesus's teaching (Neirynck 1988: 85; cf. 4:1–2); the periphrastic "he was teaching" (ἦν διδάσκων, *ēn didaskōn*; V. Taylor 1952: 45); the emphasis on the "astonishment" Jesus caused (see below); and so on. The opening "they" in 1:21 is not the indefinite "they" commonly found in Mark, but refers to Jesus and the disciples Peter, Andrew, James, and John (1:16–20). This is clear from 1:29–31 and 36–38. There is no reason to assume that Mark sought to tie this account to the same day that 1:16–20 took place, for the activities involved in 1:16–20 would not have taken place on a Sabbath.

    The city of Capernaum (Hebrew נַחוּם כְּפַר, *kĕpar nāḥûm*, village of Nahum) was located on the northwestern shore of the Sea of Galilee, about two and a half miles west of where the upper Jordan River enters the lake. It was an important city of about ten thousand people, whose ruins (Tell Ḥum) cover a strip about a mile long. Its prosperity was due to its lying on a major east-west trade route and being the site of a major toll station (cf. Matt. 9:9–13). Consequently it contained a contingent of Roman soldiers led by a centurion (cf. Matt. 8:5–13/Luke 7:1–10; cf. John 4:46–54). It possessed a major synagogue, whose black basalt foundation can still be seen below the impressive ruins of the later, fourth-century white synagogue. At the beginning of his ministry, Jesus moved from Nazareth to Capernaum (Matt. 4:13; 9:1; cf. Mark 2:1; 9:33; John 2:12), which was more centrally located for his Galilean ministry. Later in his ministry, Jesus pronounced a judgment upon the city for its lack of response to his ministry there (Matt. 11:23–24/Luke 10:15).

    One should not give any temporal significance to "And immediately" in 1:21b, for interpreting it as either "having entered immediately on the Sabbath" or "immediately he was teaching" raises more questions than it answers. It is unlikely that Mark wants to emphasize that Jesus entered the synagogue immediately at sundown, that is, that he could not wait to get in, or that the minute he entered he began to teach. It is best to see this here as a simple Markan connective lacking any distinct chronological meaning (see 1:10). (Note how Luke 4:31 omits "immediately.") Jesus's entrance into the "synagogue" refers to a building rather than a gathering of Jews on the Sabbath (cf. 3:1, where Mark adds "there" [ἐκεῖ, ekei], and 6:2). This is evident from the terms "entering into" (1:21) and "having left" (ἐξελθόντες, exelthontes; 1:29). Elsewhere Jesus is primarily found teaching outside the synagogue (2:13; 4:1–2; 6:6, 34; 8:31; 9:31; 10:1, 17; 12:35; 14:49), so that the present location in the account appears traditional. For other examples of Jesus teaching in synagogues, see 1:39; 6:2; Matt. 4:23; 9:35; 12:9; 13:54; Luke 4:15–29; 6:6; 13:10; John 6:59; 18:20. The last reference in Mark to Jesus being in a synagogue is 6:2; here and in 12:39 and 13:9 the synagogues are portrayed negatively. The verb "began to teach" (ἐδίδασκεν, edidasken) is an inceptive imperfect, describing the beginning of an action. The present account assumes Jesus's reputation as a teacher is already well established, and as a result he was invited to teach (France 2002: 101). Thus the present account is not necessarily one of the first incidents in the ministry of Jesus. Mark has placed it here, however, as a "paradigmatic illustration" (Bultmann 1968: 209) of Jesus's ministry and the amazement he created by his teaching/exorcism. No major distinction should be seen in Mark between the terms "teaching" (διδάσκω, didaskō) and "preaching" (κηρύσσω, kēryssō), as their interchangeable use in 6:12 and 30 indicates.

In 1:22 Mark emphasizes that "they" were astonished. "They" is an impersonal plural and a common Markan stylistic feature (cf. 1:30, 32, 45; 2:3, 18; 3:2, 32; 5:14, 35; 6:14, 33, 54; 7:32; 8:22; 10:13, 49; 13:9, 11, 26; 14:12). The astonishment Jesus creates is a clear Markan theological emphasis. Compare "astonished" (ἐκπλήσσομαι, ekplēssomai; 1:22; 6:2; 7:37; 10:26; 11:18); "amazed" (θαμβέομαι, thambeomai; 1:27; 10:24, 32; cf. also 9:15; 16:5, 6); "marveled" (θαυμάζω, thaumazō; 5:20; 15:5, 44; cf. also 12:17); "feared" (φοβέομαι, phobeomai; 4:41; 5:15, 33; 6:50; 9:6, 32; 10:32; 11:18; 16:8); "amazed" (ἐξίστημι, existēmi; 2:12; 5:42; 6:51); "amazement" (ἔκστασις, ekstasis; 5:42; 16:8). This often results from Jesus's teaching (1:22, 27; 6:2; 10:24, 26; 11:18; cf. also 12:17), healings (7:37), exorcisms (1:22, 27; 5:20), passion predictions (9:32; 10:32), as well as at various divine epiphanies (4:41; 6:50–51; 9:6; 16:5, 8). In the vast majority of instances, this astonishment is a positive response. That this emphasis is found so often in Mark's editorial work indicates that he is not in the least embarrassed that Jesus's ministry had a miraculous or "wonderworking" dimension to it.[1] The cause of this astonishment is Jesus's "teaching."

---

1. The idea, popular in the 1970s, that Mark sought to refute a "divine man" or θεῖος ἀνήρ (theios anēr) theology that emphasized Jesus as a miracle worker is refuted by his emphasis of this dimension in the life of Jesus. See Holladay 1977; Kingsbury 1981: 243–57; and J. Edwards 2002: 105–9 for a discussion of the issue.

This refers not so much to the content of Jesus's teaching but to his teaching ministry as a whole. Having mentioned in 1:21 that Jesus "taught" in the synagogue, Mark now points out that his "teaching" caused amazement and then adds that he "was teaching" with authority. In 1:27 he will again refer to Jesus's authoritative teaching. This heavy emphasis on Jesus's teaching appears strange in the context of an exorcism and is not found in any other exorcism account in Mark (5:1–20; 7:24–30; 9:14–29, although the title "teacher" appears in 9:17). Nor do we find it in most summary statements that refer to Jesus casting out demons (1:32–34; 3:11; 6:7, 13). The exception is 1:39 (cf. also the summary statements involving the disciples' ministry where preaching and casting out demons are placed side by side: 3:14–15 and 6:12–13). That Mark emphasizes Jesus's teaching ministry is evident (cf. 2:13; 4:1, 2; 6:2, 6, 34; 8:31; 9:31; 10:1; 11:17, 18; 12:14, 35, 38; 14:49; Stein 1970: 91–94). By doing so in 1:21–22, he ties the present account closely with the opening summary of this section (1:14–15), but the fourfold emphasis in 1:21–22, 27 would be considerable overkill if Mark were simply seeking to establish a literary tie between the present account and 1:14–15. To establish such a tie, the single reference in 1:21 would have sufficed. Even though Mark lacks most of the teachings of Jesus found in Matthew and Luke, his emphasis on the teaching ministry of Jesus is actually greater.[2] Unfortunately, no convincing theory has been put forward to explain this Markan emphasis.[3]

Mark does not explain in the present verse why Jesus was seen "as having authority" (ὡς ἐξουσίαν ἔχων, *hōs exousian echōn*), but he does so in the story that follows (1:23–28). His authority, however, is contrasted here with that of the scribes. Mark does not explain the term "scribes" (γραμματεῖς, *grammateis*). Apparently he thought this would be self-evident, as did the other Gospel writers, who also left this term unexplained.[4] A scribe was a professional person who possessed the ability to write and interpret texts. Whereas this was once a secular position, by NT times it was associated with religious duties such as interpreting biblical texts and serving as guardians of the tradition. Although a scribe could belong to any Jewish sect, or to none

2. Mark, for example, uses the term "teacher" (διδάσκαλος, *didaskalos*) 12 times (Matthew, 12 times), the verb "teach" (διδάσκω, *didaskō*) 17 times (Matthew, 14 times), and the noun "teaching" (διδαχή, *didachē*) 5 times (Matthew, 3 times). The greater emphasis of Mark in this area stands out clearly when one realizes that Matthew is two-thirds longer than Mark (18,293 words to 11,025 words; Stein 2001: 50–52), so that an equal emphasis in Matthew for "teacher" would be 20 times, for the verb "teach" 28 times, and for the noun "teaching" 8 times.

3. Some have suggested that Mark wrote his Gospel as an introduction for Q, and this is why he emphasized so strongly Jesus's teaching ministry. Others have suggested he wrote his Gospel in reaction to an overemphasis on the importance of Q. The great emphasis placed by Mark on Jesus's teaching, however, mitigates against the latter. Others have suggested that Mark emphasized this because it corresponded to the ministry of Jesus, or that he sought to ground the catechetical practice of the early church by demonstrating that these teachings ultimately went back to Jesus.

4. This should cause one to be cautious about claims that Mark's portrayal of the scribes is anachronistic (contra Dillon 1995: 94).

at all, the majority were associated with the Pharisees (2:16; Luke 5:30; Acts 23:9). In every instance but one (12:28–34), they are portrayed in Mark as bitterly opposed to Jesus (2:6, 16; 11:27–33; 15:33) and intimately involved with the elders and chief priests in the plot to kill him (8:31; 10:33; 11:18; 14:1, 43, 53; 15:1). Jesus's teaching is contrasted with that of the scribes because his teaching possessed "authority." Some have suggested that the difference between them lay in the fact that instead of basing his argument on the authority of what others had said (i.e., quoting other rabbis), Jesus's authority was seen in that he introduced his teaching with either "Amen," "Amen, Amen," or "but I say to you." For Mark, however, the authority of Jesus's teaching was intimately associated with the coming of the kingdom of God and his authority to exorcise demons (Ambrozic 1975: 115–43; Dillon 1995: 97–112). In the present account, this is evident from 1:27: his "new teaching with authority" (διδαχὴ καινὴ κατ᾽ ἐξουσίαν, didachē kainē kat᾽ exousian) is due to the fact that he commands even the "unclean spirits/demons" (τοῖς πνεύμασι τοῖς ἀκαθάρτοις, tois pneumasi tois akathartois). Other areas in which Jesus's unique authority was seen include his healing ministry, his raising the dead, and his control of nature.

"And immediately" in 1:23 serves once again as a conjunction without temporal significance (see 1:10), for it functions poorly as a temporal designation with "there was" (ἦν, ēn). If instead of "there was" we found "there entered," this would create a greater likelihood that "and immediately" should be given temporal significance. Luke's omission of "immediately" in his parallel account (4:33) should be noted. The reference to "their synagogue" (συναγωγῇ αὐτῶν, synagōgē autōn) suggests that Mark's audience was gentile (cf. 7:2–4; Hooker 1991: 63; contra Marcus 2000: 187). The expression "an unclean spirit" serves essentially as a synonym for the more Greek "demon" (δαίμων, daimōn). In Mark each expression occurs eleven times ("unclean spirit," 1:23, 26, 27; 3:11, 30; 5:2, 8, 13; 6:7; 7:25; 9:25; "demon," 1:34 [2×], 39; 3:15, 22 [2×]; 6:13; 7:26, 29, 30; 9:38), and they are used interchangeably in 3:22 and 30 as well as 7:25, 26, 29, 30.

In 1:23 Mark uses the emphatic form of the verb "cry out" (ἀνά + κράζω, ana + krazō). Such cries are frequently associated with exorcisms (3:11–12; 5:7; 9:26; cf. T. Sol. 1.13; 3.4; 4.11). The demon's cry, "What have you to do with us?" (Τί ἡμῖν καὶ σοί; Ti hēmin kai soi? lit. "What between us and you?"), is a common formula[5] and generally means "What business do we have with each other?" (Maynard 1985: 582) or "Go away and leave me alone" (France 2002: 103). It is incorrect, however, to say that this formula is always posed by an inferior or one in an inferior position (contra Guelich 1989: 56–57) because of John 2:4; 2 Sam. 16:10; 19:23 LXX. The "us" refers not to the man and the unclean spirit, but to the unclean spirits as a group. The demon's address, "Jesus of Nazareth," refers back to 1:9. The reference to Nazareth, however,

1:23–24

---

5. Mark 5:7; Matt. 8:29; Luke 4:34; 8:28; John 2:4; Judg. 11:12; 2 Sam. 16:10; 19:23; 1 Kings 17:18; 2 Kings 3:13; 2 Chron. 35:21; cf. also Josh. 22:24; Jer. 2:18; Hos. 14:9.

was probably part of the tradition, since "Jesus" was a common name and would need some sort of qualifier.[6]

The demon speaks for all the demons, "Have you come to destroy us?" Although grammatically this can be understood as an exclamation (Hooker 1991: 64), it is best interpreted as a question following the previous question (Marcus 2000: 188). The verb "come" (ἦλθες, *ēlthes*) indicates that the demons recognize that Jesus has been sent from God (1:39; 2:17; 10:45). Although one should not read the incarnational understanding of Jesus's coming found in John 1:9–14 into this verse, the emphases of Mark and John are complementary. The demons clearly recognize the superiority of Jesus (see 5:7) and his mission. He has come to "destroy them." There is no struggle or resistance on their part, for this would be useless against the one they know is the Son of God (1:1, 24d, 34d; 3:11; 5:7). The destruction of Satan's rule is a natural consequence of Jesus's bringing the kingdom of God. With his coming, the demonic world is now plundered (3:27), because the Stronger One has arrived (cf. 1:7). Jesus's coming therefore means defeat not just for this demon but also for "us," that is, all the demons.

The demon's statement "I know who you are" should be interpreted in light of the Markan editorial comment in 1:34 that the demons knew him. By this Mark indicates that the demons are reliable spokesmen for understanding who Jesus is, and because of their supernatural insight, they know better than Jesus's contemporaries his identity. Thus their description of him is of vital importance for answering, Who is Jesus of Nazareth? The demon gives the answer—Jesus is "the Holy One of God." Some have suggested that the naming of one's opponent is often a defensive (apotropaic) device by which a demon seeks to control the exorcist (cf. 9:38; Acts 19:13; Burkill 1963: 72–78; Gundry 1993: 76–77, 83–84). There is no indication of this in the present account, however, for Jesus's reply in 1:25 is not introduced by an adversative of any sort. There is no "but [no ἀλλά, *alla*, or even δέ, *de*] I know who you are." In the present account "Holy One of God" serves not as an attempt to gain control over Jesus but as a christological confession stemming from the supernatural insight and understanding of the demon (Best 1965: 17). This is clear from Mark's comment that the demons "knew" Jesus (1:34d). The present title is not used elsewhere in Mark and was probably found in the tradition that Mark inherited (Best 1986: 32–33). In light of the similar demonic confessions in 3:11 and 5:7, the title "Holy One of God" (ὁ ἅγιος τοῦ θεοῦ, *ho hagios tou theou*) was probably understood by Mark as a synonym for "Son of God" and indicated the special relationship that existed between Jesus and God. Luke, who also has "Holy One of God" in his parallel account (4:34), appears to have understood this title in the same way (1:35; 4:41). The title also appears in John 6:69. Attempts to see this title as arising from a play on the Semitic words for Nazareth (*nṣrt*) and

---

6. Bauckham (2006: 67–92) points out that "Jesus" was the sixth most common male name found among Palestinian Jews between 330 BC and AD 200.

"holy one" (*nzyr*) would have been meaningless for Mark's Greek audience (contra Guelich 1989: 57).

Although some argue that "rebuked" (ἐπετίμησεν, *epetimēsen*) is a technical **1:25–26** term for the exorcism of demons, the use of the term elsewhere in Mark indicates that it is not and that it acquires its meaning from the context in which it is found (Kee 1967–68). It is used with respect to demons in 3:12 (but not involving an exorcism) and 9:25, but it is found more frequently in contexts having little to do with demons (4:39; 8:30, 32, 33; 10:13, 48). What is constant in the use of the verb is that it is a word of authority and/or command. It has also been suggested that the command to "Be silent" (Φιμώθητι, *Phimōthēti*) is a standard part of an exorcism (Burkill 1963: 73), but here it is used not so much as part of a rite of exorcism but to show Jesus's power and authority over the demons (3:27). It is uncertain whether it functions here as an example of the "messianic secret" in Mark (cf. 1:34d). After the demon's departure from the man, as witnessed by the man's "convulsion" (σπαράξαν, *sparaxan*) and "having cried out with a loud cry" (φωνῆσαν φωνῇ μεγάλῃ, *phōnēsan phōnē megalē*; cf. 9:26),[7] nothing is said concerning the man or the demon. The healing of the man and the exorcism of the demon are important only insofar as they reveal who Jesus is. Having served this purpose, Mark leaves them without dealing with such speculations as where the demon went (cf. 5:12–13) or what happened to the man (cf. 5:15), for his Gospel is not about them but about Jesus Christ, the Son of God.

"And all were amazed" repeats the theme introduced in 1:22. The "all" (ἅπαντες, **1:27–28** *hapantes*) emphasizes the universal acknowledgment of Jesus's power and authority (cf. 1:37; 2:12; 5:20). The result of the amazement created by Jesus's action is a discussion among those in the synagogue concerning his identity. This questioning is not understood negatively as in 8:11 but positively as in 9:10 (cf. 4:41). It serves to heighten the amazement and wonder created by the actions of the Son of God. What they discuss is "What is this?" (τί ἐστιν τοῦτο, *ti estin touto*). This and other related questions (4:41; 6:2; 8:27, 29; 11:28) serve to make the reader reflect on the christological question, Who is Jesus of Nazareth? Mark, of course, is seeking to demonstrate that Jesus is the Christ, the Son of God (1:1). He does this in the present account by showing Jesus's authority over the demon and the demon's acknowledgment of Jesus's unique relationship with God. As in 1:22, Jesus's "teaching" and "authority" are linked together. The expression "with authority" (κατ᾽ ἐξουσίαν, *kat' exousian*) can be placed with what follows ("With authority he even commands the unclean spirits") or with what precedes ("A new teaching with authority!"). The fact that "even" (καί, *kai*) follows this phrase favors the rendering "A new teaching with authority! He even commands the unclean spirits" (RSV, NRSV, NIV, NASB). That "authority" is associated with "teaching" in 1:22

---

7. For other examples of the cognate dative in Mark, see 5:42; 7:13; cf. also 4:24; 12:23. See Neirynck 1988: 76–77, 237.

also supports the view that it should be so associated here. Jesus's divine "authority" in Mark is also seen in his authority to forgive sins (2:10) and to cleanse the temple (11:28–33) and in his disciples' authority to cast out demons (3:15; 6:7; J. Edwards 1994: 220–27).

The concluding Markan summary in 1:28 emphasizes Jesus's greatness. Mark gives "immediately" a temporal significance in this verse by separating it from the conjunction "and," although Luke again omits it (4:37). The different geographical descriptions of the extent of Jesus's popularity are classic examples of Markan redundancy (Neirynck 1988: 50–52; Donahue and Harrington 2002: 81)—"everywhere" (πανταχοῦ, *pantachou*) and "into all the countryside of Galilee" (εἰς ὅλην τὴν περίχωρον τῆς Γαλιλαίας, *eis holēn tēn perichōron tēs Galilaias*). Other examples of a double geographical description are found in 1:38; 4:5; 5:1, 11; 6:3, 45; 11:4; 13:3; 14:54, 66, 68. "Of Galilee" functions here as an epexegetical genitive or genitive of apposition (France 2002: 106) and helps to define "all the countryside." The summary in this verse heightens Jesus's fame and notoriety by referring to his fame (lit. "the report of him") going out "immediately," by stating that it went "everywhere," and that it went "into all the countryside" (cf. 1:33, 37, 45; 2:1–2; 3:7–9).

Summary

In this account, Mark seeks to help his readers understand who Jesus is by recounting an incident in his ministry in which he exorcised a demon. Connecting his teaching ministry with his exorcisms (and healings in the following accounts), Mark points out that Jesus possessed a unique authority that caused his contemporaries to be amazed. What makes Jesus unique is not just that he exorcised demons but also how he did this. He did not use special incantations or adjurations. He did not scream or yell. He made no special physical manipulation or appeal to God. His exorcisms were based not on technique or knowledge but on who he is. He was not an ordinary teacher or even a great teacher like Hillel or Shammai, for he possessed a unique authority that had something "new" about it. Jesus, because of who he is, not only proclaimed the arrival of the kingdom of God but in his ministry also manifested its arrival by plundering the household of Satan (3:22–29) through his exorcism of demons. The climax of the entire account comes with the demonic confession that Jesus of Nazareth is in fact the Holy One of God. The unclean spirits supernaturally know (1:34d) that he is the Son of God (3:11; 5:7), and thus are "spokesmen" for the Markan Christology. Because of his being "the Holy One of God," Jesus needs only to speak, and the demons must obey. He possesses greater power and plunders Satan's dominion (3:27) by delivering its captives (cf. Luke 4:18).

Mark's emphasis on Jesus's teaching (1:21–22, 27) does not downplay his power as an exorcist. For Mark, they are two sides of the same coin. It is true that they are not identical, but neither are they separate, unrelated entities. They are one because they all center on who Jesus is. His ministry of teaching and exorcism has unique authority because Jesus is unique. Who is this one who has power over the demons? (1:27). Who is this one who controls winds and waves? (4:41). The reader already knows. It is Jesus Christ, the one greater than John, whom both heaven (1:11) and the demons (1:24) confess is the Son of God.

Additional Notes

1:21. The expression τοῖς σάββασιν is plural in form but singular in meaning (cf. 2:23; Matt. 12:1).

1:21. Although the participle is omitted in some MSS (‫ א‬C L Δ f¹³), it should be retained because of its strong attestation in A B D W Θ f¹ (Metzger 1994: 74–75; contra France 2002: 99).

1:27. The grammar here is somewhat awkward because the subject of the infinitive συζητεῖν is not stated but implied. It may have been omitted since it is the subject of the main verb "were amazed."

1:27. There is no major difference in Mark's use of the adjectives καινός and νέος, for the latter is also used to indicate the eschatological newness of what is occurring, and the terms are used interchangeably in 2:21–22.

2. An Evening in Capernaum (1:29–34)

The present account consists of the shortest healing miracle found in the Gospels (1:29–31) and a summary of Jesus's healing activities in Capernaum (1:32–34). They form a single account and occur in the home of Simon. The miracle can be divided into the following elements: the arrival of the healer (1:29), the diagnosis of the problem (1:30a), a request for healing (1:30b), the description of the healing (1:31a–b), and the proof of the healing (1:31c–d). As in several healing stories in Mark, no mention is made of the faith of the believer (cf. 3:1–6; 7:31–37; 8:22–26). (Healing miracles where faith is mentioned are found in 1:40–45; 2:1–12; 5:21–24, 25–34, 35–43; 7:31–34; 9:14–29; 10:46–52.) A request for healing is implicit in 1:30b, "and immediately they tell him about her." There are a number of similarities between the present account and the raising of Jairus's daughter in 5:22–24, 35–43. In both, Peter, James, and John are present (1:29; 5:37), the healing/raising takes place in a home (1:29; 5:38), a woman/girl is healed (1:31; 5:23, 35, 40–42), Jesus grasps the woman's/girl's hand (1:31; 5:41), and food is served (1:31; 5:43).

Our understanding of Mark's editorial role in the composition of this material is highly dependent on whether we assume that it existed as a pre-Markan complex (see Mark 1:14–3:6 introduction). If it did, then the various chronological ties (1:21, "Sabbath . . . into the synagogue"; 1:29, "and immediately he left the synagogue"; 1:32, "that evening"; 1:35, "And in the morning") belonged to the tradition. It appears, however, that all the ties between the various accounts that make up 1:21–39 (or 1:21–45) are heavily Markan in nature. The seams (1:21–22, 29, 35, 40) and conclusions (1:28, 34, 39, 45) are almost universally seen as coming from the hand of Mark (Pryke 1978: 10–11, 138–40, 152–53; Kuhn 1971: 16–18). Also, that 1:32–34 serves as a summary of 1:21–28 and 1:29–31 supports the view that this material has been collected and organized by Mark (Gnilka 1978: 85–86). The summary nature of 1:32–34 indicates that it is not a miracle story about Jesus (V. Taylor 1952: 181), for it is difficult to imagine how this material would have been transmitted as an oral tradition.[1] Summaries tend to be the work of the final editors in the composition of their Gospels. (Cf. 3:7–12 and 6:53–56, which also focus on Jesus's healings and exorcisms.) This does not necessitate, however, that we view the material in such summaries as nonhistorical. On the contrary, they are summaries of the traditional material available to the evangelist. In the present situation it is quite possible

---

1. The attempt by Guelich (1989: 64; cf. also Marcus 2000: 198) to find a structure in this summary is unconvincing.

that one of the sources of this tradition concerning the healing of Peter's mother-in-law was Peter himself. If the author of Mark was associated with Peter, as the tradition asserts (Zahn 1909: 496–98; Bauckham 2006: 155–82; see "Authorship" in the introduction), the ties and summaries that Mark has given may very well reflect Jesus's healing of Peter's mother-in-law in Capernaum along with a general overview of his ministry in Galilee. Mark's editorial work is seen most clearly in "and immediately" and the transitional seam in 1:29a (Pesch 1980a: 128), the addition of the names James and John tying the present accounts to 1:16–20 (Gnilka 1978: 83; Guelich 1989: 61; Marcus 2000: 198), the dual temporal designation (1:32a–b), the hyperbolic description (1:33), the summary of Jesus's healing of the sick and the demonic (1:34a–b), the command to secrecy (1:34c), and the "because" (ὅτι, *hoti*) explanatory clause (1:34d).

Exegesis and Exposition

[29]And immediately having left the synagogue ⌜they entered⌝ the house of Simon and Andrew with James and John. [30]And Simon's mother-in-law was lying down with a fever, and immediately they tell him about her. [31]And having approached, grasping her hand, he raised her up. And the fever left her, and she began to serve them. [32]And evening having come, when the sun set, they were bringing to him all those who were sick and those possessed by demons. [33]And the whole city was gathered at the door. [34]And he healed many who were sick with various diseases, and he cast out many demons, and he would not permit the demons to speak because they knew ⌜him.⌝

Due to the temporal and geographical tie to the synagogue in 1:32 and 35 (cf. **1:29–31** 1:21 and 29), we should probably give full weight to the "and immediately" (καὶ εὐθύς, *kai euthys*) in 1:29. "Having left the synagogue" ties the following incident chronologically and geographically with 1:21–28. John 1:44 states that Peter and Andrew were "from" Bethsaida, which lies a short distance from Capernaum on the eastern side of the Sea of Galilee where the upper Jordan River enters, whereas Capernaum lies on the western side of where it enters. It may be that the birthplace of Peter and Andrew was Bethsaida (John 1:44), although when Jesus began his ministry, they were living in Capernaum.[2] Andrew, James, and John are not mentioned in the abbreviated accounts of the healing found in Matthew and Luke. Their names were probably omitted because they played no part in the story. They were probably added to the account by Mark because of their association with Peter in 1:16–20.

A number of traditions in Mark locate Jesus "in a house" (3:20; 7:17; 9:28, 33; 10:10; cf. 2:1). These references should not be interpreted as implying that the house in each instance was that of Peter. (Cf. 9:28, which contrasts with 9:30, 33; and 10:10, which has 10:1 as its geographical tie.) The house is specifically referred to as Peter's house in 1:29. The house popularly called

2. Compare how we today can refer to ourselves with respect to our place of birth or our place of residence.

Peter's house that was discovered in Capernaum in 1968 may very well be this house (V. C. Corbo, *ABD* 1:867–68). It is too imaginative to see here a contrast between a house, symbolizing the house churches of the early Christians, and the synagogue, symbolizing unresponsive Judaism (Guelich 1989: 62; contra Gnilka 1978: 83–84; Marcus 2000: 200). In 1:21–28 the synagogue does not carry any negative overtones, but Jesus on the contrary receives a positive reception there (1:22, 27).

Since the sick woman in the story is the mother-in-law of Simon, it is quite possible that Peter himself was the source of this story. Peter's married status is referred to here and in the parallel accounts (Matt. 8:14; Luke 4:38) as well as in 1 Cor. 9:5. Since Peter's wife is not mentioned in the account and it is his mother-in-law who serves the following meal (1:31c), this might suggest that Peter was a widower, except for 1 Cor. 9:5. Even more speculative is the suggestion that Peter was indeed a widower but by the time of 1 Cor. 9:5 had remarried. The prepositional phrase "with a fever" translates the participle "being fevered" (πυρέσσουσα, *pyressousa*). Her "lying down" heightens the severity of her fever. For the seriousness of a fever, which was considered an illness and not a symptom in the first century (Meier 1994: 754n135; Donahue and Harrington 2002: 82), see John 4:46–54. In the parallels to Mark 1:20, both Matthew (8:14) and Luke (4:38) understood "and immediately" as being a simple conjunction (see 1:10) and therefore omitted it. Although unstated, a request for healing is implied in "they tell him about her," and this request heightens the seriousness of the illness. For the impersonal plural "they," see 1:22.

Mark describes the healing in 1:31 by "and having approached, grasping her hand, he raised her."[3] In other healings in Mark, Jesus also "grasps the hand" of (5:41; 9:27), "lays his hands on" (5:23; 6:5; 7:32; 8:23, 25), "touches" (1:41; 7:33; 8:22; 10:13), or is touched (3:10; 5:27–28, 30–31; 6:56) by the person seeking healing. Being "raised" is frequently associated with healing, since the sick were often lying down (2:9, 11; 5:41; 9:27; cf. 3:3; 10:49). "And she began to serve them [διηκόνει, *diēkonei*—an inceptive imperfect] [food]" provides proof of the healing in the story rather than an example of discipleship (Gnilka 1978: 84; Meier 1994: 755n137).

1:32–34   The genitive absolute "And evening having come" ('Οψίας δὲ γενομένης, *Opsias de genomenēs*) in 1:32 is common in Mark (4:35; 6:47; 14:17; 15:42)

---

3. In the Lukan parallel (4:39) the healing is described by Jesus "rebuking" (ἐπιτίμησεν, *epitimēsen*) the fever. This is the same term used in the previous account for rebuking the unclean spirit (Mark 1:25; Luke 4:35). The suggestion that Luke interpreted the fever as demonic in origin is unlikely, however, for he is clearly able to distinguish the two (4:40–41; 6:17–19; 7:21; 8:2; 9:1; 13:32). The reason that the fever (Luke 4:38), wind and sea (4:39), Peter (8:33), unclean spirits (1:25; 9:25), and so on are rebuked is that they are to cease what they are currently doing. There is no necessity to see in all this a demonic activity (although Peter is rebuked in 8:33 for espousing the view of Satan). The verb "rebuked" is not a technical term that automatically implies gaining control of a demon. It is simply a strong command for someone or something to stop doing what they are doing (see 1:25–26).

and Matthew (8:16; 14:15, 23; 16:2; 20:8; 26:20; 27:57). In Mark 4:35 and 15:42 it functions as here as a dual temporal designation. Along with "when the sun set" (ὅτε ἔδυ ὁ ἥλιος, *hote edy ho hēlios*), the dual temporal designation is a common Markan stylistic trait (Neirynck 1988: 46–48). (We also find dual temporal designations in 1:35; 2:20; 4:35; 10:30; 13:24; 14:12, 43; 15:42; and 16:2.) Whereas 1:21–31 is described as taking place on the Sabbath, "when the sun set" indicates that the Sabbath is now over. Thus the "day" in Capernaum (1:21–31) ends at 1:32 and not 1:38, for the beginning of the Sabbath in 1:21 ends with the start of the first day of the week in 1:32. Some have suggested that Mark sought to demonstrate by this comment that Jesus did not break the Sabbath by the following healings. However, the issue of Sabbath observance has not yet arisen and will not come to the forefront until 2:23–3:6, so it is unlikely that Mark is dealing with this issue here. Furthermore, Jesus has already healed in the synagogue in Capernaum, and no one has protested its having occurred on the Sabbath (1:21–28). Later he will heal on the Sabbath and defend his action by arguing that he is able to do so because he is the Lord of the Sabbath (2:28). Although in the original setting in the life of Jesus, 1:32 might indicate that Jewish concern for the Sabbath played a role in the crowds coming for healing after the Sabbath (cf. Marcus 2000: 196–97, 200; France 2002: 108–9), it is unlikely that Mark expected his gentile readers to think along these lines (Gnilka 1978: 86).

The use of the imperfect tense (they were bringing, ἔφερον, *epheron*) emphasizes the continuing nature of Jesus's healing ministry. In effect, Mark is telling his readers that the exorcism and healing just mentioned (1:21–31) are but two examples of the many people Jesus healed. This probably assumes a greater knowledge of Jesus's healing activity by Mark's readers than simply the public exorcism miracle of 1:21–28 and the private healing miracle of 1:29–31. As a Markan summary, it reflects upon all the ministry of Jesus, with the two just mentioned serving as examples of this. For the impersonal plural "they," see 1:21–22. The expression "those who were sick" (τοὺς κακῶς ἔχοντας, *tous kakōs echontas*) is also used to describe the sick in 1:34; 2:17; and 6:55. Mark's use of "all" (πάντας, *pantas*) is hyperbolic and seeks to emphasize the greatness of Jesus's healing ministry. In 1:32 (cf. also 1:34) Mark distinguishes between sickness and demon possession. They are not identical, and this distinction reveals that it is incorrect to claim that people in the first century believed that all illness was essentially spiritual in nature. We should not assume that the Gospel writers were naive and thought that all illness was demonic in origin (Yamauchi 1986: 100–103, 105–7, 112–13, 119, 121–23, 126–27). From this Markan summary it is evident that Jesus can heal all kinds of sickness, whether physical or demonic, and the different terms used to describe the two kinds of healing (ἐθεράπευσεν, *etherapeusen*; 1:34a; and ἐξέβαλεν δαιμόνια, *exebalen daimonia*; 1:34b) also indicates this (France 2002: 109). The chiastic order of A (exorcism, 1:21–28), B (healing, 1:29–31), B′ (healing, 1:32), and A′ (exorcism, 1:32) should be noted.

The reference to "the whole city" (ὅλη ἡ πόλις, *holē hē polis*) in 1:33 refers back to Capernaum (1:21). The use of hyperbole here effectively shows the impact of Jesus's healing ministry and combined with 1:28, 37b, and 45 reveals his greatness. (See 1:5 for a similar use of hyperbole by Mark. For other examples of Jesus's popularity, see 2:2; 3:7–9, 20; 4:1; 5:21, 24; 6:14–15, 31–34; 7:24; 8:1–3; 9:14–15, 30.) The "door" (θύραν, *thyran*; cf. 2:2) is the door of Simon's house (1:29). The interchangeable use of "all" (πάντας, *pantas*) in 1:32 with "many" (πολλούς, *pollous*) in 1:34 can be seen in Matthew's reversing their order in 8:16 and by Luke's statement that Jesus healed "them," that is, "each one" who was brought (Luke 4:40; cf. Mark 3:10–11; cf. also how Paul uses these terms interchangeably in Rom. 5:15–19). Mark clearly does not intend his readers to think that Jesus Christ, the Son of God (1:1), was able to heal only some of the sick brought to him but not all (Marcus 2000: 197; contra Pesch 1980a: 134–35). The "many" here is to be understood inclusively rather than exclusively (cf. Isa. 53:12; Lohmeyer 1957: 41; J. Jeremias, *TDNT* 6:536–45, esp. 541). See 10:45. The clear distinction made between healing and exorcism is found again in 1:34. Mark probably used the term "demons" rather than "unclean spirits" in this summary because it is the more usual term he uses with the verb "cast out" (ἐξέβαλεν, *exebalen*; 1:39; 3:15, 22, 23; 6:13; 7:26; cf., however, 9:18, 28, 38). Some of the "various" (ποικίλαις, *poikilais*) diseases healed by Jesus in Mark include fever (1:30–31), leprosy (1:40–45), paralysis (2:1–12), hemorrhaging (5:25–34), deafness and speech disorder (7:31–37), and blindness (8:22–26; 10:46–52). This indicates that Jesus was a "general practitioner" and not a specialist (France 2002: 110).

The command to the demons not to make Jesus known (cf. 1:25; 3:11–12) is part of the "messianic secret." On numerous occasions those delivered from demons (1:34; 3:12), those healed of their diseases (1:44; 5:43; 7:36; 8:26), and the disciples (8:30; 9:9) are commanded not to tell others of what Jesus has done or who he is. Why on certain occasions in his ministry Jesus would have given such a command is difficult to understand, for in numerous instances a miracle of healing, exorcism, or resurrection would have been impossible to hide.[4] Such commands remain in effect until Jesus enters Jerusalem, at which point he openly proclaims his messiahship in word and deed (11:1–10; 12:1–9, 33–37; 14:61–65; 15:2, 9, 12, 16–19, 26, 32), although he remains unrecognized except for 15:39. The explosive nature of the situation in which Jesus ministered probably explains some of the commands for silence, for an open confession of Jesus's messiahship would have brought about an immediate confrontation with Rome and the Sanhedrin before his arrival in Jerusalem. Thus a confession of his messiahship had to be veiled by his use of the title "Son of Man" (see 2:28), reports of his healings and exorcisms were best downplayed, and talk about the kingdom of God, which

---

4. Gundry (1993: 88) states that Jesus did not permit the demons to speak in their self-defense, but this is speculative, and the reason Mark gives for the command to silence ("because they knew him") makes a different point.

could have been understood as a political threat to the Roman Empire, was best expressed by means of parables.

The question of why Mark sought to emphasize the "messianic secret" in his Gospel is even more difficult to understand. Some have argued that it was to explain why the Jewish people failed to recognize Jesus as the Messiah and why he was crucified. Others suggest it was to explain why the life of the historical Jesus and the Jesus traditions were so unmessianic in nature. Yet it is clear that Mark was not trying to explain why the Jesus traditions were unmessianic, for the traditions Mark inherited, and which his readers knew, were thoroughly messianic. It may be that Mark wanted to emphasize the messianic secret in order to demonstrate that Jesus's greatness could not be hidden and that he did not die because he claimed to be a messianic revolutionary. Jesus posed no political threat to Rome. On the contrary, he sought to keep his actions and messianic status under wraps. He died for one reason and one alone: it was the will of God that he should die (8:31; 9:31; 10:33–34, 45; 14:21;[5] see "The 'Messianic Secret'" in the introduction). The explanatory comment "because they knew him" (ὅτι ᾔδεισαν αὐτόν, *hoti ēdeisan auton*) is clearly Markan in origin and critical for understanding his Christology. This comment indicates that the demons possess supernatural knowledge concerning Jesus and are thus reliable "spokesmen" for the Markan Christology (contra Hengel 1985: 43). Through the witness of the demons, Mark reveals that Jesus is "the Holy One of God" (1:24), "the Son of God" (3:11), "the Son of the Most High God" (5:7).

Summary

Through two healing stories (1:21–28 and 29–31) and a summary (1:32–34), Mark reveals Jesus's universal power to heal. Both physical illness (Peter's mother-in-law in 1:29–31) and the demonic world (the man with the unclean spirit in 1:21–28) are subject to his power. This great power is emphasized in the summary (1:32–34), where Jesus heals great numbers of people. The authority and power that Jesus manifests reveal who he is. The miracles bear a christological meaning (Hooker 1991: 71–75). (Cf. 4Q521, where the Messiah is portrayed as one who would heal the sick, give sight to the blind, raise the dead, free the prisoners, and proclaim good news to the meek, etc. Cf. also Luke 4:18–19.) Although not referred to as such, these are "signs" as to who Jesus is (cf. John 6:2 with John 5:36; 10:37–38; 14:11). The christological focus of this section of Mark can be seen in that Jesus's name is not mentioned in 1:25–2:5. Mark sees

5. The discussion of the "messianic secret" came to the forefront in NT studies through the publication of Wrede's *Das Messiasgeheimnis in den Evangelien* (1901; ET: *The Messianic Secret*, 1971). For a more recent discussion of the question, see Räisänen 1990. An older article that remains useful is V. Taylor 1954b. Whereas Wrede held that the messianic secret was already in the pre-Markan tradition and that Mark developed it, Räisänen argues that the secret was a wholly Markan creation, and Taylor argues that it goes back to the historical Jesus himself.

no need for this, since the whole section (and for that matter the whole Gospel) is about him.

Regardless of how the command to silence may have functioned in the original situation of Jesus, in the present context it serves as a christological explanation of the person of Jesus. In support of his own statement that Jesus is the Christ, the Son of God (1:1), and the affirmation of the voice from heaven (1:11), Mark points out that the command to silence directed to the demons (1:34) is due to the fact that they knew who he was. Thus Mark affirms that the demonic confessions in his Gospel are correct. Jesus is "the Holy One of God" (1:24), "the Son of God" (3:11), "the Son of the Most High God" (5:7). This, along with the divine declarations at the baptism (1:11) and the transfiguration (9:7), Peter's confession (8:29), the declaration of the centurion (15:39), and Jesus's own confession (14:61–62; 15:2, 26, 32), support Mark's understanding and confession of the person of Jesus. Despite his many attempts to silence the demons and those he healed (1:44), Jesus could not remain hidden (7:24), for the more he charged others not to tell who he was and what he had done, the more zealously they proclaimed him (7:36). The veil of his humanity could not hide the reality that Jesus is the Christ, the Son of God (1:1).

Additional Notes

1:29. Although B D Θ f¹ f¹³ (cf. NAB, NJB) have the singular ἐξελθὼν ἦλθεν, it is best to follow the majority of MSS that read ἐξελθόντες ἦλθον, since it is more likely that copyists would change the plural to singular in order to focus attention on Jesus (Metzger 1994: 64) than the reverse.

1:34. Although numerous witnesses have something like αὐτὸν χριστὸν εἶναι or a variant thereof, this reading was probably derived from Luke 4:41. If original, it is difficult to explain its omission from ℵ* A (D) K Δ it vg syr. See Metzger 1994: 64.

3. Jesus's Ever-Increasing Fame (1:35–39)

Although the NA²⁷ text places 1:39 with 1:40–45, the vast majority of texts (UBS Greek text, RSV, NRSV, NIV, NEB, REB, NAB, ESV) place it with 1:35–38. That the latter is correct can be seen by the fact that Mark often introduces a new pericope with "and he comes" (καί, *kai* + the historical present) as in 1:40 (cf. 1:21; 3:13; 6:7; 7:1; 8:22; 10:46; 11:15, 27; 12:13, 18; 14:32). Luke includes Mark 1:39 (Luke 4:44) with 1:35–38 (Luke 4:42–43), inserts an independent pericope not found in Mark, and then begins a section (Luke 5:12–16) just as Mark does (Mark 1:40–45). It is difficult to conceive of Mark 1:35–39 as an independent, self-contained pericope that circulated as a unit during the oral period (V. Taylor 1952: 182).[1] Whereas one can say, "Once in the life of Jesus" and repeat 1:21–28, 40–45; 2:1–12; and so on, it is difficult to imagine repeating as a tradition, "Once in the life of Jesus" and then adding, "Jesus withdrew from Capernaum to pray, Simon and others sought him and told him that all were looking for him, and he went to neighboring towns to preach . . ."—that is, 1:35–39. This becomes even more evident when we omit from 1:35–39 the Markan editorial work, some of which involves much if not all of 1:35 (at least one of the dual temporal designations and the material that ties what follows with 1:32–34); "and those with him" (οἱ μετ' αὐτοῦ, *hoi met' autou*; 1:36; cf. 2:25; 5:40); "all are seeking you" (πάντες ζητοῦσίν σε, *pantes zētousin se*; 1:37); "in order that I may also preach [κηρύξω, *kēryxō*] there" (1:38); and 1:39, which is probably a Markan summary. Some, however, see all of 1:35–39 as a Markan composition (Bultmann 1968: 155; Gnilka 1978: 88; Pryke 1978: 11, 139, 153).

If we believe that 1:35–39 did not circulate as a pre-Markan pericope, this does not mean that the evangelist composed it out of nothing. His knowledge of various pieces of information was not limited to easily memorized, rounded traditions. Exactly how and where he obtained such information is impossible to say. Luke refers to having carefully investigated for a considerable period of time the materials handed down by the eyewitnesses (1:2–3). If, as tradition claims, the author of our Gospel was John Mark, he would have had access to various personal reminiscences and incidents learned from Peter and other eyewitnesses (cf. Acts 12:12; 13:13; 1 Pet. 5:13). Thus it may be that Mark constructed this summary of Jesus's ministry based

---

1. Guelich (1989: 68; cf. Cranfield 1959: 88) argues for a traditional, pre-Markan existence of 1:35–39 (minus 1:38b–c and 39) on the basis of certain non-Markan vocabulary ("Simon," "pursued," "other," "next towns") and thematic traits ("prayed"), but the overall redactional nature of 1:35–39 cannot be denied.

upon the traditions he reported in 1:14–34 (leaving Capernaum [1:21, 33, 35] and Peter's house [1:29–31, 33, 35]; Jesus's fame spreading [1:22–23, 37]; Peter and other disciples being present [1:14–15, 21, 29–31, 36]; Jesus's preaching ministry [1:14–15, 21–22, 27, 38] and presence in the synagogues [1:21–28, 29, 39]; his casting out demons [1:21–28, 32, 34, 39]; and the temporal ties [1:21, 29, 32, 35]). He may also have used traditions he has not yet reported in his Gospel, personal recollections of eyewitnesses he had heard in his home (Acts 12:12), in meetings of the Christian community in Jerusalem, and through his personal acquaintance with Peter, Barnabas, Paul, and others.

Exegesis and Exposition

³⁵And very early before dawn, he ⌈arose⌉ and went out, and went away into a deserted place, and there he was praying. ³⁶And Simon and those with him pursued him, ³⁷and found him and say to him, "All [the people] are seeking you." ³⁸And he says to them, "Let us go elsewhere into the neighboring towns, in order that I may also preach there; for I came out ⌈for this purpose.⌉ ³⁹And ⌈he went⌉ preaching ⌈in⌉ their synagogues ⌈throughout⌉ the whole of Galilee and casting out demons.

1:35   "Very early before dawn" (πρωῒ ἔννυχα λίαν, *prōi ennycha lian*) is another example of a duplicate temporal designation in Mark (see 1:32–34). The three consecutive adverbs found in this statement are most unusual (cf., however, 16:2). In referring to this desolate place (ἔρημον τόπον, *erēmon topon*; cf. 1:45; 6:31, 32, 35) Mark is careful to distinguish this location from the "wilderness" (ἔρημος) of 1:3–4 and 1:12. This is neither the "wilderness of Judea" (1:12) nor the eschatological wilderness of Isa. 40:3 (Mark 1:3–4). Whereas Jesus no doubt sought to be alone at times in order to pray, the comment about Jesus seeking an uninhabited place serves to show that Jesus's popularity and fame were so great that he could not be hidden. Even in deserted, unpopulated areas, people were flocking to see him. Jesus is described by Mark as seeking privacy in order "to pray" (προσηύχετο, *proseucheto*; cf. 6:46; 14:32–39). Early morning prayer was a characteristic of Jewish piety (Pss. 5:3; 88:13; 119:147). As in Mark 6:46 the content of Jesus's prayer is not given. In contrast to Luke (Stein 1992a: 51–52), although Jesus urges his disciples to pray in Mark (9:29; 11:24–25; 13:18), the evangelist does not portray Jesus as praying before the major events of his life (14:32–39 is traditional). Consequently we should not see this reference as indicating that for Mark this was a major turning point in Jesus's ministry (contra Hooker 1991: 76). The question has been raised as to whether this purpose ("to pray") in 1:35 conflicts with Jesus's purpose in 1:38 ("to preach"). For Mark, there is no conflict, because the two comments are meant to emphasize Jesus's greatness. He does this by telling his readers that during Jesus's preaching/healing mission (1:38), even when he wanted to be alone to pray (1:35), his greatness was such that all the people sought him. On the level of Jesus's personal ministry, we also need not see a conflict, because at times certain desires and wishes ("to pray") had to be subservient to his overall purpose ("to preach").

"Simon and those with him" picks up 1:16–20 and 29. For "those with him" **1:36–37** (οἱ μετ᾽ αὐτοῦ, *hoi met' autou*), compare 2:25; 5:40. Although the subject of the verb "pursued" (κατεδίωξεν, *katediōxen*) is plural ("Simon and those with him"), the verb is singular because in Greek a verb followed by a compound subject agrees with the first component of the compound subject (cf. 1:5; 3:31a; 8:27). Therefore, since "Peter" is the first component of the compound subject that follows, the verb is singular. This intensive form of the verb "pursued" (διώκω, *diōkō*) is not found elsewhere in the NT. It is reading too much into this verb to see it as indicating that this was an "unwelcome intrusion" (Hooker 1991: 76) into Jesus's period of prayer or a "friction" between Jesus and the disciples (Gnilka 1978: 89; Marcus 2000: 203; France 2002: 112; contra Gundry 1993: 100). "All are seeking you" is another example of hyperbole (cf. 1:27 ["all"], 28 ["everywhere" and "all"], 32 ["all"], and 33 ["whole"]). The reason for the disciples seeking Jesus is found in 1:34: his healing of the sick and exorcising of the unclean spirits.[2] Although "seeking" (ζητοῦσιν, *zētousin*) frequently carries a negative connotation (11:18; 12:12; 14:1; cf. also 3:32; 8:11–12), here it is used positively to show Jesus's great popularity with the people (Pesch 1980a: 138).

The question of why Jesus did not return to Capernaum to continue his successful mission there is impossible to answer. We have no means of psychoanalyzing Jesus's motives and actions. Why Mark emphasizes this, however, is easier to answer. He wants to demonstrate that it was not just all the city of Capernaum (1:33) that marveled at the actions of Jesus Christ, the Son of God (1:1). All the cities of Galilee did so as well, for 1:38 (Jesus's decision) will lead to 1:39 (going to all the cities of Galilee) and 1:45 (Jesus's fame being such that he could not enter any city of Galilee).

The emphasis of "Let us go elsewhere" is not on excluding Capernaum from **1:38–39** Jesus's mission but rather on including more cities in his healing and preaching ministry. It is highly unlikely that Mark intended his readers to understand Jesus's words as a negative judgment upon the reception he received at Capernaum or as an exhortation to missionary activity addressed to them (contra Gnilka 1978: 89; Marcus 2000: 204; France 2002: 111). On the contrary, Mark emphasizes that Jesus's ministry in Capernaum was highly successful (1:27–28, 32–34), and there is no hint that Jesus left Capernaum because of such responses as found in John 6:15 (they wanted to make Jesus a king forcibly) and 6:26 (they possessed a crass interpretation of what his miracles signified). The reference to "the neighboring towns" prepares the reader for the following accounts of

---

2. For other examples of crowds gathering around Jesus, see 1:33, 45; 2:2, 13, 15; 3:7–10, 20; 4:1, 35; 5:21; etc. For examples of Jesus seeking solitude from the pressing crowds, see 3:13; 4:35–36; 6:30–32, 46; 7:24; 8:27; 9:2, 30–31; 13:3; 14:12–26, 32–42.

Jesus's preaching and healing in Galilee. The use of the term "neighboring" (ἐχομένας, *echomenas*) with respect to a physical location is unique in the NT (but cf. Luke 13:33; Acts 13:44; 20:15; 21:26, where it is used with respect to time). In the LXX, however, ἐχομένας is frequently used for "neighboring" or "next" (V. Taylor 1952: 184). A "town" (κωμοπόλις, *kōmopolis*) was larger than a "village" (κώμη, *kōmē*) but smaller than a "city" (πόλις, *polis*) such as Capernaum (cf. Matt. 11:20 and 23).

The term "preach" (κηρύσσω, *kēryssō*) occurs twelve times in Mark; it is found only nine times each in Matthew and in Luke. In Mark "preaching" and "teaching" (διδάσκω, *didaskō*) are essentially synonyms, as their interchange in 1:14 and 2:21–22, 27, and 3:14/6:12 and 6:30 indicates. "In order that I may preach," which picks up 1:14–15, can be interpreted, "Because this Capernaum crowd is so great (and unruly) that I cannot preach here, let us go to other places where it will be possible to preach"; or "so that I can preach there also, for Capernaum has already heard the good news." The latter is much more likely, for Mark seeks to show how Jesus's fame and greatness spread throughout all Galilee, and his leaving Capernaum permits this. The content of Jesus's preaching is not given by Mark, for this has already been done in 1:15. Although elsewhere saying that Jesus "came" (ἦλθεν, *ēlthen*) possesses a christological emphasis (2:17; 10:45; cf. also 1:24 and the parallel to 1:38 in Luke 4:43), the form of the verb here is different (ἐξῆλθον, *exēlthon*),[3] and its use in 1:35 probably refers to Jesus's having come out of Capernaum (contra K. Schmidt 1919: 58; Lohmeyer 1957: 43; France 2002: 113).

In 1:39, Mark gives another summary of Jesus's ministry (cf. 1:28, 32–34): Jesus preaches in the synagogues and casts out demons throughout Galilee. The present verses serve as a summary of 1:14–38. By omitting a reference to Jesus's healing, Mark emphasizes his exorcistic ministry. Healing and exorcism are often placed side by side (cf. 1:21–28 and 29–31; 5:1–20 and 21–43), and summaries frequently contain a reference to both (1:32, 34; 3:10–11; 6:13). Mark may have omitted the reference to make a simpler summary of Jesus's preaching and healing ministry. The mention of Jesus's driving out demons in 1:39, however, emphasizes the defeat of the demonic powers (cf. 3:20–30) and thus the arrival of the kingdom of God even better than Jesus's healing ministry, although as we shall see in 1:40–45, certain healings were especially associated with the coming of the kingdom of God. As in 1:23, "into *their* synagogues" implies that the majority of Mark's readers were gentile.

Summary

In his summary of 1:14–34, Mark seeks to emphasize the greatness of Jesus of Nazareth. His fame is ever increasing. From notoriety in the synagogue caused by his exorcism (1:27) and by his healing in the home of Peter, the whole city of Capernaum gathered in excitement around him. Now because

---

3. For the use of ἐξέρχομαι (*exerchomai*) with the sense of having been sent from God, cf. John 8:42 and 16:27–28.

of Jesus's visiting other cities (1:38), his fame spreads throughout all of Galilee (1:45; cf. 1:28). Mark intends for his readers to find encouragement through their knowing this. The Jesus Christ in whom they believe is indeed the Son of God (1:1), as witnessed to by the great response to his preaching and by his exorcisms. When not influenced by the religious leadership, the people respond positively toward him with great awe and wonder. His exorcisms furthermore witness to them that he has indeed brought with him the kingdom of God (1:27, 32–34, 39; cf. Luke 11:20).

Additional Notes

1:35. ἀναστάς, translated "he arose," is lit. "having arisen."

1:38. εἰς τοῦτο is lit. "unto this."

1:39. The verb ἦλθεν and the following participles function essentially as a periphrasis, as the alternative reading ἦν in A C D W indicates (cf. Luke 4:44). See 1:4.

1:39. Both "in" and "throughout" translate εἰς. For a similar use of a double εἰς, see 11:11.

4. Jesus Heals a Leper (1:40–45)

The present pericope possesses no temporal or geographical tie to the previous accounts. As a result, 1:21–39 is frequently seen as a unified collection of traditions to which 1:40–45 has been added. However, since 1:21–39 is a collection of healing miracles and since the account in 1:40–45 is a healing miracle, 1:21–39 and 1:40–45 form a unified collection of miracles set off from what precedes and what follows. The present account is joined to 1:21–39 by various themes such as the command to silence (cf. 1:43 and 34), the location of Jesus's ministry in desolate places (cf. 1:45 and 35), and Jesus's great popularity and fame (cf. 1:45 and 32–33, 39). In the present format 1:21–45 forms a unified collection of miracles. The present account serves as a climax to what has preceded in 1:21–39, and Jesus's fame reaches a crescendo, so that he can no longer publicly enter the cities of Galilee. What had happened in Capernaum (1:33, 37) is now true for all of Galilee (1:45). The present account also serves as a bridge to the next collection of stories (2:1–3:6) by introducing the issue of the Jewish law (1:44b), which will be raised on several occasions (2:6–7, 16, 18, 24; 3:3–4).

The present account possesses many of the normal aspects found in a healing story. There is a description of the problem (1:40a), a reference to faith (1:40b), a description of the healing (1:41–42), a proof of the healing implied by the command to go to a priest (for certification of the cleansing; 1:43–44), and a concluding summary (1:45). The form of the present story, however, does not follow precisely that of a normal healing story in that it contains a reference to Jesus's anger/compassion (1:41), a stern rebuke (1:43), a command to silence (1:44a), and a reference to the Jewish law (1:44bc). The awkwardness of this miracle story has led numerous scholars to see the present account as a conflation of two separate stories—a healing story and an exorcism (Nineham 1963: 86–87; Cave 1979: 245–50).

The extent of Markan redaction in the present account is debated. Most agree that 1:45 is a Markan summary (Gnilka 1978: 91; Schmithals 1979: 1.137–38; Guelich 1989: 77; Marcus 2000: 208), as witnessed to by several Markan characteristics ("began to," "preach," πολλά, *polla* ["many things"], "deserted places," "word," etc.) and its summary conclusion (cf. 1:28, 39). Other suggested areas of Markan redaction are 1:43 and the command to secrecy in 1:44a (Bultmann 1968: 212; Pryke 1978: 11, 139–40, 153). However, the command to secrecy is most probably traditional (Gnilka 1978: 90–91; Marcus 2000: 208). As for 1:40–42, this is traditional and has been reproduced by Mark basically unchanged (Gnilka 1978: 90).

Exegesis and Exposition

⁴⁰And a leper comes to him beseeching him, ⌐kneeling down,⌐ and saying to him, "If you want to, you are able to make me clean." ⁴¹And ⌐moved with compassion,⌐ having stretched out his hand, he touched him and says to him, "I want to; be made clean." ⁴²And immediately the leprosy departed from him, and he was made clean. ⁴³And having sternly warned him, he immediately sent him away ⁴⁴and says to him, "See that you tell no one anything, but go, show yourself to the priest and bring for your cleansing what things Moses commanded for a witness to them." ⁴⁵And having departed he began to proclaim many things and spread the word, so that he [Jesus] was no longer able to enter a city openly, but stayed outside [the cities] in deserted places. And they were coming to him from everywhere.

The term "leper" (λεπρός, *lepros*), which today refers primarily to one having Hansen's disease, was understood more broadly in biblical times and encompassed various kinds of skin diseases, of which Hansen's disease was one. This is evident in that biblical leprosy was curable (Lev. 13–14; cf. Mark 1:44) whereas Hansen's disease, apart from the use of sulfone drugs, is not (D. P. Wright and R. N. Jones, *ABD* 4:277–82). The disease resulted in one being "unclean" and ostracized from society (cf. Luke 17:12) and even from one's own family and home (Lev. 13:45–46). Socially a leper was the equivalent of a corpse (Josephus, *Ant.* 3.11.3 §264). Since leprosy was often regarded as a punishment for sin (Num. 12:1–15; 2 Kings 5:25–27; 2 Chron. 26:16–21), such social ostracism was seen as having both prophylactic and moral grounds. Curing leprosy was seen as requiring a miracle equal to raising the dead (2 Kings 5:7; *b. Sanh.* 47a; cf. Luke 4:27).

1:40

From the leper's statement ("If you want to, you are able to make me clean" [ἐὰν θέλῃς δύνασαί με καθαρίσαι, *ean thelēs dynasai me katharisai*]), it is evident that the leper possesses faith in that he acknowledges Jesus's ability and power (cf. 1:27) to heal him of his disease. It is unclear whether we should read this simply as a confession of faith in Jesus's ability to heal or a confession of faith in his ability to heal along with the question as to whether Jesus was willing to do so. The twofold nature of Jesus's response (1:41) favors the latter. To be cleansed, or made "clean," can refer to being healed of the disease or being declared clean by a priest (Lev. 14). In light of Mark 1:44 and Jesus not having priestly qualifications to certify someone as clean, the request is clearly that Jesus heal the leper of his disease.

If we assume that "being angered" (ὀργισθείς, *orgistheis*) is to be read, it is uncertain if Jesus was angry because of the inconsiderateness of the leper's approaching him and possibly rendering him "unclean" (Lev. 5:3; Josephus, *Ag. Ap.* 1.31 §281), because the leper questioned his willingness to heal, or because he was moved by the poor man's suffering (John 11:33, 38; Warfield 1950: 107–22). Jesus does not elsewhere appear to be upset by the possibility of being rendered unclean (Mark 5:25–34; Luke 7:36–50; cf. Mark 2:13–17), and for Mark such an interpretation would be most unlikely in light of Jesus's

1:41–42

attitude toward the ceremonial law in 2:1–3:6; 7:1–23. Mark also gives no hint that he understood such anger as being the normal accompaniment of a healing miracle. In 3:5 the anger is directed not toward the person seeking healing but toward those opposing it due to their understanding of the ceremonial/ civil regulations, and the agitation in 7:34 (see 7:33–34) is quite different from his "being angered" in 1:41. Some suggest that Jesus's anger is directed at the leprosy and against the curse of disease brought about by the fall and/or the work of Satan (cf. *b. Ketub.* 61b, which refers to the demon of leprosy; Hooker 1991: 80; Marcus 2000: 209). Others suggest that Jesus's anger is due to his knowing that the leper will disobey the command to silence about to be given him. It is doubtful that Mark's readers were intended to understand it in the latter sense, for if they were, some hint of this would have been given to them after the leper's disobedience in 1:44 or 45. I must admit that if "being angry" is the correct reading, we simply do not possess a clear understanding of why Jesus was angry or how Mark understood it. On the other hand, "moved with compassion" has far better textual support and describes Jesus in 6:34 and 8:2 (cf. also 9:22).

For "stretching out his hand" (ἐκτείνας τὴν χεῖρα αὐτοῦ, *ekteinas tēn cheira autou*), compare 1:31; 5:41; 9:27 (also 5:23; 6:5; 7:32; 8:22). Jesus's touching of a leper should be noted. By touching the leper, he both became ceremonially unclean and exposed himself to the disease (cf. Lev. 13:45–46; Num. 12:10–15; 2 Kings 7:3–4). In including this comment, Mark wanted his readers to perceive that Jesus was troubled neither by the threat of the disease nor by possible ceremonial uncleanness. In contrast to others who became "unclean" by contact with a leper, Jesus's contact with a leper brought "cleansing" to the leper (Hooker 1991: 79; Marcus 2000: 209; J. Edwards 2002: 70). Jesus's short twofold reply to the leper (I want to; be made clean, θέλω, καθαρίσθητι, *thelō, katharisthēti*) corresponds to the two elements in the leper's statement in 1:40. Although some see "be made clean" as a divine passive (Jeremias 1971: 9–14; Marcus 2000: 206, 209), the preceding "I want to" (cf. also 1:40, "you are able to make me clean") indicates that "be made clean" is another example of Jesus's authority and power to heal (cf. 1:27). The temporal dimension "and immediately" (καὶ εὐθύς, *kai euthys*) in 1:42 should be given full weight, for by it Mark seeks to emphasize the instantaneous nature of Jesus's healing power. Since healing lepers, like raising the dead, was associated with the coming of God's kingdom (Matt. 11:5; Luke 7:22), this miracle story serves to illustrate and confirm Jesus's message that "the kingdom of God has come" (1:15).

1:43–44 The expression "having sternly warned him" (ἐμβριμησάμενος αὐτῷ, *embrimēsamenos autō*) does not appear in the parallel passage in Matt. 8:4, and Luke in his parallel (5:14) uses "commanded." Normally the term refers to being deeply angered (LXX and Mark 14:5). As a result it seems to conflict with Jesus's compassion, if σπλαγχνισθείς (*splanchnistheis*) is to be read in 1:41, and his healing of the man. Some have therefore suggested that this conflict may be due to Mark's ineptness (or someone before Mark) in combining two different healing stories. Others suggest that it may be a Markan editorial comment anticipating the leper's disobedient behavior in 1:45.[1] In an analogous passage, Matthew (9:30) uses this term in a similar way. In John 11:33 and 38, however, the term is used to describe Jesus being deeply moved rather than being angry. I will argue below that "preaching" and "spreading the word" are always understood positively in Mark, so that by using these terms to describe the leper's behavior in 1:45, Mark is not condemning his behavior (Marcus 2000: 210). It is best not to interpret "sternly warned" as a harsh, angry rebuke but, in light of how it is used in John 11:33 and 38, to see it as revealing that Jesus for some reason was deeply moved on this occasion. At the present time there is no convincing explanation of how ἐμβριμησάμενος functions in the Markan story or what caused this reaction by Jesus. As in 1:12, "sent him out" (ἐξέβαλεν αὐτόν, *exebalen auton*) need not denote hostility or anger but may convey here the urgent need to see the priest. Although frequently used in the context of the exorcism of demons (1:34, 39; 3:15, 22, 23; 6:13; 7:26; 9:18, 28, 38), here it means to send out quickly or forcefully (cf. 1:12; 5:40; 11:15; 12:8; also 9:47). See 1:12.

For a similar command to silence in a healing story, compare 5:43; 7:36 (also 8:26). The double negative (tell no one anything, μηδενὶ μηδὲν εἴπῃς, *mēdeni mēden eipēs*; lit. "tell no one nothing"; cf. 5:3; 11:2, 14; 14:25; 15:4, 5) along with the strongest possible prohibition in the Greek language (the aorist subjunctive of prohibition) emphasizes Jesus's desire for the leper not to make known to others what Jesus has done for him. Yet both the leper here and the healed deaf mute in 7:36 disobey Jesus's command, and the result is seen as positive by Mark (cf. 1:45 and 7:36). It is speculative to argue that the command to silence was intended by Jesus to hasten the leper's journey to Jerusalem and thus his testimony of Jesus having healed him (Gundry 1993: 97). There is continued discussion as to whether the command to silence in this verse was part of the tradition Mark inherited or whether this and all other such commands are due to Mark's own editorial work and emphasis. That Mark has created and added such summary statements as 1:34 and 3:11 is clear, but in this instance the command to secrecy is probably traditional (Räisänen 1990: 146–49; Marcus 2000: 208).

The similarity between the command to "go, show yourself to the priest" and the one found in the story of the healing of the ten lepers (Luke 17:14) has led some to suggest that these two accounts stem from the same incident and tradition. However, Luke has both accounts in his Gospel. Since being healed was only part of the process of a leper being accepted into society, Jesus commands the healed leper to go to a priest in order to receive the needed certification of his cleansing (Lev. 14; *m. Neg.* 3.1). Within the present story

---

1. Kee (1973: 418n123) suggests that this refers to the "growling, grumbling, muttering" by a compelling spokesman by which rebellious powers are brought under control. Such growling, however, would precede the healing, whereas here it follows it. Even less likely is the suggestion that this may be a form of sign language paraphrasing the command to silence (Jeremias 1971: 92n1).

this command provides the proof of the leper's healing, even as "serving" demonstrated the healing of Simon's mother-in-law in 1:31. In the original setting of the incident and in light of 2:15–17, 18–22, 23–28; 3:1–6; 7:1–23, Jesus appears to be less concerned with demonstrating that he keeps the law than in helping the healed leper reenter society. That Jesus commands the man to go to the priest for proof of his cleansing reveals that the heart of the story involves a healing, not an exorcism. For the command "bring for your cleansing what things Moses commanded," see Lev. 14. This would involve offering a specified sacrifice at the temple in Jerusalem.

The explanatory "for a witness to them" (εἰς μαρτύριον αὐτοῖς, *eis martyrion autois*) can be interpreted as a dative of advantage ("as a witness to them [of your healing]") or as a dative of disadvantage ("as a witness against [their hardness of hearts and unbelief]" or "as a witness against [those who say I do not keep the law]"). The same expression also appears in 6:11 and 13:9. In the former it is clearly a dative of disadvantage, and the parallel in Luke 9:5 reveals this by translating it "for a witness against [ἐπ’, *ep'*] them," but in Mark 13:9 it may be either, although it is more likely a dative of advantage in light of 13:10. In the context of 1:44, it would be too early in Mark's Gospel to interpret this as a condemnatory act directed at the priests ("them"; contra Broadhead 1992; Gundry 1993: 76–77; France 2002: 120). (Although "them" probably refers to more than the priests and therefore should probably be interpreted as referring to "the people," it refers above all to the priests.) We have, however, not yet encountered any hostility toward Jesus and his mission. Mark will begin to relate the growth of such hostility in 2:1–3:6, but the "priest(s)" are mentioned only one other time in Mark (2:26), and here they are viewed neutrally. References to the high priest(s), on the other hand, are quite negative (8:31; 10:33; 11:18, 27; 14:1ff.). Since the leper's healing involved both a physical dimension of healing provided by Jesus and a societal dimension provided by certification of the cleansing from a priest, "to them" (αὐτοῖς) is best interpreted as a dative of advantage (Gnilka 1978: 91).

1:45 The construction "began" + the infinitive is a common one in Mark (for "began to preach," ἤρξατο κηρύσσειν, *ērxato kēryssein*, compare 5:20; for "began to teach," see 4:1; 6:2, 34; 8:31; compare also 2:23; 5:17; 6:7, 55; 8:11, 32; 10:28, 32, 41, 47; 11:15; 12:1; 13:5; 14:19, 33, 65, 69, 71; 15:8, 18). It occurs twenty-six times in Mark and is a favorite Markan grammatical construction (Pryke 1978: 79–87). Although the subject of "began to preach" is not specified ("he" could refer to Jesus), the immediate antecedent in 1:44 is the leper, and the parallels in 5:20 and 7:36 indicate that Mark has the recipient of the healing, the leper, in mind.[2] The preaching and spreading of the word by the leper emulate the actions of Jesus in 1:14, 38, 39. As a result his similar action should not be considered as negative. In all the other instances in Mark (1:4, 7, 14, 38, 39; 3:14; 5:20; 6:12; 7:36; 13:10; 14:9), "preaching" is always portrayed

---

2. The attempt to interpret "having departed he began to preach" as referring to Jesus has little to commend it (Swetham 1987).

as positive, and in 7:36, where it again follows a command to silence, it also results in Jesus being glorified. In 1:34 and 3:12 the command to silence functions as a means of indicating that the demons truly know who Jesus is—he is the Son of God (cf. 5:7). The question of why Mark does not want the demons to proclaim this or, assuming the historicity of these summaries, why Jesus did not want them to proclaim this, has defied easy explanation.[3] On the level of Mark's story, the command to silence after a healing functions as follows: Even though Jesus does not seek fame and notoriety and commands those he has healed not to share what he has done for them, those who are healed cannot help but preach the good news and spread the "word" that Jesus of Nazareth is the Christ, the Son of God, and that he has inaugurated the kingdom of God. Thus the command for silence functions in Mark's story not on the level of whether those healed should or should not have preached the word about Jesus but rather to illustrate the greatness of the Son of God, who cannot be hid.[4]

Mark points out that instead of going to the priest for certification of his cleansing, the leper immediately begins to proclaim and spread "the word" (τὸν λόγον, *ton logon*; cf. 2:2) concerning what Jesus has done for him. Mark does not say whether the leper eventually went to the priest to certify the cleansing. For him, this is quite unimportant, for the Gospel and this story is not about a leper but about Jesus Christ, the Son of God (1:1). The term πολλά (*polla*) can function adverbially as "much" (cf. 3:12; 5:10, 23, 43; 6:20; 9:26) or as an accusative plural, "many things" (4:2; 6:34; 8:31; 9:41; 12:41; 15:3). It is best to interpret it here as an accusative, so that we have parallel expressions: "to preach 'many things' [accusative]" and "to spread 'the word' [accusative]." Here, as in 2:2; 4:14–20, 33; 8:32 (cf. also 7:13), the "word" is essentially a synonym for the "gospel." For Mark's readers in AD 65–70, the term would have had a more pregnant meaning than simply the "gospel/ word" of the leper's healing. They would have understood the term in the sense used in Acts 4:4, 29; 6:4; 8:4; 11:19; and so on (cf. 4:31; 6:2, 7; 8:14, 25; 11:1; 13:5, 7; etc.), and as involving the coming of the kingdom of God (Mark 1:15); the christological explanation of who Jesus was and claimed to be (14:61–62; 15:2); Jesus's teaching about his death (10:45; 14:24), his resurrection, and the coming of the Spirit; and so on. Everywhere else Mark uses this term, it is viewed positively, so that the leper's sharing the "word," despite the command of silence, functions positively to reveal Jesus's fame and glory (cf. Marcus 2000: 210).

The result of the leper's preaching is that Jesus is no longer able to enter a city. Because of 1:35–39, this should not be interpreted negatively, as if the

3. Guelich (1989: 75) argues that in the original situation the command directed to the demons to be silent functions as a counter to the demons' attempt to gain control of Jesus. This, however, is not the issue in the present form of the Markan account.

4. Hooker (1991: 67) correctly points out that the command for silence "*functions in precisely the opposite way to what one expects*: it serves as a means of revelation to the hearers/ readers of the gospel."

hostility Jesus encounters in the cities causes him to leave them (cf. 6:11).[5] No negative response has been indicated thus far in Jesus's ministry. On the contrary, Jesus's fame and popularity cause this problem. As in 1:28, 37, 39, Mark once again uses hyperbolic language. For Jesus staying (lit. "he was") "in deserted places," see 1:35. For "they were coming to him from everywhere," compare 1:33, 37. See 1:22 for the impersonal plural "they."

Summary

Mark recounts this story of Jesus healing a leper in order to provide an additional example of who Jesus is and the greatness of his power. In Judaism, healing a leper was viewed as being on a different level than other kinds of healing. It was an eschatological healing on the same level as raising the dead. As a result it witnessed to the arrival of the kingdom of God (Matt. 11:5; Luke 7:22). Whether Mark assumed that his gentile readers would have understood the healing in this manner is uncertain, but in light of Jesus's announcement of the kingdom's arrival in 1:15, it is quite likely. What is clear is that in recounting this story, Mark once again portrays Jesus as a worker of miracles who does what others cannot do (1:27) and who thus generates a tremendous response of awe and wonder throughout all of Galilee. Even despite commands to silence, the greatness of Jesus Christ, the Son of God, cannot be hid (Kertelge 1970: 74–75; Schmithals 1979: 1.138). The leper simply cannot help but preach the word concerning Jesus.

It is doubtful that Mark in his setting in life sought by this story to emphasize that Jesus kept the Jewish law, although it reveals that Jesus in his setting in life respected the Jewish law (contra Hooker 1991: 82; Marcus 2000: 210). The reference to the law in 1:44 was part of the tradition of this story that Mark inherited, and in his summary (1:45) Mark makes no mention of it. Contrary to Matthew, Mark does not appear to emphasize this. Indeed, Mark includes several passages in his Gospel that seem to suggest that he was not greatly concerned with demonstrating that Jesus respected the Jewish law (cf. 2:1–3:6; 7:1–23; Räisänen 1990: 146–48).

Additional Notes

1:40. It is questionable whether καὶ γονυπετῶν is part of Mark's text. The textual support for omitting it (B D W) is quite strong. However, both parallel accounts (Matt. 8:2, "worshiped" [προσεκύνει, *prosekyneï*]; and Luke 5:12, "falling on his face" [πεσὼν ἐπὶ πρόσωπον, *pesōn epi prosōpon*]) support its inclusion, as found in ℵ L Θ f¹ lat.

1:41. A major textual problem is whether we should read ὀργισθείς or σπλαγχνισθείς. The latter has by far the better MS support (ℵ B W and the great majority of MSS), whereas the textual support

---

5. Myers (1988: 152–54) seeks to argue that Jesus was not able to enter the towns and cities of Galilee because he had become unclean due to his physical contact with the leper (cf. also Malina 1981: 122). This, however, is certainly not how Mark wants his readers to understand his summary, for in 2:2; 3:7–8; 4:1; 5:21, 24; 6:31; etc., it is clearly Jesus's popularity that does not allow him to enter the cities of Galilee.

for the former is relatively weak (D it). The difficulty of ὀργισθείς, however, lends support to it being the original reading. The fact that σπλαγχνισθείς is not found in the Synoptic parallels (Matt. 8:3 and Luke 5:13) also suggests that Matthew and Luke found ὀργισθείς in their exemplar and chose to omit it, for they both would probably not have omitted σπλαγχνισθείς. "It is difficult to come to a firm decision concerning the original text" (Metzger 1994: 65). Most of the modern translations (RSV, NRSV, NIV, NAB) favor σπλαγχνισθείς, but the REB and NEB prefer ὀργισθείς.

D. Jesus's Mighty Acts in Capernaum and Galilee (2:1–3:6)

In 2:1–3:6 we encounter a second collection of Jesus traditions. Unlike 1:21–45, however, this collection focuses not on the healing ministry of Jesus but rather on his teachings and actions. Many see this new section as a pre-Markan collection of traditions (Kuhn 1971: 53–98). The main reasons for this are (1) the similar nature of the individual pericopes (Jesus is involved in some sort of controversy in each of the accounts); (2) the references to Jesus as the Son of Man (2:10, 28) seem too early in the Gospel, so that they are supposedly best understood as part of a pre-Markan tradition containing them; and (3) the reference to the plot to kill Jesus occurs too early in Mark and is seen as displaced because of the pre-Markan nature of the collection. That some more-recent scholars have eliminated 2:1–12 from the supposed collection (Guelich 1989: 82–83; Marcus 2000: 213) indicates some of the weaknesses of this theory. A more decisive issue with respect to the question of whether 2:1–3:6 existed as a pre-Markan collection involves the vocabulary and style of the seams that join together the individual pericopes found in this alleged collection. When one investigates the seams joining the individual stories (2:1–12, 13–17, 18–22, 23–28; 3:1–6) and their conclusions, the Markan nature of their vocabulary and style becomes apparent. The clearest Markan editorial work in 2:1–3:6 is found in the introductory seams and conclusions (cf. 2:1–2, 12, 13, 14d, 15, 18, 22; 3:1a, 6).[1] From this it appears that it was Mark who brought together these individual pericopes, for if a pre-Markan editor had joined them together, we would expect the editorial seams and conclusions to reflect his, not Mark's, vocabulary, style, and theological interests.

More important than the origin of 2:1–3:6, however, is the question of how this section functions in the Gospel. Has Mark placed them at this point to indicate the rise of conflict and controversy in the ministry of Jesus? Many hold this view, and controversy is found in each of the accounts (2:6–12, 16–17, 18–22, 24–28; 3:2–6). This controversy is also portrayed as developing in intensity (cf. 2:6, where the controversy is mental; 2:18 and 24, where it is directed at Jesus's disciples; 3:2, where it is premeditated and directed at Jesus; and 3:6, where it culminates in a plot to kill Jesus). In referring to this controversy and the plot against Jesus (2:20; 3:6) Mark prepares his readers for Jesus's passion predictions (8:31; 9:31; 10:33–34, 45) and death. Yet more important for Mark in 2:1–3:6 is his continuing demonstration of Jesus's greatness, and the high point in each account is a christological statement (2:10, 17, 19–20, 27–28; 3:4)

---

1. Pryke (1978: 11, 140, 153–54) sees all these verses (and more) as redactional in nature.

that answers the various "why(s)" (τί, *ti*; ὅτι, *hoti*; διὰ τί, *dia ti*; τί, *ti*) in 2:7, 16, 18, and 24 raised in protest against Jesus (Marcus 2000: 212–13). In 1:21–45 Mark has shown that Jesus is the Christ, the Son of God, and that he brought with him the kingdom of God by recounting his exorcisms and miracles. In this new section, Mark continues this theme by showing how Jesus's words and deeds reveal this as well (2:7–12, 28; 3:4–5). Since the Gospel has as its chief theme that Jesus is the Christ, the Son of God (1:1), this provides the key for understanding the main Markan emphasis in 2:1–3:6.[2]

Some have argued that 2:1–3:6 is an awkward intrusion into the Gospel and that it does not fit, because 3:7 follows 1:45 far better than 3:6. It has also been argued that 3:7 does follow 3:6 smoothly (Gundry 1993: 105), but it is important to remember that Mark is not in control of his story to the same extent as writers of fiction are in control of theirs. The tradition Mark used and the historical events to which that tradition referred limited his ability to fit stories together neatly and consistently at all points. Mark's use of hyperbole in 1:45 (cf. also 1:5, 28, 33, 37) should not be pressed. Clearly Jesus frequented cities (3:1, 20; 6:1–2; 7:31; 8:22, 27; 9:33), and the reference to "Capernaum" in 2:1 is probably due to the tradition that Mark inherited. As to the incident described in 2:2–4, this requires that the scene be a city. In its present context the healing and controversy found in 2:1–12 serve as an introduction to what follows and along with the healing and controversy found in 3:1–6 form an *inclusio*, giving unity to the entire section. Both accounts have similar introductions (2:1 and 3:1). In both, Jesus perceives unspoken objections (2:8, and in 3:2, 4 this is assumed), tells the sick man to "rise" (ἔγειρε, *egeire*; 2:9 and 3:3), and heals a paralytic (if we assume that the withered hand of 3:1 was paralyzed), and we read that "he says to the paralytic/man" (2:10 and 3:3). Several verbal ties in 2:1–12 unite this account with what has preceded and what follows. These include the reference to the leper and Jesus preaching "the word" (τὸν λόγον, *ton logon*; 1:45 and 2:2), Jesus's returning to Capernaum (1:35–39 and 2:1), and the presence of the crowds (1:32–34, 37, 45 and 2:2–4). See 2:1–12.

---

2. Hooker (1989: 83) states that this chapter is "not simply a collection of 'conflict stories' but a demonstration of Jesus' authority and the refusal of the Jewish religious leaders to recognize it"; and Gundry (1993: 108) adds, "What binds the stories together is the overwhelming effect of Jesus' sayings." To this can be added the overwhelming effect of Jesus's deeds.

1. Jesus Forgives the Sins of a Paralytic (2:1–12)

The present story introduces a complex of controversy stories (2:1–3:6) and serves as a bridge between 2:1–3:6 and 1:21–45. It does so by the following: Jesus returns to Capernaum (cf. 1:21, 29, 32, 35, 38 with 2:1); crowds are present due to Jesus's fame (cf. 1:32–34, 37, 45 with 2:2–4), even "at the door" (cf. 1:33 with 2:2 and 4); Jesus continues to heal (cf. 1:21–28, 29–31, 32–34, 39, 40–45 with 2:3–12); Jesus causes continued amazement by his actions (cf. 1:27 with 2:12); Jesus exercises authority (cf. 1:27 with 2:10); the preaching of "the word" continues (cf. 1:45 with 2:2); and so on. The account defies a neat classification, for it contains elements of a healing story (2:1–5, 11–12) and a controversy story (2:6–10). With regard to the former, there is a diagnosis of the problem (2:3), a reference to faith (2:4–5a), the healing proper (2:5b, 11), and the result (2:12). There is a sense in which one could omit the controversy involving Jesus's forgiveness of the man's sins (2:6–10), and it would not be missed. At the beginning of the twentieth century, Wrede suggested that the controversy element and the healing miracle were originally two separate and independent traditions and that the controversy element was later inserted into the miracle (Wrede 1904). Numerous reasons have been given in support of this view. The most important are (1) a major contradiction exists between 2:5b, which is supposedly a divine passive (see 2:5) declaring that God has forgiven the man his sins, and 2:7 and 10, where Jesus personally forgives the man his sins. (2) The reference to the Son of Man in 2:10 occurs too early in the Gospel of Mark, since all the other references except this one and 2:28 occur after the passion prediction in 8:31. Consequently 2:6–10 cannot belong in this miracle story (2:1–5, 11–12), which occurred early in Jesus's ministry. (3) The present account possesses a typical "Markan sandwich," in which one story is sandwiched between another (Marcus 2000: 219).[1] (4) Healing and forgiveness are rarely associated in the healing traditions of Jesus; John 5:14 and the present passage are the exceptions.[2]

In response to these criticisms, one should note that the first assumes that 2:5b is a divine passive, whereas in the present account it is clearly

---

1. A "Markan sandwich" involves two separate stories in which one is divided into two halves and the other inserted in between. Some examples are Mark 3:22–30 into 3:19b–21 and 31–35; 5:25–34 into 5:21–24 and 35–43; 6:14–29 into 6:6b–13 and 30–52; 11:15–19 into 11:12–14 and 20–25; 14:3–9 into 14:1–2 and 10–11.

2. Cf. Mean (1961: 348–49), who lists eight additional reasons but argues in favor of the unity of the passage; cf. also Gundry 1993: 121–23.

understood as Jesus's personal forgiveness of the paralytic's sins. We find exactly the same words in Luke 7:48, where it is also not a divine passive but a reference to Jesus's personal forgiveness of a woman's sins (cf. 7:49). To state that Jesus's words originally functioned as a divine passive assumes what it must demonstrate. On the other hand, in the present contexts in Mark 2:1–12 and Luke 7:48–49, the verbs "forgiven" are clearly not divine passives. Concerning the argument that the title "Son of Man" in 2:10 occurs too early in the Gospel, this assumes that Jesus could never have used this title of himself before his passion predictions and that 2:1–12 must have taken place early in his ministry. If Mark's arrangement of the traditions was not chronological,[3] then there is no reason why the title could not have been an original part of this story. Furthermore, 2:1–12 is not really a Markan sandwich, for in all Markan sandwiches we have in the sandwich two clearly separate stories. Here we have one single story (Doughty 1983: 162–63). Finally, although we find only two healing stories in the Gospels that connect sin and healing, this association typifies Jewish thinking in the first century (cf. John 9:2; Luke 4:18; 1 Cor. 11:27–30; James 5:14–15; 2 Chron. 7:14; Pss. 41:3–4; 103:3; cf. also the Prayer of Nabonidus [4Q242, lines 3–4] and *b. Ned.* 41a, "A sick man does not recover from his sickness until all his sins are forgiven him."). In Jewish thinking, healing involves more than simply the restoration of physical health, for sickness and disease are a symptom and result of sin (Rom. 5:12). As a result, sickness often illustrates the problem of sin, which is a more basic human problem than disease (cf. James 5:15–16; Ps. 103:3; Isa. 38:17). Frequently, God's "healing" is a synonym for his "forgiving" (Ps. 41:3–4; Isa. 57:18–19; Hos. 14:4). Thus, although disease and sin do not necessarily possess a causal relationship in the life of an individual (John 9:2–3), they are related and possess a causal relationship for humanity as a whole due to the fall. When one reads Mark 2:1–12 as it now stands, it reads as a unified whole. People over the centuries have seldom thought that it was a combination of two unrelated stories. The problem of 2:1–12 lies primarily with those who assume that during the oral period, miracle and controversy stories existed in perfect, rounded forms. Since the present account does not fit into a neat form-critical category, it is assumed that something must have happened to the original story. In 3:1–6, however, we again encounter a miracle story involving a controversy.

Mark's own hand is seen most clearly in the opening seam (2:1–2), especially in the reference to Jesus's "speaking the word" (τὸν λόγον, *ton logon*; Guelich 1989: 83; Marcus 2000: 219), although it is no longer possible to distinguish clearly the Markan redaction from the tradition in these verses (Pesch 1980a: 151). The concluding summary (2:12) also looks heavily Markan (cf. 1:27; 4:41). Although some see 2:5a, 6, 8–9, 10b (Pryke 1978: 11, 140, 153) and even 2:7 (Doughty 1983: 165) as Markan, this confuses

---

3. See "Authorship" in the introduction and the quotation of Papias.

the stylistic changes made by the evangelist in his retelling of the story with his creating this material ex nihilo. The hand of Mark can be seen in the account by the indefinite plural (2:3; cf. 1:22, 30, 32, 45; etc.); the reference to the "crowd" in 2:4 ("crowd" occurs 37 times in Mark); the dual expressions "unroofed the roof" and "having dug a hole" in 2:4; the double periphrasis (2:6; cf. 1:4, 6; 5:5; 14:54; cf. also 1:39); "reasoning in their hearts" (2:6, 9; cf. 8:16–17; 9:33; 11:31); "but God alone" (2:7; cf. 10:18); reference to the Son of Man's "authority" (2:10; cf. 1:22, 27; 3:15; 6:7; 11:28–33); and the editorial comment in 2:10 (cf. 2:15c; 7:3–4, 19c; 12:12c; 13:14b, etc.).

Exegesis and Exposition

[1]And [Jesus] having entered again into Capernaum, after some days ⌜it was reported⌝ that he was at home. [2]And many [people] were gathered so that there was no longer room, not even around the door, and he was speaking the word to them. [3]And they [some people] come bringing to him a paralytic carried by four men. [4]And not being able ⌜to bring⌝ him [the paralytic] [to Jesus] on account of the crowd, they unroofed the roof where he was, and having dug a hole, they lower the mat upon which the paralytic was lying. [5]And upon seeing their faith, Jesus says to the paralytic, "Child, your sins are forgiven." [6]And some of the scribes were sitting there and reasoning in their hearts, [7]"Why is this man speaking this way? He is blaspheming. Who is able to forgive sins but God alone?" [8]And immediately Jesus, having perceived in his spirit that they are reasoning in this manner within themselves, says to them, "Why are you harboring these thoughts in your hearts? [9]What is easier, to say to the paralytic, 'Your sins are forgiven,' or to say, 'Rise and take up your mat and walk?' [10]But in order that you may know that the Son of Man has authority ⌜to forgive sins on earth⌝," he says to the paralytic, [11]"I say to you, rise, take up your mat, and go to your home." [12]And ⌜he arose⌝ and immediately taking up [his] mat, he went out before all [of them], so that all were amazed and were glorifying God saying, "We have never seen anything like this."

2:1-2   "Again" (πάλιν, *palin*) is a frequent Markan introductory device: 2:13; 3:1, 20; 4:1; 5:21; 7:14, 31; 8:1, 13; 10:1, 10, 32; 11:27 (cf. also 7:14; 8:13, 25; 10:24; 11:3; 12:4; 14:39, 40, 61, 69, 70; 15:4, 12, 13). The reference to Jesus's returning to Capernaum serves to tie this account with 1:21–45 and Jesus's first visit to Capernaum (1:21; Peabody 1987: 22–23, 116–17). A chronological tie is created between 2:1–12 and 1:40–45 by the expression "after some days" (δι' ἡμερῶν, *di' hēmerōn*). Although Jesus did not openly enter Capernaum (1:45), even with a secret, quiet visit, he could not be hidden. Most commentators understand "at home" (ἐν οἴκῳ, *en oikō*) as a reference to Peter's home (1:29, 33, 35; Marcus 2000: 215; J. Edwards 2002: 74; Donahue and Harrington 2002: 93; France 2002: 122), but it can also refer to a home in general ("in a house"; cf. 7:24; 9:28 [note 9:30]) or Jesus's own home ("at home"; cf. Matt. 4:13 and possibly Mark 2:15; 3:20 [3:19 NRSV]; 7:17; 9:33).

Jesus continues to draw big crowds (2:2; cf. 1:32–34, 37, 45), illustrating both the truth of 1:45 and its hyperbolic nature (Jesus is in a city). The double negative in "no longer [μηκέτι, *mēketi*] room, not even [μηδέ, *mēde*] around the door" emphasizes the size of the crowd and thus heightens Jesus's greatness and fame. "No longer" (cf. 1:45) underscores the continued growth of his fame and popularity. Jesus is described as speaking the "word." In the setting of Jesus, this would have primarily involved the message of 1:15, but for Mark's readers it would imply far more in that the "word" is essentially a synonym for the "gospel" of 1 Cor. 15:3–8. Mark's use of this expression assists in tying the present account with 1:40–45 (cf. 1:45).

The reference to four men carrying the paralytic emphasizes both the plight **2:3–4** of the paralytic, in that he is not even able to crawl or hobble to Jesus, and the faith present in both the paralytic and the four men bringing him to Jesus. Jesus's great popularity and fame are again emphasized (cf. 2:2) by the paralytic's friends' difficulty in bringing him to Jesus. This prepares the reader for what the four friends are about to do. Other examples in healing stories of obstacles overcome by faith are found in 5:25–34, 21–24, 35–43; 10:46–52. The term "crowd" (ὄχλος, *ochlos*) occurs thirty-eight times in Mark and is always singular, except for 10:1.

"They unroofed the roof" (ἀπεστέγασαν τὴν στέγην, *apestegasan tēn stegēn*; cf. 14:6)[4] may be a Semitism reflecting the Aramaic origin of the story. The home in which this event takes place is a typical Galilean home, having an outside stairway or ladder leading to a flat roof. Some might see this as a destructive act in which the property of the house's owner is damaged, but this is not an issue in the story. Neither for Jesus nor for the Gospel writers are material things as important as the well-being of people. Compare 5:1–20.

The use of the redundant expressions "unroofed the roof" and "having dug a hole" is an example of Markan duality (Neirynck 1988: 102). The participle "having dug" (ἐξορύξαντες, *exoryxantes*) is used elsewhere to describe the digging of a trench or a canal and even the gouging out of an eye. It indicates that the roof was a typical mud-thatch Galilean roof, which required that the four friends dig out a hole. Luke 5:19 contextualizes this in light of the building environment of his readers and states that they lowered the paralytic "through the tiles." Both Gospel writers are saying that the paralytic was lowered through the roof (Stein 1990: 42–46). The reason for lowering the paralytic through the roof was due to the crowd at the door preventing entry into the home. It is not to prevent the demon who was afflicting the paralytic from entering the building and hindering the healing (France 2002: 123n4; contra Gnilka 1978: 97). There is no hint in the present account that the healing is an exorcism. The lowering

---

4. For other examples of the cognate accusative in Mark, see 4:41; 9:41; 10:38, 39; 13:7; 14:6; cf. also 7:7; 13:19, 20; 14:39. See Neirynck 1988: 76–77, 237.

of the paralytic serves as an unspoken request for healing.[5] The Greek term "mat" (κράβαττος, *krabattos*) is a colloquial expression (avoided by Matthew and Luke) that refers to a poor person's bed or mattress (France 2002: 123).

2:5 The reference to Jesus "seeing their faith" (ἰδὼν . . . τὴν πίστιν αὐτῶν, *idōn . . . tēn pistin autōn*) assumes that the paralytic is included in this "faith" (Lagrange 1911: 32; Williams 1994: 99–101). For other examples of how someone's faith ultimately brought healing to a sick friend or relative, see 5:21–43; 7:24–30; cf. also Matt. 8:5–13; John 4:46–53. The content of this faith was in germ form the kind of faith that brought salvation in Mark's day. It involved faith that Jesus, as God's anointed, was able to bring healing (cf. Mark 1:40) and that he brought with him the kingdom of God. For Mark's readers, "faith" would also include what Jesus accomplished through his death and resurrection. Faith is present in the healings of 1:29–31 and 40–45 and will also be present in 5:21–24, 25–34, 35–43; 9:14–29; and 10:46–52. Unlike healings described in the Greek world, faith generally precedes rather than follows the healing (Theissen 1983: 132). The importance of faith in Mark has already been stated in 1:15 and is seen in 1:30b, 40 (cf. also 5:6, 28, 34, 36; 6:5–6, 52; 7:32; 8:22; 10:47, 51–52). For "Child" (τέκνον, *teknon*) as an encouraging address, see 10:24; Luke 16:25; John 13:33; compare also Mark 5:34.

The modern reader may be surprised by Jesus's response to the paralytic—"your sins are forgiven" (ἀφίενταί σου αἱ ἁμαρτίαι, *aphientai sou hai hamartiai*)—but in the first century, sin and disease were intimately associated (France 2002: 124–25). What is unusual in the account is Jesus's action in personally forgiving the paralytic his sins. Why here, unlike in other examples of healing, Jesus specifically refers to the forgiveness of the man's sins is impossible to explain,[6] but this in no way affects the historicity of the incident. Numerous scholars interpret Jesus's words as a "divine passive" (Klostermann 1950: 23; Jeremias 1971: 11; Guelich 1989: 83–83, 93, 95–96), that is, as a way in which God's name can be omitted out of reverence for the third commandment (Exod. 20:7) by placing the verb in the passive (Stein 1994b: 64–65). Thus, it is argued, what Jesus meant when he said, "Your sins are forgiven," was, "The Lord God has forgiven you your sins." Although this is possible in a hypothetical reconstruction of what may have originally taken place, in the present context it is clear that Mark understood these words not as a declaration of God's forgiveness (as in 2 Sam. 12:13) but as a "performative utterance" (France 2002: 125) by which Jesus personally forgave the paralytic his sins (Dunn 1990: 27). The whole controversy in Mark 2:6–10 focuses on what Jesus has done in forgiving this man his sins, not on whether God has forgiven him. No attempt is made by Jesus or the evangelist to show that the scribes misunderstood what Jesus said. After being accused of blasphemy, there

---

5. For nonbiblical parallels of people being lowered through a roof, see van der Loos 1965: 441n3.

6. J. Edwards (2002: 76–77) and France (2002: 125) suggest that the account indicates Jesus's awareness that the paralytic's illness was somehow associated with his sins.

is no statement by Jesus to the effect, "You have misunderstood my words. I was not personally forgiving this man his sins. I was simply pointing out that God has forgiven him." Any attempt therefore to explain Jesus's words as a divine passive must do so on the basis of a hypothetical reconstruction of what supposedly took place. The present Markan context does not permit this, nor does the Lukan context here (5:17–26) or in 7:36–50, where Jesus says the same thing.

This unique act and claim of Jesus to forgive sins is clearly recognized in the Protestant tradition. After a congregation's public confession of sin, a pastor will declare that God, being true to his promises (cf. 1 John 1:9), has forgiven the sins of the people. In Roman Catholic tradition, where a priest, upon a penitent's confession, "forgives" sin, the high christological claim found in this verse is somewhat obscured. There is, of course, a sense in which believers forgive others (Matt. 6:14; Luke 6:37; Col. 3:13; cf. James 5:16), but this does not involve the granting of divine forgiveness. Whether John 20:23 (cf. Matt. 16:19; 18:18) involves more than the declaration of God's forgiveness and teaches that the Christian leader in the name of Jesus can bring about forgiveness is debated.[7] Regardless of how one interprets John 20:23, one should note that whatever may be the role of the Christian priests/ministers in this, forgiveness is carried out not in their name, which would be blasphemy, but in God's or Jesus's name. Jesus, on the other hand, forgave sins in his own name, and this was understood by the scribes as blasphemous. In a context in which God alone was seen as being able to forgive sins (Mark 2:7; cf. Luke 7:49), Jesus does so. When accused of blasphemy, he does not state that he was misunderstood and that what he said was a divine passive. On the contrary, in the clearest of terms Jesus states, "I shall prove to you that I, the Son of Man, have authority to do this," and proceeds to do so by healing the paralytic.

2:6–7   Because there has been no need thus far in the story, the "scribes" (γραμματέων, *grammateōn*) have not been mentioned. Whereas in 1:22 the scribes are portrayed as lacking the kind of authority Jesus possesses, here they are seen as hostile toward him. Their attitude stands in sharp contrast with that of the four men who in faith brought the paralytic to Jesus. For the scribes "reasoning in their hearts" (διαλογιζόμενοι ἐν ταῖς καρδίαις αὐτῶν, *dialogizomenoi en tais kardiais autōn*), see 2:8 and also 11:31. For similar expressions involving the disciples, see 8:16–17; 9:33. For the metaphorical use of "heart" as the center of thinking and affection, compare 3:5; 6:52; 7:6, 19, 21; 8:17; 11:23; 12:30, 33. The scribal conclusion, "he is blaspheming" (βλασφημεῖ, *blasphēmei*), indicates that Jesus's pronouncement of forgiveness in 2:5b was understood as a personal act of forgiveness on his part, not a divine passive. Jesus is accused of blasphemy not because he is directly claiming to be God or pronouncing the sacred name of God but because he acts like God. He is exercising a prerogative in forgiving sins that belongs exclusively to God (cf. John 10:33), to

7. For a helpful discussion of John 20:23, see R. Brown 1970: 1039–45.

no one but God alone (εἰ μὴ εἷς ὁ θεός, *ei mē heis ho theos*; lit. "except one, God"; cf. 10:18). Compare Pss. 51:1–3; 85:2; Midr. Ps. 17.3.[8] The christological implication of such behavior was clear to the early church (cf. John 5:18 and 10:33, which should be interpreted in light of John 1:1, 18; 20:28).

2:8–9   The reference to Jesus's "spirit" (πνεύματι, *pneumati*) does not refer to the Holy Spirit but to Jesus's own spirit (cf. 8:12). If this were a reference to the Holy Spirit, we would expect "in *the* Spirit" or "in the Holy Spirit" (cf. 12:36), not "in *his* [αὐτοῦ, *autou*] spirit." Here it serves as a synonym for "heart" (cf. the synonymous parallelism in Ps. 77:6). Mark gives no explanation of how Jesus knew what the scribes were thinking. He probably assumed that, if the prophets possessed such clairvoyance (cf. John 4:16–19), certainly Jesus Christ, the Son of God, would possess this as well (cf. Mark 5:30; 12:15; 14:18–21). Although "they were reasoning within themselves" (διαλογίζονται ἐν ἑαυτοῖς, *dialogizontai en heautois*) can be interpreted as meaning that the scribes were talking among themselves, this is unlikely since in 2:6 the locale where this takes place is the "heart." If this involved a visible whispering of the scribes among themselves, we would expect that instead of "Jesus knowing in his spirit," Mark might have written "Jesus seeing [or 'hearing']."

    The a fortiori argument that follows involves what is easier to *say*, not what is easier to *do*. Although it takes greater authority to forgive sins (only God can forgive sins, but humans can heal), it is easier to say "Your sins are forgiven" than to say "Rise, take up your bed, and walk." The reason for this is that the latter requires that a healing take place immediately or else the speaker's inability to heal will be instantly demonstrated. Anyone, however, can say that a person's sins are forgiven, for one's inability to do this cannot be shown (Marcus 2000: 217–18). It is assumed that if the man is healed, this would demonstrate Jesus's authority to forgive sins. "Your sins are forgiven" means, "I forgive you of your sins" (see 2:5).

2:10   Verse 10 is a purpose clause introduced by "but in order that" (ἵνα δέ, *hina de*), indicating that the healing that follows proves Jesus's authority to forgive sins (contra Hooker 1991: 87).[9] The stated purpose stands in an emphatic position at the beginning of the sentence (cf. Exod. 7:17). The grammar of this sentence is awkward because it is incomplete. (Cf. 14:49c for another example of an incomplete sentence, and cf. how Matthew makes it into a complete sentence [26:56].) Mark, due to the parenthetical comment ("he says to the paralytic"), leaves the sentence incomplete. (This is a more likely

---

8. Cf. Fitzmyer 1981: 585 for a possible exception.

9. Some scholars have sought to interpret the entire "but in order that . . ." clause as an editorial comment directed by Mark to his readers rather than as part of Jesus's conversation with the scribes. This seems unlikely, however, because (1) it would be the only clear editorial use of the "Son of Man" in Mark, (2) it places two unrelated editorial asides ("but in order . . ." and "he says to the paralytic") next to each other, and (3) it eliminates the main christological emphasis from the account by omitting any response to the question of Jesus's unique authority to forgive sins raised in 2:7 etc. (Dewey 1980: 78–89; France 2002: 128n15).

understanding than to make the ἵνα clause into the command: "Know that the Son of Man . . . on the earth.")

The reference to "the Son of Man" (ὁ υἱὸς τοῦ ἀνθρώπου, *ho huios tou anthrōpou*) is the first of fourteen occurrences of this title in Mark. This and 2:28 are the only two instances where it appears before the events of Caesarea Philippi (8:31, 38; 9:9, 12, 31; 10:33, 45; 13:26; 14:21 [2×], 41, 62). That Mark introduces the title without explanation indicates that his readers must have been familiar with it. There is no need to assume that the title is a Markan redactional insertion into the present context (contra Doughty 1983: 164–69); the tradition had to refer to Jesus in some way in this saying, and Jesus frequently used "Son of Man" as a title both to reveal who he was and to conceal his identity from those outside. That the title "Son of Man" occurs only four other times in the NT outside the Gospels (whereas it is found eighty-two times in the Gospels) and only once in the sense in which Jesus used it (Acts 7:56) argues for the authenticity of this title. It is unlikely that the early church would have created this rather enigmatic title and ascribed it to Jesus throughout the Gospels instead of using their favorite titles "Christ" and "Lord." The best explanation for the fact that the church's favorite titles for Jesus in Acts through Revelation are Christ and Lord, whereas Jesus's favorite self-designation in the Gospels is "Son of Man," is that this corresponds to historical reality (Stein 1994b: 146–51).

Whatever "Son of Man" may have meant in the original setting in Jesus's ministry, it cannot mean "man" in the present context. Jesus was not saying that every person has power to forgive sins. Jesus's healing of the paralytic would not prove that every man could forgive sins but only that he, the Son of Man, could do so. It should be noted that Jesus did not state that he "has been given" authority to forgive sins but that he "has" (ἔχει, *echei*) such authority. There is no evidence in other Jewish literature that any man, whether prophet, priest, king, or Messiah, had such authority to forgive sins (Hooker 1991: 87). Whereas Jesus's "authority" (ἐξουσίαν, *exousian*) has already been shown by his earlier exorcism (1:27), here and in 2:28 Jesus's unique authority is demonstrated by his exercising two divine prerogatives: forgiving sins (2:10) and being "Lord" of the Sabbath (2:28; cf. John 5:9c–18). Compare Mark 11:27–33. The expression "on the earth" (ἐπὶ τῆς γῆς, *epi tēs gēs*) modifies "to forgive sins" and indicates that already in his earthly ministry the Son of Man possesses such authority. The parenthetical comment "he says to the paralytic" is also found in the parallels in Matt. 9:6 and Luke 5:24 and is strong evidence for the view that some sort of a literary relationship exists among the Synoptic Gospels.

"I say to you" picks up the thought of 2:10, not 2:5, in both Mark and in   **2:11–12**
the Lukan parallel (5:24). The healing is described by Jesus's command to the paralytic, "Rise [ἔγειρε, *egeire*; cf. Mark 5:41], take up your mat, and go to your home." The proof of the healing and Jesus's ability to forgive sins is shown by the paralytic rising, taking up his bed, and walking away. For "all

were amazed," compare 1:22, 27; 5:42; 6:51; 12:17. The "all" includes even the hostile scribes (cf. 12:17). Although the miracle of healing is predominantly in view, Jesus's authority to forgive sins is also implicitly involved in this response. Mark's comment that they all "were glorifying" (δοξάζειν, *doxazein*) God is the only occasion in Mark where this verb in used. For "We have never seen anything like this," compare 1:27; 4:41; also see Matt. 9:33; Isa. 64:4 (64:3 MT); 1 Cor. 2:9. This functions to further heighten Jesus's authority and power. No mention is made of the scribes at this point. This does not indicate that they were not originally part of the healing story; they are not mentioned because they play no further role in the narrative. In telling the story, Mark wants to end the account with this christological confession (cf. 1:27; 4:41).

Summary

As in 1:21–45, Mark seeks in this new section (2:1–3:6) to demonstrate that Jesus of Nazareth is the Christ, the Son of God. In 1:21–45 this is demonstrated by the miracles he performed; in this new section it is shown by the overwhelming effect of his actions and sayings. The present account is one of the most important christological passages in all of Mark. Mark emphasizes the greatness of Jesus of Nazareth and that he is the Son of God in several ways: (1) He emphasizes the impact of Jesus's ministry of healing and teaching by referring to the great crowds that gather around him (2:2–4). Even though he does not openly enter Capernaum (see 2:2), he simply cannot be hidden. (2) Jesus heals a paralytic so ill and feeble that he has to be carried by four men. (3) The people are all amazed at Jesus's ability to heal (and to forgive sins; 2:12). (4) No one present has ever witnessed a man do the things Jesus does, and although not stated, the implication is that no one has ever done the things that Jesus does (2:12; cf. 1:22, 27; 4:41). (5) Jesus's ability to read the human heart (2:5 and 8) as God does (1 Sam. 16:7; 1 Kings 8:39; Ps. 7:9; Jer. 11:20; Acts 1:24; 15:8; Rom. 8:27) contains an implicit Christology concerning his divine nature (Donahue and Harrington 2002: 95). (6) Finally, and most important, Jesus exercises a divine prerogative in forgiving sins that no mere human possesses, and he proves that he has authority to do this by healing the paralytic. Luke clearly sees the christological focus of our passage by his wording in 5:21, "*Who is this* who speaks blasphemies? Who can forgive sins but God alone?" (my italics).

Along with the christological emphasis, Mark also seeks to prepare his readers for the passion and death of Jesus. He does so by showing how certain religious leaders (the scribes) are antagonistic to Jesus's words and deeds (2:6–8). They will play a major role in the plot to kill Jesus. In 1:22 their lack of authority is mentioned, but now their antagonism and hostility are pointed out. In 2:16 they are associated with the Pharisees and criticize Jesus for eating with publicans and sinners; in 2:18 the Pharisees, many of whom were scribes, criticize Jesus for not fasting, and in 2:24 they criticize him for the behavior of his disciples on the Sabbath. The high point of their hostility in this section comes in 3:6, when the Pharisees, along with the Herodians, plot how to kill (lit. "destroy") Jesus. The scribes are later linked with the chief priests (11:18; 14:1; 15:31) and the Sanhedrin (14:53, 55; 15:1), and they will be expressly mentioned in Jesus's passion predictions as bringing about his death (8:31; 10:33–34).[10] Mark wants his readers to know that it was not the people who sought Jesus's death but the religious leaders (14:1–2).

Additional Notes

2:1. The passive ἠκούσθη (lit. "it/he was heard") can be rendered "he was reported." See France 2002: 122; Cranfield 1959: 96. Cf. V. Taylor 1952: 192.

2:4. The reading προσενέγκαι follows ℵ B L Θ vg syr cop instead of προσεγγίσαι, as in A C D K Δ Π f¹ f¹³.

2:10. The translation here follows the word order in B Θ. Cf. also A K Π f¹ f¹³, where the infinitive ἀφιέναι also precedes ἐπὶ τῆς γῆς, but ἁμαρτίας ends the phrase. See Metzger 1971: 78; Marcus 2000: 218.

2:12. Here ἠγέρθη is translated as an intransitive active verb, but it can also be translated as an aorist passive, "he was raised."

---

10. For a discussion of the role of the religious leaders in the death of Jesus in Mark, see Kingsbury 1990.

2. Jesus Dines with Toll Collectors and Sinners (2:13–17)

In 2:1–12, Mark has demonstrated Jesus's personal authority to forgive sins. In the account that follows, he illustrates how Jesus came to offer that forgiveness to toll collectors and sinners. This new account, like the previous pericope, focuses on the behavior of Jesus, and once again his behavior is challenged. In the following two pericopes (2:18–22 and 23–28) Jesus will again be challenged, but the challenge will be directed at the behavior of his disciples. As pointed out earlier (see 2:1–3:6), several common themes unite these pericopes: Jesus's authority (2:10, 14–16, 18–19, 28; 3:2), his forgiving sins (2:5–11; cf. 2:16–17), the hostility of the scribes (2:6, 16, 18, 24; 3:2, 6), and a setting involving a meal (2:15, 18, 23). The present account is difficult to classify. It involves a call to discipleship (2:14) as well as a pronouncement story (2:15–17). In 2:13–14 the central character is a man named Levi, who seems to play no role in the banquet mentioned in 2:15–17. Some argue that 2:14 does not really fit 2:15–17 because the pronouncement in 2:17 focuses on "sinners," whereas Levi is a toll collector. Consequently, numerous scholars have suggested that the present account is the result of a merger of two different elements and the redactional work of Mark, and that (1) a single tradition (2:14, 16b–17) has been merged with Markan redactional work in 2:13 and 15–16a; or (2) Mark has added a calling scene (2:14) and a seam (2:13) to a single tradition (2:15–17); or (3) two separate traditions (2:14 and 15–17) have been combined by Mark, who then added 2:13 (Guelich 1989: 98; Hooker 1991: 93–94; Marcus 2000: 228).

In its present form, however, 2:13–17 is a single story (Kuthirakkattel 1990: 198), and Mark did not think it necessary to mention Levi's name again in 2:15–17. That 2:15–17 immediately follows 2:14 sufficed for Mark to indicate that Levi's presence was to be assumed. Furthermore, if "in his house" is best understood as a reference to Levi's house (see 2:15), then Levi is very much present in 2:15–17. Luke understood the present account in this manner and introduced the material in 2:15–17 with, "And Levi gave a great banquet for him [Jesus] in his house" (Luke 5:29). As to referring only to "sinners" in Jesus's proverb (Mark 2:17), Mark has done this to maintain the parallelism (well/sick, righteous/?): he needed one subject ("sinners" or "toll collectors") rather than a compound one ("toll collectors and sinners"), and "sinners" is a more comprehensive and inclusive term than "toll collectors" and thus a better antonym for "righteous." In the story "toll collectors" function as an example for a larger group (sinners), just as later healing a man with a withered hand on the Sabbath serves as an example of healing in general (cf. 3:2–3 with 4), and the tradition of washing hands serves as an example of the broader issue of the oral traditions in general (cf. 7:2–4 with 5–13; cf. also Luke 11:37–41).

It is best to understand our account as arising from Mark's use of a single tradition involving a man named Levi, who in following Jesus held a banquet for his friends. It is unlike Mark simply to create out of nothing incidents involving specific people (Best 1981: 175–76). Mark's own editorial work is most evident in the seam (2:13), the wording of the tradition in 2:14 to parallel the call of the four disciples in 1:16–20, and the "for" explanatory clause in 2:15 (Pryke 1978: 11, 140, 154; Gnilka 1978: 104–5; Marcus 2000: 228–29).

Exegesis and Exposition

¹³And he [Jesus] went out again by the sea. And all the crowd was coming to him, and he was teaching them. ¹⁴And as he was passing by he saw ⌜Levi,⌝ the son of Alphaeus, sitting at the customs booth, and he says to him, "Follow me." And he rose up [and] followed him. ¹⁵And it comes to pass that he was reclining for dinner in his house, and many toll collectors and [other] sinners were reclining for dinner with Jesus and his disciples, for they were many and were following him. ¹⁶And ⌜the scribes of the Pharisees⌝ ⌜when they saw⌝ that he [Jesus] is eating with sinners and toll collectors were saying to his disciples, "Why is he eating with toll collectors and sinners?" ¹⁷And having heard [them], Jesus says to them, "Those who are healthy have no need of a physician, but those who are sick. I have not come to call the righteous but sinners."

The introductory Markan seam in 2:13 joins the present pericope to 2:1–12 and the preceding material by several common terms: "went out" (ἐξῆλθεν, *exēlthen*; cf. 2:13; cf. also 1:35, where Jesus "went out"; cf. εἰσελθών, *eiselthōn* in 2:1); "again" (πάλιν, *palin*; cf. 2:1); "by the sea" (παρὰ τὴν θάλασσαν, *para tēn thalassan*; cf. 1:16; also 3:7; 4:1); "all" (πᾶς, *pas*; cf. 1:5, 32, 37; 2:12); "crowd" (ὄχλος, *ochlos*; cf. 2:4); "to him" (πρὸς αὐτόν, *pros auton*; cf. 1:32, 40, 45; also 1:5); and "he was teaching" (ἐδίδασκεν, *edidasken*; cf. 1:21–22). No allegorical significance should be read into the reference to the "sea." Here Mark is simply referring to the Sea of Galilee mentioned in 1:16 (cf. 4:1). We have already observed that the teaching ministry of Jesus is strongly emphasized in Mark (Stein 1970: 91–94). As in 1:21–22 (cf. also 2:2), the content of his teaching is not mentioned, for Mark has already revealed the content of Jesus's teaching in 1:15: "The time is fulfilled, and the kingdom of God has come; repent and believe in the gospel." The numerous literary ties with what precedes, however, contrast with the lack of any direct and necessary narrative link to what has preceded (France 2002: 131).

In describing the call of Levi, Mark uses similar terminology as in the call of Simon and Andrew: "passing by" (παράγων, *paragōn*; 1:16), "he saw" (εἶδεν,

2:13–14

eiden; cf. 1:16, 19), and "follow/followed" (ἀκολουθέω, *akoloutheō*; cf. 1:18, 20). This does not mean that Mark sought to make this present account conform to a specific "call story" form. One should expect certain similarities in stories of how Jesus encountered various people and called them to follow. If Mark sought to stereotype this account along the lines of 1:16–20, we would expect to find not "Levi, the son of Alphaeus, sitting at the customs booth" but rather "Levi, the son of Alphaeus, sitting at the customs booth, *for he was a toll collector*" (cf. 1:16).

The designation "Levi, the son of Alphaeus," is traditional and almost certainly authentic due to the problems it raises. This Levi is not mentioned anywhere else in the NT except in the Lukan parallel (5:27). In Mark 3:18 (cf. Matt. 10:3; Luke 6:13; Acts 1:13) James, one of the twelve disciples, is referred to as the "son of Alphaeus." Making the situation even more confusing is that in the Matthean parallel (9:9–13) the name of the toll collector is "Matthew," and in the list of the twelve disciples in Matthew's Gospel, we read of "Matthew, the toll collector." (Mark and Luke also refer to "Matthew" in their lists of the disciples, but he is not described as "the toll collector.") Matthew and Luke omit the designation "son of Alphaeus" from their description of the toll collector in their parallel accounts. Some have suggested that "Matthew" may have been a second name for "Levi," so that the same person possessed these two Semitic names. Within the NT, several people are described by two names: Simon/Peter, Saul/Paul, John/Mark, perhaps Judas the son of James/Thaddaeus, and so on. In most of these instances, however, the two names are not both Semitic; one is Semitic and the other Greek or Roman (but cf. Acts 4:36). Another suggestion is that Levi may have been the brother of James, since each is described as the son of Alphaeus (W. Lane 1974: 100n29). Nothing in the Markan account requires Levi to have been one of the twelve disciples (Best 1981: 177; Hooker 1991: 94; contra Guelich 1989: 100). The call to discipleship is often a general one addressed to any who would follow Jesus (8:34; cf. 2:15 [the "many" refers to toll collectors and sinners]; 9:38; 10:21, 28–30, 52). This, however, does not resolve the problem that Matthew refers to this person as "Matthew, the toll collector." If Matthew and Levi were the same person, then there existed among the disciples three sets of brothers: Peter and Andrew; James and John; and Matthew and James, the sons of Alphaeus.

The description of Levi "sitting at the customs booth" parallels "casting a net into the sea" in the description of the call of Simon and Andrew in 1:16. A distinction must be made between "tax collectors" and "toll collectors." The former were more concerned with income and property taxes, whereas the latter, to which Levi belonged, were engaged in "sales, customs, and road" tolls (Donahue 1971). Levi was probably an employee at a toll station on the Via Maris, a heavily traveled trade route running from Damascus to Caesarea through Capernaum, working for a man who had bought the right to collect such tolls. These tolls would have been collected for Herod Antipas, the tetrarch of Galilee and Perea. The call to Levi, "Follow me" (ἀκολούθει μοι, *akolouthei moi*), parallels the call directed to Peter and Andrew in 1:17, "Come after me" (δεῦτε ὀπίσω μου, *deute opisō mou*) and their "following" (ἠκολούθησαν, *ēkolouthēsan*) in 1:18 (cf. also 1:20). The differences, however, indicate that in the present account Mark is not applying a stereotyped call to discipleship patterned after 1:16–20, although Levi's response ("and he rose up [lit. 'rising up'] and followed him") recalls the similar description in 1:18 of Simon and Andrew following Jesus. He leaves his livelihood just as Simon, Andrew, James, and John did.

"And it comes to pass" (γίνεται, *ginetai*; cf. 4:19, 37; 11:23) ties 2:15–17 more   **2:15**
closely to 2:13–14 than the normal Markan "and it came to pass" (ἐγένετο, *egeneto*; see 1:4–6; Gundry 1993: 124), so that we need not envision an interval of time between 2:13–14 and 15–17 (contra Donahue and Harrington 2002: 101). Jesus's "reclining" (κατακεῖσθαι, *katakeisthai*) at the meal indicates that this is a banquet, since at normal meals one "sat" (cf. 14:3; Luke 5:27–29; 7:37; Jeremias 1966: 48–49).[1] At such meals one would dine lying on one's side with cushions under the arm, facing a short table on which the food was placed. The term ἀνάκειμαι (*anakeimai*) is a synonym (cf. the parallel in Matt. 9:10) and is also used to describe reclining at a banquet (cf. Mark 6:26; 14:18; Matt. 22:10; 26:7, 20; John 13:23, 29).[2] It is unclear whether Mark intends for his readers to see here an allusion to the future messianic banquet.

The antecedent of "his" in the expression "in his house" is unclear. It can be either Levi or Jesus (Malborn 1985; contra May 1993). Similarly the expression "to eat with" in 2:16 does not specify who is the host and who are the guests. As a result, the question of why Jesus ate with toll collectors and sinners can mean, "Why does Jesus eat in the homes of toll collectors and other sinners?" (Marcus 2000: 226; cf. Luke 5:30 [note v. 29]; 7:36; Acts 11:3; Gal. 2:12), or "Why does Jesus invite toll collectors and sinners to eat in his home?" (cf. Mark 14:14, 18; Matt. 24:49; Luke 22:11, 15). In favor of Jesus eating in Levi's house, we find that (1) no clear mention has been made thus far in Mark to Jesus having a house (Best 1981: 175; Marcus 2000: 225; but see 2:1); (2) Luke understood this phrase as referring to Levi's house ("And Levi held a great feast in his house for him [Jesus]," 5:29); and (3) if ritual defilement was in some way involved in the charge of the scribes against Jesus, such defilement would result from Jesus eating in the home of toll collectors and sinners but not in their eating in his home (Donahue 1971: 56). One should note the association of "toll collectors" with "extortioners" in Luke 3:13; "extortioners, unjust, and adulterers" in Luke 18:11; "harlots" in Matt. 21:32; and "gentiles" in Matt. 18:17 (cf. also Matt. 5:46–47).[3] For the

---

1. The term is also used to describe the reclining of those who are sick: 1:30; 2:4; John 5:3, 6; Acts 9:33; 28:8.

2. This explains how the woman in John 12:2–3 was able to wash Jesus's feet. She did not have to crawl under a table, because the feet of those dining were exposed and pointed outward like spokes from a hub (the short table[s] containing the food).

3. Cf. the tie with robbers, murderers, sinners, and uncleanness in *m. Ṭohar.* 7.6; *m. B. Qam.* 10.2; and *m. Ned.* 3.4, and to proprietors of brothels in Dio Chrysostom, *Orations* 14.14.

combination "toll collectors and sinners," compare Mark 2:16; Matt. 9:10, 11; 11:19; Luke 5:30; 7:34; 15:1; also Matt. 21:31–32. The term "sinners" can refer to those considered ceremonially unclean by being involved in trades considered dishonorable (camel drivers, tanners, weavers, usurers, tax collectors, etc.; Jeremias 1969: 303–12), but it more likely refers here to those who were morally unclean (adulterers, thieves, blasphemers, murderers, etc.; E. Sanders 1985: 174–211). That Mark refers to them as "sinners" in 2:15 indicates that he understood them as morally unclean according to 7:18–23 and not simply unclean by Jewish ritual standards (Marcus 2000: 226). As a result, "sinners" is a more general term and includes within it "toll collectors" (Kuthirakkattel 1990: 206). I have translated the two terms "toll collectors and [other] sinners" (Marcus 2000: 226).

The reference to the toll collectors and sinners eating with Jesus prepares the reader for the question in 2:16. Jesus's eating with such people served as a visual declaration of the offer of forgiveness such as he pronounced in 2:5. Such behavior was seen by Jesus's opponents not as a polite action in accepting the hospitality of toll collectors and sinners, but as an intentional parabolic act bearing a message (Stein 1994b: 25–26). This action by Jesus indicated that such people, not just the religious and devout, were being invited to experience divine forgiveness and to participate in the arrival of the kingdom of God.[4] In 2:15 we find the first of forty-six references to the "disciple(s)" (μαθηταῖς, mathētais) in Mark. Since they are distinguished here from the toll collectors and sinners who are present and "following" Jesus, this term does not refer to disciples in general but to "the disciples" (cf. 2:18, 23; 3:7 [note the distinction here between "the disciples" and others who "follow" Jesus], 13ff.). At the narrative level this prepares the reader for the question addressed to the disciples in 2:16 and the next two pericopes (2:18–22 and 23–28), which involve the actions of the disciples. This reference to the disciples was probably present in the tradition that Mark inherited.[5] It is unlikely that Mark is thinking here of only Simon, Andrew, James, and John (1:16–20). Mark's readers would

4. E. Sanders (1993: 225–33; cf. also 1985: 203–5) argues that the lack of any explicit mention of repentance in the passage shows that Jesus indicated God's acceptance of tax collectors and sinners apart from any necessity of repentance. His message was simply one of God's love and acceptance of them. While it is true that what many scribes and Pharisees meant by repentance for tax collectors and sinners is not mentioned (giving up their unclean and evil profession, their unkosher living, their violation of the ritual law, the constant contact with idolatrous coinage, etc.), Mark expects his readers to understand that the call to repentance that typifies Jesus's message (cf. 1:15) involves all Israel, both the "righteous" and "sinners." This is clearly how Luke understands the Markan account when he adds to Jesus's "I came" saying in 2:17 "to repentance" (5:32). Whereas Jesus did not make repentance a precondition for his love and friendship (J. Edwards 2002: 85), along with faith it was a requirement for entrance into the kingdom of God.

5. Pryke (1978: 154) excludes this from the redactional work of Mark. Marcus (2000: 229), however, argues that the reference to the "disciples" in 2:15 is probably Markan because it is unnecessary for the story itself but important for the literary framework of the chapter (2:18–22, 23–29).

not have understood "his disciples" as a reference to "one-third of Jesus's disciples." This suggests that the call of the Twelve was placed at 3:13–19 for other than chronological considerations.

The Markan comment "for they were many" (ἦσαν γὰρ πολλοί, *ēsan gar polloi*; see 1:16) is redundant and makes this comment emphatic. Who "they" refers to depends in part on how one interprets the rest of the verse. "And they were following him" is best understood as going with what precedes, that is, the "many," rather than the scribes of the Pharisees mentioned in the next verse. The verb "follow" is used eighteen times in Mark, and it is never used to describe the behavior of those hostile to Jesus. It is used both to describe the Twelve (1:17–18; 6:1; 10:28, 32; 15:41) and those outside the Twelve (3:7; 5:24; 8:34; 9:38; 10:21, 52; 11:9) who follow Jesus. Thus "they" cannot refer to the scribes of the Pharisees. On the other hand, "many" and "they" can refer to either the disciples or the toll collectors and sinners. The term "many," however, picks up the "many" toll collectors and sinners referred to earlier in the verse. Thus it is best to see this statement as referring to the toll collectors and sinners and as clarifying for the reader what is implied in their eating with Jesus. Sharing a meal with Jesus means that they were (or were considering) following him.

The reference to "the scribes of the Pharisees" (οἱ γραμματεῖς τῶν Φαρισαίων,   **2:16–17**
hoi grammateis tōn Pharisaiōn) recalls the earlier references to the scribes in 1:22, 27; 2:6. The difficulty of this reading led some copyists to change the texts to "scribes and Pharisees" as in Matt. 12:38; 23:2, 13, 14, 15, 23, 25, 27, 29; Luke 5:21; 6:7; 11:53 (reverse order in Mark 7:1, 5; Matt. 15:1; Luke 15:2), but the difficulty of the reading guarantees its authenticity. Their presence in a toll collector's home is not explained by Mark. For the combination "elders, chief priests, and scribes," see 8:31; 11:27; 14:43, 53; 15:17; for the combination "chief priests and scribes," see 10:33; 11:18; 15:31. Although "scribe" denotes an occupation rather than membership in a religious sect, many scribes were associated with the Pharisees (cf. Acts 23:9).[6] See 1:22. This is the first reference to the Pharisees in Mark. They are mentioned again in 2:18 (2×), 24; 3:6; 7:1, 3, 5; 8:11, 15; 10:2; and 12:13. The name probably means "separate ones," but it is unclear as to exactly from whom or what they were separate.[7] The Pharisees were the most influential of the three main Jewish sects. We first hear of them in the second century BC (Josephus, *Ant.* 13.10.5–6 §§283–98), but they were already at that time an established religious group. In contrast to the Sadducees, the Pharisees believed in the resurrection of the dead, the existence of angels and demons, both predestination and free will (Luke 20:27; Acts 23:6–9; cf. also Josephus, *Ant.* 18.1.2–3 §§11–15), and the validity of both the written and the oral law (Mark 7:2–5). The center of Sadducean

---

6. See, however, Marcus (2000: 523–24) for the view that most scribes in Jesus's day were of Sadducean origin.

7. Baumgarten (1983) argues that the term originally meant "specifiers," but few have followed his suggestion.

influence was located in the temple, but that of the Pharisees was located in the synagogue. As a result, when Jerusalem and the temple were destroyed in AD 70, it was the Pharisees who provided leadership for the nation (A. J. Saldarini, *ABD* 5:289–303).

Jesus's "eating with sinners and toll collectors" would clearly have been noticed by those who "separated" themselves from anything or anyone assumed morally or ritually unclean. Here the morally unclean is the most likely interpretation of "sinners" (Hooker 1991: 96). Whether Mark consciously intended the chiastic arrangement of "[A] toll collectors and [B] sinners" (2:15) and "[B'] sinners and [A'] toll collectors" (2:16) in these verses is impossible to say. The "scribes of the Pharisees" asking Jesus's disciples why Jesus ate with such people heightens their rising hostility toward Jesus. In 2:6 the opposition of the scribes toward Jesus is unstated. Here it is vocal and addressed to the disciples. In 2:18 and 24 the scribal antagonism toward Jesus, centering on the behavior of his disciples, is heightened even more by being addressed directly to Jesus, and in 3:2 and 6 it reaches its pinnacle in a plot to kill Jesus.

"Why does he [Jesus] eat with toll collectors and sinners?" can be interpreted either as a statement, "He is eating with toll collectors and sinners"[8] (with ὅτι, *hoti*, introducing direct discourse), or as a question, "Why is he eating with toll collectors and sinners?" (with ὅτι used interrogatively as "Why?"). The latter is more likely in light of the use of the "Why?" (διὰ τί, *dia ti*) that Luke (5:30) and Matthew (9:11) use to translate it. (Cf. Mark 9:11, which also uses ὅτι + a form of λέγω [*legō*] to introduce a question; cf. 9:28.) This is not an innocent question on the part of the scribes seeking clarification. It is a hostile accusation in the form of a question (cf. 2:7). To eat with someone implied acceptance of them as friends and "brothers" (cf. Matt. 15:1–2; Luke 15:1–2; 19:7; Acts 11:2–18, esp. 2–3; Gal. 2:11–14; Jeremias 1971: 115–16). Just as in the post-Easter setting the "cross" proved to be a scandal for many, so in the pre-Easter setting Jesus's eating with toll collectors and sinners was a scandal. That Jesus intentionally ate with toll collectors and sinners as a symbolic act indicating that he was offering them entrance into the kingdom of God is clear from Luke 19:5, 7. Some suggest that the present tense of "is eating" (ἐσθίει, *esthiei*) implies that this was a customary activity of Jesus (Donahue and Harrington 2002: 102).

Although the present account and such passages as 7:1–23 served as important texts in the early church to justify their acceptance of those once considered unclean (esp. gentiles), the practice of the church did not give rise to the creation of these accounts. Such an understanding confuses cause and effect. The practice of the early church in accepting into its membership the poor, maimed, lame, blind, outcasts, toll collectors, gentiles, and so on, was an effect resulting from Jesus's teachings and his practice of associating with such people during his ministry.

---

8. The use of one article for "toll collectors and sinners" in 2:16 indicates that the two terms are to be understood as making up a single group.

"Those who are healthy have no need of a physician, but those who are sick" is a common proverb that has numerous parallels in Greek and Jewish literature (Guelich 1989: 104; Donahue and Harrington 2002: 102–3) and in the literature of the early church (J. Edwards 2002: 86). It focuses on the commonly accepted fact that physicians exist to heal sick people and thus must associate with them. For "I did not come," see 1:38–39; cf. 10:45. As in other pronouncement stories, the climax of 2:13–17 comes in Jesus's concluding statement. The christological claim is that Jesus "came," that is, was sent from God to offer forgiveness and the kingdom of God to sinners. This has already been manifested in 2:7 in the exercising of his divine prerogative to forgive sins and now is witnessed to by his eating with toll collectors and sinners. For the evangelist, Jesus's divine commission was messianic in nature (1:1), and the actions of Jesus in 1:16–20, 40–45; 2:1–12; and elsewhere reveal that behind his "I came" lay a strong messianic consciousness. The metaphorical nature of the proverb is now applied to the present situation by the words "not come to call the righteous [δικαίους, dikaious] but sinners [ἁμαρτωλούς, hamartōlous]." Just as physicians work among the sick in order to bring healing, so Jesus Christ, the Son of God, who is able to forgive sins (2:10), ministers to sinners to offer them the forgiveness of sins. "Toll collectors" is omitted from the saying in order to preserve the parallelism.

Because of the parallel between the proverb and the "I came" saying (well/sick, righteous/sinners), Jesus refers to the "righteous." It is unlikely that this is an acknowledgment that there were indeed righteous people who did not need forgiveness, for Mark believed that the Son of Man gave his life as a ransom for not just some (sinners versus righteous) but for all (see 10:45; cf. also 14:24).[9] It is best interpreted ironically as referring to "those who think themselves righteous" (Marcus 2000: 228). In the proverb and the "I came" saying, we have the toll collectors and sinners associated with the sick and sinners (2:16c). This means that the well and righteous correspond to the scribes of the Pharisees (2:16a).[10] It is very doubtful, however, that either Jesus or Mark would describe them as righteous except in an ironic capacity.[11] It may be best, however, not to seek a precise meaning for the term "righteous." In our present saying, it may simply be a required member in the analogy without serving to define a specific group (France 2002: 135). Or perhaps it should be understood along the lines of Hos. 6:6, where "For I desire steadfast love and

9. Lewis (1943: 38) understands this saying well: "Christianity [and we might add Jesus] . . . has nothing (as far as I know) to say to people who do not know they have done anything to repent of and who do not feel that they need any forgiveness."

10. Support for this can be found in Ps. Sol. 13.11 and 15.6ff., where the Pharisaic authors of this work refer to themselves as "righteous."

11. Cf. Luke, who wants his readers to know that the Pharisees are not righteous but are those who "justify [themselves] in the eyes of others" (16:15) and "trusted in themselves that they were righteous and regarded others with contempt" (18:9); cf. also Matthew, who describes the scribes and Pharisees as "hypocrites" (23:13ff.), "child(ren) of hell" (23:15), "full of greed" (23:25), "whitewashed tombs . . . full of hypocrisy and lawlessness" (23:27–28), "murderers of the prophets" (23:30–31), etc.

not sacrifice" means "More than sacrifice I desire steadfast love" (Zerwick 1963: 150n445). Thus Jesus may be saying here, "I came not so much for the righteous but for sinners." For Jesus's coming for sinners, compare 10:45; Luke 4:16–19; 7:22. For other "I came" sayings, see Matt. 5:17; 10:34–35; Luke 12:49; 19:10; cf. also Mark 1:24, 38.[12] Unlike the introspective concern of the scribes of the Pharisees for personal purity under the law, Jesus's love for neighbor (12:31; cf. Matt. 7:12) dominated his mission. Consequently his concern for the "sick" outweighed any concern for ritual purity, and his eating with toll collectors and sinners was not simply an accidental feature of his mission. On the contrary, he came for this very purpose!

Summary

In this account Mark seeks to illustrate Jesus's divine authority to forgive sins by the story of Levi, the toll collector. His ability to forgive sins is shown by his calling toll collectors and sinners to follow him. Even those considered furthest from the kingdom of God are invited by Jesus to enter. This is demonstrated by his eating with the outcasts of society. Jesus is able to bring healing to the grievously sick (2:17a) and forgiveness to infamous sinners (2:17b). Jesus has authority to offer the kingdom of God even to these. The Markan explanatory comment ("for they were many") emphasizes the magnetism of Jesus in drawing such people to himself. Not only the truly just and devout are attracted to him but even the sinful and impious. How this forgiveness would be achieved is not explained by Mark until 10:45 and 14:24, but his readers no doubt would have understood this in light of their celebration of the Lord's Supper and the preaching of the early church.

Mark shares this story with his gentile readers because they were once sinners, outsiders despised by the religious leaders of Israel. Through Jesus Christ, however, despite their being dead in trespasses and sins, strangers to the covenants of promise, they had been made alive and had entered into his kingdom (cf. Eph. 2:1–22; Col. 1:21–22). The toll collectors and sinners whom Jesus called and received into his fellowship were clear evidence to Mark's readers that the barriers and walls that once separated them from God's people had been broken down. Like the toll collectors and sinners, they now broke bread with the people of God and shared in the firstfruits of the kingdom of God. Some interpret this account as reflecting a problem in the Markan community of Jewish Christians hesitating to eat with gentile believers (Marcus 2000: 231), but this is less likely if we assume that the audience of Mark is the Roman church than if we think that it is the church in the Decapolis or Syria.

Finally we should note that Jesus is seen in our story as possessing a unique divine commission. He "came" from God! The implication of this was understood more fully by Mark's readers than by the toll collectors and sinners who first heard these words. "Jesus came" would bring to their

---

12. For a detailed discussion of these sayings, see Arens 1976.

mind Jesus's preexistence and his coming from the Father as found in Phil. 2:5–11; Col. 1:15–20; John 1:1–18; and so on.

Additional Notes

2:14. D Θ f¹³ it read Ἰάκωβον, but this is almost certainly due to the influence of 3:18, where James is called "the son of Alphaeus."

2:16. Numerous MSS (A C D K Θ Π f¹ f¹³) read οἱ γραμματεῖς καὶ οἱ Φαρισαῖοι (cf. Luke 5:30). The difficulty of οἱ γραμματεῖς τῶν Φαρισαίων supports its authenticity.

2:16. Ἰδόντες is lit. "having seen."

3. Jesus and Fasting Do Not Mix (2:18–22)

Our present account is the centerpiece of the five controversy stories found in 2:1–3:6. It is placed after two narratives dealing with the forgiveness of sins (2:1–12 and 13–17) and before two narratives dealing with Sabbath regulations (2:23–28 and 3:1–6). It is tied to the previous account involving feasting (2:13–17) by the presence of the disciples of the Pharisees and the mention of fasting in 2:18. There is, however, no geographical or chronological tie between the two passages. The form of the present account is that of a pronouncement/controversy story and contains a setting (2:18a), a controversy in the form of a question (2:18b), and an extended pronouncement consisting of three parables (2:19–20, 21, 22). The last two parables are also found together in Gos. Thom. 47 but in inverted order. They have in common an emphasis on the incompatibility of the new (a cloth patch and wine) and the old (a garment and wineskin). Questions have been raised as to whether the present form of the pronouncement (2:19–22) goes back to the original incident or whether additional traditions have been added to this incident. The parables in 2:21–22 are generally acknowledged as authentic, but because they possess no direct or necessary link to 2:18–20, many presume that they were spoken at another time. Some also suggest that the subject of fasting in 2:18–20 (a cultic or ethical issue) conflicts with the theme of the arrival of the kingdom of God (a theological issue) found in 2:21–22. As for the references to Jesus's death in 2:19b–20, critical scholarship in general denies their authenticity. As a result some have suggested that the original tradition, which goes back to Jesus, involved 2:18b–19a. To this has been added the sayings concerning Jesus's death in 2:19b–20, which are pre-Markan but not authentic and reflect the early church's practice of fasting; the parables of 2:21–22, which are authentic pieces of tradition that Jesus spoke at a different time; and an editorial introduction by Mark in 2:18a (Pryke 1978: 12, 140, 154; Gnilka 1978: 112; Marcus 2000: 235). In addition, some see parts as Markan: 2:19b–20 (Schmithals 1979: 1.179; contra Gnilka 1978: 111), "the new from the old" in 2:21 (Guelich 1989: 117; Donahue and Harrington 2002: 108), and "new wine [is] for new wineskins" in 2:22 (Guelich 1989: 117).[1]

Although the parables in 2:21–22 do not directly mention fasting, they do provide the theological basis for deciding such an issue. It is precisely because Jesus in his coming brought with him the kingdom of God that the practice of fasting, washing pots and pans (7:2–4), food regulations (7:14–22), and

1. Pryke (1978: 12, 140, 154) sees only 2:18a as Markan.

ultimately circumcision (Acts 10:1–11:18) were understood by the early church as having been superseded. The parables of 2:21–22 indicate that with the coming of Jesus and the kingdom, it is impossible to maintain the old practices, because a totally new situation has occurred. The joy of the Christ's presence and the kingdom he brought make it inconceivable that the practice of fasting should continue (Stein 1994b: 109–12). Whether these parables were spoken by Jesus on this particular occasion or placed here by Mark or the pre-Markan tradition is impossible to say. Yet they are certainly not incompatible with 2:18–20. The statement of 2:19a builds precisely on what the parables in 2:21–22 affirm. Thus these two sections (2:18–20 and 2:21–22) share a common theme involving the new situation brought about by the coming of Jesus Christ, the Son of God (1:1).

The question of the authenticity of 2:19b–20 will be decided to a great extent on whether one believes that Jesus of Nazareth saw himself as the Messiah and predicted his own death. If this is denied, then not only 2:19b–20 but all of Jesus's passion predictions (8:31; 9:31; 10:33–34, 45; 14:24) must be *vaticinia ex eventu*, prophecies created by the church after the fact of Jesus's death. However, 2:19b–20 contains no messianic claim that is not already found in 2:19a. As to the passion prediction found in 2:19b–20, its subtlety should be noted. The innocuous quality of this reference to Jesus's death, which lacks any allusion to the resurrection, is not what one would expect if these sayings were the creation of the early church. Its very ambiguity favors its authenticity.

Exegesis and Exposition

¹⁸And the disciples of John and the Pharisees were fasting, and they come and say to him, "Why do the disciples of John and the disciples of the Pharisees fast, but your disciples do not fast?" ¹⁹And Jesus said to them, ⌜"The sons of the wedding hall are not able to fast while the bridegroom is with them, are they?⌝ As long as they have the bridegroom with them, they are not able to fast. ²⁰But days will come when the bridegroom will be taken away from them, and then they will fast in that day. ²¹No one sews a piece of unshrunken cloth upon an old garment. If one does, the patch tears away from it, the new from the old, and the tear becomes worse. ²²And no one puts new wine into old wineskins. If one does, the wine will burst the wineskins, and the wine ⌜ ⌝ and the wineskins will be destroyed, ⌜but new wine [is] for new wineskins⌝."

"And the disciples of John and the Pharisees were fasting" is probably a Markan seam created to introduce the tradition. No reason is given for the fasting, for this was not important to Mark. If he possessed such information, he omitted it in order not to detract from the main point of the story. The fasting of John's disciples does not involve their mourning over his death, for Mark does not report this until 6:17–29, and their fasting is paralleled to the practice of the Pharisees. What is in view is not a required OT act of fasting but a voluntary

2:18

one. If this fasting were associated with the Day of Atonement, Jesus and his disciples would have kept that fast, even as they kept the rite of the Passover (14:12–26). For John's disciples, compare 6:29; Matt. 11:2/Luke 7:18; Matt. 14:12; Luke 11:1; John 1:6–8, 15, 19–23, 35, 37; 3:25–26; 14:1–2; Acts 18:25–26; 19:1–7 (see Scobie 1964: 187–202; Ernst 1989: 349–84). The Pharisees are associated here with John and his disciples, not because any real affinity existed between them (cf. Matt. 3:7–10; cf. also Mark 11:27–33), but because of their common practice of fasting. The only major required fast in Israel was the Day of Atonement (Lev. 16:1–34, esp. v. 29; cf. Acts 27:9; *m. Yoma* 8.1–2; cf., however, Neh. 9:1; Esth. 9:31; Zech. 8:19), but certain groups added personal fast days. The Pharisees fasted twice a week, on Mondays and Thursdays (Luke 18:12; cf. *Did.* 8.1; *b. Ta'an.* 10a, 12a; and *m. Ta'an.* 2.9). This fasting did not last for twenty-four hours but from dawn to sunset. The early church fasted on Wednesday and Friday but not on Monday and Thursday, because this was when the "hypocrites" fasted (*Did.* 8.1; cf. Matt. 6:16). Fasting was a common Jewish experience. It was frequently associated with death of a loved one (1 Sam. 31:13; 2 Sam. 1:12), illness (2 Sam. 1:16; 12:21–23), bad times (Ezra 8:23; *m. Ta'an.* 1.4–7), repentance (Lev. 16; 1 Kings 21:27; Isa. 58:3–6; Joel 2:12–13), and mourning for one reason or another (Esth. 4:3; Matt. 6:16; Jdt. 8:6).

"And they come and say to him" may have been the original introduction of the pericope (Guelich 1989: 109; cf. 1:40; 2:3, 13; 5:22; 8:22; 9:33; 10:46; 11:15; etc.). The impersonal "they" is best understood as "the people" and indicates that those who come and ask the question are not disciples of John or the Pharisees, for it is unlikely that they would refer to themselves in the third person (France 2002: 138; Donahue and Harrington 2002: 105; contrast Matt. 9:14). The Pharisees technically did not have "disciples" (cf. Matthew's omission of "the disciples of" in the parallel in Matt. 9:14), but there were people outside the formal membership of the sect who followed their teaching. Such people are referred to here and in Matt. 22:16 (cf. also Matt. 23:15) as their "disciples." It is probable that the "disciples of the Pharisees" are referred to rather than the "Pharisees" in order to parallel "disciples of John" and "your disciples" and perhaps also to parallel "scribes of the Pharisees" in 2:16.[2] The spirit in which such fasting was performed was understood by Matthew (9:15) as one of mourning. The issue raised by the question in Mark 2:18b involves whether one should fast, not on what days or how often one should fast. This criticism directed at Jesus's disciples is in reality an attack on Jesus, for it was assumed that the disciples' behavior in this matter reflected his teaching and behavior (cf. 2:15–16; Matt. 11:16–19/Luke 7:31–35).

2:19–20 The expression "the sons of the wedding hall" (οἱ υἱοὶ τοῦ νυμφῶνος, *hoi huioi tou nymphōnos*; cf. *b. Suk.* 25b; *t. Ber.* 2.10) can refer to the "groom's attendants" or the "wedding guests." Although the contrast to the more general

---

2. Gundry (1993: 132) presses the terminology too far when he seeks to distinguish the disciples of the Pharisees here, who were not scribes, from those who were scribes in 2:16.

feasting of Jesus's followers and friends in 2:13–17 might suggest the latter, the criticism directed at Jesus's disciples in 2:18b favors the former. Jesus frequently used a counterquestion to answer a question (Stein 1994b: 23–25), especially if the question was hostile. The present statement answers the question of 2:18b with a christological claim. All that the OT said about fasting, the practice of Judaism in this area—all this is now put aside by one fact: Jesus of Nazareth, the Christ, the Son of God, is present, and his presence annuls this. Such a response by Jesus fits well what we have already seen in 1:7–8, 11, 22, 27, 34, 45; 2:10–12, and 17, but the enormity of this christological claim should not be missed.

"As long as they have the bridegroom with them" can refer metaphorically to the time of the wedding feast or to the time that the bridegroom is present with them. For the use of the wedding metaphor to indicate the arrival of the kingdom of God, compare Matt. 22:1–14; 25:1–13; also Rev. 19:7–9. In the present context it refers primarily to the presence of the bridegroom. Mark's Gospel, while emphasizing the coming of the kingdom of God (1:15), is centered even more on the coming of Jesus Christ, the Son of God (1:1; Guelich 1989: 110, 117; France 2002: 139). Jesus, of course, brings the kingdom with him, but it is his coming and his presence that do not allow for fasting, even as his absence will require it (2:19b–20). Whereas in the OT the image of the bridegroom or husband is used to describe God's relationship to Israel (Isa. 54:4–8; Jer. 2:2; 31:32; Ezek. 16:7–14; Hos. 2:16–20), in the NT it serves primarily as a metaphor for Christ's relationship to the church (Matt. 22:1–14; 25:1–13; John 3:25–30; 2 Cor. 11:2; Eph. 5:22–32; Rev. 19:7–9; 22:17).

It was appropriate for John's disciples to fast, for they longed for the arrival of the Promised One who would bring the kingdom of God. Using the present analogy, we could say that they longed for the time when the bridegroom would come and the wedding take place. For Jesus's disciples, the bridegroom was now present. Their hope had been realized. Thus fasting and mourning were not only inappropriate but impossible. The former times allowed for fasting. The sin and suffering endemic to it indeed required it. But now such fasting would be unsuitable and unseemly. It was time to make merry (Luke 15:24, 32), to dance (15:25), and to feast (15:23).

Although the term "bridegroom" was not used in Judaism as a technical term for the Messiah, it was used in descriptions of the coming age of salvation (Isa. 54:4–8; 61:10; 62:5; Ezek. 16:7ff.). For people awaiting the Messiah and/or the kingdom of God, the metaphor Jesus used would have been readily understood. As a result, whereas before Jesus's coming the expression was not a technical term for the Messiah, in the early church it became one, and such parables as Matt. 25:1–13 were interpreted accordingly.

"As long as they have the bridegroom with them, they are not able to fast" qualifies the "while" (ἐν ᾧ, en hō) of the previous statement. Such a statement would not have caught Mark's readers off guard, for they were fully aware of Jesus's death at the hands of Pontius Pilate and the Jewish leaders. It would, however, assist them in realizing that the events of Jesus's passion did not take him by surprise, but that he knew beforehand that this would happen. This and 2:20 prepare the readers for the plot to kill Jesus referred to in 3:6. Mention of the bridegroom's removal indicates that the bridegroom analogy refers to Jesus. That the bridegroom is not referred to as departing or leaving the feast but being "taken away" (ἀπαρθῇ, *aparthē*) alludes to the violent death that he would experience (Guelich 1989: 112; France 2002: 140; Donahue and Harrington 2002: 107). The authenticity of this saying (and 2:20) is supported by its ambiguity (contrast 8:32a). It is precisely the kind of allusion to his death that one would expect the historical Jesus to use in his conversation with outsiders. On the other hand, if this were a church creation, one would expect a more explicit reference to his death and some sort of reference or allusion to his resurrection.

The shift from the bridegroom's presence (2:19a) to his absence, when he is taken away from them, suggests to some that 2:19b and 20 were not part of the original pericope. It is speculative, however, to determine how Jesus may or may not have replied to the question of 2:18b. Such issues are ultimately decided by one's view of Jesus's messianic consciousness and the historical trustworthiness of the Gospels. The passive "will be taken away" and the fasting that results allude to something violent happening to the bridegroom; he does not simply depart but is taken away (cf. Isa. 53:8). This is probably not a divine passive (contra Jeremias 1971: 11n2) but would have been interpreted by Mark's readers in light of 3:6; compare also 14:1–2. Nevertheless, they would also have realized that in the larger context the death of Jesus was due to the preordained will of God (8:31; 10:45; 14:21, 36). "Then" (τότε, *tote*; note the emphatic position at the beginning of the statement) they shall fast in that day. The temporal contrast between the period of not fasting and that of fasting suggests to some that this present statement reflects (and perhaps derives from) the practice of fasting in the early church. Attempts to see this statement as reflecting an established practice of fasting in the early church (Marcus 2000: 235), however, are unconvincing. The practice of fasting on Good Friday apparently began in the second century, and biblical evidence to support a practice of fasting in the early church is for the most part lacking. Second Corinthians 6:5 and 11:27 refer not to a voluntary practice of fasting but to being hungry because of the unavailability of food; the fasting of Acts 13:2–3 and 14:23 has nothing to do with the sorrow, mourning, and grief associated with fasting in our passage (cf. Matt. 9:15) but is associated rather with prayer and seeking God's blessing in the commissioning of Christian leaders. Anna's fasting (Luke 2:27) is indeed an example of her piety, but this appears to be an example of OT rather than NT piety. No mention is made of the widows in Acts 6:1ff. and 1 Tim. 5:5 fasting. As to the alleged references to fasting in Mark 9:29; Acts 10:31; and 1 Cor. 7:5, these are all later scribal additions to the text. This leaves only Matt. 6:16–18 as a clear reference to fasting in the NT, and no sorrow or grief is associated with the practice. For a clear reference to fasting in the early church, one must go outside the NT to such passages as Did. 7.4 and 8.1. Although the date of the Didache is much debated, very few scholars would seek to date it before Mark.

One should also note that the early church did not think of Jesus as being away. They lived not in the sorrow of their Lord's absence but in the joy of his abiding presence. They believed not only that he was present but also that he would never leave or forsake them (Heb. 13:5). And in John the absence of Jesus is seen as being more advantageous than his earthly presence due to the gift of the Spirit (16:7). As a result, the attempt to see in Mark 2:19b–20 a hypothetical fasting practice in the early church is unconvincing. The sorrow, grief, and mourning associated with fasting in this passage find no counterpart in the experience of the early church. If anything, 2:19b–20 justifies a practice of not fasting more than a practice of fasting (Ziesler 1972: 193).

The expression "in that day" (ἐν ἐκείνῃ τῇ ἡμέρᾳ, *en ekeinē tē hēmera*) is redundant in light of the "then" (τότε), and Matthew omits it. Attempts to interpret this expression as referring to a period of time different from "days will come" or to translate it as a technical term for the eschatological final day are misguided. Even though it is singular, "that" takes as its antecedent the "days will come" in the first part of the sentence. (Note how Luke seeks to make Mark's "in that day" cohere better with its antecedent and therefore has "in those days" [ἐν ἐκείναις ταῖς ἡμέραις, *en ekeinais tais hēmerais*; 5:35].) It is best to understand "that day" as referring to the time of Jesus's arrest, death, and burial, which ended with the resurrection (cf. John 16:19, 22, and the noncanonical Mark 16:10). The time after Jesus's ascension was not thought by the early church as one in which he was "away." Jesus was always with them, to the close of the age (Matt. 28:20). After the ascension the demeanor of the early church is described as one of "great joy" (Luke 24:52; cf. Acts 8:8; 13:52). It was not at all a period typified by grief and mourning (contra Hooker 1991: 98).

The two statements in these verses are wisdom observations in parabolic **2:21–22** form. (They are found in reverse order in Gos. Thom. 47 and apart from any narrative context.) A wedding feast was an occasion for wearing special clothes (Matt. 22:11–14) and drinking wine (John 2:1–11), so that the following two parables are quite natural in this context. The imagery of this parable refers to the fact that a new piece of cloth would shrink when washed, whereas an old, outer garment or cloak (ἱμάτιον, *himation*), having been washed several times, would not shrink any more. As a result, when washed (or if it became wet), the patch would shrink and tear away from the old garment. The truth being taught by the parable is that Jesus in his coming inaugurated the kingdom of God, and this has resulted in joy and celebration, which cannot coexist with the fasting of John's disciples and the disciples of the Pharisees. Mark alluded to this contrast earlier, in 1:14, where Jesus begins his ministry (the "new") only after John the Baptist (the "old") has been arrested. "The new from the old" (τὸ καινὸν τοῦ παλαιοῦ, *to kainon tou palaiou*) may be a redundant explanation added by Mark, but it serves to emphasize the incompatibility of the arrival of the kingdom and new covenant inaugurated by Jesus with the old covenant. For "new," see 1:27. "And the tear becomes worse" may be a pun when translated back into Aramaic or Hebrew (Gundry 1993: 138).

The second parable is another wisdom observation cast in a similar form as the preceding. Although the parallelism is not perfect, we have the following: (1) "No one"—"no one"; (2) "sews a piece . . . old garment"—"puts new wine . . . old wineskins"; (3) "If one does"—"If one does"; (4) "patch tears away"—"wine will burst the wineskins"; (5) "tear becomes worse"—"wine and the wineskins will be destroyed."[3] Each also has a parenthetical comment: "the new from the old"—"new wine [is] for new wineskins." Skins were used for carrying water (Gen. 21:14–15, 19; Ps. 33:7), milk (Judg. 4:19), and wine (Josh. 9:4, 13; 1 Sam. 10:3; 16:20; Job 32:19; Jer. 13:12; cf. Jdt. 10:5).[4] The new wine's tearing the wineskin was due to the pressure on the old and brittle skin, which had already been stretched to its fullest by previous fermentations, now being unable to contain the pressure caused by the continued fermentation of the new wine.

"But new wine [is] for new wineskins" points to the fact that with the arrival of Jesus Christ, the Son of God, the behavior appropriate to and symbolic of the old age is now inappropriate, for the arrival of Jesus Christ and the kingdom of God is symbolized by feasting and celebration. Except for the time between Jesus's arrest and resurrection, the fasting practiced by John's disciples and the disciples of the Pharisees is totally unsuitable for the followers of Jesus. For "new wine" as a symbol of the new age, see Jeremias (1972: 118); Marcus (2000: 234).

Summary

The present pericope in Mark has less to do with the practice (or lack) of fasting in the Christian church than with the character of Jesus Christ and what his coming means. The coming of Jesus Christ is seen by the evangelist as an eschatological event that has changed everything. All history has now been divided into BC (before Christ) and AD (anno Domini—"in the year of the Lord"). The practice of fasting by the disciples of John and the Pharisees belongs to the BC era. It is not compatible with the coming of Jesus. The new era cannot simply be appended to the old, as the parables in 2:21–22 reveal. Mark emphasizes the arrival of this "new" (νέος, neos) era by his redundant use of this term in 2:22 and its synonym (καινός, kainos) in 2:21 and 22. The old forms of BC Judaism, which are here typified by fasting, cannot coexist with the arrival of Jesus Christ, the Son of God, and the new era he has inaugurated. How can the disciples fast at this glorious wedding? How can they fast and at the same time sing the "Hallelujah

3. Luke makes the parallelism even closer by his editorial work in 5:36, so that both the new garment and old garment are ruined.

4. For a picture of an ancient wineskin, see Millard 1990: 20.

Chorus"? Jesus's presence is overpowering and changes everything. He is the divine divide of history!

With an aside, however, there is also revealed a glimpse of a dark future event. When the prophet Simeon encountered the baby Jesus in the temple, this was an occasion of great joy (Luke 2:29–32) in which fasting would be inappropriate. Yet there was also a glance at the black and ominous future: "This child is destined for the falling and rising of many in Israel, and to be a sign that will be opposed, . . . and a sword will pierce your own soul too" (2:34–35). In a similar fashion Mark 2:19b–20 points to that ominous time. Thus Mark, like Luke, wanted his readers to understand that the death of Jesus was not a tragedy or surprise. On the contrary, Jesus knew from the beginning that a cross awaited him. This was not, however, to be understood as a tragedy but rather as the sacrifice that sealed the new covenant he came to bring (10:45; 14:24). The present behavior of the disciples should reflect the present situation. The disciples stood in the presence of the Christ, the Son of God. It was therefore a time for rejoicing, not mourning; feasting, not fasting.

Additional Notes

2:19. A negative response is expected for this question introduced by the particle μή. See BDF §427.2.

2:22. Some MSS (ℵ A C K W) add ἐκχεῖται.

2:22. The translation follows ℵ* B. The clause is omitted by D and it.

4. Jesus and the Sabbath, Part 1 (2:23–28)

In this passage we find the first criticism of Jesus involving the Sabbath. The present account is another example of a pronouncement/controversy story. We have a setting for the incident (2:23); an accusatory question (2:24; whereas in the previous account Jesus is criticized because his disciples do not perform the extra religious duty of fasting, here he is criticized because his disciples are doing something supposedly forbidden by the law); and three pronouncements (2:25–26, 27, 28), the last of which serves as the key pronouncement of the account. The first of these pronouncements is an appeal to the example of David; the second is a wisdom saying concerning the relationship of humanity to the Sabbath; and the third is a christological statement. In their present context these three pronouncements do not function as three separate reasons but form a single, unified argument. As in the previous account, they provide the rationale for the behavior being questioned. This account is connected to the two preceding ones by the reference to eating (cf. 2:15–16 and 22 with 2:23, 25–26) and the presence of the Pharisees (cf. 2:16 and 18 with 2:24). It is connected to the following account by the question of what one is permitted to do on the Sabbath (2:25, 27–28, and 3:2–4), the mention of the Pharisees (2:24 and 3:6), and the terminology "and he says/was saying to them" (2:25, 27, and 3:4). It is connected to the larger complex of 2:1–3:6 by the controversy involving the disciples' behavior (2:7, 16, 18, 24; 3:2–4) and the issue of Jesus's authority (2:10, 17, 19–22, 25–28; 3:5).

The integrity of the present account is often challenged, and numerous suggestions have been made as to how it developed. These include the following:

1. To verses 23–26, verses 27–28 were added
2. To verses 23–26, verse 27 was added (v. 28 was added later)
3. To verses 23–26, verse 28 was added (v. 27 was added later)
4. To verses 23–24 and 27, verse 28 was added (vv. 25–26 were added later)
5. To verses 23–24 and 27, verses 25–26 were added (v. 28 was added later)
6. To verses 23–24, verse 27 was added (vv. 25–26 were added later; v. 28 was added still later)
7. To verse 27, verses 23–24 were added (vv. 25–26 were added later; v. 28 was added still later)

These suggestions break down into two main categories (Neirynck 1975; Guelich 1989: 119–20):

a. Verses 23–26 are original, to which 27–28 were somehow added later (options 1, 2, and 3)
b. Verses 23–24 and 27 are original, to which verses 25–26 and 28 were somehow added later (options 4 and 5)

Through such additions, a teaching of Jesus has supposedly been changed into an apologetic for the Sabbath practice of the early church.

Support for the gradual development of the present account from two or more separate traditions is seen in "and he was saying to them" (καὶ ἔλεγεν αὐτοῖς, *kai elegen autois*; 2:27), which supposedly shows that Mark (or someone before him) added a new saying to the account at this point; a radical difference between the first pronouncement (2:25–26) and the second and third (2:27–28), which supposedly indicates that they were originally unrelated; the term "Sabbath" being plural (σάββασιν, *sabbasin*) in 2:23–26, whereas in 2:27–28 it is singular (σάββατον, *sabbaton*); and the quotation of the OT, which is frequently seen as a secondary addition into the gospel tradition. I will argue below that, whereas "and he was saying to them" does at times mark the addition of a separate saying into a pericope, at times it introduces a saying that is a necessary part of the pericope, so that it is not possible to say that everywhere we find this expression, it reveals the intrusion of a separate, independent saying into the account. See 2:27. As to the relationship of the three pronouncements, one should note that in the present account they all work together to build the case for Jesus's authority over the Sabbath. As to the term "Sabbath" being singular in 2:27–28, this makes good sense in that Jesus (or Mark) is referring not to a specific Sabbath but rather to the Sabbath as a generic entity (Gundry 1993: 143). I will also argue later (see 2:25–26) that to attribute all OT references in the Jesus traditions to the early church is impossible. It is inconceivable that Jesus as a first-century, Jewish religious teacher would not have quoted or referred to the OT.

Although some argue that the present form of the pericope originated as an apologetic out of the early church's need to defend its Sabbath practice, it is better to understand the early church's Sabbath practice as arising out of such incidents as this in the life of Jesus. It is far more likely that the Sabbath practice of the early church was the result of Jesus's teaching and actions concerning the Sabbath than that the church's practice created such traditions out of nothing. The relevance of this passage for the early church is obvious. But its relevance should not make us confuse what was the cause (Jesus's teaching concerning the Sabbath and behavior with respect to it) and what was the effect (the church's Sabbath practice). The early church's Sabbath practice and understanding was the effect whose cause lay in incidents such as this in the life of Jesus and in the resurrection of Jesus on the first day of the week.

Mark's own hand is seen most clearly in the opening seam found in 2:23 (Pryke 1978: 12, 140, 154). Numerous scholars have also attributed 2:28 to the hand of Mark (W. Lane 1974: 119–20; Pryke 1978: 12, 140, 154; Witherington: 2001: 131–32), but Matthew and Luke, while omitting verse 27, had no difficulty in including verse 28 in their accounts. This may indicate that they were already familiar with it as part of this Jesus tradition before they made use of it from Mark's Gospel. The use of "Son of Man" in 2:28 also argues against attributing the saying found in 2:28 to the early church (see 2:10). The explanatory statement in 2:26b ("which is unlawful for anyone except the priests to eat") may be Markan (C. Turner 1930: 20; Donahue and Harrington 2002: 111–12), for Mark frequently adds such explanatory material to an account to help the understanding of his gentile readers (cf. 7:3–4, 11; 12:42; etc.).

Exegesis and Exposition

[23]And it came to pass on the Sabbath that he [Jesus] was ⌜walking by⌝ the grainfields, and his disciples began to make their way, plucking ⌜grain⌝ [as they proceeded]. [24]And the Pharisees were saying to him, "Look, why are they doing on the Sabbath what is not lawful?" [25]And he says to them, "Have you never read what David did when he had need and he and the men with him were hungry? [26]How he entered into the house of God in the time of ⌜Abiathar, the high priest,⌝ and ate the bread of the presence, which is unlawful for anyone except the priests to eat, and gave [it] also to the men with him?" [27]And he was saying to them, "The Sabbath was made for man and not man for the Sabbath; [28]so that the Son of Man is also Lord of the Sabbath."

2:23   Although Mark is responsible for the wording of the present incident ("And it came to pass" [καὶ ἐγένετο, *kai egeneto*]; see 1:9; "on the Sabbath" [ἐν τοῖς σάββασιν, *en tois sabbasin*]; cf. 1:21; "began" [ἤρξαντο, *ērxanto*] + infinitive; see 1:45), the setting is almost certainly traditional and recalls a situation in the life of Jesus. It is unlikely that someone would have created this unusual setting in which Jesus and the disciples were walking by (παραπορεύεσθαι, *paraporeuesthai*) the grainfields (lit. "through the grain" [διὰ τῶν σπορίμων, *dia tōn sporimōn*]) on the Sabbath with the disciples picking grain and eating the raw kernels. Mark does not use the name "Jesus" in this introductory seam but simply refers to "he" (αὐτός, *autos*), because his readers know that he is writing about the Jesus of the previous account (2:19) and his entire work (1:1). The expression "to make a path" (ὁδὸν ποιεῖν, *hodon poiein*) can mean "to make a path by picking grain" (instrumental participle) or "to make their way, that is, to travel, picking grain as they went" (temporal participle). The latter is to be preferred because one does not make a road by picking grain but rather by plucking up the stalks or beating them down; there is no conceivable reason why the disciples would be making a road (contra Marcus 2000: 239–40, 245); and the same expression is found in Judg. 17:8 and refers to going on a journey. The unusual nature of this expression may be due to it being a Latinism, *iter facere*, which means to "make" a journey (V. Taylor 1952: 215; Gundry 1993: 140).

The question raised by the Pharisees does not involve the legitimacy of picking grain from another man's field. This was permitted (Deut. 23:25), as long as an instrument, such as a sickle, was not used (Casey 1988: 1–4). The accusation leveled against the disciples was that their picking grain and rubbing away the chaff to eat the kernels constituted harvesting or "work," and this was forbidden on the Sabbath (Exod. 34:21; Jub. 2.29–30; 50.6–13; cf. *m. Šabb.* 7.2). The time of year envisioned in the account is late April, May, or early June, which was harvesttime.

The presence of Pharisees near the grainfield on the Sabbath is not explained   **2:24**
by Mark, but this is not as improbable as it might first appear (Casey 1988: 4–5; contra E. Sanders 1985: 265). For the Pharisees, see 2:16. The charge leveled at Jesus is that his disciples are doing something that violates the OT law. In 2:18, Jesus is likewise attacked for the behavior of his disciples. This is a more serious charge than that leveled against the disciples in 2:18 because it involves not a voluntary issue of fasting but disobedience of the OT commandment concerning the Sabbath. The unlawful nature of the disciples' actions does not involve whether they have traveled more than a Sabbath day's journey (about 1,000 yards), for the Pharisees who are present would most likely also be guilty of such an infraction. Nor does it involve their taking grain from the neighbor's field, for if the Law forbade this (which it did not—see 2:23), it would be stealing, and this is wrong on any day. The unlawful act centers on the disciples doing something on the Sabbath—harvesting, which was illegal, and as a result they are, in the eyes of the Pharisees, "working" and thus profaning the Sabbath (*m. Šabb.* 7.2).

This is the first attack on Jesus in Mark that involves his alleged breaking of the Sabbath. The importance of the Sabbath and its observance for Jews in Jesus's day is hard for most Christians to understand.[1] Keeping the Sabbath was the fourth commandment of the Decalogue (Exod. 20:8–11), and the Sabbath was revered as one of Israel's greatest gifts. Along with circumcision, the Law, and the temple, it was one of the distinctives that identified Israel and set it apart from the other nations (cf. Jub. 2.19). In general only a life-threatening situation or emergency superseded the regulations surrounding the Sabbath. Among the Essenes one could not even assist a person out of a pit or assist an animal in giving birth on the Sabbath (CD 10.14–11.18). The Pharisees were somewhat less rigorous in their observance than the Essenes, but they were still strict Sabbatarians. As a result even Jesus's healing on the Sabbath was attacked by some Pharisees (3:1–6; Luke 13:10–17; John 7:22–23; 9:13–16).

As in the previous account, Jesus is attacked by means of a question directed   **2:25–26**
at his disciples, and once again Jesus answers this attack by a counterquestion

---

1. For a helpful discussion of the Jewish reverence toward the Sabbath, see E. Sanders 1990: 6–23.

(cf. 2:19): "Have you never read [οὐδέποτε ἀνέγνωτε, *oudepote anegnōte*] what David did?" (cf. 12:10, 26). The question expects a positive answer, as the οὐδέποτε indicates, for Jesus knows that the Pharisees are familiar with the incident to which he is about to refer. Some scholars argue that the reference to the OT in this verse and the next should be attributed to the early church. There is no doubt that the early church saw the OT as pointing to Jesus, and the Gospel writers often quoted various OT passages as being fulfilled in his coming (cf. Matt. 2:6, 15, 18; 4:15–16; 8:17; 12:18–21; 13:35; 21:5; etc.), but it is absurd to think that Jesus in all his teaching would never have quoted the OT. What Jewish religious teacher of Jesus's day could have or would have wanted to avoid quoting the OT? There is no reason to deny the authenticity of this OT reference or other references such as Mark 7:6–7; 11:17; 12:36; Matt. 11:10/Luke 7:27–28. That the OT reference in our passage is not directly christological in nature supports its authenticity.

Jesus's use of Scripture in this incident does not follow the technical argumentation of the scribes and rabbis. This is not an example of the *gezerah shawah* argument, because two different OT passages are not referred to; nor is this a valid scribal argument, because Jesus is not quoting from the law to establish a legal precept (halakah) but quoting from a historical book (haggadah; Cohn-Sherbok 1979). Jesus is not following the rules of rabbinic debate in his response. He is arguing rather from what he saw was a clear implication of this OT passage. Jesus refers to David's need and hunger along with "those with him." Although the OT passage does not explicitly mention David giving the bread of the Presence to his followers, this is implied by 1 Sam. 21:2, 4–5 (contra Marcus 2000: 240).

"The house of God" refers not to the temple that Solomon built but to its predecessor, the tabernacle. The statement concerning Abiathar being the high priest appears to conflict with the account in 1 Samuel 21, where the less well known Ahimelech, the father of Abiathar, is mentioned as giving the "bread of the Presence" to David. It is not surprising therefore that both Matthew (12:4) and Luke (6:4) omit the reference to "in the time of [ἐπί, *epi*; cf. Luke 3:2; Acts 11:28; also 1 Macc. 13:42] Abiathar, the high priest" and that certain MSS of Mark do so as well. There have been several attempts to explain this problem. (1) The preposition ἐπί (in the time of) should be translated "in the section of Scripture in 1 Samuel that deals with Abiathar" (see W. Lane 1974: 116n86 for objections). (2) Something such as "father of" has been lost from the original text, which read, "when the father [*abba*] of Abiathar was the high priest." This would involve the scribal error of haplography. (3) The present passage should be understood as a mistranslation for "in the lifetime of Abiathar [the later well-known] high priest" (Casey 1998: 151–52). This is reflected in the addition of τοῦ (*tou*) before "priest" or "high priest" in A C Θ f¹³ and others.[2] One must acknowledge that no satisfactory solution has

---

2. Gundry (1993: 141) argues that Mark knew that the priest David encountered was Ahimelech but intentionally changed the name to Abiathar for theological reasons. This may

come forward that resolves this problem.[3] The "bread of the Presence" or "showbread" consisted of twelve loaves of bread that were a symbol of the covenant God made with Israel (Lev. 24:5–9; cf. Exod. 25:30; Num. 4:7) and were placed each Sabbath on a table next to the holy of holies. At the end of the week they were to be eaten by, and only by, the high priest (Aaron) and his sons within the tabernacle/temple.

It is unclear whether David's actions took place on the Sabbath, although fresh bread of the Presence was placed on the table in the holy place on each Sabbath (Lev. 24:8). The point Jesus drew from the incident, however, did not involve the day on which David ate this bread, but that his eating it with his disciples was unlawful. It is uncertain whether the comment "which is unlawful . . . to eat" is a Markan explanatory comment or goes back to Jesus himself, but it serves to demonstrate that if David was able to do this unlawful act, how much more should David's Lord (12:35–37) be able to do so. Thus what is at stake in this incident is not whether what Jesus's disciples are doing is unlawful. Nor does Jesus argue that David's action demonstrates that in times of need it is permissible to break the law (J. Edwards 2002: 96). On the contrary, Jesus agrees in 2:26c that what David did was unlawful (Hooker 1991: 103; France 2002: 145). Since the Pharisees have criticized the behavior of Jesus's disciples, Jesus in his OT analogy refers to David's disciples by stating that David also gave the bread of the Presence to "the men with him" (τοῖς σὺν αὐτῷ οὖσιν, *tois syn autō ousin*). Compare "the men with him" in 2:25.

The exact point Jesus sought to make by this analogy is debated. Some suggestions are these: (1) the law allows for an exception such as in the case of David and in the present situation (W. Lane 1974: 117); (2) certain basic needs (the hunger of David and of Jesus's disciples) come before the ritual keeping of the law; and (3) if David broke the law when he and his followers ate the bread of the Presence, this serves as a precedent (J. Edwards 2002: 96; France 2002: 145–46), so that Jesus the Christ, the Son of Man, can even more freely do so. There is no reference in Mark to Jesus's disciples being hungry or in need (as in Matt. 12:1), so that no emphasis is placed in our account on a humanitarian understanding of the Sabbath (cf. *m. Yoma* 8.6). This is somewhat surprising, for such an argument is made by Jesus in the next passage (3:4; Matt. 12:11; cf. also Luke 13:14–17; 14:1–6; John 5:1–18; 7:22–24; 9:13–17; cf. also 1 Macc. 2:39–41).[4] Jesus is also not attacking a misunderstanding of the law concerning the Sabbath and seeking to provide a correct interpretation (contra Westerholm 1978: 98–99). On the contrary, he acknowledges that David's action was unlawful. The defense of his disciples' behavior focuses

---

explain why Mark may have done this, but it does not resolve the historical problem. The fact remains that Abiathar was not the priest who gave David the bread of the Presence.

3. For an example of how scholars seek to save Jesus from error by attributing the reference concerning Abiathar to Mark, see Meier (2004: 577–79), who argues that Jesus was too good a teacher to have made such a mistake.

4. This is the view of Moo (1984: 9; cf. also Marcus 2000: 239). Such a view, however, loses sight of the argument's culmination in 2:28.

rather on Jesus's authority. If David could do something that was not lawful, how much more (a fortiori) does the Son of Man have authority to do so (cf. 2:6–11). This interpretation fits best what Mark is seeking to demonstrate in 2:1–3:6—the authority of Jesus. He can forgive sins (2:7–11); he can eat with toll collectors and sinners because he has come for the sick (2:16–17). His presence turns fasting and mourning into feasting and celebration (2:19–22), and if David could break the law to feed his followers, how much more can Jesus Christ, the Son of God, the Son of Man, and David's Lord (12:36–37) break the law (Donahue and Harrington 2002: 111; France 2002: 146). The present passage is concerned not with making an apology for the Sabbath practice of the early church but with making a christological statement of Jesus's authority, as in 2:10, 17, 19a (Guelich 1989: 123; contra V. Taylor 1952: 214).

2:27–28 Whereas the phrase "and he was saying to them" (καὶ ἔλεγεν αὐτοῖς, *kai elegen autois*) serves at times as an editorial introduction to a separate tradition (cf. 4:2, 21, 24; 6:10; 9:1, 31; also 7:14), sometimes it is uncertain whether what follows is a new tradition added to the present account or part of the account itself (4:11; 6:4; 7:9). There are also a few instances where this phrase occurs in the middle of a narrative and appears to have always been part of it (cf. 8:21; also 11:17). In 2:25 the similar expression "And he says to them" is best understood as part of the tradition found in 2:23–24. Whether this and the following verse were part of the original tradition found in 2:23–26 can neither be demonstrated nor refuted; in the present context it is not simply an additional argument but part of the single point that 2:25–28 seeks to make.[5]

Some have suggested that the wisdom saying, "The Sabbath was made for man and not man for the Sabbath,"[6] may be a mistranslation of Jesus's original Aramaic saying into Greek. Several suggestions have been made on the basis that the term בַּר נָשָׁא (*bar nāšā'*) in Aramaic can mean "man" or "Son of Man." In its present form, 2:27 makes perfectly good sense. "Man," that is, humanity, was not created for the Sabbath. How could humanity have been created for the Sabbath, since humankind was created on the sixth day, whereas the Sabbath came on the seventh! Jesus did not seek to deprecate the Sabbath by this statement. He simply wanted to place it in perspective and demonstrate that humanity created in the image of God must be seen as more important than God's gift of the Sabbath to him. With this statement many rabbis would agree. Compare the statement found in Mek. on Exod. 31:13–14, "The Sabbath was delivered to you, not you to the Sabbath" (cf. also *b. Yoma*

---

5. The parallel expressions "and he says to them" (καὶ λέγει αὐτοῖς, *kai legei autois*) and "and he said to them" (καὶ εἶπεν αὐτοῖς, *kai eipen autois*) occur frequently in Mark. The former introduces a saying that is an essential part of the narrative in 1:38; 3:4; 6:50; 7:18; 10:11; 11:2; 12:16; 14:34, 41; and the latter occurs in 4:40; 9:29; 14:24. From this it is evident that "and he says/was saying/said to them" (καί + third-person singular form of λέγω + αὐτοῖς) cannot be interpreted as indicating that what follows is either a Markan or pre-Markan addition to the original narrative (cf. Guelich 1989: 205).

6. This saying is an excellent example of chiastic parallelism: "[A] The Sabbath . . . [B] for man [B'] not man [A'] for the Sabbath."

85b; 2 Bar. 14.18). There is considerable debate as to why Matthew and Luke omit this saying: perhaps because of its radical nature (cf. Hultgren 1972: 42; France 2002: 146) or their desire to heighten the christological element of 2:28 (Neirynck 1975: 230; Hultgren 1979: 112, 138n50).

Although some suggest that 2:28 is an independent saying or an editorial comment of Mark that has been added to 2:27, the "so that" (ὥστε, hōste) ties it intimately with 2:27. "So that" is used thirteen times in Mark, and in most cases it is followed by an accusative that serves as the subject of the infinitive (1:45; 2:2, 12; 3:20; 4:1, 32, 37; 9:26; 15:5). In the other four instances it takes either the subject of the preceding clause (1:27) or introduces a new subject (2:28; 3:10; 10:8). Yet in each instance "so that" introduces a conclusion that is the result of the preceding statement. Consequently, we should interpret 2:28 as the logical result of 2:27. Some have suggested that "Son of Man" here is a mistranslation of bar nāšāʾ and should be translated "man." Thus we would have the following: "The sabbath was made for man, not man for the sabbath. Therefore man is lord of the sabbath."[7] This would make a logically cohesive argument. Against such a view, however, one must note that this requires a hypothetical reconstruction of 2:28, which both Matthew and Luke leave in its Markan form. It furthermore ignores the "also" (καί) of the statement. In this chapter of his Gospel, Mark has already demonstrated Jesus's lordship in 2:10, so he is "also" Lord in 2:28. No other "lordship" has been attributed to "man" in the chapter with which the "also" can refer. The interpretation that "man is lord of the Sabbath" furthermore makes Jesus far more radical than he really is. It is inconceivable to think that Jesus said, "Man is lord of the Sabbath" (Beare 1960; Guelich 1989: 125). In the present text Mark, as well as Matthew and Luke, understood Jesus as saying that he, the Son of Man, was Lord of the Sabbath (Tuckett 1982: 59–60). The audacity of this claim should not be missed, for in the OT God is the Lord of the Sabbath because he instituted and consecrated it (Gen. 2:3; Exod. 20:8–11; 31:12–17; Lev. 23:3; etc.).

It is uncertain how Mark's Christian readers would have understood this argument. But it is quite possible that they believed that Jesus, the Son of Man, would one day return, and on that day every knee would bow before him and confess that he is Lord (Phil. 2:11), that he would reign (1 Cor. 15:25–28), and that already now God had put all things under his feet (Eph. 1:20–22). Mark's readers may or may not have been familiar with these Pauline passages, but by the late 60s they would certainly have thought of Jesus in this manner. As a result, they may very well have interpreted the passage as follows: "Since the Sabbath was made for man and not man for the Sabbath, and since Jesus is Lord of all humanity, the logical result of this is that he is therefore Lord of the Sabbath as well" (cf. V. Taylor 1952: 219; Dewey 1980: 99–100). Such

---

7. So Torrey 1933: 73. For the view that 2:27–28 should be translated, "The Sabbath was made for the Son of Man, and not the Son of Man for the Sabbath; therefore the Son of Man is Lord of the Sabbath," see Beare 1962: 91.

an interpretation does justice to the "so that" of this verse.[8] For "Lord" as a title of Jesus, see 7:28.

Such an interpretation makes sense for Mark's readers in the late 60s, but did Jesus understand this saying in this manner? The answer to this question depends on how one answers the christological question "Who is this man?" (4:41). Certainly the Jesus of Mark, who has authority to exercise the divine prerogative of forgiving sins (2:10), whose coming changes fasting to feasting (2:19), who came to seek and to save the lost (10:45), could think this way. For Jesus to say, "I, the Son of Man, am Lord of the Sabbath because I am Lord over humanity," also fits well his totalitarian claim found in such passages as 8:34–38; Matt. 10:32–34; 11:6 (Stein 1994b: 122–23).

Summary

As in each of the preceding controversy stories, the high point of the account comes in the closing pronouncement (cf. 2:10, 17, 19–22, 25–28). In repeating this story, Mark is seeking to indicate once again the great authority of Jesus. The concluding pronouncement builds on the claim that Jesus's authority is greater than that of Israel's greatest king, David (12:36–37). This is not argued but assumed. Elsewhere in the gospel tradition, Jesus is portrayed as greater than Abraham (John 8:53), Jacob (John 4:12), Jonah and Solomon (Matt. 12:38–41), the temple (Matt. 12:6), and so on, so that such an emphasis is not unique to Mark. Mark builds on this statement and continues his demonstration of Jesus's authority by pointing out that since the Sabbath was made for humanity and not the reverse, Jesus as Lord of humanity is also Lord of the Sabbath.

The greatness of Jesus Christ, the Son of God, has already been demonstrated by his divine authority to forgive sins (2:10), to call toll collectors and sinners to himself and as a consequence to grant them entrance into the kingdom of God (2:17), and to change the practice of fasting into feasting simply because he is present (2:19). Now Mark demonstrates Jesus's greatness by pointing out that he is Lord of the Sabbath and, by implication, Lord over the Sabbath commandment. Within the OT, God is repeatedly referred to as the "Lord" of the Sabbath, so that the claim of Jesus to be "Lord" of the Sabbath is a lofty one indeed. Attempts to minimize this extremely high christological understanding of Mark simply will not do.[9] Mark's Jesus is "the Lord of the Sabbath" and unique among all who came before him and who would come after him. As the example of the disciples "working" on the Sabbath indicates, allegiance to Jesus takes precedence even over the Law itself.

8. Thus, in contrast to Westerholm (1978: 97), 2:28 is not a non sequitur as it now stands.

9. Crossan (1983: 80) argues that in this account Mark portrays Jesus simply as one man among many in being lord of the Sabbath and that Jesus's lordship is something he "barely achieved." This is as complete a misunderstanding of the meaning of Mark 2:28 as can be imagined.

The controversy that leads to the pronouncement in 2:25–28 also reveals to Mark's readers the opposition that Jesus encountered and that would lead to his death. In story after story in 2:1–3:6, we encounter hostile opponents. In 2:7 it involves Jesus's claim to forgive sins; in 2:16 it has to do with Jesus's eating with the society's undesirables; in 2:18 it involves not keeping the religious leaders' ideas concerning fasting; here in 2:24 and later in 3:2 it involves Sabbath behavior. All this will lead to a plot by the Pharisees, representing the religious leaders, and the Herodians, representing the political leaders, to kill Jesus (3:6). Mark's readers were aware of all this, but Mark wants to emphasize that it was not the people who entertained such thoughts but the religious and political leaders. And he wants his readers to know that this was known by Jesus and was all according to the providence and will of God. (See the summary of 2:1–12.)

Additional Notes

2:23. The majority of uncials read παραπορεύεσθαι, and are to be followed, even though B C D have διαπορεύεσθαι (walking through).

2:23. The KJV, REB, and NJB use the terms "cornfield" and "corn" to designate grain (wheat, oats, barley, etc.). The British use of these terms is confusing for Americans, who understand "corn" as "maize," i.e., ear corn, unknown to Europe and the Middle East until the discovery of the Americas.

2:26. Due to the historical difficulty involving the mention of Abiathar, a number of textual variants have entered the textual tradition. The reference is omitted in D W syr[s]. See Metzger 1994: 68.

5. Jesus and the Sabbath, Part 2 (3:1–6)

The present account is tied closely to 2:23–28 in that both deal with criticism from Jesus's opponents about his attitude toward the Sabbath (cf. 3:2, 4 and 2:24, 27–28). Both also involve the same opponents, the Pharisees. They are mentioned by name in 2:24, but Mark refers to them as "they" in 3:2, and then in his concluding summary (3:6) he refers to them by name along with the "Herodians." The account is tied to the larger context of 2:1–3:6 by the common elements of controversy and Jesus's authority. Along with the healing of 2:1–12 (an exorcism), this miracle of healing a man on the Sabbath forms an *inclusio* for 2:1–3:6 and serves as its climax. The present account, like 2:1–12, is a combination of a healing (3:1, 3, 5) and controversy-pronouncement story (3:2, 4), and as in 2:1–12, the healing serves as Jesus's reply (cf. 2:10–11; 3:5) to his opponents' criticism (cf. 2:7; 3:2, 4). It consists of three parts: the descriptive setting (3:1–2), Jesus's challenge to the Pharisees concerning healing a man on the Sabbath (3:3–4), and Jesus's healing of the man and the resulting plot of the Pharisees and Herodians to kill Jesus (3:5–6; Marcus 2000: 251). This represents the culmination of the hostility encountered in earlier accounts (2:7, 16, 18, 24). Consequently, the audience's acclamation of wonder and awe, typical in a miracle story, is omitted. This hostility and the charge of blasphemy against Jesus (2:7) now result in the plot to kill him (3:6). Jesus is to be "destroyed" (ἀπολέσωσιν, *apolesōsin*). The more primitive nature of the Markan account is clearly revealed by a comparison with the parallel in Matt. 12:9–14. The evangelist's own hand is seen most clearly in the introductory seam (3:1a), which is made up of traditional material but possesses Markan wording, and the concluding summary (3:6; Bultmann 1968: 63; V. Taylor 1952: 220; Pryke 1978: 12, 140, 154; Schmithals 1978: 191–92; Guelich 1989: 132). The redactional nature of 3:6 is evident in that it serves as the conclusion for all of 2:1–3:6. It is also likely that the wording of 3:5a–b is Markan as well (Pryke 1978: 12, 140, 154; Gnilka 1978: 126; Marcus 2000: 250).

Exegesis and Exposition

[1]And he [Jesus] entered again into ⌜the⌝ synagogue. And a man was there who ⌜had⌝ a withered hand, [2]and they were watching him closely [to see] if on the Sabbath he would heal him, in order that they might accuse him. [3]And he says to the man having the withered hand, "Rise up [and stand] ⌜in the center of the synagogue⌝." [4]And he [Jesus] says to them, "Is it lawful on the Sabbath to do good or to do evil, to save life or to kill?" And they remained silent. [5]And looking around with anger at

them, very grieved at the hardness of their heart, he says to the man, "Stretch out your hand." And he stretched [it] out, and his hand was restored. ⁶And the Pharisees, having gone out, immediately began to conspire with the Herodians against him, how they might destroy him.

The scene for the following account implies a return to the synagogue at Ca- 3:1–2
pernaum (1:21; cf. 2:1). The vocabulary of 2:1 is decidedly Markan: "entered again" (εἰσῆλθεν πάλιν, *eisēlthen palin*; cf. 1:21; 2:1, 13), "and there was there" (καὶ ἦν ἐκεῖ, *kai ēn ekei*; cf. 1:23). For "and he entered," see 1:21 and especially 2:1. The article "the," as well as the "again," suggests that this synagogue is "the" synagogue in Capernaum (Peabody 1987: 118–20; France 2002: 149; cf. 1:21, 29; 2:1). The later statement that Jesus went with his disciples to the "sea" (3:7) fits Capernaum well. The reference to a man having a withered hand recalls the similar Markan wording in 1:23, but although Markan in wording, the statement is largely traditional (S. Smith 1994: 157). In 1 Kings 13:4 this terminology describes a paralysis. The perfect passive participle (having been withered, ἐξηραμμένην, *exērammenēn*) may suggest a prolonged illness, possibly from birth (Donahue and Harrington 2002: 115).

The unqualified "they," an impersonal plural (see 1:22), has as its antecedent the Pharisees of 2:24 (France 2002: 149). In the tradition Mark inherited, the Pharisees may have been named at this point in the account. Mark chose to name them at the end (3:6), however, in order to emphasize their involvement in the plot to kill Jesus. From the context, their "watching"¹ is malicious in nature (cf. Ps. 37:12 [36:12 LXX]), for their purpose is to bring legal charges against him (J. Edwards 2002: 98). For other examples in Mark in which Jesus's opponents seek to find fault with his actions or words, see 10:1; 12:13, 18–23. As in 2:24, their criticism of Jesus focuses on the Sabbath and their interpretation of what was and was not permitted. "On the Sabbath" (τοῖς σάββασιν, *tois sabbasin*) is in an emphatic position, beginning the clause, and this reveals that the whole incident revolves around the Sabbath and the behavior deemed appropriate for that day. In 1:21–28, Mark reports an exorcism that occurred on the Sabbath, but up to this point no healing on the Sabbath has been mentioned. That Jesus healed on the Sabbath is well attested in the tradition (Luke 13:10–17; 14:1–6; John 5:1–18; 7:23–24; 9:13–16). If this verse assumes healings on the Sabbath other than just the exorcism in 1:21–28, the placement of the present account would then be an example of Mark having written his Gospel "accurately [but not] in order."² Although healing/exorcism on the Sabbath is not prohibited in the Mishnah (*m. Šabb.* 7.2; *m. Beṣah* 5.2; contrast CD 11.9–14), it may have been assumed that when life was not in danger, one should wait until after the Sabbath (Luke 13:14; cf. *m. Yoma* 8.6; cf. also, *m. Šabb.* 14.3–4; 22.6).

---

1. Marcus (2000: 248) points out that the verb "watching" (παρετήρουν, *paretēroun*) is used with respect to the Sabbath commandment in Gal. 4:10 and Josephus, *Ag. Ap.* 2.39 §282; *Ant.* 3.5.5 §91; 14.10.25 §262.

2. See "Authorship" in the introduction for the quotation of Papias in Eusebius, *Eccl. Hist.* 3.39.15.

A spoken question is involved in a controversy in 2:16, 18, 24, but here, as in 2:6–7, Jesus perceives an unspoken question in the hearts of his opponents (cf. 2:6–8). Jesus's awareness of their hostility serves to remind readers that his passion did not catch him unawares. As in 3:22, Jesus's ability to heal is not questioned by his opponents but, rather, is assumed. The statement "in order that they might accuse him" (ἵνα κατηγορήσωσιν αὐτοῦ, *hina katēgorēsōsin autou*; cf. 15:3–4, where the same term is used) indicates that the minds of Jesus's opponents are already made up. They are not seeking to determine whether Jesus should be "destroyed" (3:6) but are seeking to accumulate evidence in order to accomplish their plan. The "they" in 3:2c picks up the "they" in the earlier part of this verse and refers to the Pharisees (cf. 2:24 and 3:6).

3:3–4   By causing the man to stand in the "middle" of the synagogue, Jesus reveals that he knows the thoughts of his opponents (cf. 2:8). The action heightens the controversy by focusing attention on the issue at hand—healing on the Sabbath and Jesus's authority. That the man did not come to Jesus seeking healing further heightens the controversy, for it indicates that Jesus intentionally confronts his opponents with this issue. Thus, one can sense the drama present in the synagogue as Jesus confronts his opponents. Everyone in the synagogue is drawn into the clash between Jesus's authority and his opponents' Sabbatarian theology. In a similar way, by indicating that Jesus's opponents are watching him closely and by noting that Jesus has the man stand in the center of the scene, Mark creates in his readers great anticipation of what is about to take place. For other examples in which Jesus uses a person as a test case for his teaching and claims, see Matt. 18:1–5; Luke 14:1–6; 19:1–10 (cf. also Gal. 2:1–3).

The charge leveled against Jesus in 2:24 (cf. 2:26) is now alluded to by Jesus himself. In his counterquestion (see 2:19)—"Is it lawful . . . ?" (ἔξεστιν; *exestin?* cf. 2:24, 26)—Jesus turns the tables on his opponents, for their opposition to Jesus's forthcoming action suggests that they think one should not do good on the Sabbath (cf. Luke 13:14). In Jesus's understanding, however, such passages as Mic. 6:8 mean that practicing justice and lovingkindness on the Sabbath is far from wrong. In fact, such passages *require* that he heal. Thus, we have two radically different views of what it means to do good and keep the Sabbath. One view, that of Jesus's opponents, involves not doing things on the Sabbath in order to avoid "working," which is forbidden. The other view, that of Jesus, sees the need to hallow the Sabbath by doing good things such as showing mercy and kindness, and this means healing the sick, delivering demoniacs from the power of Satan, and proclaiming the forgiveness of sins and the arrival of the kingdom of God. For Jesus not to do good on the Sabbath would be sin (cf. James 4:17), for "failure to do good is the same thing as doing evil" (Schweizer 1970: 75).

The phrases "to do good or to do evil" and "to save life or to kill" are individually examples of antithetical parallelism, but together they serve as an example of synonymous parallelism. The importance of saving life on the

Sabbath would not have been questioned by Jesus's opponents. When "life is in danger, and whenever there is doubt whether life is in danger this overrides the Sabbath" (*m. Yoma* 8.6; Danby 1933: 172; cf. *b. Yoma* 85a). In their understanding, however, the man with the withered hand was not facing a life-threatening emergency. Therefore Jesus's healing him would be not only inappropriate but also wrong (cf. Luke 13:14)!

The two examples of antithetical parallelism can be understood in several ways. One is that what Jesus (and Mark) meant by doing good and saving life involved Jesus's ministry of healing, casting out demons, and preaching the arrival of the kingdom of God. Doing good and saving life meant to bring wholeness from the curse of the fall and the disease and sickness that resulted from the fall. Doing evil and killing referred to his opponents' seeking to hinder Jesus's healing ministry and to their plotting on that Sabbath to kill him (3:6). If this is the proper interpretation of this saying, then the irony of their criticizing Jesus for doing good and saving life on the Sabbath while they are plotting to kill him makes the Pharisees' criticism of Jesus all the more hypocritical. Another possible interpretation of doing evil and killing may be that this is a reference to the incident in 1 Macc. 2:29–41, where, in order not to be annihilated by the Syrians on the Sabbath, Mattathias and the Hasidim decide that they will defend themselves if attacked on the Sabbath, though they would never initiate an attack on the Sabbath. Thus, it was acceptable in their thinking to "do evil" and "kill" on the Sabbath in such instances (Borg 1984: 158–59; Ellingworth 2001: 245–56). If this is the proper interpretation of this saying, then the irony of criticizing Jesus for doing good and saving life on the Sabbath while permitting the doing of evil and killing likewise makes the Pharisee's criticism of Jesus hypocritical. The silence of Jesus's opponents indicates that he has bested them in the confrontation (cf. 11:33; 12:34).

In the context of 2:23–28 and the even larger context of 2:1–3:6, the concern of our text is not simply "Can a person heal on the Sabbath?" Rather, Mark wants his readers to see the issue as "Does Jesus, the Son of Man, have authority as Lord of the Sabbath (2:28) to do good and heal on the Sabbath?" (Guelich 1989: 136–37; Donahue and Harrington 2002: 117). Jesus's question in the context of Mark is not merely seeking a more humane reinterpretation of what constitutes appropriate Sabbath behavior. Rather, it requires a decision about who Jesus is and what is the source of his authority (Banks 1975: 125).[3] "But they were silent" (οἱ δὲ ἐσιώπων, *hoi de esiōpōn*) serves as more than an interesting piece of historical information in the Markan narrative. It demonstrates Jesus's great authority because he has refuted his opponents and driven them to silence. They cannot answer the power and wisdom of his reply.

---

3. Hooker (1991: 108) and Marcus (2000: 253) argue that in healing this man by his word alone and not touching him, Jesus under the Jewish law was blameless with regard to his Sabbath behavior. The Pharisees in our account, however, do not appear to have possessed such an understanding, and with regard to Mark, this plays no part in his purpose for telling the story.

3:5–6 For the double reference to Jesus's emotions in 3:5a–b, see 1:41, 43. For "looking around" (περιβλεψάμενος, *periblepsamenos*), see 3:34; 5:32; 9:8; 10:32; 11:11. The phrase "very grieved at the hardness of their heart" explains the anger of Jesus. Συλλυπούμενος (*syllypoumenos*, very grieved) is an intensive form of the verb. In the present context it is best translated "grieved at" (V. Taylor 1952: 223; France 2002: 151) rather than "grieved for" (Schweizer 1971: 73). For "hardness of heart," see 6:52; 8:17 (cf. also 10:5; Eph. 4:18; and Exod. 7:3, 13, 14, 22; 8:15). The term "restored" (ἀπεκατεστάθη, *apekatestathē*) is also found in 8:25 and 9:12. In the latter reference, it refers to the eschatological restoration of all things at the end of time (cf. Acts 1:6). Although it cannot be demonstrated, it may be that the healing or restoration mentioned here and in 8:25 are signs that the kingdom of God has come and that, since the Christ, the Son of God, is on the scene, the restoration of all things has now already begun in part.

The action of the Pharisees and the Herodians occurs "immediately" after the healing, and the "immediately" here should be given its full temporal significance. On that very Sabbath, Jesus's opponents immediately go out to plan his death because of his doing good on the Sabbath. The irony of their action on the Sabbath and Jesus's healing on the Sabbath brings to mind Jesus's question in 3:4 (Meier 1994: 731n16; Donahue and Harrington 2002: 117). For Pharisees, see comments on 2:16–17. Along with the Pharisees, the Herodians are mentioned (cf. 12:13; also 8:15; Matt. 22:10; Josephus, *J.W.* 1.16.6 §319; *Ant.* 14.15.10 §450). The exact identity of the Herodians is uncertain. Numerous theories have been suggested (cf. Meier 2000: 741). Most likely they were not a religious sect but a political party of aristocratic families who favored the rule of Herod the Great (who ruled from 37 BC to 4 BC)[4] and his descendants rather than direct Roman rule (Hoehner 1992: 325). This preference may have been due to the fact that Herod the Great was partly Jewish. Mention of the Herodians in connection with the Pharisees makes these two groups representative of the political and religious leaders who plotted against Jesus. Despite their great ideological differences, the Pharisees and the Herodians join in common cause to destroy Jesus (J. Edwards 2002: 102). In Mark they are clearly portrayed as standing over against the people (cf. 14:1–2). In other places, those who seek to destroy Jesus are described as the "chief priests and scribes" (10:33; 11:18; 14:1) or as the "chief priests, scribes, and elders" (8:31; 11:27; 14:43, 53; 15:1). "To take counsel" (συμβούλιον ἐδίδουν, *symboulion edidoun*) may reflect a Semitic idiom. It appears in a slightly different form in 15:1 (συμβούλιον ποιήσαντες, *symboulion poiēsantes*), which may be a Latin idiom (V. Taylor 1952: 224). Along with expressions such as "they were

---

4. The "Herod" from whom these people received their name was more likely Herod the Great than Herod Antipas, tetrarch of Galilee (4 BC–AD 39). The suggestion that they were followers of Herod Agrippa (AD 41–44) is too anachronistic to fit the present context. There is no need to see their alliance with the Pharisees as reflecting the situation in Mark's day rather than the situation of Jesus (contra Marcus 2000: 250). For a discussion of the historical problems involving the "Herodians," see Meier 2000: 740–46.

seeking how" (11:18; 15:1), the phrase describes the plot of the religious and political leaders to kill Jesus. For "how they might destroy him" (ὅπως αὐτὸν ἀπολέσωσιν, *hopōs auton apolesōsin*), see 11:18 (cf. also Luke 13:33; 19:47). This is another way of saying "to kill him" (cf. 11:18; 14:1; also 12:12) by delivering him to Pilate for execution (15:1). Luke reveals this by replacing Mark's "to kill" (Mark 3:4) with "to destroy" in his parallel account (Luke 6:9).

Summary

In the present account, Mark reveals how Jesus ignores the warnings and threats of the Pharisees (2:24) and heals (3:5) because he is the Lord of the Sabbath (2:28). Mark does so by recounting one of Jesus's healings performed on the Sabbath. Thus, Mark once again demonstrates the greatness and authority of Jesus by showing that, even though the Sabbath and its regulations were one of the identifying marks of Judaism, Jesus has authority over the Sabbath. Jesus's authority is further demonstrated by the silencing of his opponents (3:4). The question "By what authority are you doing these things?" (cf. 11:28) is answered not through Jesus's superior skills of persuasion and logic but rather by his doing what God had called him as the Christ, the Son of God, to do. He manifests God's power by healing on the Sabbath. His knowledge of his opponents' thoughts also reveals a God-given, prophetic wisdom.

The controversies and hostility encountered throughout 2:1–3:6 reach their pinnacle in 3:6. Jesus's future death is planned, and the readers of Mark are shown once again that there was nothing in Jesus's behavior that brought about his death. It was through the religious and political leaders' hardness of heart that Jesus was put to death. Only their hardness of heart could condemn Jesus for doing good on the Sabbath. Yet Jesus was well aware of this possibility (2:19b–20), and his death was not a defeat or a tragedy but rather the means by which he would save the lost (10:45; 14:24).

Additional Notes

3:1. Although both ℵ and B omit τήν, all other witnesses include it, as do the parallel accounts in Matt. 12:9 and Luke 6:6. As a result, it should be deemed original (contra Sibinga 1976: 357–59 and Guelich 1989: 131). Marcus (2000: 247) suggests that the omission of the definite article from ℵ and B may be due to homoeoteleuton caused by τὴν συναγωγήν.

3:1. Ἔχων is lit. "having."

3:3. Εἰς τὸ μέσον is lit. "in the middle."

III. Who Is This Jesus? Part 2 (3:7–6:6a)

The third major section of Mark, like each preceding section (1:1–13; 1:14–3:6), begins with a Markan summary (cf. 1:1, 14–15; 3:7–12; contra Keck 1965a: 343–45). See 1:14–3:6. Just as the previous section consists mainly of a collection of miracle stories (1:21–45) and controversy stories over Jesus's authority (2:1–3:6), the present section is also built around two main collections. These are a collection of parables (4:1–34) and a collection of three miracle stories (4:35–5:43), in which Jesus demonstrates his authority over nature, demons, sickness, and death. These two collections are preceded by a summary (3:7–12; cf. 1:14–15), a call of the disciples (3:13–19; cf. 1:16–20), and a controversy over the relationship of Jesus and the prince of demons (3:20–35), and are followed by a story involving the unbelief Jesus encounters in Nazareth (6:1–6a; cf. 3:1–6).

This new section continues the subject of "Who is Jesus of Nazareth?" found in 1:14–3:6. Thus it is not surprising to find several common themes: the calling of (the) disciples (cf. 3:13–19, 33–35 with 1:16–20; 2:13–14), the message concerning the arrival of the kingdom of God (cf. 4:1–34 with 1:14–15, 35–38), Jesus's authority over the demons (cf. 3:11, 12, 20–35 with 1:21–28, 34, 39), Jesus's ministry of healing and miracles (cf. 4:35–5:43 with 1:29–34, 39, 40–45; 2:1–12; 3:1–6), the continued rise of opposition toward Jesus (cf. 3:20–21, 31–35; 6:1–6a with 2:1–3:6), and the confession that Jesus is the Son of God (cf. 5:7 with 1:1, 11, 24). This new section, however, intensifies what has preceded in several areas: Jesus's authority over the demons is shown to extend over even the prince of demons (3:23–27), and his miracle-working power extends over even nature and death (4:35–43; 5:41–43).

A. A Summary of Jesus's Ministry (3:7–12)

This is the longest summary in Mark. Some suggest that 3:7–12 is best understood as a concluding summary for the preceding section, because several themes are present that look back to what is found in 1:14–3:6. These themes include the press of the crowds (cf. 3:7–8 with 1:32–34, 37, 45), Jesus's withdrawal from the crowds (cf. 3:9 with 1:35), Jesus's healings (cf. 3:10 with 1:29–31, 34, 40–45; 2:1–12, 17; 3:1–6) and exorcisms (cf. 3:10 with 1:21–28, 34, 39), the demonic recognition of Jesus as the Son of God (cf. 3:11 with 1:24, 34b), and the command to silence (cf. 3:12 with 1:25, 34b, 44).

Although 3:7–12 does recall some of the material found in 1:14–3:6, it seems to function better as an introduction to the third section of Mark (3:7–6:6a) than as a conclusion to the second. The lack of any hint in 3:7–12 of the controversies and opposition found in 2:1–3:6 argues against it being a conclusion to 1:14–3:6. The location by the Sea of Galilee (3:7, 9), sometimes seen as a tie to what has preceded (cf. 1:16–20; 2:13), serves better as an introduction to what is to come in 3:13–6:6a (cf. 4:1–2, 35–41; 5:1–20, 21). The geographical extension of Jesus's ministry from Galilee to other regions (3:7–8) likewise fits what follows better than what has preceded, for the scene of 1:14–3:6 is exclusively Galilee, and especially Capernaum, whereas in 3:13–6:6a the scene proceeds outside these areas (cf. 4:35–5:43). Although the summary of Jesus's exorcisms in 3:11 reminds the reader of 1:21–28, 34, and 39, it likewise prepares the reader for 3:15, 23–30 and 5:1–20. It is therefore debatable whether the reference to Jesus's authority over the demons in 3:11 simply refers back to the exorcism in 1:24 and the summary in 1:34b, for it also foreshadows the future discussion in 3:22–27 and 5:7. Similarly, the reference to Jesus's healings in 3:10 looks not only backward to past healings but also forward to 5:21–43. As to the reference to the disciples in 3:7, although this does recall 1:16–20, 29–30, 36; 2:15–16, 18–20, 23–26, it fits even better the call of the disciples in the next account (3:13–19) and their presence with Jesus in 4:11–13, 34, 35–41; 5:31, 37, 40; 6:1. It is above all the reference to a boat being prepared for Jesus (3:9) that indicates that 3:7–12 is best understood as preparing the reader for what is to come. This does not look back to 1:16–20 but forward to 4:1, 35–43; 5:1–2, 21, for in 1:16–20 the boat does not involve Jesus and is left behind. From 4:1ff. the boat prepared for Jesus in 3:9 is continually used by him. There is no need, however, of choosing an either-or perspective with regard to whether 3:7–12 goes with what precedes or follows. It does recall what has preceded in 1:14–3:6 as well as serving as a bridge between

1:14–3:6 and 3:13–6:6 (Witherington 2001: 141–42; Donahue and Harrington 2002: 120–21). Nonetheless, 3:7–12 serves primarily as an introduction to 3:13–6:6a (contra Keck 1965a: 342–45), and this is why I have linked them in the commentary.

In its present form 3:7–12 would not have circulated as an independent unit of tradition during the oral period. It is rather a summary of various Jesus traditions that the evangelist includes in his Gospel, as well as others that he knew but did not include. It is not surprising, therefore, that we see the hand of Mark more clearly here than in the individual accounts he has included from the traditions he inherited. We see his hand clearly in the vocabulary and style of this summary just as we do in other summaries such as 1:14–15, 28, 32–34, 39; 2:13; 4:33–34; 6:12–13, 53–56; 9:30–32; 10:1, 30–32. We also find various Markan theological emphases (cf., e.g., 3:11 with 1:1, 11, 24, 34). A further consideration that suggests a strong Markan role in the formation of this summary is the difficulty in visualizing how a summary such as this would have circulated during the oral period. One can easily visualize how a healing miracle such as Jesus's healing of the paralytic (2:1–12), a pronouncement story involving the paying of taxes (12:13–17), or the parable of the wicked tenants (12:1–11) would have been passed on orally. This passage is not that kind of an account, however, but a summary without a unified form or content. Finally, to the extent that such summaries serve as markers or conclusions for the materials preceding and following, they must reflect the work of Mark.

There is no reason to assume that Mark created this summary out of nothing. On the contrary, he used traditional materials (Jesus's ministry by the sea, his popularity, his teaching from a boat, his healings and exorcisms, the demonic recognition of his sonship, etc.) to compose this summary. Therefore, whereas the summary is the product of the creative hand of the evangelist, the content involves traditions he inherited (Kazmierski 1979: 79). Some have attempted to see a traditional core of material in 3:7, 9–10 because of the various hapax legomena contained in them: "withdrew" (ἀνεχώρησεν, *anechōrēsen*), 3:7; "boat" (πλοιάριον, *ploiarion*), 3:9; "make ready" (προσκαρτερῇ, *proskarterē*), 3:9; "crush" (θλίβωσιν, *thlibōsin*), 3:9; "press" (ἐπιπίπτειν, *epipiptein*), 3:10; compare also "multitude" (πλῆθος, *plēthos*), which occurs only twice in Mark—3:7 and 8 (Guelich 1989: 142–44; Marcus 2000: 259). The view that all of 3:7–12 is a pre-Markan summary, however, is very unlikely (contra Pesch 1980a: 198). While there is no need to deny the historicity of the material in 3:7–12, the present composition of this summary is nevertheless best understood as the creation of the evangelist (Pryke 1978: 12, 140, 154–55, who excludes 3:10; Gnilka 1978: 133; Best 1981: 36–37; Hooker 1991: 109).

Unlike a traditional miracle or pronouncement story, the present summary has no specific form. After telling of the fame of Jesus (3:7–8), Mark prepares the reader for the coming material by telling of the preparation of a boat (cf. 3:9 with 4:1ff.), the press of the crowds due to his popularity (cf. 3:9 with

5:24, 31), the desire of the sick to touch Jesus (cf. 3:10 with 5:27–28), and his continued mastery over the demons (cf. 3:11–12 with 3:22–30; 5:1–20), who recognize him as the Son of God (cf. 3:11 with 5:7).

Exegesis and Exposition

⁷And Jesus withdrew with his disciples to the sea, and a great multitude from Galilee ⌜followed⌝; ⁸and a great multitude hearing all that he was doing came to him from Judea, and from Jerusalem, ⌜and from Idumea,⌝ and [the region] across the Jordan, and around Tyre and Sidon. ⁹And he told his disciples that a boat should be made ready for him because of the crowd in order that they might not crush him, ¹⁰for he healed many, so that all who had diseases were pressing upon him in order that they might touch him. ¹¹And whenever the unclean spirits saw him, they would fall down before him and cry out, saying, "You are the Son of God!" ¹²And he was rebuking them sternly that they should not make him known.

As in 1:14, which introduces 1:14–3:6, Mark begins this new section with the use of the name "Jesus." The reference to the disciples (cf. 2:15, 16, 18, 23) prepares the reader for Jesus's request in 3:9 and his call of the twelve disciples in the next account (3:13–19). The verb ἀνεχώρησεν (*anechōrēsen*) is best translated as "withdrew" (cf. Matt. 9:24) rather than "fled," for although the latter is a possible meaning of the word, Mark nowhere portrays Jesus as fleeing in fear from his opponents. The disciples might be afraid (9:32; 10:32), but not Jesus (14:41–42). Jesus's action here is similar to that found in 1:35, 45; 4:1 (cf. also 4:36; 6:31–32, 45), where Jesus departs or separates himself from the crowds either for privacy or to avoid the crush, as 3:9–10 states. His lack of success in 3:9–10 in avoiding the press of the crowds serves to emphasize his greatness, and the crowd's response is overwhelmingly positive and stands in sharp contrast with that of Jesus's opponents in 3:6.

The withdrawal to the "sea" (θάλασσαν, *thalassan*) sets the scene for 4:1–5:43. No spiritual significance should be attributed to the "sea" (contra W. Lane 1974: 128). It does not serve as a demonic symbol of chaos, but possesses a purely geographical and historical meaning. The following stories center on the Sea of Galilee, a frequent site of Jesus's teaching and miracles (1:16; 2:13; 4:1; 4:35–5:43; 6:32–56; 7:31–37). Matthew 12:15 associates Jesus's departure to the sea with the plot of the previous verse, but Mark makes no such connection (contra Gundry 1993: 156–57, 161). Speculation as to why Jesus went to the sea (e.g., he left official Judaism to concentrate his ministry on the common people) is simply that—speculation. From a distance of two thousand years, we have no access into the mind of Jesus for this action. Mark's purpose in referring to this is, however, clear. He is preparing the reader for traditions involving Jesus's ministry around the Sea of Galilee in 4:1ff.

The term "multitude" (πλῆθος, *plēthos*) is found in Mark only here and in the next verse. The reference to the crowds following Jesus comes from 1:28,

33, 37, 45; 2:2, 13, and reveals the success of Jesus's ministry in 1:14–3:6. Such a comment is anchored in history. Jesus was a remarkable teacher, and many people came to hear him and to be healed by him. By this comment Mark wants to show that, although official Judaism may have rejected Jesus and plotted against him (3:6), the great mass of the Jewish people gladly followed him. By this comment Mark also shows that Jesus is mightier than John the Baptist (1:7) because the crowds that followed him were greater (J. Edwards 2002: 103). See 1:5. Mark places additional emphasis on the size of the multitude following Jesus by describing it as "great" (πολύ, *poly*).

The term "followed" (ἠκολούθησεν, *ēkolouthēsen*) is frequently used in Mark as a technical term for being a "follower" of Jesus (cf. 1:18; 2:14–15; 8:34; 9:38; 10:21, 28, 52; 15:41 [?]). But in other places it refers simply to "walking behind" (cf. 5:24; 6:1; 10:32; 11:9; 14:13, 54). Here it is used in the latter sense. There are several textual variants in the tradition involving this term. Some have a plural form of the verb to agree with the sense of "multitude," whereas others use the singular form because the term is singular in Greek. (Cf. 4:1, where both a singular and a plural verb are used to describe the singular term "crowd.") The placement of the verb in the sentence is also found in different locations in various MSS. There is no theological significance to these variants.

The following text describes the crowd as coming from throughout Palestine. The only areas not mentioned are Samaria and the Decapolis. (France [2002: 154] suggests that Samaria and the Decapolis are omitted because they were "off limits for patriotic Jews.") Why certain areas are mentioned and others are not is unclear. Some have suggested that the areas mentioned possessed large Jewish populations in Jesus's day or that they possessed large Christian populations in Mark's day. Such suggestions can be neither proven nor disproven. The use of "came" (ἦλθον, *ēlthon*) to describe those outside Galilee instead of "followed" (ἠκολούθησεν) distinguishes not the degree of commitment of those involved but their geographical circumstances (France 2002: 153; cf. Kazmierski 1979: 89–90).

The people of Jerusalem are mentioned earlier, in 1:5, as coming to see John the Baptist. "Idumea" (only here in the NT) is the Greek name for "Edom," which in the first century referred to the area south of Judea bounded in the east by the Dead Sea. Politically it was part of Judea. "Across the Jordan" refers to Perea (from πέραν, *peran*, beyond) and designates the land east of the lower two-thirds of the Jordan River valley and the upper third of the Dead Sea. "Tyre and Sidon" are mentioned again in 7:24, where Jesus heals the daughter of a Syrophoenician woman, and in the summary of 7:31. They appear to have been the northernmost cities Jesus visited. They lie on the coast of the Mediterranean Sea, across from and north of Caesarea Philippi.

The "great multitude" mentioned in 3:8 is somewhat redundant in light of 3:7 and is omitted by W it syr. It should, however, be retained. It fits well Mark's tendency toward redundancy. See 1:32. Its redundancy here emphasizes the popularity and fame of Jesus. This second reference to the "great multitude" forms a chiasmus with the reference in 3:7 ([A] great multitude; [B] from Galilee; [B′] from Judea; [A′] great multitude). The causal participle (hearing, ἀκούοντες, *akouontes*) explains why the crowds in 3:7b–8 are following Jesus (cf. 1:27–28, 45; 2:12). Unlike the people of Galilee, the crowds from Judea, Idumea, across the Jordan, Tyre, and Sidon did not see the things Jesus did, but they heard about them. This is why they have come to see Jesus. In his summary, Mark is faithful to the geographical scheme found in 1:14–3:6. Consequently there is no need to see in the geographical designations allusions to sites of missionary activity in Mark's day (Guelich 1989: 145; Gundry 1993: 161–62; contra Donahue and Harrington 2002: 119–20).

Reference to a boat being made ready prepares the reader for Jesus's use of a boat in 4:1, 36, 37; 5:2, 18, 21; 6:32, 45, 47, 51, 54; 8:10, 13, 14. (There are eleven passages in Mark where a boat is mentioned: 1:16–20; 3:9; 4:1–35, 36–41; 5:1–20, 21; 6:32–44, 45–52, 53–56; 8:10, 14.)[1] Mark uses here the diminutive form of "boat" (πλοιάριον, *ploiarion*), but his frequent use of other diminutives (cf. 5:23, 39, 41; 6:9; 7:25, 27, 28; 8:7; 14:47) suggests that it often has no particular force (V. Taylor 1952: 44–45). The present tense of the verb "be made ready" (προσκαρτερῇ, *proskarterē*) alludes to the continual usage of a boat by Jesus in 4:1ff. The first ἵνα (*hina*, that) in 3:9 is best understood as epexegetical and giving the content of an indirect command (cf. 3:12; 5:18, 23, 43; 6:8, 12, 25, 56; 7:26, 36; 8:22, 30; 9:12, 30; 10:35; 11:16; 12:19; 13:19; cf. 1 John 3:11, 23; 5:3). The second ἵνα (in order that) in 3:9 is telic and reveals the purpose of the command to make a boat ready (cf. 5:24, 31). Although not stated, it is quite likely that the boat belongs to one of the disciples (cf. 1:16–20).

With the "for" (γάρ, *gar*) clause in 3:10, Mark explains why the crowds are in danger of crushing Jesus. The attempt to see in the verb "crush" (θλίβωσιν, *thlibōsin*) a reference to Jesus's later suffering should be resisted. The terms "crush" and "press" (ἐπιπίπτειν, *epipiptein*) serve not as hostile threats to Jesus's well-being but as examples of his greatness and fame (contra Marcus 2000: 258). The clause "for he healed many" should not be interpreted to mean that some who come for healing go away without healing, as though Jesus is able to heal "many" but not "all" who come to him. "Many" in a Semitic context means "all." Compare the parallel in Matt. 12:15, where Matthew translates Mark's "many" with "all," and Isa. 53:12. See Mark 10:41–45. Another way of interpreting this statement is that Jesus healed many people without this implying that some were not healed. Jesus's reputation was such that the sick (all who, ὅσοι, *hosoi*; lit. "as many as") thought merely touching him would bring healing. Thus, those with various diseases were seeking to touch him (5:27–31; 6:56; 7:37; cf. Acts 5:15–16; 19:11–12; 2 Kings 13:21). This statement prepares the reader for the story of the hemorrhaging woman who in 5:27–28

1. Keck (1965a) suggests that the miracles of 4:35–41; 5:1–20, 21–43; 6:31–44, and 45–52 that portray Jesus in a boat are part of a pre-Markan "boat cycle" (cf. also Pesch 1980a: 277–81). Although the theory is interesting, it has not convinced many (Burkill 1968; Fowler 1981: 57–68; Marcus 2000: 255–56).

is healed by touching Jesus (cf. also 6:56). The term "diseases" (lit. "scourges," μάστιγας, *mastigas*) can refer to the lashes received in criminal punishment or metaphorically to the affliction God brings in judgment. It is used here as in 5:29 and 34 for physical illness. Along with the next verse, 3:10 summarizes the healings and exorcisms described in 1:21–3:6.

3:11-12   The present summary ends with a reference to the unclean spirits, who, whenever they see Jesus, continually fall before him and cry out, "You are the Son of God!" (cf. 1:24; 5:7; also 1:1, 11; 9:7; 12:6; 13:32; 14:61; 15:39). Mark's reference to Jesus's authority over the demons and their confession of him as the Christ looks back to 1:24 and 34 and forward to 5:7 (cf. also 3:22–30). As in 1:32–34, Mark distinguishes between the healing of disease and the exorcism of demons. For "unclean spirits," see 1:23. In light of 1:34, the demonic confession of Jesus as "the Son of God" must be understood positively, for the demons serve as authoritative "spokesmen" for the Markan Christology. Some have suggested that naming Jesus "Son of God" is an attempt by the demons to control him (Reploh 1969: 40; contra J. Edwards 2002: 104). According to this view, knowing the name of a person supposedly meant having power over him. There is no hint of this, however, in the text. Mark does not understand the demons' naming of Jesus as an attempt to gain mastery over him. It is understood rather as an act of homage by the demons, whose supernatural knowledge causes them to recognize that Jesus is their master. A parallel to this kind of reluctant confession is found in Phil. 2:10, where every knee will bow in submission and confess that "Jesus Christ is Lord." In light of 1:1, 11, 24, 34; 5:7; 9:7; 15:39, the demonic confession is neither a misunderstanding nor in need of correction. Jesus is indeed the Son of God (1:1). The description of the demons falling before Jesus and confessing him to be the Son of God is a sign of humble submission before one greater than they, their conqueror. By his use of the iterative imperfects (lit. "were seeing" [ἐθεώρουν, *etheōroun*], "were falling" [προσέπιπτον, *prosepipton*], and "were crying out" [ἔκραζον, *ekrazon*]), Mark indicates that this occurs frequently. Thus Mark intends his readers to understand the two exorcisms he records (1:21–28; 5:1–20) as two examples among many. Such prostration indicates Jesus's authority over the demons (5:6; cf. Gen. 17:3; Dan. 3:5; Matt. 2:11; 4:9; 18:26; Phil. 2:9–11). Elsewhere such kneeling is often associated with a submissive request (Mark 5:33; 7:25). The act of submission by the demons is manifested by the actions of those who are possessed by them.

The command for silence assumes that in such encounters Jesus has exorcised the demon, for Mark certainly does not want his readers to think that, whereas Jesus commands the demons to be silent, he nevertheless leaves them in control of the individuals they possess (cf. 1:25—"Be silent and come out"). Yet the emphasis in this verse is not on the exorcising of the demons but in Jesus forbidding them to speak. For "making [Jesus] known" (φανερὸν ποιήσωσιν, *phaneron poiēsōsin*) after being "sternly" (πολλά, *polla*) warned not to, compare 1:45. "That" (ἵνα) is better understood as introducing an epexegetical clause revealing the content of the command than as a purpose clause. The wording of the command assumes that what the demons are saying about Jesus is true (cf. 1:34; France 2002: 155; contra Hurtado 1983: 57).

In this verse we encounter the messianic secret in Mark in its clearest form. There is no question that the messianic secret is a Markan theological emphasis. Attempts to see the messianic confession of the demon as incorrect or inappropriate because it was not yet the right time (Guelich 1989: 149; Brooks 1991: 70) conflict with the strong emphasis in Mark that Jesus is indeed the Son of God. In light of 1:34 there is no question as to the correctness of their confession. The messianic secret is part of the tradition Mark inherited and stems in part from Jesus himself. Within the situation of Jesus, the avoidance of an open proclamation of messianic and divine titles made good sense. In the tinderbox of first-century Palestine, the open acknowledgment by Jesus of his messiahship/sonship could easily have been misunderstood and fanned the revolutionary hopes of many into flame. At the least, it would have brought about an immediate confrontation with the Roman authorities. Thus the reason for Jesus's command to secrecy is easily understood.

In the situation of Mark and his readers, the messianic secret serves both to demonstrate who Jesus is (the Christ, the Son of God) and to reveal that Jesus sought to avoid a confrontation with Rome by avoiding inflammatory titles and teachings. His death therefore was due not to his publicly claiming to be the Messiah, but rather to the plot of the political and religious leadership to do away with him. Thus Mark's messianic secret serves both to reveal who Jesus is (the "Son of God") and to demonstrate that he was not in any way a political revolutionary who by his claims and teaching brought about an unavoidable confrontation with Rome. Jesus did not die due to his political activity. Rather, he sought to avoid confrontation with the authorities by teaching in parables and avoiding the open use of messianic titles. This is why Mark emphasizes that Jesus commanded the demons not to confess him as the Son of God. However, the command to secrecy also serves to indicate Jesus's greatness, for despite his command, the greatness of Jesus cannot be hidden. See "The 'Messianic Secret'" in the introduction.

Summary

Mark uses this summary to bridge "Who Is This Jesus? Part 1" in 1:14–3:6 and "Who Is This Jesus? Part 2" in 3:7–6:6a. In 3:11, the climax of the summary, he provides a christological summary of who Jesus is by the demonic confession that he is the "Son of God." The demons know (1:34; 3:12) the true identity of Jesus. This both summarizes what has preceded (1:1, 11, 24) and prepares for what is coming (5:7). For Mark, Jesus is above everything else the Son of God. The continued confession of this by the demons, whom Mark has been careful to point out truly know who he is (1:34), reveals this. In the coming section this will be revealed both by a similar confession (5:7) and by his continued miracles, which grow even more marvelous. Even nature (4:35–41), incurable disease, and death (5:21–43) are subject to Jesus. Thus, as in 1:14–3:6, Mark seeks to have his readers reflect over the question "Who is this man who . . . ?" (cf. 4:41). In our passage Mark provides a clear answer through the confession of the demons: Jesus of Nazareth is "the Son of God" (3:11).

In this passage Mark also points out that in contrast to the political and religious leadership who oppose Jesus (2:1–3:6, esp. 3:6), the people flock to him. They do so to such an extent that a boat has to be made ready (3:9) at critical times in order to rescue him. This is not a rescue from hostile enemies, however, but from friendly, overexuberant crowds. By this, Mark reveals that whatever might be the reason for Jesus's crucifixion, it was not due to the enmity of the common people.

Still another emphasis we find in our passage involves the "messianic secret." For Mark, this serves a twofold purpose. First of all, it reveals who Jesus is. Despite the command to silence, the "secret" is an open one. Jesus is "continually" commanding the demons to stop telling everyone that he is the Son of God. The command, however, does not hide from Mark's readers who Jesus is. On the contrary, it reveals that he is actually the Son of God. Thus the messianic secret serves not to hide Jesus's identity from the reader but to reveal who he is via supernatural beings who truly recognize him to be the Son of God (1:34). Second, the secret serves to show that Jesus sought to avoid notoriety and confrontation with the political authorities by refraining from publicly claiming and accepting messianic titles. Thus Jesus's death as the Christ, the Son of God, was due not to a political confrontation brought about by a public use of messianic titles, but to the divine purpose. That purpose will not be revealed until later, but Mark's readers knew this already, for in their regular celebration of the Lord's Supper, they knew that Jesus said concerning the cup, "This is my blood of the covenant, which is poured out for many" (14:24). Thus the messianic secret serves as a useful means for both revealing who Jesus is and demonstrating that his mission transcended politics.

Additional Notes

3:7. The verb ἠκολούθησεν is found in various forms in ℵ A B L P f[1] but is lacking in the Western MS tradition (D W f[13] it).

3:8. καὶ ἀπὸ τῆς Ἰδουμαίας is lacking in ℵ W Θ f[1].

B. Jesus Calls the Twelve Apostles (3:13–19)

As in 1:14–3:6 and 6:6b–8:26 after an introductory summary (1:14–15; 3:7–12; 6:6b), Mark begins this new section with an account involving the disciples (cf. 1:16–20 and 6:13–19). The placement of this account is due to Mark's desire to begin this new section (3:7–6:6) with a tradition involving the disciples. Thus, even though it does not fit the geographical scene of 3:7 (the sea and preparing a boat), the account locates Jesus on a mountain, for the tradition involving the call of the disciples had as its setting a mountain. The present account does not fit neatly any form-critical category but consists of Jesus's calling of the Twelve, their appointment to two tasks (3:13–15), and a listing of their names (3:16–19).

Mark's editorial work in the present account can be seen in several areas. It is uncertain whether Mark himself was responsible for bringing together two separate traditions—a call of the twelve disciples (3:13–14) and a list of their names (3:16–19; Gnilka 1978: 137), whether they existed together in the pre-Markan tradition (Best 1981: 180–82; Marcus 2000: 265), or whether Mark gave his own theological interpretation (3:13–15) to a traditional list of names found in 3:16–19 (Donahue and Harrington 2002: 126). His own redactional work is seen most clearly in the description of the disciples' second task (3:14b–15: preach, κηρύσσειν, *kēryssein*; authority, ἐξουσίαν, *exousian*; cast out demons, ἐκβάλλειν τὰ δαιμόνια, *ekballein ta daimonia*) and the reference to his appointing the Twelve (3:16; Pryke 1978: 12, 140, 155; Schmithals 1979: 1.206; Marcus 2000: 265). Some have suggested that 3:13 and the comment about Judas's betrayal (3:19b) should also be attributed to Mark (Pryke 1988: 12, 140, 155; Marcus 2000: 265), but it is more likely that these were part of the tradition he used. Guelich (1989: 155) sees Mark's hand most clearly in 3:15–16a, 17c, and 19b. Most agree that 3:16–19 is a pre-Markan list of the disciples.

Exegesis and Exposition

[13]And he goes up on the mountain and calls to himself those whom he wanted, and they came to him. [14]And he appointed twelve, ⌜whom he also named apostles,⌝ in order that they might be with him and in order that he might send them out to preach [15]and to have authority to cast out demons. [16]⌜And he appointed the Twelve.⌝ And he gave to Simon the name Peter. [17]And to James the son of Zebedee and John the brother of James he gave the names Boanerges, which means "Sons of Thunder." [18]And [he also appointed] Andrew, and Philip, and Bartholomew, and Matthew, and

Thomas, and James the son of Alphaeus, and Thaddaeus, and Simon the Cananaean, [19]and Judas Iscariot, who also betrayed him.

3:13 Mark refers to a mountain ten other times: 5:5, 11; 6:46; 9:2, 9; 11:1, 23; 13:3, 14; 14:26. Most of these appear to be traditional,[1] and none of them serves a clearly Markan theological purpose (Gnilka 1978: 138; Guelich 1989: 156–57; contra Donahue and Harrington 2002: 122, 127). In contrast to Matthew (cf. 4:8; 5:1; 17:1; 28:16), "mountain" does not function in Mark as a technical term for a place of divine revelation. Most times it functions as a purely geographical designation.[2] In only one instance (9:2) does a mountain appear to serve as a place of revelation, and this seems, as here, to have been part of the tradition Mark inherited. Because the reference in 3:13 to the mountain interrupts the tie between 3:7 and 4:1–5:43, it is best to see it as a part of the tradition associated with the call of the Twelve. That Mark does not eliminate the reference to a "mountain" or change it to fit the scene in 3:7 suggests that Mark was quite conservative in his use of the Jesus traditions. Although the use of the article with mountain might refer to a particular mountain, Mark here, as in 9:2, had no interest in designating which mountain is meant. For the evangelist the important thing is what happened, not where it happened, and he makes no clear tie in this verse to any OT theophany (contra J. Edwards 2002: 111n2).

The verb "calls" (προσκαλεῖται, *proskaleitai*) is generally used to summon people to listen to what is about to be said (3:23; 7:14; 8:1, 34; 10:42; 12:43), to have someone do something (6:7), or to inquire of someone (15:44). Here it has the sense of "selecting" (cf. Acts 2:39; 13:2; 16:10) or "choosing" (cf. esp. Luke 6:13; contra Gundry 1993: 167). The basis of this selection lies with Jesus alone. The intensive "himself" (αὐτός, *autos*) further emphasizes that the decision in all this lay with Jesus's own sovereign choice. Mark may want his readers to see Jesus's actions as being similar to God's sovereign calling of individuals in the OT (cf. Exod. 3:4ff.; 1 Sam. 3:4ff.; Jer. 1:5ff.). The verb ἤθελεν (*ēthelen*) can mean "wished," but here it refers not to wishing but to willing, so I have translated it "wanted." It is uncertain as to whether the "whom" refers to a larger group of disciples out of which the Twelve are appointed or whether it refers solely to the Twelve. Matthew 10:1–2 favors the latter, Luke 6:12–13 the former. Although certainty is impossible, it seems best to understand "whom" as referring to the Twelve, because Jesus's "calling"

---

1. Contra Pryke (1978: 137), who sees only three (6:46 [160]; 11:23 [168]; and 13:14 [170]) of the eleven mountain references in Mark as being traditional.

2. The portrayal of the Matthean Moses as a "new Moses" by Allison (1993: 172–80), based in large measure on the analogy of Jesus "going up on the mountain" (Matt. 5:1–2) and Moses going up on the mountain (Exod. 19:3, 12, 13; 24:12, 13, 18; 34:1, 2, 4; Num. 27:12; Deut. 1:24, 41, 43; 5:5; 9:9; 10:1, 3; 32:49), should not be read back into Mark 3:13. Jesus goes up on the mountain not to receive revelation from God like Moses did but rather to give a revelation in his choosing the twelve apostles. In Mark, such revelation occurs less frequently on a mountain than along the shore of the Sea of Galilee.

them (3:13) and his "appointing" (ἐποίησεν, *epoiēsen*) them appear to be synonymous actions. If Mark wanted to distinguish them from the Twelve, he would probably have indicated this by adding something like "from whom" (cf. Luke 6:13) to the verb "appointed" (3:14; contra Gundry 1993: 167).

Just as in 1:20 after Jesus "called" (ἐκάλεσεν, *ekalesen*) James and John, those called "came" (ἀπῆλθον, *apēlthon*—the same word in both texts) to him. This action in 3:13 by those whom Jesus called, and its parallel in 1:20 by James and John (two of the Twelve), also suggests that "whom" refers to the Twelve. Usually "came" (ἀπῆλθον) in Mark is followed by "into" (εἰς, *eis*) because the action is directed to a place or thing, but here it is followed by "to" (πρός, *pros*) because the action is toward a person (cf. 14:10). As in 1:16–20 the present sentence reveals the powerful effect of Jesus's calling and stands in sharp contrast to the rabbis. The rabbis did not call their disciples but were chosen by them because they saw their teachers as guides to following the Torah. Jesus's calling is not to the Torah but to himself (J. Edwards 2002: 112).

The verb "appointed" (lit. "made," ἐποίησεν, *epoiēsen*) is used in the sense **3:14–15** of appointing someone or something (cf. Acts 2:36; Heb. 3:2; Rev. 5:10; also 1 Sam. 12:63; 1 Kings 12:31; 13:33; 2 Chron. 2:18 [2:17 LXX]). It emphasizes Jesus's sovereign action of appointing the Twelve to be his apostles. For the "Twelve," see 3:16; 4:10; 6:7; 9:35; 10:32; 11:11; 14:10, 17, 20, 43. In Mark, this and the designation "disciples" are essentially synonymous (C. Black 1989: 273–74n5; France 2002: 158; contra V. Taylor 1952: 230; Marcus 2000: 266). The symbolism of the number "twelve" should not be missed, for the number of the disciples is more important than their names. The appointing of the Twelve was clearly a parabolic act on the part of Jesus (Stein 1994b: 25–26), but the exact meaning of this act is debated. Some have suggested that it symbolized God's judgment and rejection of Israel and its replacement with a "new Israel" (cf. Rom. 9–11). This, however, would appear to be too early for such an act in Mark's story of Jesus. Furthermore, the selection by Jesus of a gentile or a Samaritan for inclusion among the Twelve would have served such a purpose even better. Others have suggested that, since at the time Israel consisted of only two and a half tribes (Benjamin, Judah, and half of Levi), it symbolized the eschatological restoration of Israel in fulfillment of the OT (cf. Isa. 11:10–16; 49:6; 56:8; Ezek. 45:8; Mic. 2:12; also Sir. 36:11; 48:10; Ps. Sol. 17.26–32; Gnilka 1978: 139). Both of these views contain an element of truth. The arrival of the kingdom of God (see 1:15) involved the fulfillment of the OT promises and thus the "restoration" of Israel, but it did not "restore" Israel according to the national and political hopes of most first-century Jews. Similarly, a new people was indeed called into being, which included both Jew and Greek (Eph. 2:11–21), but this would become clear only after the resurrection. The christological and eschatological significance of this act should not be lost. Through the symbolism of choosing the Twelve, Jesus was proclaiming that he was bringing the long-awaited kingdom of

God to Israel. That he did not include himself as one of the Twelve reveals an understanding of his unique status and relationship to the kingdom of God (Hooker 1991: 111). The later mention of "the apostles" (οἱ ἀπόστολοι, *hoi apostoloi*) in 6:30 argues for the authenticity of their being mentioned here. The presence of the expression "whom he named apostles" in the Lukan parallel in 6:13 is better explained by Luke's having found this in his Markan source than that its presence in Mark is due to an early scribe seeking to harmonize Mark with Luke. This comment is either a pre-Markan or Markan editorial comment emphasizing the leadership role of the Twelve in the early church (cf. Eph. 2:20; Rev. 21:14).

The first reason for Jesus appointing the Twelve is "in order that they might be with him" (ἵνα ὦσιν μετ᾽ αὐτοῦ, *hina ōsin met' autou*; cf. Mark 14:67). This does not refer to a desire by Jesus for companionship. The Twelve are not chosen because "no man is an island" and Jesus craves friends. Rather, the Twelve are to accompany Jesus during his ministry (contrast 5:18–19). In so doing, they will learn from him (4:10–12, 33–34), witness his actions (4:35–5:43), and learn his teachings. As a result they will serve as his apostles and witnesses (Acts 10:39–41) and supervise the traditions concerning him (Luke 1:2). During his ministry, they will assist him (Mark 4:36; 6:41–43; 8:6–9; 11:2–7; 14:12–16) and preach/heal/exorcise in his name (3:14–15; 6:7–13). The second reason why Jesus appoints the Twelve is "in order that he might send them out" (ἵνα ἀποστέλλῃ αὐτούς, *hina apostellē autous*). The verb "send out" (ἀποστέλλω) and the noun "apostle" (ἀπόστολος) come from the same root and "connote official representation of the sender" (Donahue and Harrington 2002: 123). No mention is made here or in 6:7–13 as to where or to whom Jesus sends the apostles during his ministry. This second purpose has two subpurposes. The first subpurpose is "to preach" (κηρύσσειν, *kēryssein*). This verb is used with reference to the preaching of John the Baptist (1:4, 7), Jesus (1:14, 38–39), a healed leper (1:45), a healed demoniac (5:20), a healed deaf and mute man (7:36), the Twelve (3:14; 6:12), and the early church (13:10; 14:9). It is always used positively in Mark and refers to proclaiming the word and acts of God, that is, the "gospel" (cf. 13:10; 14:9). Mark saw no need to define the content of this preaching, because he had already done so in 1:15.

The second subpurpose for the Twelve being sent out is "to have authority to cast out demons" (ἔχειν ἐξουσίαν ἐκβάλλειν τὰ δαιμόνια, *echein exousian ekballein ta daimonia*). The parallel to Jesus's activity of preaching and casting out demons in 1:39 should be noted. In 6:12–13, in addition to preaching and exorcising demons (cf. 6:7), healing is also mentioned. ("Healing" may have been omitted in 3:15 in order to tie the present account more closely with the following, which involves the source of Jesus's exorcisms.) The Twelve are called to do what Jesus does (6:13), although in 9:14–29 they are unable to exorcise a demon that Jesus later exorcises. The wording here is awkward. (Cf. the rewording in Matt. 10:1.) One expects simply "to cast out demons." It may be that the reference to Jesus's authority in casting out the demon in the synagogue of Capernaum (1:22, 27) may have influenced Mark's wording here. In 6:7 the Twelve's authority over the demons is again mentioned. This authority is not a legal right but rather a divine power or capability. By wording the second subpurpose in this manner, Mark recalls Jesus's unique authority over the demons. Thus the Twelve's authority to cast out demons serves a christological purpose. It demonstrates the greatness of Jesus of Nazareth, who possesses such authority and is able to give it to his representatives. The importance Mark attaches to the exorcising of demons is seen in the summaries and seams where this is emphasized: 1:34, 39; 3:22; 6:13. The present reference to his authority is probably due to Mark and prepares the reader for the next account (3:20–35), which speaks of Jesus's authority over the prince of demons.

It is unnecessary to see the two purposes in 3:14–15 ("to be with him" and "to send them out in order to . . .") as being contradictory. The first purpose was not understood by Mark as a remedy for Jesus's loneliness but as an internship in which the disciples were taught by Jesus and shared in his ministry. It would be only natural that later they would assist Jesus by going out to preach and continue his ministry of healing and exorcising. We find a similar twofold understanding in Jesus's call of Peter and Andrew in 1:16–18, where they are called to follow him ("be with") in order to become fishers of men ("to send them out in order to . . ."). Thus the two purposes are to be understood as successive, not simultaneous (Best 1981: 182; Marcus 2000: 267).

Assuming that the independent clause "And he appointed the Twelve" should **3:16–19** be read, its very redundancy after 3:14a emphasizes the importance of Jesus's appointment of the twelve apostles and affirms for Mark's readers the leadership role that they possessed in the early church. Although many of "the" (note the article) Twelve are virtually unknown, as a group they exerted a symbolic and leadership role in the early church (Matt. 28:16–20; Acts 2:42; 10:40–42; Luke 1:2; Eph. 2:20; Rev. 21:14; etc.). Their importance is seen in Acts 1:12–26, where the first task of the early church after the ascension is to fill the void created by the betrayal of Judas. This indicates the importance of the symbolism of "the Twelve." Thus the healed demoniac's request to join Jesus and the Twelve in 5:18 will be denied.

"And he gave to Simon the name Peter" is a rather awkward statement in that we expect to find Simon's name in the accusative case in apposition to "the Twelve" (τοὺς δώδεκα, *tous dōdeka*), as we find in the case of the other disciples mentioned in 3:17–19. Instead we find an independent sentence. Mark does not provide any reason for Jesus's giving Simon the name "Peter" (contrast John 21:42; Matt. 16:18–19). The changing of a person's name recalls how in the OT God gave new names to certain people (cf. Abram to Abraham, Gen. 17:5; Sarai to Sarah, 17:15; Jacob to Israel, 32:38) and bears witness to the status of Jesus in renaming Simon and to the new stage in the life of the one renamed. The name "Peter" (Πέτρος, *Petros*) is the Greek equivalent of the Aramaic כֵּיפָא (*kêpāʾ*, Cephas; cf. John 1:42; 1 Cor. 1:12) and means "stone." This apparently was not a common name in either Greek or Aramaic (Fitzmyer

1979a; Bauckham 2006: 85–88). Whether Mark assumed that his readers would understand the significance of this name and the leading role that Peter played in the life of the church is uncertain but quite possible. If the Gospel of Mark was associated with Peter and the church in Rome, then the play on "Peter" and "stone" would without doubt have been understood. There is no need to deny the attribution of the name "Peter" to Jesus and attribute it to the post-Easter church (Guelich 1989: 161). As to when this name was given to Simon, the Gospels introduce the name at different times and places. Mark and Luke (6:14) assume that it was given to Simon when Jesus appointed the Twelve, although Luke uses the name earlier (5:8). According to Matthew, Jesus gave this name to Simon at Caesarea Philippi after he confessed Jesus to be the Christ (16:18), although he too uses the name earlier (4:18; 8:14; 10:2; 14:28, 29; 15:15; 16:16); and in John, Jesus gives this name to Simon at their first encounter (1:42), although John also uses the name earlier (1:40). As a result it appears that Matthew, Mark (and Luke), and John place Jesus's naming of Peter in different locations in accordance with their literary purposes. Thus, whereas Jesus's naming of Peter is witnessed to in all four Gospels, the exact time and place where this occurred is unclear. Although up to this point in Mark, "Simon" has always been used to describe this disciple (1:16, 29, 30, 36; 3:16, 18), from this point on he will always be referred to as "Peter" (5:37; 8:29, 32, 33; 9:2, 5; 10:28; 11:21; 13:3; 14:29, 33, 37, 54, 66, 67, 70, 72; 16:7), except in 14:37. Whether Jesus originally gave "Peter" as a nickname or a proper name is uncertain, but it is used in the NT as a proper name.

For "and James the son of Zebedee and John the brother of James," see 1:19, where the wording is the same except that "of James" is replaced by the pronoun "his." Both Matthew and Luke place "Andrew," the brother of Peter, second in the list rather than James. In so doing they keep the two sets of brothers together: Peter-Andrew and James-John. (Yet note that in Acts 1:13 the list of the Twelve reads: Peter, John, James, Andrew. . . .) Their agreement against Mark is quite understandable. Why Mark sandwiches James and John between Peter and Andrew is unclear. It may be that he sought to keep the names of Peter, James, and John together in the tradition (5:37; 9:2; 14:33; cf. also 13:3, where Andrew's name is added but as the fourth). Whereas the name "Peter" given to Simon signifies the role he is to play in the life of the church, "Boanerges, which means [lit. 'is'] Sons of Thunder," given to James and John seems to reveal the temperament of these two brothers (9:38; 10:35–40; Luke 9:54). The exact origin of "Boanerges" is unclear. "Boan" is not an exact transliteration for "sons of" (Heb. בְּנֵי, *bĕnê*) and "erges" is not very close to רַעַם (*ra'am*, thunder). It may be best to understand "Boanerges" as a rough transliteration into Greek of "sons of thunder." For other examples of "is" used as "means," see 7:11, 34; 12:42; 15:16, 34, 42.

For Andrew, compare Acts 1:13, where this name also appears fourth in the list. This is a Greek name. Philip is mentioned in John 1:44; 6:5; 12:21; 14:8, and is said to come from Bethsaida (John 1:44; 12:21), the same city as Peter and Andrew (John 1:44). Clement of Alexandria (*Stromata* 3.4.25) states that

Matt. 8:21–22/Luke 9:59–60 was addressed to Philip. Philip ("lover of horses") is also a Greek name. Bartholomew means "son of Tholomaios." Because of his being placed next to Philip in the list, he is often identified with Nathaniel (cf. John 1:43–51). In Matt. 10:4, Matthew ("gift of God") is described as "the toll collector." Since Matt. 9:9 in its parallel to Mark 2:14 ("Levi, the toll collector") has "Matthew, the toll collector," these may be two names for the same person. See 2:14. Although Thomas (Aramaic תְּאֹומָא, těʾômāʾ) means "twin" and is specifically alluded to as a twin (Δίδυμος, didymos) in John 11:16; 20:24; 21:2, nothing is ever said about his twin in the Gospels. Unmentioned elsewhere in Mark, Thomas plays an important role in John (cf. 11:16; 14:5; 20:24, 26–29; 21:2). Tradition associates him with the founding of the Mar Thoma Church in southwestern India (Schnabel 2004: 1.880–95). The description of James as "the son of Alphaeus" serves to distinguish this James from James the son of Zebedee and brother of John; James the Younger (15:40); and James the brother of Jesus (Gal. 1:19; 1 Cor. 15:7). Since Levi the toll collector (2:14) is also described as the son of Alphaeus, Levi (Matthew in Matt. 9:9) and James may have been brothers. If true, it is strange that Mark does not mention this. Matthew 9:9 and Luke 5:27 do not refer to Matthew/Levi as the son of Alphaeus. The name Thaddaeus also appears in the Matthean list (10:3) but is lacking in both Lukan lists (6:12–16; Acts 1:13). Instead Luke mentions in his lists Judas, the son of James (Luke 6:16; Acts 1:13), who does not appear in the Markan and Matthean lists. Apart from Judas Iscariot, in the Markan and Matthean lists no members of the Twelve have their names qualified except those who have a namesake, that is, Simon ("Peter" and "the Cananaean") and James ("son of Zebedee" and "son of Alphaeus"). It is possible that the name of Judas is qualified with "Iscariot" because he too had a namesake (cf. John 14:22). In the first century it was quite common for a man to have two names. Thus it is not at all unlikely that one of the Twelve possessed the Jewish name "Judas" (the Greek equivalent of the Hebrew name "Judah") and the Greek name "Thaddaeus" (a shortened form of Theodotos or Theodosios; Bauckham 2006: 99–100). If one of the Twelve did possess the names "Judas" and "Thaddaeus," it is not surprising that Matthew and Mark would prefer to use the second name rather than the first, as Luke did (Jeremias 1971: 232–33). (What Christian parent today would name his/her son "Judas"?) Luke describes Simon the Cananaean as "the one called the Zealot" (6:15) or simply "the Zealot" (Acts 1:13). In so doing, Luke is simply translating the meaning of the Aramaic word קַנְאָן (qanʾān, Cananaean) into Greek. Traditionally the Zealot movement is believed to have begun when Judas the Galilean led a revolt in AD 6 against the Roman attempt to collect taxes in Judea (Josephus, Ant. 18.1.6 §§23–25), which revolt led to his death (Acts 5:37). The extent of the Zealot movement in Jesus's day is uncertain, although later they were a leading cause of the Jewish revolt and the destruction of Jerusalem in AD 70. When Mark and Luke wrote their Gospels, the term would have been interpreted more as a political than a religious designation, as Luke 6:15 and Acts 1:13 indicate (France 2002: 162–63). The presence of a toll collector and a Zealot among the Twelve is remarkable, for they represent radical extremes among the Jewish people (a turncoat/traitor/collaborator and a revolutionary/superpatriot/chauvinist); only the transformation by the Spirit (1:8) could change such natural enemies and cause them to love one another (John 13:35).

Judas Iscariot is mentioned last in the list to distance him from the rest of the Twelve. The original meaning of "Iscariot" is debated. The least unlikely derivation of the term is "man" (Heb. אִישׁ, *'îš*) of "Karioth" (קְרִיּוֹת, *qĕrîyôt*), a town in Judea whose exact location is debated (cf. Josh. 15:25; Jer. 48:24; and the textual variants in John 6:71; 12:4; 13:2, 26; 14:22). If this derivation of the name is correct, then Judas was the only member of the Twelve who came from Judea.[3] (Other suggestions for the meaning of "Iscariot" are "assassin," from *sicarius*, a short daggerlike sword; "false one"; "man from Sychar," which would make him a Samaritan; "man of Issachar"; etc. [W. Klassen, *ABD* 3:1091–92; R. Brown 1994: 2.1410–18].) Mark or the tradition before him adds "who also betrayed him." Although this information was undoubtedly known to Mark's readers, the reference prepares them for Judas's role in the Passion Narrative (14:10–11, 18, 20–21, 41–44).

Some have denied the historicity of the Twelve, but it is difficult to conceive of this group as having been created by the early church, which then assigned to it a villainous traitor. Judas's presence among the Twelve guarantees the historicity of this group. The historicity of the Twelve is also supported by the mention of the Twelve in an early church creed (1 Cor. 15:5), dating perhaps from the late 30s; the importance for the early church of maintaining the symbolism of the Twelve in Acts 1:12–26; the fact that the Twelve as a group did not play any significant role in the life of the early church; and the unknown role of various members of the group (Bartholomew, Thaddaeus/Judas the son of James [?], Simon the Cananaean, Matthew).

Summary

In the present account, Mark seeks to teach his readers at least four things. First of all, he seeks to teach what it means to be a follower of Jesus. This is clear not just from this account but also from the fact that the preceding (1:14–3:6) and following (6:6b–8:26) sections in the Gospel are also introduced by a story about the disciples (1:16–20 and 6:7–13). The present story serves along with the others to indicate what following Jesus means. It means to "be" with Jesus and to carry on his mission.[4] It means to deny oneself, take up a cross, and follow Jesus (8:34). The Twelve serve as the supreme example of what it means to be a disciple, although their weaknesses and

---

3. See, however, Bauckham (2006: 106–7), who suggests that "Iscariot" was originally a description given to Judas's father.

4. Donahue and Harrington (2002: 127) rightly point out that Christian discipleship does not involve an either/or of "contemplation" or "action" but their combination, for these are inseparable and involve two aspects of one calling (3:14).

failures will soon be demonstrated. See "Theological Emphases: The Disciples" in the introduction. In hearing/reading this story, Mark's audience would have been reminded of what it means to follow Jesus.

The call of the Twelve also serves a historical purpose in explaining to Mark's readers where this group came from and how they received their leadership authority from Jesus himself. Unless the book of Acts has completely falsified the story of the church's earliest years, various members of the Twelve played a foundational role in the development of the early church. Yet some of them are essentially unknown. Nevertheless, Peter, James, and John provided leadership roles in the church, and as a group they are portrayed in the NT as being the foundation of the early church (cf. Matt. 28:16–20; Acts 1:12–26; 2:42; 8:14–25; 10:40–42; 11:1; 15:2ff.; Eph. 2:11–21; Rev. 21:14; etc.). The present account thus serves to inform Mark's readers of how this group came into existence. Through their being with Jesus, they mastered his teachings and became the guardians of the Jesus traditions (Luke 1:2), and through his empowerment they continued his ministry of preaching, healing, and exorcising.

The present account also serves a christological purpose. In calling the Twelve, one is reminded of God's sovereign calling of men and women to his service in the OT; and in renaming Peter, James, and John, Jesus performs a role that in the OT is performed by God and his angels. This, along with the prerogatives of forgiving sins (2:6), of mastery over the Sabbath (2:28; 3:4–5), tradition (2:18–22; 7:1–23), and the Law (10:2–11), naturally raise the question, "Who is this Jesus of Nazareth?" These points support Mark's introductory comment that Jesus is the Christ, the Son of God. The symbolism of appointing twelve also reveals that Jesus of Nazareth brought with him the "restoration" of Israel. He is the fulfillment and the fulfiller of the OT promises. In particular, Mark emphasizes in the present account Jesus's authority over the demons by his addition of 3:15 (cf. also 1:22, 27, 34, 39; 3:11–12, 22–27; 6:7, 12–13). This prepares the reader for the following account and emphasizes that Jesus is mightier than not only John the Baptist (1:7) but also Beelzebul, the prince of demons (3:22–27).

The last emphasis involves the reference to Judas, "who also betrayed him." The comment recalls the fate of John the Baptist (1:14), the future fate of Jesus's disciples (13:10, 12),[5] but above all that of Jesus (8:31; 9:31; 10:33–34; 14:10–11, 18, 21, 41–42, 44; 15:1, 15). Earlier in the Gospel, Jesus alluded to his death (2:19–20), and Mark has already referred to the beginning of a plot to destroy Jesus (3:6). Later the divine plan involving Jesus's death will be made explicit (8:31; 9:9, 31; 10:33–34, 45; 14:21, 24–25, 36), for Mark wants his readers to know that the death of Jesus was not an

---

5. It is speculative to assume that the treachery of Judas *Iscariot* would have caused Mark's readers to think of the terror of the Sicarii ("assassins") during the Jewish War (Marcus 2000: 269). This is based upon a debatable assumption as to the audience of Mark (Syrian Christians) and an unlikely origin for the term *Iscariot* from "Sicarii" (see 3:19).

unplanned misfortune. On the contrary, in his sovereign choice of the Twelve, Jesus knowingly chose one who would betray him (14:21). His selection of Judas Iscariot was not a tragic mistake or blunder. It was rather a deliberate choice by Jesus to help him fulfill his task (10:45). Thus Mark's readers are reminded that Jesus was fully in control of his death. In all this, Judas, the Jewish leadership, and the Roman authorities were willing but unwitting instruments in fulfilling the divine purpose.

Additional Notes

3:14. Although a number of important textual witnesses omit this phrase (A L f¹ syr), there is stronger support (ℵ B Θ f¹³) for its inclusion. The lack of the article before "twelve" (contrast 3:16, where the article refers back to 3:14) suggests that this phrase is not an early scribal insertion from Luke 6:13 (contra Marcus 2000: 263).

3:16. Although some witnesses (A C² D L Θ f¹ lat syr) omit these words, it is best to include them with ℵ B C* Δ.

C. Jesus, His Family, and Beelzebul (3:20–35)

The present passage consists of several different and independent traditions involving a story about Jesus (3:20–21, 31–35), a controversy story (3:22–26), and several sayings (3:27–30). They are connected to the preceding account (3:13–19) by the reference to Jesus giving the twelve apostles authority to cast out demons (3:15). In the present passage Mark discusses where this authority of Jesus came from. There is a variety of opinions concerning how Mark found this material in the tradition. Some suggest that he brought together three separate traditions (3:20–21, 22–30, and 31–35), two traditions (either 3:20–21 + 31–35 and 22–30 or 3:22–35 and 3:20–21), or one tradition (3:22–35) to which Mark added an introduction (3:20–21). The degree to which the traditional material in 3:20–35 has been reworked by Mark's own editorial hand is also debated.

The key issue in all this involves the relationship of 3:20–21 and 31–35. Should they be viewed as a single unit that has been split apart for the purpose of sandwiching 3:22–30 between them, or were they originally two separate units? In favor of the latter are the presence of a new introductory seam (3:31); the fact that the subjects of 3:31–35 ("Jesus's mother and brothers") appear to be different from that of 3:20–21 ("those from him"—οἱ παρ' αὐτοῦ, hoi par' autou); and the difference in the behavior of the two subjects toward Jesus (seeking to "seize him" because they think he is insane versus "calling him"). In favor of 3:20–21 and 31–35 originally existing as a single unit of tradition is their being part of a typical Markan literary form—the Markan sandwich. Mark is fond of sandwiching one tradition within another. Examples of this are found in 5:25–34, which is sandwiched into 5:21–24 + 35–43; 6:14–29 into 6:6b–13 + 30ff.; 11:15–19 into 11:12–14 + 20–25; 14:3–9 into 14:1–2 + 10–11; and 14:55–65 into 14:54 + 66–72 (Stein 1971: 193; J. Edwards 1989: 193–216). If, as most scholars believe, 3:20–35 is an example of a Markan sandwich, then 3:20–21 (A^1) and 31–35 (A^2) belong together. Such an argument, however, reverses the proper procedure. One argues from the supposed unity of what is split apart (3:20–21 [A^1] and 31–35 [A^2]) that we have a Markan sandwich. But this assumes what must be proven. To demonstrate that a passage is a Markan sandwich, one must show that what precedes and follows (A^1 and A^2) are a unity. Thus we are brought back to the question of whether 3:20–21 and 31–35 are intended to function as a unity. This docs not require that we demonstrate their original unity in the pre-Markan tradition. All that is necessary is to demonstrate that Mark intended for his readers to see 3:31–35 as the continuation of 3:20–21. In favor of this are several features: in both 3:20–21 and 31–35 Jesus is surrounded by a great crowd, which keeps him from eating (3:20) and his family from reaching him (3:31); the scene in 3:20–21 is a house and the scene in 3:31–35 appears to be a house (cf. standing outside, ἔξω στήκοντες, *exō stēkontes* [3:31]; outside, ἔξω, *exō* [3:32]); and the main actors in 3:20–21 ("those from him") are best understood as referring to Jesus's relatives (see 3:20–21), and in 3:31–35 they are "his mother and brothers." In so doing, Mark wants to have his readers note the parallel in the two accounts. Both groups interpret negatively what is taking place in the life of Jesus.

Mark probably intended his readers to see 3:31–35 as the continuation of 3:20–21; as a result 3:20–35 is an example of a Markan sandwich. Whether 3:20–21 and 31–35 existed together before Mark is less certain. As for 3:22–30, it is impossible to know whether this came to Mark as a unit (Guelich 1989: 170–71) or as a basic controversy story (3:22–26) to which Mark added three independent sayings of Jesus and a conclusion (3:27–30; Hooker 1991: 115). The presence of 3:29 at a different place in Luke (12:10) and the isolation of the parable (3:27) in Gos. Thom. 35 suggest the latter. As it now stands, however, 3:22–30 functions as a unity. The agreement of the Matthean and Lukan parallels against Mark in 3:22–27 (cf. Matt. 12:22–23/Luke 11:14 and Matt. 12:27–28, 30/Luke 12:19–20, 23) suggests that this tradition was also found in Q. Some think that Mark may have obtained his material from Q and that he omitted the Matthew-Luke agreements, but this is impossible to demonstrate.

The extent of Mark's editorial work in the wording of 3:20–35 is greatly debated. Some suggest that 3:20–22a, 23a, 28a, 30–33a, 34a, and 35b are all from the hand of Mark (Pryke 1978: 12, 140–41, 155; Gnilka 1978: 144–47; cf. also Marcus 2000: 278). Care must be taken, however, to differentiate between Mark's wording of the tradition and what he specifically created and added to it. It would appear that 3:20 (3:19b NRSV) is a typical Markan seam introducing a new pericope. "And he enters a house" (καὶ ἔρχεται εἰς οἶκον, *kai erchetai eis oikon*) recalls 1:29, 32–33; 2:1; the reference to the "crowd" (ὁ ὄχλος, *ho ochlos*) ties the present account with what has gone before (cf. 1:33, 37, 45; 2:2, 4, 13; 3:7–9; also 4:1–2); and "again" (πάλιν, *palin*) is a favorite term in the Markan seams (2:1, 13; 3:1; 4:1; 5:21; etc.). The unusual vocabulary in 3:21 (οἱ παρ᾽ αὐτοῦ, *hoi par᾽ autou*; lit. "those from him") and its harshness (the attempt to seize Jesus and the belief that Jesus was out of his mind) favor the traditional origin of this material, even though the explanatory clause (for, γάρ, *gar*) is typically Markan in style. The first part of 3:23a may indeed reflect a Markan introduction to the sayings that follow, but aside from the reference to responding "in parables" (ἐν παραβολαῖς, *en parabolais*), something like 3:23a no doubt introduced the sayings that follow. Probably, 3:30 is a Markan explanatory comment that he has added to the tradition. Whereas 3:31 reflects Mark's wording, something like this must have introduced 3:32–35. Mark's hand is seen in the meaning he attributes to Jesus's mother and brothers standing "outside" (see 3:31–35), but their location may have been part of the tradition, for Jesus is in a house and his mother and brothers are outside trying to reach him. This requires them to have been standing "outside" the house in the tradition.

As it now stands, 3:20–35 consists of an introductory statement in which Jesus enters a house and his family seeks to seize him (3:20–21). The story of Jesus and the unbelief of his family is then interrupted by an account in which scribes from Jerusalem show a similar but more hostile misunderstanding of Jesus's ministry by attributing his exorcisms to collaboration with Satan (3:22). In response, Jesus provides a defense of his ministry by showing the absurdity of such an accusation (3:23–27) and counters the charges of his opponents by pointing out that they are the ones guilty of blasphemy and an unpardonable sin (3:28–30). This is then followed by the resumption of the story about the unbelief of Jesus's family and teachings concerning what it means to be part of God's true family (3:31–35).

Exegesis and Exposition

²⁰And he enters a house. And again ⌜the⌝ crowd gathers, so that they are not even able to eat. ²¹And ⌜his family,⌝ having heard [this], came to seize him, for they were saying, "He is out of his mind."

²²And the scribes who had come down from Jerusalem began to say, "He is possessed by Beelzebul," and "By the ruler of the demons he is casting out the demons." ²³And summoning them, he began to speak to them in parables. "How is Satan able to cast out Satan? ²⁴And if a kingdom is divided against itself, that kingdom is not able to stand. ²⁵And if a house is divided against itself, that house shall not be able to stand. ²⁶And if Satan has risen up against himself and is divided, he is not able to stand but has met his end. ²⁷But no one is able, upon entering the house of the strong man, to plunder his possessions unless he first binds the strong man, and then he will [be able to] plunder his house. ²⁸Truly I say to you, all things shall be forgiven human beings, all the sins and blasphemies that they blaspheme. ²⁹But whoever blasphemes against the Holy Spirit will never be forgiven but is guilty of an eternal sin." ³⁰For they were saying, "He has an unclean spirit."

³¹And his mother and his brothers come, and standing outside they sent to him and called him. ³²And a crowd was sitting around him, and they say to him, "Look, your mother and your brothers ⌜ ⌝ are outside seeking you." ³³And he [Jesus] ⌜says⌝ to them, "Who is my mother and my brothers?" ³⁴And looking around at those sitting in a circle around him, he says, "See, my mother and my brothers. ³⁵For whoever does the will of God, this person is my brother, and sister, and mother."

"And he enters into a house" does not conclude 3:13–19 but introduces a new account (cf. 1:29; 2:1; 7:24). It is unlikely that Mark intended his readers to think that this was the home of Peter (1:29–34) or of Jesus (see 2:1–2). The latter is not very likely since it would be strange to find Jesus's mother and brothers "outside" (3:31–32) their own home and unable to enter it. If, on the other hand, Mark wanted his readers to assume that this was Peter's

3:20–21

home (Gundry 1993: 171), he could have indicated this by adding only one word—Σιμῶνος, *Simōnou*, or Πέτρου, *Petrou* (cf. 1:29). Whose house and in what city this house was located were not important for Mark, and this was probably not mentioned in the tradition he inherited. The reference to the crowd gathering again recalls 3:7–9 and 1:32–34, 37–39, 45; 2:2, 4, 13, where Jesus's popularity caused people to flock around him. It also points forward to 4:1. For "again," see 2:1, 13; 3:1; 4:1; 5:21; 7:14, 31; 8:1, 13; 10:1, 10, 32; 11:27, which are all Markan seams or summaries. For Mark, "and again" (καὶ πάλιν, *kai palin*) and "and immediately" (καὶ εὐθύς, *kai euthys*) often function as simple connectives, and a literal meaning should not be pressed. (See 1:10 and 2:1.)

The expression ἄρτον φαγεῖν (*arton phagein*, lit. "to eat bread") means "to eat" (cf. 6:37 with 44, where it involves more than just bread, and 7:2, 5, where it refers to eating in general). "They" (αὐτούς, *autous*) takes as its antecedent Jesus and the Twelve (3:13–19), who are "with him" (3:14), not the crowd, and ties the present account to the preceding. Why they were "not even able" (μὴ . . . μηδέ, *mē . . . mēde*; a double negative) to eat (too crowded, too busy, etc.) is not made clear. For Mark to explain this would detract from the purpose of this statement, which is to show Jesus's great popularity among the people and to explain why his relatives seek to seize him. The scene is similar to that found in 2:2–4; 3:7–9; 4:1–2; 5:25–31; 6:31; and so on. "Those from him" is the literal translation of οἱ παρ' αὐτοῦ, *hoi par' autou*. Nowhere else in Mark do we find this expression. Since neither Matthew nor Luke has a parallel to this verse, we receive no help from them as to its meaning. The main suggestions for who this phrase refers to are the followers of Jesus, the Twelve, and the relatives/family of Jesus. In the setting of 3:20–21, however, it cannot refer to the Twelve, since they were with Jesus in 3:13–19 and entered the house with him (3:20). As a result they would not have "heard" (ἀκούσαντες, *akousantes*) about what was going on but would have "seen" it. The phrase is probably best interpreted as referring to Jesus's family (cf. Prov. 31:21 LXX; Sus. 33 [cf. 30]). If, as seems likely, 3:20–35 is an example of a Markan sandwich, then this awkward expression must refer to the mother and brothers of Jesus mentioned in 3:31–35 (Marcus 2000: 271; France 2002: 165–66). Mark 3:21, 31–35, and 6:3 are the only references to Jesus's family found in the Gospel.

What Jesus's family "heard" is not explicitly stated, but Mark probably intended his readers to interpret 3:21 in light of 3:20. Their desire to seize Jesus involves more than simply hearing that Jesus is in a certain house (contra Guelich 1989: 172). It involves something he is doing. Mark's comment that Jesus and his followers do not have time to eat is emphatic due to the double negative and explains what Jesus's family has heard and why they try to seize him. They think he is "out of his mind" (ἐξέστη, *exestē*) and seek to seize him because, due to the crowd, Jesus is neglecting a basic human need—eating. The use of ἐξῆλθον (*exelthon*; lit. "went out") seems strange since Jesus is inside a house (3:20). This verb, however, can also mean "set out" or "came," as in 8:11, 27 (Matt. 13:49). The verb "to seize" (κρατῆσαι, *kratēsai*) occurs several times in Mark with the hostile sense of "to arrest" (cf. 6:17; 12:12; 14:1, 44, 46, 49, 51). Here, however, the term refers to Jesus's family seeking to seize "him" (αὐτόν, *auton*), which refers to Jesus, not the crowd (Marcus 2000: 271–72).[1] The explanatory "for" clause explains the behavior of Jesus's family ("they" refers back to "those from him") to Mark's readers (see 1:16). This does not require that this explanation be understood as a de novo creation of Mark, for often the content of his explanatory comments comes from the tradition (cf. 1:16; 2:15; 5:8, 42). What it indicates is that the *wording* of the explanation came from Mark. The very harshness of this clause (note its omission by both Matthew and Luke) argues for it being a piece of authentic tradition, for it is hardly likely that such a charge would have been made up by the early church. Through this comment Mark explains why the family of Jesus sought to seize him. They did so because they thought Jesus had lost his mind. Elsewhere in Mark the verb ἐξίστημι (*existēmi*) always means "were amazed" (2:12; 5:42; 6:51). In the NT it occurs only here and in 2 Cor. 5:13 with the meaning "to lose one's mind" (Dwyer 1996: 105–6).

Mark makes no attempt to explain whether the action of Jesus's family is due to sincere but misguided concern or whether it is hostile in nature. Regardless, Mark portrays the family of Jesus in this verse as outside the fellowship of Jesus's followers. The unbelieving status of Jesus's family will be developed more fully in 3:31–35 and by its association in this Markan sandwich with 3:22–30. The charge of Jesus having lost his senses has a historical basis in the life of Jesus (cf. John 7:20; 8:48, 52; 10:20), and it is clear that his family stood outside his circle of followers (John 2:3–4; 7:3–5; cf. also Luke 2:48). It goes beyond the evidence, however, to argue that Mark in his Gospel was on a vendetta to debase the character of Jesus's family, who represent James, the brother of Jesus, and the Jewish Christianity of the Jerusalem church in the 60s (Barton 1994: 82–86; Marcus 2000: 279–80; contra Crossan 1973b).

Even though Jerusalem was to the south, the scribes "had come down" (καταβάντες, *katabantes*) from Jerusalem as they went north. One always goes down when leaving Jerusalem (Luke 10:30; Acts 11:27; 25:27), and one always goes up when going to Jerusalem (10:32, 33; Luke 2:22; 18:31), because Jerusalem lies on a mountain. Thus there is no need to see any symbolism in "come down" (contra Marcus 2000: 271). Although we have encountered scribes earlier in Mark (1:22; 2:6, 16), the sinister character of this group of scribes is heightened by pointing out that they came "from Jerusalem" (cf. 7:1; 10:33–34). Instead of raising a challenging question (2:7), they now pass a judicial verdict (3:22). In the Matthean (12:22–23) and Lukan (11:14) parallels, the **3:22–23**

---

1. See Best 1975: 311, who points out that the collective singular "crowd" (ὄχλος, *ochlos*) always takes a plural pronoun, whereas the singular αὐτόν (*auton*) is used in 3:21. Cf. 2:13; 3:9–10; 3:32–33; etc. Thus the attempt to translate 3:21, "When his followers heard [it], they went out to calm it [the crowd] down, for they were saying that it [the crowd] had gone out of control in its enthusiasm," is not possible (contra Wansbrough 1972; D. Wenham 1974).

controversy that follows is preceded by an exorcism. The debate as to whether Mark omitted this exorcism or whether he used another tradition in which it was lacking is impossible to resolve, but the controversy of 3:22–26 appears to be due not so much to a particular exorcism (as in Matthew and Luke) but rather to Jesus's exorcisms in general (cf. 1:23–27, 32–34, 39; 3:11–12, 15).

The first charge continually leveled (began to say, ἔλεγον, *elegon*; an inceptive imperfect) against Jesus by the scribes accuses him of being possessed by Beelzebul (cf. Matt. 10:25). (Cf. 3:30; 5:15; 7:25; 9:17, where "to have" an unclean spirit/demon means "to be possessed" by the unclean spirit/demon.) The derivation of the name "Beelzebul" (found only here and in Matt. 10:25; 12:24/Luke 11:15; Matt. 12:27/Luke 11:18–19 in the NT) is debated. The possibilities most often mentioned are "lord of the dwelling," "lord of the dung," and "lord of the flies" (J. Lewis, *ABD* 1:638–40). In light of the reference to plundering the "house" of Beelzebul in Mark 3:27 and the reference to "house" in Matt. 10:25, "lord of the dwelling" appears to be the more likely meaning. Whatever the origin of the term, however, for the readers of Mark it was simply another name for Satan (3:23).[2] The second charge directed against Jesus accuses him of casting out demons by the prince of demons. Here is tacit acknowledgment that Jesus did in fact exorcise demons (cf. *b. Sanh.* 43a, where the charge of sorcery raised against Jesus likewise acknowledges his miracle-working activity but attributes this to sorcery [Meier 1991: 96]; also Justin Martyr, *Dial.* 69; Origen, *Cels.* 1.6).[3] The expression "ruler of the demons" serves as a synonym for Beelzebul, as Matt. 12:24 and Luke 11:15 indicate (cf. also T. Sol. 3.5).[4] A similar hierarchal understanding of the demonic world is witnessed to in T. Sol. 2.9; 3.5–6; 6.1–4; 1QS 3.20–26.

Jesus responds by "summoning" (προσκαλεσάμενος, *proskalesamenos*; cf. Mark 7:14; 8:1, 34; 10:42; 12:43) the scribes mentioned in 3:22 and begins to give (ἔλεγον is an inceptive imperfect) several parables (3:24–26) that are introduced by a question (3:23). This is the first reference in Mark to Jesus teaching in parables (cf. 4:2, 10, 11, 13 [2×], 30, 33, 34; 7:17; 12:1, 12; 13:28). Earlier Jesus had spoken in parables (2:21–22), but here Mark explicitly refers to Jesus's most famous form of teaching. In the NT a παραβολή (*parabolē*, parable) translates Hebrew מָשָׁל (*māšāl*) and refers to a broad range of literary forms. It can be used with respect to a proverb (Luke 4:23), metaphor (Mark 7:14–17), similitude (4:30–32), story parable (Luke 14:16–24), example parable (Luke 12:16–21), and allegory (Mark 12:1–11; Stein 2000). Basic to each of these literary forms is a comparison of two different things—something

2. For other names of Satan, see Davies and Allison 1991: 195–96.
3. J. Edwards (2002: 119–20) points out that Jesus's opponents did not lack evidence of God's presence in the ministry of Jesus, for they acknowledged his exorcising of demons. Due to their unbelief and hardness of heart (3:5), however, they attributed this to Satan rather than God.
4. For Mark's love of duplicate expressions in which the second intensifies the first (Donahue and Harrington 2002: 129), cf. 1:32; 11:15; 13:24; 14:12. Here it may serve to help Mark's readers understand the meaning of the name "Beelzebul."

(A) is compared to something else (B). For a discussion of why Jesus taught in parables, see 4:10–12.

Although there is no pre-Christian literary evidence that Beelzebul was a name given to Satan, in Mark the terms "ruler of the demons" (ἄρχοντι τῶν δαιμονίων, *archonti tōn daimoniōn*), "Satan" (Σατανᾶς, *Satanas*), and "Beelzebul" (Βεελζεβούλ, *Beelzeboul*) are used interchangeably in 3:22–23. Building on his listeners' assumption of a hierarchy of demons, Jesus's question in 3:23b effectively refutes the charge raised against him by the scribes. It is logically absurd to say that Satan, the ruler of the demons, is working through Jesus to cast out the very demons he sent to possess individuals.[5] Satan would not work through Jesus to undo his own work!

The first two parables are hypothetical examples drawn from war (3:24) and politics (3:25). Both illustrate the absurdity of the scribes' charge against Jesus. A nation at war with itself cannot survive. Whether Jesus intended his hearers to think of the civil strife that arose after the death of Solomon and resulted in Israel becoming two separate and often hostile nations (Samaria and Judah) is uncertain. The agreement of Matt. 12:25 and Luke 11:17 (laid waste, ἐρημοῦται, *erēmoutai*) against Mark (is not be able to stand, οὐ δύναται σταθῆναι, *ou dynatai stathēnai*) suggests that Matthew and Luke used a common source (Q). The second parable concerning a divided house not being able to stand (3:25) is in synonymous parallelism with 3:24. This example involves division within a royal family. Such internal strife often leads to the demise of that family. It may be an allusion to the rivalry over the high priesthood between the brothers Aristobulus II and Hyrcanus II, which brought an end to Jewish independence when Pompey led the Roman legions into Jerusalem in 63 BC. Other suggestions include the division of Herod the Great's kingdom among his children after his death and, for the readers of Mark, the internecine warfare among rival Jewish groups that accelerated the fall of Jerusalem in AD 70, and the internal strife in Rome following the death of Nero. The assumption of both examples is that Satan's kingdom is not collapsing from internal strife. Thus the charge that Satan is working through Jesus in direct opposition to himself is false, because his kingdom/house is not self-destructing. What was happening in Jesus's exorcisms of the demons was not the self-destruction of Satan and his kingdom from within but the overcoming of that kingdom from without by the one mightier than Satan (3:27).

The third parable concerning Satan rising up against himself (3:26) brings to a conclusion what is said in 3:24–25. The terms "is divided" (ἐμερίσθη, *emeristhē*) and "to stand" (στῆναι, *stēnai*) in 3:26 pick up the use of these terms in 3:24 and 25. There does not appear to be any difference in meaning in the two forms of the infinitive "to stand," σταθῆναι (*stathēnai*) in 3:24, 25 and στῆναι (*stēnai*) in 3:26 (Porter 1992: 72). What it means for Satan not

3:24–27

---

5. The second "Satan" in 3:23b assumes that the ruler of demons is represented by his subordinate demons. Cf. Matt. 10:40; 25:40, 45.

being able to stand is explained by the concluding statement in 3:26—"but has met his end" (ἀλλὰ τέλος ἔχει, *alla telos echei*; lit. "but he has an end"). That Satan and his kingdom still exist refutes the charge made against Jesus in 3:22. For "has an end," compare Heb. 7:3. This parable, unlike the two preceding ones, is in the form of a second-class condition, in which the "if" (εἰ, *ei*) clause assumes that the condition described is untrue.

The conclusion to the charge raised against Jesus in 3:22 comes in the form of another parable in 3:27. By his reply in 3:23–26, Jesus refutes the assertion that his exorcisms are due to the power of Beelzebul. In this verse he now gives his explanation as to the real reason why he is able to cast out demons. "But" (ἀλλ', *all'*) is a strong adversative and introduces a contrary explanation of why demons are being exorcised in the ministry of Jesus. The double negative (οὐ, *ou*, and οὐδείς, *oudeis*) gives added emphasis to the statement, as in 3:20.[6] Together with 3:22–26, Jesus's reply is as follows: "I do not cast out demons by the prince of demons. If I did, this would result in the self-destruction of Satan's kingdom, and this has not occurred [3:23–26]. But I, on the contrary, cast out demons because I am stronger than Satan [3:27; cf. also 1:7], and I have been sent from God to liberate Satan's captives, that is, to plunder his possessions." The kingdom of Satan is not self-destructing from within but is being invaded from without, and the liberation of its captives is taking place because Jesus is stronger than Satan (3:27) and has brought the kingdom of God (1:15).[7] Jesus's opponents rightly observe that something is indeed happening to Satan's kingdom (3:22). But due to their hardness of heart (3:5), they do not recognize the arrival of the kingdom of God and the beginning of the dissolution of Satan's kingdom. Jesus's casting out demons is proof that the kingdom of God has arrived (Matt. 12:28/Luke 11:20). The complete destruction of his kingdom, however, still awaits the parousia of the Son of Man (13:24–27; cf. 1 Cor. 15:24–28; cf. also T. Mos. 10.1). In this parable, the following comparisons are being made between the imagery of the parable and its meaning:

strong man	Satan
house	the world as the sphere of Satan's authority
possessions of Satan	the demon possessed
plundering of Satan's possessions	Jesus's casting out the demons and thus saving the demon possessed from the control of Satan
no one	Jesus
bind	Jesus's being stronger than Satan

6. Unlike "proper" English, where a double negative results in a positive statement, in colloquial English and in Greek a double negative results in a stronger negative statement.

7. In Jesus's explanation (3:23–27), Christology (Jesus as the "stronger one") and eschatology (the arrival of the kingdom of God) are intimately tied together, for the "stronger one" brings with him the "kingdom."

Several have attempted to interpret 3:27 as referring to a particular event in Jesus's ministry in which he, according to Mark, "bound" (δήσῃ, *dēsē*) Satan (T. Levi 18.12; Jub. 5.6; Rev. 20:2–3). The temptation is seen by some as "the" event in which this cosmic struggle and defeat of Satan took place (Robinson 1957: esp. 78, 83; Best 1965: esp. 10–15). The brevity of the temptation account in Mark, however, argues against such an elaborate interpretation, and nothing is said in that account of Satan being defeated. There is also no explicit tie between this saying and the temptation account that links the two together other than a reference to Satan. The Markan explanation of Jesus's superiority over Satan and his ability to plunder his possessions does not involve any battle or conflict in which Jesus "binds" or defeats Satan. Jesus's mere presence defeats the demons and their ruler.[8] When the Stronger One (1:7 and 3:27; cf. also Luke 11:20) comes, the weaker can do nothing but acknowledge this and submit. For a battle to be fought, there must be hope, no matter how small, of victory. In Mark's understanding, the demons and their prince have no hope. All they can do is submit and plead (cf. 5:12). Thus the emphasis in this parabolic statement lies not in the when of Satan's being bound but in the coming of a Stronger One who, because he is stronger, can plunder Satan's possessions (cf. Luke 10:18). This saying indicates to Mark's readers that Jesus did not go to the cross as a weak, unfortunate victim of circumstances, but because this was his divine calling (Mark 10:45).

After refuting the accusations leveled against him, Jesus now charges his opponents with an unpardonable sin. Mark 3:28 is the first instance in the Gospel of a saying preceded by "Truly" (Ἀμήν, *Amēn*). (Cf. also 8:12; 9:1, 41; 10:15, 29; 11:23; 12:43; 13:30; 14:9, 18, 25, 30.) In Judaism, the Hebrew אָמֵן (*'āmēn*) was used to conclude a saying, and Jesus's use of it as an introduction is striking. Its presence in a saying lends support to the saying's importance and its authenticity (Jeremias 1971: 35–36; Davies and Allison 1991: 489–80).[9] The presence of this saying in Q (Luke 12:10) and Gos. Thom. 44 lends additional support to its authenticity. The use of the passive ("shall be forgiven") in 3:28 is an example of the divine passive: "God will forgive them" (Stein 1994b: 64). This statement should not be interpreted as promising universal forgiveness of all sins and blasphemies, as 3:29 indicates, but rather as a promise that all sins and blasphemies *can* be forgiven. The expression τοῖς υἱοῖς τῶν ἀνθρώπων (*tois huiois tōn anthrōpōn*; lit. "sons of men") is idiomatic for "humanity" (cf. Matt. 12:31; Pss. 21:10; 115:16). In the Q parallel (Matt. 12:32/Luke 12:10) the saying adds a reference to the forgivable nature of sinning against the "Son of Man." The reference to sinning against "humanity" and the "Son of Man" are both possible translations of the same underlying Aramaic expression בַּר נָשָׁא (*bar nāšā'*), but it may be that two different sayings lie behind the Markan and Q versions (France 2002: 176).

3:28–30

---

8. France (2002: 173–74) rightly points out that "binding Satan" does not refer to an exorcistic methodology but is a metaphor for overpowering Satan.

9. For a refutation of the attempt to see the present saying as the creation of an early Christian prophet, see Aune 1983: 240–42.

The sweeping nature and extent of forgiveness are striking, for the forgiveness of every sin and blasphemy is offered to every human being. All sinful acts (ἁμαρτήματα, *hamartēmata*—found only here in Mark) and all blasphemies (βλασφημίαι, *blasphēmiai*) will be forgiven, that is, are capable of being forgiven. Since "blasphemies" are offenses directed against God, "sins" may refer to evil actions committed against other human beings. This understanding receives support from the twofold perspective on life frequently encountered in Jesus's teachings. Actions are viewed from a vertical (God) and a horizontal (neighbor) dimension; compare 12:30–31; Luke 15:18, 21; 18:2; also Luke 11:42, where this horizontal dimension is referred to by the term "justice."[10] The use of "sin . . . blasphemies that they blaspheme" in this verse forms a chiasmus with "blasphemy . . . sin" in 3:29.

One exception to the universal possibility of forgiveness is mentioned in 3:28, and Jesus's opponents are guilty of this. It involves the blasphemy against the Holy Spirit. This can never be forgiven. This exception does not contradict 3:28. Those who see in 3:28 and 3:29 a contradiction generally do so because either they attribute 3:28 to Jesus and 3:29 to the creation of the early church, or they assume that Jesus could not have said "all but one." Yet "all but one" is a common literary form in the Bible (cf. Gen. 2:16–17; Exod. 12:10; Jer. 7:22–23; Mark 2:17; Phil. 4:6; cf. also *m. Sanh.* 10.1; Kruse 1954: 388–89). In this form the greater the first statement—"all" (3:28), the more forceful the exception—"but" (3:29). As powerful as the statement on universal forgiveness is, the exception in 3:29 receives even greater emphasis. Thus the focus lies not on 3:28 but rather on 3:29. That 3:28–29 involves this kind of a Semitic idiom argues in favor of the authenticity and unity of these two verses. The emphatic position of "never" (lit. "not . . . forever," οὐκ . . . εἰς τὸν αἰῶνα, *ouk . . . eis ton aiōna*) adds further weight to this saying. Although "never" can mean "not for this age," the latter part of this verse (guilty of an eternal sin, αἰωνίου ἁμαρτήματος, *aiōniou hamartēmatos*) and the parallel in Matt. 12:32 ("neither in this age nor the age to come") indicates that it means "never." This particular sin has eternal consequences. Having been accused of blasphemy by the scribes in 2:7 (cf. also 14:64), Jesus now reveals that it is his accusers who are guilty of blasphemy because of their hardness of heart (3:5), because they have attributed God's work in Jesus's ministry to Satan. This is a deliberate refusal on their part to acknowledge the activity of the Spirit in Jesus's ministry. It is ironic that those (the scribes) so adept in defining what sin is and who debated what sins are unforgivable (*m. Sanh.* 10.1) were themselves guilty of the one unpardonable sin. In rejecting what the Spirit was doing in the ministry of Jesus, the scribes were rejecting God.

Over the centuries there has been a great deal of discussion concerning the "unpardonable sin." In the present context it refers to attributing Jesus's exorcisms to the work of Satan, but what is it about this that caused it to be

---

10. Contra Gundry 1993: 175, who interprets "sins and blasphemies" as an example of hendiadys for "sinful slanders."

an unpardonable sin? Perhaps it is because the act of blaspheming the work of the Spirit is to resist his work in the human heart, and without the Spirit's work, repentance and faith are impossible. Traditional Christianity, whether Roman Catholic, Lutheran, Reformed, Arminian, and so on, asserts that only through the work of the Spirit is saving faith possible. Thus to blaspheme the Spirit's work, which seeks to lead a person to faith, is unforgivable in that it makes faith impossible.[11] Mark concludes 3:22–30 with a "for" (ὅτι, *hoti*) explanatory comment that reveals why the scribes were guilty of the unpardonable sin of blasphemy against the Spirit. It serves as Mark's rewording of the scribal accusation found in 3:22 and forms an *inclusio* with it.[12]

If, as seems likely, this section resumes 3:20–21 and completes the Markan sandwich of (A) 3:20–21, (B) 3:22–30, and (A′) 3:31–35, then "those from him" in 3:21 are Jesus's mother and brothers. The lack of any mention of Joseph here and in 6:3 suggests that he died sometime during the silent years, that is, Jesus's unrecorded growing-up years (see 6:2b–3). The references to Jesus's brothers (cf. also 3:32, 33, 34, 35; 6:3; John 2:12; 7:35; Acts 1:14; 1 Cor. 9:5; Gal. 1:19) have been interpreted in three main ways: (1) younger brothers (and sisters) born to Joseph and Mary after Jesus's birth—so Helvidius; (2) sons (and daughters) of Joseph by an earlier marriage, that is, older stepbrothers (and stepsisters)—so Epiphanius; and (3) cousins of Jesus (the term "brothers" [and sisters] being understood more broadly as referring to "relatives")—so Jerome. Although John 19:26–27 lends support to the second and third views, the normal way of interpreting "brothers" is to see this as a reference to subsequent children of Joseph and Mary, that is, the first view (cf. Matt. 1:25). Matthew's wording of this verse in 12:46 argues in favor of the brothers being the sons of Mary and Joseph. If one believes in the perpetual virginity of Mary, a teaching held not only by Roman Catholicism but also by Greek Orthodoxy, Martin Luther, and John Calvin, then the Helvidian view must be rejected. However, in light of the fact that this doctrine is not found in Mark or the rest of the Bible, it appears more likely that the evangelist in 3:31–35 and 6:3 understood the brothers of Jesus as the sons of Joseph and Mary (Stein 1996: 82–84; Meier 1991: 318–32; Marcus 2000: 275–76). For the singular verb in 3:31 followed by a compound subject, see 1:36–37.

The reference to Jesus's family "standing outside" (ἔξω στήκοντες, *exō stēkontes*), which prepares the reader for the distinction of "insiders" and "outsiders" in 4:10–12, indicates that they were not within the house and that this was most likely not their home. Mark gives theological significance to this

3:31–35

---

11. The blasphemy of the Spirit should not be confused with the possibility of the believer "grieving" (Eph. 4:30) or "quenching" (1 Thess. 5:19) the Spirit. On the other hand, the "blasphemy of the Holy Spirit," "the sin unto death" (1 John 5:16–17), and "sins of a high hand" (Num. 15:30–31; Deut. 17:12) may all be different expressions of the deliberate rejection of God and his work that prohibits the possibility of repentance and faith.

12. Cranfield (1959: 143) rightly points out that the objects of Jesus's warning were the "duly accredited theological teachers of God's people," and that consequently theological teachers and leaders of the Christian church should pay particular heed to this warning.

statement. Jesus's family, unlike the crowd "sitting around" Jesus (ἐκάθητο περὶ αὐτόν, *ekathēto peri auton*; 3:32, 34; cf. 4:10), is outside the circle of Jesus's followers. The proximity of this comment to 4:10–11, where those "around him" (cf. 3:32, 34) are contrasted with "those outside" (cf. 3:31, 32), supports the symbolic nature of these words. From other references (John 7:3–5) it seems clear that before the resurrection the brothers of Jesus stood outside the circle of disciples. When placed alongside 3:21, that Jesus's family "sent to him and called him [lit. "calling him"; a complementary participle]" suggests that the attempt of Jesus's family to "seize" him probably reveals not so much a hostility toward Jesus as a genuine concern arising out of their unbelief.

The crowd of 3:32 recalls Jesus's great popularity in 1:33, 37, 45; 2:2, 4, 13; 3:7–9 and will be picked up again in 4:1–2. It is the same "crowd" referred to in 3:20. The lack of the definite article does not necessitate it being a new crowd (cf. 5:24 with 5:21 and 9:25 with 9:14–15, 17). Although the verb "seeking" (ζητοῦσιν, *zētousin*) is often used negatively in Mark (8:11, 12; 11:18; 12:12; 14:1, 11, 55), it can also be used positively (1:37; 16:6), so that there is no need to assume that Mark wanted his readers to interpret this as a hostile act. Luke 8:20 did not understand this verb negatively and added "to speak [to you]." "Look" (ἰδού, *idou*) adds emphasis to what follows (cf. 1:2; 4:3; 10:28, 33; 14:41, 42).

The reference to Jesus's mother and brothers is taken by Jesus as an opportunity to use these terms as metaphors in a question ("Who is my mother and my brothers?") concerning what it means to be part of his spiritual family. "Looking around" (περιβλεψάμενος, *periblepsamenos*) occurs frequently before an action of Jesus (3:5; 5:32; 10:23) and often adds emphasis to what Jesus is about to say or do (11:11; an exception is 9:8). From the perspective of the kingdom of God, true "relatives" are determined not by blood relationships (cf. John 1:13) but by possessing a similar commitment to follow Jesus. Note how the parallel in Matt. 12:49 makes this even clearer by referring to "those seated around him" as "his disciples." In Mark, however, this also includes the crowd sitting around him (cf. 3:32 and 34). Thus through faith one can "lose" one's physical family but receive in its place, even in this lifetime, an eternal family of brothers, sisters, parents, and children (10:29–30).

The passage concludes in 3:35 with the explanatory clause "For whoever does the will of God, this person is my brother,[13] and sister, and mother," which explains 3:34. "Father" is not mentioned since Jesus's followers have only one Father, their Father in heaven (Matt. 6:9; 23:9). It is debated as to whether 3:35 was originally attached to 3:33–34 or was added later, and it is also debated as to whether it is authentic. The authenticity of this saying is supported, however, by its inclusion in Matt. 12:50 and Luke 8:21, as well as the parallels found in John 15:14 and Gos. Thom. 99 (cf. also 2 Clem. 9.11). It also fits the criterion of correlation in that Jesus on several occasions used

13. For the use of "brother" as a fellow member of the Qumran community, cf. 1QS 6.10, 22; CD 6.20; 7.1–2.

the metaphor of family relationships to describe the meaning of discipleship (Mark 10:29–30/Matt. 19:29/Luke 18:29–30; Matt. 10:35/Luke 12:53; Matt. 10:37/Luke 14:26; Matt. 8:21–22/Luke 9:59–60; Luke 11:27–28; cf. also John 19:26–27). The uniqueness of the vocabulary in this verse ("does the will of God" occurs only here in Mark, but cf. 14:36; Matt. 6:10; 7:21; 12:50; 21:31; etc.) argues for it being at least traditional. Mark does not define in this verse what it means to do the will of God (a genitive [or ablative] of source). Apparently he did not think he needed to. To do the will of God has already been described in his Gospel. It means to "repent and believe the gospel" (1:15) and "to follow him" (1:18, 20).

Summary

In the setting of the historical Jesus, 3:22–26 served as an apologetic for Jesus's ministry of exorcisms, but in the present Markan setting it serves a different purpose. For Mark, the original emphasis was less important since his readers were not hostile critics but believers. Thus these verses now serve primarily a christological rather than an apologetic purpose. They reveal that Jesus of Nazareth is not only "stronger" than John the Baptist (1:7) but "stronger" even than the demons and the prince of demons, Satan (3:27)! Thus, in the setting of Mark's Gospel, this controversy story demonstrates the greatness of Jesus Christ, the Son of God, and his inauguration of the kingdom of God.

We cannot deny that in 3:20–35 the family of Jesus is more closely associated with the hostile scribes, who accuse Jesus of being a servant of Satan, than with Jesus's followers. Only the scribes, however, are guilty of the unpardonable sin. From Mark's portrayal of Jesus's family, we should not assume that Mark was engaged in a polemic against them or the theological position they supposedly represented in his day. Within the Bible we frequently find material that portrays its heroes in a bad light (cf. Abraham in Gen. 22:1ff. and David in 2 Sam. 12:1ff.). The biblical writers included such material not to demean these heroes but to teach through their failures what discipleship involves. Mark's purpose here was to instruct his readers in the way of discipleship, not to engage in an ecclesiastical debate with the early church (Best 1975: 317–19). No doubt there were those to whom Mark was writing who struggled with the issue of family ties and discipleship. The present account would demonstrate that just as James and John left their family to follow Jesus (1:20), so Jesus also placed obedience to the will of God above family ties. It is not membership in a particular human family that matters, but belonging to God's family (3:33–35; 10:29–30; cf. Luke 9:57–62; 12:51–53; 14:25–26). As 7:8–13 and 10:19 reveal, this does not involve an antifamily bias but focuses rather on the issue of one's priorities. One must seek first the kingdom of God (cf. Matt. 6:33; Barton 1994: 85–86).

Two other theological emphases are also found in the present account. One involves the foreshadowing of Jesus's death. This is seen in the hostility of the scribes, who, as Mark specifically points out, came from Jerusalem. For Mark's readers, who certainly knew much of the Passion Story, this would remind them of Jesus's crucifixion in Jerusalem (cf. 2:6–7, 16; 3:6; and esp. 10:33–34). Finally, Mark emphasizes the existence of a sin so terrible that it can never be forgiven. Whereas all sins against others and even all blasphemies against God are able to be forgiven, there is a sin that can never be forgiven. This unpardonable sin involves the equating of the Spirit's work in the ministry of Jesus with the work of Satan. This hardening of one's heart, against such a clear manifestation of God's grace and love in liberating the demon possessed from the domination of Satan, cuts one off from the very possibility of faith. It both inhibits and prevents the prevenient grace of the Spirit's working, which is necessary for saving faith. For those in anguish over the thought that they may be guilty of the "unpardonable sin," a word of comfort and reassurance is available. The very concern over this issue is almost a certain indication that a person has not committed this sin. Although not mentioned by Jesus, the repentance and faith he preached (1:15) will always result in forgiveness. The horror of the unpardonable sin is that it prohibits the possibility of such repentance and faith.

Additional Notes

3:20. The article ὁ should probably be read, as in ℵ¹ A B D Δ.

3:21. οἱ παρ᾽ αὐτοῦ, lit. "those from him." A few MSS (D W it) have "the scribes and others around him," but both external evidence (the MS tradition) and internal evidence (the difficulty of the attempted actions of Jesus's family and their thinking toward Jesus) assure the correctness of the reading οἱ παρ᾽ αὐτοῦ.

3:32. A D Γ it add καὶ αἱ ἀδελφαί σου, but this is not found in ℵ B C W Θ f¹ f¹³ vg and most witnesses. Cf., however, Marcus 2000: 276–77, who favors its inclusion in the Greek text.

3:33. ἀποκριθεὶς ... λέγει; lit. "answering ... he says." Cf. 6:37; 8:29; 9:5, 19; etc.

D. Jesus Teaches in Parables (4:1–34)

In this section Mark seeks to explain for his readers why the message and ministry of Jesus encountered the opposition described in the previous chapters. Why did Jesus experience opposition from the scribes when he healed the paralytic (2:6–8)? Why did they oppose his welcoming toll collectors and sinners into the kingdom of God (2:16) and complain about his disciples not fasting (2:18)? Why did the Pharisees criticize him for his disciples' actions on the Sabbath (2:23–24) and for his healing on the Sabbath (3:2)? Why did the scribes absurdly explain his exorcisms as due to his being empowered by Satan (3:22)? Why did his own family think that he had lost his mind (3:21)? And why did the Pharisees and Herodians seek to kill him (3:6)? In this section, Mark explains that "those outside" the believing community, while hearing the word and seeing the works of the kingdom, cannot understand what is taking place (4:12). God, however, has given to Mark's readers, as he did to the disciples and other followers of Jesus, the understanding and conviction that the kingdom of God had indeed come in the ministry of Jesus and that the works and deeds of Jesus were evidence of this (4:11, 34). Consequently, having been given ears to hear, they should heed (4:3, 9, 23, 24–25) and make sure that they are good soil, bearing fruit for the kingdom (4:8, 20).

This is the first of two main collections of Jesus's teaching in Mark (cf. 13:3–37) and consists of a carefully constructed complex of parables. It has an introduction (4:1–2) and a conclusion (4:33–34) and is set by the sea (4:1 and 35). It contains a lengthy parable concerning a sower, seed, and soils (4:3–9), which is given an interpretation (4:13–20). Dividing them is a saying dealing with why Jesus taught in parables (4:10–12). Following the interpretation of the parable of the sower, seed, and soils, we have two sets of parables involving the importance of hearing—that is, heeding (4:23; cf. 4:9)—the message of Jesus in light of the coming judgment (4:21–22, 24–25). Thereupon we find two more parables that also involve the growth of seed: the parable of the growing seed (4:26–29) and the parable of the mustard seed (4:30–32).[1]

The question of whether Mark 4:3–32 existed as a pre-Markan collection is much debated (Kuhn 1971: 99–146). The extent of that collection is also debated. Some suggest that only the seed parables (4:3–9, 13–20, and 26–32)

---

1. Several scholars claim to find in 4:1–34 an elaborate literary structure of "concentricity." For example, Fay (1989) sees a sevenfold chiastic structure: A (4:1–2a); B (4:2b–9); C (4:10–13); D (4:14–20); C′ (4:21–25); B′ (4:26–32); A′ (4:33–34). Such structures, however, tend to betray the genius of their authors far more than the mind of Mark.

existed together before Mark (Guelich 1989: 189). In light of the introductory Markan seam (4:1–2) and especially the Markan conclusion (4:33–34), Mark seems to be the compiler of this collection of parables. That 4:3–9 and 4:13–20 form a Markan sandwich together with 4:10–12 (J. Edwards 1989: 213–15) also argues for the present collection being primarily the work of the evangelist. Ultimately, however, whether all or some of the parables in 4:2–32 were associated together before Mark is impossible to say. Someone brought the various seed parables together, but it is uncertain whether this was the work of Mark or of someone before Mark.

Although the setting of this collection of parables involves Jesus's teaching the crowds by the sea, there appears to be a change of scene in 4:10–12, where Jesus speaks privately with his disciples. This seems at first glance to conflict with the general setting found in 4:1, where Jesus is teaching a large crowd by the sea. This scene is concluded in 4:35, when Jesus leaves the crowd and crosses the sea with his disciples in a boat. Probably Mark intended his readers to see 4:1–34 not as a chronological event in the life of Jesus but rather as a logical collection of Jesus's teachings introduced by an incident in Jesus's life in which he taught by the sea in a boat. This is suggested by the concluding summary that Mark added to the collection in 4:33–34: "By means of many such parables he [Jesus] was speaking the word to them. . . ."

Something like the following scenario seems likely. The parable of the sower was associated in the tradition with an event in which Jesus taught by the sea in a boat. To this piece of tradition, Mark then added other parables (4:21–32). Before Mark, the interpretation associated with the parable that is addressed to the disciples (4:13–20) and Jesus's explanation to them of why he taught in parables (4:10–12) were placed after the parable, even though they were said at another time. The interpretation logically followed the parable already in the pre-Markan setting. (In the pre-Markan tradition, a change of scene from 4:1 to the privacy of 4:10–20 was not a problem, for in the tradition the parable and its interpretation were not followed by 4:21–34.) As to the issue of whether 4:10–12 and 13–20 are ultimately authentic, this does not affect the understanding of the present arrangement in Mark. Mark 4:10–12 and 13–20 were, however, almost certainly not de novo Markan creations but were part of the tradition he inherited.[2]

There is a great deal of discussion concerning whether the sayings in 4:3–32 are parables, allegories, similitudes, aphorisms, and so on. However we may choose to label the various sayings in this chapter, Mark has defined them as "parables" (παραβολαί, parabolai) in 4:2, 10, and 33. That Mark understood all the sayings in 4:3–32 as "parables" is emphasized by the inclusio found in 4:2 ("And he was teaching them many things in parables . . .") and 33 ("And by means of many such parables he was speaking to them . . ."). Therefore, rather

2. Jeremias (1963: 14n11) argues that the early church added 4:10, 13–20, and 33 to an original parable source (4:3–9, 26–29, 30–32), and then Mark added 4:1–2, 11–12, 21–23, 24–25, and 34.

than referring to the various sayings found in this collection by more technical definitions that serve as subdivisions of the more inclusive term "parable," I shall use the term Mark attributes to them—"parables." I shall do so, however, recognizing that "parable" is a broad term covering various subclassifications, all of which involve some sort of a comparison. (See 3:22–23.)

1. Jesus's Parable of the Sower, Seed, and Soils (4:1–9)

Although Mark emphasizes the teaching ministry of Jesus (see 1:21–22), Mark 4:1–34 is only one of two lists of Jesus's teachings found in his Gospel. (The other is 13:3–37.) In introducing these parables, Mark refers to the crowds of people that followed Jesus (cf. 4:1 with 1:33, 45; 2:2, 13; 3:7–9, 20). The setting by the sea (4:1) picks up 3:7–12; Jesus's teaching in a boat (4:1) is prepared for by 3:9; and his teaching in parables has been alluded to in 3:23. From this we see that Mark has carefully prepared his readers for the setting of this chapter and its content. According to Mark, the present parable provides the pattern for interpreting all of Jesus's parables. This is evident from 4:13, which begins the parable's interpretation, "Do you not understand this parable? Then [lit. 'and'] how will you understand all [of the other] parables?" That the interpretation of this parable (4:14–20) is allegorical in nature is one of the reasons why the allegorical method of interpreting the parables has been so influential in the history of the church. Another reason for its popularity is that this was a common method of interpretation in Judaism, especially among the Jews of Alexandria, such as Philo. (Cf. also the allegorical interpretation of Clement of Alexandria and his successor, Origen.) Such a method was also popular among the Greeks in their attempt to make sense out of the behavior of their deities, which left much to be desired. (The question of the authenticity of the parable's interpretation will be discussed in the introduction to 4:13–20.) This parable and its interpretation function as a sandwich (4:3–9 and 13–20), between which is inserted the reason why Jesus taught in parables (4:10–12; J. Edwards 1989: 213–15).

Mark's own editorial work in 4:1–9 is seen clearly in the opening seam. Although the scene (by the sea, παρὰ τὴν θάλασσαν, *para tēn thalassan*) is probably traditional, the wording of 4:1 is clearly Markan. This is evident from the verse's literary ties with what has preceded: "again" (πάλιν, *palin*), "very large crowd" (ὄχλος πλεῖστος, *ochlos pleistos*), "boat" (πλοῖον, *ploion*), "teaching" (διδάσκειν, ἐδίδασκεν, *didaskein, edidasken*). The redundancy of the emphasis in Jesus's teaching found in 4:2 is also clearly Markan (cf. 1:21–22; Pryke 1978: 13, 141, 156; Guelich 1989: 189; Marcus 2000: 293). Whether the saying in 4:9 (Whoever has ears to hear, let him hear, ὃς ἔχει ὦτα ἀκούειν ἀκουέτω, *hos echei ōta akouein akouetō*), which is traditional, was placed at the end of the parable by Mark is, however, less certain. Within 4:3–9 the presence of Markan redaction is much more difficult to detect. The present passage can be divided into the introductory seam and setting

(4:1–2), an exhortation to pay attention to what is about to be said in the following parable (4:3), a description of the four kinds of soils (4:4–8), and a concluding exhortation forming an *inclusio* with 4:3 (4:9). As for the parable's authenticity, this is generally acknowledged (Hultgren 2000: 189).

Exegesis and Exposition

[1]And again he began to teach by the sea. And a very large crowd gathers around him, so that, having entered into a boat, he sat in the sea, and the whole crowd was by the sea on the land. [2]And he was teaching them many things in parables, and he was saying to them in his teaching, [3]"Listen. Behold, a sower went out to sow. [4]And it happened while he was sowing, part [of the seed] fell by the path, and the birds came and ate it up. [5]And part [of the seed] fell on the rocky ground, where it had little soil, and immediately it sprang up because it had no depth of soil; [6]and when the sun rose, it was scorched, and because it had no root, it withered away. [7]And part [of the seed] fell among the thorns, and the thorns grew up and choked it, and it produced no grain. [8]And other [parts of the seed] fell upon the good soil and was producing grain, ⌜rising up⌝ and growing, and it yielded thirty- and sixty- and one hundredfold." [9]And he was saying, "Whoever has ears to hear, let him hear."

By this introduction, Mark ties 4:1–34 with 3:7–9 and picks up the geographical scene of Jesus's teaching by the sea (3:7–9; cf. 2:13). (See introduction to 3:13–19 and 3:20–35.) We should not seek theological significance in Jesus's teaching by the sea, such as his having control over the powers of chaos represented by the sea (see 3:7–8). This was simply part of the tradition (3:7–12; 4:35–5:43; 6:32–56) and was the result of Jesus using Capernaum for his base of operations (cf. Matt. 4:13). For "again" (πάλιν), see 2:1. Here it refers back to Jesus being by the sea in 2:13 and 3:7–9. For "began to teach" (ἤρξατο διδάσκειν, *ērxato didaskein*), see 1:45. For the reference to the "crowd" (ὄχλος), see 2:13; 3:9, 20; compare also "the whole city" (1:33), "many" (2:2), "great multitude" (3:7–8; 5:21), "great crowd" (5:21; 6:34; 8:1; 9:14; 12:37). The use of the superlative "very large" (πλεῖστος) along with "whole" (πᾶς, *pas*) to describe the crowd emphasizes Jesus's great popularity. At this time the crowds following Jesus reach a crescendo that culminates in Jesus having to enter a boat (3:9). Unlike 4:36 and 6:45–46, here the boat serves not as a means to escape the crowd but rather as a pulpit from which to teach them. For "sat" (καθῆσθαι, *kathēsthai*), see 13:3.

"So that" (ὥστε, *hōste*) indicates that Jesus's entering the boat was the result of the large crowd gathering around him. Jesus's popularity was so great that he needed to embark in a boat (prepared for in 3:7–9) that served as a platform from which he could teach the crowd. For sitting as the normal teaching position, compare Matt. 5:1; 15:29; Mark 9:35; 13:3; Luke 4:20; also Mark 3:32, 34. The strange statement of Jesus sitting "in the sea" (ἐν τῇ θαλάσσῃ, *en tē thalassē*—omitted by Matthew and Luke) rather than in the

4:1–2

boat may be due to its paralleling the crowd being "by the sea on the land" (πρὸς τὴν θάλασσαν ἐπὶ τῆς γῆς, *pros tēn thalassan epi tēs gēs*). Although "land/ground" (γῆς) is the same term that is used in 4:8 to describe the good "soil," we should not see allegorical significance in this (contra Heil 1992: 275), because the same term is also used twice in 4:5 to describe the rocky "soil." The plural "were" (ἦσαν, *ēsan*) agrees with the sense of "crowd" rather than its number, which is singular.

"Began to teach" in 4:1 and the additional references in 4:2 to Jesus's teaching ("was teaching," ἐδίδασκεν; and "in his teaching," ἐν τῇ διδαχῇ αὐτοῦ, *en tē didachē autou*) recall 1:21–22, where we have a similar threefold reference to Jesus teaching (also involving two verbal forms and one noun). The reference to Jesus's teaching in "parable*s*" (παραβολαῖς) serves as an introduction not just to the present parable but also to the whole complex of 4:3–32. In 12:1, the plural "parable*s*" is used again even though only one parable follows. The prepositional phrase "in [ἐν, *en*] parables" is an instrumental of means. This indicates that Jesus was not teaching "parables." Contrary to recent discussion in which parables are seen as aesthetic objects possessing a vitality and power in and of themselves and thus capable of producing a "language event," Mark understood parables as a literary form that Jesus used for conveying his teaching (4:1–2); they were not an end in themselves but the means of his conveying "the word" (τὸν λόγον, *ton logon*; 4:14, 33). It is the message contained in the parabolic form that is the "word of God," not the literary form itself (Stein 2000: 34–38). Thus the proper question to ask when interpreting this (and the other parables) is, What were Jesus and Mark seeking to teach by means of this parable? See also 3:23 for another use of "in parables" as an instrumental of means. In light of 3:23, we should not translate this phrase as "in riddles" (France 2002: 188).

It is best to understand the "many things" (πολλά, *polla*) that Jesus taught as an accusative plural, as in 1:45 (Cranfield 1959: 149), rather than an adverbial accusative "much," because the content of "many things" is described in 4:3–32 (see 1:45). This reveals that although 1:15 is an extremely important summary of Jesus's teaching, there was a great deal more that Jesus taught. This comment would help explain to Mark's readers the origin of the various Jesus traditions that they had received, for it was Jesus's custom to teach (10:1). The redundancy of "and he was saying to them in his teaching" argues for its being Markan. Even though Mark contains considerably fewer teachings of Jesus than Matthew or Luke, he emphasizes Jesus's role as a teacher in his editorial work more than either Matthew or Luke (Stein 1970: 76n23). "His" in "in his teaching" is best understood as a subjective genitive (cf. 1:21), that is, "in his teaching ministry."

4:3   "Listen. Behold" (Ἀκούετε. ἰδού, *Akouete. idou*) is a rather awkward use of these two introductory imperatives. The command "Listen" (Ἀκούετε) is also found in Mark 4:9, 23; 7:14, 16(?); 9:7; 12:29; and the command "behold" (ἰδού) in 1:2; 3:32; 10:28, 33; 14:41, 42. They never appear together elsewhere in Mark, nor do they introduce a parable elsewhere either in Mark or in the other Gospels. Placed next to each other, they doubly emphasize the importance of continually heeding ("Listen" is a present imperative) the parable that follows. Whether the redundant emphasis is deemed necessary because of the greater attention and effort required to understand a parable (cf. Judg. 9:7; Isa. 28:23; Ezek. 20:47 [21:3 LXX]) or because of the importance of obeying the content of the parable depends on how one interprets the meaning of this parable (see the summary at the end of this unit). There is no reason to tie the injunction to "listen" with the Shema (Deut. 6:4), which begins, "Hear, O Israel . . ." (Guelich 1989: 192; contra Gerhardsson 1967: 167–72, 191–92; Hooker 1991: 122, 125). The addition of "Behold" makes such a tie quite improbable. Along with the exhortation in 4:9, these two imperatives form an *inclusio*.

The verb "went out" (ἐξῆλθεν, *exēlthen*) is also found in 1:35, 38; 2:13, where it describes an action of Jesus. Some therefore equate the sower with Jesus (Marcus 1986b: 37–39). The same verb, however, is also used of an unclean spirit (1:26), a report (1:28), a paralytic (2:12), and Peter (14:68); and the plural (ἐξῆλθον, *exēlthon*) is used of Jesus's family (3:21), the Pharisees (8:11), and the disciples (14:16). This very common verb would naturally come to mind when one wanted to refer to anyone or anything "going out." Therefore, although Jesus can be included in whom the sower represents, the present tense of the verb in 4:14 (sows, σπείρει, *speirei*) indicates that Mark wanted his readers to identify the sower with any and all who preach "the word." Of the three major elements in the parable (sower, seed, soils), the sower plays the least significant role. He is mentioned only here in the parable and only once in the interpretation (4:14), whereas the seed and the soils are referred to continually in 4:4–8 and 4:15–20. Thus we should name this parable not "the parable of the sower" (cf. Matt. 13:18) but either "the parable of the seed" or "the parable of the soils."

In the sowing of the first seed group, part of the seed is described as falling **4:4–8** "by the path" (παρὰ τὴν ὁδόν, *para tēn hodon*). The expression "part" (ὃ μέν, *ho men*) can be translated "a certain part of the seed" or "a seed." In support of the latter is the use of "others" (ἄλλα, *alla*) in 4:8 (cf. also 1 Clem. 24.5; Inf. Gos. Thom. 12.1). However, in favor of the former, one should note: (1) Matthew uses the plural "seeds" (cf. ἅ, *ha*) in 13:4ff. throughout the parable, and this is probably less a correction of Mark than a clarification. Luke also apparently understood ὃ μέν as part of the collective "seed" that was sown. (2) It is difficult to conceive of a sower sowing a total of six seeds (4:4, 5, 6, and 7 [3×]), and if the sower sowed more than six seeds, where did the other seeds fall? (3) It is also difficult to see how the birds (τὰ πετεινά, *ta peteina*; note the plural) could together devour a single seed (4:4b). (4) The interpretation in 4:13–20 understands ὃ μέν and "part [of the seed]" (ἄλλο, *allo*; 4:5, 7) as involving more than a single seed (cf. 4:15, 16, 17). Thus we should translate ὃ μέν as "a certain part of the seed," "some seed" (RSV,

NRSV, NAB; cf. REB), or "some" (NIV; cf. REB; contra Guelich 1989: 192–93; France 2002: 190–91).

Παρά (*para*) can mean "by" the path (cf. 4:1—"by [παρά] the sea," not "on the sea") or "on." Luke 8:5 understood it as "on" the path, for the seed is trampled underfoot by those walking on the path before the birds devour it. The picture is of a path leading through or alongside a field (cf. 2:23) upon which some seed has inadvertently been sown. Since such a path would not have a shoulder or gutter, seed sown "by" the path would not refer to seed sown in the good soil by the path but seed either in the middle of the path ("on") or on the edge of the path near the good soil ("by"). The use of παρά instead of ἐπί (*epi*, on) to describe the location of the seed favors the latter, and this is further supported by the fact that παρά with the accusative always means "by" in Mark (cf. 1:16; 2:13; 4:1; 5:21; 10:46).

It is uncertain whether the description of the birds coming and devouring this first seed group assumes the practice of sowing before plowing. If it does, the seed was intentionally sown on the path, because the path would soon be plowed up.[1] If not, the seed was sown by accident on a permanent path. In the former situation, the seed is eaten before the field is plowed; in the latter, the seed is wasted by being thrown on a permanent path, where it had no chance of growing. Regardless, birds come and devour the seed. In this verse we encounter a threefold verbal description of what happens to the seed that is repeated throughout the parable: fell–came–devoured (4:4); fell–sprang up–was scorched (4:5–6); fell–grew up–choked (4:7); fell–gave–bore (4:8; Weeden 1979: 100–101). This triadic structure is not perfect, but this basic structure also occurs later, in 4:8, in the threefold yield of thirty-, sixty-, and a hundredfold.

The second seed group described in 4:5–6 "fell upon rocky [πετρῶδες, *petrōdes*] ground." This is further described by "where it had little soil." This describes ground where only a thin layer of soil covers the substratum of rock underneath. Whether this is accidental (a mistake—he knows it is rocky ground but errantly throws some of the seed on it) or intentional (the sower is unaware of the shallow depth of soil—he thinks that it is good soil and wants to throw seed on it) is not said. Because this soil lacks depth, the seed quickly breaks through the soil, whereas seed planted more deeply in good soil will take longer to emerge (contra France 2002: 191). Furthermore, its growth is concentrated upward in outer growth rather than downward in establishing a system of deep roots, as in the case of the seed planted in good soil. As a result, it emerges and grows prematurely fast. Because of the shallowness of this soil, there is no deep subsoil moisture that the seed can reach to survive the rising of the sun and the scorching heat. Thus it "withered away" (ἐξηράνθη, *exēranthē*). In abbreviating his account of the parable, Luke simply says that

---

1. So Jeremias 1972: 11–12. Support for this is found in *m. Šabb.* 7.2; *b. Šabb.* 73b; *t. Neg.* 6.2; and Jub. 11.11, 23–24. See, however, Payne 1978; and cf. Isa. 28:24 and Jer. 4:3, where plowing precedes sowing.

the seed withered away because it had no moisture (8:6). In so doing, Luke gives the immediate cause of the seed's withering (the lack of moisture), whereas Mark gives the ultimate cause (the shallowness of its root system).

Some scholars, seeking to maintain a perfect verbal triad (fell–sprang up–was scorched), have suggested that "immediately it sprang up because it had no depth of soil" in 4:5b and "because [διὰ τό, *dia to*] it had no root, it withered away" in 4:6b are secondary additions to the parable (Crossan 1973c: 245–46; Guelich 1989: 194).[2] In support of this, they argue that these two clauses portray the problem of apostasy that the early church encountered and that the redundancy found in this verse is typical of Mark's love for duality. Yet, in his own ministry, Jesus encountered the danger of halfhearted commitment and falling away. (Note the presence of Judas among the disciples; cf. also John 6:66–71.) We cannot attribute all such sayings as 8:34–38; 9:29–30; Luke 9:57–62; 14:26–33; and John 6:66–67 to the situation of the later church. It would be incredible to think that none of those who followed Jesus "fell away" during his ministry. In both these clauses, we find διὰ τό, "because," used with the infinitive ἔχειν, "have," and these are the only two times we find this construction in all of Mark. It is difficult, therefore, to argue that they are Markan interpretive comments inserted into the text. We cannot prove or disprove the authenticity or the traditional nature of these clauses, but we should be cautious about making such decisions based on the presupposition that the more perfectly a saying fits neat form-critical classifications or forms, the more likely it is to be authentic. For the expression sowing "among thorns [ἀκάνθαις, *akanthais*]," compare Jer. 4:3.

It is possible that Mark intends us to see a progression in the various soils in that the seed is lost successively at later stages of growth (Carlston 1975: 144; Marcus 1986b: 22). The first seed group is lost before germinating in the first soil, and the second and third seed groups are lost progressively later in the second and third soils. The fourth seed group survives well in the fourth soil until the harvest (France 2002: 191). Whereas the seed is lost after germinating in the second soil, in the third soil the seed germinates and grows but due to the weeds does not bear fruit (cf. Jer. 4:3). Thus, although the parable does not emphasize the length of each seed's survival, we find the following progression: the first seed never germinates; the second seed germinates and dies shortly afterward; the third seed germinates, but at harvesttime it does not bear fruit; the fourth seed germinates, grows, and bears much fruit at harvesttime. The description of the thorns "growing up" (ἀνέβησαν, *anebēsan*) suggests that this portion of the seed was not intentionally thrown into a patch of thorns (contra Jeremias 1972: 12) but rather on ground containing thorn seeds, which, upon germinating, choked out the seed, so that it bore no fruit. The expression "produced no grain" (καρπὸν οὐκ ἔδωκεν, *karpon ouk edōken*) describes the

2. For other examples of groups of three in Jesus's parables, cf. Luke 10:31–34 (priest-Levite-Samaritan); 14:18–20 (three excuses); 19:16–21/Matt. 25:16–18 (three servants); Matt. 24:34–37 (three requests for payment).

third soil. It is not a summary description of the first three soils, as the singular "bore" (ἔδωκεν) indicates (contra Crossan 1973c: 246).

With respect to the last soil described in 4:8, the plural "other parts" (ἄλλα) of the seed corresponds to the threefold yields of thirty-, sixty-, and a hundredfold. There is a clear contrast here between the lack of yields in 4:4–7 from the three "bad" soils. We should probably not see in this, however, a carefully balanced comparison of three bad soils versus three good soils. This verse speaks of "the good soil" (τὴν γῆν τὴν καλήν, tēn gēn tēn kalēn), not the good "soils." Thus our parable talks about the four (not six) soils.[3] The overall use of triads in 4:3–8 may indicate that this threefold yield is due more to a literary style in telling stories than to a conscious attempt to contrast the three bad soils with the threefold yield of the good soil. Luke apparently thought that this was simply a matter of literary style in that he refers only to the good soil bearing fruit a hundredfold. Since no mention is made in the interpretation to the fourth seed's "rising up and increasing," we should see the Markan emphasis in the final harvest (or lack of harvest in the case of the first three soils), not on the growth of the seed in the fourth soil.

The seed falling in the good soil is described as "producing grain." The subject of "was producing" (ἐδίδου, edidou) is the seed (ἄλλα—neuter plural), not the soil, as "rising up and growing" (ἀναβαίνοντα, anabainonta, and αὐξανόμενα, auxanomena—neuter plurals) indicate. The present/imperfect tenses used to describe the continuing growth of the seed sown on the good soil should be noted (V. Taylor 1952: 253–54; France 2002: 192). The yields of the good soil are not so extraordinary that they must be interpreted eschatologically as implying the final harvest at the end of the age (Payne 1980a: 181–86; contra Jeremias 1963: 150). They are not like the enormous yields described in the eschatological contexts of 1 En. 10.19 (a thousandfold) or 2 Bar. 29.5 (ten thousandfold; cf. b. Ker. 111b–12a; Irenaeus, Haer. 5.33.4). They correspond rather to good or excellent yields described in Gen. 26:12 (a hundredfold; cf. Sib. Or. 3.263; Pliny, Nat. Hist. 18.21.95; Varro, On Agriculture 1.44.2; Guelich 1989: 195; cf., however, McIver 1994). When compared to the gigantic yields attributed to the eschatological consummation, the yields described in 4:8 seem somewhat paltry and meager if they are intended to describe the eschatological consummation. We should also remember that yields of thirty, sixty, and one hundred are for the seed sown on good soil, or one-fourth of the total seed that was sown. Thus the yield for all the seed sown is seven and a half, fifteen, and twenty-five.

4:9 The conclusion of the parable contains the exhortation "Whoever has ears to hear, let him hear," which serves along with "Listen. Behold" in 4:3 as an *inclusio* to 4:3–9. The twofold use of "hear" (ἀκούειν ἀκουέτω, akouein akouetō) is a pun in which the second "hear" refers not to physical hearing but to "heeding" (Stein 1994b: 14). The present command can be understood

---

3. Contra Marcus 1986b: 21–23, who argues for a binary structure of three bad soils (4:4, 5–6, and 7) and three good soils (4:8). Cf. France 2002: 192.

as a summons to a specific group who in contrast to others possesses the ability to hear ("those among you to whom has been given ears to hear," i.e., the disciples; Guelich 1989: 196; Marcus 2000: 297), or it can be understood as a summons to all who are listening ("those of you present within the hearing of these words," i.e., the very large crowd). This expression is always used to conclude a saying and therefore should be interpreted in light of what has preceded (4:1–8) rather than what follows (4:10–12; contra Marcus 1986b: 57–59), as 4:23; Matt. 11:15; 13:43; Luke 14:35; Rev. 2:7, 11, 17, 29; 3:6, 13, 22; 13:9 indicate. It serves to emphasize what has just been said (Derrett 2001). Generally this saying is addressed to the crowds: Matt. 11:15 (cf. 11:7 ["crowds"]); Mark 4:23 (cf. 4:33–34, where the "them" to whom this is said is contrasted with the disciples); Luke 14:35 (cf. 14:25 ["great crowds"] and 14:33, which is a general invitation to discipleship). The one exception is Matt. 13:43 (cf. 13:36). In the parallels in Matt. 13:9 and Luke 8:8, this saying also concludes the parable that is addressed to the crowds (Matt. 13:2; Luke 8:4). The saying can be used as a summons to understand some teaching Jesus was giving (Matt. 11:15) or as an exhortation to act on what Jesus has just said (Mark 4:23; Luke 14:35; perhaps Matt. 13:43). In the context of Mark 4:1–2 and the summons to "hear" in 4:3, this serves as a general exhortation to all the hearers of the parable, that is, the crowd, and not just the disciples (contra Guelich 1989: 197). Knowledge of this intended audience indicates that the focus of the parable lies with the four soils, not the seed.

Summary

Within this parable we have three different elements, each of which is seen by some as being the focus of attention: the sower, the seed, and the soils. The lack of attention given in the parable to the first of these indicates that the sower is not the focus of attention (see 4:3). By the context he gives to the parable, Mark provides a key as to how he wants his readers to interpret it. The parable involves the kingdom of God (4:11). Two possible lines of interpretation present themselves (Hultgren 2000: 188). In one the focus is on the seed, which represents the proclamation and coming of the kingdom of God. In the parable the first three soils explain why the scribes (2:6, 16; 3:22), Pharisees (2:16, 24; 3:6), and even Jesus's own family (3:21, 31–35) did not respond in faith to the proclamation of the word of the kingdom but at times vigorously opposed it. But the seed was also sown in good soil and received a positive response (1:16–20, 28, 32–34, 37–39, 45; 2:2–4, 13, 15; 3:7–12, 20; 4:1). According to this interpretation, the mystery of the kingdom (4:11) is that the kingdom of God has indeed come, and despite various setbacks, the seed will be victorious (Carlston 1975: 139–49; Hultgren 2000: 191; Marcus 2000: 295; Donahue and Harrington 2002: 144). Thus Mark's readers should understand that despite the poor response the proclamation of the kingdom of God was receiving among various soils, it is victorious nonetheless, for it is also finding good soil and bearing fruit. According to this view, the parable explains what has happened to the proclamation of the word of the kingdom in 1:1–4:2, in the rest of Mark, and in the life of the early church. As a result, Mark's readers should be encouraged to continue proclaiming the good news, since they know that there is good soil out there (Hultgren 2000: 191). This interpretation finds support in the "end stress" of the parable in 4:8. On the other hand, it needs to be pointed out that three portions of the seed out of four die and that success or failure is due not to the seed but to the soil!

A somewhat related view interprets the parable along the lines of the parables of growth (cf. Mark 4:26–29, 30–32) and understands the yields of thirty-, sixty-, and a hundredfold as being so great that they must refer to the eschatological consummation. (See 4:4–8.) According to this view, the kingdom of God has now come, but at the present time it is not recognized. From its present and apparently hopeless beginning, however, there will ultimately come a triumphant ending.[4] Yet, such an interpretation overlooks that in the parable there is no temporal contrast in what is occurring with the different soils. There is no temporal contrast between a small beginning and a large end. Nothing is said about the time of the harvest or the act of harvesting. On the contrary, all this occurs simultaneously. Thus the contrast is not between now and then, but between what is occurring now in both the bad soil and the good soil.

Another possible interpretation focuses attention on the reception of the seed by the four different soils. The ground is the primary factor (Gerhardsson 1967: 187). According to this view, the parable is an exhortation to Mark's readers to pay attention to the kind of soil they should be. The twofold exhortation found in 4:3 and 9 supports such an understanding, as does the parable's interpretation in 4:13–20. The careful descriptions of the soils and the explanations of why the first three soils did not bear fruit focus attention on the soils rather than on the seed (cf. 4:15, 17, 19). For Mark, the present meaning of the parable, whatever its original meaning may have been, focuses on the soils and on their response to the word of the kingdom. In this interpretation, the parable also serves to explain to Mark's readers why Jesus Christ, the Son of God, was rejected by some people and accepted by others. (For a discussion concerning the authenticity of 4:13–20, see the introduction to 4:13–20.) To Mark's readers, therefore, this parable would function in much the same manner as their reading of the summary of Jesus's preaching found in 1:15. To the unbelieving who may have been in attendance, it would call them to decide to become good soil, that is, "to repent and believe in the gospel"; to the majority of Mark's readers, it would serve as an exhortation to recommit themselves to their earlier decision and

---

4. So Jeremias 1972: 150, who nevertheless acknowledges that the interpretation of the parable in 4:13–20 focuses on the soils, with the resultant exhortation to the readers to make sure that they remain faithful and are good soil.

make sure that they are good soil. Such exhortations will be found later in the Gospel as well (8:34–38; 9:33–50; 10:35–45; etc.).

Along with the exhortation for self-examination, two other common Markan emphases are found in the parable. One is the great popularity of Jesus as expressed by the very large crowd that gathers around him and his need to teach from a boat (4:1). The other is the threefold emphasis in 4:1–2 on Jesus as a teacher. This recalls the similar threefold emphasis on Jesus as a teacher in 1:21–22.

Additional Note

4:8. The plural αὐξανόμενα (ℵ B) refers to "others" (ἄλλα) and is to be preferred over the more strongly attested singular αὐξανόμενον (A D L W Δ), which modifies "grain" (καρπόν). See Metzger 1994: 71.

2. Jesus's Purpose for Teaching in Parables (4:10–12)

Probably more has been written on these three verses in Mark than any other comparable passage in the Gospel. The difficulties associated with them are legion. One major problem involves how they fit into the surrounding context. In the opening verse (4:10), after teaching the crowds from a boat (4:1–2), Jesus is now alone with those around him (cf. 3:32) and the disciples, but in 4:36 (cf. also 4:33–34, where "them" refers to the crowd and is distinguished from the disciples) Jesus has apparently been teaching the crowds from the boat all along. Next Jesus is asked about the parable*s* (4:10; cf. 4:2, 33), even though he has taught only one parable (4:3–8). Jesus then tells his followers (those around him along with the Twelve, οἱ περὶ αὐτὸν σὺν τοῖς δώδεκα, *hoi peri auton syn tois dōdeka*) that they alone have been given the secret of the kingdom of God whereas those outside hear everything in parables. This at first glance seems to conflict with the fact that the disciples at times do not understand (4:13; 6:51–52; 7:17–23; 8:10–21; 9:30–32) and need explanations (4:13–20), that at times those outside understand Jesus's teaching very well (12:1–12, esp. v. 12), and that sometimes the crowds are also given explanations (see 4:11). Finally, it appears that Jesus taught in parables intentionally to keep those outside from understanding what he was saying, in order that they would not be able to repent and receive forgiveness (4:12). How does one reconcile this with such statements as John 3:16; 1 Tim. 2:4; and 2 Pet. 3:9?

Concerning the change of scene in 4:10–12, I earlier suggested that this is a problem only if Mark intended 4:1–34 to be understood as a precise, chronological sequence of events in Jesus's life. In 4:33–34, however, Mark tells his readers that 4:2–32 is a summary collection of Jesus's parables, so that the interpretation of the parable that follows in 4:13–20 is best understood as having occurred at a different time and place (alone with the disciples and those around him in a house, because the boat of 4:1 would be too small) but inserted at this point in the Gospel for logical reasons. After all, where would be a better location for the interpretation of the parable of the soils than after the parable? (See 4:1–34.)

Concerning the disciples' lack of understanding in 4:13 and elsewhere, this fits both their privileged position of being given the understanding of the mystery of the kingdom of God (4:10–12) and having that understanding mediated through Jesus's explanations to them (4:34; cf. 8:17–21). Indeed, 4:34 affirms both that Jesus's followers at times lacked understanding and that Jesus supplied this to them through private instruction (cf. 7:17–23;

10:10–12; 13:3ff.). As we shall see, what was given to Jesus's followers was not simply a cognitive perception of the content of his teaching but the inner conviction of its truthfulness as well. This God-given conviction was not possessed by "those outside." It is not attained or deciphered but "given" (J. Edwards 2002: 131; France 2002: 196).

Another major area of debate involves the question of the authenticity of these verses. Although some scholars argue that all of 4:10–12 came from the hand of Mark, most understand 4:11–12 as being traditional (Beavis 1989: 85; Marcus 2000: 301; contra Pryke 1978: 13, 141, 156; Schmithals 1979: 1.239). In favor of their pre-Markan origin are the unique vocabulary found in them,[1] the divine passives,[2] the antithetical parallelism (to you . . . to those outside, ὑμῖν . . . τοῖς ἔξω, *hymin . . . tois exō*), and the targumic nature of the OT quotation in 4:12 (see 4:12). The agreement of Matt. 13:11/ Luke 8:10 against Mark in adding "to know" (γνῶναι, *gnōnai*) and making "mystery" plural (μυστήρια, *mystēria*) also suggests that they had access to a different form of the tradition found in these verses. If, as most think, the interpretation of the parable is pre-Markan (see 4:13–20), then something like 4:10 would probably have introduced it (Tuckett 1988: 8–9).

The question of whether 4:10–12 ultimately goes back to Jesus is more difficult to answer. If, as some argue, Jesus never gave any interpretations to his parables because they were all self-evident, then 4:13–20 and 4:10–12 must be inauthentic. Yet the great number of interpretations associated with Jesus's parables[3] makes it highly improbable that every one of them is inauthentic. That Jesus explained his teaching to his followers would appear to be self-evident. What teacher does not? That his followers received an understanding that outsiders lacked is also taught in the Q tradition (Luke 10:21/Matt. 11:25–26; Luke 10:23–24/Matt. 13:16–17). Such a distinction between the followers of Jesus and those outside corresponds to the situation found in Jesus's ministry, and in a similar way the believing remnant in OT times often possessed an understanding of the prophetic message that the nation's leaders and the masses lacked.

The hand of Mark is probably most evident in the designation of Jesus's followers as "those around him along with the Twelve." Yet there is considerable debate as to whether the former ("those around him"; Guelich 1989: 202; Marcus 2000: 301) or the latter ("with the Twelve"; Gnilka 1978: 162–63; Schmithals 1979: 1.238) is due to Mark. A few see both expressions as traditional (Best 1986: 137–40). The parallel in 8:34, where we have "the

---

1. "Alone" (κατὰ μόνας, *kata monas*), "those around him along with the Twelve" (οἱ περὶ αὐτὸν σὺν τοῖς δώδεκα), "they were asking" (ἠρώτων, *ērōtōn*), "mystery" (μυστήριον, *mystērion*), "those outside" (τοῖς ἔξω, *tois exō*), "everything" (τὰ πάντα, *ta panta*), and "comes in" (γίνεται ἐν, *ginetai en*).

2. "It is given" (δέδοται, *dedotai*), "it comes" (γίνεται), and "it be forgiven" (ἀφεθῇ, *aphethē*).

3. Mark 3:27; 4:13–20, 22, 25; 7:18–23; 12:10–11; 13:29, 32–33, 35–37; Matt. 11:18–19; 13:37–43, 49–50; 18:35; 20:16; 21:31b–32; 22:14; 25:13; Luke 4:23c; 7:43–47; 10:36–37; 11:8; 12:21, 40; 13:28–30; 14:11, 33; 15:7, 10; 16:8b–13; 17:10; 18:1, 7–8, 14b; 19:11.

crowd with the disciples" (τὸν ὄχλον σὺν τοῖς μαθηταῖς, *ton ochlon syn tois mathētais*) suggests that "with the Twelve" is more likely to be a Markan addition to the tradition in 4:10. It is also easier to conceive of Mark adding the phrase "with the Twelve" to the nominative subject "those around him" that he found in the tradition, than of his changing the original subject "the Twelve" into a prepositional phrase and adding a new nominative subject, "those around him." Whether he added this to broaden the group accompanying Jesus (Marcus 2000: 301), while possible, cannot be demonstrated.

Exegesis and Exposition

¹⁰And when he was alone, those around him along with the Twelve were asking him [about] the parables. ¹¹And he was saying to them, "To you the mystery concerning the kingdom of God has been given, but to those outside everything comes in parables, ¹²in order that

seeing they may see and not perceive, and

hearing they may hear and not understand,

lest they may turn and be forgiven."

4:10   The expression "alone" (κατὰ μόνας, *kata monas*) is not found elsewhere in Mark and occurs in the other Gospels only in Luke 9:18. Mark prefers to express "alone" by κατ᾽ ἰδίαν (*kat᾽ idian*; 4:34; 6:31, 32; 7:33; 9:28; 13:3), which may suggest that κατὰ μόνας is traditional. The motif of Jesus teaching his disciples privately is a common one in Mark (Beavis 1989: 95; cf. 4:34; 7:17–23; 9:28–29, 35; 10:10–12, 32–34; 12:43–44; 13:3ff.; also 6:31–32; 7:33). The expression "those around him along with the Twelve" appears at first glance to conflict with the statement that Jesus was "alone." For Mark, these statements are not contradictory, however, but mean that Jesus is "alone" in the sense that he is apart from the "very large crowd" (4:1; cf. 9:2, where Jesus is alone with Peter, James, and John; also 4:34; 6:31–32; 9:28; 13:3). The size of the group indicates that this question was not posed in the boat (4:1). (For a discussion of the size and shape of a normal fishing boat on the Sea of Galilee in Jesus's day, see 4:37–39.) Most likely Mark intended his readers to see this as having occurred at a later time and situation (cf. 7:17; 10:10), and he placed 4:10–20 at this point to complete Jesus's teaching on the parable of the soils. After the interpretation (4:13–20) the ideal scene portrayed in 4:1–34 is then resumed. That Mark wanted his readers to see 4:1–32 as a collection of parables built around an incident in which Jesus taught from a boat seems clear from 4:33: "By means of many such parables he was speaking the word to them." The framework of 4:1–34 is thus controlled not by chronological events but by a logical arrangement of similar materials, that is, a parable collection. Once again we are reminded of Papias's statement that "Mark wrote accurately all that he remembered, not, indeed, in order" (Eusebius, *Eccl. Hist.* 3.39.15).

The expression "those around him" picks up 3:32 and 34 and reveals that the "followers" of Jesus were a larger group than just the twelve disciples and consisted of all "who do the will of God" (3:35). Thus the "secret" of the kingdom of God is given to all Jesus's followers, not just to an elite element within this group. These followers are "self-selected, rather than predestined" (France 2002: 195). For a similar expression, compare "the crowd with his disciples" (8:34). Since Jesus in 4:1ff. has taught only one parable, the plural "parables" seems strange. As a result some have sought to explain this as referring to the previous parables in 3:23–37 and 4:3–8. It is more likely, however, that Mark (or an earlier editor, if 4:2–32 is basically a pre-Markan complex) changed the singular "parable" that introduced the interpretation of 4:13–20 to the plural in light of 4:2–34 being a collection of parables (cf. 4:2, 13b–c, 33–34). In so doing, the question concerning "parables" corresponds with the parables referred to in 4:33. In Mark's understanding, the term "parables" refers to what precedes (4:3–8) and follows (4:13–32). It cannot be limited to such a narrow meaning as "riddles" (contra Jeremias 1972: 16–18; Guelich 1989: 204–5) since it refers to the parables found in 4:3–8, 21–25, 26–29, and 30, and the term "parable" is used elsewhere in Mark to describe such parables as 3:23–27; 7:14–15; 12:1–11; and 13:28. See 3:23.

Although "And he was saying" (καὶ ἔλεγεν, *kai elegen*) has been suggested   **4:11**
as being a Markan link phrase by which he inserted traditional material into his account (Jeremias 1972: 14), this is far from certain, for in 2:27; 6:4, 10; 7:9, 27; 8:21 we find this phrase within pre-Markan traditions. We cannot therefore label a saying of Jesus as either authentic, traditional, or inauthentic on the basis of it being introduced by this expression. "To you" refers to the true family of Jesus (3:34–35), who are described in 4:10 as "those around him along with the Twelve." They are contrasted with "those outside" (3:31; cf. 1 Cor. 5:12; Col. 4:5; 1 Thess. 4:12), which serves not just as a spatial designation but as a symbolic one as well. In this verse "you" corresponds with the "good" soil, whereas "those outside" correspond with the first three "bad soils" of 4:4–7.

The verb "has been given" is a divine passive: "God has given" (cf. Luke 10:21/Matt. 11:25). (For "given" used with respect to revealing divine revelation, cf. 1 En. 51.3; 68.1.) Something must be supplied to complete this verb, and both Matt. 13:11 and Luke 8:10 provide "to know." If Mark assumed that his readers would provide "to know," which seems likely, how should "know" be understood? Are Jesus's followers provided cognitive information about the kingdom of God that those outside are not privy to? Should the mystery concerning the kingdom of God given to Jesus's followers be equated with the interpretation of the parable found in 4:13–20? This would, however, conflict with the tense of "has been given" (δέδοται, *dedotai*) and restrict the meaning of "everything" (τὰ πάντα, *ta panta*; lit. "all things") too narrowly. Furthermore, there is nothing about the kingdom of God in the parable (or its interpretation) that Jesus has not already publicly proclaimed.

Both the presence now of the kingdom of God and its future consummation have already been openly announced to all (cf. 1:14–15; 2:18–22; 3:27). As a result it is difficult to think that what God has given to Jesus's followers is simply the interpretation of the parables, such as 4:13–20, that those outside are not allowed to hear. In this regard we should note that in 3:27; 12:10–11; Matt. 11:18–19; 21:31b–32; 22:14; Luke 7:43–47; 10:36–37; 13:28–30; 14:11, 33; 15:7, 10; and 18:14b interpretations of the various parables are given to "those outside."

The concept of "knowing" in the Bible can involve more than simply cognitive knowledge. In Matt. 16:17 Peter's confession that Jesus is the Christ, the Son of God, is attributed to God's having revealed this to him. In 1 Cor. 2:14 what is cognitively understood by outsiders is judged by them to be foolishness, but Paul states that through the Spirit its truthfulness is known by the believer and understood to be the wisdom of God. Similarly it may be that the mystery of the kingdom of God, which is openly proclaimed to all (1:14–15), is judged as foolishness to those outside and as a result they really do not "know" it. Jesus's followers thus "know" more than just the content of Jesus's preaching concerning the kingdom. They know that the kingdom of God has truly come and that Jesus's healings and exorcisms are a manifestation of its presence already now.

The term "mystery" should not be understood as referring to an esoteric knowledge shared by an exclusive group. Any suggestion that this should be interpreted along the lines of the Hellenistic mystery religions or Gnosticism must be rejected. The term "secret/mystery" is best understood in light of Jewish apocalyptic writings and refers here, as in the rest of the NT, to something that was hidden in the past but has now openly been made known. Thus what was once unknown is now being openly revealed to all. In 4:11 the "mystery concerning [or 'of,' a genitive of reference] the kingdom of God" refers to something about the kingdom of God that now is openly proclaimed (Marcus 1984: esp. 563–67). What is revealed about the kingdom of God is not stated in the present verse, but the context of 1:1–4:9 reveals what this is. The perfect tense of "has been given" indicates that the knowledge of the mystery of the kingdom of God has already been given to Jesus's followers.[4] They know that the kingdom of God has now come (1:14) and that, although its consummation still lies in the future, it is nevertheless now present (1:15). The manifestations of the kingdom are visible for all those with eyes to see. Lepers are being cleansed (1:40–45); paralytics are being raised (2:12); withered hands are being restored (3:1–6); demoniacs are being delivered of their unclean spirits (1:32–34); the prince of demons has met his master (3:22–27); fasting has given way to feasting (2:18–22); outcast sinners and toll collectors are finding forgiveness and life (2:13–17); and the Christ, the Son of God, is

4. Marcus (1986b: 43–47; 2000: 298) errs in seeing this as having taken place in the teaching of the parable of the soils (4:3–8), for the crowds who are not given the knowledge of the mystery of the kingdom also heard the parable (4:1–2).

present in their midst (1:1). What was once a longed-for hope is now being proclaimed for all to see. For "those around him along with the Twelve," God has revealed that what they have seen and heard is nothing other than the fulfillment of the OT promises and hopes. For others there is confusion (1:27), questioning (2:18), and misunderstanding (3:22), but for Jesus's followers, God has revealed (it "has been given" them) that Jesus is indeed the Christ, and has inaugurated the kingdom of God in his ministry. They are, of course, not aware of all the implications of this. Doubt, misunderstanding, and confusion may arise, but like the psalmist such a lament will nevertheless end in faith (cf. Pss. 13:5–6; 74:12–17). As for Mark and his readers, this mystery also included the divine necessity of the death of the Son of God, his resurrection, and future return.

As in 4:34, "everything" refers to the content of Jesus's teaching concerning the kingdom of God. (This also includes other teachings of Jesus as well, although here what he has taught concerning the kingdom of God is in the forefront, as the antithetical parallelism with 4:11b ["to you, . . . mystery of the kingdom of God; but to those outside . . . everything . . ."] reveals.) The present statement is hyperbolic in the sense that Jesus did not use only the parabolic literary form to teach. The hyperbolic nature of the statement, however, is particularly useful for Mark because of the nature of the term "parable." A parable is an illustrative metaphor or analogy that requires one to figure out its meaning. In a sense parables often function as "riddles" in being quite enigmatic (4:13; 7:17; 8:14–18). Because they do not "know" the truthfulness of what the parable teaches, those outside understand little more than the analogy itself.[5] Even when aware of the meaning of the parable, those outside judge what is being taught as foolishness (cf. 1 Cor. 2:14). "Those around him along with the Twelve," however, understand that what the parable teaches is true. God has given them eyes to *see* that what the parables teach concerning the kingdom of God is now taking place.[6]

The difficulty that the subordinate conjunction "in order that" (ἵνα, *hina*) creates is evident, for it seems to say that Jesus intentionally taught in parables *in order that* those outside would not be able to understand *in order that* they would not be able to repent and be forgiven. The question of how ἵνα should be translated is greatly debated. Some of the main suggestions are these: (1) it means "in order that," that is, it is a final (telic) clause indicating that what follows is the intended purpose of Jesus's teaching in parables (cf. NRSV); (2) it means "so that," indicating that what follows is the result (some suggested parallels are 3:9; 6:8, 12; 9:9), that is, it is a consecutive clause and not

4:12

---

5. Cf. how David could understand the analogy of Nathan's parable but did not know that he was "the man" (2 Sam. 12:7) until this was pointed out to him. The explanation along with the divine conviction of the truth of the parable allowed David to "understand" the parable.

6. For the difference between knowing cognitively the meaning of a statement (or parable) and knowing existentially its truthfulness and significance, see the comments on 9:32 and Stein 1994a: 37–46.

the purpose of Jesus's teaching in parables (cf. RSV, NAB, NIV; note how "in order that" and "so that" in English can often denote either the result or the purpose of an action); (3) it is a mistranslation of the Aramaic ד (dĕ) in the Targum of Isaiah, which should be translated by the Greek "who" (οἵ, hoi) rather than ἵνα (Manson 1955: 77–80);[7] (4) it is an abbreviation for "in order that what the Scriptures say might be fulfilled" (cf. 14:49; Jeremias 1972: 17); (5) it should be understood as causal (because [ὅτι, hoti] otherwise they would see and not perceive . . .) as in the parallel in Matt. 13:13 (Zerwick 1963: 140–41); (6) it should be interpreted as an epexegetical "that," which explains 4:11 by means of the OT quotation in 4:12 ("All things come to outsiders in parables, i.e., they see but do not perceive, hear but do not understand");[8] (7) it should be interpreted as introducing a purpose clause ("in order that"), but rather than arguing linearly from cause to effect/result (since God purposed that those outside would not repent and be forgiven, Jesus taught in parables, and as a result they did not understand, repent, and find forgiveness), the text should be understood as proceeding from the result (those outside did not turn and repent) to the cause (since Jesus's teaching in parables resulted in those outside not understanding and repenting, this must ultimately fit into the purpose and plan of God; Sutcliffe 1954: 320–27; Stein 1981: 30–31; Tuckett 1988: 19).[9]

Mark 4:12 is a quotation from Isa. 6:9–10 (cf. Jer. 5:21), whose first two lines are an example of synonymous parallelism. It differs from both the MT and LXX texts and follows the Targums in three ways: (1) it has the third person in indirect discourse rather than the second person in direct discourse; (2) it has "forgiven" rather than "heal"; and (3) it has the divine passive ("it shall be . . .") instead of the active ("I shall . . ."). This argues in favor of the pre-Markan origin of the quotation and perhaps of it even being authentic (Jeremias 1972: 15). Why the order in Isaiah of "hearing-seeing" has been reversed in Mark is unclear, although it has been suggested that it may be to have "hearing" stand closer to the explanation of the parable in which hearing (4:15–16, 18, 20) is emphasized (Gundry 1993: 201).

Just as "in order that" has been interpreted in various ways, so also has "lest" (μήποτε, mēpote). One way is as "in order that . . . not take place." This is the way it is used in its only other occurrence in Mark (14:2) and is the most common way of interpreting μήποτε in the NT. Another is as "unless" or "if perhaps." In the Tg. Isa. 6:9–10 the equivalent Aramaic expression (דְּלְמָא,

---

7. Manson's theory in effect saves Jesus from a distasteful theological teaching at the expense of Mark. More important, it does not deal with the fact that Mark wrote his Gospel in Greek, and "Nothing is more certain than that Mark wrote and intended ἵνα . . . μήποτε [the present text as it now stands]" (M. Black 1967: 213).

8. Although in the great majority of the sixty-four instances in which ἵνα is found in Mark, it introduces a purpose clause, it appears to be used in this epexegetical sense in 3:9; 5:23; 6:12, 25; 7:26; 9:12, 30; 10:35; 11:16; 12:19; 13:18 (P. Lampe 1974).

9. For a more detailed discussion of the various interpretations given to Mark 4:12, see Evans 1989b: 91–99; cf. also Beavis 1989: 69–86.

*dilmā*ʾ) is understood as promising forgiveness if Israel repented, and the rabbis understood Isa. 6:10 as a promise, not a threat (France 2002: 200). Examples of μήποτε meaning "unless" or "if perhaps" can be found in Luke 3:15; John 7:26; and 2 Tim. 2:25. A third possibility is to interpret "lest" as ironical, that is, "unless [God forbid] they should return and be forgiven" (Hollenbach 1983). In contrast to oral communication, however, it is hard to detect irony in written accounts, where it is difficult to give clear indicators of irony.

If we understand μήποτε in the sense of דִּלְמָא and ἵνα as indicating result rather than purpose, we would have: "so that Jesus's teaching in parables resulted in their seeing but not perceiving, hearing but not understanding, unless (as is hoped) they should turn and it be forgiven them." While such an interpretation is more pleasing, it requires that both ἵνα and μήποτε be given rarer and more unusual meanings. The presence of both ἵνα and μήποτε in 4:12 makes it more likely that they should both be understood as introducing the purpose for what follows—"Jesus taught in parables with the purpose (in order that) that those outside would hear and see and not understand with the purpose (lest) that they not turn and be forgiven."

Yet there seems to have been a blurring of the sense or purpose and result by the first century (Sutcliffe 1954; Moule 1959: 143), and whereas a strong predestinarian interpretation of this verse might seem at first glance to satisfy the grammar best, it too has its difficulties. If this were what Mark intended, it is difficult to understand why that part of the OT quotation in Isa. 6:9–10 that would best support such an interpretation was omitted (Manson 1955: 78–79). If 4:12 seeks to emphasize a divine hardening of "those outside" unto damnation, why does the quotation omit, "Make the mind of this people dull, and stop their ears, and shut their eyes . . ."? Such an interpretation also has difficulties with the fact that some of Jesus's parables were meant to be understood by those outside (Luke 15:1–2) and that some were in fact understood very well (Mark 12:12).

In the latter example, those outside understood the meaning of the parable on one level (cognitively) very well, but they failed to understand the truth of the parable. Their cognitive knowledge is evident in that they sought to seize Jesus (12:12) in order to put him to death (cf. 14:1); for why would they have sought to do this if they had not understood what Jesus was saying in the parable? (Few people seek to kill others for saying incomprehensible things.) Their lack of understanding the truth of the parable is revealed in their not repenting and proceeding with their plot to kill Jesus. Consequently, they do not "turn" (ἐπιστρέψωσιν, *epistrepsōsin*), a metaphorical expression to describe the act of repenting (cf. Acts 3:19 and 26:28, where it is used alongside the verb "repent"; 9:35; 11:2), and "it was not forgiven them," a divine passive for "God did not forgive them."

Summary

This passage assists Mark's readers in understanding how the coming of Jesus resulted in both the arrival of the kingdom of God on the one hand

and his crucifixion on the other. Along with the hardness of official Judaism, those outside the believing community lacked understanding of what was taking place. For believers, however, the mystery of the arrival of the kingdom and its future consummation have been "given." They "know" that God sent his Son to inaugurate the kingdom, as Jesus taught in his parables. They can also understand that, due to the obduracy of the Jewish leadership, he was crucified. The rejection by Israel's leaders, however, was all part of the divine mystery, for it was the will of God that the Son of Man come and give his life as a ransom for many (10:45; cf. 14:24). Thus the "mystery" of the kingdom of God involves a recognition of not just the eschatological nature of the events taking place but its christological nature as well (Tuckett 1988: 16–18). All that has occurred therefore fits the divine plan. There is a sense that all that has taken place—the lack of understanding by those outside, as well as their rejection of and the death of the Son of God—was part of the divine plan. Somehow all this was in accord with the will of God and has taken place "in order that" what God had decreed would find fruition. The understanding and the conviction that all this is ultimately due to the sovereign rule of God and not just a tragedy or fate is intended by Mark to provide comfort and reassurance to his readers. In light of this conviction, they should concentrate on heeding the exhortation to hear (4:3, 9; cf. also 4:23), being good soil, and bearing fruit (4:8, 20). As to those outside, their hardness of heart and unpardonable sin (cf. 2:6–7, 16, 18, 24; 3:2, 5, 22, 30) result in a further hardening of the heart.[10]

---

10. The OT provides a helpful example in showing how Pharaoh's culpability is due to his hardness of heart (Exod. 7:13–14, 22–34; 8:15, 19, 23; 9:7, 34–35; 13:15 [cf. also 3:19; 10:10]) and God's hardening of his heart (Exod. 4:21; 7:3, 13–14; 9:12; 10:1, 20, 27; 11:10; 14:8). These are interwoven without great concern as to their exact causal and temporal relationship. For NT examples of the use of Isa. 6:9–10 with respect to the refusal of some to believe the gospel message, cf. Acts 28:23–28 and Rom. 11:7–10.

3. Jesus's Interpretation of the Parable of the Soils (4:13–20)

At this point Mark introduces the second part of the Markan sandwich begun in 4:1–9. The relationship of this interpretation with the parable of the soils is greatly debated. The three main possibilities are that the interpretation is (1) a Markan creation, (2) traditional but created by the early church, and (3) authentic and stemming from Jesus himself. There is little evidence for it being a de novo Markan creation, because eight terms are found in the interpretation but not elsewhere in Mark: "joy" (χαρᾶς, *charas*; 4:16); "for a short time" (πρόσκαιροι, *proskairoi*; 4:17); "cares" (μέριμναι, *merimnai*; 4:19); "deceitfulness" (ἀπάτη, *apatē*; 4:19); "riches" (πλούτου, *ploutou*; 4:19); "desires" (ἐπιθυμίαι, *epithymiai*; 4:19); "unfruitful" (ἄκαρπος, *akarpos*; 4:19); and "welcome" (παραδέχονται, *paradechontai*; 4:20). This makes it extremely unlikely that Mark himself composed the interpretation de novo (Lambrecht 1974: 300–302; Trocmé 1977: 466).

A number of arguments are raised against attributing the interpretation of the parable of the soils to Jesus: (1) Jesus never used allegory in his teaching, and since the interpretation of the parable is an allegory,[1] he could not have taught this parable; (2) most of Jesus's parables do not have interpretations, so that it is unlikely that this one did; (3) the style of the interpretation is not Hebraic; (4) the vocabulary of the interpretation reflects a later period; (5) the interpretation assumes the situation of the early church; (6) the interpretation misses the original focus of the parable, which centers on the amazing harvest, not the soils; (7) the balance of three bad soils versus three good soils found in the parable is not carried out in the interpretation; (8) the interpretation of the parable is not found with the parable in Gos. Thom. 9; and (9) the meaning of the term "seed" is not consistent in the interpretation (see the discussion in Payne 1980a: 168–86).

These objections are uneven in weight. The first is a legacy of Jülicher (1910; 1st ed. 1888), who argued that since parables are not allegories but illustrative examples meant to clarify, they do not need an explanation. It is now evident that in opposing the allegorical method of interpretation,

---

1. The difference between an allegory and a story parable is that, whereas a story parable contains one basic analogy, an allegory contains numerous analogies. In the present parable, such details as the seed, birds, lack of roots, sun, thorns, and various soils are analogies referring to certain things, and Mark intends the reader to interpret them for their meaning. In a story parable such as the prodigal son, such details as the swine, robe, sandals, ring, fatted calf, and banquet are not analogies referring to something else, but are simply intended to serve as coloring for the parable's basic analogy.

Jülicher went too far in eliminating the possibility of allegory in Jesus's parables. This is evident from the fact that the Hebrew מָשָׁל (*māšāl*, parable) is used in the OT, the Apocrypha, and the rabbinic materials to refer not only to story parables but also to riddles, fables, proverbs, similitudes, and allegories. As a result there is no reason to assume that Jesus must have made a rigid distinction between a parable and an allegory (R. Brown 1962). On the contrary, it is probable that Jesus possessed the same understanding of a *māšāl* found in the OT, the Apocrypha, and the rabbinic writings.

The second objection is in fact incorrect. Over thirty parables in the Synoptic Gospels have interpretations associated with them (see 4:10–12), and it is unlikely that all these interpretations are inauthentic.

The third, fourth, and fifth arguments do not require that the parable be a church creation, if we permit the church (or Mark) to reword an authentic tradition in light of the situation to which it (or he) was speaking. It is extremely difficult to distinguish between an authentic gospel tradition that has been interpreted and reworded to fit the situation of the early church and a tradition created completely by the evangelist or early church (Stein 1992a: 54). Since Jesus faced situations where the deceitfulness of riches was a problem (cf. 10:17–27) and where some who earlier followed him ceased to do so (cf. Luke 9:57–62; John 6:60–71), the interpretation is not anachronistic to the situation found in Jesus's own ministry.

The sixth and seventh objections are valid only if we assume that the original parable of Jesus was substantially different from its present form (4:3–9). In the reconstructed parable the original point (supposedly) is the amazing harvest resulting from the sowing of the seed, which was (supposedly) portrayed in a balanced comparison of three bad soils versus three good soils. Yet as we observed, the present emphasis of the parable does not fall on a generous harvest but on the four different soils and their different responses to the seed. (See the 4:1–9 "Summary.") Similarly, the present parable does not focus on a comparison of three good soils versus three bad soils. There are instead three bad soils and one good soil.[2] As a result the sixth and seventh objections are based upon a hypothetical reconstruction of what Jesus supposedly said rather than what is actually in the text. As the parable and interpretation now stand, the latter fits the former very well, "as hand fits glove" (Gerhardsson 1967: 192). I have deep reservations as to how well we can reconstruct what Jesus actually said. As to why the interpretation of the parable is missing from the Gospel of Thomas, this may be due to the gnostic desire to keep the parable's meaning hidden from the uninitiated outside the gnostic community.

The final objection is based on the confusion over exactly what the seed represents. Supposedly, it refers in 4:14 to the "word of God" but in 4:15–20 to the various soils and their response to the seed. I will argue below, however, that the seed refers consistently to the four soils, which represent various groups

---

2. For the division of the world into four kinds of soils, cf. *m. 'Abot* 5.10–15.

of hearers (see 4:15–19). Although the authenticity of the interpretation is still denied by most (Jeremias 1972: 77–79; Carlston 1975: 145–46), it is not denied as dogmatically as in the past (cf. V. Taylor 1952: 259; Cranfield 1959: 158–61; Payne 1980a; Davies and Allison 1991: 396–99). For me, it is easiest to conceive of 4:13–20 being an authentic piece of tradition that the early church and the evangelist have reworked to minister to the particular needs of their communities. In so doing, they took certain themes already present and implicit in the parable and its interpretation and made them explicit.

Since the purpose of this commentary is to understand what Mark meant by this interpretation, the question of its authenticity, while interesting, is somewhat tangential. Mark possessed sufficient skill as an author so that he would not have included the interpretation of the parable if he believed it contradicted the point of the parable. We should therefore assume that for him the parable and its interpretation taught the same point. As a result we should interpret the present parable in light of the interpretation and the present interpretation in light of the parable. The present passage can be divided as follows:[3] an introductory seam (4:13–14), the three unfruitful soils (4:15–19), and the good soil (4:20).

Exegesis and Exposition

[13]And he says to them, "Do you not understand this parable? Then how will you understand all [of the other] parables? [14]The sower sows the word. [15]These are the beside-the-path people in whom the word is sown, and whenever they hear, immediately Satan comes and takes away the word that has been sown ⌜in them⌝. [16]And these are the rocky-soil people [who are] being sown [the word], who whenever they hear the word immediately with joy receive it, [17]⌜but⌝ they have no root in themselves but only endure for a short time, then when tribulation or persecution comes on account of the word, they immediately fall away. [18]And others are the thorny-soil people [who are] being sown [the word]. These are those who hear the word, [19]and the cares of this age and the deceitfulness of riches and the desires for other things enter in [and] choke the word, and it becomes unfruitful. [20]And those are the good-soil people [who] have been sown [the word], who hear the word and welcome [it] and bear fruit, thirty-, sixty-, and a hundredfold."

The opening words, "And he says to them" (Καὶ λέγει αὐτοῖς, *Kai legei autois*), pick up the inquiry of the disciples in 4:10 (cf. 4:21, 24, 25, 30) and introduce two questions addressed to the disciples. (For the presence of two rhetorical questions together, cf. 1:27; 3:7; 4:21, 30, 40; 7:18; 8:17–19 [five

4:13–14

---

3. It has been suggested that the overall organization of 4:3–20 follows the format: an ambiguous parable (4:3–8), incomprehension (4:10), critical rejoinder (4:13), and an explanation (4:14–20); and the following OT examples are given: Ezek. 17:1–24 (17:2–10 [an implied incomprehension], 11–12a, 12b–21); Zech. 4:2–10 (2–3, 4, 5b, 6–10) and 4:11–14 (11, 12, 13, 14; Lemcio 1978). Daube (1956b) gives examples of this format in the rabbinic literature.

rhetorical questions together!], 36–37; 9:19; 14:37; etc. [Neirynck 1988: 125–26].) The first—"Do you not understand this parable?"—focuses on the meaning of 4:3–8, as "this" indicates. Whether this and the second question are Markan (Pryke 1978: 13, 141, 156; Gnilka 1978: 173; Tuckett 1988: 9) or traditional is debated. The disciples' lack of understanding is a clear Markan emphasis (this is the first occurrence of this theme, but cf. 4:40–41; 6:52; 7:18; 8:14–21, 32–33; 9:5–6, 32; 10:24; 14:40), but it is also clear that historically the disciples did at times lack understanding. The reference to "this parable" (τὴν παραβολὴν ταύτην, tēn parabolēn tautēn) indicates that Jesus is referring to the parable in 4:3–8, not the saying in 4:10–12 (contra Boobyer 1961: 66–68). Even though rhetorical, this question indicates that Jesus expects the disciples to understand the meaning of the parable. (The "not" [οὐκ, ouk] in the question assumes a positive answer.) The second question—"How will you understand all the parables?"—indicates that the present parable holds the key to all the parables and is therefore fundamental for understanding Jesus's teaching concerning the kingdom of God (Hooker 1991: 130; France 2002: 204). Since the interpretation that follows is allegorical in nature, this question helped lead to the practice of interpreting all parables allegorically. It is unclear, however, how understanding this parable would provide the key for understanding all the other parables. The question can also be interpreted, "If you cannot understand this parable, how will you ever understand other parables (that are more difficult)?" The first interpretation would emphasize the importance of this parable; the second would emphasize the dullness of the disciples. The function of this twofold question is not to denigrate the disciples (contra Weeden 1971: 23, 31) but to have the disciples serve as examples whose weaknesses and failure to understand were an opportunity for Mark to teach what discipleship involves (Best 1976b: 399–401; 1983: 47).

In 4:14 the sower is defined as the one who sows "the word" (τὸν λόγον, ton logon). Although in its original setting the "sower" would have been interpreted by the disciples as referring to Jesus, Mark's readers would have understood it more broadly. It would, of course, have included Jesus, who preached the "word" (cf. 1:45; 2:2; 4:33; 8:32), but it would have also included any Christian who witnessed to or proclaimed the gospel. In the parable and its interpretation, however, little emphasis is placed on the sower. He is referred to only in 4:3 and 14. The emphasis falls instead on the proclamation of the word and the reception it receives from the various soils. The identification of the seed as the "word" is found in every verse that follows (4:15–20). That the absolute use of "word" serves as a Markan technical term for the gospel (see 1:45) suggests that he may have introduced it into the passage. The "word" is also a technical term in the vocabulary of the early church. It is "received" (λαμβάνουσιν, lambanousin; cf. 4:16 with Acts 17:11; 1 Thess. 1:6; 2:13; James 1:21) "with joy" (μετὰ χαρᾶς, meta charas; cf. 4:16 with 1 Thess. 1:6), often brings "persecution" (διωγμοῦ, diōgmou; cf. 4:17 with 1 Thess. 1:6; 2 Tim. 1:8) and "stumbling" (σκανδαλίζονται, *skandalizontai*; cf. 4:17 with 1 Pet. 2:8), and "bears fruit" (καρποφοροῦσιν, *karpophorousin*; cf. 4:20 with Col. 1:6, 10). What the original expression was that Mark found in the tradition is uncertain. It is possible that Jesus himself used the Hebrew דָּבָר (*dābār*, word) as the prophets did (R. Brown 1962: 42). If so, the meaning of the "word" would have involved the message of Jesus as found in 1:15, but for Mark's readers, the "word" would have had a more pregnant meaning and included the postresurrection understanding of the life and message of Jesus.

From this point on, the exact identification of the seed becomes more confus-   **4:15–19** ing. Numerous commentators interpret 4:15 as indicating that Mark identifies both the people ("these are the beside-the-path people"; cf. 4:16, 18, 20) and the word ("the word that they heard"; cf. 4:16, 18, 19, 29) as being represented by the seed. Whereas in 4:14 the seed is referred to as the "word," here the seed ("a certain part of the seed" in 4:4) supposedly refers both to the soil (the "path" in 4:4), which in turn refers to those on the path in whom the seed is sown, and to the "word." Thus the seed appears to refer on the one hand to "the word" and on the other to "the soil" that receives the word. Some say that this identification of the seed with the soils and their reception of the seed becomes even more explicit in 4:16ff. (Marcus 1986b: 25–26n29). One problem with this interpretation is that it equates the plural "these" (οὗτοι, *houtoi*) with the singular "seed"/"word." The antecedent of "these," however, refers to the people represented by the first kind of soil in 4:4. "These" refers to the "beside-the-path people [lit. 'ones']," where the word is sown and Satan immediately comes and takes the word sown in them. (Cf. Payne 1980b: 566–67, however, who argues from the supposed original Aramaic saying of Jesus.) This is how Matt. 13:18–23 and Luke 8:11–15 understand Mark. "'These' by the path" therefore does not refer to seeds (France 2002: 204–5; contra Cranfield 1959: 162; Guelich 1989: 221–22; Marcus 2000: 308), for, although Mark's wording is awkward, he clearly distinguishes "these, the ones by the path kind of soil . . ." from the word (seed) sown on it. "In whom" (ὅπου, *hopou*; lit. "where") and "in them" (εἰς αὐτούς, *eis autous*), where the seed is sown, are differentiated from the seed itself. (For use of the metaphor "birds" to refer to the work of Satan, cf. Jub. 11.11; Apoc. Ab. 13.3–7; 1 En. 90.8–13; *b. Sanh.* 107a.)

In the second example (4:16–17), numerous scholars again seek to make "seed" the referent of "these," but this makes nonsense of the rest of the sentence, where "these" hear the word (seed) and receive it (the word/seed) with joy. Whereas this soil/people can hear/receive the word, it makes no sense to have the word/seed receive "the word/seed." In the description of the four soils, we find the following pattern:

> "These are the beside-the-path people [οἱ παρὰ τὴν ὁδόν, *hoi para tēn hodon*]—in whom the word is sown—and whenever they hear" (4:15)

"These are the rocky-soil people [οἱ ἐπὶ τὰ πετρώδη, *hoi epi ta petrōdē*; lit. 'those on the rocky soil']—being sown—who whenever they hear" (4:16)

"Others are the thorny-soil people [ἄλλοι . . . οἱ εἰς τὰς ἀκάνθας, *alloi . . . hoi eis tas akanthas*]—being sown—these are those who hear" (4:18)

"These are the good-ground people [ἐκεῖνοι . . . οἱ ἐπὶ τὴν γῆν τὴν καλήν, *ekeinoi . . . hoi epi tēn gēn tēn kalēn*]—have been sown—who hear" (4:20)

From this comparison, it appears that the participles translated "being sown" (4:16, 18) and "have been sown" (4:20) are abbreviations for "where the word is sown" (4:15) and serve not as substantive participles ("those being sown/have been sown") describing the "seed" but as attributive participles describing the people/soil of 4:5, 7, and 8, just as "where the word is sown" describes the people/soil of 4:4. Thus we should interpret 4:16: "These refer to the people represented by the second kind of soil in 4:5–6," that is, the "rocky-soil people" who, whenever they hear the word, receive it immediately with great joy, but wither away due to lack of deep roots.[4] Since they have no root in themselves, they endure for only a short time. Those in this group, like the first and third groups, hear the word, but they also "immediately with joy receive it." They represent not simply certain followers of Jesus who during his ministry ceased following him but various followers of Jesus who throughout history have done so. The cause of their failure to continue in discipleship is that "when tribulation or persecution comes on account of the word, they immediately fall away ['are scandalized,' σκανδαλίζονται, *skandalizontai*; cf. 6:3; 9:42–47; 14:27, 29]." If Mark was written to the Roman church after the Neronian persecution, his readers would recall people who one time received the gospel message eagerly but had not counted the cost and during the persecution under Nero surrendered their faith. Jesus had warned his followers of persecution (8:34–38; 13:9–13; Luke 14:25–33), and such distress and tribulation were all too common in the early church (Rom. 8:35; 2 Cor. 4:8–9; 2 Thess. 1:4). The response of this group in the face of persecution contrasts sharply with those of the Maccabean martyrs in 4 Macc. 8–13. We should not press the expression "in themselves" to mean that this was a subjective faith in themselves and not in God.

The third group of hearers (4:18–19) is described as "others" and represents the thorny soil (4:7) being sown the word. They hear the word and like the first two soils also prove unfruitful. In this instance, the failure of this soil is

---

4. Hultgren (2000: 186, 191) argues that, unlike the other analogies that compare hearers to various kinds of soils, this analogy compares hearers with plants. This, however, loses sight of the fact that the poorly rooted plants are a product of the rocky soil, and it is therefore the rocky soil that is the ultimate cause of the seed proving unfruitful. Mark's readers would no doubt have seen the various analogies as involving four hearers represented by four kinds of soils—by-the-path soil, rocky soil, weedy soil, and good soil—not four hearers represented by three soils and a plant.

due to the cares of this age (cf. Matt. 6:24–34), the deceitfulness of riches (cf. Mark 10:17–27), and the desires for other things (cf. 7:21–23; 10:35–45), which enter in and "choke the word" (συμπνίγουσιν τὸν λόγον, *sympnigousin ton logon*) from producing its intended result; so this soil also does not produce fruit. The terms "cares," "deceitfulness," "riches," "desires," and "unfruitful" occur only here in Mark and strongly suggest a non-Markan origin of the parable's interpretation. The term "deceitfulness" can also mean "seduction" or "delight." The parallel "cares of this age," the cares that the present age has, suggests that "of riches" should be interpreted as a subjective genitive, that is, the deceitfulness that riches bring about, and this makes "deceitfulness" the more likely meaning.

The fourth and final group is described as "the good-soil people." Although the tense of the participle "sown" (σπαρέντες, *sparentes*—aorist passive) is different from that found in 4:16 and 18 (σπειρόμενοι, *speiromenoi*—present passive), this appears to be simply a stylistic feature (cf. the use of the perfect participle [ἐσπαρμένον, *esparmenon*] in 4:15). The present tense "hear" (ἀκούουσιν, *akouousin*) may imply that those who make up the good soil continually listen to the word (Guelich 1989: 223; Marcus 2000: 313). All four soils "hear" the word of God, but the difference between the first three (all aorist tenses) and the fourth (a present tense) is how they hear (cf. 4:9, 23, 24–25, 33). Whereas the first and third soils only "hear" the word (4:15, 18) and the second "hears" and "receives" (λαμβάνουσιν, *lambanousin*) it (4:16), the fourth soil continually "hears" and "welcomes [it]" (παραδέχονται, *paradechontai*) and "bears fruit." The term "welcome" is a better translation of παραδέχονται than "receive" and indicates a more heartfelt response (cf. 1 Cor. 2:14) than λαμβάνουσιν, used in Mark 4:16. The ultimate mark of the fourth soil that reveals it to be good soil is its bearing fruit (cf. 4:28; also Rom. 7:4; Col. 1:6, 10). The present tense of "welcomes" and "bears fruit" matches the present tense of the verbs in 4:16 ("receive"), 17 ("fall away"), and 19 ("choke," "becomes"), so that we should probably not see any significance in this. The yield "thirty-, sixty-, and a hundredfold" repeats 4:9. What the metaphor of "fruit bearing" corresponds to is not spelled out in the interpretation, but the readers of the Gospel, as well as the original audience, would have assumed that it involved faithfulness to Jesus and his teachings (8:34–38; cf. Matt. 7:15–20; 21:43; John 15:1–10).

4:20

Summary

The massive discussion of whether an inauthentic interpretation has altered the original meaning of Jesus's parable is a separate question from what concerns us here. (See introduction to this section.) As the parable and its interpretation now stand, they are addressed not to Jesus's original audience but to Mark's readers. The question as to the present meaning of the parable and its interpretation involves two main possibilities. Does the main point concern (1) the ultimate harvest at the end, or (2) the response of the various soils to the seed? Is the point (1) that despite everything a bountiful harvest will result from the preaching of the "word"? Or is it (2) that the preaching of the "word" elicits different responses, and Mark's readers should take heed that they are "good soil," that is, respond with faithful endurance?

In favor of the first interpretation is the rule of end stress, which argues that the meaning of a parable comes at the end, and the parable and its interpretation end with the great harvest. This interpretation usually argues, however, that the present interpretation of the parable in 4:13–20 is inauthentic and misleading and should not be used in arriving at the meaning of the parable. Another argument in favor of this interpretation is the extraordinary nature of the harvest. This places emphasis on the harvest rather than the soils. Such an interpretation also avoids an allegorical interpretation of the parable.

In favor of the second interpretation is that only one verse in both the parable and the interpretation is devoted to the harvest. In each, five verses are devoted to a description of the soils. The only variable in the parable and its interpretation is the response of the various soils, for the same seed is sown on all four soils. Consequently, it is the soils that are the focus of attention. As for the end stress, this serves primarily the purpose of ending the parable with a positive rather than a negative example; but if the order of the soils was reversed, the meaning in the present parable and interpretation would not be essentially altered. Decisive, however, is the interpretation of the parable in 4:13–20. Almost all interpreters tend to agree that it is hortatory and prescriptive, and this fits the call to "hear" in 4:3 and 9 better than the first interpretation, which is not hortatory but descriptive.

In seeking to understand the Markan message of 4:3–9 and 13–20, we must ultimately deal with the present form of the material, not some hypothetically reconstructed pre-Markan form of the parable. As it now stands, the parable and its interpretation serve a hortatory purpose. This is clear from the commands to "hear" in 4:3 and 4:9. The attempt to understand these commands as "descriptive" rather than "prescriptive" (so Guelich 1989: 224) fails to take seriously the present form of the parable and its interpretation. In its present form the parable and its interpretation serve as a warning to Mark's readers not to be hearers of the word like those portrayed by the first three soils. On the contrary, they should be concerned with being good soil, regardless of what circumstances they may find themselves in.[5] Such exhortations are found throughout Mark (cf. 8:34–38; 10:17–27; 13:9–14). One need not deny that there is present in the parable and its interpretation the implication that the proclamation of the gospel message will ultimately be successful and bear fruit. Yet whereas this is a legitimate implication of

5. There are ultimately only two kinds of soils—fruitful or unfruitful. This, however, does not mean that we should see an equal three bad versus three good soils (30, 60, 100). The much greater space devoted to the three bad soils is too disproportionate for such an interpretation.

the parable (cf. Col. 1:6, 10), it is not its main point. The main point is the exhortation to hear/heed the word of God by being good soil.

Additional Notes

4:15. The translation follows B W f¹ f¹³ by reading εἰς αὐτούς rather than ἐν ταῖς καρδίαις αὐτῶν found in D Θ 33 lat syr.

4:17. Here καί has a contrastive sense; see BDF §442.1.

4. Jesus's Parables of the Lamp and the Measure (4:21–25)

The parables of the lamp and the measure appear to interrupt the collection of seed parables found in 4:3–20 and 26–29. They are associated in theme, however, with the warnings "to hear" found in 4:9 (cf. 4:23–24) and the distinction between insiders who know the secret of the kingdom of God and outsiders who do not in 4:11–12 (cf. 4:24–25). (Cf. "insider and outsiders" in 4:10–11a and 11b–12; 4:24–25a and 25b; and "outsiders and insiders" in 4:15–19 and 20 and 4:33–34a and 34b [Marcus 1986b: 157–58].) Four distinct sayings in this passage are combined to form two parabolic sayings: 4:21—a wisdom saying from daily life introduced by "And he was saying to them" (Καὶ ἔλεγεν αὐτοῖς, *Kai elegen autois*) and its explanation in 4:22; 4:24—a proverb, also introduced by "And he was saying to them" (Καὶ ἔλεγεν αὐτοῖς), and its explanation in 4:25. Separating these two parabolic sayings are two exhortations in 4:23 and 24b. Together the parabolic sayings and exhortations form a chiasmus: (A) 4:21–22; (B) 4:23; (B') 4:24a–b; and (A') 4:24c–25.

The Markan redaction of this passage is seen most clearly in the arrangement of the material found in 4:21–25 and the arrangement of 4:21–25 within 4:3–34. Although some scholars argue that 4:21–25 had already been associated together in the pre-Markan tradition (V. Taylor 1952: 262; Jeremias 1972: 91; Pesch 1980a: 247, 251), most believe that Mark himself was responsible for bringing the individual units of 4:21–25 together and for placing them within 4:3–34 (Ambrozic 1972: 103–5; Gnilka 1978: 170–80; Marcus 2000: 315). The sayings in 4:21–25 are also found in Matthew and Luke, although in Matthew they are scattered: Mark 4:21—Luke 8:16/Matt. 5:15 (cf. Gos. Thom. 33); Mark 4:22—Luke 8:17/Matt. 10:26 (cf. Gos. Thom. 5, 6); Mark 4:24—Luke 8:18 (cf. also Luke 6:38, where we find the exhortation)/Matt. 7:2; Mark 4:25—Luke 8:18/Matt. 13:12. Additional parallels to Mark 4:21–25 can be found in Luke 11:33 (cf. 8:16); 6:38 (cf. 8:18); 12:2 (cf. 8:17); 19:26 (cf. 8:18); and in Matt. 25:29 (cf. 13:12). A possible pre-Markan connection of these sayings is seen by some in the common use of the term "measure" in 4:21 and 4:24, but it should be noted that the Greek terms are different—μόδιον (*modion*) and μέτρῳ (*metrō*), and the former refers primarily to a container and the latter to a measuring unit. Mark's frequent use of "in order that" (ἵνα, *hina*) clauses in 4:21 (twice) and 22 (twice) favors the view that Mark was the one who brought these sayings together. (There are sixty-four occurrences of ἵνα in Mark, compared to only thirty-nine and forty-six instances in the much larger Gospels of Matthew and Luke, respectively.) The presence of a "for" (γάρ, *gar*) explanatory clause in 4:25 also suggests a Markan arrangement of these materials (Stein 2001: 90–91). While the content of the γάρ clause in 4:25 was not created by Mark, as in the case of many other such clauses (see 1:16–18), the use of it to explain 4:24 suggests that it was Mark who associated these two verses together in this manner. It appears that the sayings in 4:21–25 at one time circulated as independent units of tradition and were brought together either by a pre-Markan editor or more probably by Mark himself (Marcus 1986b: 129–40) and that the more primitive forms of these sayings are the Q version of Mark 4:21–22 and 24c found in Matthew and the Markan form of 4:25 (Marcus 1986b: 140). The form of the sayings in the Gospel of Thomas is clearly secondary (Marcus 1986b: 130n28).

Some also see Mark's hand in 4:21a and 24a ("and he was saying to them"), 22a (the explanatory "for" [γάρ] clause), 23 (all), 25a (the explanatory "for" [γάρ] clause; Pryke 1978: 13, 141, 156); and others also in 4:24d (and will be further added to you, καὶ προστεθήσεται ὑμῖν, *kai prostethēsetai hymin*; Gnilka 1978: 180) and 4:21d (or under the bed, ἢ ὑπὸ τὴν κλίνην, *ē hypo tēn klinēn*; Steinhauser 1990: 210). Mark's hand and theological emphases, however, are best seen in the overall arrangement of this section and its placement after 4:10–12, 13–20, rather than in isolated individual phrases or comments that Mark supposedly added to the tradition.

Exegesis and Exposition

[21]And he was saying to them, "Does the lamp come in order that it may be placed under the basket or under the bed? [Does it] not [come] in order that it may be placed upon the lampstand? [22]For there is nothing hidden except in order that it may be made manifest, nor has anything become secret but in order that it may be made manifest. [23]If anyone has ears to hear, let him hear."

[24]And he was saying to them, "Pay attention to what you hear. By what measure you measure, it will be measured to you and will be further added to you. ⌐ ¬ [25]For [to the one] who has, it will be given to him, and [to the one] who has not, even what he has will be taken away from him."

"And he was saying to them" (καὶ ἔλεγεν αὐτοῖς), which introduces 4:21–23, also introduces 4:24–25 (cf. also 4:13, 26, and 30). "Them" (αὐτοῖς) can be understood as referring to the crowd of 4:1–2 (W. Lane 1974: 164; J. Edwards 2002: 139) or the disciples of 4:10–12 (Marcus 1986b: 140–41). The latter is supported by the fact that there is no switch from the audience of 4:10–12, 13–20, which is "those around him along with the Twelve" (4:10), and the subject matter contained in 4:21–25, and especially in 4:24–25, fits the theme of 4:10–12 and 13–20. The former suggestion is supported by the fact that in 4:33–34 "to them" (αὐτοῖς) is distinguished from the disciples and refers to the crowd of 4:1–2. That "he was saying to them" is a common introductory

4:21–22

formula for a saying (see 2:27–28) weakens the second understanding, but Mark probably wants his readers to interpret "to them" in light of the reference to the disciples in 4:10–20.

The use of the article with "lamp" (ὁ λύχνος, *ho lychnos*) contrasts with its omission in Matt. 5:15 and Luke 8:16. The presence of the article is best understood as indicating that the metaphor "lamp" refers to something definite. The most likely suggestions are that it refers to (1) the knowledge of the parable known to those "inside" (France 2002: 208); (2) the word of God (4:14; cf. Ps. 119:105; Marcus 2000: 318); (3) the coming of the kingdom of God and its association with Jesus Christ (Guelich 1989: 231); and (4) the coming of Jesus Christ, the Son of God, his identity, fate, and bringing of the kingdom of God (Cranfield 1959: 164; Hurtado 1983: 79; Hooker 1989: 133–34; Witherington 2001: 169–70; J. Edwards 2002: 139). The first suggestion would appear to be too narrow in its focus. The second loses sight of the eschatological nature of Jesus's coming and teaching. A more likely suggestion is the third, that the lamp refers to the arrival of the kingdom of God spoken of in the parable of the soils. The coming of the kingdom lies at the heart of Jesus's teachings (1:15). Yet, although openly proclaimed, the eyes of those "outside" (4:12) fail to see that the kingdom of God has indeed come. The kingdom of God, however, is only part of what has come and appears to be hidden. The bringer of the kingdom—Jesus, the Son of God—has come. His identity, like the arrival of the kingdom, is also hidden from the understanding of those outside. That the metaphor of a "lamp" can be used to refer to a person is clear (see 2 Sam. 21:17; 22:29; Zech. 4:2; Sir. 48:1; 1QSb 4.27 [cf. Rev. 21:23]). The term "come" (ἔρχεται, *erchetai*) is frequently associated in Mark with the coming of Jesus, the coming of the kingdom of God, as well as the parousia (1:7, 14, 24, 29, 39; 2:17; 3:20; 8:38; 10:45; 11:9–10; 13:26, 35, 36; 14:62). The unusual use of this verb instead of φέρω (*pherō*, to bring) suggests that the coming of the lamp is best understood as referring to the coming of Jesus upon the scene (cf. John 8:12; Rev. 21:23; contra Guelich 1989: 228). The following parables in 4:26–29 further support this view (see 4:26–29).

"In order that it may be placed" is the first of four ἵνα clauses in 4:21–22. It is best to understand it as indicating the purpose of the lamp's coming (cf., however, Gundry 1993: 212, who discusses the possibility of it indicating result). Some have suggested that the basket referred to here was a container (about two gallons in size) used to extinguish a lamp (Jeremias 1972: 120). By placing a lamp under such a container, the flame would be extinguished without creating a lot of smoke. The evidence given to support such an interpretation, however, is far from conclusive. Furthermore, since the next example has nothing to do with extinguishing a lamp, the purpose of these two examples (under a basket and under a bed) are best interpreted as examples of what one does not do with a lamp. A lamp is for illumination (v. 22), not for hiding (v. 21). The contrast in 4:21 and 22 involves hiddenness and revelation, and the basket serves as an example of hiding a lamp. The second place where a lamp is not intended to be set or hidden is "under the bed." The absence of the reference to a bed in Matt. 5:15; Luke 11:33; and Gos. Thom. 33 suggests that this may be a later addition to the original illustration. The Markan inclination to dualities (Neirynck 1988: 102), however, suggests that this may be due to the hand of Mark himself. The "not" (μήτι, *mēti*) introducing this first question anticipates a negative answer.

The second question, "[Does it] not [come] in order that it may be placed upon the lampstand [ἐπὶ τὴν λυχνίαν, *epi tēn lychnian*]?" is introduced by the negative particle οὐχ (*ouch*), indicating that, unlike the question in the first part of the verse, this question expects a positive answer. The abbreviated nature of the clause in the Greek text requires that we add the material in brackets in the translation. In contrast to the parallel sayings (Matt. 5:15; Luke 8:16; cf. also Gos. Thom. 33), the purpose of the lamp during Jesus's ministry was not to give light to those outside (cf. Mark 9:9b). Since the resurrection, however, the purpose of the lamp is to be upon a lampstand in order for all to see (cf. 9:9c; Carlston 1975: 154–55). Thus, whereas the first question deals with whether the temporary hiddenness of Jesus's coming was intended to be permanent and expects a negative answer, this question concerning the ultimate purpose and future revelation of the Son of God expects a positive one. Upon his resurrection, Jesus will indeed be manifested and set on a lampstand through the witness of the church (9:9c), so that everyone can believe that Jesus is the Christ and enter into eternal life (cf. John 21:31). Yet Mark's community knows that this "already now" manifestation since the resurrection is still in part and awaits that day when every eye will see and every tongue confess that Jesus Christ is Lord (Mark 13:26; 14:62; cf. Phil. 2:10–11; Titus 2:15).

The parallels to "For there is nothing hidden except in order that it may be made manifest" (Matt. 10:26; Luke 8:17; 12:2; Gos. Thom. 5) lack the "in order that" (ἵνα) found in Mark. Thus in the parallels this saying functions as a proverb stating that what is now hidden will one day be revealed. In Mark, however, the ἵνα implies that something has in fact been intentionally hidden for the purpose of later being made manifest. Attempts to explain the ἵνα here and in 4:12 as a mistranslation of Aramaic דְּ (*dĕ*; M. Black 1967: 76–77) fail to take seriously how it functions in the present form of the saying and its context. Mark clearly meant for his readers to take the "in order that" at face value. The opening statement in 4:22 repeats the thought found in the question of the previous statement: "For there is nothing hidden [κρυπτόν, *krypton*] except in order that it may be made manifest [φανερωθῇ, *phanerōthē*]." This is followed by another statement in synonymous parallelism: "nor has anything become secret [ἀπόκρυφον, *apokryphon*] but in order that it may be made manifest [φανερόν, *phaneron*]." Some suggest that the temporal sense of the aorist "may be made" (ἐγένετο, *egeneto*) should not be pressed because in the parallel the corresponding verb "is" (ἐστίν, *estin*) is in the present tense, but the aorist does seem to refer to a past event (Marcus 1986b: 150–51; contra Gundry 1993: 215). There was indeed a time of hiddenness, but this has come to an end (Donahue and Harrington 2002: 150). The person and work of Jesus Christ are now openly proclaimed so that all may know (13:10). And this time of proclamation will give way to an even greater revelation when all "see the Son of Man sitting at the right hand of Power and coming with the clouds of heaven" (14:62).

The problem with this saying lies in its logic. It appears to be self-contradictory. One does not normally hide something in order to make it manifest. This verse agrees with 4:21 in saying that the purpose of the lamp is not to be hidden. Yet the kingdom and the one who brought it were indeed hidden to those "outside" (4:12). This has ultimately served the divine purpose in that those for whom this was hidden unknowingly helped carry out the divine plan. They did this by fulfilling the divine necessity (8:31) that led them to crucify the Son of God (9:31; 10:33–34, 45; 14:22–25). This was, however, God's intention. Unlike the meaning of the parallel sayings in Matt. 10:26; Luke 8:17; 12:2; Gos. Thom. 5, which are a proverbial assurance that nothing will remain hidden but that God will ultimately bring all things to light, Mark reveals that God purposed this hiddenness in order to bring about his divine will. "Hiddenness *serves the purpose* of openness" (Marcus 1986b: 147); "obscurity of the word ultimately serves the purpose of revelation" (Marcus 2000: 319), so that what results is "the triumph of manifestation over hiddenness" (Gundry 1993: 213). For those given to know the secret of the kingdom of God and the identity of Jesus during his ministry (4:11), the Lamp was revealed, but since the resurrection and the proclamation of the gospel, this has been revealed more clearly. What the demons were told not to reveal concerning the Lamp (1:34; 3:11–12) can now be shouted from the housetop. Jesus is Lord and Christ, the Son of God (1:1; 3:11), and this partial revealing and making known by the believing community will one day become complete and clear to all when the Son of Man returns.

Thus Mark intends his readers in 4:21–22 to understand that the blindness of the unbelieving world to the Son of God and the arrival of his kingdom was not accidental but intentional. All this lay within the divine providence, for in their unbelief, those who opposed Jesus unknowingly carried out the divine plan that the Son of God give his life as a ransom for many (10:45). This immediate purpose, however, was simply a means to bring about God's ultimate purpose, so that the Lamp would fulfill his purpose and as a result be placed on the lampstand for all to behold (cf. Phil. 2:10–11). The time has begun to dawn in which people understand and acknowledge that Jesus Christ is Lord. This is shown by the fact that the readers of Mark's Gospel have done so. But all this simply foreshadows that glorious day (cf. 4:26–29) when all humanity will acknowledge that the Lamp is Lord and Christ.

4:23   For "If anyone has ears to hear, let him hear," see 4:9. This saying frequently concludes a saying or pericope (4:9; Matt. 11:15; 13:43; Luke 14:35; cf. Rev. 2:7, 11, 17, 29; Gos. Thom. 8, 21, 24, 63, 65, 96). The present exhortation functions less as a call to moral action or commitment (as in 4:9) than as a call to understanding and encouragement. Despite the response, or lack of response, of the world to the Lamp, God will make the Lamp manifest to all.

Thus the believing community, which has been given the understanding that Jesus Christ, the Son of God, has come and inaugurated the kingdom of God, should take heart. God will manifest to the whole world what has been made known to them. Thus 4:23 serves not primarily as a warning to heed but, in light of 4:21–22, as an encouragement.

As in 4:21 the opening saying begins with "And he was saying to them." The **4:24–25** exhortation "Pay attention to [lit. 'See'] what you hear" (βλέπετε τί ἀκούετε, *blepete ti akouete*) picks up 4:23, but whereas the exhortation in 4:23 ended the saying (as in 4:9), here it begins it. The threefold use of "hear" (ἀκούω) in 4:23–24 recalls the importance of how one hears in 4:13–20. Coming on the heels of 4:23, "hear" in 4:24 places additional emphasis on the exhortation. The use of the second-person plural in "By what measure you measure [μετρεῖτε, *metreite*] it will be measured to you and will be further added to you," as in the previous exhortation to "hear," indicates that "to measure" is a synonym for "to hear/heed." The expression "it will be measured" (μετρηθήσεται, *metrēthēsetai*) is another example of the divine passive (see 2:5). In the parallels in Matt. 7:2 and Luke 6:38 ("In what judgment you judge, you will be judged"; cf. also *m. Soṭah* 1.7; *b. Sanh.* 100a), this refers to the day when God will judge the world. In Mark the saying refers to the present understanding that the believing community possesses. Because they understand that the Lamp has already come, they will receive additional understanding concerning the person and work of the Son of God and the arrival of his kingdom. This additional statement, "[it] will be further added to you" (missing in D and W), which is not found in the Matthean and Lukan parallels, emphasizes the graciousness of God. He gives not just in proportion to one's effort but is overwhelming in his grace. The twofold "it will be measured to you [ὑμῖν, *hymin*]" and "will be further added to you [ὑμῖν]" recalls the "to you" (ὑμῖν) of 4:11. This, along with the fourfold ἵνα in 4:21–25 and the ἵνα in 4:12, indicates that 4:10–12 and 4:21–25 should be interpreted along similar lines.

The switch from the second person in 4:24 to the third in 4:25 ("For [to the one] who has, it will be given to him, and [to the one] who has not, even what he has will be taken away from him") may indicate that these two verses were originally isolated sayings of Jesus that were brought together, most probably by Mark. This proverb is found in several different places in the Gospel: at the end of the parable of the talent/pounds (Matt. 25:29; Luke 19:26); in the Lukan parallel to this saying (Luke 8:18); and in the Matthean explanation of why Jesus taught in parables (Matt. 13:12). It is a common proverb found in many cultures (cf. "The rich get richer and the poor get poorer"; "It takes money to make money"; Prov. 9:9; 2 Esd. 7:25; *b. Suk.* 46a–b; *b. Ber.* 40a: "But the Holy One, blessed be He, . . . He puts more into a full vessel but not into an empty one"; etc.). The "for" indicates that this proverb explains the saying in 4:24. Thus 4:24–25, like the parable of the soils, serve both as a warning and as a promise. They, like 4:11–12, speak of two groups: insiders who have been given the secret of the kingdom of God and outsiders who lack such knowledge.

The person who already has understanding will be further enriched by greater knowledge. Their knowledge that the Christ has come and brought with him the kingdom of God will increase even more. Whereas the parallels in Matt. 10:26/Luke 12:2 and Matt. 7:2/Luke 6:38 refer primarily to the time when in the day of judgment God will bring to light all secrets, Mark has also in mind the increase in understanding that the death and resurrection of Jesus will bring to his followers. These events and the explanations associated with them in the preaching of the early church will serve to increase the knowledge of the believing community, as Mark's readers have already experienced. Even as the original hearers of Jesus received additional light through further parables and explanations (4:33–34), so Mark's readers were privy to additional enlightenment through other teachings and sayings of Jesus found in this Gospel, as well as in the other Jesus traditions with which they were familiar. Thus 4:25 functions more as a promise than as a threat (Guelich 1989: 233). Nevertheless, for those lacking this knowledge and standing outside the believing community (4:11), their darkness will become greater still (cf. 2 Cor. 3:14–16).

Summary

In this passage, Mark shares with his readers that the kingdom of God (1:15) and the Lamp (cf. John 8:12; 9:5; 12:35) of the world have indeed come, but they have come in an unexpected way. Although others are ignorant of their coming and some even seek to thwart what God is doing, the Lamp hidden for a time according to the divine purpose cannot remain hidden. Even when ordered by the Lamp to keep his coming hidden, this was at times impossible. Both humans and demons cannot help but proclaim that the Son of God has indeed come (cf. 1:45; 3:11–12). Time and again the identity of Jesus breaks through the silence and hiddenness, and a glimpse of who Jesus truly is becomes manifest. He cannot be completely hidden. Temporally hidden for the purpose of fulfilling his divine mission, the Lamp has subsequently begun to shine more brightly through his death and resurrection and in the proclamation of the early church. Mark's readers have been given the opportunity to see this, and their understanding is continuing to grow. To them is being given greater knowledge and certainty, and to them has been given the command to proclaim this message throughout the world.

For his readers, who may have questioned why Jesus's coming and the arrival of the kingdom were not acknowledged by all, Mark points out in this passage that the hiddenness of Jesus's coming served a divine purpose. Strangely enough, Jesus was hidden in order that through that hiddenness events would take place that would bring about openness. The blindness of those outside led to opposition and death precisely in order that God's Son could give his life as a ransom for many (8:31; 9:32; 10:33, 45). In the divine mystery, the culpability of Jesus's opponents remains, but in God's sovereign will, they served his purpose. In this passage Mark does not explain how this all works out theologically, but his readers know that a divine paradox is present. The hardness of Israel's leadership toward Jesus was not only foreknown by God but used to fulfill his purpose. This is the sense of ἵνα in 4:12 and in 4:21–22. In the divine will the leaders of Israel hardened their hearts to the claims and teachings of Jesus and caused his death. This, however, was all in accordance with the ultimate plan of God. Thus, whereas the human cause of Jesus's death lies with those who opposed Jesus, and they are culpable for this, Mark wants his readers to know that the ultimate reason for all this lies with God, for "it was the will of the LORD to crush him with pain. When you make his life an offering for sin . . ." (Isa. 53:10). In light of this, they should take heart, for the manifestation of the Lamb will surely come (4:22), and take heed of the repeated warning to hear and heed the message of the parable of the soils (4:3, 9, 23, 24) and be good soil, producing much fruit.

Additional Note

4:24. Some MSS (A Θ f¹ f¹³ syr) add τοῖς ἀκούουσιν, but this appears to be a gloss added by a copyist to explain the exhortation "Pay attention to what you hear" (Metzger 1994: 71–72).

5. Jesus's Parables of the Seed Growing Secretly and the Mustard Seed (4:26–34)

At this point, Mark resumes his collection of seed parables (4:3–20), which has been interrupted by the parables of the lamp and the measure (4:21–25), with the parables of the seed growing secretly (4:26–29) and the mustard seed (4:30–32). Common to all the parables in this chapter is the "mystery concerning the kingdom of God" (4:11). Thus the present parables are connected not simply to the parables of the lamp and the measure but to the entire collection. The present "parables" (4:2, 10, 33) are technically "similitudes," although their riddle-like nature is also quite apparent.[1] The similarity of the present two parables is obvious. Both are similitudes of the kingdom of God (the only two explicit "kingdom parables" in Mark) involving seed. Both begin with the sowing of seed (4:26, 31–32), and both describe the beginning and final stage of the seed-growth process.[2] Their emphases, however, are different. The first focuses its attention on the interim stage of growth, whereas the second focuses on the final product. The present two parables complement the preceding two by showing that despite the hiddenness of the kingdom of God, growth is certain and inevitable (4:26–29), and although it may have begun insignificantly in the mind of the world, its final manifestation will be immense (4:30–32). The very purpose of the kingdom's hiddenness (4:21) has as its goal this glorious and final manifestation (4:22, 32). The entire collection of parables is then concluded by a summary in 4:33–34 ("By means of many such parables he was speaking the word to them"), which forms an *inclusio* with 4:2 ("And he was teaching them many things in parables"), indicating the unity of 4:1–34.

Numerous attempts have been made to arrive at the pre-Markan form of these two parables and the summary. Some see "And he was saying" (Καὶ ἔλεγεν, *Kai elegen*) in 4:26a and 30a as Markan (Pryke 1978: 13, 141, 156–57), but most see these as part of the pre-Markan tradition. A few see 4:27a–28 (Kuhn 1971: 105–11) or 4:28 (Crossan 1973c: 252) as Markan, and several see 4:31b ("is the smallest of all seeds upon the earth"; W. Lane 1974: 171; Crossan 1973c: 256–57; Pryke 1978: 13, 141, 157; Guelich 1989: 247) and 4:32a ("when it is sown"; Crossan 1973c: 256–57; Guelich 1989: 247; Marcus 2000: 325) as Markan. Concerning 4:33–34, the opinion is surprisingly diverse, ranging from it being traditional (Guelich 1989: 254–56), only 4:34a

---

1. For a discussion of the different subtypes that make up the genre of "parable" in the NT, see Stein 2000.

2. For additional similarities, see Lambrecht 1974: 291.

being Markan (Gnilka 1978: 190), all of 4:34 being Markan (Schmithals 1979: 1.246), to all of 4:33–34 being Markan. We find in 4:33–34 three hapax legomena: "apart from" (χωρίς, *chōris*); "to his own disciples" (τοῖς ἰδίοις μαθηταῖς, *tois idiois mathētais*); "explained" (ἐπέλυεν, *epelyen*); and to these can be added the twofold use of the conjunction δέ (*de*, and/but) rather than the more typically Markan καί (*kai*, and). Yet throughout the summary we find a strongly Markan vocabulary, style, and emphasis. We need only note how "he was speaking the word [τὸν λόγον, *ton logon*] to them" (4:33a) picks up the Markan theme in 4:11–12, and how it forms an *inclusio* with 4:2. All this argues for the summary being due to the work of the evangelist himself (Lambrecht 1974: 273–77; France 2002: 217), although it is based on traditional material and themes. The clearest understanding of the Markan redactional work in 4:26–34 is gained not by surgical attempts to dissect various verses for words, phrases, or clauses that Mark inserted, but rather by observing how the material in this section fits into the overall Markan themes and emphases found in 4:3–34.

Exegesis and Exposition

[26]And he was saying, "The kingdom of God is like this. [It is] as if a man would scatter the seed on the ground, [27]and would sleep and rise night and day, and the seed would sprout and grow, and he himself does not know [how]. [28]Of its own accord the ground bears grain, first the blade, then the ear, then the full grain in the ear. [29]And when the grain is ripe, he immediately wields the sickle, because the harvest has come."

[30]And he was saying, "To what shall we liken the kingdom of God or with what parable can we describe it? [31][It is] like a mustard seed that, when sown upon the ground, ⌐is⌐ the smallest of all the seeds on the earth, [32]and when it is sown, it grows up and becomes the greatest of all the shrubs and produces great branches, so that the birds of heaven are able to dwell under its shade."

[33]And by means of many such parables he was speaking the word to them, to the degree that they were able to hear. [34]And apart from a parable he was not speaking to them, but privately to his own disciples he explained everything.

Both this and the following parable begin with "And he was saying" (Καὶ ἔλε- **4:26–29** γεν, *Kai elegen*). For other examples, see 4:9, 30; 14:36. For "he was saying to them," see 2:27–28; for a more expanded form, compare 7:14; 8:24; 11:17; 12:35, 38; 15:12, 14. In both 4:26 and 30 no change in audience is indicated (contra Heil 1992: 282). See 4:33–34. The following parable is the only parable in Mark that has no parallel in Matthew, Luke, or the Gospel of Thomas. The banal nature of the parable (J. Edwards 2002: 142) fits well the already now–not yet dimension of the kingdom of God. "The kingdom of God is like" (lit. "So is the kingdom of God as"—Οὕτως ἐστὶν ἡ βασιλεία τοῦ θεοῦ ὡς, *Houtōs estin hē basileia tou theou hōs*) is an awkward expression and not found in the introduction of any other Gospel parable. It is not clear as to what the kingdom of God is being likened. Is it the farmer and his activity or lack of activity? The seed? The whole similitude? If it is the farmer, should we focus on his inactivity (the parable of the patient farmer—Hultgren 2000: 386) or his ignorance/unbelief (the parable of the unbelieving farmer)? Should we focus instead on the seed and how it grows secretly and irresistibly (the parable of the successful seed) or on the final harvest (the parable of the great harvest)? That this parable lies within a collection of "seed" parables favors our focusing attention upon the role of the seed and the analogy it presents to the kingdom of God. The farmer plays a rather insignificant role in the process. As in the parable of the sower (4:3–20) and in the following parable, he is present primarily to initiate and conclude the process. Nothing is said of other activities that a farmer normally does: plowing, tilling, fertilizing, weeding, and so on. He merely sleeps and rises. This, along with his not knowing how the seed grows and the seed growing of its own accord, deemphasizes his role in the parable (Gundry 1993: 220; France 2002: 213). Nor do we read of the role of the sun and rain, or of destructive elements such as drought, heat, hail, weeds, and locusts. This is true also in the following parable. The focus of this parable is upon the seed and its inevitable growth (4:28).[3]

Although "scatter" (βάλη, balē; lit. "cast") is a rather unusual verb to describe the process of sowing, it is also used in this manner in Luke 13:19. The Greek verb "cast" (βάλλω, ballō) is often used in situations where the English word "cast" would seem out of place. For example, the sick are "cast" on a bed (Matt. 9:2; Luke 16:20), wine is "cast" or poured (Mark 2:22), and peace is "cast" or brought (Matt. 10:34). The tense of the verb (aorist subjunctive) should not be pressed, since it is the normal tense for an action that is not repeated, whereas the following present subjunctives ("sleep," "rise," "sprout," "grow") indicate that these actions are seen as continuous. One does not continually sow seed in a field, but the growth of a seed is a continuous activity. We have a similar use of the aorist subjunctive to describe the harvest's arrival in 4:29 (παραδοῖ, paradoi, is ripe; cf. also the perfect παρέστηκεν, parestēken, has come) and the use of the present tense to describe the process of harvesting (ἀποστέλλει, apostellei; lit. "sends").

The description of sleeping "night and day" (νύκτα καὶ ἡμέραν, nykta kai hēmeran) may reflect a Semitic understanding of a day beginning at sundown (cf. Gen. 1:5, 8, 13, etc.). This comment, along with the ignoring of any human activities necessary in successful agriculture, emphasizes the independence of the seed's growth from any action on the part of the farmer and is meant to show that the consummation of the kingdom of God is not dependent on any human action (Marcus 2000: 326). Whether the comment was intended by Jesus (or Mark) to refute the views of revolutionaries and Zealots, who sought to bring the kingdom by force of arms, however, is unclear. Although the Hebrew term "sprout" (צֶמַח, ṣemaḥ) is used for the Messiah in Zech. 3:8;

---

3. Crossan (1973c: 252) is correct in pointing out that 4:28 shifts "the emphasis from the action of the farmer to the fate of the seed." Cf. Ambrozic 1972: 116–17.

6:12 (cf. also Jer. 23:5–6), it is unlikely that Mark's audience would have seen any such messianic allusion here (contra Marcus 2000: 322), because a different word is used in the LXX (Ἀνατολή, *Anatolē*) to translate the Hebrew term than the one found in 4:27 (βλαστᾷ, *blasta*). The marvel of the sprouting of the seed is witnessed to by the words "he himself did not know how" (ὡς οὐκ οἶδεν αὐτός, *hōs ouk oiden autos*). Among horticulturists today, the germination of a seed and its subsequent growth can elicit awe and wonder. This was even more the case in biblical times. The lack of the farmer's understanding indicates that the farmer is not to be interpreted as an allegorical reference to Jesus (Guelich 1989: 243; Gundry 1993: 226; contra Belo 1981: 123; Marcus 1986b: 177–85). Mark 13:32 does not refute this, because, whereas Jesus could be ignorant of the time of the kingdom's consummation, he was certainly not ignorant concerning the already now–not yet dimension of the kingdom of God. Furthermore, in 4:34 Mark explicitly states that Jesus was able to explain to his disciples "everything" (πάντα, *panta*) that these parables taught concerning the kingdom of God. To the "how" (ὡς, *hōs*) of 4:27, Mark assumes his readers will add "the seed sprouts and grows."

Since the kingdom of God is likened to a seed whose growth is not determined by the farmer's knowing "how" this takes place but rather to the earth "bearing grain" (καρποφορεῖ, *karpophorei*; cf. 4:20) "of itself" (αὐτομάτη, *automatē*—an adjective used adverbially), this indicates that the ultimate success of the kingdom of God does not depend on the understanding or actions of Mark's readers. The kingdom will come "of itself." For the audience of Jesus and Mark, this would have been understood to mean that God would bring about the growth of the seed, that is, God will bring the consummation of the kingdom apart from human effort.[4] "Here . . . divine causation would be taken for granted" (Hultgren 2000: 387). Compare Gen. 1:12, where the earth brings forth vegetation because God said "Let the earth put forth . . ." (1:11).

Some see the description "first the blade, then the ear, then the full grain in the ear" (πρῶτον χόρτον, εἶτα στάχυν, εἶτα πλήρης σῖτον ἐν τῷ στάχυϊ, *prōton chorton, eita stachyn, eita plērēs siton en tō stachyi*) as matching the threefold actions of the man's sowing, sleeping, and rising. Yet the present form of the parable also refers to the man "not knowing."[5] Others argue that the reference to the "grain being ripe" (παραδοῖ ὁ καρπός, *paradoi ho karpos*) in 4:29 gives a fourfold parallel to the four kinds of soils in 4:3–20 (Gundry 1993: 221). The meaning of the parable, however, is not dependent upon there being a perfect three- or fourfold parallelism. The attempt to see in this threefold description a "salvation history" (seed as Jesus's ministry; blade and ear as the period of

---

4. So Marcus 1986b: 171–73; Stuhlmann 1972: 154–56; Heil 1992: 282–83; contra Guelich 1989: 241–42, who argues that it simply refers to "without human efforts."

5. Some believe that "he knows not how" is Markan and that the original form of the parable had a perfectly matching threefold comparison. Yet if Mark has an imbalanced comparison, who is to say that the parable could not have had that same imbalance in the oral period or on the lips of Jesus himself? For the view that this expression is pre-Markan, see Guelich 1989: 241.

the church; full grain as the consummation) lacks any clear support of such a scheme elsewhere in Mark (contra Marcus 2000: 328).

"And when the grain is ripe" in 4:29 can also be translated "when [the condition of] the grain allows it" (Zerwick and Grosvenor 1981: 113). This may suggest the idea that certain things must take place before the final harvest or consummation of the kingdom. It is necessary (δεῖ, *dei*) for certain things to take place first: Elijah must come (9:11–12); the Son of Man must suffer in Jerusalem, be put to death, and rise (8:31; 9:31–32; 10:32–34); he must drink the cup given him (10:38); the disciples must experience persecution (13:9–13); the abomination of desolation must take place (13:14); the gospel must be preached to all nations (13:10); and so on (Marcus 2000: 322–23, 328–29). Much of this had already occurred for Mark's readers, and thus they probably saw little (the fall of Jerusalem—13:5ff.?) remaining before the return of the Son of Man and the final harvest.

The parable concludes not with the process of growth described in 4:28 but with the final product—the coming of the harvest (4:29). Nothing is made of the various stages of the growth cycle mentioned in 4:28. At the appropriate time ("when the grain is ripe"), the farmer is reintroduced and the harvest takes place. Since the parable is not an allegory in which the farmer represents Jesus, the disciples, or God, there is no need to find some consistent theological explanation of the farmer's behavior.[6] Attempts to interpret the harvest in terms of a realized eschatology, in which "the gradual and steady growth of crowds of people attracted by Jesus's teaching" indicates the arrival of the kingdom of God, stumble over such passages as Isa. 17:5–6; 18:5; Mic. 4:12; Matt. 3:12; Rev. 14:15; 2 Esd. 4:28–37; 2 Bar. 70.2; Gos. Thom. 21 (contra Dodd 1948: 144–46; V. Taylor 1952: 266; Heil 1992: 284–85), where the metaphor of a "harvest" is frequently used to describe the final consummation of all things. The image of the sickle being applied to the harvest is even more telling (cf. Joel 3:13 [4:13 LXX]; Rev. 14:14–19; Jer. 50:16 [27:16 LXX])[7] and may very well carry with it the sense of judgment (contra Marcus 2000: 323).

4:30–32 This parable is introduced exactly like the preceding one, "And he was saying" (see 4:26), which suggests that, before Mark, it circulated independently. It begins with a double question that is typically Markan (see 4:13–14). "To

6. Marcus (1986b: 177–85) sees in this parable an elaborate allegory in which the farmer = Jesus; seed = "word" of the kingdom; farmer's sleeping = Jesus's lack of concern for and detachment from events in his ministry; lack of understanding = Jesus's lack of understanding of events taking place; reaper = judgment of the Son of Man. It is difficult to argue that Mark intended such an interpretation in that the farmer/reaper = Jesus analogy is critically flawed. In Mark, Jesus may not know the time of the end (13:32), but he does know all about the kingdom of God. This is evident in his explaining the kingdom parables to the disciples (4:33–34). It is the disciples' lack of understanding (4:12, 33–34; 6:51; 8:32–33; 9:32; etc.), not that of Jesus, that is emphasized in Mark.

7. Marcus (2000: 329) is correct when he states, "By the time [Mark's audience] reached the final verse [4:29] they would know that it was describing the end of all things, the apocalyptic conclusion when Jesus will return on the clouds as the eschatological judge, the Son of Man." Thus one should not interpret "wields" (ἀποστέλλει) in terms of how it is used in 3:14 and 6:7.

what [πῶς, *pōs*; lit. 'how'] shall we liken the kingdom of God or with what parable can we describe it?" The existence of various Matthew-Luke agreements against Mark in their version of the parable ("which a man took and sowed," Matt. 13:31/Luke 13:19; "tree," Matt. 13:32/Luke 13:19; "branches," Matt. 13:32/Luke 13:19) suggests, if we assume Markan priority, that they had access to another version(s) of this parable along with Mark (McArthur 1971: 198–200).[8] In the analogy, the kingdom of God is compared not to the specific object mentioned (the mustard seed) but to the whole picture presented, that is, a small mustard seed that upon being planted becomes a large plant (Jeremias 1972: 101). The analogy involves a very small beginning and a great final product. Although the term "mustard seed" (σινάπεως, *sinapeōs*) is neuter, "that" (ὅς, *hos*) is masculine (4:31). This is due to the fact that it refers back to the masculine "seed" (κόκκῳ, *kokkō*). "Like a mustard seed" (ὡς κόκκῳ σινάπεως) is literally "like a seed of mustard seed," but since "mustard seed" is a genitive of description, it functions adjectivally, and we should therefore translate it "like a 'mustard seed' that. . . ." It is frequently pointed out that in the rabbinic literature mustard seeds were not planted in the garden but in the field, that is, upon the ground (*m. Kil.* 3.2; *b. Kil.* 50b). Although Jesus's audience might have been aware of this, it is unlikely that Mark's hearers/readers would have been.

The mustard seed is described as "the smallest of all the seeds on the earth." "Smallest" translates the comparative μικρότερον (*mikroteron*), which is used as a superlative, as is often the case in Koine Greek (Moule 1959: 97–98). Some have suggested that this clause is a Markan explanatory insertion. Yet it appears to be essential to the entire analogy of small to great and is probably pre-Markan and perhaps even authentic. Note that it is found in the parallel in Gos. Thom. 20. Even though the smallness of the mustard seed was proverbial (cf. *m. Ṭohar.* 8.8; *m. Nid.* 5.2; *b. Ber.* 31a; *b. Nid.* 5a, 13b, 16b, 40a, 66a; cf. also Matt. 17:20), the precision of the statement has often been challenged. The orchid seed is in fact smaller (J. C. Trever, *IDB* 3:467–77). Yet Jesus's choice of the mustard seed is due to the small beginning–large final product comparison and to his audience's experience of this analogy. To require horticultural precision of Jesus is to ignore the hyperbolic nature of Jesus's (and his cultural world's) use of language. Surely one would not expect Jesus to say, "which . . . ranks in the upper one-tenth of one percent of smallness in seed sizes."[9]

The mustard seed is described as experiencing four stages: "sown [σπαρῇ, *sparē*] . . . grows up [ἀναβαίνει, *anabainei*] . . . becomes [γίνεται, *ginetai*] . . . puts forth [ποιεῖ, *poiei*]." Attempts to determine which of these descriptions are Markan and which are authentic tend to be speculative and inconclusive. The final product of the mustard seed is described as "the greatest of all the

---

8. It may be that Matthew and Luke used the Q version of the parable but that Mark did not (Friedrichsen 2001).

9. For Jesus's use of exaggerated language, see Stein 1990: 135–220.

shrubs" (μεῖζον πάντων τῶν λαχάνων, *meizon pantōn tōn lachanōn*). Although this description is missing in both Luke 13:19 and Gos. Thom. 20, it is found in the Matthean parallel (13:32). It provides the second part of the explicit comparison—smallest to greatest (the comparative μεῖζον, "greater," is used as a superlative; cf. μικρότερον in 4:31). Although the mustard "shrub" can grow to a height of "six, twelve, or even fifteen feet" (Hultgren 2000: 395; France 2002: 216), it is an exaggeration to call it a "tree." (The use of the term "tree" in Matt. 13:32/Luke 13:19 may be due to the influence of Ezek. 17:22–23.) The result of this smallest seed is not a tree but a large shrub, but what is important in the comparison is the immense contrast between the final product and its beginning. The reference to the mustard shrub putting "forth large branches" is found also in Gos. Thom. 20 but not in Matt. 13:32 and Luke 13:19. It serves to emphasize the great contrast between the large final product and its extremely small beginning. It is this comparison with the mustard seed, not with the cedars of Lebanon, that makes the branches "large."[10] It is this size contrast, not the ordinary nature of the mustard seed and the event described, that is at play in this comparison (contra Scott 1981: 71–73). Some see in "the birds of heaven" (τὰ πετεινὰ τοῦ οὐρανοῦ, *ta peteina tou ouranou*) an allegorical reference to the inclusion of the gentiles in the kingdom of God (cf. Ezek. 17:23; 31:6; Dan. 4:12, 21; Jeremias 1972: 147; Hooker 1991: 136). No clear allusion to these OT texts is made in the parable, however, and the reference to the birds, like the reference to the large branches, makes perfectly good sense as an example of the greatness of the final product without allegorizing it. The reference to the birds making their dwelling in the shade of the shrub can mean to "nest in its branches and thus in the shade of the shrub" (cf. Luke 13:19) or to "nest under the shade of the shrub," that is, on the ground under the tree. The latter is more likely.

4:33–34 The introductory words of this summary, "by means of many such parables [καὶ τοιαύταις παραβολαῖς πολλαῖς, *kai toiautais parabolais pollais*] he was speaking the word to them," parallel 4:2—"And he was teaching them many things in parables." By this *inclusio* Mark reveals that the parables in 4:3–32 are a collection of Jesus's parables and not a chronological description of his parabolic teaching on a particular day. The particular event described in 4:1–2 serves as an introductory scene for the summary of Jesus's parabolic teachings that follow. The instrumental "by means of many such parables" indicates that the parables were not an end in themselves. They were rather a means to an end. Their end was teaching the "word" (Stein 2000: 34–38). The recipients of this parabolic teaching is "them" (αὐτοῖς, *autois*). Since the "them" is distinguished from the "disciples" in 4:34, this must refer to "those

10. The saying, "Great oaks from little acorns grow," would seem to many a better comparison of the beginning and the glorious consummation of the kingdom of God. If, however, we compare a mustard seed to the full-grown shrub, the comparison of the final product to the seed is many times greater than the comparison of a great oak to the acorn that produced it (cf. Gundry 1993: 233–34).

outside" in 4:11, who are not given the understanding of the parables (4:34). Yet Mark has not reintroduced this group in 4:13–32, and the last specific audience Mark has alluded to is "those around him along with the Twelve" (4:10–12). This suggests that the summary serves as a general explanation for Mark's readers as to why Jesus taught in parables and that 4:1–32 was not intended to be interpreted as part of a chronological sequence of events. For "word" (λόγος, *logos*), see 1:45.

"That they were able to hear" (καθὼς ἠδύναντο ἀκούειν, *kathōs ēdynanto akouein*) can be translated more literally "just as" and mean without restriction or limitation, that is, he taught in a manner and on a level to match his hearers' ability, so that they could understand everything. Or it can mean "to the degree that" or as far as they could understand it (cf. 1 Cor. 3:1). The second, more restrictive sense is favored by 4:34, in which the necessity of Jesus's explaining the parables to the disciples is described. It is also favored by the earlier references to the inability of those outside to "hear" (cf. 4:9, 10–12, 23–25). However, this verse also indicates that some understanding of the meaning of the parables was available to those "outside." That the same verb "be able" (δύναμαι, *dynamai*) is used in 4:32 as here should not be pressed (contra Marcus 2000: 331).

Mark states that Jesus did not speak to the people apart from parables. It is evident in Mark, however, that Jesus's teaching was not limited to parables (cf. 1:15; 3:28; 6:10–11; 8:34–38; 9:33–50; 10:18–19, 24–31, 42–45; 12:13–44; 13:5–37; etc.). Mark has probably used hyperbole here to emphasize the riddle-like nature of much of Jesus's teaching. The iterative nature of the verbs "was speaking" (ἐλάλει, *elalei*) and "was explaining" (ἐπέλυεν, *epelyen*) indicates that this was the general way that Jesus taught. Publicly Jesus was (continually) teaching them (the crowd of 4:1) in parables, but privately he "was [continually] explaining everything" to his own disciples, that is, "those around him along with the Twelve" in 4:10 (France 2002: 219). As a result 4:33–34a and 34b explain how 4:24 and 25 worked out in Jesus's ministry. The need to explain everything "privately" (κατ᾽ ἰδίαν, *kat' idian*; cf. 6:31–32; 7:33; 9:2, 28; 13:3) to the disciples reveals at the same time both their privileged position (4:11–12) and their lack of understanding (6:52; 8:17; cf. 4:40). Those "outside" can understand something of the meaning of the parables (4:33b), but that knowledge is only partial. To the disciples, however, Jesus explained "everything" (πάντα, *panta*).

Summary

Mark concludes his collection of parables with two parables that are meant to reassure his readers concerning the future culmination of the kingdom of God. Although the exact situation for which he writes is uncertain, the parables assure his readers that God is in full control of history. The future consummation they await and long for is certain. When the time is ripe (4:29), the final harvest will come, bringing blessing and bliss for them but judgment for those "outside." Whether Mark's readers would have been familiar with such traditions as Jesus bringing a baptism with spirit and fire (Matt. 3:10–11) and the parables of the wheat and weeds (Matt. 13:24–30) and the sheep and the goats (Matt. 25:31–46) is uncertain, but the image of the sickle being applied to the harvest would have probably raised up thoughts of judgment as well as blessing at the final harvest. Mark affirms for his audience that their initial experience of the kingdom and its firstfruits would most certainly be followed by the ultimate consummation of history, when the Son of Man returns (8:34–38; 13:24–32). The inconspicuous nature of the kingdom should not be a concern. Although at the present time hidden from the eyes of the world (4:21–22), at the consummation its final manifestation will be glorious and overwhelming! Just as a mustard seed is so very small but in its final stage becomes the largest of the shrubs, so the smallness of the kingdom at the present time should not deceive Mark's audience. At the consummation the heavens themselves will be shaken, and the Son of Man will come in great power and glory (13:25–26).

Another Markan emphasis found in this passage involves the riddle-like nature of Jesus's teachings and ministry. These were intentionally concealed from those "outside" in order that the plan of God might be realized. The divine necessity of Jesus's death (the δεῖ, *dei*, should be noted in 8:31; cf. also 9:31; 10:33–34, 45; 14:21, 36; etc.) could be accomplished only if the Lamp were covered for a time (4:21). Only in this manner could the Lord of glory fulfill his ministry (10:45; cf. 1 Cor. 2:8; Acts 13:27; John 1:10). Jesus furthermore could teach about the coming of the kingdom of God, a most incendiary subject for Pilate and Rome, only through the riddle-like nature of his parables. For Herod and Pilate, Jesus's parabolic teachings concerning the kingdom of God and its coming were not revolutionary. For them, they were simply incomprehensible. Thus they would not interfere with Jesus's ministry until in God's time "the hour had come" (cf. 14:41).

Additional Note

4:31. The grammar is awkward; I take ὄν as a concessive participle.

III. Who Is This Jesus? Part 2 (3:7–6:6a)
   D. Jesus Teaches in Parables (4:1–34)
➤ E. Jesus—Lord of Nature, Demons, Disease, and Death (4:35–5:43)
   F. Jesus Encounters Unbelief in Nazareth (6:1–6a)

E. Jesus—Lord of Nature, Demons, Disease, and Death (4:35–5:43)

The pre-Markan nature of this collection of miracle stories is much debated. Some suggest that 3:7–12, allowing for Markan expansion, was a traditional summary that introduced a pre-Markan "boat cycle" consisting of 5:35–43 as well as 6:31–52 and 6:53–56.[1] Others have argued in favor of a twofold pre-Markan tradition that consisted of 4:35–5:43; 6:34–44, 53; and 6:45–51; 8:22–26; 7:24b–30, 32–37; 8:1–10.[2] The common elements involved in 4:35–41; 5:1–20; and 5:21–43 are the presence of Jesus, the disciples, a boat, the sea, a miracle, and a christological confession of some sort (4:38, 41; 5:7, 20, 28, 42). These common elements are probably what brought these stories together, but whether it was Mark who did this or someone before him is impossible to say. The difficulty of determining if Mark used a pre-Markan complex here is shown by the fact that some scholars refer to Mark himself being the author of this pre-Markan complex.

It is not at all impossible that Mark could have arranged this material on the basis of traditions he had available.[3] We have already observed how, by his editorial comment in 3:9, he has prepared his readers for the tradition of Jesus's teaching a parable (or parables) from a boat on the Sea of Galilee (4:1ff.). Now after completing his collection of parables in 4:34, he continues with the other boat and sea stories that he possessed. Jesus stilling the storm (4:35–41) provides an excellent introduction for these miracle stories in that it concludes with the question, "Who then is this man that even the wind and the sea obey him?" (4:41). This serves to focus the attention of his readers on the christological teachings of these stories. The first reveals that Jesus is Lord over nature (4:35–41), the second that he is Lord over the demonic world (5:1–20), and the third that he is Lord over disease and death (5:21–43).

---

1. Cf. Keck 1965b; Kuhn 1971: 191–213; Guelich 1989: 142–44, 261–63; Marcus 2000: 255–56.

2. Achtemeier 1970. See Gundry (1993: 242) for a succinct but telling critique of these theories.

3. Cf. Gundry (1993: 242), who argues for the historicity and interconnectedness of these accounts. "Since Jesus ministered in Galilee and some of his closest disciples were fishers, it is reasonable to think that he really did cross the Sea of Galilee with them and that these stories occur together because the events narrated in them were historically interconnected by sea-crossings." Of course, if one denies the possibility of the miraculous, then these stories can be neither interconnected nor historical. However, such a conclusion is then based upon a priori naturalistic historical presuppositions and not on an analysis of the text or the traditions underlying them.

1. Jesus—Lord of Nature (4:35–41)

This story involves a "nature miracle," even though some of the terminology resembles an exorcism. The presence of exorcism language in the story is simply a reminder that the world of the NT is not divided into neat categories such as "exorcisms" and "nature miracles." (See 2:1–12 for a similar problem in classification: Is it a healing story or a controversy story?) All form-critical designations such as "epiphany story," "exorcism," "miracle story," or "nature miracle" are scholarly attempts to classify the story but do not affect the story itself. The meaning of the story and its use by the evangelist stand over and above any description of it and should provide the basis of its classification (Guelich 1989: 261).[1] Attempts to see a particular structure in this story have been unsuccessful. The placement of this miracle story after Jesus's teaching in parables should not surprise the reader, for word and deed go hand in hand in Mark's description of Jesus. Jesus both announces the coming of the kingdom of God in his teaching and demonstrates his authority and power by his actions (1:27; cf. 1:21–22 and 25–26).

At this point Mark continues Jesus's boat ministry (prepared for in 3:9 and described in 4:1–34) with the use of the boat to cross the Sea of Galilee. The question of why Jesus wanted to minister on the eastern side of the sea involves a highly speculative psychologizing of his mental acts. We have no access to this, and in the present account Mark makes no attempt to explain why Jesus went to the other side of the sea. Mark 1:38 ("Let us go elsewhere into the neighboring towns, in order that I may also preach there; for I came out for this purpose") is probably the evangelist's understanding. The Markan theological emphasis in the passage is reasonably clear. This story and the two that follow emphasize various christological truths that he wants to share with his readers—Jesus is Lord of nature (4:35–41), of the demons (5:1–20), of disease (5:25–34), and of death (5:21–24, 35–43).

The Markan editorial work is seen most clearly in the double chronological description in the introductory seam (4:35–36a; Pryke 1978: 13, 141, 157; Gnilka 1978: 193; van Iersel and Linmans 1978: 18–20). Mark's hand is also seen in the reference to the disciples' lack of faith in 4:40 (Gnilka 1978: 194; van Iersel and Linmans 1978: 18–20; Guelich 1989: 267–69), for this is a Markan theme found throughout his Gospel (see 4:40–41). The present account is essentially formless, but I shall treat it as a nature miracle/epiphany

---

1. Hooker (1991: 138) points out that "the difference between these [nature miracles] and healing miracles is probably more obvious to us than to Mark, for whom they are all indications of the authority of Jesus."

story containing an introduction (4:35–36), the miracle of the stilling of the storm (4:37–39), and a concluding christological confession (4:40–41).

Exegesis and Exposition

³⁵And he [Jesus] says to them on that day when evening came, "Let us cross over to the other side." ³⁶And upon leaving the crowd, they took him with them in the boat, just as he was; and other boats were with him. ³⁷And a great windstorm arose, and the waves were beginning to break over the boat, so that the boat was already filling [with water]. ³⁸And he was in the stern sleeping on the cushion, and they wake him and say to him, "Teacher, do you not care that we are perishing?" ³⁹And having awoken he rebuked the wind and said to the sea, "Quiet! Be still!" And the wind ceased and there was a great calm. ⁴⁰And he said to them, "Why are you afraid? Do you ⌜not yet have faith⌝? ⁴¹And they were filled with awe and were saying to one another, "Who then is this man that even the wind and the sea obey him?"

For the common introductory formula "and he says to them" (καὶ λέγει αὐτοῖς, **4:35–36** *kai legei autois*), see comments on 1:38–39; 2:25–26; 3:3–4; 4:13–14; and so on. Since it is unlikely that the present account began in this manner, this may be a Markan seam tying the present account with what has preceded (cf. 4:13, 21, 26, 30; van Iersel and Linmans 1978: 18–19; contra Guelich 1989: 264). The double temporal designation introducing the account ("on that day," ἐν ἐκείνῃ τῇ ἡμέρᾳ, *en ekeinē tē hēmera*; "when evening came," ὀψίας γενομένης, *opsias genomenēs*) is typically Markan, and the second designation adds specificity to the first (Neirynck 1988: 45–50 [esp. 47–48], 94). See 1:32–34. In contrast to 13:19, 24, 32; 14:25, no eschatological significance should be read into "on that day." Here the dual temporal designation simply ties 4:35–41 to 4:1–34. "Evening" should not be interpreted as an allusion to the powers of darkness that manifest themselves in the coming story. Nowhere in Mark is "evening" or "night" (νύξ, *nyx*) associated with the powers of darkness. "To them" (αὐτοῖς, *autois*) refers to the disciples of 4:34, who are distinguished from the "crowd" of 4:36 and the "them" of 4:33. For another evening boat trip in which a storm arises and the disciples need rescuing, see 6:47–52. "Let us cross over to the other side [εἰς τὸ πέραν, *eis to peran*]" is picked up in 5:1, where an incident takes place at "Gerasa" on the eastern side of the Sea of Galilee, that is, on the "other" side (see 5:21–23). Although "cross over" (διέλθωμεν, *dielthōmen*) is typically used for traveling on land, here it means traveling across water (cf. Luke 8:22; Acts 18:27).

"And upon leaving the crowd [ὄχλον, *ochlon*]" refers to the crowd of 4:1–2, 10–12, 33–34. The miracle that follows "is given" (4:11) to the disciples, so that they may perceive and understand (cf. 4:24–25, 34). As to the boat referred to in 4:36, this boat was prepared for Jesus in 3:9 and used in 4:1. It is usually Jesus who is described as "taking" (παραλαμβάνουσιν, *paralambanousin*) the disciples or someone with him (5:40; 9:2; 10:32; 14:33) rather than the reverse as here. The confusing comment "just as he was" (ὡς ἦν, *hōs ēn*) has generally been interpreted to mean "immediately" or "without returning to shore" (Nineham 1963: 148). It is unlikely that "just as" (ὡς) should be translated "when," that is, now reembarking after having disembarked in 4:10 (contra Marcus 2000: 332), for ὡς is not used in this way anywhere else in Mark. Some see in the reference to "other boats" a "genuine reminiscence" of the event (V. Taylor 1952: 274; Pesch 1980a: 270; France 2002: 223). Some assume that these other boats were sunk in the storm and that this comment serves to accentuate the severity of the storm (Theissen 1983: 102), but the lack of any further mention in this pericope or in 5:1 of these other boats or their destruction indicates that they play no role in describing the storm and its ferocity.[2] Mark probably intends the reference to the boats to be understood as evidence for Jesus's great popularity and fame (cf. 1:28, 37, 45; 2:2, 13, 15; 3:7–10, 20, 32; 4:1; etc.).

4:37–39   The first element describing the storm is that "a great windstorm arose." For hearers familiar with the OT, "a great windstorm" (λαῖλαψ μεγάλη ἀνέμου, *lailaps megalē anemou*; lit. "a great squall of wind") might recall the story of Jonah, although a different term, "great wave(s)" (κλύδων, *klydōn*), is used there (Jon. 1:4; cf., however, Jer. 32:32 LXX). The term "great" (μεγάλη) is also used in Mark 4:39, 41, and in 5:7, where the demon cries with a "great" voice when confessing Jesus as "Son of the Most High God." The second element of the storm's description is that "the waves were beginning [ἐπέβαλλεν, *epeballen*—an inceptive imperfect] to break over the boat, so that the boat was already filling." The seriousness of the storm is emphasized by the first statement and the result of the storm by the second. As in the description of the great strength of the demoniac in 5:3–5, the great strength of the storm is emphasized to demonstrate the even greater strength of Jesus (cf. 3:27).

During the storm Jesus is described as being in the stern of the boat. The 1986 discovery in the Sea of Galilee of a boat 26.5 feet long, 7.5 feet wide, and 4.5 feet deep with an elevated high stern dating from the time of Jesus helps us to understand the structure and makeup of such a boat (Wachsmann 1988). The boat could hold up to fifteen people. Jesus was probably asleep under the elevated stern platform. Here we find another analogy with the Jonah story, for Jonah was also "below." Jesus is further described as peacefully sleeping "on the cushion" (ἐπὶ τὸ προσκεφάλαιον, *epi to proskephalaion*). No comment is made in the story as to why Jesus is described as being asleep. Is it to show Jesus's faith in God's providential care? Sleep is frequently understood as a sign of such faith and trust (Pss. 3:5; 4:8; Prov. 3:24; Nineham 1963: 146; Marcus 2000: 234). The fact that in the story Jesus does not call on God to still the storm, however, argues against such an interpretation. Some suggest that it is simply a literary device to make the tradition correspond to the Jonah story. Others argue that it reveals Jesus's divine self-confidence and sovereignty

---

2. Lohmeyer (1957: 90) assumes that the text originally read, "And *no* other boats were with them." There is no textual evidence for this, however.

over the storm (Gnilka 1978: 195; Guelich 1989: 266). Mark gives no hint as to whether he intends his readers to see any theological significance in this detail. This may suggest that he found the comment in the tradition, for if he had added this to the story, one would expect that he would have given some hint as to how he intended it to be interpreted.[3] The use of the article with "cushion" may indicate that this was part of the boat's equipment, perhaps a bag of ballast, used as a pillow.

For "and they wake him" (καὶ ἐγείρουσιν αὐτόν, *kai egeirousin auton*), compare the parallel in Jon. 1:6. "Teacher" (Διδάσκαλε, *Didaskale*) is the first occurrence of this favorite address for Jesus in the Gospel (cf. 5:35; 9:17, 38; 10:17, 20, 35; 12:14, 19, 32; 13:1; 14:14). (Cf. how Matt. 8:25 uses "Lord" [Κύριε, *kyrie*] and Luke 8:24 uses "Master" [Ἐπιστάτα, *Epistata*].) If Mark is responsible for the title, this raises the question as to what title was originally found in the tradition, for some form of address must have been present. The proximity of the description of Jesus's teaching ministry in 4:1–34 (note esp. 4:1–2) may have influenced Mark at this point. Since in Mark Jesus's teaching is associated with the power to cast out demons (1:22, 27; 9:17–29), raise the dead (5:35–42), and still storms (4:35–41; 6:47–52), "Teacher" carries with it the kind of authority usually associated with a title such as "Lord." "Do you not care that we are perishing?" can be understood as an accusation (lit. "Is it no concern to you . . . ?"). If so, this would be an additional similarity with the Jonah story. Still another is the reference to the crew of the ship "perishing" (ἀπολλύμεθα, *apollymetha*; cf. Jon. 1:6, 14; 3:9). On the other hand, "Teacher, do you not care that we are perishing?" can also be understood as a request for help. The "not" (οὐ, *ou*) in the question expects a positive answer, so that the statement is best understood as a request (Gundry 1993: 246). It is difficult to think that, in the post-Easter telling of this story, these words would have been interpreted as the disciples rebuking Jesus, so this favors its being seen as a request for help here in Mark.

In Jesus "rebuking" (ἐπετίμησεν, *epetimēsen*) the wind and commanding the sea, we once again have a dual expression, although in this instance it may very well be pre-Markan. The use of the verb "rebuke" recalls 1:25, where a demon is rebuked by Jesus (cf. 3:12; 9:25) and commanded to be silent (φιμώθητι, *phimōthēti*). Yet elsewhere in Mark, people are also rebuked (8:30, 33; 10:13, 48), so that the verb is used for silencing not only evil demons but also evil actions and counsel by humans and an evil storm (cf. Pss. 18:15 [17:16 LXX]; 104:7 [103:7 LXX]; 106:9 [105:9 LXX]). In all these instances, Mark may be associating evil with Satan (cf. 8:33), but Gundry (1993: 240) points out that the contemporary literature has little evidence of demons causing storms. The twofold command, "Quiet [σιώπα, *siōpa*]! Be still (πεφίμωσο, *pephimōso*)!" is directed to a twofold adversary: the first to the wind and the second to the waves. In response to Jesus's command, the wind "ceases"

---

3. This may simply be a historical fragment referring to Jesus's weariness from the day's teaching, which then would explain his deep sleep through the storm.

(ἐκόπασεν, *ekopasen*; cf. Jon. 1:11, which describes the sea ceasing), and a great calm results. Compare the parallel in Jon. 1:15, although a totally different expression is used (cf., however, 1:12). In the account, Jesus's greatness far exceeds that of Jonah (Matt. 12:42/Luke 11:32). In the story of Jonah, the men in the boat pray to the Lord, who brings an end to the storm (cf. *b. B. Meṣiʿa* 59b), but here Jesus himself brings this about by his own word. He does what only God can do (Gen. 8:1; Job 26:11–12; Pss. 18:15; 65:7; 74:13–15; 104:4–9; 106:9; 107:25–30; Isa. 50:2; 51:9–10; Nah. 1:3–4). Like Yahweh, Jesus is also Lord over nature, and this leads to the great christological confession of 4:41. Jesus's authority permits him to bring about a "great" calm, and this will result in "great awe" (4:41).[4]

4:40–41   "Why are you afraid? Do you not yet have faith?" For the double question, see 4:13–14. One expects at this point the christological statement of 4:41 rather than Jesus's double question concerning the disciples' fear and lack of faith. Mark may have reversed the order of these two verses in order to conclude the miracle story with a high christological confession, rather than with an example of the disciples' failure. His Gospel is, after all, "the gospel of Jesus Christ, the Son of God" (1:1), not "the story of the disciples' failures" (contra Hooker 1991: 140). The disciples' lack of understanding is a Markan theological theme, and from this point onward Mark emphasizes it (cf. 6:52; 8:17, 32–33; 9:18–19, 33–37; 10:13–16, 35–45; 14:3–9, 27–31, 32–42, 53–54, and 66–72). See "Theological Emphases: The Disciples" in the introduction. The parallel in Matt. 8:26/Luke 8:25 also refers to the disciples' lack of faith. Matthew has a twofold reference such as we find in Mark, whereas Luke has no reference to the disciples being afraid. In the present account, however, the failure of the disciples serves not as the main theme of the account, but as a subplot that will ultimately have a positive resolution (14:27–28; 16:7). The disciples' lack of faith can refer to "faith in God" or "faith in Jesus" (Marcus 2000: 334). The question in 4:40 suggests that the latter is meant. For a similar use of "not yet" (οὔπω, *oupō*) with respect to the disciples' lack of faith and understanding, see 8:17, 21.

"And they were filled with awe" is the normal experience of being in the presence of God or experiencing his power. "Filled with awe" translates the cognate accusative (see comments on 2:3–4) "feared a great fear" (ἐφοβήθησαν φόβον μέγαν, *ephobēthēsan phobon megan*; cf. Luke 2:9; 1 Pet. 3:14; also Jon. 1:10; 1 Macc. 10:8). The verb "fear" is frequently used to describe a reverential or terrifying fear or awe (5:15, 33; 6:50; 9:6; 16:8; perhaps 9:32; 10:32; 11:18; cf. Jon. 1:16). Here this refers to a positive fear or "awe," whereas in 4:40 the fear

---

4. In the contemporary literature we find numerous examples of people in storms praying to God for deliverance and being rescued from the storm, but we must note that in 4:39 Jesus does not manifest his greatness and glory by praying to God and having his prayer answered by God stilling the storm. Jesus in his own power and might stills the storm! Similarly, just as we find that God alone can forgive sins (2:7) and yet Jesus demonstrates that he too can forgive sins, so here also we find that just as God alone can still the storm and control the seas, Jesus demonstrates that he too is master of storm and seas.

(a different word is used—δειλοί, *deiloi*) is negative and refers to the kind of cowardice mentioned in Rev. 21:8. For other terms used to describe a similar reaction to Jesus's words and deeds, see 1:21–22. The fear of the disciples recalls the fear of the men on board the ship with Jonah (Jon. 1:10, where we also find the cognate accusative; cf. also Luke 2:9). Whether the parallels in this account with the Jonah story are pre-Markan is uncertain. Even the matter of whether some of the similarities are intentional is far from clear. The lack of similar terminology in some of the parallels and some of the differences in the two stories should be noted. In the story of 4:35–41, there are no terminological parallels for such key terms as "great storm," "stern," the "wind ceasing," and the resulting "great calm," and between the disciples' question to Jesus and the captain's question to Jonah. This suggests that there has been no intentional effort to tie these stories together. Although the analogies in wording between the Jonah story and the present account are interesting, the differences are too great to speak of a "Jonah typology" (contra Marcus 2000: 336). If in the oral period the tradition intended, or if Mark intended, that hearers of this story should associate the present story with the story of Jonah, one would expect clearer parallels.[5] It seems best, therefore, not to see in the present account a desire on the part of Mark to have his readers associate Jesus's stilling of the storm with the Jonah story.[6]

Responding to what has happened, the disciples confess, "Who then is this man that even the wind and the sea obey him?" This question should be interpreted not as seeking an answer or as an example of the disciples' failure to understand but rather as a positive confession of the greatness of Jesus in light of this epiphany (Guelich 1989: 269). Compare 1:27; 2:7; 7:37 (also 6:2) for similar examples in which a miracle of Jesus is followed by a positive rhetorical question or statement that serves as a confession of Jesus's greatness. "Then" (ἄρα, *ara*) refers back to the stilling of the storm in 4:39. The question itself will be answered in this complex (4:35–5:43) by the demoniac's confession in 5:7: "Son of the Most High God." For the belief in Jesus's day that the heavens and the earth will obey the Messiah, compare 4Q521.

Summary

This passage has frequently been allegorized to serve as a word of encouragement to the church (as symbolized by the boat) to remain faithful during times of persecution and tribulation (the storm; cf. 13:9–13, 19), as it awaits the delayed second coming of the Son of Man (i.e., Jesus's sleeping;

---

5. See Marcus 2000: 337–38 for a discussion of the similarities and dissimilarities of the two stories.

6. We must remember that Mark's "readers" would have heard this account being read to them. They would not have had written copies of Jonah and Mark before them to compare. (Most could not read!) Furthermore, the present story would have been read to them without pauses after each verse, so that only the clearest of allusions could have been perceived as the account was being read. Mark was fully aware of this, so that if he wanted his "readers" to see an OT allusion in his text, he would have had to make this clear.

Tertullian, *On Baptism* 12; Best 1981: 230–34; Marcus 2000: 239; France 2002: 151–52). Such an allegory, however, appears to be read into the text, for Mark gives no hint that he intends such an interpretation. On the contrary, this story focuses not on the church but on Jesus.[7] The passage is meant to teach Mark's readers about the "greatness" (4:37, 39, 41) of their Lord. He is master of wind and sea, of nature (Donahue and Harrington 2002: 159–60). This finds additional support in the following two accounts (5:1–20 and 5:21–43), where Jesus's greatness and mastery over demons, disease, and death are demonstrated. The concluding verse of the present passage focuses the readers' attention upon Jesus. Mark intends his readers to reflect on who this Jesus is who possesses divine authority over nature itself. Mark's answer to this question is found throughout his Gospel. Jesus is the Christ (1:1; 8:29), the Son of God (1:1; 3:11; 15:39), the Beloved Son (1:11; 9:7), the Holy One of God (1:24), the Son of the Most High God (5:7), the Son (13:32), the Son of the Blessed (14:61–62), the Son of Man (2:10, 28; 8:31, 38; etc.), the King of the Jews (15:26, 32). The theme of the disciples' lack of understanding is also present in the passage but serves as a subplot at this point in the Gospel. It is, however, not the primary theme of the account, for the end stress of 4:41 focuses the reader's attention on the question of "who" Jesus is.

Additional Note

4:40. The translation follows ℵ B D L Δ Θ lat in acknowledging the authenticity of οὔπω ἔχετε πίστιν; contra A C K Π.

---

7. Contra van Iersel and Linmans 1978: 22–23, who see this not as a miracle story but as a summons to perseverance addressed to Mark's persecuted audience.

2. Jesus—Lord of Demons (5:1–20)

Although this account is an exorcism story (Bultmann 1968: 210), its atypical form and pattern have led some to classify it as a "tale," or *Novelle*, about Jesus (Dibelius 1934: 71–72; Burkill 1963: 86, 92; Schmithals 1979: 1.266). The unusual format of this exorcism story involves an adjuration by the demon rather than the exorcist (5:7); the strange location of the exorcist's command to the demon (5:8) and its being repeated (5:13); the unusual banishment of the demons into the swine (5:12–13); the negative response of the people who request Jesus to leave (5:17); the refusal to permit the man to follow Jesus (5:18–20); and so on. This again demonstrates that the gospel traditions often do not fit the neat classifications of form criticism.

Due to the geographical and literary problems associated with the story (the name of the region [5:1]; the description of it being near the sea [5:1–2, 13, 18]; the place being near a mountain [5:5, 11] and a steep bank [5:13]) and the apparent disjunction of various elements of the story (the location of the command of exorcism [5:8]; the "two" encounters [5:2, 6]; the differing vocabulary [different words for "tombs" in 5:2, 3–5]; the different descriptions of the man as having an "unclean spirit" and being "demonized" [5:2, 8, 13, and 15, 16, 18]), numerous attempts have been made to unravel the present account into different layers of development (cf. Marcus 2000: 347). Some suggest that an original exorcism has over time been transformed into a mission story (Craghan 1968: 534–36). This took place in several stages: (1) There was an original exorcism story of 5:1–2, 7–8, 11, 14–15, 17, 19; (2) this was embellished by midrashic allusions from Isa. 65 to describe the man's plight in Mark 5:3–6, 9, although some scholars see a greater influence being exercised on the tradition by the account of Pharaoh's defeat and the drowning of the Egyptian army in the Red Sea (Derrett 1979: 3, 6–8; Marcus 2000: 348–49); (3) when the story was added to the pre-Markan complex in which it is now found, the setting was changed in 5:1–2 and verse 18 was added, as was the drowning of the swine in 5:10, 12–13, 16; and (4) Mark added his redactional comment in 5:8 (Guelich 1989: 273). There is no textual evidence for this, however. Indeed, 5:1–20, excluding the geographical designation in 5:1, is "more textually certain than perhaps any similar section in Mark" (J. Edwards 2002: 158). It is furthermore doubtful that the scalpels of form, redaction, and historical criticism will ever be sharp enough to slice the present account into such neat parts. The lack of unanimity involved in the attempt to outline the present account (5:1–10, 11–13, 14–17, 18–20 versus 5:1–5, 6–13, 14–17, 18–20 versus 5:1–5, 6–10, 11–13, 14–17, 18–20 versus 5:1, 2–5, 6–10, 11–13, 14–17, 18–20) raises serious doubts as to the possibility of success with respect to the much more difficult task of dissecting 5:1–20 into the various, supposed layers of development.

The degree to which Mark's editorial hand is seen in the present account is heavily dependent on one's view of whether the account came to Mark as an independent pericope or whether it already existed in a pre-Markan complex. If 4:35–5:43 represents a pre-Markan miracle complex, then such editorial ties as 5:1–2, 18, 20 need not be Markan. If, however, Mark received these three (or four) miracle accounts as isolated units, then he would be responsible for such ties. Some scholars see Mark's hand primarily in 5:8 (V. Taylor 1952: 277; Klostermann 1950: 49; Koch 1975: 63–64) and 5:20 (Guelich 1989: 274, 286); others see his hand also in the seams and ties with the immediate context (5:1–2a, 18a, 20) and various editorial comments (5:8, 16).[1]

The question of a commentary's goal comes into play in all of this. Leaving aside the issue of the historical desire to unravel the *Traditionsgeschichte* of the account and to find out how its final form came into existence, what is the ultimate goal of a commentary? In light of the hypothetical (some would say "extremely hypothetical") nature of various historical reconstructions, where is the believing community to find a word from God in all this? Is it in the first stage of the tradition? The second? The third? The final? In the original event? If one brings to these questions naturalistic presuppositions, then one can seek some sort of meaning only in either the actual event, a possible accommodation of the writer(s) to his readers' mythical worldview, or in the subconsciousness that gave birth to the myth. The first possibility confronts the reader with the dilemma of discovering by means of a hypothetical reconstruction what supposedly happened and finding some religious value in this completely natural and misunderstood event. Such a rationalistic approach provides little "meaning" for the believing community. The accommodationist's attempt to discover religious value in such a text stumbles over the problem of finding value in the gross deception of the biblical authors and the fact that the authors obviously believed that what they wrote truly happened. As to the mythical interpretation, it becomes increasingly difficult to derive deep religious meaning from stories of ignorant writers who were oblivious to the religious truths they were writing, since the surface meaning of the text is so radically different from the supposed substructural meaning of the myth.[2] If the goal of a commentary, on the other hand, is to comment on what the Gospel writer was seeking to communicate to his audience by the text he has given them, then we should focus our attention on understanding the final form of the text before us. Whatever the legitimacy or value of *Traditionsgeschichte*, it presents the danger of majoring in minor issues and losing sight of the most important task of the exegete: to understand what

---

1. Marcus (2000: 347) argues that perhaps all of 5:17–20 may be Markan (cf. also Craghan 1968: 534–35; Pryke 1978: 13–14, 141, 157–58).

2. Here Frei (1974: 245–66) is especially helpful.

the biblical author is seeking to teach by the passage being investigated. It is here that we find a word from God.

For the sake of convenience I divide the present account into four sections: the introduction (5:1–5), the exorcism itself (5:6–13), the reaction of the people of the city and countryside (5:14–17), and Jesus's departure and charge to the healed demoniac (5:18–20).

Exegesis and Exposition

[1]And ⌜they⌝ came to the other side of the sea into the territory of the ⌜Gerasenes⌝. [2]And when he [Jesus] came out of the boat, immediately a man from the tombs with an unclean spirit met him. [3]⌜This man was dwelling⌝ among the tombs, and no one could bind him any longer even with a chain, [4]because he had often been bound with fetters and chains, and the chains had been wrenched apart by him and the fetters broken in pieces, and no one was strong enough to subdue him. [5]And night and day among the tombs and in the mountains, he was continually crying out and cutting himself with stones.

[6]And upon seeing Jesus from afar, he ran and knelt down before him, [7]and crying out with a loud voice, he says, "What do you want with me, Jesus, Son of the Most High God? I adjure you by God, do not torment me." [8]For he [Jesus] had been saying to him, "Come out of the man, you unclean spirit." [9]And he [Jesus] was asking him, "What is your name?" And he says to him, "Legion [is] my name, because we are many." [10]And he began to beg him earnestly in order that he would not send them out of the territory. [11]And a great herd of swine was feeding there on the mountain. [12]And they begged him, saying, "Send us into the swine, in order that we might enter into them." [13]And he gave them permission, and the unclean spirits having come out [of the man] entered into the swine, and the herd numbering about two thousand rushed down the steep bank into the sea and drowned in the sea.

[14]And those watching over them [the swine] fled and announced in the city and the countryside [what had happened], and they came to see what it is that had taken place. [15]And they come to Jesus and see the one who had been demonized sitting, clothed, and in his right mind—the one having had the legion [of demons], and they were afraid. [16]And those who had seen [this] explained to them what happened to the man who was demonized and concerning the swine. [17]And they began to beg him [Jesus] to depart from their region.

[18]And as he was getting into the boat, the one who had been demonized begged him in order that he might be with him. [19]And he [Jesus] did not permit him but says to him, "Go home [and] to your friends and tell them all that the Lord has done for you and [how] he had mercy on you." [20]And he departed and began to proclaim in the Decapolis all that Jesus had done for him, and all were marveling.

"And they came to the other side of the sea" (καὶ ἦλθον εἰς τὸ πέραν τῆς θαλάσσης, *kai ēlthon eis to peran tēs thalassēs*) continues the journey "to the   5:1–5 other side" begun in 4:35 (cf. 5:21; 6:45; 8:13) and will be completed by their returning to the western side of the Sea of Galilee in 5:17, 21. The following statement "into the territory of the Gerasenes" gives greater specificity to this designation (Neirynck 1988: 45–53, 94). "They" refers to Jesus and the disciples of 4:34–41. The textual problems associated with the geographical location are well known. Along with Γερασηνῶν (*Gerasēnōn*), or "Gerasenes" (ℵ* B D it vg cop^sa), we also have Γαδαρηνῶν (*Gadarēnōn*), or "Gadarenes" (A C K f^13 syr^p, h), and Γεργεσηνῶν (*Gergesēnōn*), or "Gergesenes" (ℵ^c L Δ Θ f^1 cop^bo). Gerasa (modern Jerash) was a city of the Decapolis (see 5:20) located thirty-seven miles southeast of the Sea of Galilee. Gadara (modern Um Qeis) was also a city of the Decapolis about five miles southeast of the Sea of Galilee that "lay on the frontiers of Tiberias" (Josephus, *Life* 9 §42). Ancient coins bearing the name of Gadara often portray a ship, indicating that its territory was seen as bordering the Sea of Galilee (Metzger 1994: 19). Although the textual evidence favors "Gerasenes," Metzger (1994: 72) gives this only a "C" rating, indicating considerable doubt as to whether this is the correct reading. The Matthean parallel (8:28) favors "Gadarenes," but this also receives only a "C" rating (Metzger 1994: 18). The Lukan parallel (8:26) favors "Gerasenes," but this reading likewise receives only a "C" rating (Metzger 1994: 121). The confusion of the textual evidence is compounded by geographical considerations. Gerasa, favored in Mark and Luke, but barely, requires too long a run (35+ miles) for pigs to the Sea of Galilee. Consequently, some suggest that the "territory of the Gerasenes" functions as a loose term for the whole of the Decapolis (France 2002: 227) or that the territory of Gerasa extended to the Sea of Galilee (J. Edwards 2002: 153). The territory of Gadara is favored in Matt. 8:28 but possesses the same kind of uncertainty as Gerasa does in Mark and Luke. This region can be understood as bordering the Sea of Galilee, but it possesses no steep banks/cliffs (5:13). Gergesa (El Kursi), identified as the site by Origen (*Commentary on John*, chap. 27), fits the geographical description best, for it is located near a steep bank on the eastern side of the Sea of Galilee (J. McRay, *ABD* 2:991–92; cf. J. Edwards 2002: 153–54), but it has the least textual support.

If, for geographical reasons, we choose Gergesa as the original city designation (Gundry 1993: 256–57), how do we explain its weak textual attestation? Did someone change its relatively unknown name for the name of the better-known Gerasa? Was "Gerasenes" added by an early copyist unfamiliar with the geographical area, or by an "ignorant" Mark, to a text that originally had no city designation? Was "Gerasenes" part of the early form of the tradition, and an ignorant redactor later added the references to the sea and the drowning of the pigs? All such suggestions are highly speculative and not without their own problems. It is probably best to interpret the present form of the story using the designation "Gerasa" for the city and territory. Apart from the geographical problem, the meaning of the Markan text is clear, but the historical evaluation of the actual site, which is dependent on the original textual designation of Mark, is best held in abeyance due to the textual confusion.

"And when he came out of the boat" (καὶ ἐξελθόντος αὐτοῦ ἐκ τοῦ πλοίου, *kai exelthontos autou ek tou ploiou*) introduces Mark's readers to Jesus's ministry to the gentiles in the Decapolis (5:1–20). This gentile ministry will be resumed in 7:24–8:10, and the Decapolis will be revisited in 7:31–37. The genitive absolute indicates that in this story, as in the previous one, Jesus ("he") is the main character. The disciples, although present in 5:18 and 31, play no significant role in this story about Jesus Christ, the Son of God (1:1). The alleged gap in time between the start of the journey ("evening" in 4:35) and the arrival on shore (crossing the Sea of Galilee would not take from evening until morning) is not a sign of the "combination of two stories that once had existed as unrelated traditional units" (contra Guelich 1989: 277) as much as the art of storytelling, which eliminates irrelevant data from the story. Upon his arrival, Jesus is met "immediately" (εὐθύς, *euthys*) by a demoniac. The location of "immediately" in the story (5:2b) is not typically Markan and suggests that its temporal quality should be taken at face value. See 1:10–11. The demoniac is described as a man "with an unclean spirit" (ἐν πνεύματι ἀκαθάρτῳ, *en pneumati akathartō*), dwelling in the tombs. This would make him unclean due to contact with the dead (cf. Matt. 23:27; the entire midrashic tractate *Oholot*). The man is unclean not only because of his contact with the dead, but even more so because he is possessed by an "unclean spirit," that is, evil demons had "swallowed him up" (Marcus 2000: 192, 342). For tombs as haunts of demons, cf. *b. Sanh.* 65b.

Verses 3–5 are for the most part not found in the parallel accounts. (Luke places an abbreviated summary of this material [Luke 8:29] after Mark 5:8.) The presence of numerous hapax legomena ("made his home" [τὴν κατοίκησιν εἶχεν, *tēn katoikēsin eichen*; 5:3]; "chain" [ἁλύσει, *halysei*; 5:3, 4]; "fetters" [πέδαις, *pedais*; 5:4]; "wrenched apart" [διεσπάσθαι, *diespasthai*; 5:4]; "subdue" [δαμάσαι, *damasai*; 5:4]) has led some scholars to argue for this explanatory material being traditional, but the nature of the story is no doubt primarily responsible for the unusual vocabulary (Watts 2000: 159n113). Attempts to see these verses as a midrashic development of the tradition based on Isa. 65:4–6 and Ps. 67:7 LXX (Guelich 1989: 277–78) or Exod. 14:1–15:22 (Marcus 2000: 349) are unconvincing due to the lack of clear terminological agreement. The different terms for "tombs" (μνημείων, *mnēmeion*) in 5:2 (cf. Ps. 67:7 LXX, τάφοις, *taphois*) and "swine" (χοίρων, *choirōn*) in 5:11 (cf. Isa. 65:4, κρέα ὕμεια, *krea hymeia*) are unlikely to have triggered in the readers' (or previous editors') minds the recollection of these OT passages, where the term "swine" (χοῖρος) does not even appear. And in these passages, we do not find any references to "fetters" and "chains" and the inability to bind the demon-possessed man. If Mark or an earlier redactor were greatly influenced by these OT texts, they would have left more distinct terminological clues than those suggested.[3] What Mark seeks to teach by these verses is quite clear and does

---

3. For further criticism of the alleged influence of Isa. 65:3–5 and Ps. 67:7 on the present account, see Gundry 1993: 258–59.

not depend upon any knowledge of OT allusions. The greater the strength of the demoniac, and he was indeed very strong, the greater must be the strength and power of Jesus, the demons' conqueror (cf. 3:27)!

"Tombs" (μνημείων) probably refers to "cave tombs" in which there would be room to stand and move around. Although awkward, a literal translation of 5:3b, "and *not* even [καὶ οὐδέ, *kai oude*] with a chain [emphatic position] *no* longer [οὐκέτι, *ouketi*] no one [οὐδείς, *oudeis*] was able to bind him," indicates the emphatic nature of the threefold repetition of the negatives οὐδέ, οὐκέτι, and οὐδείς. With this statement we have the first description of the demons' strength. Why people attempted to bind the demoniac (to keep him from harming himself or others?) is not stated and is therefore nonessential for the story. "Fetters" (πέδαις) probably refers to shackles on the feet and "chains" (ἀλύσεις) to handcuffs, and "often" (πολλάκις, *pollakis*) emphasizes the futility of human efforts to bind this powerful demoniac, because "the chains had been wrenched apart by him and the fetters broken in pieces." This is the second description of the demoniac's great strength. The verbs found here are in the passive—the chains were wrenched apart (διεσπάσθαι, *diespasthai*) and the fetters were broken in pieces (συντετρῖφθαι, *syntetriphthai*). It is uncertain whether Mark intended his readers to see these verbs as "demonic passives" (Marcus 2000; 343) in opposition to "divine passives." For divine passives, see 2:5. Note the chiasmus:

A no one could bind him (5:3b)

B fetters/chains (5:4a)

B′ chains/fetters (5:4a)

A′ no one was strong enough to subdue him (5:4b)

"And no one was strong enough to subdue him" (καὶ οὐδεὶς ἴσχυεν αὐτὸν δαμάσαι, *kai oudeis ischyen auton damasai*) is the third description of the demoniac's great strength. All human attempts to subdue him had continually (note the imperfect tense of ἴσχυεν) failed. No doubt Mark would want his readers to think back to 3:27, where similar terms are found: "no one," "bind," and "able."

In 5:5 the attention turns from the strength of the demons to the pitiful condition of the man, and this is "one of the most lamentable stories of human wretchedness in the Bible" (J. Edwards 2002: 154). "Night and day among the tombs and in the mountains, he was continually crying out." (For "night and day," see 4:26–29.) The unending tragedy of the demoniac's situation ("night and day")—his unclean and death-filled residence ("among the tombs"), his lonely (?) existence ("among the tombs and on the mountains"), and his continual crying (an imperfect periphrastic)[4] for help (cf. 9:24; 10:47–48) and/or in anger (9:26; 15:13–14)—is vividly painted for the reader. "Crying out"

---

4. Contra Zerwick and Grosvenor 1981: 115.

(κράζω, *krazō*) in Mark can also be used in the sense of shouting out a confession concerning Jesus. It is probably in this sense that we should understand its use in 5:7 (cf. also 1:23–24; 3:11; 11:9), but here it refers to his crying out in agony. Nothing is said of the man eating "swine flesh," so that the only common feature between this description and Isa. 65:4 is the man's dwelling in the tombs. The man's horrible plight is further described by his "cutting himself with stones" (κατακόπτων ἑαυτὸν λίθοις, *katakoptōn heauton lithois*). For similar self-destructive behavior caused by a demon, compare 9:22, 26. The continual nature of this action is also portrayed by the use of the imperfect periphrastic—"was continually crying out and cutting. . . ."

"And upon seeing Jesus from afar" (καὶ ἰδὼν τὸν Ἰησοῦν ἀπὸ μακρόθεν, *kai*   **5:6–13**
idōn ton Iēsoun apo makrothen) resumes the narrative of the story begun in 5:2 but interrupted by the description of the demoniac's strength and plight in 5:3–5, and begins the story of the exorcism (Donahue and Harrington 2002: 164). Despite domination by the unclean spirit, the man sees hope in Jesus. Mark's readers, of course, are well aware that Jesus has already delivered demoniacs from their unclean spirits (1:23–27, 32–34; 3:11, 22–27) and that he is therefore able to help this man as well. Like the man in the synagogue who possessed an unclean spirit (1:23–24), the demoniac, no doubt against the wishes of the demons, seeks help from Jesus (cf. 5:22–23, 33). The Greek προσεκύνησεν (*prosekynēsen*) is probably best understood as "knelt down before/prostrated himself, i.e., as an act of concession and entreaty in the face of Jesus's superior power" (France 2002: 228), rather than as "worshiped." It is too early in the relationship for the latter. For "kneeling and crying out with a loud voice and saying . . ." introducing a demoniac's confession, compare 3:11 (cf. also 1:23–24; 11:9).

Mark does not understand "What do you want with me, Jesus, Son of the Most High God?" (5:7) as an attempt by the demon to gain power over Jesus (contra Burkill 1963: 86, 89, 94). Rather, the statement indicates subservience of the demons to the Son of God (France 2002: 228). Mark has already told his readers that the demons know who Jesus is (1:34c–d), so that this demonic confession along with 1:24 ("the Holy One of God") and 3:11 ("the Son of God") come from reliable "spokesmen." What Mark has said in his opening verse (that Jesus Christ is the Son of God) is once again corroborated by the demons through their supernatural knowledge. The positive nature of the confession and the positive role it plays in advancing Mark's christological teaching make it unlikely that we should see this as a demonic attempt to thwart the exorcism (contra Gundry 1993: 250). Whether Mark's readers would have understood this title as being particularly relevant for gentiles (cf. Gen. 14:18–20; Num. 24:16; Isa. 14:14; Dan. 3:26; 4:2; 1 Esd. 2:3; 2 Macc. 3:31; 3 Macc. 7:9; Acts 16:17) is impossible to say. That this same title is found in 4Q246, where the Messiah is apparently called the Son of the Most High God, indicates that this title was not an exclusively Hellenistic name for God (García Martínez 1995: 138; Fitzmyer 1979b: 90–94, 102–7). For the meaning of the idiom "What do you want with me?" (Τί ἐμοὶ καὶ σοί; *Ti emoi kai soi?*), see 1:23–24.

In an exorcism, the technical term ὁρκίζω (*horkizō*) or "adjure" usually comes from the exorcist (cf. Acts 19:13) and is directed at the demon (Kee 1968: 246; Koch 1975: 58). Here, however, ὁρκίζω σε τὸν θεόν (*horkizō se ton theon*; lit. "I adjure you by God"; 5:7c) comes from the demon and is directed at Jesus! Speculation as to what the demon was seeking to do by this adjuration is unprofitable, for Mark does not explain this, and how is one supposed to know what is going through a demon's mind? However, what Mark wants his readers to see by this is clear. He wants to portray the power and authority of Jesus. The mighty demons (the one demon speaks for many) quail before Jesus and beg him, their superior (3:27), for a favor. Their adjuration is best understood not as an attempt to put a curse on Jesus (contra G. H. Twelftree, *DJG* 166) but as a desperate plea whose content is revealed in the next statement. For other examples of demons addressing their exorcists, see Acts 19:13–16; Jub. 10.1–9; *b. Pesaḥ.* 112b; *b. Giṭ.* 68a; *b. Šabb.* 67a; Philostratus, *Life of Apollonius of Tyana* 4.25. The request "Do not torment me" (μή με βασανίσῃς, *mē me basanisēs*) also reveals the power and might of Jesus, for the demon(s) recognize(s) that Jesus has the power to "torment" him (them). This torment can refer to their final judgment and destruction, and this is how Matthew (8:29, "before our time") and Luke (8:31, "to depart into the abyss") understand it (cf. Rev. 20:10). It can also refer to a present torment of being exiled from their current home, that is, the man (cf. van der Loos 1965: 387–88). The sending of the demons into the swine (5:12–13a) favors the latter interpretation, but Matthew's and Luke's interpretation of this request and the Markan parallel in 1:24 ("Have you come to destroy us?") weighs more heavily in favor of the former. The binding of the strong man in 3:27 indicates that we should see no sharp distinction between the present binding and the final destruction of the demons. In the account no bargaining session between Jesus and the demons is envisioned. Jesus is in total charge and command of the situation (Gnilka 1978: 204). Having read 1:1–4:41, Mark's readers would find it impossible to see here an exorcist-demon bargaining encounter. The demons plead; they do not negotiate. There is no "war" or "battle" between Jesus and the demons. From beginning to end, the scene envisions the surrender and judgment of a vanquished enemy.

The imperfect ἔλεγεν (*elegen*, he had been saying) in 5:8 is best rendered as a pluperfect (Zerwick 1963: §290; contra Donahue and Harrington 2002: 165). By this comment (see 1:16–18) Mark explains why the demon(s) both confessed Jesus and sought his mercy. Compare 5:28 and 6:18, where ἔλεγεν also explains what had occurred earlier. For a similar command to the demons to "Come out of the man" and the addition of "Be silent," see 1:25. The departure of the unclean spirits is picked up in the story at 5:13. For a similar order of a christological confession preceding the expulsion of the demon in an exorcism, compare 1:24–25. Since the command for the demons to leave the man has already been given and since the demons' name is not used to gain control over the demons, the question "What is your name?" (τί ὄνομά σοι; *ti onoma soi?*) in 5:9 does not function as part of an exorcistic formula.[5] It functions rather to demonstrate Jesus's power over the demons. "Instead of granting Jesus control over the demon(s), the question and response reveal the extent of the man's domination" (Guelich 1989: 281).

The reply by the demoniac is, "Legion [is] my name" (Λεγιὼν ὄνομά μοι, *Legiōn onoma moi*). Whether "Legion" refers to the actual name of the demon or serves as a description of the man's terrible domination by demons is uncertain. The preceding question of Jesus (5:9b) favors it being understood as a name as well as a description. A legion was a Roman military unit about the size of a modern-day brigade. Consisting mostly of infantry but including some cavalry, it could number five to six thousand men. The name is a further description of the demoniac's strength and thus serves to heighten the might and power of Jesus. Some see in the name an "unmistakable allusion" to the Roman occupation (Theissen 1983: 255; Dormandy 2000; cf. Marcus 2000: 351–52; contra Donahue and Harrington 2002: 166), but the name "Legion" functions simply to indicate the number of the demons in the man. In T. Sol. 11.3–7 the demons are called "legion," and again it is the number indicated by the word that is important. There is no specific allusion to Rome in the text, so that Mark did not seek to have his readers see in this term any allusions to the Roman occupation. "Because we are many" (ὅτι πολλοί ἐσμεν, *hoti polloi esmen*) explains the meaning and function of the name "Legion." The man is possessed by not one but thousands of demons. For examples of being possessed by more than a single demon, compare Matt. 12:45/Luke 11:26; Luke 8:2. At this point, the story begins to vacillate between the singular and the plural in the description of the demoniac. When the man is in the forefront, we have the singular ("he/him," 5:9, 10, 18, 19, 20; "the demoniac," 5:15, 16; "the man" [lit. "the one having"], 5:15, 18, 19; "you/your" [singular], 5:19). When the demons are in the forefront, we have the plural ("we/us," 5:9, 12; "they/them," 5:10, 12, 13).

The demon's subservience to Jesus is seen in his "begging him earnestly" (παρεκάλει αὐτὸν πολλά, *parekalei auton polla*). This shows that the demoniac's adjuration (5:7) was a plea for some sort of a concession. The imperfect "was begging him" indicates a continual begging of Jesus by the powerful demon(s). The superiority of Jesus over the "strong man" (3:27) is thereby heightened (cf. Matt. 18:29). Such demonic pleading is also found in T. Sol.

---

5. Gundry (1993: 251) attempts to explain the exorcism as having failed up to this point because Jesus had sought to exorcise only one demon rather than the multitude that made up the legion. There is, however, no hint of this in Mark. From the beginning Jesus has been master of the situation and has exercised complete authority over the demons. In all the other exorcisms described in the Gospels, the name of the demon is not sought or referred to (cf. Mark 1:21–28; 7:24–30; 9:14–29; Matt. 9:32–34; 12:22–32/Luke 11:14–23). Nor are names alluded to in the summaries about Jesus's exorcisms (cf. Mark 1:32–34, 39; 3:7–12; also Acts 10:38). In various nonbiblical texts, however (cf. T. Sol. 2.1; 3.6; 4.3–4; 5.1–2; 11.4–6; 13.1–4; *PGM* 4.3035–50), the name of the demon is sought.

2.6; 5.11; *b. Pesaḥ.* 112b. The concession sought by the demons is that they would not be sent out of the "territory" (χώρας, *chōras*; cf. 5:1). Why they do not want to be sent out of the territory of the Gerasenes is not explained. That it is the territory, not the "land" in contrast to the "sea," that is intended is indicated by the use of the same word in 5:1, where it refers to the territory.

That a great herd of swine were feeding on the hillside indicates the gentile nature of this region "on the other side" of the Jordan, for Jews were forbidden from raising pigs (*m. B. Qam.* 7.7; *b. B. Qam.* 79b, 82b). The "hillside" (lit. "mountain" [ὄρει, *orei*]) is one of the mountains of 5:5. The reason for the demons' request to enter the swine is unclear. Some argue that the demons wanted to remain in the territory and, if they could not inhabit the man, then the swine would do. Thus the unclean spirits dwelling in the unclean man living in the unclean tombs enter the unclean swine. Others suggest that this is the work of an editor seeking to ameliorate the subsequent loss of the swine (5:13)—the demons are to blame for this, not Jesus! Some suggest that this is part of a larger healing story. Not only is the man freed from the demons, but also the unclean land is freed of its unclean animals (Theissen 1983: 255–56). Mark gives no hint as to how he understood this command, and neither do Matthew and Luke in their parallel accounts. Jesus, the Lord over the demons, grants the request of the demons. Why he did so is not explained by the evangelists. The result, however, is that the herd (ἀγέλη, *agelē*), numbering about two thousand, rushed down the steep bank into the sea. The number two thousand seems to be traditional, for, if it was added later, one would expect the number to correspond more closely to a "legion," about five to six thousand. Even so, the number "two thousand" emphasizes the strength of the demons. For the discussion of the geography involved in this story, see 5:1–5.

The description of the exorcism proper ends with the swine/demons being drowned in the "sea." Some see an irony in this. The evil and demonic nature of the sea now destroys the evil demons. This, however, appears to read too much into this statement and involves a basic contradiction—the evil demons perish in the evil, demonic sea. Why would Satan be divided against himself (3:26)? The fate of the demons raises several unanswerable questions. Is the fate of the swine different from that of the demons? If so, what ultimately happened to the demons? Were they now simply homeless (cf. Matt. 12:43–45; Tob. 8:3)? Can demons drown? Mark probably intends his readers to see in the destruction of the swine the destruction of the demons as well (Hooker 1991: 144; contra France 2002: 231). Jesus has judged the demons! What will happen in the final day (Rev. 20:10) has proleptically happened to the demons called Legion, whose destruction is visualized by the fate of the swine. Questions of morality are often raised with respect to this exorcism. Does Jesus show indifference to the property value of the swine owners in this exorcism? Can the blame for this economic loss simply be shifted to the demons, or is Jesus in some way responsible for what happened? It may be helpful to think of how Mark's readers would have responded to the story. Would they have focused on the "crash of the stock market," or would they rather have thought more in line with such teachings of Jesus as, "For whoever wishes to save his life will lose it, but whoever loses his life for me and the gospel will save it. For what does it profit a person to gain the whole world and to suffer the loss of his life?" (8:35–36; cf. Matt. 12:12a). Such a concern would far outweigh the issue of the economic value of the swine. A man had been saved from demonic slavery. The economic value of the swine pales in comparison.[6] The question of whether the man could have been saved apart from the loss of the swine would probably not have arisen in Mark's or his readers' thinking. This is simply a description of what took place when the demons were expelled from the man and entered the swine.

At this point Mark now relates the reaction of the people of "Gerasa" to the exorcism. Although it is often the healed person who tells what has happened in a healing/exorcism story (1:45; Matt. 9:31; Luke 13:13; cf. also Mark 5:20), here it is the onlookers (1:27–28; 2:12; 7:36; Luke 7:16–17) who do so. What they recount is not so much what happened to the swine but rather the cause of what happened to the swine—the healing of the demoniac. This is clear from 5:15, where the people come to see Jesus and the demoniac (not the dead swine in the sea), and from 5:16, where what happened to the demoniac[7] is the focus of attention. For "And they come to Jesus," compare other examples in Mark of people coming to Jesus and the disciples to see for themselves what they have heard about Jesus's word and deeds in 1:45; 3:8; 5:21, 22, 27; 6:31; 7:25; 9:14–15; 10:1; also compare 2:3, 13; 3:31; 4:1; 10:47; 12:14, 18; 14:3. For the impersonal plural "they," see 1:21–22. Although what the people come to see is the healed demoniac ("what . . . had taken place"), Mark points his readers to the key figure and cause of the miraculous events. As a result he speaks of their "coming to Jesus" (5:15a). This points out that for Mark the main purpose of the account is christological.

The demoniac is described as "sitting [καθήμενον, *kathēmenon*], clothed [ἱματισμένον, *himatismenon*], and in his right mind [σωφρονοῦντα, *sōphronounta*; lit. 'right-minded']." The stark contrast between the present condition of the man and his former pathetic existence, as described in 5:3–5, reveals that something great has happened. A "great calm" (cf. 4:39) had come over his former, stormy existence. For Mark's readers, this was cause for joy because it witnessed to the man's salvation. The man is now sitting in the presence of Jesus, whereas formerly he was dwelling in the tombs. He is now clothed, which implies that he was once naked. (Luke 8:27 explicitly refers to his being naked.) Being clothed is a sign of wellness, whereas nakedness is seen as the opposite. He is now in his right mind, whereas he was once crying aloud night

5:14–17

---

6. Cf. how Paul's exorcism of the demon from a slave girl in Acts 16 also involved economic loss for her owners.

7. The present tense of the substantival participle "the man being demonized" (τὸν δαιμονιζόμενον, *ton daimonizomenon*) is technically incorrect, for the man is no longer being demonized, as 5:15c ("the one having had [ἐσχηκότα, *eschēkota*] the legion") makes clear, but the people knew the man as the one who was demonized, and as a result he is referred to in this manner.

and day and bruising/cutting himself. The description of the demoniac as "the one having had the legion" (5:15c) helps the reader recall 5:7–13. There have been numerous attempts to explain the healing of the demoniac via various psychological interpretations. The present story, however, is not about an emotionally troubled man who was healed by psychotherapy but about a man indwelt by many demons who was healed by their expulsion.

The reaction of the people is described as one of "fear" (ἐφοβήθησαν, *ephobēthēsan*). Unlike the positive fear of 4:41 (see 4:40–41), this fear must be interpreted negatively, as 5:17 reveals. The full details of what happened are told to the people of "Gerasa" by those who had seen it. Mark does not explain who these people are, but the "herdsmen" (5:14) and possibly the "disciples" (4:34–41; 5:1) are probably understood by Mark as the eyewitnesses involved in explaining what had happened (5:16). This divine visitation to the region is portrayed as a unified event. The Greek wording suggests this—"how it had happened [πῶς ἐγένετο, *pōs egeneto*] to the demoniac and concerning the swine." (Note that it is not "how it had happened to the demoniac and how it had happened to the swine.") The fate of the demon-possessed swine is an essential part of the story. The concluding statement of the people of "Gerasa" in 5:17 (the "they" refers to the "them" of 5:16) is a request for Jesus to leave "their region" (τῶν ὁρίων αὐτῶν, *tōn horiōn autōn*). There are some interesting similarities between the reaction of the townspeople and that of the demons. Both come to Jesus (5:6 and 14–15), react in fear (5:7 and 15), and plead with Jesus to do something (5:7, 10, and 17). The "fear" of the people results in their "getting rid of Jesus" by requesting that he leave their region. (Cf. 11:18 for a more sinister attempt to "get rid of Jesus" because of a similar fear.) The reason Mark gives for this request is their fear (5:15). Mark does not associate this request with the financial loss of the swine, for this issue is not raised in 5:14–17 (contra Guelich 1989: 284; France 2002: 346). Furthermore, the request to depart comes not from the herdsmen who suffered the loss of the swine but from the townspeople, and there is no hint in the account that the people of the town owned the swine. Nor is there any hint from Mark that the people of the city make this request because they attributed Jesus's exorcism to the work of Satan, as in 3:22–30 (contra Marcus 2000: 346). Their fear is a natural response to their having experienced the presence of God. How one responds varies. In some cases, the experience produces good fruit (4:20), but in others who see but do not perceive, hear but do not understand, the seed falls on bad soil (4:15–19).

5:18–20 The conclusion of the account reverses Jesus's getting out of the boat in 5:2 with "he was getting into the boat" (ἐμβαίνοντος αὐτοῦ εἰς τὸ πλοῖον, *embainontos autou eis to ploion*; 5:18) and prepares the reader for 5:21. The contrast between the attitude of the people of the city and the former demoniac is sharp and revealing. Unlike the people, the man is "good soil" (cf. 4:20). His request to "be with him [Jesus]" (μετ' αὐτοῦ ἦ, *met' autou ē*) uses the identical language found in 3:14, where Jesus chose twelve disciples to "be with him."

However, his request is refused. This is best understood, due to the similarity in language with 3:14, as a request to join the Twelve. Although this is refused, it is certainly not a rejection of his becoming a follower of Jesus, as the rest of the verse indicates. He is commissioned instead to be a missionary to his own people[8] and to "Go home [and] to your friends" (lit. "Go to your house to your friends"). Some see this as an example of the messianic secret in Mark (Wrede 1971: 140–41; Gnilka 1978: 207; Theissen 1983: 146–47). Support for this is seen in the command to go into his own house. Some argue that in Mark "house" functions as a place of secrecy (cf. 5:38–43; 7:17, 24; 8:26; 9:28; 10:10). But "house" also serves in Mark as a place of proclamation (cf. 1:29–34; 2:1–2, 15–16; 3:20–35; 14:3). There is no hint in 5:20 that the man was disobedient to Jesus's command in 5:19, for 5:20 is introduced not by the strong adversative ἀλλά (*alla*) or even by the weak adversative δέ (*de*; cf. 1:45; 7:36) but simply by καί (*kai*, and). Furthermore, it is difficult to think that the man's "proclaiming" (κηρύσσειν, *kēryssein*) should be interpreted negatively (see 1:45). These verses appear to have no direct bearing on the teaching of the messianic secret in Mark (Burkill 1963: 94–95); see 7:36. When he was possessed by demons, the man lived among the dead, was uncontrollable, screamed, and inflicted wounds upon himself. Now he is able to go home and live with his family and friends. Although the term σούς (*sous*; 5:19) can mean family or friends, 5:20 indicates that the broader meaning of "friends" is best here (V. Taylor 1952: 284; Pesch 1980a: 294).

The content of the man's proclamation is described as "tell[ing] them all that the Lord has done [a perfect tense emphasizing the abiding benefit of what had been done] for you and [how] he had mercy [an aorist referring to the act of mercy he experienced, i.e., his exorcism] on you" (V. Taylor 1952: 284; Gundry 1993: 254). The primary task given to the man is to bear witness to what the Lord did for him. All Christian preaching and teaching must involve not just the proclamation of Christian doctrine but also the telling of "how much the Lord has done" for the preacher/teacher. Although "Lord" (Luke 8:39 has "God" [ὁ θεός, *ho theos*]) may have referred originally in the setting of Jesus to God (Yahweh), Mark understands "what the Lord has done" in 5:19 as a reference in 5:20 to what "Jesus" did for the demoniac. Jesus is Lord (1:3; 2:28; 7:28; 11:3; 12:36–37; 13:35; cf. Rom. 10:9)! The request by the townspeople for Jesus to depart makes it unnecessary for him to command silence, since the resultant marveling (ἐθαύμαζον, *ethaumazon*) would not hinder his ministry. See 1:45. For commands not to tell others, compare 5:43; 7:36; 8:26 (implied), 30; 9:9.

The concluding verse telling of the man's proclamation throughout the Decapolis and the wonder that this created is a Markan summary whose

---

8. Marcus (2000: 353) comments, "It is not necessarily a sign of grace, then, but may be the opposite, when Jesus accedes to a request [note Jesus acceding to the request of the demons in 5:13], and it is not necessarily a sign of divine disapproval, but may be the opposite, when he refuses one [note Jesus's refusal of the healed demoniac's request]."

redactional nature is quite apparent: "began to" (see 1:45; cf. also 4:1); "proclaim/preach" (see 1:45; cf. also 1:14; 3:14); "all that" (ὅσα, *hosa*; cf. 3:8, 10; 6:30, 56; 9:13); "were marveling" (see 4:41). The Decapolis was less a political entity (a confederation or league) than a geographical region (cf. 7:31) consisting of Damascus, Philadelphia, Raphana, Scythopolis, Gadara, Hippo, Dion, Pella, Galasa, and Canatha (Pliny, *Nat. Hist.* 5.16).[9] The present mention of the area prepares the readers for Jesus's later mission in the Decapolis in 7:31–8:10, and the man's preaching to the gentiles is the beginning of the fulfillment of 13:10; 14:9. It is uncertain whether the chiasmus found in 5:19–20 (all that the Lord has done for you . . . all that Jesus had done for him, ὅσα ὁ κύριός σοι πεποίηκεν . . . ὅσα ἐποίησεν αὐτῷ ὁ Ἰησοῦς, *hosa ho kyrios soi pepoiēken . . . hosa epoiēsen autō ho Iēsous*) is intentional. What is clear, however, is that for Mark, the Lord of 5:19 is Jesus of Nazareth! This is evident by Mark's exact repetition of "all that . . ." (ὅσα . . .) in 5:19 and 5:20. "And all were marveling" is a frequent response to Jesus's miracles (1:27; 7:37; 16:6), teachings (1:22, 27; 6:2; 9:32; 10:24, 26; 11:18), and presence/behavior (9:15; 10:32; 15:5, 44). Mark's emphasis on the amazement that Jesus caused (cf. 5:15, 41) clearly indicates that he was not seeking to combat any "divine man" Christology (see 1:21–22).

Summary

In this account, Mark continues the christological teaching begun in 4:35–41. Whereas Jesus's great power over nature is portrayed in the former account, here Mark brings to a climax his portrayal of Jesus's authority over the demons. Having introduced this subject in the exorcism account found in 1:23–28, having alluded to other exorcisms in various summary statements (1:32–34, 39; 3:7–12), and having explained that such exorcisms require the ability to bind the prince of demons (3:22–27), Mark now describes Jesus's awesome power over a man possessed by thousands of demons. Although two additional exorcisms will be reported later by Mark in 7:24–30 and 9:14–29 (cf. also 6:7, 13), nowhere else does the evangelist spend as much time and effort to demonstrate to his readers Jesus's lordship over the demons. The prolonged description of the demoniac's strength (5:3–4) and the number of demons (5:9, 13) serve to demonstrate to his readers that, although the demons are incredibly strong, so strong that no human can control them, Jesus is stronger still, for he is Lord over the demons and the prince of demons.

Another christological emphasis that Mark has carefully prepared for is the demoniac's confession of who Jesus is. Already in 1:24 he has told us that the demons recognize Jesus as "the Holy One of God." Since this is in close agreement with his opening introduction that Jesus is the "Christ,

9. S. Parker (1975: 441) states, "In short, the term 'Decapolis' in antiquity simply served as a convenient appellation for the group of Greek cities east of the Jordan from Damascus in the north to Philadelphia in the south."

the Son of God" (1:1), the reader knows that the demon serves as a reliable spokesman for Mark's viewpoint in this regard. Yet Mark is not content to rest on the logical deduction of his readers. He adds the comment in 1:34 that Jesus did not "permit the demons to speak [note the command 'Be silent!' in 1:25], because they knew him." Then in the large summary introducing 3:7–6:6 (3:7–12), he tells his readers that "whenever the unclean spirits saw him, they would fall down before him and cry out, saying, 'You are the Son of God!'" (3:11). The demoniac's confession in 5:7 now brings the witness of these evil, supernatural beings to its pinnacle. Jesus is the "Son of the Most High God." Thus the question of the disciples in 4:41, "Who then is this, that even the wind and the sea obey him?" receives in this account a twofold answer: (1) Jesus is the mighty Lord and the conqueror of the demons, and (2) Jesus is the Son of the Most High God. Although one should not read into 5:19–20 a fully developed Nicene Christology, Mark's understanding of Jesus in this account goes far beyond such descriptions as "prophet" or even "Messiah." There exists between God and Jesus a unique relationship and unity. Jesus in his actions and deeds is the Lord (5:19), and what Jesus has done (5:20) is what God the Lord has done (5:19).

It is clear from the above that the primary purpose of Mark in this account is not missiological but christological. Nevertheless, the account does teach a missiological truth of which Mark's readers were well aware. The Messiah of Israel is for both Jew and Greek. The present account is the first clear encounter between Jesus and gentiles in Mark. For his readers this is clear from the location (5:1–2, 20–21) and the presence of the swine (5:11–13, 16). The command for the former demoniac to proclaim the good news to his people foreshadows Jesus's subsequent mission (7:24–8:10) and commission (13:10; 14:9) to the gentile world. No doubt Mark also intended his readers to see in Jesus's command to the man having had the demons to preach the good news (5:19–20) a similar command for them to do likewise.

Additional Notes

5:1. Some MSS (ℵᶜ C L Δ θ f¹³ syr) read ἦλθεν (singular) rather than ἦλθον (plural; possibly due to assimilation to the singular in the genitive absolute of 5:2 ["and when he had come out of the boat"] or to Matt. 8:28 ["And when he came to the other side"]), but the textual support for the singular is quite weak.

5:1. For a discussion of the various textual problems associated with the geographical designation, see the discussion in 5:1–5.

5:3. ὃς τὴν κατοίκησιν εἶχεν is lit. "who was having his dwelling."

3. Jesus—Lord of Disease and Death (5:21–43)

Within this passage we encounter two "healing" stories (5:25–34 and 5:21–24, 35–43), although the latter is really a raising of the dead. These are intercalated, or sandwiched together. Elsewhere, we find this well-known Markan literary technique in the placement of 3:23–30 into 3:19b–21 and 31–35; 6:14–29 into 6:6b–13 and 30ff.; 11:15–19 into 11:12–14 and 20–25; 14:3–9 into 14:1–2 and 10–11. (Cf. also 14:55–65 into 14:53–54 and 66–72; 15:16–20 into 15:6–15 and 21–32.) It is suggested that here, in contrast to the other sandwiches, one account is used not to explain the other but rather to heighten the suspense in the story of Jairus and accent the call to faith in 5:36 (Guelich 1989: 292). It is better, however, to see the account of the woman who had a hemorrhage (5:25–34) as providing a time lapse during which the little girl died (5:21–24, 35–43; Nineham 1963: 157; Meier 1994: 708; Marcus 2000: 364; contra Gundry 1993: 286), in the same way that the death of John the Baptist (6:14–29) provides a time lapse for the mission of the disciples (6:6b–13 and 6:30–31).

There are a number of similarities between the present two stories. In both we find: a woman in a hopeless situation (5:25–26 and 23, 35, 38–40); the number "twelve" (5:25 and 42); a reference to faith or the need for faith (5:28 and 34, 36); the presence of fear (5:33 and 36); an original situation of ritual impurity (a hemorrhaging woman and a dead body); a reference to touching (5:28, 30 and 41); a desire for "salvation" or healing (5:28 and 23, 34); falling at Jesus's feet (5:33 and 22); and the person healed being called a daughter (5:34 and 23; C. Marshall 1989: 93–94). It is possible that these stories were originally independent oral traditions and that they became associated because of some of these common elements. If they were originally separate traditions (Lohmeyer 1957: 109)[1] (and events), our understanding of how they were brought together depends on whether we believe that 4:35–5:43 was a pre-Markan complex (Gnilka 1978: 209–10; Kuhn 1971: 191–203), that it was part of a larger pre-Markan complex consisting of 4:35–6:44 (Achtemeier 1970: 274–81; Kee 1977: 32–34; Pesch 1980a: 279–31), or that the two were tied together before Mark but were not necessarily part of a larger complex (K. Schmidt 1919: 148). Others

---

1. Achtemeier (1970: 277) argues that this is suggested by the fact that the story of Jairus's daughter uses the historic present tense and consists of short sentences, whereas the story of the woman with a hemorrhage uses the aorist tense and consists of longer sentences (contra Gundry 1993: 288). The reference to sentence length, however, is not entirely accurate. In the story of Jairus's daughter, we have some long sentences (5:22–23, 38–39a) and in the story of the hemorrhaging woman we have some relatively short sentences (5:29, 32).

argue for a historical linking of these two passages (V. Taylor 1952: 289; Cranfield 1959: 182; France 2002: 234). The seams found in 5:24b and 35 look Markan (Pryke 1978: 14, 141–42, 158), as do the other seams that tie 4:35–5:43 together (4:35; 5:1, 21), so that it seems best to associate the editing of this entire miracle complex to Mark himself (Koch 1975: 65–67; contrary to Achtemeier 1970: 279, who claims to see "remarkably few evidences of [Mark's] redactional activity" in 4:35–5:43). This finds additional support from the presence of the Markan theme of the messianic secret (Wrede 1971: 35; Bultmann 1968: 214; Schweizer 1970: 116; Gnilka 1978: 211; Klostermann 1950: 53–54; Marcus 2000: 364; but contra Tagawa 1966: 167; Pesch 1980a: 295; Guelich 1989: 303–4).

The connection of the present two stories with 4:35–5:20 is evident. This involves the presence of the boat (4:36–37; 5:2, 18, 21 [?]), the sea (4:39, 41; 5:1, 13, 21), "the other side" (4:35; 5:1, 21), "fear" (4:41; 5:15, 33, 36), hopelessness (4:37–38; 5:3–5, 26, 35), "faith" (4:40; 5:34, 36), "Teacher" (4:38; 5:35), "beseeching" (5:10, 12, 17–18, 23), and so on. Some see the issue of ritual impurity occurring throughout 5:1–43, with the demoniac being impure by his living in the tombs and the connection with the swine, the hemorrhaging woman by the flow of her blood (perhaps menstrual blood), and the dead girl (France 2002: 235). Yet nothing is made of such ritual impurity within the present accounts (see comments on 5:24b–28, 29). If Mark is responsible for the arrangement of the present complex, issues of ritual purity and impurity did not play any significant role in these four stories being associated together in his Gospel (contrast 1:44). This is confirmed by the lack of any mention of impurity in the first story (4:35–43).

The major organization of 5:21–43 can be divided into an ABA′ "sandwich" of two healing stories: (A) the raising of Jairus's daughter (part 1; 5:21–24a); (B) the healing of the hemorrhaging woman (5:24b–34); and (A′) the raising of Jairus's daughter (part 2; 5:35–43). Further subdivisions, however, are arbitrary. I shall divide the story of Jairus as follows: Jesus encounters Jairus by the sea (5:21–24a); the report of the death of Jairus's daughter (5:35–36); Jesus travels to Jairus's house (5:37–40); and Jesus raises Jairus's daughter from the dead (5:41–43). The story of the hemorrhaging woman involves a description of the woman's terrible plight and her faith (5:24b–28), the woman's healing (5:29), and Jesus's encounter with the woman and his blessing her (5:30–34). Because Mark has retold these two accounts using his own vocabulary and style, it is not always easy to distinguish between his own contribution to the accounts and what is traditional. Although some extravagant claims have been made as to the extent of the Markan editorial work in 5:21–43,[2] Mark's own hand is seen most clearly in 5:21, 24b, 28, 34b, and 43a.

---

2. Cf. Pryke (1978: 14, 141–42, 158), who attributes to Mark's hand 5:21, 23a, 24, 25, 26, 28, 30–31, 33, 35a, 41b, 42, 43a.

Exegesis and Exposition

²¹And when Jesus had crossed over again ⌜in the boat⌝ to the other side, a great crowd gathered around him, and he was by the sea. ²²And one of the rulers of the synagogue, ⌜named Jairus,⌝ comes, and upon seeing him [Jesus], he falls at his feet ²³and begs him earnestly, saying, "My little daughter is at the point of death. Please come [and] lay [your] hands on her in order that she may be saved and live." ²⁴And he [Jesus] went with him.

And a great crowd was following him and pressing upon him. ²⁵And a woman who was hemorrhaging for twelve years, ²⁶and had suffered much at the hands of many doctors, and had spent all that she had, and had not been helped but rather had become worse, ²⁷having heard about Jesus [and] having come up behind him in the crowd, touched his garment. ²⁸For she was saying [to herself], "If I touch even his garments, I shall be saved." ²⁹And immediately the hemorrhaging ceased, and she knew in her body that she had been healed of [her] affliction. ³⁰And immediately Jesus, upon knowing in himself [that] the power had gone forth from him and turning around in the crowd, began to say, "Who touched my garments?" ³¹And his disciples were saying to him, "Do you see the crowd pressing upon you, and [yet] you say, 'Who touched me?'" ³²And he began to look around to see the woman who had done this. ³³And she, fearing and trembling, knowing what had happened to her, came and fell down before him and told him the whole truth. ³⁴And Jesus said to her, "Daughter, your faith has saved you. Go in peace, and be healed from your affliction."

³⁵While he was speaking, people come from the [home of] the synagogue ruler, saying, "Your daughter has died. Why trouble the teacher any longer?" ³⁶But Jesus, ignoring what was being said, says to the synagogue ruler, "Do not be afraid, only believe." ³⁷And he did ⌜not permit anyone⌝ to accompany him, except Peter, James, and John the brother of James. ³⁸And they enter into the house of the synagogue ruler, and he sees a commotion and much weeping and wailing. ³⁹And having entered, he says to them, "Why are you making such a commotion and weeping? The child has not died but is sleeping." ⁴⁰And they began ridiculing him. But having put them all outside, he takes the father of the child and the mother and those with him and enters into [the room] where the child was. ⁴¹And taking the hand of the child, he says to her, "Talitha koum," which means, "Little girl, I say to you, arise!" ⁴²And immediately the little girl arose and began to walk, for she was twelve years old. And ⌜immediately⌝ they were utterly amazed. ⁴³And he [Jesus] strictly charged them that no one should know this, and he told [them] to give her [something] to eat.

5:21–24a   The opening seam, "And when Jesus had crossed over again in the boat to the other side," connects the present account with 4:35–41 and 5:1–20 (cf. 4:35 and 5:1, 18). The genitive absolute that begins this verse (διαπεράσαντος τοῦ Ἰησοῦ, *diaperasantos tou Iēsou*) is a frequent Markan stylistic feature (Pryke 1978: 62–67) and may reflect the redactional activity of Mark in 1:32; 4:35; 5:2, 21, 35; 6:2, 54; 8:1; 9:9, 28; 10:17, 46; 11:11, 12, 27; 13:1, 3; 14:17–18, 22, 43, 66; 15:42. In 4:35–5:43 it occurs in 4:35; 5:1–2, 18, here, and 35, or in "every transitional seam in these miracle stories" (Guelich 1989: 294). The presence of such genitive absolutes throughout this complex favors the view that the evangelist himself is responsible for the arrangement of this material (contra Guelich 1989: 294). The vocabulary found in 5:21 is also Markan (Koch 1975: 65n2; Pryke 1978: 14, 141, 158), and has numerous parallels within 4:35–5:43 (Guelich 1989: 294).

The "other side" (εἰς τὸ πέραν, *eis to peran*) picks up this expression found in 4:35 and 5:1 (cf. 6:45; 8:13). The expression is not a technical term for "the eastern side of the Sea of Galilee" (Friedrich 1964: 11) but simply refers to the other side from where Jesus presently is (4:35) or was (5:1, 21). As a result, whereas in 4:35 and 5:1 it refers to the eastern side of the Sea of Galilee, here it refers to returning "again" to the western side. The Aramaic "Talitha koum" in 5:41 and the presence of a ruler of the synagogue in 5:22 all point to the western, more Jewish, side of the Sea of Galilee. In this verse, Mark concentrates his attention on the central figure in the story, that is, Jesus, and only later in the account (5:31, 37–38) refers to the disciples.

The "great crowd gathered about him" (συνήχθη ὄχλος πολὺς ἐπ᾽ αὐτόν, *synēchthē ochlos polys ep' auton*) refers not to the people of Gerasa (5:14) but to the crowds mentioned in 4:1 and 36. If the reference to the "sea" (θάλασσαν, *thalassan*) was part of the pre-Markan form of this tradition, it may be one of the reasons why 5:21ff. was placed together via this word association with 4:35–5:20. "One" in "one of the rulers" (εἷς τῶν ἀρχισυναγώγων, *heis tōn archisynagōgōn*) here may simply mean "a certain," that is, the εἷς may serve as an equivalent for τίς, *tis* (Moule 1959: 125), as in 10:17 and 12:28. If "one" is the preferred interpretation, this indicates that there were several rulers of that particular synagogue, as in Acts 13:15 (France 2002: 235). Such an official was in charge of the financial and physical well-being of the synagogue, representing the Jewish community to the outside world, and regulating such worship activities as the reading of the Torah, having someone lead in prayer, inviting people to preach (cf. Acts 13:15), and so on. The office at times appears to have been an elected position and at times a hereditary one (C. J. Setzer, *ABD* 5:841–42). It is unusual to find a name such as Jairus associated with a healing miracle (cf., however, "Bartimaeus" in 10:46), and Matthew in his abbreviated version of the story omits it. Luke, however, who has abbreviated Mark's account less drastically, includes it. On form-critical grounds some scholars see the name as secondary because of the tendency of the tradition to add names (Bultmann 1968: 215; cf. E. Sanders 1969: 88–189). Yet no ironclad rules exist for the transmission of the gospel material. At times they became longer and more detailed and at times shorter and less detailed.[3] A play on the name "Jairus" based on it being a transliteration of the Aramaic יָאִיר (*yāʾîr*, he enlightens) or יָעִיר (*yāʾîr*, he awakens) is overly subtle (Guelich 1989: 295) and loses sight of the fact that it is Jesus, not Jairus, who "awakens" the girl.

---

3. E. Sanders (1969: 272) states, "*Dogmatic statements that a certain characteristic proves a certain passage to be earlier than another are never justified*" (italics his).

Such a play on the name "Jairus" would be possible only in an environment in which people were fluent in both Greek and Aramaic, and Mark's readers knew no Aramaic, as the explanation of all his Aramaic expressions reveals (see 5:41–43). That the wordplay on the well-known name "Jesus" (Matt. 1:21; cf. also 1:23) is explicitly explained by Matthew makes it highly unlikely that Mark intended his readers, without an explanation, to see such a play on words with the less-familiar name "Jairus." The description of Jairus falling at Jesus's feet may describe an attitude of submission (3:11; 5:33) or petition (here and 7:25) and reveals that not all Jewish leaders were opposed to Jesus. In the present context, Jairus's actions reveal his sense of helplessness and need (C. Marshall 1989: 95).

Verse 23 begins the verbalization of Jairus's action of falling at Jesus's feet (cf. 7:25–26). For similar beseeching, compare 1:40; 5:10, 12, 18; 6:56; 7:32; 8:22. For the adverbial use of "much" in Mark, see 1:45. Jairus seeks for Jesus to heal his daughter. This will require a great miracle, for his daughter is at the point of death (ἐσχάτως ἔχει, eschatōs echei; lit. "has finally").[4] He will receive the benefit of a far greater miracle, for his little daughter will be raised from the dead. The Greek term for "daughter" (θυγάτριον, thygatrion) can refer to a young girl or a girl of marriageable age or (as here) be a term of endearment without respect to age. As in 7:25 the term is far from specific with respect to the girl's age. The ambiguity of the age of Jairus's daughter, however, is resolved by Mark's editorial comment in 5:42. For similar examples of a parent seeking healing for their child, see 7:25–27; 9:17–24. Jairus's request is "that" (ἵνα, hina) Jesus come and lay his hands on her. This ἵνα clause can be understood as introducing a request (cf. 10:51; 12:19; Moule 1959: 144; Zerwick 1963: §415) or as a purpose clause. There is little difference in their meaning in the present verse, although the former is more likely (see 3:9–10). This symbolic act of "the laying on of hands" (ἐπιθῆς τὰς χεῖρας, epithēs tas cheiras) often involves passing on a blessing (10:16; Matt. 19:13, 15; Acts 6:6; 8:17, 19; 9:17; 13:3; 19:6; 1 Tim. 5:22) or bringing about a healing (1:31, 41; 5:41; 6:5; 7:32; 8:23, 25; Luke 4:40; 13:13; 22:51; Acts 9:12, 17; 28:8; cf. Mark 3:10; 5:28–30; also 16:18). The use of this act in healing was common in the ancient world (Theissen 1983: 62–63, 92–93; cf. Gen. 48:14–17, 20; 1QapGen 20.20–22, 28–29; Fitzmyer 1966: 119, 124). The second ἵνα clause (in order that she may be saved and live, ἵνα σωθῇ καὶ ζήσῃ, hina sōthē kai zēsē) describes the purpose of the preceding request and the particular blessing that Jairus seeks through Jesus's laying hands on his daughter. The terms "saved" and "live" may be an example of hendiadys (Guelich 1989: 296), in which two expressions are used to describe the same thing, rather than as a twofold request for salvation and healing. For "saved" (σωθῇ) used in the sense of healing, compare 3:4; 5:28, 34; 6:56; 10:52; 15:30–31. The term can also be used of salvation from the danger of eternal destruction (cf. 8:35; 10:26; 13:13, 20).

---

4. For the similar expression "has badly" (κακῶς ἔχοντας, kakōs echontas) to describe a person being sick, cf. 1:32, 34; 2:17; 6:55.

Even when used with respect to healing, however, it often carries overtones of salvation. The first part of the story of Jairus's daughter concludes with Jesus proceeding to Jairus's home.

The story of the hemorrhaging woman begins with a reference to the "great crowd" (ὄχλος πολύς, *ochlos polys*) of 5:21 that is following Jesus. The term "was following" (ἠκολούθει, *ēkolouthei*) is not used here in the sense of following him as disciples (1:18; 2:14–15; 6:1; 8:34; 10:21, 28, 52; 14:54) but in the sense of walking with or accompanying him (3:7; 10:32; 11:9; 14:13; 15:41). See 3:7–8. In light of the varied use of this term throughout Mark, it is unwise to see this as indicating that it was part of a pre-Markan miracle collection involving 3:7, 9–10; 4:35–5:43; 6:32–56 (contra Guelich 1989: 296). At this point the second healing story begins with a description of the plight of a woman hemorrhaging for twelve years. Just as the sandwiched account of the death of John the Baptist in 6:14–29 allows time for the mission of the disciples (6:6b–13), so here the sandwiched account of the hemorrhaging woman (5:24b–34) allows time for Jairus's daughter to die (5:35). Verses 25–28 make up a single sentence in Greek. In it the plight of the woman and her healing is described by a string of seven participial clauses. The first clause (5:25) explains that she was "hemorrhaging [for] twelve years" (οὖσα ἐν ῥύσει αἵματος δώδεκα ἔτη, *ousa en rhysei haimatos dōdeka etē*; lit. "having a flow of blood twelve years"). Her continuing hemorrhaging would make her ceremonially unclean (Lev. 12:1–8; 15:19–30; cf. the entire mishnaic tractate *Niddah*), especially if the hemorrhaging involved her menstruation. Nothing, however, is made of the issue of her being ceremonially unclean in the account. It plays no part in the miracle story (contra Selvidge 1984; D'Angelo 1999). The woman's plight is highlighted by the length of her suffering—twelve years! Although the number possesses great symbolism in the Bible, there is no reason not to interpret the number literally. Understood literally, the number serves to heighten the seriousness of her condition.

The second clause (5:26a), "had suffered much at the hands of [lit. 'under'] many doctors" (πολλὰ παθοῦσα ὑπὸ πολλῶν ἰατρῶν, *polla pathousa hypo pollōn iatrōn*), heightens the tragic situation (note the double "much" [πολλά]—"many" [πολλῶν]) in that the woman had sought medical help from not merely one but many physicians. In the process she had suffered much under their medical care. Compare Tob. 2:10; Sir. 38:15 LXX; *m. Qidd.* 4.14; and 1QapGen 20.20 for the inability of physicians to heal and the harm they often inflicted. Some ancient medical treatments were both painful and harmful (cf. *b. Šabb.* 110a–b). The third clause (5:26b) states that she "had spent all that she had" (δαπανήσασα τὰ παρ' αὐτῆς πάντα, *dapanēsasa ta par' autēs panta*). Her seeking help from physicians had resulted in three tragic consequences. Two were much suffering and the loss of all her financial resources. The fourth and fifth clauses (5:26c–d) describe the third tragic consequence. She "had not been helped [μηδὲν ὠφεληθεῖσα, *mēden ōphelētheisa*] but rather had become worse [ἀλλὰ μᾶλλον εἰς τὸ χεῖρον ἐλθοῦσα, *alla mallon eis to*

5:24b–28

cheiron elthousa]." Her physical health had actually become worse under the care of the doctors. As in the case of the demoniac, human help (5:3–4) was of no avail; human help actually harmed.

Whereas the first five participles are attributive and describe the woman, the sixth and seventh participles (5:27; having heard, ἀκούσασα, *akousasa*; coming, ἐλθοῦσα, *elthousa*) are adverbial and circumstantial and describe what the woman does as her last hope. Like the Gerasene demoniac, she has lost all hope in others. But she has heard about Jesus. Mark assumes that the woman would know of such teachings of Jesus as found in 1:14–15, 22, 38; 2:18–22, 23–28; 3:20–30; 4:1–34; and also of such healings as 1:23–28, 29–34, 39, 40–45; 2:1–12; 3:1–6, 10; 4:35–41; 5:1–20. Mark does not expect his readers to assume that the woman knew all of the above, but rather that these were the kinds of things that she had heard. Because of what she had heard (cf. 7:25), she came and "touched his garment" (ἥψατο τοῦ ἱματίου αὐτοῦ, *hēpsato tou himatiou autou*). Why she surreptitiously touched Jesus's garment rather than directly asking him for healing is not explained. Whatever the reason—fear, being impure and ceremonially unclean (Marcus 2000: 357–58; cf., however, Gundry 1993: 269), feeling unimportant or outcast, concern for violating normal male-female relationships, etc.—Mark does not think it necessary for understanding the story, for he makes no attempt to explain why she took this approach rather than another. He explains rather what the woman thought touching Jesus's garment would do (cf. 6:56; Luke 6:19; Acts 5:15; 19:12). The appearance of the verb "touched" after the string of seven participles appears to heighten the woman's act (Marcus 2000: 367).

The reason the woman sought to touch Jesus's garment is explained in 5:28 by a typical Markan γάρ (*gar*) explanatory clause (Pryke 1978: 126–35; Gnilka 1978: 1.213; contra Guelich 1989: 297; see 1:16–18). Having heard about Jesus, the woman "believed" (5:34) that Jesus, unlike the physicians, could help her. He possessed "healing power" (δύναμιν, *dynamin*; 5:30), and she believed that just touching him would bring her healing. Many commentators discuss issues of ceremonial purity with respect to this account (the woman's touching Jesus would make Jesus ceremonially impure) and the following (touching the dead girl would make Jesus ceremonially impure). Whatever the situation in the original setting in Jesus's life, Mark makes no clear reference to this issue in any of the three miracle accounts found in this chapter. Thus it plays no role in what he wants to share with his gentile readers. At times Mark explains Jewish customs in order to help his readers understand what he is writing (cf. 7:3–5, 11), but not in the present chapter. As a result, if we want to understand what he sought to convey to his readers through these accounts, we should concentrate on what the text tells us rather than speculate on the hypothetical mental activities of the woman. Mark uses a γάρ explanatory clause to tell his readers that the woman believed that if she "even" (κἄν [*kan*] is best translated as "even" rather than "just") touched Jesus's outer garment, she would be healed. And she did so and was healed!

The "And immediately"[5] that begins this sentence is meant to show the great   **5:29**
power of Jesus in that the woman's twelve-year medical condition was resolved,
and she was healed instantly by Jesus of her affliction (μάστιγος, *mastigos*;
see 5:34; cf. 3:10). It has been suggested that the words "the hemorrhaging
ceased" (ἐξηράνθη ἡ πηγὴ τοῦ αἵματος αὐτῆς, *exēranthē hē pēgē tou haimatos
autēs*; lit. "the fountain of her blood was dried up") is a wordplay on Lev.
12:7 (LXX), and this implies that despite her ritual impurity, the woman was
able to touch Jesus without defiling him (Guelich 1989: 297). It is difficult,
however, to conceive of how these words could have caused Mark's hearers
to reflect on Lev. 12:7, issues of ritual purity and impurity, how the woman's
healing affected this, and so on, and at the same time could allow them to
concentrate on the rest of the narrative that continued to be read to them. It is
also important to realize that speculations about pure versus impure issues in
this statement and Lev. 12:7 could not have taken place in the setting of Jesus,
since the present description in 5:29 is editorial in nature and the alleged allusion is based on the Greek text of Lev. 12:7 found in the LXX. It is not based
on Aramaic (or Hebrew), the native tongue of Jesus and his audience. Since
Mark makes no reference to such issues in his account, the issue of purity
and impurity could only have taken place in a hypothetically reconstructed
setting during the period between Jesus's ministry and Mark's writing his
Gospel. On the other hand, for Mark's readers/hearers the meaning of these
words was clear. Even the touch of the Son of God's garment brought instant
and complete healing after twelve years of hopeless suffering! The woman is
described as aware that she has been healed because she "knew" (ἔγνω, *egnō*)
this in her body. How she "knew" that her hemorrhaging had ceased is not
explained. Various translations (KJV, NIV, RSV, NRSV, NASB, NAB, NJB)
assume that this knowledge came from her "feeling" it (Gundry 1993: 270).
It is probably wiser to translate ἔγνω as "knew" (so REB) and leave open the
question of how she knew.

As a result of the woman's healing, Jesus "immediately" perceives in himself   **5:30–34**
(ἐπιγνοὺς ἐν ἑαυτῷ, *epignous en heautō*) that divine power has gone forth
from him (5:30). In Mark, healing can come through Jesus touching someone
(1:31, 40–45; 7:31–37; 8:22–26) or by someone touching him (3:10; 6:56; cf.
Acts 5:15; 19:11–12). It has been suggested (Kuhn 1971: 193–200) that an
early Christian view of Jesus as a wonder-worker or θεῖος ἀνήρ (*theios anēr*)
resulted in references to "Jesus's healing touch" being read back into the
Gospels. It seems more likely, however, that, if anything, the opposite would
be true. "Jesus's healing touch" later gave rise to a disproportionate emphasis
on Jesus as a wonder-worker. For "perceiving in himself," see 2:8. Elsewhere in
Mark, "power" can serve as a substitute for God (14:62), a reference to mighty
works (6:2, 5; 9:39), in a prepositional phrase as an adverb, "powerfully" (9:1;
cf. 13:26), a term for heavenly bodies (13:25), or a reference to God's power

---

5. The "immediately" (εὐθύς, *euthys*) here and in 5:30 and 42 should be given its full value
as a temporal designation.

(12:24), but here and in 6:14 it refers to the divine, supernatural force within Jesus by which he could perform mighty deeds (cf. 6:2, 5, 14; 9:37; also 1:40, 45; 2:7; 3:23, 27; etc.). The question "Who touched my garments?" should be understood as an example of Jesus's supernatural knowledge resulting from his "perceiving in himself" that his supernatural power had healed someone who touched him. Compare 2:8; 3:5; 5:32; 8:17; 12:15.

"And his disciples were saying to him" (καὶ ἔλεγον αὐτῷ οἱ μαθηταὶ αὐτοῦ, *kai elegon autō hoi mathētai autou*; 5:31) is the first explicit reference to the disciples since 4:34, although their presence has been indicated by the "they" of 4:35–41; 5:1, 16 (?). The press of the great crowd (5:24, 31) makes the disciples think that Jesus's question is ludicrous, because the whole crowd has been brushing, touching, pressing against him all along. From the Markan perspective, this reveals a failure of the disciples. They have been with Jesus long enough that they should possess "understanding" (cf. 7:18). Jesus's supernatural knowledge thus stands in sharp contrast with the ignorance of the disciples. The theme of the disciples' lack of understanding will be emphasized by Mark in the coming chapters (cf. 6:52; 7:18; 8:4, 14–21; Räisänen 1990: 97–101, 195–222).

Through supernatural knowledge, Jesus recognizes not only that he has been touched but also that it was a woman who had touched him (contra W. Lane 1971: 193n50; Zerwick and Grosvenor 1981: 118). This is shown by the singular feminine article, which with the feminine participle (τὴν τοῦτο ποιήσασαν, *tēn touto poiēsasan*) is translated as "the woman who had done this" (5:32). In 5:33 Mark returns to the woman of 5:29 and describes her as fearful and trembling due to her miraculous experience of healing and as falling down before Jesus (cf. 5:22). The response of "fear" toward Jesus and his mighty power has already been referred to in 4:41 and 5:15. Here, unlike in 5:15 (cf. also 16:8), it refers to a positive response and appropriate awe in experiencing the mighty, healing power of the Son of God. See 4:40–41. "Fear and trembling" is described in Phil. 2:12 as the appropriate manner in which Christians should "work out" their salvation (cf. also 1 Cor. 2:3; 2 Cor. 7:15; Eph. 6:5; also Mark 16:8). She then tells Jesus "the whole truth" (πᾶσαν τὴν ἀλήθειαν, *pasan tēn alētheian*). Included in the "whole truth" is her desire to be healed and why she touched his garment. Since issues of impurity have not been referred to by Mark, it is best in understanding the present account from the Markan perspective not to assume that the evangelist believed his gentile readers would read this issue into the "whole truth."

Jesus gives a fourfold response of encouragement to the woman. First, he addresses her as "Daughter" (cf. Ruth 2:2, 8, 22; 3:1, 10, 16, 18; also 1:11–13). In later Jewish writings, "daughter" is often a respectful and affectionate address to women regardless of age or relationship (Marcus 2000: 360). Second, he commends her faith. In miraculous healings, wellness ("being saved," σέσωκεν, *sesōken*; see 5:21–24a) is often associated with faith (Guelich 1989: 85–86). Compare 2:5 for the association of faith and forgiveness and for the use of a similar affectionate address, "Child" (Τέκνον, *Teknon*). Mark sees the touching of Jesus's garment as the manifestation of the woman's faith. It is not, however, just the touch of Jesus's garment that brings healing, for the whole crowd was continually pressing against and touching him (5:24b, 31). It was rather the "touch of faith." In the Greek world, faith was seldom a prerequisite for such healing (Theissen 1983: 132, 140). The expression "Your faith has made you well" (σέσωκέν σε, *sesōken se*; lit., "has saved you") is also found in 10:52; Luke 7:50; 17:19. (There are a number of interesting parallels between this account and Luke 7:36–50; cf. Marcus 2000: 367.) Third, Jesus tells her, "Go in peace" (ὕπαγε εἰς εἰρήνην, *hypage eis eirēnēn*), a common Semitic greeting and blessing as well as farewell.[6] The expression generally involves less a wish for "peace of mind" than a wish for divine peace that is a foretaste of eschatological salvation. Finally, since healing has already taken place (cf. 5:29), Jesus adds, "and be healed from your affliction" (ἴσθι ὑγιὴς ἀπὸ τῆς μάστιγός σου, *isthi hygiēs apo tēs mastigos sou*). This statement functions as a word of assurance, ratifying what has already taken place and guaranteeing that her healing is permanent (Donahue and Harrington 2002: 176).

"While he was still speaking, people come [lit. 'they come'—an impersonal plural; see 1:21–22] from the [house] of the synagogue ruler, saying . . ." resumes the story of Jairus and his daughter. The genitive absolute (Ἔτι αὐτοῦ λαλοῦντος, *eti autou lalountos*) is typically Markan (contra Guelich 1989: 300) and serves as a seam uniting the third part of this sandwich (5:35–43) with the first two parts (5:21–24 and 25–34). See 5:21–24a. "From the home of the synagogue ruler" is literally "from the synagogue ruler" (ἀπὸ τοῦ ἀρχισυναγώγου, *apo tou archisynagōgou*). This is probably an example of ellipsis in which the term "home" has been omitted. They bring the message that Jairus's daughter has died, and since Jesus (they assume) cannot possibly help now, he should not be troubled any further. The insertion of the story of the hemorrhaging woman into the story of Jairus's daughter allows time for her to die (cf. John 11:3–7). These two statements prepare the reader for the rest of the story and heighten the forthcoming miracle (Bultmann 1968: 214). Having described the hopelessness of the disciples in the storm (4:38), of the demoniac (5:3–5), and of the hemorrhaging woman (5:25–26), Mark now describes the utter hopelessness of Jairus's situation. His daughter is no longer sick and at the point of death. She has died! It is now too late. At this point not even "the teacher" can help. The readers of Mark, however, unlike the messengers from the house of Jairus, have learned in the preceding chapters of the Gospel that no situation is hopeless for Jesus, the Son of God, for he, like God, possesses mastery over nature, demons, and illness. In anticipation

5:35–36

6. Cf. Exod. 4:18; Judg. 18:6; 1 Sam. 1:17; 20:42; 25:35; 29:7; 2 Sam. 15:9; 2 Kings 5:19; also 2 Sam. 3:21; Tob. 10:13; Jdt. 8:35. It also appears in the abbreviated form of "Peace" or "Shalom." It occurs as a greeting in the NT in Matt. 10:13; Luke 10:5–6; John 20:19, 21, 26; Rom. 1:7; 1 Cor. 1:3; 2 Cor. 1:2; Gal. 1:3; Eph. 1:2; Phil. 1:2; Col. 1:2; 1 Thess. 1:1; 2 Thess. 1:2; 1 Tim. 1:2; 2 Tim. 1:2; Titus 1:4; Philem. 3; 1 Pet. 1:2; 2 Pet. 1:2; 2 John 3; Jude 2; Rev. 1:4 (in the OT see Judg. 6:23; 19:20; cf. Tob. 12:17) and as a farewell in 1 Cor. 16:11; Gal. 6:16; Eph. 6:23; 1 Pet. 5:14; 3 John 15. For "go in peace," compare Luke 7:50; Acts 16:36; James 2:16.

they await to learn what this mighty Son of God will do. After all, did not Elijah (1 Kings 17:17–24) and Elisha (2 Kings 4:18–37) raise the dead? And one greater than Elijah and Elisha is present! Within the Dead Sea Scrolls we find the view that the Messiah would heal, raise the dead, and preach good news to the poor (4Q521 [2.12]). See 4:37–39 for a discussion of the use of "teacher" in the context of Jesus's miracle-working ministry.

The term παρακούσας (*parakousas*) in 5:36 can mean to "overhear" or to "ignore." The seven times that it is used in the LXX and the only other use of the term in the NT (Matt. 18:17) all have the sense of "ignore" (Guelich 1989: 291n1). It is best, therefore, to translate it similarly here, even though "overhear" fits the context well. The expression τὸν λόγον (*ton logon*, lit. "the word"), which is translated "what was said," does not have the technical sense of "the gospel" here as it does in 1:45; 2:2; 4:14ff.; and 8:32, but simply refers to the message brought to the synagogue ruler by the messengers.

The present tenses of Jesus's two imperatives, "Do not fear, only believe" (μὴ φοβοῦ, μόνον πίστευε, *mē phobou, monon pisteue*), imply that Jairus should stop his present fearing (a present imperative of prohibition) brought about by the news of the messengers and continue his believing in Jesus, which began even before 5:22–23. "Fear" is used here in the negative sense of being frightened and lacking faith. As in 6:50 (cf. Matt. 1:20; 10:26, 28, 31; 17:7; 28:5, 10; Luke 1:13, 30; 2:10; 5:10; 12:4, 32), the command serves as a word of encouragement. The command to "believe" can have as its object "something" (Mark 1:15 [the gospel]; 13:21 [false reports]) or "someone" (11:24 [God, as the divine passive "it will be to you" indicates], 31 [God's messenger—John the Baptist]; 15:22 [Jesus]). Here Jairus is urged to believe "someone." Whether Jesus meant God or himself, Mark does not see any difference. To believe in the Lord God is to believe in the Lord Jesus (5:19–20). For Mark, faith in the Son of God and faith in the God and Father of our Lord Jesus Christ (cf. 2 Cor. 1:3) cannot be separated. To believe in the one is to believe in the other (see the summary to 5:1–20). Whereas Jairus and the hemorrhaging woman serve as positive examples of such faith, the people of Nazareth in the next story (6:1–6a), like the people of Gerasa (5:17), provide a negative example of the lack of such faith.

5:37–40 Although 3:16–17 lists Peter, James, and John together, this is the first clear reference to them in Mark as a core group of the disciples. The use of a single article (τὸν Πέτρον καὶ Ἰάκωβον καὶ Ἰωάννην, *ton Petron kai Iakōbon kai Iōannēn*) for the three names indicates that they are understood as a group— "the three." They will be mentioned again in 9:2 (the transfiguration) and 14:33 (the Garden of Gethsemane). Compare 13:3, where Andrew is also mentioned with the three, but once again, as in 3:16–17, after Peter, James, and John. Their importance can be seen in the account of Jesus's calling them to follow him (1:16–20), for no other disciple's call is so described. (See 2:13–14 for a discussion of the call of Levi and his relationship to the Twelve.) That these three disciples do not function as a leadership core within the Gospel (or the history of the early church) argues for the historicity of the various accounts in which they appear. Their presence here is not used to heighten the miracle. Mark's mention of them is probably due to their presence in his tradition of the account (Pesch 1980a: 307). This in turn is probably due to Jesus's choice of the three as his inner core. For Mark's readers, they serve as eyewitnesses to the present incident (Gnilka 1978: 217; Meier 1994: 779), just as the herdsmen and disciples serve this function for the people of Gerasa in 5:16.

The scene at Jairus's house (commotion and much weeping and wailing, θόρυβον καὶ κλαίοντας καὶ ἀλαλάζοντας πολλά, *thorybon kai klaiontas kai alalazontas polla*; 5:38) confirms the report of the messengers: the child has died (5:35). The traditional mourning has begun, and in typical Semitic style there is a great outpouring of grief. Jairus's leadership position in the community would have guaranteed "much" weeping and wailing. (For the adverbial use of πολλά, see 1:45.) Professional mourners would often be hired to assist in such mourning (cf. Josephus, *J.W.* 2.1.3 §6; 3.9.5 §437; Safrai 1976: 774–75). Matthew 9:23 mentions flute players being present (cf. Jer. 9:17–20; Luke 23:27; Josephus, *J.W.* 3.9.5 §437; and *m. Ketub.* 4.4: "Even the poorest in Israel should hire not less than two flutes and one wailing woman [in such circumstances]"). The mourning of the people highlights the desperate and hopeless situation. On the basis of Jesus's statement, "The child has not died but is sleeping" (τὰ παιδίον οὐκ ἀπέθανεν ἀλλὰ καθεύδει, *to paidion ouk apethanen alla katheudei*; 5:39), some scholars have argued that the girl was not dead but in a coma (V. Taylor 1952: 285–86, 295). Her salvation is not from death but from premature burial. This was a common interpretation during the height of rationalistic attempts to explain the biblical miracles in the mid-nineteenth century (Strauss 1972: 478–80; cf. Meier 1994: 781–84). With his ability/gift of healing, Jesus revived a comatose child, and later the early church transformed this act into a miracle of resurrection. The tradition (and Mark), however, clearly understood the account as a raising from the dead, as the messengers (5:35), the mourners (5:38), the mocking (5:40), and the fact that Jesus has not yet even seen the child all reveal. Matthew's account also contains the words "She has not died but is sleeping" (9:24), but this must be understood in light of the father's earlier explicit statement in 9:18, "My daughter has died."

The metaphor of "sleep" is frequently used to describe death (Matt. 27:52; John 11:11; Acts 7:60; 13:36; 1 Cor. 7:39; 11:30; 15:6, 18, 20, 51; 1 Thess. 4:13–15; 5:10; 2 Pet. 3:4; cf. Dan. 12:2; Ps. 87:6 LXX). The similarity between sleep and death is self-evident, and the use of "sleep" as a metaphor for death is self-explanatory. The statement means that the girl is not "dead" in the sense of awaiting only the final, eschatological resurrection, but "dead," that is, asleep, in the sense of no longer experiencing human life, but soon to experience such life once again. Her temporary experience of physical death will be so short that it will seem as though she has only taken a nap, a short sleep (cf. Davies and Allison 1991: 131–32). All the miracles of raisings from the dead (Luke 7:11–17; John 11:1–44; Acts 9:36–43; cf. Matt. 27:52–53; 1 Kings

17:17–23; 2 Kings 4:18–37) are not resurrections in the eschatological sense but resuscitations to this present life that leave the recipients still susceptible to the experiences of sorrow, disappointment, tears, disease, and physical death once again.

The mourners respond cynically to Jesus's words and ridicule him. They know that the girl is not literally sleeping, and they cannot interpret Jesus's use of "sleeping" as a metaphor for death, for this would lead to the absurd "The child is not dead but dead ['sleeping']." Thus their response is quite natural, and since they did not believe in Jesus, they could not conceive that even as those raised by Elijah (1 Kings 17:17–24) and Elisha (2 Kings 4:18–37) were not ultimately dead but only temporally dead, that is, "sleeping," so in the presence of Jesus, the Son of God, Jairus's daughter was not ultimately dead but only "sleeping." For those "outside" (4:11), the riddle-like nature of Jesus's words was "hearable" but not "understandable" (4:12). In Mark, faith leads to understanding (4:25a, 34); unbelief leads to confusion and misunderstanding (4:25b). The mocking of the mourners, however, will be refuted by the girl's rising from the dead; this scene anticipates the mocking of Jesus in 14:65 and 15:16–20, which will be refuted by Jesus's rising from the dead.

As in certain other miracle stories (7:31–37, esp. v. 33; 8:22–26, esp. v. 23; cf. also Acts 9:36–43, esp. v. 40), Jesus puts the scoffers outside. This miracle will be performed in private (cf. 1 Kings 17:19; 2 Kings 4:4, 33). Those weak in faith (cf. "I believe; help my unbelief," Mark 9:24) can share in the witness of God's/Jesus's glorious power, but those who offer nothing but disdain and ridicule are excluded. Jesus takes with him only the girl's parents and "those with him," that is, Peter, James, and John. The home of the synagogue ruler was large enough that the child was in a separate room (ὅπου ἦν τὸ παιδίον, *hopou ēn to paidion*). The description of the following miracle does not borrow from the OT accounts of Elijah and Elisha raising children from the dead (cf. 1 Kings 17:17–23; 2 Kings 4:18–37).

5:41–43   For Jesus's use of touch (taking the hand of the child, κρατήσας τῆς χειρὸς τοῦ παιδίου, *kratēsas tēs cheiros tou paidiou*; cf. 1:31) in healing miracles in Mark, see 5:30–34. Issues of defilement in touching a dead body do not play a role in Mark's telling of this story (see 5:24b–28). The Semitic expression "Talitha koum" (cf. 3:17, 22; 7:11, 34; 9:43; 10:46; 14:36; 15:22, 34; Matt. 5:22; 6:24; John 1:42), which means, "Little girl, . . . arise" (Τὸ κοράσιον, . . . ἔγειρε, *To korasion, . . . egeire*; cf. 12:26; 16:6), suggests, among other things, that Jesus's mother tongue was Aramaic (Meier 1991: 255–68). The Greek translation that follows (and, of course, the whole Gospel) reveals that the native language of Mark's readers is Greek. The Aramaic expressions found in Mark do not function as magical incantations (Gundry 1993: 274–75; contra Mussies 1984: 427). Even less do they serve as secret "gnostic" formulas, since they are openly stated along with their interpretations. Nor are they used "to demonstrate the superior power of eastern words of healing" (Theissen 1983: 254), since the expressions in Mark are used mostly in nonmiracle settings (cf. 3:17; 7:11; 14:36; 15:34; also Matt. 5:22; 6:24; John 1:42). (Only two Aramaic expressions are found in the setting of a healing miracle, here and 7:34.) It is best to understand these expressions as remnants of the Aramaic traditions with which Mark was familiar (Gnilka 1978: 211). In their abbreviations of Mark, Matthew and Luke omit them (except for Matt. 27:46).

Unlike the frequent Markan "and immediately" found throughout the Gospel (see 1:10–11), the temporal sense plays an important role in "And immediately the little girl arose and began to walk" (5:42). In this instance it functions not so much to tie what follows with what precedes but rather to show the greatness of Jesus. He has power to raise the dead "immediately." It takes only two Aramaic words, and instantly the dead girl comes to life again. Proof of return to life is seen in her rising up and beginning to walk (an inceptive imperfect). The term "arose" (ἀνέστη, *anestē*) is used with respect to Jesus's own rising from the dead in 8:31; 9:9–10, 31; 10:34 (cf. Luke 18:33; 24:7, 46), as well as the general resurrection of the dead in 12:23, 25. As a result, it would probably have brought to the minds of Mark's readers Jesus's own rising from the dead.

The "for" (γάρ, *gar*) clause ("for she was twelve years old") contains traditional material, but the wording is probably Markan. It explains why the girl was able to get up and walk. The term θυγάτριον (*thygatrion*) in 5:23 and the synonym κοράσιον in 5:41–42 are not very precise, and the "for" clause clarifies this imprecision. The lack of any specific theological function for the number twelve in this account suggests that it was part of the pre-Markan tradition, even though the explanatory clause is Markan in form. The appearance of this number in both stories (here and 5:25) may be one of the elements that caused them to be joined together. Such word associations were undoubtedly at play in the oral period and caused certain sayings and stories to be combined together. The result of the girl getting up and walking is that "they," that is, the parents and the three disciples, "were utterly amazed" (5:42; see 1:21–22). "Utterly amazed" (lit. "were astonished with great astonishment") is a cognate dative consisting of the verb ἐξέστησαν (*exestēsan*) and the noun ἐκστάσει (*ekstasei*; see comments on 1:25–26). Like the "And immediately" found earlier in this verse, the second "And immediately" should be given its full temporal significance.

The "that" (ἵνα, *hina*) in "And he strictly charged them that no one should know this [μηδεὶς γνοῖ τοῦτο, *mēdeis gnoi touto*]" can be understood as introducing a purpose clause or the content of the command (see 3:9–10). The latter is more likely here. As in 1:44 and 7:36, a command to keep silent is given (cf. 8:26, 30; 9:9). This does not refer to keeping the Aramaic expression "Talitha koum" secret (contra Gundry 1993: 284) but rather the miracle. How this rising from the dead could be kept secret, however, is unclear. The commands to silence in 1:34, 44; 7:36; 8:26, 30; 9:9 are feasible, but the crowd of mourners has seen Jesus enter the room of the dead girl, and when he leaves, the dead girl is alive. Thus it is difficult to understand how something like this could be kept secret.[7] This verse is one of the most important examples of the messianic secret in Mark (Räisänen 1990: 42). See the introduction to this unit.

The function of Jesus's command to give the girl something to eat is uncertain. Some suggest that it serves to assure the readers that the girl is not just some sort of a phantom spirit but has truly been raised from the dead (Bultmann 1968: 215) and possesses a real body (cf. Luke 24:41–43). Others suggest that it originally served in a large, pre-Markan complex to introduce the feeding of the five thousand (6:35–44), which immediately followed these words but is now separated by 6:1–34 (Achtemeier 1970: 279). If so, the present command to give the girl something to eat served originally as a command to give the crowds something to eat (6:37). However, there is no reference to the girl actually eating, as in 6:42. Most scholars agree that 6:1–30 breaks any connection between the present account and the feeding of the five thousand, so that in the present statement found in Mark, there is no connection of this command with the feeding of the five thousand. The statement seems to emphasize that the mighty Son of God not only is Lord over nature, demons, illness, and death but also cares for the physical needs of his followers (Cranfield 1959: 191). For Mark's readers, it may have reassured them that their heavenly Father knows that they have need of such things (Matt. 6:32), and that is why they pray for their daily bread (Matt. 6:11).

Summary

The present two stories continue Mark's christological teaching concerning the greatness of the Son of God begun in 4:41. Having shown that Jesus is the Lord of nature (4:35–43) and Lord of the demons (5:1–20), he now continues to tell of the lordship of the Son of God. In the story of the hemorrhaging woman, he shows how Jesus is Lord and master of illness and, in the story of Jairus's daughter, how he is Lord over even death itself. As in the two earlier accounts where Mark has heightened the problems (4:37–38; 5:3–5) in order to show the greater might and power of Jesus, so here also he describes in great detail the hopeless plight of the hemorrhaging woman (5:25–26) and Jairus's daughter (5:23, 35, 38–40). Yet the mere touch of Jesus's garment can bring healing (5:28–30), and his words can raise the dead (5:41–42). "Who is this one who possesses such divine power?" The answer to this question in 4:35–5:43 is found in the confession of the demon(s) in 5:7: this Jesus is "the Son of the Most High God!"

A secondary emphasis of Mark that appears in this passage (and the whole complex) is the importance of faith. The disciples are criticized for their lack of faith (4:40); the demoniac shows it by coming to Jesus (5:6); the woman is commended for it (5:34); and Jairus is urged not to lose it (5:36). It is unclear why Mark emphasizes the need for faith and what specific situation of his readers (if any) caused him to emphasize this. The theory

---

7. See Gundry (1993: 276–77), who argues that the command is historical and was intended to allow "a getaway" for Jesus. Cf. John 6:15.

that he did so because of persecution being experienced by his readers will always remain speculative, for this cannot be demonstrated from the present text. What is clear is that Mark emphasizes to his readers the importance of faith. This faith is based on the greatness of the one in whom they are to have faith. This Jesus in whom they believe is worthy of faith, for he is Lord over nature, demons, illness, and death. What need they fear if they remain faithful to him? In light of their knowing that the Son of God has "saved" them (cf. 5:34) and can continue to do so and will "raise" them (5:42) from the dead, they are encouraged not to fear but to trust (5:36).

Additional Notes

5:21. The question of whether ἐν τῷ πλοίῳ should be read is uncertain. It is included by ℵ A B C K L Δ W f^{13} vg but not found in $\mathfrak{P}^{45}$ D Θ f^{1}.

5:22. Although ὀνόματι Ἰάϊρος is not found in D $it^{a, e, ff(2), i}$, it is overwhelmingly supported by $\mathfrak{P}^{45}$ ℵ B C L N Δ $it^{b, c, l, q}$ vg syr cop and should be included (Metzger 1994: 73–74).

5:37. Note the double negative: οὐκ . . . οὐδένα.

5:42. εὐθύς is omitted by $\mathfrak{P}^{45}$ A W Θ f^{1} f^{13} lat syr but found in ℵ B C L Δ bo.

F. Jesus Encounters Unbelief in Nazareth (6:1–6a)

Some see the present account as "a typical example of how an imaginary situation is built up out of an independent saying" (Bultmann 1968: 31; cf. Koch 1975: 149). (The saying in 6:4 is found both in the parallel account in Matt. 13:57 and as an independent saying in Luke 4:24; John 4:44; Gos. Thom. 31; and P.Oxy. 1.6.) Others view the account as an earlier tradition that has been maintained virtually intact (Pesch 1980a: 315–16). It is unlikely that the early church would have created an account de novo in which Jesus is limited in his ability to heal (6:5; Donahue and Harrington 2002: 187), and most consider 6:2b–6a as consisting of a traditional core (6:2b–3, 4b–5) that has been modified by Mark at 6:4a and 6a (Pryke 1978: 14, 142, 158–59), and that the introduction in 6:1–2a is due to Mark as well (Guelich 1989: 306, 308; Grässer 1970: 9–12).

Within the text itself, several internal tensions are present: there is the "obvious discrepancy" between the positive reaction toward Jesus in 6:2 and the negative one in 6:3 (Crossan 1973b: 99); 6:1–3 refers to Jesus's hometown but 6:4 to his relatives and family; 6:5a implies that Jesus did not heal anyone, but 6:5b implies that he healed some; Jesus is surprised at his rejection in 6:6a, but in 6:4 he utters a proverb saying that this is to be expected; and so on. Due to such internal tensions, some believe that the present account is the product of various traditions and editorial redactions (Grässer 1970: 4–9; Koch 1975: 151–52; Mayer 1978). The strong redactional influence of Mark in the present account cannot be denied. Yet regardless of its origin,[1] the present account must have made sense in its present form to Mark. If this is so, it is difficult to assume that the same internal tensions could not have made sense to others in a pre-Markan setting. The exegete's main goal is to discover how Mark himself understood this account and what he was seeking to teach his readers through it.

The present account is tied to the preceding material by way of a startling contrast between the faith of the woman in 5:34 (cf. also 5:36) and the lack of faith that Jesus encounters in Nazareth (6:6a). Another tie involves the reference to the "power" (δύναμιν, *dynamin*) of Jesus to heal in 5:30 and the "mighty works" (δυνάμεις, *dynameis*) of Jesus referred to in 6:2 and 5 (cf. also 6:14–16). Others suggest that geographical and chronological concerns are the reason for the present account's placement (Gundry 1993: 294). By the placement of this account, Mark picks up the theme that despite his

---

1. See Gundry (1993: 298) for arguments supporting the overall historicity of the account.

teaching (4:1–32) and mighty works (4:35–5:43), Jesus was greeted with a lack of understanding (4:10–12, 33–34), rejection (5:17), and ridicule (5:40). The rejection of Jesus's word and work in Nazareth (6:3–6a) is a frank reminder that the hostility Jesus had already encountered (cf. 2:6–7, 16, 18, 24; 3:2, 6, 22, 30) would continue to dog his steps and eventually lead to his death. Golgotha and the cross should not take the readers of Mark by surprise. The evangelist has already shown numerous foreshadowings of this and in the present account gives still another.

Even as the preceding section (1:14–3:6) ends with a negative, concluding story in which the Pharisees and Herodians seek to kill Jesus (3:1–6), so the present section ends similarly with a negative story in which Jesus encounters amazing unbelief in his hometown of Nazareth (6:1–6a). Mark's editorial work is seen most clearly in the placement of the present account at the end of 3:7–6:6a, in the introductory seam (6:1), in the emphasis on Jesus's teaching and the astonishment that this creates (6:2a), in the introduction to Jesus's response (6:4a), and in the concluding summary (6:6a). The story can be divided into the opening introductory seam in which Jesus arrives in Nazareth and teaches in the synagogue (6:1–2a), the reaction of the people of Nazareth (6:2b–3), and Jesus's response (6:4–6a).

Exegesis and Exposition

[1]And he [Jesus] departed from there and comes to his hometown and his disciples are following him. [2]And when the Sabbath came, he began to teach in the synagogue, and many hearing were amazed, saying, "Where did this man get all this? And what is the wisdom that is given to this man? And [what are] these mighty works being accomplished through his hands? [3]Is not this ⌜the carpenter, the son of Mary⌝ and brother of James, Joses, Judas, and Simon? And are not his sisters here with us?" And they were taking offense at him. [4]And Jesus was saying to them, "A prophet is not without honor except in his [own] hometown, and among his [own] relatives, and in his [own] family." [5]And he was not able to do any mighty work there except that he laid his hands upon a few sick people [and] healed [them]. [6a]And he was marveling at their unbelief.

"And he departed from there and comes to his hometown" (καὶ ἐξῆλθεν . . . καὶ ἔρχεται . . . , kai exēlthen . . . kai erchetai . . .) serves to sew the present account to what has preceded. "From there" (ἐκεῖθεν, ekeithen; cf. 7:24; 9:30; 10:1) means "from Jairus's house." This term and "departed" (ἐξῆλθεν—1:35; 2:13; 8:27; cf. also 7:31; 8:11; 9:30; 14:26) reveal the editorial nature of this transitional seam (Pryke 1978: 14, 142, 158). Although πατρίς (patris) in classical Greek literature tends to mean "fatherland, homeland," in the NT it tends to refer to one's "hometown" (Marcus 2000: 374). This is most evident in Luke 4:23, where Jesus is requested to do in his "hometown" (πατρίδι), Nazareth (4:16), what he did in Capernaum. (Cf. also Heb. 11:14–16, where the heavenly

6:1–2a

"homeland" [πατρίδα] being sought is referred to as a "city" [πόλιν, polin].) This view receives support from the difficulty of defining exactly what a first-century Jew considered his "homeland." Would it include Galilee? Samaria? The Decapolis? The lack of a specific reference to "Nazareth" in the present account may indicate that Mark assumed his readers were familiar enough with the gospel traditions that they knew that Jesus's hometown was Nazareth. On the other hand, he might simply have assumed that they would have concluded this from 1:9 and 24 (cf. 10:47; 14:67; 16:6). The reference to the synagogue (singular rather than plural as in 1:39; 12:39; 13:9) supports the view that πατρίδα refers to "hometown" rather than "homeland."

The reference to the disciples' following Jesus picks up 5:31 and 37. For "are following" (ἀκολουθοῦσιν, akolouthousin), see 3:7–8. Here it probably means "accompanied." As in 5:1–20, the disciples play no role in the account, although mention of them prepares the readers for 6:7–13, where Jesus sends them out on a mission. Their presence here does not surprise the reader, however, for Jesus had called them to be "with him" (3:14). "And when the Sabbath came" (καὶ γενομένου σαββάτου, kai genomenou sabbatou) introduces the third and last account in Mark where Jesus is present in a synagogue (cf. 1:21–28; 3:1–6; also 1:39). Whereas the first synagogue incident is positive in nature, here, as in 3:1–6, the incident in the synagogue results in a negative response toward Jesus (cf. 12:38–40; 13:9). For "began to teach" (ἤρξατο διδάσκειν, ērxato didaskein), compare 4:1; 6:34; 8:31 (also "began to say/speak" in 10:32; 12:1; 13:5). This suggests that, although the location and event may be traditional, the wording of this opening statement is probably Markan (Pryke 1978: 14, 142, 158). Compare 1:15, and for the Third Evangelist's understanding of the content of such teaching, see Luke 4:18–21. Here, however, Mark focuses the reader's attention on the response to Jesus's teaching rather than on its content.

6:2b–3 The reaction of the crowd is one of astonishment (they were amazed, ἐξεπλήσσοντο, exeplēssonto; cf. 1:22; 7:37; 10:26; 11:18). In all these occurrences in Mark except 10:26, "astonishment" describes a positive response toward Jesus.[2] In 10:26 it reflects neither a positive nor a negative response toward Jesus but rather a perplexed bewilderment about what he had said. In light of the following statements in 6:2b–3 (cf. also 1:22a and 27), it is best to understand Mark as indicating a positive reaction on the part of the "many" (Grässer 1970: 5–6, 12–14; contra Gundry 1993: 290; Guelich 1989: 308). This receives further support from the fact that the "many" (πολλοί, polloi; 2:2, 15; 3:7–8; 6:31; 11:8) and the "crowd" (2:13; 4:1; 5:21, 24; 6:34, 45; 8:1–2, 6, 34; 9:14–15; 10:1; 11:18, 32; 12:12, 37; 14:2) are almost always portrayed in Mark as being positive toward Jesus. "Many" here refers to "all" (see 1:32–34 and 3:9–10).

---

2. A number of scholars have argued that the astonishment passages in Mark should be interpreted negatively, but this is due to their view that Mark was seeking to combat a θεῖος ἀνήρ (theios anēr) Christology, a view that is now generally discredited.

"Where did this man get all this?" (Πόθεν τούτῳ ταῦτα, *Pothen toutō tauta*) introduces a string of five questions. The first three are positive (Marcus 2000: 377–39; contra Donahue and Harrington 2002: 184) and concern the person and work of Jesus. The first, more general question (lit. "From where [have come] these things to this man?") introduces the second and third questions, which define "these things" (ταῦτα; C. Marshall 1989: 192). It assumes that the wisdom of Jesus's teaching and his power to work miracles "came" to him and raises the question of its source. Unlike the negative conclusion of 3:22 (from Beelzebul, the prince of demons), the assumed conclusion here is "from God." (Cf. the positive nature of the similar questions in 1:27 and 4:41 [contrast 11:28] that occur after similar responses of reverential fear and amazement.)[3] Those who seek to interpret this question as disparaging (Donahue and Harrington 2002: 183) must add something like, "who is no different from what we are." Yet this is not in the text, and the positive nature of the questions in 1:27 and 4:41 inclines the reader to interpret this question positively. The attempt to interpret "this man" (τούτῳ) as derogatory (Gundry 1993: 290; France 2002: 242) stumbles on its positive use in 4:41. The question of Jesus's occupation/education and family arises not at this point but in the next verse. Just as in 6:14, where the "powers" at work in John the Baptist are assumed by Mark to have come from God, so here the same conclusion is expected. Mark expects his readers to answer this question, "From God!" (cf. 11:30). In the second question the passive participle "given" (δοθεῖσα, *dotheisa*) is a divine passive (cf. 4:11), "What is the wisdom that God has given to him?" (V. Taylor 1952: 299; C. Marshall 1989: 192). It is possible that Jesus's possession of wisdom might be an allusion to Isa. 11:2, where the future shoot of David is described in this manner (cf. also Ps. Sol. 17.23). For the reader of Mark, the combination of teaching (wisdom, σοφία, *sophia*) and healing (mighty works, δυνάμεις, *dynameis*) recalls 1:22, 27. This is the only occurrence of "wisdom" in Mark and suggests that this saying probably came to Mark from the tradition. For the combination of wisdom and power in the OT, compare Isa. 10:13; Jer. 10:12; 51:15; Dan. 2:20, 23.

The next response of the people, "What are these mighty works being accomplished through his hands?" can be understood as a question (REB, NJB, NASB, KJV) or as an exclamation (RSV, NAB, NRSV, NIV).[4] The fact that it is preceded by two questions and followed by two questions, however, argues for the former. "Mighty works" picks up the reference to "power" in 5:30 and is referred to again in 6:5 (cf. also 6:14; 9:39), but what "mighty works" does this question refer to? Does it refer to some mighty works Jesus has just performed in the synagogue and that are referred to in 6:5b (Gundry 1993: 293; France 2002: 242)? What may or may not have happened on this occasion is impossible to discover. Although the portrayal of this synagogue

---

3. See Marcus (2000: 378) for a helpful comparison of 6:2 and 1:21–28.

4. The lack of any clear indications that the third response is a question (contrast Πόθεν [*Pothen*], τίς [*tis*], and the particles οὐχ [*ouch*] and οὐκ [*ouk*] that anticipate a positive answer to a question) suggests to some that it is best interpreted as an exclamation.

event is greatly abbreviated by Mark, what Mark is seeking to teach by the account is reasonably clear. He assumes that his readers/hearers would think of what they had been taught about Jesus and especially what they had just heard read to them in 1:1–5:43. This would serve as the framework for their interpreting this verse (cf. Luke 4:23).

Although "Is not this the carpenter, the son of Mary and brother of . . ." and the following question expect positive answers because of the presence of "not" (οὐχ, *ouch*) and "not" (οὐκ, *ouk*), the tone of both questions is negative as revealed by the concluding "And they were taking offense at him" (καὶ ἐσκανδαλίζοντο ἐν αὐτῷ, *kai eskandalizonto en autō*). The voice from heaven (1:11) and even the demons (1:24; 3:11; 5:7) recognize Jesus as the Son of God, but the people of Nazareth recognize him only as the son of Mary and brother of James, Joses, Judas, Simon, and various unnamed sisters. The change in attitude between these two questions and the preceding three (Marcus 2000: 377–79; contra Gundry 1993: 295; Donahue and Harrington 2002: 184) is both sudden and unexpected. Mark does not explain what has happened between 6:2 and 6:3. Yet for a similar sudden switch from a positive to a negative evaluation of Jesus, compare Luke 4:22 and 23–30 (cf. also Acts 14:8–18 and 19–20 for a similar incident in the life of Paul). In Mark there is not a lot of time between the "Hosannas" of Palm Sunday (11:9) and the "Crucify him" of Good Friday (15:13–14).

The use of the article ("the" carpenter, ὁ τέκτων, *ho tektōn*) indicates that Jesus was well known to the townspeople. The term "carpenter" or "wood-worker" can refer to someone who worked with wood (a carpenter) or to someone who worked with stone (a stonemason; cf. 2 Sam. 5:11 LXX; Meier 1991: 280–85). Justin Martyr (*Dial.* 88; contra Origen, *Cels.* 6.36) states that Jesus made "plows and yokes," but it is unclear as to whether he had deduced this from the present text in Mark or possessed additional information. The nearby construction in Sepphoris would have supplied work for a carpenter/stonemason (Batey 1984; 1991: 29–103; cf., however, E. Sanders 1993: 104).

The reference to Jesus as the "son of Mary" is strange.[5] In a Semitic culture, one expects "son of Joseph" (cf. Luke 3:23; 4:22; John 1:45; 6:42). This was true even when the father was dead. The unusual nature of the present expression in Mark is most evident in the Matthean parallel, where it appears as "the carpenter's son" (13:55; cf. also Luke 4:22; John 1:45; 6:42). Numerous suggestions have been made to explain this unusual expression: (1) a veiled reference to the virgin birth (but both Matthew and Luke, who possess virgin birth accounts, refer to Jesus in their parallel accounts as the son of the carpenter [Matt. 13:55] or son of Joseph [Luke 4:23]); (2) an attack on Jesus's legitimacy (Marcus 2000: 375);[6]

---

5. Cf. Hartman 2004, who lists a number of examples in Greek literature where a son is defined by means of a reference to his mother.

6. Such charges can be found in Origen, *Cels.* 1.28–32, 39, 69; cf. *b. Sanh.* 67a; John 8:41 (Wilson 1995: 187–89). Do the changes in Matt. 13:55 and Luke 4:22 suggest that they saw in this expression some sort of a slur? See, however, Ilan (1992) for evidence that "son of [woman's name]" was not a slur or odium.

(3) a preference to mention his mother's higher pedigree (Ilan 1992: 42–45); (4) to distinguish Jesus from his brothers and sisters via an early marriage of Joseph (the Epiphanian view; Bauckham 1994a: 698–700); (5) to indicate that Joseph had died (Gundry 1993: 291; cf. Meier 1991: 226–27); (6) a lack of interest in Joseph by Mark (Crossan 1973b: 102); and so on. None of these explanations is compelling, but the fifth suggestion is the least unlikely. The use of a single article for "the son of Mary and brother of . . ." argues in favor of the Helvidian view that Jesus's brothers and sisters were the natural children of Joseph and Mary.

For a discussion of the brothers and sisters of Jesus, see 3:31–35. The names of the brothers are Hebraic and allude back to the OT patriarchs: Jacob (James) and his sons Joseph (Joses), Judas, and Simon. The biblical nature of all the names suggests that Jesus was raised in a devout, religious home (Meier 1991: 208). Of the four brothers, only two are mentioned elsewhere in the NT.[7]

The concluding editorial comment in 6:3c, "And they were taking offense ['were being scandalized'] at him" reveals that the previous two questions, unlike the first three, are negative in tone. Mark gives no explanation of why they took offense at Jesus, and all suggested explanations (offense at Jesus's humble background [W. Lane 1974: 201; cf. John 1:46; 7:41, 52]; familiarity breeds contempt, etc.) are speculative. In Mark, Jesus's mighty works do not necessarily result in faith. For those lacking understanding (4:10–12, 21–25) the result of Jesus's mighty works is confusion and often hostility (cf. 3:6, 22; 5:17), and the people of Nazareth, as well as his relatives and family, belong to "those outside," who hear but lack ears to understand (4:9, 23; 8:18). This negative response ironically serves for Mark as proof that Jesus is indeed a prophet, as 6:4 demonstrates (Marcus 2000: 379). The present statement anticipates the ultimate rejection of Jesus in 14:43–15:39, as foreshadowed in 3:6, 21–35. The verb might well raise in the minds of Mark's readers thoughts of how Jesus and the gospel were still a "scandal" (cf. 1 Cor. 1:23; 1 Pet. 2:8) in their day.

The proverb "A prophet is not without honor except in his [own] hometown, and among his [own] relatives, and in his [own] family [lit. 'house']" is also found in Luke 4:24; John 4:44; Gos. Thom. 31 ("No prophet . . . is acceptable in his village; no physician works cures . . . on those who know him");[8] P.Oxy. 1.6; and Plutarch, *De exilio* 604D.[9] This indicates that the proverb circulated as an independent saying in the early church.[10] The intimate tie between the saying and the present account is evident by the fact that 6:1–6a **6:4–6a**

---

7. James: Matt. 13:55; Acts 12:17; 15:13; 21:18; 1 Cor. 15:7; Gal. 1:19; 2:9, 12; James 1:1; Jude 1 (cf. also Josephus, *Ant.* 10.9.1 §200); and Jude: Matt. 13:55; Jude 1. Cf., however, Mark 15:40, 47, where some argue that Mary the mother of James the younger and Joses is Mary the mother of Jesus.

8. For the view that the latter part of the saying in Gos. Thom. 31 is secondary, see Grässer 1970: 8; Koch 1975: 148.

9. For additional parallels, see Davies and Allison 1991: 459–60.

10. For the rejection of the prophets, cf. 2 Chron. 24:19; 36:16; Neh. 9:26–30; Jer. 35:15; Ezek. 2:5; Dan. 9:6, 10; Hos. 9:7; Matt. 5:12; 23:29–31, 34–35; Luke 6:23; 11:47–51; 13:33–34; Rom. 11:3; 1 Thess. 2:15; Heb. 11:32–38; Rev. 11:1–10; 16:6; 18:24.

is a pronouncement story and the saying in 6:4 is the pronouncement (Marcus 2000: 376). The threefold description—"hometown" (πατρίδι, *patridi*), "relatives" (συγγενεῦσιν, *syngeneusin*), and "family" (οἰκίᾳ, *oikia*)—is unique to Mark and may reveal his own hand (Marcus 2000: 377). Matthew 13:57 mentions "family" but not "relatives," and Luke 4:24; John 4:44; and Gos. Thom. 31 lack both "relatives" and "family." Up to this point in Mark, Jesus's own family (3:21, 31–35) belong to "those outside," and this may very well reflect the historical situation (cf. John 7:1–5). The present saying assumes that Jesus is indeed a prophet (Mark 6:14–15; 8:28; cf. Matt. 21:11, 46; Luke 7:16; 13:33; 24:19; John 4:19; 6:14; 7:40, 52; 9:17; Acts 3:22–23; 7:37), but in Mark he is, of course, more. The description "prophet" by itself is inadequate (6:15; 8:28) because Jesus is more than a prophet (cf. Matt. 12:6; John 4:12; 8:53). He is the Son of God (see Mark 1:1)!

Because of the tie in Mark between faith and healing (cf. 2:5; 5:34, 36; 9:23–24; 10:52; 11:22–24; also 4:40), the lack of faith in Nazareth prohibits the manifestation of Jesus's mighty works (6:2). Thus "he was not able to do any mighty work there" (οὐκ ἐδύνατο ἐκεῖ ποιῆσαι οὐδεμίαν δύναμιν, *ouk edynato ekei poiēsai oudemian dynamin*). The lack of such miracles, emphasized by the double negative (not, οὐκ; not any, οὐδεμίαν), is not due to Jesus's lack of power. Rather, it was because he was not free to exercise his power in the present situation in Nazareth due to the unbelief of the townspeople (W. Lane 1974: 204). Jesus's miracles were not theatrical performances but demonstrate the coming of the kingdom of God in Jesus's ministry. To enter into the kingdom of God and experience its power, however, one must repent and believe (1:15). Nevertheless, some people were healed in Nazareth, for Jesus "laid his hands upon a few sick people and healed them." For "laid his hands" (ἐπιθεὶς τὰς χεῖρας, *epitheis tas cheiras*; lit. "having laid his hands"), see 5:23. The "except" (εἰ μή, *ei mē*) serves as a qualification for the general nature of the first statement in this verse. This is a common literary construction in Mark (cf. 2:26; 5:37; 6:4; 8:14; 9:9, 29; 10:18; 11:13; 13:32). No explanation is given or implied by Mark as to the relationship between 6:5a and 5b. Some suggestions are these: Jesus did encounter some faith in Nazareth and as a result was able to heal "some" (Guelich 1989: 311–12; Grundmann 1977: 158); Mark seeks to soften the story's treatment of the people of Nazareth; Mark does not want to let it appear that Jesus was incapable of performing miracles in Nazareth; Jesus arbitrarily worked some miracles based on his mercy and not on faith; Jesus did some minor miracles but no mighty works. It may be best, however, to see 6:5b as qualifying 6:5a much like 5:8 explains 5:6–7, that is, Jesus had earlier performed a few healings in Nazareth but in general "he could do no mighty work there." (Cf. also 8:14b, which qualifies 8:14a.)

The account concludes in 6:6a with the brief summary, "And he was marveling at their unbelief" (καὶ ἐθαύμαζεν διὰ τὴν ἀπιστίαν αὐτῶν, *kai ethaumazen dia tēn apistian autōn*). In 5:20; 15:5; and 15:44, "marveling" describes the reaction of others toward Jesus, but here it refers to Jesus's reaction to them.

In all the other passages in Mark that speak of amazement, astonishment, fear, marveling, and so on (see 4:41), it is always used to describe the response of others to Jesus. This is the only place where Jesus is described as amazed. Even though Jesus knew that "a prophet is not without honor . . . ," he was nevertheless amazed at the "unbelief" (ἀπιστίαν, only here and 9:24 in Mark, but cf. 9:19) he encountered. This statement functions less as an indication of Jesus's "humanness" (contra Guelich 1989: 312; Marcus 2000: 377), perhaps in opposition to a θεῖος ἀνήρ (*theios anēr*) theology (Grässer 1970: 22–23), than as a foreshadowing of the dark cloud descending upon the Son of God, which will eventually lead to the cross.

Summary

Mark ends this major section (3:7–6:6, esp. 4:35–5:43) with this concluding account. (Cf. how 1:14–3:6 ends with 3:1–6.) In the present account he resumes the theme of Jesus's rejection. He has been rejected by the Pharisees and Herodians (3:6), his family (3:21 and 31–35), the scribes (3:22), and the gentile city of Gerasa (5:17). Now he is rejected by his townspeople, relatives, and family. The theme of Jesus's rejection by his family is emphasized by Mark (3:31–35), but it was no doubt part of the tradition and historical (cf. John 7:1–5). Mark may emphasize this because of the present situation of his readers. They too may have been experiencing ostracism and rejection (13:12–13; cf. also 1:16–20; 10:28–31).[11] Yet the present account looks not only at the human side of Jesus's rejection but also at the divine. Seen from God's side, all this fits his preordained purpose and will. What this foreshadows is the fulfillment of God's will. There is a divine necessity for Jesus to die in Jerusalem (8:31; 9:31; 10:33–34, 45; 14:23–24). Growing opposition to Jesus in 7:1–13 and 8:11–13 should not take Mark's readers by surprise. The problem of Israel's rejection of the gospel was a problem for the early church (cf. Rom. 9–11). This account is symbolic of Israel's failure to respond to the gospel (Hooker 1991: 152), and Mark wants his readers to know that rejection was part and parcel of Jesus's ministry and the divine plan. Another theme found in the account involves the importance of faith. The positive dimension of faith has been and will continue to be emphasized by Mark (2:5; 4:40; 5:34, 36; 9:23–24; 10:52). The negative side of unbelief found in the present passage (6:6a) serves to emphasize the importance of faith. Those lacking faith will not experience healing and salvation, but those who come to Jesus in faith will find their needs met (2:5; 5:34; 10:52).

11. The view that Mark reveals a hostility to the relatives of Jesus because they represent the Jerusalem mother church that sought to manifest "doctrinal and jurisdictional hegemony" over the Markan community (Crossan 1973b: 112–13) reads too much into Mark 3:21–22, 31–35 and 6:1–6a. Should we read the same tension between Jerusalem and the Johannine community because of John 7:1–5? Much of this seems to be based upon a Hegelian dialectic that revives once again the Tübingen Hypothesis, with its Jewish church/apostles/Jesus's family theological antagonism toward the Christianity of the gentile church/Paul/Mark.

Additional Note

6:3. The reading ὁ τοῦ τέκτονος υἱὸς καὶ τῆς Μαρίας is found in 𝔓⁴⁵ f¹³ it, but ὁ τέκτων, ὁ υἱὸς τῆς Μαρίας is found in all the uncials (Metzger 1994: 75–76) and should be accepted (Meier 1991: 225–26).

IV. Mission and Misunderstanding: Part 3 (6:6b–8:21)

The fourth section of Mark, like 1:1–13; 1:14–3:6; and 3:7–6:6a, begins with a transitional summary statement in 6:6b (cf. 1:1; 1:14–15; 3:7–12). This is then followed, as in sections two and three, by a story concerning the mission of the disciples in 6:7–13 (cf. 1:16–20 [the call of Peter, Andrew, James, and John]; 3:13–19 [the call of the twelve disciples]; cf. also the story of Jesus's forerunner, the "disciple" John the Baptist, in 1:2–8). Like the preceding two sections, it ends negatively with misunderstanding and hardness of heart. In 8:14–21 this involves the disciples, whereas in 3:6 it involves the Pharisees and Herodians conspiring to kill Jesus, and in 6:1–6a the rejection of Jesus by his hometown, relatives, and family.

After the introductory statement (6:6b), Mark recounts the mission of the disciples (6:7–13), whose importance for the later passing down of the gospel traditions after the death and resurrection of Jesus is emphasized in Luke 1:2; Acts 1:21–26; 4:33; 5:32; 10:39–42; and so on; see 6:7. Sandwiched between their going out on a mission and their return (6:30–34) is an account of the death of John the Baptist (6:14–29; F. Maloney 2001). Then Mark tells the story of Jesus's feeding of the five thousand (6:35–44). This is followed by another stormy crossing of the Sea of Galilee (6:45–52) in which the miracle of Jesus's walking on the water is related, and a summary is given of Jesus's healing ministry on the plain of Gennesaret (6:53–56). At this point Mark inserts a lengthy controversy-pronouncement story (7:1–23) involving the issues of clean and unclean that he may have placed here in order to prepare for the following mission of Jesus to the gentiles, that is, the unclean world (7:24ff.). This mission involves the exorcism of an unclean spirit in the city of Tyre (7:24–30). Upon returning from the Decapolis, Jesus heals a deaf man (7:31–37). This is then followed by Jesus feeding the four thousand. (See 7:31 and 8:1, where I will argue that the healing of the deaf man and Jesus's feeding of the four thousand take place not in the Decapolis but in Galilee.) The section then ends negatively, with a pronouncement story involving the Pharisees' demand for a sign (8:11–13) and a story of the disciples' lack of understanding (8:14–21).[1]

Within 6:6b–8:21 a number of common themes appear. One involves food. Throughout this section the subject of food appears time and time again. It

---

1. Although some see this section as ending at 8:26 (Guelich 1989: 316; Hooker 1991: 28), it appears best to end it at 8:21 (Marcus 2000: 381; France 2002: 11–15). This allows the present section to end with a negative account (cf. 3:6; 6:1–6a; 8:14–21) and the next section to begin with a miracle story serving as an introductory summary (cf. 1:14–15; 3:7–12; 6:6b; 8:22–26).

figures predominately in the feeding of the five thousand (6:35–44) and of the four thousand (8:1–10), but it is also present in 6:52, where the disciples' lack of understanding concerning the miracle of Jesus's walking on the water is explained as due to their having forgotten "about the loaves." In 7:1–23, it comes up in the discussion of clean and unclean with respect to eating, and in the exorcism in 7:24–30, the conversation between Jesus and the gentile woman involves the eating of the children's food and its crumbs (7:27–28). After the feeding of the four thousand (8:1–9), Jesus has a lengthy discussion concerning the "leaven" of the Pharisees and Herod, which recalls the feeding of both the five and the four thousand (8:14–21). To the examples listed above can be added the story of John the Baptist's martyrdom, since it involves a banquet (6:14–29). Whether Mark brought these accounts together because of the common theme of food is difficult to say. The presence of this theme, however, is quite obvious.

Another theme found throughout this section involves the misunderstanding of the disciples. Their lack of understanding seems to deepen in this section (cf. 6:35–37, 52; 7:17–18; 8:14–21), even though they play an increasingly important role in Jesus's ministry (6:7–13, 35–44; 8:1–10). The theme of hostility toward Jesus shows up as well. The death of John the Baptist clearly foreshadows the death of Jesus in Mark, for if a prophet like John is without honor and is put to death, how much more will Jesus, who is the greatest of the prophets and the Son of God, face a similar fate! The continued hostility of the Pharisees toward Jesus is described in 7:5–13 and 8:11–13.

Yet this section, like every section in Mark, is not primarily about food, the hostility of Jesus's opponents, or the misunderstanding of the disciples. It is about Jesus, the Son of God (1:1). The question "Who then is this?" (4:41) continues to be answered in this section. Jesus's supernatural power over disease continues to be revealed by his healing of the sick (6:55–56) and the deaf man (7:31–37). His authority over the demons is demonstrated once again by his exorcism of an unclean spirit (7:24–30). His rule over nature is shown by his multiplication of the bread and fish in the feeding of the five thousand and the four thousand (6:34–44; 8:1–10) and by his walking on the sea and stilling the storm (6:45–52). Although Jesus rejects a request to perform a sign (8:11–13), the miracles in this section do function as signs for Mark's readers that he is indeed the Son of God.

A. A Summary of Jesus's Ministry and the Mission of His Disciples (6:6b–13)

The fourth section of Mark begins with a summary statement concerning Jesus teaching in the villages near Nazareth (6:6b; cf. 6:2). It is tied thematically to Jesus's rejection in Nazareth (6:4–6a), his warning the disciples in his missionary charge that they might have a similar experience (6:11a), and the instructions he gives to them (cf. 6:11b with 6:5a). Immediately after the introductory summary, the disciples take center stage. This follows the pattern found in the preceding two sections (1:14–3:6 and 3:7–6:6a), where a summary statement (1:14–15 and 3:7–12) and topographical description (1:14 and 3:7) are followed by an account featuring the disciples. In the second section this involves the call of Peter, Andrew, James, and John (1:16–20), and in the third it involves the choosing of the Twelve (3:13–19). In the present section, it consists of the mission of the Twelve, which entails certain instructions (6:8–11) sandwiched within the narrative of their being sent out (6:7, 12–13).

It is debated whether the present account was constructed by Mark himself out of diverse traditional materials (V. Taylor 1952: 302; Best 1981: 190–92) or whether it existed pretty much in its present form before Mark (Lohmeyer 1957: 113; Pesch 1980a: 326–27). Only an extreme skepticism denies the historicity of such a mission by the Twelve (6:7, 12–13),[1] and it is difficult to imagine that Jesus did not give them instructions for such a mission. Similarly, the instructions found in 6:8–11 imply the existence of a mission such as that described in 6:7, 12–13 (Gundry 1993: 307).

Many have noted the close tie in vocabulary between the present account and the call of the Twelve in 3:13–19. Compare "to send" (ἀποστέλλειν, *apostellein*) in 3:14 and 6:7; "preached" (ἐκήρυξαν, *ekēryxan*) in 3:14 and 6:12; "was giving authority [ἐδίδου ἐξουσίαν, *edidou exousian*] over/to cast out [demons/unclean spirits]" in 3:15 and 6:7 (cf. 6:13); and "calls" (προσκαλεῖται, *proskaleitai*) in 3:13 and 6:7. This strongly suggests the presence of the hand of Mark in both accounts (Reploh 1969: 52–58). This redactional work by the evangelist, however, does not imply that the incident

---

1. Cf. the famous statement by Manson (1937: 73): "The mission of the disciples is one of the best-attested facts in the life of Jesus." Cf. also: "There can be no reasonable doubt that we are dealing with authentic sayings of Jesus. The Mission Charge is better attested than any other part of the gospel record" (Caird 1969: 41). Even if there may be a degree of exaggeration in these statements, the historicity of the disciples' mission during the lifetime of Jesus is well established. The lack of any common mission by the disciples after the resurrection lends support to the historicity of this mission (Gundry 1993: 306–7).

is fictional (Guelich 1989: 320), and the instructions found in 6:8–10 are almost certainly based upon tradition (Best 1981: 190). The places that show the hand of Mark most clearly are 6:6b–7, 10a and the summary in 6:12–13 (Pryke 1978: 14, 142, 159; Gnilka 1978: 236–37). I divide the account into an introduction (6:6b–7), Jesus's instructions to the Twelve (6:8–11) concerning traveling (6:8–9) and staying in homes (6:10–11), and a summary report of the mission of the Twelve (6:12–13).

Exegesis and Exposition

⁶ᵇAnd he was going around the [surrounding] villages teaching. ⁷And he calls the Twelve and began to send them out two by two, and he was giving them authority over the unclean spirits. ⁸And he instructed them that they should take nothing for the journey except only a staff—no bread, no bag, no money in [their] belt[s], ⁹but they were to wear sandals and not to wear two tunics. ¹⁰And he was saying to them, "Wherever you enter into a house, remain there until you leave from there. ¹¹And whatever place does not welcome you and they do not listen to you, ⌜leave there⌝ [and] shake off the dust from under your feet as a witness against them." ¹²And they went out [and] preached that they [people] should repent, and ¹³they were casting out many demons, and were anointing many sick people with oil and healing [them].

6:6b–7   The account begins with a summary: "And he was going around the [surrounding] villages teaching." Although "was going around" (περιῆγεν, periēgen, found only here in Mark) and "among" (κύκλῳ, kyklō; cf. 3:34 and 6:36) are not especially Markan in nature, the summary nature of the statement appears to come from Mark (Best 1981: 190; Gnilka 1978: 236–37; Pryke 1978: 14, 142, 159; contra K. Schmidt 1919: 158–59). It fits well the Markan emphasis of Jesus's teaching found in such Markan seams, summaries, and insertions as 1:21–22, 27; 2:13; 4:1–2; 6:2, 34; 8:31; 9:31; 10:1; 11:17, 18; 12:35, 38; 14:49. Since no geographical designation is specified in 6:6b, Mark no doubt expects his readers to supply after "among the villages" something like "around his hometown of Nazareth." The imperfect "was going around" implies a teaching mission of some duration.

"And he calls the Twelve" (καὶ προσκαλεῖται τοὺς δώδεκα, kai proskaleitai tous dōdeka) recalls 3:14, but whereas in 3:14 Mark narrates Jesus's calling of the Twelve in order that he might "send them out" (ἵνα ἀποστέλλῃ, hina apostellē), now he describes Jesus beginning "to send [them] out" (ἀποστέλλειν, apostellein). The verb "call" is often found introducing a pronouncement of Jesus or a new scene (Guelich 1989: 321). Compare 3:23; 7:14; 8:1, 34; 10:42; 12:43. For "the Twelve," see 3:14–15; for "began" with the infinitive, see 1:45. The importance of this event for the future passing on of the gospel traditions cannot be overestimated. In this mission the disciples, as Jesus's representatives, replicate their teacher's healing/exorcism and teaching/preaching ministry. As a result they would have repeated the teachings they had heard from Jesus's lips and given reports of what they had seen Jesus do. That the mission involved a period of time is indicated by the imperfect tense of the verbs ("were . . .") in 6:13. Repeating Jesus's teachings and deeds over and over as they went from place to place would have indelibly stamped in their minds the traditions they would later "deliver" in the postresurrection situation as eyewitnesses and ministers of the Word (cf. Luke 1:2). Whether Jesus sent the disciples out on missions on several occasions (France 2002: 246) is uncertain. Mark seems to see this charge and sending as part of a single event. Being paired together (two by two, δύο δύο, *dyo dyo*) would have provided the practical benefit of firming up in their own understanding exactly what Jesus said and did, so that they would be reliable eyewitnesses of what they had seen with their own eyes and heard with their own ears (cf. 1 John 1:1–3; Schürmann 1960; Stein 2001: 209–11).

Jesus probably had several reasons for sending out his disciples "two by two." Whether Jesus did so to fulfill the OT requirement for the need of having two witnesses (Hooker 1991: 155; cf. Num. 35:30; Deut. 17:6; 19:15; also Matt. 18:16; John 8:17; 2 Cor. 13:1; 1 Tim. 5:19) cannot be demonstrated, but probably this and other considerations (mutual protection, assistance in preaching, moral support, companionship, etc.) all played a part (cf. Eccles. 4:9–12). The practice of sending out Christian missionaries in pairs is found in Acts 8:14; 9:38; 11:30; 13:1–3; 15:22, 39–40; 1 Cor. 9:6, and in the Gospels in the sending out of the seventy(-two) (Luke 10:1; cf. also Mark 11:1; 14:13; Luke 7:18). It is also implied by the listing of the disciples in pairs in Matt. 10:2–4 and Acts 1:13. A similar Jewish practice is found in Tob. 5:3ff.

To equip them for their mission, Jesus gave the Twelve "authority over the unclean spirits" (ἐξουσίαν τῶν πνευμάτων τῶν ἀκαθάρτων, *exousian tōn pneumatōn tōn akatharton*), so that what was envisioned in 3:15 is now to be fulfilled (cf. T. Levi 18.12). The imperfect "was giving" (ἐδίδου, *edidou*) may refer to the act of giving this authority successively (an iterative imperfect) to each pair (V. Taylor 1952: 303) or to their continually casting out demons during the mission. It may also imply that during their mission the disciples were given an authority that was not present later, as in 9:14–29, when the disciples were not able to cast out a demon. Nothing is mentioned here as to the preaching and healing dimension of this mission. This, however, will be referred to in 6:12–13. The authority of Jesus (1:27; 2:10) is such that he can even pass his own authority on to others. He does not have to pray for God to bestow such authority upon them. He can simply share his own (Lohmeyer 1957: 113–14). Contrast 2 Kings 2:9–10.

The instructions that follow in 6:8–9 are concerned less with what they should **6:8–11** take on their mission journey (a staff, sandals) than what they should not take (bread, bag, money, two tunics). The charge "to take/not take" is proceeded by a "that" (ἵνα, *hina*), which introduces not a purpose or telic clause ("in order to take") but the content of the command (V. Taylor 1952: 304; Guelich 1989: 321). This occurs frequently in Mark (cf. 3:9; 5:18, 43; 7:26, 32, 36; 8:22,

30; 9:9, 12, 18; 10:48; 13:34; 14:35; and later in the present account in 6:12). "For the journey" translates εἰς ὁδόν (*eis hodon*; lit. "in the way"), which is a typical Markan expression (Best 1981: 15–18; Marcus 1992b: 31–45; cf. 8:3, 27; 9:33, 34; 10:17, 32, 52; 11:8). The mission charge here is also found in Matt. 10:9–10 and Luke 9:3. A similar charge appears in Luke 10:4 in the sending out of the seventy(-two). Some interesting differences become apparent when one compares the parallel accounts:[2]

a staff (ῥάβδον, *rhabdon*), for walking and protection, 6:8; *no* staff in Matt. 10:10 and Luke 9:3

no bread (ἄρτον, *arton*), 6:8; Luke 9:3

no bag (πήραν, *pēran*), a kind of knapsack to carry things, 6:8; Matt. 10:10; Luke 9:3; 10:4

no money (χαλκόν, *chalkon*, a copper coin of small value) in their belts, 6:8; Matt. 10:9 (Matt. 10:9 also mentions "no silver" [cf. Luke 9:3] and "no gold")

sandals (σανδάλια, *sandalia*), 6:9 (why Mark places the strong adversative "but" [ἀλλά, *alla*] before "sandals" is unclear); *no* sandals in Matt. 10:10; Luke 10:4

not to put on two tunics[3] (χιτῶνας, *chitōnas*, an undergarment worn under a cloak), 6:9; Matt. 10:10; Luke 9:3

Some suggest that the charge in Mark is worded to correspond to Exod. 12:11, where the people of Israel are commanded to be ready for their exodus with sandals on their feet and staff in hand (W. Lane 1974: 207n31; Marcus 2000: 389). The LXX uses a different word for "staff" (βακτηρίαι, *baktēriai*), however, and if Mark were seeking to have his readers recall Exod. 12:11, one would expect that he would have used that term.

The differences between the various accounts stand out rather clearly. In Mark the disciples are instructed to take a staff and to wear sandals, whereas in Matthew and Luke they are instructed not to take a staff or sandals. Some have suggested that Matt. 10:9–10, "Take no . . . staff" (μὴ κτήσησθε . . . ῥάβδον, *mē ktēsesthe . . . rhabdon*), means "Do not acquire" and assumes that the disciples should not acquire a new staff and sandals but use the staff and sandals they already possess (Carson 1984: 245). It is also suggested that Matthew and Luke may be referring to a different kind of staff, which was heavy and burdensome to carry, whereas Mark refers to a lighter walking stick (Calvin 1980: 1.293).[4] The problem with this explanation is that Matthew and Luke

2. Marcus (2000: 386–87) provides a useful synopsis of these four accounts.

3. It is unclear whether this refers to wearing two tunics under the cloak (for warmth?) or to bringing an extra tunic for a change. Matt. 10:10 and Luke 9:3 understand it as the latter.

4. Does the textual variant "staffs" (ῥάβδους, *rhabdous*) in C W et al. and the Koine text-types of Matt. 10:10 suggest that certain scribes understood that Jesus forbade taking two tunics, two pairs of sandals, and two staffs? This would still not eliminate the problem of the forbidding of

use the same term for "staff" that Mark does. Others suggest that perhaps the command in Matthew and Luke forbids taking an extra staff (Bock 1994: 816). With respect to the differences regarding the sandals, it is possible that Matt. 10:14 and Luke 9:5 assume that shaking off the dust from your "feet" may mean "the dust from the sandals on your feet." If this is so, then the prohibition in Matthew and Luke involves not bringing an extra pair of sandals (France 2002: 249). No fully convincing explanation has yet arisen that explains these differences.[5]

The exclusion of normal traveling needs and supplies (bread, bag, money, extra tunic) indicates that the disciples were to travel light. They were to proceed on their mission unencumbered, depending on the common hospitality practiced in Israel (Koenig 1985: 15–20; idem, *ABD* 3:299–301), which would provide lodging and food and eliminate the need for small change, and on God's providential care (Grundmann 1977: 124). This provides a more convincing rationale for the commands than that Jesus (and Mark) intentionally sought to outdo the strict mission style of wandering Cynic and Stoic preachers (cf. Hengel 1981: 27–33).[6] Nevertheless, it appears that Jesus himself normally took some of these items on his own mission (cf. Mark 8:14; Luke 22:36; John 4:8; 12:6).

Having instructed the Twelve concerning what to bring and what not to bring (Mark 6:8–9), Jesus now gives instructions on how they should act with respect to the hospitality they will encounter on their mission. "Wherever you enter into a house, remain there until you leave from there." At this point the indirect discourse of 6:8–9 turns to direct discourse. Since this change did not trouble Mark, it is unnecessary to assume that this difference is due to the use of different sources. An editor of a source before Mark could also have combined direct and indirect discourse.[7] For "And he was saying to them" (καὶ ἔλεγεν αὐτοῖς, *kai elegen autois*), see 2:27–28. The present instruction, found also in Matt. 10:11; Luke 9:4 (cf. Luke 10:7), is to avoid moving up the social ladder to better and more luxurious housing (and cuisine; Luke 10:7). The ambassadors of Jesus were to live a modest lifestyle off the gospel (Matt. 10:10; an admonition that needs to be repeated throughout the history of the Christian church!). The abuse of such Christian hospitality by early missionaries is witnessed to in Did. 11.4–6. The difference in the teaching found in

---

a staff in Luke 9:3 and sandals in Luke 10:4. The attempt to distinguish the "sandals" in Mark 6:9 from "shoes" in Matt. 10:10 and Luke 10:4 is untenable due to the presence of the participle "wear" (ὑποδεδεμένους, *hypodedemenous*; lit. "wearing"), which comes from the verbal form of the noun ὑποδήματα (*hypodēmata*) used in the parallel in Matthew and Luke.

5. See Gundry (1993: 308–9) for various explanations as to why Jesus gave such instructions to his disciples. See Bock (1994: 815–16) for various attempts to harmonize the differences among the accounts.

6. It is unlikely that these instructions should be interpreted in light of Stoic and Cynic wandering preachers (cf. Marcus 2000: 383–84, 388–89; J. Edwards 2002: 179–80).

7. Cf. BDF §470.2: "It is quite impossible for a NT author to do what is so common in classical Greek (still more so in Latin), namely, to maintain indirect discourse in an extended passage." They give as examples our present text; Luke 5:14; Acts 1:4; 23:22; 25:4ff.

the Didache and here in Mark may be due to the present mission's purpose in establishing new faith communities, whereas in the Didache the situation involves itinerant missionaries overstaying their visits in established churches (Guelich 1989: 322).

Jesus prepares the Twelve in 6:11 for two possible responses they may encounter on their mission. Any place that does not receive them and where the people do not heed their message is to receive the parabolic act of the disciples shaking off the dust of the village from their feet. The switch in verb number from "it" (i.e., the place) not receiving the disciples to "they" (i.e., the people) not hearing them is somewhat confusing, but the meaning is clear. The expression "the dust from under your feet" (τὸν χοῦν τὸν ὑποκάτω τῶν ποδῶν ὑμῶν, *ton choun ton hypokatō tōn podōn hymōn*) may refer to the dust under their feet that has been kicked up in their walking and now lies on their clothes (Gundry 1993: 309–10; cf. Neh. 5:13; Acts 18:6). On the other hand, it seems more likely in light of Matt. 10:14; Luke 9:5; 10:11 (cf. Acts 13:51) that it is "the dust on the bottom of their sandals" that is to be shaken off. (Cf. the common practice of footwashing in the early church to remove the dust that clung to their feet and sandals.) The parabolic act described here has been interpreted variously as treating the place as a gentile area (Grundmann 1977: 169; Gnilka 1978: 240; J. Edwards 2002: 181), a symbolic act terminating contact with the place (Marcus 2000: 384) and thus withholding the blessings of the kingdom of God, washing their hands of any responsibility for the future judgment of the place (Cranfield 1959: 201; cf. Acts 18:6), declaring or pronouncing divine judgment upon the place for their rejection of the good news (Gundry 1993: 310), a warning of future judgment in the final day or in the near future (cf. Caird 1969: 41 and N. Wright 1996: 329–33, who see Jesus as giving an urgent political warning to Jewish cities to change their ways in order to avoid the disaster with Rome looming ahead), and so on. In light of the following statement ("as a witness against them," εἰς μαρτύριον αὐτοῖς, *eis martyrion autois*), it is best to see the parabolic act as a declaration of the judgment awaiting them on the final day (cf. Luke 10:10–12). As Mark 9:37 reveals, the response of the place toward the disciples and their message signifies their response toward Jesus, for they are his disciples/representatives/ambassadors, and to refuse the practice of hospitality to the disciples and to reject ("not hear") their message is to reject Jesus.[8]

The act of shaking off the dust of an unreceptive village serves as a "witness against them." This can also be interpreted in several ways: positively

---

8. Rogers (2004: 169) has argued that "the dust-shaking is best understood as a testimony that their feet were not washed according to the customs of hospitality." This, however, confuses hospitality per se with hospitality not shown because they are disciples of Jesus. Not to welcome or listen (6:11) to the disciples of Jesus means to reject Jesus (8:37; Matt. 10:40; 25:31–45; Luke 10:16; John 13:20). The disciples were not sent out to preach that people should practice hospitality but that they should repent and believe the gospel (Mark 1:15), and that gospel centers on Jesus Christ, the Son of God (1:1). We should not confuse the result of their action (lack of hospitality toward the disciples) with its cause (rejection of Jesus's message and person).

(dative of advantage—"to them"), as a witness to the availability of God's grace; neutrally, as a warning to repentance (cf. W. Lane 1974: 209; Caird 1969: 41—a positive warning, not a threat); or negatively (dative of disadvantage— "against them"), as a witness against them in the day of judgment (Pesch 1980a: 329–30; Gnilka 1978: 240). The addition in the Matthean parallel (10:15; cf. also 11:23–24) clearly sees this as a witness against the "house" in the final judgment when Sodom and Gomorrah will fare better than those who rejected the good news preached by the disciples. The Lukan parallel (10:12), which also has the saying concerning Sodom and Gomorrah, understands these words similarly. As Jesus's disciples, their mission was essentially the extension of Jesus's mission. Thus, to receive them was to receive Jesus and to reject them was to reject Jesus (Mark 9:37; Matt. 10:40; Luke 10:16; cf. Matt. 18:5; 25:31–46; John 13:20).

The concluding summary of the mission of the Twelve picks up 6:7 and completes the sandwich: (A) 6:7; (B) 6:8–11; (A′) 6:12–13. The fulfillment of the disciples' calling to preach in 3:14 is now described along with its verbal content: "And they went out and preached that people should repent [ἐκήρυξαν ἵνα μετανοῶσιν, ekēryxan hina metanoōsin]." Like Jesus, the disciples "went out" (lit. "going out"; 1:38; 6:1) and "preached" (1:14, 38, 39; cf. also 1:4; 5:20) that people should "repent" (1:15; cf. also 1:4). No doubt Mark's readers would fill in the remaining, "The time is fulfilled, and the kingdom of God has come; repent and believe in the gospel," which they knew was the essence of Jesus's message (1:14–15). As in 6:8, the "that" (ἵνα, hina) of 6:12 is best interpreted as introducing the content of their preaching rather than the purpose.

6:12–13

In addition the disciples during their mission "were casting out many demons" (δαιμόνια πολλὰ ἐξέβαλλον, daimonia polla exeballon). This describes the carrying out of the commission of 6:7c and of their calling in 3:15. Like Jesus (1:21–28, 32–34; 3:11–12, 22, 26–27; 5:1–20), they exorcised "many" (cf. 1:34; 5:9ff.) demons and unclean spirits. The use of "unclean spirits" in 6:7c and "demons" in 6:13 indicates that these expressions are synonyms in Mark (cf. 3:22 and 30; 5:2, 8, 13, and 15, 18; also 1:23–24, 26–27 and 5:8 with 1:34). The success of their mission (many, πολλά) stands in contrast to what happened in Nazareth (few, ὀλίγοις, oligois; 6:5) and as a result heightens the unbelief that Jesus encountered in his hometown. The problem in Nazareth therefore lay not with Jesus's authority/power to heal but with the city's unbelief. Along with their ministry of exorcism, the disciples were also "anointing many sick people with oil and healing [them]" (ἤλειφον ἐλαίῳ . . . ἐθεράπευον, ēleiphon elaiō . . . etherapeuon). As in 3:10–11, Mark observes a distinction between healing disease and exorcising demons, so that 6:13a and 13b are not an example of synonymous parallelism. See 1:32–34. The reference to anointing with oil in healing occurs only here in the Gospels (cf., however, James 5:14–15) and argues for Mark's use of tradition. The oil probably functioned less as a healing medicine (a kind of antibiotic) than as a symbol of God's blessing coming upon a person (Gnilka 1978: 240; France

2002: 250–51). Whereas Jesus in 6:5 healed few sick due to the unbelief of Nazareth, here the disciples heal many sick.

Summary

In this account, Mark portrays the twelve disciples as agents of Jesus who extended the ministry of the Son of God. Their calling to be "fishers of men" (1:17) and "apostles" (3:13–14) at this point turned from a future plan and mission to a present reality. What the disciples "began" (6:7a) in this mission would continue after the resurrection. As a result the Markan community's experience of the power and benefits of the kingdom of God through the mission of the Twelve (whether directly or indirectly by their successors) stood in direct continuity with this earlier mission and with the ministry of Jesus who sent them.

The specifics of the mission charge in 6:8–10 experienced various revisions over time (cf. Luke 22:35–36; Rom. 15:24, 28–29; Phil. 4:10–20; 3 John 5–8), but the principles contained in it remained. Those who go out in Jesus's name should do so unencumbered by the goods of this world, that is, bringing only what is necessary and useful for their mission. The accusation of love of money or luxurious living should never find an opportunity of arising with respect to ministers of the gospel. Exactly how this was meant to relate to the Markan community is uncertain. Whether we should apply a mirror reading here and see Mark rebuking the abuse of Christian hospitality (cf. Did. 11.4–6) and of these principles is uncertain. Mark may have included this traditional material for a prophylactic purpose to prevent future abuse. Regardless, Christians who proclaim the gospel message in Jesus's name need to be continually reminded of this mission charge. The description of the disciples in the present account indicates that forthcoming passages that speak of their lack of understanding (6:52; 7:18; 8:14–21) and even of their hardened heart (6:52; 8:17–18) should not be interpreted as indicating that Mark is on a vendetta to sully and destroy their reputation. Mark 14:28 and 16:7 prove this. Nevertheless, the passages that speak of the disciples' lack of understanding and hardness of heart indicate that the present passage should not be so romanticized that we lose sight of the fact that the twelve disciples were sinners saved by grace. Yet despite their flaws and sins, Mark describes them as followers of Jesus Christ. This offers hope today to others who seek to follow Jesus Christ that we too, despite our flaws and sins, can be of service to him.

Also present in our passage is a christological dimension that should be noted. Jesus is portrayed by Mark as one who possesses sufficient authority that he can bestow this authority upon his disciples (6:7b). He does not pray to God that authority to heal, exorcise, and proclaim the gospel may come upon those he has chosen. He directly bestows his authority, which is considerable (1:27; 2:10), upon them. Furthermore, the eternal fate of those who hear his disciples will depend on their response to them. The reason for this is not immediately clear, but from 9:37 onward it is evident that this is due to the fact that they represent Jesus, and to reject Jesus will result in judgment worse than that which befell Sodom and Gomorrah. To be sure, the reference to Sodom and Gomorrah does not appear in our account (cf., however, Matt. 10:15; 11:23–24; Luke 10:12; 17:29), but Mark's readers were well aware that rejecting the warning to repent had dire consequences.

Additional Note

6:11. ἐκπορευόμενοι ἐκεῖθεν is lit. "proceeding out from there."

B. The Death of John the Baptist (6:14–29)

The account of John the Baptist's death is intimately tied to the mission of the disciples (6:7b–13) in at least two ways. First, the present flashback to his arrest and death (cf. 1:14a) forms the middle part of a Markan sandwich (6:14–29) and provides a literary time period for carrying out of the disciples' mission (6:7b–13 and 30ff.). Second, it picks up the theme of Jesus's power and authority (6:14) as a result of the disciples' successful mission in 6:7b–13 (cf. also 5:30; 6:2, 5). The successful mission and exercise of this power and authority by the disciples (6:12–13, 30) is seen as evidence of Jesus's authority and power (W. Lane 1974: 211; Reploh 1969: 55–56; contra Hooker 1991: 159) because the disciples' mission is essentially the continuation and extension of the work and words of Jesus. The fate of John the Baptist is also used by Mark to foreshadow the fate of Jesus, who soon would also be handed over (cf. 1:14a with 9:31; 10:33; 14:21, 41) and put to death (cf. Schenk 1983: 470). The experience of Jesus in Nazareth (6:4–5), the warning given to the disciples in their missionary charge (6:11), and now the fate of John the Baptist all point ominously to the fate of Jesus. Since Mark's readers are already aware of that fate, these accounts are clear forebodings of Jesus's death.

Although the literary ties between the present account and what has preceded are clear, the question of the pre-Markan form of this tradition is far from certain. In the present account it consists of two parts: a report of Jesus's fame coming to Herod Antipas (6:14–16) and the death of John the Baptist (6:17–29). In isolation from the Markan context, the story of the death of John the Baptist "is a legend exhibiting no Christian characteristics" (Bultmann 1968: 301). How would such a tradition have originated and circulated?[1] Was it passed down by followers of John the Baptist (Bultmann 1968: 301; W. Lane 1974: 215; Pesch 1980a: 343)? This seems unlikely (Schenk 1983: 470; Guelich 1989: 326–27). Did it circulate as an example of "Jewish martyrdom accounts" (Gnilka 1973: 85–87; Dormeyer 1974: 43–47; contra Gundry 1993: 314)? Even if it circulated within the Christian community, it was certainly not passed on with the zeal and frequency of the stories about Jesus. This and 1:4–8 are the only stories in Mark without a direct reference to Jesus. Its value in Mark is primarily due to its placement here by the evangelist (note the sandwich) and its foreshadowing of Jesus's death. Outside its Markan context, the account of John's death does not serve nearly as well to foreshadow the death of Jesus.

1. Cf. Hoehner (1972: 120): "It is extremely difficult to know exactly from where this story is derived."

Attempts to reconstruct the stages of development that led to its present form in Mark are highly speculative (Guelich 1989: 326–28). Mark appears to have recorded the tradition substantially unchanged from the form in which he had received it (Marcus 2000: 397–98; contra Pryke 1978: 14–15, 142, 159, who sees 6:14–16, 17a, 18, 20a–c, 21, 22, and 29 as redactional). His own editorial work appears to have involved the placement of the tradition within a Markan sandwich, the wording of the introductory seam (esp. the "for" [γάρ, *gar*] clause in v. 14b), the γάρ clauses in 6:17 and 18, the wording of the suggestions as to who Jesus is in 6:14b–15 (cf. 8:28 and Matt. 16:14), and the term "Baptizer" in 6:14, 24 (cf. 1:4). The various theories concerning the development of the tradition before Mark are quite hypothetical. As to 6:14–16, it is unlikely that it circulated in its present form as an isolated unit (Gnilka 1978: 245; Guelich 1989: 327) or that it had been added to 6:17–29 before Mark wrote his Gospel. It is uncertain whether it was attached to some other tradition and placed here by Mark, whether Mark composed 6:14–16 from various pieces of information known to him (Marcus 2000: 398; Donahue and Harrington 2002: 200–201), or whether these verses were part of a pre-Markan tradition. As to the origin of 6:17–29, it is possible that it came to the early church and thus to Mark (cf. Acts 12:12) through the reports of Joanna (Luke 8:3) or Manaen (Acts 13:1). The account will be divided into the following sections: the introductory transition (6:14–16), the arrest and imprisonment of John the Baptist (6:17–20), Herod's birthday party (6:21–26), and the death and burial of John the Baptist (6:27–29).

Exegesis and Exposition

[14]And King Herod heard [about it], for his [Jesus's] name had become well known, and ⌜they were saying⌝, "John the Baptizer has been raised from the dead, and because of this these powers are working in him." [15]And others were saying, "He is Elijah," and others were saying, "[He is] a prophet like one of the prophets [of old]." [16]But Herod, upon hearing [this], was saying, "John, whom I beheaded, this one has been raised [from the dead]."

[17]For Herod himself had sent out [and] seized John and bound him in prison on account of Herodias, the wife of his brother Philip, because he had married her. [18]For John was saying to Herod, "It is not lawful for you to have the wife of your brother." [19]And Herodias was holding a grudge against him [John] and wanted to kill him, but she was not able to. [20]For Herod feared John, knowing that he [was] a righteous and holy man, and he was protecting him, and hearing him ⌜he was greatly perplexed,⌝ and he was hearing him gladly.

[21]And an opportune day having arrived when Herod gave a banquet on his birthday for his noblemen, military officers, and the leading men of Galilee, [22]and when ⌜his⌝ daughter Herodias entered and danced, she pleased Herod and his guests. The king said to the girl, "Ask me whatever you wish, and I will give it to you." [23]And he swore a strong oath to her, "Whatever you ask me I will give you, up to half of my kingdom."

²⁴And ⌜she went out⌝ [and] said to her mother, "What should I ask for?" And she said, "The head of John the Baptizer." ²⁵And immediately having entered with haste to the king, she asked [him], saying, "I wish that you give me at once the head of John the Baptist on a platter." ²⁶And although the king became very distressed, he did not want to refuse her on account of his oaths and his guests.

²⁷And immediately the king sent for an executioner [and] commanded [him] to bring his head. And he went and beheaded him [John] in prison, ²⁸and brought his head on a platter and gave it to the girl, and the girl gave it to her mother. ²⁹And when his [John's] disciples heard [about it], they came and took his body, and placed it in a tomb.

6:14–16 The present story begins abruptly with "And King Herod heard [about it], for his name had become well known" (Καὶ ἤκουσεν ὁ βασιλεὺς Ἡρῴδης, φανερὸν γὰρ ἐγένετο τὸ ὄνομα αὐτοῦ, *Kai ēkousen ho basileus Hērōdēs phaneron gar egeneto to onoma autou*). This Herod was Herod Antipas, born in 20 BC to Herod the Great and Malthace, a Samaritan. Upon his father's death in 4 BC, he became tetrarch (a ruler of a fourth part of his father's kingdom) of Galilee and Perea (the territory east of the Jordan River and the Dead Sea between Pella and Machaerus). He never received the title "king" from Rome and indeed was removed as tetrarch in AD 39, when he went to Rome seeking the title. There is no clear evidence that Mark is using this title ironically (contra Marcus 2000: 398–99). The present designation probably represents a popular designation rather than an official one, and it is unlikely to be due to a comparison with King Ahasuerus in the story of Esther (Aus 1988: 41–66). Compare Matt. 14:1, where Herod is correctly referred to as a "tetrarch" (cf. also Luke 9:7), and Matt. 14:9, where he is referred to as a "king." Herod is mentioned in passing in Mark 8:15, and his followers are mentioned in 3:6 and 12:13. He also appears at the trial of Jesus in Luke 23:6–16 (cf. Acts 4:27–28). Some suggest that in the pre-Markan form of the tradition, Herod heard about Jesus's ministry directly. In the context of Mark's Gospel, however, what Herod heard is 6:12–13, that is, the successful mission of Jesus's disciples.[2] This mission spread abroad Jesus's name (or "fame"). The successful nature of six different missions within Galilee and Perea by six teams of Jesus's disciples would have made Jesus's name well known to the ruler and people of these regions. This contrasts with what Jesus encountered in Nazareth and proves the point of 6:4.

In response to Jesus's great fame, people ("they"—an impersonal plural; see 1:21–22) were saying, "John the Baptizer [βαπτίζων, *baptizōn*] has been raised from the dead [ἐγήγερται ἐκ νεκρῶν, *egēgertai ek nekrōn*]." The

---

2. It is debated whether what Herod heard should be understood as the mission of the disciples (6:12–13) or the opinions expressed in 6:14–15. Marcus (2000: 392) argues that historically Herod probably learned directly about Jesus from reports about his ministry, not indirectly through reports of what his disciples were doing. He admits, however, that in the present context of Mark, "heard" refers to the preceding mission of the disciples in 6:12–13.

similarities between Jesus and John the Baptist might lead to such an association because both were about the same age; both were popular itinerant preachers not associated with any established religious group; both preached an eschatological message of repentance and the arrival of the kingdom of God; both were extremely popular; and, according to the following statement, both worked "powers." The difficulty that is raised by this statement is how Jesus could be confused with John the Baptist since they were contemporaries (cf. Matt. 11:2–6/Luke 7:18–23, who both record this same identification of Jesus with John). It is difficult to assume that the ruler of Galilee and Perea would not have known this. What is envisioned is probably either (1) that just as Elijah's spirit (רוּחַ, *rûaḥ*) came to rest upon Elisha (2 Kings 2:1–15), so the spirit of John the Baptist had come to rest upon Jesus (France 2002: 253); or (2) that Herod was simply saying in exasperation, "This is John the Baptist all over again" (Hooker 1991: 159). Compare Mark 8:28, where Jesus is again considered to be John the Baptist.

For the reference to "the powers" (αἱ δυνάμεις, *hai dynameis*) at work in Jesus, compare 5:30; 6:2, 5; also 6:12–13, 30; 9:39. It is unclear whether this report assumes that John the Baptist also worked such miracles even though none are recorded in the Gospels (suggested by Luke 1:17, but contrast John 10:41; Gnilka 1978: 247; Pesch 1980a: 334), or whether it assumes that because of his resurrection, John the Baptist would have possessed such powers (Lohmeyer 1957: 116; Grundmann 1977: 171; Marcus 2000: 393). The difficulty of Herod believing that Jesus was actually John the Baptist raised from the dead (see above) favors the former view. As in 3:22, Jesus's miracles are acknowledged by his opponents. A second explanation (6:15) is that Jesus was the prophet Elijah, and a third that he was "a prophet, like one of the prophets" ("of old" is implied; contra N. Turner 1965: 66). The first suggestion recalls the prophecies in Mal. 3:1 and 4:5–6 concerning the return of Elijah in the last days. Since Elijah was expected to return in the last days, and since Jesus was considered a prophet (Mark 6:4; Luke 7:16; Matt. 21:46) and preached that the kingdom of God had arrived, his being considered Elijah was quite natural. Reports of Jesus's raising the dead (Mark 5:21–43) would have recalled Elijah's raising the dead (1 Kings 17:17–24). For Elijah in Mark, see 8:28; 9:4–5, 11–13; 15:35–36. The final suggestion is that a different OT prophet had been raised from the dead (cf. Matt. 16:14; also Deut. 18:15, 18; Acts 7:37). Since it was generally considered that the period of the prophets had ceased (1 Macc. 4:46; 9:27; 14:41; 2 Bar. 85.1–3; *t. Soṭah* 13.3; Josephus, *Ag. Ap.* 1.8 §41; Sommer 1996), the excitement created by the appearance of a prophet would have been great. While flattering in one sense in that these views attribute to Jesus a high status, they are inadequate, for he is more than a prophet—he is the Son of God (Mark 1:1). Here no suggestion is raised that Jesus might be the Messiah/Christ. The lack of this possibility reveals the apolitical nature of Jesus's ministry and suggests that up to this point Jesus had not revealed even to his disciples that he was the Christ (8:27–30). The similarity between the views represented here and 8:28 raises the issue of whether these two passages are possible pre-Markan variants of the same tradition (Pesch 1980a: 332), whether Mark has repeated a single tradition in both places (Schweizer 1970: 132; Gnilka 1978: 244–45; Schenk 1983: 471), or whether similar opinions of Jesus arose in different circumstances based in part on similar messianic expectations.

Herod's explanation in 6:16 is the same as one of the suggestions in 6:14—"John, whom I beheaded, this one has been raised" (Ὃν ἐγὼ ἀπεκεφάλισα Ἰωάννην, οὗτος ἠγέρθη, *Hon egō apekephalisa Iōannēn, houtos ēgerthē*). This tie between Jesus and John the Baptist makes the fate of John all the more foreboding and serves as a portent of what ultimately awaits Jesus. The verse prepares for John the Baptist's death and the circumstances leading up to it in 6:17–29. Since a ruler is responsible for the orders he gives (6:27), Herod's statement acknowledges that he is responsible for the death of John the Baptist. There is no reason to assume that the emphatic "I" (ἐγώ) should be understood as boastful (contra Marcus 2000: 393). The passive "has been raised" serves as a divine passive, meaning "God has raised John" (cf. 6:14; Acts 2:23–24; 3:15).

6:17–20 With a typical "for" (γάρ, *gar*) clause, Mark now begins to explain why Herod beheaded John, and provides more information concerning 1:14a: "For Herod himself had sent out and seized John and bound him in prison." "Seized" (ἐκράτησεν, *ekratēsen*) and "bound" (ἔδησεν, *edēsen*) are common terms used to describe the arrest of John the Baptist, but their appearance in the story of Jesus's arrest (δέω, *deō*; 15:1; κρατέω, *krateō*; 14:1, 44, 46, 49) would cause Mark's readers to see Jesus's fate as following the pattern of what happened to John. Herod's "sending out" (ἀποστείλας, *aposteilas*) to seize John stands in sharp contrast to Jesus's sending out the disciples to preach, exorcise, and heal (6:7b, 12–13). Herod having "bound [John] in prison" can be understood as Herod having seized John, brought him to prison, and then bound him, or that he seized and bound John and put him in prison.

Mark here seeks to focus the blame for John's death on Herodias, the wife of Herod's brother Philip. The account of John the Baptist's death in Josephus (*Ant.* 18.5.2 §§116–19) conflicts with the account in Mark in several places. Josephus attributes John's death to Herod's fear that John's great popularity might start a revolution. Yet the differences between the moral-religious reasons recorded in Mark and the political ones found in Josephus may involve two different ways of viewing the same event.[3] It has also been suggested that Herod's reason for arresting John was fear of his popularity and a possible revolt by his followers (as Josephus states), but that after being arrested, and only after that arrest, John told Herod that it was wrong for him to marry his

---

3. Note how Jesus's guilt before the Sanhedrin is based on religious grounds in 14:63–64, whereas the charges brought against him before Pontius Pilate are political (15:2; cf. Luke 23:2–3). Likewise the accusations against Paul change from religious ones (Acts 21:28; 22:21–24; 23:29) to political ones when he is brought before political leaders (24:5), and the religious charge becomes a kind of postscript in 24:6a (Hoehner 1972: 136–46).

brother's wife (as in Mark 6:17–18). This, however, requires that we see Mark as having "advanced [in time] what John said directly to Herod after imprisonment" (Gundry 1993: 319), and this plays havoc with the reading of the text. Mark says John was arrested because (γάρ) he rebuked Herod for marrying his brother's wife (6:18). Some scholars believe that the differences between these two accounts are too great to be reconciled (Marcus 2000: 399–400), but it would be quite natural for Josephus to concentrate on the political grounds for John's death and for Mark to focus on the moral and religious ones. It is doubtful that the story of John's death, involving Herodias, her mother, and Herod is a fiction created de novo. On the other hand, information about the circumstances of his death could have come to the early church through the presence of Joanna (Luke 8:3) and Manaen (Acts 13:1) in Herod's court.

Mark refers to Herodias as the wife of Herod Antipas's brother Philip. Josephus, however, states that Herodias was married to another Herod, the half-brother of Herod Antipas, who was the son of Herod the Great and Mariamne II. Josephus also refers to another half-brother, Philip the Tetrarch, who was the son of Herod the Great and Cleopatra of Jerusalem. This Philip married Salome, the daughter of Herodias (*Ant.* 18.5.4 §136). Tracing the descendants of Herod the Great is no easy task, for he had ten wives (two possessing the same name: Mariamne I and Mariamne II) and numerous sons (many possessing the name "Herod"), and various incestuous marriage relationships existed between the descendants of Herod the Great. With the messed-up family relationships resulting from this, Herodias's daughter was in effect Herod Antipas's "niece (on her father's side), his grandniece (on her mother's side), and his step-daughter" (Marcus 2000: 395). This creates a great deal of confusion, and some scholars claim that this led to an error on Mark's part. The same confusion, however, could have also led Josephus to err. The suggestion that the Herod who married Herodias was actually Herod "Philip" and that Mark refers to this "Philip," not Philip the Tetrarch (Luke 3:1), as the former husband of Herodias (Hoehner 1972: 132–36; H. W. Hoehner, *DJG* 323–24)[4] is attractive but unproven.

The statement "because he had married her" (ὅτι αὐτὴν ἐγάμησεν, *hoti autēn egamēsen*) in 6:17c (reiterated in 6:18) explains why Herod placed John the Baptist in prison. What John earlier had said to the people about the illegality of Herod's marriage to Herodias (cf. Luke 3:19) is now directed to Herod himself in 6:18, "It is not lawful for *you* to have the wife of *your* brother" (οὐκ ἔξεστίν <u>σοι</u> ἔχειν τὴν γυναῖκα τοῦ ἀδελφοῦ <u>σου</u>, *ouk exestin <u>soi</u> echein tēn gynaika tou adelphou <u>sou</u>* [my emphasis]). Mark explains John's imprisonment with another "for" (γάρ) clause. Except in the case of a levirate marriage (raising up children for a childless wife of a deceased brother, Deut.

---

4. W. Lane (1974: 216) states that "nearly every son of Herod the Great bore the name 'Herod' as a family designation" (e.g., Herod Archelaus, Herod Philip, Herod Antipas, and the grandson Herod Agrippa). He suggests that Josephus simply forgot to provide the second name, Philip, for the Herod who was the husband of Herodias.

25:5–10), marrying a brother's wife was forbidden by the law (Lev. 18:16; 20:21; cf. also *b. Yebam.* 55a). Compare CD 5.8–11, which forbids a man marrying his niece. In order to marry Herodias, Herod Antipas sent home his first wife, the daughter of Aretas IV, king of Nabatea. Aretas IV was offended by this, went to war with Herod, and defeated him. According to Josephus (*Ant.* 18.5.2 §§116, 119), the people saw this defeat as God's judgment upon Herod for having put John the Baptist to death.

In Matthew, the desire to kill John the Baptist is attributed to Herod (Matt. 14:3–5). The abbreviated nature of the Matthean account may have caused him to simplify the details of how this murderous couple put John the Baptist to death; Mark, devoting more space to the account, concentrates the responsibility on the murderous "Jezebel" (cf. 1 Kings 19:1–3): "And Herodias was holding a grudge against him and wanted [ἤθελεν, *ēthelen*—a tendential imperfect indicating a continual desire that had been frustrated up to this point] to kill him, but [lit. 'and'] she was not able to" (6:19). In so doing, Mark draws a close parallel between Jesus and John the Baptist. Both are put to death by a reluctant political leader who knows that they are innocent (cf. 6:20 and 15:6–10, 14a) but against his better judgment succumbs to the wishes of his opponents (6:25–28 and 15:14b–15). In both instances Herod Antipas and Pontius Pilate bear witness to the righteous character of their victims. Mark describes Herod as "fearing [ἐφοβεῖτο, *ephobeito*] John," knowing that he was "a righteous and holy man" (ἄνδρα δίκαιον καὶ ἅγιον, *andra dikaion kai hagion*; cf. Josephus, *Ant.* 18.5.2 §§117–18), and "protecting him" (6:20). This description of Herod Antipas is not meant to excuse his horrible act of putting a man to death whom he knew was an innocent ("righteous") servant of God ("holy man"; cf. 11:32; also Acts 3:14). The turmoil in Herod's mind makes his action all the more damnable. This verse serves to show Mark's readers that the death of John the Baptist, and later the death of Jesus (cf. 15:9–15), was not due to any crime that they had done. On the contrary, they proclaimed God's truth, and evil men loved the favor and acclaim of this world over that of God (6:26; 15:14–15). The question of why Jesus, the Son of God, was crucified is in part answered by this pericope. This is often the fate of God's servants. John the Baptist's death proves this. Of course, for Mark Jesus's death has far greater meaning still, but this awaits further disclosure (cf. 10:45; 14:24).

In contrast to Herodias, Herod is described in 6:20 as fearing John, knowing that he was a righteous man, protecting him, hearing John gladly (note the imperfect ἤκουεν, *ēkouen*), and being greatly perplexed. If the reading "was much perplexed" is correct (see additional note on 6:20), it implies that Herod reacted to John in a typically Markan fashion: he was perplexed, amazed, astonished, astounded, and so on (cf. 15:5 and see 4:41). This, however, does not necessarily imply a positive response (cf. 5:15). According to 6:20, Herod opposed John the Baptist due to 6:18 (cf. Matt. 14:5), but he was nervous about what to do with him, that is, "he was much perplexed." If we choose the reading πολλὰ ἐποίει (*polla epoiei*, "was doing many things"—perhaps a translation Semitism for "[he was hearing him] often"; see BDF §414.5), Herod is portrayed as hearing John often and protecting him from Herodias until she tricked him into doing what he did not want to do (Marcus 2000: 394). The latter interpretation would support the Herod Antipas/Pontius Pilate parallels in their actions to protect/free John the Baptist and Jesus. The use of πολλά as an adverb ("much") or as an accusative ("many things") are both Markan (see 1:45; contra Metzger 1994: 76–77), so that it functions well with either reading. The last comment in this verse ("was hearing him gladly") and 6:26 favor the reading "was doing" found in the Majority text. It is impossible to be dogmatic concerning either reading. The more difficult reading, πολλὰ ἠπόρει (*polla ēporei*, was greatly perplexed), however, is the more likely reading (see the additional note on 6:20). For the expression "he was hearing him gladly," compare 12:37.

Verses 21–22 are a single sentence containing three genitives absolute: "an op- **6:21–26** portune day having arrived" (γενομένης ἡμέρας εὐκαίρου, *genomenēs hēmeras eukairou*; "for Herodias" [6:19] being understood); and "Herodias's daughter having entered" (εἰσελθούσης τῆς θυγατρὸς αὐτοῦ Ἡρῳδιάδος, *eiselthousēs tēs thygatros autou Hērōdiados*); and "having danced . . ." (ὀρχησαμένης, *orchēsamenēs*). For "and an opportune day having arrived," compare 14:11. The audience includes "noblemen" (μεγιστᾶσιν, *megistasin*), who made up the inner circle of Herod's government; "military officers" (χιλιάρχοις, *chiliarchois*; lit. "tribunes"); and "leading men [πρώτοις, *prōtois*] of Galilee" or the local aristocracy. Their presence caused Herod to act contrary to his better judgment (6:26). Such a gathering seems more likely in Tiberias than at the fortress of Machaerus, on the eastern side of the Dead Sea, where Josephus places the incident, although the latter is not impossible (Cranfield 1959: 208).[5] A number of questions arise with respect to 6:21–22. For one, it is unclear whether the daughter is described by Mark as "his" (αὐτοῦ, *autou*) or "her" (αὐτῆς, *autēs*) daughter. The textual evidence (‭א‬ B D L Δ) favors "his," but the parallel in Matt. 14:6 refers to the "daughter of Herodias," and this suggests that the copy of Mark possessed by Matthew may have read "her daughter." Compare also the latter references in Mark 6:24, 28 to "her mother." She was the daughter of Herodias and the stepdaughter of Herod Antipas. The name "Herodias" also causes problems, for the text can be interpreted "her [or his] daughter [who was named] Herodias, came in." Thus both the mother and the daughter would possess the same name (cf. Origen, *Commentary on Matthew* 10.22). Perhaps the "least unsatisfactory" interpretation is "his daughter, Herodias" (Metzger 1994: 77). Those who choose "her" do so primarily on historical grounds (Cranfield 1959: 211–12). The name "Salome" for the daughter of Herodias is not found in the Gospel accounts, but comes from Josephus (*Ant.* 18.5.4 §136). Another question involves the historical

---

5. Gundry (1993: 313–14) points out that archaeological investigation of Machaerus has discovered a prison and two dining rooms, a large one for Herod and his friends and a smaller one for Herodias and the women.

probability of a "king's" daughter dancing a seductive dance in such a setting (V. Taylor 1952: 315; Guelich 1989: 332). The nature of such birthday parties was deprecated by Jews (*m. 'Abod. Zar.* 1.3), but Herod Antipas was far from being a noble example of moral virtue (Josephus, *Ant.* 18.2.3 §§36–38), so that the description of his daughter's dancing is not at all impossible. Yet the use of the term "girl" (κορασίῳ, *korasiō*) to describe the daughter implies that she is fairly young, perhaps about twelve years old (cf. 5:41–42). It may be best, therefore, to think of this not as a sensuous dance but as a "child's performance" (Donahue and Harrington 2002: 198–99).

The dance of the daughter Herodias so pleased Herod (and his guests; lit. "those dining with him") that he offered to give her whatever she wished (6:22c–d), even to half of his kingdom (6:23). The latter recalls the words of King Ahasuerus to Esther in Esth. 5:3, 6; 7:2 (cf. also 1 Kings 13:8; Luke 19:8). The language is surely hyperbolic, but it does imply that Herod would grant just about anything that the girl asked. The character of Herodias's "daughter" is remarkably different from the other "daughters" we read about in stories surrounding this account (cf. 5:24–34 [esp. 34] and 7:24–30 [esp. 25–26, 29]). The grisly request of Herodias, upon the advice of her mother (6:24), is "I wish that you give me at once the head of John the Baptist on a platter." Her taking counsel with her mother indicates that the dance was not planned in order to bring about the death of John the Baptist, but that it provided an unexpected opportunity for this. The description of her entrance (immediately with haste, εὐθὺς μετὰ σπουδῆς, *euthys meta spoudēs*) and her request that this be done "at once" (ἐξαυτῆς, *exautēs*) reveal the eagerness with which the mother Herodias and her daughter want to have John the Baptist killed, and the request for the head of John the Baptist would serve as proof of his death.

The description of the king's sadness ("And although the king became [γενόμενος, *genomenos*; a concessive participle] very distressed [περίλυπος, *perilypos*]"; cf. 14:34; also 10:22) is a result of his knowing that John was a righteous and holy man (6:20). Like Pontius Pilate, Herod Antipas is trapped between what is right (releasing John) and what is expedient for his personal reputation. As a result of his "oaths" (ὅρκους, *horkous*) and the presence of his guests who had heard his oaths, Herod is in a terrible bind, for he does not want to break his word. Although the two expressions can be interpreted as an example of hendiadys, "because of the oath that he had sworn in the presence of his table guests" (Gundry 1993: 321), it is probably best to interpret them as two separate reasons for Herod's subsequent action: (1) his oaths (6:22–23, 26) and (2) the presence of his guests (6:21, 26). The keeping of an oath was vested with far more importance in biblical times than today. An oath or vow was generally deemed irrevocable (Num. 30:2; Judg. 11:29–40). Even horrible oaths were seen as binding (cf. Judg. 11:34–40). The second reason for Herod's subsequent fulfillment of the daughter's request is the presence of his guests, before whom he did not want to lose face (cf. Josephus, *Ant.* 18.5.11–18.7.2

§§239–56).[6] Tragically, the nature of his guests was such that he would lose face by not killing John the Baptist as the girl requested (cf. 1 Cor. 15:33).

In response to Herodias's request, Herod "immediately" (cf. 6:25) sends a **6:27–29** σπεκουλάτορα (*spekoulatora*), a Latin loanword found only here in the NT. Some translate it according to his position ("one of his staff"; "a soldier of the guard"), others by his function ("executioner"). In the present context, the latter rendering is probably better, for he is sent to behead John. The executioner carries out Herod's order, and John the Baptist is beheaded. Then his head is brought on a platter and given to the girl. The impression is that all this takes place within a matter of minutes. If the banquet took place in the fortress of Machaerus (W. Lane 1974: 217; Hoehner 1972: 146–48) and John was imprisoned there as Josephus (*Ant.* 18.5.2 §119) states, there is no problem. However, if the banquet was in Tiberias (see 6:21–26), located on the western side of the Sea of Galilee, and John was martyred in Machaerus, located on the eastern side of the Dead Sea, the sending of an executioner from Tiberias to Machaerus and his subsequent return would have taken days. Yet there is no necessity from the text itself to see the beheading as occurring at the time of the banquet. No mention is made of the guests or the banquet in 6:28. The collapsing of the time between the command (6:27a) and the carrying-out of the command (6:27b–28) may be a literary device used to heighten the telling of a story. There would be no reason why Mark, if there were a time gap between the command and its fulfillment, would have written, "And after *x* days, the executioner arrived at Machaerus and beheaded John. Then *y* days later, having arrived back at Tiberias, he showed the head to Herod, placed it on a platter, and gave it to the girl."

The story ends with John's disciples coming to Herod (this is assumed), receiving his body, and taking it and laying it in a tomb. The similarity between this and Jesus's death and burial (15:43–46) is obvious. As a result, once again the fate of John the Baptist serves to foreshadow the forthcoming death of Jesus. The disciples of John continued to exist after their teacher's death until at least the third century (Scobie 1964: 187–202; Ernst 1989: 359–84; see 2:18), and we read of them in Acts 18:24–19:7.

Summary

For Mark, the story of John the Baptist's death provides a temporal interlude (6:14–29) for the mission of the disciples (6:6b–13 and 30ff.). Yet it serves a christological function as well, for it emphasizes the success of the disciples' mission (6:14). Consequently, it emphasizes the greatness of Jesus, for their mission was an extension of his preaching and healing ministry. Thus the greater their success, the greater must be the one who sent them. (In a similar way the greater the strength of the demon[s] possessing the man in 5:3–5, the greater must be their conqueror, Jesus.)

6. See Marcus (2000: 402) for numerous extrabiblical examples.

Throughout the account the role of John the Baptist as Jesus's forerunner is continually emphasized. Not only does John precede Jesus in the proclamation of the kingdom of God and the need to repent (cf. 1:2–9 and 14–15), but his death also foreshadows the death of the "one mightier than he" (1:7). In his description of the death of John, Mark prepares his readers for the death of Jesus. Like John, Jesus's death is due to pressure placed upon a political leader by others. Both Herod and Pilate, however, acknowledge the innocence of their victims. Both choose to gain the favor and acclaim of the world in exchange for their souls (8:36). For both, the concerns of this world choked out the Word they had heard from John and Jesus. Mark makes no attempt to dissociate Jesus from John the Baptist (contrast John 1:20), for although Mark certainly understands Jesus to be far greater (1:7–8), he makes no attempt to hide their identification in 6:14 and 8:28.

Additional Notes

6:14. The reading "they were saying" (ἔλεγον) is supported by B (D) W it; the reading "he was saying" (ἔλεγεν) appears in ℵ A C L Θ f¹ f¹³ Majority text lat syr cop. Whereas ἔλεγεν has better textual support, the better reading is ἔλεγον because it is the more difficult reading; it fits well the Markan style and the two following uses of ἔλεγον in 6:15; and the singular ἔλεγεν may have been a scribal attempt to harmonize the verb with the third-person singular, "(he) heard." See Metzger 1994: 76.

6:20. A major textual problem is found here. The reading "he was doing" (ἐποίει) is found in A C D f¹ f¹³ Majority text lat syr, whereas the reading "he was perplexed" (ἠπόρει), a hapax legomenon in Mark, is supported by ℵ B L W Θ. The fact that ἠπόρει is a much more difficult reading argues for it being the more likely. See, however, D. Black 1988: 141–45.

6:22. For the textual problem involving whether we should read "his" (αὐτοῦ) or "her" (αὐτῆς), see the comments on 6:21–26.

6:24. ἐξελθοῦσα is lit. "she going out."

C. Jesus Feeds the Five Thousand (6:30–44)

The present passage returns to and concludes the mission of the disciples (6:6b–13) and contains the miracle of the feeding of the five thousand. The exact demarcation of where the one ends and the other begins, however, is far from clear. Various suggestions range from 6:30–31, 32–44; 6:30–32, 33–44; 6:30–33, 34–44; to 6:30–34, 35–44 (Guelich 1989: 336). The passage is tied to the context by

1. the return (6:6b–13) of the apostles (cf. 6:30a [ἀπόστολοι, *apostoloi*] and 6:7 [ἀποστέλλειν, *apostellein*]);
2. the report of the disciples' mission, which involved "doing" and "teaching" (cf. 6:30b and 6:7, 12–13 ["preaching" and "exorcising/healing"]);
3. the disciples' facilitation of Jesus's ministry (cf. 6:6b–13 and 37–43);
4. various references to the "boat" (6:32; cf. 3:9; 4:1, 36; 5:2, 18, 21; 6:45), "bread" (6:37ff.; cf. 6:8, 52; the term is used seventeen times in 6:8–8:19), the "sea" (cf. 6:33–34 [implied by 6:32 and 45]; 4:1, 35–41; 5:1–2, 13, 18, 21; 6:45–51), and so on.

The Markan redactional work can be seen in

1. the introductory seam and the desire for privacy (6:30–31);
2. the reference to teaching (6:30; cf. 1:22) and its use to introduce a miracle story (6:34; cf. 1:21–22);
3. the expressions "began to teach" (ἤρξατο διδάσκειν, *ērxato didaskein*; 6:34; cf. 4:1; 6:2; 8:31; also 1:45; 5:20; 12:1; 13:5); "gather" (συνάγονται, *synagontai*; 6:30; cf. 2:2; 4:1; 5:21); "all that" (πάντα, *panta*; 6:30; cf. 11:24; 12:44);
4. the (γάρ, *gar*) explanatory clause (6:31b; see 1:16–18);
5. "much/many/all" (ὅσα, *hosa*; 6:30b, 31b, 33 [2×], 34 [2×]);
6. the use of the dual expression "by yourselves [lit. 'alone'] to a deserted place" in 6:31a, repeated in 6:32 in reverse (chiastic) order (cf. also 6:35), and so on (Masuda 1982: 192–96; Pryke 1978: 15, 142, 159–60).

Whereas Mark's hand can clearly be seen in 6:30–35, this is due not to the de novo creation of this material but rather to his free reworking of the traditions he reports (Guelich 1989: 337). The remaining material (6:36–44) shows little evidence of Mark's editorial work.

The miracle of Jesus's feeding of the five thousand is the only miracle found in all four Gospels (6:34–44; Matt. 14:13–21; Luke 9:10–17; John 6:1–15). The traditional basis of the Markan account is demonstrated by the appearance of the same account independently in John (Stein 1992b: 486–88; Marcus 2000: 53–54). All four accounts agree on the number five thousand (Matt. 14:21 makes even more explicit that the "men" [ἄνδρες, *andres*] were males by adding "besides women and children"), the reference to five loaves and two fish, the excess of fragments left over, the mention of twelve baskets, Jesus pronouncing a blessing/thanksgiving, the command to the disciples to make the people recline/sit down, the disciples' lack of understanding concerning the need for food, and so on. In three Gospels additional agreements are found in reference to a boat (implied in John 6:1) used in crossing the sea (not in Luke), a reference to Jesus's healing (not in Mark), the lateness of the hour (not in John), and so on.[1]

The parallel account of the feeding of the four thousand (Mark 8:1–10) has raised the issue of whether these two feeding miracles are doublets of the same tradition (Fowler 1981: 68–90; Masuda 1982; Meier 1994: 956–58) or two totally different traditions. Although the accounts have several similarities, there are a number of significant differences: the number five thousand versus four thousand, five loaves versus seven, two fish versus a few small fish, twelve baskets of fragments versus seven, and so on (see the introduction to 8:1–9.) Even more important, both Mark and Matthew (Matt. 14:13–21 and 15:32–39) understood these as two different events. This is evident not only from their presenting them as two separate events but also from Mark 8:19–20 and Matt. 16:9–10, where reference is made to both feeding miracles. Thus, at least for these two evangelists, the two feeding miracles refer to two separate traditions and events.

Whether 6:34–44 came to Mark as part of a pre-Markan complex of miracle stories (Keck 1965b: 348–52; Kuhn 1971: 203–10, 217–18) cannot be known with any certainty. Similarities such as the command that Jairus's daughter be fed and the command that the five thousand be fed are interesting, but 6:34–44 does not follow closely the command to feed Jairus's daughter. It is separated by a considerable amount of nonmiraculous material. Also, the attempt to see ties between Elijah/Elisha raising a dead little girl and feeding people with these two events in the life of Jesus is not immediately convincing. Whether some of the material found in 4:35–6:44 was found in a pre-Markan complex cannot be demonstrated. Whatever common themes there are within these accounts that argue for the existence of a pre-Markan complex can also be understood as reasons for Mark's having chosen to arrange this material in his Gospel in their present form and place.

1. See Marcus (2000: 412–13) for a helpful synopsis of the four accounts.

The account can be divided as follows: 6:30–31, the return of the apostles; 6:32–34, the introduction to the miracle of the feeding of the five thousand; 6:35–37, a description of the problem; 6:38–41, the miracle described; and 6:42–44, the concluding proof of the miracle.

Exegesis and Exposition

[30]And the apostles gather around Jesus and reported to him all that they had done and all that they had taught, [31]and he says to them, "Come alone by yourselves to a deserted place [with me], and rest for a little while." For many were coming and going, and they did not even have an opportunity to eat.

[32]And they departed in the boat alone into a deserted place. [33]And many saw them departing and recognized [them], and from all the cities they ran on foot and arrived there ahead of them. [34]And when he got out [of the boat], he saw a great crowd, and he had compassion on them, for they were like sheep not having a shepherd, and he began to teach them many things.

[35]And when the hour had already become late, his disciples ⌜came⌝ to him [and] began to say, "This is a deserted place and the hour is already late. [36]Send them away, so that they ⌜may go⌝ into the surrounding countryside and villages [and] purchase for themselves something to eat." [37]And he answered [and] said to them, "You yourselves give them [something] to eat." And they say to him, "Should we leave and purchase two hundred denarii worth of bread and give [it] to them to eat?"

[38]And he says to them, "How much bread do you have? ⌜Go,⌝ see." And when they found out, they say, "Five [loaves], and two fish." [39]And he ordered them to have all [the people] recline in companies on the green grass. [40]And they reclined in groups of hundreds and fifties. [41]And having taken the five [loaves of] bread and the two fish, having looked up into heaven, he blessed and broke the [loaves of] bread and was giving [them] to his disciples, so that they might distribute [them] to them [the people], and he divided the two fish for all. [42]And all ate and were filled. [43]And they gathered up twelve baskets full of fragments [from the bread] and from the fish. [44]And those having eaten ⌜the [loaves of] bread⌝ numbered five thousand men.

At this point Mark completes the sandwich, begun in 6:6b–13 and interrupted by the story of John the Baptist's death, with the return of the "apostles" (ἀπό-στολοι, *apostoloi*). For Mark's readers the expression "apostles" was clearly a technical term for the twelve disciples whom Jesus named "apostles" ("sent ones," 3:14, ἀποστόλους, *apostolous*) and who had been "sent out" (ἀποστέλ-λειν, *apostellein*) in 6:7 (Best 1981: 193). Mark may have chosen this term rather than "disciples" not only to emphasize that they were Jesus's "sent-out ones" but also to avoid confusion with the disciples of John the Baptist mentioned in 6:29. Their return "to Jesus" (πρὸς τὸν Ἰησοῦν, *pros ton Iēsoun*) reveals the source of the disciples' authority and that their mission was in effect an extension of Jesus's own ministry. Having been sent out in Jesus's name and with his authority, their preaching, healing, and exorcising were in effect Jesus's

6:30–31

preaching, healing, and exorcising. They now report "all that they had done and taught" (πάντα ὅσα ἐποίησαν καὶ ὅσα ἐδίδαξαν, *panta hosa epoiēsan kai hosa edidaxan*). "Had done" corresponds to their exorcising and healing, and "taught" corresponds to their preaching the need of repentance (6:7, 12–13). The chiastic order in 6:12–13 ("preached," "exorcised/healed") and 30 ("did," "taught") should be noted. The interchange of "teaching" (ἐδίδαξαν, *edidaxan*; 6:30) and "preaching" (ἐκήρυξαν, *ekēryxan*; 6:12) indicates that these terms are essentially synonymous for Mark. By their mission the disciples replicated and extended Jesus's teaching and preaching.

Jesus's call for privacy, "Come alone by yourselves [emphatic—ὑμεῖς αὐτοί, *hymeis autoi*] to a deserted place, and rest for a little while," recalls 1:35; 6:46; 7:24; 9:2–8; 14:32–42. The term "rest" (ἀναπαύσασθε, *anapausasthe*) may allude to Ps. 23:2 (cf. also Mark 6:34 ["shepherd"], 39 ["green grass"], and 41–42 [the presentation of a meal; Ps. 23:5]). The expression "lonely place" (ἔρημον τόπον, *erēmon topon*) also occurs in 1:35, 45; 6:32, 35. Although ἔρημος is often used in the sense of "desert" or "desert-like," here it means "lonely" or "deserted," as indicated by the references to the countryside and villages round about (6:36; cf. also 6:33) and to their being next to a freshwater lake. With a typical γάρ (*gar*) clause in 6:31c, Mark explains why Jesus gave the preceding command: "For many were coming and going." The "many" (πολλοί, *polloi*) witness to the success of the disciples' mission (and thus of Jesus's own mission) in the same way as Herod's having heard about Jesus witnesses to the successful mission of the disciples (6:14–15). As in 3:20–21, the disciples as Jesus's representatives were also finding no time to eat.

6:32–34   Mark now describes Jesus and the disciples going to a lonely place by themselves (6:32). Note the chiasmus:

> A by yourselves [lit. "alone"] (6:31)
>   B to a lonely place (6:31)
>   B′ to a lonely place (6:32)
> A′ by themselves [lit. "alone"] (6:32)

The "boat" (πλοίῳ, *ploiō*) picks up the "boat" of 3:9; 4:1, 36–41; 5:2, 18, 21; cf. also 6:45. The "many" of 6:33 who see Jesus and the disciples leaving are the "many" of 6:31. They recognize Jesus and the disciples as they leave, and people from all the towns run after them on foot. We should probably envision Jesus and the disciples proceeding eastward along the northwestern shoreline of the Sea of Galilee (contra Boobyer 1953: 78–80) in an area west of Bethsaida (Luke 9:10; cf. John 6:23), and the crowds hurrying along the shoreline with the boat in sight. The use of the hyperbolic "from all the towns" emphasizes the great fame and magnetism of Jesus, and where the five thousand of 6:44 came from. The verb "ran" (συνέδραμον, *synedramon*) also emphasizes Jesus's great popularity. According to Mark, even when seeking privacy, Jesus cannot be hid. He is too great.

Upon disembarking, Jesus "saw a great crowd, and he had compassion [ἐσπλαγχνίσθη, *esplanchnisthē*] on them" (6:34). It is probably at this point (after the editorial "And when he got out," Καὶ ἐξελθών, *Kai exelthōn*; cf. 5:2) that the tradition of the five thousand begins (Koch 1975: 99). Mark does not mention the disembarking of the disciples. Although this is assumed in 6:35, he does not mention this here in order to focus the readers' attention on the key figure of the story—Jesus. The suggestion that 6:34 was originally connected to the story of Jairus's daughter (Achtemeier 1970: 281; Pesch 1980a: 346–47) stumbles over the fact that it is extremely unlikely that the feeding of the five thousand took place on "Jairus's front lawn" (Gundry 1993: 323). Jesus's compassion has already been referred to (1:41) and will be mentioned again in the feeding of the four thousand (8:2). In the latter instance it is due to the crowd not having eaten for three days. Here it is due to their lack of a shepherd to guide them: "for they were like sheep not having a shepherd" (ὅτι ἦσαν ὡς πρόβατα μὴ ἔχοντα ποιμένα, *hoti ēsan hōs probata mē echonta poimena*). This recalls numerous OT allusions to Israel's need of a shepherd to lead them (Num. 27:17; 1 Kings 22:17; 2 Chron. 18:16; cf. Jer. 31:10; Ezek. 34:5, 8; Zech. 10:2; 13:7; also Jdt. 11:19) and the promise that God would one day provide a shepherd to do so (Ezek. 34:23). David and his successors are often portrayed as shepherds of God's people (Ps. 78:70–72; Ezek. 34:23). The christological nature of this saying may be especially apparent in Num. 27:16–17, where Moses' request for someone to lead Israel is answered in Joshua (Num. 27:18–23). Now a greater Joshua ("Jesus" in Greek), who possesses even more of the Spirit of God (cf. Num. 27:18 and Mark 1:10), has come to lead Israel (cf. Heb. 4:8). The promised shepherd of Ezek. 34:23 would "feed" Israel, and Jesus now feeds his people. This editorial comment comes, of course, from the "omniscient editor," who informs his readers of Jesus's inner feelings and thinking. That Jesus thought of himself as a shepherd receives support from Mark 14:27 (cf. John 10:1–18, 27–28; Heb. 13:20–21; 1 Pet. 2:25; 5:1–4). Mark concludes his introduction of the miracle story with a typical Markan theme: Jesus "began to teach them many things" (καὶ ἤρξατο διδάσκειν αὐτοὺς πολλά, *kai ērxato didaskein autous polla*). A similar Markan editorial comment is found introducing the exorcism in 1:21–27 and Jesus's miracles in Nazareth (6:2–6a; cf. also 4:1–2; 8:31). In Jewish literature the "feeding" of Israel is often associated with their being taught the Torah (2 Bar. 77.13–15). By this editorial comment Mark indicates that Jesus supplied the spiritual needs of his hearers by teaching (1:14–15); shortly, he will relate how Jesus would meet their physical needs by feeding them.

6:35–37 All three Synoptic Gospels contain a reference to the miracle taking place late in the day (cf. Matt. 14:15; Luke 9:12). "And when the hour had already become late" (καὶ ἤδη ὥρας πολλῆς γενομένης, *kai ēdē hōras pollēs genomenēs*). The genitive absolute is frequently used in Mark to designate time (1:32; 2:1; 14:17; 15:33, 42; 16:1). The double expression of the late hour in this verse ("when the hour had already become late . . . and the hour is already late [καὶ ἤδη ὥρα πολλή, *kai ēdē hōra pollē*]") is an example of Markan redundancy (Neirynck 1988: 116). Since a number of events would still transpire (arranging the crowd, feeding them, collecting the leftovers, sending the disciples away, dismissing the crowd, climbing the mountain to pray) before nightfall (6:47; cf. 15:42), it is probably best to interpret this temporal designation as referring to sometime in the late afternoon (Gundry 1993: 324, 329), during the normal dinner hour (Gnilka 1978: 259; France 2002: 265). The Johannine parallel lacks any temporal designation. Since the disciples suggest that the people be dismissed to buy food in the surrounding countryside and villages (6:36), the "lonely place" should not be envisioned as the deserts of Sinai or Saudi Arabia but as the fields and slopes along the northwest corner of the Sea of Galilee.

The disciples' suggestion (note that "disciples" in 6:35 and "apostles" in 6:30 are used interchangeably) that Jesus dismiss the crowd so that they can purchase food for themselves in the surrounding countryside (τοὺς κύκλῳ ἀγρούς, *tous kyklō agrous*; cf. 5:14) and villages (κώμας, *kōmas*) seems like a reasonable and considerate suggestion on their part. However, it loses sight of the fact that Jesus is the "good shepherd" (cf. 6:34) and that his miracles in 1:21–6:6 indicate that he can and will feed his sheep. In contrast to the disciples' suggestion that the people should buy food for "themselves" (ἑαυτοῖς, *heautois*; 6:36), Jesus tells them, "You yourselves [emphatic—ὑμεῖς, *hymeis*], give them [something] to eat" (6:37). Jesus's command assumes that the disciples should serve as extensions of his own miracle-working power and authority. The disciples, however, seek to understand Jesus's command in terms of what they themselves are capable of doing. "Should we leave and purchase two hundred denarii worth of bread?" There is no need to assume that Mark wants his readers to interpret the disciples' reply as sarcastic (contra Marcus 2000: 407, 415, 418; France 2002: 266). A denarius (δηνάριον, *dēnarion*) was the equivalent of a day's wages (Matt. 20:2, 13). Whether the disciples had this amount of money with them or whether this is a purely hypothetical question is uncertain. Exactly how many loaves of bread a denarius could purchase is not important. Mark 6:37 and John 6:7, and those who earlier repeated this tradition, assume that approximately 200 denarii would be needed to provide bread for the five thousand.

6:38–41 In response to Jesus's question, the disciples seek to find the resources available to them. They have five loaves and two fish. What they have forgotten, however, is that they are in the presence of Jesus Christ, the Son of God (1:1)! Mark gives no hint to his readers that the numbers "five," "two," "twelve" (6:43), "five thousand" (6:44), "seven" (8:6), or "four thousand" (8:9) possess any symbolic significance. It is best, therefore, not to see any specific symbolism in them ("five loaves" = the Torah; "twelve" = the twelve tribes of Israel [see 6:43–44]; etc.). The later reference in the feeding of the four thousand to a "few fish" (8:7) suggests that Mark is not interested in promoting symbolic significance in these numbers (contra Marcus 2000:

411, 418), and the difficulty of finding symbolism in the numbers "two," "five thousand," and "four thousand" weakens the alleged symbolism of the other numbers (contra Thiering 1970: 4–5). The emphasis on the loaves (referred to twice in this verse and central to Jesus's question) may be due to its symbolism in recalling the Lord's Supper (Meier 1994: 962; Marcus 2000: 407, 419–20).

"And he ordered them [the disciples] to have all [the people] recline in companies on the green grass" (6:39). To "recline" or "sit down" (ἀνακλῖναι, *anaklinai*) was the normal position for eating a banquet meal (Luke 12:37) and is used with respect to the messianic banquet in Matt. 8:11/Luke 13:29. Note the disciples' role in carrying out Jesus's command and later in the distribution of the miraculous food. Here, as in their mission (6:6b–13), they serve as extensions of Jesus's ministry. The mention of "the green grass" (τῷ χλωρῷ χόρτῳ, *tō chlōrō chortō*) has drawn a great deal of comment. Some see this as a sign that the messianic age had arrived and the desert was now blossoming (Isa. 35:1; 2 Bar. 29.5–8; Marcus 2000: 408; contra Schweizer 1970: 139); others see it as a personal and thus historical reminiscence (V. Taylor 1952: 321); still others see it as a reflection of Jesus's role as a shepherd leading his sheep to green pastures (Ps. 23:2; Pesch 1980a: 350; Guelich 1989: 341). The last interpretation encounters difficulty in that the actual verbal correspondence between "green pastures" (τόπον χλόης, *topon chloēs*; Ps. 23:2 [22:2 LXX]) and "green grass" (χλωρῷ χόρτῳ) is not great. If this reference is historical, then the event must have taken place in the spring, near the time of Passover (cf. John 6:4, 10), since green grass cannot be found in the countryside during the rest of the year. Mark provides his readers with no indication as to how he wanted this reference to be interpreted. Thus, although the feeding of the five thousand should not be interpreted as a "Lord's Supper" (Pesch 1980a: 352–53; Gnilka 1978: 261), its similarities (cf. 6:41) would later bring to mind the Lord's Supper, and both would call the readers' attention to the future messianic banquet.

"And they reclined in groups of hundreds [κατὰ ἑκατόν, *kata hekaton*] and fifties [κατὰ πεντήκοντα, *kata pentēkonta*]" along with the reference to sitting down in "companies" (συμπόσια συμπόσια, *symposia symposia*) and "groups" (πρασιαὶ πρασιαί, *prasiai prasiai*), has generated a great deal of discussion. Some have suggested that this is meant to recall the camps formed during the exodus (Exod. 18:21, 25; Deut. 1:15; cf. 1QS 2.21–22; 1QSa 1.14–15; 1.29–2.1; 1QM 4.1–5.16; CD 13.1), but the numbers in the alleged parallels are thousands, hundreds, fifties, and tens, so that the parallel is far from exact. Even more speculative is the view that Mark wanted his readers to think of one large square consisting of fifty rows of one hundred people each (Gundry 1993: 325). That "companies" and "groups" are found only here in the NT makes it unwise to interpret them as technical terms for "eating parties/groups" and "garden beds" (cf. Marcus 2000: 407–8). They are probably another example of Markan duality (Neirynck 1988: 121) and simply mean "groups of between fifty and one hundred."

"And having taken the five [loaves of] bread and the two fish,[2] having looked up into heaven, he blessed and broke the [loaves of] bread and was giving [them] to his disciples." The similarities between these words and those of the Last Supper are quite apparent.[3] In both we find a late hour (6:35; 14:17), "taking" (λαβών, labōn), "bread" (ἄρτους/ἄρτον, artous/arton), "blessed" (εὐλόγησεν/ εὐλογήσας, eulogēsen/eulogēsas), "broke" (κατέκλασεν/ἔκλασεν, kateklasen/ eklasen), "gave" (ἐδίδου/ἔδωκεν, edidou/edōken), "to the disciples/to them" (6:41; 14:22). Also the word order of the verbs is identical. Compare also 6:39, "sit down" (ἀνακλῖναι; lit. "recline"), and 14:18, "sat at table" (ἀνακειμένων, anakeimenōn; lit. "reclined"). If, as seems reasonable, the readers of Mark were Christians, it is quite likely that the wording of the present account would have brought to mind their experience of eating the Lord's Supper. During the oral period the retelling of these two accounts probably acquired a similar introductory rewording in the blessing, breaking, and distribution of the bread. In this respect we should note that Matthew and Luke in their parallel accounts of the feeding of the five thousand are freer in their reporting of the rest of the account than in 6:41–42, and this may imply that Mark's wording was due to the analogy of these verses with the institution of the Lord's Supper (Tagawa 1966: 136–37; Marcus 2000: 409). Also, the common use of "breaking bread" in the early church to describe the sharing of a communal meal and the Lord's Supper (cf. Acts 2:42, 46; 20:7, 11; 1 Cor. 10:16–17; 11:23) would probably have caused the readers/hearers of the present account to think about the Lord's Supper.

The differences that exist between the present account and the Lord's Supper (fish versus wine, extra food left over, etc.) indicate that these were separate and distinct traditions, and although a similarity in wording developed, the two accounts were seen as referring to two different events and remained two separate traditions. If the celebration of the Lord's Supper was understood by Mark's readers as a proleptic experience of the messianic banquet (14:25), it is quite possible that the feeding of the five thousand was also seen as a proleptic anticipation of that future banquet.[4] The reference to Jesus looking up to heaven is found before the performance of a miracle in 7:34 and John 11:41. (Cf. Luke 18:13; John 17:1; Ps. 123:1; also 1 En. 13.5.) It is uncertain whether the object of blessing in this verse is God or the bread. Compare the ancient Jewish blessing: "[Blessed are you] . . . who brings forth bread from the earth" (m. Ber. 6.1; cf. b. Ber. 38a). Yet in Mark 8:7, Jesus blesses the fish, and

---

2. Mark has no interest in describing the kind of bread (contrast John 6:9, 13) or fish (salted? dried?) involved.

3. Fowler (1981: 134–47) objects that the first-time hearers of the Gospel of Mark had not yet heard the story of the Last Supper in 14:22–25, so they would not have seen a correspondence in terminology. This, however, loses sight of the fact that the hearers were Christians and that the story of the Last Supper would have been one of the better-known accounts in the life of Jesus.

4. See Gen. Rab. 88.5; Exod. Rab. 25.7; and Num. Rab. 21.21, which understand Ps. 23:5 as a symbolic portrayal of the messianic banquet.

Luke 9:16 understands the object of the blessing as being "them," the loaves and the fish. Compare also 1 Cor. 10:16, where Paul refers to the blessing of the cup (contra Gundry 1993: 325–26, 332).

The verb "was giving" (ἐδίδου) has been seen as symbolizing the inexhaustible supply of messianic bread (Marcus 2000: 410; cf. John 6:34–35). It is best, however, to see this as an iterative imperfect in which Jesus was continually giving bread to his disciples as they distributed what they had been given and continually returned for more. Whereas the bread is "broken" (κατέκλασεν), the fish is "divided" (ἐμέρισεν, emerisen). The difference in the verbs matches the differences in the two kinds of food. It is unlikely that Mark's readers would associate the two fish with dining upon the evil sea monster, Leviathan, as in 2 Bar. 29.3–8; 2 Esd. 6:51–52 (contra Davies and Allison 1991: 481).

The conclusion of this miracle story involves three statements that serve to **6:42–44** heighten the miraculous nature of the incident. The first is that they all ate and were satisfied (6:42). Marcus (2000: 420) points out, "It is difficult for modern-day readers who live comfortably . . . and have never gone hungry to imagine the impact these statements may have had on some of their first hearers, who may have known hunger frequently; it is not for nothing that one of the most frequent biblical images of the bliss of the age to come is a *banquet*, in which the participants will be able to eat as much as they wish (see e.g. Isa. 25:6–9)." The second statement heightening the miracle is that after eating, the disciples took up "twelve baskets full of fragments [from the bread] and from the fish." The superlative nature of this miracle is seen in the excess of leftovers. Not only did all get something to eat and were filled (ἐχορτάσθησαν, echortasthēsan; cf. 8:8), but there also were twelve baskets of uneaten bread and fish left over! This emphasis on the superabundance of the food is probably intended to allude to the arrival of the kingdom of God and its bringing an abundance of blessing. The "twelve" baskets do not have any direct, symbolic value. They simply indicate that after their distribution, the twelve disciples collected twelve "baskets" (κοφίνων, kophinōn, a basket particularly associated with the Jews [see Juvenal, *Satires* 3.14]) of leftovers. Whatever symbolism there may be in the number twelve comes from Jesus having chosen twelve disciples (3:14), not to there being twelve baskets. These baskets may have normally been kept in the fishing boat (6:34) as containers for the catch in times of fishing. It is possible that the twelve baskets refer not to actual baskets but to the quantity of fragments left over (France 2002: 268).

The third statement of the astonishing nature of the miracle is that those who ate the loaves numbered (lit. "were") "five thousand men" (πεντακισχίλιοι ἄνδρες, pentakischilioi andres). If "the [loaves of] bread" should be read, this (and the omission of any mention of the "fish") would serve as another allusion to the Lord's Supper. The number of men fed emphasizes the exceptional nature of the miracle. This mighty work of Jesus (6:2) makes Elisha's feeding one hundred people with twenty loaves (2 Kings 4:42–44) seem almost trivial (cf. also 1 Kings 17:8–16). Jesus feeds fifty times more with one-fourth of what Elisha had and has a greater surplus left over! The term "men" (ἄνδρες) refers not to "people" (ἄνθρωποι, anthrōpoi) but to "males," as Matt. 14:21, which mentions additional women and children, clearly indicates.[5] If Mark expected his readers to assume that women and children were present, it is unlikely that he wanted them to think that this group went hungry. Matthew 14:21 assumes that they were fed along with the men.

In the account, no mention is made of the reaction of the crowd to this miracle; contrast Mark 1:27, 45; 2:12; 4:41; 5:15–17, 20, 42. Instead, 6:42–44 confirms the miracle. As in 1:31; 3:5; 5:29–34, the miracle is confirmed not by the crowd's reaction but by a description of what happened: Peter's mother-in-law gets up and serves; the man's hand is restored; the woman with the hemorrhage is healed; and here five thousand men are fed and satisfied, and there are many leftovers. The lack of any mention of the crowd's reaction is in sharp contrast to John 6:14–15.

Summary

The Markan christological emphasis in the present account is seen in several ways. For one, the massive nature of the miracle reveals the greatness of Jesus. Other miracles of feeding by Elijah (1 Kings 17:8–16) and Elisha (2 Kings 4:42–44) pale in comparison. Only God's provision of manna in the wilderness to the children of Israel surpasses it. Clearly Jesus's greatness is highlighted in the present account. His greatness is such that he simply cannot be hidden (cf. 1:35–37, 45 with 6:33–34). To what extent the crowd in the original situation in the life of Jesus was aware of this miracle is unclear.[6] For Mark's readers, however, once again Jesus is seen as Lord over nature (cf. 4:35–41). An additional christological image is introduced in this account. This involves the portrayal of Jesus as Israel's "shepherd"

5. Some scholars (Montefiore 1961; Brandon 1967: 352–53; France 2002: 261–62) have suggested that the original situation described in the Gospel accounts involved a gathering of five thousand men who sought to engineer a messianic uprising in which Jesus would be made king (cf. John 6:14–15). It must be pointed out, however, that such a scenario is not obtained from the present account in Mark (or Matthew or Luke), and France (2002: 261–62) admits that the account in Mark "reads more like an ad hoc picnic than a military manoeuvre." It is furthermore unlikely that Herod Antipas or Pontius Pilate would have tolerated such a large gathering of males of military age, and at the trial of Jesus when charges were sought against him (cf. 14:55–61; 15:3–4), nothing is mentioned of this supposed attempt to make Jesus a king and organize a messianic uprising. This is strange if this event had militaristic and messianic hopes associated with it. That all four Gospels refer to the five thousand as "men" (ἄνδρες) is unusual, but Matthew adds that there were also women and children present (14:21).

6. Numerous rationalistic explanations have been suggested to explain what actually happened on this occasion in the life of Jesus: the example of a boy's willingness to share his food (John 6:9) caused everyone to share what they had brought, and thus there was more than enough for everyone; Jesus had access to large food stores located in a nearby hidden cave; etc. All the Gospel accounts portray the feeding of the five thousand as a remarkable nature miracle. To understand the Markan message, we must interpret what Mark is seeking to teach through this miracle story by means of the text he has given us, not by a hypothetical reconstruction of earlier forms of the text or of the event itself.

(6:34). The promise of a coming "shepherd" whom God would send to his people (Ezek. 34:23; Ps. Sol. 17.30–44) has now been fulfilled.

Another theme found in this account involves the disciples' lack of understanding (6:36–37). Although this theme is not altogether new (cf. 4:13, 40–41), it will receive greater and greater emphasis in the coming chapters (7:18; 8:4, 14–21, 31–33; 9:5–7, 32; 14:37–40). Yet this must be interpreted along with such passages as 3:13–19; 6:6b–13, 30; 14:28; 16:7. We should also note that in the present passage, despite their lack of understanding in 6:36–37, they are Jesus's chosen apostles and assist him in the miraculous feeding of the five thousand.

A third emphasis found in our passage involves the coming of the kingdom of God. Not only is the one who performs the miracle greater than any who have preceded him, but the miracle also reveals that indeed the kingdom of God has arrived (1:15), and its firstfruits are manifesting themselves. Elsewhere it has shown itself in the laying waste of Satan's house and the freeing of the demonized (3:20–30), in the sick being healed, and in the dead being raised. In the present passage the arrival of the kingdom is seen in the lost sheep of Israel having received their shepherd (6:34), who feeds them spiritually by teaching them (6:34) and physically by providing food (6:37–44). The kingdom of God has come, and already the messianic banquet is being tasted. The excessive emphasis and allegorization that the shepherd theme has received from some exegetes does not require a denial of its presence in this account. Mark wants his readers to know that Jesus is indeed the shepherd of God's people (cf. 14:27). Nevertheless, the extraordinary miracle-working power of the Son of God receives more emphasis in the account than that of his being the promised shepherd (Koch 1975: 104).

Additional Notes

6:35. προσελθόντες is lit. "having come."

6:36. ἀπελθόντες is lit. "going."

6:38. The translation follows ℵ B D L W f¹. "And" (καί) is found in A Θ f¹³ lat.

6:44. The textual support concerning whether "the [loaves of] bread" (τοὺς ἄρτους) is part of the Markan text is divided. Favoring its inclusion are A B L 33 Majority text syr^{p,h} bo; favoring its exclusion are 𝔓⁴⁵ ℵ D W Θ f¹ f¹³.

D. Jesus Walks on the Sea (6:45–52)

The exact nature of this pericope is unclear. Is it an epiphany in which Jesus reveals himself as the "I am" (6:48c–50; Theissen 1983: 94–95; Meier 1994: 907–8); a rescue story in which the miracle (6:48b, 51a) is the main point (Theissen 1983: 99–103); or are aspects of a sea rescue and an epiphany "inextricably intertwined" (Fleddermann 1983: 393; cf. also Heil 1981: 17; Dwyer 1996: 130)? The difficulty in deciding the nature of the story is compounded by 6:48, which implies that Jesus "comes to" (ἔρχεται, *erchetai*) the disciples because of the difficulty they are encountering on the sea but then means "to pass by them" (παρελθεῖν αὐτούς, *parelthein autous*). The present account defies any simple attempt to classify it and place it into a neat category.[1] Theories of how the present account came into existence abound. Was it a rescue story that developed into an epiphany story? Was it an epiphany story that developed into a rescue story (Guelich 1989: 346)? Were they originally two separate stories that were combined? Also much debated is whether the story came to Mark (1) as an isolated unit, (2) in combination with the feeding of the five thousand (cf. John 6:1–21), or (3) in a complex of miracle stories. If we assume the independence of Mark and John (R. Brown 1966: 236–50, 252–54), their combination in John apart from the other miracles found in Mark 4:35ff. argues in favor of the second possibility. The attempt to deny the rescue element of the present story (Gundry 1993: 342) is unconvincing due to the Matthean parallel (Matt. 14:24), the ceasing of the wind in Mark 6:51, and the various parallels that remind the readers of 4:38–39.

The present connection with the preceding feeding miracle is strained. The account begins with the disciples going by boat to the "other side," toward Bethsaida. If the "lonely place" of 6:32 is the eastern side of the Sea of Galilee, this seems contradictory, because they would already be on "the other side" (εἰς τὸ πέραν, *eis to peran*) near Bethsaida. It is more likely, however, that the feeding of the five thousand took place on the western side of the Sea of Galilee (see 5:21–24a and 6:45–47). The temporal designation associated with the account ("And when evening came," 6:47) also seems to conflict with 6:35 ("And when the hour had already become late . . . the hour is already late"), for it is difficult to fit between these two similar time designations all the events of 6:35–46 (seating the crowd, feeding them, collecting the leftovers, the departure of the disciples, dismissing the crowd, going up the mountain to pray). See, however, 6:35–37. Is it possible that

---

1. For similarities between the present account and Jesus's stilling of the storm (4:35–41), see Marcus 2000: 428–29.

originally the feeding of the five thousand and Jesus's walking on the sea were two independent incidents that were later joined before Mark and John wrote their Gospels? If, however, the designation in 6:35 can refer to mid- or late afternoon (Gundry 1993: 324, 335; France 2002: 265), the chronological necessity that these be unrelated events is eliminated (see below). Topically the ties between the stories involve the boat (6:32, 45), the crowd (6:34, 45), two nature miracles, bread (cf. 6:38), and the disciples' lack of understanding (6:37–38, 51–52). The last is clearly a Markan theme and is not found in the Johannine parallel (cf. John 6:16–21). Because of the independent parallel in John (Meier 1994: 993–94n110), which is also tied to the account of the feeding of the five thousand, these two accounts were apparently associated together before Mark wrote his Gospel (Gnilka 1978: 266; Meier 1994: 906, 922; contra Achtemeier 1970: 282).

Mark's own hand is seen most clearly in the introductory seam (6:45) and concluding explanation (6:52; Quesnell 1969: 65–66; Gnilka 1978: 266–67; Guelich 1989: 347). It is also possible that the explanatory "for" (γάρ, gar) clause in 6:50a comes from Mark. Pryke (1978: 15, 142, 160) also sees 6:47–48 as Markan, but this is unlikely. The account consists of three almost equal parts: the connecting seam and introduction (6:45–47); the miracle/epiphany proper (6:48–50); and the ending of the miracle story and the Markan conclusion (6:51–52).

Exegesis and Exposition

[45]And immediately he [Jesus] made his disciples get into the boat and go ahead of him ⌜to the other side⌝, toward Bethsaida, while he himself dismisses the crowd. [46]And after having taken leave of them [the disciples], he went away to the mountain to pray. [47]And when evening came, the boat was ⌜ ⌝ in the middle of the sea, and he himself [was] alone on the land. [48]And when he saw them being hard pressed while rowing, for the wind was against them, around the fourth watch of the night he comes walking toward them on the sea, and he wanted to pass by them. [49]But when they saw him walking on the sea, they thought that it was a ghost, and cried out. [50]For all saw him and were terrified. But immediately he spoke with them and says to them, "Have courage; it is I; stop being afraid." [51]And he entered into the boat with them, and the wind ceased. And they were utterly ⌜astonished⌝ within themselves, [52]for they did not understand about the [loaves of] bread, but [on the contrary] their heart had been hardened. ⌜ ⌝

The account begins with a typically Markan "And immediately" (καὶ εὐθύς, kai euthys). Here it is best not to see in the phrase "a sense of urgency" (Guelich 1989: 347–48), but to see it as a typical Markan construction joining this account with the preceding. See 1:10–11. Jesus is usually portrayed as traveling in a boat with the disciples (4:35–41; 5:1–2, 18; 6:31–34; 8:10, 14; cf. 4:1–2), but here Jesus makes his disciples enter into the boat and go before him to the

6:45–47

other side, toward Bethsaida. The verb "made" (ἠνάγκασεν, *ēnankasen*) occurs only here in Mark. The redactional nature of this verse raises the question of why Mark chose this verb, but unfortunately he gives no suggestion as to why. It can mean to "compel" or "force," but here it may mean to "urge strongly." That Jesus compelled the disciples to leave in order to squelch a potential messianic uprising (cf. John 6:15; W. Lane 1974: 234–35; J. Edwards 2002: 197) is to read John's Gospel into Mark. Mark's earliest readers had no access to John, and thus, whatever the historical reason for Jesus's actions, Mark did not intend his readers to understand the verb in this manner.

The "other side" (εἰς τὸ πέραν) probably refers to the eastern, or "other" side (see 5:21–23), of the Sea of Galilee. The exact location of Bethsaida, the home of Peter and Andrew according to John 1:44, is debated (J. F. Strange, *ABD* 1:692–93), but the suggested site is north of the Sea of Galilee and on the eastern side of the Jordan River as it flows into the sea.[2] If the Jordan River and the middle of the Sea of Galilee divide one side from the "other side," then traveling from the previous side (west of Bethsaida and the Jordan River) across the Jordan toward Bethsaida would be going to the "other side." If in 6:53 "crossed over" refers to a return after a period of time to the western side of the Sea of Galilee, there is no need to accuse Mark of ignorance concerning the geography of Galilee.[3] The doubling of the topographical references in this verse is typically Markan (Neirynck 1988: 95). "While he himself dismisses the crowd" (ἕως αὐτὸς ἀπολύει τὸν ὄχλον, *heōs autos apolyei ton ochlon*) serves as a tie to the previous story but plays no role in the present account, even though the crowd is mentioned in passing in the next verse.

Having dismissed the crowd and taken leave of them, Jesus departs to "the" mountain to pray. It is strange that the parallel in Luke does not mention this, since the praying of Jesus is a strong Lukan theological emphasis (Stein 1992a: 51–52), but this is part of his "great omission" of the Markan material found in 6:45–8:26. A number of scholars see in the reference to "the mountain" an interpretive clue by Mark indicating that what follows should be interpreted as an epiphany (Pesch 1980a: 360). A mountain is a favorite place for God to appear to his people (Exod. 19:3, 20; 24:15; 31:18; Deut. 33:2; Hab. 3:3). If a specific mountain is intended, we might be inclined to think of Mount Sinai (Exod. 24:15–18), because of the possible allusions to the exodus in the account (the miracle of feeding the people = manna; the miracle of walking on the sea = crossing the Red Sea; Moses going up Mount Sinai to commune with God = Jesus "praying" on the mountain; Marcus 2000: 422–23), but the scene is a mountain overlooking the Sea of Galilee (Mark 6:45–46) from which Jesus sees the disciples toiling on the sea on their way to Bethsaida (6:47). In the account of the feeding of the five thousand in John, "the mountain" is

2. There is no reason to think that there were two cities by that name near each other (Gundry 1993: 339).

3. Cf. Guelich (1989: 348), who suggests that Mark envisions a trip from the west side of the Sea of Galilee northeast toward Bethsaida and landing at Gennesaret (cf. also Gundry 1993: 338–39).

referred to twice (6:3, 15), so that there as here the miracle of Jesus walking on the sea is preceded by a reference to his being on "the" mountain. Thus the reference appears to be traditional. None of the Gospel writers, however, makes any attempt to identify the mountain. As in 1:35 (cf. also 14:32–39) Jesus takes time to be alone and pray, and as in 1:35 the content of the prayer is not mentioned. There is no indication, as some suggest, that through prayer Jesus is seeking power to work miracles.

I have already alluded to the difficulty of reconciling this temporal designation, "And when evening came" (καὶ ὀψίας γενομένης, *kai opsias genomenēs*), and those in 6:35 (see the introduction to the present unit). Some have seen this as evidence that the present account and the preceding one originally existed independently of each other, but the reference to the coming of evening in the Johannine parallel (6:16) makes it probable that this temporal designation was part of the tradition, and the occurrence of the miracle at night in both stories (Mark 6:48; John 6:17) lends additional support to the traditional nature of the time designation. The Johannine story of the feeding of the five thousand, however, does not have any temporal reference and therefore lacks the difficulty created by Mark 6:36. It is not impossible, however, for the events of 6:35–44 to have taken place within a three- or four-hour period (see 6:35–37). The introductory part of the account ends with the disciples in the boat "in the middle of the lake" (ἐν μέσῳ τῆς θαλάσσης, *en mesō tēs thalassēs*) under duress and Jesus alone on the land.

Mark does not explain how Jesus was able to see the plight of the disciples   **6:48–50** "hard pressed in the rowing" (βασανιζομένους ἐν τῷ ἐλαύνειν, *basanizomenous en tō elaunein*). Does Mark assume Jesus's supernatural ability and "telephoto" vision? Was the night clear, and did Jesus's vantage point on the mountain enable him to see what was happening? Yet the disciples were in the middle of the sea, if ἐν μέσῳ is to be taken literally, some three to four miles away! What mountain was he on? For Mark such questions are irrelevant. All his readers need to know is that in response to his disciples' plight, Jesus came to them, for he would never leave them or forsake them (cf. Heb. 13:5). For a description of such a boat, see Mark 4:37–38. Mark gives the reason for the disciples' painful progress by an explanatory γάρ (*gar*) clause, "for the wind was against them" (ἦν γὰρ ὁ ἄνεμος ἐναντίος αὐτοῖς, *ēn gar ho anemos enantios autois*). The Markan explanatory γάρ clause appears to be based on tradition, due to the reference to the wind in the Johannine parallel (6:18). Earlier the disciples experienced a similar problem of wind (and waves) in Mark 4:37, 39, but there they could turn to Jesus. Here Jesus is absent. The description of the wind and the problem it caused suggest that the present account was never a pure epiphany story, although an epiphany was associated with it.

"Around the fourth watch" (περὶ τετάρτην φυλακήν, *peri tetartēn phylakēn*) of the night, Jesus comes to the disciples, walking "on the sea" (ἐπὶ τῆς θαλάσσης, *epi tēs thalassēs*). Unlike the Jewish reckoning of time, which involved three watches, the Roman reckoning of time involved four watches (Josephus, *Ant.* 5.6.5 §223; 18.9.6 §356), and the fourth watch would be 3 a.m. to 6 a.m. This lends support to the traditional view that Mark was written for the church in Rome (cf. 13:35). See "Audience" in the introduction. The miracle of Jesus's walking on the sea has undergone many rationalistic explanations: Jesus was walking along the shore (i.e., "beside," not "on," the sea), and a mist obstructed the disciples' view; Jesus was wading through the surf near the hidden shore (V. Taylor 1952: 327); Jesus was walking on a floating raft; Jesus was walking on a shallow mud flat reaching out into the sea (Derrett 1981); and so on. The attempt to interpret "on" the sea as "beside" the sea (cf. this use of ἐπί in John 21:1) encounters the insurmountable problem that the same preposition (ἐπί) is used with the same genitive case in 6:47, and there it must mean "on (the land)." Thus here it must mean "on the sea." Clearly, the Gospel writers understood this story as a nature miracle in which Jesus walked on top of the sea. That the incident does not take place near the shore but in the middle of the sea (6:47) makes this absolutely clear. As a result, whereas one can speculate as to "what actually happened," the meaning of the evangelists is clear. They are telling their readers that Jesus walked on the sea!

The statement that Jesus "wanted to pass by them" (ἤθελεν παρελθεῖν αὐτούς, *ēthelen parelthein autous*) has no parallel in the other two Gospel accounts and is confusing. If Jesus came to the disciples because he saw their distress, why does he now want to "pass by them" (6:48d)? Some interpret "wanted" (ἤθελεν) as an auxiliary verb with a future meaning reflecting the disciples' thinking, that is, they thought that Jesus was about to pass them by (Cranfield 1959: 226; France 2002: 272); but this use of the verb lacks any parallel in the NT (Guelich 1989: 350). Furthermore, the preceding "he comes walking" indicates that Mark does not expect his readers to provide an unstated "and the disciples thought that" before "he wanted." Also, in the majority of instances in Mark, "want" (θέλω) refers to an attained (or attainable) desire (Gundry 1993: 341). It has also been suggested that "pass by them" should be interpreted as "to save" (Fleddermann 1983).[4] Other interpretations include these: Jesus intended to test the disciples' faith by passing by (Schweizer 1970: 142); Jesus intended to walk alongside the disciples (Hill 1988); Jesus intended to walk ahead and lead the disciples, so they could "follow" him (van Iersel 1992: 1074–76).

An interpretation gaining more and more advocates is that the verb παρέρχομαι is "almost a technical term for a divine epiphany in the Septuagint" (Heil 1981: 69–72; Meier 1994: 914–19; Marcus 2000: 426). The OT evidence for this appears in Exod. 33:17–34:6; 1 Kings 19:11–13; cf. Dan. 12:1 and Gen. 32:31–32 (Lohmeyer 1957: 133–34; Guelich 1989: 350; contra van Iersel 1992:

---

4. This view is based on the interpretation of παρέρχομαι (*parerchomai*) in Amos 7:8 and 8:2, where God says that he will no longer "pass by" Israel but will save them. But this interpretation, while possible, is most unusual, and it is highly unlikely that Mark's readers would have interpreted παρέρχομαι in this manner (cf. van Iersel 1992: 1072).

1068 and 1071, who defines an epiphany more narrowly). Additional support for this interpretation is seen in the following: an indication of time is frequently associated with an epiphany (Mark 6:47–48; cf. 16:2; Matt. 28:1; Luke 1:8, 26; 2:8; 24:1; John 20:1, 19, 26; 21:4); the sudden and unexpected nature of the event is often associated with a form of the verb "to come" (Mark 6:48; cf. Matt. 14:25; 28:2; Luke 1:28; John 20:19, 26); a reaction of fear is frequently present (Mark 6:49c–50a; cf. 16:5, 8; Matt. 28:4; Luke 1:12–13, 29; 2:9; 24:5, 37), as well as a word of encouragement not to fear (Mark 6:50b–c; cf. 16:6; Matt. 28:5, 10; Luke 1:13, 30; 2:10; Heil 1981: 11–12). If we interpret Jesus's words "It is I" or "I am" as a revelation formula, this further supports such an interpretation.

In light of the above, it may be that the least unlikely interpretation of "he wanted to pass by them" is "he came to them, walking on the sea, and he desired to manifest himself to them" (by this epiphany . . . and rescue them [6:51]). Yet it is unclear whether Mark's readers/hearers would have understood it in this way during the initial reading/hearing. Whether they possessed a sufficient knowledge of the OT and the technical use of "pass by" to refer to an epiphany is uncertain. (In the vast majority of instances where παρέρχομαι occurs in the LXX, it does not bear this technical meaning.) We must furthermore remember that this understanding would have had to take place during the continuous reading of the Gospel, without pause or time for reflection. For many, the reaction to these words might have been that of most present-day readers and hearers of the passage. They may not have understood the meaning of "he meant to pass by them," but the christological teaching of the account would nevertheless have stood out clearly. Jesus, the Son of God, once again demonstrates that he is Lord over nature!

The response of the disciples to this epiphany in 6:49 is that they thought it "was [lit. 'is'] a ghost" (φάντασμά ἐστιν, *phantasma estin*). The reaction of the disciples is quite natural. They did not recognize the figure as Jesus (note the need for identification in the next verse—"It is I" [ἐγώ εἰμι, *egō eimi*]), for humans cannot walk on water. But "weightless ghosts" can. Ghosts, however, tend to frighten people, not reassure them (6:50). The word used for "ghost" (φάντασμα) is not the common term for "spirit" (πνεῦμα, *pneuma*) and is found in the NT only here and in the Matthean parallel. Seeing a ghost, the disciples quite naturally "cried out" (ἀνέκραξαν, *anekraxan*). Although this verb can be used positively to indicate reverential awe in the presence of deity or Jesus (1:23; Luke 4:33; 8:28; cf. Mark 3:11; 5:7; 9:24; 10:47–48), here in conjunction with "terrified" and "Have courage" in the next verse, it is used negatively to mean "cried out in terror." Mark explains the reason for this crying out in 6:50a by the γάρ clause: "For all saw him and were terrified" (πάντες γὰρ αὐτὸν εἶδον καὶ ἐταράχθησαν, *pantes gar auton eidon kai etarachthēsan*). The "him" refers, of course, to Jesus, but the disciples did not recognize "him" and thought that they saw an "it," a ghost. The result is that they were "terrified" (ἐταράχθησαν, a hapax legomenon in Mark).

Although this is a typical Markan γάρ explanatory clause and explains why the disciples cried out, its content is traditional, as the parallel in Matt. 14:26 (cf. also John 6:19) indicates.

Jesus seeks to encourage the disciples and to allay their fears by an immediate word of reassurance: "Have courage!" (θαρσεῖτε, *tharseite*). The "immediately" here should be given its full temporal meaning. This is due to the fact that we have "but" (δέ), not "and," preceding "immediately." "Have courage" also serves as a word of encouragement in 10:49 (cf. also Matt. 9:2, 22; John 16:33; Acts 23:11). It means "Be of good cheer," "Take heart," and so on. Jesus continues his encouragement by identifying himself to the disciples, "It is I [ἐγώ εἰμι]; stop being afraid" (μὴ φοβεῖσθε, *mē phobeisthe*). In the original setting of the story, "It is I" probably served as an identification formula with an emphasis on the pronoun "I" (Mark 13:6; 14:62; Matt. 26:22, 25; John 9:9; Acts 10:21). The disciples should not fear, for it was not a phantom approaching them but Jesus. Clearly the terror of the disciples left little opportunity for their reflecting on the theological significance of this identification. However, Mark may intend his readers to see a more pregnant meaning in these words. In numerous places in the OT, God identifies himself with the words "I am" (Exod. 3:14; Deut. 32:39; Isa. 41:4; 43:10; 46:4; 51:12; cf. 47:8, 10; 48:12; also John 8:58; 18:5–6). As a result this expression has a "solemn and sacral use in the OT, as well as the NT, Gnosticism, and pagan Greek religious writings" (R. Brown 1966: 533; cf. also 534–38). This, along with the fact that in the OT, God is portrayed as walking on the waters (Job 9:8; 38:16; Ps. 77:19; Isa. 43:16; Hab. 3:15; cf. also Sir. 24:5–6), would further give to "It is I" (lit. "I am") a theophanic sense (contra van Iersel 1992: 1070). The Christology of Mark's readers was far more developed than that of the disciples during Jesus's ministry. As a result it is quite possible that Mark expected them to see in the "I am" of this verse a reference to Jesus's divine nature. Whether they knew all the OT background for this title is unclear, but they had already read in the Gospel about Jesus's divine sonship; his lordship over disease, demons, and nature; his divine prerogative to forgive sins; and so on. Mark's Christian readers would also have brought to the reading/hearing of the Gospel other christological teachings. Thus it is not at all impossible that they would have understood the "I am" as a reference to Jesus's divine nature. As a result of who Jesus is, the command, "Have courage," is reassuring. Their previous rescue from the stormy sea by Jesus (4:35–41) should have given the disciples additional encouragement not to fear. For a similar command by Jesus, see 5:36. For Mark's readers, as for readers today, Jesus's words are likewise reassuring and comforting in times of distress and turmoil.

6:51–52   The presence of Jesus and his entrance into the boat results in the wind ceasing (6:51). Whereas in 4:35–41 Jesus commands the wind and the sea to be still, here his simple presence in the boat causes the wind to cease. This may very well have been the traditional ending of the story (cf. John 6:21; Matt. 14:32

[v. 33 looks like a Matthean comment]).[5] This indicates that the miracle-rescue dimension of the account is integral to the story. Although Mark does not directly state that Jesus was responsible for the wind ceasing, he clearly implies this by describing it as ceasing when Jesus enters the boat and by the disciples' reaction, "And they were utterly [lit. 'very, exceedingly'] astonished within themselves" (καὶ λίαν ἐκ περισσοῦ ἐν ἑαυτοῖς ἐξίσταντο, *kai lian ek perissou en heautois existanto*). Whereas in 6:50 "terrified" is negative, "astonished" (ἐξίσταντο) in 6:51 need not be (Dwyer 1996: 131–34). Elsewhere (2:12; 5:42; contra 3:21) it is used positively (see 1:21–22; 4:41), and this is clearly how Matt. 14:33 understands the disciples' response. Mark portrays the disciples as experiencing astonishment and awe as they see the greatness and glory of the Son of God. The degree of astonishment is emphasized by the twofold use of the terms "very" (λίαν) and "exceedingly" (ἐκ περισσοῦ; see Neirynck 1988: 103). Astonishment is a legitimate response when experiencing Jesus's miracle-working powers, but the disciples should be familiar with this by now. In light of all they have experienced, they should not be surprised and astonished. The explanatory expression that follows in 6:52 reveals that this astonishment should be interpreted negatively (Guelich 1989: 352; Donahue and Harrington 2002: 214). It is produced less by a reverential awe than by a lack of understanding and hardness of heart.

The reference to the disciples' lack of understanding concerning the loaves (6:52; 6:37, 38, 41, 44) supports the view that Jesus's walking on the water and the feeding of the five thousand were associated together in the pre-Markan tradition. The assumption that the disciples were sitting among twelve baskets of bread in the boat (Gundry 1993: 338) involves questions concerning the original setting of the story in the life of Jesus, that is, the first *Sitz im Leben*. Mark, however, does not mention this.[6] What is said concerning their not understanding "about the loaves" could equally be said about the stilling of the storm (4:35–41), the healing of the demoniac (5:1–20), the raising of Jairus's daughter (5:21–24, 35–43), or the healing of the hemorrhaging woman (5:25–34). The feeding of the five thousand may have been singled out because it is the only miracle story since 6:1ff. and immediately precedes the present account. (Cf. Hooker 1991: 169, who sees their association as being due to the connection between the crossing of the Red Sea and the miraculous feeding of the Israelites with manna in the story of the exodus.) By now the disciples should know the answer to the question "Who then is this?" (4:41). Their lack of understanding is seen by Mark as culpable. They do not truly believe that Jesus is the Son of God or understand what the implications of this are. If they did, they would have understood the great might and power of the Son of

---

5. It is also possible that the concluding part of 6:51, if interpreted positively, could have served as the original ending of the story.

6. If Mark had intended his readers to reflect on the presence of this bread in the boat, after "about the loaves" he could have simply added something like "among them." Of course, if one denies the miracle of 6:30–44, any reference to real loaves is ludicrous.

God and not have feared their circumstance (6:48–50) or have been surprised and astonished (6:51) over this experience.

Mark states that, instead of recognizing the implications of the miracle of the feeding of the five thousand, "their heart had been hardened" (ἦν αὐτῶν ἡ καρδία πεπωρωμένη, ēn autōn hē kardia pepōrōmenē). One tends to expect that the Markan explanatory clause begun earlier in this verse might end with a reference to their eyes being blind (4:12; 8:18; cf. also 7:18). "Hardened hearts" have been mentioned as a quality of Jesus's opponents (3:5), but here and in 8:17 it is a quality of the disciples. The use of the singular "heart" probably emphasizes the corporate nature of the disciples' response in these two instances. They possess a single, hardened heart.

Summary

The Markan christological emphasis can be clearly seen in the present account. Once again, Jesus demonstrates that he is Lord of nature (cf. 4:35–41; 6:30–44). The question "Who is this man?" raised in 4:41 is answered once more by the manifestation of the authority and power of the Son of God. For Mark, however, Jesus's walking on the sea involves more than simply a miracle of great power. This miracle must be interpreted in the context of all the miracles and confessional statements recorded thus far. In addition, the feeding of the five thousand and the walking on the sea reminds Mark's readers that these are the kinds of things that God does in the OT. He provides manna for his people and roams over the seas. If the interpretation suggested in 6:48c is correct, Mark wants his readers to see in this event a revelation and epiphany of Jesus's divine nature. This is further revealed in Jesus's use of the divine "I am" to identify himself. Clearly for Mark, Jesus transcends all of the available categories such as teacher, prophet, Christ, Son of God, and so on. He is absolutely unique. He is the "only" Son of God and possesses some sort of "divinity."[7]

Several implications flow out of the Markan Christology. It should be evident by now to the readers of Mark that Jesus's crucifixion, with which they are familiar, was not due to weakness or helplessness on the part of the Son of God. The Christ portrayed by Mark in 4:35–6:52 is no feeble and frail subject of the Roman authorities. He is a mighty Christ, who is Lord over disease and death, demons and nature. Although Mark has not yet explained to his readers why Jesus was crucified, there must be some important reason why. That answer does not lie in this mighty Son of God being unable to resist or overcome those who eventually put him to death. Jesus's crucifixion is clearly not a result of weakness! Along with the christological teachings of this passage, there is also an eschatological dimension. The kingdom that Jesus announced as having come is indeed manifesting itself in the person and work of Jesus Christ, the Son of God.

7. Cf. Marcus (2000: 432), "Although . . . Mark never explicitly says that Jesus is divine, he comes very close to doing so here."

Still another Markan emphasis that appears in the present account and plays an increasingly important role involves the disciples' lack of understanding. This becomes brutally clear in 6:52, where Mark states that their ignorance is due to their "hardness of heart." Despite their unique calling (1:16–20; 3:13–19), privileged instruction (3:31–35; 4:13–20, 34), commissioning, gift of miracle-working power, and participation in Jesus's ministry (6:7–13, 30, 35–44), they still do not understand. Like the Pharisees (3:5) and Pharaoh of old (Exod. 7:3, 13, 22; 8:15; cf. also Israel's hard heart in Ezek. 11:19), the disciples continue to fail. This failure will come to a climax in Jesus's verbal rebuke in 8:14–21 and in their behavior in 14:32–50, 66–72. Mark, however, does not point out their weaknesses and failures because he is on a vendetta against the disciples. On the contrary, they will be restored, and Jesus will lead his sheep (14:27–28; 16:7) after the resurrection. Mark is aware that their failures are part of the historical account, but the failures of the disciples also serve a pastoral function of providing hope to his readers. Even though the disciples failed time and time again, they were nevertheless Jesus's servants and apostles. Thus Mark's readers, despite their failures, can also through repentance and faith continue to be Jesus's servants. And for present-day readers, it gives hope that our failures can be forgiven and that despite our weakness God may still use us to proclaim the good news of Jesus Christ and bring healing and hope to a hurting world.

Additional Notes

6:45. "To the other side" (εἰς τὸ πέραν) is missing in 𝔓⁴⁵ W f¹, but the omission is probably due to a scribal attempt to smooth out the geographical difficulties (Guelich 1989: 346).

6:47. Some MSS (𝔓⁴⁵ D f¹) add "already" (πάλαι), but this is not found in ℵ A B K L W f¹³ it vg.

6:51. "Astonished" (ἐξίσταντο) is found in ℵ B L Δ vg. Other MSS (A D K W Θ f¹³) add "and were marveling" (καὶ ἐθαύμαζον). The latter may be due to a scribe's familiarity with Acts 2:7 (ἐξίσταντο … καὶ ἐθαύμαζον).

6:52. José O'Callaghan (1972) shook the world of NT scholarship by claiming that a Qumran fragment (7Q5) was in reality a fragment of Mark 6:52–53 (cf. also Thiede 1992). The alleged identification is based on only ten Greek letters that can be read clearly and requires a textual emendation in the second line. Nearly all textual critics reject the supposed identification (cf. Stanton 1995: 20–32; Gundry 1999). Donahue and Harrington (2002: 214) make the astute comment that it would be strange indeed to find in a community that so strongly stressed ritual purity a fragment of a section of Mark that precedes Jesus's mitigation of OT purity regulations (7:1–23).

E. A Summary of Jesus's Healings at Gennesaret (6:53–56)

The present account is a summary report betraying a heavy Markan hand. Source-critical proposals concerning the origin of the report include its being a pre-Markan tradition (Guelich 1989: 355), a pre-Markan tradition heavily reworked by Mark (Marcus 2000: 437), and a summary created by Mark from earlier reported traditions and miscellaneous information that he possessed (Hooker 1991: 171). Numerous Markan grammatical and stylistic traits are found throughout the summary. These include the genitive absolute (6:54; cf. 5:2), the impersonal plural (6:55), "began" (ἤρξαντο, ērxanto) + the infinitive (6:55), "sick" (τοὺς κακῶς ἔχοντας, tous kakōs echontas; 6:55; see 1:32–34), "and . . . immediately" (καὶ . . . εὐθύς, kai . . . euthys; 6:54; see 1:10), "mats" (κραβάττοις, krabattois; 6:55; cf. 2:4); "as many as" (ὅσοι, hosoi; 6:56; cf. 3:10); and so on.

Along with the heavily Markan nature of the present summary (Pryke 1978: 15, 142, 160; Gnilka 1978: 271–72), two other factors favor this being a Markan summary created from earlier reported traditions and information. First, this summary alludes to previous accounts reported in Mark: arriving by boat (5:1, 21, 32–34, 45), people bringing the sick on mats (2:1–12; cf. 1:32), and the sick touching Jesus's garment and being healed ("saved," ἐσῴζοντο, esōzonto; 6:56; cf. 5:28; also 3:10). To argue that these allusions came from stories and summaries already joined together in a pre-Markan complex is less convincing than that Mark himself created the summary out of the various traditions that he had incorporated into his Gospel. (In most reconstructions of this pre-Markan complex and its editorial work, the editorial work looks very much like Mark!) Second, it is unlikely that a summary such as this would ever have been passed down as an isolated piece of tradition. That Mark created the present summary is much easier to conceive than that Mark possessed a pre-Markan complex of 4:35–5:43 and 6:32–52 that began with a summary (3:7–12) and concluded with a summary (6:52–56; forming an *inclusio*) and that looks extremely Markan in style, grammar, and content.

With this summary Mark concludes his "boat" traditions (4:1, 35–5:43; 6:32–52; cf. 3:9) and will soon tell of Jesus's mission to the gentiles (7:24–37). Why Mark placed 7:1–23 between the "boat" and "gentile mission" traditions is not clear. See the introduction to 7:1–23. The present account consists of three parts: (1) the completion of the voyage of Jesus and the disciples (6:53), (2) the people flocking to Jesus and bringing their sick (6:54–56a), and (3) a description of Jesus's great healing ability (6:56b–d).

Exegesis and Exposition

[53]And having crossed over, they came ⌜to land⌝, to Gennesaret, and they anchored [there]. [54]And when they got out of the boat, they [the people] immediately recognized him [55][and] ran throughout all that countryside and began to bring the sick on their mats to wherever they were hearing that he [Jesus] was. [56]And wherever he was entering, whether villages, cities, or the countryside, they were placing the sick in the marketplaces and were begging him that they might touch even the tassel of his garment. And as many as touched him were being healed.

This introductory seam ties the present summary to the preceding incident. **6:53** The Markan meaning of "having crossed over" (διαπεράσαντες, *diaperasantes*) is unclear. Does it mean "crossed over" from Bethsaida or from the middle of the sea (6:47) back to the western side? Either is possible, for "voyaging to the middle of the sea and back again covers enough water to count as a crossing" (Gundry 1993: 346). "Gennesaret" is probably a Greek rendering of Hebrew גִּינֵיסַר (*gînîsar*, Gennesar; 1 Macc. 11:67; Josephus, *J.W.* 3.10.7 §506) and refers to a fertile plain, three and a half miles long and one and a half miles wide, lying on the northwest coast of the Sea of Galilee between Capernaum and Tiberias. A geographical problem arises due to the fact that the goal of the previous voyage is stated as being Bethsaida (6:45). If 6:53 refers to the conclusion of this earlier voyage, a serious question arises, for instead of "having crossed over" and landing at Bethsaida, they, "having crossed over," land at Gennesaret. Several suggestions have been put forward: (1) The disciples were blown off course by the wind (6:48) and, although their intended destination was Bethsaida, they landed at Gennesaret (J. Edwards 2002: 202). (2) This verse assumes a successful completion of the journey to Bethsaida and a subsequent recrossing from Bethsaida to Gennesaret. (3) Mark 6:45 should be understood as referring to a journey "toward," in the direction of, Bethsaida. The Greek term πρός (*pros*, toward) does not assume a landing at Bethsaida. Mark uses the term εἰς (*eis*, at) to designate a landing, as in 6:53 ("at Gennesaret") and 8:22 ("at Bethsaida"). There is therefore no contradiction between 6:53 and 6:45, for Mark says only that the disciples were sailing toward the direction of Bethsaida (Pesch 1980a: 359; Gundry 1993: 346). (4) The two geographical designations in 6:53 (Gennesaret) and 45 (Bethsaida) are traditional, but Mark has clumsily placed together the two different sea-voyage traditions possessing these designations and created a geographical conflict (Marcus 2000: 437; cf. Guelich 1989: 356–57). Frequently, the last view assumes that Mark was either ignorant of the geography of Galilee or indifferent toward such geographical concerns.[1] Alternative 1 or 3 seems the most likely.

---

1. Hooker (1991: 171) argues that originally 6:32–52 was followed by 8:22–26, but in John 6:1–14 the feeding of the five thousand and Jesus's walking on the sea (6:16–21) are associated together, just as in Mark (cf. 6:30–44 and 45–52), and the latter incident concludes at Capernaum (John 6:17, 24), that is, on the plain of Gennesaret.

6:54–56a "And when they got out of the boat" (καὶ ἐξελθόντων αὐτῶν ἐκ τοῦ πλοίου, *kai exelthontōn autōn ek tou ploiou*) is a typical Markan genitive absolute (Pryke 1978: 62–67) and along with the following "and immediately" is identical to the Markan seam in 5:2. The only difference is that in the former instance the subject is singular, whereas here it is plural. The people (lit.) "immediately having recognized him" (εὐθὺς ἐπιγνόντες αὐτόν, *euthys epignontes auton*) recalls 6:33 (possibly Markan), where Jesus is "recognized." From this point onward in the summary, the disciples recede into the background, and Mark focuses on Jesus. This again reminds us that the theme of Mark's Gospel is Jesus Christ, the Son of God (1:1), not the disciples! "They ran throughout all that countryside" (περιέδραμον ὅλην τὴν χώραν, *periedramon holēn tēn chōran*) is an example of the impersonal use of the third-person plural in Mark (V. Taylor 1952: 47; see 1:21–22). This summary resembles the Markan summaries in 1:32–34 and 3:10 and suggests the Markan origin of the present account. "All that countryside" (cf. 1:5; 5:1, 10) emphasizes the spiritual magnetism of the Son of God (Donahue and Harrington 2002: 217), as does the double use of "wherever" (ὅπου, *hopou*) in 6:55 and 56. "And wherever he was entering" (καὶ ὅπου ἂν εἰσεπορεύετο, *kai hopou an eiseporeueto*) alludes to the various places mentioned in earlier accounts: "villages" (κώμας, *kōmas*) in 6:6 (a Markan summary), 36; "cities" (πόλεις, *poleis*) in 1:33, 45 (a Markan summary); 5:14; 6:33 (a Markan comment?); "countryside" (lit. "fields," ἀγρούς, *agrous*) in 5:14; 6:36; and "marketplaces" (ἀγοραῖς, *agorais*); compare 7:4 (also 12:38). Their bringing the sick to Jesus recalls 1:34; 2:2–3; 3:10; 5:24b–34; reference to the crowds recalls 1:32–34, 37–39, 45; 2:1–2, 13, 15, 18; 3:7–10, 20, 31–32; 4:1, 10, 36; 5:14–17, 21, 24b–31, 38–39; 6:2, 31, 33–44, 54–55.

6:56b–d The people's "begging" (παρεκάλουν, *parekaloun*) Jesus recalls 1:40; 5:10, 12, 17, 18, 23 (cf. also 7:23; 8:22). "That" (ἵνα, *hina*) introduces the content of their petitions rather than the purpose (see 3:9–10). The request is that they might touch even "the tassel of his garment" (τοῦ κρασπέδου τοῦ ἱματίου αὐτοῦ, *tou kraspedou tou himatiou autou*). This recalls 3:10 and builds on the words of the hemorrhaging woman in 5:28, "If I touch even his garment, I shall be saved" (cf. Matt. 9:20 and Luke 8:44, who add "tassel" [κρασπέδου]). The κρασπέδου refers to one of the four tassels worn by Jewish men on their robes in accordance with Num. 15:38–39 and Deut. 22:12 (κράσπεδα in the LXX). Compare Matt. 23:5 (cf. also Let. Aris. 158; *b. Ta'an.* 22a; *b. Menaḥ.* 43a; Sifre on Num. 15:38 [§115]). This incidental comment indicates that Jesus was a law-abiding Jew (Booth 1986: 31–32).

The Markan emphasis here is christological in nature. Emphasis on the faith associated with touching Jesus in 5:27–34 should not be read into the present summary (contra Guelich 1989: 357). As in 3:10, the emphasis falls on Jesus's miraculous power to heal, not on the importance of human faith (cf. Acts 5:15; 19:11–12). The presence of faith is assumed by the desire to touch Jesus's garment, but it is not emphasized. Since this Gospel is about Jesus

Christ, the Son of God, Mark focuses on Jesus and his great power to heal. "Even" (κἄν, *kan*) further emphasizes the healing ability of Jesus.

The account concludes with "And as many as touched him [or 'it,' the garment] were being healed [lit. 'saved']" (καὶ ὅσοι ἂν ἥψαντο αὐτοῦ ἐσῴζοντο, *kai hosoi an hēpsanto autou esōzonto*). This statement ties the present summary even more closely to the healing of the hemorrhaging woman in 5:27–28, where the term "saved" (σωθήσομαι, *sōthēsomai*), rather than "healed" (ἐθεράπευσεν, *etherapeusen*; cf. 3:10), is also used. The use of the imperfect "were being healed/saved" here and throughout 6:55–56 emphasizes the continuing and enduring ability of Jesus to heal. Mark wants his readers to understand that the healings of Jesus were not rare or occasional occurrences but an ongoing ministry.

Summary

In the present summary, Mark emphasizes once again Jesus's great ability to heal. He heightens his description of Jesus's healing ministry at Gennesaret by referring to the "whole" countryside coming (6:55), and that healing took place "wherever" Jesus went (6:55, 56a), whether villages, cities, fields, or marketplaces (6:56b). The great healing power of Jesus extended even to the fringes of his garments (6:56c), and everyone ("as many as") who touched even the tassels of his garment was healed (6:56d). The continuing nature of this healing ministry is further emphasized by the use of the imperfect tense throughout 6:55–56. By his summary Mark seeks to "give the impression of a ministry that is broader and more influential than the few brief examples of healings . . . [he has] narrated" (Hedrick 1984: 311). Mark is not the least bit embarrassed over the wonder-working ability of Jesus.[2] In the present account Mark also emphasizes the great fame and magnetic personality of Jesus. In Mark, the people are almost always supporters of Jesus, and this indicates that the death of Jesus must be understood as contrary to the people's wishes and desires (14:2). See the unit summary for 3:7–12. This stands in sharp contrast to what Jesus experienced in Nazareth (6:1–6a).

The present summary makes no mention of the preaching/teaching dimension in Jesus's ministry or of his expulsion of demons. This lack has caused some to see the present summary as being based on tradition (Gundry 1993: 345). Yet in an account in which the hand of Mark is so clearly present (see the introduction to this unit), it would have been very easy for the evangelist to have added such a reference, if he desired. Within the various summaries of Mark, we discover healing and exorcism associated (1:32–34; 3:10–11); preaching and exorcism associated (1:39; 3:14–15); teaching and exorcism

---

2. It is surprising that the view that Mark sought to oppose a θεῖος ἀνήρ (*theios anēr*) Christology that portrayed Jesus as a wonder-worker ever received as much press as it did. Mark clearly seeks to emphasize Jesus's great miracle-working power and the astonishment this created (see 1:21–22). In our present account, just touching the fringe of his garment brings healing.

associated (1:21–27); teaching and healing associated (6:2, 5); and preaching, healing, and exorcism associated (6:12–13). Why one or more of these dimensions may be omitted by Mark in an editorial comment is unclear. It is unlikely, however, that in so doing Mark is seeking to minimize these aspects of Jesus's ministry, for references to Jesus's teaching are found throughout 7:1–14:43, and two additional exorcisms by Jesus are reported in 7:24–30 and 9:14–29. Probably Mark expected his readers/hearers to assume that each of these editorial comments should be interpreted inclusively in light of what is said in the others.

Some have suggested that Mark intends to contrast the faith of the people described in the present account with the disciples' lack of understanding in the previous one (Guelich 1989: 358; Brooks 1991: 112). According to this interpretation, the people's recognition of Jesus in 6:54 stands in sharp contrast to the disciples' lack of such a recognition (6:49–50). Yet Mark makes no clear tie between these two events. If he wanted his readers to see such a contrast, he could have added something like, "*And they did not recognize him but* thought it was a ghost" (6:49). Mark makes no such link between these two incidents. Furthermore, the disciples' lack of understanding involves a theological flaw and misunderstanding, whereas the crowd's understanding involves simply a cognitive recognition that the person in front of them is Jesus of Nazareth. The key Markan emphasis in the present account is once again a christological one. The great miracle-working power of Jesus of Nazareth demonstrates once again that he is the Christ, the Son of God (1:1).

Additional Note

6:53. "To land" (ἐπὶ τὴν γῆν) can describe the participle "having crossed over" (διαπεράσαντες) or the verb "came" (ἦλθον). It makes better sense to have it describe the verb, for "having crossed over" refers to travel by sea (cf. 5:21).

F. Jesus and the Tradition of the Elders (7:1–23)

The present account appears in Mark as a unified pericope. It has no necessary tie with the preceding material. This indicates that it (or its component parts) circulated as an isolated unit without a specific geographical or chronological tie to another account. It assumes only a context such as "Once in the ministry of Jesus . . ." (K. Schmidt 1919: 196). The introduction (7:1–2a) begins with an incident in which Jesus's disciples are observed as eating without having first followed the ritual cleansing prescribed by the tradition of the elders. This is followed by a Markan explanation of this Jewish tradition to his gentile readers (7:2b should be included in this) that breaks the flow of the account. The narrative resumes with a question addressed to Jesus by the Pharisees and scribes as to why his disciples (and he by implication) do not keep the traditions (7:5). Jesus's response consists of two parts. The first (7:6–13) centers on two OT passages and involves a two-part attack on the tradition of the elders (7:6–8 and 9–13). Each part is introduced by "And he said/was saying to them" (ὁ δὲ εἶπεν αὐτοῖς/καὶ ἔλεγεν αὐτοῖς, *ho de eipen autois/kai elegen autois*; 7:6a and 9a), followed by an OT quotation (7:6b–7 and 10), and concludes by contrasting the tradition of the Pharisees, stemming from men, and the commandment/word of God (7:8–9 and 11–13). The second part deals with Jesus's teaching on what defiles and what does not defile (7:14–23). This involves a parable addressed to the crowds (7:14–15) and the private explanation of the parable to the disciples (7:17), which consists of two parts (7:18–19 and 20–23).

Many commentators show less interest in discussing the present form of the account than in seeking to reconstruct a *Traditionsgeschichte* or history of how the present form of the account came into existence (cf. Guelich 1989: 360–62; Marcus 2000: 447–48).[1] Some scholars argue that the present account, minus the Markan redaction in 7:2b, 3–4, 19c, existed as a unity before Mark (Cranfield 1959: 230). Some see two separate traditions lying behind the present account. One centering on the "tradition of the elders" consisted of 7:1–8 (or 1–13), and the other tradition centering on the issue of "clean and unclean" consisted of 7:14–23.[2] The former was a controversy

---

1. The present account is an excellent example of C. S. Lewis's criticism of reviewers or commentators: "Until you come to be reviewed yourself you would never believe how little of an ordinary review is taken up by criticism in the strict sense: by evaluation, praise, or censure, of the book actually written. Most of it is taken up with imaginary histories of the process by which you wrote it" (Lewis 1975: 114).

2. For a defense of the essential historicity of 7:14–23, see Stettler 2004.

story with a pronouncement (7:6–8 or 6–13) directed to the Pharisees and scribes (7:1–2, 5); the latter was a teaching narrative addressed to the people (7:14–15), with private instruction to the disciples (7:17–23). Others see an original historical core (7:1–2, 5, 15) to which have been added scriptural expansions (7:6–8, 9–13), secondary teachings concerning eating unclean food (7:18b–19), a list of the sins that come out of the heart (7:20–23), and Markan editorial work (7:3–4, 14, 19c, with additional Markan shaping of traditional material in 15, 17–18a; Marcus 2000: 447–48).[3] Others see a great deal more Markan redactional activity throughout the passage (Pryke 1978: 15–16, 143, 161; Booth 1986: 52–53).

I have serious questions as to whether the tools of historical and literary criticism are precise enough to distinguish between a unified tradition going back to a situation in the ministry of Jesus that has been heavily reworked by Mark, a two- or three-stage formation of the tradition that Mark subsequently heavily reworked, and various independent traditions that were put together by and heavily reworked by Mark. That Mark (or a pre-Markan editor) saw no conflict between the beginning of the pericope involving the Pharisees and scribes (7:1–2, 5) and the later involvement of the crowd (7:14–15) and disciples (7:17–23) weakens historical reconstructions based on the supposedly contradictory nature of the subject matter found in the present account. There is no need to assume that the reference to the Pharisees and scribes in 7:1–2, 5 excludes the presence of the crowd (7:14–15; cf. 3:1–6 and 10:1–2, where both groups are together). As to the view that two different issues (the "tradition of the elders" and "clean and unclean") are being dealt with in the present account, these are certainly not contradictory issues. They are in fact intimately related, for the question of not keeping the "tradition of the elders" raised in 7:5 involves the basic issue of what defiles a person in 7:15, that is, what is "clean and unclean." If Mark were simply a scissors-and-paste editor, the laser surgery performed by various literary critics would be more credible, but this naive form-critical assumption is out of date. The present account is not a neat quilt of distinct pieces of tradition sewn together. Rather, it is a holistic account that flows together from the hand of Mark. Whatever the original form of the tradition(s) Mark incorporated, the reconstruction of the form of these traditions before Mark used them is highly speculative.

Although no necessary chronological or geographical ties exist between the present account and the immediate context, there are several literary ones. One involves the word association between the loave(s) "of bread" in 7:2, 5 and 6:30–44, 52; 7:27; 8:1–9. I will argue that Mark does not intend his readers to think that the bread of 7:2 and 5 are the same loaves as in 6:30–44 and 52 (see 7:2), but it may very well be that the association of these various accounts is due to the common appearance of this term. A second literary

---

3. Some see this Markan editorial work as being the work of a pre-Markan editor, but once again the alleged pre-Markan editorial work looks remarkably Markan.

tie between the present account and its context involves the incomprehension of the disciples (cf. 7:18–19a with 6:52 and 8:17; also cf. 4:13, 40–41). A final literary tie between the present account and what follows involves the issue of clean versus unclean. Jesus's teachings in 7:2, 5, 15, 20, 23 help prepare Mark's readers for Jesus's mission to "unclean dogs" (7:24–30). The present account introduces an ominous change (contrast 6:31–56 and 7:1–2, 5) in which the Jewish leadership in Jerusalem begins to concentrate its attack against Jesus.

Exegesis and Exposition

[1]And the Pharisees and some of the scribes having come from Jerusalem ⌜gather around⌝ him [Jesus], [2]and because ⌜they saw⌝ [that] some of his disciples eat bread with unclean hands, that is, with unwashed [hands]—[3](for the Pharisees and all the Jews, unless they wash their hands with the fist, do not eat because of holding to the tradition of the elders, [4]and [when they come] from the marketplace, unless they wash themselves, they do not eat, and there are many other traditions they have ⌜received and observe⌝ [such as] the washings of cups and pitchers and bronze vessels ⌜ ⌝). [5]And the Pharisees and the scribes were asking him, "Why do your disciples not walk according to the tradition of the elders but eat bread with unclean hands?" [6]And [Jesus] said to them, "Well prophesied Isaiah concerning you hypocrites, as it is written, 'This people honors me with their lips, but their heart is far distant from me. [7]Vainly they are worshiping me, teaching [as] teachings precepts of men.' [8]Abandoning the commandment of God, you hold the tradition of men." [9]And he was saying to them, "How well you nullify the commandment of God in order that you may establish your tradition! [10]For Moses said, 'Honor your father and your mother,' and 'The one who speaks evil of father or mother, let him certainly die.' [11]But *you* say, 'If a man should say to [his] father and mother, Whatever you should have benefited from me is Corban, that is, a gift [to God],' [12]you no longer permit him to do anything for [his] father or mother, [13][and thus you are] making void the word of God by your tradition that you pass down. And you do many similar things."

[14]And having again called the crowd, he began to say to them, "Listen to me, all of you, and understand. [15]There is nothing outside a person that, entering into him, is able to make him unclean, but the things coming out of a person are the things making him unclean." ⌜ ⌝ [17]And when he entered into a house away from the crowd, his disciples were asking him [to explain] the parable. [18]And he says to them, "So are you also without understanding? Do you not know that anything [from] outside that enters into a person is not able to make him unclean, [19]because it does not enter into his heart but into his stomach and passes out into the latrine?" ([This he said] cleansing all foods.) [20]And he was saying, "That which comes out of a person, that makes him unclean. [21]For from inside, out of the human heart, proceed evil thoughts, fornications, thefts, murders, [22]adulteries, covetings, evils, deceit, licentiousness, envy, slander, arrogance, folly. [23]All these evil things from within proceed out and make the person unclean."

7:1–2   The mention of "the Pharisees" recalls earlier references to the Pharisees, who directed hostile questions toward Jesus (2:16, 24; cf. also 3:6), and "some of the scribes having come [down] from Jerusalem" (τινες τῶν γραμματέων ἐλθόντες ἀπὸ Ἰεροσολύμων, *tines tōn grammateōn elthontes apo Hierosolymōn*) recalls 3:22, where they responded with hostility toward Jesus's exorcisms. The listing of both groups gathering together against Jesus is especially sinister (Marcus 2000: 440). The generalization "the Pharisees" (οἱ Φαρισαῖοι, *hoi Pharisaioi*) is not intended by Mark to imply that the entire sect of the Pharisees were present on this occasion but only that the Pharisees present represented the Pharisees as a whole (for "Pharisees," see 2:16–17). "Gather around" (συνάγονται, *synagontai*) is used positively in 2:2; 4:1; 5:21; 6:30, but here it gives the sense that they were ganging up against Jesus (cf. 3:6). Mark's description of the scribes having come from Jerusalem indicates that they have come from the center of opposition toward Jesus and represent the leaders of Israel. Whether they were on an official mission to spy out Jesus cannot be determined.

The reference to "some of Jesus's disciples" eating with unclean (lit. "common," κοιναῖς, *koinais*) hands does not necessarily imply that within the Markan community certain Christians practiced the Jewish traditions concerning defilement and others did not (contra Hultgren 1979: 118; Marcus 2000: 452–53). That Mark has to explain this "Jewish" issue to his readers suggests that this was not a problem that concerned them (Gundry 1993: 348). "They eat bread" (ἐσθίουσιν τοὺς ἄρτους, *esthiousin tous artous*; lit. "they eat the breads") is unusual. One expects the singular "bread" (ἄρτον, *arton*) as in 7:5, but without the article. It is uncertain whether "the breads" in 7:2 is intended to refer back to "the breads" left over in 6:43 and perhaps taken to Gennesaret in 6:52 (Gundry 1993: 348). The use of the singular "the bread" in 7:5, where it refers simply to eating food (Lohmeyer 1957: 139n1), weakens such a connection. The reference to "bread(s)" in 6:37–38, 41, 44, 52; 7:2, 5, 27; 8:4–6, 14, 16, 19 may have caused these accounts to be associated together by word linkage, but it does not require that Mark be referring to the same bread(s) in 6:37–52 and 7:2, 5. If this pericope originally existed as an isolated unit in the oral period (see the introduction to this unit), then at this stage it had no tie to the bread of the feeding miracles in 6:30–44 and 8:1–10. As in 2:18, 23–24, the behavior of Jesus's disciples provides a convenient means for attacking Jesus.

At this point Mark begins to explain this unfamiliar Jewish custom to his readers by clarifying what "unclean" (κοιναῖς)[4] or "defiled" hands means with a typical "that is" (τοῦτ' ἔστιν, *tout' estin*; cf. ὅ ἐστιν [*ho estin*] in 3:17; 7:11, 34; 12:42; 15:16, 42). They are "unwashed" in the sense of being ceremonially unwashed and therefore ritualistically unclean (cf. Lev. 11:32; 15:11–12). Hygienic issues are not to be read into the situation. The issue is ritual cleanness. A further, more detailed explanation of this practice follows in 7:3–4 with a typically Markan γάρ (*gar*, for) clause (V. Taylor 1952: 335; contra Guelich 1989: 363).

---

4. For a similar use of κοιναῖς, cf. 1 Macc. 1:47, 62; Josephus, *Ant.* 11.8.7 §346.

The following Markan explanation reveals that the evangelist's audience was primarily non-Jewish and unfamiliar with the clean-versus-unclean Pharisaic traditions.[5] This is further demonstrated by the reference to "all the Jews" (πάντες οἱ Ἰουδαῖοι, *pantes hoi Ioudaioi*) as a group distinguished from his readers, and by the omission of 7:3–4 in the Matthean parallel, since Matthew was written to an apparently Jewish-Christian audience familiar with such traditions. If interpreted literally, "all the Jews" is an incorrect statement. It was the Pharisees and their followers who were most closely associated with keeping the tradition of the elders. One must allow room for some hyperbole or generalizing at this point on the part of Mark. Certainly one would not expect Mark to write, "The Pharisees and approximately *x* percent of the Jewish people . . . ," or even, "The Pharisees and many Jews. . . ." To gentiles one of the most distinctive features of the Jewish people was their concern for kosher living, and no clear distinction would be made by gentiles between the Pharisaic rules of defilement based on tradition and the Jewish food and eating regulations based on the OT (Lev. 11:46–47). Both would have been seen as Jewish boundary markers. Compare, for example, Let. Aris. 305: "And as is the custom of all the Jews, they washed their hands in the sea and prayed to God and then devoted themselves to reading and translating the particular passage *upon which they were engaged*" (Charles 1913: 120; cf. also Luke 11:37–38; John 2:6; Jdt. 12:7; Sib. Or. 3.591–93; *m. Yad.* 1.1–2.4; *m. Ḥag.* 2.5–6).

7:3–4

The understanding of "defilement" referred to in 7:2 is said to originate from "the tradition of the elders" (τὴν παράδοσιν τῶν πρεσβυτέρων, *tēn paradosin tōn presbyterōn*; cf. Josephus, *Ant.* 10.4.1 §51). This expression (cf. Gal. 1:14) refers to the traditions, supposedly given orally by God to Moses on Mount Sinai (*m. ʾAbot* 1.1ff.; Josephus, *Ant.* 13.10.6 §297), that were codified into the Mishnah (ca. AD 200), which along with its Aramaic commentary, the Gemara, make up the Jerusalem Talmud (ca. AD 400) and the larger Babylonian Talmud (ca. AD 500). Jesus, in his defense against the specific teaching concerning defilement (7:2, 5), first directed his attack against the cause and origin of the teaching, that is, the tradition of the elders (7:6–13). The issue of whether eating with unwashed hands can defile a person would be addressed later, in 7:14–23. The practice of ceremonially washing hands, even though not prescribed by the Torah (so *b. Ber.* 52b), clearly existed in Jesus's day (Neusner 1976: 494–95; Booth 1986: 189–203; Baumgarten 1987: 71–72), yet the meaning of "washing their hands with the fist [πυγμῇ, *pygmē*]" is unclear.[6] Suggestions abound and include washing: to the elbow, to the wrist, with the fist, with a fistful of water, with a cupped hand (Hengel 1969; Guelich 1989: 364; Marcus 2000: 441). However, "What πυγμῇ is supposed to mean no one

---

5. This reference alone is sufficient to refute Marxsen's thesis that the Gospel of Mark was written to the Jewish church in Palestine, warning them to flee the coming Romans in AD 70 (Marxsen 1969: 166–89).

6. The RSV and REB do not even attempt to translate the term. The NAB and NASB translate it "carefully"; the NRSV "thoroughly"; and the NIV "give their hands a *ceremonial washing*."

knows" (Wellhausen 1909: 54). Although the specific meaning of πυγμῇ is uncertain, the basic practice to which it refers is clear. "The Pharisees and all the Jews" did not eat unless they performed some sort of ritualistic washing, believing that not to do so involved eating with unclean hands, and (it is assumed) this would result in their defiling themselves (7:15).

The reason the Pharisees performed this washing "[when they come] from the marketplace" is also unclear, as is the subject of "come." Does it refer to *what is brought* from the marketplace being washed, or does it refer to their washing *themselves* when they come from the marketplace? If it is the latter (this receives support from the reference to personal washing in 7:3 and from the fact that there is little evidence for the ceremonial washing of food [Donahue and Harrington 2002: 221]), it assumes that the individual became defiled by physical contact with the people and things of the marketplace. Although there is no clear evidence that the Pharisees thought that contact with the marketplace required ceremonial cleansing, we find an analogy to something like this in Jdt. 12:7; Tob. 7:9 (cf. also Let. Aris. 305). It is probably best to interpret βαπτίσωνται (*baptisōntai*) as a middle ("they wash themselves") rather than a passive ("they are washed"), because (1) it does not require a change of subject in the verbs "wash" and "eat"—that is, "unless they wash themselves, they do not eat," rather than "unless they [the items brought from the marketplace] are washed, they [the Pharisees] do not eat"—and (2) the "and many other things" (καὶ ἄλλα πολλά, *kai alla polla*) seems to refer to additional traditions of washing other things distinct from that just mentioned ("washing themselves"). The "cups, pitchers, and bronze vessels" are all utensils involved in eating food,[7] so that the "tradition of the elders" (7:6–13) and the issue of eating (7:14–23) are intimately associated. For the textual issue of whether "and beds" should be included in the text, see the second additional note on 7:4.

7:5   This verse picks up 7:2 rather awkwardly. The lengthy explanatory clause in 7:3–4 has resulted in 7:2 being an incomplete sentence, and in 7:5 Mark resumes and refers again to the Pharisees and the scribes.[8] The question addressed to Jesus concerning "your disciples" (note that the "some" [τινάς, *tinas*] in 7:2 is omitted for brevity) is an indirect attack on Jesus, for a teacher was responsible for the behavior of his disciples (Daube 1972). (For similar attacks, cf. 2:18, 23–24; also 2:16; Matt. 21:15–16.) It appears here that the Pharisees and scribes assumed that their ritualistic practice of washing was obligatory for all Jews (cf. *m. 'Ed.* 5.6). To "walk" (περιπατοῦσιν, *peripatousin*) means to live in accordance with the traditions of the elders. (The term *halakah*, used to describe the kinds of teachings that deal with moral living, comes from

7. For the ceremonial washing of cups, pitchers, and bronze vessels, cf. Matt. 23:25–26; Luke 11:39; *m. Kelim* 8.3–11.3.
8. The rough grammatical break between 7:2 and 5 is more easily understood if 7:3–4 is due to Mark, for if 7:1–5 existed together before Mark, it is more likely that the grammatical awkwardness would have been rectified by Mark or by someone before him.

the Hebrew equivalent of the Greek περιπατέω, *peripateō*, to walk.) There is no need to see any conflict or disjunction between the reference to eating with defiled hands and the question concerning not keeping the tradition of the elders. The former involves the practice taught in the latter, as the reference to eating with "unwashed hands" in both 7:2 and 5 reveals. The strong adversative ("do not walk according to the tradition of the elders but [ἀλλά, *alla*] eat bread with unclean hands") also demonstrates the intimate relationship between the two. As a result, this does not require a later "adjustment . . . in the formative stages of the primitive Church" (contra Guelich 1989: 366). Unless we attribute all of 7:9–13 (cf. also Matt. 23:4, 16–24) to the early church, Jesus must have had heated discussions with the Pharisees concerning the traditions of the elders.

In 7:6–13, Jesus focuses his attention on the traditions of the elders, and his response centers on OT quotations from Isa. 29:13 and Exod. 20:12; 21:17. (Matthew shows the Jewish nature of his Gospel by reversing the order, so that the quotation from the Law [Matt. 15:4 quoting Exod. 20:12; 21:17] precedes the quotation from the Prophets [Matt. 15:8–9 quoting Isa. 29:13]). As one might expect, the form of these quotations follows more closely the Bible of Mark's readers, the LXX, than the Hebrew Bible, but no significant differences exist between them (Guelich 1989: 368). Although the prophet Isaiah was not consciously thinking of the Pharisees of Jesus's day when he wrote Isa. 29:13 but had in mind rather the people of Israel in his own day, Jesus saw an implication in the prophet's accusation that fit his own situation. His words probably meant, "Isaiah described people like you very well when he said. . . ." Both Jesus and the LXX built on the implications already contained in Isaiah's text (Gundry 1993: 351; France 2002: 284). The Isaiah quotation served Jesus's purpose well in that it deals with the discrepancy between the words and teachings that come from the Pharisees' mouths and lips and the practice that comes from their hearts (Mark 7:9–13; cf. Josephus, *Ant.* 17.2.4 §41; 1QH 4.7–20).[9]

In 7:8 a sharp contrast is made between the commandment of *God* (τὴν ἐντολὴν τοῦ θεοῦ, *tēn entolēn tou theou*) and the tradition of *men* (τὴν παράδοσιν τῶν ἀνθρώπων, *tēn paradosin tōn anthrōpōn*). This same contrast is found again in both 7:9 ("the commandment of God" versus "your tradition" [τὴν παράδοσιν ὑμῶν, *tēn paradosin hymōn*]) and 7:13 ("the word of God" [τὸν λόγον τοῦ θεοῦ, *ton logon tou theou*] versus "your tradition that you pass down" [τῇ παραδόσει ὑμῶν ᾗ παρεδώκατε, *tē paradosei hymōn hē paredōkate*]). See comments on 1:25–26. What was earlier referred to as the "tradition of the elders" (7:3, 5) is now described with respect to its ultimate source—"the commands and teachings of *men*" (cf. Col. 2:22). Exactly what

7:6–8

---

9. Marcus (2000: 444) points out an important difference between Jesus's criticism of the Pharisees and the Qumran community's criticism of them. Jesus criticized them for making the law more severe than it was (Matt. 23:4); the Qumran community criticized them for making it easier (CD 1.18)!

the "commandment of God" refers to is not clear. Some suggest the command to love God with all one's heart, soul, mind, and strength and one's neighbor as oneself (Mark 12:30; Deut. 6:5; Pesch 1980a: 373), but here it may be best not to think of a specific commandment but rather of the principle of God's actual commandments in Scripture being ignored and even rejected because of human tradition.

7:9–13 With an ironical "well" (καλῶς, *kalōs*; 7:9) that connects what follows with the "well" (καλῶς) that introduces the Isaiah quotation in 7:6, Jesus gives a specific example (for, γάρ, *gar*) that demonstrates how the Pharisaic tradition nullifies the commandment of God. Whereas in 7:8 the tradition causes the Pharisees to "abandon" (ἀφέντες, *aphentes*) God's commandment, here it causes them to go further and "nullify/annul" (ἀθετεῖτε, *atheteite*) it in order to (ἵνα, *hina*) establish their tradition. The Scriptures have as one of the Ten Commandments "Honor [τίμα, *tima*] your father and mother" (Exod. 20:12; Deut. 5:16; note "honor" [τιμῶσιν, *timōsin*] in Isa. 29:13), and Jesus emphasized the seriousness and severity of disobeying this commandment by adding, "The one who speaks evil of father or mother, let him certainly die" (Exod. 21:17; Lev. 20:9). By placing Exod. 20:12 and 21:17 together, Jesus reveals the same eschatological intensification of the OT commandments that we find in such passages as Matt. 5:21–48 (Marcus 2000: 444). This is what Moses (and God, for Moses received the commandment from God; cf. the parallel in Matt. 15:4) commanded.

The "you" in "But you say" (ὑμεῖς δὲ λέγετε, *hymeis de legete*; 7:11) is emphatic both in its location at the beginning of the sentence and by the fact that it is unnecessary since the verbal form (λέγετε) already contains the second-person plural designation. It sharpens the contrast between "Moses/God said" and "But *you* say." The term "Corban" (Κορβᾶν, *Korban*) transliterates the Hebrew-Aramaic term and means an "offering" or "vow" (cf. Josephus, *Ant.* 4.4.4 §§72–73; *Ag. Ap.* 1.22 §167; Baumgarten 1984). In typical fashion Mark explains this term to his Greek readers: "that is, a gift" (ὅ ἐστιν, δῶρον, *ho estin, dōron*).[10] It is uncertain whether the support that was due to one's parents because of God's commandment was in fact already given to the temple, so that it was not even theoretically available for the parents, or whether it had been vowed to the temple, so that even though the gift/support was still in the son's possession, it was no longer available to the parents but reserved for God. Regardless, the commandment of God was made void, and the son was no longer honoring his father and mother by providing for them (7:13). Thus what is a capital offense in the law (7:10) is not only permitted but even required by the Pharisaic tradition! The practice of the Pharisees in personally doing this was bad enough, but worse still, they encouraged/made others follow their practice (cf. Rom. 1:32).

---

10. There is an almost exact parallel to Jesus's words in Mark 7:11 in an ossuary lid found near Jerusalem ("All that a man may find to his profit in this ossuary [is] an offering to God from him who is within it"); see Fitzmyer 1959. Cf. also *m. Ned.* 8.7.

One should not read into the present account a conflict over whether the scriptural injunction to keep one's vows (Num. 30:2; Deut. 23:21–22) takes priority over the scriptural injunction to honor one's parents (Gundry 1993: 363; contra Hooker 1991: 177). The issue in our present account involves whether a Pharisaic tradition concerning this oath can nullify one of God's Ten Commandments. For Jesus, the answer was obvious. Through their tradition the Pharisees not only "abandoned" (ἀφέντες) God's commandment (7:8) to honor one's parents, but they also "no longer permit[ted]" (οὐκέτι ἀφίετε, *ouketi aphiete*), that is, forbade (!), a person from keeping God's commandment (7:12). (Note the emphatic double negative: "no longer . . . nothing," οὐκέτι . . . οὐδέν, *ouketi . . . ouden*.) In other words, the issue at hand is whether the human traditions of the Pharisees coming from men (7:8, 9, 13) should overrule the clear command of Scripture coming from God (cf. T. Levi 14.4; T. Ash. 7.5).

The accuracy of Jesus's statement in 7:11–13 has been called into question due to *m. Ned.* 9.1, which argues that duty to one's parents overrules any vow (cf. Josephus, *Ant.* 5.2.12 §169). Yet the very discussion of this issue in *m. Ned.* 9.1 implies that some Pharisees and scribes held the view portrayed here in Mark (Guelich 1989: 370). Furthermore, it is quite possible that the situation in Jesus's day (AD 30) was more rigid than when *m. Ned.* 9.1 was written (ca. AD 200; Marcus 2000: 445–46, 520–24). The concluding comment in 7:13 points out that this was not an isolated example, for the Pharisees did "many similar things" (παρόμοια τοιαῦτα πολλά, *paromoia toiauta polla*; cf. 7:4b). The progression from the Pharisees and scribes "abandoning" (ἀφέντες; 7:8), to "nullifying" (ἀθετεῖτε; 7:9), to "making void" (ἀκυροῦντες, *akyrountes*; 7:13) God's word should be noted. The expression "word of God" is best understood as a synonym for "commandment of God" (7:8, 9) rather than as a reference to the OT Scriptures as a whole (France 2002: 288).

The verb "having called" (προσκαλεσάμενος, *proskalesamenos*) frequently **7:14–15** introduces a new pericope or teaching (cf. 3:13; 6:7; 8:1, 34), but it can also serve as an introduction to a teaching within the same pericope (cf. 3:23; 10:42; 12:43; also 15:44). It functions in the latter way here. In 7:6–13, Jesus attacked the "tradition of the elders" as a source of authority for defining the condition of the person eating; in 7:14–23, he attacks the specific issue of being defiled from external contact, that is, by the character of what is being eaten (Hooker 1991: 178). "Listen to me, all of you, and understand" recalls earlier commands to hear (4:3, 9, 23, 24) and to understand (8:17, 21; cf. also 6:52). It recalls the "Hear, O Israel" that introduces the Shema (Deut. 6:4) and indicates that the saying that follows is especially significant. Its use here and in the two surrounding chapters emphasizes the theme of the disciples' lack of understanding. The proverbial nature of the saying in 7:15 is evident, and its appearance in Gos. Thom. 14 apart from the present context has led some scholars to assume that it originally circulated as an isolated saying (Guelich 1989: 374–75). Yet many of Jesus's proverbs are intimately tied to specific contexts (cf. Mark 2:17; 3:24–25; 6:4; 9:40; 10:25, 43; Matt. 26:52; Luke 14:11; 16:10; etc.). The present saying can be classified as a proverb (Stein 1994b: 18); an example of antithetical parallelism/poetry (Stein 1994b: 28); a riddle (Stein 2000: 43); or, due to its metaphorical nature, a parable. Although the original issue involved *how* to eat (unclean hands), Jesus expanded this more broadly to *what* to eat. For a similar progression, compare Luke 10:29–36, where the original question "Who is my neighbor?" (10:29) is expanded to "What does it mean to be a neighbor?" (10:36).

From 7:18–19 it is clear that the "nothing" (οὐδέν, *ouden*; 7:15) that enters into a person refers to food. We should not see any unified meaning in the term "man" (ἄνθρωπος, *anthrōpos*) in 7:7, 8, 11, and 15 because the term is used very differently in the various statements (contra Marcus 2000: 454). The question has been raised as to why the church struggled so greatly over the issue of what one could or could not eat (Acts 10:14–15; 15:28–29; Rom. 14:14, 20; Gal. 2:11–14; Col. 2:20–22), if Jesus had indeed said 7:15. We must note, however, that the comment in 7:19c is a Markan interpretive comment explaining an implication of Jesus's teaching in these verses. It is not a comment made by Jesus himself. Mark 7:15 is not an isolated legal ruling uttered by Jesus. In the original context it was probably understood as meaning, "There is nothing outside a person that enters into him via *defiled hands* that defiles him." The implication from this saying that the OT food regulations were being done away with by Jesus due to the arrival of the kingdom of God is far from self-evident. For Jesus's hearers, it appeared that he was rejecting the Pharisaic traditions concerning defilement and saying, "A person is not *so much* defiled by what enters him from outside as by what comes from within" (Marcus 2000: 453). Compare also the message of the OT prophets (Isa. 1:11–17; Hos. 6:6; Amos 5:21–27), where the spiritual meaning and the literal observance are seen not as contradictory but as supplementary. What Jesus's audience probably understood by these words was the importance of inner purity stemming from the heart. This was far more important than any outer ceremonial purity. This has already been shown in Mark by various actions of Jesus: his contact with a leper (1:41), a hemorrhaging woman (5:27–29), a dead body (5:41), and, in the following account, a gentile woman (7:24–30). The full implication of Jesus's teaching was not immediately apparent to the disciples (7:17–18) and even less so to the crowd. In its present form, along with the editorial comment in 7:19c, however, Mark clearly indicates that Jesus was passing down a christological ruling: the kingdom of God had arrived and the food regulations of the OT had come to an end (Witherington 2001: 228–31; Stettler 2004; contra Rudolph 2002).[11]

7:17–19 For a discussion of 7:16, see the additional note on 7:15. For Jesus's withdrawal from the crowd in order to teach the disciples privately, compare 3:13; 4:10; 6:31. We have already encountered a house as the scene of Jesus's public teaching in 1:32–34; 2:1–2, 15, but a house can also provide a place for privacy

---

11. Cf. Gen. 1:29–30; 9:3–4; and Lev. 11:1–47 for earlier changes in food regulations.

(5:37–40; 7:24; 9:28, 33; 10:10; 14:3; cf. also 6:31; 8:23), in order that Jesus can explain the "parable" (7:17) to his disciples (cf. 4:10, 33–34). As in Luke 4:23, the broad range of the Greek term παραβολή (*parabolē*) in the NT (and of Hebrew *māšāl* in the OT) is apparent. The reference to the disciples' lack of understanding in 7:18 (ἀσύνετοι, *asynetoi*) recalls 4:13 and 6:52 and will appear in 8:17, where both the lack of "understanding" (οὐδὲ συνίετε, *oude syniete*) and "knowing" (νοεῖτε, *noeite*) again occur together (cf. also 4:40–41; 8:32–33; 9:5–6, 32; 10:24; 14:40). The disciples are no worse than the crowds in their lack of understanding, but in light of their privileged position (3:14–15) and special instruction (4:10–12, 33–34), *they* (the "you" [ὑμεῖς] in 7:18 is emphatic) should understand by now. The privileged position of the disciples, however, allows them to receive additional instruction.

The argument in these verses involves a simple physiological fact in the form of a question and expects a positive answer (note the οὐ, *ou*). All food (even food considered unclean by the Pharisees) enters merely into the physical-digestive part of a person, the stomach (τὴν κοιλίαν, *tēn koilian*; cf. Rev. 10:9–10). It does not enter the moral-ethical-spiritual part, the heart (τὴν καρδίαν, *tēn kardian*). Thus food cannot defile a person, because (ὅτι, *hoti*) it enters a person's stomach (or digestive tract), not the heart (or spiritual being). Then it leaves the body and enters the latrine. Since the digestive system lacks contact with the heart, whatever one puts into the mouth cannot make a person unclean. This explanation of the parable/proverb given in 7:15 appears to be an example of wisdom based on a truth of nature. The digestive system of the human body does not allow what is eaten, whether it is "clean" or "unclean," to touch the moral part of a person, that is, one's heart. Yet this explanation seems to argue for what has always been true: because of the physiological truth mentioned in 7:18–19, all foods have always been clean. This would mean that all food laws, such as those found in Lev. 11:1–47, were never really binding. But this seems to conflict with the fact that Jesus clearly accepted Moses's authority as a teacher of the Word of God (cf. Mark 1:44; 7:10; 10:3; 12:26; cf. Matt. 5:17–20). Jesus's words here must be interpreted in the context of the entire Gospel of Mark. They must be understood in light of the eschatological fact that the kingdom of God has come (1:15) and in light of the authority of Jesus Christ, the Son of God, to pronounce the will of God (1:1, 27; 2:23–28; 7:19c; 10:2–12; cf. Matt. 5:33–37). With the coming of the kingdom of God, the period of tutelage under the Law has come to an end. Thus regulations given by Moses concerning food have given way to the freedom of divine sonship (Gal. 3:23–26). In the kingdom of God, regulations concerning clean versus unclean food, like the practice of fasting (Mark 2:18–22), have now given way to joy and freedom, and discipleship sets new priorities.

The participial clause "cleansing [καθαρίζων, *katharizōn*] all foods" (7:19c) agrees with "he [Jesus]" of 7:18 in both number and case (nominative singular). It is best to understand it as a Markan interpretive comment (V. Taylor 1952: 345; Marcus 2000: 455) concerning the implications of Jesus's words in 7:15 and 18b–19—"Thus Jesus [through these words] now cleansed, that is, declared as 'clean,' all foods" (cf. Acts 10:14–15, 28; 11:8; Rom. 14:14, 20; Gal. 2:11–14). By this comment Mark seeks to explain to his gentile readers why the OT kosher rules concerning clean and unclean food were no longer binding and that this was already implied in Jesus's words in 7:15. It is better to see this comment not as polemical and reflecting a problem within the Markan community but as didactic and explaining from where the community's present practice and understanding ultimately derive.[12]

7:20–23 After discussing what cannot defile a person (i.e., food), Mark picks up the second part of 7:15 and discusses from where moral defilement really comes and what causes it. It is the heart (7:21), the very innermost nature of one's being, that is the problem. The cause of sin and moral defilement is not found in external "things" but in our "carnality" (cf. Rom. 7:14–25; Ps. 51:7; also 1QH 12.25).[13] The catalog of sins that follows has similarities to other vice lists (Rom. 1:29–31; 1 Cor. 5:10–11; 6:9–10; 2 Cor. 12:20–21; Gal. 5:19–21; Col. 3:5–8; 1 Tim. 1:9–10; 2 Tim. 3:2–5; 1 Pet. 4:3, 15; cf. also Wis. 14:25–26; 3 Bar. 4.17; 1 En. 91.6–7; Jub. 23.14; 4 Macc. 1:2–8; 1QS 4.9–11). The parallel in Matt. 15:19–20 is shorter than in Mark and rearranges the Markan order to conform to the Hebrew order of the commandments in Exod. 20:13–15 (murder, adultery, stealing) rather than that of the LXX as in Mark (adultery, stealing, murder).

The thirteen kinds of defilement listed begin with seven plural actions followed by six vices (V. Taylor 1952: 345). If the first, "evil thoughts," serves as an overarching category such as the "evil inclination" (*yēṣer hārāʿ*; Gundry 1993: 355–56; Marcus 2000: 459–60; France 2002: 292), then we have two distinct lists consisting of six actions in the plural and six vices in the singular. For the most part, the plural actions are prohibited in the Decalogue: fornications, thefts, murders, adulteries, covetings, and evils (a broad term that may act as a summary of the preceding sins). The six vices in the singular are deceit, licentiousness, envy (lit. "an evil eye," ὀφθαλμὸς πονηρός, *ophthalmos poneros*—in the sense of jealousy rather than placing a hex on someone), slander (lit. "blasphemy," βλασφημία, *blasphēmia*—of others, not God, as in 14:64), arrogance, and folly (ἀφροσύνη, *aphrosynē*—this may serve as a summary of the preceding vices). Aside from the division into plural and singular nouns, there does not seem to be a clear organizational principle for the list.

Mark 7:23 serves as a summary conclusion to 7:20–22 (and 7:15b) and concludes that the evil actions and vices listed in 7:20–22 that defile a person do not result from what is eaten (food) or how it is eaten (with defiled hands) but from one's "unclean" nature. Mark does not explain the remedy for this,

---

12. Cf. Guelich (1989: 380): "We have no evidence that any of the issues ('defile hands,' 'tradition of the elders,' or even 'foods') per se concerned Mark or his community"; and Booth (1986: 113): "It is unlikely that handwashing was ever an issue between the Gentile and the Judaizing Christians." France (2002: 278) points out that by his comment Mark "is doing no more than any other intelligent reader of Jesus' epigram might have done" (cf. Hooker 1991: 179).

13. See Holm-Nielsen 1960: 198.

but elsewhere in the NT, we read of the need for "being born again" (John 3:3–8), "becoming a new creation" (2 Cor. 5:17), "walking according to the Spirit" (Rom. 8:4), "dying with Christ" (Rom. 6:1–14), and so on.

Summary

Within the present account, several Markan theological emphases can be found. One involves an explanation of the origin of the community's freedom concerning food regulations. Mark's readers were well aware of the Jewish practice of refraining from eating certain foods, and they were well aware of the scriptural commandments concerning such matters. After all, their Bible was the OT! The present account explained to them that freedom from the issue of clean versus unclean foods stemmed from Jesus himself. He said that it was not what enters into a person's stomach that defiles one but what comes out of one's heart (7:21). Thus, as Mark points out, he declared all food clean to eat (7:19c). Consequently, the readers' present practice stems from the teachings of Jesus Christ, the Son of God.[14]

A second theme emphasized by Mark involves the incomprehension of the disciples. Based on history and tradition, Mark portrays the disciples as lacking understanding, but despite this they have been especially chosen and trained by Jesus to be his apostles. The *why* of this emphasis by Mark is unclear. He does teach it, however, and the disciples' human frailty and incomprehension (so far, 4:13, 40–41; 6:52; 7:18) will crescendo in the coming events all the way up to the time of the crucifixion (8:14–21, 32–33; 9:5–6, 32; 10:24; 14:10). But the disciples are still Jesus's chosen "apostles," and restoration was promised and later took place (14:27–28 and 16:7).

More important than the disciples' lack of understanding, however, is the demonstration of Jesus's christological authority as the Son of God to pronounce not only the illegitimacy of the Pharisaic traditions but, more important, even the termination of certain commandments found in Scripture itself. He can do what the elders in practice did by their traditions: abrogate parts of the OT. The traditions in practice nullified OT commandments (in the present instance, a cardinal moral and ethical commandment), even though the Pharisees and scribes would never agree to having done so. Jesus also nullified certain OT commandments (in the present instance, the cultic regulations concerning clean versus unclean foods). Mark's Jesus, however, is the Son of God and thus is able to terminate the cultic rules of Scripture concerning clean versus unclean that have served their purpose but are now superseded by the greater freedom of the new covenant, which enables one to concentrate more fully on what comes out of the heart. Such authority again raises the question, "Who is this man who . . . ?" (4:41).

14. For Peter, Jesus's words in 7:14–23, along with the heavenly vision of Acts 10:10–16 and witnessing the Spirit come upon Cornelius by faith apart from circumcision (Acts 10:34–48; 11:4–18), would have served to confirm the truth that neither circumcision nor keeping the food regulations of the OT was essential for the Christian life.

Another emphasis found in the account involves the growing hostility toward Jesus. The Pharisees and scribes who come from Jerusalem, and the national leadership represented by them, are gathering against Jesus (7:1). Their accusations continue (7:5), and Jesus's criticism of them is becoming harsher. They are "hypocrites" (ὑποκριτῶν, *hypokritōn*; 7:6) whose external religion (their lips) says one thing, but their inner being (their heart) is opposed to God. Such strong condemnation, his damning of their traditions (7:8–9, 13), and the implication that even cultic regulations stemming from Scripture are no longer binding will result in a confrontation in Jerusalem that will ultimately lead to his crucifixion. Thus Mark's readers, who were well aware of Jesus's death at the hands of the Jerusalem leadership, are again reminded that their Lord's death was not for crimes that he had done. The human cause of his death was due to the hostility of those who honored God with their lips but whose heart was far from him. The divine cause for Jesus's death still awaits explanation, but this will come shortly (8:31).

Additional Notes

7:1. συνάγονται πρός is lit. "gather together to."

7:2. ἰδόντες is lit. "having seen."

7:4. παρέλαβον κρατεῖν is lit. "received to hold."

7:4. The textual support for including "and beds" in the translation comes from A D W Θ f¹ f¹³ latt. Its omission is supported by 𝔓⁴⁵ ℵ B L Δ. Although the difficulty of a textual reading is usually support for its originality, in this instance "and beds" (καὶ κλινῶν) appears to be too difficult. See, however, Crossley (2003) for a strong defense of "and beds" as the original reading.

7:15. Some MSS (A D W Θ f¹ f¹³ latt syr) at this point add v. 16, "If anyone has ears to hear, let him hear." It is best omitted, following ℵ B L Δ, and understood as a scribal addition due to the similarity to 4:9, which also comes after a parable. The absence of these words in the Matthean parallel (15:10–12), despite Matthew's fondness for this expression (11:15; 13:9, 43), favors their omission in the Markan account.

G. Jesus and the Syrophoenician Woman (7:24–30)

The present account has been described as a pronouncement story (V. Taylor 1952: 347), a miracle story (Nineham 1963: 198), a teaching narrative (Gnilka 1978: 291), a distant healing narrative (Pesch 1980a: 385–86), and a combined pronouncement-miracle story (Koch 1975: 85–86) in which either the dialogue in 7:27–28 was added to the miracle story or the miracle story was added to or grew out of the dialogue (cf. Marcus 2000: 466). Once again we are confronted with a tradition that does not fit neat form-critical categories, and it is clear that the account is dominated by its content rather than its form, for the miracle and the dialogue are intimately associated together (Gnilka 1978: 290). The account possesses a number of similarities with the story of the healing of the centurion's servant (Luke 7:1–10; Matt. 8:5–10; Pesch 1980a: 386). Mark's hand is seen most clearly in the introductory seam (7:24–25a; cf. 10:1) with its "messianic secret" motif (Klauck 1978: 273, 279–80; Marcus 2000: 466). The chronological ordering of salvation history in 7:27a (note the "first" that is missing in the parallel in Matt. 15:24–26) may also be due to Mark (Pryke 1978: 16, 143, 161). The historicity of the present account is supported by the apparent conflict between Jesus's words in 7:27 and 29 (Marcus 2000: 466).

Mark has prepared his readers for the present account by the extended discussion of what is "clean and unclean" in 7:1–23. Jesus now (7:24) enters an unclean gentile area (Tyre), has contact with an unclean gentile woman (7:25–26), and casts out an unclean spirit/demon (7:25, 30). Marcus (2000: 466) points out that Chrysostom (*Homily on Matt.* 52.1) long ago observed a similarity between the present account and Acts 10, where a mission to the gentiles is preceded by teachings concerning "clean and unclean" food. The reference to the "bread" of children (7:27) ties the present account by word association to both the preceding (6:30–44, 52; 7:2, 5) and following references to bread (8:1–9, 14–21). "To be filled" (χορτασθῆναι, *chortasthēnai*) in 7:27 also recalls the superabundance of food and the reference to being filled in the two feeding miracles (6:42 and 8:8).

The account consists of three parts. The first (7:24–26) involves a transitional seam (7:24–25a) consisting of an introductory encounter between Jesus and a Syrophoenician woman, and a request for healing (7:25b–26). This is followed by a dialogue and repartee between Jesus and the woman (7:27–28). The story concludes (7:29–30) with a pronouncement concerning the faith of the woman (7:29a), the distant exorcism of the demon from her daughter (7:29b), and the proof of the exorcism (7:30).

Exegesis and Exposition

[24]And having risen, he departed from there into the regions of Tyre, ⌐ ¬ and having entered into a house, he was wishing [that] no one would know [that he was there], and he was not able to escape notice. [25]But immediately a woman, ⌐whose daughter¬ had an unclean spirit, having heard about him, ⌐came¬ [and] fell at his feet. [26]And the woman was a Greek, a Syrophoenician by race. And she was asking him ⌐to¬ cast the demon out of her daughter. [27]And he began to say to her, "Permit first the children to be filled, for it is not right to take the bread of the children and to throw it to the dogs." [28]But she answered and says to him, "⌐ ¬ Lord, even the dogs under the table eat from the scraps of the children." [29]And he said to her, "On account of what you said, go. The demon has gone out of your daughter." [30]And having departed to her house, she found the child lying upon the [her] bed and the demon having departed.

7:24–26 The change of scene "from there" (ἐκεῖθεν, *ekeithen*) probably refers to having departed from the house of 7:17 (Pesch 1977: 387; cf. 6:1 and 5:38; 6:11 and 10; 9:30 and 28; 10:1 and 9:33). The close similarity between this seam and 10:1 suggests that their similarity is due to the hand of Mark. "Into the regions of Tyre" (εἰς τὰ ὅρια Τύρου, *eis ta horia Tyrou*) probably refers to the city and the surrounding areas under its control. There was little love lost between the people of Galilee and people of Tyre, who were "notoriously our [the Jews'] bitterest enemies" (Josephus, *Ag. Ap.* 1.13 §70; cf. also *Ant.* 14.12.3–5 §§313–22; *J.W.* 2.18.5 §478). There has been much speculation as to why Jesus went to Tyre. Some suggestions are as follows: to preach to the gentiles (but note 7:24b; cf. also Matt. 10:5–6), for privacy and rest (cf. 7:24b with 1:45; 6:31), for privacy to teach the disciples (cf. 9:28, 30–31, 33; 10:10), to reflect on the success (or lack of success) of his mission, or to escape the hostility of Herod Antipas. Mark provides no explanation for Jesus's going to Tyre but says only that he did not wish anyone to know (οὐδένα ἤθελεν γνῶναι, *oudena ēthelen gnōnai*; cf. 9:30–31). This indicates that for Mark the trip was not for the purpose of a gentile mission. Yet despite Jesus's desire for secrecy, he "was not able to escape notice" (οὐκ ἠδυνήθη λαθεῖν, *ouk ēdynēthē lathein*). By this comment "Mark heightens the power and numinous presence of Jesus" (Donahue and Harrington 2002: 232). Jesus was too great to be hidden. His fame was already known in Tyre and its environs (3:8), so that the knowledge of his presence results in his being unable to escape notice.

Although the young girl is later described as having a "demon" (δαιμόνιον, *daimonion*; 7:26, 29, 30), in 7:25 she is described as possessing (lit. "was having") an "unclean spirit" (πνεῦμα ἀκάθαρτον, *pneuma akatharton*). Even though this term ἀκάθαρτον (unclean) is not used in 7:1–23, Mark may have chosen to use "unclean spirit" here in order to link the present account with the preceding discussion of "unclean/clean" (κοινός/καθαρίζων, *koinos/katharizōn*; 7:18–19). "Unclean spirit" is found also in 1:23, 26, 27; 3:11, 30; 5:2, 8, 13; 6:7; 9:25; "demon" is found in 1:34 (2×), 39; 3:15, 22 (2×); 6:13;

9:38. Elsewhere they occur in the same pericope only in 3:20–30. The change to "demons" in 7:26 may be due to a Markan preference for using "demons" with the verb "cast out" (ἐκβάλλω, ekballō; cf. 1:34, 39; 3:15, 22; 6:13; 9:38; but also 9:18, 28; Guelich 1989: 56), or it may be due to its presence in the tradition Mark used.

The woman's "falling at his feet" (προσέπεσεν πρὸς τοὺς πόδας αὐτοῦ, prosepesen pros tous podas autou; cf. 3:11; 5:33; also 5:22) demonstrates physically the urgency of her request, even as the durative imperfect (was asking, ἠρώτα, ērōta) reveals the intensity of her supplication. As in the case of Jairus (5:22), so here the woman beseeches Jesus for her daughter's healing/exorcism. Mark describes her as a "gentile" (Ἑλληνίς, Hellēnis). In light of 7:27–28, this should be understood as indicating that she was non-Jewish (cf. Rom. 1:16; 2:9, 10; 3:9; 10:12; 1 Cor. 1:24; 10:32; Gal. 3:28; Col. 3:11), rather than indicating her linguistic (Greek; cf. Acts 7:1–6) or cultural (Hellenistic) background. It is unlikely that Mark wanted his readers to conclude that she was a "God-fearer" or "half-convert" to Judaism but not a proselyte[1] in the sense of Acts 10:2, 22; 13:16, 26; 16:1, 3; 17:4, 12; 18:12 (contra Marcus 2000: 464), for in the present account Ἑλληνίς serves to contrast the children of God (Deut. 14:1–2; Isa. 1:2; Hos. 11:1; Ps. 82:6; etc.; cf. m. 'Abot 3.15) and those outside the family of God, the gentiles. The woman is further described as Syrophoenician by race. It is unclear whether Mark seeks to distinguish between a Phoenician from Syria and one from northern Africa (Hengel 1985: 29, 137–38; Donahue and Harrington 2002: 233) or between someone living in the coastal area of Syria and someone living in the central part (Coele-Syria; Marcus 2000: 462–63). Knowing Jesus's reputation (cf. 3:8) and learning of his presence in her area (7:25a), she came and besought him to cast out the unclean spirit/demon from her daughter. Mark makes no mention of the father of the child, and it is purely speculative to ask why he is not mentioned. Ultimately, the father (whether alive or dead, opposed to or in favor of the woman coming, etc.) is unimportant for Mark's purpose in telling the story. What Mark considers important for understanding the story is included in the account.

7:27–28   Jesus's reply to the woman (probably in Greek [Stein 1994b: 4–6; but cf. Meier 1991: 294–95n41) appears at first like a harsh refusal of her request. Attempts have been made to soften Jesus's words by pointing out that the term κυναρίοις (kynariois) in our text is a diminutive ("puppies") of the normal term κύνες (kynes; V. Taylor 1952: 350; Cranfield 1959: 248; W. Lane 1974: 262; Brooks 1991: 121; Gundry 1993: 374–75, 378), but it is uncertain whether κυναρίοις should be interpreted as a diminutive (Guelich 1989: 386–87; Marcus 2000: 463–64).[2] In understanding the present account, we should not read into it our

---

1. See S. McKnight, DNTB 846.
2. The presence of other diminutives in the pericope (daughter, θυγάτριον, thygatrion [7:25]; scraps, ψιχίων, psichiōn [7:28]; child, παιδίον, paidion [7:28, 30]) weakens the argument for the diminutive sense of "puppies" (κυνάρια) in 7:27–28.

modern-day affection for dogs (Marcus 2000: 463–64). In biblical times, dogs were seen more often than not as "curs" or wild scavengers that lived outside the cities and towns and fed on carrion. They were not generally thought of as lovable, domesticated pets ("man's best friend"). Note their association with pigs (Matt. 7:6) and heretics (Phil. 3:2; 2 Pet. 2:22; Rev. 22:15). The woman's reference to the "dogs [κυνάρια, *kynaria*] under the table," however, suggests that she understood them as household pets, not wild scavengers (cf. Tob. 6:1; 11:1 [some MSS]; *b. ʾAbod. Zar.* 54b; *b. Šabb.* 155b; Midr. Ps. 4.11).

France (2002: 296) rightly points out that what Jesus was doing in the conversation with the woman is often misunderstood when it is not interpreted in light of the account as a whole, and the account ends very positively in 7:29–30. From the account it is clear that the woman was not put off by Jesus's statement in 7:27. She sees this rather as an opportunity to interact and enter into a repartee (7:28).[3] The term "first" (πρῶτον, *prōton*) in Jesus's reply is intended to indicate that she as a gentile is not excluded from God's mercy, but that there exists a divinely established temporal priority in which the Jew is "first" (Rom. 1:16; cf. Acts 13:46; also Isa. 42:1; 49:6). In Mark, "first" in its neuter form is always used to describe some sort of a divinely ordained historical time line: 3:27 ("first" Satan is bound before the plundering of his house); 9:11–12 ("first" Elijah comes before the Messiah); 13:10 ("first" the gospel must be proclaimed before the end comes); and here ("first" the Jew hears, then the gentiles; cf. Rom. 1:16; Marcus 2000: 463). In the present account, the term brings hope to the woman. (Note how different the statement reads if "first" is omitted.) Gundry (1993: 378) points out that 7:27b should be understood not as an absolute refusal that stands in contradiction to 7:27a with its "first" but rather as an explanation (note the "for," γάρ, *gar*) of why the children should be fed "first." It is most unlikely that Mark would have included this story in his Gospel if he thought that it would have a negative effect on his gentile readers (France 2002: 296). It is also unlikely that Mark intended his readers to see the woman "besting" Jesus and forcing him to "capitulate" (contra Van den Eynde 2000; Donahue and Harrington 2002: 234–35, 237). How does one "best" and force the Christ, the Son of God, the Lord, to "capitulate"? It is also unlikely that Mark intended his readers to see in 7:27b a socioeconomic tension based on the Tyrian "dogs'" oppression of Galilean "children" by their domination of the agricultural products of Galilee and that Jesus is arguing against the unfairness of taking away the children's bread in Galilee and giving it to dogs in Tyre (contra Theissen 1991: 72–80; Marcus 2000: 462).

The contrast between the imagery or picture part of this parable (Stein 1981: 20; "children" and "dogs") and the meaning or reality part involves "Jews" and "gentiles," not "Jesus's disciples" and "gentile children" (contra Gundry 1993: 373). For the association of gentiles with "dogs," compare 1 En. 89.42, 46–47,

---

3. The inceptive imperfect "he began to say" (ἔλεγεν, *elegen*) indicates that Jesus's reply to the woman in 7:27 is the beginning of a conversation between them.

49. The privileged position of the children is clear: they are to be "filled" first. The verb "filled" is found in only two other places in Mark—in the two feeding miracles (6:42; 8:8). Some have suggested that the present saying indicates that not only this verse but also the two feeding miracles were understood by Mark as portraying the eschatological scheme of salvation being offered to the Jew first (6:30–44) and then to the Greeks/gentiles (8:1–10; Klauck 1978: 273, 279–80; Quesnell 1969: 224–28; contra Guelich 1989: 386). This scheme, however, ignores Mark's description of the feeding in 8:1–10 as taking place in Galilee (see 7:31 and 8:1). The saying of Jesus gives temporal priority ("first") to the Jew but not exclusive rights. This encourages the woman to see Jesus's words not as a rejection of her request but as a test and to respond with a witty riposte. She (and, of course, Mark) did not see Jesus's words as a "flat refusal" or rejection (contra Guelich 1989: 386–87, who is referring here to the original historical situation). Jesus's words in Mark are not a refusal but a test of faith (Pokorny 1995: 328–29; Marcus 2000: 468–69).

The woman's address of Jesus as "Lord" (Κύριε, *Kyrie*) even in the original historical setting was more than a simple polite "Sir." Her address of Jesus as "Lord" was not as pregnant with meaning as it was for Mark's readers, who would probably associate with this title ideas such as found in Phil. 2:9–11; Rom. 10:9; Rev. 17:14; 19:16; and so on. Mark's readers had already heard this title used of Jesus in 1:3; 2:28; and 5:19, and it would become even more prominent in the remaining part of the Gospel (11:3; 12:9, 11 [?], 36 [2×], 37; 13:35). For the woman, it probably involved the idea that Jesus was the one whom the Jews had looked for and awaited, the Messiah. Her reply acknowledged the truth of Jesus's previous statement. The Jew held a privileged position in the divine order of salvation history, but with great wit (and faith) she responded that she was not seeking to take away the children's bread but, like a dog, merely to share in their leftover crumbs. She believed that Jesus could bring healing for her daughter. If Elijah could perform a miracle for a gentile woman (1 Kings 17:8–24), how much more could Jesus do so in inaugurating the kingdom of God! With the coming of the kingdom, God's good news of salvation could no longer be contained within Israel but would extend to the gentiles. She sought only some of the overflow of that divine manifestation for her daughter. This clear temporal order of the "first" in 7:27 was, of course, clearer to the Markan readers than to the woman. Nevertheless, the presence of Tyrians and Sidonians in 3:8 indicates that these regions had heard of Jesus's preaching concerning the arrival of the kingdom of God. This gave hope to the woman that Jesus's coming to her region might in some way bring blessing to gentiles as well.[4] That the gentiles would benefit in the coming of

---

4. Guelich (1989: 387) argues that the woman's reply indicates that she understood Jesus's statement in 7:27 as implying an "exclusive" rather than a "temporal" privilege for Israel. However, Mark wants his readers to assume that what the woman heard of Jesus (7:25) involved the coming of the kingdom of God (1:14–15) and his offer of salvation to the outcasts (lepers, tax collectors, demoniacs, the unclean, etc.). Those once excluded were *now* being offered the kingdom. It does not seem at all impossible that she would see this *now* as also bringing good news

the kingdom of God to Israel is clearly taught in the OT (Isa. 2:2–4; 11:10; 42:1–9; 51:4–5; 55:1–5; 56:6–8; 60:1–3; Mic. 4:1–5; Zech. 8:20–23; 14:1–21), and there is no need to deny that Jesus himself foresaw and taught a future mission to the gentiles (Mark 4:30–32; 12:9; 13:10; 14:9; Matt. 8:11–12; 22:8–14; 25:31–46; Luke 11:29–32; 14:15–24; cf. Jeremias 1958).

7:29–30   Jesus responded to the woman that "on account of what you said" (διὰ τοῦτον τὸν λόγον, *dia touton ton logon*; lit. "because of this word" ["of faith" is implied]; cf. 2:5; 5:34; 9:23–25; 10:52; also the Matthean parallel in 15:28) he had healed her daughter. Already the demon had been exorcised. Even from a distance, apart from physical contact, Jesus had healed her. In Luke 7:1–10/ Matt. 8:5–13/John 4:46–54 we find a similar healing of Jesus performed at a distance, and there it also involves a gentile. (Cf. *b. Ber.* 34b and the Life of Apollonius 3.38 for other examples of healing from a distance.) Some suggest that this may have been due to the inappropriateness of a Jewish religious teacher entering into a gentile house (France 2002: 297). However, Jesus on numerous occasions seemed to be oblivious to, and even consciously rejected, the regulations concerning clean versus unclean (cf. Mark 1:41–42; 2:14–17; 5:25–34, 40–42; 7:1–23; etc.), so that this suggestion is unlikely. The account ends with the woman returning home and finding her daughter (lit. "child") lying (lit. "cast") on her bed and the demon expelled (7:30). The use of the verb "lying/cast" (βεβλημένον, *beblēmenon*) appears somewhat strange. It is used at times to describe sick people (Matt. 9:2; Rev. 2:22), but here it describes a healed person. Is this a sign of the demon's departure (cf. 1:26; 9:26), or is it possible that "cast" is intentionally used here by Mark due to its appearance in 7:27? Is the "casting" of bread to the dogs now taking place in the healing of the child? The analogy is not perfect, but the use of the verb here seems to draw attention to its earlier use in 7:27.

Summary

The Markan christological emphasis in this passage centers on two themes. One involves Jesus's inability to be hidden. Despite his attempt to remain incognito (7:24; cf. 7:36–37; see 1:45), his reputation and fame do not permit this. The report of his words and works have preceded him even into gentile territory, so that he simply cannot be hid. The messianic secrecy motif in our passage serves to show Mark's readers that Jesus did not seek notoriety. Thus he did not seek to establish any situation that might be misconstrued as rebellious or politically dangerous. His fame arose, despite all attempts to the contrary, because of the words of hope he preached and the mighty works of healing and compassion he performed. In addition, Mark reports a mighty miracle of Jesus in the present account. A child was healed and her demon exorcised without Jesus even being present! The Son of God

---

to "dogs" as well. Clearly Mark wanted Jesus's words and the woman's reply to be interpreted in light of the temporal "first" of 7:27.

possesses such healing power and authority over demons that he can heal without a physical presence or word (see van der Loos 1965: 328–33 for a discussion of distant healing). He can simply will the child's healing and it takes place.

A second theological emphasis that Mark makes in the present account involves the coming of the kingdom of God to the gentile world. This is especially apparent if Mark intends his readers to focus their attention on the dialogue in the account (France 2002: 299). When read in the light of the situation of Mark's readers, it is easy to see how relevant this account would be. Having just explained how Jesus brought an end to the clean versus unclean distinctives of Judaism (7:1–23, esp. 7:19), Mark goes on to show his readers that Jesus in his ministry had already prefigured the church's later mission to the gentiles by healing a gentile girl. Mark's readers, even as gentiles, possessed an assured place in salvation history. Jesus taught that the Jews possessed a temporal priority. They were indeed "first," as God's call of Abraham and his offspring demonstrates, but this divine order of "first to the Jew and then to the gentile" (Rom 1:16; see also Acts 13:46) has resulted in salvation coming to the readers of Mark's Gospel. And this, just like the ending of the clean versus unclean regulations, is not due simply to some arbitrary church decision. It was Jesus's doing from the start! There is no need to see in this teaching a particular problem in the Markan church. Such a mirror reading is far less likely than that Mark wanted to demonstrate how the present understanding of the Markan church in this area had its roots in the words (7:1–23) and deeds (7:24–30) of Jesus. The coming of the new covenant (14:24; 1 Cor. 11:25; 2 Cor. 3:6; Heb. 8:8–13) involves not the rejection of the Abrahamic covenant (the error of Marcion and certain extreme forms of Lutheran and dispensational theology) but its glorious fulfillment with the ingrafting of the gentiles into the kingdom of God (Rom. 11:1–24).

Additional Notes

7:24. Although the best MS tradition favors the addition of καὶ Σιδῶνος (and of Sidon; א A B K f¹ f¹³ and the early translations), it is much easier to understand why "and of Sidon" would have been added by a later scribe in order to agree with the Matthean parallel in 15:21 and with Mark 3:8, where Tyre and Sidon occur together (cf. also 7:31), than to understand why "and of Sidon" would have been dropped.

7:25. The text reads "whose daughter of her," which may be due to Semitic influence (Zerwick 1961: §201).

7:25. ἐλθοῦσα is lit. "having come."

7:26. Although ἵνα can be understood as providing the purpose of the woman's asking, it is best to interpret it here as introducing the content of what she was asking. See 3:9–10.

7:28. א A B H L Δ f¹ lat and the majority of witnesses have ναί, but despite this strong textual support, it should be omitted, as in 𝔓⁴⁵ W Θ f¹³. It has probably been added to agree with the parallel in Matt. 15:27 (contra France 2000: 295). Ναί is not found anywhere else in Mark.

H. Jesus Heals a Deaf Mute (7:31–37)

The present account, found only in Mark, is a good example of a healing miracle. After the introductory seam involving a geographical change in scene (7:31), we find the typical elements of a healing miracle: a description of the problem and request for healing (7:32), the healing itself (7:33–34), the proof of the healing (7:35), and the reaction of the crowd (7:37). Mark's own hand is seen most clearly in the introductory seam and travel journey (7:31), the command to secrecy (7:36a), the breaking of that command by the "preaching" (ἐκήρυσσον, *ekērysson*) of the miracle (7:36; cf. 1:45; 5:20), the inability of Jesus's healing ministry to remain hidden (7:36b–c; cf. 7:24b), and the subsequent amazement (7:37; see 4:41; cf. Pryke 1978: 16, 143, 161–62). The pre-Markan tradition is seen most clearly in 7:32–35 and 37b (Guelich 1989: 390). The traditional nature of 7:32–35 and 37b can be seen by the unusually high number of terms that occur only here in Mark: "hardly speak" (μογιλάλον, *mogilalon*; 7:32); "having taken aside" (ἀπολαβόμενος, *apolabomenos*), "fingers" (δακτύλους, *daktylous*; 7:33); "sighed" (ἐστέναξεν, *estenaxen*), "*Ephphatha*" (ἐφφαθά), "Be opened" (διανοίχθητι, *dianoichthēti*; 7:34); "were opened" (ἠνοίγησαν, *ēnoigēsan*), "chain" (δεσμός, *desmos*), "correctly" (ὀρθῶς, *orthōs*; 7:35); and "exceedingly" (ὑπερπερισσῶς, *hyperperissōs*; 7:37). "This is a remarkably large amount of non-Markan vocabulary for one compact seven-verse story" (Meier 1994: 758n154). The story of the healing of the deaf mute is tied to the preceding account by the geographical reference to Tyre (cf. 7:24 and 31).

The similarity between this healing miracle and the healing of the blind man in 8:22–26 is striking. This is seen in the similar ordering of the events and the common vocabulary. (Cf. Fowler 1981: 105–8; Marcus 2000: 476–77 for helpful comparisons.) Some scholars have suggested that these two healing miracles were paired together in reverse order before Mark wrote his Gospel and that 7:37 served as a conclusion for both miracles (Gnilka 1978: 296; Guelich 1989: 390). The probable allusion in 7:37 to Isa. 35:5–6, where God heals the blind and the deaf, is seen as favoring the pre-Markan association of these two miracle stories. The strongest argument in favor of 7:37 being an allusion to Isa. 35:5–6 is the presence of "scarcely speak" (μογιλάλον) in these two accounts, for these are the only two places in the entire Bible where this term occurs. Although this argues for an allusion to the Isaiah passage in the present account, it does not demonstrate that Isa. 35:5–6 and Mark 8:22–26 were tied together in the pre-Markan tradition. For one thing, the wording of 7:37 and Isa. 35:5–6 is not really that close.

Furthermore, the Isaiah passage refers to healing the blind first, and it also refers to healing the lame. Neither of these is mentioned in 7:37. The various suggestions as to why Mark might have chosen to separate the two healing miracles (Marcus 2000: 477), while interesting, are highly speculative.

Exegesis and Exposition

[31]And having departed from the regions of ⌜Tyre, he again came to the Sea of Galilee by way of Sidon⌝ through the middle of the Decapolis. [32]And they bring to him a deaf man [who could] hardly speak and plead with him in order that he might set the [= his] hand upon him [to heal him]. [33]And having privately taken him aside from the crowd, he put his fingers into his [the man's] ears, and having spat, he touched his [the man's] tongue, [34]and having looked up into heaven, he sighed and says to him, "*Ephphatha,*" which means, "Be opened." [35]And ⌜ ⌝ his ears were opened, and his tongue was unchained, and he began speaking correctly. [36]And he commanded them ⌜that⌝ they should tell [this] to no one, but the more he was commanding them, the more zealously they were preaching [it]. [37]And they were exceedingly astonished, saying, "He has done all things well. He makes both the deaf to hear and the mute to speak."

The difficulty of Jesus's itinerary described here is obvious when one traces the journey on a map. Jesus leaves Tyre to go to the Sea of Galilee (which is southeast of Tyre) by way of Sidon (which is about 22 miles north of Tyre) and through the middle of the Decapolis (which is east of Sidon and north of the Sea of Galilee). Some analogies given involve going from New York City to Chesapeake Bay by way of Boston (Guelich 1989: 391) or going from Portland to Denver via Seattle and the Great Plains (Marcus 2000: 472). (The distances in the analogies are disproportionately large.) This itinerary and the location of Gerasa by the Sea of Galilee (5:1) have resulted in numerous suggestions: Mark was simply ignorant of the geography of Palestine and made geographical blunders in these instances; Mark mentions these "off the beaten path" gentile areas in an attempt to provide historical grounding for the existence of Christian congregations in these locations in Mark's day (Marcus 2000: 472; cf. Acts 21:3–6; 27:3); Mark may be giving a compressed summary of a journey that he believes Jesus made but whose details he may not have known (Hooker 1991: 185); the journey is historically accurate and accords better with Jesus's desire for privacy than a direct journey to the Sea of Galilee (Brooks 1991: 122; J. Edwards 2002: 223–24, who offers 2 Kings 2:2–6 and 23–25 as similar hairpin journeys); and so on.

The exact geographical location where the following miracle and the feeding of the four thousand in 8:1–10 take place is debated. Do these occur in the Decapolis or in the area of Jesus's earlier ministry around the Sea of Galilee (1:14–4:41; 5:21–7:23)? Some argue that Mark intended his readers to understand these two accounts as involving gentile audiences in the Decapolis. This

7:31

is supposedly due to Mark's placing last in the geographical listing the locale for what follows. Mark 10:1 and 11:1 are suggested as supportive evidence. Yet in 10:1 it is unclear whether the following incident takes place in the region of Judea or beyond the Jordan (mentioned last). If anything, Judea is more likely, due to the presence of the Pharisees in 10:2ff. and as the "to" (εἰς, *eis*) suggests (see below). As for 11:1, Mark mentions Jerusalem first because it is Jesus's ultimate goal, and the other locations (Bethphage, Bethany, the Mount of Olives) essentially refer to the environs of Jerusalem. In 7:31 it appears that Jesus passes through Sidon and the Decapolis in order to arrive at his goal, the Sea of Galilee. The supposedly Hellenistic nature of the miracle story is also mentioned as supporting the view that the present account took place in a gentile environment, but see 7:33–34.

Far more important in understanding Mark's geographical description in 7:31 is the Markan use of "he came to" (ἦλθεν εἰς, *ēlthen eis*). In every other instance in Mark where we find "he/they came to" (1:14, 29, 39; 5:1; 6:53; 8:10; 9:33; 14:16), the following incident/event takes place in the location described by the "to" (εἰς). Similarly, wherever we find the historical present "he/they come to" (ἔρχεται εἰς, *erchetai eis*; 3:20; 5:38; 6:1; 8:22; 10:1, 46; 11:15, 27; 14:32), the following incident takes place in the location described by the "to." There is no reason for believing that Mark wants his readers to interpret 7:31 differently. Thus the miracle of 7:32–37 takes place, according to Mark, after Jesus passed by way of Sidon through the middle of the Decapolis and came to the Sea of Galilee (cf. Gundry 1993: 382). This is clearly how Matt. 15:29 understands the Markan itinerary. This conclusion receives additional support from the fact that the feeding in 8:1–10 takes place by the Sea of Galilee (8:10 [note the boat], 22; cf. Matt. 15:39) and from the presence of the Pharisees in the area (8:11). Usually when Mark describes Jesus crossing from the western ("Jewish") side of the Sea of Galilee (or the Jordan River) to the eastern ("gentile") side (or vice versa), he uses the expression "across" (πέραν, *peran*; 3:8; 10:1) or "to the other side" (εἰς τὸ πέραν, *eis to peran*; 4:35; 5:1, 21; 6:45; see 5:21–24a).[1] No such terminology is used for Jesus leaving the site of the feeding of the four thousand to go to Dalmanutha in 8:10, which suggests that 8:1–9 took place on the same side of the Sea of Galilee as 8:11–13, where Jesus encountered the Pharisees.

A final argument in support of this view involves the interpretation of the adverb "again" (πάλιν, *palin*). Does it modify the participle "having departed" or the verb "came"? In Mark, when this adverb is used in a sentence containing a single participle and a verb, we find that when we have the order participle + πάλιν + verb, the πάλιν modifies the participle (2:1, "having entered again into Capernaum"; 5:21, "having crossed again to the other side"; 7:14, "having called again the crowd"; 10:32, "having taken again the Twelve"), but

---

1. Although Bethsaida was a Jewish city, it lay on the eastern side of the Jordan River as it entered the Sea of Galilee, and apparently the river separated one side of the lake from "the other side."

when we have the order πάλιν + participle + verb, the πάλιν modifies the verb (14:39, "and having departed he again prayed the same words"; 14:40, "and having come he again found them sleeping").[2] It is therefore probable that in 7:31 πάλιν should also be interpreted as modifying the main verb. This lends additional support to the view that the following miracle took place in the locale to which Jesus "came again," that is, the area around the Sea of Galilee where most of his ministry has occurred so far (Räisänen 1990: 153–54; contra France 2002: 301–2).

The similarity between this verse and 8:22 is obvious. This raises the question **7:32** of why these verses (and the rest of the two miracle stories in 7:31–37 and 8:22–26) look so much alike. The presence of a Markan vocabulary (bring, φέρουσιν, *pherousin* [an impersonal plural; see 1:21–22]; "plead with him" [παρακαλοῦσιν, *parakalousin*] + ἵνα [*hina*, in order that] and the subjunctive; cf. 5:10; 6:56), style (the historical present), theology (the secrecy motif involving a private healing and the command to secrecy, and the astonishment the miracle produces), and the similar order and content (the description of the trip, bringing the deaf mute, beseeching Jesus, a private healing involving spitting, a command to secrecy) suggest that these two traditions, already possessing a similar vocabulary and format, were edited by Mark, resulting in an even greater similarity between the two accounts. It is not possible, however, to demonstrate that these two accounts were linked in the pre-Markan tradition.

The man brought to Jesus is described as "deaf" (κωφόν, *kōphon*),[3] and he could "hardly speak" (μογιλάλον, *mogilalon*). There is no indication that the man is a gentile (contra Guelich 1989: 394; Marcus 2000: 472). Such a conclusion is the result of assuming that this event took place in the Decapolis, but Mark describes it as taking place at the Sea of Galilee (see 7:31). The man's hearing problem is absolute. He is deaf. His speaking problem is not. He can speak but not correctly, that is, he has a speech impediment (as "speaking correctly" [ἐλάλει ὀρθῶς, *elalei orthōs*] in 7:35 suggests), a problem that may have resulted from his inability to hear. The man's healing will result in an ability to hear and to speak correctly (7:35). Those who brought the man to Jesus are described in the account by an impersonal "they" (cf. 1:22, 32; 2:3; etc.). "They" beseech Jesus on behalf of their friend in order to have him "set his hand upon him" (see 5:21–24a). There is no reason to interpret this expression as implying that they wanted Jesus to "bless" the man but did not expect Jesus to "heal" him (contra W. Lane 1974: 266). In the mind of Mark's readers, such a bifurcation would be impossible. To bless the deaf mute would mean to heal him. In every other instance but one in Mark, "setting his hand(s)

---

2. Mark 10:24 and 15:12 are not included in the examples because of the idiomatic nature of the participle-verb combination "having answered he said"; Mark 8:1 and 13 are not included because of the presence of multiple participles.

3. The word "deaf" (κωφόν) can indicate that a person is either "deaf" or "mute," but in light of the following comment that he could "hardly speak" (μογιλάλον), it must mean "deaf" here.

on someone" involves an act of healing (5:23; 6:5; 8:22, 25; cf. also 1:31, 41; 5:41; 9:27; the exception is 10:16).

7:33–34   The healing of the deaf mute is performed "privately" (κατ' ἰδίαν, *kat' idian*), away from the crowd, as in 5:40–43 and 8:23 (cf. also 4:34; 6:31–32; 9:2). In Mark, this is part of the overall messianic secret motif, although here this may very well have been part of the tradition. In the ministry of Jesus, the present healing was an act of mercy and grace. It was not meant to serve as a sign to the people (8:11–12) that he was the Christ, the Son of God. For the Markan reader, however, this miracle and Jesus's other miracles do serve as signs that Jesus is the Son of God. The description of the man's healing involves six actions: Jesus taking him aside; putting (lit. "casting," ἔβαλεν, *ebalen*) his fingers into his ears (to cure his deafness), spitting, touching the man's tongue (to cure his speech impediment), sighing, and saying, "Be opened." There is no reason to assume that the more detailed description of this healing implies that this was a "particularly difficult" miracle (contra Gundry 1993: 383; but cf. also France 2002: 300). The elements that raise the most questions involve spitting and sighing. Why does Jesus spit? Where does he spit (on the ground, on his fingers, on the man's tongue)? The only other place in Mark where Jesus spits is in 8:23, where he spits on the eyes of the blind man in curing his blindness. This may favor the view that Jesus spat on the man's tongue (cf. *t. Sanh*. 12.10), but whereas in 8:23 the eyes are specifically mentioned, here the place of spitting is not described (Donahue and Harrington 2002: 240). The use of spittle in healing (cf. John 9:6) is well documented (cf. Gundry 1993: 389; Marcus 2000: 473–74).

The "sighing" of Jesus has been described as a standard magical healing technique (Bonner 1927: 172–74), a sigh of compassion for the man (V. Taylor 1952: 355), a prayer-like gesture (cf. Exod. 2:24; 6:5; Judg. 2:18; also Tob. 3:1) seeking God's power for healing, and so on. In light of its association with "having looked up into heaven" (ἀναβλέψας εἰς τὸν οὐρανόν, *anablepsas eis ton ouranon*), it is best to see Jesus's sighing as an emotional, prayer-like gesture (cf. 6:41, where "looking up into heaven" is associated with "blessing" the bread; also John 11:41). A later reference in Mark in which Jesus tells his disciples that a demon that caused muteness (9:25) could only be cast out by prayer (9:29) gives additional support to this interpretation.

There have been a number of attempts to interpret the healing activities described in these two verses as "a Hellenistic healing story" reflecting its origin in a Hellenistic situation in life or as a Christian contextualization of the story for preaching it in the Greek world (Guelich 1989: 390, 395; Donahue and Harrington 2002: 242; contra Gundry 1993: 389). Yet we can find parallels in the Jewish literature for each of the elements found in the present account, and the presence of the Semitic ἐφφαθά (*ephphatha*) indicates that the original setting of the story was most likely Jewish. Even if it is not impossible that such an expression could have been uttered in the regions of Tyre and Sidon or the Decapolis, it is far more likely that it would have been uttered in a Jewish setting on the western side of the Sea of Galilee (see 7:31).

All the preceding actions are preliminary to Jesus's word of healing. There is debate as to whether ἐφφαθά is a transliteration of an Aramaic (Jeremias 1971: 7n4; Morag 1972; Meier 1991: 266; Marcus 2000: 474) or Hebrew (Rabinowitz 1962; 1971) expression. The greater likelihood appears to favor it coming from Aramaic. It is easier to explain the presence of an Aramaic (or Hebrew) expression in the account if we assume that Jesus is addressing an Aramaic-speaking audience in Galilee rather than a Greek-speaking audience in the Decapolis. If the audience were Greek, we would also have to assume that the Aramaic expression was added later in the retelling of the tradition.[4] As elsewhere, Mark's retention of the Aramaic term is due not so much to it being a special or secret incantation possessing magical power (contra Pesch 1980a: 396; Theissen 1983: 64)[5] as to his conservative handling of the traditions available to him (see 5:41–43). As usual, Mark provides a Greek translation of the expression (διανοίχθητι, *dianoichthēti*) for his readers, indicating that ἐφφαθά was not understood by him as a secret, magical term. Mark intends his readers to understand the command "Be opened" as a word of power initiating the healing of the man's deafness and enabling him to speak correctly (Donahue and Harrington 2002: 240).

The healing is now described. The man's ears (ἀκοαί, *akoai*; lit. "hearings") are opened, that is, he is able to hear, and (lit.) the "chain of his tongue was loosed." The latter describes the man's ability to speak "correctly" (ὀρθῶς, *orthōs*). Mark makes no implication that the man's former inability to speak was due to demon possession. In 9:14–29 this is clearly the case (9:17–18, 20, 25–26, 28–29), but the present healing miracle is not an exorcism (contra Deissmann 1978: 307). Mark is clearly aware of the difference (see 1:32–34). **7:35**

The command for secrecy following this healing recalls 1:44 and 5:43 (cf. also 8:26). We have also come across such commands for secrecy in several summary statements (1:34; 3:12). The command to silence, however, like Jesus's desire that his whereabouts not be known (7:24), cannot be kept. Jesus cannot be hidden. His words and works cannot be concealed. Mark does not portray "them" (αὐτοῖς, *autois*; it is uncertain whether this refers to the man's friends or to the crowd) or the leper in 1:45 as disobedient and insubordinate. On the contrary, the cleansed leper "preaches" and disseminates "the word," and "they preach" (ἐκήρυσσον, *ekērysson*). These are both positive expressions in Mark. (Cf. how John the Baptist "preaches" in 1:4 and 7; Jesus "preaches" in 1:14–15, 38–39; the disciples "preach" in 3:14 and 6:12; the early church is to "preach" in 13:10 and 14:9; and the man healed by Jesus "preaches" in 5:20.) Furthermore, they have done exactly what Mark's readers are expected **7:36**

4. It is not impossible that Jesus could have uttered an Aramaic command to an Aramaic-speaking Jew in the Decapolis, but there were far more Aramaic-speaking Jews in Galilee.
5. Meier (1994: 550) points out, "Perhaps nothing makes one feel more the difference in tone and spirit between the spells of the Greek magical papyri and the Gospel miracles than to read through a collection like Betz's *The Greek Magical Papyri in Translation* and to encounter regularly spells like "A EE ĒĒĒ IIII OOOOO YYYYYY . . . NIPOUMICHMOUMAŌPH.""

to do—bear witness to the good news of Jesus Christ, the Son of God. Once again, Mark portrays Jesus as not seeking notoriety or fame but despite this receiving great fame and notoriety. Jesus, the Son of God, is too great to be kept hidden. He may command that his name not be made manifest, but the more he commands, the more exceedingly (lit. "much more") still is he proclaimed. Mark does not define what the man's friends are not to tell. Was it the technique Jesus used to heal? Was it the secret/sacred magical term ἐφφαθά? And so on. By his use of "preach" to describe their activity, Mark probably wants his readers to understand this broadly as "preach about the greatness and power of Jesus Christ, the Son of God" (cf. 5:20) and the arrival of the kingdom of God (cf. 1:14–15).

7:37 The result of the healing (7:37 refers back to 7:35 not 7:36) brings a familiar response (see 4:40–41). The people are "exceedingly astonished" (ὑπερπερισσῶς ἐξεπλήσσοντο, *hyperperissōs exeplēssonto*—a double superlative). Whereas this expression describes their emotional response, the verbal response "He has done all things well" (Καλῶς πάντα πεποίηκεν, *Kalōs panta pepoiēken*) indicates that Jesus, like God, does all things well (Gen. 1:31; Eccles. 3:11). Like God, he gives speech to humans (Exod. 4:11). This is then explained by the summary statement, which may allude to Isa. 35:5–6: "He makes both the deaf [plural] to hear and the mute [plural] to speak." Mark may intend his readers to interpret the present tense in this saying as a durative or progressive present: in the time of Mark's readers, Jesus is still making the deaf hear and the mute speak (cf. Matt. 11:5/Luke 7:22).

Summary

In this passage, two Markan themes are intimately related. The healing of the deaf mute bears witness both to the coming of the kingdom of God and to the character of the one who brings the kingdom. The former is seen both in the miracle and in the allusion in 7:37 to the miracle of healing the deaf promised in Isa. 35:5–6 when the kingdom comes. The healing of the deaf mute also focuses attention on the one who brings such healing and like God "does all things well" (Mark 7:37; cf. Gen. 1:31). The messianic secret and its violation further serve to show the greatness of Jesus. He simply cannot be hidden (cf. Mark 1:34 with 3:11–12 and 5:7; 1:44 with 45 and 2:1–2; etc.).

A number of attempts have been made to see in this passage allusions to the disciples' lack of understanding (Fowler 1981: 107–8; Guelich 1989: 391; Donahue and Harrington 2002: 242–43). Often this involves a symbolical interpretation of "hearing" in this story and "seeing" in 8:22–26 (Marcus 2000: 476–77). Do these symbolize having ears to hear the implications of Jesus's teachings in 7:1–30 and having eyes to understand the messianic teaching in 8:31–10:45? An "opened ear" was a symbol for receiving divine revelation and truth (1QH 1.21; Tg. Isa. 35:5). The strongest evidence for such a symbolic interpretation is found in 8:18, where seeing and hearing refer to something more than physically seeing and hearing. Yet in both the present miracle (as well as the healing of the Syrophoenician woman's daughter that precedes it) and the healing of the blind man in 8:22–26, the disciples are not mentioned. If Mark intends his readers to see in the present account an allusion to the disciples' lack of understanding, why does he not mention the disciples anywhere in the entire account? Why the subtlety?

Still another attempt to find a Markan emphasis in the present account involves seeing in it implications for the gentile mission. Numerous scholars have argued that the site of this miracle was the Decapolis and as a result that the deaf mute was a gentile. Thus this miracle, like the healing of the Gerasene demoniac (5:1–20) and the Syrophoenician woman's daughter (7:24–30), is interpreted as a proleptic example of the future gentile mission. There is little doubt that the healing of the Gerasene demoniac and the Syrophoenician woman's daughter function in this way, but the attempt to interpret the present healing as another gentile healing by Jesus stumbles over how one should interpret 7:31. We have sought to show that Mark expects his readers to understand that the present miracle took place in the area on the western side of the Sea of Galilee and not in the Decapolis (see 7:31). Thus the present account does not serve as an example of the future gentile mission of Mark's day.

Additional Notes

7:31. A number of MSS read Τύρου καὶ Σιδῶνος ἦλθεν ($\mathfrak{P}^{45}$ A W f¹ f¹³ syr) instead of Τύρου ἦλθεν διὰ Σιδῶνος (ℵ B D L Δ Θ lat). The former is probably either a copyist's attempt to ameliorate the difficult itinerary described in 7:31 or due to the common expression "Tyre and Sidon."

7:35. Some MSS add "immediately" (εὐθέως) at this point ($\mathfrak{P}^{45}$ A W Θ f¹ f¹³). It is lacking in ℵ B D L Δ it. "Immediately" (εὐθύς) occurs forty-one times in Mark, but εὐθέως occurs nowhere in Mark except in this disputed passage. It is best therefore not to see it as part of the original text of Mark.

7:36. "That" (ἵνα) is best interpreted as indicating the content of the command rather than its purpose (see 3:9–10).

I. Jesus Feeds the Four Thousand (8:1–9)

One cannot read the present account of Jesus's feeding of the four thousand without noting the many similarities that exist between it and the account of the feeding of the five thousand (6:34–44): Jesus's compassion for the crowd (6:34; 8:2); the location in a desert place (6:35; 8:4); the question on how to feed the people (6:37; 8:4); the exact same question concerning the amount of food available (6:38; 8:5); a command for the people to recline (6:39–40; 8:6a); a similar order and vocabulary involving the giving of thanks/blessing, breaking the bread, and the giving of it to the disciples for distribution (6:41; 8:6b–d); a reference to fish being eaten (6:38b, 41e; 8:7); all the people eating and being filled (6:42; 8:8a); the baskets of leftovers collected (6:43; 8:8b); the number of people being fed (6:44; 8:9); and the dismissal of the crowd (6:45b; 8:9b). In both feeding miracles the next pericope begins with a change of scene to another place along the Sea of Galilee (6:45; 8:10).

As a result of these similarities, numerous scholars argue that the present account is a "doublet" or duplicate of the same tradition. Some claim that Mark has created the earlier account in 6:30–44 on the basis of the present one (Fowler 1981: 43–90).[1] Others claim that Mark created 8:1–9 on the basis of the earlier account (Donfried 1980). Yet the presence of numerous hapax legomena in Mark that appear in 8:1–9 ("have remained," προσμένουσιν, *prosmenousin* [8:2]; "will faint," ἐκλυθήσονται, *eklythēsontai* [8:3]; "hungry," νήστεις, *nēsteis* [8:3]; "desert," ἐρημίας, *erēmias* [8:4]; "remaining," περισσεύματα, *perisseumata* [8:8]; and "baskets," σπυρίδας, *spyridas* [8:8]) argues against it being a Markan creation.[2] Although Mark has created various seams and summaries and inserted his own editorial comments into certain accounts, we have no reason to assume that he created entire accounts de novo. Even if we grant that he did, it would be impossible to distinguish such an account from a Markan retelling of a traditional account in which he heavily used his own vocabulary and style (Stein 1991: 54). That the feeding of the five thousand in John 6:1–14 is literarily independent of the accounts of the feeding miracles in Mark and Matthew and yet has parallels to both feeding miracles indicates that both these accounts existed

---

1. Rather than Mark creating the tradition of 6:34–44, it is far more likely that he "used [the] traditional material creatively" (Hooker 1991: 189).

2. "In view of the *hapax legomenon* [sic] in the second account [8:1–9], it is no longer argued that the second account is the editorial work based on the first account" (Masuda 1982: 200; cf. also Pesch 1980a: 400).

in the pre-Markan tradition (Marcus 2000: 491, 493–95).[3] The pre-Markan nature of the two feeding accounts receives further support from the numerous differences found in the two accounts. These include the amount of bread (5 loaves [6:38] versus 7 loaves [8:5]); the different number of fish (2 fish [6:38] versus a "few" fish [8:7]); "blessing" (εὐλόγησεν, eulogēsen) the bread and fish (6:41) versus "thanking" (εὐχαριστήσας, eucharistēsas) for the bread (8:6) and "blessing" (εὐλογήσας) the fish (8:7); the amount of leftovers (12 "baskets" [κοφίνων, kophinōn; 6:43] versus 7 "baskets" [σπυρίδας, spyridas; 8:8]); the number of people (5,000 "men" [ἄνδρες, andres; 6:44] versus 4,000 [8:9]); the location ("desert place" [ἔρημος . . . τόπος, erēmos . . . topos; 6:35] versus "desert" [ἐρημίας; 8:4]); the location of the following event (Bethsaida [6:45] versus Dalmanutha [8:10]). (Cf. also the mention of green grass [6:39], the organized sitting [6:40], the separate blessing and distribution of the fish [8:7], etc.) Clearly Mark (6:34–44; 8:1–9, 19–20) and Matthew (14:14–21; 15:32–39; 16:9–10) understood them as two separate accounts.

The historical question of whether there were two feeding miracles is raised by the disciples' lack of understanding in 8:4. If they had witnessed Jesus's miraculous feeding of the five thousand in 6:34–44, how could they have reacted in such unbelief and have asked how these people could be fed in the wilderness? Clearly this fits the Markan motif of the dullness of the disciples very well (see "The Disciples" under "Theological Emphases" in the introduction), but is such a response from the disciples credible if they had earlier witnessed the feeding of the five thousand? Yet such "dullness" is found throughout the Bible. Compare how the people of Israel forget so quickly the mighty works and miracles that they had witnessed (contrast Exod. 7:1–15:27 with 16:1–3) and how Elijah is afraid of Jezebel after he had witnessed God's awesome power and might (contrast 1 Kings 17:1–18:46 and 19:1–3). More important for deciding the historical question than the credibility of the disciples' lack of understanding is the issue of the presuppositions that are brought to the study of the account. If one is closed to the possibility of the supernatural occurring in history, if miracles cannot happen, then neither feeding account can be historical, for both affirm that a great miracle took place. If one is open to the possibility of one of the feeding miracles being historical, arguments against the historicity of the second are not that weighty.

A number of scholars have argued that this account and the feeding of the five thousand introduced an extensive and similar pre-Markan complex of stories (Quesnell 1969: 28–32; Fowler 1981: 7–11; contra Kuhn 1971: 29–32). This can be seen in the following synopsis (W. Lane 1974: 269; Brooks 1991: 124):

3. France (2002: 307) concludes that "there were two such incidents, separately remembered and passed down in tradition, but, naturally enough, told in increasingly similar terms as time went on, except only that the different sets of numbers were faithfully preserved."

1. 6:34–44	Feeding the 5,000/4,000	8:1–9 (cf. John 6:1–15)
2. 6:45–56	Crossing the Sea of Galilee	8:10 (cf. John 6:16–21)
3. 7:1–23	Dispute with the Pharisees	8:11–13 (cf. John 6:30)
4. 7:24–30	Discussion about bread	8:14–21 (cf. John 6:22–59)
5. 7:31–36	Healing involving spittle and laying on of hands	8:22–26
6. 7:37	A confession of faith	8:27–33 (cf. John 6:60–69)

These parallels are interesting, but upon closer examination they are far from exact. The Johannine parallel lacks a healing miracle (5) and has the debate with the Pharisees (3) out of Markan order. As for the Markan parallels, the crossing of the Sea of Galilee (2) in 6:45–56 is quite extensive and involves a miracle, where the parallel in 8:10 does not. Here the Johannine parallel is much closer to Mark 6. It may well be that (1), (2), and (4) were associated together in the pre-Markan tradition, but elements (3), (5), and (6) seem less certain. The immediate tie of the present account with the preceding material is loose. "In those days" (Ἐν ἐκείναις ταῖς ἡμέραις, *en ekeinais tais hēmerais*; 8:1) provides a loose chronological tie with the preceding (cf. 1:9), and the common locale, the Sea of Galilee (cf. 7:31 with 8:10), also provides a loose tie. As to the following material, the reference to "bread" in the present account (8:5–8) ties it to the warning concerning the leaven of the Pharisees and Herod, and with the reference to the bread of the two miraculous feedings in 8:14–20.

The present story consists of four parts: (1) a brief seam introducing the problem (8:1); (2) a description of the problem, consisting of a conversation between Jesus and the disciples (8:2–4); (3) the resolution of the problem by means of a feeding miracle (8:5–7), using language similar to the earlier feeding miracle (6:41) and the Last Supper (14:22); and (4) a conclusion (8:8–9), revealing the superabundance of God's miraculous provision by the crowds being filled, the amount of leftovers collected (8:8), and the number of people fed (8:9). Although some see the Markan editorial activity primarily in 8:1 ("again" [πάλιν, *palin*]; the opening genitive absolute ["when again there was a great crowd and they did not have anything to eat"]; "great crowd" [πολλοῦ ὄχλου, *pollou ochlou*]; and "having called" [προσκαλεσάμενος, *proskalesamenos*]; Pryke 1978: 16, 143, 162; Gnilka 1978: 301; Guelich 1989: 402), Markan vocabulary and style are present throughout the account. This is due not so much to his creation of extensive new material as to his retelling of the tradition in his own words and style (Masuda 1982: 196–98) and to the influence on this account of the wording of the earlier feeding (6:34–44) and the tradition of the Last Supper (14:22–25).

Exegesis and Exposition

¹In those days when again there was a great crowd and ⌜they did not have⌝ anything ⌜to eat⌝, having called the disciples, he [Jesus] says to them, ²"I have compassion for

the crowd, because for ⌜three days⌝ they have remained with me and they do not have anything to eat. ³And, if I should send them away hungry to their home[s], they will faint on the way, and some of them have come from a great distance." ⁴And his disciples answered him, "How will anyone be able here in the desert to provide these people with bread?" ⁵And he was asking them, "How much bread do you have? And they said, "Seven [loaves]." ⁶And he commands the crowd to recline on the ground, and having taken the seven loaves of bread [and] having given thanks, he broke [them] and was giving [them] to his disciples so that they might distribute [them], and they distributed [them] to the crowd. ⁷And they also had a few ⌜small fish⌝, and having blessed ⌜these⌝, he said that they also should be distributed. ⁸And they ate and were filled, and they gathered up ⌜seven baskets of the remaining fragments.⌝ ⁹And there were about four thousand people, and he sent them away. ⌜ ⌝

The present account is tied to the preceding one by two phrases, "In those days" and "when again there was a great crowd" (πάλιν πολλοῦ ὄχλου ὄντος, *palin pollou ochlou ontos*). The former is used in an introductory seam only in 1:9, where it serves as a loose temporal indicator. The degree to which it should be seen as bearing eschatological significance is debated. In 13:17, 24 (cf. 13:19) the eschatological dimension is clear from the immediate context, but, although anything in Jesus's ministry involves the coming of the kingdom of God and is thus eschatological in nature, here the eschatological emphasis appears to be minimal. To the degree that the feeding miracle alludes to the Last Supper, the event also has eschatological overtones (cf. 14:25). The second phrase is more specific and reveals that Mark wants his readers to remember the last time when a "great crowd" was present. The preceding healing of the deaf mute (7:31–37) mentions a crowd (7:33), but not a "great crowd." There is no crowd present in the healing of the Syrophoenician woman's daughter (7:24–30); and no "great crowd" is mentioned when Jesus teaches concerning clean and unclean (7:1–23), in the summary of Jesus's healings (6:53–56), or in the miracle of his walking on the water (6:45–52). The last reference to a "great crowd" is 6:34, when Jesus feeds the five thousand (6:30–34). The similarity in content between the present account and the former feeding miracle, the specific verbal tie to the "great crowd," and the word "again" indicate that Mark wants his readers to recall the previous feeding miracle as they read/hear the present account (Guelich 1989: 403; Gundry 1993: 392–93; Donahue and Harrington 2002: 235–36). Mark prepares his readers for the coming miracle in the opening verse by mentioning that this great crowd did not have anything to eat.

8:1

The location of the story is the Sea of Galilee (8:10). The attempt to see this feeding as occurring in the Decapolis, and therefore among gentiles, is due primarily to a misreading of 7:31 (see 7:31), but "the story itself contains no indication of place, . . . [and] Mark makes no reference to his [i.e., Jesus's] being on Gentile territory. Nor does he indicate that the crowd consisted of Gentiles" (Hooker 1991: 188; cf. Fowler 1981: 60–61). This contrasts with

7:26, where Mark clearly wants his readers to know that the woman was a gentile. He does so there by stating that she was a "Syrophoenician by race," even though there are already present several indicators that the woman is a gentile (she comes from Tyre [7:24], is not a child but a dog [7:27], and acknowledges that she is not one of God's children [7:28]). In an account where all such indicators are missing, it would be strange not to add to "from a great distance" (8:3) something like "from Tyre and Sidon and throughout the Decapolis," if Mark wanted his readers to assume a gentile audience. The suggestion that in 8:10 Mark indicates that the present account is meant to be understood as taking place on the eastern side of the Sea of Galilee possesses three major problems: (1) although the location of the following sea journey, Dalmanutha, is unknown (Marcus 2000: 498), it is on the western side of the lake as indicated by the presence of the Pharisees in 8:11; (2) no mention is made of going "to the other side" (εἰς τὸ πέραν, eis to peran; cf. 5:1, 21; 6:45; 8:13; see 5:21–23) or of "crossing over" (διαπεράσαντος, diaperasantos; cf. 5:21; 6:53) from the site of the feeding of the four thousand to Dalmanutha; and (3) the subsequent journey from Dalmanutha "to the other side" (8:13) ends at Bethsaida (8:22), which is on the eastern side of the Sea of Galilee. Thus Mark does not give any clear evidence that he wants his readers to understand the present account as a miraculous feeding of gentiles in the Decapolis (Friedrich 1964: 10–12).

8:2–4 "Having called" (προσκαλεσάμενος; 8:1; see 3:13) the disciples, Jesus expresses his compassion for the crowd. In 6:34 this compassion is directed to their lost, shepherdless condition, but here it is due to their hunger. These should be seen not as contrasting but as complementary concerns, since Jesus cares for the entire person. Mark emphasizes the plight of the crowd in several ways: they have nothing to eat (8:1); they have been (lit. "are remaining") with Jesus for three days (8:2); as a result of their time with Jesus, the phrase "they have nothing to eat" (8:2) is repeated; if dismissed, "they will faint on the way" (8:3); and "some of them have come from a great distance" (8:3), so that they are a long way from home (cf. Gundry 1993: 393).

The expression "three" in "three days" (ἡμέραι τρεῖς, hēmerai treis) is frequently associated in Mark with the resurrection of Jesus (8:31; 9:31; 10:34; 14:58; 15:29), but it can also mean a "short period of indeterminate length" (Marcus 2000: 487, listing Acts 28:7, 12, 17 as examples). In the present instance, since the time reference is associated with the crowd rather than with Jesus, it is best not to see any symbolism in it. Numerous scholars see in the comment that some had come a great distance an allusion to the gentile nature of the audience (Danker 1963; Guelich 1989: 404; Marcus 2000: 487). Yet in the other instances in Mark where "from a great distance" (ἀπὸ μακρόθεν, apo makrothen) occurs (5:6; 11:13; 14:54; 15:40), it has nothing to do with "gentileness" but simply indicates distance. Mark gives no indication in the present account that he intends his readers to assume that they came from distant gentile locations. In the present account, the expression serves to explain the hunger of the people and the dynamic power of Jesus, which caused them to forget such a basic need as food just to be with him. As a result, "from a great distance" functions in Mark as a christological statement concerning the great magnetism of Jesus rather than as a description of the ethnic makeup of the crowd.

The reply of the disciples in 8:4 serves to magnify the miracle-working power of Jesus. Its primary purpose is not to emphasize the dullness of the disciples, for in contrast to 8:17–21, nothing negative is made of their statement. The emphasis is on their question, "How [lit. 'from where'] will anyone be able here in the desert to provide [lit. 'feed'] these people with bread?" God was able to provide manna for the children of Israel in the wilderness, but what human can do so?[4] The subsequent miracle, like the miracle of the feeding of the five thousand, indicates that Jesus Christ, the Son of God, can do what God does! He is able to do what no other person, only God alone, can do (2:7; 3:27; 5:3; 9:22–23, 28–29). To be sure, the disciples who had witnessed and participated in the feeding of the five thousand should have known that Jesus could and would feed the great crowd as before, but Mark makes no allusion here to this. As a result, whereas the dullness of the disciples is a real issue on the historical level, on the literary level the present question functions primarily christologically, to demonstrate the greatness of Jesus (Gundry 1993: 393).

As in the feeding of the five thousand (6:38), Jesus asks a question concerning the amount of bread available. The relationship between the numbers, five bread and two fish versus seven bread and a "few" fish, along with the other numbers in the two accounts, has engendered a great deal of discussion. Various kinds of symbolic significance are seen in the numbers:

    8:5–7

5 bread—the five books of the Law; to be combined with the seven bread to equal twelve disciples or twelve tribes of Israel

7 bread/baskets—the seven "Hellenistic" deacons of Acts 6:3 (who were, however, Jews, not gentiles); the seven Noachic commandments given to the whole world, according to Jewish tradition;[5] the seven nations of Canaan (Deut. 7:1; Acts 13:19); the multiple of seven in the seventy peoples of the world (and thus the gentiles) or the seventy disciples (Luke 10:1–20); a general sense of completeness (seven seals, bowls, trumpets, etc.)[6]

---

4. For numerous analogies between the present account and the exodus, see Marcus 2000: 483–86. Watts (2000: 178), however, sees the parallels as "superficial," and to see the question of the disciples as analogous to the grumbling of the Israelites in Exod. 16:3 is not at all convincing.

5. These involve the prohibitions against worshiping other gods, blaspheming the name of God, cursing judges, murder, incest and adultery, theft, and eating meat with its blood (Gen. 9:4–7).

6. The vast majority of instances in which the number "seven" appears in the Bible have absolutely nothing to do with gentiles (Marcus 2000: 489).

4,000—the four thousand gatekeepers and musicians of the temple (1 Chron. 23:5), the four winds (Mark 13:27), the four corners of the earth (Rev. 7:1), the four parts of the compass

12 baskets—the twelve disciples, the twelve tribes of Israel, and so on

The lack of any consensus on the alleged symbolism and the fact that in our present account no number is given to the "few fish" suggest that none of the numbers carries any real symbolic significance (Gundry 1993: 397).

Just as in the feeding of the five thousand (Mark 6:39–40), Jesus instructs the people to recline in 8:6. The following miracle shows great similarities in wording with the previous feeding miracle and the Last Supper (14:22–23):

Feeding of 5,000 (Mark 6:41)	Feeding of 4,000 (Mark 8:6–7)	Last Supper (Mark 14:22–23)
he blessed εὐλόγησεν *eulogēsen*	having given thanks εὐχαριστήσας *eucharistēsas*	having blessed εὐλόγησας *eulogēsas*
he broke κατέκλασεν *kateklasen*	he broke ἔκλασεν *eklasen*	he broke ἔκλασεν *eklasen*
he was giving ἐδίδου *edidou*	he was giving ἐδίδου *edidou*	he gave ἔδωκεν *edōken*
	having blessed [the fish] εὐλογήσας *eulogēsas*	having given thanks [the cup] εὐχαριστήσας *eucharistēsas*

The interchangeable nature of "giving thanks" and "blessing" can be seen by the fact that both occur in the present account and the account of the Last Supper but in reverse order (8:6 = 14:23; 8:7 = 14:22; Patsch 1971: 217–19) and that Mark uses them interchangeably in the giving thanks/blessing of the bread (cf. 8:6 and 6:41).

As in the earlier feeding account, the disciples play a key role in the distribution of the bread and fish (8:6 and 6:41) and the collection of the leftovers (8:8 and 6:43). This makes their historical dullness in 8:15–21 all the more culpable. Although the present feeding miracle is much shorter than the previous one, greater emphasis is placed upon the blessing (lacking in the feeding of the five thousand) and distribution of the fish. Whether this was done in order to align the two elements (bread and fish) more closely with the two elements in the Last Supper (bread and wine; Pesch 1980a: 404) is uncertain. Even more uncertain is whether this is due to the hand of Mark or whether it was already in the pre-Markan tradition.

The surpassing greatness of Jesus's miracle is emphasized by the people "eating" and being "filled" (ἐχορτάσθησαν, echortasthēsan; cf. 6:42) and the collecting of an abundance of leftovers (cf. 6:43). The difference in the term used for baskets (κοφίνων, kophinōn, in 6:43; σπυρίδας, spyridas, in 8:8) suggests that the two accounts came to Mark as separate traditions. No theological significance, however, should be read into the use of these two different terms. An additional indicator of Jesus's great miracle-working power is the number of people fed—four thousand. Despite all attempts, no convincing symbolism has been found in the number.

8:8–9

Summary

Numerous attempts have been made to see in the present account a Markan emphasis on Jesus's ministry to the gentiles. We have noted, however, that Mark gives no clear evidence that he wanted his readers to interpret the feeding of the four thousand as a gentile counterpart to the feeding of the five thousand Jews. On the contrary, the healing of the deaf mute and the feeding of the four thousand take place by the Sea of Galilee, not in the Decapolis (see 7:31; the summary in 7:31–37; 8:1 and 8:2–4). Another alleged Markan emphasis seen in the present passage involves the dullness of the disciples. One cannot deny that the present account does serve in this capacity in 8:14–21, especially in verse 21. But Mark makes no direct allusion to this theme in the present account itself (contrast 4:40; 6:50; 8:14–21). Furthermore, the dullness of the disciples in 8:14–21 has nothing to do with their inability to accept the gentiles into the church apart from circumcision (contrast Acts 10–11, 15), but has to do with their christological blindness.

The main Markan emphasis in this passage can be seen by noting its location in the middle of a collection of miracle stories (cf. 7:24–30, 31–37; and 8:22–26). "Mark wants in this story in chap. 8 to report a miraculous feeding and nothing else" (Friedrich 1964: 14). The compassion of Jesus for the people is emphasized in 8:1, but the story of the feeding of the four thousand is told to highlight the mighty miracle-working power of Jesus. The question "How will anyone be able here in the desert to provide these people with bread?" is meant to elicit the response, "No human being can." Yet just as God was able to feed the children of Israel with manna in the wilderness, so the Son of God is able to do the same. The degree to which "in the desert" is meant to recall the events of the exodus is uncertain, but Mark's emphasis on the divine miracle-working ability of Jesus is clear. Once again the question "Who is this man . . . ?" (4:41) comes to the forefront. Mark's answer is clear: this Jesus is the Christ, the Son of God!

Additional Notes

8:1. The plural ἐχόντων particularizes the individuals making up the "crowd" (ὄχλου is singular; V. Taylor 1952: 357).

8:1. Here and in v. 2, φάγωσιν is lit. "they might eat."

8:2. An awkward "parenthetical nominative" (BDF §144).

8:7. "Small fish" (ἰχθύδια, *ichthydia*) is best interpreted as a true diminutive due to the modifying ὀλίγα, *oliga*, "few" or "small."

8:7. αὐτά is lit. "them."

8:8. περισσεύματα κλασμάτων ἑπτὰ σπυρίδας is lit. "the remainders of the fragments, seven baskets."

8:9. Mark 8:10 is best understood as introducing 8:11–13 (cf. 6:45). See the introduction to 8:10–13.

IV. Mission and Misunderstanding: Part 3 (6:6b–8:21)
    I. Jesus Feeds the Four Thousand (8:1–9)
➤ J. Jesus Is Asked for a Sign (8:10–13)
    K. Jesus's Miracles of the Two Feedings Recalled (8:14–21)

J. Jesus Is Asked for a Sign (8:10–13)

The present account is a brief pronouncement story or conflict story (Guelich 1989: 410; contra Marcus 2000: 502). The extent to which it existed as an independent, pre-Markan story is debated. The existence of a similar saying and incident in the Q material (Matt. 12:38–39/Luke 11:29) in which the "sign of Jonah" is mentioned and the presence of significant Markan editorial work[1] have led some scholars to argue that the present account is a Markan creation. However, the presence of several hapax legomena[2] argues for the existence of a pre-Markan tradition lying behind the present account (Guelich 1989: 411).[3] In light of the above, it seems best to understand the present account as being due to a Markan retelling of a tradition in which Jesus rejected a demand for a sign. Whether that tradition included the saying concerning the sign of Jonah is debated. (Did Mark omit the Jonah saying in his retelling of the tradition [V. Taylor 1952: 361; Marcus 2000: 502, 505], or did Mark's source lack the saying [Schweizer 1970: 158; R. Edwards 1971: 83–87; Gnilka 1978: 305]?) Mark's own hand is seen most clearly in the introductory and concluding framework in 8:10 and 13 (Gnilka 1978: 305).

As in the earlier feeding of the five thousand, the feeding of the four thousand is followed by a crossing of the Sea of Galilee (cf. 6:30–44 + 45 and 8:1–9 + 10). The parallel in John (cf. 6:1–15 + 16–21), in which the feeding of the five thousand is also followed by a crossing of the Sea of Galilee, supports the view that this was rooted in the tradition. Closely associated in all these accounts is a dispute. In Mark 7:1–23 it involves Jesus's rejection of the Pharisaic traditions, but in 8:11–13 it involves a Pharisaic demand for a sign. In John 6:30 it also involves a demand for a sign. (For a discussion of these parallels, see the introduction to 8:1–9.) In Mark and John, each

---

1. Cf. "immediately" (εὐθύς, *euthys*; 8:10); "boarded" (ἐμβάς, *embas*; 8:10, 13); "boat" (πλοῖον, *ploion*; 8:10; cf. 8:13); "with the disciples" (μετὰ τῶν μαθητῶν, *meta tōn mathētōn*; 8:10); "argue" (συζητεῖν, *syzētein*; 8:11); "tempting him" (πειράζοντες αὐτόν, *peirazontes auton*; 8:11); cf. 10:2; also the similar use of the explanatory participle "cleansing" in 7:19; "again" (πάλιν, *palin*; 8:13); "to the other side" (εἰς τὸ πέραν, *eis to peran*; 8:13); see Marcus 2000: 502; Pryke 1978: 16, 143, 162.

2. See "Dalmanutha" (8:10), "region" (μέρη, *merē*; 8:10), "sighed deeply" (ἀναστενάξας, *anastenaxas*; 8:12); and Semitic stylistic features (circumlocution of "heaven" [οὐρανοῦ, *ouranou*; 8:11] for "God"; the divine passive, "shall be given" [δοθήσεται, *dothēsetai*; 8:12]; "verily" [ἀμήν, *amēn*; 8:12]; the "if" [εἰ, *ei*] oath formula [8:12]; "this generation" [ἡ γενεὰ αὕτη, *hē genea hautē* + τῇ γενεᾷ ταύτῃ, *tē genea tautē*; 8:12]).

3. "The early Aramaic or Semitic quality of Mark's version is quite clear" (R. Edwards 1971: 75; cf. also 75–80).

feeding, sea journey, and dispute is also followed by a discussion of some sort concerning bread (cf. 7:24–30; 8:14–21; John 6:22–59).

The present account consists of an introductory seam involving a sea journey (8:10); a brief pronouncement or controversy story (8:11–12), which contains a negative demand for a sign (8:11) and Jesus's pronouncement rejecting the demand (8:12); and a concluding sea journey across the Sea of Galilee (8:13). It is best to see 8:10 as an introduction to the present account rather than as a conclusion to the preceding miracle (contra various translations such as RSV, NRSV, REB, NASB, NIV). Changes of location usually introduce the following account (cf. 5:1, 21; 6:1, 45, 53; 7:24, 31), and this allows the previous account, like the feeding of the five thousand, to end with a description of the number of people who were fed (cf. 6:44 and 8:9). Similarly, "and immediately" (καὶ εὐθύς, *kai eythus*), which begins 8:10, more often introduces a pericope (cf. 1:12, 21, 23, 29; 6:45; 9:15; 14:43; 15:1) than concludes one (cf. 1:18, 28 [word order different]; 2:12 [word order different]; 3:6 [word order different]; 10:52). In the latter (concluding) examples, one should note that the temporal dimension of "immediately" is emphasized, whereas in the former (introductory) passages "and immediately" serves as a connecting link possessing no real temporal significance (see 1:10–11).

Exegesis and Exposition

[10]And immediately ⌜having boarded⌝ the boat with his disciples, he [Jesus] went into the regions of Dalmanutha. [11]And the Pharisees went out and began to argue with him, seeking from him a sign from heaven. [They did this] to test him. [12]And having sighed deeply in his spirit, he says, "Why does this generation seek a sign? Truly, I say to you, [May God's judgment fall upon me], if a sign will be given to this generation!" [13]And having left them [and] having again boarded ⌜ ⌝, he departed to the other side.

8:10   The Markan vocabulary and style of this introductory seam is quite apparent (cf. 6:45). The goal of the journey is Dalmanutha. The presence of Pharisees in 8:11 suggests that Dalmanutha lay on the western or "Jewish" side of the Sea of Galilee. Since no indication is made that Jesus and the disciples "crossed to the other side" in order to get to this location, this suggests that the previous incident took place on the western side of the Sea of Galilee as well. (See 7:31.) Despite all the attempts to discover the location of Dalmanutha, no mention of a town by this name is found in any of the literature outside our present text. Instead of Dalmanutha, the Matthean parallel has Magadan/Magedan/Magdala, an important fishing center located one mile north of Tiberias. Numerous suggestions have been made concerning Dalmanutha: a Markan misinterpretation of an Aramaic expression, a small anchorage misunderstood as a town, and so on. There is no scholarly consensus, however, regarding to what Dalmanutha refers. It may be that Mark is referring here to a town that has left no traces in contemporary sources (Marcus 2000: 498).[4] Mark provides no explanation of how a boat was so readily available for Jesus and the disciples (cf., however, 3:9). It is not relevant to his purpose (France 2002: 309).

Jesus is immediately confronted by a group of hostile Pharisees. The antagonism of the Pharisees toward Jesus has already been seen in 2:16–18, 24; 3:6; 7:1–5 and will come to the forefront again in 10:2; 12:13–15. They come to "argue" (συζητεῖν, *syzētein*, a favorite Markan term [1:27; 9:10, 14, 16; 12:28]), not to "discuss" (1:27; 9:10). Here, as in 9:14, 16, and 12:28, the "arguing" is hostile in nature. The Pharisees want Jesus to prove his authority to speak on God's behalf. The request for a sign is not always evil. Gideon asked for a sign (Judg. 6:36–40), as did Hezekiah (2 Kings 20:8–11), and they were not rebuked for doing so. It should also be noted that Ahaz was commanded by God to ask for a sign (Isa. 7:10–12) and was disobedient for not doing so. Yet in the great majority of instances, the request for a sign is seen as an act of disobedience and a tempting of God (Matt. 12:39; 16:4; John 2:18–19; 6:30; cf. *b. Sanh.* 104a).

8:11–12

The "sign" (σημεῖον, *sēmeion*) requested does not involve the working of a miracle. In Mark and the other Synoptic Gospels, miracles are referred to not as "signs" but as "mighty works" (δυνάμεις, *dynameis*) involving healings, exorcisms, or nature miracles (see 6:2, 5, 14; 9:39; cf. 5:30), whereas "sign" refers to an event of wonder (13:22). What the Pharisees seek is not a specific healing or nature miracle, for there have been many of these: 4:35–5:43; 6:30–56; 7:24–8:9. Jesus's ability to work miracles was well known (1:32–34, 45; 3:7–12; 6:53–56), and they were acknowledged by the Pharisees (3:22). Additional exorcisms or miracles would not change anything. What they now seek is a sign "from heaven" (ἀπὸ τοῦ οὐρανοῦ, *apo tou ouranou*). The latter prepositional phrase serves not adjectivally for "cosmic," that is, a "cosmic" sign (cf. Matt. 24:30; Luke 21:11, 25; Rev. 12:1, 3; 15:1), or for "apocalyptic," that is, Israel's eschatological deliverance and the judgment of the nations (contra Gibson 1990: 42–53), but as a circumlocution for God, that is, a "sign from God" (Pesch 1980a: 407; Gnilka 1978: 306; Guelich 1989: 413–14). This is evident from 8:12, where "will be given" is a divine passive for "God will give," and from 11:30–31, where the almost identical expression "from heaven" (ἐξ οὐρανοῦ, *ex ouranou*) stands in opposition to "from men" (ἐξ ἀνθρώπων, *ex anthrōpōn*) and serves as a circumlocution for "from God" (contra Gibson 1990: 43). The sought-for sign would involve an act by which God would reveal his approval of Jesus in an irrefutable way. Yet as 3:22 has demonstrated, no miracle or sign is irrefutable. To those whose hearts are open, the blind

---

4. Guelich (1989: 413) comments, "Since Mark does not create specific place names elsewhere in his redaction and since one is more likely to use a well-known rather than a rare place name when creating a scene, this geographical reference most likely belongs to a pre-Markan tradition." Cf. also Pesch 1980a: 406.

seeing, the lame walking, the lepers being cleansed, the deaf hearing, the dead being raised (Luke 7:22) are convincing signs that Jesus is the Christ, the Son of God. For those outside (Mark 4:11–12) whose hearts are hardened (3:5), nothing can function as a sign, for it can always be attributed to Satan (3:22; Matt. 9:34). The latter attribution may at times have merit (Mark 13:22; Deut. 13:1–5; Rev. 13:11–15).[5]

The evil intention of the Pharisees is indicated by "to test him" (a participial phrase; lit. "testing him"). This is probably a Markan interpretive comment (10:2; cf. the similar use of a participial clause [καθαρίζων πάντα τὰ βρώματα, *katharizōn panta ta brōmata*] in 7:19) revealing the purpose of the Pharisaic demand. It was intended to "test" him, as in 10:2 and 12:15 (cf. Luke 11:16; 1 Cor. 1:22). The role of the Pharisees in testing Jesus places them in partnership with Satan, the great tester/tempter, who at the beginning of Jesus's ministry tempted Jesus (Mark 1:13; cf. Matt. 4:3; 1 Thess. 3:5). The connection between seeking a sign, tempting God, and this generation recalls the association of these elements in Exod. 17:1–7 (esp. vv. 2, 7), where Israel in the wilderness tempted the Lord (Deut. 6:16; 9:22; 33:8; cf. Num. 14:1–11, 22; Ps. 95:8–11 [LXX 94:8–11]; also Heb. 3:1–4:13, esp. 3:7–11).[6]

Jesus's response involves a deep sighing (ἀναστενάξας, *anastenaxas*, is a hapax legomenon in the NT, but cf. 7:34) in "his" (αὐτοῦ, *autou*) spirit (not the Holy Spirit). This has been interpreted variously as a painful emotional reaction of anger or grief (V. Taylor 1952: 362; W. Lane 1974: 277; Hooker 1991: 192), a struggle with a demonic obstacle (Marcus 2000: 501, 504), a struggle of Jesus involving his faithfulness to God (Gibson 1996), the author's attempt to focus his readers' attention on the following pronouncement (Donahue and Harrington 2002: 248), a gathering of inner power to give a forceful prophetic action or pronouncement (Gundry 1993: 404; Pesch 1980a: 408; Guelich 1989: 414), and so on. The last receives support from such passages as Isa. 21:2; Ezek. 21:12 (LXX 21:11–12); John 13:21; compare also 2 Macc. 6:30; Sus. 22. Jesus's response is further intensified by the introductory "Verily" (ἀμήν, *amēn*). See 3:28–30. In his reply, Jesus refers to the Pharisees as representing "this generation." Although this expression can be used in a neutral sense (13:30), here, as in most cases, it refers to something like "this adulterous and sinful" (8:38) or "faithless" (9:19) generation (cf. also Luke 11:29/Matt. 12:39; Matt. 16:4; Matt. 17:17/Luke 9:41; Acts 2:40). In the OT this expression is used to describe the evil generation of Noah's day (Gen. 7:1; cf. Gen. Rab. 30.1; Midr. Ps. 1.12) and the generation of the wilderness sojourn (Ps. 95:10 [LXX 94:10]; cf. Deut. 32:5, 20; also Jub. 23.14, 16; Lövestam 1995: 8–17).

5. See Gray (1993: 112–44) for a discussion of contemporary false prophets mentioned by Josephus who worked signs. For a general discussion on miracles and signs, see C. Brown 1984.

6. Marcus (2000: 504) argues that 8:1–13 follows the order of events in Exod. 16:1–17:7, but whereas Mark's readers may have seen the analogy between 8:10–13 and Israel's tempting God in the wilderness, it is doubtful that they would have perceived a correspondence in the order of events.

Both these generations were thought of as not being worthy of sharing in the world to come (*m. Sanh.* 10.3).

Jesus's reply concludes with an oath. The oath is Semitic in style, and its protasis ("If . . .") lacks an apodosis ("May God . . ."). Examples of this form of an oath are found in Gen. 14:23; Num. 32:11; Deut. 1:35; 1 Sam. 3:17; 1 Kings 3:14; 2 Kings 6:31; Ps. 95:11 (LXX 94:11); Heb. 3:11; 4:3, 5. The unexpressed apodosis assumes a self-imposed curse such as "May God do . . . to me" to complete the "If. . . ." An example of this is found in 2 Kings 6:31, "So may God do to me, and more, if. . . ." The verb "will be given" (δοθήσεται, *dothēsetai*), a divine passive, recalls its earlier use in 4:25, where more "will be given [by God]" to those who have, but to those who have not and are "outside," nothing more "will be given [by God]," but their ignorance and darkness will increase.

The pronouncement of Jesus is followed by his departure "to the other side" **8:13** via the boat of 8:10. As pointed out earlier (see 5:21 and 7:31), "to the other side" (εἰς τὸ πέραν, *eis to peran*) is not a technical term for the eastern side of the Sea of Galilee. It can refer to traveling from the eastern to the western side of the Sea of Galilee or vice versa. Since the goal of the journey is Bethsaida (8:22), which is on the eastern side of the lake, it involves departing "to the other side." Although "again" (πάλιν, *palin*) can modify "having left them [i.e., the Pharisees]" (ἀφεὶς αὐτούς, *apheis autous*), it is best to interpret it as modifying "having boarded," since "having boarded" occurs in 8:10 and the "again" recalls this earlier boarding. For a previous encounter with the Pharisees, we would have to go back to 7:1–23. The textual variants associated with "again" indicate that some copyists understood it as qualifying "having boarded."

Mark does not indicate that at this point Jesus ended his public ministry in Galilee or that he had rejected the Jews in Galilee and was turning elsewhere to preach the gospel (contra Guelich 1989: 415–16) or that this was a symbolic abandoning of any further attempt to reach the Pharisees (contra France 2002: 310, 313). The expression "having left" (ἀφεὶς) is not a technical term for such a rejection. This verb is used over thirty-five times in Mark with a broad range of meanings ("depart from," "forgive," "set aside," "permit," "forsake," "leave," "expire," etc.), but it is never used in the sense of permanently ending a mission or rejecting a people. If Mark wanted his readers to understand that Jesus's departure marked an end to his Galilean ministry and involved a rejection of the Jewish people in Galilee, he could have indicated this very easily by a gesture (cf. 6:11) or a phrase (cf. Acts 13:46). No such indication is found in the present account.

Summary

The main Markan emphasis in this passage involves the continued and growing hostility that Jesus faced in his ministry. The religious leadership represented by the Pharisees, like the rebellious generations in Noah's day and during the wilderness sojourn, tempt the Lord by demanding a sign. Thus the readers of Mark should not be surprised that Jesus met death at the hands of the religious leadership of Israel. Whatever the flaws of the disciples—and the next account will provide a blatant example of their blindness—they are not hostile to the Son of God. They can be taught. Even if at times their hearts are hardened (6:52; 8:17), theirs is not an unpardonable sin. They do not understand the significance of Jesus's miracles, but they know that the miracles are from God. Thus their eyes can be opened, but this is not true of the religious leadership. These leaders are guilty of an unpardonable sin, for they are unwilling to see that the exorcisms, healings, and nature miracles of Jesus are indeed signs that he is the Christ, the Son of God. Instead, they attribute his works to Satan (3:22). Thus they exclude the possibility of having their blindness healed. There is also a christological emphasis in the passage that a superficial reading of the passage may not see. The request for a sign in the OT and the tempting by this evil generation are directed toward God. In the present passage they are directed toward Jesus! Faith and unbelief in God are understood by Mark to focus on Jesus. Thus to tempt Jesus (8:11) is to tempt God.

Additional Notes

8:10. ἐμβάς is lit. "having entered."

8:13. "Into the boat" (εἰς τὸ πλοῖον) is found in $\mathfrak{P}^{45}$ A D W Θ f[1] f[13]. It is best, however, to follow its omission in ℵ B C L Δ and see this as a scribal addition to make the text conform to 5:18; 6:45; 8:10 (cf. also 4:1).

K. Jesus's Miracles of the Two Feedings Recalled (8:14–21)

The classification of the present account is difficult. It consists primarily of teaching material (8:15, 17–21) involving an interaction between Jesus and the disciples (Gnilka 1978: 310; Beck 1981: 51–52). The Markan flavor of the passage has led most scholars to see it as a Markan construction. The redactional nature of the account includes a recalling of the two feeding miracles (6:34–44; 8:1–9); the detailed references to the two accounts involving not just the numbers (5 loaves, 5,000, 12 baskets; and 7 loaves, 4,000, 7 baskets—8:19–20) but even the distinctly different terms used for the baskets (κόφινος, *kophinos*, and σπυρίς, *spyris*); numerous Markan verbal characteristics (Pryke 1978: 16, 143, 162); and several Markan theological emphases, such as the dullness of the disciples (cf. 4:13, 41; 6:37, 52; 7:18; 8:4, 31–33; 9:6; etc.); the importance of "seeing" (βλέπετε, *blepete*; 8:15, 18; cf. 4:12, 24; 8:22–26; 10:46–52; 13:2, 5, 9, 23, 33), "hearing" (ἀκούετε, *akouete*; 8:18; cf. 4:3, 9, 10–13, 14–20, 23, 24, 33; 7:14; 9:7), and "understanding" (συνίετε, *syniete*; 8:17, 21; cf. 6:52; 7:14); and the reference to "hardened hearts" (πεπωρωμένην . . . τὴν καρδίαν, *pepōrōmenēn . . . tēn kardian*; 8:17; cf. 3:5; 6:52; also 7:6).

Although some scholars argue for the historicity of the incident (Gundry 1993: 411–16) and some for the account being an entirely Markan creation based on a traditional saying (8:15; Gnilka 1978: 310; Räisänen 1990: 200), most understand the present account as consisting of a traditional core (8:14, 16) that has been edited and reworked by Mark to fit the present context (Quesnell 1969: 105–6; Beck 1981: 55). The awkwardness of 8:15 and its interruption of 8:14 and 16 are often used as arguments to support the traditional nature of 8:14b and 16 and dispute the unity of 8:14–16. Whether these materials originally existed independently of each other but were associated together in the pre-Markan tradition is also debated. It appears best to understand the present account as a heavily reworked Markan retelling[1] of a tradition involving Jesus and the disciples crossing the Sea of Galilee, which included a discussion concerning their lack of bread and a saying concerning "the leaven of the Pharisees" (τῆς ζύμης τῶν Φαρισαίων, *tēs zymēs tōn Pharisaiōn*; 8:15). The emphasis on the disciples' dullness, while rooted in the tradition, is given added emphasis in the present account by the evangelist.

---

1. Guelich (1989: 426) refers to the present account as "bear[ing] the most redactional marks of any pericope so far."

The account possesses numerous ties to its present context. The reference to the "leaven of the Pharisees" (8:15) recalls the Pharisees' demand for a sign in the preceding incident (8:10–13). The account refers in detail (8:18–21) to the two feeding miracles (6:34–44; 8:1–9), and the lack of understanding by the disciples, which is repeated twice (8:16–17, 21), recalls numerous earlier examples of their dullness (see above). The superlative miracle-working power of Jesus manifested in the feeding miracles (8:19–20) brings to mind Jesus's many healings (1:29–31, 32–34, 40–45; 2:1–12; 3:1–6, 10; 5:21–43; 6:5, 53–56; 7:31–37), exorcisms (1:21–28, 32–34; 3:11–12; 5:1–20; 7:24–30), and nature miracles (4:35–41; 6:45–52; cf. also 1:10–11) reported earlier.[2] The reference to Herod recalls 3:6 and 6:14–29 (cf. 12:13).

The present account contains the following elements: (1) an introduction (8:14–16) referring to the disciples' lack of bread (8:14, 16) that sandwiches Jesus's warning concerning the leaven of the Pharisees and Herod (8:15); (2) a dialogue between Jesus and the disciples involving seven questions and two responses by the disciples centering on the numbers "twelve" and "seven" (8:17–20); and a concluding question (8:21) that refers to the disciples' dullness and repeats the second question (cf. 8:21 and 17c).

Exegesis and Exposition

[14]And they had ⌜forgotten⌝ to take loaves of bread, ⌜and except for one loaf of bread, they had no other [loaves of bread]⌝ with them in the boat. [15]And he was admonishing them, saying, "Look! Beware of the leaven of the Pharisees and the leaven ⌜of Herod⌝." [16]And they began to ⌜discuss⌝ among themselves, ⌜"[Did he say this] because they had no bread?"⌝ [17]And knowing [this], he [Jesus] says to them, "Why are you discussing that you do not have loaves of bread? Do you not yet perceive or understand? Do you have hardened hearts? [18]Having eyes, do you not see, and having ears, do you not hear? ⌜And do you not remember?⌝ [19]When I broke the five loaves of bread for the five thousand, how many full baskets of fragments did you take up?" And they say to him, "Twelve." [20]"When ⌜I broke⌝ the seven [loaves] for the four thousand, the contents of how many full baskets of fragments did you take up?" And they say [to him], "Seven." [21]And he was saying to them, "Do you not yet understand?"

8:14–16   The scene for the following account involves a dual reference to a lack of bread (Neirynck 1988: 113). The awkwardness of the second part of 8:14 has already been discussed (see the introduction to this unit; also the second additional note on 8:14). Since the singular and plural "bread" and "breads" is unclear in English, I translate them "loaf of bread" and "loaves of bread." The importance of the exception clause, "except for one loaf of bread," is debated. The idea that it is to be interpreted symbolically as a reference to

2. To these can be added the healings and exorcisms performed by Jesus's disciples (6:13).

Jesus the "one bread" (cf. John 6:35) and that the bread of the Lord's Supper is in mind has numerous supporters (Pesch 1980a: 414–15; Beck 1981: 49–56; Marcus 2000: 509–10) but also detractors (Guelich 1989: 421; Gundry 1993: 410–11; France 2002: 315n19). (The idea that the one loaf implies the unity of Jews and Greeks within the church [Boobyer 1953: 84–85; Kelber 1979: 40–41; Donahue and Harrington 2002: 254] finds no textual support in the present passage.) The importance of the exception clause should not be minimized (contra Räisänen 1990: 202). This is evident from the emphasis that "except" (εἰ μή, ei mē) clauses receive elsewhere in Mark (2:7; 5:37; 6:4; 9:9, 29; 10:18; 13:20, 32; cf. also 6:5, 8; 11:13). Mark makes no clear reference to Jesus as the "bread of life" or to the bread of the Lord's Supper in the present passage. It may be that this exception clause and the number "one" are "a traditional splinter" (Guelich 1989: 421) that Mark incorporates from his source material. It probably serves here to tie the present incident more closely with the feeding of the five thousand and four thousand, where an inadequate number of loaves (five and seven, respectively) were broken to feed the multitude. The mention of "one" (ἕνα, hena) loaf continues the analogy of an inadequate number of loaves of bread (five, seven, and now "one") and a great need of food for a large group (five thousand, four thousand, and now "the disciples"). The dullness of the disciples involves their not understanding that in Jesus's presence one loaf, just as earlier the five and seven loaves, is enough to feed them. Just as their need and limited resources earlier led to Jesus's miraculous provision of food, so they should know by now (note the "not yet" [οὔπω, oupō] in v. 17) that Jesus could miraculously provide food.

Verse 15 seems to interrupt the flow of 8:14 and 16. The "they had [lit. 'have'] no bread" (ἄρτους οὐκ ἔχουσιν, artous ouk echousin) in 8:16 seems to follow 8:14 smoothly. Yet 8:16 assumes a previous saying of Jesus whereas 8:14 is not such a saying. It is simply a statement of fact. If 8:14 and 16 were part of the pre-Markan tradition, Mark omitted either some statement ("I hope you brought bread to eat") or a question ("Do you have any bread to eat?") and inserted Jesus's saying about the leaven of the Pharisees and Herod (8:15) in its place. In many ways 8:15 and 16 fit together more logically than 8:14 and 16. Furthermore, we must remember that 8:14 is a Markan redactional seam, so that the pre-Markan form of the tradition was probably more like 8:15–16 than 8:14, 16.[3] The warning of Jesus in 8:15 is emphatic, as the double "Look! Beware [lit. 'See'] . . ." indicates. The reference to "leaven" (ζύμης, zymēs) refers not to yeast but to unbaked dough containing the yeast culture that when added to new dough would cause it to rise. Although "leaven" can function symbolically in a positive sense (Matt. 13:33/Luke 13:20–21), it is usually understood negatively as a symbol of evil or an evil influence (cf. Luke 12:1, where it symbolizes "hypocrisy" [ὑπόκρισις, hypokrisis]; 1 Cor.

---

3. Note Gundry (1993: 411), who states, "It is mystifying why the framework of the disciples forgetting to take enough bread for a lake-crossing should be thought unsuitable for Jesus' warning against the leaven of the Pharisees and against that of Herod." Cf. Pesch 1977: 412.

5:6–8; Gal. 5:9). The fact that at the Passover celebration all leaven was to be removed from the house gave to it a negative association with the bondage and slavery of Egypt (*m. Pesaḥ.* 10.5). In contemporary Jewish literature it was used to refer to the evil inclination within humans (Gen. Rab. 34.10; 1QS 5.4–5; Marcus 2000: 510–11).

It is far from clear what the "leaven of the Pharisees and the leaven of Herod" refers to. (For "Herod," see 6:14–16; cf. also 3:6 and 12:13 for a similar pairing.) Mark provides no clear explanation. In the Matthean parallel (16:12) it refers to the "teaching of the Pharisees and Sadducees," and in Luke (12:1) it refers to the "hypocrisy of the Pharisees." Numerous suggestions have been made that include the sign-seeking attitude of the Pharisees (8:11–12) and of Herod (Luke 23:8; cf. 6:14; Gundry 1993: 408; Donahue and Harrington 2002: 252), a politically dangerous nationalism (Lohmeyer 1957: 157; Pesch 1980a: 413; Gnilka 1978: 311), the evil impulse that has hardened the heart of the Pharisees and Herod (Marcus 2000: 510; cf. Hooker 1991: 195) and refuses to recognize and accept the truth, and unbelief reflected in one's response to Jesus (Quesnell 1969: 254–57; Guelich 1989: 423–24; J. Edwards 2002: 239). The nature of the questions in 8:17–18 and 21 favors the last interpretation.

Although symbolic in nature, Jesus's words in 8:15 are interpreted literally by the disciples (cf. Matt. 16:12), who assume that Jesus said this because they lacked bread. (For similar literal interpretations of symbolic imagery, note John 3:3–4; 4:10–15; 6:31–34; 7:35). The lack of a clear explanation in Mark of why and how the disciples interpreted Jesus's statement suggests that their dullness is not the main emphasis of this passage. What Mark wants to emphasize is Jesus's great miracle-working power, and the confused response of the disciples in 8:16 serves as a foil for this (Gundry 1993: 408).

8:17–20 Jesus's knowledge of the disciples' conversation may serve as an allusion to his supernatural knowledge (cf. 2:6–8, where the discussion takes place "in their hearts"; also 9:33–34; and 5:28 and 6:26, where the omniscient author also possesses such knowledge), but in the crowded and confined situation of the boat, it can also be understood as due to Jesus overhearing their discussion (Gundry 1993: 409; contra Marcus 2000: 508). The first question ("Why are you discussing that you do not have loaves of bread?") mentions for the third time in the account (cf. 8:14a and b) the disciples' lack of bread. Although the main emphasis of this account does not fall upon the disciples' dullness, this dullness is emphasized in Jesus's second and third questions: "Do you not yet perceive or understand [note the duality of verbs; cf. 7:18; Neirynck 1988: 92]? Do you have hardened hearts [lit. 'your hearts hardened']?" In light of the disciples having not only witnessed but also participated in the two feeding miracles, their ignorance is inexcusable for Mark, but it is neither damning nor unpardonable. It is an "at the present time" ignorance or "not yet" understanding (8:17, 21), and Mark's readers know that this was not permanent or damning, for the disciples later provided the core leadership of the early church, just as Jesus intended (3:14–19). The question concerning "hardened hearts" recalls 3:5 and 6:52. The fact that in 8:17 it is found in the form of a question makes it less severe than the statements in 3:5 and 6:52. In 6:52 we find a similar combination of not understanding and hardness of heart.

The fourth compound question, in 8:18, resembles the wording found in Jer. 5:21 and Ezek. 12:2 (cf. also Isa. 40:21, 28), and recalls the quotation of Isa. 6:9 found in Mark 4:12. It also alludes back to the healing of the deaf mute (7:31–37), and forward to the healing of the blind man in Bethsaida (8:22–26). The difference between the order of these healings and the order of seeing and hearing in 8:18 weakens the argument that these miracles are meant to be interpreted symbolically as involving the disciples' lack of hearing and seeing. The fifth question is introduced by "Do you not remember?" (οὐ μνημονεύετε, *ou mnēmoneuete*), which ties the present incident to the two other incidents in which the disciples lacked bread and faced a great need: the feeding of the five thousand and of the four thousand. It is apparent from the discussion in 8:15–17 that although the two miraculous feedings were in the memory bank of the disciples, they did not understand their implications for the present situation, that is, they did not "remember" (cf. Geddert 1989: 67).

The wording of the sixth and seventh questions recalls with great precision the two accounts of Jesus's miraculous feedings in 6:34–44 and 8:1–9. Numerous attempts have been made to see symbolic significance in the numbers found in these verses (Quesnell 1969: 270–74; Drury 1987: 414–15). Mark provides no tie between the numbers given and any supposed referent that they are supposed to symbolize. No clear symbolical significance exists for the numbers five, five thousand, and four thousand in the OT, and the numbers seven and twelve can refer to many different things (Marcus 2000: 513–14). Their presence here is due to their earlier use in the two feeding miracles. They serve simply to recall the magnitude of these two miracles. The emphasis in these two verses falls upon the numbers "twelve" and "seven," which correspond to the superabundance of food that Jesus miraculously provided in the two feeding miracles (6:43 and 8:8).[4] They focus not so much on eschatological fulfillment (contra Marcus 2000: 514) but on the christological greatness of Jesus Christ, the Son of God; and the emphasis on these numbers argues against seeing in 8:17–21 a Markan reference to the Lord's Supper. In these two feedings, Jesus was more than able to supply what was lacking. By implication the disciples should know that he is able now as well to supply the bread that is lacking. If these numbers possess any symbolic significance here, it is due to the symbolic significance that they received in the earlier accounts. In the earlier accounts, however, I argued against interpreting these numbers symbolically (see 6:38–41, 42–44; and esp. 8:5–7). If they lacked symbolic significance in the feeding miracles, then they clearly lack it here.

---

4. One should not see in 8:19–20 a "lessening of effectiveness from the first feeding to the second" (contra Countryman 1985: 645–50). Mark is simply following the order of the two feeding miracles at this point.

8:21 The final question ending the account repeats both the issue of the disciples not understanding (συνίετε, *syniete*) and the "not yet" (οὔπω, *oupō*) mentioned in 8:17 (cf. 4:13, 40; 6:52; 7:18; 9:18–19). It ends with a clear portrayal of the disciples' present failure to grasp the implications of what they have seen and experienced. They know the miracles that Jesus has performed, and they believe that they are worked through the power of God, but they do "not yet" understand. Nevertheless, Jesus's very question, "Do you *not yet* understand?" implies that a time would come when they would understand. Mark's readers, of course, already knew this.[5] They knew that Easter brought understanding to the disciples (contra Kelber 1979: 41; Tolbert 1989: 102–3, 199–200).

Summary

Most commentators see the primary Markan message in the present account as involving the dullness of the disciples (Guelich 1989: 427). The interpretation of the "leaven of the Pharisees and the leaven of Herod" as referring to unbelief in Jesus (see 8:14–16) lends support to this interpretation. The dullness of the disciples, however, is not permanent. They do "not yet" (8:17, 21) understand, but they are still his chosen disciples (1:16–20; 3:13–19; 6:7–13), and in time they will understand (Marcus 2000: 508). The questions of Jesus are furthermore not primarily intended to condemn but to enlighten and teach. Thus, while the dullness of the disciples is indeed a Markan emphasis found in the account, it is not his primary emphasis.

The main emphasis in the entire string of Jesus's questions in 8:17–20 is found in the answers provided by the disciples. "Twelve" and "seven" call attention not to the misunderstanding of the disciples but to the mighty miracle-working power of Jesus manifested in the two feeding miracles (Hooker 1991: 196). It is not the dullness of the disciples that receives the main emphasis in the passage, but what the disciples are dull about. From the very beginning of his Gospel, Mark has told his readers that he intends to tell them about "Jesus Christ, the Son of God" (1:1). It is helpful therefore to ask ourselves once again how the present passage helps us understand that Jesus is the Christ, the Son of God. The rebuke of the disciples in the passage is due to the fact that they do not understand, "Who then is this man . . . ?" (4:41). Who is this Jesus who heals the sick, raises the dead, exorcises the demon possessed, and is master of nature? Who is this Jesus of Nazareth who like God can abundantly feed the multitudes miraculously in the wilderness? Truly, he must be the Christ, the Son of God!

---

5. "The disciples may not [yet] understand, but the entire Gospel breathes with the confidence that they will eventually understand, that they will repent and be forgiven. The difference between those outside and the disciples is to be sought primarily in this: the disciples will be converted and forgiven, those outside will not" (Ambrozic 1972: 69).

Additional Notes

8:14. ἐπελάθοντο is a culminative aorist, lit. "forgot."

8:14. The awkwardness of the Greek is smoothed out in 𝔓⁴⁵ (W) Θ f¹ (f¹³) to "having only one bread" (ἕνα μόνον ἄρτον ἔχοντες), but the more difficult reading is to be preferred.

8:15. Some MSS (𝔓⁴⁵ W Θ f¹ f¹³) read "of the Herodians," but this is no doubt due to a scribal attempt to make the present text conform to 3:6 and 12:13.

8:16. διελογίζοντο is an inceptive imperfect.

8:16. The Greek describing the disciples' response is quite confusing. The portion following "And they began to discuss among themselves" can be translated in a variety of ways. Among them are the following:

> "We have no bread." (This translation regards the ὅτι as *hoti recitativum* and accepts the reading ἔχομεν found in ℵ A C L Θ f¹³ [cf. Matt. 16:7].)
> "[He said this] because [ὅτι] they had no bread."
> "why [ὅτι] they had no bread."
> "that they had no bread."

"They have" (ἔχουσιν) is found in 𝔓⁴⁵ B W f¹, and "they had" (εἶχαν) in D it. Despite variant readings and some uncertainty about how to translate this verse, the general meaning of the passage is evident.

8:18. This question and the next (v. 19) are sometimes connected into a single question ("Do you not remember when . . . ?"). It is best, however, to interpret them as two separate questions. This allows the question of v. 19 to stand in synonymous parallelism with v. 20.

8:20. Mark expects the reader to provide here the "I broke" (ἔκλασα) of 8:19.

V. On the Way to Jerusalem: Part 4 (8:22–10:52)

In the previous three sections in Mark (1:14–3:6; 3:7–6:6a; 6:6b–8:21), we have encountered a recurring pattern. Each began with a summary (1:14–15; 3:7–12; 6:6b) that was followed by a call or sending out of the disciples (1:16–20; 3:13–19; 6:7–13) and, after various intervening Jesus materials (1:21–3:5; 3:20–5:43; 6:14–8:20), ended with a reference to the unbelief Jesus encountered (3:6, from the Pharisees and Herodians; 6:1–6a, at Nazareth; 8:14–21, from the disciples). The beginning of the new section is debated. Some suggest that the healing of the blind man in Bethsaida concludes 6:6b–8:21 (Nineham 1963: 223; Hooker 1991: 28; Guelich 1989: 316; Evans 2001: 3–4). Others see it as "bridging" 6:6b–8:21 and 8:27–10:52 (France 2002: 321–22), but it seems best to understand 8:22–26 as beginning a new section (Best 1970: 325; Brooks 1991: 34; Marcus 2000: 381; Donahue and Harrington 2002: 49). This allows the preceding section to end, like the two previous ones, with a reference to unbelief (3:6; 6:1–6a; 8:14–21), and for the new section to begin, after an introduction (1:14–15; 3:7–12; 6:6b; 8:22–26), with an episode centering on the disciples (8:27–30), as in the three previous sections (1:16–20; 3:13–19; 6:7–13). It also allows the healing of the blind man in Bethsaida in 8:21–26 to form an *inclusio* with the healing of blind Bartimaeus in 10:46–52.

The construction of 8:22–10:52 is built around three cycles that contain a threefold pattern. These follow the major turning point of Mark's story of Jesus. That turning point takes place at Caesarea Philippi, where the disciples confess that Jesus is the Christ (8:27–30), and Jesus begins to disclose the purpose and goal of his ministry (8:31). The pattern that follows involves

1. a passion prediction by Jesus: 8:31; 9:30–32; 10:32–34[1]
2. an error by the disciples: 8:32–33; 9:33–34; 10:35–37
3. Jesus's teachings concerning Christian discipleship: 8:34–9:1; 9:35–10:31; 10:38–45

Much of the other material included in these three cycles may have already been associated in some way in the pre-Markan tradition (9:2–8 with 8:27–30; see 9:2–3), or Mark may have included it because it fit thematically (9:14–29

---

1. Each of these also involves a geographical reference: 8:27; 9:30; 10:32 (Brooks 1991: 132).

supports the dullness/error of the disciples as does 9:38–41, and 10:1–31 picks up the teachings on discipleship begun in 8:34–9:1). Interwoven throughout this section of Mark is Jesus's explanation of his mission as the Christ, the Son of God, centering on three passion predictions and the example they provide for Christian discipleship.

A. Jesus Heals the Blind Man of Bethsaida (8:22–26)

The present account is a healing miracle and possesses numerous similarities with the healing of the deaf mute in 7:31–37. These similarities include

1. a change of scene (8:22; 7:31);
2. similar wording:
    2.1. "And they brought to him" (καὶ φέρουσιν αὐτῷ, *kai pherousin autō*; 8:22; 7:32);
    2.2. "and plead with him" (καὶ παρακαλοῦσιν αὐτόν, *kai parakalousin auton*; 8:22; 7:32);
    2.3. "in order that [ἵνα, *hina*] he might . . . touch/set his hand on" (ἅψηται/ἐπιθῇ, *hapsētai/epithē*; 8:22; 7:32);
3. taking the man away (ἐπιλαβόμενος/ἀπολαβόμενος, *epilabomenos/apolabomenos*) privately from the crowd/out of the village (8:23; 7:33);
4. the common use of spittle (πτύσας, *ptysas*) in the healing (8:23; 7:33);
5. a command to "secrecy" (8:26; 7:36); and so on (Fowler 1981: 105–6).

The presence of these similarities has evoked a great deal of speculation as to how the accounts may have been related. Some suggestions are these: the two accounts were composed by the same community or the same author (E. Johnson 1979: 374); they are duplicate accounts of the same incident; they were two independent accounts centering on Isa. 35:5 brought together before Mark.[1] All this is highly speculative and cannot be verified. Furthermore, in the discussion of 8:18, I pointed out that the order of the healings (deaf mute, then blind man) is the opposite of that found in the OT passages cited in 8:18 (seeing, then hearing).

The healing of the blind man in Bethsaida, however, is also unlike the healing of the deaf mute in 7:31–37. It is unlike any other healing miracle in the Gospels in that the healing involves two stages (8:23–24 and 25). Also, instead of a command like "Come out of him" (1:25), "Be made clean" (1:41), "Stretch out your hand" (3:5), "Be healed" (5:34), "Arise" (5:41),

---

1. These are the only two miracles in Mark that are omitted by both Matthew and Luke. V. Taylor (1952: 352, 369) and Cranfield (1959: 254) suggest that this may be due to the use of spittle and touch in the healing and the apparent difficulty Jesus encountered in healing the blind man.

"Be opened" (7:34), we have a question: "Do you see anything?" (8:23). It is also somewhat atypical in that it lacks a response from the crowd/disciples (contrast 1:27, 45; 2:12; 4:41; 5:20, 42; 6:51; 7:37; but cf. 1:31; 3:6; 5:34; 6:44; 7:30; 8:10; 10:52). Mark's own hand is seen most clearly in the location of the present story in the Gospel, the change in scene (8:22a), various verbal similarities with 7:31–37 (see above), and the command to secrecy (8:26b; Pryke 1978: 16–17, 143, 162; E. Johnson 1979: 370–74; Guelich 1989: 429, 436).

The story consists of (1) a change of scene (8:22) with the arrival of Jesus and the disciples in Bethsaida (8:22a) and people bringing a blind man to Jesus for healing (8:22b); (2) the healing (8:23–25), which consists of two stages (after the removal of the man from the village [8:23a], we have a partial healing involving a conversation between Jesus and the blind man [8:23b–24] and then the complete healing [8:25]); and (3) after the healing, the narrator concludes the story with a dismissal of the man and a command to secrecy (8:26).

Numerous writers interpret this miracle story (and the healing of the deaf mute in 7:31–37) allegorically. They see Mark using it as a symbolic description of the disciples' blindness concerning Jesus as described in 8:14–21 and their gradual "seeing" and understanding resulting from Jesus's teaching concerning his passion in 8:31–10:52 (Best 1981: 134–39; Guelich 1989: 430–31; France 2002: 323). I have earlier pointed out (see the introduction to 7:31–37) that interpreting the healings of the deaf mute and the blind man symbolically encounters the problem that one of the key passages used to support such an interpretation (8:18) has the healings in reverse order. If Mark intended these miracles to be interpreted as symbolizing the deafness and blindness of the disciples, why did he not assist his readers by reporting these two miracles in the same order as found in 8:18? An even more serious problem for this symbolic interpretation of the two miracles is that at the end of this section, in Mark 10:52, the disciples are still deaf and blind. They still do not understand. In fact, they do not see or hear correctly even by 16:8. Thus the healing of the deaf mute and the blind man appear to stand not as analogies to but in contrast to the deafness and blindness of the disciples (Räisänen 1990: 203–4).

Exegesis and Exposition

²²And they come into Bethsaida. And they bring to him [Jesus] a blind man and plead with him in order that he might touch him. ²³And having taken the hand of the blind man, he brought him outside the village, and having spat into his eyes [and] having set [his] hands upon him, he was asking him, ⌜"Do you see anything?"⌝ ²⁴And having regained his sight, he was saying, ⌜"I see men, for I see [them] walking like trees."⌝ ²⁵Then again he set his hands upon his eyes, and he saw clearly, and was healed, and he was seeing all things plainly. ²⁶And he sent him to his home, saying, "Do not enter into the village." ⌜ ⌝

8:22   Earlier Jesus and the disciples had set out unsuccessfully for Bethsaida (6:45); here they finally arrive. It is doubtful, however, that their arrival in Bethsaida is to be understood as the fulfillment of Jesus's goal in 6:45 (contra Myers 1988: 240; Matera 1989: 167–68). The wording "And they come into" (Καὶ ἔρχονται εἰς, *Kai erchontai eis*) occurs also in 10:46 ("Jericho"); 11:15 ("Jerusalem"), 27 ("again . . . Jerusalem"); and 14:32 ("a place . . .").[2] This suggests that the style and wording is Markan, although the geographical location may be traditional (Pesch 1980a: 417; Best 1981: 135; Gundry 1993: 420). Attempts to associate Bethsaida with the gentile world and interpret the miracle as part of a collection of gentile miracles (Guelich 1989: 430–31) reads into Mark something that the evangelist does not state. John 1:44 (cf. also 12:21) refers to Bethsaida as the home of Peter, Andrew, and Philip. Elsewhere Bethsaida is referred to in the Synoptic Gospels only in Matt. 11:21/Luke 10:13, where it is the recipient of a judgmental woe that contrasts Bethsaida and Chorazin with the gentile cities of Tyre and Sidon, and in Luke 9:10. Thus in the Gospels, Bethsaida does not evoke the idea of a gentile city but the opposite. The present story begins with a typically Markan impersonal plural ("they"; see 1:21–22) and two historical presents ("bring" [φέρουσιν] and "plead" [παρακαλοῦσιν]). Although the ἵνα (*hina*) following the verb "plead" can introduce the content of their pleading ("that") or the purpose ("in order that"), the latter is more likely here (see 3:9–10). For the use of touch in Jesus's healings, see 5:21–24a.

8:23–25   As in 7:33, Jesus "takes" (ἐπιλαβόμενος, a hapax legomenon in Mark) the man who is to be healed by the hand and "brought him out" (ἐξήνεγκεν, *exēnenken*, a hapax in Mark) of the village and away from the crowd. The description of Bethsaida as a "village" (κώμη, *kōmē*) is somewhat strange. Matthew 11:20–21; Luke 9:10; and John 1:44 refer to it as a "city" (πόλις, *polis*). Some explain this as due to Mark's careless insertion of a city name into a tradition about a healing in an unidentified village (Lohmeyer 1957: 158; Nineham 1963: 219). Others suggest that the term "village" is used to link the present account with the following one, which tells of an incident that took place in the "villages" of Caesarea Philippi (Gundry 1993: 417). Despite being a "city," Bethsaida apparently remained organizationally a village (Guelich 1989: 432). Although Bethsaida was technically part of Gaulanitis, it was popularly considered part of Galilee (John 12:21). Before being relocated, elevated to city status, and renamed Julias by Philip the Tetrarch (Josephus, *Ant.* 18.2.1 §28), Bethsaida was a small fishing village. It may be that the old fishing village (el-ʿAraj) is being referred to here rather than the city (et-Tell/Julias) built by Philip.

    The use of spittle in the healing recalls 7:33. Why Jesus used spittle is not stated, and suggestions like "to remove the dirt and dried secretions from the eyelids preparatory to the healing" (Howard 1984: 165) are highly speculative.

---

2. As in 10:46; 11:15, 27; and 14:32 (cf. also 1:21; 11:1), it is best to associate the place designation with what follows rather than what precedes (Guelich 1989: 430). See the introduction to 8:10–13.

Spittle is also used in the healing of the blind man in John 9:6–7.[3] The healing action of Jesus is twofold. It involves spitting into the blind man's eyes (ὄμματα, *ommata*, a hapax legomenon in Mark) and putting his hands upon him. The latter is a synonymous expression for "touching him" (8:22; cf. 7:32 and 33). The use of a question, "Do you see anything?" is unique in a healing miracle, and the reply indicates that the healing has begun but is incomplete. The man's ἀναβλέψας (*anablepsas*; lit. "looking up") refers not to his "looking upward" as in 6:41; 7:34; 16:4 but to his "regaining his sight" as in 10:51–52 (cf. also Matt. 11:5/Luke 7:22; John 9:11, 15, 18; Acts 9:12, 17, 18; 22:13; E. Johnson 1979: 376–78). Yet the man's description of what he sees indicates that he sees imperfectly. Attempts to diagnose the man's optical problem either before or after the first stage of the healing (severe nearsightedness [Hurtado 1983: 134], severe cataracts [Howard 1984: 168–69], displacement of the man's eye lens [M. Sussman, *ABD* 6:12], etc.) are speculative (cf. Gundry 1993: 423). There is no reason to assume that the blind man was not born blind based on the comparison that he gives between men (probably those who brought the man to Jesus) and trees (contra W. Lane 1974: 285; Gnilka 1978: 314; Hurtado 1983: 134; Donahue and Harrington 2002: 256) or on an overly literal interpretation of "healed" (ἀπεκατέστη, *apekatestē*; lit. "restored"; Gundry 1993: 418).[4] The man's words are simply meant by Mark to indicate that he was now able to see but not perfectly.

The imperfect sight of the man leads to a second (again, πάλιν, *palin*) laying of hands upon his eyes in 8:25. The use of a different word here for "eyes" (ὀφθαλμούς, *ophthalmous*) may be a conscious attempt by Mark to parallel 8:18. The term ὄμματα used in 8:23 is rare, found in the NT only this one time in Mark and in Matt. 20:34, so that in 8:25 Mark may simply have preferred the usual term found elsewhere in his Gospel and a total of a hundred times in the NT. The use of three different words in the present account for "seeing" (βλέπω, διέβλεψεν, and ἐνέβλεπεν [*blepō, dieblepsen,* and *eneblepen*]), two different terms for "regaining sight" (ἀναβλέψας) and "being healed/restored" (ἀπεκατέστη), and two different terms for "touching" (ἅψηται, *hapsētai*) and "setting hands on" (ἐπιθεὶς τὰς χεῖρας/ἐπέθηκεν τὰς χεῖρας ἐπί, *epitheis tas cheiras/epethēken tas cheiras epi*; lit. "set the hands upon") also suggests that Mark may simply have preferred using synonyms to avoid repetition. The plurals "hands" and "eyes" in 8:25 indicate that one hand was placed upon each eye. The result is a threefold description of the man's complete healing: he is able to "see clearly" (διέβλεψεν), is "healed/restored" (ἀπεκατέστη), and "was seeing [imperfect] all things plainly" (ἐνέβλεπεν τηλαυγῶς [*tēlaugōs*, a hapax legomenon in the NT] ἅπαντα [*hapanta*]). The emphatic forms διέβλεψεν and ἐνέβλεπεν, in contrast to βλέπω in 8:24, witness to the man's complete healing, and this is further emphasized by the threefold description of his healing.

3. See Pesch (1980a: 417–18) for extrabiblical examples of the use of spittle in healing.

4. Howard (1984: 164) argues that the absence of a statement that he was born blind (cf. John 9:1) implies that he was not born blind.

Whatever may have been the situation of the first stage of his healing, now he is completely and perfectly able to see.

The two-stage aspect of the man's healing has been interpreted symbolically by numerous scholars. Many see the two stages as symbolic of a two-stage, gradual healing of the disciples' blindness and lack of understanding. Others see the two stages as evidence of the greatness of the miracle (Klostermann 1950: 78; Gundry 1993: 423; cf. John 9:32). There is no evidence in the story itself that the two stages imply any inadequacy on the part of Jesus, for he is completely in control throughout the miracle. The complete healing of the man is never in doubt; it simply involves two stages. The two-stage description of the healing is probably pre-Markan, and the question of how the two stages of the account function in the Gospel of Mark and why the original account possessed a two-stage healing are two distinct questions. In the pre-Markan tradition it may have simply borne witness to the unusual form that the healing actually took (Gnilka 1978: 314).

In its present location in Mark, however, many scholars interpret this healing symbolically.[5] It is interpreted as symbolizing the present blindness and lack of understanding of the disciples and their future "healing." They have a "bad case of myopia," are "almost as blind as the 'Pharisees,'" and need a "'second touch'" (Guelich 1989: 434). This healing supposedly has as its first stage Peter's confession in 8:27–30 (Lightfoot 1934: 91; Richardson 1941: 86; Best 1970: 325). But in response to this interpretation, note that nothing happens to heal the disciples' blindness in 8:27–30, as 8:32–33 clearly reveals (E. Johnson 1979: 381–82). After Jesus's teaching, they still do not understand. Indeed, nothing happens in 8:27–16:8 that brings understanding and heals the disciples' blindness (contra Matera 1989: 169–70). Healing, the "second touch," comes only after Easter (Guelich 1989: 434 admits this). Are we to assume that Mark intended his readers to understand a symbolical two-stage healing of the disciples' blindness not on the basis of anything found recorded in Mark 8:27–16:8,[6] but upon their knowledge of the post-Easter experience of the disciples (Guelich 1989: 434, 436)?[7]

5. Some of the reasons given in favor of interpreting the healing symbolically are the following: (1) its location after 8:13–21 and esp. 8:18; (2) its similarity to the healing of the deaf mute; (3) its location before 8:27–9:1; (4) the symbolic use of "blindness" for ignorance elsewhere (8:18; Matt. 15:14; 23:16–26; cf. Luke 1:79 and 4:18); (5) the various verbal ties with the surrounding materials (desire for privacy, 8:23 and 8:26; "ask," 8:23 and 8:27, 29; "see," 8:23, 24 and 8:18; "eyes," 8:25 and 8:18; the command to secrecy, 8:26 and 8:30); etc.

6. I will argue later (see 16:1–8, "The Ending of Mark") that, although we do not possess any authentic material after 16:8, Mark did not originally end there and that the ending contained a resurrection account in which Jesus met the disciples in Galilee (14:27–28; 16:7). To argue, however, that this lost ending of Mark possessed clues that it was the fulfillment of the symbolism of "seeing" in 8:22–26 is far too speculative.

7. E. Johnson (1979: 381–83) sees the difficulty involved in interpreting 8:27–9:1 as the first stage of the disciples' healing and argues that before 8:27–33 the disciples already have partial understanding (first-stage sight). They will see clearly (second-stage sight) after the resurrection.

That the disciples are dull and blind in certain respects is evident in Mark (cf. 4:10, 13, 40; 6:37, 52; 7:17; 8:4, 14–21). But they are still dull and blind in 8:22–10:52 (note the triple cycle involving passion prediction, disciple error, and Jesus's teachings on discipleship in this section [see 8:22–10:52]), and they remain blind throughout 11:1–16:8. Mark's readers know that the disciples will understand, as is clear from 14:27–28 and 16:7. Yet where is the *two-stage* progression of this healing described in Mark? There is only one stage—Jesus meeting the disciples after his resurrection. Mark 8:27–9:1 is not a first stage of his "healing" process. In contrast to 8:24, there is no "seeing" at all. There is no response by Jesus to Peter after his confession such as, "Now you are beginning to see. . . ." On the contrary, there is even greater blindness: "Get behind me, Satan!" (8:32–33). If Mark wanted his readers to interpret 8:22–26 symbolically as portraying a two-stage enlightenment of the disciples leading to complete understanding, we should expect some reference to this in 8:27ff. We find no such reference. The healing of the blind man certainly does not prepare the reader "for the continued focus on [the disciples'] myopia that follows" (Guelich 1989: 436). On the contrary, a symbolic interpretation of the blind man's healing prepares for the opposite—the gradual understanding of the disciples at 8:27–33, but this does not happen (Gundry 1993: 421; cf. also Williams 1994: 130–32).

The story concludes with Jesus sending the man to his home and a command **8:26** not to enter the city. Mark is not interested in supplying information as to how the man got home (friends guided him, he asked for directions, he closed his eyes and remembered how he had come, etc.) or where the man lived (outside the village, on the outskirts of the village, etc.). While interesting, these questions are not important for Mark's telling of this mighty miracle of Jesus. Being sent home does not require the presence of a secrecy motif (cf. 2:11–12; 5:19–20; 7:29–30). A home is not necessarily a place of privacy (1:32–34; 2:1–2, 15), although it can serve that purpose (7:24; 9:28, 33; 10:10). However, in association with the command not to enter the village (perhaps the village "square" or center of the village's activity) and due to numerous other commands to secrecy (1:34b, 44; 3:12; 5:43; 7:36; 8:30; 9:9), it is probably best to interpret 8:26 as an example of the secrecy motif in Mark (Wrede 1971: 35; Pesch 1980a: 410; Theissen 1983: 69, 148–49; contra Gundry 1993: 419; E. Johnson 1979: 373). This is true whether the command is traditional (Luz 1983: 78; E. Johnson 1979: 373) or not.

Summary

Many present-day commentators see the main Markan message in this passage as involving a symbolical interpretation of the blindness and healing of the blind man. Thus Mark is seen as teaching through this healing miracle that, despite the present lack of understanding by the disciples, they will eventually be enlightened and their blindness healed. I have discussed the difficulties of such an interpretation above (see 8:23–25). Despite the proclivity to symbolical and allegorical interpretation on the part of the early church fathers, such an interpretation is rarely, if ever, found among them.[8] The normal function of a miracle story in Mark is to reveal who Jesus is and to show his power and greatness (Gundry 1993: 421–22; cf. 1:1). The latter is often emphasized by the amazement that the miracle creates (1:27; 2:12; 4:41; 5:20, 42; 6:51; 7:37). The lack of such a reference in the present account may appear to weaken this christological emphasis. Yet numerous other miracle stories also lack a reference to such amazement (1:31, 40–45; 5:30–34; 6:44; 8:10) and conclude with a reference to the person going home (5:34; 7:30; cf. 10:52). Even if one were to interpret Mark's purpose as involving a symbolic interpretation of the miracle, the healing of the blind man still functions as a mighty miracle describing the greatness of Jesus and witnesses to his being the Christ, the Son of God (1:1; cf. John 9:30–34, 38). Like God (Ps. 146:8), Jesus can open the eyes of the blind, and for those readers familiar with Isa. 35:5–6, such a miracle is associated with the coming of the messianic age (cf. also Isa. 29:18).

Additional Notes

8:23. εἴ τι βλέπεις is lit. "If you see anything." "If" (εἰ) here introduces a direct question (France 2002: 324). Cf. Matt. 12:10; 19:3; Luke 13:23; Acts 1:6; 7:1.

8:24. The translation of these words is difficult. Some have suggested that the difficulty is due to the mistranslation of the original Aramaic, but Mark is not here translating an Aramaic source. One would expect that in the retelling of this story in Greek during the oral period, the description of what the man saw would have been smoothed out.

8:26. The addition "and tell no one in the village" (μηδενὶ εἴπῃς εἰς τὴν κώμην; D) and its variants (A C Majority text) is a secondary addition and should not be read (Metzger 1994: 84; contra Ross 1987).

---

8. Cf. Thomas Aquinas's references to earlier interpretations of Mark 8:22–26 in *Catena Aurea*.

B. Peter's Confession and Jesus's First Passion Prediction (8:27–33)

In the first half of his Gospel (1:1–8:21), Mark has shared the story of the "good news of Jesus Christ, the Son of God" (1:1). Now he comes to the turning point or "watershed" of the Gospel (Hooker 1991: 200). As they proceed to Caesarea Philippi (8:27),[1] Jesus asks his disciples who they believe him to be. Invited by Jesus to reflect on who they had come to think that he is (8:27b–28), Peter, acting as the spokesman for the disciples, confesses that he is the Christ (8:29). This is then followed by a stern warning not to tell who he is to others, to those "outside" (cf. 4:11). Intimately tied to this confession is the first of Jesus's passion predictions (Bayer 1986: 165–66). At this point in his ministry, Jesus begins to teach (8:31) the disciples concerning his future death and vindication. Because of possible misunderstanding concerning his messiahship, Jesus begins to explain to his disciples that his role as the Son of Man involves his giving his life as a ransom for many (cf. 10:45). (The passion predictions in 8:31; 9:31; and 10:33–34 are later explained theologically by 10:45 and 14:24.) Attempts to relocate the passion prediction at a later time and place (after Palm Sunday in Jerusalem; cf. Evans 2001: 11–12) stumble over the intimate connection with Peter's confession and the location of this incident in Caesarea Philippi. The passion prediction is then followed by teachings on discipleship in 8:34–9:1. This completes the first cycle of passion prediction, disciple error, and discipleship teaching (see 8:22–10:52).

The historicity of the present passage is much debated. Peter's confession of Jesus as the Christ is thought by some to be a theological fiction created either by the early church or Mark (Wrede 1971: 238–41; Bultmann 1968: 257–59; Catchpole 1984: 327–28) but as historically reliable by others (V. Taylor 1952: 374–75; Bayer 1986: 155–57; Evans 2001: 9–12). In favor of its historicity are several considerations: (1) The reticence of Jesus to have this title that Mark emphasizes (1:1) openly proclaimed. The lack of the title "Son of God" (cf. 1:1; 14:61) in Peter's confession also argues that Mark is being faithful to his tradition at this point. (2) The negative portrayal of Peter in the account (he is called "Satan" in 8:33) supports the historicity of the account. Attempts to argue that this negative portrayal is due to Mark's attempt to vilify Peter and the disciples (Tyson 1961; Weeden 1971) stumble over such passages as

---

1. It is best to understand 8:27a as beginning this pericope (Bayer 1986: 154) rather than ending the previous one (Bultmann 1968: 257). Geographical designations generally introduce a new section (cf. 1:21; 2:1; 4:1; 5:1; 6:45; 7:24, 31; 8:22; 9:2, 30; 10:1, 46; 11:1, 12, 15, 27).

3:13–19; 14:27–28; 16:7 and the fact that for nineteen hundred years no one has interpreted Mark in this manner. In light of the early church's reverence for Peter and the disciples, if Mark had wanted to portray Peter negatively, he would have had to be far more explicit. As we shall see, Peter's confession must be understood positively (cf. 1:1; 14:61–62; also Matt. 16:17), so that the rebuke of Peter is best understood as a historical reminiscence (Cranfield 1959: 267). (3) If the confession was fabricated by the early church, one would expect a confession more along the lines of Matt. 16:16 and a corresponding commendation (16:17). (4) If the confession were created by the early church, it is difficult to understand why the site was designated as Caesarea Philippi, since this city is never mentioned elsewhere in the NT or in the writings of the early church. (5) It would have been inevitable that the question of messiahship would have arisen during Jesus's ministry, and this is confirmed by the charges brought against him at his trial and crucifixion (14:61; 15:2, 18, 26). (6) Finally, to argue that such a Jewish confession could not have taken place outside Jewish territory (Best 1981: 20) makes one think of what Jesus and the disciples would have discussed in Tyre, Sidon, the Decapolis, and so on. Would it have been only "non-Jewish things"? Indeed, leaving Galilee for Caesarea Philippi would have provided an excellent opportunity to discuss privately on the way (8:27) the disciples' understanding of who Jesus was.

There is a similar division of opinion concerning the historicity of the passion prediction (8:31). Critical scholarship denies the historicity of such predictions (Wrede 1971: 87; Bultmann 1968: 152). "But can there be any doubt that they [the passion predictions] are all *vaticinia ex eventu*?" (Bultmann 1951: 29; cf. Perry 1986: 638). Yet more and more scholars are willing to acknowledge that Jesus foresaw the possibility of his death and shared this with his disciples (Hooker 1991: 204–5; Evans 2001: 10–11; even Crossan 1991: 353). In light of the martyrdom of John the Baptist, it would be incredible, from simply a psychological point of view, for Jesus not to have reflected on a similar possibility. He had too many enemies in high places. If Jesus saw his future as containing rejection and death and if he believed that he was following God's preordained path, he could also have thought that his future involved a future vindication. When suffering for righteousness' sake, any devout Jew assumed divine vindication would come (Allison 1985: 137–40). The framing of the present passion prediction in terms of the "Son of Man," which is not the title one would expect if created by the church (cf. 1 Cor. 15:3; 1 Tim. 1:15; etc.), and the lack of any developed theology of atonement in the prediction also argue in favor of its historicity (Witherington 2001: 243). Ultimately the question of historicity on both these issues depends heavily on whether one believes Jesus made any messianic claims.[2] That Jesus claimed to be the Messiah seems to be

2. Hooker (1991: 202) correctly points out, "Our decision regarding the historicity of this narrative will in fact depend ultimately on our judgment about Jesus' 'messianic self-consciousness.'" Cf. Catchpole 1984: 327.

affirmed by his having been crucified on political grounds as a messianic pretender (14:61–64; 15:2, 18, 26) and that even belief in his resurrection would not have provided a basis for the disciples' conviction that Jesus was the Christ. The resurrection would have confirmed an earlier understanding of this during Jesus's ministry, but it would not have caused a de novo creation of this view.

Mark's own hand in the present account is most apparent in his wording of the tradition. Most see 8:27b–29, 31, 32b, and 33 as being traditional (Best 1981: 25; Bayer 1986: 157, 163–65; Räisänen 1990: 177; contra Pryke 1978: 17, 143, 163, who sees all of 8:27–33 as Markan). Various terminology appears to be Markan: "went out" (ἐξῆλθεν, *exēlthen*; 8:27 [38 times in Mark]); "Jesus and the disciples" (ὁ Ἰησοῦς καὶ οἱ μαθηταί, *ho Iēsous kai hoi mathētai*; 8:27; cf. 3:7b; 10:46b); "in the way" (ἐν τῇ ὁδῷ, *en tē hodō*; 8:27; cf. 9:33; 10:17, 32); to "order" (ἐπετίμησεν, *epetimēsen*, followed by ἵνα, *hina*; 8:30; cf. 3:12; 10:48); "began to teach" (ἤρξατο διδάσκειν, *ērxato didaskein*; 8:31; "began" followed by an infinitive appears 26 times in Mark; see esp. 4:1; 6:2, 34); "the word" (τὸν λόγον, *ton logon*; 8:32; cf. 1:45; 2:2; 4:14–20, 33).

The unusual use of "rise again" (ἀνίστημι, *anistēmi*; 8:31; 9:9–10, 31; 10:34) instead of the more common "rise" (ἐγείρω, *egeirō*) favors the traditional nature of the term (Gundry 1993: 429–30; Evans 2001: 12). Although 8:30 is a clear example of the "messianic secret" and therefore, in the minds of many scholars, Markan in origin (Best 1981: 21–22; Luz 1983: 82), arguments for it being traditional can also be brought forward (V. Taylor 1952: 377; Dunn 1981: 124, 127; Bayer 1986: 157–59). In 8:27–33 we seem to have a combination of traditional materials that Mark has retold in his own language and style, and with respect to the passion prediction, he has repeated the tradition in light of his knowledge of its fulfillment.

The present account consists of a story about Jesus (8:27–30) connected to Jesus's first passion prediction and the response of his disciples (8:31–33). It will be divided into (1) a Markan seam based on a traditional location (8:27a), (2) a preliminary question and answer (8:27b–28), (3) the primary question and answer (8:29), (4) a command to secrecy (8:30), (5) Jesus's first passion prediction (8:31–32a), and (6) an error by the disciples followed by a rebuke by Jesus (8:32b–33).

Exegesis and Exposition

[27]And Jesus and his disciples ⌜went out⌝ into the villages of Caesarea Philippi, and as they were proceeding he was asking his disciples saying to them, "Who do people say that I am?" [28]And they ⌜said⌝ to him, "John the Baptist, and others [say] Elijah; and others [say] one of the prophets." [29]And he was asking them, "But *you*, who do you say that I am?" Peter answering says to him, "You are the Christ ⌜ ⌝." [30]And Jesus strictly ordered them ⌜that⌝ they should not tell anyone concerning him.

³¹And he began to teach them that it is necessary [for] the Son of Man to suffer many things, and to be rejected by the elders and the chief priests and the scribes, and to be killed and after three days to rise [from the dead]. ³²And he was speaking the word [to them] plainly. And having taken him aside, Peter began to rebuke him. ³³But having turned and seen his disciples, he [Jesus] rebuked Peter and says, "Get behind me, Satan, because you are setting your mind not on the things that come from God but on the things that come from people."

8:27a   The present account begins with Jesus being mentioned before the disciples because he is the central figure. The geographical location, "villages" (τὰς κώμας, *tas kōmas*) of Caesarea (lit. "of") Philippi is somewhat awkward. One expects either the "territory of" (χώραν, *chōran*; 5:1), the "regions of" (μέρη, *merē*; 8:10), or "regions of" (ὅρια, *horia*; 7:24, 31; 10:1; cf. 5:17). Caesarea Philippi was situated on the southern slopes of Mount Hermon some twenty-five miles north of the Sea of Galilee. Earlier it was called Panion or Paneas. It was enlarged and renamed Caesarea by Philip, the son of Herod the Great (Josephus, *Ant.* 18.2.1 §28; *J.W.* 2.9.1 §168). It is distinguished from the larger and more famous Caesarea Maritima built by Herod the Great on the Mediterranean coast. (Many cities were named "Caesarea" to gain favor with the emperor.) This geographical designation must be a historical reminiscence since there is no known theological or political reason for the designation (Hooker 1991: 202; Gundry 1993: 425–26; Evans 2001: 10, 13; contra Schmithals 1979: 1.381).

8:27b–28   The following conversation takes place "as they were proceeding" (lit. "in the way"). In light of the use of "the way" (ἡ ὁδός, *hē hodos*) to identify the early Christian church (Acts 9:2; 16:17; 18:25–26; 19:9, 23; 22:4; 24:14, 22), a number of scholars see the expression as a technical term describing Christian discipleship (Best 1981: 15–18; France 2002: 320–21; contra Gundry 1993: 441–42). Although it seems quite possible that the expression is to be understood this way in 10:52 ("follow him in the way"), and perhaps in 10:32, it is far less certain that it has this sense here, in 9:33–34, and in 10:17. As a result I have translated it "as they were proceeding." The "people" referred to in Jesus's question are not the people of 8:24 (contra Gundry 1993: 443) but the Jewish people in general. Nothing negative should be read into the term, such as "humans" in contrast to "God." The question as to the identity of Jesus is the central theme of the entire Gospel of Mark (Donahue and Harrington 2002: 264; cf. 1:27; 2:12; 4:41; 6:2, 14–16; 7:37; 14:61; 15:2; etc.) and confronts every reader of the Gospel.

    The opinions of the people in 8:28 recall those given by Herod in 6:14–16. Both the names and their order are identical (cf. John 1:21). How Jesus could have been considered John the Baptist is puzzling since their careers overlapped (1:9–11; Luke 7:18–35; John 3:22–30; 4:1–2; see Mark 6:14–16). Elijah is named as a possibility because of the common view that he would return at the end time (Mal. 4:5–6; Sir. 48:1–10). One way of understanding Elijah's return was that he would personally be raised from the dead and return to Israel. For Jesus and the NT writers, however, the prophecy was understood figuratively. Someone like Elijah (i.e., John the Baptist) would return and carry out Elijah's prophetic ministry. This is how Mark 9:11–13; Matt. 11:12–14; 17:10–13 (esp. v. 13) understand the prophecy. By his dress it appears that John the Baptist also understood the prophecy in this manner (see 1:4–6). "One of the prophets" probably has Deut. 18:15–19 in mind. The parallel in Matt. 16:14 lists Jeremiah as a suggestion (cf. 2 Esd. 2:18). The parallel in Luke 9:19 agrees with the Markan listing. That Jesus was understood to be a prophet is clear from Mark 6:4; 14:65; Luke 7:16, 39; 13:33–34; 24:19.

In the question that Jesus asks his disciples, the "but" (δέ, *de*) is contrastive **8:29** and the "you" (ὑμεῖς, *hymeis*) is emphatic. In contrast to what people in general think, Jesus asks the opinion of his disciples, expecting a better answer. In their association with Jesus, what have they learned concerning who he is? Peter, representing the disciples (cf. 9:5; 10:28; 11:21; 14:37), confesses that Jesus is the "Christ" (see 1:1). The confession is correct (cf. Matt. 16:16–17). Jesus is in fact the Christ. No attempt is made by Jesus to modify this confession. The use of the title "Son of Man" in 8:31 is not a correction of this confession (see 8:31–32a). The comprehension of the disciples, and especially Peter, as to what Jesus's messiahship may have involved was erroneous, but the confession is correct. It confirms Mark's understanding in 1:1, and later in 14:61–62 Mark records a clear affirmation of this title by Jesus himself. Jesus is indeed the Christ.[3] The lack of a commendation of Peter for his confession (cf. Matt. 16:16–17) is probably due to the fact that the evangelist did not think it was necessary to affirm this. The readers already know that Jesus is the Christ from the opening statement of Mark (1:1).

Several attempts have been made to interpret this verse as either Jesus's or **8:30** Mark's rejection of Peter's confession in 8:29 as being Satanic (Hahn 1969: 223–28; Weeden 1971: 64–69). Such attempts, however, are impossible for the following reasons.[4] (1) The Gospel begins with a statement affirming Jesus as the Christ, the Son of God (1:1). (2) The predisposition of the Markan readers is that Jesus is the Christ, and Mark supports such a view throughout his Gospel (1:1; 14:61–62; etc.). Thus, if Mark is seeking to refute Peter's confession that Jesus is the Christ, he would have to do this explicitly and clearly. He does not do this, as the first nineteen hundred years of Markan interpretation reveals.[5]

---

3. Räisänen (1990: 179) rightly points out: "No passage in the gospel suggests that Mark regarded the Christ title as in any way questionable. . . . If Mark had doubts about the Christ title, he would certainly not have used it programmatically in the title of his work (1:1)."

4. In the following discussion, arguments against the view that Jesus rejected Peter's confession or that Mark is rejecting Peter's confession are not distinguished, because many of them refute both viewpoints.

5. C. S. Lewis rightfully points out, "The idea that any man or writer should be opaque to those who live in the same culture, spoke the same language, shared the same habitual imagery and unconscious assumptions, and yet be transparent to those who have none of these advantages, is in my opinion preposterous" (1975: 112).

(3) In 14:62 Jesus clearly affirms before the Sanhedrin that he is the Christ (cf. 9:41). In fact, Jesus acknowledges his messiahship more boldly and clearly in Mark than in the parallel accounts (cf. Matt. 26:63–66; Luke 22:67–71). (4) Jesus was condemned and crucified by Rome as the king of the Jews, that is, the Christ (15:2, 12, 18, 26). (5) Peter is called "Satan" in 8:33 not because of his confession (cf. Matt. 16:17–18) but because of his rejection of Jesus's teaching concerning his forthcoming passion. Note that 8:33 follows right after 8:31–32, not 8:29 (Gnilka 1979: 13; Räisänen 1990: 177–78). (6) Jesus charges Peter and the other disciples in 8:30 not to tell anyone "concerning him" (περὶ αὐτοῦ, peri autou). If he were forbidden to tell the supposedly false confession that "Jesus is the Christ," one would expect a command not to tell "this" (τοῦτο, touto). But the command is not to tell "concerning him," that is, that he is truly the Christ (cf. Gundry 1993: 445). (7) Jesus's warning in 8:30 involves the same term used in the rebuke of the demons in 1:25 and 3:12.[6] Yet Mark has gone out of his way to tell his readers (1:34) that the demons are reliable spokesmen for his view. Thus they truly know who he is. The command to Peter in 8:30 must be interpreted in a similar way. Peter, like the demons, is a reliable spokesman for the Markan christological understanding of Jesus (Gundry 1993: 427). (8) Finally, the following story of the transfiguration (9:2–8) provides divine approval of Peter's confession in that the voice from heaven calls Jesus "My beloved Son" (9:7), and the title "Son of God" is intimately tied to the title "Christ" (1:1; 14:61). In light of the above, it is remarkable that interpreting 8:27–30 as a rejection of Peter's confession that Jesus is the Christ/Messiah has received as much support as it has.[7]

Within the ministry of Jesus, such a prohibition makes sense (Gundry 1993: 427; Evans 2001: 15). Rome would not have tolerated an open proclamation of messiahship by so popular and influential a leader. Regardless of Jesus's understanding of what messiahship means, this would not be accepted by Rome. It was not accepted by his own disciples even after he explained it to them (8:31–33)! Would not the crowds be even less able to understand that Jesus's messiahship involves dying as a ransom for many (10:45)? The predominant understanding concerning the coming of the messiah involved political and revolutionary hopes of liberation from Roman rule (cf. Ps. Sol. 17–18; CD 19.10–11). Jesus needed to be careful not to stir up such false hopes (cf. John 6:15). Such false expectations later inflamed the revolutionary fervor of the masses and brought disaster in both AD 70 and 135.

Many scholars argue that the command to silence in 8:30 is a Markan redactional insertion involving the "messianic secret." The vocabulary and thought is clearly Markan (cf. 3:12 and the use of "rebuke" in 1:34). The present

---

6. Although Schweizer (1970: 174) and Witherington (2001: 240) argue that the "rebuke" of Peter in 8:30 reveals that he has no better understanding of who Jesus is than the demons in 3:11 and 5:7, Mark explicitly states that the demons truly know who Jesus is (1:34)!

7. Hooker (1991: 201) remarks, "It seems hard to believe . . . that an indignant rejection by Jesus could have been transformed by degrees into the enthusiastic acceptance that we have in Matthew's account of the scene."

verse, however, is probably better understood as a Markan rewording of the traditional ending to the pericope. Its appearance in the Matthean (16:20) and Lukan (9:21) parallels lends support to it being traditional. Furthermore, without this verse the account lacks a proper ending. Note that even Matthew, whose commendation of Peter and the famous "key" statement (16:17–19) would provide an excellent conclusion to the narrative of Peter's confession, ends his version of the story with Jesus's prohibition not to tell others that he is the Christ (16:20).

Some argue that the construction "began to . . ." serves simply as a loose **8:31–32a** connective (Best 1981: 23). Yet it appears that here "began to teach" should be understood as marking a new stage in the ministry of Jesus (Hooker 1991: 205; France 2002: 327). This is how Matthew understood it: "From that time he began . . ." (Ἀπὸ τότε ἤρξατο, *Apo tote ērxato*; 16:21). There have been a few, veiled allusions to Jesus's forthcoming passion (Mark 2:19–20; cf. 3:6), but now this becomes explicit and a focus of Jesus's teaching (8:31; 9:31; 10:33–34, 45; 12:1–11; 14:3–9, 24–25). From 8:31 to the end (16:8), the Gospel of Mark becomes an extended "Passion Narrative," and the necessity of Jesus's death is emphasized. It is necessary because (1) Scripture teaches this (9:12; 14:21, 27), and (2) it is a divinely preordained necessity (δεῖ, *dei*; cf. 8:31; 9:11; 13:7, 10). (The expression "it is written" [9:12; 14:21, 49] and δεῖ share the same connotation—God's word and will must take place.) The divine purpose of Jesus's ministry as the Christ is to fulfill the divine plan and to offer himself as a ransom for many (10:45). As a result, Mark wants his readers to understand that the death of Jesus should be thought of not "as the triumph of the opposition but as the fulfillment of the divine purpose [and thus] to be welcomed rather than bewailed" (France 2002: 333).

Jesus's passion prediction in 8:31 switches from the title "Christ" to the more familiar yet enigmatic "Son of Man" (see 2:10). This is Jesus's favorite self-designation (Stein 1994b: 135–51) and was probably found by Mark in the passion prediction. It is an error to see the switch of terms as a "correction" of Peter's confession in 8:29, for according to Mark, Jesus is the Christ (1:1). As the Christ/Son of Man, Jesus must suffer "many things" (πολλά, *polla*). Although πολλά can be translated "much," it seems that the manner of Jesus's suffering, which is described in the rest of the verse, is more in mind than the severity of his suffering. The general term "suffering" (παθεῖν, *pathein*) is defined by his being "rejected" (ἀποδοκιμασθῆναι, *apodokimasthēnai*; cf. 12:10) and "killed" (ἀποκτανθῆναι, *apoktanthēnai*). This suffering will come from "the elders" (τῶν πρεσβυτέρων, *tōn presbyterōn*), "the chief priests" (τῶν ἀρχιερέων, *tōn archiereōn*), and "the scribes" (τῶν γραμματέων, *tōn grammateōn*). Mark emphasizes the individuality of each of these groups by the repetition of the article. The order of the three groups differs from what we normally find in Mark. Usually we find the "chief priests" mentioned first (11:27; 14:43, 53; cf. 10:33; 11:18; 14:1; 15:1). This naming pattern, as well as the use of "rise again" (ἀναστῆναι, *anastēnai*) instead of the more traditional "rise" (ἐγείρω, *egeirō*), the use of "kill" (ἀποκτανθῆναι; cf. 9:31 [2×]; 10:34) instead of "crucify" (σταυρόω, *stauroō*; cf. 15:13, 14, 15, 20, 24, 25, 27; 16:6), and the unusual "after three days" (μετὰ τρεῖς ἡμέρας, *meta treis hēmeras*; 9:31; 10:34) instead of "on the third day" (τῇ τρίτῃ ἡμέρᾳ, *tē tritē hēmera*; cf. Matt. 16:21; 17:23; 20:19; 27:64; Luke 9:22; 13:32; 18:33; 24:7, 46; 1 Cor. 15:4; etc.), suggests that Mark is dependent on tradition in this passion prediction (Best 1981: 24). The temporal designation does not function as an expression for the rapidity of Jesus's resurrection (contra Gundry 1993: 430) but as a description of the length of time, as the parallels reveal (cf. Matt. 16:21/Luke 9:22; Matt. 17:23; Matt. 20:19/Luke 18:33; also Luke 24:7, 46; Acts 10:40). The apologetic change to "on the third day" by both Matthew and Luke indicates that they understood "after three days" as a specific temporal designation and not as a general reference for "quickly." Some have sought to see the temporal designation as arising out of the early church's reflection on Hos. 6:2, but it is more likely that it is authentic. The extent to which Hos. 6:2 plays a role in this temporal designation is uncertain (see Evans 2001: 17–18 for a discussion). "After three days," "on the third day," and after "three days and three nights" (Matt. 12:40) are all ways of describing a Friday afternoon death, a Saturday stay in the tomb, and a Sunday morning resurrection (Stein 1990: 119–21).

The close agreement between the passion prediction in 8:31 and the subsequent events surrounding Jesus's death and resurrection has caused numerous scholars to argue that the prediction is a *vaticinium ex eventu*. It is obvious that in retelling the passion prediction(s) of Jesus, the early church was aware of the course of events surrounding Jesus's death and resurrection. It is also possible, perhaps even probable, that this knowledge shaped the subsequent retelling of the prediction(s). However, the suggestion that the original form of Jesus's passion prediction was "to suffer many things and be treated with contempt" (Strecker 1968) is too extreme.

The technical use of the term "word" (λόγος, *logos*) in Mark (2:2; 4:12–20, 33; cf. also 7:13) indicates that Jesus was now clearly teaching the disciples the gospel message concerning his death and resurrection. Unfortunately, such translations as the KJV, RSV, NRSV, NIV, NASB, REB, and NAB do not recognize the technical use of "the word" in Mark in their rendering of this expression (cf., however, Best 1981: 24; France 2002: 337). Jesus now teaches "the word" with clarity. This new clarity indicates that "began to teach" in 8:31 should be understood literally as indicating the beginning of a new stage in the Gospel. The subtle and few allusions to his death found earlier in Mark now give way to a concentrated period of teaching on this subject.

8:32b–33   "Having taken him aside" (προσλαβόμενος . . . αὐτόν, *proslabomenos . . . auton*) may portray a gesture of superiority or patronization by Peter (Wiarda 2000: 75–76). His rebuke of Jesus indicates that despite his correct understanding that Jesus is the Christ, he does not accept Jesus's interpretation of the messianic role. It stands in stark contrast and opposition to his own thoughts (and that of most Jews) about what the Messiah would do. Unfortunately, his correct understanding of who Jesus is is accompanied by a complete misunderstanding of what Jesus, the Messiah, will do. This "misunderstanding" does not involve an incorrect mental grasp of what Jesus is saying (Peter could have told others what Jesus had just said) but an unwillingness to accept what Jesus is saying. Only the resurrection will enable him to accept Jesus's teaching about this.

Mark explains Jesus's vocal rebuke of Peter as being caused by his "having turned and seen" (ἐπιστραφεὶς καὶ ἰδών, *epistrapheis kai idōn*) the other disciples. This can be understood as indicating that Peter was acting as the spokesman for the other disciples (Hooker 1991: 206) or that Peter's rebuke of Jesus's teaching in 8:32 was seen by the other disciples, so that Jesus had to respond to it publicly. "Get behind me" (ὕπαγε ὀπίσω μου, *hypage opisō mou*) can be understood as meaning that Peter should join the rest of the disciples behind Jesus and follow him (Gundry 1993: 443; Evans 2001: 19), but it more probably means something like "Get out of my sight" (Osborne 1973; Hooker 1991: 206; Wiarda 2000: 76–77; cf. Matt. 4:10). Peter is called "Satan" (see 1:13) not because he is indwelt by Satan or satanically possessed so that Satan is using him to tempt Jesus away from the divine plan.[8] Rather, Jesus is best understood as saying that Peter is acting like Satan and representing a satanic-like attitude. Other common names used for Satan include Beelzebul, Beelzebub, Belial, Beliar, Mastema, and the devil. One expects that Jesus's rebuke would refer to Peter's thinking "the things that come *from Satan*." Instead, Jesus rebukes him for thinking "the things that come *from people*" (τὰ τῶν ἀνθρώπων, *ta tōn anthrōpōn*). In the NT, however, these are essentially synonymous expressions. Like Paul, Jesus and Mark probably understood Satan as the "god of this world" (2 Cor. 4:4; cf. John 12:31; also Rom. 8:5–9; Col. 3:2), so that the fallen world's values reflect satanic values.

Summary

In the present passage Mark supports his christological understanding (1:1) by recounting the tradition of Peter's confession. Those who were associated with Jesus and witnessed his healings, exorcisms, and teachings recognized that Jesus was the Christ (8:29), and Jesus himself will confirm this before the Sanhedrin (14:61–62), before Pilate (15:2), and by his crucifixion (15:26). In addition, Mark shows his readers that Jesus predicted his suffering and death (8:31; cf. 9:9, 31; 10:33–34, 45; 12:1–12; 14:24–25). This reveals Jesus's great predictive power in knowing both the fact and the manner of his death. It also assists the Markan readers in understanding that the crucifixion was not a tragedy or mistake but the plan of God. A divine necessity (δεῖ, *dei*;

8. Witherington (2001: 241) argues that this is one of three crucial instances in which Jesus encounters temptation in Mark. The others are at the temptation (1:12–13) and in the Garden of Gethsemane (14:32–43). Yet the terms "tempt" and "temptation" are not mentioned here, and Mark gives no hint that Jesus was in any way experiencing temptation by Peter's words.

8:31) lies behind these events. The atoning purpose of Jesus's death is not yet revealed in Mark, but the readers probably brought with them to the reading of the Gospel the explanation given in their celebration of the Lord's Supper (cf. 1 Cor. 11:23–26) and the various early church confessions (cf. 1 Cor. 15:3–8), and Mark would share this later (10:45; 14:24).

Whether Mark emphasizes the close tie between Jesus's messiahship and his suffering due to a misunderstanding among his readers is impossible to say. Such a mirror reading is speculative. Nevertheless Mark does emphasize that Jesus is the Christ, the Son of God, the Son of Man, whose mission (it is necessary, δεῖ [8:31]; came, ἦλθεν, ēlthen [10:45]) involved giving his life for his followers. His death sealed the coming of the kingdom of God and the new covenant (14:24). Those who have no room for sacrificial death, atonement, ransom, and so on in their theology of Jesus are warned by Mark that their understanding is more in line with Satan and fallen humanity than with God (8:33). Mark glories both in the amazement and wonder that Jesus elicited by his mighty acts *and* in his sacrificial death. He does not minimize one for the sake of the other. However, we cannot be sure that Mark emphasizes this because he is combating an error in the community to which he wrote. What is clear is that Mark wants to portray Jesus Christ, the Son of God, as both "mighty in deed and word" (cf. Luke 24:19) and fulfilling the divine plan by dying as "a ransom for many" (λύτρον ἀντὶ πολλῶν, *lytron anti pollōn*; 10:45).

Additional Notes

8:27. The singular verb ἐξῆλθεν agrees with the first of the compound subjects that follow (see 1:36–37).

8:28. εἶπαν ... λέγοντες is lit. "said ... saying."

8:29. Some MSS (ℵ L W f¹³) add "Son of God" or "Son of the living God," but this is clearly secondary and based on the parallel reading in Matt. 16:16.

8:30. The ἵνα can be interpreted as epexegetical "that" or telic/purpose "in order that" (see 3:9–10). There is not a great deal of difference here between these two possibilities, but the former seems more likely.

C. Jesus's Invitation to Discipleship (8:34–9:1)

The present account consists of five separate sayings of Jesus that were either brought together by Mark or already existed together in the pre-Markan tradition (Best 1981: 31). Their originally isolated nature is suggested by the fact that some of them are found as doublets in different locations in Matthew and Luke (Mark 8:34 in Matt. 10:38 and Luke 14:27 [cf. Gos. Thom. 55b]; Mark 8:35 in Matt. 10:39 and Luke 17:33 [cf. John 12:25]; Mark 8:38 in Matt. 10:33 and Luke 12:9). They were brought together because of their common theme of discipleship. The present arrangement is quite logical in that an invitation to discipleship in the form of a conditional statement (8:34) is followed by four explanatory (γάρ, *gar*) clauses (8:35–38) explaining why one should follow Jesus. The four explanatory clauses form a chiasmus:

> A For whoever (ὃς γὰρ ἐάν, *hos gar ean*; 8:35)
>   B For what . . . ? (τί γάρ, *ti gar*; 8:36)
>   B′ For what . . . ? (τί γάρ, *ti gar*; 8:37)
> A′ For whoever (ὃς γὰρ ἐάν, *hos gar ean*; 8:38)

Verses 35–36 are also linked together by the terms "losing/forfeiting [ἀπολέσει/ζημιωθῆναι, *apolesei/zēmiōthēnai*] one's life." In addition, 9:1 has been added to these teachings on discipleship (probably by Mark; see Best 1981: 28–31) to provide a climactic word of encouragement (Perrin 1967: 199; Gnilka 1979: 22–23) and to show how the transfiguration was a proleptic foretaste of the coming of the kingdom of God with power (Nardoni 1981: 381–84).

    The opening words "And having called the crowd along with his disciples, he said to them" (Καὶ προσκαλεσάμενος τὸν ὄχλον σὺν τοῖς μαθηταῖς αὐτοῦ εἶπεν αὐτοῖς, *Kai proskalesamenos ton ochlon syn tois mathētais autou eipen autois*; 8:34a) suggest the beginning of a new pericope (cf. 3:13, 23; 6:7; 7:14; 8:1; 10:42). Mark was probably the one who joined this material (teachings on discipleship) with the preceding passion prediction (8:31) and example of the disciples' failure (8:32–33), for this is a recurring pattern in 8:27–10:52 (see 8:22–10:52). Along with this recurring cycle, the present account is tied to 8:27–33 by the parallel between Jesus's own fate and the warning that discipleship may involve a similar fate (take up his cross, ἀράτω τὸν σταυρὸν αὐτοῦ, *aratō ton stauron autou*; 8:34) and the common reference to the future activity of the Son of Man (8:31 in his crucifixion, and 8:38 in his parousia).

The hand of Mark is seen most clearly in the introductory statement (8:34a), to which Mark has probably added the reference to the disciples (Gundry 1993: 453; cf. 4:10; contra Evans 2001: 25, who thinks that Mark has added the reference to the crowd); the placement of 9:1 with 8:34–38 and the placement of the entire passage with 8:27–33 (Kümmel 1957: 25; Best 1981: 30–31); and the reference to the "gospel" (εὐαγγελίου, euangeliou) in 8:35 (V. Taylor 1952: 382; Keck 1965a: 357–58). Other suggested Markan additions to these sayings include "and my words" (καὶ τοὺς ἐμοὺς λόγους, kai tous emous logous; Gundry 1993: 438) and "this adulterous and sinful" (ταύτῃ τῇ μοιχαλίδι καὶ ἁμαρτωλῷ, tautē tē moichalidi kai hamartōlō) in 8:38 (Gundry 1993: 456). There is no reason to attribute 9:1 to Mark (contra Perrin 1967: 200–201). The "Truly" (ἀμήν, amēn) argues strongly for a dominical origin (Jeremias 1971: 35–36), as does the unlikelihood that the early church would create a saying that appears to have been unfulfilled (J. Edwards 2002: 259).

Exegesis and Exposition

34And having called the crowd along with his disciples, he said to them, "If anyone wishes to ⌜follow⌝ me, let him deny himself, and let him take up his cross, and let him continually follow me. 35For whoever wishes to save his life will lose it, but whoever loses his life for me and the gospel will save it. 36For what does it profit a person to gain the whole world and to suffer the loss of his life? 37For what might a person give in exchange for his life? 38For whoever is ashamed of me and my ⌜words⌝ in this adulterous and sinful generation, the Son of Man will also be ashamed of him, when he comes in the glory of his Father with the holy angels." 9:1And he was saying to them, "Truly, I say to you that there are certain [of you] standing here who will ⌜by no means⌝ ⌜die⌝ until they see the kingdom of God having come with power."

8:34   The awkwardness of the opening statement, "the crowd with his disciples," recalls "those around him along with the Twelve" in 4:10. As in the former instance, Mark is probably responsible for the reference to the "disciples/Twelve" (Best 1981: 28–29; Gundry 1991: 453), who are usually distinguished from the crowd (5:31; 7:17; 10:10). In so doing, he has applied Jesus's invitation given to the unconverted to those who are already followers of Jesus. Luke has done this even more explicitly by his addition of "daily" (καθ' ἡμέραν, kath' hēmeran; 9:23) to "take up his cross."

Although "following" Jesus is not a technical term for being a disciple throughout Mark, in 8:22–10:52 it is frequently used in this sense (cf. 8:34; 9:38; 10:21, 28, 52; Luz 1983: 84; contra Gundry 1993: 453). Following Jesus is described as involving three requirements. One must (1) "deny himself" (ἀπαρνησάσθω ἑαυτόν, aparnēsasthō heauton). This involves not the denial of things (e.g., "giving up something for Lent") or some sort of asceticism or self-discipline. It is far more radical than this, for it is not the denial of "something" but of "someone"—oneself! It requires the denying or saying no to the self as the determiner of one's goals, aspirations, and desires. (Cf. 10:28, where the disciples state that they have left "everything" [πάντα, *panta*].) The use of the aorist tense here and in the following requirement focuses attention on the act of becoming a disciple. In including the disciples in the invitation, Mark wants his readers to recall the earlier commitment they made to follow Jesus and to renew it (cf. Luke 9:23).

One must also (2) "take up his cross." Even before Jesus's crucifixion, the image of bearing one's cross to the place of execution (Plutarch, *De sera numinis vindicta* §554b) was well known both to Jesus's and Mark's audiences (Hengel 1977: 62; contra Nineham 1963: 230). The imagery implies both death and shame (Heb. 12:2), for crucifixion was reserved for the most hardened criminals and for revolutionaries committing treason against the state. That the primary meaning here is metaphorical and not literal is evident from Luke's adding "daily" in his parallel (9:23) and by the fact that 8:38 assumes that the Christian community will continue to exist until the parousia. To be sure, the possibility of martyrdom is present here, as well as in the expression "loses his life" (ἀπολέσει τὴν ψυχὴν αὐτοῦ, *apolesei tēn psychēn autou*) in the following verse. Taking up one's cross, however, probably serves to reinforce and intensify what it means to deny oneself (W. Lane 1974: 307). One should not think that the second requirement is concerned with the normal sufferings of life brought about by illness, disability, death, and so on. It involves rather the experience of denying oneself even to the point of death because of being a follower of Jesus. Like the first command, "taking up one's cross" refers back to the act of becoming a Christian and denying oneself, as the aorist tense of the verb "take up" (ἀράτω, *aratō*) indicates. The authenticity of this requirement is now more readily accepted by even critical scholarship (cf. Crossan 1991: 353). The fact that in the Synoptic Gospels Jesus is not described as carrying his cross (Simon of Cyrene does this; cf. 15:21 and the Matthean and Lukan parallels) supports its authenticity.

The last requirement is (3) to follow Jesus. The repetition of "follow" (ἀκολουθείτω, *akoloutheitō*) as a specific requirement for "following" Jesus in the opening protasis (If anyone wishes to follow me, Εἴ τις θέλει ὀπίσω μου ἀκολουθεῖν, *Ei tis thelei opisō mou akolouthein*; lit. ". . . follow after me") is somewhat clumsy, but we have encountered a similar double use of the verb in 2:14. Unlike the aorist tenses found in the opening two requirements for becoming a disciple, the present imperative found in the third requirement emphasizes the continual nature of following Jesus. Thus the "act" of denying oneself and taking up one's cross is followed by the process of following Jesus (Best 1981: 32). This continual process also indicates that the preceding requirement of taking up the cross must be understood metaphorically. What is being emphasized is not the road to martyrdom but the continual following of Jesus until his return (13:32–37; 14:25) and enduring to the end (13:13; Matt. 10:22; 24:13). The first reference to following in 8:34b is used comprehensively to refer to all three requirements, but in 8:34c "follow" is more specific. Although not defined in the Gospel, Mark's readers would have thought that it meant keeping Jesus's teachings (both those mentioned in the Gospel and those known to them via the oral tradition), experiencing the initiatory act of baptism, sharing regularly in the breaking of bread, keeping the moral teachings of the OT, faithfully confessing the lordship of Jesus (Matt. 10:32–33/Luke 12:8–9), proclaiming the gospel to all nations (13:10; Matt. 28:18–20; Luke 24:46–49), and so on.

8:35   The presence of "For" (γάρ, *gar*) indicates that 8:35 provides a rationale for accepting the invitation for discipleship found in 8:34. The verse involves several puns in that the crucial terms ("save," "lose," "life") possess double meanings (contra Best 1981: 41). "Save" (σῴζω, *sōzō*) is used first in the negative sense of not denying oneself and then in the positive sense of achieving eternal salvation in the final day (cf. 8:38). "Lose" (ἀπολέσει, *apolesei*) is first used negatively in the sense of not acquiring eternal salvation and then in the positive sense of denying oneself and acquiring eternal salvation. "Life" (ψυχή, *psychē*) is first used to describe human, physical existence that does not deny personal goals and desires, that is, does not repent (1:15), and then it is used to describe one's personal being, that is, the real self that continues to exist after death.[1] "Losing one's life" must be understood in the sense of denying oneself, taking up one's cross, and following Jesus, as referred to in 8:34. It is described as taking place "for me [Jesus Christ, the Son of God] and the gospel." Since in other places in Mark "gospel" appears to be due to the editorial work of Mark (1:1, 14–15; 10:29; 13:10; 14:9) and since both parallels (Matt. 16:25; Luke 9:24) lack it here,[2] "gospel" is probably an insertion by the evangelist into the saying. Mark sees the person of Jesus ("me") and the message concerning Jesus ("the gospel") as intimately related. He knows nothing of a distinction between a historical Jesus ("me") and a kerygmatic Christ ("the gospel"; cf. Hooker 1991: 209). For Mark's readers, the addition "gospel" helps describe and clarify what loyalty to the person of Jesus involves. For his readers, the "gospel" involved not just the message that Jesus proclaimed but also the preached gospel of the early church (Witherington 2001: 245; contra Evans 2001: 26; cf. 1 Cor. 15:1–11; see Mark 1:15).

The authenticity of "for me" (ἕνεκεν ἐμοῦ, *heneken emou*) will be determined in part by one's preconception of Jesus's messianic self-consciousness. Support for its authenticity, however, is found in other sayings of Jesus in which one's eternal fate is dependent on one's attitude or relationship to him (Matt. 7:21–23/Luke 13:25–27; Matt. 10:32–33/Luke 12:8–9; Matt. 10:35–36/Luke 12:51–53; Matt. 10:37–39/Luke 14:26–27; Matt. 11:6/Luke 7:23). The chiastic parallelism found in the present verse can still be seen in most translations ([A] "save"; [B] "lose"; [B′] "lose"; [A′] "save").

---

1. For Jesus's frequent use of puns in his teaching, see Stein 1994b: 12–14.
2. Cf. also Mark 10:29, where we have a similar pairing "for me and the gospel," and both Matthew (19:29) and Luke (18:29) again lack "gospel" (εὐαγγελίου, *euangeliou*) in their parallels.

Although some see 8:35–38 as consisting of a series of four consecutive reasons for obeying Jesus's call to discipleship (Gundry 1993: 434, 439–40; Evans 2001: 24), it is best to see the "for" of 8:36 as explaining 8:35 and not as a separate reason supporting 8:34 (V. Taylor 1952: 382). The reason why one should be willing to "lose" one's life is because of the surpassing worth of gaining eternal life. This is more valuable than possessing the whole world (cf. Matt. 4:8–9/Luke 4:5–6). To acquire all the world and yet lose one's life, that is, not acquire eternal salvation, is a terrible loss. This is why one should be willing to lose one's life "for [Jesus] and the gospel" (Mark 8:35). The common nature of this proverb can be seen in Ps. 49:7–8; 2 Bar. 51.15. Just as Mark 8:36 explains 8:35, so 8:37 explains 8:36. When you have lost your life (8:36), nothing can ever buy it back (8:37). Both questions in these two verses are left unanswered because they are so obvious. Both assume an answer like "Nothing at all!"

8:36–37

This verse gives the second reason for accepting Jesus's invitation to follow him (8:34). Unlike 8:35 and its supporting arguments in 8:36–37, which are addressed to the "crowd" of 8:34a, this argument is aimed at those who are already disciples. (Cf. the context of the parallel saying in the Q tradition in Matt. 10:33/Luke 12:9, where the parallels lack the title "Son of Man.") Both Matthew (16:27) and Luke (9:26), however, have the title in their parallels to the Markan account. There are sufficient differences between the Q saying and our present one to suggest that they are separate sayings, as both Matthew and Luke assume. The reference to the coming of the Son of Man refers not to the ascension but to the return of the Son of Man at the parousia when he comes with the angels (cf. 2 Thess. 1:7; contra France 2002: 342–43).

8:38

The reference to "the Son of Man" (ὁ υἱὸς τοῦ ἀνθρώπου, *ho huios tou anthrōpou*) coming "in the glory of his Father" (ἐν τῇ δόξῃ τοῦ πατρὸς αὐτοῦ, *en tē doxē tou patros autou*) ties this title and the title "Son of God" intimately together (cf. also 14:61–62). Although some suggest that "of his Father" is Markan (Hooker 1991: 210), its inclusion in Matthew and Luke suggests that it is traditional. It is clear that all three evangelists understood the Son of Man in the saying to refer to Jesus and not to some other person. It is furthermore unlikely that Jesus ever distinguished between himself and the Son of Man (contra Bultmann 1968: 112, 151–52; Tödt 1965: 57–60, 224–26, 339–44), for nowhere in the teachings of Jesus does he give the slightest hint that he expected someone greater than himself to follow him. Jesus's answer to John the Baptist's question "Are you he who is to come or do we expect another?" (Matt. 11:3) is not that there is in fact another one coming greater than he—that is, the Son of Man—but rather that his deeds and actions prove that he is the promised Messiah awaited by Israel (Matt. 11:4–15). The authenticity of Mark 8:38 is supported by the fact that the expression "Son of Man" does not occur in early Christian confessions identifying who Jesus is (Gundry 1993: 456). For a similar use of the third person to describe oneself, compare 2 Cor. 12:2–5.

Whether the reference to "my words" is traditional or Markan (Best 1981: 43; Gundry 1993: 438) is uncertain. Mark uses the singular "word" twenty times, whereas the plural occurs only here and in 10:24 and 13:31. In favor of it being Markan is the similar pairing of "me and the gospel/my words" in 8:35, 38; and 10:29. For "adulterous and sinful generation," compare 9:19/ Matt. 17:17/Luke 9:41; Matt. 12:39/Luke 11:29; Matt. 12:45; 16:4; also Phil. 2:15. The term "ashamed" (ἐπαισχυνθήσεται, epaischynthēsetai) is found only here in Mark. It refers not so much to internal emotions, such as feeling embarrassed with respect to the person of Jesus and his teachings, but rather to one's actions. It means to deny[3] Jesus in times of persecution (cf. Matt. 10:33/Luke 12:9) in contrast to confessing him (cf. Matt. 10:32/Luke 12:8). The consequence of being ashamed of/denying Jesus is that at the final judgment he will be ashamed of/deny us!

9:1 The introductory phrase (And he was saying to them, καὶ ἔλεγεν αὐτοῖς, kai elegen autois) frequently sets up a new saying added to what has preceded. The saying itself is best understood as "a climactic promise" (Perrin 1967: 199; cf. also Kilgallen 1982; Hatina 2005: 21–26) concluding the preceding sayings. The difference in theme between this saying and the preceding verses (seeing the kingdom of God coming in power versus teachings on discipleship) suggests that they were originally uttered on different occasions. The similarity of the event envisioned (the coming of the Son of Man in glory in 8:38 and seeing the kingdom of God having come in power in 9:1), however, helps tie them together. If, as we shall see, Mark understands this saying as being in some way fulfilled in the following account of the transfiguration, this further explains its location here by Mark.

The importance of this saying is emphasized by the opening "Truly" (ἀμήν, amēn; see 3:28–30) and the double negative "by no means" (οὐ μή, ou mē). It is intended to provide encouragement, explaining why Mark's readers should continue following Jesus. The statement that there are "certain [of you] standing here who will by no means die until they see the kingdom of God having come with power" (τινες ὧδε τῶν ἑστηκότων οἵτινες οὐ μὴ γεύσωνται θανάτου ἕως ἂν ἴδωσιν τὴν βασιλείαν τοῦ θεοῦ ἐληλυθυῖαν ἐν δυνάμει, tines hōde tōn hestēkotōn hoitines ou mē geusōntai thanatou heōs an idōsin tēn basileian tou theou elēlythuian en dynamei) has received a great deal of discussion, for it appears that this prophecy was not fulfilled (cf. 13:30). This verse appears to say that some of Jesus's hearers would live to see, in the near future, the coming of the kingdom of God in power that is associated with the parousia of the Son of Man (Kümmel 1957: 27). However, the ultimate consummation of the kingdom and glorious appearing of the Son of Man to judge the world did not occur in their lifetime. The disciples all died, that is, tasted death (Heb. 2:9; cf. also 2 Esd. 6:26), without apparently seeing the Son of Man come in/with his kingdom (Matt. 16:28). Numerous attempts have been made to

---

3. In Matt. 10:33 and Luke 12:9 the synonym "deny" ([ἀπ]αρνήσηται, aparnēsētai) is used to describe what it means to be ashamed of Jesus.

resolve this difficulty (cf. Brower 1980). These include seeing the kingdom of God coming in power as referring to (1) the resurrection of Jesus from the dead (J. Edwards 2002: 260); (2) the coming of the Spirit upon the church at Pentecost; (3) the fall of Jerusalem in AD 70 (McKnight 1999: 128–30); (4) perceiving or becoming aware of the fact that the kingdom of God "has already come" (ἐληλυθυῖαν, elēlythuian), that is, has been realized (Dodd 1961: 37–38; cf. Evans 2001: 28–30; France 2002: 344–45); (5) experiencing the realized dimension of the kingdom's arrival (Pesch 1980b: 66; Brower 1980: 37–41), which would include options 1, 2, and 3; (6) the transfiguration as a proleptic preview and preliminary fulfillment of the coming of the kingdom (Cranfield 1959: 287–88; Pesch 1980b: 67; Nardoni 1981: 381–84; Gundry 1993: 469; Evans 2001: 29); and (7) the parousia, and thus Jesus erred (Hooker 1991: 212); and so on.[4]

Suggestions 5 and 6 seem to be the most likely of these possibilities. If 9:1 is treated as an isolated saying of Jesus (cf. 13:30), option 5 involves a better understanding of "see" (ἴδωσιν) than suggested in option 4, and it understands "some standing here" in the most natural sense as Jesus's hearers. In its present setting just before the account of the transfiguration, however, option 6 appears to capture best the Markan meaning. Because of their presence at the transfiguration, some of the disciples (Peter, James, and John [9:2]) experienced "already now" a foretaste of the "not yet" of the kingdom's future consummation at the parousia of the Son of Man (see 1:15).[5]

Summary

The strong christological emphasis found in this passage is apparent. The eternal destiny of human beings is dependent on their relationship to Jesus. Saving one's life depends upon becoming his disciple (8:34, 38). Nothing else matters. Losing one's life results from ignoring Jesus's call and having him be ashamed of them in the final judgment. To assert that the eternal destiny of all humans depends on their relationship to Jesus is a fantastic claim. Such a claim on the lips of anyone else is damnable (Stein 1994b: 122–23). Yet Jesus can make this claim because he is the Son of Man of Dan. 7:13, who will soon die for the sins of the world (Mark 10:45; 14:24) and one day come to judge it.

Closely related and stemming out of the Christology of the passage are Jesus's teachings on discipleship. Although 8:34–38 is devoted to explaining what it means to be a disciple, these teachings are dependent on who Jesus is, that is, on Christology (Gundry 1993: 434; Evans 2001: 30). Thus

4. Cf. also Bird (2003), who argues, unconvincingly in my mind, that it refers to the crucifixion.

5. The attempt by Hatina (2005) to interpret "certain [of you] standing here" as referring to "those ashamed of me and my words" (8:38) is unconvincing because Mark interprets 9:1 by 9:2–8, and the "certain" of 9:1 therefore involves Peter, James, and John; and "[you] standing here" refers back not to a hypothetical "whoever" of 8:38 but to the crowd and the disciples of 8:34a.

because of who Jesus is, Mark's hearers must make sure that they have a right relationship to him. If, as suggested, the reference to "with his disciples" (8:34) is due to Mark's own editorial work, this indicates that he is emphasizing to the believing community the importance of renewing their commitment to Jesus. Being a follower of Jesus is dependent on an act of the will. It does not depend on birth, religiosity, or position. One must "will" (θέλω, thelō; 8:34–35) to follow Christ. For the crowd, this means the act of conversion involving repentance ("denying oneself") and commitment ("taking up one's cross") and following Jesus continually. For the believing community, it involves reaffirming their earlier commitment, for what is decisive is not merely confessing Jesus as Christ and Lord (Matt. 7:21–23) but also following him in obedient discipleship (Hooker 1991: 208).

Additional Notes

8:34. "Come" (ἔλθειν) is found in ℵ A B K L f¹³, whereas "follow" (ἀκολουθεῖν) is found in 𝔓⁴⁵ D W Θ f¹ lat. Most probably "come" has entered the MS tradition due to assimilation to the parallel in Matt. 16:24.

8:38. "Words" (λόγους) is not found in 𝔓⁴⁵ and W. It was probably omitted by a copyist due to haplography, i.e., having written "my" (ἐμους) and looking back at the MS he was copying, he focused on the -ους in the next word, λόγους, and assumed that he had already copied this word.

9:1. The expression "by no means" translates the emphatic double negative οὐ μή.

9:1. γεύσωνται θανάτου is lit. "taste death."

D. Jesus Is Transfigured (9:2–8)

The present account is tied closely to 8:27–9:1 in both time and theme. In 9:2, it is tied to the preceding account by "after six days" (μετὰ ἡμέρας ἕξ, *meta hēmeras hex*), a rare Markan temporal tie (cf. 14:1 for the only other real example of such a tie). This suggests that it is traditional (Stein 1976: 83; Gnilka 1979: 31). The temporal designation may refer to three possibilities in 8:27–9:1: the confession of Peter (8:27–30), Jesus's passion prediction (8:30–33), or Jesus's teachings on discipleship (8:34–9:1). The temporal tie is less likely to connect the present account with a series of sayings (8:34–9:1) than with an event (Best 1981: 55).[1] This is especially true if Mark is responsible for the placement of 8:34–9:1 in its present location (see the introduction to 8:34–9:1) and if the temporal tie is traditional. Most likely 9:2–8 was connected to either 8:27–30 or 8:31–33, or to both in the pre-Markan tradition. If, as has been suggested (see the introduction to 8:27–33), 8:27–33 already existed together in the pre-Markan tradition (and is perhaps historical), then the temporal tie connects 9:2–8 to 8:27–33. This is also supported by the thematic tie that exists between the two passages.

The transfiguration is tied to 8:27–34 by two themes: Peter's christological confession (8:27–30) and Jesus's passion prediction (8:31–33). The voice from heaven corroborates Peter's confession at Caesarea Philippi as to Jesus's identity. Although the titles are different ("Christ" in the confession and "Son [of God]" by the voice), these are understood by Mark as complementary. Jesus is "the Christ, the Son of God" (1:1; 14:61–62). Thus the divine voice from heaven confirms what Peter has said about Jesus in the preceding account and serves as the second heavenly endorsement of Jesus's divine sonship (cf. 1:11). The other thematic tie with the preceding materials is found in the second part of the message from heaven, "Hear him." This does not refer back to the teachings on discipleship found in 8:34–9:1 (contra Best 1981: 57–58) or to the entire complex of sayings in 8:31–9:1 (contra Gundry 1993: 457) but more specifically to Peter's refusal to "hear" Jesus's teaching concerning his future passion in 8:31–33 (Schweizer 1970: 182; Pesch 1980b: 77).[2] This means that the two parts of the heavenly message

---

1. Cf., however, Nardoni (1981: 375), who argues that the time indication ("after six days," 9:2) provides "a good sign of literary and thematic connection" with the prophetic saying in 9:1.

2. Mark placed 8:34–9:1 between 8:27–33 and 9:2–8 not primarily because of its ties to the latter passage but because of its ties to the former. It is placed here to complete the cycle of passion prediction, disciple error, and teachings on discipleship (see the introduction to 8:34–9:1).

function as a confirmation of Peter's confession in 8:27–30 and a rebuke of Peter's rejection of Jesus's passion prediction in 8:31–33 (see 9:5–6).

It is difficult to delineate the exact nature of Mark's editorial work in the present passage. The temporal tie as well as the geographical tie (cf. 2 Pet. 1:16–18, which is an independent account of the transfiguration and refers to the location as "the holy mountain" [1:18]) appear to be traditional. There is no clear evidence that Mark added the reference to Peter, James, and John (cf. Best 1981: 57–58), for the account continually refers to their presence ("them," 9:2, 4, 7, 8; "they," 9:6; "you [plural]," 9:7), so that their presence seems to be part of the story. On several other important occasions, these three are present with Jesus (5:37; 14:33; cf. also 1:16–20; 13:3). The use of "we" in 2 Pet. 1:16–18, which stands in notable contrast to the "I" in 1:12–15, argues against the view that only Peter was originally present in the account (contra Bultmann 1968: 260). "Privately by themselves" (κατ᾽ ἰδίαν μόνους, kat' idian monous; 9:2) may be Markan (Best 1981: 56) because of its redundancy and the use of κατ᾽ ἰδίαν in typically redactional settings (4:34; 6:31, 32; 7:33; 9:28; 13:3), and the explanatory "for" (γάρ, gar) clause (9:6) looks Markan as well (see 1:16–18; Best 1981: 56). Some see the command "Hear him" (ἀκούετε αὐτοῦ, akouete autou; 9:7) as a Markan addition (Best 1981: 57), but this is uncertain.[3]

The origin of the present account is much debated. Numerous scholars have suggested that it was originally a resurrection account read back into the life of the historical Jesus (see Stein 1976: 79–80 for a listing of scholars advocating this). Reasons given in support of this include these: (1) the "mountain" of 9:2 supposedly refers to the mountain associated with the Great Commission (Matt. 28:16); (2) the "cloud" supposedly refers to the cloud associated with the ascension (Acts 1:9); (3) the temporal designation "after six days" supposedly refers to an event taking place six days after Easter, since many specific temporal designations ("after three days," "in the first day," "during forty days") are associated with the resurrection; (4) the verb "appeared" (ὤφθη, ōphthē; 9:4) is associated with a resurrection appearance in 16:7; and so on.[4] There are serious problems with such a view: the use of "Rabbi" (9:5) to describe the risen Christ;[5] the need for a command to "hear" (ἀκούετε, 9:7) the risen Lord seems anachronistic in a resurrection narrative; there are marked differences between the form of the present account and that of the resurrection narratives (Dodd 1955: 25); nowhere in any resurrection account are Peter, James, and John (9:2) singled out,

---

3. Pryke (1978: 17, 144, 163) is surely wrong in attributing most of 9:2 and 7 and all of 9:3 and 6 to Mark. Contrast Gnilka (1979: 32), who sees 9:6 as the primary Markan redaction.

4. Carlston (1961: 235) even goes so far as to claim that the burden of proof is upon those who argue that the transfiguration is not a misplaced resurrection account. He says this despite the fact that Matthew, Mark, and Luke in their Gospels present it as a nonresurrection account.

5. Evans (2001: 37) states, "Addressing Jesus as ῥαββί, 'Rabbi,' lends the story an important element of verisimilitude, for it is not likely that in an invented story, or in an Easter appearance story, Jesus would be addressed by such a pedestrian epithet."

whereas in the narratives of the historical Jesus they are mentioned in 5:37; 14:33 (cf. 1:16–20; 13:3), and the earliest list of resurrection appearances (1 Cor. 15:5–8) says nothing of such an appearance; it is doubtful that such an error as honoring Jesus, Moses, and Elijah equally (9:5) would ever be made in a resurrection setting; and so on (Stein 1976: 90–96). The origin of the transfiguration in a misplaced resurrection narrative is unconvincing (Gundry 1993: 471–73).

It is even less convincing to believe that someone in the early church created the transfiguration account out of nothing when they one day read Exod. 24:16. Although the Exod. 24 account may have influenced the subsequent retelling and wording of the transfiguration account, the de novo creation of the account from Exod. 24 is extremely unlikely (cf. Gundry 1993: 475–76).[6] Some historical event must lie behind the present account (Hooker 1991: 214). One's view of the historicity of the present account is greatly influenced, of course, by whether one is open to the possibility of the miraculous in history.

The present story about Jesus can be divided as follows: (1) a change of location followed by Jesus's transfiguration (9:2–3), (2) the appearance of Elijah and Moses (9:4), (3) Peter's foolish response (9:5–6), (4) the voice from heaven (9:7), and (5) "Jesus only" (9:8).

Exegesis and Exposition

²And after six days Jesus takes Peter and James and John and leads them up into a high mountain privately by themselves, and he was transfigured before them. ³And his garments became glistening, intensely white, such as no ⌐earthly¬ bleacher is able to whiten. ⁴And there appeared to them Elijah with Moses, and they were speaking with Jesus. ⁵And Peter ⌐responds¬ to Jesus, "Rabbi, it is good for us to be here. ⌐ ¬ Let us make three booths—one for you, one for Moses, and one for Elijah."⁶[He said this] because he did not know what he should say, for they were terrified. ⁷And a cloud ⌐overshadowed¬ them, and a voice came out of the cloud, "This is my beloved Son. Hear him!" ⁸And suddenly, having looked around, they no longer saw ⌐anyone¬ but Jesus only with them.

The temporal designation ("after six days") is not understood by Mark in terms of a Semitic literary device pointing to a climactic event occurring on the seventh day (contra McCurley 1974). A possible allusion to Moses's six-day experience on Mount Sinai (Exod. 24:16), in which on the seventh day a voice speaks to Moses out of a cloud, is suggested by some (Best 1981: 59–60; Hooker 1987: 60). However, though the Exodus account may have influenced the shaping of the present account, "after six days" is not intended to focus

9:2–3

6. Note the following connections: "six days" (Exod. 24:16), "cloud" (24:16; cf. 40:35), "voice" from a cloud (24:16), three companions (24:1, 9); cf. also a transformation of appearance (34:30) and the reaction of fear (34:30).

the attention of Mark's readers/hearers on Exod. 24:16, for there is no reference to a seventh day in the present account. It focuses rather on the preceding account (Mark 8:27–9:1) that they have just heard read to them (Caird 1956: 291). Thus six days after 8:27–9:1 (perhaps on the sixth day [Gundry 1993: 474; contra McCurley 1974: 74, 81]), the present account takes place.

The scene is a "high mountain" (ὄρος ὑψηλόν, *oros hypsēlon*). Tradition identifies this as Mount Tabor, a "hill" 1,843 feet above sea level, standing in striking isolation above the Plain of Esdraelon and located about ten miles southwest of the Sea of Galilee. Mount Tabor is not a high "mountain," however, and in Jesus's day it was probably occupied by a Roman garrison (Josephus, *J.W.* 2.20.6 §573; 4.1.8 §§54–61). Other suggestions include Mount Carmel, on the Mediterranean coast overlooking modern-day Haifa, and Mount Hermon, the only truly "high mountain" in the area, having an elevation of 9,100 feet above sea level. In favor of the latter is both its height and the fact that Caesarea Philippi (8:27) is located on its slopes. None of the evangelists (or 2 Peter) identifies the actual site. Thus all suggestions are speculative. For the Gospel writers, it was not where the event took place but rather what took place that was important. The high mountain functions in the story as a "suburb of heaven" where one encounters God and deceased saints (Gundry 1993: 457).

The incident takes place for Peter, James, and John "privately by themselves" with Jesus. It thus involves only "some" of the disciples and serves as the fulfillment of 9:1 (Gundry 1993: 457–59). The verb "was transfigured" (μετεμορφώθη, *metemorphōthē*) is a divine passive indicating that God is responsible for the transfiguration. Exactly what is meant by Jesus being "transfigured" is unclear. The various descriptions include the following: "his garments became glistening, intensely white [στίλβοντα λευκὰ λίαν, *stilbonta leuka lian*], such as no earthly bleacher [γναφεύς, *gnapheus*] is able to whiten [λευκᾶναι, *leukanai*]" (9:3; cf. Dan. 7:9); "his face shone like the sun" (Matt. 17:2); "his garments became white as light" (Matt. 17:2); and "the appearance of his face was altered" (Luke 9:29). Second Peter refers to his appearance as "majestic" and "glorious" (1:16–17).[7] The miraculous, divine transformation is explained by the biblical writers through various this-world analogies. This transformation occurs before the three disciples alone. (Note the emphatic redundancy of "privately by themselves.") It is evident from this and the other references to the disciples that the event is described by Mark as taking place for "them" (9:2, 4, 7, 8; cf. "they" in 9:6; and "you" [plural] in 9:7; also "This is . . ."), whereas at Jesus's baptism it takes place for "Jesus" (see 9:7).

The transfiguration is described by Mark in 9:3, but its meaning is not explained. Two frequent suggestions are made: (1) The preincarnate glory of

---

7. For OT and intertestamental references to physical transformations of appearance, see Exod. 34:30; Dan. 12:3; 2 Esd. 7:97, 125; 1 En. 39.7; 104.2. For references to the transformation of clothing, see 2 Esd. 2:39, 45; 1 En. 62.15; cf. also Rev. 4:4. Evans (2001: 36) points out that in light of the parallels in Jewish literature, there is no need to seek for a Hellenistic (or more specifically a mystery religion) origin for the transfiguration account.

the Son of God broke through the veil of his humanity (cf. John 1:14; 17:5). Yet nothing in the account suggests that Jesus possessed before the transfiguration a hidden glory that was veiled up to this point. (2) It is a proleptic glimpse of the glory of the Son of Man/Son of God in his future coming (8:38), when the kingdom comes in power (9:1). In light of the understanding of the transfiguration in Matt. 16:28 and 2 Pet. 1:16–18 as a foreshadowing of the parousia, and above all by Mark's placement of 8:38 and 9:1 before the present account, it seems best to understand the theological meaning of the transfiguration as an anticipation of the future manifestation of the Son of Man/Son of God when he comes in glory and thus as the fulfillment of the promise made in 9:1 (Boobyer 1942; Cranfield 1959: 287–88; W. Lane 1974: 313–14; Pesch 1980b: 67; contra Thrall 1970: 309–17, who sees the transfiguration as foreshadowing the resurrection).

The wording "Elijah with Moses" is both awkward and unusual. This is evident by the fact that both Matthew (17:3) and Luke (9:30) reverse the order to "Moses and Elijah." This is what one would expect given that Moses and the Law preceded Elijah and the Prophets.[8] The traditional interpretation of their presence is that they represent the two divisions of the OT, the Law and the Prophets (Matt. 5:17; 7:12; 11:13; Luke 16:16; John 1:45; etc.).[9] Other explanations include these: both were faithful servants who suffered due to their obedience (cf. Mark 8:34–9:1); both did not see death (Elijah, 2 Kings 2:1–12; Moses, Josephus, *Ant.* 4.8.48 §326, despite the fact that Deut. 34:5 records his death [cf. Marcus 1992b: 88–90]); both experienced theophanies on a mountain (Exod. 20–34; 1 Kings 19:9–18). None of these explanations, however, accounts for why Elijah is mentioned first. One suggestion is that it is because Elijah is Jesus's forerunner (Hooker 1987: 62, 67) and inaugurates the end time (Gnilka 1979: 37). It may be, however, that Mark places his name first and gives him greater emphasis because of his being referred to in 8:28 and 9:11–13.[10] What these two OT saints discussed with Jesus is not mentioned by Mark or Matthew. Luke, however, states that they "spoke of his departure [ἔξοδον, *exodon*] that he was about to fulfill in Jerusalem" (9:31). The suggestion that they talked about the coming of the kingdom of God and Jesus's relationship to this (Evans 2001: 37) is possible, but Mark does not state this. Apparently what was discussed was not important for him (or for Matthew).

9:4

Peter's leadership role among the disciples is seen in his response to the theophany and the silence of James and John. At times Peter does well (8:29), but at times he errs (8:32; 9:5). His address to Jesus, "Rabbi" (see 14:44–46), immediately reveals a failure in his understanding (Hooker 1987: 64; contra

9:5-6

---

8. For the order Elijah and Moses, cf. Mal. 3:22–24 LXX.

9. Luke suggests this by his addition in 9:31.

10. Hooker (1987: 68–69) suggests that Moses represents the OT (the "Law" is sometimes used to describe the whole OT; cf. John 10:34; 12:34; 15:25; 1 Cor. 14:21), so that his presence symbolizes the OT witness to Christ.

Viviano 1990: 211) that the voice from heaven will address. Peter's statement "it is good for us to be here" (καλόν ἐστιν ἡμᾶς ὧδε εἶναι, *kalon estin hēmas hōde einai*), is capable of several interpretations. Two of the most common are (1) it is good because they are able to build three booths (Cranfield 1959: 291), and (2) it is good because they are able to see the kingdom come in power via the transfiguration. Mark's intended meaning by these words is unclear. A second error of Peter involves his suggestion to build three booths—one for Jesus, one for Moses, and one for Elijah.[11] This ignores both his earlier confession (8:29) and the fact that only Jesus, not Moses or Elijah, was transfigured. Peter's reply takes none of this into consideration (Heil 2000: 127, 149). In a typical explanatory comment, Mark tells his readers that Peter's suggestion is a mistake. He did not know what to say, because "they" (Peter speaks for James and John as well) were "terrified" (ἔκφοβοι, *ekphoboi*; cf. 4:41; 6:50). This fear was not because of what he was about to say and the future divine rebuke; rather, fear is quite natural and often accompanies a theophany. The real sense of being in the presence of God is often not ecstasy and delight but a holy awe and even terror, for at such times human weakness and sin stand in sharp contrast to the holiness and omnipotence of God (cf. 4:41; 5:15, 33; 6:49–50; Luke 5:8; Rev. 1:17). Thus Mark's comment serves less to emphasize the foolishness of the disciples than to heighten the glory of Jesus.

9:7 The mistake made by Peter is not that he prematurely assumed that the messianic age had completely arrived or that he sought to prolong the experience. Rather, it is that he did not recognize the uniqueness of Jesus and his great superiority over Moses and Elijah. This is made clear by the voice coming out of the cloud.[12] The voice corrects Peter's statement by pointing out the uniqueness of Jesus—"This is my beloved Son" (Οὗτός ἐστιν ὁ υἱός μου ὁ ἀγαπητός, *Houtos estin ho huios mou ho agapētos*).[13] Moses and Elijah are God's servants; Jesus is God's beloved Son (Mark 12:6; Heb. 1:1–2). The voice also confirms Peter's confession in Mark 8:29 that Jesus is more than a prophet, even the great prophet Elijah. He is greater than the prophet like unto Moses (Deut. 18:15), for he is the Christ. In 1:1 Mark has pointed out that the Christ is the Son of God, and Jesus himself at his trial will confirm that he is the "Christ, the Son of the Blessed" (14:61–62). Thus the voice affirms to Peter, James, and John, as well as to Mark's readers, that the confession of 8:29 is correct and rebukes Peter for his suggestion in 9:5 that forgets this. Whereas in 1:11 the

---

11. Booths were shelters made of branches and leaves and were usually associated with the celebration of the Feast of Tabernacles (Lev. 23:33–43; Num. 29:12–38; cf. Neh. 8:14–17), a yearly harvest festival that lasted seven days. As time went on, the festival began to be seen as anticipating the coming messianic age. Here the three booths are seen as honoring three distinguished persons.

12. A cloud is often associated with the glorious presence of God: Exod. 16:10; 19:9; 24:15–18; 33:7–11; 40:34–38; Num. 9:15–22; 1 Kings 8:10–13; Isa. 4:5; cf. also Ezek. 1:28; 11:23. For the divine voice coming out of a cloud, cf. Exod. 19:19; 24:16; 34:5ff.; Num. 11:25; 12:5–6; Deut. 31:15–16.

13. See Guelich (1989: 34) for the view that ἀγαπητός may have overtones of "only."

voice from heaven affirms to Jesus his sonship ("You are [σὺ εἶ, *sy ei*] . . ."), here the voice affirms Jesus's sonship to the disciples ("This is [οὗτός ἐστιν] . . ."; see 1:10–11). The revelation (of Jesus's transfiguration and the voice from heaven) is for the benefit of the disciples, not Jesus (Evans 2001: 38).

The second aspect of the voice's message, "Hear him," is often interpreted as an allusion to Deut. 18:15 (Marcus 1992: 81) and a reference to the need to listen to Jesus's teachings on discipleship found in 8:34–38. It is better, however, to interpret this as a rebuke of Peter's (and the disciples') refusal to accept Jesus's teachings concerning his passion, that is, to 8:32b–33 (J. Edwards 2002: 268). This allows the tone of the message to be consistent (a twofold rebuke) rather than containing two rather different messages (a rebuke and a general command to discipleship). This also allows the present reference to "hear" (ἀκούετε) to agree with its previous usage in 8:18, a rebuke of the disciples.[14]

The transfiguration account ends with a visual affirmation of the voice's confession that Jesus is the Son of God. The disciples now see "Jesus only" ('Ιησοῦν μόνον, *Iēsoun monon*). Moses and Elijah disappear. Whether Mark expected his readers to see in this concluding statement Jesus's superiority over Moses and Elijah because he alone remains is uncertain. Nevertheless, he emphasizes that at the end only the Son of God remains (Gundry 1993: 461–62), and this has strong christological implications. The good news centers on Jesus Christ, the Son of God, not Moses or Elijah!

9:8

Summary

The present passage contains a heavily christological message. This Markan emphasis is seen in a number of areas. The voice from heaven, "This is my beloved [only] Son" (9:7), confirms the earlier confession of Peter that Jesus is the Christ (8:29). It is the second divine affirmation from heaven of Jesus's sonship (cf. 1:11) and supports Mark's introductory statement that Jesus is the Christ, the Son of God (1:1). It also supports the demonic recognition of Jesus as the Son of God (1:34; 3:11; cf. 1:24; 5:7). This will be confirmed later by Jesus's own acknowledgment that he is the Christ, the Son of the Blessed (14:61–62), and by the confession of the centurion (15:39). The transfiguration was to be understood by Mark's readers as a further sign of Jesus's divinity (Gundry 1993: 458–59; Baltensweiler 1959: 134–36).

14. Evans (2001: 38) correctly sees the command "Hear him" as a rebuke, but he interprets it as a rebuke to "hear Jesus" rather than Moses or Elijah. This contradicts, however, the need to "hear" Moses found elsewhere in Mark (cf. 1:44; 7:9–13; 10:19; etc.). It is best seen as a rebuke of Peter's and the disciples' refusal to "hear" Jesus's teachings concerning his passion (8:32–33). To see this as a command for the disciples to "hear" Jesus because he is the prophet Moses referred to in Deut. 18:15, 18 (Cranfield 1959: 295–96; Lohmeyer 1957: 177; W. Lane 1974: 321) is less likely than that the three disciples should heed what Jesus, the Son of God, had just told them with respect to his coming passion (8:31), which they had rejected (8:32–33).

By locating the transfiguration immediately after 8:38 and 9:1, Mark reassures his readers that Jesus will one day come as the Son of Man to judge the world and that the kingdom, which has already been realized in part, will be consummated in power. The transfiguration is a divine confirmation of this in which "some" (9:1) were privileged to see a proleptic vision of the surpassing glory of Jesus in that day (2 Pet. 1:16–17). The resurrection, ascension, and glorious appearing of Jesus are all part of his ultimate vindication and are foreshadowed in the transfiguration. The great predictive power of Jesus is also revealed at the transfiguration by the fulfillment of the prophecy in 9:1. Thus the readers of Mark can be assured that the promise of his return to consummate the kingdom will also take place.

A third christological teaching found in our passage involves the absolute uniqueness of Jesus. Elijah and Moses appear and speak to Jesus, but they are not transfigured. Only Jesus is! The voice says nothing about these great OT saints, but it singles out and announces Jesus as God's only Son. When the miraculous event ends, Mark points out that Jesus alone remains. For Mark, the Christian faith involves "Jesus only." There is no room for anyone else to share his glory. Christian faith centers not on the saints of old or the heroes of the present. Christian ministries that focus on great Christian personalities, whether past or present, are clearly misguided. The good news of the Christian faith is about Jesus Christ, the Son of God. It centers on Jesus alone! Thus the Christian faith must always be a faith based on the grace of God found uniquely in Jesus Christ, his Son. The Christian faith must always remain above all things CHRISTianity.

A second Markan emphasis in our passage involves the central place of the cross. The voice from heaven affirms Jesus's teaching concerning his passion. The command "Hear him" refers not to the teachings on discipleship found in 8:34–9:1, although these are extremely important in Mark. It focuses rather on the divine necessity of Jesus's death. Peter's rejection of this teaching in 8:32–33 receives a divine rebuke. He needs to heed Jesus's teachings concerning his suffering, death, and resurrection. The death of Jesus is by no means a tragedy or mistake, or a withdrawal of God's favor. On the contrary, the voice reveals that this is indeed a divine necessity, a divine "must" (δεῖ, *dei*; 8:31) that includes the resurrection and parousia. The divine voice continues to warn us today that the sacrificial death of the Son of God is at the heart of the Christian faith. Those who are offended by such a theology (cf. Rom. 1:16–17; 1 Cor. 1:18) need to heed this command.

Additional Notes

9:3. It is best to interpret the prepositional phrase "earthly/upon earth" (ἐπὶ τῆς γῆς) as adjectivally modifying "bleacher" (γναφεύς; Evans 2001: 35) rather than adverbially with the verb "is able" (contra Gundry 1993: 458), because ἐπί adverbial phrases follow the verb by a ratio of roughly five to one, and here ἐπὶ τῆς γῆς precedes the verb.

9:5. "Responds" translates "having answered, he says." Here "having answered" (ἀποκριθείς) refers not to Peter answering a question addressed to him but rather to Peter responding to a situation. Cf. 10:24, 51; 11:14; 12:35; 14:48 for a similar use of this participle.

9:5. It is best to leave the "and" (καί) untranslated.

9:7. This translates a periphrasis involving ἐγένετο. See additional note on 1:4, which contains a similar periphrasis involving ἐγένετο with the same word order (contra Gundry 1993: 480).

9:8. οὐδένα is lit. "no one."

V. On the Way to Jerusalem: Part 4 (8:22–10:52)
    D. Jesus Is Transfigured (9:2–8)
➤ E. The Son of Man and the Return of Elijah (9:9–13)
    F. Jesus Performs a Difficult Exorcism (9:14–29)

E. The Son of Man and the Return of Elijah (9:9–13)

Few passages in Mark raise more contextual and interpretive questions than this one. Some of these questions include the following: (1) What was the relationship of 9:9–10 and 9:11–13 in the pre-Markan tradition? Were they originally independent of each other? What is Mark's role in the present organization of these materials and their wording? (2) How were 9:9–10 and 9:11–13 related to the transfiguration (9:2–8) in the pre-Markan tradition? Was 9:9–10 connected to 9:2–8, whereas 9:11–13 was an independent unit? (3) In the present context of Mark, how are these passages related to each other and the preceding materials? (4) Where is it written that the Son of Man and Elijah would suffer and be treated with contempt? (5) In what way is Elijah's return (9:11–13) related to the resurrection of the Son of Man from the dead (9:9–10) and his suffering (9:12)?

Although 9:9–10 is heavily Markan in flavor,[1] something like 9:9–10 probably concluded the transfiguration account in the pre-Markan tradition (Best 1981: 62–63). At least Matthew (17:9) and Luke (9:36b) assume this. I argued in 8:30 that the command to the disciples not to publicize Jesus's messiahship makes good sense historically (see 8:30). Since the transfiguration confirms Jesus's messiahship (9:7), a similar command here also makes good sense historically, and the reflection of the disciples in 9:10 better fits a pre- rather than a postresurrection setting. To compose such a saying after the resurrection would require a skill in writing historical narrative that is relatively modern (cf. Lewis 1975: 108). The Markan editorial work in 9:11–13 is generally seen as centering on the two scriptural allusions in 9:11b and 13b–c (Best 1981: 63), but the use of the title "Son of Man" in 9:12 (as in 9:9) argues in favor of the authenticity of this material. The attempts to delineate 9:9, 12, and 13 as Markan and 9:10 and 11 as traditional (Pryke 1978: 17, 144, 164) or 9:11–13 as Markan (Schmithals 1979: 1.404) are too drastic.

In the present context 9:9–13 is related to what precedes by several linguistic and thematic ties: Son of Man (9:9, 12 and 8:31), rising from the dead (9:9–10 and 8:31), Elijah (9:11–13 and 8:28; 9:4–5), suffering and rejection

---

1. Note the introductory genitive absolute; "commanded" (διεστείλατο, *diesteilato*; cf. 5:43; 7:36 [2×]; 8:15); a command to secrecy (cf. 3:11–12); "rise" (ἀναστῇ, *anastē*; cf. 8:31); the term "the matter" (τὸν λόγον, *ton logon*), although it is not used in a technical sense as elsewhere in Mark (see 1:45); "to themselves" (πρὸς ἑαυτούς, *pros heautous*; cf. 1:27; 10:26; 11:31; 12:7; 14:4; 16:3); "questioning" (συζητοῦντες, *syzētountes*; cf. 1:27; 8:11; 9:14, 16; 12:28); a failure on the part of the disciples to understand (cf. 6:49–52; 8:14–21).

(9:12–13 and 8:31), death (9:13 and 8:31), a command to secrecy (9:9 and 8:30), Jesus's messiahship (9:9 and 8:29–30; 9:7), the coming of the kingdom of God in power (9:12 and 9:1 and the proleptic experience of this in the transfiguration), and the OT promise (Mal. 4:5–6; 3:22–23 LXX; 3:23–24 MT) of the coming of Elijah as a forerunner of the end times (Mark 9:11–13 and 9:5–6).

Exegesis and Exposition

⁹And, as they were coming down from the mountain, he [Jesus] commanded them ⌜that⌝ they should not tell ⌜anyone⌝ what things they had ⌜witnessed⌝ until the Son of Man should rise from the dead. ¹⁰And they kept the matter to themselves, questioning what this rising from the dead meant. ¹¹And they were asking him, saying, "⌜Why⌝ do the scribes say that it is necessary for Elijah to come first?" ¹²And he said to them, "Elijah indeed ⌜will come first and restore⌝ all things. Yet how [come] it is written concerning the Son of Man that he should suffer many things and be treated with contempt? ¹³But I say to you that Elijah has ⌜already⌝ come, and they did to him whatever they wanted, just as it is written concerning him."

Verse 9 is the only place in Mark where a temporal limitation is placed on the command to keep Jesus's messiahship a secret. It provided for Wrede the key for interpreting all the commands to secrecy in Mark (Wrede 1971: 67–69; cf., however, Räisänen 1990: 188–89, who argues that 9:9 is uniquely tailored and fits only the transfiguration). Wrede argued that the early church, and especially Mark, sought by this passage to explain why Jesus's earthly ministry was so unmessianic. Jesus, according to Wrede, never claimed to be the Messiah. Such claims and beliefs were later read back into the life of Jesus via the "messianic secret." Wrede's theory, however, does not arise from the text of Mark. Rather, it is superimposed on the Markan text to explain how Jesus's supposedly unmessianic and nonmiraculous earthly life was reinterpreted to harmonize with the early church's resurrection faith in Jesus Christ, the Son of God. Yet it is clear that the pre-Markan Jesus traditions in the early church were thoroughly supernatural and messianic in nature. Only a priori naturalistic presuppositions require scholars to assume that the life of Jesus was "originally" nonsupernatural and unmessianic. The text gives no support for such a view.

9:9–10

The command to keep secret (9:9) the divine confirmation of Jesus's messiahship/sonship at the transfiguration (9:7) parallels Jesus's command to Peter not to tell anyone that he is the Messiah (8:30; cf. also 5:43; 7:36). Jesus's particular understanding of the messianic role was so different from what was popularly held that a public declaration of his messiahship could only cause confusion and misunderstanding (see 8:30). Telling others what happened at the transfiguration before Jesus's resurrection would also cause confusion, for the way of vindication and glory for the Son of Man was via the suffering of the cross (8:31). It was already clear that the disciples thought that the messiahship of the Christ did not or could not involve a cross (8:32), and some of Mark's readers may have had a similar misunderstanding. However, Good Friday must precede the fulfillment of what the transfiguration points to. The Son of Man must first give his life as a ransom for many (10:45) before he comes in glory (8:38).

The tradition of the transfiguration first became known to the followers of Jesus (and the other disciples) after the resurrection. Only then would it make sense. It is unlikely that Mark was seeking to explain to his readers why they were unfamiliar with the story of the transfiguration. It is even more unlikely, in fact impossible, that he was attempting to explain to his readers why the Jesus traditions with which they were familiar were so nonsupernatural and unmessianic. Neither Mark nor Luke (nor Matthew nor John, for that matter) is a radical reworking of supposedly nonsupernatural and unmessianic traditions known to their readers. Like Luke, Mark was seeking to confirm to his readers the certainty of the messianic and miraculous Jesus traditions with which they were already familiar (Luke 1:4).

Verse 10 can be interpreted in several ways. It can mean, "They kept the matter [τὸν λόγον][2] to themselves, questioning what this rising from the dead meant" (cf. Evans 2001: 42); or, "They kept the matter, questioning among themselves what this rising from the dead meant" (cf. V. Taylor 1952: 394; Hooker 1991: 219; France 2002: 356–57). In favor of the former is that whenever the prepositional phrase "to themselves" (πρὸς ἑαυτούς) is found in Mark in the same order (verbal form + prepositional phrase + participle), the prepositional phrase goes with the preceding verbal form (cf. 1:27; 11:31). In 10:26, when Mark wants to have the prepositional phrase modify the participle, he uses this order: verbal form + participle + prepositional phrase. Assuming that the prepositional phrase modifies the verb "kept," this indicates that Peter, James, and John heeded Jesus's command in 9:9 and did not share their experience of the transfiguration even with the other disciples (Bayer 1986: 166; Räisänen 1990: 184–85; cf. also Cranfield 1959: 297, who states, "It would be time enough to tell the other disciples about this experience when they themselves had begun to understand it"). Yet the three disciples did discuss among themselves what Jesus meant by "this [lit. 'the'] rising from the dead." This refers not to the general rising of the dead (contra Öhler 1999: 464n12) but specifically to "the" rising of the Son of Man from the dead. (The article "the" [τό, to] refers back to the rising of the Son of Man in 9:9; see Luke 2:19 and 51 for Mary's similar pondering over the meaning of sayings concerning/by Jesus.)

If Mark 9:11–13 was historically associated with 9:9–10, then the subsequent question in 9:11 indicates that the disciples wondered how the resurrection of the Son of Man related to the OT tradition of the return of Elijah (Evans 2001: 42). By their present location in the Gospel, the evangelist seeks to tell his

2. Τὸν λόγον is not used here in the technical sense of "the word" as in 1:45; 2:2; 4:14–20, 33; 8:32.

readers how these two events are related. If 9:9–10 and 9:11–13 were originally separate traditions, however, in the historical setting of Jesus the question of the disciples in 9:11 would probably have involved their seeking to understand the scribal objection (see 9:11) of how the return of Elijah fit Jesus's teaching concerning the claim that the kingdom of God had arrived (1:14–15).

The relationship of this question with the preceding two verses is unclear. **9:11–13** The question appears to introduce an abrupt change of subject (Hooker 1991: 219). It has been suggested that originally 9:11–13 followed the saying found in 9:1 (Bultmann 1968: 124). If Mark is responsible for its present location, he may have placed it here because of the references to Elijah found in 8:28 and 9:4–5. The tie between 9:11 and 9:9–10, however, is quite logical. If Jesus's death, resurrection, and return (8:31, 38; 9:9) are intimately associated with the coming of the kingdom of God in power (9:1, 2–8), and if the OT promise (Mal. 4:5–6) says that Elijah would return before that time (i.e., the day of the Lord) to restore all things (Mark 9:12; cf. Sir. 48:10; *m. B. Meṣiʿa* 1.8; 2.8; 3.4–5; *m. ʿEd.* 8.7), then why has Elijah not returned?[3] Since the disciples are quoting a question raised by the "scribes," who are portrayed in Mark as opposing Jesus (cf. 1:22; 2:6, 16; 3:22; 7:5; 8:31; 10:33; 11:18, 27; 12:38; 14:1, 43, 53; 15:1, 31 [12:32 and 35 are the lone exceptions]), the question probably involved an objection to Jesus's claim that the kingdom of God had come (cf. 1:14–15). How can Jesus claim that the kingdom of God (i.e., the restoration of all things) was here, since Elijah has not yet returned? Scripture (Mal. 4:5) states that he must come "first," before these things take place. As it now stands in Mark, however, the evangelist is seeking to teach his readers, by means of this question, the relationship between this known teaching about the return of Elijah, the coming of the kingdom of God, the proleptic appearance of its coming in power at the transfiguration, and Jesus's resurrection from the dead.

Jesus's reply to the disciples' question in 9:12 consists of two parts. The first is a statement that the view that Elijah will return at the end time is correct. For several reasons, it is best to interpret 9:12a as a statement in which Jesus answers the question addressed to him in 9:11 (Cranfield 1959: 298; J. Edwards 2002: 274) rather than as a counterquestion (Hooker 1991: 220; Marcus 1992b: 99). For one, 9:12 contains a clear reference to the OT (it is written, γέγραπται, *gegraptai*), and the great majority of such references in Mark occur in statements. Second, the emphatic "indeed" (μέν, *men*) fits a statement better than a question. Third, Matthew (17:11) understands it as a statement. In Mark 9:12a Jesus affirms that the scribes (9:11) are correct about Elijah returning.

---

3. Although there is no clear connection in the Jewish literature before Mark between the coming of Elijah and the coming of the Messiah (Faierstein 1981; Fitzmyer 1985c), they are each associated with the restoration of all things, the day of the Lord, the coming of the kingdom of God, the last things, and so on. As a result, the connection of the two of them together in our passage is not as strange as it might appear. For the expectation of Elijah's return, see Öhler 1999: 461–64.

But, as 9:13 reveals, they are wrong in thinking that this is a future event. The dialogue of 9:11–13 may be paraphrased as follows:

> Disciples: "Why do the scribes say that Elijah must come first (before the kingdom of God arrives and the resurrection of the Son of Man takes place)?" (9:9–10)
>
> Jesus: "They are right. Elijah will come first. . . . But he has already come [in the form of John the Baptist] and . . ."

The second part of Jesus's reply in 9:12b is in the form of a rhetorical question reminding the disciples of the necessity of his death. The reference to the Son of Man in the question picks up the earlier reference in 9:9. It thus refers to Jesus's sufferings. The attempt to interpret the "Son of Man" as a reference to John the Baptist (Casey 1998: 121–37; Evans 2001: 43–44) is based upon a hypothetical reconstruction of an earlier Aramaic form of the saying. In the Greek text of Mark, however, the "Son of Man" clearly refers to Jesus, so that the question in 9:12b follows the statement of 9:12a somewhat awkwardly by switching from Elijah to the Son of Man. What is clear is that 9:12b indicates that Elijah's return to restore all things is intimately associated with the suffering and resurrection of the Son of Man. Both are eschatological events of the end time. Thus the scribes are correct. If Jesus's death and resurrection and the coming of the kingdom of God are end-time events, then Elijah's return must in some way be associated with them. The scribal objection, however, errs in not recognizing that Elijah has already returned (9:13). In its present form the question of Elijah's having to return first does not cast doubts on why the Son of Man must suffer. On the contrary, the opposite is true. Since the Son of Man must suffer in accordance with the Scriptures (and for Mark's readers this had already occurred), then Elijah must have returned.

As in 14:21 and 49, no specific OT reference is given in support of the statements—just "it is written" (9:12, 13). Paul similarly states that "Christ died for our sins according to the Scriptures" and "rose on the third day according to the Scriptures" (1 Cor. 15:3 and 4) without specifically mentioning the Scripture passages to which he is referring. Because of Mark's and his readers' belief that Jesus is the Christ, the Son of God, the Son of Man, David's Son, the Servant of the Lord, and so on, any reference to the suffering of one of these figures (Pss. 22; 89:39; 118:22; Isa. 53; etc.) is applicable to the others (Gundry 1993: 486).

Having referred to Elijah's coming in 9:12, Jesus corrects the view that this coming is a future event with a strong "but" (ἀλλά, *alla*) in 9:13. Elijah has already come! He has already successfully accomplished his task of preparing the way of the Lord (1:3). Did not all Jerusalem and Judea go out to be baptized by him in preparation for the coming of the kingdom of God (1:4–5)? As a result, Elijah has already "restored" the people through his calling Israel to repentance (Mal. 4:5; Sir. 48:10; W. Lane 1974: 326; Hooker 1991: 220; contra

Nineham 1963: 240–41 and Gundry 1993: 464–65, 484–85, who interprets 9:12a as referring to a still-future coming of Elijah).

Although Elijah was not martyred but ascended into heaven without tasting death, the suffering mentioned in this verse probably refers to his treatment by Jezebel in 1 Kings 19:1–3 (cf. Rom. 11:2–3; cf. also 1 En. 89.52). What Jezebel tried unsuccessfully to do, however, was accomplished by Herodias (6:19, 22, 25–26).[4] Elijah has already returned in the person of John the Baptist. Although John the Baptist is not specifically named in this verse as filling the role of the returning Elijah, the reference to Elijah's suffering and abuse must refer to the martyrdom of John the Baptist. Matthew (17:13) clearly interprets Mark 9:13 in this manner, "Then the disciples understood that he was speaking to them about John the Baptist." The mention of Elijah's/John the Baptist's suffering in this verse confirms that Jesus must also suffer, because this is what the Scriptures teach concerning both (9:12, 13). (Note how in describing the attire of John the Baptist in 1:6, Mark has prepared his readers for Jesus's identifying John the Baptist with Elijah.)

It is evident that Jesus and the NT writers often interpreted OT prophecy in a nonliteralistic way. They understood the prophets as using metaphorical and impressionistic language to proclaim their prophetic message. They used the tools of a poet rather than those of a photographer to convey their divine message (Stein 1994a: 91–95).[5] They understood the "literal meaning" of the prophets as involving what the prophets meant to convey by their words, not what a literalistic interpretation of the words (used figuratively by the biblical author) means. Thus Mal. 4:5 refers to one who would fulfill the role of the prophet Elijah, that is, John the Baptist (see 1:4–6). The dress of John the Baptist indicates that he also saw himself as the fulfillment of the prophecy in Mal. 4:5–6.

Summary

Two Markan emphases are found in our present passage. One involves a salvation-historical explanation of the relationship of Jesus's mission and the OT promise of Elijah's return. This centers on the scribal comment that Elijah must first return before the end-time events take place (9:11). Mark gives Jesus's explanation of how this event promised in the OT (Mal. 4:5) fits with the events surrounding Jesus's ministry. How can the kingdom of God be present (Mark 1:14–15), and how can the Son of Man rise from the dead (both end-time events), if Elijah has not yet returned? Mark points out that Jesus agreed concerning Elijah returning first but notes that he had already returned in the mission and ministry of John the Baptist. The OT promise

4. Although some scholars argue that Rev. 11:2–8 alludes to a tradition that the returning Elijah would experience suffering, no Jewish literature before Mark refers to Elijah suffering when he returns.

5. For some examples of how NT writers interpret OT prophecies in a nonliteralistic fashion, see Luke 1:51–55, 68–79; 3:4–6; 4:18–19; Acts 2:16–21.

had thus been fulfilled. Consequently the promise of Elijah's return does not refute the claims of Jesus but on the contrary supports them.

A second Markan emphasis involves the necessity of Jesus's passion and death. What Jesus had begun to explain to the disciples in 8:31 is reaffirmed again in our passage. It is mentioned in 9:9–10 when Jesus gives the command to Peter, James, and John not to tell even the other disciples about the transfiguration until after his resurrection. Since Jesus's resurrection assumes his death and since this alludes back to 8:31, where Jesus's death and resurrection are explicitly mentioned, "resurrection" in 9:9–10 is an abbreviation for "death and resurrection." In 9:12–13 Jesus's suffering and being treated contemptuously are mentioned again alongside Elijah's/John the Baptist's similar treatment. The death of Jesus, the Christ (8:29), the Son of God (9:7), is foretold in Scripture (9:12), and what happened to Elijah/John the Baptist indicates that this must "also" happen to the Son of Man. For Mark, however, the emphasis is not on the death of Jesus but on his resurrection, as indicated by the addition "from the dead" (ἐκ νεκρῶν, *ek nekrōn*) in 9:9 and 10 and its being placed before the verb (Gundry 1993: 462).

Additional Notes

9:9. Here and in v. 12, "that" (ἵνα) introduces not a purpose clause but the content of the command. See 3:9–10.

9:9. μηδενί is lit. "no one."

9:9. "Seen" (εἶδον) is an abbreviation for "seen and heard" (cf. 9:7–8). I therefore translate it "witnessed."

9:11. ὅτι here introduces a question and is best translated "Why?" (V. Taylor 1952: 394; Cranfield 1959: 297; France 2002: 357). Cf. 2:16; 9:28.

9:12. ἐλθὼν πρῶτον ἀποκαθιστάνει is lit. "having come first, restores." The present tense ἀποκαθιστάνει (א² A B L W f¹) is to be preferred and translated as a futuristic present.

9:13. καί is used here adverbially in the sense of "also" or "already" (Donahue and Harrington 2002: 272; REB).

F. Jesus Performs a Difficult Exorcism (9:14–29)

The present account is the fourth and last exorcism found in Mark (cf. 1:21–28; 5:1–20; 7:24–30). Some scholars think that the present story is made up of two distinct miracle stories. One involved an account in which the disciples were unable to perform an exorcism (9:14–19, 28–29). The other was an exorcism involving a beseeching father that centered on the necessity of faith (9:20–27). Some of the reasons given in support of this are the presence of (1) two separate descriptions of the child's illness (9:18 and 21–22); (2) two separate references to a crowd gathering and coming (9:14–15 and 25); (3) two references to the child foaming at the mouth (9:18 and 20); (4) the presence of the disciples in 9:14–19 and 28–29 but not in 9:20–27; (5) the description of the spirit as a "mute spirit" in 9:17 but as "unclean" and "mute and deaf" in 9:25; (6) the symptoms of the boy's illness (9:18, 20, 22) having nothing to do with his being mute (9:17, 25) or deaf (9:25) because of the demon; and so on (Kertelge 1970: 174–75). These separate accounts were supposedly brought together because of the similarity of the illness and healing (an exorcism) either before Mark wrote his Gospel (Bultmann 1968: 211–12; Achtemeier 1975: 476; Best 1981: 68; Latourelle 1988: 150; Hooker 1991: 222) or by Mark himself (Koch 1975: 114–26). Others, however, see the vivid imagery and wealth of detail in the account as a mark of its historicity (V. Taylor 1952: 395).

The extent of the Markan redaction in the account is debated. Some see it primarily in its placement (all the other exorcisms in Mark occur before 8:27ff.). Others see the concluding verses (9:28–29) as Markan (Best 1981: 66–67; Schmithals 1979: 1.409), because they lack the normal reference to amazement or praise typically found at the end of an exorcism (cf. Luke 9:43) and contain typically Markan terminology (privately, κατ᾽ ἰδίαν, *kat' idian* [see the introduction to 9:2–8]; entering into, εἰσελθόντος αὐτοῦ εἰς, *eiselthontos autou eis* [cf. 1:21b, 45; 2:1, 26; 3:1, 27; 5:12; etc.]; the repetition of a compound verb with the same preposition [εἰσελθόντος . . . εἰς; cf. 1:16, 21a, 42; 5:17; 6:56; 7:15, 18, 19; 11:2; etc.]; the instruction of the disciples in a house [see 9:28–29; etc.]). Yet the reference to prayer (9:29) is not a strong Markan emphasis. Most probably the Markan contribution to 9:28–29 involves the rewording of the tradition and the emphasis on teaching the disciples privately. Other Markan activity can be seen in the evangelist's rewording of the opening seam (9:14–15; Gnilka 1979: 45; Best 1981: 67). The greatest consensus on the Markan editorial work involves the present location of the account in Mark and 9:14–16, 26–27, and 28a (cf. Achtemeier 1975: 475–76; Pryke 1978: 17, 144, 164; Sterling 1993: 481–84).

A number of elements in the account appear to be traditional: the description of the illness (9:18a–b, 20, 22, 26); the use of "able/strong enough" (ἴσχυσαν, *ischysan*) in 9:18 (the three other occurrences of which in Mark are all in nonredactional settings: 2:17; 5:4; 14:37) instead of "able" (δύναμαι, *dynamai*; 33 times in Mark); "generation" (γενεά, *genea*) in 9:19 (found elsewhere in Mark only in nonredactional settings: 8:12 [2×], 38; 13:30); various unfamiliar themes such as the rebuke of the crowd and the inability of the disciples to heal look pre-Markan (Best 1981: 67); the connection of faith with exorcism (9:22b–24), which is not found in any other Markan exorcism, although it is found in association with physical healings (2:5; 5:34; 10:52); an emphasis on prayer that, unlike Luke (Stein 1992a: 51–52), is unusual; and the description of the boy "foaming at the mouth" (ἀφρίζει, *aphrizei*), a term found only in 9:18 and 20 in the NT.

In contrast to Luke 9:37 there are no necessary ties between this event and the transfiguration such as a reference to a mountain or to Jesus's glorious transformation. Attempts to see such a tie in the amazement caused by Jesus's approach (9:15; Gundry 1993: 487–88) are forced. See 9:15. The present account may have been placed here because (1) it illustrates the themes of passion prediction, disciple error, and teachings on discipleship found in 8:31–10:52; and (2) it requires a separation of Jesus from the disciples (9:14–18), and the transfiguration provides this (Best 1981: 68). The story probably came to Mark as a unity lacking the normal, rounded form of other exorcisms. This, plus Mark's own editorial work, resulted in its present form and location.

The account as it now stands is tied to its context by Jesus's separation from his disciples (9:2 and 14), an error on the part of the disciples (8:32–33; 9:5–7 and 17–19), christological considerations (8:29; 9:7; and Jesus's exorcism of a difficult demon), the distinguishing of Jesus from others (transfiguration: Jesus from Moses and Elijah; exorcism: Jesus's ability from the disciples' inability), a reference to the scribes (9:11 and 14), and the use of "speaking/arguing" (συζητοῦντες, *syzētountes*; 9:10 and 14, 16). Attempts to see a tie with 8:31 and 9:9 by interpreting 9:27 as foreshadowing the resurrection (cf. Evans 2001: 48) are unconvincing (see 9:26–27).

The present account is an unusual combination of an exorcism and a pronouncement story. In addition, there are several elements not usually present in an exorcism account: the inability of the disciples to exorcise the demon, a necessity for faith (this often appears in healing stories [5:34, 36; 6:5–6] but not in exorcisms), a teaching on the importance of prayer for exorcising demons, and so on. As a result the form of the present account is irregular (Meier 1994: 654–55). I divide it as follows: (1) Jesus's arrival on the scene (9:14–15), (2) a description of the disciples' inability to heal a father's demonized son (9:16–19), (3) the demoniac being brought to Jesus and the demon convulsing the boy (9:20–22a), (4) the father beseeching Jesus to heal his demonized son (9:22b–24), (5) Jesus's exorcism of the demon (9:25–27), and (6) Jesus's concluding pronouncement (9:28–29).

Exegesis and Exposition

[14]And ⌜having⌝ come to the disciples, they saw a great crowd around them and scribes arguing with them. [15]And immediately all the crowd ⌜having seen⌝ him [Jesus] were utterly amazed and running up were greeting him. [16]And he asked them, "⌜What⌝ are you arguing with them?" [17]And one man out of the crowd answered him, "Teacher, I brought my son to you because he ⌜has⌝ a mute spirit. [18]And wherever it seizes him, it throws him down [on the ground], and he foams at the mouth and grinds his teeth and becomes rigid. And I ⌜asked⌝ your disciples ⌜to cast it out,⌝ but they could not." [19]And he, answering, says to them, "O faithless generation, how much longer will I be with you? How much longer shall I put up with you? Bring him to me." [20]And they brought him to him, and when the spirit ⌜saw⌝ him [Jesus], he immediately threw him [the boy] into convulsions, and having fallen on the ground, he was rolling around foaming at the mouth. [21]And he [Jesus] asked his father, "How long has this been happening to him?" And he replied, "From childhood. [22]And frequently it has also cast him into fire and into ⌜water⌝ in order that it might destroy him, but if you are able, have pity on us and help us." [23]And Jesus said to him, "⌜If⌝ you are ⌜able?⌝ All things are possible⌝ for the one who believes." [24]Immediately the father of the child cried out and was saying ⌜ ⌝, "I believe. Help my unbelief." [25]And because Jesus saw that a crowd was running together [toward him], he rebuked the unclean spirit, saying to it, "Mute and deaf spirit, I command you, come out of him and never enter into him again." [26]And having cried out and having caused much convulsing, he went out, and he [the boy] became as [if he were] dead, so that many were saying, "He is dead." [27]But Jesus grasped his hand and raised him up, and he arose. [28]And when he [Jesus] entered into the house, his disciples privately were asking him, "⌜Why⌝ were we not able to cast it [the demon] out?" [29]And he said to them, "This kind [of demon] is not able ⌜to be cast out⌝ by anything except prayer ⌜ ⌝."

The present story is connected to the transfiguration by Jesus, Peter, James, and John rejoining the other disciples. No necessary tie, however, exists in the story itself between the present exorcism and the transfiguration. Although in 9:10 the participle συζητοῦντες (*syzētountes*) refers to the three disciples "discussing" together what Jesus meant by his rising from the dead, here the same participle must be interpreted negatively as "arguing," because the general character of the scribes in Mark is negative (see 9:11–13). The scribes are disputing with the disciples. "Around them" (περὶ αὐτούς, *peri autous*) and "with them" (πρὸς αὐτούς, *pros autous*) are best interpreted as referring to the same group, and the first prepositional phrase must refer to the disciples, since they are distinguished from the "great crowd" (ὄχλον πολύν, *ochlon polyn*) and "the scribes" (γραμματεῖς, *grammateis*). The presence of the crowd after the transfiguration may be an allusion to Exod. 34:30, where Moses encounters the

9:14–15

people of Israel after he has met the Lord on Mount Sinai (Hooker 1991: 223). Others see the presence of the crowd as another example of the magnetism of the Son of God (Gundry 1993: 502). No reason is given for the presence of the scribes, who play no role in 9:15–29. The suggestion that they were there to gather information against Jesus (Witherington 2001: 265) is not stated in the present account but is based on such passages as 3:1–6 and their general hostility toward Jesus.

Although the three disciples accompany Jesus, the crowd sees only Jesus (cf. 9:8), that is, "him" (αὐτόν, *auton*), and run to "him" (cf. 10:17). Their reaction to seeing Jesus is that they "were utterly amazed" (ἐξεθαμβήθησαν, *exethambēthēsan*). This response is unusual because such a response normally comes after a great miracle, a surprising teaching, or a theophany (1:27; 5:15; 10:24; 16:5–6; cf., however, 10:32; see 1:21–22). Some explain this as due to the crowd's observance of the lingering effects of Jesus's transfiguration, and in particular his glistening garments (Gundry 1993: 487; Hooker 1991: 222–23; Witherington 2001: 266; Evans 2001: 50; contra Cranfield 1959: 300; van der Loos 1965: 398; Best 1981: 68). Mark, however, does not give a reason for this amazement. If the story were originally an independent exorcism unconnected to the transfiguration, such an interpretation would be due to Mark's editorial work in placing this account right after the transfiguration and his description of this reaction. The disappearance of the cloud and the heavenly witnesses, however, seem to designate the end of the transfiguration experience (9:8; cf. Matt. 17:8; Luke 9:36), and the command to silence in 9:9 would be pointless if Jesus still radiated the glory of the transfiguration (J. Edwards 2002: 276). Thus it may be that Mark is simply seeking to emphasize the amazement that Jesus creates by his appearance on the scene.

9:16–19   There are two "them(s)" in 9:16, and the antecedent in each case is unclear. It appears best to interpret the two references, "And Jesus asked them [the crowd of 9:15 running and greeting him (Cranfield 1959: 300–301; contra Evans 2001: 50)], 'Why are you [the crowd] arguing with them [the disciples; note the πρὸς αὐτούς in 9:14]?'" It is not one of the disciples but someone in the crowd who responds. He is the father of a demon-possessed boy who brought his son to Jesus to be healed. In Jesus's absence the disciples sought to perform the exorcism. Their attempt to do so was due to the fact that they were Jesus's disciples, had been commissioned by him, and had already successfully performed such exorcisms (6:7, 13, 30). In the present context, Jesus's absence is due to his being on the Mount of Transfiguration with Peter, James, and John.

For the address "Teacher" (διδάσκαλε, *didaskale*), see 4:37–38. Note that Matt. 17:15 changes the address to "Lord" (κύριε, *kyrie*). In the first diagnosis of the child's malady in 9:17c, the father describes him as having a "mute spirit," that is, a demon that caused him to be mute. It is unclear whether the muteness was continual or occurred only during the demonic attacks (Gundry 1993: 488). Jesus in his exorcism gives a more comprehensive description of the child's malady (9:25): the demon causes muteness and deafness. In 9:18 the father describes the results of the malady. "Wherever" (ὅπου ἐάν, *hopou ean*) the demon attacked the boy, he threw him down on the ground, caused the child to foam at the mouth, grind his teeth, and become rigid. These acts are often symptoms of epilepsy, and Matthew (17:15) may describe the boy as having epilepsy (σεληνιάζεται, *selēniazetai*).[1] Yet Mark clearly emphasizes to his readers that the cause of the boy's malady is due to demon possession (9:17–18, 25–26, 28; Evans 2001: 52).

The father then explains that the disciples were unable to cast out the demon. Although this statement, along with Jesus's reply in the next verse and in 9:28–29, is another example of the failure of the disciples, the main emphasis in these verses focuses not on their inability but on the great ability of Jesus. In the present account, the disciples' inability serves primarily to emphasize the surpassing power and greatness of Jesus Christ, the Son of God. Whether Mark intended his readers to think back to John the Baptist's description of Jesus as "stronger than he" (1:7; cf. 3:27; Gundry 1993: 489) is uncertain. The intended audience of Jesus's exasperated address, "O faithless generation" (cf. Deut. 32:5, 20), is unclear. This can be interpreted as being addressed to (1) the unregenerate, that is, the crowd and/or the father (along with the scribes), but not the disciples (Gundry 1993: 489; J. Edwards 2002: 278);[2] (2) the disciples (Cranfield 1959: 301); or (3) the entire group (Hooker 1991: 223; Witherington 2001: 267). In favor of the latter is the broad, sweeping indictment of the unbelieving generation. The difficulty in determining the exact addressee is compounded by the fact that, whereas in 9:22–24 it is the lack of faith on the part of the father that is singled out, in 9:28–29 it is the lack of prayer by the disciples and the particular kind of demon (τοῦτο τὸ γένος, *touto to genos*, this kind) that is the reason for the failed exorcism. It is probably best to see the indictment as involving the entire group and not excluding the disciples, because immediately after the statement of their inability in 9:18 comes 9:19: "How much longer will I be with you? [ἕως πότε πρὸς ὑμᾶς ἔσομαι; *heōs pote pros hymas esomai?*] How much longer shall I put up with you? [ἕως πότε ἀνέξομαι ὑμῶν; *heōs pote anexomai hymōn?*]." These questions not only reveal Jesus's exasperation but also indicate that "his hour" is near at hand. What was alluded to in 2:19–20 and explicitly referred to in 8:31; 9:9, 12 is close at hand. "How long?" in Mark's story means "Soon!"

The reaction of the evil spirit on seeing Jesus is violent but, unlike 1:24; 5:7, and 9–10 (cf. 1:34; 3:11–12), nonverbal. (The exorcism described in 7:24–30 is atypical because it is performed at a distance and no direct encounter between

9:20–22a

---

1. For a survey of the view that the boy was suffering from epilepsy, see van der Loos 1965: 401–5. See, however, France (2002: 362–63) for the opposing view.

2. Gundry restricts the rebuke to the crowd and the father because it is their lack of faith that has hindered the disciples in their attempted exorcism. The account, however, places emphasis on the disciples' inability to heal due to their lack of prayer (9:28–29) and the particular nature of this demon.

Jesus and the demon takes place.) The nonverbal nature of the present encounter may be due to the demon causing muteness (Hooker 1991: 224). The power of the demon is seen in his bringing about the behavior in 9:20 that has already been described in 9:18. Jesus's question in 9:21 leads to the father's description of the seriousness of the boy's condition: the boy has been possessed by this demon "from childhood" (ἐκ παιδιόθεν, *ek paidiothen*; 9:21) and the demon has frequently sought to destroy him by burning him to death or drowning him (9:22). The length (9:21–22; cf. 5:25–26) and severity of the demonic possession (cf. 5:3–5) serve to describe the unusual strength of "this kind" (9:29) of demon and thus reveal the surpassing greatness of Jesus, who easily casts it out.

9:22b–24 The father pleads for his son, "But if you are able, have pity on us and help us." The earlier confidence in Jesus's ability to heal his son (9:18) appears to have been shaken by the disciples' inability to exorcise the demon (contrast 1:40). A person's understanding of Jesus is often shaped by what they see Jesus's followers do or not do, and the father's early faith wavered due to the inability of the disciples to heal his son. Jesus's response, "If you are able?" (Τὸ εἰ δύνῃ; *To ei dynē?*) reveals a degree of exasperation. How can one talk about possibility with God? In his reply, Jesus uses hyperbole for emphasis: "All things [emphatic position] are possible for the one who believes" (πάντα δυνατὰ τῷ πιστεύοντι, *panta dynata tō pisteuonti*; cf. 11:22–24).[3] The opposite has already been shown in 6:5. Lack of faith hinders the work of God. Thus the shift from Jesus's ability to heal to the question of the father's ability to believe is not as abrupt as it first appears. The father's "I believe" exhibits a "mustard-seed-like" faith (Matt. 17:20), and he pleads for Jesus to help his "unbelief" (ἀπιστία, *apistia*). He does so in order to acquire a faith that will facilitate the healing of his son. Just as the inability of the disciples to heal his son may have resulted in the weakening of faith, so Jesus's healing would result in greater faith.

9:25–27 Because of the crowd running toward him, Jesus brings the exorcism to a speedy conclusion. The reference to the crowd seems redundant in light of 9:14–17. The impression is that Jesus sought to perform the healing as privately as possible (cf. 1:34, 44; 3:11–12; 5:43; 7:36; 8:26; also 8:30; 9:9). The relationship between the participial phrase "When Jesus saw [ἰδών, *idon*]" and the main verb "he rebuked" (ἐπετίμησεν, *epetimēsen*) is not just temporal but causal. Thus we can translate their relationship, "Because Jesus saw the crowd running, . . . he (immediately) rebuked the unclean spirit. . . ." Jesus's

---

3. Gundry (1993: 499) points out that the issue is not that all things are possible to do *by* the one who has faith (either the disciples or Jesus), for these words are addressed to the father of the child, not to the disciples. It is the father, not the disciples, who manifests faith in 9:24. Similarly, Jesus's faith is not the issue because it is not referred to. Jesus's words should be translated, "All things [are] able [to be done] *for* the one who believes." For similar exhortations to faith in God's all-powerful ability, cf. 5:36; 10:27; 14:36. For various views on how to interpret this verse, see Meier 1994: 669–70n37.

command is emphatic, "I [ἐγώ, egō] command you [ἐπιτάσσω σοι, epitassō soi]." This, along with the inability of the disciples to perform the exorcism, heightens Jesus's personal authority over the demon.

In Jesus's addressing the spirit, we learn that the spirit caused the boy to be not only mute but also deaf. It is doubtful that Mark intended his readers to attribute unique authority over the demon to Jesus because he knew what the demon was able to do (contra Gundry 1993: 491). The father also knew what the demon did, but he had no authority over it. Jesus's authority is manifested not in his address of the demon but in his all-powerful, twofold command to the demon to leave the boy and never to return. The command to the demon never to enter the boy again implies that an exorcism could be temporary (cf. Matt. 12:43–45/Luke 11:24–26; cf. also Josephus, *Ant.* 8.2.5 §§45, 47). The description of the healing in 9:26–27 reveals both the strength of the demon and the success of the exorcism. The last, departing attack of the demon is so violent that it leaves the boy as if he were dead (cf. 9:18). For a similar convulsing and corresponding calm after an exorcism, compare 1:25–26 (cf. also 5:15; 7:30). The language used to show his healing, "arose" (ἀνέστη, anestē), is used in 8:31; 9:9–10, 31; 10:34 to describe Jesus's resurrection from the dead (cf. also 12:23, 25), but here the boy is only described "as if [ὡσεί, hōsei] he were dead." Furthermore, in the majority of instances the verb "arise" in Mark refers to rising and standing up (cf. 1:35; 2:14; 5:42; etc.), as here. In recounting the healing of the boy, Mark uses much of the terminology found in the account of the raising of Jairus's daughter from the dead (grasping, κρατήσας, kratēsas [5:41; see 1:29–31]; lifting up, ἔγειρε, egeire [5:41]; and arose, ἀνέστη [5:42]).

Mark concludes the account with a private pronouncement to the disciples in a **9:28–29** house (cf. 7:17–23; 9:33–37; 10:10–12; 14:3–8; also 1:29–31; 2:1–12; 4:10ff., 34; 5:37–43; 6:31–32; 7:33–37; 13:3ff.). The Markan description of Jesus frequently being in a home with the disciples is often both traditional and historical, so that in his conclusion of the account, Mark did not necessarily create this scene out of nothing (Gundry 1993: 500–501). The conclusion, which is heavily Markan in terminology, emphasizes Jesus's surpassing ability to heal. He is greater than the disciples, just as at the transfiguration he is greater than Moses and Elijah. Whereas others can cast out demons, "this kind" of demon that the Son of God can cast out easily (he is stronger: 1:7; 3:27), others (the disciples) can cast out only with great difficulty, if at all, and with much prayer.

The reference to the importance of prayer in these verses is both surprising and strange. Nowhere in the present account, except in these concluding verses, is prayer referred to and the importance of prayer in this kind of exorcism mentioned. Earlier in the account, the importance of faith is emphasized (9:23–24), but prayer is not. In fact, prayer is not referred to in any of the earlier exorcisms recorded in Mark. The only close tie between prayer and faith in Mark occurs later, in 11:22–26. The attempt to relate prayer to the present exorcism by stating that whereas other kinds of exorcism did not require prayer, this particular kind did (Gundry 1993: 501–2), is not convincing, nor are other explanations that speculate concerning the situation of the Markan community that the evangelist was seeking to address by this comment.

Summary

As in all the exorcism accounts in Mark, we find a strong christological emphasis in the present passage (Evans 2001: 54). Jesus's surpassing greatness is found in that he performs a most difficult exorcism. The failure of the disciples to expel the demon serves to heighten the fact that Jesus, who easily expels it, is stronger and greater than they and the demon. By its location in Mark, the present exorcism serves to prove Jesus's sonship that was declared at the transfiguration (Nineham 1963: 242); just as Jesus's greatness places him on a different level than Moses and Elijah, so here he is also on a different level than the disciples. Other aspects in the account that emphasize Jesus's greatness and glory are the amazement he causes by his appearance (9:15) and the great crowd that gathers together (9:15, 25) because of his reputation and power to heal. That the crowd sees only "him" (9:15) and not Peter, James, and John serves to focus the reader's attention on Jesus as the central figure in the narrative. In light of the suggestions in the next paragraph that the main Markan emphasis is to be found elsewhere, we need to remind ourselves that the Gospel of Mark is about "Jesus Christ, the Son of God" (1:1).

A second Markan emphasis found in the account involves the importance of faith (9:19). The father's cry, "I believe. Help my unbelief," no doubt would resonate with many of Mark's readers as it has with believers through the centuries. In a similar manner the need for prayer (9:28–29) is also emphasized. No clear relationship between faith and prayer is made in the account, but in 11:22–24 they are associated. It would be incorrect, however, to see the main Markan emphasis in the account as being the need for faith (contra C. Marshall 1989: 116–18; and Myers 1988: 253–56, who gives to the account the subtitle "The Struggle for Faith")[4] or on the failure of the disciples to perform the exorcism (9:18, 28–29; Nineham 1963: 242; Achtemeier 1975: 478). The present account fits well the cycle of Jesus's passion teaching, disciple error, and teachings on discipleship found in Mark 8:27–10:52 (Kertelge 1970: 178–79; Achtemeier 1975: 476, 478; Hooker 1991: 222; Myers 1988: 253–56), but the account is primarily about Jesus, as Mark points out in 9:8 ("Jesus only") and 9:15 ("the crowd having seen Jesus").

Additional Notes

9:14. It is best to follow ℵ B L W Δ (Metzger 1994: 85) and read the plural "having come" (ἐλθόντες), since it is the harder reading, i.e., the one that is less likely to be due to scribal emendation.

4. Gundry (1993: 496) rightly states that to "identif[y] the point of the story as the disciples' inability rather than as Jesus' ability puts things in reverse."

9:15. Although the subject, "crowd" (ὄχλος), is singular, the participles and verbs are plural due to the sense of the collective noun. Most times "crowd" (ὄχλος) takes a singular verb, but compare 4:1; Matt. 21:8; Luke 6:19; John 6:22; 7:49; 12:12–13.

9:16. Although Τί can be translated as "Why" instead of "What," i.e., as an adverb rather than a direct object, most commentators translate it "What" (contra Gundry 1993: 488).

9:17. ἔχοντα is lit. "having."

9:18. εἶπα is lit. "said."

9:18. The ἵνα + subjunctive ("in order that they might cast it out") functions essentially as an infinitive (Zerwick 1963: §407).

9:20. The masculine participle ἰδών agrees with the neuter "spirit" (πνεῦμα) in sense (V. Taylor 1952: 398).

9:22. The plural "waters" (ὕδατα) may be Semitism, but it more likely refers to the various occasions that the demon had thrown the boy into water in the attempt to kill him.

9:23. The presence of the article Τό before "If you are able" reflects a classical usage of the article before quoted words (BDF §267.1).

9:23. The play on words between δύνῃ and δυνατά is difficult to maintain in translation. There are two possible ways of doing this: "If you are *able*? All things are *able* (to be done)," and "If you *can*? All things *can* (be done)."

9:24. Some MSS (D Θ f¹ f¹³ lat) add "with tears" (μετὰ δακρύων).

9:28. Although ὅτι is usually translated "that," here it abbreviates something like τί ἐστιν ὅτι. See the additional note on 9:11.

9:29. The active infinitive "go/come out" (ἐξελθεῖν) should be interpreted as a passive, such as "to be cast out" (V. Taylor 1952: 401; Donahue and Harrington 2002: 280).

9:29. Some MSS (𝔓⁴⁵ A C D L W f¹ f¹³ lat) add "and fasting." It is best to see this as a secondary gloss reflecting the emphasis of the early church on fasting (Metzger 1994: 85).

G. Jesus's Second Passion Prediction (9:30–32)

The present passage begins the second cycle of passion prediction (9:30–32), error by the disciples (9:33–34), and teaching concerning discipleship (9:35–10:31). See 8:22–10:52. The arrangement of these cycles that all begin with a passion prediction concentrates the readers' attention on the suffering, death, and resurrection of Jesus (Hooker 1991: 225). The question of the historicity of the passion predictions is generally determined by one's understanding of the messianic self-consciousness of Jesus and his foreknowledge of coming events. The death of John the Baptist and the OT prophets, along with the hostility of much of the religious establishment toward Jesus, however, would make it highly likely that he thought about and foresaw an inevitable clash that would lead to his death. Convinced of his having been sent from God, Jesus would have understood such a death as a divine calling. As a result, in Caesarea Philippi (8:27), Galilee (9:30), and on the road to Jerusalem (10:32), Jesus taught his disciples concerning his coming death.

The term "saying" (ῥῆμα, *rhēma*; 9:32) is the only clear non-Markan term found in the passage (Best 1981: 74), and most scholars assume that the majority of 9:30–32 (except "The Son of Man is delivered into the hands of men," due to its Semiticisms [Bayer 1986: 169–71]) is redactional (Pryke 1978: 17, 144, 164; Gnilka 1979: 53). The form of the second passion prediction is Markan (Achtemeier 1976: 178–79), but it is probably constructed on the basis of pre-Markan tradition (V. Taylor 1952: 402). Because 9:31 is the least developed of the three passion predictions (note the general "human hands" [εἰς χεῖρας ἀνθρώπων, *eis cheiras anthrōpōn*]), some have argued that it is likely the most primitive of the three (Evans 2001: 56), although 8:31 has also been suggested as being the most primitive (Strecker 1968: 429–35; cf. the discussion in Bayer 1986: 177–81). Like 10:33–34, the present passion prediction occurs in direct discourse, in contrast to the indirect discourse of 8:31.

Exegesis and Exposition

[30]And having departed from there, they were proceeding through Galilee, and he was not wishing that anyone know [it], [31]for he was teaching his disciples and was saying to them, "The Son of Man ⌜will be delivered⌝ into human hands, and they will kill him, and having been killed, ⌜after three days⌝ he will rise [from the dead]." [32]But they did not understand the saying, and they were afraid to ask him.

Jesus and the disciples departed (lit. "having gone out" [ἐξελθόντες, *exelthon-**tes*]) from "there" (Κἀκεῖθεν, *Kakeithen*), that is, the house Jesus had "en-tered" (εἰσελθόντος, *eiselthontos*) in 9:28. Compare 6:1 (note 5:38–39), 10; 7:24 (note 7:17); and 10:1 (note 9:33), where ἐκεῖθεν (*ekeithen*) + a form of the verb ἦλθον (*ēlthon*) refers to leaving a house (the verb in 10:1 is ἀνίστημι). They will continue to proceed through the region of Galilee, heading toward Capernaum (9:33), where they will remain until 10:1, when they begin their journey to Jerusalem. During this time Jesus sought privacy (cf. 7:24), and Mark informs his readers that this was "for" (γάρ, *gar*) the purpose of teaching his disciples (9:31). Although there are times in 8:27–10:52 when Jesus is portrayed as ministering to and teaching the crowds (8:34–38; 9:14–27; 10:1–9, 13–22, 46–52), the focus of his ministry at this time involves teaching the disciples. Since they would be most affected by his passion, death, and resurrection, he concentrates his attention on preparing them for this and for their subsequent ministry as his apostles (cf. Matt. 28:16–20; Luke 1:1–2; Acts 1:8).

9:30

The use of the iterative imperfect (was teaching, ἐδίδασκεν, *edidasken*) indi-cates that the subject of Jesus's future passion, death, and resurrection had been a constant theme of his teaching since 8:31 (France 2002: 371; Donahue and Harrington 2002: 283; contra Gundry 1993: 505). Thus the variation in the passion predictions (8:31; 9:31; 10:33) could have a historical basis in Jesus's having taught this "theme with variations." The use of the futuristic present tense "will be delivered" (παραδίδοται, *paradidotai*) indicates the certainty of this future event (V. Taylor 1952: 403). In the plan of God, his Son is already delivered over to death. Although the term "deliver" can mean "betray" (3:19; 14:18–21, 42, 44), here it means to deliver over (1:14; 10:33; 13:9; 15:1, 10, 15), for the focus of the passion predictions lies not with Judas and his betrayal but with God's purpose in sending his Son to give his life as a ransom for many (10:45; note the δεῖ [*dei*] of 8:31; cf. John 3:16–17; Rom. 8:32; also Isa. 53:6 LXX). The passive voice ("will be delivered") serves here as a divine passive, meaning "God will deliver" (Hooker 1991: 226; Evans 2001: 57; Witherington 2001: 268–69; J. Edwards 2002: 284; contra Gundry 1993: 506). Whatever the origin of the title "Son of Man" and the idea of his being delivered over to death (Schaberg [1985] suggests a tie between Dan. 7:13 and 25, but cf. Gundry 1993: 506), for Mark's readers this connection lies less with their familiarity with possible OT allusions to this than with their knowledge of the Christian traditions concerning the passion, death, and resurrection of Jesus, the Son of Man.

9:31

The major similarities between the first and second passion predictions involve the use of the title "Son of Man," his being killed, the temporal designa-tion "after three days," and the Son of Man's rising from the dead. The differ-ences involve "will be delivered" instead of "necessary to suffer, be rejected"; being delivered "into human hands" instead of to "the elders, chief priests, and scribes"; and the repetition of the verb "killed." Mark expects his readers to interpret "into human hands" in light of the reference to the "elders, chief priests, and scribes" in 8:31 and the "chief priest and scribes" in 10:33, but here the culpability of all humanity is probably to be understood as well.

9:32 Once again Mark describes the inability of the disciples to understand (see 4:40–41). A distinction must be made between a cognitive understanding of the words Jesus was speaking to the disciples and an acceptance of what Jesus was saying. If the disciples were asked, "What did Jesus say?" they would have been able to respond with something like, "He talked again about his being delivered into the hands of men, killed, and rising from the dead. We wish that he would stop saying such things." The content and meaning of the words Jesus spoke were understood by the disciples, but the truth and divine necessity of what he said were not. Yet they were afraid to ask for further clarification. As in other instances of Jesus's mighty words and acts, so here the response to the teaching about his death is incomprehension (cf. 8:32) and fear. The text gives no hint that this fear is the result of the disciples' concern for their own possible martyrdom (contra Best 1981: 73; Evans 2001: 57–58). A better suggestion is that it is a "holy fear" (Dwyer 1996: 150) inspired by Jesus (cf. 4:41; 5:15, 33; 6:50; 11:18 [?]; 16:8), as the emphatic position of the "him" (αὐτόν, *auton*) suggests (Gundry 1993: 504).

Summary

The key Markan message found in this passage involves a correct understanding of the death of Jesus. Whatever may have been the situation in the ministry of Jesus, Mark is not seeking to correct a false, nationalistic, messianic hope. He is writing to gentile Christians, who never entertained such hopes (Gundry 1993: 503). Mark seeks rather to assure his readers that the death of Jesus is not a tragedy or catastrophe. On the contrary, Jesus, as the Son of God, possessed a clear foreknowledge of his death and the circumstances surrounding it. He furthermore believed that what was to take place was divinely ordained. There was a divine necessity for what was about to occur, and God himself would deliver his Son into human hands. In contrast to the disciples' confusion and fear, Jesus was resolved to carry out the will of his Father. As the Son of God, he would obediently fulfill the role ordained for him (10:45). Thus his death is not to be construed as unfortunate or tragic, but as the great redemptive act by which a new covenant would be sealed (14:22–25) and sinful humanity ransomed (10:45).

Additional Notes

9:31. This translates the futuristic present "is delivered" (παραδίδοται).

9:31. The translation follows ℵ B D L Δ it, instead of "on the third day" (τῇ τρίτῃ ἡμέρᾳ) in A N W Θ f¹ f¹³ vg.

H. Jesus's Teachings on Discipleship (9:33–50)

Just as Jesus's first passion prediction (8:31) is followed by an error on the part of the disciples (8:32–33) and by teachings on discipleship (8:34ff.), so the second passion prediction (9:30–32) is followed by an error by the disciples (9:33–34) and teachings on discipleship (9:35–10:31; see 8:22–10:52). In the present instance the disciples' error does not involve a comment directed at Jesus concerning his passion, for they are afraid to ask him concerning this (9:32). It involves rather their inability to see the implications of Jesus's passion for their own lives (9:33–34; Hooker 1991: 227). Whether 9:33–50 came to Mark as a unit (V. Taylor 1952: 408–9; Bultmann 1968: 149; Best 1981: 75; Hooker 1991: 230–31) or was brought together by the evangelist himself (Kuhn 1971: 32–36; Pesch 1980b: 101–2) is uncertain. In favor of the former is that the sayings in 9:35–50 do not fit well the Markan emphasis of this section. This might be an example of Mark using a pre-Markan collection of sayings whose beginning relates well to his purpose and theme, whereas the final sayings do not.[1] On the other hand, that these sayings are found scattered in Matthew (18:1–5; 10:42; 18:6–9; 5:13; 5:29–30) and Luke (9:46–50; 17:1–2; 14:34–35) argues in favor of the latter. The difficulty in understanding how Mark 9:35–50 originated and that much of it was brought together by catchword association rather than logical reasoning helps make this section "the most obscure part of Mark" (McDonald 1980: 171).

Regardless of who was responsible for the present arrangement of the material, its present order is due less to chronological or logical reasons than to catchword linkage.[2] Compare "in (my) name" (ἐπί/ἐν τῷ ὀνόματι, *epi/en tō onomati*; 37, 38, 39, 41); "cause to stumble" (σκανδαλίζω, *skandalizō*; 42, 43, 45, 47); "child/little one" (παιδίον, *paidion* + μικρῶν, *mikrōn*; 36, 37, 42); "hell" (γέεννα, *geenna*; 43, 45, 47); "salt" (ἁλισθήσεται, *halisthēsetai* + ἅλας, *halas*; 49, 50); "whoever" (ὃς ἄν, *hos an* + ὅς, *hos*; 37 [2×], 39, 40, 41, 42); "if" (εἰ, *ei* + ἐάν, *ean*; 35, 42, 43, 45, 47); "one of" (ἕν, *hen* + ἕνα, *hena*; 37, 42); "it is better" (καλόν ἐστιν, *kalon estin*; 42, 43, 45, 47, 50); "be thrown into" (βέβληται, *beblētai* + βληθῆναι, *blēthēnai*; 42, 45, 47); and "fire" (πῦρ, *pyr*; 43, 48, 49).

---

1. Best 1981: 91n8 states, "The difficulty commentators seem to find in relating the verses of our sequence to one another or to their context is an indication that Mark is using material of which only a part, the first part, was really suitable for his purpose. As often, instead of dropping the less relevant material, he preserves the whole unit." Cf. Ambrozic 1972: 174–75.

2. Cf. Mark 2:14 and 15–17 for a similar catchword linkage involving "toll office" (τελώνιον, *telōnion*) and "toll collector" (τελῶναι, *telōnai*). Cf. also 4:3–9, 13–20, 26–29, 31–32 with respect to the word "sowing" (σπείρω, *speirō*).

Mark's own redaction is seen clearly in 9:33–34 (Best 1981: 76; Gnilka 1979: 55). Compare the structure: "and [καί, *kai*] + verb of motion + into [εἰς, *eis*] + place name" (Fleddermann 1981: 58; cf. 1:21; 8:22; 11:11, 15, and 27); "he was asking" (ἐπηρώτα, *epērōta*; 5:9; 8:23, 27, 29); "in the house" (ἐν τῇ οἰκίᾳ, *en tē oikia* + εἰς τὴν οἰκίαν, *eis tēn oikian*; 2:15; 7:24; 9:33; 10:10; 14:3; cf. 1:29); "discussing" (διελογίζομαι, *dielogizomai*; 2:6, 8 [2×]; 8:16, 17; 11:31); "in the way" (ἐν τῇ ὁδῷ, *en tē hodō*; 8:3, 27; 10:32, 52); "were silent" (ἐσιώπων, *esiōpōn*; 3:4); the explanatory "for" (γάρ, *gar*) clause in 9:34b; and so on. However, most regard 9:43–48 as well as 9:38–41 as traditional. The hand of Mark is seen most clearly, though, in the pattern of passion prediction, disciple error, and discipleship teachings.[3]

Exegesis and Exposition

[33]And they entered into Capernaum. And when he was in the house, he was asking them, "What were you discussing in the way?" [34]But they were silent, for they had ⌜discussed⌝ with one another in the way who was the ⌜greatest⌝. [35]And having sat down, he called the Twelve and says to them, "If anyone wishes to be first, he ⌜must be⌝ last of all and servant of all." [36]And having taken a child, he stood it in the middle of them, and having put his arms around him, he said to them, [37]"Whoever receives ⌜one child like this⌝ for my sake receives me, and whoever receives me, receives not [just] me but the one who sent me."

[38]John said to him, "Teacher, we saw someone casting out demons in your name, ⌜and we tried to forbid him because he was not following us⌝." [39]But Jesus said, "Stop forbidding him, for there is no one who will do a miracle in my name and will quickly be able to speak evil of me. [40]For whoever is not against us is for us. [41]For whoever gives to you a cup of water to drink in [my] name because you are of Christ, truly I say to you that he shall not by any means lose his reward. [42]And whoever should cause one of these little ones who believe ⌜in me⌝ to stumble, ⌜it is better⌝ for him if a large millstone were placed around his neck and he were cast into the sea.

[43]And if your hand is causing you to stumble, cut it off. It is better for you to enter into life maimed than to go into hell, into the unquenchable fire, having ⌜your⌝ two hands. ⌜ ⌝ [45]And if your foot is causing you to stumble, cut it off. It is better for you to enter into life lame than to be cast into hell having your two feet. ⌜ ⌝ [47]And if your eye is causing you to stumble, pluck it out. It is better for you to enter the kingdom

---

3. Fleddermann (1981: 58) sees an "extensive Marcan redaction and composition" in 9:33–50. For instance, 9:33b–35 has been created by Mark from the material in 10:35–45, 9:36–37 from 10:13–16, and 9:38–39, 41 (?), and 50b were also created by Mark (pp. 73–74). In 9:42–49 the only material that he believes is traditional is 43, 45, and 47 (p. 71). Contrast Derrett (1973: 366–67), who sees 9:42–50 as a pre-Markan unity. Pryke (1978: 17–18, 144, 164–65) sees most of 9:33–37 as being Markan. We must note, however, that similarity in wording does not require that either passage be secondary. It would be strange if similar incidents and sayings that Mark found in the tradition did not appear with similar wording in his Gospel.

of God with one eye than to be cast into hell having two eyes, [48]where their worm does not die and the fire is not extinguished.

[49]For everyone will be salted with fire. [50]Salt is good, but if the salt should become saltless, with what will you season it? Have salt in yourselves, and be at peace with one another."

For Capernaum, see 1:21–22 and 2:1–2. Mark does not state if this took place **9:33–34** in Peter's house (cf. 1:29–31), Jesus's own home, or some other house, for his focus is not on the where but on the what that takes place. Although 9:32 might suggest that the disciples were discussing among themselves in 9:33 Jesus's second passion prediction, Mark clarifies for the reader the content of this discussion with a typical "for" (γάρ) explanatory clause in 9:34b (cf. Gos. Thom. 12). The disciples' misunderstanding of Jesus's first passion prediction involved an unwillingness to accept the divine necessity of Jesus's death (8:32–34); here it involves their misunderstanding of how Jesus's death revolutionizes the essence of leadership. Jesus's messiahship and sonship meant for him being a servant (10:42–45), but the disciples thought that their unique role involved lordship and mastery over others. They did not see the implications of Jesus's death with respect to their own leadership roles.[4] This involves not so much greatness in the kingdom of God (Matt. 18:1) but greatness among themselves (Donahue and Harrington 2002: 284). This issue will come up again in 10:35ff. The silence of the disciples to Jesus's question (cf. 3:4) reveals that they were aware that he would not have approved of their pursuit and discussion of human greatness (Hooker 1991: 227; Evans 2001: 61). For another example of Jesus's discussion of this issue, compare Luke 14:7–11; for the extensive discussion of this at Qumran, where rank was very important, see 1QS 2.20–23; 5.20–24; 6.3–10; 1QSa 2.11–21. For OT and intertestamental parallels, consult Prov. 25:6–7 and Sir. 3:18, 20.

The series of sayings that follow are spoken after Jesus sat down (cf. Mark **9:35–37** 4:1–2; 12:41; 13:3; Matt. 5:1; 13:1–3; Luke 4:20; 5:3; John 8:2) and assumed the role of a "teacher" (διδάσκαλε, didaskale; 9:38). The saying in 9:35 was well known within the early church, as the parallels in 10:43–44/Matt. 20:26–27; Matt. 23:11; Luke 22:26 (cf. also Luke 9:48 and the various "first-last" sayings in Mark 10:31; Matt. 20:16; and Luke 13:30) indicate. In these parallels the first-last/slave comparison involve: great-slave, first-servant, great-servant, greatest-servant, greatest-youngest, and leader-servant.

The saying in Mark 9:35 is illustrated in 9:36 by a parabolic act (Pesch 1980b: 106–7; Stein 1994b: 25–26). The sudden appearance of a child is surprising, and the way 9:36–37 relates to 9:35 is unclear. Does the child serve as an example of the humble (Matt. 18:3–4; Mark 10:15–16), of needy humanity, of the most needy within the Christian community, of Christians in general

---

4. Best (1981: 77) points out that "the cross faces the believer with a challenge to his self-importance as much as it warns him about martyrdom."

(1 John 2:12–13), of Christian missionaries (Matt. 10:40; Luke 10:16; John 13:20; Matt. 25:31–46, esp. 40 [cf. Stein 1981: 137–40]), and so on? Furthermore, the example appears to involve receiving the humble (a child), whereas the context seems to be concerned with being humble.[5] Yet the fact that 9:36 involves a real child suggests that the illustration refers not abstractly to a child as a metaphor but to an actual child. The meaning of 9:37 is best understood in light of the position of children in the ancient world. Unlike the present-day idealization of children, the first century was not a child-oriented time. Children were not romanticized as examples of innocence and purity. On the contrary, unable to keep the law, little children were seen in Judaism at best as "weak" and not yet "people of the covenant." Thus to receive such insignificant people means to humble oneself and become last and servant of all (Best 1981: 79). This understanding best fits the context of 9:33–35 in that receiving a child involves humbling oneself and serving those who normally would be expected to serve the "first" (Von Wahlde 1985: 54–55).

The phrase "for my sake" (ἐπὶ τῷ ὀνόματί μου, *epi tō onomati mou*) is literally "in my name." It can refer to the child himself, who comes "in my name," that is, who comes as a Christian (Gundry 1993: 510), or it can refer to the one receiving the child "on account of my name," that is, who as a Christian receives such a child (Best 1981: 80; Hooker 1991: 228). In favor of the former is that in the parallel account in Matt. 18:3–5, the "child" serves as a metaphor for being a Christian, and in Mark 9:42 "little ones" are specifically referred to as believing in Jesus. Also in the other parallels to 9:37, where we find "to receive/reject *x* is to receive/reject me, and to receive/reject me is to receive/reject the one who sent me" (cf. Matt. 10:40; Luke 10:16; John 13:20), the *x* always refers to a Christian (cf. also Mark 9:41). It is best, however, not to seek an either-or (a real child or metaphor for a believer) resolution of the saying in 9:37. Since the parallels to 9:37 all involve receiving/rejecting believers and since in 9:42 the "little ones" are believers, it is best to understand the child of 9:37 as a literal child who believes in Jesus. Serving such a child, the least in the Christian social ladder, means to be servant of all other believers (cf. 10:43–45; Luke 22:27). Receiving such a child would of course mean receiving the one in whose name they believe and into whose name they were baptized (C. Marshall 1989: 156–57). The saying in Mark 9:37 is an example of step parallelism (Stein 1994b: 29–30), in which the second parallel line advances the thought found in the first line. It is best understood as follows: When a Christian receives (serves) a socially unimportant person in the believing community such as a child (i.e., when he has become servant of all), he receives (serves) Jesus, and receiving (serving) Jesus means to receive (serve) the one who sent him (J. Edwards 2002: 288). (The saying assumes the ancient understanding that an emissary is to be treated with the same respect and dignity due the one

5. Hooker 1991: 228 suggests that originally the example of the humble child in Mark 10:15 was associated with 9:36, but that it was replaced (actually "misplaced") by Mark or someone before him by the example of receiving a humble child now found in 9:36.

sending him.) For Jesus being "sent" (ἀποστείλαντα, *aposteilanta*), compare 12:6; Matt. 10:40; 15:24; 21:37; Luke 4:18, 43; 9:48; 10:16; and so on.

These verses consist of three parts: (1) an incident involving an unknown **9:38–42** exorcist not associated with the disciples ("not following us") who was successfully casting out demons in Jesus's name (9:38–40); (2) a saying concerning giving a drink of water (cf. Matt. 10:42) to a person because that one is a follower of Jesus (9:41); and (3) a warning against causing Christians to stumble (9:42). The first two parts are associated with the preceding material by the expression "in your/my name" in 9:38, 39, and "in (my) name" in 9:41 (cf. 9:37), whereas the third part is associated with the preceding materials by the common reference to "children" (παιδίων, *paidiōn*) in 9:37 and "one of these little ones" (ἕνα τῶν μικρῶν τούτων, *hena tōn mikrōn toutōn*; 9:42). The authenticity of the incident is assured by its tension with the situation of the early church recorded in Acts 19:13–17, for it is unlikely that the early church would have created an account of a successful exorcist who was not within the apostolic circle (Hooker 1991: 229; Gundry 1993: 520–21; Evans 2001: 64). (Cf. Num. 11:27–29 for a similar account in the OT.)

The authenticity of the saying in 9:41 is much debated. Some see it as a post-Easter creation (Evans 2001: 66) or as an authentic saying of Jesus that, like 9:40, occurred in a different setting (Hooker 1991: 231). Many emend the authentic form of the saying to "in (my) name because you are mine [ἐμοῦ, *emou*]" instead of "in (my) name because you are of Christ [Χριστοῦ, *Christou*]" (V. Taylor 1952: 408). If this is correct, it would not involve a change in meaning but an early church's clarification that doing something for someone because they are followers of Jesus means to do this because they are followers of Jesus who is the Christ (Hooker 1991: 231). The arguments that 9:40 and 41 were later editorial additions of Jesus's sayings to 9:38–39 because they "fit" or are "relevant" can also be used to argue in favor of considering them part of the original incident. It is likely that Mark found them associated in the tradition he was using (Best 1981: 80–82). It is speculative to do a mirror reading of this passage and assume that it reflects a dispute within the Markan community in which some leaders tried to exercise a monopoly on certain gifts (contra Hooker 1991: 229). The role of John, one of the "sons of thunder" (3:17), recalls a similar incident in which he and his brother James were out of touch with the mind of Christ (cf. 10:35–45; Luke 9:51–55). Here John serves as a spokesman for the other disciples as the threefold we/us (9:38) indicates. This is the only instance in Mark where he is mentioned alone. The address "Teacher" may allude to the teaching position Jesus assumed back in 9:35, but in Mark, when used of Jesus, "Teacher" carries with it the power and authority associated with "Lord" (see 4:37–38).

The identity of the exorcist is uncertain. Was he a syncretistic, unbelieving exorcist who simply used Jesus's name for pragmatic reasons (cf. Acts 19:13–17; Matt. 7:21–23), because it worked (Evans 2001: 64)? Or was the exorcist a true follower of Jesus, and the disciples saw themselves as the only ones "authorized" by Jesus (3:15; 6:7, 30) to do such exorcisms (W. Lane 1974: 343–44; Painter 1997: 138; Evans 2001: 65)?[6] The irony of the disciples' opposition to the successful exorcist is all the more striking because of their own lack of success in 9:14–29. Mark gives no hint of any deficiency on the part of the exorcist, and in light of the exorcist's success in 9:39, it is best to see him as a follower of Jesus who carried out his ministry outside the circle of the Twelve (cf. 1 Cor. 12:3). This may be the first time, but certainly not the last, in which ecclesiastical leaders have sought to hinder those who would minister in the name of Christ independently of their authority.

Jesus's rebuke of the disciples consists of a twofold explanation. The first (9:39) involves the pragmatic reason that a person who performs a "miracle" (δύναμιν, dynamin, mighty work) in Jesus's name is not suddenly going to slander (lit. "speak evil of," κακολογῆσαι, kakologēsai) him. The switch from the "we/us" of 9:38 to the "me" of 9:39 should be observed. Ministry, such as that of this exorcist, that brings glory to the name of Jesus should not/must not be hindered, even when it ignores "we/us," for what is important is "he/him," not "we/us"! The second explanation involves the proverb, "For whoever is not against us is for us" (9:40).[7] The saying in Luke 11:23 ("He who is not with me is against me"; cf. also Matt. 12:30) should not be seen as standing in contrast with Mark 9:40 but rather as complementing it, for Luke contains both proverbs (cf. 9:50 and 11:23). Thus it is evident that he did not see them as contradictory. Furthermore, the proverb in Mark 9:40/Luke 9:50 involves an exorcist casting out demons in Jesus's name. Such a "not against Jesus's activity" is certainly "for him."[8]

Verse 41 is associated with the preceding by means of word association: "in [my] name" (cf. 9:37–39) and the "for" clause (cf. 9:39–40) introduced by the relative pronoun "whoever" (ὅς, hos; cf. 9:40). Its thought, however, is closer to 9:37 (Fleddermann 1981: 66–67). We should probably not seek in 9:33–41 (and 9:33–50) "too rigorous a logical progression of thought" (Best 1981: 83), since much of this material was brought together by catchword association. Probably 9:41 serves to bridge the reference in 9:37 to receiving a child (an act which involves being last of all and servant of all; 9:35) and the warning in 9:42 not to offend the little ones (a metaphor for those who believe in Jesus [cf. Matt. 18:3–6] or itinerant missionaries who go out in Jesus's name [cf. Matt. 10:40–42; 25:40]). Verse 41 is one of the rare occurrences in which Jesus

6. For other suggestions concerning the identity of the strange exorcist, which include the apostle Paul, the Twelve, leaders of the Markan community, and others, see Best 1981: 84.

7. Cf. the similar saying in Cicero, Oratio pro Ligario 11 (33): "For we have often heard you assert that, while we held all men to be our opponents save those on our side, you counted all men your adherents who were not against you."

8. Evans (2001: 65) points out, "The 'whoever is not against us' saying applies to a man who makes positive use of Jesus' name to carry on the fight against Satan's kingdom. The 'whoever is not with me' saying refers to those who criticize and oppose Jesus' exorcisms." Cf. Cranfield (1959: 311) for a different explanation.

refers to himself as the "Christ." Note that this occurs after Peter's confession in 8:39 and in the privacy of a home to the disciples.

The question of whether 9:42 goes better with 9:38–41 or 9:43–48 is much debated. Those who argue for it being placed with 9:43ff. do so because of the common catchword "to cause to stumble" (σκανδαλίζω, skandalizō; Pesch 1980b: 101; Deming 1990: 131). I favor placing it with 9:38–41 because of the similar use of a relative clause introduced by "whoever" (ὅς . . . ἄν, hos . . . an); because it forms a kind of antithetical parallelism with 9:41, with the negative statement following the positive one (cf. 2:19–20; 3:28–29; 4:25; 7:15; also Matt. 10:32–33; 12:35; etc.; contra Fleddermann 1981: 67); and because of its tie to 9:37 by "child/little ones." Thus it functions as a parallel statement to 9:41, making 9:41–42 into an example of antithetical parallelism that compares the blessing that awaits those who show kindness to those who follow Jesus (9:41) with the warning of the horrible judgment that awaits those who harm them (9:42). (Cf. Rom. 14 and 1 Cor. 8–9 for similar teachings concerning Christians not causing other believers [cf. the "weak" in 1 Corinthians and Romans with the "little ones" here] to stumble.)

Verse 42 can be understood either as a word of encouragement or as a warning to believers. The former sees this as a word of comfort to the church in knowing that justice will triumph. They will be vindicated and their persecutors punished (Reploh 1969: 152–53). Since the following "stumble" materials are all warnings, however, it is best to interpret 9:42 also as a warning (Best 1981: 85). The warning is a stark one indeed. If it is better to drown in the sea wearing a giant millstone (lit. "a donkey-pulled millstone") as a collar than to experience the fate of those who cause believers to stumble, how horrible indeed must be the fate awaiting such people! As great and magnanimous as the "reward" (μισθόν, misthon; used only here in Mark) is for even so small an act of kindness as giving a believer a drink of water (9:41), equally great and horrible is the act of causing a believer to stumble. How one might cause a believer to stumble is not delineated.[9] Does it refer back to the attempt to forbid the work of other Christians, such as the unknown exorcist of 9:38–40, who were not "following" the disciples (W. Lane 1974: 345; Best 1981: 85; Gundry 1993: 512–13)? Yet it is far from clear how forbidding such an exorcist to continue his ministry would of necessity cause him to stumble and lose his faith. The arrangement of 9:33–50 by catchword association should warn against seeing too tight a logical argumentation and connection among all these verses.

These verses consist of a string of sayings that warn against believers stumbling due to temptations coming from within them. In contrast to 9:42, which warns against causing believers to stumble, the three sayings in 9:43, 45, and 47 warn against personal stumbling. All use a conditional clause (a "more

9:43–48

---

9. Neither Mark nor Jesus specifies whether the person envisioned as causing this is a believer or unbeliever. They simply emphasize that "whoever" (ὅς . . . ἄν) causes a believer to stumble and lose his/her faith is in danger of being cast into hell.

probable future condition") introduced by "if" followed by the subjunctive of σκανδαλίζω (*skandalizō*). The parallelism should be noted. All have the format "If your hand/foot/eye is causing you to stumble" followed by a "cut it off/pluck it out. It is better for you to enter life/the kingdom of God crippled/lame/with one eye than to go/be cast into hell having two hands/feet/eyes." Together they form a threefold series of synonymous parallelism.

Attempts to see 9:43–48 as dependent on the imagery in 2 Macc. 7 lose sight of the fact that, whereas in our passage the mutilation of the body (understood metaphorically, not literally) was self-inflicted for a good purpose, in 2 Macc. 7 the mutilation of the body is a form of torture inflicted by evil people who seek the harm and not the good of those who are suffering. In Mark 9:43–48 the purpose of such self-discipline is to prevent sinning and stumbling from the temptations coming from within a person (cf. 7:18–23). In 2 Macc. 7 it comes from without and seeks to cause seven brothers to sin by breaking God's law. The continual nature of the temptations in Mark 9:43–48 (cf. Sir. 9:5; 23:8; Ps. Sol. 16.7) is emphasized by the use of the present tense, which I have translated "is causing to stumble" (σκανδαλίζῃ, *skandalizē*).

The exact nature of the three temptations is unclear. Do the hands serve as an instrument for violence, the feet as a means of running to do evil, and the eyes as the vehicle for covetousness? Should they all be grouped together as referring to sins in general, violations of community rules (cf. 1QS, the *Manual of Discipline* of the Qumran community), or sexual sins? The similarity of 9:43, 45, and 47 to Matt. 5:29–30 supports the last interpretation. The similarity in vocabulary is quite striking, for in both passages the eyes serve (1) to "scandalize" and (2) should be plucked out in order (3) to avoid being thrown into hell. However, the Matthean parallel makes no mention of hands or feet. In *m. Nid.* 2.1 and *b. Nid.* 13b, the hand is associated with "adultery of the hand" (i.e., masturbation), and the foot is seen as a euphemism for the penis and thus associated with adultery (Deming 1990: 130–41; Gundry 1993: 524). Yet the eyes are not mentioned in *m. Nid.* 2.1 or *b. Nid.* 13b, and it is very unlikely that Mark expected his reader to be familiar with this rabbinic imagery.[10] Since Mark does not delineate the exact nature of these sinful tendencies, he probably intended them to be understood as referring to any temptation that might cause a follower of Jesus to be "scandalized."

The seriousness of stumbling is emphasized in 9:43–48 by the nature of the consequences: going to hell or *Gehenna* (γέεννα, *geenna*). Gehenna, an Aramaism, refers literally to the Valley (Aramaic גֵּי, *gê*) of Hinnom (Aramaic הִנֹּם, *hinnām*), on the southwestern slopes of the city of Jerusalem. In OT times it was associated with the sacrificing of children to the Canaanite gods Molech and Baal. Later it was used as a refuse dump, and the continual burning of the refuse gave rise to its metaphorical use as a symbol for the eternal, fiery

---

10. There is always a problem in assuming that a teaching found in the Mishnah and Talmud existed centuries earlier in a common oral tradition known to Jesus and/or the Gospel writers.

judgment awaiting the wicked (2 Esd. 7:36; 1 En. 27.2–3; 90.24–27; 103.8; 2 Bar. 59.5–11). It is used in this sense twelve times in the NT. With the exception of James 3:6, all the remaining references are sayings of Jesus found in the Synoptic Gospels (Matt. 5:22, 29–30 [2×]; 10:28; 18:9; 23:15, 33; Mark 9:43, 45, 47; Luke 12:5). *Gehenna* is best translated by the term "hell." It is described in the NT as a place of eternal punishment (Matt. 25:41, 46), consisting of unquenchable fire (Mark 9:43, 48), whose most famous occupants are the devil and his angels (cf. Matt. 25:41; Rev. 20:10; D. F. Watson, *ABD* 2:926–28). In Mark 9:43 to go "into hell" is described by the appositional phrase "into the unquenchable fire" (εἰς τὸ πῦρ τὸ ἄσβεστον, *eis to pyr to asbeston*) and in 9:48 by the phrase "where their worm [ὁ σκώληξ αὐτῶν, *ho skōlēx autōn*] does not die and the fire is not extinguished [οὐ σβέννυται, *ou sbennytai*]."[11] These two additional descriptions (cf. Isa. 66:24) indicate that the punishment of hell is an eternal, continuing punishment (Donahue and Harrington 2002: 288; contra Hooker 1991: 232, who argues that it envisions annihilation). A horrific place and fate indeed!

These sayings use hyperbolic and metaphorical language. Literally cutting off one's hand or leg and plucking out one's eye would not resolve the "cause" of the problem. A one-handed, one-footed, one-eyed person can still be tempted, sin, and thus stumble. So too can people with no hands, no feet, and no eyes. The human dilemma is that the sinful nature is part of a person's innermost being (7:18–23), and thus it cannot be removed by any form of amputation. The sayings are a hyperbolic attempt by Jesus (and Mark) to warn his audience that there is no sin worth going to hell for. Better to repent, no matter how painful that repentance may be, and follow Jesus, whatever the cost, than to perish in hell. The seriousness of this warning is emphasized in several ways. The use of hyperbole is quite intentional. One uses such exaggerated language when what one is seeking to say is urgent. The threefold repetition of this teaching drives home its importance. The reward for repentance and the faithful exercise of self-discipline is described as "entering life [ζωήν, *zōēn*]" (9:43 and 45) or "entering the kingdom of God [τὴν βασιλείαν τοῦ θεοῦ, *tēn basileian tou theou*]" (9:47);[12] the alternative is described as being "cast into hell" (βληθῆναι εἰς τὴν γέενναν, *blēthēnai eis tēn geennan*).

9:49–50 These two verses are associated together by the common term "salted/salt." They were probably independent sayings (Cranfield 1959: 315; Evans 2001: 72) that became associated with 9:42–48 because of the term "fire" (cf. 9:49 with 9:43, 48). The meaning of 9:49 is unclear. Suggested allusions to various OT passages (Lev. 2:13; Num. 18:19; Ezek. 43:24) are unlikely (contra Carlston 1975: 174; Fleddermann 1981: 71; Evans 2001: 73), as is the view that the reference to "salt" and "fire" suggests the idea of sacrifice (J. Edwards 2002:

---

11. For the association of "worm" and "fire," cf. Jdt. 16:17; Sir. 7:17.

12. The parallel between possessing (eternal) life and entering the kingdom of God is also found in 10:17, 23; John 3:3, 5 and 15, 16.

295–96; France 2002: 383–84). The suggestion that it refers to the purifying fires of purgatory finds little support in the NT. More likely is the idea that it refers to the final judgment, for the preceding verses refer to "fire" in this manner (9:43, 48; cf. also 1 Cor. 3:10–15). Yet "salted" is better understood as a metaphor involving purification (Ezek. 16:4; 43:24), and in Matt. 5:13 "salt" is understood positively.[13] Thus it is best to interpret this verse as a reference to the purifying experiences of Christians (contra Gundry 1993: 515, 527) in their journey to life/the kingdom of God (Hooker 1991: 233; Evans 2001: 73). These experiences may involve persecution (Nauck 1952: 171–73; Reploh 1969: 154; McDonald 1980: 175), for "fire" is often a metaphor for persecution (1 Pet. 1:7; 4:12; Rev. 3:18). This interpretation allows 9:49 to continue the theme of following Jesus in 9:42–48 and also allows the "for" to function as a normal causal conjunction. The passive "will be salted" (ἁλισθήσεται, halisthēsetai) may be a divine passive. If so, it means that in God's permissive will, such experiences are allowed to occur (Nauck 1952: 173) and that in them God works for the believer's ultimate good (Rom. 8:28).

The meaning of "salt" in 9:50 appears to be different from that in 9:49. This should not be altogether surprising because these verses are associated together less by logic than by catchword linkage (Best 1981: 87–88). Here salt serves as a metaphor for the characteristics of discipleship (cf. Matt. 5:13). In Palestine "saltless [ἄναλον, analon] salt," often a mixture of salt and impurities such as gypsum, was mined from the Dead Sea and frequently appeared as perfectly good salt (Hooker 1991: 233). Yet such "saltless salt" was worse than useless, for it was not only unusable but also presented a disposal problem (Luke 14:34–35).

The concluding two imperatives in 9:50b ("Have salt . . . be at peace . . .") are an example of synonymous parallelism in which the second imperative interprets and makes specific the preceding general one (Gundry 1993: 528). They build on the preceding analogy in 9:50a and reveal that 9:50a should be interpreted in light of 9:50b and not 9:49 (Nauck 1952: 175). The disciples, like salt, are worthless unless they possess the qualities of "saltness," the characteristics of true discipleship. "Have salt in [among] yourselves" probably means for the disciples to possess salt-of-the-earth (Matt. 5:13) characteristics that cause them to "be at peace with one another." Such characteristics involve removing anything from their lives that would hinder them from entering life/the kingdom of God (9:42–48), not demanding or claiming exclusivity (9:38–40), and not seeking selfish gain or status (9:33–37). As a result, these characteristics would lead to their being at peace with one another (Carlston 1975: 176–78). The last imperative in 9:50 forms a kind of *inclusio* with 9:35 and brings the sayings in 9:35–50 to a conclusion.

---

13. Whereas in Matt. 5:13 "salt" is a metaphor for the "disciples" (cf. Matt. 5:1–2), in the present verse it is not a synonym for the disciples, for here "everyone" is referred to as "being salted," not as being "salt."

Summary

Two main Markan emphases can be found in this passage. Most evident is the emphasis on Christian discipleship. The teachings of 9:33–50 are part of the threefold pattern of passion prediction, disciple error, and teachings of discipleship begun in 8:31 (see 8:22–10:52). The cost and reward in following Jesus and the warning of the consequences found in 8:34–38 are repeated in 9:35–50 and will be repeated again in 10:1–31 and 42–45. The specific dangers discussed in our passage involve seeking personal greatness (9:33–37), discriminating against followers of Jesus who are not under the leadership of the twelve disciples (9:38–41), causing other Christians ("little ones") to stumble (9:42), and removing anything from one's life that would cause one to stumble (9:43–50). Yet there is also a promise to those who follow Jesus. This involves receiving God (9:37), reward (9:41), and (eternal) life (9:43, 45), that is, the kingdom of God (9:47).

Our account also has a strong christological emphasis. Acts done for Jesus are acts done for God (9:37). The exorcisms done in Jesus's name by someone not directly associated with the disciples reveal the authority and power of Jesus as well. Most important, the Markan Christology in our passage involves the fact that in 9:37 (cf. also 41), as in 8:34–38, human destiny is primarily dependent on one's relationship with Jesus. How one should treat others is not based on anthropology—the value of the human soul or their treatment of the image of God that resides in humanity. It is based rather on Christology—one's attitude toward Jesus. Being received by God is determined by one's attitude toward the "name of Jesus" (9:37), whether one has faith in Jesus. Human actions are ultimately not judged on the basis of the value of human life, the infinite value of the human soul, the laws of creation, and so on. Rather, they are based on whether they are done in faith for Jesus's sake (9:41).

Additional Notes

9:34. Although different terms are used in 9:33 (διελογίζεσθε from διαλογίζομαι) and 34 (διελέχθησαν from διαλέγομαι), they function essentially as synonyms (contra Gundry 1993: 508).

9:34. The comparative μείζων functions here as a superlative.

9:35. ἔσται is lit. "shall be."

9:37. ἓν τῶν τοιούτων παιδίων is lit. "one of such children."

9:38. The present translation follows ℵ B Δ Θ Ψ. See Metzger 1994: 86. The other variants involve primarily differences in tenses and in the order of the clauses. Ἐκωλύομεν is a tendential/conative imperfect.

9:42. The present translation follows A B L W Θ Ψ f¹ f¹³ against ℵ D Δ it, which omit "in me."

9:42. καλόν ἐστιν . . . μᾶλλον is lit. "good is . . . more." I also translate καλόν as "better" in vv. 43, 45, 47.

9:43. The article τάς functions here as a possessive.

9:43. Both here and in 9:45 the translation follows ℵ B C L W Δ f¹, which omit vv. 44 and 46, "where their worm does not die and the fire is not extinguished." The latter expressions were most probably added by later copyists from 9:48 to make 9:43 and 45 parallel 9:47–48 more closely (Metzger 1994: 86).

9:45. As the note to 9:43 indicates, v. 46 is absent from important early witnesses.

I. Jesus's Teaching concerning Divorce (10:1–12)

The following account involves a change of location (from Capernaum in Galilee [9:33] to Judea and across the Jordan [εἰς τὰ ὅρια τῆς Ἰουδαίας καὶ πέραν τοῦ Ἰορδάνου, *eis ta horia tēs Ioudaias kai peran tou Iordanou*; 10:1]) and audience (from disciples [9:31–50] to the crowds [ὄχλοι, *ochloi*; 10:1]). The focus of the teaching, however, remains upon the disciples, as 10:10–12 reveals. Although some suggest that 9:33–10:31 existed as a pre-Markan complex, the heterogeneity of the material argues against this (Best 1981: 99). The suggestion that 10:1–31 came to the evangelist in the form of a pre-Markan complex has more to commend it, for there appears to exist a common thread of marriage (10:1–12), children (10:13–16), and possessions (10:17–31; Best 1981: 99). On closer look, however, the supposed commonality is only superficial, for the passage concerning children does not involve how parents should raise their children. Children serve rather as a metaphor for the character required to enter the kingdom of God (Kuhn 1971: 37; contra Witherington 2001: 274).

Whether Mark has combined a controversy story (10:2–9) with a pronouncement story (10:10–12; V. Taylor 1959: 415; Reploh 1969: 179–85; Witherington 2001: 274) or whether they were connected before Mark (Gnilka 1979: 69; Best 1981: 100) is much debated. In its present form 10:2–12 functions as a pronouncement story consisting of an introductory question by the Pharisees (10:2), a counterquestion by Jesus (10:3), a response by the Pharisees (10:4), and Jesus's concluding pronouncement consisting of his response to the Pharisees (10:5–9) and his teaching on the subject to the disciples (10:10–12). The heart of the account focuses on the Pharisaic search for exceptions to the divinely ordained "till death do us part" intention of marriage (10:6–9) and the concession God permits in the OT (10:3–4) due to human sinfulness (10:5). True discipleship, Jesus teaches, is not to be lived out in light of concessions given due to the fallen nature of humanity but in light of the ultimate divine intention. Therefore divorce is excluded and remarriage after divorce becomes adultery (10:10–12). Thus 10:10–12 is understood by Mark (and Jesus) not as contradicting the Law (cf. Deut. 24:1) but as revealing its true purpose (Hooker 1991: 235).

Mark's editorial work is most apparent in 10:1 (cf. 7:24) and 10 (Pryke 1978: 18, 144, 165; Best 1981: 100; Evans 2001: 81–82, 84–85). Most commentators see 10:2–9 as being for the most part traditional (Best 1981: 100; Evans 2001: 82). There is much debate as to whether 10:12 is authentic, a pre-Markan tradition, or Markan. I will argue below (see 10:10–12) that

10:12 is traditional and may very well go back to Jesus himself. Mark includes the present account at this point to explain what discipleship involves in the area of marriage. For those contemplating following Jesus (8:34), Mark emphasizes the future implications of this with respect to marriage. This emphasis, necessary in Mark's day, is even more necessary in our own. For those who seek to follow Jesus, divorce is not an option. Part of taking up the cross and following Jesus (8:34) involves maintaining the divine purpose of marriage with one person until death.

Exegesis and Exposition

¹And having risen up from there, he comes into the regions of Judea ⌜and⌝ across the Jordan, and again crowds gather around him; and as he was accustomed, he was again teaching them. ²⌜And the Pharisees came up⌝ [and] were asking him if it was lawful for a man to divorce his wife. They said this in order to test him. ³⌜And he answered⌝ and said to them, "What did Moses command you?" ⁴And they said, "Moses permitted [a man] to write a certificate of dismissal and to divorce [his wife]." ⁵And Jesus said to them, "For the sake of your hard heart he wrote this commandment for you, ⁶but from the beginning of creation [God] made them male and female. ⁷Because of this a man shall leave his father and mother ⌜and shall be joined [by God] to his wife⌝, ⁸and the two shall be one flesh. As a result they are no longer two but one flesh. ⁹What therefore God ⌜has joined together⌝, let no man separate." ¹⁰And [when] the disciples [were] again in the house, they were asking him about this. ¹¹And he says to them, "Whoever divorces his wife and marries another commits adultery against her, ¹²and if she, having divorced her husband, marries another man, she commits adultery."

10:1 Jesus's "rising up" (ἀναστάς, anastas) recalls his "sitting down" (καθίσας, kathisas) in 9:35, and "from there" (ἐκεῖθεν, ekeithen) refers to leaving "Capernaum," named in 9:33 (Gundry 1993: 528–29; Evans 2001: 82). The route described is from Galilee toward Judea (and ultimately Jerusalem) via the eastern side ("across") of the Jordan River. It was common for devout Jews traveling from Galilee to Judea/Jerusalem to cross the Jordan River and proceed south to a point opposite Jericho, where they would cross the Jordan again. In so doing, they would avoid traveling through Samaria. The order of "into . . . Judea and across the Jordan" is somewhat puzzling, since this is the reverse of the actual order traveled. Mark may have chosen to place "Judea" first, however, to emphasize the ultimate goal of the journey (Gundry 1993: 529). (See 7:31, and compare the order in 11:1, where the ultimate goal, Jerusalem, is placed first.) Mark emphasizes Jesus's popularity and fame by his reference to the "crowds." This plural is found only here in Mark. In the other thirty-seven instances of "crowd" in Mark, it is always singular. The "again" (πάλιν, palin) recalls the previous references to crowds gathering around Jesus (2:4, 13; 3:9, 20, 32; 4:1, 36; 5:21, 24, 30; 6:34, 45; 7:14, 33; 8:1; 9:14; 10:46; 12:37).

"As he was accustomed [εἰώθει, *eiōthei*]" emphasizes the Markan theme of Jesus's teaching ministry (see 1:21–22).

Along with the crowds, Pharisees are also present who approach him and ask **10:2** a question as to whether it is "lawful" (ἔξεστιν, *exestin*) for a man to "divorce" (ἀπολῦσαι, *apolysai*) his wife. (Matt. 19:3 adds "for any cause.") The question is hostile in nature, as Mark's "in order to test him" (πειράζοντες αὐτόν, *peirazontes auton*; lit. "testing him") indicates. The appearance of πειράζοντες αὐτόν here and in 8:11 (cf. also 12:13–15 and 7:5 for the similarity in theme and 7:19 for a similar use of a participial clause by Mark) indicates that this is probably a Markan explanatory comment. The comment indicates that this was not a sincere theological question but an attempt to entrap Jesus (cf. 2:16, 18, 24; 7:5; 8:11; 12:13). In so doing, they were carrying out the work of Satan (1:12–13). It may very well be that behind this question lay a dangerous political issue (Evans 2001: 82). John the Baptist had been put to death by Herod Antipas for criticizing his marriage to Herodias, who had divorced her husband to marry him (see 6:17–20). John the Baptist may have been beheaded at Machaerus (see 6:21–26 and 27–29), which was "across the Jordan." If this is true, the Pharisees' testing Jesus "across the Jordan" may have involved less a desire to learn Jesus's theological position on the issue of divorce and remarriage than an attempt to ensnare him in a statement that would have angered Herod. This may be why the question is worded as it is. If this were simply an in-house Jewish question, one might expect a question concerning the just causes for divorce (Hooker 1991: 235; cf. Matt. 19:3).[1]

Jesus's counterquestion asks what Moses commanded in the Torah. For Jesus **10:3–4** (1:44; 7:10; 10:3; 12:26), as well as for the Pharisees (10:4; 12:19), Moses was the author of the Law/Pentateuch. Instead of quoting what Moses and the Law "command" (ἐνετείλατο, *eneteilato*; 10:3) concerning marriage, as Jesus does in 10:6–9, the Pharisees quote what God "permits" (ἐπέτρεψεν, *epetrepsen*; 10:4; Schweizer 1970: 203). There was much debate within Judaism about the meaning of the expression "something indecent/objectionable/offensive" (עֶרְוַת דָּבָר, *'erwat dābār*), which, according to Deut. 24:1, justified divorce. The school of Shammai interpreted the expression conservatively and permitted divorce only in the case of sexual unchastity by the wife. The school of Hillel interpreted it more liberally and permitted divorce for such things as a wife spoiling her husband's supper or his finding someone more attractive than her (*m. Giṭ.* 9.10; *b. Giṭ.* 90a–b). In the Talmud a lengthy tractate (*Gittin*) is devoted to the issue of divorce. Clearly, to focus on what God "allows" (but disapproves of) due to the hardness of the human heart (10:5), rather than on what he commands and wills, reveals a

---

1. Some have argued from CD 4.21 and 11QTemple[a] 57.17–19 that divorce and remarriage were prohibited by the Qumran community, but it appears more likely that this refers to the prohibition of polygamy (Instone-Brewer 2002: 61–72).

misguided focus.[2] France (2002: 390–91) points out that Deut. 24:1–4 does not even "permit" divorce but rather seeks to "regulate" it. It may also seek to discourage hasty divorces.

10:5–9   Jesus's reply to the Pharisees is twofold. The first part (10:5) responds to the answer given by the Pharisees and points out that the OT reference quoted (Deut. 24:1) was not imperative in nature but concessive. It does not set forth the absolute and perfect will of God but his will in light of human sin (Cranfield 1985: 229–30). It was a concession that God permitted due to sin, due to the "hardness of human hearts" (σκληροκαρδίαν, sklērokardian or "cardiosclerosis"),[3] for the sake of the woman (Pesch 1980b: 123; R. Collins 1992: 95).[4] It was meant to limit the problem of divorce, not to serve as license for this practice (Witherington 2001: 276). By adding "your" (ὑμῶν, hymōn) to his explanation, Jesus moves the discussion from the abstract "hardness of the human heart" to the sinful attitude manifested by the Pharisees in their discussion (cf. the hardening of Pharaoh's heart in Exodus). Their reply focused on what God permitted in such instances due to sin rather than what God's purpose and intention is in marriage. Why do they quote Deut. 24:1 instead of Gen. 1:27 and 2:24 (cf. also 5:2)? (Cf. CD 4.21, which also quotes Gen. 1:27 in arguing for the permanence of marriage; cf. also 11QTemple[a] 57.17–19.) Why not quote Mal. 2:16?[5]

The second part of Jesus's reply (10:6–9) consists of his understanding of the divine intention for marriage. As the basis of his argument, Jesus appeals to the divine purpose "from the beginning of creation" (ἀπὸ ἀρχῆς κτίσεως, apo archēs ktiseōs; note its emphatic position at the start of 10:6) found in Gen. 1:27. Jesus does not appeal to the new eschatological situation brought about by the arrival of the kingdom of God (contra Donahue and Harrington 2002: 294) but rather to God's purpose in creation. God created humanity as male and female, and "because of this" (ἕνεκεν τούτου, heneken toutou), that is, God's creation of them (R. Collins 1992: 97; not the woman's origin from man [contra V. Taylor 1952: 418]), a man shall leave (καταλείψει, kataleipsei; an imperatival future) his father and mother and be joined (a divine passive implying "by God," as 10:9 indicates) to his wife. This joining, witnessed above all in their sexual union (cf. 1 Cor. 6:16), results in the two becoming one flesh.

---

2. Cranfield (1985: 231) rightly states, "We ought to resist every temptation to tamper with the absoluteness, the perfection, of God's requirement which confronts us in the Genesis verses quoted by Jesus." Cf. also Hooker 1991: 235: "Because [Jesus's] concern is with what God wills, rather than with what the Law allows, he stands in opposition to legalism, which is concerned with definitions rather than with wholehearted obedience"; and J. Edwards 2002: 302: "The divine intention for marriage cannot be determined from a text on divorce."

3. The term "hardness of heart" is found in the NT only here and in the parallel in Matt. 19:8, but cf. Mark 3:5; 4:10–12; 6:52; 8:17.

4. Gundry (1993: 538) argues that the purpose of Deut. 24:1 was not as a concession but rather to incite people like the Pharisees to divorce their wives and disobey God's ordinance. This, however, reads Paul's understanding of the Law into the present situation.

5. Even b. Giṭ. 90b acknowledges the great sorrow that divorce brings to God.

Thus, according to the divine purpose, they are no longer two[6] (a male and a female) but one (a couple, or better, "a coupled one"). In light of this "oneness" rather than "twoness," divorce destroys the unity of the divine purpose. Jesus ends his response to the Pharisees with a warning. Since it is God who has created male and female and their oneness in marriage, "you shall not sever" this divinely created unity. Thus no one created by God should seek to undo and separate, that is, divorce (Painter 1997: 141), what God, the Creator, has created in marriage by making the two into one (Gundry 1993: 531). The "man" of 10:9 almost certainly refers to the man contemplating divorce (Hooker 1991: 236). The idea of the "man" being a lawyer suing for divorce for his client is anachronistic, since a Jewish male could divorce his wife by simply saying to her, "You are free to marry whomever you wish" (*m. Giṭ.* 9.3).[7]

In 10:10 Mark changes the scene "again" to a house where the disciples ask Jesus concerning the previous teachings and Jesus instructs them in private (cf. 7:17; 9:28, 33; also 4:34 [see 7:17–19]). It is uncertain whether 10:11–12 is an independent teaching of Jesus (cf. Matt. 5:32; Luke 16:18; 1 Cor. 7:10–11) that has been added to 10:2–9. If it is, there is then uncertainty as to whether it was Mark or the pre-Markan tradition that brought them together. In favor of Mark having joined them is the seamlike nature of 10:10 (Crossan 1983: 210; contra Best 1981: 100). As it stands, 10:10–12 turns Jesus's general teaching of the crowds and Pharisees (10:1–2) on the subject into instruction on discipleship in this area. This causes 10:10–12 to fit well the pattern of passion prediction, an error by the disciples, and teaching on discipleship found in 8:31–10:45 (see 8:22–10:52).

10:10–12

We find parallels to Jesus's teachings on divorce (10:11–12) in Luke 16:18; Matt. 5:32; 19:9; and 1 Cor. 7:10–11. The Markan form of the teachings in 10:11 is generally considered to be more authentic than the two parallels found in Matthew (5:32; 19:9) that contain the famous exception clause that prohibits divorce "except for fornication [πορνεία, *porneia*]." There are several reasons for this. For one, the Markan wording is more difficult, since it does not appear to allow divorce for any reason. Thus it is easier to see Matthew helping his readers adapt Mark's teaching to their situation than Mark making Matthew's form of the saying more difficult. Second, the Lukan version agrees with Mark in that he too lacks any exception. Third, Paul's version of Jesus's teaching on divorce also agrees with Mark more closely than with Matthew. Although he apparently allows for divorce in the case of desertion by an unbelieving partner (1 Cor. 7:12–15), Paul appears to be unfamiliar with Matthew's exception clause.[8]

---

6. Although "the two" of Mark 10:8 is not found in Gen. 2:24 MT, the LXX has "the two," which simply makes explicit what is implied in the Hebrew text.

7. There is no reason to doubt that this rabbinic saying goes back to the time of Jesus, for the debates on divorce between Hillel and Shammai indicate that this issue was already much discussed toward the end of the first century BC.

8. For the view that Mark 10:11–12 better reflects Jesus's actual words and that Matthew in 5:32 and 19:8 and Paul in 1 Cor. 7:12–15 provide an application of Jesus's teaching to their

According to Mark 10:11, for a man to divorce his wife and marry another is an act of adultery against his first wife. The Greek expression ἐπ' αὐτήν (*ep' autēn*) is best translated "against her" (cf. 3:24–26; 13:8, 12; 14:48) rather than "with her," that is, with the second wife (Gundry 1993: 541–42; Witherington 2001: 277–78). This permits the feminine singular pronoun "her/she" (αὐτήν/αὐτή) in 10:11–12 to refer to the same woman. Jesus's saying is quite remarkable, for in Israel a man was generally considered an adulterer only when he had an extramarital sexual relationship with a married woman, and he was guilty of adultery against the husband of this woman, not his own wife. However, if a woman had an extramarital sexual relationship with a married man, she was guilty of adultery against her husband. Jesus points out that by an extramarital affair a married man was just as guilty of adultery as a married woman (Gundry 1993: 532–33), for there is no difference between "male" and "female" (cf. Gal. 3:28). There is no need to see a conflict between Mark 10:9, which forbids divorce, and 10:11, which forbids remarriage after divorce. In Judaism, divorce always included the right to remarry. The very act of divorce assumes that remarriage can follow: "You are free to marry whomever you will" (*m. Giṭ.* 9.3).[9] Thus, there is no conflict between 10:9 and 10:11 but rather a difference in emphasis on the act of divorce-remarriage.

Many scholars believe that 10:12 is a secondary addition to 10:11, reflecting the situation of the church in the Roman world (Best 1981: 100–101; R. Collins 2000: 25–26), for Jewish women could not divorce their husbands in Israel (Josephus, *Ant.* 15.7.10 §§259–60; 18.5.4 §136; *m. Yebam.* 14.1). Divorce was both possible and common, however, among Roman women (cf. Rom. 7:2–3). While it was generally true that Jewish women could not divorce their husbands in Israel, there were exceptions (cf. Sir. 23:22–23; Brewer 1999). More important, however, is that a very famous example of Mark 10:12 existed in Galilee. This involved the case of Herodias, who divorced her husband and married Herod Antipas. John the Baptist was ultimately martyred for rebuking Herod Antipas for marrying a woman who had divorced her husband (who was actually a brother of Herod). Thus it is quite possible that, just as John the Baptist spoke of the adulterous nature of such a union, Jesus also rebuked such a union in 10:12 (Burkitt 1906: 99–101; J. Edwards 2002: 304–5), and the fact that 10:11–12 forms a kind of synonymous parallelism argues in favor of its authenticity. The rebukes of Jesus and John the Baptist stand in sharp contrast to today's concern that

---

own situation, see R. H. Stein, *DJG* 196–98. This view interprets Jesus's words as an overstatement to emphasize the indissoluble nature of marriage and that divorce is an affront to the divine plan. Thus Jesus deals with the basic issue of the legitimacy of divorce in general, not with questions concerning the legitimate grounds for divorce as a "less worse" situation (as we find in Matt. 19:3, 9).

9. For an example of such a certificate of divorce, cf. Donahue and Harrington 2002: 293; Instone-Brewer 2002: 86–90.

would seek not to be condemnatory and would see Herod's and Herodias's lifestyle as quite acceptable.

Summary

Two clear Markan themes can be found in this passage. One involves Christology. Jesus by his magnetic personality once again draws not just "a" crowd but "crowds" (10:1). His unique authority is witnessed to in the passage not by miracles or exorcisms but by his authoritative teaching of the Scriptures (cf. 1:22; 7:1–23; 12:18–37). His teaching provides the definitive word on the Scriptures. One might expect that the climax of Jesus's teaching would come in his quotation of what the Law teaches on the subject in 10:6–8. However, it comes not here but in his personal pronouncement of what he claims the Law teaches in 10:9, 11–12 (Hooker 1991: 234). Jesus's pronouncement is ultimately based not on a logical deduction from Scripture but rather on his declaration of the will of God with respect to Scripture (J. Edwards 2002: 302). The christological question once again arises: "Who is this man" who teaches like this? Where does this "norm-shattering authority with which Jesus teaches" (Gundry 1993: 535) come from? Mark teaches that it comes from God himself, who anointed Jesus, his Son, as the Christ (1:1, 10–11).

A second Markan theme involves what it means to be a disciple and follow Jesus with respect to marriage. Although the principle given in 10:2–12 is applicable to all people because the Creator has determined that this is how his creation should live, Mark intends that 10:2–12 should be understood in light of the call to discipleship in 8:34 (cf. 10:10–11a). The followers of Jesus cannot live a life based on what God has conceded (Deut. 24:1) due to human sinfulness (Mark 10:5). "Divorce . . . no matter how nuanced its defense or how cleverly justified, violates God's design for human marriage" (Evans 2001: 84) and is not permissible for Jesus's followers. Those who are thinking about following Jesus must commit themselves to a life of monogamy and fidelity. This teaching is not based on a higher standard brought about by the arrival of the kingdom of God. Nor should we see here a special, higher standard given to the church to fulfill its priestly and royal function (contra Evans 2001: 86). Jesus calls rather for a wholehearted commitment to do what God ordained at creation with respect to marriage. Mark, following Jesus, is not interested in speculating when a divorce may be a "less worse" situation than a "bad marriage." There is no such thing as a "good divorce." Every divorce witnesses to a failure of God's purpose in marriage. Perhaps in a dangerous and abusive marriage, divorce may be a lesser evil, but Mark intentionally leaves Jesus's teaching on this subject in its unqualified hyperbolic form.[10]

10. In their application of Jesus's teaching on divorce to their own situations, Matthew (5:32; 19:9) and Paul (1 Cor. 7:12–15) explicitly allow for divorce and remarriage in case of sexual immorality and desertion by an unbelieving spouse. Are there other instances in which divorce is

Additional Notes

10:1. The translation follows the Alexandrian witnesses of ℵ B C* L Ψ, which include "and" (καί), rather than D W Δ f¹ f¹³ latt, which omit it. Cf. Metzger 1994: 87–88.

10:2. Although Metzger and Wikgren see the reference to καὶ προσελθόντες Φαρισαῖοι (lit. "and the Pharisees having come to") and its variants as an intrusion into the text from the parallel in Matt. 19:3, it should probably be retained (see discussion in Metzger 1994: 88).

10:3. ὁ δὲ ἀποκριθείς is lit. "but he having answered."

10:7. There is great uncertainty as to whether "and shall be joined to his wife" belongs to the original text. Cf. Metzger 1994: 88–89.

10:9. The term "joined together" (συνέζευξεν) draws on the imagery of two animals in a "yoke" (ζεῦγος) together.

---

permitted? What about physical abuse of a wife and sexual abuse of children? In such cases, is divorce permissible? (I know of a pastor who, while counseling a woman whose husband was physically abusing her, suddenly had his counseling come to an end when the woman's husband killed her.) One should not expect in the twenty-two words of Mark 10:11–12 a ruling that can cover every hypothetical situation that might present itself. In light of the frequency of divorce today, should we not, like Jesus, emphasize the permanency of marriage in the divine plan rather than seeking "good reasons for divorce"? For those contemplating divorce, it is important to consider, How will I explain to a holy and righteous God why I chose to divorce my husband/wife despite Jesus's teachings in 10:11–12? There are instances, I believe, where divorce is a "less worse" alternative, but every divorce witnesses to a failure of the divine purpose in marriage, and surely the burden of proof must always rest with those claiming that their situation constitutes an exception to 10:11–12.

J. Jesus Blesses the Children (10:13–16)

Jesus's blessing of the children is loosely associated with Jesus's teaching on divorce (10:1–12) by the fact that marriage commonly leads to children. Thus the placement of these two traditions together is fairly logical, even though there is no clear geographical or chronological tie between them (Reploh 1969: 186). The only connection between 10:13–16 and 10:1–12 is a simple "and" (καί, *kai*), and the bringing of children to Jesus for blessing does not fit particularly well the "house" of 10:10 (contra Gundry 1993: 546). Whether it was Mark or the pre-Markan tradition (Best 1976a: 119–27) that first brought these two traditions and 10:17–25 (or 31) together is uncertain. The former is favored by the theme of discipleship found in 9:33–50; 10:2–12, 13–16, 17–32, and 35–45.

There are a number of parallels between the present account and 9:35–37, such as the references to child/children (παιδίον, *paidion*; 9:36, 37, and 10:13) and above all the rare expression "put his arms around" (ἐναγκαλισάμενος, *enankalisamenos*, found only in 9:36 and 10:16 in the NT). There is no reason, however, to see these two accounts as doublets of a single event (Evans 2001: 91). Their similar vocabulary is probably due to the "Markanizing" of the two traditions by the evangelist. As it now stands, 10:13–16 is best classified as a pronouncement story (Bultmann 1968: 32; Stein 2001: 181). It is associated with what follows (10:17–22 and 23–31) by the common theme of entrance into eternal life/the kingdom of God (10:14–15, 17, 23, 24, 25; cf. also 9:43–47).[1] The hand of Mark is most frequently seen in the "for" (γάρ, *gar*) explanatory clause at the end of 10:14 (Best 1981: 106–7; contra Pesch 1980b: 132; Pryke 1978: 18, 144, 165). Yet almost all the Markan γάρ explanatory clauses occur in narrative portions of Mark (see 1:16–18) and not in the sayings material. Explanatory γάρ clauses found in the sayings of Jesus are almost always traditional and even dominical (cf. 1:38; 7:21, 27; 9:39; 10:27; 12:44; 13:11). Few scholars dispute the traditional nature of 10:13–16 (Witherington 2001: 278), although the fact that 10:15 is found in a different location in Matthew (18:3; cf. also John 3:3, 5) and seems to interrupt the transition from 10:14 to 10:16 suggest that it may have originally existed as an independent saying (Gnilka 1979: 80; Best 1986: 88–92; Witherington 2001: 278; contra Gundry 1993: 548–49).

In the history of the church this passage has often been used to support the practice of infant baptism (Jeremias 1960: 48–55). There is no hint in the

---

1. In Gos. Thom. 22 (cf. also 46) we have a heavily gnosticized parallel of the present passage that seems to borrow additional elements from Matt. 23:25–26; Mark 9:43–47; John 8:23; Gal. 3:28; and Eph. 2:15 (Evans 2001: 91–92).

account, however, that for Mark the issue at hand involved whether infants should be baptized. The question of whether infants should be baptized arose later (Beasley-Murray 1962: 320–29; Best 1976a: 130–31; Hooker 1991: 238; cf., however, A. Lane 2004).

Exegesis and Exposition

¹³And they were bringing children to him in order that he might touch them, but the disciples rebuked ⌜them⌝. ¹⁴But Jesus, having seen [this], became indignant and said to them, "Allow the children to come to me. Stop forbidding them, for to such as these belongs the kingdom of God. ¹⁵Truly, I say to you, whoever does not receive the kingdom of God like a child will never enter into it." ¹⁶And having put his arms around them [and] having placed his hands upon them, he was blessing [them].

10:13–14 The account begins abruptly with an impersonal plural, "they were bringing" (προσέφερον, *prosepheron*; Best 1981: 106; see 1:21–22). In light of the disciples' rebuke of this action, the verb "were bringing" is best understood as a conative/tendential imperfect—"were trying to bring" (Gundry 1993: 544; France 2002: 395). Their purpose is to have Jesus bless the children (10:16; cf. Gen. 48:14), not heal them (as in Mark 1:41; 3:10; 5:28–31; 6:56; 7:33; 8:22). The age of the children is not given, but the same term (παιδίον, *paidion*) is used of a twelve-year-old child in 5:41–42 and an eight-day-old child in Gen. 17:12 LXX. The verb "bring" is frequently used of leading someone (Matt. 4:24; 8:16; 9:32; 14:35; Mark 2:4; cf. 9:17) or something (a donkey, Mark 11:7) and not necessarily carrying them. The strongest support for the view that they were infants (βρέφη, *brephē*) is that the parallel in Luke 18:15 uses this term βρέφη to describe the children and then uses παιδία/παιδίον in 18:16 and 17 (cf. also Gos. Thom. 22, which refers to nursing children in its apparent parallel). "Allow the children to come to me," however, may imply that the children are able to come by themselves to Jesus (Blinzler 1969: 42).

The disciples' rebuke is most likely directed to the parents ("them" [αὐτοῖς, *autois*]) rather than the children (contra J. Edwards 2002: 306). No reason is given as to why the disciples sought to keep the parents from bringing their children to Jesus. Some suggestions are that they thought they would be disruptive and cause a distraction (Evans 2001: 93); children were thought of as less important than adults (Witherington 2001: 279; cf. *m. 'Abot.* 3.11; 4.20); the disciples thought that they possessed exclusive access to Jesus and were to serve as intermediaries (cf. Hooker 1991: 238). For Mark, it was not necessary to explain this to his readers in order to emphasize the point of the passage. If any of these explanations is correct and the incident recorded in 10:13 occurred after that of 9:33–37, this reveals once again the dullness of the disciples and their inability to understand the implications of true discipleship (France 2002: 396).

Mark 10:14 reveals Jesus's great love of children (cf. 5:41–43; 9:36–37, 42). He "became indignant" (ἠγανάκτησεν, ēganaktēsen; cf. 1:43; 3:6; 8:12, 17–21; and 9:19 for earlier displays of Jesus's emotion and exasperation) at the disciples' attitude toward them and orders them to "stop forbidding" (μὴ κωλύετε, mē kōlyete) parents from bringing them to him. The verb is a present imperative of negation (cf. 9:39) that orders them to cease hindering the parents who sought to bring their children to Jesus. Although "to such" can be interpreted "to these children [and not just adults]" belongs (lit. "is") the kingdom of God, it is best to interpret it as "to people like these children," to such a class or group of people like this, as 10:15 suggests (Best 1981: 107; Witherington 2001: 279). It is uncertain what characteristic Jesus is appealing to in these children that results in their possession of the kingdom of God (Blinzler 1969: 43–45). Matthew suggests that it involves humbling oneself (18:3–4, i.e., being poor in spirit [cf. the wording of Matt. 5:3b with 19:14c]). Other suggestions include receiving the kingdom of God as one receives a child or receiving the kingdom of God simply, graciously, humbly, as children frequently receive things (Best 1981: 107).

Mark's own understanding of what the characteristic(s) of such a class of people described in 10:14 involves must be understood in the context of 10:15. It involves how children receive the kingdom of God. The importance of 10:15 in the present account is witnessed to by the introductory "Truly" (ἀμήν, amēn; see 3:28–30) and by the fact that it explains why the kingdom of God belongs to childlike individuals in 10:14. In the present verse, a child's behavior serves as the model for adult behavior in respect to entering the kingdom of God (Gundry 1993: 545). Unfortunately, what it means to receive the kingdom of God as a child (ὡς παιδίον, hōs paidion) is not self-evident. Numerous suggestions have been made as to the point of the "childlike" analogy (Via 1985: 129). According to one interpretation, it means that people are to receive the kingdom of God as they receive a child. This view understands παιδίον as the direct object of the implied verb "receive." Generally this interpretation involves a romanticizing of children as innocent and/or precious that fits our present day but not the first century (Hooker 1991: 239). Such common practices as child exposure (P.Oxy. 744.8–10: "If you bear a child, if it is a boy, let it be; if it is a girl, expose it"), and the general view in Judaism that male children could not lead a holy life until they were entrusted with the Law at their thirteenth year (when they were bar mitzvahed) make such an interpretation unlikely. Thus the analogy of receiving the most precious and valuable possession, the kingdom of God, with receiving a child seems anachronistic. The most likely interpretation is that people are to receive the kingdom of God as children receive things (Best 1981: 107–8; France 2002: 397–98), that is, without questioning, without presumption of one's self-importance, in simple obedience (Evans 2001: 94), in humility and faith/trust (Hooker 1991: 239; Gundry 1993: 550–51), in helplessness (J. Edwards 2002: 307). They are to receive the kingdom as

10:15

children receive a gift.[2] The reference to "receiving" (δέξηται, *dexētai*) the kingdom of God alludes to receiving the offer of the kingdom of God through repentance and faith (1:15). One receives the kingdom now in the present time, but "entering it" (εἰσέλθῃ, *eiselthē*) lies in the future. This illustrates well the "already now–not yet" dimension of the kingdom. The long-awaited kingdom has come in the ministry of Jesus, and it must be received "now" (cf. 2 Cor. 6:2). Its presence and benefits are to be experienced now, even though its consummation still lies in the future. Thus one receives the kingdom that Jesus initiated at the present time and lives already now in the power of its firstfruits (the Spirit), which is the "earnest" or "guarantee" of the kingdom's future realization (cf. 2 Cor. 1:22; 5:5; Eph. 1:14). See 1:15.

The importance of receiving the kingdom or reign of God now is emphasized by the following statement that if one does not receive the kingdom of God now with the humble simplicity and faith of a child, one will not in any way enter that reign in the future (Marcus 1986a: 672–74).[3] This subjunctive of emphatic negation (οὐ μὴ εἰσέλθῃ, *ou mē eiselthē*) is the strongest possible negation in Greek. Thus the translation "He/she will never enter it" does not adequately reveal the forcefulness of the statement. Something like "There is no way in the world that he/she will ever enter it" expresses the meaning of the text better.

10:16   The account ends with a parabolic act of Jesus (Stein 1994b: 25–26) illustrating the truth of 10:14–15. Jesus goes beyond the expectations of those who led their children to him by putting his arms around them and blessing them. Mark emphasizes Jesus's blessing of the children by using an intensive form of the verb "bless" (κατευλόγει, *kateulogei*) not found elsewhere in the NT. The participial phrase "putting his hands upon them" describes the manner in which the blessing was administered. For other examples where the laying on of hands involved either healing or blessing, see 5:21–24a.

Summary

There have been numerous suggestions as to what Mark is seeking to teach in this passage. Some of these include a criticism of the narrowness of church leaders toward children, exclusivistic attitudes of superiority by some church leaders, denying baptism to children (cf. Hooker 1991: 239), and a concern for the weak and vulnerable within the church (Witherington 2001: 280). Others suggest that the Markan emphasis falls upon the understanding of what is involved in discipleship and is not about children at all (Blinzler 1969: 52; contra Reploh 1969: 190). This seems to be correct,

---

2. Other suggestions as to the point of the childlike analogy include modesty, dependence, trustfulness, simplicity, unconditionality (Witherington 2001: 279–80), with "freshness," and so on. See Via 1985: 129–32 for a helpful discussion.

3. There is no need to choose between seeing the kingdom of God as a "reign" or a "realm." The future reign involves a realm, but here the dynamic dimension of the "reign" of God seems to be dominant.

but here too there is a difference of opinion. Is the emphasis on what is involved in becoming a disciple (Via 1985: 128–29) or in what is involved in living out the life of discipleship (Best 1976a: 123)? The terminology of "receiving" and "entering" in 10:16 suggests that the issue at hand involves primarily what it means to become a disciple of Jesus. The theme of the following account (10:17–31), which involves inheriting eternal life (see esp. 10:17, 23–26, 30) and entering the kingdom of God (10:23) supports this understanding. Mark emphasizes that to receive/enter the kingdom of God, one must do so as children do: receive God's offer of the kingdom in humility and simple faith.

Another Markan emphasis in the passage involves the dullness of the disciples. In 9:36–37 Jesus used the examples of receiving a child (who possessed low status in first-century society) to illustrate attaining great status in the kingdom of God. Our present passage reveals that the disciples failed to understand this teaching. The very "children" whom in 9:36–37 the disciples were encouraged to receive they are now seeking to send away and prevent from coming to Jesus. Whether this is the primary emphasis in the passage (so France 2002: 395) is debatable, but the Markan emphasis on the disciples' dullness is clearly stressed in 10:13–16.

One other Markan emphasis should be noted in the present account. It involves the authority of the one who states without qualification or hesitation that one must become like a child if one wants to enter the kingdom of God. "With an authority such as only God can claim, [Jesus] promises the Kingdom to those whose faith resembles the empty hand of a beggar" (Schweizer 1970: 207). Who is this Jesus who speaks so dogmatically on God's behalf? Who is this Jesus who equates receiving the kingdom of God with coming to him? For Mark and his readers, the one who speaks this way is none other than the Christ, the Son of God (1:1).

Additional Note

10:13. The reading "them" (αὐτοῖς) in ℵ B C L Δ Ψ is to be preferred over "those who were bringing [the children]" in A D W Θ f¹ f¹³ lat. See Metzger 1994: 89.

K. Jesus, the Rich Man, and Eternal Life (10:17–31)

The present account consists of four distinct subsections: the story of the rich man who came to Jesus (10:17–22), Jesus's teaching about riches (10:23–27), the promise of reward for following Jesus (10:28–30), and a concluding proverb (10:31). This makes a simple classification of the account difficult, if not impossible. In the Synoptic Gospels all four subsections are found in the same order (cf. Matt. 19:16–30 and Luke 18:18–30) and in the same context. The only difference is that Matthew places the parable of the laborers of the vineyard (Matt. 20:1–16) between this account and Jesus's third passion prediction (Mark 10:32–34; Matt. 20:17–19; Luke 18:31–34). Matthew may have inserted this here because of the parable's similar ending (cf. Mark 10:31/Matt. 19:30 with Matt. 20:16). A few scholars argue that these four sections came to Mark essentially as a unity and reflect a single incident in the life of Jesus (V. Taylor 1952: 425), but most believe that Mark was the first to bring them all together (Schweizer 1970: 209–10; Pesch 1980b: 135; Best 1981: 112–13; Evans 2001: 92–93). Although most scholars agree that 10:17–22 came to Mark as a unit and that 10:23–27 and 10:28–30 consist of traditional and for the most part dominical materials, their placement, especially that of 10:28–30, is probably Markan (Cranfield 1959: 325–26; Gnilka 1979: 91; Best 1981: 113). The placement of Jesus's proverb (10:31), which seems to have been a free-floating tradition (cf. Matt. 20:16; Luke 13:30; also Mark 9:35; Matt. 20:8; Gos. Thom. 4), is almost certainly due to Mark (V. Taylor 1952: 433).

In its present context, the account continues the theme of discipleship and entrance into the kingdom of God, which appears after the second passion prediction in 9:33–10:16. The present story of the rich man whose wealth proved an insurmountable hurdle for following Jesus in simple, childlike faith (Evans 2001: 91; France 2002: 399) serves as a stark contrast to the previous example of the childlike faith that leaves everything in order to receive/enter the kingdom of God (10:13–16).

Mark's own hand is seen most clearly on the macrolevel in his organization of these materials into the framework of passion prediction, disciple error, and discipleship teachings found in 8:31–10:52. The present account concludes the second block of discipleship teaching begun in 9:35 (see 8:22–10:52). On the microlevel Mark's hand is seen in the opening seam (10:17a) connecting this passage with the preceding context (Pryke 1978: 18, 144, 165). The rest of 10:17–22 betrays little evidence of the evangelist's editorial work (Best 1981: 110) other than the explanatory "for" (γάρ, *gar*) clause (10:22b). Probably 10:23a and 24a are also Markan, whereas the rest of 10:23–25 is likely traditional (Gnilka 1979: 84; Best 1981: 111; contra Evans 2001: 91). Although 10:26a and 27a reflect Mark's own wording, the rest of these verses and 10:28–31 are most likely traditional, except for "for my sake and for the gospel" (10:29), which recalls 8:35 and looks Markan (contra Best 1981: 113–14, who attributes vv. 28 and 31 to Mark). The location of 10:28–31 after 10:17–27 is probably due to Mark.

Exegesis and Exposition

¹⁷And as he was proceeding on the way, a man ran up and knelt before him [and] began to ask him, "Good Teacher, what must I do in order that I may inherit eternal life?" ¹⁸And Jesus said to him, "Why do you call me good? No one is good except God alone. ¹⁹You know the commandments: Do not murder; do not commit adultery; do not steal; do not give false testimony; ⌜do not defraud;⌝ honor your father and mother." ²⁰And he said to him, "Teacher, all these things I have kept from my youth." ²¹And Jesus, having looked at him, loved him and said to him, "One thing you lack. Go—whatever you have, sell and give to the poor, and you will have treasure in heaven—and come, follow me." ⌜ ⌝ ²²And he became sad at this saying [and] went away grieving, for he had many possessions.

²³And having looked around, Jesus says to his disciples, "How difficult it will be for those having riches to enter into the kingdom of God!" ²⁴And the disciples were amazed at his words, but Jesus again says to them in reply, "Children, how difficult it is ⌜ ⌝ to enter the kingdom of God. ²⁵It is easier for a ⌜camel⌝ to go through the eye of a needle than for a rich man to enter into the kingdom of God." ²⁶And they were exceedingly astonished, saying to ⌜themselves⌝, "Then who can be saved?" ²⁷Having looked at them, Jesus says, "For humans [it is] impossible, but not for God. All things [are] possible for God."

²⁸Peter began to say to him, "Look, we have left everything and have followed you." ²⁹Jesus said, "Truly I say to you, there is no one who has left house or brothers or sisters or mother or father or children or fields for my sake and for the gospel, ³⁰who will not receive a hundred times more now in this time houses and brothers and sisters and mothers and children and fields with persecutions and in the coming age—eternal life. ³¹But many [of those who are] first shall be last, and the last [shall be] first."

"As he was proceeding on the way" (καὶ ἐκπορευομένου αὐτοῦ εἰς ὁδόν, *kai* **10:17–18** *ekporeuomenou autou eis hodon*) probably refers back to Jesus's entrance into a house in 10:10 (Gundry 1993: 552) because all the other uses of the verb "proceeding/going out" (ἐκπορεύομαι) in Mark involve a change of location (cf. 1:5; 6:11; 7:15–23; 10:46; 11:19; 13:1). The "way" (ὁδόν) here denotes more than going on a journey. Here it bears the nuance of the "way" to Jerusalem (10:32) and the cross. As he proceeds, Jesus is approached by a certain man who is described as "rich," that is, having many possessions (ἔχων κτή-ματα πολλά, *echōn ktēmata polla*; 10:22). In Matthew, he is also described as "young" (νεανίσκος, *neaniskos*; 19:20, 22), and in Luke as a "ruler" (ἄρχων, *archōn*; 18:18)—hence the traditional title "the rich young ruler." The address "Teacher" occurs frequently in Mark (see 4:37–38), but "Good Teacher" is unusual, and no clear parallels have been found in the first or previous centuries (Evans 2001: 95). The use of "Good Teacher" shows the young man's respect for Jesus, as well as his sincerity. That Jesus saw him as sincere is indicated in 10:21a (France 2002: 403; contra Nineham 1963: 270). The rich man's concern is a good one and involves his desire to be sure that he possesses eternal life, and his eagerness to know this is revealed by his (literally) running to Jesus and kneeling (cf. 1:40).

It is incorrect to see in the rich man's question, "What must I do in order that I may inherit eternal life?" (τί ποιήσω ἵνα ζωὴν αἰώνιον κληρονομήσω; *ti poiēsō hina zōēn aiōnion klēronomēsō?*), an attempt on his part to earn or merit salvation. The question is not treated negatively by Jesus any more than the question on this same issue, "What shall we do?" (τί ποιήσωμεν; *ti poiēsōmen?* the same Greek term), is understood negatively by Peter in Acts 2:37 (cf. also 16:30: τί με δεῖ ποιεῖν ἵνα σωθῶ; *ti me dei poiein hina sōthō?*). In Mark the expressions "inheriting eternal life" (10:17), "having treasure in heaven" (10:21), "entering the kingdom of God" (10:23), and being "saved" (10:26) are essentially synonyms. Compare also 9:45 ("to enter into life") and 47 ("to enter the kingdom of God"). In John 3:3, 5 and 3:15–16 entering the kingdom of God and inheriting eternal life are also understood as synonyms. The reference to "eternal life" in Mark 10:17 and 30 and "follow" in 10:21 and 28 may form a chiasmus (Lang 1976: 329).

Jesus's response in 10:18, "Why do you call me good? No one is good except God alone" (τί με λέγεις ἀγαθόν; οὐδεὶς ἀγαθὸς εἰ μὴ εἷς ὁ θεός, *ti me legeis agathon? oudeis agathos ei mē heis ho theos*) has troubled exegetes through the centuries. The emphatic position of "me" (με) in the sentence heightens the problem—"Why *me* do you call good?" Matthew (19:17) has sought to ameliorate the problem by rewording the question, "Why do you ask me concerning what is good?" But the difficulty of the Markan saying guarantees its more authentic nature. What Jesus objects to in the rich man's address is unclear. (1) Is he objecting to the application of the designation "good" in the sense of "perfect" to any human being, even himself (i.e., ultimate goodness and perfection belong to God the Father alone)? In other words, is he seeking to have the man rethink the idea of goodness, since there is no one that is ultimately good/righteous (Rom. 3:10) but God? Is he saying that one should focus one's attention upon God, without in any way implying that he (Jesus) himself is not good (Evans 2001: 96)? (2) Is he probing the sincerity of the man's address? (3) Is it possible that Jesus is denying that he is good, because like any other human he too has sinned and fallen short (Rom. 3:23)? Nowhere in the rest of the NT, however, is sin attributed to Jesus (2 Cor. 5:21; Heb. 4:15; 7:26; 1 Pet. 1:19; 2:22; etc.), and clearly Mark, at least, did not understand Jesus's response as a confession of personal sin (Nineham 1963: 274; Hooker 1991: 241). (4) Or is Jesus, far from acknowledging that he is not good, pointing out that the logical conclusion of the man's correct address is to acknowledge his own divine goodness (Gundry 1993: 553)? The first suggestion is more likely, and Jesus is contrasting God's absolute goodness to his own, which was subject to growth (V. Taylor 1952: 427; cf. Banks 1975: 160–61). There is no basis for thinking that Jesus's response involved an initial negative attitude toward the man that changed and became positive in 10:21 (contra Donahue and Harrington 2002: 303).

It is evident from his reply to the young man that Jesus believed that the true keeping of the Law in the sense and manner that God intended would result in eternal life. (Cf. the parallel in Luke 10:25–28.) A legalistic interpretation of Jesus's words in 10:19 misinterprets his understanding of God's commandments. To love the Lord God with all one's heart, soul, mind, and strength (Mark 12:30) involves trusting God's grace. It involves trusting in the sacrificial death of Jesus (10:45; 14:24), even as OT believers trusted in the grace of God provided through the Day of Atonement and the OT sacrifices. We should not read into this passage the controversies that Paul addressed in Romans and Galatians (cf. also Acts 15).

10:19–22

Jesus quotes five of the Ten Commandments, to which he adds "do not defraud" (μὴ ἀποστερήσῃς, mē apostereses). Because the command not to covet is missing from Jesus's list of commandments, some have suggested that "do not defraud" is the equivalent of "do not covet." It is more likely, however, that it should be understood as a variant of "do not steal" (V. Taylor 1952: 428; France 2002: 402).[1] For the most part, the order of the commandments follows Exod. 20: do not murder, do not commit adultery, do not steal, and do not give false witness are commandments six through nine. Jesus completes the list with honor your father and mother, which is the fifth commandment.[2] The placement of honoring parents (cf. Mark 7:10) last may be due to it being associated with long life (Exod. 20:12), which ties closely with the rich man's desire for eternal life in Mark 10:17 (cf. Gundry 1993: 561). For Jesus's own understanding of the implications of these commandments, one must read Matt. 5:21–48, and it is quite likely that this understanding was widespread in the early Christian community. Speculation as to why other commandments were omitted is of little value (contra Witherington 2001: 282). The man's reply that he has kept all these commandments from his youth[3] is not made arrogantly (cf. Phil. 3:6). In light of his having come to Jesus uncertain of his future, his response assumes that he lacks something. He lacks both eternal life and a proper understanding of what it means to keep the commandments. Nothing should be made of his addressing Jesus in 10:20 as "Teacher," since

---

1. For the less likely view that it alludes to the teachings on divorce in Exod. 21:10 and Jesus's discussion on the subject in 10:2–9, cf. Evans 2001: 97.

2. The order of the first four commandments mentioned by Jesus (murder, adultery, stealing, bearing false witness) follows the Hebrew OT, not the LXX (adultery, stealing, murder, bearing false witness). This supports the authenticity of 10:19.

3. This seems to imply that the rich man was not "young" (but cf. Matt. 19:20, 22).

this was the normal way of addressing him, and Jesus's response (10:18) to the earlier address of "Good Teacher" would no doubt have discouraged his being addressed like this again.

In 10:21, Jesus does not enter into an elaborate discussion of what it truly means to keep the commandments but instead zeroes in on the specific issue that reveals the man's basic problem. He lacks "one" thing. This "one thing" (ἕν, *hen*) stands in the emphatic position in the sentence and contrasts with "all these things" (ταῦτα πάντα, *tauta panta*) in the young man's reply (10:20). He lacks obedience to the first table of the Ten Commandments. He loves his riches more than God. Thus Jesus bids him to get rid of what is keeping him from God and from inheriting eternal life by "selling it all" (ὅσα ἔχεις πώλησον, *hosa echeis pōlēson*; the aorist tense may imply an act of divesting himself of his possessions), giving ("it all" is implied) to the poor, and "following" (ἀκολούθει, *akolouthei*) Jesus. In so doing, he would be removing what is "scandalizing" him (9:43–47) and keeping him from entering the kingdom of God (9:47; 10:23–25). In 8:34, Mark has already shown what following Jesus means (cf. 1:17–18, 20; 2:14; 9:38; also 10:52; 15:41) and will do so again later in the account (10:28). The command of Jesus to the rich man is best understood not as a universal command for all potential followers, as such passages as 15:42–46; Luke 8:1–3; 19:1–10; Acts 5:3–4; 28:30–31 indicate.[4] It is best understood as a particular teaching, directed to this particular situation, indicating for the rich man what repentance (1:15) would entail for him. Jesus singles out the main problem that keeps the man from eternal life and the kingdom (W. Lane 1974: 367; Gundry 1993: 563). He needs to repent, and the key sin that he needs to repent of is his greater love for riches than for God. In 10:29 other areas that could possibly stand in the way of following Jesus are mentioned, and this supports the view that Jesus focused on the issue of the man's wealth because he knew that this was his particular problem. The true test of the man's relationship to God is revealed in his response to Jesus's invitation and command, "Sell all, give to the poor, and follow me."[5] The former two commands do not involve meritorious service but rather describe for this man the essence of repentance. For the twofold nature of discipleship that involves both a negative and a positive demand, compare 1:15 (repent and believe; cf. also Acts 20:21; Heb. 6:1), 18 (left nets and followed), 20 (left father and followed), 8:34 (deny self

4. The command to sell all and give to the poor contrasts with the demands of the Qumran community, which involved selling all and giving it to the community. Cf. Josephus, *J.W.* 2.8.3 §122; 1QS 1.11–13; 6.13–23. Contrast, however, the rabbinic teaching that forbade giving away all one's possessions (Hengel 1974: 20–23; cf. *m. ʿArak.* 8.4; *b. Ketub.* 50a; *b. Taʿan.* 24a).

5. Contra T. Schmidt 1987: 111, who argues that it was not the rich man's love of his possessions that was the problem but rather the fact that he had possessions. This loses sight of the fact that the Markan emphasis in 10:21 is not on the verbs "sell" and "give" but on the verb "follow" (W. Lane 1974: 368). The least important part of Jesus's command involves "giving to the poor," for this is not mentioned in 10:23ff. or 28. Contrast Crossley (2005: 399): "The obvious must not be avoided: in a world of extreme social and economic inequality Jesus damned the rich."

and take up cross/follow); 10:28 (left everything and followed); also Acts 2:38 (repent and be baptized).

Mark poignantly describes the result of the man's not following Jesus, despite the offer of treasure in heaven in 10:22. He became "sad" (στυγνάσας, *stygnasas*; lit. "having become sad"; in the NT only here and Matt. 16:3, where it describes the weather as "gloomy") and departed grieving, experiencing already now separation from God and his kingdom. Despite his not altogether superficial piety (10:20) and despite his being loved[6] by Jesus (10:21), he does not follow him and goes away sorrowful, for he knows that he has chosen earthly riches over the heavenly riches (10:21)[7] of eternal life (10:17, 23). (There does not seem to be any significant difference between the terms used for wealth [κτήματα (*ktēmata*), χρήματα (*chrēmata*), and πλούσιον (*plousion*)] in 10:22, 23, and 25 [contra J. Edwards 2002: 313–14].) Contrary to the thinking of this world, the rich man's "many possessions" (κτήματα πολλά, 10:22), far from being a blessing and good fortune for the rich man, were rather a curse that kept him from eternal life and the kingdom of God.

Jesus's "looking around" (περιβλεψάμενος, *periblepsamenos*) indicates that what he is about to say is a response to the unspoken thoughts of the disciples. (For similar private instruction to the disciples, cf. 4:10–12, 34; 7:17–23; 10:10–12.) His comment as to the difficulty of those with riches entering (lit. "How difficultly those having riches shall enter") the kingdom of God indicates that his instruction to the rich man should not be interpreted as a challenge to enter into a new level of discipleship in his relationship with God. The issue is not becoming "sanctified" or being "baptized by the Spirit" after one's experience of salvation. It is not entering into a "deeper spiritual life," or "receiving Jesus as Lord" after receiving him as "Savior," or "placing Jesus on the throne of their heart," and so on. What is at stake is entering the kingdom of God or not entering it (10:24), receiving eternal life or not receiving it (10:17), being saved or not being saved (10:26). The issue here is not ethical in nature but soteriological. The man kept his possessions and this world but lost his life (8:36; cf. also 4:19), for one cannot serve God and things (Matt. 6:24; Luke 16:13). He failed to exchange his riches for the pearl of great price (Matt. 13:45–46). The disciples' amazement at Jesus's words reflects the contemporary view of that day (and tragically often among Christians today) that wealth and prosperity are usually an indication of God's favor and blessing.[8] For this man, however, they were a curse leading to his damnation.

Jesus's use of the term "children" (τέκνα, *tekna*; 10:24) in addressing the disciples is unique (but cf. 2:5; Luke 16:25) and may betray an affectionate

10:23–25

---

6. It is speculative to assume that this involved a hug or caress (contra Nineham 1963: 274–75; Gundry 1993: 554).

7. For "heavenly riches" in Jewish literature, cf. Tob. 4:8–9; Ps. Sol. 9.5; Sir. 29:10–12; 2 Esd. 7:77; in the NT, cf. Matt. 6:19–21; Luke 12:21, 33–34; 1 Tim. 6:17–19.

8. To be sure, there is a tradition in the Psalms and in the Beatitudes of Jesus that identifies the humble poor with the pious and the haughty rich with the ungodly (Luke 6:20–26), but all too often religious people neglect such teaching for a gospel that promises health and wealth.

form of address (Gundry 1993: 556; France 2002: 404). The difficulty of entering the kingdom of God is repeated in 10:24 and, although not stated, "for a rich man" is assumed. This is evident from 10:25, where "a rich man" (πλούσιον, *plousion*) is repeated. Numerous copyists understood 10:24 in this manner and added "for those who trust in riches" (see additional note on 10:24). Although these words are not part of the original Markan text, it is correct to understand 10:24 as implying "for a rich man" because this verse is sandwiched between two statements (10:23 and 25) that speak of the difficulty of a rich man entering the kingdom of God. The implications of Jesus's teaching in 10:23–25, of course, go far beyond the issue of riches. To enter the kingdom of God, one must give up anything that stands in the way (Via 1985: 137; cf. 9:43–47).

In describing the great difficulty of entering the kingdom of God, Jesus uses a hyperbolic comparison (contra Crossley 2005: 399). (For a similar Greek construction [easier . . . than, εὐκοπώτερον . . . ἤ, *eukopōteron . . . ē*], cf. Luke 16:17.) It is easier for a camel to go through the eye of a needle than for a rich man to enter the kingdom of God. The authenticity of this saying is supported by a very similar rabbinic saying involving "an elephant going through the eye of a needle" (cf. *b. Ber.* 55b; cf. also *b. B. Meṣiʿa* 38b). That hyperbole was a favorite literary form Jesus used in teaching (Stein 1990: 143–210) also supports the authenticity of the saying. The difficulty of taking these words literally is evident. Since some rich people do enter the kingdom of God whereas a camel, the largest land animal native to Palestine, cannot go through the eye of a needle (the smallest hole imaginable), numerous, often fanciful interpretations have arisen. The best-known tend either to reduce the camel to a "rope" or to enlarge the eye of the needle to a "gate." The former argues that the present term "camel" (κάμηλον, *kamēlon*) is a mistranslation of the original term "cable" or "rope" (κάμιλον, *kamilon*). This, however, while lessening the degree of hyperbole, nevertheless still leaves a literally impossible comparison, for a "rope" cannot pass through the eye of a needle. Another attempted solution involves the claim that the "Eye of a Needle" was the name of a gate in Jerusalem through which a camel could proceed only with great difficulty, but evidence for such a gate has never been found (Gundry 1993: 565), and the parallel rabbinic saying about an elephant going through the eye of a needle refutes such an interpretation. Once one becomes aware of the frequent appearance of hyperbole in Jesus's teachings, one can understand 10:25 as an emphatic warning about the terrible obstacle that riches can present to entering the kingdom of God.

10:26–30   The hyperbolic statement of Jesus in 10:25 resulted in the disciples being "exceedingly astonished" (περισσῶς ἐξεπλήσσοντο, *perissōs exeplēssonto*; see 1:21–22). If it is impossible for a pious rich man to be saved when he possesses the leisure and means to perform various charitable acts and his wealth apparently witnesses to God's blessing and favor (Evans 2001: 101; Donahue and Harrington 2002: 304–5), how can anyone be saved? The term "saved" (σωθῆναι, *sōthēnai*;

cf. 8:35; 13:13) is synonymous with inheriting eternal life, having treasure in heaven, and entering the kingdom of God (10:17, 21, 23). Once again looking at the disciples (cf. 10:23), Jesus now responds with an example of antithetical parallelism (10:27b–c) and a proverb (10:27d). Probably such passages as Gen. 18:14; Job 42:2; and Zech. 8:6 form the context for the proverb.

Exactly what it is that makes salvation impossible for humans but not for God (10:27; cf. 14:36) is unclear. To be sure, Jesus is referring to the "gift" character of salvation, but what exactly is the nature of this gift? Is Jesus arguing that human efforts cannot merit salvation but God can graciously bestow it as a gift (Hooker 1991: 243)? In other words, should we see in these verses the Pauline teaching of justification as a gift of God through faith alone (cf. Eph. 2:8–9)? Or does the issue involve the gift of prevenient grace that enables humans, and especially the rich, to sell all that they have, give to the poor, and follow Jesus—that is, to repent and believe (Gundry 1993: 566; J. Edwards 2002: 315)? The former involves the inability of humans to merit salvation; the latter involves the human inability to respond to God's invitation. The former is favored by the disciples' assumption that the rich man is just the kind of person who would most likely be saved because of his greater ability to do good works. The latter interpretation is favored by the special difficulty that a rich man has of being saved because of his wealth and by Peter's response in 10:28. Unfortunately, Mark does not provide enough information to determine which, if either, of these interpretations is closer to his understanding. He is simply content to emphasize to his readers that salvation involves God's gracious activity without being specific.

Peter's words in 10:28 stand in sharp contrast to the actions of the rich man. The disciples have indeed left everything and "followed" (note the perfect tense of ἠκολουθήκαμεν, *ēkolouthēkamen*) Jesus (1:16–20). Although Peter and Andrew still possessed a home (1:29) and a boat (3:9; 4:1, 36; cf. John 21:3), their commitment to Jesus was total. Whatever Jesus told them to leave, they left (1:17–18) in following him. In response, Jesus gives an emphatic word of reassurance (note the "Truly" [ἀμήν, *amēn*]; see 3:28–30) in 10:29 that no doubt was encouraging for the readers of Mark's Gospel as well. Leaving house, brothers, sisters, and mother recalls both Jesus's own commitment (3:31–35)[9] and that of his disciples (1:18, 20; cf. also Luke 14:26; Matt. 10:37; and Luke 9:57–62; 12:49–53). "Father or children or fields" completes the list. The omission of "wife" from the list may reflect the indissoluble nature of marriage taught by Jesus in 10:2–12 (T. Schmidt 1987: 115). In light of the redactional character of the term "gospel," it is probable that "for the gospel" (ἕνεκεν τοῦ εὐαγγελίου, *heneken tou euangeliou*) and also "for my sake" (ἕνεκεν ἐμοῦ, *heneken emou*) come from the hand of the evangelist here, as in 8:35. Although it would be going too far to say that for Mark "Jesus is the gospel," they are intimately connected and inseparable.

---

9. Joseph had almost certainly already died before Jesus began his ministry (see 6:2b–3).

Those who have left the things described in 10:29 are promised all these a hundredfold in the fellowship of the church (10:30). The gaining of a new family (brothers, sisters, mothers [cf. Rom. 16:13], children [cf. Philem. 10]), and hospitality (houses and lands) already now in the present time/age is a foretaste of the greater family in the age to come (cf. T. Job 4.6–9).[10] What is gained far outweighs (a hundredfold!) even in this life ("now in this time" [νῦν ἐν τῷ καιρῷ τούτῳ, *nyn en tō kairō toutō*]) what is lost! Omitted from the second list is "fathers," due to the believer already having a heavenly Father (11:25; cf. Matt. 23:9), but Mark adds his own editorial comment, "with persecutions" (μετὰ διωγμῶν, *meta diōgmōn*). It is tempting to do a mirror reading and see in this a word of encouragement to the Markan community in the midst of the Neronian persecution (Evans 2001: 103; J. Edwards 2002: 316). However, the warning of future persecutions seems to have been an integral part of Jesus's message (8:34–38; 10:38–39; 13:9–13), and although Markan, this phrase may not have the Neronian persecution particularly in mind. The eschatological understanding of Jesus and the early church is clearly seen in 10:30 (cf. Luke 20:34–35; Matt. 12:32; 13:39–40, 49; 24:3) and follows the traditional Jewish understanding of the two ages: this time (καιρῷ) and the age (αἰῶνι, *aiōni*) to come. The duality ("now in this time") is typically Markan (Neirynck 1988: 45–53, 94–96). The high point of encouragement for the disciples comes with the final eight words of 10:30: καὶ ἐν τῷ αἰῶνι τῷ ἐρχομένῳ ζωὴν αἰώνιον, *kai en tō aiōni tō erchomenō zōēn aiōnion*, and in the coming age—eternal life. "Eternal life" teams with the same expression in 10:17 to form an *inclusio* for 10:17–30.

10:31   The account ends with a common proverb contrasting the radical difference between God's evaluation and judgment and humanity's. Using chiastic order, Jesus says that (A) the *first* (in this world's judgment) (B) will be *last* (in God's judgment), and (B′) the *last* (in this world's judgment) (A′) will be *first* (in God's judgment). The same thought in chiastic form but in reverse order is found in Matt. 20:16 and Luke 13:30. For those with eyes to see and ears to hear (Mark 4:12; 8:18), the great reversal is already taking place in Jesus's ministry (cf. Luke 3:4–6; 14:15–24; 16:19–31; etc.). Already now the kingdom has come and is bringing about a great overturning of the values of this world.

Summary

Several Markan theological emphases are found in this account. One that stands out clearly involves the teaching on what it means to become a disciple and enter the kingdom of God. This involves an exposition less on ethics than on soteriology. This is clear from the opening question, "What must I do in order that I might inherit eternal life?" (10:17). Jesus's comment on the difficulty of entering the kingdom of God (10:23) and the

---

10. Gundry (1997: 473) argues that the order in 10:29 is determined by "an ascending scale of economic value in agrarian culture," but this is questionable (cf. T. Schmidt 1992: 618n9).

references to entering the kingdom of God (10:24), being saved (10:26), and receiving eternal life (10:30) make this still clearer. In the second discipleship section of 8:31–10:52 (see 8:22–10:52), we encounter a cluster of terms used to describe the results of following Jesus. True discipleship results in eternal life (10:17, 30), treasure in heaven (10:21), entering the kingdom of God (10:23–25), and being saved (10:26). Yet the demands of discipleship are total in nature. In the present account, a rich man who possesses great piety (10:20) and is loved by Jesus (10:21) loses his soul due to his love of riches (10:22; cf. 8:35–37). Christian discipleship demands a radical reorientation of life and priorities. The example of the rich man is a continual warning that placing anything ahead of following Jesus will result in grief and eternal loss. However, following Jesus will result in reward and blessing far beyond anything that this earth provides (a hundredfold more). And this is not simply a future, "next world" hope. Although it is certainly this, already now in this present age some of those rewards and blessings can be experienced in the family and fellowship of Jesus's followers.

A strong christological emphasis can also be found in this account. The popularity and drawing power of Jesus is seen in the rich man's hurried and reverent approach to Jesus (10:17). He acknowledges by his question that Jesus is the supreme teacher on the most important subject in the world—"What must I do to inherit eternal life?" The consummate role of Jesus in human salvation is seen in that human destiny is ultimately determined by a person's relationship to him. What one does "for [his] sake," which is another way of saying "for the gospel" (10:29; cf. 8:35), ultimately determines one's eternal existence. Because of this, Jesus can make the totalitarian claim that he comes before mother, father, brothers, sisters, and children (10:29; cf. Luke 14:26). Once again the reader of the Gospel is faced with the question "Who is this man who does such things and says such things?" (cf. 4:41).

One final Markan emphasis in the passage concerns Jesus's understanding of the OT. Salvation involves keeping the OT commandments (10:19). This teaching can be found throughout the Gospels (cf. Luke 10:25–27, esp. v. 28; Matt. 5:17–20). The sharp disjunction between law, that is, keeping the commandments, and grace found in certain theological systems is not found in the present account. To truly keep the commandments and love God with all one's heart does not involve the idea of merit, for it is based on the gift of God's grace (10:27). It is based on the understanding that before the commandments came the covenant. Before Sinai came the experience of God's grace of being saved through the exodus from Egypt. Understood properly, not legalistically like the Judaizers of Acts and Galatians did, the commandments lead to life. Misunderstood as a means to earning merit, they lead to death. Yet it is not the commandments themselves that are the cause of this but rather the misunderstanding and misuse of the commandments.

Additional Notes

10:19. This command is not found in B* K W Δ Ψ f¹ f¹³ and the parallel accounts in Matthew and Luke. This may be due to the fact that it is not one of the Ten Commandments, and thus it may have appeared inappropriate to Matthew and Luke and later copyists for it to be listed along with those that are part of the Ten Commandments. I include it in the translation because of its better textual support (א A B² C D Θ lat) and the difficulty of explaining why copyists would have inserted it into a listing of some of the Ten Commandments. On the other hand, its omission can be easily understood.

10:21. A f¹ f¹³ and TR add at this point "take up your cross." However, it should not be read, as indicated by its omission in א B C D Θ Ψ lat.

10:24. Some MSS (A C D Θ f¹ f¹³; cf. also W) add "for those who trust in riches." This is best seen as a scribal attempt to soften the statement or perhaps to make it apply more directly to the context, which refers to a rich man (10:22).

10:25. A few MSS have "rope" (κάμιλον) instead of "camel" (κάμηλον), but this is clearly a later scribal attempt to ameliorate this hard saying.

10:26. The MSS א B C Δ have πρὸς αὐτόν (to him), but the reading πρὸς ἑαυτούς (to themselves; A D W Θ f¹ f¹³ lat) is more difficult and thus more likely to be original.

L. Jesus's Third Passion Prediction (10:32–34)

The third passion prediction is far more detailed than the previous two (cf. 8:31; 9:31; cf. also 9:9, 12) and contains numerous details found in the coming passion account:

> Behold, we are going up to Jerusalem (cf. 11:1)
> and the Son of Man will be delivered over (cf. 14:42–53; also 1 Cor. 11:23)
> to the chief priests and to the scribes (cf. 14:1, 10, 43, 53, 55; 15:1; also 11:18, 27–33)
> and they will condemn him to death (cf. 14:64; 15:1; also Acts 2:23)
> and deliver him over to the gentiles (cf. 15:1, 10; also Acts 2:23; 4:27–28)
> and they will mock him (cf. 15:17–20, 31–32)
> and spit upon him (cf. 14:65; 15:19)
> and scourge him (cf. 15:15; also John 19:1)
> and kill [him] (cf. 15:24; also Acts 2:23)
> after three days he will rise (cf. 16:1–2, 6; also 1 Cor. 15:4; Evans 2001: 106; Gundry 1993: 572)[1]

Because of the greater detail found in this passion prediction and its close correlation to the passion account in Mark, numerous scholars argue that it is a *vaticinia ex eventu* coming primarily from the hand of Mark (Strecker 1968: 434–35; contra Cranfield 1959: 334–35; McKinnis 1976: 89–100; Bayer 1986: 172–74). The likelihood of there having existed three passion predications such as 8:31; 9:31; and 10:33–34 circulating as independent and separate traditions, while not impossible, also raises questions (Strecker 1968: 433). There are several indications, however, that the present passion prediction contains traditional features. These include "hand over" (παραδίδωμι, *paradidōmi*), "kill" (ἀποκτενοῦσιν, *apoktenousin*) instead of "crucify," and "after three days" (μετὰ τρεῖς ἡμέρας, *meta treis hēmeras*; Best 1981: 24). There are also indications that the present passion prediction is not simply a summary based on the forthcoming Passion Narrative. These include the lack of references to the elders (14:43, 53; 15:1) and false witnesses

---

1. Some scholars see in this prophetic description various allusions to the suffering servant of Isaiah and argue for its origin going back to Jesus's own self-understanding or to the theology of the evangelist (Marcus 1992: 186–90; Watts 2000: 265–69; France 2002: 413). A stronger argument for such allusions can be found in Mark 10:45 (Watts 2000: 269–87; Witherington 2001: 288–90). However, for a succinct critique, see Hooker 1991: 248–51.

(14:57–59), the use of different terms for scourging in 10:34 (μαστιγώσουσιν, *mastigōsousin*) and in 15:15 (φραγελλώσας, *phragellōsas*), and a difference at times in the order of events.

It is possible that in the three passion predictions found in 8:31; 9:31; and 10:33–34 Mark is repeating a historical tradition (Evans 2001: 106–7; see the introduction to 8:27–33) in which Jesus prophesied of his future death and resurrection and that the tradition taught that he foretold this to his disciples on several occasions. What we have in 10:33–34 is Mark's repeating of this tradition in greater detail in light of his knowledge of the event itself.[2] This would account for both the traditional nature of the material in 10:33–34 as well as the Markan redactional elements. Within 10:32–34 the hand of the evangelist is seen most clearly in verse 32, which is traditional in the sense that Jesus did go with his disciples to Jerusalem, but its present form is due to the hand of Mark (McKinnis 1976: 82–88; Gnilka 1979: 95). This is evident from such things as "in the way" (ἐν τῇ ὁδῷ, *en tē hodō*); the imperfect periphrases ("were proceeding up" [ἦσαν ... ἀναβαίνοντες, *ēsan ... anabainontes*] and "was going ahead" [ἦν προάγων, *ēn proagōn*] [V. Taylor 1952: 45]); the reference to "following" (ἀκολουθοῦντες, *akolouthountes*; see 1:16–18); "began to say" (ἤρξατο ... λέγειν, *ērxato ... legein*; see 1:45); the theme of amazement and fear (see 1:21–22; 4:41; Pryke 1978: 166; Best 1981: 120–21).

The extent of Mark's hand in verses 33–34 is impossible to determine. That the wording and detail of these verses comes from Mark is clear, but it is difficult (impossible?) to distinguish a Markan rewording and elaboration of a traditional passion prediction from a Markan creation of such material (Stein 1991: 54).

Exegesis and Exposition

[32]And they were going up in the way to Jerusalem, and Jesus was going ahead of them. And they were amazed, and those following were afraid. And having taken aside the Twelve again, he began to tell them the things [that] were about to happen to him, [33]"Behold, we are going up to Jerusalem, and the Son of Man will be delivered over to the chief priests and to the scribes, and they will condemn him to death and deliver him over to the gentiles, [34]and they will mock him, and spit upon him, and scourge him and kill [him], and after three days he will rise."

10:32 With the specific mention of Jesus and the disciples proceeding toward Jerusalem and the clearest mention so far as to what will occur there, there is a sense that the Passion Narrative begins at this point (Hooker 1991: 244). This is heightened by the amazement and fear that these things bring about. It is doubtful that Mark's readers would have associated "going up [ἀναβαίνοντες, *anabainontes*]

---

2. Cf. Evans (2001: 106): "The third prediction of Jesus' passion bears the most obvious marks of post-Easter editing." He further comments, however, "The prediction has been edited, but it has not been created *ex nihilo*" (109).

to Jerusalem" with the idea of a religious pilgrimage (contra Pesch 1980b: 148; Best 1981: 121n6). Although numerous scholars see "the way" as a technical term (Hooker 1991: 245; France 2002: 411), there is no need to interpret it as such here (Gundry 1993: 573; see 8:27b–28). Similarly, although "going ahead" (προάγων, *proagōn*) is found in two future prophecies/promises (14:28 and 16:7), no significance should be seen in this, for the time (after the resurrection), the place (Galilee), and the purpose (meeting the disciples) associated with the verb are quite different (Gundry 1993: 574; contra Evans 2001: 107).

The exact makeup of the group proceeding with Jesus is unclear. Besides Jesus, several are mentioned: "they" (the indefinite plural of the verbs "were going up" and "were amazed"), "those following," and "the Twelve." Some interpret these as three separate groups. Others understand the above references as indicating two groups consisting of "they," that is, "the Twelve," who are "going up" and are "amazed," and "those following" (Cranfield 1959: 335; Gundry 1993: 569–70, 573; Evans 2001; 107; France 2002: 412). The main argument in favor of this involves the understanding of the second δέ (*de*) in verse 32 as adversative and thus contrasting two groups.[3] However, the first δέ in the sentence is not adversative but a continuative "and," and this weakens the argument. The third interpretation understands all three designations as referring to a single group, the Twelve (Best 1981: 120; Hooker 1991: 244–45). Yet "and those following" would be a most awkward way of referring to the same group mentioned earlier in the verse. If Mark wanted to do this, he could have written, "And Jesus was going ahead of them, and the Twelve, who were following, were amazed and afraid. And taking them aside, Jesus began to say. . . ." As a result, it is best to see Mark as describing two distinct groups in this verse: those following Jesus (οἱ ἀκολουθοῦντες, *hoi akolouthountes*), who are afraid; and the "Twelve," who are going up (ἀναβαίνοντες) to Jerusalem behind Jesus and are amazed (Bauckham 2006: 160).

The description of the "Twelve" (δώδεκα, *dōdeka*) being "amazed" (ἐθαμβοῦντο, *ethambounto*) is elsewhere associated with a sense of astonishment at what Jesus had said (1:27; 10:24), but here it involves his behavior. His sense of destiny and desire to fulfill God's will (note the divine "it is necessary" [δεῖ, *dei*] in 8:31) result in a reverential awe (France 2002: 412). On the other hand, the response of the second group does not involve a positive sense of awe, although "fear" (ἐφοβοῦντο, *ephobounto*) can have this sense (cf. 4:41; 5:33; 9:32 [?]; 11:18; 16:8), but rather a negative sense of being fearful and afraid (cf. 5:15, 36; 6:20, 50; 11:32; 12:12; McKinnis 1976: 85–86; contra Gundry 1993: 570–71; Evans 2001: 108). Their fear is due to Jesus's heading up toward Jerusalem, for as Mark's readers know, death awaits him there, and they will experience hostility there as well (Best 1981: 120). Despite the positive references to Jerusalem in 1:5 and 3:8, the negative references in 3:22 and 7:1 and the reader's knowledge of the passion tradition indicate that evil awaits Jesus and his followers in Jerusalem.

---

3. The MS tradition omitting the second δέ is very weak.

Once "again" (πάλιν, *palin*) Jesus takes the disciples aside (see 7:31) and provides them with private teaching concerning his future passion (cf. 8:27–33; 9:9–10, 30–32; also 2:18–20). Jesus's prophecy concerning "the things [that] were about to happen to him" (τὰ μέλλοντα αὐτῷ συμβαίνειν, *ta mellonta autō symbainein*) is not portrayed by Mark as coming via a revelation from God. There is no "Thus says the Lord." His direct knowledge of the future and his precise knowledge of the various details (vv. 33–34) portray him as more than a prophet. This is further demonstrated by his certainty of what is about to take place. There is no "might happen" or "possibly" in his prophecy. The christological significance of all this is evident, and its apologetic value is also clear. Mark wants to emphasize to his readers that Jesus's death was neither a tragedy nor an unfortunate turn of events. Jesus went to Jerusalem knowing full well that he would be put to death. He knew the precise details of what would be involved, but he nevertheless went because this was a divine necessity (8:31; cf. 14:21a), and he desired to fulfill his Father's will (14:36).

10:33–34 The death of Jesus is described as involving two distinct groups. One is the Jewish leadership (the "chief priests and the scribes" [τοῖς ἀρχιερεῦσιν καὶ τοῖς γραμματεῦσιν, *tois archiereusin kai tois grammateusin*]—*not* the Jewish people, who are in reality a hindrance to the plans of the Jewish leadership [14:1–2, 10–11]). These leaders will condemn Jesus and deliver him over. The other is the gentiles, that is, the Roman authorities led by Pontius Pilate, who will mock him, spit upon him, scourge him, and kill him. Behind all these actions, Mark wants his readers to know that the Jewish leadership and the gentiles did "whatever [God's] hand and plan had predestined to take place" (Acts 4:27–28). The reference to Jesus as the Son of Man is found in all three passion predictions (8:31; 9:31; 10:33) and lends support to their authenticity (see 2:10). In the prediction of Jesus's scourging, Mark uses the term μαστιγώσουσιν, but in the passion account in 15:15 he uses φραγελλώσας. This suggests the use of different sources, but the terms function in Mark as synonyms. A flogging/scourging normally preceded crucifixion (cf. Josephus, *J.W.* 2.14.9 §306). Thus it occurs before "kill" in the prediction.

The concluding four words of the passion prediction are essentially identical in all three passages (after three days he will rise [again], μετὰ τρεῖς ἡμέρας ἀναστήσεται, *meta treis hēmeras anastēsetai*). In each instance Matthew (16:21; 17:23; 20:19) and Luke (9:22; in the second prediction [9:44] he omits the temporal designation; 18:33) replace the temporal designation with "on the third day" (τῇ τρίτῃ ἡμέρᾳ, *tē tritē hēmera*). Nevertheless it is clear that these are temporally identical in meaning (V. Taylor 1952: 378; cf. Stein 1990: 119–21). Because the Markan designation is unusual and contrasts with the more traditional "on the third day," it is probable that it was found in the evangelist's pre-Markan tradition (Strecker 1968: 429). The three-days tradition referred to in 14:58 and 15:29 uses different prepositions. The suggestion that the temporal designation in our passages refers to Jesus's death taking place three days after his being delivered over (McKinnis 1976: 97–98) is unconvincing, because of its location immediately after the verb "kill [him]" (ἀποκτενοῦσιν).

Summary

Two clear Markan emphases are found in the third passion prediction. One is that the death of Jesus is to be understood as part of the sovereign plan of God, who rules over history. For the readers, who had been raised in a context in which crucifixion was associated with criminals and shame, the passion predictions served as a word of reassurance. The crucifixion of their Lord was not a tragedy but part of the predetermined counsel and will of God. Although in 10:33–34 the human agency of the Jewish religious leaders and the gentiles is in the forefront, the divine agency of God behind all this has already been affirmed (the δεῖ of 8:31), and the reason and necessity of Jesus's death will become clearer through such passages as 10:45 and 14:24. Furthermore, it is quite likely that the Markan readers already understood the death of Jesus in terms of an atoning sacrifice through their regular celebration of the Lord's Supper, and if as suggested (see "Audience" in the introduction) the Gospel was written to the church in Rome, perhaps through such traditions as Rom. 3:21–26.

Our passage also has a strong christological emphasis. Not only does Jesus possess a clear knowledge of his future fate, but this knowledge is also not mediated through a vision or voice from heaven but is due to his own unique ability to know the future. The precision of his knowledge is also to be noted. In addition, the Son of God displays a total dedication and obedience to the will of God. At Gethsemane this becomes even more clear when, despite his own desire to have this "cup" removed, he affirms, "but not what I will but what you [will]" (14:36). The amazement of Jesus's disciples (10:32) emphasizes the Son's obedience and commitment to the Father's will and contrasts with the fear of his followers.

M. The Misguided Request of James and John (10:35–45)

As in the case of the first two passion predictions (8:31 and 9:31), the third (10:33–34) is followed by an example of failure on the part of the disciples (10:35–45; cf. 8:32–33; 9:32–41). The present account consists of two parts. The first involves the request of James and John (10:35–40), consisting of the request of the two brothers (10:35–37) and Jesus's reply to them (10:38–40). Coming right after the second passion prediction and the teachings of 9:33–37, the brothers' request heightens Mark's portrayal of the disciples' dullness, for their request in 10:37 is totally oblivious to what Jesus has said in 9:35. The second consists of Jesus's response to the Twelve and various teachings concerning what it means to be a leader in the kingdom of God (10:41–44) and concludes with the example of Jesus's own vicarious death (10:45). Although it is possible to see 10:41 as concluding 10:35–40, it is best to see it as introducing what follows.

Several arguments have been advanced to suggest that originally the materials in these two parts existed independently of one another, and that Mark placed an independent collection of sayings (10:42b–45) at this point in his Gospel (Best 1981: 123, 128; Hooker 1991: 246). In support of this is that 10:42b–45 is found in a different location in Luke (cf. 22:24–27). This, however, may have been due to Luke's desire to place the teaching of Jesus's servanthood right after his account of the Last Supper (22:14–23). That Matthew in his Gospel has the present account in the same place as Mark (cf. Matt. 20:17–19 and 20–28) suggests that Luke's placement of the disciples' dispute on greatness and of Jesus's teachings on servanthood elsewhere is due to his own redactional interests. Another argument given in favor of the original independence of 10:35–40 and 41–45 is that the former deals with issues concerning the end of the age, whereas the latter deals with life in the present age. The relationship of 10:35–40 and 41–45 seems quite natural, however, for the eschatological hope of the not-yet dimension of the kingdom of God vitally affects how one lives and serves in the already-now of the kingdom. As it now stands, the present passage makes sense. Unless one denies to Jesus a messianic consciousness and awareness of his forthcoming death, there is no need to deny the unity of 10:35–45 (Gundry 1993: 581–82; Casey 1998: 193–218; Evans 2001: 114).

There does not seem to be a great deal of redactional work by Mark in 10:35–40 (Pryke 1978: 18–19, 145, 166; Best 1981: 123).[1] Most of the debate centers on whether 10:41–42a comes from Mark (Best 1981: 123–24; Gnilka 1979: 98–99; Pryke 1978: 166 attributes 10:41c–42a and 45c to Mark), whether 10:45 is Markan or traditional (and if traditional, whether its placement is Markan or traditional), and whether the placement of the two parts (10:35–40 and 10:41–45) is due to the hand of Mark. Although some of the words in 10:41–42a, such as "and having called them" (καὶ προσκαλεσάμενος αὐτούς, *kai proskalesamenos autous*; Evans 2001: 114 refers to this as "the only clearly Markan addition"; cf. 3:23) may be due to Mark's wording of the tradition, there is no justification to assume that they are entirely the creation of Mark. The debate over the authenticity of 10:45, which is notorious, must be distinguished from the question of whether it is Markan (Pryke 1978: 166 lists only 10:45c as Markan). The latter question is more easily answered. Mark 10:45 is not the creation of Mark (Best 1981: 125–27), as indicated by the fact that "ransom" (λύτρον, *lytron*) appears nowhere else in Mark. Indeed, it may be historical (Wilcox 1996).

The general impression of the present account favors its historicity. It fits well the general tenor of Jesus's teachings on servanthood in the kingdom of God and the portrait of the disciples found throughout the Gospels. Furthermore, why would the early church create an account in which the leaders of the church are portrayed so poorly? The entire account looks like "a fragment of embarrassing but authentic tradition" (Evans 2001: 114). As to the reference to the "sons of Zebedee" in 10:35, this seems traditional because it is entirely unnecessary; James and John have already been referred to as such in 1:19 and 3:17 (Best 1981: 123).

Exegesis and Exposition

[35]And James and John, the ⌜ ⌝ sons of Zebedee, come to him [Jesus], saying to him, "Teacher, we want you to do for us whatever we ask you." [36]And he said to them, "What do you want me ⌜to do⌝ for you?" [37]And they said to him, "Give us [the right] that one [of us] may sit on your right hand and one on your left in your glory." [38]And Jesus said to them, "You do not know what you are asking. Are you able to drink the cup that I ⌜[am about to]⌝ drink or to be baptized with the baptism that I am [about to be] baptized with⌝?" [39]And they said to him, ⌜"We are able."⌝ And Jesus said to them, "The cup that I drink you will drink, and the baptism with which I am baptized you will be baptized with, [40]but to sit on my right hand or left hand is not ⌜in my power⌝ to give, but is [reserved] ⌜for those⌝ [for whom] it has been ⌜prepared⌝."

[41]And when the ten heard [this], they began to be indignant at James and John. [42]And Jesus, having called them, says to them, "You know that those ⌜recognized

---

1. The way that the conversation is reported in 10:36–39 with a straightforward "And he/ they said to them/him" in 10:35 supports this. Pryke (1978: 145, 166) lists only the introductory seam, "And . . . to him," as Markan.

as rulers⌐ over the gentiles lord it over them and their great men exercise authority over them." ⁴³It ⌐is⌐ not [to be] so among you, but whoever wants to become great among you will be your servant, ⁴⁴for whoever wants to be first among you shall be the slave of all. ⁴⁵For even the Son of Man came not to be served but to serve and to give his life as a ransom for many."

10:35–37   The third example of disciple failure that leads to teachings on discipleship (see 8:22–10:52) involves a request by the disciples James and John. This is the only time in Mark outside of their call to discipleship (1:19–20; 3:19) that they are mentioned apart from Peter (5:37; 9:2; 14:33; and 1:29; 13:3, where Peter's brother, Andrew, is also mentioned) or the Twelve. The address "Teacher" is often found on the lips of the disciples (4:38; 9:38) and others (5:35; 9:17; 10:17, 20; see 4:37–39). In the Matthean parallel the request of James and John is found on the lips of their mother (20:20–21), but Jesus's reply in 20:22–23 is addressed to the brothers. Some suggest that Matthew has sought to ameliorate the error of the two disciples by placing the request on the lips of their mother. However, we have a related example in the account of the healing of the centurion's servant. In Luke it is Jewish elders who speak on behalf of the centurion (7:3–6), whereas in Matthew the spokesmen are omitted and the centurion speaks directly to Jesus (8:5–13). (Compare how translators are never mentioned in reported conversations of international leaders who cannot converse in the same language.) It is therefore possible that Mark may simply have omitted mentioning the intermediary of the message, because the conversation is ultimately between Jesus and the two disciples (cf. how in both Matt. 20:22 and Mark 10:38 Jesus's reply is addressed to the brothers).

The indirect way (10:35) of presenting their specific request (10:37) may reveal that James and John realized its impropriety (France 2002: 415), but since they were approaching Jerusalem (10:32), they may have risked making such a request.[2] The specific nature of the request is uncertain. It may refer to being given the best seats in the messianic banquet (cf. Matt. 22:1–10; Luke 14:15–24; also 1 Kings 2:19; Ps. 110:1; 1 Esd. 4:29; Sir. 12:12; Josephus, *Ant.* 6.11.9 §245) or to sitting at Jesus's side when he was to be enthroned as the supreme judge of the world (cf. 8:38; 13:26–27; 14:62; Matt. 19:28; 25:31–46).[3] That James and John want to "sit" at Jesus's right and left hand, whereas at a banquet one usually reclined, favors the latter view (France 2002: 415). Yet whatever view is taken, the brothers' request reveals both a correct and an incorrect understanding of Jesus's messianic role. They recognize correctly that Jesus is indeed the Messiah, as Peter's confession (8:29), the transfiguration (9:2–8, esp. v. 7), and Jesus's teachings concerning his coming glory and the coming of the kingdom (8:38–9:1) indicate. But they refuse to accept Jesus's

2. France (2002: 416) suggests that perhaps James and John thought that as Jesus was approaching Jerusalem "he may yet be coaxed back to take the more sensible way [to fulfill his role as Messiah]." This, however, is highly speculative. For Mark, at least, Jesus knows no other possibility as Messiah except to "give his life as a ransom for many" (10:45).

3. Cf. Luke 22:28–30, which combines images of the messianic banquet and judgment.

repeated teaching concerning his coming passion (8:31; 9:31; 10:33–34). Thus they are correct on the *who* question: "Who then is this man?" (4:41). Jesus is the Messiah, who will one day enter his glory and judge the world (8:38). But they are totally wrong on the *what* of his present messianic task (J. Edwards 2002: 322). Mark uses this misunderstanding of James and John, that of Peter in 8:32, and that of the disciples in 9:33ff. to teach his readers that suffering precedes glory both for the Christ and for his followers.

Jesus's reply reinforces the passion prediction of 10:33–34 and reveals that **10:38–40** the Markan Jesus knows full well that Jerusalem involves for him suffering, not earthly glory. The statement "You do not know what you are asking" was certainly true of James and John, but the readers of Mark were clearly aware of what the "cup and baptism" meant for James (Acts 12:1–2), what it meant for Jesus, and what it implied with respect to their own fate as well. The references to the cup and baptism are examples of synonymous parallelism (Stein 1994b: 27) and point to Jesus's forthcoming death foretold in his three passion predictions (8:31; 9:31; 10:33–34). Although the metaphor of a "cup" can refer to experiencing blessing (Pss. 16:5; 23:5; 116:13), it refers far more frequently to experiencing suffering and even death (Ps. 75:8; Isa. 51:17, 22; Jer. 25:15; 49:12; Lam. 4:21; Ezek. 23:31–35; Hab. 2:16; cf. Ps. Sol. 8.15; Mart. Isa. 5.13). In the NT it is used in the latter way on numerous occasions (Mark 14:23–24, 36; John 18:11; Rev. 14:10; 16:19). For the expression "cup of death," see Tg. Neof. on Gen. 40:23 and Tg. Neof. on Deut. 32:1. What the cup meant for Jesus was well known to Mark's readers (10:33–34; 14:23–24, 36), and their drinking the cup at communion would recall Jesus's death (1 Cor. 11:26).

The metaphor of "baptism" to describe one's terrible fate is not as familiar as the imagery of being overwhelmed by a watery flood (Ps. 42:7; Isa. 43:2). Whether Jesus expected James and John to understand this saying in light of their baptism is doubtful (Donahue and Harrington 2002: 311), but for the Markan readers "baptism" might have recalled their own "baptism" into Jesus's death (Rom. 6:3–5). There is no need to choose between understanding the two metaphors as referring to either the martyrdom of James and John (Acts 12:1–2) or to the Christian sacraments of baptism and communion (contra Best 1981: 124). For Mark's readers, real or possible martyrdom is implied in their dying with Christ in baptism, and sharing the cup in communion recalls Jesus's teaching that following him involves "losing one's life" (8:35), both figuratively and often literally. The order of cup first and baptism second in 10:38–39 may be due to the fact that the cup in the Lord's Supper has a more vivid tie to Jesus's vicarious death than does his baptism. The cup and baptism that the sons of Zebedee would share are not identical with the cup and baptism of Jesus (Muddiman 1987: 56). Their experience would involve suffering and martyrdom (the latter at least in the case of James), but Jesus's sacrificial and vicarious suffering as a "ransom for many" (10:45; cf. 14:22–25) was unique. Thus Mark's readers would not have understood Jesus's cup and baptism in 10:38 as identical to that of James and John in 10:39. What the metaphors had in common in both instances is that they involved suffering and martyrdom, not vicarious, sacrificial suffering and martyrdom.

The authenticity of the sayings concerning the "cup and baptism" has often been denied and seen as a *vaticinium ex eventu* (Bultmann 1968: 24), a prophecy after the fact. However, a number of factors argue against this. For one, although James's martyrdom was probably known to the readers of Mark, the fate of his brother John was not. Indeed, if we take the church tradition seriously, John did not experience martyrdom at all. Thus at the time when the cup and baptism sayings were supposedly created, they were evidently not true with respect to John. The creation of such an apparently "unfulfilled" prophecy is less likely than that it is authentic and goes back to Jesus himself (E. Sanders 1985: 147; Hooker 1991: 247; Gundry 1993: 584–85). A second factor arguing for the authenticity of 10:38–39 is that they are intimately tied to 10:40, in which Jesus claims that he does not possess the authority to grant the disciples' request. Such a limitation of Jesus's authority (cf. 13:32) is unlikely to be a church creation, for the tendency of the early church was to intensify the miracle-working power of Jesus (back to his infancy!) and to remove or ignore the limitations of his power found in the Gospels (cf. 1:34; 3:10; 6:5 and their parallels in Matthew and Luke). The use of the divine passive "has been prepared" (ἡτοίμασται, *hētoimastai*) in 10:40 (made explicit in Matt. 20:23—"by my Father") also argues for the authenticity of 10:38–40. The alleged creation of these sayings by the early church also encounters the problems that the early church had no special interest in the question of who would sit at Jesus's right and left hand and that one would expect a later church creation to be more specific and accurate (Evans 2001: 117).

10:41–45 The reason for the angry response of the ten toward James and John is not explained, but it was probably due to their own desire for such special places of honor in the kingdom. The selfish requests of the brothers and the response of the other disciples serve as an occasion for Mark to teach his readers what true greatness in the kingdom of God involves. Jesus provides a truism (France 2002: 418) as a negative example of what Christian discipleship should not be. Gentile rulers (probably a reference to the Romans, since Israel was ruled by Rome)[4] use their authority to lord it over their subjects, but Christian greatness does not lie in such behavior. It involves more than being a just master over one's subjects instead of an unjust one. The secular world may think that rulers should be good and fair rather than evil and oppressive, but Christian leadership is far more radical. Jesus teaches that leadership in the kingdom of God is totally different. It does not involve being *master* over others at all; instead, it involves being their *servant*.[5] True greatness involves being a servant

---

4. Note that in the third passion prediction in Mark (10:33), Jesus is delivered to the gentiles (clearly Rome), who put him to death.

5. Evans (2002: 119) points out: "In the Greek world διακονία, 'service,' was the opposite of happiness, as Plato says: 'How can one be happy when he has to serve [διακονεῖν] someone?' (*Gorgias* 491e)."

and slave (8:34; 9:35; 10:31), as the two examples of synonymous parallelism (Stein 1994b: 27) in 10:43b–44 illustrate. Greatness in the kingdom of God does not involve public honor and the authority to command others but "humble, unrewarded service" (Best 1981: 126–27).[6]

Mark 10:45 may be the most disputed verse in all of Mark (Evans 2001: 119). This is due not only to questions concerning its interpretation but even more to questions concerning its authenticity. The latter are multiple and complex. Concerning the authenticity of the saying itself, three possibilities arise: is it (1) the creation of Mark, (2) the creation of the pre-Markan church, or (3) the creation of Jesus himself (and thus authentic)? To this can be added another question: is its location (1) due to Mark, (2) due to the pre-Markan church, or (3) due to Jesus? It seems reasonably clear that 10:45 is not the creation of Mark. Its Palestinian coloring (Best 1981: 126), the indirect way that it serves a doctrine of atonement, and its unusual vocabulary ("ransom") argue against its being Markan. Its lack of any mention of the resurrection (contrast the passion predictions: 8:31; 9:31; 10:33–34) argues against its being a purely Markan or church creation. It has also become evident that previous arguments holding that the doctrine of substitutionary ransom or atonement found in 10:45 is a late idea have now been discredited (cf. Exod. 13:13–16 LXX; 1 Macc. 2:50; 6:44; 2 Macc. 7:37–38; 4 Macc. 6:27–29; 17:21–22; 1QS 5.6; 8.3–10; 9.4; Lindars 1983: 78–79). The question of whether 10:45 is due to the theological reflection of the early church or came from Jesus himself tends ultimately to be answered according to one's preconceptions concerning the historical Jesus. If one assumes that the historical Jesus was radically different from the Jesus of the Gospels, then one is predisposed, almost compelled, to deny the authenticity of this verse. Yet it is not easy to see how the early church could have created de novo the picture of Jesus as the suffering servant whose death served as a ransom for many if this were diametrically opposed to the life and teachings of the historical Jesus. It is much more likely that Jesus saw his mission along the lines of the suffering servant of Isaiah (cf. esp. Isa. 53:7, 10–12)[7] and that the present verse ultimately goes back to Jesus himself.[8]

As to whether Mark already found this verse as the conclusion of 10:42–44, this seems probable for several reasons. Rather than appearing to be a foreign body added to 10:42–44, it is intimately associated with the previous verses

---

6. "At no place do the ethics of the kingdom of God clash more vigorously with the ethics of the world than in the matters of power and service" (J. Edwards 2002: 325).

7. Although Jesus's understanding of himself as the suffering servant of Isa. 53 has been exaggerated in the past (as pointed out by Barrett 1959 and Hooker 1959: 74–79; 1991: 248–49), there seems to be a growing consensus that Jesus did understand his ministry in terms of the suffering servant of Isaiah (France 1971: 110–32; Wilcox 1996; Watts 1998; 2000: 270–87).

8. Many argue that 10:45c is inauthentic because its parallel in Luke 22:27 speaks only of "one who serves." For some brief, helpful summaries in favor of the authenticity of this verse, see V. Taylor 1954a; Witherington 2001: 288–90; Evans 2001: 120–23; and Riesner 2003, who argues that both Luke (cf. 19:10; 22:27; Acts 20:28, 34) and Paul (Rom. 5:15; 15:1–8; 1 Cor. 7:22–23; 9:19; 10:33; Gal. 1:10; 2:17, 20; 3:13; 4:5; Phil. 2:6–11; Col. 1:13–14; 1 Tim. 2:5–6) reflect in these passages knowledge of a pre-Markan form of the ransom saying found in Mark 10:45.

and serves as the key to the whole passage (Donahue and Harrington 2002: 315). As argued earlier (see the introduction to this unit), the entire passage (10:35–45) may well be a unified whole going back to a situation in the life of Jesus. If we grant that Jesus did see himself as a prophet awaiting a fate similar to that of the OT prophets and John the Baptist, there is a logical unity in the passage that argues strongly for the historicity of the incident and sayings.

Verse 45 serves as a concluding example of the teachings of 10:42b–44. For Mark, the best example of what greatness and being a servant in the kingdom of God means is found in Jesus, the model leader (cf. Luke 22:27; John 13:4–16). In perhaps the clearest example of an *imitatio Christi* found in Mark, the evangelist shows how greatness (Jesus is the Christ, the Son of God) involves becoming a servant (Jesus gives his life as a ransom for many). Yet while 10:45 serves as a conclusion for the teachings on discipleship in 10:42b–44, it also reveals Mark's understanding of the purpose of Jesus, the Son of Man. The verse explains why he came (cf. 1:38; 2:17; 9:37; 12:6; also Matt. 10:40; 11:18–19) and his God-given commission. This commission is expressed both negatively and positively (V. Taylor 1952: 444). He has been sent from God (lit. "came" [ἦλθεν, *ēlthen*]), not to lord it over others like the Romans do, but rather to give his life as a ransom for many.

The expression "ransom for many" (λύτρον ἀντὶ πολλῶν, *lytron anti pollōn*) has been much discussed, for each word is capable of several possible meanings. To Mark's Greek readers, "ransom" would evoke the idea of a payment to secure the release of a slave or captive (A. Collins 1997). It is an image and metaphor often used in the NT to describe the purpose or result of Jesus's death (cf. Luke 24:21; Eph. 1:7; Col. 1:14; 1 Tim. 2:6; Titus 2:14; Heb. 9:12; 1 Pet. 1:18; also Rom. 3:24–25; 1 Cor. 1:30; 6:20; 7:23; Heb. 9:5; 1 John 2:2). Neither here nor anywhere else in the NT, however, does this imagery deal with the question that later arose: To whom was this ransom paid? Origen's theory that Jesus paid this ransom to Satan is not found in the NT. The fact that in 14:24 Jesus's death is seen as a sacrifice sealing a covenant with God argues against Origen's view.[9]

By its location the expression "for many," an allusion to Isa. 53:12, defines the noun "ransom," not the verb "give." The preposition "for" (ἀντί, *anti*) can mean "instead of" (i.e., as a substitute for) or "for the sake of." If the former is correct, we have an example of Jesus's death being described as substitutionary and his standing in the place or stead of those he ransomed.[10] If "for the sake of" is correct, Jesus's death is described in more general terms as bringing about the ransom of the "many" but without a description of how this ransom is accomplished. The former interpretation is probably preferable here, for a "ransom" served as a replacement or substitute to the slave owner

9. It also argues against Witherington (2001: 280), who sees the idea of a possible ransom from the devil in Mark's strong emphasis on Jesus's ministry of exorcism.

10. The preposition ἀντί is used with this sense in Matt. 2:22; 5:38; Luke 11:11; Rom. 12:17; 1 Thess. 5:15; Heb. 12:16; 1 Pet. 3:9; cf. also Prov. 17:13; Tob. 1:15, 21; 1 Macc. 3:1; 9:31; etc.

for the slaves freed in the process of manumission. The expression "many" can be understood exclusively as "a large number but not all" or inclusively as "all." Although the term "the many" is used at Qumran to describe the sect (1QS 6.1, 7–25; CD 13.7; 14.7), it is uncertain as to whether it refers to the sect in distinction from others or whether it refers to them as all the people of God. In Semitic usage "many" tends to be used inclusively as a synonym for "all" (E. Maloney 1981: 139–42). This is how 1 Tim. 2:6 understands Jesus's ransom (ἀντίλυτρον ὑπὲρ πάντων, *antilytron hyper pantōn*, a ransom for all), and the interchangeable use of "many" and "all" in Rom. 5:15, 18–19 proves this (Gnilka 1979: 104). In support of this understanding of the present verse, note that the contrast is not between "many" and "all" but between the "one" (Jesus) and the "many." The question of whether God intended Jesus's ransom to be for the "elect" or "the whole world" goes beyond Mark's intended meaning of the passage. Mark's readers were well aware that the ransom for "many" was effective only for those who "deny themselves and take up the cross" (8:34–38), but neither Mark nor his readers were thinking about the question of a limited or unlimited atonement.

Summary

A number of Markan emphases can be found in this passage. As in the previous passion predictions (8:31; 9:31), where a collection of sayings involving Christian discipleship follows (8:34–38; 9:33–50), so here we find sayings of Jesus concerning discipleship (10:35–45) following the third passion prediction (10:33–34). Once again a misunderstanding of the disciples (10:35–40; cf. 8:32–33; 9:33–34) serves as the occasion to teach the ethic of the kingdom of God. In stark contrast to this world's value system (10:42), Jesus teaches that greatness in God's kingdom involves not being master or lord over others but being a servant or slave (10:43–44). Unfortunately, over the centuries the model for Christian leadership, which is Jesus's own servanthood unto death (10:45), has been lost sight of and ignored, and the desire for honor, prestige, and power has dominated. In the present day, when the pattern often suggested for Christian leaders is that of a CEO ruling over a corporation, the model of Jesus as a servant leader cannot be emphasized enough. Those who aspire to greatness in the kingdom of God should have this example of Jesus for their model. For a Christian, there is less need to reflect on the hypothetical question of "What would Jesus do?" than to reflect on the actual "What has Jesus done?" We should be careful not to let our familiarity with the gospel story dull the revolutionary nature of this teaching. It is the way of the cross (8:34), the way of servanthood and slavery, that leads ultimately to glory!

Several christological emphases also appear in this passage. One involves Jesus's knowledge of the future. Although this is not absolute (13:32), it goes far beyond that of other human beings. Jesus knew not only his own fate (10:38) but that of his disciples as well (10:39). Jesus's authority is not absolute (10:40; God has prepared [the Greek verb is a divine passive] and will appoint those who will sit in the chief places in his kingdom), yet Jesus's unusual and unique authority is indicated by the questions of James and John in 10:35 and 37. Finally, although Mark has on numerous occasions alluded to the forthcoming suffering and death of Jesus (2:19–20; 8:31; 9:31; 10:33–34), he here (and again in 14:24) clearly teaches the purpose of that suffering and death. Jesus does not die the death of a martyr. He dies rather a vicarious and substitutionary death for "many." His death serves as a ransom for the world. Thus his death is not only the supreme example of what it means to be "great" in the kingdom of God, that is, being a servant and slave of all; it is also the once-for-all sacrifice (cf. Heb. 7:27; 9:28) by which he vicariously ransomed humanity from sin and death. This, Mark tells his readers, is why Jesus went up to Jerusalem (10:33).

Additional Notes

10:35. Here and in 10:37 B and C add "two" (δύο), but the majority and best MSS lack the term.

10:36. ποιήσω is lit. "I should do."

10:38. The present tenses used in 10:38–39 (πίνω, βαπτίζομαι) should be understood as futuristic presents emphasizing the certainty of Jesus's fate. For the cognate accusative "the baptism with which I am baptized," see the comments on 2:3–4.

10:39. Jesus's words in 10:38–39 should not be interpreted as laying down a condition for the privileged seats in the kingdom of God, as 10:40 clearly points out.

10:40. ἐμόν is lit. "mine."

10:40. Some versions (it syr[s] cop[sa]) read ἄλλοις (for others), but this is a less likely reading and probably resulted in a misreading ΑΛΛΟΙΣ for ἄλλοις instead of ἀλλ' οἷς. See Metzger 1994: 91.

10:40. For God preparing a place for his followers, cf. Matt. 25:34; 1 Cor. 2:9; Heb. 11:16; also John 14:3; Rev. 21:2.

10:42. οἱ δοκοῦντες ἄρχειν is lit. "who are supposed to rule." Gundry (1993: 579) rightly points out that δοκοῦντες does not mean to only "seem" to rule. They do in fact rule.

10:43. Some MSS (A C[3] f[1] f[13]) read ἔσται (will be).

V. On the Way to Jerusalem: Part 4 (8:22–10:52)
   L. Jesus's Third Passion Prediction (10:32–34)
   M. The Misguided Request of James and John (10:35–45)
➤ N. Jesus Heals a Second Blind Man (10:46–52)

N. Jesus Heals a Second Blind Man (10:46–52)

The healing of the blind man of Jericho is the last healing miracle recorded in the Gospel of Mark. It is the only one in which the person healed is named. (In 1:30 the name of the son-in-law of the person healed is given [Peter], and in 5:22 the name of the father is given [Jairus].) Because Mark arranged his Gospel geographically (Galilee, journey to Jerusalem, Jerusalem), he had little choice as to where the present account could be placed, since Jericho is the last city in the Jordan River Valley before Jerusalem (Räisänen 1990: 232; contra Robbins 1973: 238–39). Yet the present healing serves as an "appropriate climax" (Hooker 1991: 252) to this section and along with the healing of the blind man in 8:22–26 forms an *inclusio* for 8:22–10:52 (Brooks 1991: 172; Meier 1994: 686; see 8:22–10:52). The present healing also serves as a bridge to Jesus's entrance into Jerusalem as Israel's Messiah in 11:1–11 (France 2002: 421), for the title "Son of David" (Υἱὲ Δαυίδ, *Huie Dauid*; 10:47–48) prepares the reader for the story of the triumphal entry in which the "kingdom of our father David" (11:10) is mentioned. The present story also prepares the reader for Jesus's messianic judgment of Israel's worship in 11:12–25 and the exercise of his messianic authority in 11:27–12:44 (Hooker 1991: 252).

The classification of the form of this pericope is debated (Steinhauser 1986; Gundry 1993: 596). Is it a miracle story, or is it a call (to faith and discipleship) story? The lack of a traditional reference to the amazement caused by the healing normally found in a miracle story and its replacement by the statement that the blind man "began to follow [Jesus] in the way" (ἠκολούθει αὐτῷ ἐν τῇ ὁδῷ, *ēkolouthei autō en tē hodō*; 10:52b) suggests that this is a call story. The blind man's ability to follow Jesus also functions as a proof of his healing. The account serves well as an example of what discipleship involves and thus is an excellent conclusion to 8:22–10:52, which emphasizes the requirements of Christian discipleship. We must remember, however, that Mark is above all a Gospel "concerning Jesus Christ, the Son of God" (1:1), and this healing miracle emphasizes this in two ways.[1] Not only does Jesus have the power and ability to heal the blind man, but he is also the recipient of a messianic confession. He is the "Son of David"! We are faced once again with a purist's desire for an either-or designation concerning form and the problem that the account being discussed does not neatly fit an either-or classification (Meier 1994: 735n38). In its present form, it is a mixed type. It is a healing story, and as such emphasizes a christological

---

1. Contrast Kingsbury (1983: 103) and C. Marshall (1989a: 125), who see the main emphasis as being the great faith of Bartimaeus.

point, and it is also a story that teaches about Christian discipleship. If Mark could accept the mixed nature of the present form of the account, there is no reason to deny that the pre-Markan form of the tradition could also have existed in such a mixed form. The account consists of four parts: the introductory seam (10:46), the cry for help (10:47–48), Jesus's call to come (10:49–50), and the healing proper (10:51–52).

There is considerable debate and divergence of opinion as to the extent of the Markan redaction in the passage. Some see the entire account as being primarily pre-Markan, so that the hand of Mark is seen mainly in the introductory "And they come into Jericho" (Καὶ ἔρχονται εἰς Ἰεριχώ, *Kai erchontai eis Ierichō*; 10:46a) and the concluding "And immediately [καὶ εὐθύς, *kai euthys*] . . . he began to follow him in the way" (Achtemeier 1978: 119; Best 1981: 139).[2] Others see 10:47–49 as being Markan (Robbins 1973: 234–36), but several considerations mitigate against this. These verses lack a heavily Markan style and vocabulary: the use of "call" (φωνήσατε, *phōnēsate*) and "jumped up" (ἀναπηδήσας, *anapēdēsas*—only here in the NT) are non-Markan; the double reference to Jericho is unusual; and several atypical theological emphases are present ("Son of David" occurs only here in all of Mark).[3] In addition, the command to silence comes from the crowd, not Jesus, and occurs before the miracle. It also appears that 10:50–52 requires something like 10:47–49 to explain why the man threw off his cloak and came to Jesus (10:50). There is no convincing reason to attribute 10:47–49 to Mark (Achtemeier 1978: 118–19; Best 1981: 141); indeed, several arguments favor the traditional and even historical nature of the entire pericope. These involve the Palestinian nature of the account (the location—Jericho, the name "Bartimaeus" and its explanation "the son of Timaeus" (ὁ υἱὸς Τιμαίου, *ho huios Timaiou*), the title "Son of David," the description of Jesus as "the Nazarene," and the address "Rabbouni" (Ῥαββουνί, *Rhabbouni*) suggest at least a traditional origin in early Jewish Christianity (Gnilka 1979: 108; Meier 1994: 688–90), and there is a sense in which the vividness of the account appears to reflect a historical incident (V. Taylor 1952: 446–47; Evans 2001: 129).

Some have argued that in Jesus's day it was no longer possible to successfully trace one's lineage back to David. Yet the emperors Vespasian, Domitian, and Trajan sought out the family of David in order to assure that no royal Davidic heir might arise and trouble their reigns (Eusebius, *Eccl. Hist.* 3.12, 19–20; 3.32.1–4), and the Talmud assumes that Davidic descendants could trace their lineage back to David (*b. Šabb.* 56a; *b. Ketub.* 62b). One should note how Paul points out that he is a descendant of Benjamin (Phil. 3:5) and that Josephus reproduces his own genealogy (*Life* 1 §3). The

---

2. Contrast Pryke (1978: 167), who sees all of 10:46–52 as redaction except 10:47b–49a and 51b–c.

3. It is strange that some scholars (Robbins 1973: 234–36) argue for it being a Markan redaction. See, however, E. Johnson 1978: 195–97; Olekamma 1999: 232–37.

Davidic lineage of Jesus was well known (note this claim in the pre-Pauline tradition in Rom. 1:3) and was never challenged by the church's opponents (Evans 2001: 129–30).

Exegesis and Exposition

⁴⁶And they come into Jericho. And as he, and his disciples, and a great crowd are proceeding out of Jericho, the son of Timaeus, Bartimaeus, a blind ⌜beggar⌝, was sitting by the road. ⁴⁷And having heard that ⌜Jesus the Nazarene was coming⌝, he began to cry out and say, "Son of David, Jesus, have mercy on me." ⁴⁸And many began to ⌜rebuke⌝ him in order that he should be silent. But he all the more continued to cry out, "Son of David, have mercy on me." ⁴⁹And Jesus, having stopped, said, "Call him," and they call the blind man, saying to him, "Take heart, rise, [for] he is calling you." ⁵⁰And having thrown off his [outer] cloak, he jumped up and came to Jesus. ⁵¹And Jesus answered and said to him, "What do you want that I should do for you?" And the blind man said to him, "Rabbouni, ⌜that⌝ I might see." ⁵²And Jesus said to him, "Go, your faith has saved you." And immediately he received his sight and began to follow him in the way.

The journey begun in 10:1 toward Jerusalem (10:32) now leads to Jericho. **10:46** The original city of Jericho (Tell es-Sultan) lies approximately seventeen miles northeast of Jerusalem in the Jordan River valley. In Jesus's day the city was no longer located on the original tell but was five miles west of the Jordan River and six miles northwest of where the Jordan River enters into the Dead Sea. It is a fertile oasis fed by several springs in the midst of a hostile desert area. Because it is 825 feet below sea level, its temperature in the summer is very hot but in the winter very mild. It may well be the oldest continually occupied city in the world (since around 9000 BC). The NT Jericho had been enlarged by Herod the Great, who built three separate palaces and an elaborate hippodrome complex (T. A. Holland and E. Netzer, *ABD* 3:723–41). It is the last major city in the east before the steep road to Jerusalem. The difference in elevation between Jericho and Jerusalem is about 3,500 feet.

The introductory seam, "And they come into Jericho," reveals a Markan hand (the wording is identical to 8:22; 11:15, 27; 14:32; cf. also 9:33), but it is difficult to think that the traditional story started abruptly with a reference to leaving Jericho (καὶ ἐκπορευομένου αὐτοῦ, *kai ekporeuomenou autou*; Pesch 1980b: 169; Gundry 1993: 598; cf., however, Matt. 20:29). The location of the story is traditional (Olekamma 1999: 245), as the second reference to Jericho in the sentence indicates. The story takes place as Jesus departs from the city (cf. Matt. 20:29); but Luke, due to his inclusion of the Zacchaeus story, places it in Jericho as Jesus was passing through (Luke 19:1). Accompanying Jesus are his disciples, who are present throughout the chapter (10:10, 13, 23, 24, 46; cf. also 26–31, 32–34, 35–40, 41–45) and a "great" crowd. "Great" (ἱκανοῦ, *hikanou*; 1:7; 15:15) is not the usual term Mark uses for a "large" (πλεῖστος, *pleistos*) or "great" (πολύς, *polys*) crowd (cf. 4:1; 5:21, 24; 6:34; 8:1; 9:14; 12:37). Although it may very well be that the crowd consisted of fellow pilgrims heading to Jerusalem to celebrate the Passover (W. Lane 1974: 386–87; France 2002: 422), in Mark they serve primarily to emphasize Jesus's magnetic personality and charisma (Gundry 1993: 593; Evans 2001: 131).

The designation "the son of Timaeus, Bartimaeus," is unusual for several reasons. "Timaeus" may be not an Aramaic name but a Greek one (Donahue and Harrington 2002: 317; cf., however, Cranfield 1959: 344; Evans 2001: 131; France 2002: 423). If so, we have a mixed Aramaic (*Bar*)–Greek (*Timaeus*) name explained in Greek. Normally Mark places the alleged Aramaic name or phrase first and then introduces the Greek explanation with "which is" (ὅ ἐστιν, *ho estin*; 3:17; 7:11, 34; 12:42; 15:16, 42; cf. also 14:36) or "which means" (ὅ ἐστιν μεθερμηνευόμενον, *ho estin methermēneuomenon*; 5:41; 15:22, 34). Mark may have changed the order to balance the order of Bartimaeus's address, "Son of David, Jesus," in 10:47 (Gundry 1993: 593). Attempts to explain who Bartimaeus was or represents (cf. J. Edwards 2002: 329n70) are highly speculative.

Whereas "in the way" (ἐν τῇ ὁδῷ) in 10:52 is symbolic (see below), here "by the road" (παρὰ τὴν ὁδόν, *para tēn hodon*) lacks any such figurative meaning (Donahue and Harrington 2002: 317; contra J. Edwards 2002: 329). It simply locates the beggar on the road where Jesus is traveling and permits the following encounter. Together, along with "they come" (10:46a) and "he began to follow" (10:52c), they may form an *inclusio* (Olekamma 1999: 40). It is possible that Bartimaeus was "by the road" because it was a good location for collecting alms, for religious pilgrims going up to celebrate the Passover in Jerusalem would have been in a pious mood for helping a needy blind man (Gundry 1993: 600). Mark, however, makes no mention of this.

10:47–48   That Jesus is described as "the Nazarene," the one from Nazareth, to distinguish him from others with the same name (cf. 1:24; 14:67; 16:6), probably reflects a historical situation, because it would have been totally unnecessary to add such a superfluous detail in the time and situation of Mark or the early church. Hearing that Jesus of Nazareth was approaching, Bartimaeus addresses him, "Son of David, Jesus" (Υἱὲ Δαυὶδ Ἰησοῦ, *Huie Dauid Iēsou*; 10:47). This and its repetition in the next verse are the only two occurrences of "Son of David" in Mark and betray a non-Markan origin. There have been attempts to understand this title as referring to the healing and exorcistic authority of Jesus. This is based on the idea that the title refers to Solomon, the son of David, who is described in the intertestamental literature as possessing a great ability to heal and cast out demons (Duling 1975; Chilton 1982: 92–97; Charlesworth 1996). Such an allusion is unconvincing, however, for a connection here with Solomon is extremely tenuous (Gundry 1993: 600). For Mark's readers, the most likely understanding of the title "Son of David" would have been as a reference to the promised royal descendant of Israel's greatest king, Jesus Christ, the long-awaited Son of David (Olekamma 1999: 69–81). The introduction to the Gospel (1:1), Peter's confession (8:29), the tie with the coming events in Jerusalem and the temple (11:1–11), and the inscription on Jesus's cross—"the King of the Jews" (15:26; cf. also 15:18)—all point to this (Marcus 1992b: 137–39).

The challenge to this normal understanding of the Son of David (cf. Ps. Sol. 17.21) in 12:35–37 is not that this is an incorrect understanding of Jesus Christ, but that it is an inadequate one. It is "not big enough!" (Marcus 1992b: 144). The NT understanding of the person and work of Jesus does not deny that he is the Son of David (Matt. 1:1, 17, 20; 9:27; 12:23; 15:22; Luke 1:27, 32, 69; 2:4, 11; Acts 13:22–23; Rom. 1:3; 2 Tim. 2:8; Rev. 5:5; 22:16). It points out that he is this and more. The wording of the address, "Son of David, Jesus," places the title in the emphatic position. This and its twofold repetition indicates that Mark wants to emphasize that Jesus is indeed the Son of David.[4] The wording of Bartimaeus's cry, "Have mercy on me" (ἐλέησόν με, eleēson me) appears frequently in the LXX: Pss. 9:14 (9:13 Eng.); 24:16 (25:16 Eng.); 25:11 (26:11 Eng.); 26:7 (27:7 Eng.); 30:10 (31:9 Eng.); 40:5 (41:4 Eng.); 50:3 (51:1 Eng.); 56:2 (57:1 Eng.); 85:3 (86:3 Eng.); Isa. 30:19. The content of this cry is revealed by Mark in 10:51. It is the desire to be healed of his blindness. As Jesus's words in 10:52 reveal, Bartimaeus receives this and much more. Mark does not explain how Bartimaeus had heard of Jesus and his ability to heal even the blind (8:22–26; cf. also Matt. 9:27–31; 11:5; 12:22; 21:14; John 9:1–41), but the account assumes that the knowledge of Jesus's healing ministry was extensive (cf. 1:32–34, 45; 2:1–2, 13; 3:7–12, 20; 4:1–2, 36; 5:21–34; 6:12–13, 30, 31–44, 55–56; 7:24–30, 31–37; 8:1–10, 22–26; 9:14–27; 10:1, 13–16).

Bartimaeus is commanded to "be silent" (σιωπήσῃ, siōpēsē—an ingressive aorist). This, however, is not an example of the "silence motif" in Mark (see 1:44), for it is issued not by Jesus but by the crowd; the motive is different. It would prevent a possible miracle, not avoid its proclamation, and it occurs before the miracle, not after it (Räisänen 1990: 230–32). Mark does not identify the "many" who rebuke the blind man (there is no tie with the "many" [πολλῶν, pollōn] of 10:45, as the lack of the article reveals) or explain why they rebuke him to be silent (cf. 3:12; 8:30). For Mark, such information was not vital to the story. Suggestions include they thought Jesus had more important things to do than to spend time with a blind beggar lacking any real status (France 2002: 424), they sought to avoid the exuberance of the crowds getting out of hand (Evans 2001: 132–33), and they did not want to hinder or delay

4. The idea that Bartimaeus's blindness indicates that the confession of Jesus as the Son of David is incorrect and misguided (Kelber 1974: 95; Via 1985: 162) is extremely improbable (Kingsbury 1983: 102–7). See C. Marshall 1989: 127. The confession is not only acknowledged by Mark as being correct, but it is also emphasized, for in the account Jesus commends Bartimaeus for his saving faith: "Your faith has saved you." This refers not simply to his belief that Jesus could heal him but also to the reason why Jesus could heal him: he is the Son of David, i.e., the Christ. As the Christ, Jesus brings with him the messianic kingdom and the benefits of that kingdom, which include salvation and eternal life (cf. 10:17, 23, 26). As in 8:31–9:1, confession and following Jesus go hand in hand (Eckstein 1996: 50).

Jesus's setting up his messianic kingdom in Jerusalem, but these suggestions are speculative and impossible to demonstrate. Furthermore, spending time on such speculations moves one's attention from what the evangelist thought was important and sought to emphasize.

10:49–50   As Jesus proceeds out of the city (10:46), he stops (lit. "having stood," in contrast to proceeding out), and states, "Call him." The subject of the imperative, a plural, is not specified. It can refer to the disciples, the large crowd of 10:46, or the "many" of 10:48. Probably it refers to the "many," since this is the nearest antecedent. The verb "call" (φωνήσατε, *phōnēsate*) is unusual. One expects the verb προσκαλέσατε (*proskalesate*; 3:13, 23; 6:7; 7:14; 8:1, 34; 10:42; 12:43) or καλέσατε (*kalesate*; 1:20; 2:17; but cf. 9:35). This and its threefold usage in 10:49 argue for the traditional nature of the verse. In response to Jesus's words, the "many" of 10:48 now turn from being a hindrance to being an encouragement to Bartimaeus, and they call him. Whether the imperative φωνήσατε is to be understood as a command indicating Jesus's authority (Gundry 1993: 594; France 2002: 424; Donahue and Harrington 2002: 318) or a request is uncertain, but the "many" tell the blind beggar, "Take heart [Θάρσει, *Tharsei*; cf. 6:50], rise [ἔγειρε, *egeire*], [for] he is calling you [φωνεῖ σε, *phōnei se*]."

The response of Bartimaeus is better understood as descriptive (France 2002: 424) than as symbolic (C. Marshall 1989: 141–44; Williams 1994: 156–57). Casting aside his outer cloak (ἱμάτιον, *himation*) has been understood as portraying a historical circumstance (it was spread out on the ground or on his lap to receive alms [V. Taylor 1952: 449]) or as a symbolic act (leaving all to follow Jesus [Williams 1994: 157; cf. 1:18, 20; 2:14; 10:21, 28], putting off the old man/life [Culpepper 1982]), but it is best understood as a spontaneous act of joy and anticipation. "Jumped up" (ἀναπηδήσας, *anapēdēsas*; a hapax legomenon in the NT; lit. "having jumped up") further describes the haste (cf. 2 Kings 7:15) and anticipation of the blind man (Olekamma 1999: 207–8) and builds up the expectation of Mark's readers for what is about to happen. The lack of any mention of assistance in the blind man's coming to Jesus has led some to suggest that he was not totally blind (V. Taylor 1952: 449). Some have argued that since the text does not mention that he was born blind, this also suggests that he was not totally blind (Gundry 1993: 603), but this is an argument from silence. Thus, we are not told whether the man partially seeing approached Jesus by himself, in total blindness stumblingly approached the direction of Jesus's voice, or was assisted to Jesus by some of the crowd. Mark thought that such information was unnecessary and unimportant for understanding the story.

10:51–52   It is best to see "answered and said" (ἀποκριθεὶς . . . εἶπεν, *apokritheis . . . eipen*; lit. "having answered . . . said") as an idiomatic expression for "said" rather than as Jesus's answering Bartimaeus's call for attention (Evans 2001: 133), since no question has been asked.[5] Jesus's question to Bartimaeus is

---

5. See the first additional note on 9:5.

identical to the one addressed to James and John in 10:36. The address "Rabbouni" (Ῥαββουνί, *Rhabbouni*) is a heightened form of "Rabbi" (9:5; 11:21; 14:45) and means "my rabbi/master." It occurs only here and in John 20:16. The request is what one expects from a blind man who has faith—to see! Without such faith one might seek alms for surviving in the present state of blindness. Although Jesus appears to have understood his mission in terms of Isa. 61:1, which included the restoration of sight to the blind (Luke 4:18; Matt. 11:5/Luke 7:22), it is improbable that Bartimaeus's hope was based on this OT promise.[6] It was most probably based on reports of Jesus's healing ministry that he had heard.

Jesus's response, "Go, your faith has saved you" (ὕπαγε, ἡ πίστις σου σέσωκέν σε, *hypage, hē pistis sou sesōken se*), recalls 5:34 (Matt. 9:22; Luke 8:48; cf. also Luke 7:50; 17:19). As in Mark 7:24–30 (cf. also Luke 7:1–10/Matt. 8:5–13/John 4:46–54; Luke 17:11–19), the healing is performed without touch (contrast 8:22–26). Jesus needs only to speak for healing to take place. The term "saved" can refer to both physical healing (3:4; 5:23, 28, 34; 6:56; cf. also 13:20; 15:30–31) and spiritual healing, the gift of salvation (8:35; 10:26; 13:13). Here both meanings are present. The account ends with a reference to the fact of his healing, "And immediately he received his sight" (καὶ εὐθὺς ἀνέβλεψεν, *kai euthys aneblepsen*; lit. "and immediately he saw"), and to the proof of his healing, "and he began to follow him [an inceptive imperfect—cf. 1:31] in the way." The reference to his "following [ἠκολούθει, *ēkolouthei*; 1:18; 2:14–15; 6:1; 8:34; 9:38; 10:21, 28, 32] Jesus in the way [ἐν τῇ ὁδῷ, *en tē hodō*; 1:2–3; 8:27; 9:33–34; 10:32]" contains two terms often used in Mark to describe Christian discipleship. Their presence here suggests not only that Bartimaeus is cured and able to walk but also that he becomes a follower of Jesus (Best 1981: 143; Evans 2001: 134; France 2002: 425; contra Kingsbury 1983: 104–5).

Summary

The twofold theological emphasis in this account is evident from the difficulty encountered in trying to classify it. As a healing miracle, it possesses a christological emphasis. The power and ability to heal a blind man reveal Jesus's unique authority to heal. This is heightened by several details. The healing is accomplished by Jesus's word alone, and it takes place immediately. If "Call him" in 10:49 is to be interpreted as an imperative, this also emphasizes Jesus's authority. The presence of a great crowd stresses Jesus's great popularity and charismatic personality. The most unique christological emphasis found in the account, however, is the twofold confession that Jesus is the Son of David. This is not simply a statement that Jesus was somehow related to the line of David. Rather, it is understood by Mark as indicating that Jesus of Nazareth is "the" Son of David, that is, the promised royal Messiah for whom Israel longed. Mark wants his readers to know that Jesus

---

6. The reference to "the recovery of sight to the blind" is found in the LXX of Isa. 61:1, but is not in the Hebrew text. Cf., however, Isa. 29:18; 35:5.

is Israel's long-awaited king, the one greater than David himself (12:35–37). And Jesus is more than this. He is the Son of God and the Son of Man, who came not to be served but to serve and to give his life as a ransom, so that a blind Bartimaeus might be saved physically and spiritually.

The account also serves to teach what Christian discipleship involves. To truly "see" involves faith to understand that Jesus is the Christ, the Son of David. The action of Bartimaeus is a paradigmatic example of what it means to be a Christian. Like Simon and Andrew, he follows Jesus (cf. 10:52 and 1:18) in the way of the cross (8:34). In sharp contrast to the story of the rich young ruler, he possessed saving faith (cf. 10:52 with 10:26c), as is shown in his following Jesus in the way (cf. 10:52 with 10:21–22). Similarly, in sharp contrast to the previous story in which the disciples still do not see that discipleship means following Jesus in being a servant, Bartimaeus "sees" clearly and follows Jesus in the way to Jerusalem.

Additional Notes

10:46. Some MSS (A C² D W Θ f¹ f¹³ lat) read προσαιτῶν (was begging). The translation follows ℵ B L Δ Ψ: προσαίτης.

10:47. Ἰησοῦς ὁ Ναζαρηνός ἐστιν is lit. "Jesus the Nazarene it is."

10:48. ἐπετίμων is an inceptive imperfect.

10:51. The translation assumes that the ἵνα is imperatival (Morrice 1972: 327).

VI. Jesus's Entry into Jerusalem: Part 5 (11:1–13:37)

The material found in Mark 11–16 can be organized in several ways. It can be arranged according to a temporal outline involving seven days: Day 1 (Sunday), 10:46–11:11; Day 2 (Monday), 11:12–19; Day 3 (Tuesday), 11:20–26; Day 4 (Wednesday), 11:27–13:37 (?); Day 5 (Thursday), 14:1–16; Day 6 (Friday), 14:17–15:41; Day 7 (Saturday), 15:42–47; and Day 8 (Sunday), 16:1–8. Whether all the material in these six chapters occurred in a period of a single week is, however, doubtful. Furthermore, some of the material seems to have been grouped together for topical rather than chronological reasons, as the collection of controversy stories in 11:27–12:25 and the eschatological teachings in 13:1–37 suggest (Hooker 1991: 255–56; Witherington 2001: 307; J. Edwards 2002: 332–33).[1] Whether Mark intended his readers to understand all of 11:1–16:8 as taking place within this tight chronological framework is unlikely. By the fourth century, however, the organization of this material into a passion week scenario became a popular catechetical device for teaching.

A more useful way of organizing the material of Mark 11–16 is to see it as consisting of two main parts: Jesus's entry into Jerusalem centering on his actions and teachings in the temple (11:1–13:37; cf. esp. 11:11, 15, 27; 12:35, 41; 13:1–2, 3ff.) and the suffering, death, and resurrection of Jesus (14:1–16:8; Dowd 2000: 117). A superficial glance at the present section might suggest that Jesus's entry into Jerusalem was a highly triumphal one (11:1–11) in which the crowd received him as the one who came in the name of the Lord to bring the messianic kingdom (11:9–10). He purifies the temple (11:15–18), refutes his opponents handily (11:27–33; 12:13–40), and teaches (13:1–37) concerning the near and more distant future: the destruction of Jerusalem and his coming as the Son of Man to judge the world. Yet a closer look at this material reveals a much more sobering and negative picture. Jesus's popular welcome into Jerusalem is quite superficial, and his cleansing (actually "cursing"; see 11:12–14) of the temple reveals the poverty and hypocrisy of the faith of the Jewish leadership. They do not welcome Jesus as the Christ, the Son of God (1:1), but rather oppose him (11:27–12:40) and seek his death (11:18; 12:6–8, 10, 12; cf. the earlier references to Jerusalem's attitude toward Jesus in 3:22 and 7:1). Only one miracle is recorded in this entire section, and none in the following (14:1–16:8), revealing the lack of faith that Jesus encounters in

---

1. The famous quotation of Papias, "Mark . . . wrote accurately all that he remembered, not, indeed, in order, of the things said or done by the Lord" (Eusebius, *Eccl. Hist.* 3.39.15), comes to mind at this point.

Jerusalem (cf. 6:5–6a). Furthermore, the miracle itself—the cursing of the fig tree—serves as a parabolic act symbolizing Jesus's judgment of the temple and the religious leadership of Israel (11:12–14, 20–21).

Within this section, the question of who Jesus is (4:41) is constantly raised (Hooker 1991: 253–54). He is portrayed as the one who brings with him the awaited kingdom of David (11:1–11), has authority to pronounce judgment on the temple (11:20–21), claims authority from heaven to do "such things" (11:27–33), claims a unique relationship to God as God's "beloved son" (12:6–7), refutes the leaders of the nation by his superior wisdom (12:13–40; cf. esp. vv. 17, 34c, 37b), and pronounces judgment on the nation for their rejection of him (13:1–37; cf. others coming "in my name," v. 6; "for my sake," v. 9; "for my name's sake," v. 13; "the Son of Man," v. 26; "truly, I say to you," v. 30; "son," v. 32; "what I say to you, I say to all," v. 37).

A. Jesus's Messianic Entry into Jerusalem (11:1–11)

According to the geographical organization of Mark, the present account records the first and only time Jesus enters Jerusalem. John, on the other hand, refers to several such visits in 2:13–4:45; 5:1–47; 7:1–10:40; and 12:12–20:31, and Luke suggests more than one such visit to Jerusalem in 13:34 (cf. Mark 14:49). Some have suggested that this event fits better the autumn Feast of Tabernacles due to the presence of pilgrims, branches (11:8), and the shouts of "Hosanna" (Manson 1950–51; Donahue and Harrington 2002: 322). Others suggest that it fits better the celebration of Hanukkah in December, which commemorated the cleansing of the temple by the Maccabees in 164 BC (Burkitt 1916: 139–44; Mastin 1969). Yet all the Synoptic Gospels and John as well (cf. 12:1, 12ff.), who has several visits of Jesus to Jerusalem, associate the "triumphal" entry into Jerusalem with the Passover Festival. All also associate the triumphal entry with the cleansing of the temple (cf. John 2:13–25).

Numerous scholars have suggested that the present account is an early Christian myth created and read back into the life of Jesus on the basis of the church's reading of Zech. 9:9 (Bultmann 1968: 261–62; Dibelius 1934: 121–22). It is unlikely, however, that the reading of Zech. 9:9 created the account in Mark, since this verse is not quoted by Mark. It is more likely that this event in Jesus's life later resulted in the church seeing in Zech. 9:9 a prophecy of this event (Gundry 1993: 632). This is supported by the fact that it is the later Gospels that explicitly connect the prophecy to the account (Matt. 21:5; John 12:15; Hooker 1991: 257). Furthermore, it is quite unlikely that a story supposedly created to teach a christological truth would end as anticlimactically as we find in 11:11 (V. Taylor 1949: 151; Evans 2001: 138).

There are numerous reconstructions as to how the present account came into existence. Some suggest that an original story of Jesus's entrance into Jerusalem (11:1a, 8–11) was expanded with a story (11:1b–7) created from Zech. 9:9. Others suggest that an original story (11:1–6) was augmented later by 11:7–11. The lack of agreement among many of the hypothetical reconstructions weakens confidence in such suggestions (Evans 2001: 138–39). There are good reasons for assuming the pre-Markan unity of the material found in 11:1–11 (V. Taylor 1952: 451–53; Catchpole 1984: 325). As it now stands, the account consists of two parts: Jesus's procurement of a colt (11:1b–6), and Jesus's entrance into Jerusalem (11:7–11). Although some see extensive Markan editorial work in 1:1–2a, 3c, 9a, 10, and 11 (Pryke

1978: 19, 145, 167), outside of the introductory seam (11:1a), which is based on tradition, and the conclusion (11:11), the Markan editorial work in the account seems to be minimal (Gnilka 1979: 114–15; Evans 2001: 140–41). The account has several close literary ties with the preceding story: "way" (ὁδός, *hodos*; 10:46, 52; 11:8), taking off garments (10:50; 11:7–8), the theme of salvation (10:52; 11:9–10), following Jesus (10:52; 11:9), and Jesus as the Son of David bringing the coming kingdom of David (10:47–48; 11:10; Catchpole 1984: 319).

In seeking to understand what actually happened when Jesus entered Jerusalem on this occasion, we must recognize that several different perspectives of the event are present: Jesus's understanding and intention; the understanding of the crowd and of the disciples, which may not have been identical; and the understanding and interpretation of the evangelists. In the commentary, I will argue that Jesus intentionally arranged for a colt to be available for him to ride into Jerusalem and that this was a conscious messianic act (pilgrims normally entered into Jerusalem by foot) in fulfillment of Zech. 9:9 (Stein 1996: 178–81). For the crowd, made up mostly of disciples, other followers of Jesus, and Galilean pilgrims, the event was understood more as an enthusiastic welcome and greeting (along the lines of Ps. 118) of a pilgrim who was a famous religious teacher. It was not understood by the crowd as an overt messianic act. The lack of any Roman opposition and of any mention of this event at Jesus's trial indicates this (cf. Mark 14:55–15:5). Even John, who unlike Mark has Jesus addressed at his entrance as "the king of Israel" (12:13), comments that Jesus's own disciples did not understand what was taking place until later, when Jesus was glorified (12:16). The messianic and yet hidden nature of this event was clearly understood by Mark, even though he does not quote Zech. 9:9 directly in his account and records no clear messianic title as being uttered by the crowd (cf. 11:9–10 with Matt. 21:5 and 9).

Exegesis and Exposition

[1]And when they are approaching Jerusalem, to Bethphage and Bethany at the Mount of Olives, he sends two of this disciples [2]and says to them, "Go into the village opposite you, and immediately as you are entering into it, you will find a tethered colt upon which no one has yet sat. Untie it and bring [it]. [3]And if anyone should say to you, 'Why are you doing this?' say, 'The Lord has need of it, and immediately ⌐he will send it back here again⌐.'" [4]And they departed and found a colt tethered at a door outside in the street, and they untie it. [5]And some of those standing there were saying to them, "What are you doing, untying the colt?" [6]And they told them just as Jesus had told them to, and they permitted them [to take the colt]. [7]And they bring the colt to Jesus and place their garments on it, and he sat on it. [8]And many spread their garments on the road and others, having cut off leafy branches from the fields, [spread them]. [9]And those proceeding and those following were shouting,

"Hosanna! Blessed is the one coming in the name of the Lord! ¹⁰Blessed is the coming kingdom of our father David! Hosanna in the highest!" ¹¹And he [Jesus] entered into Jerusalem, into the temple, and having looked around at everything, because it was already evening, he went out to Bethany with the Twelve.

The order of the geographical designations "Jerusalem . . . Bethphage and Bethany" seems strange. Although the exact location of Bethphage is debated, it is generally thought to be close to the summit of the Mount of Olives, whereas Bethany (modern-day El-Azariah) lies two miles east of Jerusalem, on the eastern slopes of the mountain. While in Jerusalem during "Holy Week," Jesus apparently stayed in Bethany (11:11–12; 14:3–9). The order of these cities is due less to Mark's supposed geographical confusion than to his desire to list the ultimate goal of Jesus (Jerusalem) first (10:32), and since Bethphage was nearest Jerusalem, it is mentioned second (Cranfield 1959: 348; W. Lane 1974: 394; Evans 2001: 141). See 7:31 and 10:1 for similar examples.[1] The Mount of Olives lies east of Jerusalem and overlooks the city. It consists of a mountain ridge two miles long and at its northern summit is 2,963 feet above sea level. Opposite the temple area it possesses a height of 2,700 feet. Jerusalem stands about 2,600 feet above sea level. According to Zech. 14:4 the Mount of Olives would be the site of the final judgment, and it was associated by some with the coming of the Messiah (Ezek. 11:23; 43:1–5; cf. Josephus, *Ant.* 20.8.6 §§169–70). For the sending out of the disciples by twos, see 6:6b–7.

11:1

Jesus's words to the disciples have been interpreted as an example of either his supernatural knowledge or his prior arrangements for his entrance into Jerusalem. Jesus's prophetic knowledge of the future has been observed on numerous occasions (2:8; 3:5; 5:30, 32; 8:17, 31; 9:31; 10:33–34; cf. also 12:8, 15; 13:3–36; 14:7–8, 18–21, 27–30), and this could be another such example. There is also precedent for commandeering an animal for a limited time (Derrett 1971; Witherington 2001: 308–9), and the return of the colt is promised in 11:3d. (Cf. the impressment of Simon of Cyrene by the Romans in Mark 15:21 and Matt. 5:41.) If this is the correct understanding, it would be an example once again of Jesus's supernatural knowledge and lordship (Hooker 1991: 258; Gundry 1993: 624). On the other hand, the exactness of the details, the reply "The Lord has need of it," the specific description and nature of the colt (unridden, ἐφ᾽ ὃν οὐδεὶς οὔπω ἀνθρώπων ἐκάθισεν, *eph' hon oudeis oupō anthrōpōn ekathisen*; lit. "on which no one from men has yet sat"; 11:2c), and the acquiescence of the people in letting the two disciples take the colt suggest that Jesus probably prearranged the acquisition of this colt for his entry into Jerusalem (W. Lane 1974: 395; Evans 2001: 142; Donahue and Harrington 2002: 321–22; France 2002: 432). If this is correct, then Jesus intentionally

11:2–3

---

1. For the view that the journey from Jericho to Jerusalem would have originally passed through Bethphage, bypassing Bethany, cf. J. Edwards 2002: 334, who suggests that Bethany is mentioned simply to prepare the reader for 11:11.

planned to enter Jerusalem riding on a colt in fulfillment of Zech. 9:9 and to present himself as Israel's longed-for king, and this makes the event a highly messianic act.

Several additional interpretive questions arise in these verses: the exact location of the city in which the colt was found, the meaning of the term "colt" (πῶλον, *pōlon*), and to whom "the Lord" (ὁ κύριος, *ho kyrios*) in this passage refers. The village is not named but is simply described as the one "opposite you" (τὴν κατέναντι ὑμῶν, *tēn katenanti hymōn*). This could refer to Bethphage, Bethany, or an unnamed village. Although Bethphage is more likely (Evans 2001: 142; Donahue and Harrington 2002: 321), some suggest Bethany (Gundry 1993: 624). That Mark does not name the village indicates that where this took place is unimportant for him. What took place and what this in turn reveals about Jesus are primary. (See 9:2–3.) As to the term "colt," this can refer to a colt of a horse, and some argue that this is how Mark's readers would have understood the term (Bauer 1953; Gundry 1993: 626; Evans 2002: 142). However, in the LXX the term can refer to a donkey or its offspring (Gen. 32:15; 49:11; Judg. 10:4). Matthew specifically refers to it as a donkey (21:2, 5, 7), as does John (12:14–15). If Mark's readers were Christians, they would probably have been familiar with the OT account of Zech. 9:9 (cf. also Gen. 49:11) as well as the Jesus traditions, so that the evangelist in light of this probably intended them to interpret "colt" as a young donkey (Witherington 2001: 308; France 2002: 431). The unique nature of the colt (never before ridden) indicates that it was a special animal qualified for the sacred task of carrying Israel's king (cf. Num. 19:2; Deut. 21:3; 1 Sam. 6:7; also *m. Sanh.* 2.5).[2] No allusion is made to the "unbroken" nature of the animal or to Jesus's mastery over it (contra Gundry 1993: 625; Evans 2002: 142).

The term "Lord" (κύριος) has been interpreted in three ways, as referring to the donkey's human owner (V. Taylor 1952: 454–55; W. Lane 1974: 391–92n3), God (cf. Evans 2001: 143; France 2002: 432), or Jesus (Gundry 1993: 624, 628; Hooker 1991: 258; J. Edwards 2002: 335). Against the view that its human owner is meant, one should note that none of the four Gospel accounts refers to him, and the promise in 11:3 that the "Lord" will immediately return the colt makes no sense if the "Lord" is the owner, for to whom would he return the colt? To himself? Mark has already used the term "Lord" for Jesus in 1:3; 2:28; 5:19 and will do so again in 12:36, 37. Furthermore, for Mark's Christian readers it was clear that "Jesus is Lord" (Rom. 10:9; Phil. 2:11), so that it is best to interpret the "Lord" of 11:3 as referring to Jesus.

11:4–6 In accordance with Jesus's words (11:2–3), everything takes place exactly as he said. The colt is found "tethered" (δεδεμένον, *dedemenon*), and Mark adds "at a door outside in the street" (πρὸς θύραν ἔξω ἐπὶ τοῦ ἀμφόδου, *pros thyran exō epi tou amphodou*). He does not feel it is necessary, however, to repeat the virginal nature of the colt mentioned in 11:2.

---

2. Cf. the use of a *virgin* tomb for the burial of Jesus (Matt. 27:60; Luke 23:53; John 19:41) and Jesus's *virgin* birth (Matt. 1:18–25; Luke 1:26–2:7).

Since the animal does not have a saddle of any sort (it is an unridden donkey), **11:7–10** they (referring to at least the two disciples of 11:1) place their "outer garments" (ἱμάτια, *himatia*) or cloaks on the animal as a makeshift saddle. In addition, cloaks and leafy branches or tall blades of grass (στιβάδας, *stibadas*; only here in the NT) are placed before Jesus to ride on as he proceeds toward Jerusalem. (The reference to "palm branches" and thus to "Palm Sunday" comes from John 12:13.) The scene recalls 1 Kings 1:38–48, where Solomon rides to his coronation, but even more so 2 Kings 9:13, where cloaks are placed on the ground for Jehu when he is anointed as king. The scene is further heightened by the shouts of the people preceding and following, that is, the people accompanying Jesus, some of whom were in front and some behind, who cry, "Hosanna! Blessed is the one coming in the name of the Lord!" (Ὡσαννά· Εὐλογημένος ὁ ἐρχόμενος ἐν ὀνόματι κυρίου, *Hōsanna! Eulogēmenos ho erchomenos en onomati kyriou*). This comes from Ps. 118:26a [117:26 LXX], a Hallel pilgrim psalm. "Hosanna" is Hebrew for "Save now!" By the first century, however, its use in Ps. 118 was no longer understood literally as a cry by those shouting it for God (or on this occasion, perhaps for Jesus) to now save the people of Israel from their enemies. Being repeated by pilgrims each year at the various major festivals, it had become more idiomatic in nature and was by then an expression of joy and jubilation, much as in the use of the word today (Pesch 1980b: 183; Fitzmyer 1987; Hooker 1991: 260; contra Evans 2001: 145). A present-day example is the now-idiomatic nature of the expression "Praise the Lord." This is not understood as command (or even request) to do something but a statement of thanksgiving.

"Blessed is the one coming in the name of the Lord!" in this pilgrim psalm was addressed from the temple to every pilgrim entering Jerusalem (France 2002: 434), as Ps. 118:26b indicates: "We bless you from the house of the Lord." Thus the shout of blessing is not specifically messianic in nature. The remaining "Blessed is the coming kingdom of our father David!" stands in poetic parallelism with the first cry in 11:9. It lacks any clear, close Jewish parallel (Hooker 1991: 260; J. Edwards 2002: 337; cf., however, Evans 2001: 145–46)[3] but is certainly not a Christian creation (Pesch 1980b: 185). Whether this cry is historically tied to the cry of Bartimaeus in Jericho, "Jesus, Son of David" (10:47, 48; France 2002: 434), is uncertain, although Mark intends his readers to interpret 11:10 in light of 10:47 and 48. The second "Hosanna" in 11:10 balances the first in 11:9 and forms an *inclusio* with it. "In the highest" (ἐν τοῖς ὑψίστοις, *en tois hypsistois*; cf. Luke 2:14; Job 16:19; Ps. 148:1) is an example of circumlocution in which a synonym or synonymous phrase is employed to avoid using God's name (Stein 1994b: 63–64).

In seeking to understand this event, it appears that Jesus prepared for a virginal colt to be ready for him to ride into Jerusalem. Nowhere do we read of Jesus riding an animal in any other Gospel account. Weariness is certainly not the reason for the use of the colt, because not only has Jesus prepared for it

---

3. Gundry (1993: 631) correctly points out that this does not mean that this expression is un-Jewish.

beforehand, but having walked from Jericho to this point, the remaining journey is less than two miles and all downhill. (If Jesus originally left Bethany for Jerusalem, there would be even less reason to be weary.) Furthermore, pilgrims did not ride into Jerusalem; they walked. The special nature of the colt (never "ridden") emphasizes its unique function. Jesus intended to enter Jerusalem as the king of Israel. The actions and adulation of his followers must not be understood as standing in contradiction to Jesus's own understanding of his actions, because he in no way hinders them (cf. Luke 19:39–40). Similarly, the adulation and confession of the crowds, like that of Bartimaeus (10:47–48), does not stand in opposition to Mark's own christological understanding and emphasis (contra Kelber 1974: 94–97). The use of a donkey should not be understood as a symbol of lowliness and meekness (Hooker 1991: 257). A donkey was a fit vehicle for a king (Zech. 9:9; cf. also *b. Ber.* 56b, where a donkey is associated with kingship due to Zech. 9:9). Matthew describes Jesus coming humbly as a king (21:5), yet his humility is not because of his riding a donkey but because of his character (cf. Matt. 11:28–29).

For the disciples and crowds, Jesus's entry into Jerusalem was an exuberant experience that brought much excitement. The normal welcome given pilgrims was exploited by them to the fullest. The crowd saw all this as a deserved honoring of the great prophet Jesus from Nazareth of Galilee (Matt. 21:11); others saw it as an overexuberant welcome (Luke 19:39–40; John 12:19); but not even his disciples truly understood the significance that Jesus gave to this event (cf. John 12:16). As in the cleansing of the temple, we should not overestimate the number of people involved. The lack of any Roman intervention in both instances and the fact that these events were apparently never brought up as accusations at Jesus's trial (Hooker 1991: 256) strongly suggest that the number of people involved in these events was much smaller than generally portrayed in Christian art and thought. It also suggests that the full messianic significance that Jesus attributed to his actions was not understood by the crowd, authorities, or even the disciples. Furthermore, what happened in one part of the temple during the cleansing did not necessarily affect what was going on in the rest of the temple, and what took place on one part of the road leading to Jerusalem did not affect all the people traveling on that road. Thus what was highly significant and messianic to Jesus (his coming as Israel's messianic king) was seen by the crowds, Jesus's opponents, the Romans, and even the disciples as not much more than a confusing, enthusiastic welcome of the famous religious teacher, Jesus of Nazareth. Later (cf. John 12:13, 15, 19; Matt. 21:5, 11) the messianic nature of the event was more clearly recognized and heightened (Evans 2001: 140).[4]

11:11   The account ends surprisingly and anticlimactically with Jesus entering Jerusalem and the temple, where the religious leaders of Israel do not greet him or

---

4. Contrary to Duff (1992), Mark does not heighten the story of Jesus's entry into Jerusalem with allusions to Zech. 14 and Greco-Roman entry processions. When one compares the Markan account with those of Matthew (21:5, 11) and John (12:13, 15, 19), Mark's account looks remarkably "unheightened."

welcome him (cf. Luke 19:39–40). Having looked around the temple, due to the late hour (lit. "the hour already being evening") Jesus leaves, the crowds disappear, and Jesus proceeds to Bethany with the twelve disciples. The entrance into the temple and Jesus's looking around (a kind of inspection tour? [Pesch 1980b: 186; Witherington 2001: 311]), however, prepare readers for the next account, the "cleansing" of the temple.⁵ The anticlimactic nature of Jesus's entrance into Jerusalem and the temple supports the suggestion that the events surrounding Jesus's arrival in Jerusalem (11:1–10) were not understood as messianic by the people (Hooker 1991: 260). It is not what happens when Jesus enters Jerusalem and the temple on this day that is so noteworthy but what does not happen (J. Edwards 2002: 338)!

Summary

The entrance of Jesus into Jerusalem is understood by Mark as a messianic act. Although the later accounts make this more explicit with the quotation of Zech. 9:9 (Matt. 21:5; John 12:15) and/or references to Jesus as "king" (Luke 19:38; John 12:13), the messianic nature of the event in Mark is clear. "Jesus Christ, the Son of God" (1:1), has just been acknowledged twice in the preceding account as the "Son of David" (10:47 and 48), and his healing of the blind man who confesses this (10:52) confirms the truth of this title. Whatever the original crowd's understanding of the acclamation "Hosanna! Blessed is the one coming in the name of the Lord! Blessed is the coming kingdom of our father David! Hosanna in the highest!" Mark wants his readers to interpret this as addressed to Jesus, the Son of David. He has come in the name of the Lord (cf. 1:3) and is Lord (11:3). He, the Son of David, has come and has brought the messianic kingdom of David, as he has proclaimed from the beginning (1:15).

Yet Mark's readers are well aware that Jesus's bringing of the messianic kingdom is quite different from that expected by most of the Jewish people (cf. Ps. Sol. 17–18). He comes to deal with the real need of humanity, which is not freedom from Rome but freedom from sin, guilt, and the devil (10:45; 14:24). They know that God has ordained Jesus's death (8:31; 9:31; 10:33–34) as a ransom for sin (10:45), and this will be accomplished by his dying as the Son of David, the King of the Jews (15:2, 9, 12, 18, 26, 32).

Additional Note

11:3. ἀποστέλλει is a futuristic present. Some MSS have the future ἀποστελεῖ and others omit "again" (πάλιν), but this is probably due to scribal attempts to conform Mark to the parallel in Matt. 21:3 (Metzger 1994: 92).

---

5. "Looking around" (περιβλεψάμενος, *periblepsamenos*) is found seven times in the NT. Six of these are in Mark and usually involve looking around in a discerning manner (3:5, 34; 5:32; 10:23; cf. also 9:8).

B. Jesus's Judgment of the Fig Tree and the Temple (11:12–25)

Few texts in Mark have as many questions associated with them as this one. Numerous questions arise concerning the history behind the text, the history of the text itself, and the Markan meaning of the present text. The first issue involves such questions as these: Did Jesus really cleanse the temple? If he did, was his intention reformatory (to rid it of impure elements), judgmental (a symbolic action foretelling God's judgment upon the temple and Israel), or both (Evans 1989a: 269)? Was there one cleansing or two, and if there was one, did it occur at the beginning (John 2:13–22) or at the conclusion of Jesus's ministry (Mark 11:12–25/Matt. 21:12–22/Luke 19:45–48)? How extensive was the cleansing, and why did the authorities (Jewish and/or Roman) not interfere? Did everything in Mark 11:12–25 occur in Jerusalem and in that particular order? Did Jesus really behave in the way described in the present account, violently driving out the merchants and money changers in the temple (11:15; cf. John 2:15), and cursing a fig tree for not having fruit at a time of year when it did not normally bear fruit? Does Jesus's behavior appear to be out of character with what we know of him elsewhere? (Contrast Luke 13:6–9.) Do the OT quotations "My house shall be called a house of prayer for all the nations" (Isa. 56:7) and "but you have made it a den of robbers" (Jer. 7:11) go back to Jesus himself, or is it an early church addition to the narrative?

The present account consists of a story about Jesus's cleansing of the temple (11:15–19), sandwiched between a miracle story of Jesus's cursing the fig tree (11:12–14, 20–21) and a conclusion consisting of a series of Jesus's teachings concerning the importance of faith and its bearing on prayer (11:22–25). Numerous questions arise as to the pre-Markan form of this material. Were the teachings of 11:22–25 always associated with the story of the cursing of the fig tree? Were they originally linked together, or were they later joined together by various word associations centering on "faith" and "prayer"? Was the story of the cursing originally associated with the cleansing of the temple? Were the two stories associated together before Mark? Is the sandwiching of these two accounts due to Mark, or was it pre-Markan? What is the extent of the Markan editorial work in the account? And so on.

Finally, there is the question of what Mark is seeking to teach by this material. Does he understand the cleansing of the temple primarily as an act of reformation or as an act of judgment? If it is the latter, is it an act of judgment condemning the temple and those in charge of the temple cult

(Evans 2001: 154; J. Edwards 2002: 343–44), or is it an act of judgment condemning the nation (Hooker 1991: 261–66; Stein 1991: 127–33)?[1] How does Mark understand the relationship between the cleansing of the temple and the cursing of the fig tree? How are we to interpret the Markan explanatory clause ("For it was not the season for figs" [11:13])? Does it assist in answering the previous question? How does Mark understand the teachings of 11:22–25 in relation to what has preceded? These are only a few of the questions associated with the present account. It is, of course, impossible to deal with all of these questions in any detail.[2] Various historical issues will be discussed in the comments below, but we shall concern ourselves primarily with seeking to understand what Mark sought to teach by Mark 11:12–25. To the extent that various tradition-historical issues play a role in this, we shall also deal with questions concerning the pre-Markan form of the tradition and the editorial work of the evangelist.

The present account consists of a miracle story involving the cursing of the fig tree (11:12–14, 20–21), a story about Jesus in which he cleanses the temple (11:15–19), and a series of teachings concerning prayer (11:22–25). It is associated with the preceding story of Jesus's entrance into Jerusalem (11:1–11) by various geographical ties (Jerusalem [11:11, 15]; Bethany [11:1, 11, 12]; the temple [11:11, 15]); the Markan editorial comment, "and having looked around at everything [in the temple]" (11:11), which prepares the reader for what Jesus will do as a result of what he saw in the temple; and the chronological note ("and on the following [day]," 11:12). It is tied to the following material by geography (Jerusalem and the temple [11:27; 12:35, 41; 13:1ff.]) and the theme of God's judgment upon the temple and Israel (12:1–12 [cf. Matthew's understanding of the parable in 21:43]; 13:1–37; 14:58; 15:29, 38).

The Markan editorial work is seen most clearly in his sandwiching of the cleansing of the temple (11:15–19) between the miracle of the cursing of the fig tree (11:12–14, 20–21). In both Mark and John the cleansing of the temple (Mark 11:15–19; John 2:13–22) is associated with the Passover (Mark 14:1ff.; John 2:13) and a question concerning Jesus's authority (Mark 11:28; John 2:18; cf. also Matt. 21:12–13, 23 and Luke 19:45–46; 20:2). This suggests that the miracle of the cursing of the fig tree may not originally have been associated with the cleansing of the temple in the pre-Markan tradition.

---

1. E. Sanders (1985: 61–71) sees the cleansing of the temple as a symbolic act of destruction that "looks towards the restoration" (71). The term "restoration," however, is a strange word to use to describe an act that includes the destruction of Jerusalem. Few Jews (even Jewish Christians) would have understood such an event as a "restoration." It would have been understood more as a "judgment," just as 587 BC was a judgment. Furthermore, "restoration" is an inadequate term to describe the replacement of the old covenant with the new because the new covenant "surpasses," not simply "restores," the old.

2. For a helpful survey of these issues, see E. Sanders (1985: 61–71), Meier (1994: 884–96), and Evans (2001: 149–53, 164–71, and 185–86). For a more detailed discussion, see Telford 1980.

That the sandwiching of two separate accounts is a favorite Markan literary device (see the introduction to Mark 3:20–35) argues strongly that, even if the two accounts were associated together in the pre-Markan tradition, their sandwiching is the result of Mark's editorial work (contra Pesch 1980b: 190).

Mark's editorial hand should probably also be seen in the chronological designations tying together the following sections:

11:1–11	because it was already evening ὀψίας ἤδη οὔσης τῆς ὥρας *opsias ēdē ousēs tēs hōras* (11:11)
11:12–14	on the following day τῇ ἐπαύριον *tē epaurion* (11:12)
11:15–19	And they enter into Jerusalem καὶ ἔρχονται εἰς Ἱεροσόλυμα *kai erchontai eis Hierosolyma* (11:15)
	and when evening came καὶ ὅταν ὀψὲ ἐγένετο *kai hotan opse egeneto* (11:19)
11:20–26	early [in the morning] πρωΐ *prōi* (11:20)
11:27–32	And they come again into Jerusalem καὶ ἔρχονται πάλιν εἰς Ἱεροσόλυμα *kai erchontai palin eis Hierosolyma* (11:27)

Additional editorial work by Mark can be found in the introductory seam (11:12); the "for" (γάρ, *gar*) explanatory clause in 11:13c; perhaps the comment "And his disciples were hearing it" (καὶ ἤκουον οἱ μαθηταὶ αὐτοῦ, *kai ēkouon hoi mathētai autou*) in 11:14b; the introductory "And they enter into Jerusalem" (καὶ ἔρχονται εἰς Ἱεροσόλυμα) in 11:15a (V. Taylor 1952: 461; Evans 2001: 165); and the conclusion in 11:18–19 (V. Taylor 1952: 461; Evans 2001: 165; cf. Pryke 1978: 19, 145, 167–68). It is also possible that 11:20–22a reflects Mark's reworking of traditional material (Pryke 1978: 19, 145, 169; Gnilka 1979: 133).

The awkward connection of Jesus's sayings on prayer (11:22–25) with the miracle of the cursing (11:12–14, 20–21) and the fact that they, or similar sayings, appear elsewhere in the gospel tradition as isolated sayings[3] suggest that these sayings were originally independent and only later connected by word association to the miracle of the cursing of the fig tree. Compare how the saying on prayer in 9:29 is connected to the miracle story found in 9:14–28 as an example of what faith can do. That the sayings in 11:22–25 do not

---

3. Mark 11:23—cf. Matt. 17:20/Luke 17:6; 1 Cor. 13:2; also Gos. Thom. 48, 106; Mark 11:24—cf. Matt. 7:7–8/Luke 11:9–10; also John 14:13–14; 15:7, 16; 16:23–24; Mark 11:25—cf. Matt. 5:23–24; 6:14–15; 18:21–35.

support the Markan emphasis that the cursing miracle and the cleansing of the temple are symbolic acts of judgment argues in favor of their association being pre-Markan (Gnilka 1978: 133; Evans 2001: 151, 185–86).[4]

Exegesis and Exposition

[12]And on the following [day], after they departed from Bethany, he was hungry. [13]And having seen from a distance a fig tree having leaves, he went [to see] if by chance he might find anything [to eat] on it, and having come upon it, he found nothing except leaves. For it was not the season for figs. [14]And he answered and said to it, "May no one any longer ⌜eat⌝ fruit from you ever again," and his disciples were hearing [this].

[15]And they enter into Jerusalem. And having entered into the temple, he began to cast out those selling and those buying in the temple, and he overturned the tables of the money changers and the seats of those selling pigeons, [16]and he did not allow anyone to carry a vessel through the temple. [17]And he was teaching and saying to them, "Is it not written, 'My house shall be called a house of prayer for all the nations'? 'But *you* have made it a den of robbers.'" [18]And the chief priests and the scribes heard [this] and were seeking how they might destroy him, for they were fearing him, for all the crowd was astonished at his teaching. [19]And when evening came, ⌜they began to proceed⌝ out of the city.

[20]And while passing by early [in the morning], they saw the fig tree withered from the roots up. [21]And Peter having remembered [Jesus's words] says to him, "Rabbi, look! The fig tree that you cursed has withered!" [22]And Jesus answered and says to him, "⌜Have faith⌝ in God. [23]Truly, I say to you that whoever should say to this mountain, 'Be taken up and be cast into the sea,' and does not doubt in his heart but believes that what he is saying is coming about, it will be [done] for him. [24]Therefore I say to you, all things whatsoever you pray and ask for, believe that you have received it, and it will be [done] for you. [25]And whenever you stand praying, forgive, if you have anything against someone, in order that your Father who is in heaven also might forgive you your trespasses." ⌜ ⌝

"On the following day" (τῇ ἐπαύριον) is found only here in Mark and ties what follows to the conclusion of 11:11, as does the reference to Bethany.[5] Although in 2:23–28 we read of an incident in which the disciples were hungry, this is the only place in Mark were Jesus is so described. There is no reason to interpret Jesus's hunger as a "spiritual" hunger to find godly fruit in Israel. The parabolic act of cursing the fig tree involves a real, physical hunger by Jesus. This is proven

11:12–14

---

4. Dowd (1988: 40–45) rightly criticizes the attempt of Telford (1980: 54–55, 58, 79–80, 108–10, 239) to attribute Mark 11:24–25 to a post-Markan scribe.

5. Gundry (1993: 634–35) and France (2002: 436, 442) argue that 11:11 does not serve as the conclusion for 11:1–10 but as the introduction for 11:12–25. Verse 11, however, is better understood as the conclusion of the journey to Jerusalem and the conclusion of the day begun at 11:1. Verse 12 begins a new day and a new episode in the life of Jesus.

by the fact that the incident involves a real fig tree (11:13b, 14a, 20; cf. also Matt. 21:19–20) and a real cursing of that tree. Mark portrays the cursing of the fig tree as a real event that serves as the interpretive guide for the meaning of another real event, the cleansing of the temple. Questions as to why Jesus was physically hungry are unanswerable on the historical level, but on the literary level this comment serves to prepare the reader for the following story. Mark's placement of the cursing miracle before the cleansing of the temple is intentional (contrast Matthew, who places it [21:18–22] after the cleansing [21:12–13]). The intercalation of the cleansing account between the cursing miracle is also intentional. By this arrangement and his editorial comment to his readers in 11:13b, Mark indicates that Jesus's action with respect to the fig tree is a parabolic act serving as the interpretive guide for understanding Jesus's cleansing the temple (J. Edwards 2002: 339). Such prophetic acts were part and parcel of the OT prophetic repertoire (Isa. 20:1–6; Jer. 13:1–11; 19:1–13; Ezek. 4:1–17), and Jesus made frequent use of this teaching device as well (2:15–16; 3:14–19; 11:1–11; 14:61a; Stein 1994b: 25–26).

Upon seeing a fig tree having leaves, Jesus approaches it to see if he might find on it something to eat. That it had leaves indicates that it was alive and perhaps contained something edible. The fig tree was one of the most common fruit trees in Israel. Its leaves sprout in late March and fall off in the late fall. Normally it yields two harvests. The second and later harvest of figs takes place between mid-August and mid-October. In the fall the fig tree develops buds that remain undeveloped until early spring, when they swell into green knops, or *paggim*. The leaves of the fig tree develop after this (Pliny, *Nat. Hist.* 16.49). The knops, which are edible even if not very palatable (France 2002: 440), develop into the earlier harvest of figs (Song 2:13; Isa. 28:4; Jer. 24:2; Hos. 9:10; Mic. 7:1) that takes place at the end of June. It was these early green knops that Jesus apparently looked for. The idea that Jesus was looking for leftover figs from the second harvest of figs in the fall (Manson 1950–51: 279–80) is contradicted by the general setting of the account found in Mark and Matthew, that is, the Passover season; the comment that Jesus was looking for fruit because he saw leaves on the fig tree; Jesus's turning over of the tables of the money changers in the temple, which could only take place between the twenty-fifth of Adar and the first of Nisan (W. Lane 1974: 405); and above all the Markan comment that it was not the season for figs.

Although the Markan explanatory comment (see 1:16–18), "For it was not the season for figs" (ὁ γὰρ καιρὸς οὐκ ἦν σύκων, *ho gar kairos ouk ēn sykōn*), is the key for understanding both Jesus's cursing of the fig tree and his cleansing of the temple, its meaning is greatly debated. If it was not the season for figs, why did Jesus curse the fig tree for what it was incapable of doing? It is not surprising that numerous scholars have denied the historicity of various aspects of the present account. This is true of even moderate and conservative scholars (Manson 1950–51: 279; Meier 1994: 896; Evans 2001: 152). For some scholars, that the accounts report a "nature miracle" automatically brings a verdict of nonhistorical because of the presupposition that history is a closed continuum of time and space in which miracles do not occur. Various exorcisms and healing "miracles" are accepted as historical events since they can be explained rationally as psychosomatic events (they were not really miracles but healings worked by means of Jesus's great psychological insights into the human condition). Nature miracles, however, lie outside this possibility. For other scholars, the supposed picture of an irate, vindictive Jesus cursing an innocent fig tree is aesthetically unpleasing. As a cursing, it seems out of character with how Jesus is portrayed in the rest of the Gospels. His action is "irrational and revolting" (Bundy 1955: 425), a "tale of miraculous power wasted in the service of ill-temper" (Manson 1950–51: 279).[6] But the response of Jesus in 11:14 is not in any sense described as irate. Nothing is said of Jesus's emotional condition (contrast 1:43), and the description of Jesus's "cursing" the fig tree loses much of its supposed vitriolic flavor when we realize that this "cursing" has nothing to do with profanity and obscenity but refers rather to a symbolic act of condemnation and judgment.

How exactly should we understand Mark's interpretive comment? We should first recognize that the comment is directed to the readers of Mark (cf. 7:19b; 13:14b). Although some scholars have attempted to associate the comment with an earlier statement in the sentence ("He went [to see] if by chance he might [lit. 'shall'] find anything [to eat] on it," ἦλθεν εἰ ἄρα τι εὑρήσει ἐν αὐτῇ, *ēlthen ei ara ti heurēsei en autē*; Cotter 1986: 65–66; cf. Meier 1994: 891–92), the most natural interpretation of the explanatory comment is that it explains what immediately precedes, that Jesus did not find figs but only leaves on the fig tree. It is intended by its very incongruity to help the reader understand that Jesus's action must be interpreted symbolically. Mark is telling his readers that Jesus did not curse the fig tree because it was hopelessly barren (contrast Luke 13:6–9). His parabolic action is no more a lesson on horticulture than is the parable of the fig tree in Luke 13:6–9. The explanatory comment is meant to help Mark's readers realize that what Jesus is doing in the story is not about a fig tree at all. It is rather a symbolic act, an acted-out parable (Hooker 1991: 262; Donahue and Harrington 2002: 327), that explains the meaning of the cleansing of the temple sandwiched within the two parts of this parabolic event.

This understanding is further supported by the fact that the "fig tree" was frequently used as a symbol in prophetic pronouncements of judgment upon God's people (Telford 1980: 132–37). It is so used in judgment statements against Israel (Isa. 28:4; Hos. 2:12; 9:10; Joel 1:7; Mic. 7:1), Judah (Jer. 5:17; 8:13; 24:1–10; 29:17; Hab. 3:17), Nineveh (Nah. 3:12), and the nations in general (Isa. 34:4). In Mark 13:28 Jesus again uses a fig tree, this time in a parable to signify the forthcoming destruction of Jerusalem and the temple.

6. After World War II, in which sixty million people were killed, in a day when terrorists delight in how many innocent victims they have killed, when millions die each year from hunger and diseases that can be prevented, when the lives of tens of millions of unborn children are aborted each year, it seems extremely critical, to say the least, to condemn and revile Jesus for using one of the planet's trillions of trees to serve as a parabolic lesson.

It is clear that Mark does not want his readers to think that what Jesus does in 11:14 is due to anger or rage. There is no hint of this in the verse. On the contrary, just as his "looking around" in 11:11 indicates that the cleansing of the temple was a carefully thought-out and planned prophetic act, so his coming to the fig tree and finding no leaves indicates that the cursing miracle is also a thought-out symbolic act, a dramatized prophecy (J. Edwards 1989: 208). The fig tree represents Israel (Jer. 8:13; Hos. 9:10, 16–17; Mic. 7:1) and is judged by its Messiah because, despite its appearance and religious activity (symbolized by the leaves), Israel has failed to produce the appropriate fruit (Hooker 1991: 261).

Describing Jesus's reply as "answered and said" is a classic example of the idiomatic nature of this expression. Here Jesus is not answering a question at all, for none has been asked. He is rather responding to the situation (see the first additional note on 9:5). Jesus's words in 11:14 have been understood as a prophetic declaration of what would happen to the fig tree because of the arrival of the messianic age (Hiers 1968: 397–98), and 14:25 is suggested as a parallel. Often associated with this view is an attempt to interpret "ever again" as "unto/until the age to come" and the idea that Jesus thought the age to come would take place before the coming harvest of figs (Hiers 1968: 395, 398–40).[7] Thus Jesus's words are understood not as a curse but as a statement that no one would eat the fruit of this fig tree until the age to come arrived, and this would be coming soon. Such interpretations, however, are not based on the present form of the text, in which the fig tree withers overnight, but on a supposed reconstruction of the historical event and the original form of the underlying Aramaic saying (Hooker 1991: 267). In the present Markan text, 11:14 is clearly understood as a curse, as Peter's response, "The fig tree you cursed" (ἡ συκῆ ἣν κατηράσω, hē sykē hēn katērasō), in 11:21 indicates; and though in 14:25 we have a subjunctive of emphatic negation stating a fact, in 11:14 we have an optative expressing a wish on the part of Jesus. In addition we should note that the expression εἰς τὸν αἰῶνα (eis ton aiōna; lit. "unto/until the age") normally means "forever" or "to eternity." Although many prophecies of judgment are intended as warnings, and it is understood that repentance will avert the judgment, for Mark and his readers the pronounced curse was understood as a certain and unavoidable judgment (Hooker 1991: 266; Witherington 2001: 312). It was not a warning but an absolute announcement of what would soon take place (Caird 1980: 56–57).

The first part of the cursing miracle concludes with a reference to the disciples listening to Jesus's words. Although some have sought to attribute a deeper meaning to these words (evidence of the disciples' dullness or their privileged position [4:11–12, 33–34]), it is best to understand this statement as simply providing a literary tie to the second half of the sandwich, where

7. Hiers's view is based on a reconstruction of the event that has little support in the text. If Mark understood Jesus's words in 11:14 as Hiers does, he would not have commented, "For it was not the season for figs" (11:13) but rather "For it was not *yet* the season for figs."

Peter remembers what Jesus had said, observes the result of Jesus's words, and comments about the cursed fig tree (11:21).

The story of the cleansing of the temple consists of three parts: the cleansing **11:15–17** itself (11:15b–16), Jesus's teaching and use of the OT (11:17), and the response of Jesus's opponents (11:18). It is introduced (11:15a) and concluded (11:19) by an introductory Markan seam and conclusion. The scene of the incident is the temple in Jerusalem, one of the most magnificent structures in the world of that day. Excelling even Solomon's temple in grandeur, the rebuilt temple of Zerubbabel had been massively renovated and largely rebuilt by Herod the Great. Built upon a huge raised platform, the entire temple complex consisted of four sections. As a total complex, it was the largest such site in the ancient world. Built in the shape of a trapezoid, its north-south walls were about 500 yards long and its east-west walls about 325 yards long, although the northern wall was longer than its southern counterpart. The total temple platform was 172,000 square yards, or about thirty-five acres. The perimeter of the temple contained a covered portico built of huge columns thirty-five feet in height, whose base was so large that it took three men joining hands to encircle one. It was within this portico that the events described in 11:15–16 took place. The largest area of the temple, in which the portico was located, was the Court of the Gentiles. Within this court and separated by a fence with a series of steps leading up to it lay the Court of the Women; the Court of Israel, which only Jewish men could enter; and the temple itself, with its holy place and holy of holies. No gentile could enter through the fence into these courts, upon pain of death.

Whereas various scholars once denied the historicity of the cleansing episode, the great majority of scholars, both conservative and liberal, today accept its historicity (Evans 2001: 166). Integral to the worship carried on in the temple were the offering of sacrifices and the once-a-year collection of the temple tax. This half-shekel tax was collected from each Jewish male who was twenty years of age or older (Exod. 30:11–16; Neh. 10:32–33; Josephus, *Ant.* 18.9.1 §§312–13). Payment had to be made by using the Tyrian silver half-shekel (the silver didrachma of Tyre; Murphy-O'Connor 2000: 46–50). To facilitate this, money-changing tables were set up in the provinces surrounding Jerusalem on the fifteenth day of Adar, the month preceding Passover. On the twenty-fifth of that month, they were set up in the Court of the Gentiles (*m. Suk.* 1.1, 3) so that the tax could be paid by the first of Nisan (the next month), although late payment was common (*m. Suk.* 6.5). All this, of course, did not take place on a nonprofit basis (*m. Suk.* 1.6), and the exchange of moneys involved a charge of about 4–8 percent. To facilitate the offering of blemish-free sacrifices, "certified/approved" sacrifices were sold year-round in the Court of the Gentiles within the temple itself. This was apparently quite a profitable venture under the control of the priests, whose character was highly criticized in Jewish writings (cf. 1QpHab 1.13; 8.8–13; 9.9; 11.4; 12.1–15; CD 5.6–8; 6.12–17; Ps. Sol. 2.3–9; 8.11–13; Josephus, *Ant.*

20.9.4 §213; *b. Pesaḥ.* 57a) for robbing the poor (1QpHab 8.12; 9.5; 10.1; 12.10; T. Mos. 7.6–10; 2 Bar. 10.18; Josephus, *Ant.* 20.8.8 §§180–81; 20.9.2 §§205–7) and accumulating wealth (1QpHab 8.8–12; 9.4–5).[8]

Jesus's action in the temple was directed against both those selling and those buying, those exchanging money, and those selling pigeons—the sacrifices of the poor (Lev. 12:6–8 [cf. Luke 2:22–24]; Lev. 14:22; John 2:14 adds "those who were selling oxen and sheep"). It is evident from other incidents in the life of Jesus that he was not opposed to the sacrificial system (Mark 1:44; Matt. 5:23; Luke 17:14; cf. Mic. 6:6–8, which is now recognized not as an attack on the sacrificial system as such but an attack on the abuse of it), nor is he portrayed as being opposed to paying the temple tax (Matt. 17:24–27). Consequently his "cleansing" should not be understood as an attack on these practices mandated by the OT. The early Jewish church did not interpret it this way (cf. Matt. 5:17–19; Acts 21:20–26; also Acts 2:46; 6:7c). That both the sellers and buyers are driven out indicates that Jesus's action is not primarily directed against the exploitation and corruption of the chief priests and their agents in the transaction of this business. Rather, it is directed at the very fact that this activity was taking place in the temple itself (Betz 1997, esp. 461–62). This was not what the temple, and the Court of the Gentiles in particular, were intended for (France 2002: 444). Such transactions could and were already being done elsewhere, outside the temple. This understanding of Jesus's action receives additional support from the fact that he would not allow anyone to carry (lit. "that anyone might carry") a vessel through the temple (11:16). The temple was a sacred place and not to be used as a shortcut for carrying things (lit. "vessel")[9] from one place to another (cf. *m. Ber.* 9.5; Josephus, *Ag. Ap.* 2.8 §§106, 109; yet see J. Edwards 2002: 342n23). Thus Jesus's actions serve both as a symbolic act of cleansing illustrating what should or should not be done in the temple and as a prophetic act foretelling the coming of judgment upon the temple and upon the nation (Witherington 2001: 315–16).

A number of factors suggest that the area in the temple affected by Jesus's cleansing may not have been as large as popularly envisioned. One is the great size of the temple courtyard. Only a portion of it was devoted to the sale of animals and the exchange of money. What was done, for example, in the southern porticos would not have been visible to the people in the northern porticos. The lack of interference by the temple police or the Roman soldiers stationed in the Fortress of Antonia (a fortress attached to the northwest part of the temple wall that overlooked the temple area and had direct access to it) suggests this as well. Finally, at the trial of Jesus, when there was a desperate search for witnesses to testify against him (14:55–56), this action is never mentioned. This suggests that Jesus's cleansing of the temple involved not

---

8. Although many of these references apply to the decades closer to the fall of Jerusalem in AD 70, they probably reflect, to a certain degree at least, the situation in Jesus's day as well.

9. There is no reason for understanding "vessel" (σκεῦος, *skeuos*) as referring to liturgical vessels involved in sacrifice (Gundry 1993: 642–43).

a massive attempt to stop the entire activity of buying and selling sacrificial animals and exchanging money but rather a symbolic act of judgment by Jesus upon the nation (J. Edwards 2002: 342; cf. E. Sanders 1985: 69–71).[10]

This action of Jesus is associated with his teaching (11:17). The imperfect "he was teaching and saying" (ἐδίδασκεν καὶ ἔλεγεν, *edidasken kai elegen*) suggests that the teaching may have taken place while he was casting out those guilty of making the temple a den of robbers. The content of Jesus's teaching in Mark 11:17 consists of two OT quotations. The first (Isa. 56:7) is in the form of a question expecting a positive reply (as indicated by the οὐ, *ou*). "Is it not written, 'My house shall be called a house of prayer for all the nations'?" (οὐ γέγραπται ὅτι ὁ οἶκός μου οἶκος προσευχῆς κληθήσεται πᾶσιν τοῖς ἔθνεσιν, *ou gegraptai hoti ho oikos mou oikos proseuchēs klēthēsetai pasin tois ethnesin*). Although numerous scholars attribute this (E. Sanders 1985: 66–67) and the next quotation to the early church, if according to 11:11 Jesus had carefully looked the temple over the night before, and if the activity described in 11:15–16 was a carefully thought-out activity, this argues in favor of the authenticity of the OT quotations (Evans 2001: 174–75). What religious teacher in Israel would not seek to justify his actions by means of the OT? The critical denial of the authenticity of OT quotations found on the lips of Jesus in the Gospels and their attribution to the early church makes Jesus a strange Jewish teacher indeed. He would essentially be the only great Jewish teacher of his day who did not quote the OT! This does not mean, however, that the introduction ("As it is written") could not be Markan (cf. 1:2). Nor does it mean that the early church and the evangelists would not have used the form of the quotations (the LXX) with which their readers were most familiar.

In the Markan context the emphasis of the Isaiah quotation falls upon "for all the nations."[11] The denigration of the Court of the Gentiles by the commercialism surrounding the sale of sacrifices and exchanging of money conflicted radically with its intended purpose. The irony of Jesus's actions should not be missed. Popular messianic hopes and expectations looked for the Messiah to rid Jerusalem and the temple of the gentiles (esp. the Romans), but Jesus's action criticizes the Jewish leadership for hindering the gentiles' access in the temple. It was God's purpose for gentiles to occupy (in worship, of course) the temple (cf. Isa. 2:2–4; 66:18–24). Jesus's criticism falls not on the "cursed" gentiles but on the leadership of Israel for demeaning their rightful place in the temple. France (2002: 445–56) is correct, however, in pointing out that this may not have been the main emphasis of Jesus in cleansing the temple. It is uncertain whether Mark's readers would have known the geographical makeup of the temple well enough to associate Jesus's cleansing of the temple as having taken place in the Court of the Gentiles. Nor does Mark emphasize

10. Buchanan (1991) does not acknowledge this possibility. For him the cleansing was either a large violent military confrontation (282–83; cf. Brandon 1967: 331–34) or simply a later fictional creation of the church (283–86; cf. Seeley 1993, who thinks it is a purely Markan composition).

11. Why Matt. 21:13 and Luke 19:46 omit this phrase found in the Isaiah text is uncertain.

this clearly in his text. What is clear is that for both Jews and gentiles, the temple was intended by God as a sacred place for prayer and worship, and the commercialism of the temple hindered this greatly.

The second OT quotation (Jer. 7:11) is in the form of a statement.[12] The temple leadership had made the temple a "den [lit. 'cave'] of robbers" (the emphatic "you" [ὑμεῖς, *hymeis*] includes not only those participating in the commercialization of the temple but also those behind this, the chief priests and the scribes,[13] who perhaps provided the scriptural justification for such behavior). The term "robbers" (λῃστῶν, *lēstōn*) is used in Mark 14:48 of Jesus and in 15:27 of the two thieves crucified along with Jesus. It generally describes brigands and revolutionaries. As France (2002: 446) points out, it appears here not because it is particularly appropriate, but because it was the term used in the Jeremiah passage. In the present context it probably alludes to the profiteering taking place in the sale of sacrifices and the exchanging of moneys (cf. *m. Ker.* 1.7). The large scale of these business enterprises provided great profits for the temple leadership (Josephus, *J.W.* 6.9.3 §§423–24; *m. Šeqal.* 4.7–9; 5.3–5).

11:18–19   The reference to "the chief priests and the scribes" (οἱ ἀρχιερεῖς καὶ οἱ γραμματεῖς, *hoi archiereis kai hoi grammateis*) and their plot to destroy Jesus recalls the passion predictions of 8:31 and 10:33 and the early attempts by the Pharisees and Herodians in 3:6 to "destroy" him. The "chief priests" consisted of the high priest, the "other priest" who was to assume the role of the high priest in case of emergency, the retired high priests, the captain of the temple, and the temple treasurer (Evans 2001: 179–80). The sinister role that the chief priests and scribes (3:22; 7:1) play in the death of Jesus comes to the fore again in 11:27 ("elders" also mentioned); 14:1, 43 ("elders" also mentioned), 53 ("elders" also mentioned); compare also 12:12. The imperfect "were seeking" (ἐζήτουν, *ezētoun*) is best understood as iterative ("continually seeking") rather than inceptive ("began to seek") due to these other references. The reason given for the desire to kill Jesus is that they were afraid of him (ἐφοβοῦντο γὰρ αὐτόν, *ephobounto gar auton*; 11:18b). Although additional reasons may have played a role (fear that Jesus and/or his followers might start a rebellion and bring destruction on the nation; cf. John 11:49–50), the reason given here is fear due to the popularity of Jesus and his teachings (Mark 11:18c; cf. 11:32; 12:12; 14:1–2). For other examples of Jesus evoking such fear, see 4:41; 5:15, 33; 6:50; 9:32; compare also 16:8. For the astonishment created by Jesus's teachings, see 1:22, 27.

The account of the cleansing of the temple ends with Jesus and the disciples leaving the city and presumably returning to Bethany (11:11; cf. also 14:3). There is no reason to see in Jesus's "proceeding out of the city" any symbolism, such as Jesus now separating himself from the temple and Jerusalem (contra

---

12. Cf. Jesus ben Ananias's use of Jer. 7 to declare judgment upon Jerusalem and the temple in the 60s of the first century AD. See Evans 2001: 176–78.

13. Brandon (1967: 332) correctly emphasizes this.

J. Edwards 2002: 345), for in 11:27 Jesus returns to both and will remain there for some time (11:27–13:1). The verb "began to proceed" (ἐξεπορεύοντο, *exeporeuonto*) is plural, referring to Jesus and the disciples, and it is an inceptive imperfect that does not suggest such a decisive departure.[14]

The second part of the cursing miracle concludes on the following day. Upon seeing the fig tree, Peter speaks on behalf of the disciples and responds to this and the curse he heard the previous day: "Rabbi [ῥαββί, *rhabbi*; Hebrew for 'Teacher' (cf. John 1:38)], look!" See 14:44–46. The curse Jesus pronounced had been fulfilled. The fig tree was totally withered, "from the roots up" (ἐκ ῥιζῶν, *ek rhizōn*). The dead fig tree and the temple action that it interprets are recipients not of an attempted therapeutic action but rather of a curse of judgment by the Son of Man (J. Edwards 2002: 346). This judgment is furthermore not a divine passive ("May God see to it that you never bear fruit"), but an act of judgment by Jesus Christ, the Son of God. Peter points out for Mark's readers that it is Jesus who has cursed the fig tree: "The fig tree that you cursed [ἣν κατηράσω, *hēn katēraso*] has withered." It is Jesus himself who will bring judgment on the temple (14:58; 15:29; cf. John 2:19; Acts 6:14) and the world (cf. Mark 8:38; 13:26–27; Matt. 7:21–23; 10:32–33; 13:36–43; 25:14–30, 31–46; etc.).

11:20–21

In the introduction to this unit, I argued that the sayings in 11:22–25 were not originally associated with the cursing of the fig tree, for 11:12–21 has little to do with faith, prayer, or forgiveness, which are the theme of 11:22–25 (Hooker 1991: 269). They probably became associated together in the pre-Markan tradition. In 11:22, Jesus's command, "Have faith in God," serves as the introductory theme for the sayings that follow. The expression "faith in God" (πίστιν θεοῦ, *pistin theou*) is an objective genitive and refers to a faith whose object is God (cf. Acts 3:16; Rom. 3:22, 26; Gal. 2:16; contrast the subjunctive genitive in Rom. 3:3, "the faithfulness of God"). What such trust in God entails is illustrated by Mark 11:23–25. The importance of what follows is emphasized by the "Truly" that introduces the verses (see 3:28–30).

11:22–25

The faith commanded is described as a faith that can remove mountains (11:23; cf. 1 Cor. 13:2). The numerous parallels to this saying found in the tradition (Matt. 17:20/Luke 17:6; 1 Cor. 13:2; Gos. Thom. 48, 106) argue for the authenticity of the saying. In its present form in Mark (cf. also Matt. 21:21), there is an explicit reference to "this" mountain being cast into the sea. The debate as to which specific mountain is being referred to centers on either the Mount of Olives (W. Lane 1974: 410; cf. Zech. 4:7), on which the cursing of the fig tree takes place (Mark 11:12–13, 15), or the Temple Mount (Hooker 1991: 269–70; N. Wright 1996: 334–35; Evans 2001: 188–89), that is, the mountain of the Lord's house (Mic. 4:1). When this saying circulated independently apart from its present context, the question of which mountain was being referred

---

14. Gundry (1993: 647) suggests that the imperfect is an iterative imperfect building on the earlier departure of 11:11. However, the use of a different verb in 11:11 weakens this possibility.

to would have been meaningless. In the present context, however, "this" must be taken seriously. Here Jesus speaks of the temple's destruction, and in the following materials he talks about the "vineyard" being given to others (12:9) and at great length about the destruction of Jerusalem and the temple (13:1–37). This and the twofold reference to Jesus's saying concerning the destruction of the temple (14:58; 15:29) strongly suggest that "this mountain" refers to the Temple Mount.[15] The "sea" (θάλασσαν, *thalassan*) is not specified, so that there is no need to discuss whether it was the Sea of Galilee, the Dead Sea, or the Mediterranean Sea. It could refer to any real or hypothetical sea.

Similar acts of faith, such as what Jesus will do with respect to the temple and Jerusalem (11:23), are promised to his disciples. The idiomatic and hyperbolic nature of this saying (Stein 1994a: 117–21, 123–35) indicates that its meaning is to be found not in a literalistic interpretation of the words but rather in what Jesus and the biblical authors meant by their use of these words. They intended to emphasize and encourage the importance of faith and prayer. The present tense, "is coming about" (γίνεται, *ginetai*), adds additional emphasis and encouragement to seek the kind of faith commanded. Through such a faith, God can accomplish great things. On the other hand, lack of faith hinders God from doing great things (6:5–6a).

The second saying (11:24), found in variant forms in Matt. 7:7–8/Luke 11:9–10; John 14:13–14; 15:7, 16; 16:23–24, is tied to the preceding by a "Therefore" (διὰ τοῦτο, *dia touto*). This indicates that the possession of the faith described in 11:23 assures believers that anything (lit. "all things whatsoever," πάντα ὅσα, *panta hosa*) they pray and ask for (these serve as synonyms; cf. Matt. 7:7) "will be [done] for [them]." As in the previous verse the saying is emphasized (I say to you, λέγω ὑμῖν, *legō hymin*) and contains a condition: "believe that you have [already] received it" (πιστεύετε ὅτι ἐλάβετε, *pisteuete hoti elabete*), which serves as a synonym for "does not doubt in his heart" (μὴ διακριθῇ ἐν τῇ καρδίᾳ αὐτοῦ, *mē diakrithē en tē kardia autou*) in 11:23. The aorist-tense "received" (the equivalent here of a Hebrew prophetic perfect) indicates confidence that the prayed-for request is already answered.

The final verse (11:25) is associated with 11:22–24 not by the term "believe"/"faith" (πιστεύω/πίστις) but by the term "pray" (προσευχόμενοι, *proseuchomenoi*). It is even further removed from the main theme of 11:11–21.[16] Standing for prayer was a common posture among Jewish people (Matt. 6:5; Luke 18:9–14; 1 Kings 8:14, 22; Ps. 134:1; Jer. 18:20). This saying gives an additional condition for having one's prayers answered, especially the prayer

15. In my opinion the suggestion by Dowd (1988: 45–55) and C. Marshall (1989: 163–74) that 11:23 refers figuratively to the replacement of the temple by the new "house of prayer," i.e., the praying community of believers, finds little textual support in Mark 11:22–25.

16. Evans (2001: 194) is probably correct when he states, "Since it is highly unlikely that the Markan evangelist would have introduced this independent saying on forgiveness into his literary context, a context that speaks at most of faith and prayer (11:15–19), he most likely would have found it as part of a traditional complex of isolated sayings around the fig tree story formed and used in the early church as a prayer catechism."

for personal forgiveness. Those who want to be forgiven of their "trespasses" (παραπτώματα, *paraptōmata*) must forgive those who have offended them. A well-known parallel to this is found in Matt. 5:23–24 (cf. also 18:21–35), and the reference to forgiving others of their "trespasses" and the expression "your Father who is in heaven" recall the Lord's Prayer and the accompanying sayings found in Matt. 6:9, 12, 14–15. It is quite clear that for both Jesus and the evangelists, being forgiven by God and forgiving others go hand in hand. Sometimes our forgiving others may be portrayed as preceding God's forgiving us (11:25; Matt. 5:23–24; 6:12, 14; Luke 6:37), sometimes as being simultaneous with God's forgiving us (Luke 11:4), and sometimes as following God's forgiving us (Luke 7:41–43, 47b; cf. Eph. 4:32; Col. 3:13). What is clear from all this is that forgiveness and forgiving cannot be separated (Matt. 6:15).

For the view that 11:26 is not part of the Markan text but a later scribal addition, see the additional note on 11:25.

Summary

The message that dominates this section of Mark (and continues in the following chapters) involves the divine judgment that is soon to fall on the nation of Israel. It is quite possible that the cleansing of the temple was not understood in the pre-Markan tradition as simply a reformatory attempt by Jesus to purify the temple practices, for there are too many other Jesus traditions that spoke of the divine judgment about to fall upon Israel, and in particular on the temple and Jerusalem. Mark, however, clearly and forcefully emphasizes that the cleansing of the temple was a prophetic act of Jesus telling of the forthcoming judgment of the nation. By bringing the cursing of the fig tree and the cleansing of the temple together, above all by inserting the latter into the former, Mark tells his readers that Jesus clearly foretold of the judgment (for Mark's readers—now befalling?) Jerusalem. Additional Jesus traditions are given in the coming chapters to support this teaching of the coming judgment upon the temple, Jerusalem, and the nation. The parable of the vineyard (12:1–12) states that the privileged position of the nation of Israel will be taken away and given to others. In chapter 13, Mark gathers together various teachings of Jesus concerning the destruction of Jerusalem, and a description of the horror soon to come is given: "For those days will [bring] tribulation, such as has never been from the beginning of creation . . ." (13:19). At his trial and crucifixion (14:58; 15:29) Jesus's prophetic claim that he would destroy the temple is quoted. Finally, Mark refers to an incident that illustrates all this. At the crucifixion the curtain of the temple is torn in two from top to bottom (15:38).

A strong christological emphasis permeates all this as well. This is seen in Jesus's casting out from the temple those who bought and sold and those exchanging money. He does this single-handedly, and no one offers resistance. It is seen in the cursing of the fig tree that quickly withers from the roots up. It is seen in the power of Jesus's teaching and his popularity with the people (11:18). It is seen above all in the fact that the cursing of the fig tree and the corresponding destruction of the temple and Jerusalem are not merely prophecies of Jesus. They are also something *he* will do. It is he who cursed the fig tree (11:21: "The fig tree that you cursed has withered"). Similarly, the destruction of the temple and Jerusalem is not something Jesus predicts God will do, but something he will do. "We heard him [Jesus] saying, '*I* will destroy this sanctuary . . . and after three days will build another . . .'" (14:58). "Ha! [You who would be] the destroyer of the sanctuary and rebuilder [of it] in three days . . ." (15:29). Unlike the prophets of old, Jesus does not proclaim God's future judgment of the nation of Israel. The Markan Jesus proclaims his own future judgment of it! An additional christological emphasis is found in our passage, if the "my" found in the Isa. 56:7 quotation ("my house") was understood by the evangelist as referring to Jesus himself (Gundry 1993: 640).

A final Markan emphasis found in the passage comes from the traditional sayings of Jesus on prayer associated with the traditions he used. In them there is present the need for single-mindedness and wholehearted trust in God by the believing community. The encouragement to pray using the hyperbolic example of removing mountains through prayer is uttered, however, in a context in which the lack of such faith (9:24), failure (9:28–29), and unanswered prayer (14:32–43) are openly acknowledged. Some of the conditions required for effective prayer are more easily achieved than others. Forgiving others (11:25), in light of God's forgiveness of us in Christ, should be relatively easy. However, not doubting in one's heart (11:23) and believing that one's requests are granted even before they come to fruition (11:24) are more difficult. All too often in the pilgrimage of faith, Christians have learned to identify with the father of 9:24 and cry out, "I believe. Help my unbelief."

Additional Notes

11:14. An optative expressing a negative wish (BDF §384): φάγοι.

11:19. The textual evidence is almost equally divided between the singular ἐξεπορεύετο (ℵ C D Θ f¹ f¹³ lat) and the plural ἐξεπορεύοντο (A B K W Δ Ψ). No great issue is at stake in these textual variants, but the plural reading is probably to be preferred (Metzger 1994: 92).

11:22. Some MSS (ℵ D Θ f¹³) read, "If (εἰ) you have faith. . . ." This, however, appears to be a scribal addition due to the influence of Luke 17:6 and Matt. 21:21.

11:25. A few MSS (A C D Θ f¹ f¹³ lat) add v. 26 at this point, "But if you do not forgive, neither will your Father who is in heaven forgive your trespasses." Its omission in ℵ B L W Δ Ψ indicates that this was added by an early copyist in imitation of Matt. 6:14–15 (Metzger 1994: 93). Since the versification in the English Bible first occurred in the translation known as the Geneva Bible (1560), and since the Greek MSS used in it and the later King James Version (1611) are inferior to ℵ B L W Δ Ψ, etc., they contain this scribal addition.

C. Jesus Questioned concerning His Authority (11:27–33)

The present account is intimately related to the events of Jesus's messianic entry into Jerusalem (11:1–11) and his parabolic act of judgment, popularly called "the cleansing of the temple" (11:15–19). The whole account centers on two questions by the chief priests, the scribes, and the elders: "By what authority are you doing these things? . . . Who gave to you this authority to do these things?" (11:28). The theme of Jesus's authority permeates the whole account in that it begins with this twofold question concerning Jesus's authority (11:28); the issue of Jesus's authority is repeated in 11:29; and the account concludes with a reference to Jesus's authority in 11:33, forming an *inclusio*. As already pointed out (see the introduction to 11:12–25), the Johannine account of the cleansing of the temple (2:13–17) is also followed by a question concerning Jesus's authority to do this (2:18). This supports the view that in the pre-Markan tradition the question concerning Jesus's authority was already associated with the account of his cleansing the temple. Thus the two questions about doing "these things" (ταῦτα ποιεῖς/ποιῇς, *tauta poieis/poiēs*; 11:28) in the present context of Mark involve primarily Jesus's authority to judge/cleanse the temple (Hultgren 1979: 71–72). However, that the plural "these things" (ταῦτα) is repeated in each of the two questions in 11:28 indicates that the cleansing of the temple is seen as one of several things Jesus had done that required special authority.

The present account is in the form of a controversy story (V. Taylor 1952: 468) and introduces a block of five controversy stories (11:25–12:37; cf. 2:1–3:6). It starts with a description of the occasion (11:27), proceeds to the controversial questions (11:28), and concludes with Jesus's response (11:29–33; Shae 1974: 10; Evans 2001: 197). The response includes a counter-question by Jesus (11:29–30), the opponents' reply (11:31–33a), and Jesus's concluding statement (11:33b). Numerous suggestions have been made as to the earliest form of the tradition. These include that it consisted of 11:28–30 (Bultmann 1968: 19–20); 11:27b, 28b, 29a, and 30 (Hultgren 1979: 70); and 11:28b, 29a, and 30 (Shae 1974: 10–13). Evans (2001: 198) points out that these attempts generally argue for a different setting for the account than the cleansing of the temple (cf. Bultmann 1968: 20; Gnilka 1979: 140). Yet the present location makes good sense, and in the pre-Markan tradition it was already associated with the cleansing of the temple (cf. John 2:13–17 and 18ff.). There is no need to deny the essential historicity of the account (V. Taylor 1952: 469; Cranfield 1959: 362; Evans 2001: 198).[1]

It is difficult to delineate the Markan editorial work in the present account. The introductory seam (11:27a) is probably Markan in wording (Shae 1974: 4–5; Gnilka 1979: 137), although the location of the account (Jerusalem and the temple) is traditional. The question in the Johannine parallel (2:18) also occurs in the temple (2:14–21). Similarly, whereas the reference to the chief priests, the scribes, and the elders recalls Mark 8:31; 14:43, and 53, it is very unlikely that the tradition would have referred to those coming to Jesus and asking the questions on authority simply by an indefinite "they." Although the threefold description of opponents of Jesus in the account is Markan, the tradition probably mentioned one or more of these groups in the incident.[2] The Johannine parallel (2:18) also argues in favor of the pre-Markan origin of the question(s) concerning Jesus's doing "these things." Another suggestion as to the Markan editorial work involves the double question found in 11:28. Hultgren (1979: 69–71) sees only the second (11:28b) as being original and the first (11:28a) as Markan (contra Shae 1974: 5–6, who sees both questions as authentic). The omniscient editorial comment in 11:31–32a need not be Markan (contra Pryke 1978: 19, 145, 168), for Jesus's counterquestion in 11:30 requires some sort of response. If something like 11:33a was the response, there would be a need in telling the story to have something like 11:31–32. On the other hand, the comment "they were afraid of the crowd" (ἐφοβοῦντο τὸν ὄχλον, *ephobounto ton ochlon*; 11:32b) looks Markan (cf. 12:12; also 6:20; 9:32; 11:18), as does the explanatory "for" (γάρ, *gar*) clause (11:32c; Gnilka 1979: 137). Nevertheless, if 11:31–32a is traditional, something like 11:32b–c was probably associated with it in the pre-Markan tradition. The clearest evidence of Mark's editorial work is found in 11:27a and 32c (Shae 1974: 7–9).

Exegesis and Exposition

[27]And they come again into Jerusalem, and as he [Jesus] was walking in the temple, the chief priests and the scribes and the elders come to him, [28]and were asking him, "By what authority are you doing these things?" Or "Who gave to you this authority

---

1. The lack of any distinct christological teaching in the account tends to argue for its historicity. In Jesus's question concerning the baptism of John (11:30), his authority is portrayed as parallel to that of John. Nothing is present here concerning John being the forerunner of the mightier one coming after him (1:7), whose baptism would be greater still (1:8). Meier (1994: 166) therefore suggests that the account has a strong historical claim because it satisfies the criterion of embarrassment as well as the criterion of multiple attestation. Moreover, "nothing argues strongly that the core of the tradition was a creation of the early church" (Meier 1994: 167).

2. Meier (1994: 165) points out that the chief priests and scribes fit well the type of group that would have felt embarrassment with respect to Jesus's counterquestion. Unlike the Herodians, they would have been embarrassed to say that John's baptism was from "men" because of the general consensus of the Jewish people that John was a prophet. They would have also been embarrassed to say that John's baptism was from "heaven" since they did not believe in him.

⌜to do these things⌝?"²⁹But Jesus said to them, "I shall ask you one question, and ⌜you answer me⌝ and I shall tell you by what authority I do these things. ³⁰The baptism of John, was it from heaven or from men? Answer me." ³¹And they were discussing [this] among themselves, ⌜saying,⌝ "If we say 'From heaven,' he will say, 'Why [then] did you not believe him?' ³²But [if] we say, 'From men'?"—They were afraid of the crowd, for all regarded John as truly a prophet. ³³And ⌜they answered⌝ Jesus, "We do not know." And Jesus says to them, "[Then] neither will I tell you by what authority I do these things."

In the previous section I have argued that Mark has sandwiched the cleansing **11:27–28** of the temple (11:15–19) in the middle of the cursing of the fig tree (11:11–14, 20–25). I also argued that in the pre-Markan tradition the account of the cleansing of the temple and the present account were associated together in the pre-Markan tradition (see the introduction to 11:12–25). Therefore by his "And they [Jesus and the disciples being understood] come again into Jerusalem" (καὶ ἔρχονται πάλιν εἰς Ἱεροσόλυμα, *kai erchontai palin eis Hierosolyma*), Mark indicates the connection of the present account to the cleansing of the temple. The repetition of "Jerusalem" in this chapter (11:1, 11, 15) is intentional and reminds the reader that we have reached the place where Jesus predicted that he would be crucified (France 2002: 453). As Jesus "was walking in the temple,"[3] the site of the previous day's cleansing, the chief priests, the scribes, and the elders come to ask (lit. "say to") him two questions. Just as the present reference to Jerusalem reminds the reader of Jesus's forthcoming passion, so also does the reference to the chief priests, scribes, and elders (cf. 8:31; 10:33 [elders not mentioned]; also 14:43, 53; 15:1). These three groups made up the leadership of the Sanhedrin, the ruling body of the nation. Presided over by the high priest, the Sanhedrin consisted of seventy-one members made up of the chief priests, scribes, and elders. They had authority over all religious matters and, within the boundaries set by the Romans, over various political issues as well.

Jesus is confronted by his opponents with two questions. The questions are not sincere but are an attempt to embarrass Jesus and perhaps even intimidate him before the crowd. In 11:33, their refusal to respond to Jesus's question reveals their insincerity. The reader already knows that one element of this group, the scribes, had already come to the conclusion that Jesus was "possessed by Beelzebul" and "by the prince of demons . . . [was] casting out demons" (3:22). Because of the major similarities in their two questions (both ask about Jesus's "authority" [ἐξουσία, *exousia*] to do "these things" [ταῦτα]), it is best to understand them as essentially synonymous (C. Marshall 1989: 197n2; Evans 2001: 203; contra Hultgren 1979: 69–70). The repetition of the first question alone in 11:29 and 11:33 demonstrates this. In the present context they refer above all to Jesus's "authority" for "these things" that he

---

3. Mark probably wants his readers to understand that Jesus was engaged in a teaching ministry in the temple during the week (cf. 14:49 and 11:27–13:37).

had done in the temple on the previous day, that is, his cleansing/judging the temple (V. Taylor 1952: 469–70; Hurtado 1983: 189).[4] In Mark the term "authority" never involves permission or authorization from a human power or agency. In 1:27 (cf. also 1:22) and 2:10 it refers to Jesus's God-given authority to cast out demons and to forgive sins. In 3:15 and 6:7 it refers to the authority of Jesus, the Son of God, to bestow on his disciples authority to cast out demons. The ultimate source of this authority in 1:27 and 2:10 is God, and in 3:15 and 6:7 Jesus himself. Even in the last instance where the term is used (13:34), the parable speaks of the authority that the "master," who returns as "lord of the house," gives his servants. Here too this authority refers either to the authority of God or to the authority of the Son of God. It seems clear, therefore, that Mark expects his readers to answer the questions "By what authority?" and "Who?" in 11:28 with "By God's authority" and "God" (J. Edwards 1994: 220–27). Neither Mark nor his readers would have thought of the historical question of whether originally the chief priest, scribes, and elders were asking Jesus about whether he had received permission from them to cleanse the temple.[5]

11:29–30 Jesus's response to his opponents involved one "question" (λόγον, *logon*; lit. "word") or thing. It was a counterquestion. This was a common rabbinic technique (Evans 2001: 203–4), and Jesus used it frequently (Stein 1994b: 23–24). In Mark we have already seen Jesus's use of a counterquestion in 2:8–9, 19, 25–26; 3:4, 23; 10:3, 38; cf. also 12:16. Jesus's use of a counterquestion differs from the practice of the rabbis. In rabbinic usage, it was assumed that the questioner and those questioned would agree on the same answer. Here, however, they differ radically. Jesus tells his opponents that he will answer their question(s) "and explain by what authority I do these things" on the condition that they answer his question first. Mark's repetition and summarization of Jesus's opponents' question here and in 11:33 emphasize the source of John the Baptist's and Jesus's authority.

The question of Jesus is crisp and clear, and it builds upon the crowd's belief that John the Baptist was a prophet sent from God. "The baptism of John, was it from heaven [a circumlocution for 'God'] or from men [ἐξ οὐρανοῦ ἦν ἢ ἐξ ἀνθρώπων, *ex ouranou ēn ē ex anthrōpōn*]?" Fleshed out more fully, the question Jesus asks is: "The prophetic ministry of John the Baptist, calling the nation to repent and be baptized because there was coming one who was mightier than he, did it have God as its origin and source, or was it a purely man-made ministry?" (cf. 8:33). Jesus then concludes with an abrupt "Answer me" (ἀποκρίθητέ μοι, *apokrithēte moi*; 11:30b), which is omitted in the parallels in Matthew and Luke. If they believed John was a prophet, then they would

---

4. The view of Gundry (1993: 657) that "these things" along with the present tense of "you are doing" (ποιεῖς/ποιῇς) should be interpreted as meaning that Jesus was continuing to cleanse the temple just as he did the day before is grammatically possible but very unlikely in that no other act of cleansing is mentioned in 11:27ff.

5. See Evans (2001: 199–203) for a more detailed discussion.

believe in the one who he announced would follow him (Hooker 1991: 272). They would also believe that both John and Jesus had received their authority from God. That Jesus himself had come to John the Baptist and been baptized by him has already been reported in Mark (1:9–11). Thus he and John shared a common prophetic ministry and divine authorization (1:2–15; 6:14–29; 8:28; 9:11–13). Yet their ministries, although both were divine in origin, were not equivalent, for John pointed to Jesus as the Lord (1:3), whose way he was to prepare. Jesus was mightier than John (1:7), and his baptism would be more wonderful still (1:8).

Clearly Jesus's question placed the chief priests, scribes, and elders on the horns of a dilemma. At this point the omniscient editor helps us understand what was going through the minds of the chief priests, scribes, and elders.[6] If they acknowledged (lit. "If we should say" [ἐὰν εἴπωμεν, *ean eipōmen*]—a deliberative subjunctive) that John's ministry was authorized by God, then Jesus could reply, "Then why did you not believe him?" (and as a result repent and receive his baptism [1:4]), and by implication, "Why then do you not accept me as the one greater than John, whom he foretold as coming?" (1:2–3, 7–8). To answer Jesus's question positively would in effect answer the questions they addressed to Jesus, for those who would accept the messenger (John) would accept the Lord who followed (W. Lane 1974: 413–14; Hooker 1991: 271; cf. J. Edwards 1994: 227). On the other hand, to say that John's ministry was not from God but that his ministry had a purely human origin would infuriate the crowd, for they considered or "regarded" (εἶχον, *eichon*; lit. "were having") John the Baptist as a prophet.[7] The result of this would be not only a loss of credibility with the people but their scorn and anger as well. (For the popularity of John the Baptist, cf. 1:5 and Josephus, *Ant.* 18.5.2 §118.) The break in grammar that leaves the sentence "But if we say, 'From men'" incomplete heightens the drama and reveals the great dilemma in which the religious authorities found themselves (C. Marshall 1989: 196–97).

The insincerity of the chief priests, scribes, and elders becomes most evident in their reply: "We do not know" (οὐκ οἴδαμεν, *ouk oidamen*). It is a cowardly answer that seeks to save face. But instead of saving face and embarrassing Jesus with their questions in 11:28, they have embarrassed themselves by their hypocrisy and refusal to answer Jesus's question. If they were unable to conclude whether John the Baptist was a true or false prophet, they had forfeited the right to be the religious leaders of the nation. Jesus's question would have required only a single-word (ἓν λόγον, *hen logon*) answer from his opponents, and he provided the two possibilities: from "God" or from "men." As a result

11:31-32

11:33

---

6. Although the omniscient editor may have been Mark, it is also possible that there was such an editorial comment in the pre-Markan telling of the story.

7. This γάρ explanatory clause in 11:32c looks typically Markan (Evans 2001: 207). If it is, Mark is here explaining to his readers why the chief priests, scribes, and elders were afraid to say that John's baptism was from men. Normally Mark explains traditional material with his γάρ clauses. This suggests that "they were afraid of the crowd" may be traditional.

of refusing to answer the question Jesus had asked them, Jesus's opponents forfeited the right to expect an answer from him. He will not answer their question(s). Yet the way Jesus responds, "[Then] neither will I tell you by what authority I do these things," assumes that he does have a unique authority to do these things. Mark's readers, of course, already know the source of this authority. It comes from the same source as John the Baptist's authority. It is the God who sent his messenger John (1:2) who has sent Jesus his Son (1:11; 9:7). Mark's readers have known this from the very beginning (1:1). The chief priests, scribes, and elders, because of their hardness of heart (cf. 3:5; 7:6),[8] see but do not perceive, hear but do not understand (4:12). Because of their deliberate refusal to accept the truth, Jesus saw that further discussion would be fruitless, and so he refused to answer their question(s). They had refused to meet the only condition Jesus had given (11:29–30).

Summary

As is evident from the fourfold repetition of the question (11:28 [2×], 29, 33), the main thrust of the present account centers on the fact and source of Jesus's authority. What is the source of Jesus's authority that enables him to cast out demons (1:27), to forgive sins (2:10), to enter Jerusalem as its messianic king (11:1–11), to cleanse/judge the temple (11:15–19), and so on? By what authority does Jesus do "these things," and many other things as well? For Mark's readers, the answer has been evident from the earliest words of the Gospel. Jesus is the Christ, the Son of God! His authority to cast out demons, to offer the kingdom of God to outcasts (2:13–16), to give the definitive interpretation of the Sacred Scriptures (7:1–23), to present himself as Israel's king, to judge the temple, to offer himself as a ransom for many (10:45), and so on comes from God. It is God himself who has said to him "You are my beloved Son" (1:11) and has declared to the disciples "This is my beloved Son" (9:7)! Later it would become even more clear that "all authority in heaven and on earth has been given to [him]" (cf. Matt. 28:18; Eph. 1:20–23; Phil. 2:9–11; etc.).

An additional christological emphasis found in the passage involves the portrayal of Jesus's dominating presence throughout the account. He is not intimidated by his many opponents or their positions. Mark points out that the amazement, wonder, and even fear that Jesus creates by his ministry and presence continue even in this hostile environment (see 1:21–22). The attempt by the chief priests and the scribes and the elders to embarrass Jesus does not succeed at all. On the contrary, just the opposite occurs! Jesus overpowers his opponents in the theological debate with an awesome display of wisdom. This will continue in the four controversy stories found in 12:13–40.

8. The hardness of heart that the disciples at times possessed (6:52; 8:17) was more cognitive in nature and involved a dullness and lack of understanding that the resurrection of Jesus would remedy. The hardness of the chief priests, scribes, and elders, however, was volitional in nature and therefore unpardonable.

Mark also continues to prepare his readers for the inevitability of Jesus's death. The hostility of the chief priests, scribes, and elders is clearly evident in the account. Earlier in the Gospel we have come across similar hostility (2:6–7, 16, 18, 24; 3:2, 22; 6:3–4; 7:5–8; 8:11–12; 10:2; etc.) and even a plot to kill him (3:6; cf. 12:13; 14:1–2; etc.), along with Jesus's various attempts to prepare his disciples for this (2:19–20; 8:31; 9:12, 31; 10:33–34, 45). Mark's readers know the fact of Jesus's death, of course, so this is nothing new. Mark wants his readers to know, however, that whatever might have been the human causes that brought about Jesus's death, they must keep in mind that the ultimate cause was to be found in the will of God. There was a divine necessity (δεῖ, *dei*; 8:31) for the Son of Man to give his life as a ransom (10:45) and to pour out his blood for many (14:24). For this purpose "he came" (10:45); this was the cup he came to drink (14:36).

Additional Notes

11:28. The ἵνα ταῦτα ποιῇς (lit. "that you may do these things") is probably best understood as epexegetical (Zerwick and Grosvenor 1981: 146).

11:29. The imperative "you answer me" (ἀποκρίθητέ μοι) may reflect a Semitic usage and function as the protasis of a conditional sentence (Evans 2001: 197, 204).

11:31. The translation follows 𝔓⁴⁵ ℵ A B C K L W etc. rather than the reading τί εἴπωμεν; (What should we say?) found in D Θ f¹³ (Metzger 1971: 110).

11:33. ἀποκριθέντες . . . λέγουσιν is lit. "having answered . . . say."

D. Jesus's Parable of the Vineyard (12:1–12)

The present parable in Mark (the only major parable outside chap. 4) is intimately associated with the question of Jesus's authority (11:27–33) by "And he began to speak to them in parables . . ." (Καὶ ἤρξατο αὐτοῖς ἐν παραβολαῖς λαλεῖν, *Kai ērxato autois en parabolais lalein*; 12:1a). The material in 11:27–12:44 is all envisioned as occurring in the temple (13:1). Luke follows Mark closely in this regard (cf. 20:1–21:4). In Matthew the geographical context remains the temple (21:23), and the parable (21:33–46) follows the question of Jesus's authority (21:23–27), but Matthew has placed the parable of the two sons (21:28–32) between them. After the parable of the vineyard, Matthew places the parable of the marriage feast (22:1–14) and then follows Mark (cf. Mark 12:13–37 with Matt. 21:15–46), but he considerably enlarges Jesus's concluding denunciation of the scribes in Mark 12:38–40 with Matt. 23:1–36. All of Matt. 21:23–23:39 likewise takes place in the temple (24:1). Mark 11:27–12:37 consists of a series of conflict stories centering on Jesus's authority for his actions and teachings. The parable of the vineyard is so closely associated with the preceding question of Jesus's authority that some scholars treat 11:27–12:12 as a single incident with two parts: the challenge to Jesus's authority (11:27–33) and Jesus's reply (12:1–12 [Gundry 1993: 656]).

The parable tells of a man who builds a vineyard and leases it out to tenants. He then departs to another country (12:1). At the appropriate time the absentee landlord sends a servant to receive his rental fees (part of the "fruit of the vineyard" [τῶν καρπῶν τοῦ ἀμπελῶνος, *tōn karpōn tou ampelōnos*]). Instead of receiving the agreed-upon rental fees from the tenants, the servant is beaten and sent back empty-handed (12:2–3). Thereupon the owner of the vineyard sends another servant, and this time the servant is hit in the head and shamefully treated (12:4). The owner sends a third servant, and this time the servant is killed. The owner continues to send many others, and they receive similar treatment. Some are beaten; some are killed (12:5). Finally, the owner sends his beloved son, assuming that the tenants will certainly respect him; but the tenants, realizing that he is the heir, kill him and throw his body outside the vineyard, expecting that as a result the vineyard will become theirs (12:6–8). Jesus then asks rhetorically, "What therefore will the lord of the vineyard do?" and answers his own question, "He will come and destroy the tenants and give the vineyard to others" (ἐλεύσεται καὶ ἀπολέσει τοὺς γεωργοὺς καὶ δώσει τὸν ἀμπελῶνα ἄλλοις, *eleusetai kai apolesei tous geōrgous kai dōsei ton ampelōna allois*; 12:9). The parable then ends with a question, "Have you not read this scripture," and a quotation from Ps. 118:22–23 (Mark 12:10–11). The account concludes as "they" (referring back to the "them" in 12:1 and ultimately back to the chief priests, scribes, and elders in 11:27) are attempting to arrest Jesus because "they" know that Jesus told the parable against them. But due to their fear of the multitude, "they" leave Jesus and go away (12:12).

Numerous questions are encountered in this parable, which is one of the *"most debated—and misunderstood—parables of Jesus"* (Snodgrass 1998: 187). One involves the question of the parable's authenticity. Does the parable ultimately stem from Jesus, or is it entirely the creation of the early church (so Jülicher 1910: 2.406; Carlston 1975: 183–84, 186–87)? At one time the simple presence of allegorical details in this parable (or any parable) was sufficient to deny the parable's authenticity. While this was a natural overreaction to the allegorical method of interpreting the parables, it was nevertheless still an overreaction.[1] If the early church and the evangelists could have accepted the presence of allegorical details in the parables of Jesus, there is no good reason for denying that Jesus could have also accepted such details in his own parables.

Others have argued against the authenticity of the parable on the basis that the behavior of the owner and tenants is so irrational and the supposed situation so unrealistic that it could not have made any sense to Jesus's hearers. Thus it must be inauthentic (Carlston 1975: 187; Kloppenborg Verbin 2000). There are good reasons, however, for seeing the situation portrayed in the parable as reflecting the farming situation in Galilee during Jesus's ministry (Snodgrass 1983: 31–40; Evans 2001: 215–31). The supposedly incoherent and utterly unrealistic behavior that some scholars claim is found in the parable and argues against its authenticity loses sight of at least three important factors: (1) This is a parable, and parables often portray unrealistic behavior. (Does a shepherd really leave ninety-nine sheep in the wilderness to find the lost one [Luke 15:4]? Do rich owners really commend dishonest stewards who swindle them [Luke 16:1–8]? Do people really forgive servants of debts as large as a thousand talents [Matt. 18:24, 27]? etc.) (2) Why do Mark, Matthew, and Luke tell their readers this parable if it is so unrealistic? It must have made sense to the evangelists, and they must have believed that it would have made sense to their readers.[2] Finally, (3) the "unrealistic" behavior of the landowner and the tenants in the imagery of the parable corresponds exactly with the "unrealistic," but *true*, behavior of the God of Israel and the people of Israel in the interpretation of the parable. God had indeed sent his servants to his vineyard, time and time again, only to find that they were tortured, mocked, scourged, imprisoned, stoned, sawn in two, killed, and so on (Heb. 11:35–37). What some scholars

---

1. France (2002: 457) rightly comments, "The days are long gone when it was axiomatic that Jesus never used allegory and that his parables were simply moral lessons." Cf. also Snodgrass 1983: 13–26.

2. See Evans (2001: 220–22) for several interesting rabbinic parallels.

criticize as absurd and unrealistic is in reality the inconceivable "amazing grace" of God!

While the majority of scholars today are willing to accept the present parable as stemming from Jesus (Hultgren 2000: 361; Evans 2001: 216, 223), they nevertheless still raise questions about the extent to which the present parable stems from him. Some scholars claim that the attempts to remove all the allegorical details from the present parable (cf. Dodd 1948: 124–32; Jeremias 1972: 70–77) in order to find the original parable of Jesus have been confirmed by the discovery of the Gospel of Thomas (Arnal 2000: 138–41). The form of the parable found in Gos. Thom. 65 is much like the "de-allegorized" form suggested by Dodd and Jeremias. This "more authentic" form of the parable supposedly consisted of 12:1b–3, 5a, 6–9a. Yet the claim that the Gospel of Thomas presents a more primitive version of the parable than Mark has been seriously challenged (Snodgrass 1989; Evans 2001: 217–19). Though the parable in Gos. Thom. 65 ends abruptly with the killing of the son and an exhortation to hear, the following saying in Gos. Thom. 66 is composed from Ps. 118:22 (cf. Mark 12:10–11). Its location and the fact that the Gospel of Thomas has a strong anti-OT bias argues in favor of the view that the tradition upon which Gos. Thom. 65 is based had the psalm quotation concluding the parable. It is also evident that one cannot remove all of the allegorical material from this parable, because the image of Israel as a vineyard ultimately stems from the allegory/parable found in Isa. 5:1–7 (Hooker 1991: 274).

Numerous scholars have suggested that the association of Ps. 118:22–23 with the parable was due to a pun in Hebrew/Aramaic. The rejected "son" (*ben*) in the parable corresponds to the rejected "stone" (*'eben*) of the psalm and suggests an intentional tie originating in a Hebrew-Aramaic environment (M. Black 1971: 11–14; Snodgrass 1983: 63–65, 113–18; N. Wright 1996: 499–501) and not a Hellenistic one. As a result, if the early church was responsible for this association, it was not the Hellenistic, Greek-speaking church that did this, nor Mark, but it must be due to the early Jewish church or Jesus himself. This is supported by the fact that some of the parable's allusions to Isa. 5:1–7 do not come from the LXX but instead follow the MT (Evans 2001: 224–26). If Jesus saw himself as rejected by the "builders," that is, the religious leadership of Israel,[3] and believed in his ultimate vindication, and if he understood himself as the "Son" sent by the Father, then it is not at all unlikely that the tie between Ps. 118:22–23 and the parable was made by Jesus himself.[4] As in many other cases, the presuppositions one

3. For examples of "builders" referring to religious leaders, see CD 4.19; 8.12, 18; Acts 4:11; 1 Cor. 3:10; *b. Ber.* 64a; *b. Šabb.* 114a.

4. N. Wright (1996: 498) points out that Ps. 118 was a psalm sung by pilgrims coming to Jerusalem and the temple. As a result it was probably as well known as "anything in the scriptures." This familiarity with the psalm and the setting within the temple fit exactly the situation in the Gospels, where during the high season of pilgrimage Jesus is teaching in the temple. Wright thinks, therefore, that Mark 12:10–11 goes back to Jesus himself (501).

holds concerning Jesus's messianic self-consciousness play an important (perhaps the decisive) role in this matter.

While it is true that proving that the parable and its OT quotation did not stem from a Hellenistic environment but a Hebrew-Aramaic one does not prove that they are authentic and stem back to Jesus, we must admit that we have no substantial reason for denying their essential authenticity. Whereas their origin in a Hellenistic environment would disprove their authenticity, we cannot ultimately prove their authenticity.[5] More often than not, such a decision depends upon the presuppositions one brings to the discussion.[6] As to the Markan redaction, the best candidates are 12:1a (the wording is Markan but the scene [the temple] and the association with the question concerning Jesus's authority [11:27–33] need not be), perhaps 12:5b–c, and finally 12:12 (the summary nature of the conclusion and the portrayal of the leadership's antagonism and the people's positive response look Markan as well; Pryke 1978: 19, 145, 168; Best 1981: 218–19; Marcus 1992b: 111–14; Evans 2001: 231; Donahue and Harrington 2002: 337).

Exegesis and Exposition

[1]And he began to speak to them in parables, "A man planted a vineyard and he built a fence around [it] and dug [a pit for] a winepress and built a tower and ⌜leased it out⌝ to tenants and he departed. [2]And he sent to the tenants a servant in due course in order that he might receive from the tenants [some of] the fruit of the vineyard. [3]And they ⌜took⌝ and beat him, and sent him away empty-handed. [4]And again he sent to them another servant, and that one they beat on the head and treated shamefully. [5]And he sent another and that one they killed, and [he sent] many others, ⌜some of whom they beat and some of whom they killed⌝. [6]And he had still one, a beloved son. He sent him last of all to them, ⌜thinking,⌝ 'They will respect my son.' [7]But those tenants said to one another, 'This is the heir. Come, let us kill him, and the inheritance will be ours!' [8]And they took and killed him and cast his body out of the vineyard. [9]What ⌜therefore⌝ will the lord of the vineyard do? He will come and destroy the tenants and give the vineyard to others. [10]Have you not read this scripture: 'The stone that the builders rejected, ⌜this stone⌝ has become the head of the corner; [11]this [head

5. See the discussion between Evans (2003: 105–10) and Kloppenborg Verbin (2002; 2004) over the Septuagintal character of the parable. Kloppenborg Verbin argues that the parable's reference to Isa. 5:1–7 cannot be authentic, because it is based on the Septuagintal version of the parable in Isa. 5:1–7 and not the MT. Evans, however, argues that the overall Semitic flavor of the parable "provides evidence that [while] the tradition has passed through Greek hands [before reaching Mark] . . . Greek hands [did not] create it in the first place" (2003: 106).

6. Snodgrass (1998: 208) comments: "Three factors lead to failure in understanding this parable: (1) ignoring its OT and Jewish context; (2) the desire [on the part of interpreters] to avoid any thought of judgment; (3) the desire to avoid any connection to Jesus." Contrast Milavec (1990: 30), who approaches the parable as a "post-Holocaust" scholar opposed to "supersessionist instincts." Yet the present account is no more anti-Semitic than the OT prophets' messages of judgment upon Israel (cf. Isa. 3:14; Jer. 12:10–13).

stone] came from the Lord and it is marvelous ⌜to behold⌝?"⌝ [12]And they were seeking to arrest him, ⌜but⌝ they feared the crowd, for they knew that he had spoken the parable against them. And they left him and went away.

12:1   For "And he began" (ἤρξατο, ērxato) followed by an infinitive, see 1:45. This is a common Markan construction and suggests that the wording, if not the content, is due to the evangelist. For "in parables" (ἐν παραβολαῖς, en parabolais), compare 3:23; 4:2, 11. In 4:2, 11, and here the plural "parables" is used, but only a single parable is referred to (cf. Matt. 22:1). Note that the parallels in Matt. 21:33 and Luke 20:9 use the singular. The prepositional phrase, used adverbially here, and the plural "parables" suggest that the phrase has become an idiom for "parabolically" (cf. Matt. 22:1; France 2002: 458; contra Gundry 1993: 683). "To them" (αὐτοῖς, autois) is not indefinite but refers back to the "to them" in 11:33 and ultimately to the chief priests, the scribes, and the elders in 11:27.

"A man planted a vineyard" (ἀμπελῶνα ἄνθρωπος ἐφύτευσεν, ampelōna anthrōpos ephyteusen) recalls the parable of the vineyard in Isa. 5:1–7: a "vineyard" (ἀμπελών; 5:1) "I planted" (ἐφύτευσα; 5:2 LXX) and "put a fence around it" (φραγμὸν περιέθηκα, phragmon periethēka; 5:2 LXX; cf. 5:5 MT); "I dug out a pit for a wine vat" (προλήνιον ὤρυξα, prolēnion ōryxa; 5:2); and the question "What shall I do?" (τί ποιήσω; ti poiēsō? Isa. 5:5/Mark 12:9); and so on.[7]

Since in the OT analogy "the vineyard of the LORD of Hosts" is described as "the house of Israel and the people of Judah, . . . his pleasant planting" (Isa. 5:7), the hearers of the parable would immediately have known that the parable Jesus was telling was about the Jewish people. New in Jesus's parable is that he "leased it out to tenants and went into another country" (καὶ ἐξέδετο αὐτὸν γεωργοῖς καὶ ἀπεδήμησεν, kai exedeto auton geōrgois kai apedēmēsen). At this point, those familiar with the OT parable would have had their interest piqued for what Jesus was about to say concerning them.

The practice of leasing out farmland by an absentee landlord was common in Israel.[8] What is uncommon is the behavior of the landlord and the tenants in Jesus's parable. Yet in a parable/allegory it is this uncommon quality that makes it interesting. Various allegorical analogies are found in this verse: a man = God; the vineyard = Israel;[9] and the tenants[10] = the leaders of Israel:

7. See Weren (1998: 6–13) for a helpful comparison of Mark 12:1–12 and Isa. 5:1–7.

8. "The story would have been unexpected, possibly even shocking, but it fits in the first-century Palestinian narrative world. Conflicts over farming agreements were an all-too-common occurrence" (Snodgrass 1998: 197). For more information, see Jeremias 1972: 74–75; Derrett 1970: 286–312.

9. A "vineyard" is a frequent OT metaphor for Israel (cf. Ps. 80:8–19 [79:9–20 LXX]; Isa. 1:8; 27:2; Jer. 2:21; Ezek. 19:10; also 3 Bar. 1.2), and the prophets frequently criticized the leaders of the nation for their abuse of God's vineyard (cf. Isa. 3:14; Jer. 12:10).

10. It is uncertain whether the "tenants" in the parable refer to agricultural workers who physically took care of the vineyard or to middle-management people who supervised and managed the vineyard but hired others to do the actual physical labor.

the chief priests, scribes, and elders. In the following verses we have servants = the prophets (12:2–5); beloved son = Jesus, the Son of God (12:6–11); and killing the son = the crucifixion of Jesus, the Son of God (12:7–8). In addition, some scholars (Brooke 1995: 271–72) find allegorical significance in the winepress = the altar of the temple (cf. *t. Me'il.* 1.16; *t. Suk.* 3.15); the tower = the temple (cf. 1 En. 89.50–73; *t. Suk.* 3.15; 4Q500). It is unclear how broadly the symbolism of the last two metaphors was known to Jesus's hearers, but it is unlikely that Mark's gentile readers would have known them. Other attempts to see allegorical significance in the owner's departure and the hitting of a servant in the head involve allegorizing, that is, reading allegory into nonallegorical aspects of the parable.

The meaning of "in due course" (τῷ καιρῷ, *tō kairō*) is uncertain. It may mean **12:2–5** after the new vineyard would produce its first crop, that is, after about four years (Evans 2001: 233; France 2002: 459), or after the requirements in Lev. 19:23–25 concerning a new vineyard are met (Donahue and Harrington 2002: 338). At the appropriate time the owner sends a servant to receive his share of the "fruit of the vineyard." This refers to the agreed-upon portion of the grape harvest that the owner would be paid by the tenants. We should not envision, however, that this would have been paid in baskets of grapes or wineskins filled with wine. Rather, it refers to the cash equivalent of what the owner's share of the crop would be. The servant, however, is not given the agreed-upon payment of the lease due the owner but instead is beaten and sent away with nothing (12:3).[11] Another servant is sent to the tenants, and this one receives worse treatment. He is beaten on the head and treated shamefully (12:4b). Although the meaning of "beat on the head" (ἐκεφαλίωσαν, *ekephaliōsan*) is uncertain, it cannot refer to his being beheaded, for he is also shamed after this. Some have seen in ἐκεφαλίωσαν a reference to the beheading of John the Baptist (Crossan 1973a: 87), but if this were intended, the treatment of this servant would have been placed last in the list of servants sent by the owner. That other servants follow means that Mark did not interpret this servant as John the Baptist. Another servant is sent, and the evil of the tenants increases again; this servant is killed (12:5a). The owner sends more servants, and the tenants beat or kill all of them (12:5b).

The high point of the evil behavior of the tenants is now reached. The owner, **12:6–8** having apparently run out of servants to send, still has one person left, his "beloved [ἀγαπητόν, *agapēton*] son." Upon hearing this expression, Jesus's audience might well have thought of Gen. 22:2, where Abraham is told to sacrifice his "beloved son." Mark's readers, however, would have recalled earlier references in the Gospel where God refers to Jesus as "my beloved Son" (1:11; 9:7). For Jesus's original hearers, the expression "a beloved son" might not have had messianic overtones, but for the readers of Mark's Gospel it would have.

11. For an interesting parallel from the Zenon papyrus archive, see Evans 2001: 233; cf. also Evans 1995: 381–406.

Much of the confusion involved in the discussion of the meaning of "beloved son" is due to a failure to distinguish clearly the situation in life being referred to, the situation of Jesus or of Mark.[12] The owner's sending his beloved son to the tenants on the assumption that they would respect him seems foolhardy, to say the least, in light of the treatment given the servants. Many scholars therefore conclude that Jesus could not have told the parable in this present form. Yet in telling the parable in its present form, Mark, as well as Matthew and Luke, must have thought that it made sense. Other scholars refer to the use of extreme hyperbole and exaggeration in the present parable. However, the picture part of the parable is not at all exaggerated when one compares it to the reality part. The absurdity of the owner's and tenants' behavior is only exceeded by the absurdity of God's and the children of Israel's behavior in real life. God (the owner) had time and time again sent his prophets (the servants) to the people of Israel and their leaders (the tenants), and they were persecuted (1 Kings 19:10–14; 2 Chron. 36:15–16; Matt. 5:12) and killed (1 Kings 18:13; 2 Chron. 24:20–27; 36:15–16; Neh. 9:26; Jer. 26:20–23; Matt. 23:29–36/Luke 11:47–51; Matt. 23:37/Luke 13:33–34; 1 Thess. 2:15). And they treated the "Son" similarly!

The arrival of the son causes the tenants to think that by killing him they will gain possession/ownership of the vineyard (12:7). The wording of the tenants' plot, "Come, let us kill him" (δεῦτε ἀποκτείνωμεν αὐτόν, *deute apokteinōmen auton*) recalls the plot of Joseph's brothers against him in Gen. 37:20. There has been much speculation as to why the tenants assume that the son's death would allow them to take possession of the property. Whatever the reason (possibly the assumption that the son's coming meant that the father has died, and with the son's death, ownership would fall to those who have been working the vineyard for years), in a fictional parable, a legitimate, legal rationale for their thinking is not required. The story as it now stands must have made sense to Mark's readers, and Matthew (21:38) and Luke (20:14) repeat the same reasoning of the tenants for their readers. When the son arrives, the tenants seize and kill him, and they throw his body (lit. "him") outside the vineyard. Not to give someone a decent burial was shameful; not to give the son any burial at all heightens the tenants' evil and shamelessness. Matthew (21:39) and Luke (20:15) reverse the order of events found in Mark. They have the tenants first cast the son out of the vineyard and then kill him. They probably did this in order to make the son's death fit the death of Jesus, the Son of God, more precisely, for Jesus was crucified outside the city of Jerusalem (John 19:17–20; Heb. 13:12–13; contra Snodgrass 1998: 202). In so doing, they reveal the more primitive character of the Markan narrative.

12:9–11   The parable concludes with two rhetorical questions (12:9 and 10–11). Other examples of Jesus's use of this kind of question in Mark are found in 3:23,

---

12. Contrast V. Taylor (1952: 475) and Evans (2001: 235), who do not attribute messianic overtones to "beloved son," with Nineham (1963: 312) and Anderson (1976: 272), who do. Cf., however, Hooker (1991: 276), who sees the two different situations-in-life clearly.

33; 4:13, 21, 30, 40; 7:18; 8:12, 17–18, 21, 36–37; 9:19, 50; 11:17; 12:24; 13:2; 14:6, 37, 41, 48. The first, "What therefore will the lord of the vineyard do?" corresponds to "the LORD of Hosts" (Isa. 5:7) saying in Isaiah's parable of the vineyard, "And now I will tell you what I will do to my vineyard" (5:5).

Up to this point in the parable, the possessor of the vineyard is simply described as "a man" (ἄνθρωπος; 12:1), but here he is called the "lord" (κύριος, *kyrios*) of the vineyard. Most translations interpret κύριος as "owner" (RSV, NRSV, REB, NAB, NIV, TNIV, NASB). It is best, however, to interpret it as "lord," for at this point the picture part of the parable is giving way to the reality part. Thus the allegorical reference to "a man" is now being interpreted by Jesus. The "man" is the "Lord," and as in Isa. 5:5–7, the "LORD of Hosts" will bring judgment upon Israel (Donahue and Harrington 2002: 339; J. Edwards 2002: 359). The judgment of the tenants in the parable, however, would not simply fall upon the leadership of Israel. The destruction of the temple, alluded to in Jesus's cleansing of the temple (Mark 11:15–19) and the clear prophecy of its destruction in 13:1–37, was fulfilled in AD 70 and came upon not only the leaders of the nation but the people of Israel as well. In the OT, the prophetic message was not directed only to the leadership of the nation (1 Kings 18:1–4, 13; 22:1–28; 2 Chron. 16:7–10; Jer. 20:1–30; 26:20–23; 37:11–16; 38:4–6). It was even more often directed to the people of Israel (1 Kings 19:10, 14; 2 Chron. 24:20–21; Neh. 9:26; Jer. 2:30; 11:21; 25:1–11; Marcus 1992b: 128n47).

Jesus himself answers the rhetorical question.[13] The Lord will come, destroy the tenants, and give the vineyard to others. Since in the allegory the man/lord is clearly distinguished from the "son," the "lord" here must refer to God, the Lord of Hosts. As a result of the tenants' behavior, he will come in judgment. This judgment involves two things: destruction of the tenants and transfer of the vineyard to others (12:9b–c). The identity of the tenants is clear. They are the "them" of 12:1 and the "they/them" of 12:12. Their antecedent is the chief priests, scribes, and elders of 11:27–33. The identity of the "others" (ἄλλοις, *allois*) is more debated, and suggestions vary: not identifiable (V. Taylor 1952: 476), Jesus and the disciples (Gundry 1993: 688–89; Evans 2001: 153–54, 237; Donahue and Harrington 2002: 339, 342), the church or "new Israel" (Nineham 1963: 313; Best 1981: 219–20; Brooks 1991: 191; Aus 1996: 62; France 2002: 462), the gentiles (Hooker 1991: 191; Marcus 1992b: 122–24, 128–29; J. Edwards 2002: 359–60; contra Evans 2001: 237: "The Markan Jesus is not saying that Israel is about to be replaced by Gentiles"; cf. also France 2002: 462n17). Matthew 21:43 refers to the vineyard being "taken away from you and given to a people [ἔθνει, *ethnei*] that produces the fruits of the kingdom," which suggests that the new covenant would involve a community whose ethnicity would consist of both Jew and Greek. By the time of the evangelists, it may very well have come to contain more gentiles than Jews.

---

13. Although Matthew has the audience answer Jesus's question (21:41), in Mark there is no indication that there is a change of speakers. Luke makes it even more clear that Jesus is speaking by having his audience respond to his words of judgment (20:16b).

The second rhetorical question involves a scriptural quotation (cf. 2:25; 12:26). Jesus quotes Ps. 118:22–23, a favorite Christian proof text (Acts 4:11; 1 Pet. 2:4, 6–7). The question "Have you not read this scripture?"[14] expects a positive response, as indicated by the "not" (οὐδέ, *oude*). The religious leaders had read this portion of Scripture, of course, but they did not accept what it meant with respect to the present situation. In rejecting Jesus (God's Son), they (the tenants in charge of God's vineyard) were rejecting the very cornerstone of God's new temple. Without their acknowledgment, they were doing the will of God, and this is marvelous to behold. They had indeed read this scripture, but because they did not accept what it taught, they were misled in their thinking and actions (12:24). As expected, in quoting Ps. 118:22–23, Mark follows the LXX (Ps. 117), the Bible of his Greek-speaking readers. The stone described as the head of the corner is probably not a cornerstone in the foundation of a building (the use of "head" does not fit well a stone that would be buried), but either a capstone at the top of a building marking its completion or a capital that sits on top of a column (Cahill 1999; France 2002: 463). Whatever the specific meaning, the stone referred to is the most important one of all. The rejection of this stone was, ironically enough, ultimately the Lord's doing. It fulfilled the divine necessity (the δεῖ, *dei*; 8:31) for which the Son of Man was sent (10:45). The evil actions of the religious leaders in conjunction with Pontius Pilate were in fact according to the definite plan and foreknowledge of God (Acts 4:28). Thus the providential rule of God in these events is evident. All of this, along with the vindication of the son/stone, is marvelous to contemplate and behold.

12:12 The parable ends with a Markan conclusion in which the chief priests, scribes, and elders ("they") are "seeking to arrest" (lit. "seize") Jesus (cf. 3:6; 14:1). The reason Mark gives for this is that they understand the parable to be about them. They are the evil tenants of God's vineyard. Jesus's great popularity with the crowd, however, thwarts the leaders' attempt. Not able to do anything while Jesus is in the temple surrounded by an adoring crowd, they leave (complementary participle) him and go away. In the following accounts, however, they, along with the Pharisees, attempt to refute Jesus by posing various questions (12:13–40). In this too they will be thwarted.

Summary

The importance of this passage with regard to the question of the messianic self-consciousness of Jesus has long been recognized and much debated. With respect to the Christology of Mark, the issue is clearer. In the account the Markan Jesus is clearly unique and distinguished from the OT prophets, even the most venerated of the OT prophets. In the parable the prophets are "servants" of God (12:2–5). The Markan readers would recognize that

---

14. The plural "Scriptures" is found in 12:24 and 14:49. The singular is found only here in Mark. (Cf. 15:28, where the singular is found in a few MSS but lacks solid textual support.)

Jesus is more than this. He is the "Son" of God. The stress on the end of the account also means that, despite what the parable may say about the judgment of the evil tenants, the emphasis of the present account falls upon the vindication of the "stone" or "Son." Thus the parable is less a "parable of the wicked tenants" than it is a "parable of the Rejected Son" (M. Black 1971: 12–13). Despite his death at the hands of the evil tenants, the stone rejected by the builders has become the head of the corner. He has become the most important part of the new people of God. Using the words of Paul, he who "humbled himself and became obedient to the point of death, even death on a cross . . . has [been] highly exalted . . . and [received] . . . the name that is above every name, so that at the name of Jesus every knee should bend, in heaven and on earth and under the earth, and every tongue should confess that Jesus Christ is Lord, to the glory of God the Father" (Phil. 2:8–11). Mark's readers would recognize that Jesus's vindication or exaltation (Phil. 2:9) came through his resurrection from the dead (see Mark 8:31; 9:31; 10:33–34; and other church traditions they had been taught; cf. Rom. 1:4).

The account also affirms once again what Jesus has taught in the Markan passion predictions, that Jesus's death was a divine necessity (8:31). Thus the death of Jesus was not simply a great tragedy that Jesus could not avoid but rather the divine purpose for his life. He came to give his life as a ransom for all (10:45). Later in the Gospel the readers will be reminded that Jesus came to seal a new covenant with his blood (14:24). This was not accomplished by accident or chance. On the contrary, this all "came from the Lord" (παρὰ κυρίου ἐγένετο αὕτη, *para kyriou egeneto hautē*; 12:11a), and to those who understand this it is indeed "marvelous to behold" (θαυμαστὴ ἐν ὀφθαλμοῖς ἡμῶν, *thaumastē en ophthalmois hēmōn*; 12:11b).

This account, like Mark 11:15–19 and 13:1–37, speaks of a coming judgment. Most clearly this judgment involves the chief priest, the scribes, and the elders, who are told the parable and recognize that it was addressed to them. Numerous passages in Mark, however, indicate that this judgment is not so selective that it will fall only on the leaders of the nation, the Sanhedrin. Judgment is coming upon the nation, Jerusalem, and the temple (13:1–31; 15:29). As in the OT, the prophetic message against the nation's leadership involves the whole nation as well. And the "others," to whom the vineyard is given (12:9), would have been understood by Mark's readers to involve not a new group of chief priests, scribes, and elders and not just Jesus and the disciples but also the new Israel of God, the church. The exclusivity of the people of Israel in the old covenant would be abolished in the new covenant (14:24). In the "others," Mark's readers would almost certainly have seen the church, and its gentile element in particular. This understanding is supported by Matthew's understanding of Ps. 118:22–23 in his parallel account (21:43), and Luke suggests this in his parallel account as well (20:16c). Jesus's concern for gentiles encountered so far in the Gospel (Mark 5:1–20; 7:24–30; and above all in the cleansing of the temple and the place of the gentiles in it [11:17]) would have inclined Mark's readers to interpret the present account in light of the present makeup of their gentile-dominated church.

One final Markan emphasis in the account that comes to the surface is the division that Jesus created in Israel (cf. Matt. 10:34–36). The religious leaders are offended by him and seek his death (cf. 2:1–12, 15–3:6 [esp. 3:6], 22–30; 6:1–6a; 7:1–23; 8:11–12; 10:2–9; 11:15–19 [esp. 11:18], 27–33; 12:13–27; 14:1–2, 10–11, 43ff.). In Jesus's passion predictions (8:31; 10:33–34), except the most abbreviated one (9:31), they are singled out as the human cause of Jesus's death. On the other hand, the people (or "crowd") hold Jesus in esteem and prove a major obstacle in the leaders' attempt to do away with Jesus (11:18; 12:12b; 14:2). The usual portrayal of the people/crowd(s) in Mark is one of amazement, astonishment, reverential fear, and awe. Only in 15:11–15 and 29 are the crowds portrayed negatively in Mark.

Additional Notes

12:1. The term "to give out" (ἐξέδετο) is used here in the technical sense of leasing something to someone.

12:3. λαβόντες is a complementary participle here and in v. 8.

12:5. οὓς μὲν δέροντες, οὓς δὲ ἀποκτέννοντες is lit. "some beating, others killing."

12:6. λέγων is lit. "saying."

12:9. Although "therefore" (οὖν) is omitted by B L and some of the Syriac, Sahidic, and Bohairic MSS, it is found in ℵ A C D W Θ f¹ f¹³ lat and most of the Syriac, Sahidic, and Bohairic MSS.

12:10. οὗτος is lit. "this one."

12:11. ἐν ὀφθαλμοῖς ἡμῶν is lit. "in our eyes."

12:12. The καί is best translated as "but" (Zerwick 1963: 455β).

VI. Jesus's Entry into Jerusalem: Part 5 (11:1–13:37)
    D. Jesus's Parable of the Vineyard (12:1–12)
➤ E. The Pharisees and Herodians Seek to Trick Jesus (12:13–17)
    F. The Sadducees Seek to Trick Jesus (12:18–27)

E. The Pharisees and Herodians Seek to Trick Jesus (12:13–17)

After the parable of the vineyard (12:1–12), we find a series of four incidents involving questions. The first three consist of questions asked of Jesus by the Pharisees and Herodians (12:13–17), the Sadducees (12:18–27), and a scribe (12:28–34). Of these, the first two are clearly hostile in intent, but the third is less certainly so (see the introduction to 12:28–34). The fourth question is asked by Jesus and involves the nature of the Messiah (12:35–37). Although there exist several rabbinic parallels to these four questions (Daube 1956a; Hooker 1991: 278–79) involving legal/halakah (12:13–17) and nonlegal/haggadah (12:18–37) questions, it is unlikely that the present arrangement in Mark is dependent on such a rabbinic pattern (Gundry 1993: 695). Mark's gentile readers would clearly have been unaware of such parallels.

The context for this incident is provided by the controversy story found in 11:27–33. Although some see a chiastic pattern—(A) 11:27–33, (B) 12:1–12, and (A′) 12:13–17[1]—it is best to see 11:27–33 as introducing an illustrative parable (12:1–12) followed by a string of stories (12:13–37). These are mostly controversy stories exemplifying the lack of fruit found in the temple (representing Judaism and especially the Jewish leadership of Jesus's day). In this series of controversy stories, the main groups making up the religious leadership of Israel and the Sanhedrin are all represented: the chief priests, the scribes, and the elders (11:27; 12:12); the Pharisees and Herodians (12:13); the Sadducees (12:18); and the scribes (12:28, 38). The parable is placed at the beginning of these stories to illustrate this lack of fruit and the resulting judgment coming upon Israel that was earlier symbolized by Jesus's cursing of the fig tree and cleansing of the temple (11:12–26). The string of five stories (11:27–33; 12:13–37) concludes with a teaching summary concerning the hypocrisy of the religious establishment (represented by the scribes in 12:38–40) and the story of the poor widow, which illustrates true piety (12:41–44). This will then be followed by a long excursus in 13:1–37 on the judgment soon to fall upon Israel, and in particular on Jerusalem, and the vindication of the Son of Man.

The present account is both a controversy story and a pronouncement story (Bultmann 1968: 26; V. Taylor 1952: 477–78) that may be the most famous of all of Jesus's pronouncement stories. Failing to arrest Jesus (12:12), his opponents (the "they" of 12:13 refers back to the "they" in 12:12 and the "them" of 12:1, which have as their antecedent the chief priests, the

---

1. For a different chiastic pattern, see Myers (1988: 306) and Witherington (2001: 318).

scribes, and the elders of 11:27) send some of the Pharisees and Herodians to Jesus (12:13). After some flattery, they ask him, "Is it lawful [for Jews] to pay taxes to Caesar or not?" (12:14). In so doing, they think that they have placed Jesus on the horns of a dilemma. If he answers yes, he will lose favor with the people, for they despise the Roman taxation. If he answers no, he will be advocating rebellion against Rome and force the Roman authorities to take immediate action against him. Unlike the chief priests, the scribes, and the elders, who refused to answer when Jesus placed them in a similar dilemma (11:28–32), Jesus brilliantly replies, "Bring me a denarius in order that I might look [at it]" (φέρετέ μοι δηνάριον ἵνα ἴδω, *pherete moi dēnarion hina idō*), and then asks his opponents, "Whose image and inscription [is this]?" (τίνος ἡ εἰκὼν αὕτη καὶ ἡ ἐπιγραφή; *tinos hē eikōn hautē kai hē epigraphē?* 12:16). When they respond, "Caesar's" (12:16), Jesus states, "The things that belong to Caesar give to Caesar, and the things that belong to God give to God" (τὰ Καίσαρος ἀπόδοτε Καίσαρι καὶ τὰ τοῦ θεοῦ τῷ θεῷ, *ta Kaisaros apodote Kaisari kai ta tou theou tō theō*; 12:17a). The account ends with his opponents witnessing to the great wisdom of Jesus by their utter amazement (12:17c).

The present account is found in variant forms in Egerton Papyrus 2 (see Evans 2001: 243) and Gos. Thom. 100. In comparison, the Markan account appears to be more primitive, for the addition of "and give to me what is mine" in the Gospel of Thomas is clearly a secondary expansion, and the same can be said of the Egerton Papyrus form of the tradition, which is a mixture of Johannine (John 3:2) and Synoptic traditions (Mark 7:6–13; Evans 2001: 243; contra Crossan 1985: 73–75; Koester 1990: 205–16). Mark's own hand is seen in the placement of the account (see 12:13) and the introductory seam that ties the account to 11:27ff. (12:13a) and indicates the hostile intent of the question (12:13b; Gnilka 1978: 150–51). It is possible that the reference to Jesus "knowing their hypocrisy" (12:15b) is also Markan, but the concluding reference (12:17c) to the utter amazement of Jesus's opponents clearly is (see 1:21–22; Pryke 1978: 19, 145, 169; Hultgren 1979: 76). Bultmann (1968: 26), however, sees Mark's hand only in 12:13. The account consists of an introductory seam joining the present story to the preceding one (12:13), a question introduced with flattery but attempting to either destroy Jesus's popularity with the people or force a dangerous confrontation with Rome (12:14–15a), Jesus's counterquestion (12:15b–16), and Jesus's amazing pronouncement refuting his opponents (12:17).

Exegesis and Exposition

¹³And they send to him some of the Pharisees and of the Herodians in order that they might trap him in [his] speech. ¹⁴And having come, they say to him, "Teacher, we know that you are an honest man and you are not concerned with the opinion of others, ⌜for you do not show partiality⌝ but teach the way of God truthfully. Is it lawful to pay taxes to Caesar or not? Should we pay it or should we not?" ¹⁵But knowing

their hypocrisy, he said to them, "Why are you ⌐ ⌐ testing me? Bring me a denarius in order that I might look [at it]." [16]And they brought [one]. And he says to them, "Whose image and inscription [is this]?" And they said to him, "Caesar's." [17]And Jesus said to them, "The things that belong to Caesar give to Caesar, and the things that belong to God [give] to God." And they were utterly amazed at him.

The subject "they" is not indefinite but in the present context refers back to the "they" of 12:12, the "them" of 12:1, and ultimately to the chief priests, the scribes, and the elders of 11:27. Having failed in their attempt to arrest Jesus (12:12a), they seek to entrap[2] him (cf. Luke 20:20) by his speech (λόγῳ, logō—an instrumental of means), by having him say something unpopular with the people or politically revolutionary with respect to the authorities. The Pharisees and Herodians (see 3:5–6) are sent to ask a dangerous and explosive question. The reader already knows from the earlier incident in 3:6 (cf. also 8:15) that these two groups had teamed up to "destroy" Jesus.[3] The Pharisees and Herodians were not natural allies, and the appearance of the Herodians in Jerusalem seems strange in that Herod Antipas was the tetrarch of Galilee and Perea and had no authority in Jerusalem/Judea, which was ruled by the Roman governor, Pontius Pilate (cf., however, Luke 23:6–7). As a result some suggest that this incident may have originally taken place in Galilee (Evans 2001: 244). If this is true, Mark may have placed the account in its present location to show the hostility of this group, along with the Sadducees (12:18) and the scribes (12:28, 38), that led up to Jesus's death and the judgment of Israel (12:1–12; 13:1–37). Yet the Herodians could have been present in Jerusalem at the time of the Passover, even as Herod Antipas was (Luke 23:6–12; Donahue and Harrington 2002: 343–44). Since such a tax was apparently not imposed on Galilee (Gundry 1993: 697), the question seems more applicable in a Judean setting, such as the present one, than in a Galilean one.

12:13

The flattering comments addressed to Jesus in 10:14 are in the form of a chiasmus: (A) "you are an honest man" (lit. "you are truthful"); (B) "you are not concerned with the opinion of others" (lit. "it is not a care for you concerning no one"); (B′) "you do not show partiality" (lit. "you do not look at the face of a man"); and (A′) "you teach the way of God truthfully" (lit. "you teach the way of God according to the truth"). For the address "Teacher," see 4:37–39. The flattery addressed to Jesus by the Pharisees and Herodians (cf. their "we know" [οἴδαμεν, oidamen; 12:14] with respect to Jesus and the "we do not know" [οὐκ οἴδαμεν; 11:33] with respect to John the Baptist) is insincere, but the content of their flattery is true with respect to what it says about Jesus. Jesus is truthful; he is not concerned with the opinion of others; he does not

12:14–15a

---

2. The term ἀγρεύω, agreuō, found only here in the NT, is often used to describe snaring and trapping animals. Cf. Prov. 5:22; 6:25–26.

3. The hostility of the Pharisees toward Jesus has in addition been seen in 2:16, 24; 7:1–5; 8:11; 10:2.

show partiality; and he truly teaches the way[4] of God. The flattery of Jesus's opponents, however, does not lessen the hostility of their forthcoming question. The question "Is it lawful[5] to pay taxes to Caesar[6] or not? Should we pay it or should we not?" (ἔξεστιν δοῦναι κῆνσον Καίσαρι ἢ οὔ; δῶμεν ἢ μὴ δῶμεν; *exestin dounai kēnson Kaisari ē ou? dōmen ē mē dōmen?*) is insincere in that it is not seeking the truth on this issue but rather seeks to trap Jesus. Because of this, it is hypocritical (ὁ δὲ εἰδὼς αὐτῶν τὴν ὑπόκρισιν, *ho de eidōs autōn tēn hypokrisin*; 12:15).

The question places Jesus on the horns of a dilemma. If he says yes, he will alienate the people who despise the taxes they are forced to pay to Rome. It is difficult to imagine Jesus saying anything that would anger the general populace more than to advocate and support paying taxes to those subjugating the people of Israel. If, on the other hand, he says no, he will be siding with the Zealots and nationalists, and this would result in an immediate confrontation with Rome and his arrest, for the Roman authorities would not tolerate such a clear act of insurrection. Regardless of whether Jesus would answer yes or no, the Pharisees and Herodians would succeed in bringing an end to his popularity and ministry. As to the Pharisees' and Herodians' own views on this issue, it is obvious that the latter would have supported the payment of taxes to Rome. Since they supported Herod Antipas, who owed his rule to Rome, they had to be in favor of supporting Rome by paying imperial taxes. Although some scholars argue that the Pharisees probably opposed the payment of such taxes, at least in theory (Evans 2001: 244; Donahue and Harrington 2002: 344), it appears probable that they held a view similar to, if more reluctant than, the Herodians (Hooker 1991: 280). Their alliance here and in 3:6 suggests that they were most likely in agreement on this issue, for this was not a small, abstract, theoretical question. For Jews, this was a serious and deeply impassioned issue.

The term "tax(es)" (κῆνσον) is a Latin term that probably refers to a poll tax, or head tax, but it can also refer to a tax on agricultural goods (Schürer 1973–87: 1.401–4; France 2002: 465n28). The imposition of such a tax in AD 6 based on the census of Quirinius (Luke 2:1–2; Acts 5:37) resulted in a Jewish uprising under Judas the Galilean (Josephus, *J.W.* 2.8.1 §118; *Ant.* 18.1.1 §§1–10; 20.5.2 §§100–104). Although this was quickly crushed by the Romans, the issue of paying taxes to Caesar (i.e., to Rome) was a continual irritant to the Jews of Palestine (Josephus, *Ant.* 17.11.2 §308). It was a continual reminder of their captivity to the Romans, and along with other grievances led to the Zealot revolt of AD 66 and its disastrous consequences.

4. For the "way" (ὁδός, *hodos*) as a description of the Christian movement, cf. Acts 9:2; 18:25; 19:9, 23; 22:4; 24:14, 22 (cf. also Mark 1:2–3); and for the Qumran community's use of this term in describing itself, see 1QS 8.13–14; 9.18–20.

5. In all the other instances in Mark (2:24, 26; 3:4; 6:18; 10:2), "Is it lawful?" (ἔξεστιν; *exestin?*) involves whether something is permitted under divine law as revealed in the OT or according to the scribal traditions (France 2002: 468).

6. Although originally a family name (e.g., Julius Caesar), "Caesar" was in Jesus's day, and even more so in Mark's, a title for the Roman emperor.

The comment "knowing their hypocrisy" is probably not an allusion to Jesus's omniscience, for any wise teacher would have known that the earlier flattering comments were not in harmony with the politically loaded and dangerous question asked. Matthew 22:18 makes this clear by changing Mark's "hypocrisy" to "malice" (πονηρίαν, *ponērian*). Jesus clearly understood that the question was an attempt to "trap/trick" (πειράζετε, *peirazete*)[7] him into giving an answer that would result in a loss of popularity with the people or put him in political danger. His response involves a request for a denarius (12:15c), a question concerning the coin (12:16), and a brilliant pronouncement (12:17a).

The coin that Jesus specifically asked for was the Roman denarius (δηνάριον, **12:15b–16** *dēnarion*; cf. 6:37; 14:5), which was used to pay the Roman poll tax. Apparently the poll tax had to be paid in Roman coinage (Bruce 1984: 258). This silver coin was worth the equivalent of a day's salary (Matt. 20:2). The request to bring a denarius may indicate that Jesus and his disciples did not possess one (Donahue and Harrington 2002: 345; J. Edwards 2002: 363). Matthew 17:24–27 may lend support to such a view (cf. also Mark 6:8). There is no need, however, to assume that Jesus's opponents did not have one (W. Lane 1974: 423; Gnilka 1979: 153; Gundry 1993: 698). The parallel accounts in Matthew (22:19) and Luke (20:24) seem to assume this in their use of the term "Show me" (ἐπιδείξατέ/δείξατέ μοι, *epideixate/deixate moi*) rather than "Bring me" (φέρετέ μοι). It is quite possible that Jesus wanted his opponents to produce the denarius from their own pockets in order to strengthen his pronouncement in 12:17b. If in their daily lives they used the coinage of Caesar (i.e., the Roman Empire), they then should not object to giving back to Caesar what was his. The words "that I might look [at it]" (ἵνα ἴδω, *hina idō*) should not be interpreted as implying that Jesus had never seen a denarius. His work as a carpenter in Galilee of the gentiles and probably in the Greek city of Sepphoris (Batey 1991: 65–82; Meier 1991: 284) make it highly unlikely that Jesus had never seen or possessed such a coin. Furthermore, Jesus's whole pronouncement and response to the question of the Pharisees and Herodians depends on his knowledge of the appearance of the denarius, its "image and inscription."[8]

Upon being shown the denarius, Jesus asks whose image and inscription are on the coin. The image was almost certainly that of Tiberius Caesar, who reigned AD 14–37, and the inscription was TI[BERIUS] CAESAR DIVI AUG[USTI] F[ILIUS] AUGUSTUS—"Tiberius Caesar Augustus, Son of [the] Divine Augustus" (Hart 1984). On the other side was the title PONTIF[EX] MAXIM[US]—"High Priest." Jesus does not refer to the image and inscription in order to allude to the commandment prohibiting the making of graven

---

7. Cf. 1:13, where Jesus is "tested" (πειραζόμενος) by Satan, and 8:11 and 10:2, where he is "tested" (πειράζοντες) by the Pharisees.

8. Contrast Rabbi Menaḥem, who was considered holy because he would not look at the image of a coin (*b. Pesaḥ.* 104a).

images or idols (Exod. 20:4; Evans 2001: 247; contrast Pesch 1980b: 227), for the terms used in the LXX text are entirely different. As in 11:27–33, Jesus answers his opponents' questions (12:14d–e) with his own (12:16b). Here, however, his opponents feel free to answer his question because they do not think it places them on the horns of a dilemma, as in 11:30–33.

12:17   Their answer, "Caesar's," results in Jesus's pronouncement, "The things that belong to Caesar give to Caesar, and the things that belong to God give to God."[9] Although Gundry (1993: 694) sees Jesus's answer being more a clever tour de force than a persuasive, logical deduction, Jesus's reply is a logical implication drawn from the coin's image and inscription. The possession of this Roman coin by the Pharisees and Herodians indicated that they accepted the economic system that the Roman Empire provided. In doing so, they had the obligation of paying (ἀπόδοτε, apodote; lit. "pay back") to that system the taxes that belonged to it (Witherington 2001: 325; Donahue and Harrington 2002: 345, 346; contra Myers 1988: 312). Jesus's opponents were not forced to have in their possession a Roman coin. (Note the use of Tyrian coinage in 11:15; see 11:15–17.) But "those who use Caesar's money are obliged to pay tribute when he demands it" (Hultgren 1979: 77). It is not surprising, therefore, that one of the first acts in the Jewish revolt was to mint new coins (Reiser 2000: 465–66).

Some scholars have sought to interpret Jesus's words as a Zealot-like response denying that Jews should pay taxes to the hated Romans (Brandon 1967: 345–50; contra Bruce 1984: 259–60). According to this view, ultimately all things belong to God and nothing belongs to Caesar, so that Jesus's statement was in reality a rejection of paying taxes to Caesar.[10] It is very unlikely, however, that any Zealot would ever have said, "The things that belong to Caesar give to Caesar, and the things that belong to God give to God" (contra Brandon 1967: 347–48).[11] Jesus was clearly opposed to the Zealot cause (cf. Matt. 5:9, 39, 41; 26:52; etc.). On the other hand, his words are not a simple pro-Roman statement. In general the NT does not understand the Roman rule as innately evil (Rom. 13:1–7; 1 Tim. 2:1–4; Titus 3:1; 1 Pet. 2:13–17; cf. how the Roman governmental authorities rescued Paul from danger on several occasions: Acts 17:1–9; 18:12–17; 19:21–41; 21:27–25:27; etc.; also Justin Martyr, *1 Apol.* 17). In normal situations the compatibility of Jesus's two commands were presumed. Yet experience has shown that at times Caesar demands not only the things that legitimately belong to Caesar but also the

9. The expression τὰ τοῦ θεοῦ (ta tou theou, the things of God) is also found in 8:33, where it is opposed to τὰ τῶν ἀνθρώπων (ta tōn anthrōpōn, the things of men) and refers to God's purpose for Jesus to suffer and die in Jerusalem and rise on the third day from the dead. Here it refers to the honor, glory, and obedience that humans owe God (contra Gundry 1993: 694; and Evans 2001: 248, who see this as a reference to following Jesus).

10. For a short, helpful summary and critique of this view, see Pilgrim 1999: 67–69.

11. Although Luke 23:2 (Jesus is said to forbid giving tribute to Caesar) might seem at first glance to support such a view, it should be observed that Jesus's accusers here and in the previous statement (Jesus is said to be perverting the nation) are false witnesses (Derrett 1970: 337–38).

things that belong to God. In the NT this is seen clearly in Rev. 18:1ff. In such cases the church has always recognized that the first commandment of all is, "You shall love the Lord your God with all your heart, and with all your soul, and with all your mind, and with all your strength" (Mark 12:30). The Pharisees and Herodians had asked Jesus about a less important issue in order to trap him, but he calls to their attention the more important issue of whether they were giving to God what belongs to him (Tannehill 1975: 175–76). From what Jesus had said in the previous parable (12:1–12), it is obvious that they were not. In the past, during the time of the prophets, they did not (12:2–5); now, in the time of the Son, they were not (12:6–8). Thus judgment is soon to fall upon the nation (12:9; 13:1–37).

The account ends with the Markan comment, "And they were utterly amazed at him" (καὶ ἐξεθαύμαζον ἐπ' αὐτῷ, *kai exethaumazon ep' autō*). The term "utterly amazed" is an intensive form of θαυμάζω and is found only here in the NT. The parallels in Matt. 22:22 and Luke 20:26 also refer to the amazement of Jesus's opponents at his response, but they use the latter verbal form. Once again the greatness of Jesus is seen in that even his bitter opponents marvel at him and in so doing acknowledge his great wisdom and authority (cf. 2:12).

Summary

In the present account we encounter two frequent Markan themes. One involves the greatness and authority of Jesus as a teacher. Asked about the basis of his authority for cleansing the temple (11:28), Jesus reveals this by his teaching in 12:13–17 and 12:18–38. The wisdom and utter astonishment that even his opponents experience witness to Jesus's authority. In the present account as in previous instances (see 1:21–22), there is a sense of amazement, wonder, and awe. This sense is emphasized here by the fact that even his enemies bear witness to Jesus's divine wisdom by their reaction (12:17b; cf. 2:12) and by Mark's use of the intensive form "utterly amazed" to describe this. In the contest of wits with his opponents, Jesus totally defeats his enemies. He does so to such an extent that they themselves bear witness to the surpassing wisdom of the Son of God.

For his readers, Mark provides guidance by this account on how they as members of the kingdom of God are to live as members of the kingdom of Caesar. Jesus's pronouncement is far more than "a comment on the relative insignificance of the issue in light of the inbreaking dominion of God" (contra Witherington 1990: 102). If we assume that Mark's readers are Christians living in Rome, in light of the Jewish revolt of AD 66–72 and in light of their experience during the Neronian persecution, Jesus's teaching provided a fundamental guide as to how to live in these two worlds. Although Christians have at times wished that their Lord's command was more specific with respect to their particular situation, in the vast majority of instances, "The things that belong to Caesar give to Caesar, and the things that belong to God give to God" has provided a basic guide for living as members of the kingdom of God in the political domain of Caesar.

Additional Notes

12:14. The idiomatic nature of this expression can be seen by such references in the OT as Lev. 19:15; Deut. 10:17; Ps. 82:2; Prov. 18:5; Mal. 2:9; and in the NT as Acts 10:34; Rom. 2:11; Eph. 6:9; Col. 3:25; James 2:1, 9. Its idiomatic nature makes it unlikely that Jesus intended a pun here concerning the face or image of the denarius referred to in 12:16. The terms "face" (πρόσωπον) and "image" (εἰκών) are quite different (contra Gundry 1993: 693).

12:15. The MSS 𝔓[45] N W Θ f[1] f[13] add ὑποκριταί. This is clearly secondary, however, and comes from the Matthean parallel in 22:18. This noun is found only once in Mark (7:6) but fourteen times in Matthew.

VI. Jesus's Entry into Jerusalem: Part 5 (11:1–13:37)
    E. The Pharisees and Herodians Seek to Trick Jesus (12:13–17)
➤   F. The Sadducees Seek to Trick Jesus (12:18–27)
    G. A Scribe Asks Jesus about the Great Commandment (12:28–34)

F. The Sadducees Seek to Trick Jesus (12:18–27)

The third pronouncement/controversy story (12:18–27) follows the second (12:13–17) without interruption. Although it is unlikely that all the events and teachings in 11:27–13:37 occurred consecutively in the temple (11:27–12:44) and on the slopes of the Mount of Olives facing Jerusalem (13:1–37), it is quite possible, if not probable, that the present incident took place in the temple in Jerusalem. All the references to the Sadducees in the NT are located in the temple (12:18–27/Matt. 22:23–33/Luke 20:27–40; Acts 4:1–3; 5:17 [cf. 5:12]; 22:30–23:10 [?]) or Judea (Matt. 3:7 [cf. 3:1]), except one, which is located in Galilee (Matt. 16:1–12 [cf. 15:39]). Although some scholars argue that the present account is a creation of the early church (Bultmann 1968: 26), it is difficult to conceive of the early church creating a dialogue on the facticity of the resurrection without alluding in some way to the resurrection of Jesus.[1] The lack of such an allusion argues strongly in favor of the authenticity of the incident (V. Taylor 1952: 480; Meier 2000a; Evans 2001: 251), as does the fact that the portrayal of the Sadducees fits well what we know of them.

Even as the Pharisees had come seeking to trap Jesus with a political question (12:14c–15a), so now the Sadducees come seeking to trick him with a theological one. If they can embarrass Jesus by showing that his belief in the resurrection[2] (Mark 8:31; 9:9, 31; 10:34; 14:28; 16:6–7; Luke 14:14; John 5:29; 11:24–26; etc.) is absurd, they hope that his authority as a teacher will be weakened. Their question (12:19–23) has been carefully thought out and crafted. Moses (cf. 1:44; 7:10; 10:3–4) gave a command that, if a man dies leaving a wife and no children, his brother should marry her and have children with her (Deut. 25:5–6; cf. Gen. 38:6–11; Ruth 4; Tob. 6:10–13; 7:9b–13; Josephus, *Ant.* 4.8.23 §§254–56). The Sadducees then give a

---

1. Cf. how Paul's argument concerning the resurrection of the dead in 1 Cor. 15:12–58 is based on the fact of Jesus's resurrection (15:12–28).

2. The question of the Sadducees involves not just the specific doctrine of the resurrection but also the general doctrine of life after death. The resurrection from the dead, in the technical sense of the resurrection of the body, was seen as a future event occurring at the end of history (12:23: "in the resurrection, when they rise"). The fact that Jesus argues that Abraham, Isaac, and Jacob were alive (12:27) deals more with the doctrine of life after death. Since the Sadducees denied both, the demonstration of either would refute their denial of life after death. Jesus himself apparently believed that upon death the righteous entered into a conscious relationship with God (12:27; Luke 16:19–31; 23:43; Mark 8:35–38; John 8:51–52) but that "the resurrection from the dead" was a future event that would take place at the end of history (Mark 12:25a; Matt. 12:41–42; Luke 14:14; John 11:24).

hypothetical example of this happening to a man having six brothers. Upon his death the second brother married the widow and died, also leaving no children. This happened with all seven brothers. All had the same woman as a wife and left no children. Since the law about levirate marriage (from the Latin *levir*, "brother-in-law") is commanded by Moses in Deut. 25:5–6 and since in the supposed resurrection state the woman cannot be wife of seven different men at the same time, they believe that Moses in the Torah denies the doctrine of the resurrection.[3] Thus this refutes Jesus's (and the Pharisees') belief in the resurrection. Since in light of this carefully worked-out illustration Jesus will not be able to defend his belief in the resurrection, they believe that they will have refuted such a belief, and as a result his reputation and authority as a teacher will be severely damaged.

Jesus's reply involves two parts. The first involves the Sadducees' ignorance of the Scriptures (12:24c), for Moses, who recorded God's command in Deut. 25:5–6, also records God referring to himself as the God of Abraham, Isaac, and Jacob (Exod. 3:6, 15, 16). In so doing, Moses indicates that Abraham, Isaac, and Jacob, who had died, are alive (contra Gundry 1993: 703, 708–9), for God does not cease being their God upon their death. The "everlasting" covenant God made with them (Gen. 17:7, 19) involved an "everlasting" relationship that cannot be terminated by death (Dreyfus 1959; Hooker 1991: 285). The second part of Jesus's reply involved the Sadducees' ignorance of the power of God (12:24d). This caused them to think that the resurrection life would be basically no different from this present life. Marriage, however, is "until death do us part." In the resurrection life, believers are more like the angels in this regard (12:25c) than present-day humans. Since there is no death, there is no need to reproduce. Also, their need for companionship that is fulfilled in the present life by marriage will be more than satisfied by fellowship with the multitude of fellow believers in the resurrection life (10:29–30). Having proven that the patriarchs are alive, the consequence is that there will be a resurrection in the future. "Prove the first [that the patriarchs are still alive], and (within the worldview assumed by both parties in the debate, and any listening Pharisees) you have proved the second" (N. Wright 2003: 425).

Mark's hand is seen primarily in the present location of the pericope (Pesch 1980b: 229; Donahue 1982: 575). It is unlikely that the present collection of controversy stories (11:27–33; 12:13–37) and the parable (12:1–12) that follow the cleansing of the temple/cursing of the fig tree (11:12–25), as well as the following collection of material concerning the destruction of Jerusalem (13:1–37), all existed together in the pre-Markan tradition. They fit well, however, Mark's own theological scheme found in the passion

---

3. There were several reasons for the institution of levirate marriage. A childless widow held a precarious position in ancient society. By means of a levirate marriage, however, a widow could maintain the name of her deceased husband (Deut. 25:6) and her relationship with her husband's family, maintain the husband's inheritance, and have children who could take care of her when she became old.

predictions (8:31; 9:31; 10:33–34) by showing the continued and heightened opposition of the Jewish leadership against Jesus and the coming judgment of the nation. It is difficult in the present account to separate the redactional work of Mark from the form of the account in the tradition he received. Although some scholars believe that originally the present account consisted of two separate traditions—12:19–23, 25 and 12:26–27a (Hultgren 1979: 130; Gnilka 1979: 156–57; Donahue 1982: 576)—and that Mark combined them, the present form of the account does not seem to have experienced any major modification (Pesch 1980b: 229). The wording of 12:18 may be Markan (Pryke 1978: 20, 145, 169; Gnilka 1979: 156; Donahue 1982: 575), and its identifying clause "who say there is no resurrection" (οἵτινες λέγουσιν ἀνάστασιν μὴ εἶναι, hoitines legousin anastasin mē einai) may also be (cf. similar explanations in 15:7 and 7:3–4 that come from the hand of Mark). Nevertheless, something like 12:18 must have introduced the pre-Markan form of the pericope. In 12:23 the redundancy of "when they rise" (ὅταν ἀναστῶσιν, hotan anastōsin) following "In the resurrection" (ἐν τῇ ἀναστάσει, en tē anastasei) looks typically Markan (Neirynck 1988: 105; Meier 2000a: 6). The explanatory clause, "for all seven had her as a wife" (οἱ γὰρ ἑπτὰ ἔσχον αὐτὴν γυναῖκα, hoi gar hepta eschon autēn gynaika) in 12:23b, however, is probably not Markan, for the explanation is not directed by Mark to his readers, as in the case of most Markan explanatory clauses, but is directed by the Sadducees to Jesus. That it forms a carefully worked-out *inclusio* with the "seven" of 12:20 suggests it is pre-Markan in origin (Meier 2000a: 7).

The present form of the pericope consists of three parts: (1) an introductory seam joining the present account to the preceding pronouncement/controversy story (12:18a); (2) a question from the Sadducees that seeks to refute Jesus's personal belief and teaching concerning the resurrection of the dead (12:18b–23); and (3) Jesus's reply confounding their attempt to defeat him in debate, which refutes the Sadducees by revealing their ignorance of the Scriptures and their limiting the power of God according to their erroneous preconceptions (12:24–27).

Exegesis and Exposition

[18]And Sadducees, who say there is no resurrection, come to him, and they ⌜were asking him⌝, [19]"Teacher, Moses wrote for us that if someone's brother should die and leave behind a wife but leave no ⌜child⌝ ⌜that⌝ his brother should take the wife and raise up ⌜children⌝ for his brother. [20][Now] there were seven brothers, and the first took a wife and when he died he left no children. [21]And the second ⌜married⌝ her and died, leaving behind no children. And the third [did] likewise. [22]And ⌜all⌝ seven [married her and] left no children. Last of all the wife also died. [23]In the resurrection, ⌜when they rise⌝ [from the dead], whose wife will she be, for all seven had her as a wife?" [24]Jesus said to them, "Is not this the reason that you are wrong—because you do not know the Scriptures or the power of God? [25]For when they rise from the

dead, they neither marry nor are given in marriage, but they are like [the] angels in heaven. [26]And as for the dead being raised, have you not read in the book of Moses in the passage about the [burning] bush how God said to him, 'I [am] ⌜the⌝ God of Abraham, and ⌜the⌝ God of Isaac, and ⌜the⌝ God of Jacob?'[27][Consequently] he is God not of the dead but of the living. You are very wrong."

12:18a Without interruption, Mark follows the preceding controversy story involving the Pharisees and Herodians with one involving the Sadducees. This is the only account in Mark that mentions them. The earliest reference to the Sadducees is connected with the reign of John Hyrcanus (135–104 BC; Josephus, *Ant.* 13.10.6 §§293–97), but from the way they are introduced, they must have existed as a group for some time (cf. Josephus, *Ant.* 18.1.2 §11). The origin of the name is debated. Although some suggest that it was derived from "righteous" (צַדִּיק, *ṣaddîq*), most scholars believe that it comes from the name "Zadok," who was high priest during the reigns of David (2 Sam. 8:17; 15:24; 1 Kings 1:8) and Solomon (1 Kings 1:34; 1 Chron. 12:28). The Sadducees were associated primarily with the priestly aristocracy (Acts 4:1–2; 5:17) and were not closely associated with the Jewish people (Josephus, *Ant.* 13.10.6 §§296–97; 18.1.4 §§16–17; *J.W.* 2.8.14 §166). This is why they appear surprisingly infrequently in the NT in comparison to the Pharisees. With the fall of Jerusalem and the destruction of the temple in AD 70, the Sadducees disappear from the scene.

Their theological views are generally described by contrast to that of the Pharisees (Saldarini 1988: 79–237, cf. esp. 110, 112–13). In contrast to the Pharisees, they denied the doctrine of the resurrection and of personal life after death in general (12:18b; Acts 23:8a; Josephus, *Ant.* 18.1.4 §§16–17; *J.W.* 2.8.14 §165; cf. also Acts 4:1–2),[4] the authority of the oral traditions and probably of the Prophets and Writings of the OT, holding only the books of Moses as authoritative (Josephus, *Ant.* 13.10.6 §297; 18.1.4 §16); the existence of spirits and angels (Acts 23:8b); and the sovereignty of God with respect to such matters as fate and predestination in favor of an emphasis on human freedom (Josephus, *J.W.* 2.8.14 §§164–65). According to the rabbinic literature, there was also a major difference between the Pharisees and Sadducees over issues of purity, what is clean and unclean (G. G. Porton, *ABD* 5:892–93).

12:18b–23 For his readers, Mark describes two identifying characteristics of the Sadducees: they say that there is no resurrection (12:18b; cf. Acts 23:8a; 4:1–2), and they base their arguments on the books of Moses (Mark 12:19). Like the Pharisees and Herodians (12:13), although this is not specifically stated, they came seeking to trap Jesus with a question. As in the preceding narrative, Jesus is addressed as "Teacher" (see 4:37–39). The Sadducees were fond of

---

4. Compare the later Pharisaic statement, "These are they that have no share in the world to come: he that says that there is no resurrection of the dead prescribed in the Law" (*m. Sanh.* 10.1).

debating with religious teachers, for "they reckon it a virtue to dispute with the teachers of the path of wisdom that they pursue" (Josephus, *Ant.* 18.1.4 §16). Their question is not asked until 12:23 but is prepared for by the hypothetical situation described in 12:19–22. The situation involves the command in Deut. 25:5–10 concerning levirate marriage. The illustration is carefully crafted. Although at first it would appear that any remarriage in the case of the husband's death might serve as an illustration, the careful description of seven men as brothers is far more powerful. In the former instance, whereas remarriage by the woman is permissible (cf. Tob. 7:11), in the case of brothers, if there are no children, it is specifically commanded in Scripture. Because it is commanded, the Sadducees argue that this command refutes a doctrine of life after death, and in particular the doctrine of the resurrection, because of the absurdity that would result. The well-thought-out nature of the illustration can further be seen in that not even the last brother had a child with the woman. As a result no brother had any special claim on the woman as his wife in the resurrection. The cynical nature of the question is evident. Like the question of the Pharisees and Herodians, it is hypocritical and seeks not enlightenment on the issue but rather to embarrass and humiliate Jesus.

The number "seven" recalls two similar stories found in the Apocrypha. One involves seven successive husbands of the same woman. They each die on their wedding night before consummating the marriage, leaving the wife childless (Tob. 3:7–15; 6:14–15; 7:11). The other involves seven brothers who are martyred possessing hope of the resurrection (2 Macc. 7:1–41, esp. vv. 11, 14, 28, 29). The present illustration, however, is not dependent on either of these two accounts. The former does not mention the resurrection, and the latter does not mention the brothers being married. "Seven" is a favorite number in Jewish literature, designating a sense of completeness. As a result it serves well in the present illustration. The statement "for all seven had her as a wife" indicates that in each instance there was a sexual consummation of the marriage. Although a monogamous marriage continuing until the death of both the husband and the wife might be expected to continue in the resurrection, no such circumstance seems conceivable in the present situation. If, as would be expected, the other six brothers had their own wives before entering into the levirate marriage, the situation is even more difficult to imagine. Thus the Sadducees believed they had demonstrated that Moses (i.e., the Scriptures) argues against a doctrine of the resurrection.

Jesus's response involves a twofold reply. The Sadducees are wrong,[5] and Jesus gives two reasons why they are wrong (lit. "being led astray," πλανᾶσθε, *planasthe*; a "planet" was [supposedly] a "wandering/straying" star), which form a chiasmus. They are wrong first of all because (A) they do not know (lit. "not knowing") the Scriptures (12:24c). In the OT, the doctrine of the

12:24–27

5. The οὐ (*ou*, not) in the question in 12:24 expects the positive answer "Yes," as in 12:26a. The "for this reason" (διὰ τοῦτο, *dia touto*) refers here not to what has just been said in the previous verses but rather to what follows (France 2002: 474; contra Gundry 1993: 705–6).

resurrection is most clearly taught in the Prophets (Isa. 26:19; Ezek. 37:1–14) and the Writings (Dan. 12:2; Pss. 16:9–11; 49:15; 73:23–26; Job 19:26). (Cf. also the ascension of Enoch and Elijah into heaven, which implies a continued fellowship with God and not "there they died"!) Jesus knew, however, that the Sadducees did not accept the Prophets and Writings of the OT as being as authoritative as the Torah. Therefore he argues from the book of Moses or Torah (A′), which the Sadducees accepted as authoritative (12:26–27). The second reason the Sadducees err is that (B) they do not know the power of God (12:24d). With respect to the latter, they do not know that (B′) the resurrection life is no mere continuation of the present life (12:25). Whereas marriage on earth is for the purpose of procreation (Gen. 1:28) and companionship (Gen. 2:18, 23), in the resurrection there is no longer a need for procreation (cf. *b. Ber.* 17a: "In the future world there is no . . . propagation"), for there is no more death (cf. Luke 20:36). Nor is there necessity for marriage to fill the need of companionship, for there one will have an uncountable number of brothers, sisters, mothers, children (cf. Mark 10:30), and a heavenly Father. As a result in the resurrection men will no longer marry and women will no longer be given in marriage (12:25b). The Sadducees limited God's power to what they knew about this life. Like the Corinthian Christians, they erred by thinking that the resurrection life is essentially a continuation of the present one (1 Cor. 15:35–50). In contrast to the frailty and needs of human existence in this life, however, believers in the life to come will be more like the "angels[6] in heaven" (lit. "in the heavens"; cf. 2 Bar. 51.5, 10; 1 En. 104.4, 6; 1QSb 4.24–26), that is, they will be like angels, who do not marry and have children.[7] Whereas "love" is eternal, for God is love, marriage and the sexual relationship (contra Belo 1981: 189) are temporal.[8] The reunion of married partners in the resurrection leads to greater joy and fulfillment than can be imagined, but marriage, as we know it here on earth, will cease to exist (cf. 1 En. 15.7). The Sadducees' denial of this possibility was in reality a denial of God's power.

The second cause of the Sadducees' error in denying that the dead *are*[9] raised is that (B) they did not know the power of God (12:24d). No doubt Jesus's statement that they erred because they did not understand God's power or the

6. Although the Sadducees are said not to have believed in angels (Acts 23:8), the Torah refers to angels (Gen. 6:2, 4 [?]; 16:7–12; 18:1–33; 28:12; 33:1–2; Deut. 32:8 [?]; 33:2; etc.). See Daube (1990: 495–97), who believes that their mention alludes to the issue of life after death.

7. N. Wright (2003: 422) points out that the likeness to angels referred to in 12:25 is not *ontological* or *locational* in nature but *functional* in the sense that angels do not marry.

8. Witherington (1984: 34–35) seeks to argue that, whereas in the resurrection state no more marriages will take place, the marriage state nevertheless continues. However, this does not resolve the problem of the Sadducees' illustration. How can the marriage state of the woman continue simultaneously with all seven brothers?

9. The verb "are raised" (ἐγείρονται, *egeirontai*; 12:26) is a divine passive. The resurrection of the dead is not a quality of human nature. In contrast to Greek thinking that considered immortality an attribute of the soul, the Judeo-Christian tradition understands the resurrection from the dead as a gift of God. It is not something owed to humanity or a quality of human nature, but a gracious gift bestowed on those who trust in God (Gundry 1993: 704; Donahue

Scriptures would have been extremely insulting, for as the priestly aristocracy, they exercised authority over the populace (within the parameters allowed by Rome), and they thought of themselves as the interpretive guides of the Scriptures (i.e., the Torah). Jesus thus attacked their alleged greatest strength.[10] Since the Sadducees accepted only the Torah as authoritative, Jesus refutes them from the very source they claimed supported their denial of the resurrection. Indeed, he uses as his proof text one of the most famous passages in all the OT. In the time before the Bible was divided into chapters and verses, he denotes the passage in Exodus by referring to "the book of Moses in the passage about the [burning] bush" (Exod. 3:1ff.; cf. "in [the story of] Elijah," Rom. 11:2). For Jesus, this statement proves that there is life after death for the righteous (V. Taylor 1952: 484; Donahue and Harrington 2002: 351).[11] The covenantal relationship God established with the patriarchs and the fact that long after their death he still identifies himself as their God indicates that they are alive and in fellowship with him.[12] God's promises and his relationship with the patriarchs and prophets are not broken by death, for they are alive (Luke 16:19–31; Matt. 8:11–12; 13:17; John 8:56; cf. 4 Macc. 7:19; 13:17; 16:25; cf., however, Gundry 1993: 703, 708–9). Jesus culminates his reply with a pronouncement based upon an implication of this Exodus text: "[Consequently] he is God not of the dead but of the living." Jesus then concludes his argument by repeating the statement made in 12:24 that the Sadducees are wrong, only here he is even more emphatic, "You are very wrong" (πολὺ πλανᾶσθε, *poly planasthe*; 12:27c). Just as the Sadducees' question (12:20–23) is framed by an *inclusio* ("seven" in 12:20 and 23), so Jesus's reply (12:24–27) is likewise framed by an *inclusio* ("you are wrong/very wrong" in 12:24 and 27).

Summary

As in the previous account, Jesus once again demonstrates his great wisdom. Although Mark lacks the ending found in Matthew ("And when the crowd

---

and Harrington 2002: 351) or a terrible punishment for those who have rejected God's grace. See note 11 below.

10. Cf. J. Edwards (2002: 367): "Scripture (the Torah) and power (the Sanhedrin) were precisely the Sadducees' stock-in-trade, the two matters in which they majored" (cf. also France 2002: 474).

11. The argument of Jesus neither proves nor disproves the resurrection of the unrighteous unto judgment, since his argument for the resurrection is based on the covenantal relationship of God with Abraham, Isaac, and Jacob. Elsewhere, however, Jesus teaches that the unrighteous also live after death (Matt. 25:31–46; Luke 16:19–31).

12. Jesus's argument in Mark is not based primarily on the "am," for there is no "am" in the Greek text of 12:26 or in the Hebrew text (Hooker 1991: 285; France 2002: 471). Matthew (22:32), following the LXX, includes "am" (εἰμί, *eimi*), but although implied, neither Mark nor Luke has this. Jesus's argument is based primarily on the eternal nature of God's covenant with Abraham, Isaac, and Jacob, which cannot be broken by death. A similar argument is found in *b. Sanh.* 90b: "R. Simai said: Whence do we learn resurrection from the Torah?—From the verse, *And I also have established my covenant with them* [namely, the patriarchs], *to give them the land of Canaan*: '[to give] you', is not said, but '*to give* them' [personally]; thus resurrection is proved from the Torah."

heard it, they were astonished at his teaching" [22:33]) and Luke ("And some of the scribes answered, 'Teacher, you have spoken well.' For they no longer dared to ask him anything" [20:39–40; v. 40 is no doubt borrowed from Mark 12:34]), Jesus's authority as a teacher is clearly seen. He is able to refute the Sadducees at their own game and on the basis of their own Scriptures. He clearly demonstrates his greater authority as a teacher, and he tells them, "You are wrong. . . . You are very wrong!" (12:24, 27). The culmination of Jesus's debates with his opponents will come in 12:34d, "And no one any longer was daring to ask him [any more questions]." With this conclusion Mark reveals that Jesus's victory over his opponents in 11:27–12:37 is absolute.

A second Markan emphasis involves the encouragement that the passage provides for his readers with respect to the hope of the resurrection from the dead. For a community having experienced expulsion of its Jewish members from Rome in AD 49 during the reign of Claudius (Acts 18:2; cf. Suetonius, *Claudius* 25.4) and the horrors of the Neronian persecution in the mid-60s, the hope of the resurrection (cf. Acts 23:6; 24:15) would provide courage and fortitude, as it did for the seven Maccabean brothers (2 Macc. 7:1–41). The "doctrine" of the resurrection provided this for the seven brothers, yet there was more than this for Mark's Christian readers. That God is a God not of the dead but of the living (Mark 12:27) had been demonstrated most emphatically. Jesus, who taught the resurrection of the dead, experienced the resurrection! He who refuted the Sadducees not only taught that he would rise from the dead (8:31; 9:9, 31; 10:34) but in fact did so. His tomb is forever empty (16:1–8), and he appeared to his followers (14:28; 16:7; Matt. 28:1–20; Luke 24:1–53; John 20:1–21:23; cf. 1 Cor. 15:4–8). What he taught has been verified by his own resurrection. The power of God of which the Sadducees were ignorant (Mark 12:24, 27) has raised Jesus from the dead and will raise his followers (and we who believe!) as well (1 Cor. 6:14; cf. Mark 14:62). Through this hope Mark encouraged his readers to "conquer" and share in the resurrection life (cf. Rev. 2:7, 11, 17, 26; 3:5, 12, 21).

Additional Notes

12:18. ἐπηρώτων αὐτὸν λέγοντες is lit. "asking him, saying."

12:19. The MSS A D f¹³ and the Latin and Byzantine traditions read "children" (τέκνα).

12:19. "That" (ἵνα) here introduces not a purpose clause but the content of Moses's command (see 3:9–10).

12:19. σπέρμα is lit. "seed," as also in vv. 20–22.

12:21. ἔλαβεν is lit. "took."

12:22. οἱ is lit. "the."

12:23. "When they rise" (ὅταν ἀναστῶσιν) is omitted by ℵ B C* D L W Δ but found in A Θ f¹ lat. The duality resulting from this phrase is typically Markan (Neirynck 1988: 105), and its omission by early copyists is quite understandable (Metzger 1994: 93; Donahue and Harrington 2002: 350).

12:26. There is confusion among the witnesses as to whether one, two, or all three occurrences of the article ὁ should be omitted. While a textual problem, this does not affect the interpretation of the passage.

G. A Scribe Asks Jesus about the Great Commandment (12:28–34)

The present account is joined closely to the preceding incident (12:18–27) by both its placement and the transitional statement "after hearing them disputing [and] seeing that he answered them well" (ἀκούσας αὐτῶν συζητούντων, ἰδὼν ὅτι καλῶς ἀπεκρίθη αὐτοῖς, *akousas autōn syzētountōn, idōn hoti kalōs apekrithē autois*; 12:28). After the transitional statement, a scribe asks Jesus the fourth question in the series (11:28; 12:13–15, 19–23), "Which is the first commandment of all?" (ποία ἐστὶν ἐντολὴ πρώτη πάντων; *poia estin entolē prōtē pantōn?*). For several reasons, one is predisposed to interpret the scribe's question as being hostile. For one, all three previous questions in the present context have been hostile (11:28; 12:13–15, and 19–23), and all have been asked by religious leaders (11:27; 12:13, and 18). That the present question is asked by a "scribe" (γραμματεύς, *grammateus*) also prepares the reader for a hostile question because of earlier references in Mark to the scribes' hostility toward Jesus (2:6–7, 16; 3:22; 7:1, 5; 8:31; 9:14; 10:33; 11:18, 27). In addition, after the next account, in which Jesus asks the scribes a question concerning the relationship of the Messiah to David (12:35–37), Jesus warns the crowd concerning the hypocrisy of the scribes (12:38–40). Thus one is predisposed to see the question of this scribe in 12:28 as hostile in intent. This is how Matthew understands it in his parallel account (22:35). In Luke, where we find a similar account with a different context, a "lawyer" (νομικός, *nomikos*; cf. Luke 10:25; Matt. 22:35) engages Jesus with a question involving the same OT passage (Deut. 6:4–5; Lev. 19:18), and the intent is once again hostile, although in the Lukan parallel it is the scribe who quotes the OT passages rather than Jesus.

The question in the present account, however, cannot be seen as hostile in intent (contra Gundry 1993: 710) for at least four reasons: (1) the scribe is positively inclined toward Jesus, not insolent (contra Trocmé 1975: 96; 12:28, 32); (2) he praises Jesus (12:32–33); (3) he is described as having answered Jesus "wisely" (νουνεχῶς, *nounechōs*; 12:34a); and (4) he is praised by Jesus for not being far from the kingdom of God (12:34b). Thus in Mark the present account is not a controversy story but a pronouncement story or *Schulgespräch* (Bultmann 1968: 51; Donahue and Harrington 2002: 356).

As to its origin, it is difficult to imagine the early church creating an account in which Jesus repeats the Shema (Evans 2001: 261). It is also unlikely that the positive portrayal of the scribe is due to Mark's editing (Ambrozic 1972: 177–81). The question of whether Luke's or Mark's form of the story is more primitive is greatly debated. Did Mark receive his tradition in the present form (Nineham 1963: 324; Bultmann 1968: 51), or did he receive it as a controversy story and change it? "The former is possible, the latter requires explanation" (Hooker 1991: 287). The intimate association of the Lukan account (10:25–28) with the parable of the good Samaritan (10:29–37) argues for either a separate incident or a separate tradition (Tuckett 1983: 126). (For Jesus, as a religious teacher, to have spoken on more than one occasion concerning the question of the greatest commandment is not at all unlikely [Evans 2001: 262].) Despite the suggestion that the incident took place in Galilee (V. Taylor 1952: 485), the reference to "whole burnt offerings and sacrifices" (τῶν ὁλοκαυτωμάτων καὶ θυσιῶν, tōn holokautōmatōn kai thysiōn; 12:33) fits the present context of the temple (11:27; 12:41; 13:1) particularly well.

The account itself consists of (1) a scribe's approaching Jesus and asking him a question concerning the greatest commandment (12:28); (2) Jesus's twofold answer based upon the Shema (Deut. 6:4–5) and the command to love one's neighbor (Lev. 19:18; Mark 12:29–31); (3) the scribe's positive response to Jesus's answer and his repetition of the two commands (12:32–33); (4) Jesus's reply to the scribe, acknowledging that he is not far from the kingdom of God (12:34a–b); and (5) Mark's closing comment (12:34c), which serves as a conclusion not only to 12:28–34 but to all the questions and challenges directed at Jesus in 11:27–33 and 12:13–34. Mark's own hand is seen most clearly in the present location of the account. The inclusion of a story about a friendly scribe in a possible pre-Markan collection of controversy stories found in 11:27–33; 12:13–17; and 12:18–27 is unlikely. It is more likely that it was Mark who placed this account in its present context (Daube 1956: 162–63). Mark's redactional work is also seen in the concluding statement of the account (12:34c; V. Taylor 1952: 490; Nineham 1963: 328; Pryke 1978: 20, 145, 169; Marcus 1992b: 135). Note the "no one any longer" (οὐδεὶς οὐκέτι, oudeis ouketi) in 12:34 and in 5:3; 7:12; and 9:8. The introduction (12:28) also looks like a Markan rewording of the original introductory seam (Nineham 1963: 326; Pryke 1978: 20, 145, 169; Gnilka 1979: 163).

Exegesis and Exposition

[28]And one of the scribes, having come [to Jesus], after hearing them disputing [and] seeing that he answered them well, asked him, "⌜Which⌝ is the first commandment of ⌜all⌝?" [29]Jesus answered, "The first is, 'Hear, [O] Israel, The Lord our God is one Lord; [30]and you ⌜shall⌝ love the Lord your God with all your heart, and with all your soul, and with all your mind, and with all your strength.' [31]The second [is] this, 'You shall love your neighbor as yourself.' There is no other commandment greater than these." [32]And the scribe said to him, "Well [said], Teacher. You have truly stated that he [God] is one, and there is no other than he; [33]and to love him with all your heart, and with all your understanding, and with all your strength, and to love your neighbor as yourself is ⌜much greater than⌝ all the whole burnt offerings and sacrifices." [34]And Jesus, seeing

⌜him⌝ that he answered wisely, said to him, "You are not far from the kingdom of God." And no one any longer was daring to ask him [any more questions].

12:28   References to the scribes have been quite negative up to this point (see the introduction to this unit). For a discussion of the role of scribes in the time of Jesus, see 1:21–22. On this occasion "one" (εἷς, *heis*) of the scribes approaches Jesus and asks him a question. Whether the singular "one" is emphasized to contrast him with the hostility of the scribes as a group (France 2002: 476) is impossible to say. The question Jesus was asked was often debated among Jewish religious teachers. Since the Torah contained 613 separate commandments (*b. Mak.* 23b), of which 248 were positive and 365 were negative, it was natural to discuss if some of the commandments were more important ("heavier") than others ("lighter"). Elsewhere Jesus seems to allude to such a division in his own thinking when he spoke of the "least of these commandments" (Matt. 5:19) and when he criticized the Pharisees for tithing mint, dill, and cummin, but neglecting the weightier matters of the law: justice and mercy and faith (Matt. 23:23). One is, of course, to do the "heavier" commandments (justice, mercy, faith) without neglecting the others. Yet it is best to understand this question as an attempt to identify not which commandments are unimportant and need not be kept but rather which commandment is the most fundamental one from which all the other commandments arise (Hurtado 1983: 207; Hooker 1991: 287–88). Matthew seems to understand the question in this manner when he concludes the account, "On these two commandments depend all the law and the prophets" (22:40). Paul in a similar manner states that "love is the fulfillment of the law" (Rom. 13:10).

Within the Second Temple period, we find several attempts to answer the question addressed to Jesus. Perhaps the most famous is found in *b. Šabb.* 31a, in which Shammai and Hillel are challenged by someone, "Teach me the whole Torah while I stand on one foot." Hillel then replies, "What is hateful to you, do not do to your neighbor: that is the whole Torah, while the rest is the commentary thereof." This "silver" rule, which is a negative form of the "golden" rule (Matt. 7:12), is also found in Tob. 4:15. Other parallels are found in *b. Mak.* 24a, where the law is seen as being reducible to the eleven principles found in Ps. 15, the six found in Isa. 33:15–16, the three found in Mic. 6:8, the two found in Isa. 56:1, and the one found in Amos 5:4b and Hab. 2:4b. In *b. Ber.* 63a the basis for all the essential principles contained in the Torah is found in Prov. 3:6. In another rabbinic text we read, "Charity and righteous deeds outweigh all other commandments in the Torah" (*t. Pe'ah* 4.19).

12:29–31   Jesus's own answer to which commandment is greatest of all involves two separate commandments from two widely separated sections in the Torah. The first may be the best-known verse in the whole of the Jewish Scriptures, for the Shema (Deut. 6:4–5), named because the first word in these two verses is the Hebrew word שְׁמַע (*šĕmaʿ*, hear), was repeated twice each day (Deut. 6:7) by pious Jews. The first part of the Shema is not a command but a preamble affirming that the LORD (*YHWH*), the God of Israel, was the one and only God. It was a pillar for Jewish and Christian monotheism.

The first commandment involves four elements. These are to love God with all one's heart, soul, mind, and strength. The Matthean parallel (22:37) contains the first three elements in the same order, but lacks "strength." Luke (10:27) contains all four elements, but the order of the last two is reversed. All three accounts agree against the MT and targumic texts, which lack "mind." The LXX texts are mixed. Some have "heart" but not "mind," and some have "mind" but not "heart." No LXX MS of this passage appears to have both. The agreement of the Synoptic Gospels against both the Hebrew, Aramaic, and LXX forms of Deut. 6:5 is probably best explained by a literary interdependence (Stein 2001: 45–46). The four areas mentioned are the "heart" (καρδίας, *kardias*; see 2:6–7), which is the center of one's thinking and affections; the "soul" (ψυχῆς, *psychēs*), which serves here not as a reference to physical life as in 8:35–36 but to the source of one's desires and feelings; the "mind" (διανοίας, *dianoias*; only here in Mark), which involves thinking and understanding; and "strength" (ἰσχύος, *ischyos*), which serves as a reference to one's energy or strength and is almost a synonym for "power" (δύναμις, *dynamis*), although the last term is used in Mark primarily to describe the power of God (9:1; 12:24; 14:62) or of Jesus (5:30; 6:2, 5, 14; 9:39; 13:26). In combination these four terms refer to loving God totally with all one's energy and being (Donahue and Harrington 2002: 355). It is clear that the command to love God (cf. Luke 11:42; Rom. 8:28; 1 Cor. 2:9; 8:3; 16:22; 1 John 4:20–21) sees God as a person and not as some sort of an abstraction such as "the prime mover," "the first cause," "the force," and so on. Like all such commands, this command is not understood as a means for entering into a covenantal relationship with God but rather as a stipulation deriving from and resulting from such a covenantal relationship. The Shema was given to a covenantal people who had been redeemed out of Egypt. We love God because he first loved us (1 John 4:19).

The first commandment corresponds to the first table of the Decalogue and deals with a person's vertical relationship with God. As "first," it possesses priority (note Matt. 22:38: "great[est]" [μεγάλη, *megalē*] and "first") over the second (Furnish 1982: 330; France 2002: 480; contra Furnish 1972: 26–27). The second commandment corresponds to the second table of the Decalogue and deals with a person's horizontal relationships to fellow human beings (Allison 1994).[1] The second commandment is based on the natural inclination of people to care for and look after themselves.[2] It does not command self-love (J. Edwards 2002: 372n49) but rather assumes that people love themselves and that this kind of love should be extended to one's neighbor. Its importance in

---

1. For other examples of Jesus's pairing of these two commandments, cf. Luke 15:18, 21; 18:2; also see 11:42.

2. Thus one's willingness to lose one's life for the sake of Jesus and the gospel (8:35) also reveals one's self-love for one's own future (8:34–38).

the NT and in the early church can be seen by its frequent repetition (Matt. 5:43; 19:19; Rom. 13:8–10; Gal. 5:14; James 2:8; Did. 1.2; 2.7; 2 Clem. 3.4; Gos. Thom. 25; etc.). Although in its original context in Lev. 19:17–18, one's "neighbor" refers to one's relatives and fellow Israelites, Jesus's understanding of who is a neighbor extends to enemies (Matt. 5:43–48/Luke 6:27–36) and even the hated Samaritans (Luke 10:29–37). Such "love" is to be understood not as an abstract emotional feeling but as active obedience toward God and acts of loving-kindness to one's neighbor.

There are several examples of the pairing of these two commandments in Jewish literature. In T. Iss. 5.2 we read, "Love the Lord and your neighbor" (cf. T. Benj. 3.3); and in T. Iss. 7.6, "I loved the Lord; likewise also every man with all my whole heart" (cf. T. Dan 5.3). Philo in *Spec. Laws* 2.15 §63 divides all human duty and responsibility under the heads "duty to God . . . [and] duty to men" (cf. also *Dec.* 22 §§108–10). Compare also Jub. 36.7–8. These references vary in date, and some of the references may even be later Christian interpolations. It is uncertain therefore whether anyone clearly linked these two commandments before Jesus (J. Edwards 2002: 372; contra Allison 1994). Even if some teachers did link these two commandments together before Jesus, the emphasis and centrality that they receive from him is unique and unlike any possible earlier associations (Piper 1979: 92–94).

Jesus's summary of the law by these two commandments is a clear indication that he "came not to abolish the law and the prophets" (Matt. 5:17). He did not see any conflict between the moral teachings of the old covenant and those of the new. In Mark 12:30–31 he summarizes the law by means of two commandments. The two commandments are held together by the imperatival future "you shall love" (ἀγαπήσεις, agapēseis). There is a priority and order in the twofold command. The "first" (πρώτη, prōtē) involves one's relationship with God. Obeying this commandment provides the desire and ability to obey the "second" (δευτέρα, deutera). Isolating one command from the other can lead to a religious mysticism that ignores the needs of one's neighbor or to a humanistic concern based on a false sentimentality. Together they provide a basis for understanding life as first of all consisting of loving God and as a result loving one's neighbor, who is created in the image of God, is loved by God, and is one for whom Christ died. There is a sense in which these two separate commands are brought together by Jesus and form a single command. This is seen in 12:31, where Jesus says that no other commandment (singular) is greater than these (Witherington 2001: 330–31), and in 12:33, where the scribe repeats Jesus's two commandments and says that this "is" (ἐστίν, estin) greater than all whole burnt offerings and sacrifices. All the other commandments can be understood as an explication of this one, two-part command. Thus Jesus's twofold commandment does not seek to abrogate the remaining 611 commandments in the Law but to prioritize them and show that the foundation upon which all the other commandments rest is this two-part commandment to love God and one's neighbor (Donahue and Harrington 2002: 357).

The response of the scribe is not found in the parallel accounts in Matthew **12:32–33** and Luke. They may have chosen to omit it because of the redundancy in repeating Deut. 6:4–5 and Lev. 19:18, or they may have omitted it to make it fit better the normal form of a pronouncement story in which Jesus's pronouncement appears at the end as the culmination of the story. The scribe's reply, "Well [said], Teacher" (καλῶς, διδάσκαλε, kalōs, didaskale) is clearly positive in tone and reminds Mark's readers once again of Jesus's wisdom and authority as "Teacher." The address, "Teacher," is also found in the two previous stories (12:14, 19). For "Teacher," see 4:37–39. The scribe affirms Jesus's opening statement of the Shema (Deut. 6:4; cf. 4:35) concerning God being one (Mark 12:32b)[3] and again commends Jesus by saying to the one who is the "truth" (John 14:6) that he has spoken the truth on this issue (Mark 12:32; cf. 12:14).

The scribe concludes his affirmation of Jesus's twofold command by repeating it. In so doing, however, he omits "with all your soul" and changes "with all your mind" (διανοίας) to "with all your understanding" (συνέσεως, syneseōs). The differences are minor, and Mark attributes no significance to them. The scribe adds to his summary of Jesus's love command his own value judgment that doing this command is greater than "all the whole burnt offerings and sacrifices," an expression found over a hundred times in the LXX (see 1 Sam. 15:25; Pss. 39:7 [40:6 Eng.]; 50:18–19 [51:19 Eng.]; Isa. 1:11; Jer. 6:20; Hos. 6:6; Amos 5:22; etc.). The comment by the scribe serves in Mark as an endorsement of Jesus's act of judgment in the temple (11:12–23; Hooker 1991: 289). The expression "whole burnt offerings" refers to sacrifices in which the whole offering was burned on the altar; the expression "sacrifices" refers to various sacrifices and offerings in which part of the sacrifice was burned on the altar but part was given to the priest and part was eaten by the worshipers.

The account ends with Jesus's commendation to the scribe for his "wise/ **12:34** intelligent" (νουνεχῶς, nounechōs) answer. This refers not to his repetition of Jesus's two-part love command in 12:32–33a but to his understanding that in light of this command "all the whole burnt offerings and sacrifices" are of less importance (12:33b). Love is more important than ritual (Mic. 6:6–8; cf. b. Suk. 49b; 1QS 9.3–5). In the context of Jesus's prediction of the temple's destruction (Mark 11:12–23; 12:1–12; 13:1–37; 14:58; 15:29) and his teaching in 12:29–31, the scribe's wise statement (12:32–33) would take on great importance for the reader of Mark. With the coming destruction of the temple and its cult in AD 70, the scribe's words would provide understanding for both Jewish and gentile Christians that the once-for-all sacrifice of Jesus (14:22–25; cf. Heb. 7:27; 9:12; 10:10) and the twofold love command provided them with what was necessary for holy living.

3. For similar statements, cf. Deut. 4:39; 2 Sam. 7:22; 1 Kings 8:60; 2 Kings 19:19; 2 Chron. 33:13; Isa. 37:20; 43:10.

Jesus's reply to the scribe in 12:29–31 recalls his reply to the rich young ruler in 10:18 (cf. 12:29) and 19 (cf. 12:30–31).[4] There we also encounter a positive response of Jesus toward the young man ("Jesus, having looked at him, loved him" [10:21a]), just as here ("You are not far from the kingdom of God"). Unfortunately, in the case of the rich young ruler, the command to love God totally (found in the form "Whatever you have, sell and give to the poor, and you will have treasure in heaven—and come, follow me" [10:21c–d]) was too difficult because he had many possessions. As a result he left grieving and not having entered the kingdom of God (10:22). The scribe's nearness to the kingdom of God[5] and his fate are left unresolved in the account. He is "not far from the kingdom of God" in the sense that he is in the presence of the one who has brought the kingdom of God, he understands the meaning and spirit of Jesus's teachings, and he knows the way into the kingdom. But did he love God totally, so that he was willing to "repent and believe in the gospel"? (1:15); leave all to follow Jesus? (1:18, 20); deny himself, take up his cross, and follow Jesus? (8:34). The account ends without telling us. This may be intentional, for Mark may want his readers to wrestle with the question "Have I entered the kingdom of God?" "Nearness" to the kingdom is not enough. Being close is good in some sports (archery, horseshoes, etc.), but it is tragically inadequate with respect to the kingdom of God.

The account ends with the Markan comment "And no one any longer was daring to ask him [any more questions]" (καὶ οὐδεὶς οὐκέτι ἐτόλμα αὐτὸν ἐπερωτῆσαι, *kai oudeis ouketi etolma auton eperōtēsai*). This serves as a conclusion not only to the present account but also to the whole series of controversies and questions begun in 11:27ff. As in the other instances, it reveals Jesus's great wisdom and superiority over his opponents. Although it brings the present series of questions to a conclusion, it also prepares for 12:35–37, where Jesus will ask the questions.

Summary

The present passage contains several Markan emphases involving theology, ethics, Christology, and soteriology. A major theological teaching for Mark's original readers involves the monotheistic teaching of the Shema: "The Lord our God is one Lord!" While this served for centuries as a foundational statement of monotheism for the descendants of Abraham, it was an especially appropriate reminder for Mark's gentile readers, who came out of a polytheistic and idolatrous background and still lived in such a culture. The monotheistic presuppositions that the modern-day readers of Mark bring

---

4. Williams (1994: 175) thinks that Mark deliberately contrasts the scribe here with the rich young ruler.

5. The kingdom of God is portrayed here as a present reality and not in its future, consummated form, for the scribe's being "near" the kingdom refers not to a chronological nearness but to the fact that the scribe was close/near to entering the kingdom that Jesus announced as being present (see 1:15).

with them to the reading of the text should not obscure that this was being said in an environment in which it might be tempting to place the God and Father of Abraham and our Lord Jesus Christ alongside the other deities dominating the landscape of idolatrous Rome. But this was not possible, for "the Lord our God is one Lord," and there is no other than he.

The ethical teachings found in the account would also have been helpful for Mark's readers. The present situation in Jerusalem (if Mark was written before AD 70) or the recent destruction of the city and its temple (if Mark was written afterward) should not catch Mark's readers off guard. Jesus had predicted the destruction of the temple and thus the end of the sacrificial system (cf. also 7:18–19). Even before the events of AD 70, gentile Christians were less inclined than their Jewish counterparts to attend the temple in Jerusalem and offer sacrifices. Had not Jesus designated the temple primarily as a house of prayer (not sacrifice) for all nations (11:17)? The primary importance of the love commandments and the lesser importance of burnt offerings and sacrifices also indicated that the Jerusalem temple was of minimal importance. True piety and the Christian ethic did not center on the rituals of the temple. Jesus's own sacrifice (10:45; 14:22–25), once for all (Heb. 7:27; 9:12; 10:10), was all that was necessary. Thus one should focus on the twofold love command, which summarizes all God's commandments.

As for Christology, once again the great wisdom of Jesus enables him to answer successfully all the questions asked him. With respect to his opponents, he demonstrates complete mastery and superiority and answers their hostile questions in a way that often elicits awe and even admiration. With respect to the sincere, he provides true counsel for entering the kingdom of God. Just as his miracles of healing result in awe and wonder (1:27, 45; 2:12; 4:41; 6:51; 7:37; 9:28), so do his teachings (11:18; 12:17, 34; cf. also 11:29–33). Such awe and wonder is just what one would expect the Christ, the Son of God (1:1), to elicit.

With respect to soteriology, we have in this present account a repetition of the emphasis found in the story of the rich young ruler (10:17–31). When asked the question "What must I do in order that I might inherit eternal life?" Jesus answers with a list of commandments dealing with loving your neighbor as yourself (10:19). In the Lukan parallel to our account, after the lawyer quotes the twofold commandment (Luke 10:27), Jesus states, "Do this and you will live" (Luke 10:28). "Doing this" means first of all to "love the Lord your God with all your heart, and with all your soul, and with all your mind, and with all your strength." This involves acknowledging our need to repent (Mark 1:15) and trusting in the grace God has provided in the death of his Son (8:31; 9:31; 10:32–34), whom God has provided as a ransom by which we can be saved (10:45; 14:24). To love God in this way means to accept his view of us (we are sinners) and to accept his provision for our sin (Christ's death and resurrection), that is, to trust and believe in God's grace. The love of our neighbor is a natural consequence of experiencing

God's love for us in Christ (1 John 4:19). It is our natural and required response to loving God (1 John 4:20–21), for his love is poured out in our hearts (Rom. 5:5).

Additional Notes

12:28. "Which" (ποία) functions here as the equivalent of "what" (τίς), as "first" (πρώτη) indicates (V. Taylor 1952: 485; France 2002: 479).

12:28. "All" (πάντων) here is used idiomatically and means "of all the commandments" (France 2002: 479; contra Gundry 1993: 714; J. Edwards 2002: 370).

12:30. "Shall" is used here and in 12:31 to express the imperatival nature of the future tense.

12:33. "Much greater than" or "much more than" translates the comparative περισσότερον (cf. France 2002: 281).

12:34. "Him" (αὐτόν) is omitted by ℵ D L W Δ Θ f¹ f¹³ lat but is found in A B Ψ and the majority of Greek MSS. Its awkwardness argues for its authenticity.

H. Jesus's Question concerning the Messiah (12:35–37)

This account is connected to the immediate context by several verbal ties. It is located in the "temple" (ἱερῷ, *hierō*; 12:35; cf. 11:11, 15–16, 27; 12:41: temple treasury, γαζοφυλάκιον, *gazophylakion*); Jesus has just "answered" (ἀποκριθείς, *apokritheis*; 12:35) the previous questions addressed to him (cf. 11:29–30; 12:15b–17a, 24–27, 29–31); he is "teaching" (διδάσκων, *didaskōn*; 12:35; cf. 12:1–11 [a parable], 14, 19 and 32 [Jesus is called "Teacher"], 38; also 14:49); the account centers on the designation "Son of David" (12:35, 37; cf. 10:47, 48; 11:10); and the "scribes" (γραμματεῖς, *grammateis*) are referred to (12:35; cf. 11:27; 12:28, 38). Still another tie with the immediate context is Jesus's use of Scripture to refute his opponents and in his teaching (12:36; cf. 12:26, 29–31). After Jesus answers his opponents' questions and silences them (12:34c), it is now his turn to ask a question. Classifying the present account is difficult. It is variously classified as an apothegm (Bultmann 1968: 66), pronouncement story (V. Taylor 1949: 78), or controversy story (Marcus 1992b: 132), but these classifications are often based on its supposed original form rather than on the present form of the account in Mark (Evans 2001: 271). The reconstruction of the alleged earlier form of the present account, however, is extremely hypothetical.

Many deny the authenticity of the account. Some do so because of its unusual form (question by Jesus [12:35b], an OT quotation [12:36], and a concluding question by Jesus [12:37a]).[1] When Jesus is asked a question and responds in return with a question, it is usually in the form of a counter-question (2:19, 25; 10:3; 11:28–30; 12:16; cf. also 2:8–9; 3:2–4, 22–23). Yet we encounter instances where Jesus initiates the discussion with a question (8:27; cf. also Matt. 17:25; 21:31; Luke 10:36). Jesus also used rhetorical questions in his teaching (Stein 1994b: 23–25). The attributing of the present account to the early church (Bultmann 1968: 136–37; Hooker 1991: 291) is due not only to its unusual form but also to the belief that Jesus never made

---

1. Gundry (1993: 719) sees the pericope as consisting of the following chiasmus:

  A And Jesus, having answered, was teaching in the temple.
    B "How [is it that] the scribes say that the Messiah is the Son of David?
      C David himself said by the Holy Spirit, 'The Lord said to my Lord, Sit at my right hand, until I place your enemies under your feet.'
      C′ David himself calls him Lord,
    B′ so how is he his son?"
  A′ And the great crowd [of people] was hearing him gladly.

See Marcus 1992b: 130–31 for a different form of the alleged chiasmus.

any explicit messianic claims.[2] On the other hand, is it likely that the early church would cast doubt on the Davidic descent of the Messiah? The Davidic descent of Jesus and the Messiah was readily and widely acknowledged by the early church. Along with the references in 10:47–48 and 11:10, we find this emphasized in Rom. 1:3–4; 2 Tim. 2:8; Matt. 1:2–16, 20; Luke 1:27, 32, 69; 2:4, 11; Rev. 3:7; 5:5; 22:16; cf. also Acts 2:30; Rom. 15:12. It would be unlikely that the early church, which took for granted that Jesus the Messiah was the Son of David, would create an account that appears to question this. The Davidic lineage of Jesus and the Messiah does not seem to have been an issue in the Jewish-Christian debates or within the Christian community (Hooker 1991: 291). Thus it is unlikely that the present account is a creation by the early church (Cranfield 1959: 381; Bock 2000: 220–22).[3] Its creation would only raise questions and doubts concerning the church's established belief that Jesus was the Davidic Messiah. Furthermore, the present account does not seem to meet a clear christological need of the Christian community, so that its creation by the early church is doubtful.

Mark's own hand is seen most clearly in the vocabulary of 12:35a (Pryke 1978: 20, 146, 169; Gnilka 1979: 169; Marcus 1992b: 131; contra Pesch 1980b: 250). The reference to Jesus's "teaching" (διδάσκων) is a clear Markan redactional emphasis (see 1:21–22), and its unnecessary redundancy also argues for its Markan origin. In a similar way the concluding "And the great crowd was hearing him gladly" (12:37c) also looks Markan (Pryke 1978: 20, 146, 169; Marcus 1992b: 131; contra Pesch 1980b: 250), for the expression "great crowd" (πολὺς ὄχλος, polys ochlos) occurs frequently in Markan seams (5:21, 24; 6:34; 8:1; 9:14). Similarly, "were hearing him gladly" (ἤκουεν αὐτοῦ ἡδέως, ēkouen autou hēdeōs) recalls the Markan explanatory clause found in 6:20. The lack of any necessary connection in the account with the preceding or following material suggests that Mark is probably responsible for placing this tradition in its present location.

Exegesis and Exposition

[35]And Jesus, having answered [his opponents' questions], ⌜was teaching⌝ in the temple, "How [is it that] the scribes say that the Messiah is the Son of David? [36]David himself said by the Holy Spirit, ⌜'The⌝ Lord said to my Lord, Sit at my right hand, until I place your enemies ⌜under⌝ your feet.' [37]David himself calls him Lord; so ⌜how⌝ is he his son?" And ⌜the⌝ great crowd [of people] was hearing him gladly.

12:35   It is easy to understand why the scribes say that the Messiah (lit. "Christ") is the "Son of David." The "messianic" promises of the OT refer to him as a

2. Nineham (1963: 330–31) denies the authenticity of the account because he believes that in the account Jesus denies the Davidic lineage of the Messiah, and if Jesus had said this, the early church would not have proclaimed his Davidic lineage so strongly.

3. The view of Crossan (1983: 262–66) that all of 12:35–37a is a creation of Mark has even less to commend it.

"branch" of David (Jer. 23:5–6; 33:15–16) and a "branch" from Jesse's (David's father's) stump (Isa. 11:1ff.; cf. Isa. 9:2–7; Ezek. 34:23–24; 37:24–28). This "branch" is also referred to in Zech. 3:8 and 6:12. In Ps. Sol. 17.21 the coming king who will rule over Israel is expressly called the "Son of David," and in the rabbinic literature as well the Messiah is referred to as the "Son of David" (*b. 'Erub.* 43a; *b. Sanh.* 38a; *b. Yoma* 10a; *b. Suk.* 52a; see Evans 2001: 272 for additional examples). The widespread use of this title to describe the Messiah in the pre-Christian literature and the NT makes it very unlikely that Jesus's question seeks to show that the scribes are poor exegetes because nowhere in the OT is it explicitly stated that "the Messiah is the Son of David" (contra Gundry 1993: 718, 723). For Mark, the purpose of the passage is to describe the nature of the Messiah.

The meaning of the question addressed to the great crowd (12:37c; in Matt. 22:41 it is addressed to the Pharisees) is far from self-evident. We must furthermore distinguish between what Jesus meant by the question and what Mark intended his readers to understand by the question. For Mark, the question is clearly not a denial that Jesus is the Messiah or that he/the Messiah is of Davidic descent. This is clear from the confession of blind Bartimaeus that Jesus is the "Son of David" (10:47, 48), a confession viewed positively by Mark. The greeting Jesus receives as he enters Jerusalem, "Blessed is the coming kingdom of our father David!" (11:10), is also viewed positively by Mark. In addition, we must take into consideration that the audience of Mark believed that Jesus was indeed the Son of David (cf. Rom. 1:3–4), and the incorporation of this pericope by Matthew and Luke into their Gospels indicates that they saw no conflict between this question and their genealogies tracing Jesus's lineage to David. If Mark therefore was seeking to teach in this account that Jesus was denying his Davidic descent, he was singularly inept (cf. Hooker 1991: 292; France 2002: 484).[4]

Another suggestion is that Mark intended his readers to understand by this account that Jesus rejected any nationalistic or political understanding of his messiahship. Mark supposedly wanted to make sure, especially in light of the events of the Jewish revolt (AD 66–70), that his readers harbored no such false understanding. The Jewish hopes of the coming Son of David as portrayed in Ps. Sol. 17 are indeed radically opposed to Mark's understanding that Jesus came to suffer and give his life as a ransom for many (10:45; Marcus 1992b: 146–49). Though this suggestion about Mark's intention may be partially correct, it is insufficient. More likely is the view that Mark understands the present text as teaching that the Messiah is the Son of David, but that such an understanding by itself is inadequate. Jesus is far more. The question of Jesus in this verse is meant to evoke the response, "The Messiah is not just

---

4. Chilton (1982) argues that the title "Son of David" is not a messianic title for Jesus but claims that he understood himself as the "Son of David" in the sense that he was a Solomonic healer of the sick (cf. also Duling 1975). However, the tie in Mark between the title "Son of David" and healing is found only in 10:47 and 48. In 11:10 and 12:35–37 there is no hint of healing (Marcus 1992b: 151–52), and in 11:1ff. no mention is made of Jesus's healing or exorcising.

the Son of David but is indeed the Son of God!" Matthew understands the question in this manner: "What do you think of the Messiah? Whose son is he?" (22:42). In the Jewish tradition of the first century, the Messiah, or Christ, was primarily identified as the Son of David, but Mark wants to indicate that he is much more. Jesus is the Messiah–Son of David, but more important, he is the Messiah–Son of God (1:1; 14:61–62; Marcus 1989a: 135–37)!

The matter of what Jesus meant by this question, assuming its authenticity, is highly dependent on one's view of Jesus's messianic self-consciousness. The Jesus of Mark and the other Gospels, however, claims that he is the Son of Man and the Son of God and acknowledges that he is the Christ (8:27–30; 14:61–62; 15:2) and the Son of David (10:47, 48). This suggests that Jesus could have meant by this question exactly what Mark means. He who heard the heavenly voice, "You are/This is my beloved Son" (1:11; 9:7), who "came . . . to give his life as a ransom for many" (10:45) and believed that he would one day be "sitting at the right hand of Power" (14:62; cf. 8:38) clearly thought of himself as much more than just the Son of David.[5]

12:36 "David himself said by the Holy Spirit" emphasizes not only the prophetic nature of the following scriptural quotation but that the "Messiah" (lit. "Lord," κύριος, *kyrios*) was in reality his (my, μου, *mou*) Lord. Jesus and Mark, along with their contemporaries, assumed that David was responsible for this psalm (note the psalm's superscription: "Of David: A Psalm") and that he was divinely inspired (cf. 2 Sam. 23:2; Acts 1:16; 4:25; *b. Ber.* 4b; *b. Suk.* 52a; see Evans 2001: 273 for additional rabbinic examples). There is no reason for interpreting the reference to the Holy Spirit as contrasting with the lack of the Spirit in the scribes' view (contra Gundry 1993: 718; Evans 2001: 273). As in each of the preceding two controversy stories, Jesus uses Scripture to prove his point (12:26, 29–31; cf. also 7:6–7; 10:5–8).

The Davidic text that Jesus quotes comes from Ps. 110:1 (109:1 LXX), the most-quoted OT verse in the NT (Hengel 1995: 133).[6] In contrast to the rest of the NT, which emphasizes the second line of the verse ("Sit at my right hand, until I place your enemies under your feet"; cf. 14:62; Acts 2:34–35 and note v. 36; Rom. 8:34; 1 Cor. 15:25; Eph. 1:20, 22; Col. 3:1; Heb. 1:3; 8:1; 10:12–13; etc.), in Mark 12:36 the key part of Jesus's argument is found in the first line ("The Lord said to my Lord"). This is clear from Jesus's question in 12:37a, "David himself calls him Lord; so how is he his son?" In Hebrew the first line reads, "The Lord [יהוה, *YHWH*] said to my Lord [אֲדֹנִי, *ʾădōnî*]." In the LXX, the two terms "Lord [*YHWH*]" and "Lord [*ʾădōnî*]" are both translated as κύριος (*kyrios*). In Jesus's actual quotation of the psalm in Aramaic, he

---

5. Even if one denies that Jesus possessed a messianic self-consciousness, it is impossible to believe that he was here denying the Davidic lineage of the Messiah (V. Taylor 1952: 491).

6. For the direct quotation of Ps. 110:1, see the parallels to 12:36 in Matt. 22:44 and Luke 20:42–43; Acts 2:34–35; Heb. 1:13; for partial quotations or allusions, see Mark 14:62/Matt. 26:64/Luke 22:69; Rom. 8:34; 1 Cor. 15:25; Eph. 1:20, 22; Heb. 1:3; 8:1; 10:12–13. See Hay 1973: 45–46 for additional examples.

would have used מָרִי (*mārî*; cf. 1 Cor. 16:22) for both (Fitzmyer 1979b: 90, 131, 141n71). Since this is a psalm of David—that is, David is speaking—the terms of the present text should be understood, "The Lord [God] said to my [David's] Lord [the Messiah]." Nothing in the LXX translation or the Hebrew text disallows this interpretation (France 2002: 486–87), and in Mark this is how it should be translated. Jesus asks, "How can the Messiah be simply David's son, since David himself [the αὐτός, autos, is emphatic], calls him 'my Lord'?" This is not a denial that the Messiah is the Son of David (i.e., David's descendant), but the affirmation that he is much more.

The remaining part of the OT quotation continues to follow the LXX closely. The only difference is that Mark (and Matt. 22:44) has "under" (ὑποκάτω, *hypokatō*; cf. Ps. 8:6 [8:7 LXX]) rather than "a footstool for" (ὑποπόδιον, *hypopodion*; cf. Luke 20:43). The textual problems associated with the Markan and Matthean texts here witness to scribal attempts to harmonize these texts with that of the LXX (Metzger 1994: 94). The idea of Jesus sitting at the right hand of God (κάθου ἐκ δεξιῶν μου, *kathou ek dexiōn mou*) will be repeated in 14:62 and occurs frequently in the NT (cf. Acts 2:34; Rom. 8:34; Eph. 1:22; Heb. 10:12; etc.). It describes the unique relationship and privileged position of Jesus, the Messiah, with respect to God (cf. Mark 10:37). "Until I place your enemies under your feet" (ἕως ἂν θῶ τοὺς ἐχθρούς σου ὑποκάτω τῶν ποδῶν σου, *heōs an thō tous echthrous sou hypokatō tōn podōn sou*) refers to God's defeat of all the Messiah's enemies (both human and demonic; cf. Phil. 2:9–11; Rom. 14:11). For the reader of Mark, this would bring to mind Jesus's triumph over sin and death by his death and resurrection, and his coming to judge the world (8:38; 13:26–27; cf. Matt. 7:21–23; 10:33; 13:40–43; 25:31–46).

The point that Jesus sought to make in 12:35b now comes in the form of another question: How can David's Lord simply be his son? (καὶ πόθεν αὐτοῦ ἐστιν υἱός; *kai pothen autou estin huios?* lit. "and how is he his son"). He must be more. For Mark, that Jesus is more than the "Messiah–the Son of David" is evident from the very beginning of his Gospel. He is the "Messiah–Son of God" (1:1), as God himself has declared (1:11; 9:7). This has been acknowledged by the demons (3:11; 5:7; cf. 1:24) and will be by others (15:39) and by Jesus himself (14:61–62). Mark ends the account with the comment, "[the] great crowd was hearing [Jesus] gladly." The use of "great" seeks, of course, to emphasize the size of the crowd, and their hearing him "gladly" (ἡδέως, *hēdeōs*) contrasts their view of Jesus with that of the chief priests, scribes, elders, Sadducees, and Pharisees in 11:27–12:40. Josephus, in a much-disputed passage (*Ant.* 18.3.3 §63), refers to Jesus as being a "teacher of such people as accept the truth gladly."

12:37

Summary

The primary emphasis in this passage is christological in nature and involves the correct understanding of the nature and mission of the Messiah. In previous accounts, Jesus has been shown to be greater than the prophets

(8:27–29; 12:1–12); here he is shown to be greater than David. The common nationalistic hope of the people of Israel that the Messiah–Son of David would restore national independence and greatness to Israel, as during the time of King David and King Solomon, was both inadequate and incorrect (Marcus 1989a: 136–37). Our passage does not deny the Davidic descent of Jesus and the Messiah. Instead, it points out that thinking along such lines is insufficient, for such a view of the Messiah does not do him full justice.[7] "Jesus' divine dignity outstrips Jewish notions of the messiah as David's son" (Hay 1973: 114). The Messiah is "Lord" not just of the Jewish nation but also of the whole earth. Ultimately every knee will bow and every tongue will confess that "Jesus Christ is Lord" (Phil. 2:11). The whole world will know that Jesus Christ is "King of kings and Lord of lords" (Rev. 19:16). His victory involves the humiliation and shame of the cross, but it results in victory over sin and death, evil and the demonic world. The implications of this for Mark's readers probably resulted in both comfort and apprehension. It would bring comfort, because this great Messiah/Christ had promised them eternal life in God's kingdom (10:29–30; cf. 8:34–38). But to confess "Jesus is Lord" might well bring confrontation with Rome, where the emperor falsely claimed that he was "Lord."

Two other Markan emphases that appear in the text are (1) the continued emphasis on Jesus's "teachings" and his role as a "teacher," and (2) the great popularity of Jesus with the people. His great wisdom as a teacher easily allows him to rebut the hostile questions of the religious leaders of Israel. He totally refutes and silences them (12:34). And in contrast to their hostility, the people gladly hear him (12:37). Once again Mark emphasizes the acceptance and approval of Jesus by the multitudes.

Additional Notes

12:35. ἔλεγεν διδάσκων is lit. "was saying as he was teaching."

12:36. The article is omitted in B D but is found in ℵ A L W Θ Ψ f¹ f¹³ lat syr.

12:36. Instead of "under" (ὑποκάτω) found in B D W, "a footstool for" (ὑποπόδιον) is found in ℵ A L Θ f¹ f¹³ lat, which follow the LXX (Ps. 109:1 [110:1 Eng.]).

12:37. πόθεν is used here in the sense of πῶς or "how?" (V. Taylor 1952: 492; contra Gundry 1993: 722–23, who interprets it "from where [what source]?").

12:37. The article "the" (ὁ) is found in A B L Ψ f¹ but omitted in ℵ D W Θ f¹³. In favor of the latter is that everywhere else in Mark "great crowd" (πολὺς ὄχλος) lacks the article (cf. 4:1; 5:21, 24; 6:34; 8:1; 9:14).

---

7. Marcus comments that "a messianic hope that has been fashioned along strictly Davidic lines is simply not big enough to embrace the one whose resurrection to God's right hand implies his participation in the divine majesty" (1992b: 144). Cf. also Boobyer 1939, who understands 12:35–37 as implying the preexistence of Jesus; V. Taylor 1952: 492; Witherington 2001: 333.

I. Jesus's Denunciation of the Scribes (12:38–40)

The present passage is tied to the preceding by the term "scribes" (γραμματέων, *grammateōn*; 12:38; cf. 11:18, 27; 12:28, 32, 35), who are the object of Jesus's teaching in the account. The account continues the negative portrayal of this group in Mark (cf. 1:22; 2:6, 16; 3:22; 7:1, 7; 8:31; 9:11, 14; 10:33; 11:18, 27–28; also 14:1, 43, 53; 15:1, 31). The lone exception (12:28–34) reminds us that one should not universalize the description of the scribes found elsewhere in Mark (Hooker 1991: 294). Nevertheless, there must have been a sufficient number of scribes who fit the description given in this and the other Gospel accounts to warrant Jesus's condemnation of them (cf. Matt. 23:1–36). The present account is also tied to 11:27ff. by the reference to Jesus's continued teaching (12:38a) in the temple (cf. 12:41; 13:1). It is associated with the following account by the term "widows" (χηρῶν, *chērōn*; cf. 12:40 with 42–44) and by the contrasting behavior of the scribes and a poor widow in the present account. The former provides a negative example of what discipleship is not; the latter furnishes a positive example of what it is. Although this and the following account function as a diptych contrasting these two kinds of people (Donahue and Harrington 2002: 364; France 2002: 488–89), it is best to treat them as two separate accounts whose association is probably due to the hand of Mark. In the parable of the rich man and Lazarus (Luke 16:19–31), we find such a contrast in a single account, but here the contrast is due to Mark's having placed two separate accounts together.

The account consists of an introductory seam describing Jesus's continued teaching (in the temple; 12:38a),[1] a warning concerning the scribes (12:38b), a description of the behavior of the scribes that elicited the warning (12:38c–40b), and a concluding pronouncement of judgment (12:40c). If 12:40 originally stood independently of 12:38–39 (Gnilka 1979: 173; Pesch 1980b: 257), it is impossible to know if they were joined together in the pre-Markan tradition or by Mark. Regardless of whether 12:38–39 and 12:40 were originally independent sayings, there seems to be little reason for denying their authenticity (Evans 2001: 277). The clearest Markan editorial work is found in the opening seam in 12:38a (Pryke 1978: 20, 146, 169; Gnilka 1979: 173; cf. "in his teaching" [ἐν τῇ διδαχῇ αὐτοῦ, *en tē didachē autou*]

---

1. It is best to understand 12:37b as concluding the preceding account (contra Cranfield 1959: 383; Fleddermann 1982: 53–54). This allows 12:38–41 to begin with a similar introduction ("And in his teaching he was saying . . .") as 12:35–37 ("And Jesus, having answered, was teaching . . .").

with 4:2; also 1:22; 11:18; and cf. "beware" [βλέπετε, *blepete*] with 8:15). Mark may also be responsible for the present location of the account and perhaps also for the explanatory relative clause in 12:40a ("who devour the houses of widows and for show pray long [prayers]," οἱ κατεσθίοντες τὰς οἰκίας τῶν χηρῶν καὶ προφάσει μακρὰ προσευχόμενοι, *hoi katesthiontes tas oikias tōn chērōn kai prophasei makra proseuchomenoi*; Pryke 1978: 20, 146, 169).

Exegesis and Exposition

[38]And in his teaching he was saying, "Beware of the scribes, who like to walk around in long robes and [to receive] ⌜ ⌝ greetings in the marketplaces [39]and seats of honor in the synagogues and places of honor at banquets [40][but] ⌜who devour the houses of widows and for show pray long [prayers]⌝. These [scribes] will receive greater condemnation!"

12:38–39 Jesus continues his teaching ministry to the great crowd (12:37b) in the temple with a harsh condemnation of the scribes (for "scribes," see 1:21–22). The warning "Beware of the scribes" (βλέπετε ἀπὸ τῶν γραμματέων, *blepete apo tōn grammateōn*) recalls "Beware of the leaven of the Pharisees and the leaven of Herod" (8:15). The warning to beware of the scribes involves their violation of the two great commandments (12:30–31). They violate the first by their ostentatious dress and behavior. They wear long flowing robes (στολαῖς, *stolais*), possibly priestlike robes or tallith, which were worn by religious men (Hooker 1991: 295; Evans 2001: 278), but more likely "distinguished garments of men of eminence and standing and/or of wealth, rather than a specifically scribal robe" (Schams 1998: 156; cf. also Fleddermann 1982: 55–56; Gundry 1993: 727). Their arrogance and false piety causes them to desire being singled out in the marketplaces and perhaps being called "Rabbi" (Matt. 23:7; cf. *y. Ber.* 2.1 [IV]; contrast, however, the attitude of Joḥanan ben Zakkai [*b. Ber.* 17a], who was always the first to give a greeting in the street to a person he met, even if the other was a heathen). In addition, they liked to receive the seats of honor (lit. "first seats," πρωτοκαθεδρίας, *prōtokathedrias*) in the synagogues (cf. James 2:2–4). These were probably the seats at the front of the synagogue that faced the congregation (J. Edwards 2002: 378; cf. *t. Meg.* 3.21) and were located before the ark containing the scriptural scrolls. They liked the "places of honor" (πρωτοκλισίας, *prōtoklisias*) at banquets as well (cf. Luke 14:7–10; also *b. Ber.* 46b; *t. Ber.* 5.5). Yet such behavior violates the first commandment to love God and give to him alone the kind of respect and adoration that the scribes liked to receive for themselves (W. Lane 1974: 439).

12:40 Jesus levels another charge at the scribes by singling out their violation of the second commandment (12:31). Their behavior toward widows clearly reveals that they did not love their neighbors as themselves. The expression "devour [κατεσθίοντες, *katesthiontes*; lit. 'eat up'] the houses of widows" is capable of being interpreted in several ways. Scribes do this by (1) accepting payment from widows for legal aid and advice, even though this was forbidden (*m. 'Abot* 1.13); (2) cheating widows in their roles as guardians of their husband's estates; (3) sponging off the hospitality of widows; (4) mismanagement of widows' estates; (5) taking money from widows for lengthy prayers made on their behalf; (6) taking houses as pledges for debts that could not be paid; and so on (Fitzmyer 1985b: 1318; cf. also Derrett 1972; Schams 1998: 156–57). Even though it is uncertain exactly what this expression means, it is clear that the scribes were in some way taking financial advantage of vulnerable and needy widows. Despite the numerous commands of Scripture expressing God's concern for widows (Deut. 14:29; Pss. 68:5; 146:9; Isa. 1:17; Jer. 7:6; 49:11) and the criticism of those who mistreat them (Isa. 1:23; Ezek. 22:7; Zech. 7:10; Mal. 3:5), the scribes preyed upon needy widows. And they hypocritically clothed their behavior with a religious veneer or piety (note their dress [12:28b] and long prayers [12:40b; cf. Matt. 6:5–6; Luke 18:11–12]). Thus they compounded their religious hypocrisy by actions toward widows that revealed a total disregard of the commandment to love one's neighbor. If the rich man was condemned and cast into Hades for his neglect of poor Lazarus (Luke 16:19–31), how much more certain would be the condemnation of scribes who did not simply neglect needy widows but stole their property!

In the parable of the vineyard (12:1–12), the judgment pronounced upon the evil tenants seems to refer to the events of AD 70 (cf. 12:9–11). Similarly, the judgment alluded to in the cursing of the fig tree and the cleansing of the temple (11:12–21) and the judgment described in 13:1–37 seem to refer primarily to AD 70 as well. However, it is best to understand the judgment referred to in 12:40c as involving the final, eschatological judgment referred to in 9:42–48 (Evans 2001: 279). The words of Jesus in Luke 14:11 seem to fit the behavior of the scribes quite well: "For every one who exalts himself will be humbled."

Summary

Although there are allusions to several Markan themes in this account (Jesus as a teacher, the authority of Jesus of Nazareth, etc.), the key emphasis concerns Christian discipleship. In our passage, the scribes by their behavior provide an example of what a follower of Jesus ought not to be like (Fleddermann 1982: 66). They seek their own glory and honor (12:38–39), whereas Jesus has taught his followers that greatness in the kingdom of God involves being servant of all (10:42–45). Jesus's followers are to seek the gain not of this world but of the next (8:36–37). As a result this passage serves as a powerful example to the Christian leaders of the Markan community not to seek their own glory (Pesch 1980b: 260) but to be servants of the community, especially the needy such as the widow mentioned in 12:42 (cf. Acts 6:1–6). Like the rich young ruler, the scribes serve as examples of those who do not love God with all their heart, soul, mind, and strength

(12:29–30). In addition, they also serve as examples of those who do not love their neighbors as themselves (12:31). Mark's readers must beware of being like such people!

Additional Notes

12:38. Cf. Luke 20:46, which adds "loving" (φιλούντων).

12:40. The nominative participial clause ("who devour the houses of widows and for show pray long [prayers]") follows awkwardly the genitive "scribes" in 10:38, but it is best seen as referring back to "scribes" as a *constructio ad sensum* (V. Taylor 1952: 495; France 2002: 491; contra N. Turner 1965: 55–56; Gundry 1993: 720, 728).

J. Jesus's Teaching concerning the Widow's Great Gift (12:41–44)

The story of the widow's great gift is connected to the preceding material by the term "widow" (χήρα, *chēra*; 12:42–43; cf. 12:40) and its geographical location. It takes place at the temple treasury (12:41, 43), located in the part of the temple (cf. 11:11, 15–16, 27; 12:35) called the Court of the Women. It is also tied to the preceding account by the contrast between the behavior of the scribes (12:38–40) and that of the widow (12:42–44; Hooker 1991: 296; Brooks 1991: 202–3). It is connected to the following chapter by its location (cf. 13:1) and the continued teaching ministry of Jesus (13:5–37).

The historicity of the account is often denied on the basis that Jesus could not have known how much the widow contributed to the treasury or that the widow had contributed all that she had (Haenchen 1966: 432–33). In addition, some claim that the present account was originally a parable that has been transformed into a historical account (Dibelius 1934: 261; Nineham 1963: 334–35). Yet Jesus might have known of the amount of the widow's gift by overhearing the attending priest, who would have examined the widow's offering and directed it to the appropriate receptacle. All that transpired would have been spoken out loud (Gundry 1993: 731–32; J. Edwards 2002: 380–81). The widow's appearance may also have betrayed her situation (Evans 2001: 284). As for the amount donated, this may have been ascertained by the small sound of the two coins as they were deposited in the treasury receptacle (Donahue and Harrington 2002: 364; J. Edwards 2002: 381).

The account is in the form of a pronouncement story (V. Taylor 1952: 496; Bultmann 1968: 32–33; Evans 2001: 281). After the introductory seam tying the present account to the preceding one (12:41a), a situation is described in which the large gifts of the rich are contrasted with the small, apparently insignificant gift of a poor widow (12:41b–42). This is followed by Jesus calling his disciples, uttering a pronouncement (12:43), and explaining the pronouncement (12:44). The clearest Markan redactional comment in the account is the explanation "which is [the equivalent of] a penny" (ὅ ἐστιν κοδράντης, *ho estin kodrantēs*; 12:42c). Mark's explanation of the value of the two "small copper coins" (λεπτά, *lepta*) by the Latin term "penny" (κοδράντης), a Roman monetary unit, while not proving that the Gospel was written to the church in Rome, does support such a view (Donahue and Harrington 2002: 364; Incigneri 2003: 98). The explanatory "for" (γάρ, *gar*) clause in 12:44 was probably part of the tradition Mark received, although the concluding appositional clause ("all she had to live on" [ὅλον τὸν βίον αὐτῆς, *holon ton bion autēs*]) could be Markan (Gnilka 1979: 176). The only other Markan redaction in the account is its location in the present context.[2]

The traditional understanding of the meaning of this account is that it gives Christians a positive model for sacrificial giving and stands in sharp contrast to the self-indulgent behavior and false piety of the scribes in 12:38–40 (Witherington 1984: 18). Since the 1980s, this interpretation has been challenged by one that sees the widow's action not as commendable but as a tragic example of how the scribes by their teaching devour the homes of widows (12:40; A. Wright 1982: 256–65; Fitzmyer 1985b: 1320–21; Myers 1988: 321; Evans 2001: 282–83). Yet in the present account the scribes are not mentioned. In the Markan form of the account, the contrast between the rich people and their giving and the poor widow and her giving is meaningless unless the action of the poor widow is being commended. As a pronouncement story the emphasis falls on the pronouncement (note the "Truly" [ἀμήν, *amēn*]) in which the widow is described by Jesus as having given more than the rich (12:43). Surely the readers of Mark would have understood this pronouncement as a commendation. The reference to her putting in more than the rich would be entirely misleading if her action is being decried by Jesus. Furthermore, the woman's action involves her doing exactly what Jesus told the rich young ruler to do (10:21). She gave "all that she had" (πάντα ὅσα εἶχεν, *panta hosa eichen*; 12:44), perhaps to the poor, in contrast to the rich young ruler (Williams 1994: 178), who did not obey Jesus's command to give "whatever you have" (ὅσα ἔχεις, *hosa echeis*; 10:21; cf. all, πάντα, *panta* in 10:28). Her action follows exactly what Jesus taught the disciples.[3] One must love God with all one's heart, soul, mind, and strength and follow Jesus (12:30). This involves leaving/ giving up nets (1:18), father (1:20), plans and life (8:34–35), everything (10:28–29).[4] As to the placement of the account, Mark had little choice but to place it somewhere between 11:15 and 13:1 due to the reference to the temple treasury (12:41, 43). Since the account does not center on a question asked of Jesus (11:27–33; 12:13–34), its placement was even more limited. Moreover, if word association plays a role in Mark's placement, his choice was still further limited, because the term "widow" appears only in the

---

2. Best (1981: 155) argues that certain words ("much" [v. 41], "having come" [v. 42], "having called" [v. 43]) are Markan, but although they are favorite Markan words, they may not be so much additions to the narrative as the use of his own terminology to express what the tradition said in another way. For the view that there is no recognizable Markan redaction in this passage, see Pesch (1980b: 260). He is much nearer to the truth than Pryke (1978: 20, 146, 169), who sees almost all of 12:41–44 as Markan.

3. Williams (1994: 177–78n3) rightly asks, "Why should it be exemplary for the rich man to give away all that he has (10:21) but lamentable for the poor widow to do the same (12:44)?" Cf. how the disciples are commended in 10:29–31 for having given away "all" (10:28). Cf. Di-Cicco 1998: 442–43.

4. See Gundry (1993: 730–31) for additional criticism of A. Wright's interpretation that views the widow's action as tragic.

preceding account (12:40). Thus one must be careful not to determine the meaning of the account primarily on the basis of its location. Its content is far more important.

Exegesis and Exposition

[41]And having sat down opposite the treasury, he was watching how the crowd put ⌜money⌝ into the treasury, and many rich people were putting in large amounts. [42]And a poor widow ⌜came⌝ [and] put in two small coins, which is [the equivalent of] a penny. [43]And he [Jesus], having called his disciples, said to them, "Truly I say to you that this poor widow put in more than all [the others] who contributed [money] into the treasury, [44]for all [the others] contributed out of their abundance, but she out of her poverty contributed all that she had, all she had to live on.

It is uncertain whether the word "treasury" (γαζοφυλακίου, *gazophylakiou*) refers to a building in the temple's Court of the Women in which the temple moneys were stored (Neh. 12:44; 1 Macc. 14:49; 2 Macc. 3:6; Josephus, *J.W.* 5.5.2 §200; 6.5.2 §282; *Ant.* 19.6.1 §294) or the collecting chests into whose trumpet-like openings various kinds of gifts were put (*m. Šeqal.* 6.5).[5] There were thirteen such chests, and each chest referred to a specific kind of offering: new shekel dues, old shekel dues, bird offerings, young birds for whole offerings, wood, frankincense, gold for the mercy seat, and six freewill offerings. In our account, it is more likely that "treasury" refers to these money chests. Although many rich people are referred to as having put (lit. "threw") large amounts of money into the money chests, Jesus's attention fell upon a (lit. "one"; cf. 5:22; 9:17; 10:17) poor widow (note the connection with the preceding account, which refers to "widows" in 12:40). Jesus notices that the poor widow put two small copper coins (λεπτά, *lepta*) into one of the chests. A λεπτόν was a small coin less than a centimeter in diameter. Mark explains the value of the two λεπτά for his readers by converting them into more familiar Roman coinage. Two λεπτά equal the smallest Roman coin, the quadran. (The Latin term is transliterated into Greek as κοδράντης.) A quadran equals one-quarter of the value of the next Roman coin, the assarion, or "as," which in turn is worth one-sixteenth of a denarius. Thus the widow's contribution was the equivalent of one sixty-fourth of a denarius; a denarius was the normal pay for a day's work (Matt. 20:1–16).

12:41–42

For "calling" (προσκαλεσάμενος, *proskalesamenos*) the disciples as an introduction to Jesus's teaching, see 3:23; 6:7; 8:1; 10:42. As an introduction to teaching the crowds, see 7:14; 8:34 (disciples included). Because of the paradoxical nature of what he was about to say, Jesus secures his disciples'

12:43–44

5. The wealth of the Jerusalem temple was enormous (2 Macc. 3:6; Schürer 1973: 2.270–74). Besides the half-shekel temple tax that each Jewish man twenty years or older contributed each year to the temple (Matt. 17:24–27), Jews, both rich and poor, contributed generously to the temple treasury. The temple also served as a bank (1 Macc. 14:49; 2 Macc. 3:1–40).

attention by beginning "Truly" (see 3:28–30). The poverty of the widow is emphasized by the attributive position of the adjective "poor" (ἡ χήρα αὕτη ἡ πτωχή, hē chēra hautē hē ptōchē, this widow, this poor), but no reason is given to explain her poverty. Poverty was an all-too-common experience for widows in ancient times. Although Jesus's knowledge that the woman was a poor widow may be supernatural, it may also have been due to Jesus's observance of her appearance and the sound made by her two λεπτά as they fell down the trumpet-like openings of the money chest (Donahue and Harrington 2002: 364). Although the knowledge that the two coins were "all that she had to live on" (lit. "her whole life") appears to be due to Jesus's supernatural knowledge, it must be pointed out that, while this is a legitimate historical question, the narrative betrays no interest in the source of Jesus's knowledge (V. Taylor 1952: 498).

By this world's thinking, the pronouncement that this widow gave more than all the rich contributed (lit. "threw") is simply wrong. No one would name a building or even a room in a building for the widow because of the two coins she contributed. On the other hand, church buildings and chapels are often named after rich contributors, even when their moral character is questionable, because whereas "the LORD looks on the heart, . . . [this world] looks on the outward appearance [of things]" (1 Sam. 16:7). As a result, Jesus must explain why the poor widow's offering is greater, even though smaller. The gifts of the rich came out of their great abundance and surplus (περισσεύοντος, perisseuontos). The widow gave not out of her excess but out of her poverty and lack (ὑστερήσεως, hysterēseōs). She had only two tiny λεπτά, and she gave not one of them but both. Thus she manifests her total love for God (cf. Mark 12:30) by giving to him all she had (cf. 14:3–9 for a similar act of generous love). The rabbinic literature contains an interesting parallel in which a priest looks scornfully at a woman's gift of a handful of flour. Later, the priest received this message in a dream: "Do not despise her! It is regarded as if she had sacrificed her own life" (Lev. Rab. 3.5).[6]

Summary

The purpose of the present account is not to discredit the scribes of 12:38–40 for devouring widows' houses but rather to provide a model of Christian discipleship (see the introduction to this unit). In contrast to the ostentation, deviousness, and evil of the scribes, the poor widow provides a positive contrast and example of a sincere, devout, and generous follower of Jesus (Donahue and Harrington 2002: 365). For the poor of Mark's church, and for the humble and poor through the centuries, our passage reveals that God looks upon their meager offerings of love with great delight and pleasure. No gift to God is insignificant when given in love and devotion. All humanity stands equal before the command to love God with all one's heart, soul, mind, and strength. The rich have no special advantage in this. In fact, as

6. For additional rabbinic parallels, see Pesch 1980b: 263.

in the case of the rich young ruler, riches may be a disadvantage. This poor widow's example will be remembered throughout history for the great and generous gift of her two small λεπτά.

Additional Notes

12:41. The term "money" is χαλκόν and refers to the metal copper. It can also refer to a "copper coin." Here it refers to money in general.

12:42. ἐλθοῦσα is lit. "having come."

K. Jesus's Eschatological Discourse (13:1–37)

The thirteenth chapter of Mark brings the present section (11:1–13:37) to its conclusion. The failure of Israel, especially of its leadership, to fulfill its mission; its lack of fruit (11:12–26; 12:38–40); and its hostility toward God's anointed (11:1–11, 27–33; 12:13–17, 18–27) all lead to the inevitable judgment resulting in the destruction of the temple and Jerusalem. The present chapter brings to a climax Jesus's teachings on the coming judgment begun in Jesus's "cleansing" of the temple (11:12–26), warned about in the parable of the wicked tenants (12:1–12), and now spoken of at great length in chapter 13 (cf. also 14:58; 15:29, 38; Hooker 1991: 301). Chapter 13 is the longest continuous series of teachings found in Mark. Elsewhere the longest speech of Jesus consists of six sentences (8:34–38). Even Mark 4, the closest analogy to the present chapter, consists of various short teachings (4:3–9, 11–12, 13–20, 21–25, 26–29, 30–32) interrupted by short narratives (4:1–2, 10, 33–34) and introductions (4:11a, 13a, 21a, 26a, 30a). Furthermore, what unites the material in Mark 4 is primarily the similarity in literary form—parables.[1] The thirty-nine sentences of Mark 13 (Grayston 1973–74: 375) are united by a similar eschatological theme: the destruction of the temple/Jerusalem and the coming of the Son of Man.

The genre of this chapter is frequently debated. Although it resembles such apocalyptic passages as 1 En. 37–71 and 2 Esd. 13 and is often referred to as "the Markan Apocalypse,"[2] it lacks a number of features associated with apocalyptic literature. We find no heavenly vision, no review of human history, no angelic mediator, no portrayal of heavenly or earthly battles, no resurrection, no final judgment involving rewards and punishment, no bizarre imagery, and so forth, usually associated with such literature.[3] There is furthermore no distinct line that distinguishes apocalyptic literature from prophecy. This is evident from the fact that the most apocalyptic book in the NT is expressly called a "prophecy" (Rev. 1:3; 22:7, 10, 18–19; cf. also 22:6). Ultimately little is gained in debating the question of whether Mark 13 should be classified as prophetic or apocalyptic literature, because the use of exaggerated, metaphori-

---

1. The content of Mark 4:1–34 revolves broadly around the theme of the kingdom of God (4:11, 26, 30).

2. Other titles given to this chapter are "The Olivet Discourse" (due to its location [cf. 13:3]) and "The Eschatological Discourse" (due to its dealing with the "last [Greek ἔσχατα, *eschata*] things").

3. Cf. France (2002: 499), who comments, "A discourse which is constructed primarily around second-person imperatives addressed to the disciples [cf. 13:5, 7, 9, 11, 18, 21, 23, 28, 29, 33 (2×), 35, 37] does not look like what is normally understood by 'apocalyptic.'" Cf. Hatina 1996: 45–49.

cal language is common to both. Attempts have also been made to classify this chapter as a kind of testament or farewell discourse, as is found in Gen. 49:2–27; Deut. 32; Josh. 23–24; 1 Chron. 28–29; John 13–17; Acts 20:17–38 (cf. the pseudepigraphical Testaments of the Twelve Patriarchs; Gaston 1970: 42). Unlike such testaments, however, Mark 13 does not reflect on the past, the setting lacks a summoning by the one giving the supposed testament, it lacks moral instruction (Evans 2001: 289–90), and the impending death of Jesus is not the immediate occasion of the speech (A. Collins 1996: 9; Witherington 2001: 342). Attempts to classify this chapter into one of the classical categories of rhetoric are also unconvincing (A. Collins 1996: 10–13). Ultimately "the label we put on this chapter matters little" (Hooker 1991: 299).

In the past, much effort was expended on seeking to reconstruct the main source (or sources) of the present chapter. Colani (1864) argued that the chapter was based on an early Jewish-Christian apocalypse consisting of 13:5–8, 9–13, 14–31 (Beasley-Murray 1993: 32–33).[4] Although the composite nature of Mark 13 is evident (V. Taylor 1952: 499; Hooker 1991: 298; Evans 2001: 291–92),[5] the reconstruction of its earlier stages of formation is highly speculative. The authenticity of the material in the discourse and its pre–AD 70 flavor is supported by the lack of certain features that occurred in AD 70 but are not found in the discourse. These include the lack of mention of the part that fire played in the destruction of the city (cf. Josephus, *J.W.* 6.4.5–6.5.1 §§249–80; Grundmann 1977: 351), the intramural fighting in the city among various rival Jewish groups during the siege, the many Jews (thousands of them!) crucified by the Romans, and the lack of a clear explanation of the abomination of desolation (13:14; Hengel 1985: 14–28; Evans 2001: 290–92). Furthermore, the reference to praying that the destruction not take place in the winter (13:18) would be quite strange as a *vaticinium ex eventu* since the city and temple were destroyed in the summer of AD 70. Since the task of the present commentary is to understand the Markan message found in this chapter, the various attempted reconstructions of the pre-Markan nature of the material in this chapter are of questionable value. To understand what the evangelist Mark is seeking to teach in Mark 13, we need to investigate the present form of the chapter. It is the present form of the text before us that reveals Mark's understanding of Jesus's teaching concerning the destruction of the temple and Jerusalem and the coming of the Son of Man.[6]

4. For example, Bultmann (1968: 122) attributes 13:7, 8, 12, 14–22, 24–27 to this early Jewish apocalypse; Hartman (1966: 207–8) attributes 13:5b–8, 12–16, 19–22, 24–27 to a "midrashic substrate"; Pesch (1968: 207–11) attributes 13:6, 7b, 8, 12, 13b–17, 18 (?), 19–20a, 22, and 24–27 to an apocalyptic "Flugblatt" (leaflet); Grayston (1973–74: 383–85) attributes 13:7, 9, 11, 14–16, 18, 21, 23 to the source; and Dyer (1998: 27–66, esp. 63–64) attributes 13:7–8, 11d–13a, 14–20, and 22 to a pre-Markan Aramaic source. The most common elements in the alleged Jewish-Christian apocalypse lying behind this chapter are 13:7–8, 14–20, and 24–27 (Bristol 1939; V. Taylor 1952: 498).

5. Grayston (1973–74: 375) argues that the lack of any other lengthy discourse in Mark suggests that the present chapter was probably pre-Markan in origin.

6. Cf. Geddert (1989: 19): "*Our goal will be to uncover the intentions of the author of Mark's Gospel as they can be known by studying Mark 13 in its Gospel context*" (his italics). See also

There is no reason to think that Mark has recorded the sayings of Jesus found in this chapter simply due to historical interests. The chapter contains instructions that Mark believes are important for his intended readers. This is evident by the fact that it is the longest sustained collection of Jesus's sayings in the whole Gospel. If Mark simply wanted to tell his readers that Jesus predicted the destruction of the temple and the city of Jerusalem, he could have done this in less than thirty-seven verses (cf. 14:58; 15:29). The warnings directed against false messianic pretenders and prophets (13:5–6, 21–23), of coming persecution (13:9–13), of the need to be watchful concerning the appearing of the Son of Man (13:33–37), and other numerous warnings (13:5, 7, 9, 11, 14 [2×], 15 [2×], 16, 18, 21, 23, 28, 29, 33 [2×], 35, 37) indicate that Mark has more than a simple historical interest for recording what Jesus taught on this subject. Above all, the direct editorial appeal of Mark to his readers in 13:14 to understand what he has written is directed to his audience in the late 60s and not to Jesus's audience in the late 20s. What that message is will be discussed in the summary of each of the following sections.

The present chapter is a self-contained unit, as the new introduction in 14:1–2 indicates, and will be divided into five sections:

1. Jesus's prediction of the destruction of the temple (13:1–4)
2. The coming destruction of the temple and Jerusalem described (13:5–23)
3. The coming of the Son of Man (13:24–27)
4. The lesson of the fig tree (13:28–31)
5. The coming of the Son of Man and the call to watchfulness (13:32–37)

The following oversimplified survey shows how sections 2 through 5 are interpreted by various scholars:

Option 1[7]

13:5–23	The destruction of the temple and Jerusalem	AD 30–70
13:24–27	The coming of the Son of Man	parousia
13:28–31	The lesson of the fig tree	AD 70
13:32–37	The unknown time of the end	parousia

Option 2[8]

| 13:5–13 | The destruction of the temple and Jerusalem | AD 30–70 |
| 13:14–23 | The great tribulation before the parousia | parousia |

France 2002: 499–500. Cf., however, Donahue and Harrington (2002: 379), who see the "great critical question" as involving the issue of the origin of the material in Mark 13.

7. Cf. W. Lane 1974: 466, 474–75, 478, and 481–82; and Witherington 2001: 340.

8. Cf. J. Edwards 2002: 385.

13:24–27	The coming of the Son of Man	parousia
13:28–31	The lesson of the fig tree	AD 30–70
13:32–37	The unknown time of the end	parousia

Option 3[9]

13:1–31	The destruction of the temple and Jerusalem, the coming of the Son of Man, and the lesson of the fig tree	AD 30–70
13:32–37	The unknown time of the end	parousia

Option 4[10]

13:1–37	The destruction of the temple and Jerusalem	AD 30–70

Two key issues must be dealt with in order to understand how these sections relate to one another: How are the two questions in 13:3 and 4 to be understood? Are they two separate questions in which the second extends the subject matter found in the first (these things, ταῦτα, *tauta*), or does the second (all these things, ταῦτα . . . πάντα, *tauta . . . panta*) serve essentially as an example of synonymous parallelism repeating the first question? A second issue involves the extent to which the terminology in 13:24–27 can be understood metaphorically to mean the destruction of Jerusalem and the spread of the Christian mission in the world. Or was the expression "the coming of the Son of Man" already a technical term in the early church for the parousia? Along with several other issues, how we answer these questions will determine how we understand this chapter.

9. Cf. France 1971: 231–39; 2002: 500–505.
10. Cf. Gould 1896: 240–55 (esp. 240–41); Hatina 1996; N. Wright 1996: 339–66. Contrast Gundry (1993: 733–50), who argues that only 13:1–4 refers to the fall of Jerusalem in AD 70 and the events leading up to it and that all the rest of chap. 13 (13:5–37) refers to the parousia and the events associated with it.

1. Jesus's Prediction of the Destruction of the Temple (13:1–4)

At this point, Mark brings to a conclusion Jesus's activity in the temple described in 11:1–12:44.[1] Although some scholars see in Jesus's departure from the temple a symbolic rejection of the temple (Grundmann 1977: 350), Mark makes no allusion to this. As a result it is best to read the opening words of 13:1 as simply a transitional phrase by which Jesus leaves the temple for the Mount of Olives, where he will deliver a series of eschatological teachings, some of which were associated in the tradition with this site (cf. Mark 13:3; Matt. 24:3; also Luke 21:5–6, which implies this). Jesus's prediction of the temple's destruction is precipitated by a comment concerning the temple's beauty and magnificence. Scholars debate the relation of Jesus's prediction in 13:2 and the one alluded to in 14:58 ("We heard him saying, 'I will destroy this sanctuary made with hands and after three days I will build another not made with hands'") and 15:29 ("Ha! [You who would be] the destroyer of the sanctuary and rebuilder [of it] in three days"). Some argue that they are two versions of the same saying (Bultmann 1968: 120; Pesch 1968: 91), but they are more likely different sayings (Beasley-Murray 1993: 378–79). The latter better explains that 13:2 is directed to the disciples and in private (13:3), whereas 14:58 and 15:29 were apparently spoken publicly. There seems to be agreement that another such prophecy (Luke 19:44) comes from an independent tradition (Pesch 1980b: 271; Evans 2001: 294–95). Compare also Matt. 23:37–39/Luke 13:34–35; Acts 6:14; John 2:19. The destruction of the temple and the city of Jerusalem are intimately associated in Mark (Hooker 1991: 304–5). One cannot conceive of the one occurring without the other (cf. Luke 13:34–35/Matt. 23:37–38; Luke 19:44).[2]

The authenticity of Jesus's prediction in 13:2 is widely acknowledged (V. Taylor 1952: 501; Lohmeyer 1957: 268; Grundmann 1977: 351; Bultmann 1968: 120–21, 128). Various scholars point to the lack of mention of the devastating fire that destroyed the city and temple (cf. Josephus, *J.W.* 6.4.5–6.5.1 §§249–80) as arguing for it not being a *vaticinium ex eventu*, or prophecy after the fact (contra Pesch 1980b: 271). Also in light of the fact that the city

---

1. Although some scholars see 13:1–2 as the conclusion of chap. 12 (Lambrecht 1967: 68–69; Pesch 1968: 83; Grayston 1973–74: 373), it is best to understand it as introducing chap. 13 (Hooker 1991: 303). Changes of location usually introduce the following account (cf. 1:21, 29; 2:1, 13; 3:1, 7, 13; 4:1, 35; 5:1, 21; 6:1, 45, 53; 7:24, 31; 8:10, 22, 27; 9:2, 9, 30, 33; 10:1, 17, 32, 46; 11:1, 12, 15, 27). Cf., however, France (2000: 402), who argues that it serves as both.

2. Other predictions of Jesus in Mark can be found in 2:20; 8:31; 9:9, 31; 10:32–34; 12:1–12; 14:9, 17–21, 25, 27–30.

was destroyed in August and September of AD 70, the warning in 13:18 to pray that this event not take place in winter would be strange if the prophecy was created after the fact. Other prophecies concerning the approaching destruction of Jerusalem by the Romans were quite widespread. See 13:2.

Mark 13:1–4 is extremely important for understanding this chapter. The prophecy concerning the destruction of the temple (13:2) and the two questions addressed to Jesus by the disciples (13:4) provide the main key for interpreting the rest of the chapter (see 13:1–37). Therefore 13:4 will be discussed in detail below. The passage consists of a change of scene (13:1a), an exclamation by one of the disciples (13:1b), a prophecy of Jesus concerning the destruction of the temple (13:2), and a twofold question by the disciples as to when Jesus's prediction would be fulfilled and what the sign of its approaching would be (13:3–4). Although some classify 13:1–2 as a pronouncement story (V. Taylor 1952: 500; Bultmann 1968: 36; Hartman 1966: 219; Pesch 1968: 84; Gaston 1970: 10), the present account is not a pronouncement story, for Jesus's pronouncement (13:2) does not come at the end of the account but in the middle. Furthermore, the key verse in 13:1–4 is 13:4, for 13:5–37 focuses on the two questions of the disciples concerning the time and sign of the destruction of Jerusalem and the coming of the Son of Man.

The Markan redaction in this section is difficult to determine. Some see all four verses as being redactional (Pryke 1978: 20, 146, 170; cf. Lambrecht 1967: 68–91). It seems clear that the opening six words of 13:1 have been created by Mark as a transitional seam (V. Taylor 1952: 500; Gnilka 1979: 181). As for the seam in 13:3a, the wording looks Markan, but the scene may very well be traditional. The wording and style of 13:1b–c and 13:2 is also Markan (Pesch 1968: 84–85), but the content is based upon tradition, whose ultimate source is the disciples. This is almost certainly true of Jesus's prophecy of the temple's destruction in 13:2. The unusual reference to the four disciples, rather than the inner three (5:37; 9:2; 14:33), argues for the traditional nature of 13:3b (contra Gnilka 1979: 182). As for 13:4, the double question is typical of the Markan propensity toward duality (Neirynck 1988: 126, 129), and the reference to "these things" (ταῦτα, *tauta*) in 13:29 (cf. 13:4a) and to "all these things" (ταῦτα πάντα, *tauta panta*) in 13:30 (cf. 13:4b) argues for at least the wording of these two questions being Markan. However, it is unlikely that they are totally Markan creations (V. Taylor 1952: 501–2).

Exegesis and Exposition

¹And as he [Jesus] was proceeding out of the temple, one of his disciples says to him, "Teacher, look what [huge] stones and what [beautiful] buildings!"²And Jesus said to him, "Do you ⌜see⌝ these great buildings? There will ⌜not⌝ be left ⌜here⌝ one stone upon another that will not be thrown down." ³And as he was sitting on the Mount of Olives opposite the temple, Peter and James and John and Andrew privately ⌜began

to ask⁊ him, ⁴"Tell us, when will these things be and what [will be] the sign when all these things are about to be accomplished?"

13:1   As Jesus leaves the temple (note how Mark focuses his readers' attention on the main character, Jesus), probably through the Golden Gate in the Eastern Wall of the city, and proceeds across the Kidron Valley toward the Mount of Olives, a disciple draws his attention to the massive "stones" (λίθοι, *lithoi*) and the "buildings" (οἰκοδομαί, *oikodomai*) made from these stones. There is no reason to interpret the disciple's comment as an expression of an awestruck tourist's gawking over the city (contra France 2002: 496; J. Edwards 2002: 388; Donahue and Harrington 2002: 368), for, ever since they entered the city (11:1), they would have proceeded early each day from Bethany to Jerusalem over the Mount of Olives to the temple, where Jesus taught (11:12–12:44), and returned the same way later that day. Furthermore, unless they had been nonobservant Jews before they met Jesus, they would have celebrated numerous Passovers in Jerusalem.

The magnificence of the city and temple complex cannot be exaggerated. The majesty and grandeur of the temple complex would have made even some of the seven wonders of the world pale in comparison. In one place (*J.W.* 5.5.1, 6 §§189, 224) Josephus describes one of the extremely large stones that served as building blocks for the temple as 45 × 5 × 6 cubits (a cubit is approximately eighteen inches), and in another place (*Ant.* 15.11.3 §392) he mentions stones 25 × 8 × 12 cubits in size. Even allowing for exaggeration, some of the stones were massive indeed. In the latter part of the twentieth century, a large stone on the second tier of the western foundation wall was discovered whose dimensions are approximately 42 feet long × 14 feet wide × 11 feet tall. Its weight is estimated to be about 600 tons (Bahat 1995: 39). Two other stones nearby are 40 and 25 feet long. Josephus states that from the top of the Mount of Olives, the whiteness of the stones, its gold trim, and gold-covered roof of the temple sanctuary made the Temple Mount look like a snow-capped mountain and was a blinding sight (*J.W.* 5.5.6 §§222–23). Compare also the rabbinic saying in *b. Suk.* 51b: "Our Rabbis taught, . . . he who has not seen the Temple in its full construction has never seen a glorious building in his life."[3]

For "Teacher" as a title for Jesus, see 4:37–39.

13:2   Jesus's prophecy concerning the destruction of the temple and its various structures is the first reference to this event so far in Mark. God's judgment upon Israel has been alluded to on several occasions (11:12–19; 12:1–12), but there has been no clear statement about the destruction of the temple or Jerusalem up to this point. The language of "not . . . one stone left upon another" recalls such passages as 2 Sam. 17:13 LXX and Hag. 2:15 (the language is also found on Jesus's lips in Luke 19:44), and the destruction of Jerusalem brings

---

3. See Ritmeyer and Ritmeyer (1989) for a helpful description of the Herodian temple. Josephus (*Ant.* 15.11.3 §396) says of the walls supporting the temple platform that "the wall itself was the greatest [work] ever heard of by man."

to mind such passages as Mic. 3:9–12 and Jer. 7:14; 9:1–11; 26:6, 16–19, which refer to the destruction of Jerusalem in 587 BC. Contemporary prophecies concerning the forthcoming destruction of the temple in Jesus's day are found in Josephus, *J.W.* 3.8.3 §§351–52; 4.3.2 §128; 6.5.4 §311; T. Jud. 23.1–5; T. Levi 10.3; 15.1–3; and so on.[4]

Evans (2001: 299) points out the stunning nature of Jesus's prediction, for the great size of the buildings and walls of Jerusalem and the massive nature of stones used in them gave the impression of permanence, not of impending disaster. In most judgment prophecies, whether stated or not, the assumption is that if the people will repent, the judgment will be averted (Jer. 18:7–8; cf. Mic. 3:12 and Jer. 26:18–19; 1 Kings 21:20–29; Jon. 3–4, esp. 4:1–2; Stein 1994a: 90–91). However, there are also times when the prophet knows that there will be no repentance and that the judgment is unavoidable. In such instances a judgment prophecy functions not as a warning but as a prediction (Caird 1980: 56–57). Jesus's prophecy of judgment here and in the rest of the chapter is an example of the latter. Tragically, judgment and catastrophe lay ahead for Jerusalem and the temple, and they could not be escaped.

As in most prophecies, Jesus makes use of hyperbolic language to express his message (Stein 1994a: 91–95). Some interpreters question whether this prophecy was fulfilled, since some foundation stones are still lying one on top of the other (E. Sanders 1993: 257); others argue that the prophecy refers to the sanctuary only and that this was literally fulfilled. Such a debate completely misunderstands the poetic and hyperbolic nature of prophecy.[5] The genres of prophecy and apocalyptic literature are extremely fond of using exaggerated and hyperbolic language. As a result, it is foolish to expect Jesus in AD 30 to use the scientific language of the twenty-first century and say, "Do you see these great stones . . . 92.6854 percent of them will be thrown down." In AD 71, anyone who visited Jerusalem and saw the wreckage of the temple and city caused by the fires and the systematic attempt by the Roman army to raze them down to the ground (Josephus, *J.W.* 6.9.1 §413; 7.1.1 §§1–4) would say that Jesus's prophecy was "literally" fulfilled, that what Jesus meant by his prophecy had literally occurred. Also, it is linguistically impossible to limit Jesus's prophecy in 13:2 to just the temple sanctuary. The normal term for the sanctuary of the temple is ναός (*naos*; 14:58; 15:29, 38). The term used in 13:1 and 3 is ἱερόν (*hieron*), which refers to the whole temple complex (walls; the extensive portico and its columns surrounding the inside walls of the temple complex; the other buildings on the Temple Mount including the

---

4. In addition, Evans (2001: 296–97) lists the following: T. Levi 16.4; Sib. Or. 3.657–700; Lives of the Prophets 10.10–11 (Jonah); 12.11 (Habakkuk); Josephus, *J.W.* 6.2.1 §§109–10; 6.5.3 §§300–309; *b. Yoma* 39b; Lam. Rab. 1.5 (1 §31); cf. also 1 En. 90.28–29.

5. The poetic sections of prophecy can be recognized in most modern translations of the Bible by the uneven right margins and the indention, usually every other line, used to translate them. Compare poetic books such as Psalms and Proverbs for similar print. On the other hand, nonpoetic books such as Genesis through Esther, Acts, and the letters of the NT are printed with both margins even.

temple sanctuary, the Court of the Gentiles, and the Court of the Women; the entire Temple Mount and its foundations; etc.). The references in Jesus's prediction to the "stones and . . . [beautiful] buildings" (my emphasis) cannot refer only to the sanctuary.

13:3–4   Although some place these verses with 13:5–13 or 13:5–23, it is best to see them as part of the Markan introduction (13:1–4) to Jesus's entire eschatological discourse (13:5–37). Jesus's "sitting" (καθημένου, *kathēmenou*) on the Mount of Olives and teaching recalls the only other long teaching discourse in Mark, where Jesus sat in a boat (4:1). It also recalls Jesus sitting down and delivering the Sermon on the Mount in Matt. 5:1. Sitting "opposite" (κατέναντι, *katenanti*) the temple and the city of Jerusalem adds drama to the scene and to what Jesus is about to say. That the Mount of Olives is often associated with the temple and Jerusalem in prophecy (Ezek. 11:23; 43:1ff.; Zech. 14:1–11; T. Naph. 5.1; Josephus, *Ant.* 20.8.6 §§169–72) adds further drama. The addition of Andrew to the trio of Peter, James, and John completes the two sets of brothers (1:16–20; cf. also 3:16–18) but seems strange in light of his omission in 5:37; 9:2; 14:33. Its unusual nature argues in favor of the authenticity of the scene. For Jesus teaching his disciples privately, see 4:10.

Jesus's prophecy of the destruction of Jerusalem elicits two questions from the disciples involving the time "when" (πότε, *pote*) and the "sign" (σημεῖον, *sēmeion*) associated with "these things" (ταῦτα, *tauta*) and "all these things" (ταῦτα πάντα, *tauta panta*). The use of the plural "these things" (ταῦτα) and not "this thing" (τοῦτο, *touto*) indicates that the destruction of the temple, the antecedent of "these things," is understood as part of a complex of events associated with it (Grayston 1973–74: 374; Beasley-Murray 1993: 386–87; Evans 2001: 304). Although some argue that the second question ("all these things") looks beyond the first question ("these things") to the end of the age (Pesch 1980b: 275; Ernst 1981: 370; Hooker 1991: 302–3, 305; Beasley-Murray 1993: 387; A. Collins 1996: 13), it is best to see them as essentially an example of synonymous parallelism (W. Lane 1974: 455), with the first question focusing on the time and second on the sign associated with "these things/all these things" (France 2002: 506–7; Donahue and Harrington 2002: 368). This is how Luke 21:7 understands it, for he omits "all" (πάντα) from the second question and simply repeats "these things" (ταῦτα) in both questions. The close association of "these things" and "all these things" in 13:29–30 also argues in favor of this interpretation, for the antecedent of "all these things" in 13:30 is "these things" in 13:29. The difference in the two questions therefore involves not a difference in the events referred to but rather different aspects of the same event: the time (πότε) and the sign (σημεῖον) associated with it. The second question does give a "sense of climax" in contrast to the first (Pesch 1968: 104; Neirynck 1988: 54; cf. also Hartman 1966: 221), so that the two could possibly be understood as showing step parallelism.

The two questions of the disciples are natural and legitimate (contra Geddert 1989: 57; J. Edwards 2002: 389–90). Jesus does not rebuke the disciples for asking them. Even the request for a sign does not receive a rebuke (Such 1999: 21–23; France 2002: 506), for it does not seek an apocalyptic timetable of the end events, nor does it ask Jesus for a sign to validate his message. Rather, it seeks information as to how they can be forewarned and prepare for "these things" (Evans 2001: 304–5). After warning in 13:5–13 against possibly misinterpreting naturally occurring events as signs, Jesus gives such a sign in 13:14–23 and 28–31.

The term "accomplished" in "when all these things are about to be accomplished" (ὅταν μέλλῃ ταῦτα συντελεῖσθαι πάντα, *hotan mellē tauta synteleisthai panta*) should not be understood as a technical term referring to the end times (contra Gaston 1970: 12; J. Edwards 2002: 390). It is best understood as referring to the accomplishment of the destruction referred to in 13:2 (France 2002: 507–8). There is no need to interpret this in light of Matt. 24:3, which was not yet written and thus unknown to Mark's readers. It is best interpreted in light of the context in which it is found in Mark, and that context is Jesus's prophecy of judgment in 13:2. Matthew 24:3 sees the second question as extending beyond the first and referring to the "parousia and the end [συντελείας, *synteleias*] of the age," for he is writing after AD 70. As a result, Matthew looks back at the destruction of the temple and emphasizes what is still future: the parousia, or second coming of Christ. He therefore adds to his Markan material a series of traditions dealing with the parousia. In addition to the material he received from Mark (13:24–27/Matt. 24:29–31; Mark 13:33–37/Matt. 25:13–15), he adds Matt. 24:37–41, 42–44, 45–51; 25:1–13, 14–30, 31–46. Writing before AD 70, however, Mark concentrates his emphasis on the destruction of Jerusalem.

Summary

In our passage, Mark shares with his readers Jesus's prediction concerning the destruction of Jerusalem and the events associated with it. Like the OT prophets, Jesus knew that Jerusalem and its temple, one of the glories of the people of Israel (along with the Sabbath and the Law), would soon be utterly destroyed. Not a stone would remain on another. All would be thrown down (13:2). Jesus's knowledge of coming events reveals God's sovereign control of history. Here Mark is revealing an important theme in his Gospel. All is taking place "as is necessary" (δεῖ, *dei*), that is, according to the divine plan (8:31; 13:7, 10, 14). Mark also seeks to teach a christological truth here. As in the passion predictions (8:31; 9:31; 10:32–34), Jesus is well aware of and in control of these events. Even as he is fully conscious that by his death he is giving his life as a ransom for many (10:45), so he knows about the coming destruction of Jerusalem and the temple. The prophecy of the temple's destruction in 13:2 is not simply a neutral prediction of what will soon take place (Gnilka 1979: 183), for Jesus is well aware that in some way he is responsible for bringing it about (11:15–25; 12:1–12; 14:58; 15:29). Therefore, Mark wants his readers not to be disturbed by what is taking place in Jerusalem and Judea. Jesus both knew and was in control of these things.

Mark also reveals that Jesus, like the prophets, was not impressed with the architectural beauty of human structures such as Herod's temple. He was more cognizant of the underlying values and practices associated with them. (Note Paul's similar reaction to the architectural beauty of the Athenian Acropolis in Acts 17:16.) God's eschatological judgment on this marvel of the world was not simply a tragic caprice of fate but the result of Israel's failure to fulfill its divine calling. Instead of godly fruit, it produced nothing except leaves (11:13). Instead of welcoming God's anointed, its leadership brought about his death (12:7–8; 14:1–2). Jerusalem and the temple were like whitewashed tombs whose magnificence and beauty could not conceal the dead bones and barrenness of the religious infidelity of Israel's leadership.

Additional Notes

13:2. It is best to interpret βλέπεις as a question, "Do you see those great buildings over there?" (5:31) rather than an implied rebuke, "Are you marveling at those great buildings over there?" (contra Gundry 1993: 735–36; France 2002: 496).

13:2. Here and at the end of the sentence, the "not" (οὐ μή) is part of a subjunctive of emphatic negation, the strongest negation possible in Greek.

13:2. Certain MSS (primarily Byzantine) omit "here" (ὧδε).

13:3. ἐπηρώτα is best interpreted as an inceptive imperfect.

2. The Coming Destruction of the Temple and Jerusalem Described (13:5–23)

In this section, I seek to demonstrate that 13:5–23 is a unit dealing with the destruction of Jerusalem and the temple in AD 70 and the events leading up to this (so Luke 21:20, 24; W. Lane 1974: 447, 478; Witherington 2001: 340, 343–47; France 2002: 497–505). The entire section appears to have been arranged in the form of a chiasmus (Lambrecht 1967: 173; Grayston 1973–74: 374; Gundry 1993: 733):

A Deceivers who claim to speak for Jesus (13:5–6)
  B Reports of fighting and natural disasters (13:7–8)
    C Persecution of believers (13:9–13)
  B′ The onset of fighting in Judea and resulting tribulation (13:14–20)
A′ Deceivers who claim to be the Christ (13:21–23)

Within this framework is a strong emphasis on distinguishing normal events taking place (13:5–13) and "the end" (τὸ τέλος, to telos; 13:7)—the destruction of Jerusalem and the temple (13:2, 4). Three warnings appear in our passage: "Watch out" (βλέπετε, blepete) in 13:5; "Watch out" (βλέπετε; note the emphatic "you," ὑμεῖς, hymeis) in 13:9; and "Watch out" (βλέπετε; note the emphatic "you," ὑμεῖς) in 13:23 (cf. also 13:33).[1] The first and the last warnings form an *inclusio* indicating that 13:5–23 is a unity. One of the problems in understanding 13:5–23 involves Mark's use of traditions and warnings that go back to the historical Jesus. His faithfulness to these traditions creates difficulties when we seek to interpret them in light of the time and situation of Mark and his readers. It is clear that Jesus predicted the destruction of Jerusalem and the temple (13:2; cf. 14:58; 15:29) and that he knew that this would take place in the not-too-distant future (13:30). Both Jesus and Mark, however, did not seek to provide their hearers with a prophetic time chart of end-time events to satisfy their audiences' intellectual curiosity. Nor did Mark record what Jesus said to his disciples about the destruction of Jerusalem in AD 70 simply to provide historical information about this event for posterity's sake. His purpose in 13:5–23 was to exhort his readers to be faithful in the present time amid deceptions, trials, and

---

1. Cousar (1970: 322–23) points out that these are addressed to different dangers: false pretenders (13:5), persecution (13:9), concerning all that has been said (13:23), and the return of the Son of Man (13:33). Other imperatives are found in 13:7b, 11b–c, 14c, 15, 16, 18, 21d.

suffering (J. Edwards 2002: 386). In the original historical setting of these sayings, Jesus sought (1) to warn the disciples (13:3) that the coming of false messianic claimants, wars and rumors of wars, and natural disasters were not signs of the destruction of the temple/Jerusalem (13:5–13); and (2) to warn them to flee Jerusalem when they saw *the* sign, the "abomination of desolation" (13:14–20), that would precede their destruction. Despite the appearance of false messiahs, wars and natural catastrophes, and persecution, "the end" (τὸ τέλος, 13:7), when all these things spoken of in 13:2 were about to be accomplished (συντελεῖσθαι, *synteleisthai*; 13:4), was "not yet" (οὔπω, *oupō*; 13:7). The meaning of "the end" is debated. Some interpret it as a reference to the events of AD 70 (France 2002: 508–9), but the majority interpret it as a reference to the parousia of 13:24–27 and 32–37 (Hooker 1991: 308; Evans 2001: 307; Donahue and Harrington 2002: 369). The latter interpretation has a number of difficulties associated with it. One is that the setting for 13:5ff. involves the destruction of the temple/Jerusalem (13:2 and 4), not the parousia. Another is that 13:14–20 is best understood as referring to the events of AD 66–70 and not the parousia.

The major argument in favor of interpreting "the end" as referring to the parousia is that, in the setting of Mark and his readers, it is difficult to understand how in the late 60s, when Mark was written (and this is even more so if Mark was written in the early 70s), the destruction of the temple/ Jerusalem could be said to be "not yet." These events were "already now" taking place. Thus numerous scholars believe that what was "not yet" and was not to be confused with the events of 13:5–13 was the parousia of the Son of Man, which would bring history to its end. Rather than indicating that the parousia was imminent, Mark urged his readers not to misunderstand what was happening and be led astray. The "end" or the parousia of the Son of Man was still future (13:7). It was not yet. For Mark's readers, some of the events Jesus spoke of had already occurred, but others were taking place in Judea in their day, and the destruction of Jerusalem was approaching, but the parousia lay in the more distant future (see 13:24–27). Some scholars believe that Mark may have emphasized this to dampen a second-coming excitement among his readers (Hooker 1991: 299; Donahue and Harrington 2002: 368–69). Since such excitement had already manifested itself in the life of the church (cf. 2 Thess. 2–3), Mark may have intended this to serve as prophylactic warning and to head off such eschatological excitement and frenzy among his readers. Mark's readers were instead to prepare themselves for a difficult time of persecution (13:9–13) and to arm themselves with the assurance that those who would persevere in faith to their personal end, that is, until death, would be saved (13:13b).

The understanding of 13:5–23 that I present in the commentary differs from those who see this passage as referring entirely to events preceding the coming of the Son of Man (Gundry 1993: 733–37) or in part to events preceding his coming (Donahue and Harrington 2002: 378). In the latter instance, 13:5–13 is usually associated with the destruction of Jerusalem in AD 70 and 13:14–23 with the events preceding the coming of the Son of Man (Ernst 1981: 379–84; Evans 2001: 328–29; J. Edwards 2002: 385–86, 395–401).[2] The first interpretation is not held by many. That 13:5–23 involves Jesus's response to questions (13:4) raised by the disciples concerning the destruction of the temple (13:2) requires that 13:5–23 must deal, at least in part, with the destruction of the temple/Jerusalem. There is no hint at all in Mark that after "And Jesus began to say to them" (13:5a) Mark's readers were to add, "Your questions about the time and sign of the temple's destruction are out of place, and I will not answer them. Instead I want to talk to you about the events preceding the coming of the Son of Man. Take heed. . . ." In addition, the warnings to those in Judea to flee to the mountains (13:14–16), the woe announced to those pregnant or nursing (13:17), and the prayer that "it" not be in winter (13:18) make little sense if associated with events preceding the coming of the Son of Man. The separation of the sheep and the goats at the coming of the Son of Man (Matt. 25:31–46) is not affected in any way if one is in Judea rather than somewhere else, whether one is pregnant or not, or whether it is summer or not. On the other hand, such issues would be important if associated with the events leading up to AD 70.

Those who interpret 13:14–23 as referring to the coming of the Son of Man usually do so for several reasons. One is that they understand the "abomination of desolation" (τὸ βδέλυγμα τῆς ἐρημώσεως, *to bdelygma tēs erēmōseōs*; 13:14) as a technical term for someone like Paul's "man of lawlessness" (2 Thess. 2:3–4), who appears before the coming of the Son of Man. In 1 Maccabees, the abomination of desolation spoken of in Dan. 11:31 and 12:11 (cf. also 9:27) is referred to as taking place in 167 BC (1 Macc. 1:54), when Antiochus IV Epiphanes desecrated the temple by profaning the altar (1 Macc. 1:59), which indicates that there is no need to interpret the reference in Mark 13:14 as an eschatological event associated with the coming of the Son of Man (see comments on 13:14–20 for further discussion). The argument presented in the previous paragraph—that the events associated with the abomination of desolation in 13:14–18 make more sense if describing events leading up to and including AD 70 rather than the coming of the Son of Man—also counts against the view that 13:14–23 refers to events preceding the parousia.

Some see the language of 13:19–20 as favoring the view that 13:14–23 refers to the coming of the Son of Man. Such language, it is argued, can refer only to an event bringing history, as we know it, to an end. However, this loses sight of the fact that exaggerated and hyperbolic language is part of the vocabulary of prophecy (Stein 1994a: 91–95).[3] This is demonstrated by the language the prophets use to describe the destruction of Babylon in

2. There are numerous variations of this. Hooker (1991: 315–16) sees 13:5–18 as describing the events surrounding AD 70 but 13:19–20 as preceding the parousia.
3. For the use of various stock expressions in these verses, see 13:14–20.

Isaiah (13:9–11; cf. 13:1, 19), of Jerusalem in Jeremiah (15:5–9), of Pharaoh's army in Ezekiel (32:1–16), and so on. This is surely how Luke understood such passages as Joel 2:28–32 (cf. Acts 2:14–21) and Isa. 40:3–5 (Luke 3:4–6). In light of this, the language used by Jesus in Mark 13:19–20 would probably have been understood by his hearers as referring to the destruction of Jerusalem and the temple. Mark's placing this material in the context of 13:2, 4 indicates that he wants his hearers to understand it in this manner.

Still another argument sometimes used by those who interpret 13:14–23 as referring to the coming of the Son of Man is the concept of a *sensus plenior* (Stein 1994a: 96–98). This involves the idea that texts often have a "deeper" meaning than the author was consciously thinking—a fuller, divine meaning (cf. Evans 2001: 316–17; J. Edwards 2002: 399–400). Thus, though Mark and Jesus may have been thinking about the destruction of Jerusalem in these verses, there is an additional and "fuller" meaning in the text that involves the events preceding the coming of the Son of Man (cf. Cranfield 1959: 401–2). The idea of a *sensus plenior* is frequently employed to explain the NT interpretation of certain OT passages in ways apparently different from that intended by the OT author. With respect to our passage, we should note that the idea of a *sensus plenior* assumes that the description of the destruction of Jerusalem and the temple in these verses has not just a literal meaning but also a deeper reference to the coming of the Son of Man. This understanding of the *sensus plenior* maintains that in some way 13:14–23, with its reference to the abomination of desolation and its hyperbolic language, refers to AD 70! Once this is conceded, there is then no need for finding a "fuller" sense. In the discussion below, we shall attempt to understand all of 13:5–23 in light of Jesus's statement in 13:2 and the disciples' questions in 13:4. The coming of deceivers who claim to speak for Jesus (13:5–6) and the coming of wars, rumors of wars, and natural disasters (13:7–8) are not signs of the end (13:7). Neither is the persecution that believers will experience (13:9–13). They are not signs of the coming destruction of the temple/Jerusalem. The sign of this will be "the abomination of desolation" (13:14a), but this requires wisdom to understand, as Mark's parenthetical comment "(let the reader understand!)" indicates (Such 1999: 30, 91–92, 96).[4] "Then" (τότε, *tote*) the residents of Judea and Jerusalem are to flee from the coming destruction and tribulation (13:14–20). Associated with Jerusalem's destruction will be the appearance of messianic-like figures, and believers are warned not to follow them (13:21–23).

The attempt to reconstruct the pre-Markan form of 13:5–23 and distinguish the unique Markan material in it is difficult. Some of the material makes little sense for the readers of Mark who were gentiles and did not

---

4. Hooker (1991: 300) rightly argues that Mark gives no sign in chapter 13 for the parousia (cf. 13:32–37), but if 13:5–23 refers to the fall of Jerusalem in AD 70, then he does give a sign (13:14a). Thus the sign asked for in 13:4b with respect to Jerusalem's impending destruction is given in 13:14.

live in Judea. By implication they have significance for them (Donahue and Harrington 2002: 372), but Mark would certainly not have created out of nothing material that was localized in a different geographical area than that in which his readers lived. This would be especially true if Mark wrote to Christians in Rome. It is much more natural to understand such material as 13:9 (delivered over to councils [συνέδρια, *synedria*] and synagogues [συναγωγάς, *synagōgas*]), 14 (those in Judea), 15 (the flat roofs of houses describe a Palestinian house), and so on as being traditional. The editorial hand of Mark is apparent throughout 13:5–23, but it is not always easy to distinguish Markan insertions into the traditions he inherited and his modification of these traditions or rewriting of them in his own style and vocabulary (cf. Pesch 1980b: 277). One need only compare the suggested Markan redaction of this passage in Lambrecht (1967: 256–58) and Pryke (1978: 20–21, 146, 170). Mark's editorial work is seen most clearly by Lambrecht in 13:5a, 7–8, 10, 13, 14, 17, 20, and 23 and by Pryke in 13:5a, 6b, 7c, 8c, 9a, 10, 11b, 13, 14b, 19a, and 23. The clearest examples of Markan redaction in this passage are most probably 13:5a, 10 (although see Pesch 1980b: 285), and 14b. Other examples probably include 13:13 and 23.

Exegesis and Exposition

[5]And Jesus began to say to them, "Watch out that no one leads you astray. [6]Many will come in my name, saying, 'I am [he]!' and will lead many astray. [7]And when you hear of wars and reports of wars, do not be ⌜troubled⌝; [such things] must take place, but [it is] not yet the end. [8]For nation ⌜will rise up⌝ against nation and kingdom against kingdom. There will be earthquakes in various places. There will be famines. These [are] the beginning of birth pangs. [9]As for yourselves, watch out! They will deliver you ⌜over to⌝ councils, and you will be beaten ⌜in⌝ synagogues, and you will stand ⌜before⌝ governors and kings because of me for a witness to them. [10]And in all the nations it is necessary first that the gospel be preached. [11]And when they hand you over and lead you [to trial], do not worry beforehand what you should say, but whatever is given you at that hour, say this, for you yourselves are not the ones speaking but the Holy Spirit. [12]And brother will deliver brother over to death, and a father [his] child, and children will rise up against parents and have them put to death. [13]And you will be hated by all because of my name. But the one who perseveres unto the end, this one will be saved.

[14]But when you see the abomination of desolation standing where he should not (let the reader understand!), then those in Judea must flee into the mountains, [15]the one on the housetop must not go down to enter to get anything out of his house, [16]and the one in the field must not turn back to get his cloak. [17]And woe to those who are pregnant and to those nursing in those days. [18]Pray that it does not take place in winter. [19]For those days will [bring] tribulation, such as has never been from the beginning of creation, which God has created, until now and will never be [again].

²⁰And if the Lord had not shortened those days, no one would be saved, but for the sake of the elect whom he has elected, he has shortened the days.

²¹And then if anyone should say to you, 'Look, here is the Messiah! Look, there [he is]!' do not believe [it]. ²²For false messiahs and false prophets will arise, and they will perform signs and wonders to deceive, if possible, the elect. ²³You watch out! I have told you all [these] things beforehand."

13:5–6 For "began to say" (ἤρξατο, *ērxato* + infinitive), a construction used twenty-six times in Mark, see 1:45. For βλέπετε as an imperative, compare also 4:24; 8:15; 12:38; 13:9, 23, and 33. In these verses we find the first "not yet" (13:7) concerning the signs that might be mistaken as indicating the destruction of Jerusalem and the temple. This involves the coming of false messianic claimants. There will be many (πολλοί, *polloi*) false claimants who will profess to come in the name of or claiming to be Jesus. The phrase "in my name" can mean that false prophets and teachers will come claiming to represent Jesus and to have his authority (cf. Acts 19:13–17) or that they are claiming to be the risen Christ himself returning from heaven (cf. 8:38; 13:24–27, 32–37; 14:62; V. Taylor 1952: 503–4; Donahue and Harrington 2002: 369). Another explanation is that these are Jewish claimants (cf. Acts 5:36–37; Josephus, *Ant.* 17.10.5–8 §§271–85; 20.5.1 §§97–98; 20.8.6 §§167–72; *J.W.* 2.13.5 §§261–63) who assert that they are the Jewish Messiah or the agents of the Jewish Messiah (Hooker 1991: 306–7; A. Collins 1996: 14–17; France 2002: 510–11). The latter explanation is more likely and better fits the events of the first century (W. Lane 1974: 457; France 2002: 508–9; contra J. Edwards 2002: 390). It probably refers to messianic-like claimants such as Theudas, Judas the Galilean, Simon son of Gioras, John of Gischala, and Menaḥem; compare also Bar Kokhba in AD 135 (A. Collins 1996: 16–18; Evans 2001: 306).

The further assertion of the false claimants' "I am" (ἐγώ εἰμι, *egō eimi*) recalls God's self-description as the "I am" (Exod. 3:14; Deut. 32:39; Isa. 41:4; 43:10), although we should not interpret it here as an allusion to the divine name (Evans 2001: 305–6). It also recalls Jesus's use of ἐγώ εἰμι in 6:50 and 14:62.[5] These false claimants will "lead astray" (πλανήσουσιν, *planēsousin*; 13:5, 6; cf. also 12:24, 27) many. This concluding comment (13:6), an all-too-frequent reality in history, explains and emphasizes the command, "Watch out" (13:5). As 13:7c indicates, however, the appearance of such false messianic individuals does not indicate that the end, that is, the destruction of the temple/Jerusalem, has arrived (France 2002: 508–9).

13:7–8 The second non-sign that does not indicate that the destruction of the temple/ Jerusalem is imminent involves wars and natural disasters (contra A. Collins 1996: 18–19). Luke's substitution of "insurrections" (ἀκαταστασίας, *akatastasias*;

5. Matthew 24:5 makes the "I am" more explicit by adding "the Christ," and Luke 21:8 adds, "the time has come." The latter makes explicit what is implicit, i.e., that the coming of the Messiah would bring the consummation of the kingdom of God.

21:9) for "reports of wars" (ἀκοὰς πολέμων, *akoas polemōn*) is probably an attempt to tie the words of 13:7a more closely with the events of AD 70 (Evans 2001: 306). Wars and rumors of wars, nations and kingdoms warring against one another (cf. Isa. 19:2),[6] are all part of history since the fall, and this must happen. But Mark's readers must not be troubled and think that history has run amok. God still reigns. The use of "must take place/it is necessary" (δεῖ, *dei*) here and in 13:10 indicates that in God's sovereign and active supervision of history, he has allowed all this to take place according to his divine plan (Witherington 2001: 343; Donahue and Harrington 2002: 369). (See 8:3–32a.) Additional tragedies of nature such as earthquakes (the destruction of Pompeii in AD 62?) and famines (cf. Acts 11:28) would also take place (France 2002: 512). Wars (cf. 2 Esd. 13:31) and natural disasters do not mark the end but are the birth pangs[7] of the end (France 2002: 509). Even as the birth pangs of a woman ultimately ends in birth, so the birth pangs described in 13:7–8 will ultimately be followed by the destruction of Jerusalem, and in the more distant future the coming of the Son of Man (13:26) to gather God's elect (13:27; cf. gathering in the wheat [Matt. 13:24–30] and the sheep [Matt. 25:31–46]).[8]

The second warning to "watch out" (βλέπετε δὲ ὑμεῖς ἑαυτούς, *blepete de hymeis heautous*; lit. "you, see to yourselves") occurs in 13:9 (cf. 13:5, 23, 33). A third set of dangerous circumstances, of a different kind than the first two in 13:5–6 and 7–8, is now mentioned. This involves persecution (cf. 6:11; 8:34–38; 10:30; also 4:17). The warning is not given in order that believers may seek to escape such persecutions (as in 13:14–20) but in order to prepare for them.[9] Jewish Christians will be brought before councils (συνέδρια) and "beaten in synagogues" (συναγωγάς).[10] The former refers to local councils of Jewish leaders exercising authority over Jewish communities, not to the

13:9–13

---

6. For a litany of such wars and uprisings at the end of the first century, see Tacitus, *Histories* 1.2. Cf. also N. Taylor 1996: 27–29.

7. For the use of this imagery, cf. Isa. 13:8; 26:17–21; 66:7–9; Jer. 6:24; 22:23; Hos. 13:13; Mic. 4:9–10. There is no evidence, however, that at the time of Jesus or Mark, "birth pangs" was a technical term for the end times (France 2002: 512–13).

8. For Mark, just as the resurrection of Jesus and his parousia are both eschatological events intimately associated together and part of the same chapter of divine history, so the destruction of Jerusalem and the temple in AD 70 (13:5–23 and 28–32) and the coming of the Son of Man (13:24–27 and 33–37) are eschatological events intimately associated together. Both Jesus's resurrection and Jerusalem's destruction are end-time events that are completed only by the parousia of the Son of Man. Like engagement and marriage, they are necessarily connected, even though a time period separates them. So for Mark the events of AD 70 and the parousia are united and yet separated in time. Mark was probably unaware of how long a time would separate them. He may even personally have thought that the parousia would soon follow the fall of Jerusalem, but he does not state this. He did believe, however, that the parousia would take place "after" (μετά, *meta*; 13:24) the destruction of Jerusalem.

9. This is very different from the popular view that Christians will be spared from persecution and tribulation and be "raptured" out of them. On the contrary, Mark emphasizes that his readers, like Jesus, will (cf. 8:31; 10:33) be "delivered over" (13:9; see 1:14) to trial and persecution.

10. Paul's beatings described in 2 Cor. 11:24–25a were probably inflicted by leaders of such councils in the local synagogues. Cf. Acts 5:40; 22:19.

Sanhedrin in Jerusalem (14:55; 15:1), as indicated by the plural (only here and in Matt. 10:17; but the singular [συνεδρίῳ, synedriō] in Matt. 5:22 refers to such a council). All believers, both Jews and gentiles, however, would be susceptible to arrest and trials before governors such as Pontius Pilate (cf. Mark 15:1ff.), Felix, and Festus (cf. Acts 23:26–30; 24:10–27; 25:1–26:32; also 8:12–17), and kings such as Herod Agrippa II (cf. Acts 25:13–26:32). Such trials are not envisioned as due to Christian wrongdoing (cf. 1 Pet. 4:15) but because of their faithfulness to Jesus (ἕνεκεν ἐμοῦ, heneken emou; cf. Mark 13:9, 13; also 1 Pet. 4:14, 16). At such trials they will "witness to them" (εἰς μαρτύριον αὐτοῖς, eis martyrion autois). Although this expression can be understood negatively ("for a witness against them" [Mark 6:11]) or positively ("for a witness to them" [1:44]), in light of 13:10 it is most probably meant here to be understood positively.

Verse 10 seems to interrupt the flow of the argument, for verse 11 follows verse 9 more naturally. Many scholars see its placement here as a Markan insertion (V. Taylor 1952: 507; Hooker 1991: 310; Beasley-Murray 1993: 402–3; cf., however, Pesch 1980b: 285; Gundry 1993: 768). Since the vocabulary and style is very Markan, this may well be true. If so, then Mark seeks to explain how, by the uncomfortable means of persecution (France 2002: 516), the Christian witness before governors and kings will help bring about the preaching of the gospel to all nations. Although some have argued that "And in all the nations" (καὶ εἰς πάντα τὰ ἔθνη, kai eis panta ta ethnē) should be interpreted as the conclusion of 13:9 (Kilpatrick 1955), it is best understood as introducing 13:10 (Gundry 1993: 768; Evans 2002: 310). The term "first" (πρῶτον, prōton) can be interpreted as "first, before you are arrested" (the text has πρῶτον δεῖ; lit. "first it is necessary"), but in light of the present context it is better understood as "first, before the destruction of Jerusalem and the temple" (France 2002: 516). This is how Matt. 24:14 understands it. To interpret "in all the nations" as referring to all the world's "people groups" is to define what Mark means by this expression through twenty-first-century glasses. In the mind of the NT writers, the concern of Jesus to bring the gospel to all nations began already in the ministry of Jesus (Mark 5:1–20; 7:24–30; cf. 3:8; 11:17; 14:9; also Matt. 28:19–20) and could be said to have been accomplished already at the time Mark wrote his Gospel (France 2002: 516–17). Paul writes that the gospel had been "made known to all nations" (Rom. 16:26; Col. 1:6, 23; cf. also Rom. 1:5, 8; 10:18; 15:19, 23). For Mark's readers, the "gospel" would have been understood not simply in light of Jesus's message that "the time is fulfilled and the kingdom of God has come" (1:14–15) but would also include the message about Jesus himself, that is, his death, resurrection, and future parousia. See 1:15.

In 13:11 the theme of 13:9 is picked up, and a promise of support and encouragement is given. When delivered over and brought before governors and kings, they need not worry beforehand as to what they are to say, for at that hour the Holy Spirit will provide the words that they will need. The generally uneducated and powerless nature of the early church (cf. 1 Cor. 1:26; Acts 4:13) would have caused many believers great anxiety and fear when appearing and defending themselves before powerful leaders and judges. (Cf. Moses's fear in such situations in Exod. 4:10–17.) Thus this promise would have provided great comfort and encouragement to them (Donahue and Harrington 2002: 370–71; France 2002: 517).[11] What is prohibited here is not so much thinking about what they should say as being anxious over it (V. Taylor 1952: 508).

In 13:12–13 the persecution spoken of in verses 9 and 11 is enlarged to include the family as well (cf. Mic. 7:6; Isa. 19:2).[12] Brothers will deliver brothers over to death, fathers will do the same with their children, and children will rise up against parents. (Cf. Matt. 10:35–36/Luke 12:51–53, where this warning/prediction is found in the Q material in the context of Jesus's missionary discourse; also Gos. Thom. 16.) We should probably understand this as occurring primarily within natural families, but such persecution would also arise within one's spiritual family (Mark 3:33–35; J. Edwards 2002: 393–94). The warnings concerning persecution conclude with "And you will be hated by all because of my name" (καὶ ἔσεσθε μισούμενοι ὑπὸ πάντων διὰ τὸ ὄνομά μου, *kai esesthe misoumenoi hypo pantōn dia to onoma mou*; 13:13a; cf. John 15:19). "All" here refers not to every human being but rather to every element of society: rulers, religious leaders, citizens, slaves, criminals, philosophers, one's own family, and so on. The mention of one's family members as a source of persecution emphasizes its universal and all-inclusive nature. Such hatred is due to one reason—being a follower of Jesus, as "because of my name" (a synonym for "because of me"; 13:9; cf. also 9:37–41) indicates. The gospel they bear witness to is bound to offend due to such teachings as the universality of sin, the worthlessness of human works for earning eternal life, salvation by grace alone, the totalitarian claims of Jesus (8:34–38), a morality that is critical of many kinds of lifestyles, and so on.

The middle section of 13:5–23 (see the introduction to this unit) concludes with a word of encouragement. It is a promise. Those who "persevere unto the end" (ὑπομείνας εἰς τέλος, *hypomeinas eis telos*) in their commitment to Jesus will be saved. The word "end" refers here not to the "end" when "all these things are about to be accomplished" (mentioned in 13:4) or to the "end" mentioned in 13:7 (i.e., to the destruction of the temple/Jerusalem) but to the end of their life (i.e., until death; cf. John 13:1).[13] An alternative interpretation is that "end" refers to the destruction of Jerusalem and the temple and means

11. Jesus's word of encouragement in 13:11 is directed not to pastors and teachers who have failed to prepare for their preaching and teaching responsibilities but to potential martyrs who in the midst of their suffering have neither the time nor the ability to defend themselves.

12. For additional examples of internecine struggles, see Evans 2001: 312, who lists among others 2 Esd. 6:24; 1 En. 100.1–2; Jub. 23.19; 3 Bar. 4.17. For examples of how such persecutions befell Christians in the latter part of the first and the early part of the second century, see Hengel 1985: 23–24; Tacitus, *Annals* 15.44.4; and Pliny the Younger, *Ep.* 10.96.5–6.

13. It is not always easy to know if a commentator is referring to the present meaning of the word in Mark or the meaning in the pre-Markan source. Hooker (1991: 312–13), for example, argues that the original meaning of "end" in the pre-Markan source was to physical death but in the present Markan text refers to the parousia.

that persecuted Christians who persevere would not physically die (13:20) but would survive the destruction of Jerusalem in AD 70 (cf. Witherington 2001: 345). Yet earlier in the Gospel, Jesus says that "saving" (σῴζω, sōzō) one's life comes from losing it (8:35), and the same expression in Matt. 10:22 (ὑπομείνας εἰς τέλος) is associated with being put to death (10:21). Those who persevere are promised that they "will be saved" (σωθήσεται, sōthēsetai) in the sense of inheriting eternal life, or as the parallel in Luke 21:19 words it, "gain[ing] their souls." For similar promises, compare Rev. 2:7b, 10, 17b–c, 26–28; 3:5, 12, 21.

13:14–20 Having warned his disciples about misconstruing the coming of deceivers (13:5–6), wars and natural disasters (13:7–8), and persecution (13:9–13) as signs of the coming destruction of the temple/Jerusalem (13:2), Jesus now gives "the" sign requested by the disciples in 13:4 (Such 1999: 205–9). This is evident when one compares the two corresponding expressions "when [ὅταν, hotan] you hear, . . . do not be troubled . . ." (13:7) and "when [ὅταν] they hand you over and lead you, . . . do not worry . . ." (13:11) with the statement "when [ὅταν] you see, . . . then [τότε, tote, which answers the 'when' (πότε, pote) of 13:4] those in Judea must flee [lit. 'let those in Judea flee'] into the mountains" (13:14). Whereas in 13:5–13 the readers are told not to be excited or alarmed, now they are told to be alarmed and flee (A. Collins 1996: 21). Furthermore, here the distress points to a particular event, the abomination of desolation, not to various and sundry events (many deceivers, wars, earthquakes, famines, persecutions) as in 13:5–13 (Hooker 1991: 302, 313). The sign is described as seeing "the abomination of desolation standing where he should not" and locates the event in the temple, the place above all places where such an abomination should not be located (see, however, J. Edwards 2002: 398–99, who gives to this sign a double referent, the temple in AD 70 and the antichrist at the end time).

The meaning of the expression "abomination of desolation" was no doubt clearer for Mark's readers than for us today. Nevertheless, Mark urges his readers by his comment, "let the reader understand!" (ὁ ἀναγινώσκων νοείτω, ho anaginōskōn noeitō), to decode what the expression "the abomination of desolation standing where he should not" means.[14] This indicates that it will require some thinking on their part to recognize the present realization of the event referred to as the abomination of desolation in Dan. 9:27; 11:31; 12:11 (cf. 1 Macc. 1:54, 59), for the meaning of the expression lies below the surface level (France 2002: 524). This Markan comment is addressed either to the actual reader of the Gospel,[15] perhaps to note or explain the masculine

14. Hooker (1991: 314) is correct in seeing this as directed to the readers/hearers of the Gospel, but why Mark was not more explicit is unclear. Most attempts to explain this—the dangerous political situation (V. Taylor 1952: 512); Mark did not understand what this expression in the tradition meant (Hooker 1991: 314); Mark is calling his readers to interpret the abomination of desolation in light of Daniel's prophecy (ibid., 315)—are speculative.

15. The attempt to interpret this as a comment by the historical Jesus for his audience as they read the book of Daniel has few supporters. Most commentators see this as a Markan

participle ("he"), or more likely to the audience hearing Mark read to them (Evans 2001: 320; Donahue and Harrington 2002: 372). The masculine participle "standing where *he*" (ἑστηκότα ὅπου, *hestēkota hopou*) is surprising in that the antecedent "abomination" is neuter. However, it may be that what is being referred to is the person most responsible for the abomination of desolation. Some of the suggested explanations of what the abomination of desolation refers to are the following:

1. Caligula's attempt in AD 39–40 to erect a statue of himself in the temple. This was never carried out but nevertheless caused great turmoil in Judea (Josephus, *Ant.* 18.8.2 §261; 18.8.3 §§269–71; cf. Manson 1937: 329–30; Gaston 1970: 25–27; also N. Taylor 1996: 20–21, who sees this meaning in the pre-Markan source used by the evangelist).
2. The attempt by Pontius Pilate to have Roman soldiers march into Jerusalem displaying their standards, which the Jews considered idolatrous (Josephus, *J.W.* 2.9.2–3 §§169–74; *Ant.* 18.3.1 §§55–59).
3. The atrocities committed in the temple by the Zealots under John of Gischala and Eleazar son of Simon in AD 67–68 (Josephus, *J.W.* 4.3.6–8 §§147–57; 4.3.9 §160; Marcus 1992a: 454–56; Witherington 2001: 345–46).
4. The role of Titus in the destruction of Jerusalem and his forceful entrance into the temple sanctuary in AD 70 (Josephus, *J.W.* 6.4.7 §260; Lührmann 1987: 221–22; Hooker 1991: 314; Such 1999: 96–102, 206).
5. The Roman soldiers setting up their standards in the temple and sacrificing to them as they proclaimed Titus "emperor" (Josephus, *J.W.* 6.6.1 §316; Ford 1979: 158). The masculine pronoun "he" thus refers to the man behind the act.
6. The events leading up to the siege of Jerusalem by the Roman army in AD 70 (Luke 21:20; Gould 1896: 246; Ford 1979: 166–69).
7. The destruction of the temple (Pesch 1980b: 292; Beasley-Murray 1993: 411).
8. A future event involving the antichrist and preceding the parousia (2 Thess. 2:3–4; V. Taylor 1952: 511; Evans 2001: 320; J. Edwards 2002: 398–99).

France (2002: 520) rightly points out that the context (both literary and historical) places various constraints upon any interpretation of what Mark means by "the abomination of desolation":

• It must have some interpretive continuity with Dan. 9:27; 11:31; 12:11; and 1 Macc. 1:54, 59, where the expression "abomination of desolation" is used. This would be the linguistic context out of which Jesus

---

comment to his readers (W. Lane 1974: 467; Hooker 1991: 314; A. Collins 1996: 22, 25; J. Edwards 2002: 496; et al.). By now the readers of Mark are quite accustomed to seeing Markan editorial comments inserted into the tradition (see 1:16–18 for the many Markan "for" clauses; cf. also 1:34d; 2:10; 3:30; 7:11, 19d, etc.).

and his audience and Mark and his readers would have interpreted the expression. This context involves the Jerusalem temple, its altar, and its sacrificial ritual.

- The "abomination of desolation" must be recognizable enough that those living in Judea could flee to safety.
- The "abomination of desolation" must occur before the Roman armies advanced toward the city of Jerusalem and laid siege to it, for once that occurred, flight for those in Judea would no longer be possible.
- The masculine participle "standing" indicates that the abomination of desolation most likely refers to a person rather than a thing.

In light of this literary and historical context, the following interpretations listed above are unconvincing: Events 1 and 2 occurred too early (over two decades too early) for Mark's readers to think that they were a sign to flee Judea. They were furthermore never carried out. Events 4, 5, and 7 occurred too late, for there would be no time or possibility of fleeing to safety after these events. Item 6 refers to a "thing" rather than a person. Regarding item 8, the persecution and horrors associated with the coming of the antichrist will not be localized in Judea, and I have earlier argued (see the introduction to this unit) that 13:5–23 is best interpreted as referring to the destruction of the temple/Jerusalem in AD 70. The best interpretation of the "abomination of desolation" involves item 3, the events associated with the Zealots and their leaders John of Gischala and Eleazar in AD 67–68. At that time they appointed Phanni to the high priesthood, even though he was unqualified. They were also involved in numerous sacrileges in the temple, including internecine warfare among various Jewish factions (Josephus, *J.W.* 4.3.6–4.6.2 §§147–376). This seems to fit best the literary context (the setting in the temple and events involving the altar and sacrifice), the historical context (it allows time to flee Judea before the Romans occupied Judea and sealed off the city in AD 69–70), and the grammatical context (it involves a person, not a thing). It also keeps from confusing the "sign" of the coming disaster (the abomination of desolation) from the disaster to which it pointed (the destruction of Jerusalem and the temple).

What follows at this point are three specific imperatives. The first (13:14b) commands flight to the mountains for those living in Judea. Eusebius (*Eccl. Hist.* 3.5.3) speaks of an oracle preceding the destruction of Jerusalem that led Jewish Christians to flee to the city of Pella for safety. Some scholars see Mark 13:14–16 as a reference to this (W. Lane 1974: 468; Sowers 1970: 316–20; Pesch 1980b: 292, 295), but the majority argue against this (Beasley-Murray 1993: 412–13; Evans 2001: 320; France 2002: 526). The first of these imperatives is that those in Judea, upon seeing (i.e., learning of) the abomination of desolation, should flee "into the mountains" (cf. εἰς τὰ ὄρη, *eis ta orē*; 1 Macc. 2:28; 2 Macc. 5:27). Pella, however, is not located in the mountains but lies northeast of Jerusalem in the Jordan River valley, some 3,000 feet below Jerusalem. There is no reason to allegorize the term "Judea" (Evans 2002: 320; contra Grundmann 1977: 359), since elsewhere in Mark it always refers to a geographical location (cf. 1:5; 3:7; 10:1). The two additional imperatives ("must not go down to enter" and "must not turn back to get") in 13:15–16 heighten the necessity of the command for immediate flight (13:14b). The person relaxing on the flat roof of his Palestinian home, upon learning of the abomination of desolation, should not even come down to enter the house[16] to gather necessary provisions but should flee immediately (13:15). The person working in the field should not return home to retrieve his "cloak/coat" (ἱμάτιον, himation; 13:16). Such imagery is to be understood as hyperbolic examples urging the necessity of immediate flight without delay. In reality, the Roman armies did not practice Blitzkrieg. Their movement was usually slow and methodical, so that there would be time to flee, but those who played a waiting game might delay and wait too long. "Go; flee; don't take any chances! Destruction, terror, and death await those who tarry too long" (cf. Gen. 19:26).

The intensity of the future suffering surrounding the destruction of Jerusalem is shown by a woe placed upon the most vulnerable, those pregnant and nursing (13:17). The joyous anticipation of motherhood (cf. Luke 1:25, 57–58; 11:27) and the delight of nursing the newborn will in that day be a curse. The terrors and suffering of flight will be even worse if in winter, for the cold and the swollen wadis will make life and travel unbearable (13:18). So the hearers are told to pray that this does not take place in winter (lit. "But pray that it is not winter"). One is not encouraged to pray or think that, as in the case of the judgment pronounced upon Nineveh (Jon. 3:1–10), the divine judgment of Jerusalem can be averted. The destruction of the temple/Jerusalem was inevitable. There would be no escape for the city. One can only pray or wish (depending on how 13:18 is to be understood) that this would not take place in the cold of winter, the rainy season when many wadis would be flooded. Furthermore, in winter one might be tempted to stay in the warmth of the city and be doomed by this. The flight envisioned in these verses would make more sense in AD 67–68 than in AD 69–70, when the Roman army had occupied Judea and the siege of Jerusalem had begun. This lends support to the interpretation of the abomination of desolation as involving the desecration of the temple by such people as John of Gischala and Eleazar in AD 67–68 (Marcus 1992a: 454–56; but see A. Collins 1996: 24–25).

"Those days" (ἐκείναις ταῖς ἡμέραις, ekeinais tais hēmerais) in 13:17 and 19 is not to be understood as a technical term for the "last days" despite such references as 2 Esd. 4:51 and 1 En. 80.1 (contra J. Edwards 2002: 400), as the noneschatological use of this expression in Mark 1:9; 8:1; and 4:35 indicates (cf. also Matt. 3:1; Luke 2:1; 4:2; 5:35; 9:36; etc.). The language of this verse

---

16. The commands μὴ καταβάτω μηδὲ εἰσελθάτω (mē katabatō mēde eiselthatō; lit. "do not go down" and "do not enter") are probably best understood as a combined command "do not go down and enter" or "do not go down to enter" (cf. 13:16). The first command was necessary, however, if one were to flee into the mountains.

again witnesses to Jesus's frequent use of hyperbole (Stein 1994a: 123–35; 1994b: 8–12). The horror of the war is described as "such as has never been from the beginning of creation, which God has created, until now and will never be [again]" (13:19). The idiomatic nature of this description can be seen by the numerous linguistic parallels (Exod. 9:18; 11:6; Deut. 4:32; Dan. 12:1; Joel 2:2; 1 Macc. 9:27; T. Mos. 8.1; 1QM 1.11–12; Rev. 16:18; etc.). Its idiomatic wording suggests its hyperbolic nature (Stein 1994a: 117–21; contra Gaston 1970: 31, who interprets this as introducing the last great woe before the end). Such use of hyperbolic language is far more expressive and emotive than the use of any scientific or statistical language.[17] W. Lane (1974: 472) points out that "will never be" assumes that time will continue after this event and that this hyperbolic language does not refer to the great tribulation preceding the last days. Geddert (1989: 230–39, 253–55), however, argues that Mark intentionally left this issue ambiguous.

Another statement indicating the horror of the events surrounding the destruction of Jerusalem in AD 70 follows in 13:20. Only God's shortening of those days (lit. "the days"), that is, the length and period of the war and siege, would allow any human being to be "saved" (lit. "all flesh would not be saved").[18] The latter expression refers to physical survival, to remaining alive (W. Lane 1974: 472; Hooker 1991: 316). The reason given for God's shortening those days is "for the sake of the elect" (διὰ τοὺς ἐκλεκτούς, dia tous eklektous; 13:20, 22, 27).[19] This shortening does not involve a sudden change and modification by God of his divine plan for history but reflects a limit that God has set from the beginning on the suffering of his elect (Hooker 1991: 316). The meaning of the term "elect" (13:20, 22, 27) depends on a number of factors. If one concludes that 13:14–23 refers to the events preceding the coming of the Son of Man, then the "elect" refers to Christians (Hooker 1991: 316; Donahue and Harrington 2002: 373). For the use of "elect" to describe Christians, compare Rom. 8:33; Col. 3:12; 2 Tim. 2:10; Titus 1:1; 1 Pet. 1:1; Rev. 17:14. If, however, as I have argued in this commentary, it refers to the events preceding the fall of Jerusalem, such an interpretation has difficulty, for it is unclear as to what extent Christians were in Jerusalem during the events immediately preceding and during its destruction. Since most of the material used by Mark in this chapter is traditional in nature and reflects the teachings of Jesus, the language may reflect Jesus's meaning of these words for his audience in AD 30, that is, for the four disciples referred to in 13:3. In the OT, the "elect" frequently describes

17. Compare this sterile restatement: "This time of suffering will rank in the upper 98 percentile of similar events that have occurred or will occur in the known world." Yet outside Galilee and Judea and its immediate borders, the Roman world was little affected by the war and sufferings going on in Jerusalem.

18. For God's shortening his timetable of history, cf. 1 En. 80.2; 2 Bar. 20.1; 54.1; 83.1; 2 Esd. 2:13; Sir. 36:10; 4Q385, fragment 3; b. B. Meṣiʿa 85b; etc. (Evans 2001: 322–23).

19. There are two Semitisms in this and the preceding verse: "from the beginning of *creation*, which God *has created*," and "for the sake of the *elect* whom he *has* [lit.] *elected*" (V. Taylor 1952: 514). For Mark's use of the cognate accusative, see the comments on 2:3–4.

the people of Israel or the "remnant" among the people of Israel (cf. Ps. 105:6; Isa. 42:1; 43:20; 65:9–11, 15; cf. 1 En. 1.1). Consequently, France (2002: 528) argues that in Mark 13:20 it refers to Jewish Christians living among the Jewish community and suffering along with them. Their suffering is in fact the reason for the "shortening" of the time. France may well be correct. It is for the sake of the followers of Jesus caught up in the events of AD 70 that God will "shorten" the suffering of the time.[20]

This section concludes the chiasmus of 13:5–23 with (A′) a warning of coming deceivers (13:21–23) that matches the earlier warning (A) in 13:5–6 (cf. Grayston 1973–74: 374; A. Collins 1996: 27). In 13:5–6, the appearance of messianic deceivers is associated with the normal course of events; here they are associated with the destruction of Jerusalem in AD 70 (contra Hooker 1991: 316–17). Along with false messiahs (Josephus, *J.W.* 2.17.8–9 §§433–48, esp. §§434, 444; 4.9.3–8 §§503–44, esp. §510; cf. also 1 John 2:18), there will be false prophets (Josephus, *J.W.* 6.5.2–3 §§285–300; cf. also Jer. 6:13; 14:14; 23:32; Zech. 13:2; Matt. 7:15; 1 John 4:1; etc.). These false deceivers will perform "signs and wonders" (σημεῖα καὶ τέρατα, *sēmeia kai terata*; cf. Deut. 13:2–3; 28:46; 29:2–3; 34:11; Isa. 8:18; John 4:48; Acts 2:19, 22; Rom. 15:19; etc.) to lead astray, if possible, the elect.[21] Believers should not be misled into thinking that the Messiah/Christ had returned (cf. 2 Thess. 2:2) and go out to see him (Mark 13:21), for the Messiah/Son of Man will come from heaven (13:26; 14:62; cf. Acts 1:11; 1 Thess. 4:16–17; 2 Thess. 1:7), all will see him (cf. Rev. 1:7), and he will judge the world (Mark 13:27, 35–36; cf. Matt. 16:27; 25:31–32). The section concludes (13:23) with the third "watch out," which forms an *inclusio* with the same warning in 13:5, and "I have told you all [these] things beforehand" (προείρηκα ὑμῖν πάντα, *proeirēka hymin panta*; cf. Acts 1:16; Rom. 9:29). The "you" in the original historical context refers back to the four disciples, Peter, James, John, and Andrew, of 13:3. The purpose of these verses was to not let false hopes and claims, such as caused many Jews to hope foolishly in a messianic deliverance from the Romans, distract believers from fleeing Jerusalem (W. Lane 1974: 472–73).

13:21–23

Summary

In Mark 13:5–23, it is easy to intermix the meaning of Jesus for his audience and that of the evangelist for his readers. Such a fusion of these two separate horizons, however, leads to confusion. For the disciples (13:3), Jesus's message involved a prediction of the coming destruction of Jerusalem, and a twofold warning not to be confused by various events (13:5–13) into thinking that the destruction of Jerusalem was imminent. Instead, the disciples and the Jewish believers who became followers of Jesus through

---

20. Even if the events associated with the Pella tradition are correct, this would not mean that every single Jewish Christian in Judea fled to Pella.

21. See Josephus, *Ant.* 17.10.8 §285, for the harm done by such false prophets and messiahs.

their preaching were to await the sign of the abomination of desolation. Upon seeing this, they were immediately to flee Judea and Jerusalem to seek safety. Jerusalem and its leaders would inevitably be punished for their sins (11:12–25; 12:1–12, 13–27), but by fleeing Judea the followers of Jesus could avoid the suffering and tribulation associated with this.

Mark builds upon Jesus's words and teachings and draws out various implications of this for his readers. Although they do not reside in Judea or Jerusalem (contra Marxsen 1968: 181–83)[22] and the command to flee Judea has no direct application, they too need to "watch out that no one leads [them] astray" (13:5). In this section, Mark does not seek "to provide a timetable or blueprint for the future [let today's readers understand!] so much as to exhort readers to faithful discipleship in the present" (J. Edwards 2002: 384). The readers of Mark are not to allow themselves to be led astray by false prophets, teachers, or messiahs (13:5–6, 21–23; cf. Matt. 7:15; John 10:12–13; Acts 20:28–31; 1 John 2:19). Nor are they to misinterpret various events and circumstances and enter into a parousia frenzy (cf. 2 Thess. 2:1–12; 3:6–13). Rather, they are to prepare themselves for persecution (Mark 13:9–13). Mark 13:5–23 serves for Mark's readers (and also for today's readers) as a commentary on Jesus's teachings on discipleship found in 8:34–38.

Mark also intends for his readers to find encouragement in this passage. They are to understand that despite any appearance to the contrary, God reigns supreme over history. All that is occurring "must take place" (13:7; cf. 13:10). The future tenses found throughout this chapter reveal God's sovereign control of history. Even in the midst of persecution (13:9–13), Mark's readers should realize, "Our God reigns!" The happenings of history are but the daily fulfillment of the divine calendar (13:20). Mark also encourages his readers with the promise that if they "persevere unto the end, [they] will be saved" (13:13b–c). In the midst of all this, they are promised God's presence. They need not even fear or worry over what they should say when brought before hostile courts, for the Holy Spirit will give them the words to say at that time (13:11). The risen Christ has promised his followers, "I am with you always, to the end of the age" (Matt. 28:20), and God has given them his word, "I will never leave you or forsake you" (Heb. 13:5).

Still another Markan emphasis found in this passage is christological in nature. Jesus is portrayed as a great prophet who sees the future clearly (13:23). Despite appearances, the massive walls and stones do not promise security to Jerusalem. Jesus knows that within the lifetime of the present generation (13:30), it would be utterly destroyed (13:2). Mark also wants his readers to recognize that Jesus is the true Messiah and that all other claimants are false (13:5–6, 21–22). Salvation is to be found in his name

---

22. The various Aramaic expressions (3:17; 5:41; 7:11; 15:34; etc.) and explanations of Jewish customs (7:3–4) to Mark's readers makes no sense if his readers were Jews living in Judea and Jerusalem.

only (13:9, 13; cf. Acts 4:10–12), and he has promised that those who take up his cross and follow him (8:34) will share in his power and glory at his parousia (13:26–27).

Additional Notes

13:7. A few MSS (D) read a synonymous term such as "alarmed" (θορυβεῖσθε).

13:8. France (2002: 512) points out that the future tenses of the verbs in 13:8 have the same effect as the "must" (δεῖ) of 13:7.

13:9. The translation associates a prepositional phrase with each verb (V. Taylor 1952: 506; France 2002: 514; contra Gundry 1993: 765).

3. The Coming of the Son of Man (13:24–27)

The interpretation of this passage centers on two related questions. The first involves the meaning of 13:26. The traditional understanding of this verse is that it describes the coming or return of the Son of Man from heaven, the second coming, the parousia (Cranfield 1959: 405–7; Ernst 1981: 385–88; Hooker 1991: 319; Beasley-Murray 1993: 422–34; Evans 2001: 328–30; J. Edwards 2002: 402–4). An alternative understanding is that it describes the destruction of Jerusalem in AD 70 and the vindication of the Son of Man (Gould 1896: 240–41, 250–52; Hatina 1996; N. Wright 1996: 360–65; France 1971: 231–39; 2002: 500–503, 530–37). I will present the arguments for both in the comments below, where I will advocate the traditional view. The second question involves the relationship of 13:24–27 to the destruction of Jerusalem described in 13:2–23. How closely associated with 13:2–23 is "in those days after that tribulation" (ἐν ἐκείναις ταῖς ἡμέραις μετὰ τὴν θλῖψιν ἐκείνην, en ekeinais tais hēmerais meta tēn thlipsin ekeinēn) and the events described in 13:24b–27? Are they essentially contemporaneous, or does a lengthy period of time intervene? This also I will discuss below in the comments. Integrally related to both of these questions is the issue of how one is to interpret the cosmic imagery found throughout this passage.

The tradition history of this passage is much discussed and debated. In general, most scholars understand these verses as coming from a pre-Markan tradition, but there is little unanimity as to the extent to which it comes from the historical Jesus (Grundmann 1977: 361 argues that none of it comes from Jesus; cf., however, Gundry 1993: 785–86) or whether it was associated before Mark with the preceding material (Pesch 1980b: 301 says it was; Lohmeyer 1957: 279 says it was not). This in turn is intimately associated with the question of whether Mark 13 is based on an early Jewish-Christian apocalypse (see 13:1–37). As to the extent of the Markan editorial work found in this passage, it appears to be fairly minimal. The most likely is his addition of either "after that tribulation" (μετὰ τὴν θλῖψιν ἐκείνην; Pryke 1978: 21, 146, 170; Beasley-Murray 1993: 422–23) or "in those days" (ἐν ἐκείναις ταῖς ἡμέραις; Gnilka 1979: 199–200), as the Markan love of duality suggests (Neirynck 1988: 95; cf. however, Pesch 1980b: 301, who thinks that they may both be traditional). "After that tribulation" is more likely Markan since "in those days" is a fairly traditional formula. The passage consists of three sections: (1) a description of a series of cosmic events occurring "in those days after that tribulation" (13:24–25); (2) the coming of the Son of Man in clouds with great power and glory (13:26); and (3) the sending of angels to gather the elect from the end of the earth (13:27).

Exegesis and Exposition

[24]"But in those days after that tribulation, the sun will be darkened and the moon will not give its light, [25]and the stars will be falling from heaven and the powers in the heavens will be shaken. [26]And then they will see the Son of Man coming in clouds with great power and glory. [27]And then he will send out ⌜his⌝ angels and gather ⌜his⌝ elect from the four winds, from the end of the earth to the end of heaven."

The expression "in those days" is often used to describe a theophany or divine intervention in history involving either judgment or restoration (A. Collins 1996: 29). (For examples of this terminology, see Jer. 3:16, 18; 5:18; 31:29; 33:15–16; Joel 2:29 [3:2 LXX]; 3:1 [4:1 LXX]; Zech. 8:23.) We have already seen, however, that the expression is not a technical term with a consistent eschatological meaning (see 13:14–20). In itself the terminology does not require any predetermined eschatological meaning. In 13:24, it refers to the preceding events and the destruction of Jerusalem. Since this is an eschatological event and is associated with the parousia of the Lord (see note 8 under the comments on 13:7–8), there is a sense in which "those days" are part of the events of the end time, but they are not necessarily a sign of the imminent return of the Son of Man. "After that tribulation" refers to the tribulation associated with the destruction of Jerusalem in 13:14–23. We should not assume that the term "tribulation" (θλῖψιν) is a technical term for "the great tribulation." The term "tribulation" is used forty-five times in the NT, and in only one instance do we find the expression τῆς θλίψεως τῆς μεγάλης (*tēs thlipseōs tēs megalēs*, the great tribulation; Rev. 7:14). Four times it is used with the adjective "great," but only in Rev. 7:14 and possibly Matt. 24:21 is it used in the sense of "the great tribulation."

13:24–25

The traditional interpretation of this passage is that it refers to the parousia, which lies in the distant future, whereas Mark 13:14–23 refers to the destruction of Jerusalem in AD 70. Some argue that the "but" (ἀλλά, *alla*) introducing 13:24 is a strong adversative and indicates a major change of subject from the destruction of Jerusalem to the distant future (W. Lane 1974: 473n87; Gnilka 1979: 200; Pesch 1980b: 302). It is true that ἀλλά indicates a change or contrast with what has preceded, but this contrast need not be one of time (France 2002: 531–32). Others have sought to find some sort of time gap in the words "in those days" (see Geddert 1989: 229–31 for a discussion of this, and 310n9 for a list of those who hold this view; cf. A. Collins 1996: 29), assuming that it is a technical term for the last days.[1] I have argued above against this interpretation. The nearest antecedent to this phrase is the identical wording in 13:17, "in those days" (ἐν ἐκείναις ταῖς ἡμέραις), and 19, "those days" (αἱ ἡμέραι ἐκεῖναι), referring to what is to happen in Judea and Jerusalem in AD

1. Gundry (1993: 782) rightly points out that the phrase "in those days" obtains its meaning solely from its context. Geddert (1989: 310n8) states, "All it [13:24a] says is that the End is more distant in time than the events of 13:5–23."

70. "That tribulation" (τὴν θλῖψιν ἐκείνην) in 13:24a therefore refers to the tribulation mentioned in 13:19. For Mark, the events of 13:14–23 and 24–27 are intimately associated, and it is unlikely that he saw a great gap of time between them.[2] They are intimately associated in that they are part of the same great divine act of history.[3] This includes Jesus's coming, ministry, death, and resurrection, which bring the kingdom of God; the divine judgment on Jerusalem in AD 70; and the parousia of the Son of Man, which brings history to its conclusion and goal. Seen from the vantage point of the prophets and evangelists, these events are perceived as a two-dimensional portrait that lacks the perspective of depth, much like a spectator in the centerfield stands of a baseball stadium sees through a pair of binoculars. Through the binoculars, one can see the centerfielder, second baseman, pitcher, batter, catcher, and umpire clearly, but they appear to be standing together. The binoculars provide no real sense of the distance between the people and events that are seen (cf. Caird 1980: 258–59; J. Edwards 2002: 404). Geddert (1989: 231, 235–39) argues that Mark intentionally left the issue of time unclear.

The cosmic language in 13:24b–25 comes from OT passages such as Isa. 13:10; 34:4; Ezek. 32:7–8; Joel 2:10, 31 (3:4 LXX); and Amos 8:9, although Mark does not quote any of them directly.[4] It involves standard OT apocalyptic imagery (France 1971: 74; cf. Rev. 6:12–13; 8:10; also As. Mos. 10.5; 2 Esd. 5:4; 1 En. 80.3–7; Sib. Or. 3.796–805). That such cosmic terminology is frequently used to describe divine interventions via "normal" historical events and means is evident from such passages as Isa. 13:9–11 (the destruction of Babylon [13:1, 19] by the Medes [13:17–18]); Jer. 4:23–28; 15:9 (the destruction of Jerusalem by Babylon [4:11; 5:1; 15:5]); Ezek. 32:7–8 (the destruction of Pharaoh's army [32:2, 12, 18, 20]); and Amos 8:9 (the destruction of Samaria). Additional "cosmic" language is found in the use of the verb "shaken" (σαλευθήσονται, *saleuthēsontai*; cf. Judg. 5:5; Job 9:6; Ps. 18:7 [17:8 LXX]; 46:6 [45:6 LXX]; 77:18 [76:19 LXX]; 82:5 [81:5 LXX]; 114:7 [113:7 LXX]; Amos 9:5; Mic. 1:4; Nah. 1:5; Hab. 3:6; also T. Levi 4.1; etc.).[5]

The question of whether verses 24b–25 (I will discuss vv. 26–27 separately) should be interpreted "literally" or "metaphorically" is overly simplistic (Ernst 1981: 385). The key issue is rather whether (1) these cosmic descriptions should

---

2. Cf. Matt. 24:29, which has "Immediately [Εὐθέως, *Eutheōs*] after the tribulation of those days. . . ."

3. Cranfield (1954: 288) says it is important to realize "that the Events of the Incarnation, Crucifixion, Resurrection, Ascension and Parousia are in a real sense one Event."

4. Beasley-Murray (1993: 423) believes that Mark 13:24 essentially follows Isa. 13:10; Mark 13:25a follows Isa. 34:4; and Mark 13:25b follows Isa. 34:4; Joel 2:10; 3:15–16. For additional OT parallels to Mark 13:24–27, see Hartman 1966: 156.

5. There is no reason to assume that Mark intended his readers to interpret this cosmic language to mean "the end of the idols of the Greco-Roman pantheon" (contra van Iersel 1996: 89). This would be but one consequence of the divine theophany described in this passage. The content of this theophany, however, is not provided by the cosmic language of 13:24–25. The cosmic imagery reveals only that a theophany is being described. Mark provides the content of the theophany in 13:26–27.

be interpreted primarily as events associated with the coming of the Son of Man at the parousia, or (2) whether they should be interpreted as metaphorical descriptions of the coming of the Son of Man in the destruction of Jerusalem in AD 70. If Mark interpreted the cosmic terminology found in his tradition in the same way that the OT prophets understood such terminology, then he probably regarded it as metaphorical language to show God's intervention into history by the return of his Son, the Son of Man. If he did not, then Mark probably understood the language as describing actual events associated with the final coming of the Son of Man. J. Edwards (2002: 402), who favors the latter, understands them as describing a metahistorical event that "includes history but subsumes and supersedes history." There is additional cosmic and metaphorical imagery in the NT associated with the coming of the Son of Man such as an archangel's call (1 Thess. 4:16) and the sound of a trumpet (1 Thess. 4:16; Matt. 24:31). Regardless of whether Mark's description in this passage should be interpreted literally, one thing is clear: the metaphorical language refers to a real historical event. The coming Son of Man is understood as the personal return of Jesus of Nazareth: "This Jesus, who has been taken up from you into heaven [cf. Acts 1:9; Luke 24:50–51], will come in the same way as you saw him go into heaven" (Acts 1:11). If one takes a more literal approach to interpreting Mark 13:24b–25, then it of course cannot refer to the destruction of Jerusalem. On the other hand, if one takes seriously the use of this exact same kind of language to describe the fall of Babylon, Jerusalem, Pharaoh's army, and Samaria, then it is possible to interpret these verses as referring to AD 70. The way one interprets 13:26 will ultimately be the determining factor as to how one interprets 13:24–25.

Those who argue that this verse refers to the vindication of the Son of Man in the destruction of Jerusalem do so for the following reasons: (1) the language of 13:26, like 13:24b–25, should be understood as the prophets of the OT would have understood it, that is, metaphorically; (2) the reference in this verse to Dan. 7:13–14 involves the Son of Man "going to," not coming from, God;[6] (3) this interpretation is the best way of resolving the problem of 13:30, where Jesus says, "Truly, I say to you, this generation will in no way pass away until all these things will have taken place." There are, however, a number of serious problems with such an interpretation. For one, it moves the vindication and exaltation of Jesus primarily from the resurrection of Jesus to the destruction of Jerusalem (France 2002: 500–501).[7] This is not how the early

13:26

---

6. France (2002: 503) argues that the primary source for understanding the meaning of 13:26 is what the author of Daniel meant by Dan. 7:13–14. This is, however, incorrect. Far more important for our understanding of what Mark meant by 13:26 is how the NT writers understood Dan. 7:13–14, and they understood it not as the Son of Man going to God but rather coming from God and going to earth.

7. N. Wright (1999: 269) recognizes this and states, "The early church clearly believed that Jesus had been vindicated by the resurrection. . . . The resurrection was more important to them than any other single event" (cf. also 1996: 660). Despite this, he maintains that 13:24–27 refers to the events of AD 70.

preaching of the church understood it (Acts 2:24, 33–36; 4:10–12; 5:30–31; 7:55–56; 13:30–39; Rom. 1:4; 8:34; Eph. 1:20; Phil. 2:8–11; Col. 3:1; Heb. 1:3, 13; 8:1; 10:12; 12:2; 1 Pet. 3:22). The great emphasis placed on the destruction of Jerusalem in this interpretation is simply not found in Acts–Revelation, and this makes one question the extent to which the events of AD 70 should play a role in the interpretation of 13:26.

More important, the language of 13:26 cannot be so "demetaphorized" that it is interpreted radically differently from passages concerning the parousia, or second coming, elsewhere in the NT that use similar language and terminology. Compare, for example, the following passages:

Matthew 13:41 refers to the "close of the age" (13:39) and the final judgment and furnace of fire (13:41) and uses the same terms found in Mark 13:26–27 (*Son of Man, will send, angels*) to describe this.

Matthew 16:27 (cf. Mark 8:38; Luke 9:26) refers to the final judgment of everyone as individuals (contra France 1971: 139–40; 2002: 342–43, 500–503) and uses the terms *Son of Man, will come, angels.*

Matthew 25:31 refers to the coming of the Son of Man and a judgment that involves eternal punishment or eternal life (25:46; contra France 1971: 143–44) and uses the terms *Son of Man, comes, glory,* and *angels.*

Mark 14:62 (cf. Matt. 26:64) refers to Jesus's enthronement (cf. Acts 2:33; 5:31; Ps. 110:1) and may refer to his subsequent coming (Hooker 1991: 362; Donahue and Harrington 2002: 423; contra France 1971: 140–42; 2002: 611–13) and uses the terms *see, Son of Man, coming, power,* and *clouds.*[8]

It would be difficult for the readers of the Gospels to interpret two similarly worded descriptions of the Son of Man's coming as referring to two different events (cf. Adams 2005). As to the language of the final judgment in Matt. 13:41; 16:26; and 25:31ff., this portrays a judgment, the final judgment, that goes far beyond the events of AD 70.

In addition, in his use of Mark 13 Matthew introduces the discourse with a question concerning the parousia and the "end of the age" (συντελείας τοῦ αἰῶνος, *synteleias tou aiōnos;* 24:3; cf. 28:20). He also refers to this as παρουσία (*parousia*) in 24:27, 37, and 39. Since this is frequently a technical term for the second coming (France 2002: 501n22; cf. 1 Thess. 2:19; 3:13; 4:15; 5:23; 2 Thess. 2:1, 8; 1 Cor. 15:23; James 5:7, 8; 2 Pet. 1:16; 3:4; 1 John 2:28; also Rev. 1:7),[9] Matthew appears to have understood the reference in Mark 13:26 in the traditional sense as referring to the parousia or second coming of Christ. Finally, in light of numerous other sayings in the church referring to

---

8. In light of 13:24–25, the present verse is portrayed as a theophany. As a result, if one asks the question of the direction of the "coming" of the Son of Man, it must be from heaven (Beasley-Murray 1993: 430). A theophany comes from heaven to earth, not from earth to heaven.

9. The term "parousia" is never associated in any clear way with the events of AD 70.

a second coming of Jesus (cf. μαράνα θά [*marana tha*] in 1 Cor. 16:22 and its Greek translation in Rev. 22:20), Mark's readers would have been predisposed to interpret 13:26 along similar lines and not as a reference to the destruction of Jerusalem in AD 70. Mark gives no clear clue, no "let the reader understand!" to interpret it otherwise. As a result, the traditional interpretation of this verse is more persuasive.

The purpose of the coming of the Son of Man is given in this verse. He will **13:27** send his angels to gather his "elect" (ἐκλεκτούς, *eklektous*), those who believe in him, from throughout the world. The gathering of God's elect in the last days has numerous OT roots (Isa. 11:11–16; 27:12–13; 43:5–7; 49:12; 60:1–9; Pss. 107:2–3; 147:2; Jer. 31:10; Ezek. 11:16–17; 39:27; Neh. 1:9; 1 En. 1.1; 62.8).[10] The extent of this gathering is described by two phrases: "from the four winds" (ἐκ τῶν τεσσάρων ἀνέμων, *ek tōn tessarōn anemōn*; Zech. 2:6) and "from the end of the earth to the end of heaven" (ἀπ᾽ ἄκρου γῆς ἕως ἄκρου οὐρανοῦ, *ap᾽ akrou gēs heōs akrou ouranou*; Deut. 13:7; 30:4; Isa. 48:20; 62:11; cf. also Jer. 3:18). The dual description emphasizes that no believer anywhere will be forgotten and miss out on this great event. All will be gathered and share in the great messianic banquet.

The coming of the Son of Man is described only positively in Mark 13:26–27. It is salvific, oriented toward the elect. Elsewhere his coming is described as involving judgment as well (8:38; 13:32–37; Matt. 13:41–43; 16:27; 24:36–44, 45–51; 25:1–12, 31–46). Some have attempted to see Mark 13:14–23 as referring to the judgmental dimension of the coming of the Son of Man (A. Collins 1996: 29–30), but I have argued above that 13:14–23 describes not the coming of the Son of Man at the end of history but the destruction of Jerusalem in AD 70 (see the introduction to 13:5–23). In light of the persecution of the elect in 13:9–13, it is not surprising that the positive aspect of the parousia is emphasized in 13:24–27 (cf. 1 Thess. 4:13–18). One should not expect that a description of the parousia should always be comprehensive and include all that is associated with that event. Note that Mark and Matthew (Mark 13:41–43; Matt. 25:31–46) do not include any reference to the resurrection in their description of the parousia, even though they believed in it (cf. Mark 12:18–27 and Matt. 22:23–33).

Summary

In this passage Mark seeks to assure his readers that despite persecution (13:9–13) and world chaos (13:5–8, 14–23), they need not fear. Their faithfulness will be rewarded. A day is coming when the Son of Man will return (14:25; cf. John 14:1–3) and gather his elect from the end of the earth. After that day there will be no more sorrow or weeping (cf. Rev. 7:17; 21:4). Those

10. Cf. E. Sanders 1985: 95: "The motif of the restoration of Israel figures more prominently in Jewish literature than that of the restoration or reconstruction of the temple." Cf. also Ps. Sol. 8.34; 11.1–4; 17.28; Tg. Isa. 53:8; Tg. Hos. 14:8; Tg. Mic. 5:1–3; Matt. 8:11/Luke 13:29; Justin Martyr, *Dial*. 76.4–5; etc.

who endure will be saved (Mark 13:13; cf. Rev. 2:7b, 10, 17b–c, 26; 3:5, 12, 21). The words of Mark 13:24–27 are intended to provide comfort (1 Thess. 4:18) for Mark's readers amid their trials and tribulation (Hooker 1991: 319; Evans 2001: 330). The negative side, which involves being ashamed of Jesus in this adulterous and sinful generation, has already been stated (Mark 8:38) and is not repeated here.

A second Markan emphasis found in 13:24–27 is christological in nature. Jesus's foreknowledge and the return of the Son of Man reveals that he is truly a great prophet. More important, however, is that Jesus in this passage is the subject of a theophany. In the OT, God is the subject of a theophany; here the subject of the theophany (13:24–25) is Jesus, the Son of Man (13:26–27)! There is no need for heralding him (13:21–22), for he comes in the clouds (often associated with God in the OT [Exod. 34:5; Lev. 16:2; Num. 11:25; Isa. 19:1; etc.]) with great power and glory (Ps. 63:2; 1 Chron. 29:11; cf. also Dan. 2:37; 4:30), and everyone will see him (Gundry 1993: 783). All ("they") will see the Son of Man in his glory, and for the elect it will mean salvation (Mark 13:13). For others it will mean judgment, but regardless, "every knee will bow . . . and every tongue confess that Jesus Christ is Lord" (Phil. 2:10–11).

Additional Notes

13:27. "His" (αὐτοῦ) is not found in B D L W it, but I include it in the translation due to its presence in ℵ A C Θ Ψ f¹ f¹³ lat syr.

13:27. The translation follows ℵ A B C Θ Φ f¹³ lat syr, which have "his" (αὐτοῦ). Cf. Matt. 24:31.

4. The Lesson of the Fig Tree (13:28–31)

The present account consists of a parable (13:28–29) and two sayings (13:30 and 31). Its composition is much debated. Although most scholars attribute the parable to Jesus (V. Taylor 1952: 520; Lohmeyer 1957: 281–82; Evans 2001: 333; cf., however, Bultmann's ambivalence [1968: 123 and 125]), there is uncertainty as to its original setting in the life of Jesus. Similarly, the original setting of the two sayings and the extent of the Markan redaction in this passage are also debated. Mark's hand is probably seen most clearly in the placement of this material after 13:1–27, the introductory seam in 13:28a (Pryke 1978: 21, 146, 170; Gnilka 1979: 203), and the rewording of 13:29 and 30 to correspond to the disciples' question in 13:4 (cf. Gnilka 1979: 206, who attributes "all" [πάντα, *panta*] to Mark), although some see 13:30a as Markan (Pryke 1978: 21, 146, 170). It is probably wise to follow the advice of Donahue and Harrington (2002: 379), who state concerning Mark 13 in general, "Many learned attempts . . . at unscrambling the various elements have revealed the difficulty of the undertaking and the wisdom of reading the text as it now stands in Mark's Gospel and as a literary unit."

The tie with the previous material is seen most clearly in the terms "these things taking place" (ταῦτα γινόμενα, *tauta ginomena*; 13:29a; cf. 13:4a) and "all these things" (ταῦτα πάντα, *tauta panta*; 13:30; cf. 13:4b). If, as argued previously, the two questions of the disciples in 13:4 involve Jesus's prediction of the destruction of Jerusalem in 13:2 and vv. 5–23, then in the lesson of the fig tree a fig tree's branches becoming tender and sprouting leaves as a harbinger of summer is likened to the appearing of the abomination of desolation (13:14) as a harbinger of the destruction of Jerusalem. The lesson or analogy of the parable involves not the parousia (contra Pesch 1980b: 308) but rather the fall of Jerusalem. The two sayings, as they stand in the present context, add two additional comments concerning the destruction of Jerusalem and the temple: (1) it will take place in "this generation" (ἡ γενεὰ αὕτη, *hē genea hautē*), and (2) the elements of the universe—"heaven and earth" (ὁ οὐρανὸς καὶ ἡ γῆ, *ho ouranos kai hē gē*)—will one day pass away, but Jesus's words concerning the destruction of Jerusalem will not.

Exegesis and Exposition

²⁸"From the fig tree learn [the lesson of] the parable. As soon as its branch becomes tender and sprouts leaves, ⌜you know⌝ that summer is near. ²⁹So also, when you see these things taking place, *you* know that ⌜it is near⌝, at the very gates. ³⁰Truly, I say

to you, this generation will in no way pass away until all these things will have taken place. [31]Heaven and earth will pass away, but my words will never pass away."

13:28–29   Verse 28b–c is called a "parable" (παραβολήν, *parabolēn*). It is in reality an extended simile (Stein 1981: 19; France 2002: 537). See 3:22–23. The use of a fig tree in this parable recalls the use of a fig tree in the parabolic action of Jesus in 11:12–14, 20–21. In the former instance the parable involves the destruction of Jerusalem (see the introduction to 11:12–25). Whether Mark wanted his readers to interpret the present parable in light of, or in contrast to (Hooker 1991: 320), the former parabolic action is debated. Jesus's parable may use the budding of the fig tree here simply as an example of a sign that something is to follow. The fig tree served this purpose because it was one of the few deciduous trees in Palestine, and the Mount of Olives was famous not only for its olive trees but also its fig trees (W. Lane 1974: 479). Whether its budding is meant to be interpreted positively as a sign of hope in light of the parousia (Hooker 1991: 320) or of judgment in light of the destruction of Jerusalem (as in 11:12–25) can be determined only by the context.

Normally a fig tree, "the most characteristic springtime tree" (Telford 1980: 215), would begin to experience the swelling of its branches and the sprouting of leaves in March and April. When this happened, this indicated that summer (θέρος, *theros*; not θερισμός, *therismos*, harvest) was near. In a similar manner, when you see "these things taking place" (13:29), you know that "it" is near, "at the very gates."[1] Many commentators prefer to translate ἐγγύς ἐστιν (*engys estin*) as "he is near," but "these things" in 13:29 refers back to "these things" in 13:4a, which has as its antecedent the destruction of Jerusalem foretold by Jesus in 13:2 (Telford 1980: 217–18; Cranfield 1982: 502) not the parousia saying in 13:24–27 (contra Wenham 1984: 327).[2] This is made even more clear by "all these things" in 13:30, which refers back to "all these things" in 13:4b (W. Lane 1974: 479–80; Witherington 2001: 348–49; France 2002: 540; contrast Donahue and Harrington 2002: 376). That the order "these things—all these things" in 13:29 and 30 follows exactly the order of "these things—all these things" in 13:4a and b indicates that the lesson of the fig tree involves the fall of Jerusalem, not the parousia. This is further supported by the appearance of "when you see" (ὅταν ἴδητε, *hotan idēte*) here and in 13:14, which speaks of seeing the abomination of desolation. The readers of Mark, and Jesus's original audience, were to be aware that, just as seeing the budding of the fig tree meant that summer was

---

1. Some scholars (Hooker 1991: 321; Gundry 1993: 788) have argued that the expression "at the very gates" implies the pronoun "he." "At the doors/gates," however, is idiomatic language (J. Jeremias, *TDNT* 3:173–74), so that this argument has little weight. It is the immediate context involving 13:2, 4, 14–23 that is determinative, and this favors "it is near" as the correct translation.

2. Cranfield (1982: 502) rightly points out that to make "these things" include the parousia would involve interpreting 13:29 like this: "When you see the Son of Man coming in the clouds with great power and glory [13:26]. . . , you know that *he* is near." Such a statement would be pointless.

near, so seeing the abomination of desolation (13:14) meant that Jerusalem's destruction was at hand.

The first saying associated with the parable is a saying of Jesus emphasized   **13:30–31**
by "Truly" (ἀμήν, *amēn*). "All these things" will take place before the generation of Jesus would pass away. If 13:28–31 is interpreted as dealing with the
parousia rather than the destruction of Jerusalem in AD 70, this creates an
evident problem. Jesus's parousia has not yet taken place, and Jesus's generation has for the most part died. This has resulted in numerous attempts
to explain "this generation" as referring not to Jesus's generation but to the
continued existence of the Jewish people, to "that" (last) generation of the
end time, to the continued existence of the human race, to the continued existence of Jesus's followers (i.e., Christians), and so on. The expression "this
generation" elsewhere in Mark (8:12 [2×], 38; cf. 9:19), however, refers to the
contemporaries of Jesus and should be interpreted similarly here (W. Lane
1974: 480; France 2002: 539; cf. Geddert 1989: 239–45).[3] There is no need to
seek some esoteric interpretation of this expression, once we realize that the
event being referred to by "these things" and "all these things" in 13:29–30 is
the same as "these things" and "all these things" in 13:4—Jesus's prediction
of the destruction of Jerusalem in 13:2 (Telford 1980: 217; Beasley-Murray
1993; 444–49; contra Bayer 1986: 244–49).[4] Like the "some" of 9:1 who would
not taste death before they saw the kingdom of God come with power, "this
generation" would also not taste death before they saw "all these things" take
place. For the former this was fulfilled in the experience of Jesus's transfiguration; for the latter it was fulfilled in the destruction of Jerusalem.

In verse 31 Jesus places his personal guarantee on the truthfulness of what he
has said in 13:30. Heaven and earth will one day pass away (cf. Ps. 102:25–27;
Isa. 40:6–8; 51:6; Matt. 5:18; Luke 16:17; 2 Pet. 3:7, 10; Rev. 20:11; 21:1),[5]
but Jesus's words will never pass away. The words of Jesus Christ, the Son of
God, are more enduring than creation itself. Such a christological claim should
not go unnoticed. What "words" are intended is not made explicit. They can
refer to 13:28–30 (Evans 2002: 336 favors only 13:30), the entire apocalyptic
discourse in 13:2, 5ff., or the totality of Jesus's teachings (Cranfield 1959:
410; Gnilka 1979: 206). For Mark's readers, the last would at least be implied,
even if 13:28–30 was meant. It would not have been possible for Mark and his
readers to conceive of the teachings in 13:28–30 enduring forever but other

3. For Jesus's use of "this generation" elsewhere in the Gospels, cf. Matt. 11:16; 12:41,
42, 45; 23:36; 24:34; also 12:39; 16:4; 17:17; Luke 7:31; 11:29, 30, 31, 32, 50, 51; 17:25; 21:32;
and 9:41.

4. Geddert (1989: 243–44) argues that for Mark to have placed 13:30 before the parousia
saying in 13:24–27 would have implied that Jesus's generation would not experience the coming
of the Son of Man, and neither Mark nor Jesus was prepared to do this (cf. 13:32).

5. Contra France (2002: 541), who believes that Isa. 51:6 (?); 54:9–10; Jer. 31:35–36; and
33:20–21 assume the permanence of the created order. He understands Mark 13:31 in the sense
of an a fortiori "Even if heaven and earth were to pass away (and they will not), my words will
never pass away."

teachings of Jesus Christ, the Son of God, passing away. Like the Torah (Matt. 5:18; Luke 16:17; Bar. 4:1; Wis. 18:4; 2 Esd. 9:36–37), Jesus's words are eternal (Beasley-Murray 1993: 451; cf. Stein 1994b: 120–24).

Summary

The main emphasis found in this passage involves the recognition of Jerusalem's forthcoming destruction. The parabolic analogy is that just as the budding of the fig tree is a harbinger and herald that summer is near, so when "these things" spoken of in 13:14–23 take place, especially the abomination of desolation, the destruction of Jerusalem is near. Thus Jesus's original hearers should flee from Judea and the city. For Mark's readers, it indicated that what was taking place in Palestine was foreseen by Jesus and that the commands, warnings, and exhortations he gave (13:5, 7, 9, 11, 13b, 14–16, 18, 21, 23) should be heeded. "These things" must take place in their generation. Yet in the next section, Jesus warns against the danger of calculating the exact time of the parousia. Mark's readers are to be alert and watch, but they are not to panic or allow themselves to be overcome with eschatological frenzy.

The high Christology found in these verses is quite striking. With an authoritative "Truly" (13:30), Jesus boldly claims that the destruction of the mighty city of Jerusalem will take place within his generation. This is more certain than the continued existence of heaven and earth! Like God's word, his own words will never pass away (13:31). They are more sure than the foundations of the universe. Mark's readers were probably beginning to see the fulfillment of Jesus's prediction of Jerusalem's destruction, which would have reinforced their faith in the authority of Jesus Christ, the Son of God. He who foretold these things also promised them succor and aid (13:11) and that faithfulness in their time of crisis would result in eternal salvation (13:13).

Additional Notes

13:28. Some MSS (B² D L W Δ Θ) read "it is known" (γινώσκεται).

13:29. ἐστίν can also be translated "he is near."

5. The Coming of the Son of Man and the Call to Watchfulness (13:32–37)

Although some scholars and translations interpret 13:32 as the conclusion of 13:28–31 (Pesch 1980b: 305–13; Gnilka 1979: 203–7; Evans 2001: 330–37; Aland 2001: 406; NASB; etc.), it is best to understand it as the introduction to 13:33–37 (W. Lane 1974: 480–84; Hooker 1991: 322–24; Gundry 1993: 747–50; A. Collins 1996: 32–35; J. Edwards 2002: 406–9; France 2002: 541–46; RSV; NRSV; NIV; TNIV; etc.).[1] Not knowing the exact time of "that day" (13:32) fits better the call to watchfulness (13:33–37) because one does not know the time of the Lord's coming (13:35) than it does the emphasis on knowing that "all these things" will occur in "this generation" (13:28–31). Likewise, Mark 13:32 and its emphasis on not knowing fits better the need to be ready for a future, more distant crisis (13:33–36) whose time is unknown (Hooker 1991: 322) than with the sign that will mark when "these things" take place (13:29). Clearly the "resounding certainty" (France 2002: 541) of Jesus's "Truly, I say to you" concerning "these things/ all these things" (13:29–30) stands in sharp contrast to his not knowing "that day or hour."

The introductory "But concerning" (Περὶ δέ, *Peri de*) of 13:32 is best understood as signaling a switch to a new subject, as in 1 Cor. 7:1, 25; 8:1; 12:1; 16:1; 1 Thess. 4:9; 5:1 (so France 2002: 541). This switch is also suggested by the new expression "that day" (τῆς ἡμέρας ἐκείνης, *tēs hēmeras ekeinēs*), which has not appeared previously in this chapter.[2] The attempt to see this as referring back to the plural "those days" (αἱ ἡμέραι ἐκείναι, *hai hēmerai ekeinai*) in 13:17, 19, 24 (cf. 13:20; J. Edwards 2002: 406) loses sight of the fact that no particular day has been singled out in 13:5–24. The only "day" that provides a suitable antecedent for 13:32 is "in those days after that tribulation" (ἐν ἐκείναις ταῖς ἡμέραις μετὰ τὴν θλῖψιν ἐκείνην, *en ekeinais tais hēmerais meta tēn thlipsin ekeinēn*) when the Son of Man comes (see 13:24–25). Thus it is best to interpret 13:5–23 and 28–31 as referring to the events preceding and including the fall of Jerusalem in AD 70, and 13:24–27 and 32–37 as referring to the parousia of the Son of Man.

The composition of 13:32–37 and the extent of the Markan editorial work is uncertain. The overall form and location of the material betray the hand and purpose of Mark. Suggestions of the Markan redaction include

---

1. Some translations are ambiguous on this and place 13:32, sometimes with 13:33, as (an) independent saying(s) between 13:28–31 and 13:33/34–37. Cf. REB, NJB, NLT.

2. For the use of this expression and "the day of the Lord" in the OT, cf. Isa. 2:11–22; 3:7, 18; 4:1–2; Jer. 46:10; Ezek. 13:5; Amos 5:18–20; Zeph. 1:7–18; Zech. 14:1–21.

the present placement of 13:32 (V. Taylor 1952: 522; Beasley-Murray 1993: 453); "or hour" (ἢ τῆς ὥρας, *ē tēs hōras*; Gnilka 1979: 205) in 13:32; much or most of 13:33 (Bultmann 1968: 130, 174; Pesch 1980b: 313; Pryke 1978: 21, 146, 171; Gnilka 1979: 208); 13:34a (Pryke 1978: 21, 146, 171); 13:35a (Pesch 1980b: 315; Pryke 1978: 21, 146, 171); the four temporal designations of 13:35 (Gnilka 1979: 208); most or all of 13:37 (Pesch 1980b: 313; Pryke 1978: 21, 146, 171; Gnilka 1979: 208); and all the imperatives found in 13:32–37 (Gnilka 1979: 208). The main linguistic tie that exists with the rest of the chapter involves the presence of various warnings: "watch out" (βλέπετε, *blepete*) in 13:33 (cf. 13:5, 9, 23); "be alert" (ἀγρυπνεῖτε, *agrypneite*) in 13:33; and "watch" (γρηγορεῖτε, *grēgoreite*) in 13:34, 35, and 37. These parallel other commands found in 13:5 ("see"), 7 ("be not troubled"), 9 ("see"), 11 ("be not anxious"), 14 ("flee"), 15 ("do not come down to enter"), 16 ("do not return"), 18 ("pray"), 21 ("do not believe"), 23 ("see"), 28 ("learn"), and 29 ("know"). The presence of these imperatives here, as well as in the previous material, indicates that Mark is not presenting this material to satisfy his readers' curiosity concerning the end times. They are meant rather to warn, exhort, encourage, and prepare his readers for Christian living in light of the destruction of Jerusalem and the parousia. There is a difference, however. The earlier commands tended to warn about misconstruing normal events as indicating that the destruction of Jerusalem was at hand and to reveal that Jesus predicted this event; now Mark exhorts his readers to be ready for "that day" when the Lord returns, and since they do not know when that day will be, they should live in accordance with the expectation that it could occur at any time (France 2002: 543).

As it now stands, the present passage begins with an introductory warning statement (13:32) about end-time speculation. No one, no angel, not even the Son knows the time of "that day." Only the Father knows this. In light of their not knowing when the Son of Man will return, there is a warning to watch out and be alert (13:33). This warning is followed by a parable in the form of a similitude (13:34), which is then interpreted and applied for the readers (13:35–36): they need to watch, because they do not know the time of "that day" (13:35), so that the returning Lord will not find them unprepared (13:36). The passage then ends with an appeal that goes beyond the original hearers of Jesus to all Christians who read/hear these words (13:37). They are to watch, to be ready, for the parousia of the Son of Man.

Exegesis and Exposition

[32]"But concerning that day or hour no one knows, not even the angels in heaven, nor the Son, but only the Father. [33]Watch out, be alert ⌜ ⌝! For you do not know when the time will come. [34][It is] like a man [who], going on a journey, left his house and gave authority to his servants, to each one for his work, and he commanded the doorkeeper that he should watch. [35]Watch, therefore, for you do not know when the lord of the house is coming, whether in the evening, or at midnight, or at the cock's

crowing, or early, ³⁶lest he ⌐should come⌐ suddenly [and] find you sleeping. ³⁷What I am saying to you I say to all, 'Watch.'"

Although some scholars question the authenticity of this verse due to doubts that **13:32** Jesus spoke so openly of himself as "the Son" (ὁ υἱός, *ho huios*; Bultmann 1968: 123; Jeremias 1971: 131n1; Hooker 1991: 323), "its offence seals its genuineness" (V. Taylor 1952: 522; van Iersel 1964: 117–20; Meier 1991: 169; Evans 2001: 336; J. Edwards 2002: 407n56; Donahue and Harrington 2002: 376). The embarrassment of the statement that "the Son" does not know the day or the hour, the omission of this verse from the parallel passage in Luke, and the omission of "the Son" in certain MSS of the Matthean parallel in 24:36 (ℵ¹ L W f¹ vg syr) reveal how unlikely it is that anyone in the early church would have created this saying limiting the wisdom and omniscience of the "Son." As in Mark 12:6 and Matt. 11:27/Luke 10:22, the so-called Johannine thunderbolt, Jesus refers to himself as "the Son" without qualification.³ The case for the authenticity of 13:32 is especially strong due to it going counter to the early church's tendency to magnify, not qualify, the divine attributes of Jesus. (Cf. such a work as the Infancy Gospel of Thomas and the absolute use of the title "the Son" in John 3:17, 35, 36 [2×]; 5:19 [2×], 20, 21, 22, 23 [2×], 26; 6:40; 8:35, 36; 14:13; 17:1 [2×].)

The emphasis on God's knowing everything, even the future (Isa. 46:10; Zech. 14:7; 2 Bar. 21.8; Ps. Sol. 17.21), and the angelic and human lack of such knowledge (2 Esd. 4:51–52; Eph. 3:10; 1 Pet. 1:12; Tg. Qoh. 7:24) fits well the Jewish tradition. In contrast to God's omniscience, Mark tells his readers that even the Son, the Christ, the Son of God (cf. 1:1, 11, 24; 3:11; 5:7; 9:7; etc.), does not know the time of the parousia (Beasley-Murray 1993: 458–61).⁴ Yet we must not lose sight of the fact that in Mark the purpose of the saying is not primarily to teach a christological truth but to serve as a ground for exhorting the church to be ready at all times for the parousia, "that day," because no one knows when the Lord of the house will come (13:33, 35).

The statement in 13:32 serves as the basis for the conclusion in 13:33b. Since **13:33–36** only the Father knows "that day or hour," Jesus can say, "You do not know

---

3. Gundry (1993: 794–95) points out that the absolute use of "the Son" here is probably due to the absolute use of "the Father" immediately following. On the Johannine thunderbolt, see Fitzmyer 1985b: 866.

4. Whereas in 10:40 the Son speaks of a lack of authority, in 13:32 he speaks of a lack of omniscience. These passages, and others like them, are better understood along the lines of Phil. 2:6–11 as being due to the "self-emptying" (ἐκένωσεν, *ekenōsen*) of the Son (Donahue and Harrington 2002: 376; cf. also Erickson 1984: 710–11), than that the Son of God is referring here to his human nature and that as the son of Mary he lacked such knowledge and authority, whereas as the Son of God he did not lack them (Grudem 1994: 561–63). On the contrary, it is the "Son," distinct from humanity ("no one") and the angels, who does not know! (The very difficulty that some theologians have in accepting the plain meaning of 13:32 is proof of the saying's authenticity. Who would have created such a saying in the early church, and why would Mark and Matthew have included this saying in their Gospels, unless its authenticity was well established? Contrast John's emphasis on Jesus's omniscience in 1:48; 2:24–25; 5:6; 6:6, 61, 64; 8:14; 9:3; 11:11–15; 13:1–3, 11; 18:4; 19:28.)

when the time [a synonym for 'that day or hour'] will come [lit. 'is']" (οὐκ οἴδατε γὰρ πότε ὁ καιρός ἐστιν, *ouk oidate gar pote ho kairos estin*). This in turn provides the ground (for, γάρ, *gar*) for the double exhortation "Watch out, be alert!" The duplication of the exhortation places added emphasis on the importance of being on guard and not letting the parousia catch one unprepared. Jesus's followers are to be vigilant.

The similitude in 13:34 is an incomplete sentence, and we must provide something like "It is" to make "like a man . . ." into a complete sentence. It has been suggested that the parable (or similitude) may be a Markan version of Luke's parable of the watchful servants (12:36–40), the parable of the pounds (19:12–27/Matt. 25:14–30), or the parable of the wise and foolish servants (Matt. 24:45–51; Bultmann 1968: 119; Lambrecht 1967: 249–51; Hooker 1991: 323–24; Evans 2001: 340–41). Some have pointed out that the similitude presents a rather odd picture, since the lord of the house would normally not be traveling and returning during the night (Hooker 1991: 323; France 2002: 545–56), but this is a parable and parables often portray unrealistic situations (Stein 1981: 40–41). The emphasis in the similitude is not that the return of the Lord is unexpected (cf. Matt. 24:45–51; 25:1–13, 14–30; Luke 12:36–38; 19:12–27) or uncertain,[5] but that there will be no sign or warning of his coming. This is emphasized by the repetition of "you do not know when the time will come" (13:33b) and "you do not know when the lord of the house is coming" (οὐκ οἴδατε γὰρ πότε ὁ κύριος τῆς οἰκίας ἔρχεται, *ouk oidate gar pote ho kyrios tēs oikias erchetai*; 13:35b). These clauses place great stress on the commands "Watch out, be alert!" in 13:33. The additional threefold command to "watch" (γρηγορέω, *grēgoreō*; 13:34, 35, 37) is paralleled by a similar threefold command in the Gethsemane story (14:34, 37, 38). Compare also the reference to "sleeping" (καθεύδοντας, *katheudontas*) in 13:36 and the threefold reference to sleeping in 14:37, 40, 41.

By the time of Mark's Gospel, the similitude would have been interpreted allegorically with respect to at least two details. The return of the "lord" (13:35) would have been understood as the return of the "Lord Jesus Christ, the Son of God," and the "servants" would have been interpreted as referring to the Christian community (Hultgren 2000: 266–67). The tendency to interpret the doorkeeper as the apostles or Peter, however, is a post-Markan development, for in Mark the doorkeeper disappears from the scene after 13:34 and is not referred to in the application (13:35; Hultgren 2000: 267). The four temporal periods described in 13:35b (evening, ὀψέ, *opse*—an adverb;[6] midnight, μεσονύκτιον, *mesonyktion*—accusative of time; the cock's crowing, ἀλεκτοροφωνίας, *alektorophōnias*—genitive of time;[7] early, πρωΐ, *prōi*—an

---

5. Cf. 1QpHab 7.7–10: "The final age will be extended and go beyond all that the prophets say, because the mysteries of God are wonderful. Though it might delay, wait for it; it definitely has to come and will not delay."

6. Cf. 11:19; also 1:32; 4:35; 6:47; 14:17; 15:42.

7. Cf. 14:30, 68 (?), 72 (2×).

adverb)[8] represent the conventional Roman division of the twelve hours of night into four quarters or watches of three hours each (6–9 p.m., 10 p.m.–12 a.m., 1–3 a.m., 4–6 a.m.; cf., however, Martin 2001, who argues that while the fourfold designations reveal a Roman reckoning of the four watches that make up the night, the names given to the four watches are not Roman but Jewish). See 6:48–50. Numerous scholars point out that three of these watches are referred to (probably intentionally) in the Passion Narrative: 14:17; 15:42 ("evening"), 72 ("cock's crowing"); and 15:1 ("early"; Lightfoot 1950: 53; Hooker 1991: 324; J. Edwards 2002: 409; Geddert 1989: 89–103, however, presses the analogy too far).

The passage ends with the application of Jesus's teachings and exhortations,   **13:37** originally addressed to the disciples (you, ὑμῖν, *hymin*; 13:37; cf. 13:3–5), to the readers of the Gospel (all, πᾶσιν, *pasin*). This verse thus provides a fitting conclusion to the entire discourse found in Mark 13. The earlier warnings concerning the destruction of Jerusalem were addressed primarily to those in Judea in the late 60s of the first century (13:14a) and to Mark's Christian readers concerning the meaning of the events occurring there (13:14b). Now the final exhortation is addressed to Christians everywhere and at all times who live on this side of the parousia. Watchfulness is commanded. For the early church, this watchfulness served less as a threat and warning that they should not be caught unprepared than as a joyous anticipation of the blessed hope (Titus 2:13) for which they prayed and longed. "*Marana tha*" (1 Cor. 16:22; cf. Rev. 22:20) and "Thy kingdom come" (Matt. 6:10) were daily in their prayers and produced hope, comfort, and expectation (1 Thess. 4:18). What was true of the early church is also true today for all who "love his appearing" (2 Tim. 4:8).

Summary

The Markan emphasis in this passage is clear from the high number of imperatives urging the readers to be vigilant and watchful. "That day," the coming of the Son of Man, should not catch them unawares. They are to "watch out" (13:33), "be alert" (13:33), and "watch" (13:34, 35, 37). These commands demonstrate that the evangelist's warnings against misconstruing normal events as indicating the time of the destruction of Jerusalem (13:5–13) do not lessen in the slightest the need for watching and being prepared for the return of the Son of Man. Mark sees the need to watch, not as an activity of a fringe group of the Christian church, but as one in which "all" (13:37) should be engaged. A Christian faith that lacks the daily praying of "*Marana tha*" and "Thy kingdom come" is clearly not the faith envisioned in Mark 13 or the rest of the NT (1 Thess. 4:13–18; 2 Tim. 4:8; Titus 2:11–14; Rev. 22:20; etc.).

Although not the primary emphasis of Mark, we find an important christological teaching in 13:32. Here we find mentioned in an ascending order

8. Cf. 1:35; 11:20; 15:1; 16:2.

(France 2002: 543; contra Donahue and Harrington 2002: 376) humanity ("no one"), the angels in heaven, the Son, and the Father. The order indicates that, for Mark, "Jesus Christ, the Son of God" (1:1, 11; 9:7; 12:6), stands in a position high above all other human beings and even the angels. He stands next to God himself. Although in function he stands below the Father (John 14:28) in authority (Mark 10:40; cf. 1 Cor. 15:28) and knowledge (Mark 13:32), being second only to God the Father is a high Christology indeed!

Additional Notes

13:33. Although a number of MSS (‏א‎ A C L W Θ Ψ f¹ f¹³ lat syr) add at this point "and pray" (καὶ προσεύχεσθε), this is probably due to 14:38. If it was part of the original text, its omission from B D and some Old Latin MSS is difficult to explain.

13:36. ἐλθών is lit. "coming."

VII. The Passion Narrative: Part 6 (14:1–16:8)

The final section of Mark is the Passion Narrative. All the events in this section center in or around Jerusalem and occur in a tight chronological sequence covering a period of less than a week ("Passion week"). The early form critics argued that "during the oral period, the narratives and sayings, with the exception of the Passion Narrative, circulated mainly as single and self-contained detached units, each complete in itself" (Redlich 1939: 37). They all tended to see the Passion Narrative as an exception, which was understood to have circulated early as a continuous story (K. Schmidt 1919: 303–6; Dibelius 1934: 178–217; Bultmann 1968: 275–84; Redlich 1939: 37, 161–79; V. Taylor 1949: 44–62; 1952: 524–26; Theissen 1991: 166–99). There are a number of reasons for this opinion. Along with the close chronological (14:1, 12, 17, 22, 26, 32, 43, 53, 66; 15:1, 8, 15, 20c–21, 33, 34, 42, 43; 16:1, 2) and topographical ties (14:3, 26, 32, 53–54, 66; 15:1, 16, 21, 22, 41, 46; 16:2), there is a shortage of identifiable oral forms (Kelber 1983: 186–87), and pericope follows pericope as a matter of course. There does not seem to be any place within the narrative where one can satisfactorily end. After each pericope one is led to ask, "Then what happened?" Even the tradition of the Lord's Supper, which was passed on as an isolated account by Paul of what he received and delivered (1 Cor. 11:23a), begins with, "On the night in which he [Jesus] was betrayed . . ." (1 Cor. 11:23b), and one either knows or wants to know how Jesus was betrayed and what happened after this. The story of Jesus in the Garden of Gethsemane ends with Jesus being seized (Mark 14:42–50), and one wants to know what happened next. The cock crowing associated with Peter's denial requires an association with the trial of Jesus late at night (R. Brown 1994: 1.54). And so it goes. What happened at the trial? What happened before the Roman governor? What happened after the crucifixion? Furthermore, the description of Judas in 14:10 and 43 and its needless repetition of information already given in 3:19 strongly suggests that Mark was following a source in these instances (Soards 1994: 1522–23).

Voices have been raised against this thesis (Donahue 1973: esp. 237–40; Kelber 1976a; 1983: 184–99; Hooker 1991: 324–25; et al.). The difficulty of reconstructing the exact composition of the pre-Markan Passion Narrative is one reason for this. Even the early form critics believed that Mark added various traditions to his Passion Narrative. Those most often seen as having been added by Mark are Jesus's anointing (14:3–9), the preparation for the Passover (14:12–16), elements of the story of Jesus in the Garden of Gethsemane (14:39–42), elements added to the trial account (14:59–65), mention of the young man fleeing naked (14:51–52), and part of the account of Jesus's resurrection and the empty tomb (16:1–8; Dibelius 1934: 178–217; Bultmann 1968: 262–84). One of the places where Mark's hand is most clearly seen is in the Markan sandwiches found in the narrative. These include 14:3–9 into 14:1–2 and 10–11; 14:22–26 into 14:17–21 and 27–31; 14:55–65 into 14:53–54 and 66–72; and 15:42–46 into 15:40–41 and 15:47–16:6 (J. Edwards 2002: 410–11, 421–22, 441, 484).[1]

The exact makeup of the Passion Narrative is uncertain. V. Taylor (1952: 653–64) argues that it arose in two stages. The first stage consisted of 14:1–2, 10–11, 12–16 (?), 17–21 (?), 26–31, 43–46, 53, 55–64; 15:1, 3–5, 15, 21–24, 26, 29–30, 34–37, 39, 42–46; 16:1–8. The second stage, which he believed could be detected by the presence of Semitisms, was 14:3–9, 22–25, 32–42, 47–52, 54, 65, 66–72; 15:2, 6–14, 16–20, 25, 27, 31–32, 33, 38, 40–41, 47. Pesch (1980b: 1–27), who sees Mark as a conservative editor, thinks that little of Mark's hand should be seen in 14:1–16:8 and that the pre-Markan Passion Narrative consisted of 14:1–16:8 essentially as we now have it. A. Collins (1992: 92–118) thinks that the pre-Markan Passion Narrative consisted essentially of 14:32–15:39. Others tend to see the size of the pre-Markan Passion Narrative as somewhere in between (Senior 1984: 9–11; Green 1988: 214–17, 221–313; et al.). The confidence of V. Taylor in reconstructing so precisely the pre-Markan Passion Narrative and the stages by which it came into being is now generally questioned, and R. Brown (1994: 1.55; cf. also Soards 1994: 1523–24) is probably correct in saying that the reconstruction of the original or even the pre-Markan form of the Passion Narrative is impossible. The existence of a pre-Markan Passion Narrative is acknowledged by most, but the pre-Markan Passion Narrative was no doubt shorter than it now stands in Mark.

The material in Mark's Passion Narrative is arranged as follows:

A. The plot to kill Jesus, and his anointing by an unnamed woman (14:1–11)
B. The Last Supper and Jesus's prediction of the denial of the disciples (14:12–31)
C. Jesus prays in the Garden of Gethsemane (14:32–42)
D. Jesus is seized (14:43–52)
E. Jesus is tried by the Sanhedrin (14:53–65)
F. Jesus is denied by Peter (14:66–72)
G. Jesus is tried by Pontius Pilate (15:1–15)
H. Jesus is crucified (15:16–41)
I. Jesus is buried (15:42–47)
J. Jesus is raised from the dead (16:1–8)

---

1. Heil (1990), however, sees too many Markan sandwiches (seven) in 14:1–52 alone, with some individual sandwiches making up larger sandwiches.

A. The Plot to Kill Jesus, and His Anointing by an Unnamed Woman (14:1–11)

The present account sets the scene for the following events of Jesus's "Passion" (from the Latin for "suffering"). It does so chronologically by giving the time when the following events begin: "two days before the Passover and the Feast of Unleavened Bread" (τὸ πάσχα καὶ τὰ ἄζυμα μετὰ δύο ἡμέρας, *to pascha kai ta azyma meta dyo hēmeras*; 14:1). It speaks once again of the plot of the religious leadership to kill Jesus (14:1–2, 10–11; cf. 3:6; 11:18; 12:12) and contrasts this with the actions of an unnamed woman who recognizes Jesus as the Messiah and prepares his body for burial (14:3–9). The material reveals the hand of the evangelist by its arrangement as a "Markan sandwich" (14:3–9 into 14:1–2 and 10–11). See the introduction to 3:20–35. The extent to which the hand of Mark is seen in this section varies. Pryke (1978: 21–22, 146, 171) sees it in 14:1a, 2a, 3a, 4a, 5a, 7a, 8–11; Gnilka (1979: 219, 222, 228–29) sees it in 14:1–2, 3a, 7b, 9, 10–11. Mark's hand is seen most clearly in the Markan arrangement of this material (the sandwich is almost certainly Markan); the introductory seams to the two parts of the sandwich (14:1a and 3a); the saying about the "gospel" (εὐαγγέλιον, *euangelion*; 14:9; cf. 1:1, 14–15; 8:35; 10:29; 13:10, where the term in each instance is probably due to the hand of Mark); "preached" (κηρυχθῇ, *kērychthē*; 14:9; cf. 1:14, 39, 45; 3:14; 5:20; 6:12; 7:36; 13:10, where the term appears to be part of Markan editorial comments); "in the whole world" (εἰς ὅλον τὸν κόσμον, *eis holon ton kosmon*; cf. 13:10) in 14:9; and the concluding summary (14:10–11), which uses traditional material expressed in a Markan style and vocabulary.

The account of Jesus's anointing (14:3–9) has parallels in all the other Gospels (Matt. 26:6–13; Luke 7:36–50; John 12:1–8). For all intents and purposes, the Markan and Matthean accounts are identical, and the parallel in John is probably a variant form of the same tradition. The anointing takes place in Bethany during "holy week" (Mark 14:1; John 12:1); the description of the perfume as "ointment, pure nard, [and] very expensive" (14:3; John 12:3) is essentially identical (μύρου νάρδου πιστικῆς πολυτελοῦς/πολυτίμου, *myrou nardou pistikēs polytelous/polytimou*); there is criticism of the woman's act (14:4–5; John 12:4–5); the cost of the ointment in both is three hundred denarii (δηναρίων τριακοσίων, *dēnariōn triakosiōn*; 14:5; John 12:5); there is a similar comment that the ointment should have been sold and the proceeds given to the poor (14:5; John 12:5); in both Jesus defends the actions of the woman (14:6; John 12:7); and the statement "You always have the poor with you, . . . but me you will not always have [with you]" (πάντοτε γὰρ τοὺς πτωχοὺς ἔχετε μεθ' ἑαυτῶν, . . . ἐμὲ δὲ οὐ πάντοτε ἔχετε, *pantote gar tous ptōchous echete meth' heautōn*, . . . *eme de ou pantote echete*; 14:7; John 12:8) is almost identical in wording. The main differences between the two accounts involve the exact time (two days before the Passover [14:1] and six days before the Passover [John 12:1]), the name of the host (Simon the leper [14:3] and Lazarus [John 12:2]);[1] the anonymous woman in Mark is named "Mary" in John 12:3; it is the head that is anointed in 14:3 but the feet in John 12:3; and the anonymous "some" who protest the extravagant waste in 14:4 is Judas Iscariot in John 12:4. Despite these differences, most scholars believe that the accounts in Matthew, Mark, and John are variants of the same tradition.

The account in Luke, however, is significantly different. Like Mark, it includes an anointing by an unnamed woman (14:3; Luke 7:37), Jesus's reclining at a meal (14:3; Luke 7:36), the ointment being described as in an alabaster jar (14:3; Luke 7:37), the host's name being Simon (14:3; Luke 7:40), objections to the woman's actions (14:4–5; Luke 7:39), and Jesus's defense of the woman (14:6; Luke 7:40–48). On the other hand, there are a number of significant differences: the location of the account in Luke is Galilee (7:1, 11), not Bethany (Matthew, Mark, and John), for in Luke Jesus does not enter Judea until the end of his ministry (19:28ff.); the event takes place early in Jesus's ministry, not at the end; as in John, Jesus's feet are anointed, not his head, whereas in Matthew/Mark it is his head (14:3; Luke 7:38); the objection made against the woman comes from Simon, not the anonymous "some" (14:4; Luke 7:39–40); Simon is described as a Pharisee rather than a leper (14:3; Luke 7:39); and the objection is based upon the woman's character, not her waste of money, and is directed at Jesus, not the woman (14:4–5; Luke 7:39). We are probably dealing here with two separate traditions (Matthew/Mark/John and Luke; cf. J. Edwards 2002: 413), and during the oral period the two traditions experienced a certain standardization of terminology (France 2002: 550). This is more likely than that we have three separate traditions (Matthew/Mark, Luke, John) of the same incident.

Exegesis and Exposition

[1]It was two days before the Passover and the Feast of Unleavened Bread, and the chief priests and the scribes were seeking how they might seize Jesus by subterfuge [and] kill him. [2]For they were saying, "Not during the feast, lest there be a riot by the people."

1. The description of Lazarus in John 12:2 ("And Lazarus was one of those reclining at the table with him [i.e., Jesus]") suggests that he was a guest at the meal rather than the host (R. Brown 1966: 448). Morris (1995: 511) comments, "This is perhaps a more natural remark if the meal were in another house than Lazarus' own. His presence among the guests could be assumed in his own home." Cf. also J. N. Sanders (1954: 39), who suggests that Simon the leper (14:3) may have been the father of Mary, Martha, and Lazarus.

³And while he was in Bethany in the house of Simon the leper, as he was reclining to eat, a woman came carrying an alabaster jar of ointment, [which was] pure nard, [and] very expensive. After breaking the alabaster jar, she poured [it] on his head. ⁴But ⌐some [of those present] were indignant [and said]¬ among themselves, ⌐"Why was this ointment wasted?"¬ ⁵For this ointment could have been sold for over three hundred denarii and given to the poor. And they were berating her. ⁶But Jesus said, "Leave her alone. Why are you troubling her? She has done a good thing for me. ⁷For you always have the poor with you, and whenever you want you can do [something] good for them, but ⌐me¬ you will not always have [with you]. ⁸What she was able to do [for me], she has done. She has in anticipation anointed my body for burial. ⁹⌐Truly,¬ I say to you, wherever the gospel is preached in the whole world, what she did will also be spoken in memory of her."

¹⁰And ⌐Judas Iscariot¬, one of the Twelve, went to the chief priests in order that he might deliver him [Jesus] over to them. ¹¹When they [the chief priests] heard [this], they were delighted and promised to give him money. And he [Judas] began to seek for an opportunity to deliver him [Jesus] over [to them].

The plot of the chief priests (see 11:18–19) and scribes (οἱ ἀρχιερεῖς καὶ οἱ γραμματεῖς, *hoi archiereis kai hoi grammateis*; cf. 8:31; 10:33; 11:18, 27; 14:43, 53; 15:1, 31) to seize Jesus and kill him, already referred to in 3:6; 11:18; and 12:12, now comes to a climax. Mark gives a precise chronological designation at this point. "It was two days before the Passover and the Feast of Unleavened Bread." Up to the Passion Narrative, the only temporal designation is in 9:2, but in the Passion Narrative we encounter a number of them (14:12, 17; 15:1, 25, 33, 34, 42; 16:1, 2). To understand this and the other temporal designations that follow, we must remember that in the Jewish reckoning of time a day was reckoned from sunset to sunset (from 6 p.m. to 6 p.m.), not from midnight to midnight (12 a.m. to 12 a.m.; R. Brown 1994: 2.1352–53). Thus the third hour (15:25), sixth hour, and ninth hour (15:33, 34) refer to hours from 6 a.m. onward (9 a.m., noon, and 3 p.m.). The Feast of Unleavened Bread was a celebration lasting seven days (Exod. 12:15–20; 34:18; Num. 28:17), from the fifteenth to the twenty-first of Nisan. It commemorated the exodus of Israel from Egypt, when during their deliverance the Israelites ate unleavened bread. The Passover occurred on the first day of the Feast of Unleavened Bread, and they are mentioned together in 2 Chron. 35:17 (cf. Josephus, *Ant.* 14.2.1 §21; 17.9.3 §213). The Passover celebrated the passing of the death angel over the homes of the Israelites because the blood of the Passover lamb had been smeared on the doorposts and lintels of their homes. Thus that night the firstborn males of Israel were spared, whereas the firstborn males of Egypt were killed, and this finally led to the deliverance of the Israelites from Egypt (Exod. 11:1–13:22; Num. 9:2–14; Deut. 16:1–8). The Passover had to be celebrated in Jerusalem and was the nation's most important religious festival.

The expression μετὰ δύο ἡμέρας (lit. "after two days") is not as precise as we might think. It can be understood inclusively; compare how "after three days" (μετὰ τρεῖς ἡμέρας) in 8:31; 9:31; 10:34 refers to a time period beginning the day before the Sabbath (15:42)—late Friday afternoon (day 1), Friday 6 p.m. to Saturday 6 p.m. (day 2), and Saturday 6 p.m. to Sunday 6 a.m. (the first day of the week, our Sunday morning; 16:1, day 3). The Passover meal was eaten on the fifteenth of Nisan (from Thursday 6 p.m. to Friday 6 p.m. in AD 30). Understood inclusively, "after two days," that is, "the day after," would mean that 14:1 refers to the thirteenth of Nisan (from Tuesday 6 p.m. to Wednesday 6 p.m.; Hooker 1991: 325–26; Gundry 1993: 801; J. Edwards 2002: 411; Donahue and Harrington 2002: 384; France 2002: 548). If "after two days" is interpreted exclusively, then this would refer to the twelfth of Nisan (from Monday 6 p.m. to Tuesday 6 p.m.). A related question involves whether Mark is thinking of the more traditional dating of the Passover, which involved the eating of the Passover on the fifteenth of Nisan or the day of the sacrificing of the Passover lambs and the searching of the houses for leaven, which took place on the eve of the Passover or the fourteenth of Nisan (see 14:12). It is not possible to be dogmatic as to the exact day being referred in 14:1. It was probably either from Tuesday 6 p.m. to Wednesday 6 p.m. (the thirteenth of Nisan; more likely) or from Monday 6 p.m. to Tuesday 6 p.m. (the twelfth of Nisan; less likely). If the former is true, 14:1 took place sometime Wednesday morning or afternoon.

The opponents of Jesus realize that Jesus must be seized[2] "by subterfuge" or stealth. The reason for this is given in 14:2 by Mark, the omniscient editor, who knows the thinking of the chief priests and scribes. To seize Jesus openly would cause a riot "by" (an ablative of source) the people, for Jesus was popular with the people (11:7–10, 18c; 12:12, 37b). The Passover was an especially dangerous time for the possibility of such riots (Josephus, *Ant.* 17.9.3 §§213–15), for the city, swollen perhaps fourfold in population by pilgrims, was filled with nationalistic feelings and hopes of deliverance from the bondage of the Romans due to their reliving the story of the exodus in the Passover celebration. As a result, both Roman and Jewish officials were extremely sensitive concerning this situation and sought to avoid anything that might ignite a riot. Thus the chief priests and scribes did not seek actively to seize Jesus at the Passover even by subterfuge. This would change, however, by the opportunity provided by one of Jesus's disciples, Judas Iscariot (14:10–11; Hooker 1991: 326).

14:3–5 The account of the woman's anointing of Jesus consists of four parts: (1) the description of the anointing (14:3), (2) the rebuke of the woman's act by "some" (14:4–5), (3) Jesus's defense of the woman's anointing (14:6–8), and

---

2. Donahue and Harrington (2002: 385) point out that for most readers the word "arrest" suggests various legal procedures (obtaining a warrant, etc.) leading up to an "arrest." Mark refers here more to a lynch mob seeking to seize Jesus and kill him. The trial that follows is understood by Mark as seeking to accumulate evidence in order to justify what they have already agreed on doing, killing Jesus. It is not understood as an attempt to gather and weigh evidence to see whether Jesus is guilty. Thus "seize" (lit. "having seized") describes their desire better than "arrest."

(4) his memorializing of what the woman did (14:9). The incident takes place in Bethany (modern El-Azariyeh), where Jesus apparently stayed during his time in Judea (11:1, 11, 12). Bethany was located about two miles east of Jerusalem, on the lower eastern slope of the Mount of Olives. The host is Simon the leper. Since lepers (see 1:40) were isolated from society to prevent the spread of the disease, Simon's hosting a banquet meal (indicated by Jesus's "reclining to eat," κατακειμένου, *katakeimenou*) presupposes that he had been healed of his leprosy (J. Edwards 2002: 412–13), possibly by Jesus himself (cf. 1:40–45).[3] A less likely view is that he became a leper after this incident. During the banquet an unnamed woman[4] brazenly entered the dining area carrying a sealed alabaster jar. Whether the jar was made of alabaster itself or of some other semiprecious, translucent material is uncertain. It was a small jar without handles, used for holding precious perfume/ointment (Pliny, *Nat. Hist.* 13.3.19). Within the jar was a very expensive perfume, "nard" (cf. Song 1:12; also 4:13), which was derived from a plant native to India (Donahue and Harrington 2002: 386). Its purity is emphasized by the term "pure" (πιστικῆς, *pistikēs*). To access the costly perfume, the woman broke the neck of the alabaster jar and poured the entire amount on Jesus's head. For examples of similar anointings in the OT, compare Exod. 29:4–7; 1 Sam. 10:1; 2 Kings 9:1–6; also Pss. 23:5; 133:2. The breaking of the alabaster jar was not because this was the only way of pouring out the perfume, for it could have been poured out in the same manner as it was poured into the jar (Gundry 1993: 813). Its "breaking" (συντρίψασα, *syntripsasa*) dramatizes the total outpouring of this valuable perfume, container and all, for Jesus. Hooker (1991: 329) points out that such ointment jars, when used for anointing the dead, were often purposely broken and left in the tomb.

"Some" (τινές, *tines*) present (the disciples in Matt. 26:8; Judas Iscariot in John 12:4) become indignant (ἀγανακτοῦντες, *aganaktountes*). In Mark 10:14 this same verb is used to describe Jesus's being indignant at the disciples, and in 10:41 it is used to describe the ten disciples being indignant at James and John. Although Mark frequently recalls the failure of the disciples (see the summary at 6:45–52 and "The Disciples" under "Theological Emphases" in the introduction), he does not do so here. The anonymity of the "some" is not to protect the disciples but to focus the account totally on the objection itself (Painter 1997: 182) and to emphasize the christological significance of the woman's action. Thus Mark is content simply to say that "some" people present were indignant over the "waste" of the perfume. "Waste" is a better translation of ἀπώλεια (*apōleia*) than "destruction" (the usual meaning of this Greek word), for the perfume was not destroyed. It remained perfume on the head of Jesus, as its aroma would have made apparent.

3. The Temple Scroll (11QTemple[a] 46.17–18) indicates that lepers lived east of Jerusalem.

4. In John 12:3 she is Mary, the sister of Martha and Lazarus (12:2). The tradition that the unnamed woman, called a "sinner" in the parallel account in Luke (7:39), was Mary Magdalene dates from the fourth century.

The explanation for this indignation involves two considerations. The first consists of the value of the jar and its contents (14:5a). It was worth over three hundred denarii, or a year's wages for the average working man (cf. the wage of a denarius for a day's work in Matt. 20:2). The second consideration builds upon the first and raises the issue of what could have been done with the three hundred denarii. This could have helped many poor people. Passover, of all times in the year, was a time in which the poor were to be remembered (*m. Pesaḥ.* 10.1; cf. John 13:29; W. Lane 1974: 493). The idea that "some" were thinking of the financial needs of the new government that Jesus would soon inaugurate (Evans 2001: 361) is highly speculative. It furthermore ignores what the text itself says could have been done with the money that the perfume would have brought—it could have been given to the poor (14:5b).

14:6–8   Jesus's defense of the woman, "But . . ." (14:6), involves a command (Leave her alone, ἄφετε αὐτήν, *aphete autēn*), a question (Why are you troubling her? τί αὐτῇ κόπους παρέχετε; *ti autē kopous parechete?* lit. "making trouble for her"; for the terminology, cf. Luke 11:7; 18:5; Gal. 6:17), and a statement ("She has done a good thing [lit. 'worked a good work'; see 2:4] for me"). The "good" or "honorable" (Donahue and Harrington 2002: 387) thing that the woman has done has been interpreted in several ways. Some suggest that it is an act of charity along the lines of Ps. 41:1 (Danker 1966; W. Lane 1974: 494). She has shown kindness to the poor Jesus of Nazareth. This is unlikely, however, for the criticism of the woman in 14:5 contrasts her action to Jesus with helping the poor (Evans 2001: 361). Her good deed is explained differently by Jesus in 14:8b. Jesus states concerning the poor that they are always present (cf. Deut. 15:11). This in no way minimizes the importance of ministering to the poor, which was clearly a vital concern of Jesus and Mark (10:21; cf. Luke 4:18; 7:22; 14:13, 21; 19:8; etc.), as 14:7b indicates. The statement "Whenever you want you can do [something] good for them" (ὅταν θέλητε δύνασθε αὐτοῖς εὖ ποιῆσαι, *hotan thelēte dynasthe autois eu poiēsai*) emphasizes the continual opportunity and necessity to help the poor (cf. *b. Šabb.* 63a: "For the poor will never cease out of the land"). It does not suggest that if one wanted to do something for the poor, one could not do so. On the contrary, by making the action done to Jesus an exception, the account makes concern for the poor obligatory (Painter 1997: 182). The poor will continue to be present, but the opportunity to minister to Jesus was limited. It involved only hours![5] As to the woman, she did the only thing that "she was able to do" (lit. "what she had"). She is concerned for no one and nothing but Jesus alone; like Mary in Luke 10:38–42, the unnamed woman chose the best thing she could do with her perfume. As in Mark 2:18–20, there is a contrast between required religious duties (fasting and almsgiving) and the "now" of Jesus's presence. The current "now," a short period, causes Jesus's followers to act in unusual ways (Hooker 1991: 329; France 2002: 554). The unnamed woman, knowing

---

5. Donahue and Harrington (2002: 387) point out that 14:7c constitutes another "Passion prediction."

that to "love the Lord your God with all your heart, and with all your soul, and with all your mind, and with all your strength" (12:29) is the first commandment (12:29; cf. Matt. 22:38), expresses her love to God's Son by this lavish act of love and devotion.

In 14:8b Jesus interprets what the woman has done. What she did was clearly more than a customary anointing of a guest at a feast (Pss. 23:5; 141:5; cf. Luke 7:46), for none of the other guests was anointed. Some suggest that the woman's action was motivated by a desire to anoint Jesus as the Messiah (Elliott 1974: 107; Evans 2001: 359, 360; cf. Donahue and Harrington 2002: 388, who give this as one of the multiple reasons for the anointing). Several factors argue against this interpretation. For one, the words translated "anoint" (μυρίσαι, *myrisai*) in 14:8 and "poured" (κατέχεεν, *katecheen*) in 14:3 are not the ones normally used to describe the anointing of a king. The customary word for "anoint" is χρίω (*chriō*; from which we get *Christ*), found in Luke 4:18, where Jesus says, "The Spirit of the Lord is upon me because he has anointed me." Also, such an anointing would involve oil (1 Sam. 10:1; 2 Kings 9:1–13), not perfume (Gundry 1993: 813; J. Edwards 2002: 416). On the other hand, perfume was used for burial purposes (Witherington 2002: 367). For Mark, the meaning of the anointing is explained in 14:8b: the woman anointed Jesus's body beforehand (lit. "she has anticipated to anoint") for burial. That she was aware of Jesus's imminent death and consciously sought to prepare his body beforehand for burial (cf. *m. Šabb.* 23.5) is unlikely (V. Taylor 1952: 533; Cranfield 1959: 415; France 2002: 550). Mark, however, states that her loving act did serve this purpose.[6]

The story of the anointing concludes with Jesus's words emphasized by the opening "Truly" (ἀμήν, *amēn*). The language of this saying is clearly Markan, but this does not mean that it is a de novo creation of the evangelist. The absence of the woman's name in a saying that speaks of her deed being forever remembered argues for its authenticity (Evans 2001: 362). The "Truly," which is characteristic of Jesus's utterances (see 3:28–30), also argues in favor of its authenticity. This statement—along with 14:7 (cf. also 13:24–27 and 14:25), in which Jesus states that his followers will not always have him present with them but they will always have the poor—indicates that Mark and Jesus envisioned an interval of time between Jesus's death and the parousia in which ministering to the poor and preaching the gospel throughout the inhabited world would take place (Cranfield 1959: 417–18). During this period the good deed of the woman would be forever remembered as this account in the Gospels was read and proclaimed (cf. *b. B. Bat.* 21a; *m. Yoma* 3.9). The woman will

14:9

---

6. Some scholars seek to explain the interpretation of 14:8b as a rectification of what was lacking in the actual burial of Jesus (15:45–47; Nineham 1963: 372; Elliott 1974: 106). Yet most readers of Mark would not think that something was missing at the burial of Jesus. If there was, this would have been taken care of by the women in 16:1ff. Hooker (1991: 330) rightly points out that the resurrection faith of the early church would not have seen any need for a proper preparation for Jesus's burial. What purpose would it have served? He would rise from the dead in less than two days!

be remembered, not because of her name, which is unimportant, but for her act (Hooker 1991: 330) of service to Jesus Christ, the Son of God.

14:10–11 In these verses, Mark returns to the plot to kill Jesus (see 14:1–2) and completes his sandwich. What was lacking for the chief priests in order that they could seize Jesus by subterfuge is now serendipitously provided by Judas Iscariot (see 3:16–19), one of the Twelve.[7] The reader is well aware of Jesus's selection of the Twelve and that Judas Iscariot was one of them, both from what they have already read in 3:14–19 and from the Christian tradition they had been taught. The historicity of Judas Iscariot and his betrayal of Jesus is guaranteed by the fact that the early church would hardly have created a character who, as one of the Twelve, betrayed Jesus. The story of Jesus's betrayal by one of the Twelve, whom Jesus promised would sit on twelve thrones and judge the twelve tribes of Israel, would be a most unlikely church creation. The account of Judas's replacement in Acts 1:15–26 is also better understood as a historical incident than as a myth built on top of another myth.

Numerous speculations exist as to why Judas betrayed Jesus. Was it because when Jesus spoke of his death in 14:7–8, Judas became disillusioned and finally gave up hope that Jesus was the messianic deliverer who would free Israel from the Romans? Or was it because he wanted to assist Jesus in his offering himself as a ransom for many (10:45), and he was the only disciple who loved him enough to assist him in this by betraying him to the chief priests (so Kazantzakis 1960: 411–25 [chap. 28]; cf. also the mid-second-century apocryphal Gospel of Judas). Surely the latter is totally refuted by Jesus's words in 14:21: "For the Son of Man goes just as it has been written concerning him, but woe to that man by whom the Son of Man is betrayed. [It would have been] better for him if he had never been born." Such a fictional and romantic explanation of Judas's action is shipwrecked on 14:21 and the many references to Judas's "betraying" Jesus (Matt. 10:4; 26:14–16, 21–25, 46–50; Mark 14:10–11, 18, 21, 41–42, 44; Luke 6:16; 22:3–16, 47–48; John 6:71; 12:4; 13:2, 21–30; 18:2–5; Acts 1:15–26; etc.). As to Judas having become disillusioned and betraying Jesus as a result, there is no evidence for this, and it is ultimately only speculation. Another suggestion is that Judas betrayed Jesus for money. This is stated in Matt. 26:15 (cf. John 12:6), but it is not found in Mark. We must acknowledge that no clear explanation is given in Mark as to why Judas chose to betray Jesus. In the sovereign plan of God, he does so,[8] but his personal reasoning and thinking was either not known to Mark or considered unimportant for the telling of the story.

---

7. France (2002: 557) sees the "one" (εἷς, *heis*) as serving to contrast Judas from the rest of the Twelve.

8. Note "For the Son of Man goes just as it has been written concerning him" (14:21a); and cf. the divine necessity in the δεῖ (*dei*) of 8:31, which 9:31, 10:33–34, and 10:45 assume (cf. also 1 Cor. 15:3 and Acts 2:23). In Luke 22:3 and John 13:2, 27, Satan is seen as causing Judas to betray Jesus. Nevertheless, in all these passages the personal responsibility of Judas for what he did is not ignored or minimized, as Mark 14:21 indicates.

As to what Judas betrayed, this is reasonably clear. Although some suggest that what Judas betrayed was the "messianic secret" (i.e., that Jesus was privately claiming to his disciples that he was the Messiah; Schweitzer 1910: 396; E. Sanders 1985: 309; cf. also Evans 2001: 365 and France 2002: 557, who suggest that this was part of what Judas betrayed), this finds little support from the text itself. Judas's absence from the trial of Jesus (14:55–65), where such evidence was desperately sought, argues strongly against this (Hooker 1991: 331). What Judas betrayed to the religious leaders was how Jesus could be seized by stealth while away from his support base, the people. Judas supplied this information because he knew where Jesus would spend the night of the Passover. After the Passover was eaten in Jerusalem, he would spend the night on the Mount of Olives, where he could be seized apart from the crowds. This information delighted the chief priests, and Judas's promise of betrayal was sealed by an unspecified sum of money (lit. "silver"). (In Matt. 26:15 and 27:3, 9 it is specified as thirty pieces of silver.) The money serves less as a motive for Judas's betraying Jesus than as a sealing of the agreement (France 2002: 556). Thus from then on, Judas sought an opportunity to "betray" (παραδοῖ, *paradoi*; cf. 3:19; 9:31; 10:33; 14:10–11, 18, 21, 41–42, 44) Jesus. This betrayal involves not what Jesus is teaching (the "messianic secret"), but rather finding an "opportunity" (εὐκαίρως, *eukairōs*) to betray him. If Judas betrayed "information," this could have been done at his first meeting with the chief priests. What he betrayed was still future and required the presence of an opportunity to do so. This is most easily understood as betraying the time and place (John 18:2) where the religious leadership could seize Jesus apart from the people (cf. 14:48–49; Luke 22:6; France 2002: 557). The Jewish people were clearly the major stumbling block in the chief priests' desire to kill Jesus. Thus one would totally misunderstand Mark if one blamed the Jewish people for the death of Jesus. It was the religious leadership and the Roman authorities who were the immediate cause of this death, but the ultimate cause is humanity; God sent his Son to be a ransom for its sin (10:45).

Summary

Within this Markan sandwich at least three Markan themes are present. One involves the contrast between "insiders" and "outsiders" and the reversal of positions brought about by the coming of Jesus. Those who were considered by society as insiders to God's kingdom, the chief priests and scribes, are portrayed as rejecting the kingdom of God and seeking Jesus's death (14:1–2, 10–11). They are now outsiders, who not only refuse to enter the kingdom of God but also seek to hinder others from entering it (cf. Matt. 23:4, 13). On the other hand, those often thought of as outsiders, a leper (14:3; cf. 1:40–45) and an unnamed woman (14:3–9), reveal by their actions that they are now insiders and have entered the kingdom of God and possess eternal life (10:17, 24). Like other women in Mark (cf. 5:25–34; 7:24–30; 12:41–44; 15:40–41, 47; cf. also 16:1ff.), this unnamed woman serves as a model of faith (Beavis 1988). The sandwiching of her action (14:3–9) between that of the chief priests and scribes (14:1–2, 10–11) heightens the contrast between her great act of love and the treachery of Judas Iscariot and the murderous hatred of the religious leaders. Whereas for her faith she sacrifices her money (more than three hundred denarii), Judas Iscariot sacrifices his faith for money (cf. Heil 1990: 313). As a result, her action is memorialized. If one omits the self-contained Olivet Discourse (13:1–37), we have two pericopes side by side (12:41–44; 14:3–9) in which two unnamed women, known only to God, serve as eternal examples of love and devotion to God and his Son, Jesus Christ. Both show, in contrast to Judas and the chief priests and others such as the rich young ruler (10:17–31), what it means to follow God/Jesus with singleness of heart.

A second Markan emphasis found in this passage involves God's sovereign control of history. The anointing by the woman points to Jesus's imminent death. Mark, however, does not portray this as a cruel twist of fate or as a tragedy, but rather as the fulfilling of God's plan for Jesus, the Son of God. What is about to happen is divinely ordained (note the δεῖ of 8:31). The Son of Man came for the very purpose of offering his life as a ransom for many (10:45), and this would be accomplished by his pouring out his blood (14:24) to establish a new covenant. Mark has prepared his readers for Jesus's forthcoming death (2:18–20; 3:6; 8:31; 9:9, 31; 10:33–34, 45; 11:18; 12:12), so that it would not catch them by surprise. The choice that Judas made, for which he is culpable (14:21), lies within God's sovereign providence and control of history. As in the case of Pharaoh (Exod. 7–14), Judas Iscariot's evil and hard heart will serve the divine purpose. In reality Judas and the chief priests are "only subsidiary characters in the real drama" (Hooker 1991: 330) in which God and his Son are the main ones.

A final Markan emphasis in this passage involves Christology. Concerning Jesus's statement in 14:7, "You always have the poor with you, and whenever you want you can do [something] good for them, but *me* you will not always have [with you]," J. Edwards (2002: 415) comments, "We can, perhaps, justify such a statement from the mouth of God, but it is hard to imagine a justification for such a statement from a mere mortal." In placing himself above concern for the poor, Jesus is placing himself above the commandment to "love your neighbor as yourself" (12:31). Once again, we are forced to ask, "Who is this man who says and does such things?" (cf. 4:41). In the Markan context this has already been answered in the opening verse of the Gospel. This man is "Jesus Christ, the Son of God" (1:1). But he is the Christ–Son of God who comes to serve and minister to the most basic and important of all human needs. He comes to give his life as a ransom for the salvation of humanity (10:45).

Additional Notes

14:4. A few MSS replace "some" with "the disciples" and add "saying" (A C² D Θ W f¹ f¹³ lat), but this is probably due to the influence of the parallel in Matt. 26:8.

14:4. εἰς τί ἡ ἀπώλεια αὕτη τοῦ μύρου γέγονεν; is lit. "Why has this waste of ointment taken place?" τοῦ μύρου is lacking in W and f¹.

14:7. "Me" is emphatic by its location.

14:9. The δέ is best left untranslated here since it functions simply as a connective.

14:10. Numerous MSS add the article ὁ before Ἰσκαριώθ. Its omission in ℵ B D and the greater likelihood that later copyists would add the article in order to balance the article after Ἰσκαριώθ argue for its being a later addition.

B. The Last Supper and Jesus's Prediction of the Denial of the Disciples (14:12–31)

After the Markan sandwich in 14:1–11, in which the anointing of Jesus (14:3–9) is wedged between developments in the plot to kill Jesus (14:1–2 and 10–11), we have another Markan sandwich. This consists of the Last Supper (14:22–25) sandwiched between the prediction of Judas's betrayal (14:17–21) and the denial of the disciples (14:26–31). This new sandwich is introduced by the preparation of the Passover meal (14:12–16), which serves as the setting for the Last Supper. The description of the preparations for the Passover meal recalls the preparations for Jesus's entry into Jerusalem in 11:1–6, and the wording in several places is identical:

1. "And he sends two of his disciples and says to them, 'Go into the city/village and'" (14:13; 11:1b–2b—many words in Greek are identical: ἀποστέλλει δύο τῶν μαθητῶν αὐτοῦ καὶ λέγει αὐτοῖς· ὑπάγετε εἰς τὴν πόλιν/κώμην καί, *apostellei dyo tōn mathētōn autou kai legei autois, hypagete eis tēn polin/kōmēn kai*)
2. "Say . . . 'The Teacher/Lord'" (εἴπατε . . . Ὁ διδάσκαλος/κύριος, *eipate . . . ho didaskalos/kyrios*; 14:14a; 11:3c)
3. "And they entered/departed . . . and found" (καὶ ἦλθον/ἀπῆλθον . . . καὶ εὗρον, *kai ēlthon/apēlthon . . . kai heuron*; 14:16b; 11:4)
4. "just as he/Jesus said . . . and" (καθὼς εἶπεν [ὁ Ἰησοῦς] καί, *kathōs eipen [ho Iēsous] kai*; 14:16b; 11:6a; see V. Taylor 1952: 536; Evans 2001: 370)

This similarity in wording does not require that one or both of these two accounts are Markan creations but suggests that Mark in retelling these traditions used his own vocabulary and style (V. Taylor 1952: 536).

In Mark and the other Synoptic Gospels, the Last Supper is clearly understood as being associated with a Passover meal (14:1, 12 [2×], 14, 16; Matt. 26:2, 17, 18, 19; Luke 22:1, 7, 8, 11, 13, 15; cf. 1 Cor. 5:7). Later that same night, the events of Gethsemane (14:32–42), the betrayal of Judas (14:43–50), the trial before the Sanhedrin (14:51–65), and Peter's denial take place (14:66–72). In the morning of that day (15:1), Jesus is brought before Pontius Pilate, condemned to death (15:2–20), and crucified (15:21–39). In the afternoon (15:33, 34) he dies, and late in the afternoon toward evening he is buried (15:40–47). All 14:17–15:47 is portrayed as taking place on the fifteenth of Nisan (i.e., between 6 p.m. Thursday and 6 p.m. Friday). The next day was the Sabbath. The chronology of events in John, however, is different. According to John, the trial of Jesus took place *before* the Passover (18:28; cf. 13:1), and he was crucified on the eve of the Passover (19:14, 31), when the Passover lambs were being slain in preparation for the Passover meal (i.e., the fourteenth of Nisan). This apparent conflict in chronology between the Passover and the death of Jesus in the Synoptic Gospels and in John is one of the most, if not *the* most, debated chronological problems in all of the Bible.

Numerous attempts have been made to explain the difference in chronology (France 1986: 43–54; R. Brown 1994: 2.1361–73). These options can be arranged as follows:

1. The Synoptic Gospels are correct. The Last Supper was a Passover meal, and the term "Passover" (πάσχα, *pascha*) in John 18:28 refers not to the Passover meal itself but to other feasts associated with the Feast of Unleavened Bread (2 Chron. 30:22; *m. Pesaḥ.* 6.3; 9.5; B. Smith 1991: 40–44).
2. John is correct. Jesus did not eat the customary Passover meal with his disciples, because he knew that he would be dead before then. Therefore, he anticipated the meal and celebrated it earlier (V. Taylor 1952: 664–67; I. Marshall 1980: 67–78; France 2002: 560–62). John 18:28 refers to the time of the actual Passover meal.
3. Both the Synoptic Gospels and John are correct (cf. R. Brown 1994: 2.1362–64):
   3.1 There was confusion that year as to the beginning of the month of Nisan, and the Pharisees (Jesus and the Synoptic Gospels) thought that the month started a day earlier than the Sadducees (the priests and John's Gospel)[1] did.
   3.2 There were so many lambs that needed to be slaughtered for the Passover that it took two days for this to be accomplished (Chenderlin 1975). The first day the lambs were slaughtered for pilgrims coming to Jerusalem (Jesus and the disciples—so the Synoptic Gospels), and the second day they were slaughtered for the residents of Judea and Jerusalem (the priests—so John; Pickl 1946: 121–22).
   3.3 In Jesus's day two separate calendars were operational in Israel. The one was a lunar calendar followed by most of the people, and the other was a solar calendar followed by the Qumran community, the book of Jubilees, and Jesus and the disciples (Jaubert 1965; cf. R. Brown 1994: 2.1366–68).
   3.4 That year the Passover fell on the Sabbath, and the Pharisees decided to celebrate it a day earlier (Jesus and the Synoptic Gospels), whereas the Sadducees decided to celebrate it at

---

1. Hoehner (1977: 86–90) argues for a variation of this in which the Pharisees (and Galileans) used a calendar in which the day began at sunrise, and the Sadducees (and Judeans) used a calendar in which the day began at sunset.

the normal time (John 18:28 and the priests; Chwolson 1908: 20–44). Compare also Shepherd (1961: esp. 125), who argues that Jews in Palestine observed the Passover that year on the Sabbath (John), whereas Dispersion Jews observed it on Friday (Mark and the other Synoptic Gospels).

Unfortunately, there is little evidence for 3.1, 3.2, and 3.4, and most of the reasoning is speculative. Explanation 3.3 has some support, but the idea that Jesus and the disciples followed the solar calendar of the Essene community is speculative and unlikely. At the present time no truly satisfactory explanation has come forth.

A number of indications within the Gospel accounts support the view that the Last Supper was associated with the Passover meal (Jeremias 1966: 41–62; I. Marshall 1980: 58–62):

1. The Passover meal had to be eaten within the walled city of Jerusalem (Deut. 16:2; *m. Pesaḥ.* 7.9; *t. Pesaḥ.* 8.2; Sifre Num. §69), and that day Jesus and the disciples did not return to Bethany as usual to eat and spend the night (cf. 11:11, 12, 19, 27; 14:3) but ate the Last Supper within the walled city of Jerusalem (14:13, 17, 26).
2. The night of the Passover had to be spent in Jerusalem. Since the great crowd of pilgrims[2] could not find lodging within the walled city, the rabbis, to accommodate the large influx of pilgrims, ruled that the night could be spent in "greater Jerusalem," which included the slopes of the surrounding hills facing Jerusalem. Consequently, that night Jesus and the disciples did not return to Bethany but spent the night in the Garden of Gethsemane on the western slope of the Mount of Olives, facing Jerusalem (Jeremias 1969: 101n4).
3. The disciples and Jesus ate in a "reclining position" (ἀνακειμένων, *anakeimenōn*; 14:18; *m. Pesaḥ.* 10.1; Bahr 1970: 190–91). It was customary to recline at banquets (Matt. 22:10, 11; 26:7; Luke 22:27; cf. also Mark 2:15; 14:3; John 12:2; 13:23, 28; and esp. Luke 7:37, which can be visualized only if Jesus was reclining and the woman was standing behind him), and the Passover was a banquet meal.
4. The people of Israel normally ate two meals a day. The first was in the late morning (10–11 a.m.) and the second in the late afternoon. The Last Supper was eaten in the evening (14:17;

---

2. Estimates of the normal population of the city of Jerusalem in Jesus's day vary considerably. Jeremias (1969: 83n24) suggests about 55,000, as does Wilkinson (1974). Murphy-O'Connor (1998: 34) estimates that at Passover about 120,000–140,000 pilgrims would be added.

1 Cor. 11:23), and the Passover had to be eaten at night (Exod. 12:8; Jub. 49.12).

5. The Last Supper ended with the singing of hymns (14:26), and the Passover ended with singing (probably the last part of the Hallel Psalms [Pss. 114/115–18]).

6. While celebrating the Passover, it was customary to interpret the meaning and significance of the various elements in the meal (Exod. 12:26–27), and this was done with the elements of the Last Supper. The interpretation of the Last Supper furthermore builds upon the analogy of the interpretation of the elements of the Passover (covenant, blood of the Passover lamb/Christ our Passover [cf. 1 Cor. 5:7], a call for continual remembrance, etc.).

7. The drinking of four cups of wine in celebration of God's four promises in Exod. 6:6–7 was part of the Passover celebration (*m. Pesaḥ.* 10.1), and the Last Supper has as one of its two basic elements a cup. Furthermore, wine was generally drunk only on special occasions, such as the celebration of the Passover (Jeremias 1966: 50–52).

Although none of these arguments is conclusive to prove that the Last Supper was part of a Passover meal, together they strongly support this conclusion. However, several objections have been raised against this interpretation. One is that the accounts of the Last Supper do not refer to the eating of the Passover lamb or other parts of the Passover meal (the bitter herbs, the paste or haroseth that reminded the participants of the bricks they made in their captivity in Egypt, the bowl of salt water, etc.; Evans 2001: 372). Yet the writers of the Synoptic Gospels have already clearly stated that this was a Passover meal (14:1, 12, 14, 16; Matt. 26:2, 17, 18, 19; Luke 22:1, 7, 8, 11, 13, 15), and the focus of the evangelists is not on the Passover meal and the symbols of the old covenant rite but on the new. It is therefore to be expected that the focus of the Last Supper would be on the new festival that supersedes the old. Some have also suggested that Luke 22:15–16 indicates that Jesus's desire to eat the Passover went unfilled, so that the Last Supper was not part of a Passover meal (Evans 2001: 372). However, this is certainly not how Luke interpreted these verses, which he clearly understood as being spoken during a Passover meal (Luke 22:1, 7, 8, 11, 13, 15). "This Passover" in Luke 22:15 ("I have greatly desired to eat this Passover with you") is therefore best interpreted as a reference by Jesus to the present Passover meal that he and the disciples were eating. Finally, the argument that the expression "Christ, our Passover," in 1 Cor. 5:7 requires that Jesus must have been crucified on the fourteenth of Nisan, before the Passover celebration at the time when the Passover lambs were slain (as John seems to suggest), is unconvincing, for the expression could just as easily have arisen if Jesus had died during the Passover celebration. It does not require that he died when the Passover lambs were slain.[3]

The extent to which scholars see the hand of Mark in this account varies considerably. Pryke (1978: 22, 146–47, 171–72) sees the evangelist's hand in 14:12a, 17–21, 22a, 25a, 26, 27–31. Gnilka (1979: 231, 235, 252) sees it in 14:12a, 17, 18 ("and eating" and "one eating with me"), 20 ("one of the Twelve"), 27c–d, and 28. Pesch (1980b: 345–46; 1996: 17), on the other hand, sees 14:12–26 as a pre-Markan passion prediction with little Markan editorial work. Whether, and the degree to which, one believes that Mark used a pre-Markan Passion Narrative in writing this section of Mark will greatly affect the extent to which one sees the hand of Mark in the present account. The sandwich of 14:22–25 between 14:17–21 and 26–31 may very well be Markan (V. Taylor 1952: 539; J. Edwards 1989: 198, 211), but it is unlikely that Mark created the accounts of the prediction of Judas's betrayal and the disciples' denial. It is more likely that he used pre-Markan traditions, possibly already associated with the Last Supper, and arranged them according to his predilection into a sandwich or intercalation.

The present account has several ties to both the preceding and the following material. With respect to 14:1–11, it picks up and develops the theme of Judas's betrayal (cf. 14:10–11 and 14:17–21), and Jesus's anointing for his death (14:8) will be picked up in the words of the Last Supper, where Jesus describes his giving his life to seal a new covenant for many (14:22–25). These same themes will be picked up in the following account in which Jesus prays that, if possible, the Father will take the cup from him (14:36), for the consequences involved in his shedding his blood to inaugurate the new covenant (14:22–25) are so terrible that he asks if another way might be found. The betrayal of Judas begins to reach its terrible climax with his leading the representatives of the chief priests, scribes, and elders to the Garden of Gethsemane, where he knows Jesus and the disciples were planning to spend the night (14:42). The desertion of the disciples also begins to reveal itself: they fail to support Jesus in his agony three times (14:37, 40, 41), and they do not "watch out" (γρηγορέω, grēgoreō; 13:34, 35, 37; 14:34, 37, 38), so they will shortly desert and deny him.

Exegesis and Exposition

[12]And on the first day of [the Feast of] Unleavened Bread, when they were sacrificing the Passover lamb, his disciples say to him, "Where do you want us ⌜to go and prepare⌝, so that you might eat the Passover?" [13]And he [Jesus] sends two of his disciples and says to them, "Go into the city, and a man carrying a jar of water will meet you. Follow him, [14]and wherever he enters, say to the owner of the house, 'The Teacher says, "Where is my ⌜guest room⌝ where I may eat the Passover with my disciples?"'" [15]And he

---

3. For a more complete discussion of such objections, see Jeremias 1966: 62–84; I. Marshall 1980: 62–66.

will show you a large upper room furnished [and] ready. ⌜ ⌝ There make [everything] ready for us." ¹⁶And the disciples set out and entered the city and found [things] just as he told them, and they prepared the Passover.

¹⁷And when evening came, he [Jesus] arrives with the Twelve. ¹⁸And as they were reclining and eating, Jesus said, "Truly, I say to you that one of you will betray me, one who is eating with me." ¹⁹[And] they began to be distressed and to say to him, one after the other, "Surely it is not I, is it?" ²⁰And he said to them, "[It is] one of the Twelve, one who is dipping [bread] ⌜in the bowl⌝ with me. ²¹For the Son of Man goes just as it has been written concerning him, but woe to that man by whom the Son of Man is betrayed. [It would have been] ⌜better⌝ for him if he had never been born."

²²And while they were eating, ⌜he⌝ having taken bread and blessed [God *or* it], broke [it], gave [it] to them, and said, "Take, this is my body." ²³And having taken ⌜a cup⌝ [and] having given thanks, he gave [it] to them, and they all drank out of it. ²⁴And he said to them, "This is my blood of ⌜the covenant⌝ that is poured out for many. ²⁵Truly, I say to you that I will never again drink of the fruit of the vine until that day when I drink it new in the kingdom of God!"

²⁶And after singing, they went out to the Mount of Olives. ²⁷And Jesus says to them, "You will all fall away, because it is written, 'I will strike the shepherd, and the sheep will be scattered.' ²⁸But after ⌜I rise up⌝, I will go before you into Galilee." ²⁹But Peter said to him, "Even if all [the others] would fall away, I [will] not." ³⁰And Jesus says to him, "Truly, I say to you, ⌜Today⌝, this very night, before the cock crows twice, *you* will deny me three times. ³¹But he [Peter] vehemently ⌜was insisting⌝, "If it is necessary for me to die with you, I will never deny you." And all [the others] were saying ⌜the same thing⌝.

The first section (14:12–16) of the complex involving the Last Supper consists of the preparations for the Passover meal including (1) the time and setting (14:12), (2) Jesus's sending of the two disciples to prepare for the Passover along with the instructions as to where it should be prepared (14:13–15), and (3) the preparation of the Passover meal itself (14:16). The similarities between 14:13–16 and 11:1–6 are striking (see the introduction to this unit) and witness to Mark's tendency to use the same terminology when recording similar accounts (cf. 6:34–44 and 8:1–10; 7:31–37 and 8:22–26). Although some see this section as being legendary and a "fairy tale" (Nineham 1963: 376; Bultmann 1968: 263–64), it is difficult to conceive of it as ever having existed and circulated as an independent unit. It has no value apart from the celebration of the Passover meal, and no Passover meal is mentioned in our Gospels other than the present one, which took place "on the night in which Jesus was betrayed" (1 Cor. 11:23).

14:12

The temporal expression "on the first day of [the Feast of] Unleavened Bread, when they were sacrificing the Passover lamb" (τῇ πρώτῃ ἡμέρᾳ τῶν ἀζύμων, ὅτε τὸ πάσχα ἔθυον, *tē prōtē hēmera tōn azymōn, hote to pascha ethyon*) has elicited much discussion. Frequently in Mark the second temporal (or geographical) reference defines the first (1:32, 35; 4:35; 13:24; 14:30; 15:42; 16:2;

V. Taylor 1952: 536; Neirynck 1988: 45–53, 94–96). Technically the sacrifice of the Passover lamb took place on the fourteenth of Nisan along with the ritual search to remove all leaven from the house. The first day of the Feast of Unleavened Bread, which lasted seven days, was the fifteenth of Nisan, and this was the day in which the Passover meal was eaten. However, just as for many families today the celebration of Christmas begins on Christmas Eve, so the first day of the Feast of Unleavened Bread was popularly understood as beginning with the events of the fourteenth of Nisan. Compare Josephus (*J.W.* 2.1.3 §10; 5.3.1 §§98–99; *Ant.* 14.2.1 §21; 17.9.3 §213; 18.2.2 §29; 20.5.3 §106), who refers to the fourteenth of Nisan as the beginning of the Feast of Unleavened Bread.[4]

Although some scholars argue that "they were sacrificing" refers to Jesus and the disciples sacrificing the Passover lamb (Casey 1998: 223; Evans 2001: 373), it is best to interpret this as an example of one of Mark's many impersonal plurals (V. Taylor 1952: 47; see 1:21–22). In 14:12d–13 Jesus sends the two disciples (Peter and John, according to Luke 22:8) to prepare (ἑτοιμάσωμεν, *hetoimasōmen*) for the Passover; after they found the room furnished and ready (14:15a),[5] they then prepared the Passover meal (14:15b–16). This indicates that it was these two disciples, not Jesus and the entire twelve, who went to the temple to prepare the lamb for the Passover meal. The command to "Go into the city" is furthermore best understood as being uttered in Bethany (14:3), not in the temple (France 2002: 564; contra Casey 1998: 227). The reference to making all things ready in order that Jesus might eat the Passover focuses the readers' attention here and in all of 14:12–31 on Jesus. Although the Twelve/disciples[6] are involved in all that takes place, "everything centres on Jesus" (Hooker 1991: 334; cf. J. Edwards 2002: 420; cf. 1:1).

14:13–15 The instructions Jesus utters in these verses remind the reader of 11:2–6 and suggest that here, as in the procurement of the unridden colt on Palm Sunday, Jesus had prearranged having a room available to eat the Passover (W. Lane 1974: 499; Evans 2001: 373). This prearrangement is strongly implied by the two disciples being told to meet a man carrying a jar of water; the title "*The Teacher*" (ὁ διδάσκαλος, *ho didaskalos*), which indicates that Jesus was known to the owner of the house; a large room being available and ready in Jerusalem during the most crowded night of the year; the owner's lack of surprise

4. Another attempt at reconciling the twofold temporal designation is to see Mark as using the Roman understanding of time at this point, in which the day began and ended at midnight, so that the slaughtering of the Passover lambs took place in the afternoon (the 14th of Nisan), and the Feast of Unleavened Bread (the 15th of Nisan) took place the evening of the "same" day by the Roman reckoning of time (Witherington 2001: 371).

5. It is probably best to understand these two terms as synonymous and reflecting Mark's love of duality (Neirynck 1988: 80, 105).

6. In 14:12, 13, 14, and 16 we read of the "disciples"; in 14:17 and 20 we read of the "Twelve." Although some suggest that this indicates the use of two different sources, it may be that the reference to the "Twelve" is used in 14:17 and 20 because of the central role of Judas, who was "one of the Twelve" (cf. 3:14 and 19; 14:10) in 14:17–21.

by the disciples' request; and Jesus's words, "Where is *my* guest room?" (τὸ κατάλυμά μου, *to katalyma mou*). Prior arrangements are also suggested by the fact that Jesus knew where to go in Jerusalem in 14:17 to join Peter and John and eat the Passover. The two disciples are told to meet a man in a very crowded city, but he will be easy to find, for he will be carrying a jar of water. This would cause him to stand out, for carrying a jar of water was the work of women, and if a man carried water, it would usually be in an animal skin rather than a jar (V. Taylor 1952: 537; Donahue and Harrington 2002: 393). The clandestine nature of all this was probably to ensure that Jesus would have a time of privacy with his disciples to celebrate the Passover and institute the Last Supper (Hurtado 1983: 220–21; Pixner 1996: 88; contra Hooker 1991: 335). For Jesus's identification as "The Teacher," see 4:37–39. The guest room was a large upper room already "furnished [and] prepared," that is, the rugs, carpets, cushions, and couches for reclining were arranged, and short tables for the food were set up. All that was lacking was the food itself, and this the two disciples were told to prepare.

14:16 Upon following Jesus's instructions, the two disciples "found [things] just as [Jesus] told them" (εὗρον καθὼς εἶπεν αὐτοῖς, *heuron kathōs eipen autois*). This once again shows Jesus's mastery of the situation. He is in charge of what is taking place. The two disciples then prepared the Passover meal. This would include the Passover lamb (slaughtered, skinned, cleaned, and roasted over a fire), unleavened bread, a bowl of salt water, a bowl of bitter herbs, a fruit puree or haroseth, and enough wine[7] for each participant to drink four cups in celebration of God's fourfold blessing in Exod. 6:6–7 (see Bahr 1970: 190–202).

14:17–18 Verse 17 serves as a seam joining 14:17–31 to the preparations made by the two disciples for the celebration of the Passover (14:12–16). Although no mention is made of the Passover meal in 14:17–31, it is evident that for Mark the meal that follows (14:18, 20, 22–25) is the Passover, due to 14:12, 14, 16. That it was a Passover meal I have argued in the introduction to this unit. Jesus and the Twelve[8] join the other two disciples in the large upper room in the evening (the beginning hours of the fifteenth of Nisan). While "reclining" (ἀνακειμένων [*anakeimenōn*] indicates that the meal is festive and fits well the Passover setting of 14:12–16) and eating, Jesus announces that one of the Twelve will betray (παραδώσει, *paradōsei*; lit. "hand [him] over"; cf. 3:19; 9:31; 10:33 [2×], 14:10, 11, 18, 21, 41, 42, 44; also 1:14; 13:9, 11, 12; 15:1, 10, 15). The explanatory comment "one who is eating with me" emphasizes the heinous nature of this betrayal (cf. Ps. 41:9, which is quoted in John 13:18; Ps. 55:12–14; also 1QH 13.23–25). Although the reader has been aware since 3:19 (and perhaps even earlier due to their knowledge of the gospel traditions)

---

7. This was a mixture of wine and water (about one part wine to three parts water; Stein 1990: 233–38).

8. The term "Twelve" refers here to the ten members of the twelve disciples who did not go to prepare the Passover.

that Jesus would be betrayed by one of the Twelve, this is the first time that the Twelve are themselves made aware of it.

France (2002: 574) outlines the relationship of the three following predictions of Jesus and their fulfillment as follows:

> A Prediction of Judas's betrayal (14:18–21)
>   [The Passover meal (14:22–25)]
>   B Prediction of the disciples' desertion (14:26–28)
>   C Prediction of Peter's denial (14:29–31)
>   [Jesus prays in Gethsemane (14:32–42)]
> A′ Fulfillment of Judas's betrayal (14:43–49)
>   B′ Fulfillment of the disciples' desertion (14:50–52)
>   [The Sanhedrin "trial" (14:53–65)]
>   C′ Fulfillment of Peter's denial (14:66–72)

14:19–20 The response of the Twelve is one of shock and sadness. They are "distressed." (Cf. 10:22, the only other instance in which this word is found in Mark, where the rich young ruler leaves Jesus grieved because he chose his money over following Jesus.) One by one they ask, "Surely it is not I, is it?" The question expects a negative answer, as the Greek particle μήτι (*mēti*) indicates. Each hopes that Jesus will say, "No, it is not you." The anonymity of the betrayer, however, is maintained by Jesus. The betrayer is simply referred to as one of the Twelve[9] who is presently sharing Jesus's food.[10] In Matt. 26:25 Judas's question is answered affirmatively by Jesus, but it is assumed in Matthew that this was said privately and not overheard by the others, as the lack of response by the other disciples suggests (cf. John 13:25–30).

14:21 Jesus's concluding remark about his betrayal indicates that the fate awaiting him is according to the Scriptures ("as it has been written concerning him" [καθὼς γέγραπται περὶ αὐτοῦ, *kathōs gegraptai peri autou*]). Once again the reader is reminded that there is a divine necessity for Jesus's passion and death (8:31; 9:31; 10:33–34, 45). Exactly what Scripture is being referred to is not specified (cf. 14:49; also 1 Cor. 15:3, 4). It is unnecessary, however, to assume that the OT Scripture must have specifically referred to the Son of Man (contrast Evans 2001: 377), for Jesus used this title to refer to himself, and any Scripture that refers to his giving his life as a ransom for many or his being killed would qualify (cf. Isa. 53; Zech. 13:7 [cf. Mark 14:27]; Ps. 41:9; Dan. 9:26; etc.). Despite the fact that his death is divinely foreordained, Jesus adds a severe, twofold condemnation[11] upon the one who by his action fulfills the

---

9. J. Edwards (2002: 422n18, 424) suggests that "one of the Twelve" would be unnecessary if the Twelve were the only ones present at the meal.

10. Cranfield (1959: 424) suggests that the "bowl" refers to the bowl of bitter herbs that was part of the Passover meal.

11. We see in 14:18 ("one of you . . . one who . . ."), in 14:20 ("one of . . . one who is . . ."), and here ("woe to that man . . . better for him if . . .") examples of Mark's love of duality (cf. Neirynck 1988: 100).

divine necessity of Jesus's death: "Woe to that man . . . better for him if. . . ."[12] Such a severe condemnation forever refutes any and all attempts to exonerate Judas or to commend him for his action. Judas is clearly culpable for his horrific crime. Here the willful act of Judas is seen as standing side by side with the divine sovereignty of God, which directs history (cf. *m. 'Abot* 3.16). Jesus and the Gospel writers (Matt. 26:24; Luke 22:22; cf. also Matt. 18:7 and Luke 17:1) do not explain how human freedom and divine sovereignty exist together side by side, but they do not compromise one for the sake of the other. Both exist together (cf. John 19:11).

Many who maintain that the Last Supper was not part of a Passover meal **14:22** point out that there is no necessary connection in Mark between the account of the Last Supper in 14:22–25 and the preparations for the Passover in 14:12–16 (Evans 2001: 372, 385). In 1 Cor. 11:23–26 this is clearly true, but in the context of the regular celebration of the Lord's Supper among gentile Christians, it is to be expected that any original ties with the once-a-year Jewish Passover would gradually be diminished. In Mark, however, even though the elements of the Passover meal are not mentioned in 14:22–25, the Last Supper is intimately associated with a meal (14:22) that is festive in nature (14:18: "reclining and eating") and is expressly referred to as a Passover meal (14:12, 14, 16). As it stands, 14:22–25 forms a unity intimately connected to 14:17–21 and 26–31 (Pesch 1980b: 354, 377) and consists of (1) a blessing, distribution, and word about the bread (14:22); (2) a thanksgiving, distribution, and drinking of a common cup (14:23); (3) an interpretive word about the cup (14:24); and (4) Jesus's statement that he would not drink wine again until he did so in the kingdom of God (14:25).

The Passover meal began with a blessing over the group followed by the drinking of a cup of wine. Then the youngest child or member of the group would ask the question, "Why is this night different from other nights?" (*m. Pesaḥ.* 10.4). This was followed by the father or host (in this case Jesus) recounting the events of the Passover (cf. Deut. 26:5–9; cf., however, Saldarini 1984: 36, who places this after the meal). In this retelling, the symbolism of the various elements would be interpreted: Passover lamb—the blood of the sacrificial lamb that protected the people of Israel from the angel of death; unleavened bread—the quickness of God's deliverance; bowl of salt water—the tears shed in bondage and in crossing the Red Sea; bitter herbs—the bitterness of captivity; four cups of wine—the four promises of Exod. 6:6–7; and so on. Within the reliving of the Passover experience, the celebrants would recall the covenant that God made with Abraham and renewed with Isaac, Jacob, and Moses. The recounting of the glorious events of liberation in the Passover story ended with the drinking of a second cup of wine, which would mark the

---

12. For additional examples of such "woes" in the Gospels, cf. 13:17; Matt. 11:21; 18:7; 23:13–36; Luke 6:24–26; 11:42–52; 17:1; for such woes in the OT, cf. Isa. 5:8, 11, 18, 20–22; 28:1; Hos. 7:13; Amos 5:18; 6:4; Mic. 2:1. For examples of the expression "better . . . never to have been born," cf. 1 En. 38.2; 2 En. 41.2; *m. Ḥag.* 2.1.

beginning of the Passover meal itself. Toward the end of the meal, Jesus probably used the third cup of wine as part of the institution of the Last Supper, which speaks of the beginning of the (new) covenant. Toward midnight there would be the singing of the Hallel Psalms (114/115–18) and the drinking of the fourth cup of wine (Bahr 1970: 188, 198–200).

The first part of the Last Supper involves a blessing associated with the bread (cf. 6:41; 8:6). The term "bread" (ἄρτος, artos) is not the specific term used for "unleavened bread" (ἄζυμος, azymos) yet it is often used to refer to unleavened bread (Josephus, Ant. 3.6.6 §143; cf. §142; 3.10.7 §256) and is the designation the LXX uses to describe the unleavened showbread (Exod. 40:23; 1 Sam. 21:7; 1 Chron. 9:32; etc.). It is not specified whether Jesus "blessed" (εὐλογήσας, eulogēsas) the bread or God (Hooker 1991: 340; Donahue and Harrington 2002: 395). Unlike our present-day custom of "blessing the food" we eat, Jews in Jesus's day tended to "bless God" for the food they were about to eat. Compare m. Ber. 6.1: "Blessed are you, O Lord our God, King of the universe, who brings forth bread from the earth." Some suggest that this was the very blessing Jesus used on this occasion (V. Taylor 1952: 544; Hooker 1991: 340). Note, however, 1 Cor. 10:16, where the cup is the recipient of the blessing. The parallel expression in Mark 14:23, "having given thanks" (εὐχαριστήσας, eucharistēsas), where God is probably the object, lends support to the view that God is also the object of the blessing (cf. Josephus, J.W. 2.8.5 §131).

Jesus's interpretation of the bread is "This is my body" (τοῦτό ἐστιν τὸ σῶμά μου, touto estin to sōma mou). Luke 22:19 and 1 Cor. 11:24 have the addition, "which is given/is for you." This indicates that here and in the addition, "Do this in remembrance of me" (Luke 22:19; 1 Cor. 11:24), they witness to an independent tradition of the Lord's Supper. Whether "which is for you" is authentic is debated,[13] but if not, it makes explicit what was already implicit in Jesus's words. The close association of the cup with the bread indicates that "body" should be interpreted in light of the sacrificial imagery in Mark 14:24 (Gundry 1993: 831). The bread and cup ("body and blood") are "two ways of expressing the total self-gift of Jesus 'for the sake of the many'" (Donahue and Harrington 2002: 395). It is extremely unlikely that the Twelve would have understood these words to mean that the bread was actually Jesus's body, since Jesus's body was present with them (Gundry 1993: 831).[14] This is even more likely of the statement "This is my blood" (τοῦτό ἐστιν τὸ αἷμά μου, touto estin to haima mou). See 14:23–24. The bread represents the person of Jesus, not simply a part of him, such as his "flesh" in contrast to his "blood," and portrays Jesus as giving himself in death as a ransom for many (10:45; contra Evans 2001: 390). The act of "breaking" the bread should not be pressed as

13. Gundry (1993: 831–33) and Evans (2001: 390) think that the words are authentic and that Mark has omitted them.

14. The probable lack of the verb "is" in the original Aramaic saying (France 2002: 569; Donahue and Harrington 2002: 395) also suggests this. I. Marshall (1980: 86) states concerning Jesus's words, "One might compare how a person showing a photograph of himself to a group of friends could say, 'This is me.'"

referring to Jesus's body being broken (cf. the scribal addition of "broken" in א² C³ D² G K P Ψ in 1 Cor. 11:24), for tradition emphasized the lack of any bones being broken in the death of Jesus (John 19:33, 36). The breaking of bread was simply part of the process involved in distributing bread during the meal (Gundry 1993: 840).

The "thanksgiving" (εὐχαριστήσας), like the "blessing" of the bread, is prob- **14:23–24** ably directed to God (see comments on 14:22). From it we obtain one of the biblical names associated with the Last Supper—the Eucharist. Other names derived from the Bible are the breaking of bread (Acts 2:42, 46; 20:7, 11), the table of the Lord (1 Cor. 10:21), communion (1 Cor. 10:16), and the Lord's Supper (1 Cor. 11:20). (The term "Mass" comes from the Latin ending of the rite—*Ite, missa est* ["Go, you are dismissed"].) The interchangeable nature of the "blessing" and the "giving thanks" (I. Marshall 1980: 41; B. Smith 1992: 172) can be seen in Luke's use of "giving thanks" for both the cup in 22:17 and the bread in 22:19, as well as by the implied "giving thanks" in 22:20 ("likewise"). Similarly, 1 Cor. 11:24 has "giving thanks" associated with the bread and also implies that the same "giving thanks" is given with respect to the cup by the "likewise" in 11:25. If, as argued, the Last Supper was associated with a Passover meal (see the introduction to this unit) in which four cups of wine were drunk, the cup of the Last Supper was probably the third cup in the Passover ritual (J. Edwards 2002: 426; cf. Donahue and Harrington 2002: 395). All drank from a single cup. Although there are hygienic reasons for the use of individual cups in the present celebration of the Lord's Supper, that the disciples drank from a common cup emphasized the oneness of the church as the body of Christ in a powerful way that is lacking in drinking from small individual cups.

In 10:38–39 the term "cup" (ποτήριον, *potērion*) was used to describe the future death of Jesus (cf. also 14:36). The interpretive word associated with the cup is more detailed than that given with the bread: "This is my blood of the covenant that is poured out for many." Given the strong prohibition in the OT against eating and drinking blood (Lev. 3:17; 7:26–27; 17:14; etc.), the lack of protest on the part of the Twelve in drinking the cup indicates that they did not believe that the wine in the cup was the actual blood of Christ (Hooker 1991: 342). This is true even though the interpretation is given after they have drunk the cup. (Cf. Peter's strong protest in Acts 10:9–16 to God's command to eat unkosher meat.) Even more dramatically than the bread, the cup's contents represent/symbolize the sacrificial nature of Jesus's death. "Blood" refers to the giving up of life (cf. Lev. 17:14 NIV: "For the life of every creature is its blood"), and the "blood of the covenant" (Exod. 24:8; Zech. 9:11; cf. Heb. 9:18–22; 10:29) refers to the surrender of the life of the sacrificial victim whose blood (i.e., death) seals a covenant. The death of Jesus, his giving his life as a ransom for many (10:45), is understood as a sacrificial act sealing a covenant. Luke 22:20 and 1 Cor. 11:25 refer to "the new covenant," and numerous MSS of Mark include "new" (καινῆς, *kainēs*) in the interpretation of the cup. However, ℵ B C L Θ Ψ lack it, and it is much easier to understand why copyists would tend to add "new" to the Markan tradition because of the Lukan and Corinthian parallels, than to understand why copyists would have tended to omit it. Regardless, "the covenant" that Jesus inaugurates with his sacrificial death would have been understood as a "new covenant" from the beginning, for the covenant of Exod. 24:8 and Zech. 9:11 had already been sealed by the blood of the Passover lamb in the time of Moses.[15] The idea of a new covenant brings to mind Jer. 31:31–34 (38:31–34 LXX) and the Qumran community, which believed that it was the people of a "new covenant" that God had established with the Teacher of Righteousness and them (CD 6.19; 19.33–34; 20.11–12; 1QpHab 2.1–4; etc.).

The last interpretive remark concerning the blood of the covenant is that it is poured out "for many" (ὑπὲρ πολλῶν, *hyper pollōn*). This recalls the "for many" (ἀντὶ πολλῶν, *anti pollōn*) of 10:45, and both allude to Isa. 53:12.[16] "Many" can refer to "some, but not all," or to "all" (V. Taylor 1952: 546; Donahue and Harrington 2002: 396). (Cf. the interchangeable use of "many" and "all" in Rom. 5:15–19.) As a result this verse cannot serve as a proof text for the view that the death of Christ had as its purpose a "limited" or a "universal" atonement. For "poured out" (ἐκχυννόμενον, *ekchynnomenon*) and its use in describing OT sacrifice, compare Lev. 4:7, 18, 25, 30, 34.[17]

14:25 The concluding statement begins with an emphatic "Truly" (ἀμήν, *amēn*), which occurs frequently in Jesus's sayings (see 3:28–30). The distinctive nature of Jesus's use of the expression is recognized by most scholars (Guelich 1989: 177–78). Although numerous attempts have been made to interpret the Lukan parallel (22:16) as indicating that Jesus had desired (though unsuccessful) to eat the Passover meal with the disciples on the next day, so that the Last Supper was not a Passover meal (Hooker 1991: 332; Evans 2001: 395), this is certainly not how Luke understood the saying. In the preceding verse (22:15), he records Jesus's words, "I have eagerly desired to eat this Passover with you before I suffer." In this verse, Luke refers to Jesus's realized desire of eating the present Passover meal (Fitzmyer 1985b: 1395–96; Bock 1996: 1719–21). In Mark 14:25 and Luke 22:16, Jesus refers to a future eating of the Passover at the messianic banquet in the kingdom of God. In light of this and 14:12 ("that you [Jesus] might eat the Passover") and 14 ("I shall eat the Passover"), the "never again" in 14:25 should be interpreted, "after this Passover I shall never again eat until . . ." (cf. W. Lane 1974: 508). The present verse in Mark should not be interpreted as indicating that Jesus did not partake of the Passover meal but fasted (contra Jeremias 1966: 209–12; Donahue and Harrington 2002:

---

15. B. Smith (1992: 180–82) suggests that "new covenant," while not part of the original Markan text, may actually be more authentic.

16. The expressions "for many" in 10:45 (ἀντὶ πολλῶν) and here (ὑπὲρ πολλῶν) are essentially synonyms.

17. For examples of the atoning quality of a righteous man's death, a number of which would have been known to Jesus's audience, see Evans 2001: 386–88.

397). "While they were eating" in 14:22 is best interpreted inclusively (i.e., as referring to Jesus's and the disciples' eating), rather than exclusively (i.e., to the disciples' but not Jesus's eating). In addition, the expression "never again" and the future "I shall drink" suggest that Jesus's abstinence will begin after the Passover meal and Last Supper, not before (France 2002: 571n63). There is little in the text to suggest that Jesus's vow was a nazirite vow of abstinence (Gundry 1993: 843; Evans 2001: 395; contra Cranfield 1959: 428), and France (2002: 571n63) rightly points out that the emphasis in 14:25 is not on "abstaining until" but "feasting then."

The term "new" (καινόν, *kainon*) is ambiguous and permits several possible interpretations. It can be interpreted adverbially ("I will drink it again/anew"; Gundry 1993: 834) or adjectivally, describing "it" (the fruit of the vine or wine; cf. *m. Ber.* 6.1; "I will drink the new wine in the kingdom"; France 2002: 572) or "I" (i.e., Jesus) having been renewed (resurrected; cf. V. Taylor 1952: 547; Evans 2001: 395), or as describing the "new" world of the kingdom (W. Lane 1974: 508). Earlier in Mark, Jesus had referred to the kingdom of God as a reality already present in his coming (see 1:15), but here the future, not-yet aspect of the kingdom is meant (Meier 1994: 302–9). This future dimension is described in the imagery of the messianic banquet (Isa. 25:6–9; 55:1–2; 2 Esd. 6:49–52; 1 En. 62.13–16; 2 Bar. 29.3–8; Matt. 8:11–12; Rev. 19:9). Each NT account of the Last Supper involves a positive statement concerning the future (Mark 14:25; Matt. 26:29; Luke 22:16; 1 Cor. 11:26). Thus the celebration of the Lord's Supper should not be simply a sorrowful, backward recollection of Jesus's suffering and death but should also conclude with a hopeful looking forward to and joyous anticipation of that glorious day when believers will share with Jesus the "new" wine/food of the messianic banquet (R. H. Stein, *DJG* 449).

Although this verse can be interpreted as concluding 14:22–25 (NAB, NIV, TNIV, NLB, ESV), it is best understood as beginning a new section (RSV, NRSV, NEB, REB, NJB). In Mark, geographical and chronological changes usually serve as introductions to what follows[18] rather than as conclusions to what precedes (1:39; 11:11, 19). After (1) the setting (14:26), we have (2) Jesus's prediction of the disciples' denial (14:27); (3) a prophecy concerning the future reconciliation of Jesus and the disciples in Galilee after the resurrection (14:28); (4) Peter's protest (14:29); (5) Jesus's predicting Peter's threefold denial (14:30); and (6) the continuing protest of Peter and the other disciples (14:31). Along with 14:17–21, Mark 14:26–31 forms a parallel bookend that sandwiches 14:22–25. (See the introduction to this unit.) Although some deny the historicity of the account (Bultmann 1968: 306), others have defended it as an eyewitness report stemming from Peter himself (V. Taylor 1952: 548; Cranfield 1959: 428–29). The difficulty of understanding why Mark or someone before

14:26

18. Cf. 1:9, 16, 21, 29, 35; 2:1, 13, 23; 3:1, 7, 13, 19c; 4:1, 10, 35; 5:1, 21; 6:1, 6b, 45, 53; 7:1, 24, 31; 8:22, 27; 9:2, 14, 30, 33; 10:1, 17, 32, 46; 11:1, 12, 15, 20, 27; 12:35; 13:1, 3; 14:1, 3, 10, 12, 17, 32, 53; 15:1, 16, 42; 16:2.

him would make up a story magnifying the failures of the disciples argues for the account's historicity (Donahue and Harrington 2002: 405).[19]

"And after singing" (ὑμνήσαντες, *hymnēsantes*) probably refers to concluding the Passover meal by singing the Hallel Psalms (Pss. 114/115–18; contra R. Brown 1994: 1.123). For other instances of singing in the NT, compare Acts 16:25; 1 Cor. 14:26; Eph. 5:19; Col. 3:16; Heb. 2:12; and James 5:13. After the completion of the Passover meal, which had to be eaten within the walled city of Jerusalem, Jesus and the disciples left the crowded city to spend the night on the Mount of Olives, which was part of "greater Jerusalem" (Hooker 1991: 344). That the meal was eaten within the walled city of Jerusalem and that the night was spent on the Mount of Olives rather than in Bethany argue strongly in favor of the Last Supper being associated with a Passover meal.

14:27–28 The setting for the following prediction is the journey of Jesus and the disciples from the upper room across the Kidron Valley to Gethsemane, on the Mount of Olives (cf. 14:26 and 32). Jesus's sad prediction that "all" (πάντες, *pantes*) the disciples would "fall away" (be scandalized, σκανδαλισθήσεσθε, *skandalisthēsesthe*) recalls earlier appearances of this term in Mark (cf. 4:17; 6:3; 9:42, 43, 45, 47; also 14:29). It is uncertain whether Zech. 13:7 is the source of Jesus's prediction (Scripture says this will happen, so Jesus knew that his disciples would fall away) or served as supporting evidence to what he already knew (my disciples will fall away, and this is in accordance with what Scripture in Zech. 13:7 says).[20] However, the divinely ordained nature of Jesus's passion and death is shown in the quotation by "It is written" (γέγραπται, *gegraptai*; cf. 1:2; 7:6; 9:12; 11:17; 14:21) and the words "I will strike the shepherd." It is God himself who is ultimately the cause of his Son's suffering and death.

Along with his disturbing prediction, Jesus has a word of encouragement (14:28). Introduced by an emphatic "but" (ἀλλά, *alla*), Jesus states that the death of the shepherd and the falling away of the disciples will not be the end of the story. The resurrection of Jesus will involve not only his own vindication by God but also the restoration of the disciples as Jesus's apostles. It is quite possible that Mark inserted 14:28 into his tradition at this point, for its omission allows 14:29 to follow smoothly after 14:27. The same is also true with respect to 16:7. Although Markan in location, wording, and style (Stein 1973), 14:28 is probably based upon pre-Markan tradition that told of the meeting and reconciliation of Jesus and the disciples in Galilee (cf. Matt. 28:16–20; John 21:1–23; R. Brown 1994: 1.142–43). In Mark it serves as another resurrection prediction and reveals how, despite their failures and even their denial of Jesus, the disciples came to be leaders of the church. The reference to Jesus "going before" the disciples into Galilee is best interpreted as indicating

---

19. The radical idea that Mark was on a vendetta seeking to discredit Peter and the other apostles (Weeden 1971) is now rightfully rejected by the vast majority of NT scholars. The strong Markan comments found in 14:28 and 16:7 clearly show the unlikely nature of such a radical view.

20. For Mark's heavy use of Zechariah in his Passion Narrative, see Marcus 1992b: 154–64.

that Jesus would go before (precede) them into Galilee and there await them (as 16:7, "there you will see him," requires; Gundry 1993: 845; Witherington 2001: 377; France 2002: 577) rather than that he would personally lead them into Galilee as a shepherd (cf. 10:32 for προάγων and 14:27 for the image of a shepherd; Hooker 1991: 345; Evans 2001: 401–2).[21]

Peter's protest and Jesus's rebuke recalls 8:31–33, where Peter denies what Jesus **14:29–31** has said (8:32; cf. 14:29) and Jesus rebukes him (8:33; cf. 14:30). The present rebuke is more serious than the former. In 8:32 Peter is rebuked for refusing to accept what Jesus was saying about his death, but here Peter is rebuked because of his forthcoming, threefold denial of Jesus. The term "deny" (ἀπαρνήσῃ, *aparnēsē*) is a synonym for "being ashamed" (ἐπαισχύνομαι, *epaischynomai*; cf. 8:38). It is also the opposite of "confess" (ὁμολογέω, *homologeō*; cf. Matt. 10:32–33 and John 1:20). Jesus's reply, "Truly, I say to *you* [σοι, *soi*] that *you* [σύ, *sy*] . . ." corresponds to Peter's emphatic protest, "I [will] not" (lit. "but not I"; Donahue and Harrington 2002: 403). "Today, this very night, before the cock crows,"[22] Peter would deny Jesus three times.[23] There is no reason not to take this as a reference to an actual rooster crowing (J. Edwards 2002: 430n39). Since such a crowing would take place very early in the morning, perhaps even late at night (*m. Yoma* 1.8; *m. Tamid* 1.2), this indicates that the denial would take place very soon. Peter's vigorous denial of what Jesus said (14:31a) recalls 8:32b–c. It may have been well intended, and his profession of a willingness to die (cf. 2 Macc. 6–7) may have been sincere, but his professed superiority over the other disciples ("Even if all [the others] would fall away, I [will] not") is shameful. His boasting makes his denial all the more sad and tragic. But Peter is not alone. All the other disciples also profess a willingness to die rather than deny Jesus, and they too will fall away.

Summary

Within the present passage we encounter several Markan themes. One is God's sovereign control of the events surrounding the death of the Son of God. The divine necessity (δεῖ, *dei*) spoken of earlier in 8:31 (cf. also 9:31; 10:33–34, 45) is reinforced by Jesus's words in 14:21. His betrayal by one of his disciples fulfills a divine necessity because this "has been written concerning him." Despite human betrayal, Mark does not want his readers to conceive of Jesus's death as an ironic or tragic twist of fate. This is all God's doing. He is ultimately the one in charge. He is the one who will

21. Van Iersel (1982: 365–70) argues that "I will go before you into" should be translated "I will lead them [once again] in Galilee." He further argues, however, that Galilee does not refer to a geographical location but means that the disciples will remember what Jesus said and did in Galilee.

22. Cranfield (1959: 429) points out the ascending order of specificity in the temporal designations. For the view that the second cockcrow marked the rising of the sun, see R. Brown 1994: 1.137.

23. Cf. the threefold denial Romans required of Christians in Pliny the Younger, *Ep.* 10.96.2–3.

strike the shepherd (14:27). Yet this does not in any way excuse the human agents responsible for this. On the contrary, their culpability is strongly emphasized and condemned (14:21b–c).

On the other hand, though Judas's betrayal is unforgivable, the denial of the disciples can be forgiven (R. Brown 1994: 1.141–42). Jesus knows that they will fail (14:27–31). Not a single one of them will remain true. By their words or by their desertion, all will deny the Lord for whom they have professed a willingness to die (14:31; cf. John 11:16). Yet there is a promise of restoration (14:28; cf. 16:7). Some would later suffer martyrdom for Jesus, and all would prove faithful. Whether Mark's emphasis reflects a situation that existed in his day (denial by some Christians during Nero's persecution?) is impossible to say. Yet through the centuries the restoration of Peter and the other disciples has provided encouragement for numerous Christians who have failed their Lord and found similar forgiveness and restoration. The Christian faith is for sinners, and it should be remembered concerning two of the greatest heroes of the Christian church that one denied his Lord three times (14:66–72) and the other was a persecutor of Jesus and the church (1 Cor. 15:9; Acts 8:1; 9:4–5; Donahue and Harrington 2002: 406).

The present passage also contains both a soteriological and an eschatological emphasis. Along with 10:45, the account of the Last Supper provides a strong soteriological understanding of the death of Jesus. In 10:45 Jesus's death is understood as serving as a ransom for many. Here the sacrificial nature of Jesus's death is portrayed by the pouring out of his blood to seal a (new) covenant "for many" (14:24). Jesus would leave to his apostles the fuller description of what this means. With respect to eschatology, we see both the now ("blood of the [new] covenant"; 14:24) and the not yet ("that day when I drink it new in the kingdom of God"; 14:25). Jesus is not only the proclaimer of the kingdom of God in Mark (1:14–15). He is also the inaugurator of the (new) covenant that comes with the kingdom of God (14:24), and he will be the consummator of the kingdom as well (14:25; cf. 8:38).[24]

The christological element found in the present passage should also be recognized. Jesus is the prophet par excellence. He knows that Judas, one of the disciples, will betray him (14:18–21). He knows that Peter will deny him three times that very night (14:30). He knows that the other disciples will desert him (14:27, 31). Earlier he has spoken of his death (8:31; 9:31; 10:33–34) and resurrection (8:31; 9:31; 10:33–34; cf. also 9:9; 14:28). In all these things the readers, like the two disciples in 14:16, find it "just as he told them." Mark's readers know that Jesus is a prophet who can be trusted.

24. Although 10:45 and 14:24 are the only two clear references in Mark to the soteriological significance of the death of Jesus, it would be incorrect to think that this is an unimportant theme in Mark. In both instances the sayings are the culmination of the section in which they are found. Mark 10:45 is the culmination of 8:22–10:52, which centers on the theme of the divine necessity of Jesus's death and resurrection, and 14:24 marks the climax of the Last Supper (Hengel 1985: 37).

They can trust that he, the Son of Man, has indeed "give[n] his life as a ransom for many" (10:45) and by his blood inaugurated a (new) covenant (14:24). Because of this, they know that they, like the disciples, will one day eat and drink in the kingdom of God (14:25) with Jesus their Lord, who is the Christ, the Son of God, and the Son of Man.

Additional Notes

14:12. ἀπελθόντες ἑτοιμάσωμεν is lit. "going we should prepare."

14:14. The term κατάλυμα can refer to an inn (Luke 2:7), but here it refers to a guest room, as the expression "large upper room" in 14:15 (cf. Luke 22:11–12) indicates.

14:15. The καί need not be translated here.

14:20. Some MSS (B C* Θ) read "in the one bowl."

14:21. καλόν functions in this verse as a comparative—"better."

14:22. My translation follows ℵ¹ B D W, although ℵ* A C L Θ Ψ f¹ lat read "Jesus" (ὁ Ἰησοῦς).

14:23. The codices A K P W have "the cup."

14:24. Numerous MSS (A Δ 𝔐 f¹ f¹³ lat syr) read "the new covenant," but this is probably due to assimilation to Luke 22:20 and 1 Cor. 11:25.

14:28. For this translation, see 16:5–7.

14:30. "Today" (σήμερον) is omitted in D Θ f¹³ and the Old Latin MSS.

14:31. ἐλάλει is lit. "was saying."

14:31. ὡσαύτως is lit. "similarly."

C. Jesus Prays in the Garden of Gethsemane (14:32–42)

This passage is intimately tied to the preceding and following accounts. Literarily, it is tied to the preceding by the introductory seam (14:32a), in which Jesus and the disciples leave the scene of the Last Supper (14:12–31) in Jerusalem and proceed to a place called Gethsemane on the Mount of Olives (14:26). The agony of Jesus in 14:33–36 builds on the "cup" (ποτήριον, *potērion*; 14:23–24, 36)[1] he is about to drink. The failure of the disciples to "watch" (γρηγορέω, *grēgoreō*; 14:34, 37, 38) alludes to the command to "watch" in 13:34, 35, 37, and their failure in this passage builds on Jesus's prediction of their falling away in 14:27–31. The possible (delivered over, παραδίδοται, *paradidotai*; 14:41) and explicit (the one betraying me, παραδιδούς, *paradidous*; 14:42) mention of Judas recalls what Jesus has said in 14:18–21 and what Mark has told his readers in 14:10–11 (cf. also 3:19). This and the disciples' failure will be described more fully in the next account, which tells of Jesus's arrest (14:43–52).

Some scholars have sought to distinguish two (or more) separate sources lying behind the present account due in part to the presence of various "doublets," but such attempts have not been convincing (Pesch 1980b: 386; R. Brown 1994: 1.218–23; contra Barbour 1969: 232–34; Murphy-O'Connor 1998). As for the Markan redaction, Pryke (1978: 22, 147, 172–73) sees Mark's hand in 14:32a, 33, 38, 39, 40, 41, and 42, but Gnilka (1979: 257) sees only 14:32c, 33a, and 40b as Markan. The style of the account is heavily Markan (R. Brown 1994: 1.223n10). This can be seen in the use of the introductory "and" (καί, *kai*) followed by a historical present tense (14:32 [2×], 33, 34, 37 [2×], 41); "began" (ἤρξατο, *ērxato*) followed by an infinitive (14:33; see 1:45); "and again" (καὶ πάλιν, *kai palin*) in 14:39, 40 (see 2:1–2); the "for" (γάρ, *gar*) explanatory clause in 14:40 (see 1:16–18); the similar wording in the explanations of 14:40 and 9:6; the use of the double participle (14:39); and so on. It is best to see this, however, as the retelling of the Gethsemane tradition by Mark in his own vocabulary and style rather than as his creation of a large portion of the present account (contra Kelber 1972: 169–76). The pre-Markan tradition lying behind the present account is witnessed to by the presence of numerous Markan hapax legomena (Pesch 1980b: 386;[2] cf. R. Brown 1994: 1.223–27). Bultmann (1968: 267–68) has

---

1. France (2002: 585) seeks to differentiate between the "cup" mentioned in 14:23–24 and that mentioned in 14:36. The close proximity of these two references, however, argues against this.

2. Pesch lists χωρίον (*chōrion*), οὗ τὸ ὄνομα (*hou to onoma*), Γεθσημανί (*Gethsēmani*; 14:32); μικρόν (*mikron*) to denote distance (14:35); αββα (*abba*), παρένεγκε (*parenenke*; 14:36); πειρασμόν

argued that the present account is a legend, but its historical nature is witnessed to by the negative portrait of Jesus found in the account. Who in the early church would have portrayed Jesus as so terrified by his approaching death (Hooker 1991: 346; R. Brown 1994: 1.224n12; Evans 2001: 408)? The account's historicity is also supported by its multiple attestation here, in John (12:27; 14:31; 18:11), and in Hebrews (5:7–10), as well as by the divergent pattern from the redaction by the evangelist (Stein 1991: 179–81), who has been emphasizing all along Jesus's resolute acceptance of God's sovereign plan for his life, which included his death (Hooker 1991: 346).

The story of Jesus in Gethsemane can be divided as follows: (1) The arrival of Jesus and the disciples in Gethsemane (14:32); (2) Jesus's selection of Peter, James, and John to share his personal agony by watching with him (14:33–34); (3) Jesus's prayer that his Father might remove the cup from him (14:35–36); (4) Jesus returning and finding the disciples sleeping (14:37–38); (5) Jesus praying a second and third time and returning each time to find the disciples sleeping (14:39–41a); and (6) Jesus and the disciples going to meet Judas (14:41b–42).

Exegesis and Exposition

³²And they proceed into a place ⌜that is called⌝ Gethsemane, and he [Jesus] says to his disciples, "Sit here while I pray."³³And he takes with him Peter and James and John, and he began to be deeply distressed and troubled, ³⁴and he says to them, "My soul is extremely sorrowful—even to death. Remain here and watch."³⁵And having proceeded a little further, he fell on the ground and began to pray that if it were possible, the hour might pass from him, ³⁶and he was saying, "Abba, Father, all things are possible for you. Take away this cup from me. But not what I will but what you [will]."³⁷And he comes and finds them sleeping and says to Peter, "Simon, are you sleeping? Were you not able to watch [with me] one hour? ³⁸Watch and pray that you not enter into temptation. The spirit [is] willing but the flesh [is] weak."³⁹And leaving them, ⌜he again⌝ prayed, ⌜saying the same thing,⌝ ⁴⁰and having come, he again found them sleeping, for their eyes were very heavy, and they did not know ⌜what they should say to him⌝. ⁴¹And he comes the third time and says to them, "Are you still sleeping and resting? It [the money] ⌜is paid⌝. The hour has come; behold, the Son of Man is being delivered over into the hands of sinners. ⁴²Rise up, let us go. Behold, the one who is betraying me ⌜has come⌝."

The name Gethsemane, which is Aramaic for "oil press," is spelled differently in various MSS: Geth-, Get-, Ges-, Ged-, Gēth-, and -sēmanei, -semanei, -sēmani, -simanē. These all refer to the same place on the Mount of Olives, which contained an olive grove. John 18:1 describes the place as a "garden," and we learn from John 18:2 that Jesus frequently visited this place (cf. also

14:32

(peirasmon), πρόθυμον (prothymon), ἀσθενής (asthenēs; 14:38); καταβαρυνόμενοι (katabarynomenoi; 14:40); τὸ τρίτον (to triton), τὸ λοιπόν (to loipon; 14:41).

Luke 22:39). Such a garden was probably enclosed with walls, as their proceeding "into" (εἰς, *eis*) it suggests. Upon their arrival, Jesus tells the disciples to "sit." Although this term can mean "remain" (cf. 14:34), there is no reason to reject the normal meaning "to sit," and the command "Rise up" (ἐγείρεσθε, *egeiresthe*) in 14:42 assumes that they were sitting. For other examples of Jesus praying alone, compare 1:35 and 6:46.

14:33–34 On several other important occasions, Jesus took Peter, James, and John with him: to witness the raising of Jairus's daughter (5:37–43); to witness his transfiguration (9:2–9); and, along with Andrew, to be the recipients of his eschatological teachings concerning the destruction of Jerusalem and the coming of the Son of Man (13:3–37). Now those who bravely claimed their willingness to suffer for Jesus (10:38–39; 14:29, 31) would have the opportunity to prepare for this, just as Jesus would prepare for his suffering, by watching and praying in Gethsemane. At Gethsemane, Jesus seeks the fellowship and encouragement of his disciples as he faces the most difficult experience of his life. He wants them to recognize his turmoil and suffering and to watch with him (cf. Matt. 26:38) in this (Mark 14:34). Jesus is described as being "deeply distressed" (ἐκθαμβεῖσθαι, *ekthambeisthai*; an intensive form of θαμβέομαι, *thambeomai*) and "troubled" (ἀδημονεῖν, *adēmonein*). This dual use of expressions (Neirynck 1988: 106) adds emphasis to the description of Jesus's agony. To this is added Jesus's own words, "My soul[3] is extremely sorrowful [περίλυπος, *perilypos*; an emphatic form of λύπος, *lypos*]—even to death."[4] Some OT parallels to the soul being grieved can be found in Pss. 42:5–6, 11 (41:6–7, 12 LXX); 43:5 (42:5 LXX); cf. 1QH 8.32. For "grieved unto death," compare Jon. 4:9 LXX and Sir. 37:2. This extreme sorrow unto death can mean a sorrow that is almost killing him; a sorrow so great that he wants to die; a sorrow that will last until he dies, when at last he is delivered from it; and so on (R. Brown 1994: 1.154–55). In the last two interpretations, death is a longed-for liberation from such grief and sorrow, but in Gethsemane Jesus prayed not for death but to be delivered from death (Pesch 1980b: 389–90). Thus the best interpretation is that the grief Jesus was experiencing was almost killing him.

In light of Jesus's agony, Peter, James, and John are asked to remain with him and to watch. Since Jesus's sorrow, distress, and extreme sorrow have been in the forefront of the preceding verses, the command to remain and watch should be understood as a request that the three disciples agonize with and for Jesus during this terrible time. The rebuke of Peter in 14:37 involves his failing to pray on behalf of Jesus. In 14:38, however, the object of concern

---

3. "My soul" is essentially a synonym for "I." Cf. Ps. 42:2, 5–6, 11.

4. The idea that Jesus in his agony sweat great drops of blood is based upon a misinterpretation of a dubious textual reading in Luke 22:44 found in ℵ D L Θ f¹ lat but lacking in 𝔓⁶⁹ 𝔓⁷⁵ ℵ¹ A B W f¹³ sa bo. As to the MSS in which Luke 22:43–44 is found, these state that Jesus's sweat became "like" (ὡσεί, *hōsei*) great drops of blood. The simile "like great drops of blood" indicates that they were not actual great drops of blood.

for the disciples' prayer changes. Now Jesus tells them to watch and pray for their own concerns and needs, and the content of what they should pray for is given in 14:38b by an epexegetical ἵνα (*hina*). They are to pray that they not enter into temptation, for at such times their inner being (the spirit) may be willing, but their weakness as humans (the flesh) may cause them to stumble and fall away.

The description of Jesus's agony in Gethsemane continues with the state- **14:35–36**
ment "He fell [lit. 'was falling'] on the ground and began to pray. . . ."[5] Luke 22:41 describes the distance that Jesus advanced from Peter, James, and John as "a stone's throw." Since normally one prayed out loud, the three disciples probably overheard Jesus praying. One should not assume that the disciples fell asleep from the moment Jesus left them to the moment he returned. They would have heard bits and pieces of Jesus's prayer (France 2002: 583). The normal position for prayer was standing (Mark 11:25; Matt. 6:5; Luke 18:11, 13). There are, however, numerous examples of people in distress or in the presence of God who are portrayed as falling on their face (Gen. 17:1–3; Lev. 9:24; Num. 14:5; 16:4, 22, 45; 20:6; Matt. 17:6; Luke 5:12; 17:16; 24:5; 1 Cor. 14:25). For an example of prayer in this position, see Jos. Asen. 14.3. The content of Jesus's prayer is given in indirect discourse and introduced by an epexegetical "that" (ἵνα). As in 14:38, ἵνα introduces the content of the verb "to pray" (προσηύχετο, *proseucheto*; Gundry 1993: 872).[6]

Jesus's prayer is that "if it were possible, the hour [ὥρα, *hōra*] might pass from him." In the next verse this prayer is repeated in direct discourse, "Abba, Father, all things are possible for you. Take this cup from me. . . ."[7] "If it were possible" (εἰ δυνατόν ἐστιν, *ei dynaton estin*; 14:35) should be interpreted in light of God's omnipotence ("all things are possible" [9:23]; "all things [are] possible with God" [10:27]) as "all things are possible for you" (πάντα δυνατά σοι, *panta dynata soi*; 14:36). Consequently, this is not a question concerning God's ability but a request. For Jesus, the issue is not whether God "can" remove the "hour" and "cup" but whether God "wills" it. The two metaphors "hour" and "cup" are synonyms (Donahue and Harrington 2002: 408). The former emphasizes the eschatological moment in history of Jesus's passion and death (14:35, 41),[8] whereas the latter emphasizes the suffering Jesus will experience (14:36; cf. 10:38–39) in that eschatological event (Stanley 1980:

---

5. The imperfect ἔπιπτεν (*epipten*) is unusual. Gundry (1993: 854) suggests that the imperfect is used to indicate that each time Jesus prayed (14:35, 40, 41), he prayed in this manner.

6. Cf. 3:9; 5:23, 43; 6:8, 12, 25, 56; 7:26, 36; 8:30; 9:9, 12, 18, 30; 10:35, 37, 48, 51; 11:16; 12:19; 13:18, 34; 14:35, 38. It is at times very difficult to determine whether ἵνα functions primarily epexegetically or to indicate purpose.

7. Cf. the indirect description of Jesus's agony in 14:33 and the direct description in 14:34.

8. Although some commentators see a tie here with the "hour" of 13:32 (R. Brown 1994: 1.167–68), the two passages refer to two different moments in the divine economy, the crucifixion and the parousia. In 14:35 the "hour" of Jesus's death is known to him. It is but moments away. But in 13:32 the "hour" of his parousia is not known to him. The one "hour" Jesus seeks to avoid; the other he looks forward to (14:25).

137–39). Despite his personal desire to avoid the forthcoming passion, Jesus submits himself to the will of God with an emphatic, "But not what I will but what you [will]" (ἀλλ' οὐ τί ἐγὼ θέλω ἀλλὰ τί σύ, all' ou ti egō thelō alla ti sy). Herein lies faith: the ability to request openly another destiny than the one God has chosen but ultimately submitting to God's will whatever this may involve (2 Sam. 15:25–26; cf. also 1 Macc. 3:58–60).[9]

Jesus's address, "Abba, Father," contains the actual Aramaic term he used for God (אַבָּא, 'abbā') and the Greek translation of it (ὁ πατήρ, ho patēr, Father; cf. Rom. 8:15; Gal. 4:6). Jesus's use of the term *Abba* to address God (cf. Luke 11:2) is quite unique. Jeremias (1965: 9–30) has argued that no Jew before Jesus addressed God in this way. This claim may need to be qualified somewhat (Fitzmyer 1985a; R. Brown 1994: 1.172–75; Evans 2001: 412–13) in light of 4Q372 1.16 ("My Father, my God") and 4Q460 5.6 ("My Father and my Lord") (Evans 2001: 413). Yet it can still be said that Jesus's use of this term as *the* way he addressed God (contra D'Angelo 1992: 630) was extremely rare and "striking and unparalleled" (France 2002: 584) in Jesus's day. It was furthermore an extremely intimate way of addressing God; it was not simply a childlike term but was used by grown children as an address for their fathers. In the Mishnah and Targums, it is used primarily by adult children. Thus the expression "Daddy" is not as correct a translation of *Abba* as "Father" (Barr 1988; Stein 1994b: 83–86). The God of Jesus is not an abstraction (a force, first cause, unmoved mover, etc.) but a person. He is furthermore not the god of Deism, who is unconcerned and uninvolved in the lives of his children or the events of history. On the contrary, he is a Father whom one can love and pray to.

That Jesus was deeply distressed, troubled, and sorrowful unto death is evident from the passage. What caused this turmoil and agony is also evident. It is the "hour" and "cup" he is facing. What is not stated in the account, however, is why Jesus feared the hour and cup so terribly. R. Brown (1994: 1.217–18) rightfully speaks of the "scandal" of the portrayal of Jesus in this account. If Jesus is quailing at the thought of physical death, he is a poor example for his followers of how they should face death and martyrdom. Contrast the noble examples in Heb. 11:32–38; Acts 7:54–60; Phil. 1:20–30; compare also 2 Macc. 6–7; Josephus, *J.W.* 1.33.3 §653; 2.8.10 §153; 7.10.1 §§417–18; and so on. Some have sought to explain Jesus's turmoil and dread as due to his being abandoned by Judas and the disciples, inner doubts as to the ultimate value of his death, the additional guilt his death would bring upon those responsible, his unique understanding of how human death is a curse and not intended in God's plan, and so on. The answer, however, is rather to be found in "the" death that Jesus was to experience. His hour and cup involves giving his life as a ransom for many (10:45) and his sacrificially pouring out his blood to seal the new covenant (14:24). It is not the physical sufferings he will have to endure

---

9. J. Edwards (2002: 436) comments, "What profound irony Gethsemane conceals, for when Jesus feels most excluded from God's presence he is in fact closest to God's will!"

that trouble Jesus (Stanley 1980: 133). Rather, it is that he would become sin for us even though he knew no sin (2 Cor. 5:21) and a curse for us (Gal. 3:13) that we might escape the wrath of God (Feldmeier 1987: 176–85). He feared "the" death that no one else would ever need to or be able to experience. He would experience God's wrath in order that those who believe in him would not have to face it. His cry of dereliction and abandonment, "My God, my God, why have you forsaken me" (15:34), reveals what Jesus fears.[10]

As Jesus returns the first time from prayer, he finds the disciples sleeping. This **14:37–38** emotional abandonment of Jesus foreshadows their literal abandonment that will soon take place (Evans 2001: 414). The use of the old name "Simon" is seen by some as symbolic of Peter's failure to be a true disciple of Jesus (Kelber 1976b: 54–55; cf. Hooker 1991: 349; J. Edwards 2002: 435), but the change in name may simply be to avoid repetition, since the name "Peter" is used immediately before this (Donahue and Harrington 2002: 409). Furthermore, it is the name "Peter," not Simon, that is used in the account of his denial (14:54, 66, 67, 70, 72; R. Brown 1994: 1.195). Note also how "Simon" is used positively in Matt. 16:17. Jesus's words, "Simon, are you sleeping?" (14:37c), are best understood not as a question, for Jesus already knows that Peter has been sleeping (14:38a), but as a rebuke. The second question also functions as a rebuke: "Were you not able [lit. 'strong enough'] to watch [with me] one hour?" (οὐκ ἴσχυσας μίαν ὥραν γρηγορῆσαι; *ouk ischysas mian hōran grēgorēsai?*).[11] The "one hour" is probably meant to be interpreted as an approximate chronological length of time (contra R. Brown 1994: 1.196).

The plural commands, "Watch and pray" (γρηγορεῖτε καὶ προσεύχεσθε, *grēgoreite kai proseuchesthe*), indicate that what is being said to Peter is meant for all the disciples as well. Whereas the "Watch" in 14:37 involved watching in the sense of sharing Jesus's agony and turmoil (cf. 14:34), the "watch and pray" in 14:38 refers to the need for the disciples to watch and pray for themselves (cf. 1 Pet. 5:8). The content of their prayer is indicated by another epexegetical "that" (ἵνα; see 14:35–36). They are to pray continually (this is the sense of the present imperative) that they not enter into temptation. This recalls a similar petition in the Lord's Prayer: "lead us not into temptation" (Matt. 6:13a). There is no need, however, to give "temptation" the same eschatological connotation here as in Matt. 6:13a/Luke 11:4 (Gundry 1993: 871–72). What faces Peter and the disciples is the immediate test of denying Jesus (cf. Mark 14:50, 66–72). The prayer is that they not confront this temptation, so that they will not succumb to it (Gundry 1993: 873). The reason for seeking to avoid the temptation is that the "flesh" (not fallen humanity

10. Cf. Cranfield 1959: 433: "In his identification with sinful men [Jesus] is the object of the holy wrath of God against sin, and in Gethsemane as the hour of the Passion approaches the full horror of that wrath is disclosed." Cf. Cranfield 1947; J. Edwards 2002: 433.

11. If this were a pure question, the οὐκ would expect a positive reply: "Yes I was able to watch . . ."; it is Peter's weakness, not his strength, that Mark wants to emphasize (Gundry 1993: 855).

in its depravity but the general weakness and vulnerability of humanity) is weak, even though the "spirit" (not the Holy Spirit[12] but the human spirit in its being able to will but not necessarily accomplish [cf. Rom. 7:18b, 22a]) is willing (R. Brown 1994: 1.198–99).[13]

14:39–41a In these verses, Mark records in abbreviated form the second and third instances of Jesus's prayer at Gethsemane and the disciples' sleeping. The content of Jesus's prayer the second time is mentioned as being literally "the same word" as the first. Nothing is said about the content of his third time of prayer, but Mark intends his readers to assume that it was the same as in the first two instances. (If he wanted them to think that it was different, he would have indicated this.) After each time of prayer, the disciples are described as sleeping, and this recalls Jesus's prediction of Peter's threefold denial (14:30) and the denial itself (14:66–72). Mark's "for" (γάρ, *gar*) explanatory clause ("for their eyes were very heavy") does not serve as an excuse for the disciples sleeping, as the following phrase indicates (cf. 9:6, where Peter's statement in 9:5 is explained but not excused; also 9:34). It serves rather as an example of the weakness of the flesh (14:38; R. Brown 1994: 1.206; Donahue and Harrington 2002: 410).

14:41b–42 Jesus's words to the disciples in 14:41b can be interpreted as (1) imperatives ("Sleep and rest!"), (2) exclamatory indicatives ("You are sleeping and resting!"), or (3) interrogatives ("Are you sleeping and resting?"). Since two imperatives follow ("Rise up, let us go"), some see it as supporting the first possibility, but the actions commanded in the two imperatives in 14:42 are the opposite of those described by the two verbs in 14:41b. Some suggest that we should understand that immediately after Jesus said "Sleep and rest!" he saw Judas coming and countermanded the first two imperatives with the two imperatives in 14:42 (France 2002: 588). It is unlikely, however, that Mark expected his readers to supply this missing data to make the imperatival interpretation of these two verbs credible. It is best to interpret the two verbs as interrogatives (cf. RSV, NRSV, REB, NAB, NIV, TNIV, NLT, NASB, ESV). The expression τὸ λοιπόν (*to loipon*) is confusing. Generally it means "from now on," but the fact that the disciples do not sleep after this makes such an interpretation difficult. The more popular interpretation of the expression is "still," but it must be admitted that this is an unusual sense for it (France 2002: 588). Some suggest that it be interpreted as a "vague" connective such as "So then (or 'Therefore'), are you sleeping . . . ?" (R. Brown 1994: 1.208).

The most difficult exegetical problem in this passage involves the verb ἀπέχει (*apechei*; see additional note on 14:41). Many scholars have despaired

---

12. So Hooker 1991: 349; R. Brown 1994: 1.199; Evans 2001: 415; contra W. Lane 1974: 520; Witherington 2001: 380. One should not read into this passage the Pauline description of the struggle of the Christian between the Holy Spirit and fallen flesh (cf. Gal. 5:16–21).

13. There is no reason to believe that Mark wanted his readers to understand this saying as applying to Jesus as well as to the disciples (Cranfield 1959: 434; contra Stanley 1980: 143; R. Brown 1994: 1.199–200).

of coming to any real resolution of its meaning (Lohmeyer 1957: 318; Holleran 1973: 56; France 2002: 589). The translation "He is paid" best fits the common monetary use of this term. "He [i.e., Judas] is paid" fits the following statement that the hour, which Jesus so dreaded (14:35), had come. The "hour" refers not just to the immediate arrival of sinners and Jesus's arrest, but that the passion and all that is involved with it has now begun. The hourglass of time has turned over, the passion has begun, Judas is here. By his twofold "Behold" (ἰδού, *idou*; 14:41, 42), Mark emphasizes the divine "giving over" (παραδίδοται, *paradidotai*) of the Son of Man in order to give his life as a ransom for many (10:45). The verb παραδίδοται serves here as a "reverential passive" (Holleran 1973: 63) in which the delivering over of Jesus by Judas (14:42b) fulfills the divine giving over (9:31; 10:33).[14] Jesus is delivered into the hands of "sinners" (14:41), that is, given over to their power. Earlier these have been described by their occupation (chief priests, scribes, elders; 8:31; 10:33; 14:1, 10) or their humanity (men; 9:31), but here they are described by their moral character, "sinners." It is ultimately not a difference in eschatological expectations and hopes, or of interpretations concerning the Law and the oral traditions, or of the role of the Messiah, or of their attitudes toward Rome, and so on that causes Jesus's opponents to seek to destroy him. It is their sin! Yet there is irony in all this, because despite what their sin will cause them to do, Jesus came to call sinners (2:17).

Jesus's words, "Rise up, let us go" (ἐγείρεσθε ἄγωμεν, *egeiresthe agōmen*), indicate Jesus's acceptance of the will of God (14:36). He seeks not to escape by flight those who seek his death. On the contrary, he initiates the encounter as he goes out to meet his betrayer and those he leads. It is not a weak, effeminate Jesus of much Christian art who goes out to meet his enemies but the conquering Son of Man/Son of God! It is the one who is Lord of nature (4:35–41), of the demons (5:1–20), of disease (5:24b–34), and of death (5:21–24a, 35–43). Yet he defeats his enemies by dying for them! That he includes his disciples with him as he goes out to meet those approaching him indicates that Mark is not on a vendetta to discredit the disciples (R. Brown 1994: 1.213–15).[15]

Summary

We encounter three common Markan themes in this account. One involves God's sovereign control of the events surrounding Jesus's life. God is in complete charge. All things are possible with God (14:36; cf. 9:23). The hour and cup that Jesus will experience (14:35–36b) are God's will (14:36c). The

14. See R. Brown (1994: 1.211–13) for a discussion of how Jesus is "given over" to death by human beings, God, and Jesus himself.

15. Contrast Kelber (1972: 184), who argues that Gethsemane was "the very last chance offered to the disciples" and that Mark is writing an apologetic against the "Peter-Christians" in the early church (187). Yet 14:28 and 16:7 refute this. That the discovery of this supposed Markan apologetic against Peter and the disciples was never noticed until nineteen centuries after Mark wrote his Gospel makes such an interpretation highly unlikely.

passion will occur because God has willed it. He has delivered Jesus over to death (14:41d; cf. 9:31; 10:33); he is the one who will strike the shepherd (14:27); this is what God's Word has decreed (14:21a). Jesus's prayer to have God remove the hour/cup from him (14:35–36) reveals that God is the one in charge of Jesus's fate, not his enemies. The theoretical question of whether the Father could have brought the kingdom of God (1:15; 14:25) apart from the death of Jesus mistakenly conceives of the kingdom as merely a political, even if eschatological, entity. The kingdom, however, also involves the ransom of sinful humanity (10:45; 14:24) and the saving of lost sinners (2:17). The forgiveness of sins, according to the OT, involves the death of a sacrificial victim and the shedding of its innocent blood (Lev. 17:11; Heb. 9:15–22). In the divine economy the sacrificial death of Jesus is necessary for the ransom of humanity. Thus it is God and his will that have ordained the death of Jesus. The human actors in bringing this about are but pawns in the divine plan. They will bear a terrible responsibility for the part they play in this (Mark 14:21), but they are simply the means, not the ultimate cause, of Jesus's suffering and death. God is the ultimate cause; the redemption of sinful humanity is the reason.

A second theme encountered in our passage involves Christian discipleship. The contrast between the faithful, noble, and heroic Jesus and the unfaithful, weak, and cowardly disciples is very apparent. Jesus watches and prays and, although deserted by all, successfully prepares for the terrible events that lie before him. The disciples do not watch and pray, and thus they are unprepared for the coming events. As a result they will fail and deny their Lord (14:50, 51–52, 66–72). Jesus, on the other hand, provides a pattern for Mark's readers. He submits to the will of God ("what you [will]"; 14:36) as an obedient son. This would have recalled to Mark's readers the prayer that Jesus taught his followers to pray and the third petition, "Your will be done" (Matt. 6:10). (Although not found in Mark, the Lord's Prayer was almost certainly known to Mark's readers.) Jesus fulfills God's will by watching and praying. So Mark's readers are to watch and pray (14:38; cf. 13:34, 35, 37; also v. 33). The failures of the disciples, unlike Judas's betrayal, are forgivable. This is seen in that Jesus takes his disciples with him to meet Judas and those with Judas (14:42), and after their failure he will restore them (14:28; 16:7). For the readers of Mark, the failure and restoration of the disciples serves as a source of encouragement and hope, for like the disciples, Mark's readers are assured that "if we confess our sins, he who is faithful and just will forgive us our sins and cleanse us from all unrighteousness" (1 John 1:9).

Since Mark has told his readers from the beginning that his Gospel is about "Jesus Christ, the Son of God" (1:1), it is not surprising that our passage provides additional building materials for constructing a Markan Christology. The predictions of Jesus, the great prophet, are already beginning to be fulfilled. His disciples are already slipping down a slope that will lead to their deserting and denying Jesus (cf. 14:27–31 and 37–38, 40–41,

50, 51–52, 66–72). Judas, as predicted, has arrived and is about to fulfill the predicted betrayal (cf. 14:18–21 and 14:42b). The hour referred to in Jesus's passion predictions (8:31; 9:31; 10:33–34) has come (14:41, 43ff.). Jesus even knows without seeing that Judas, his betrayer, has arrived. Thus other things that Jesus has prophesied and promised can be trusted to take place as well. Mark also reveals that Jesus is the obedient Son of God. He submits to the will (14:36, 39) of his Father (14:36a). He will drink the cup God has ordained for him and offer his life sacrificially to ransom humanity (10:45) and seal the new covenant (14:24).

Additional Notes

14:32. οὗ τὸ ὄνομα is lit. "whose name is."

14:39. See the discussion of πάλιν at 7:31.

14:39. The participial phrase τὸν αὐτὸν λόγον εἰπών, lit. "saying the same word," is omitted by D and it. Although some suggest that this may be a gloss (a "Western non-interpolation"; Hooker 1991: 349; Evans 2001: 416), its omission is weakly supported and is probably the result of a scribal error (Metzger 1994: 96; France 2002: 580).

14:40. "What [τί] they should say to him" can also be translated as "How they should answer him."

14:41. The meaning of the verb ἀπέχει is notoriously difficult, and Matt. 26:45 omits it. For discussions of possible meanings, see Holleran 1973: 52–56; R. Brown 1994: 2.1379–83. Some who favor the present interpretation (It [the money] is paid) are R. Brown 1994: 1.208–9; and Donahue and Harrington 2002: 410 (see 14:41b–42).

14:42. The verb "has come" (ἤγγικεν) is the same verb found in 1:15 ("The kingdom of God has come"). This lends support to the view that in 1:15 ἤγγικεν is better translated as "has come" than as "is near."

D. Jesus Is Seized (14:43–52)

The present account is closely tied to the preceding one (14:32–42) by "and immediately" (καὶ εὐθύς, *kai euthys*) and "while he was still speaking" (ἔτι αὐτοῦ λαλοῦντος, *eti autou lalountos*; 14:43a; cf. 5:35). The intimate connection between them has caused some to see them as "one single episode" (van Iersel 1998: 432). The present account is also closely tied to the following account of Jesus's trial (14:53–65), resulting from Jesus's arrest (Gnilka 1979: 267). It is possible that all of 14:43–72 is to be understood as consisting of an A-B-A′ pattern in which we have (A) the betrayal of Judas and desertion of the disciples (14:43–52), (B) the trial of Jesus (14:53–65), and (A′) the denial of Peter (14:66–72). The present account can also be divided into a similar pattern: (A) the seizing of Jesus (14:43–46), (B) the wounding of the chief priest's servant and Jesus's rebuke of his opponents' cowardice in arresting him at night (14:47–49), and (A′) the flight of the disciples and a young man (14:50–52; Donahue and Harrington 2002: 418). The loose connection of 14:47–52 to 14:43–46 is seen by the fact that 14:53–65 flows smoothly when read after 14:43–46. If one reads 14:43–46 and 14:53–65 without interruption, one would not think that something had been left out. Within the account, only two characters are named, Judas and Jesus. This focuses the reader's attention on them and not on the subsidiary characters. Even Judas immediately fades from the scene after his role in betraying Jesus (14:43–45; France 2002: 591–92).[1] The reason for this is evident. The Gospel of Mark is not about Judas but about Jesus Christ, the Son of God (1:1).

It has been suggested that Mark has used two sources in composing this passage (R. Brown 1994: 1.307–10). One (A) consists of 14:43b–46, to which Mark has added 14:43a as an introductory seam. The other (B) consists of 14:47–52. There is widespread unanimity that Mark found 14:43b–46 in his source(s), but it is debated whether 14:47–52 existed together in this or another pre-Markan source or whether Mark has brought together diverse traditions at this point. The extent of Mark's own editorial work is also debated. Pryke (1978: 22, 147, 173) attributes 14:43a, 47a, 48a, 49, 50, 51–52 to Mark; but Gnilka (1979: 267) attributes only 14:43a, perhaps the references to the scribes and elders in 14:43c, and 14:49a to Mark.

The historicity of the present account is strongly supported by the fact that Jesus's betrayal by one of his disciples and the desertion of the other

---

1. That Judas is not referred to after his betrayal of Jesus in Gethsemane indicates that what he betrayed was how and where Jesus's opponents could seize him quietly, away from the crowds and without causing a riot. There was no need for Judas's presence at the trial of Jesus (see 14:10–11).

disciples are unlikely to have been fictional creations of the early church (Evans 2001: 421–22). The wounding of the chief priest's servant (14:47) finds additional attestation in John 18:10. Although some argue that the historicity of Judas's kissing Jesus cannot be proven or disproven (Fitzmyer 1985b: 1449; R. Brown 1994: 1.255), the large part that the kiss plays in the Synoptic accounts of the seizing of Jesus and the fact that it serves no theological purpose but only functions as a means of identifying Jesus in the darkness of Gethsemane argue in favor of its historicity. Many tend to think that Jesus's reference to the fulfillment of Scripture (14:49c) is secondary; yet in contrast to Matthew and Luke, Mark does not greatly emphasize the fulfillment of Scripture in his Gospel. Thus the reference appears to be traditional and perhaps even dominical (Evans 2001: 422). With respect to the story of the flight of the young man, the difficulty in finding any theological point in it (although there have been numerous unsuccessful attempts) is attested by its omission by Matthew and Luke, which argues for its being a piece of historical tradition. The chief priests' violent usage of various Sanhedrin officials and their desire to get rid of any threats to their authority are sufficiently attested in the first century that the arrest has a true-to-life ring about it. (See Evans 2001: 422–23, who lists as examples Josephus, *J.W.* 6.5.3 §§308–9; *Ant.* 20.8.8 §181; 20.9.2 §§206–7; *b. Pesaḥ.* 57a; *b. Yebam.* 86a–b; *b. Ketub.* 26a; 1QpHab 8.8–12; 9.4–12; 12.8–10.)

Exegesis and Exposition

[43]And immediately while he was still speaking, Judas ⌜ ⌝, one of the Twelve, comes accompanied by a ⌜crowd⌝ from the chief priests and the scribes and the elders [armed] with swords and clubs. [44]And the one betraying him had given them a sign, saying, "The one whom I kiss is ⌜the one⌝; seize him and lead him away securely." [45]And coming immediately [and] approaching him [Jesus], he says, "Rabbi," and kissed him. [46]And they laid hands on him and seized him.

[47]But one of those who had been standing nearby, having drawn his sword, struck the servant of the chief priest and cut off his ear. [48]And Jesus ⌜in response⌝ said to them, "Have you come out as against a revolutionary with swords and clubs in order to arrest me? [49]Daily I was with you in the temple teaching, and you did not seize me. But [let it be] in order that the Scriptures may be fulfilled." [50]And abandoning him, they all fled. [51]And a certain young man was following him wearing [only] a linen garment. And they seized him. [52]But leaving his garment behind, he fled away ⌜ ⌝ naked.

For "And immediately" here and in 14:45, see 1:10–11. Judas is referred to as **14:43** "one of the Twelve." Some have suggested that this appears as if Judas is being identified to the readers for the first time and indicates Mark's use of a source (Soards 1994: 1522–23), but it is more likely that this description is intentional and emphasizes Judas's treachery (Hooker 1991: 351; R. Brown 1994: 1.246). Of the nine times that the expression "one of the Twelve" (εἷς τῶν δώδεκα, *heis tōn dōdeka*) is found in the Gospels, in eight instances it refers to Judas (Mark 14:10, 20, 43; Matt. 26:14, 47; Luke 22:47 [cf. also Luke 24:3]; John 6:71; 12:4; the exception is John 20:24). It was therefore associated with the name Judas in the Christian tradition and emphasizes the treacherous nature of his betrayal. The arrival of Judas "accompanied by" (lit. "and with him") those who seek to arrest Jesus catches the reader somewhat by surprise. It is not surprising that Judas will betray Jesus, for the reader has known this ever since 3:19 (cf. 14:10, 18–21). However, unlike John 13:27–30, Mark has not told the reader that Judas left Jesus and the disciples during the celebration of the Passover and Last Supper.

The coming crowd is described as armed with "swords" (μαχαιρῶν, *machairōn*; probably short swords [not knives], as the reference to someone unsheathing his sword suggests [Mark 14:47; Matt. 26:52]) and "wooden clubs" (ξύλων, *xylōn*).[2] The use of clubs has led some to suggest that this was a mob of rabble gathered quickly for seizing Jesus (Hooker 1991: 351; Evans 2001: 422–23), but the Gospels describe the crowd as officially sanctioned and coming "from" (παρά, *para*) the chief priests, the scribes, and the elders (Blinzler 1959: 61; R. Brown 1994: 1.247; France 2002: 592). That "clubs" were at times used as weapons by Roman soldiers is evident from Josephus (*J.W.* 2.9.4 §176). The role of "the chief priests and the scribes and the elders" does not surprise the reader here because of earlier references to them (cf. 8:31; 11:27; 14:53; 15:1; also 10:33; 11:18; 14:1, 55). That they were the leaders of the temple is evident from Jesus's words to them: "Daily [καθ' ἡμέραν, *kath' hēmeran*] I was with you [πρὸς ὑμᾶς, *pros hymas*] in the temple [ἐν τῷ ἱερῷ, *en tō hierō*]" (14:49). The prepositional phrase "with you" also emphasizes that whatever the Roman involvement in Jesus's arrest may have been, it is the Jewish character of the group that is being emphasized.

The makeup of those who came to arrest Jesus is described differently in the various Gospels: Mark 14:43 has a crowd from the chief priests, the scribes, and the elders (cf. Matt. 26:47); Luke 22:47, 52 has a crowd consisting of chief priests, officers (στρατηγούς, *stratēgous*) of the temple, and elders; and John 18:3, 12 has a cohort (σπεῖρα, *speira*), generally 600–1,000 men (Josephus, *J.W.* 3.4.2 §§67–68), although some suggest that this refers to a "maniple" of two hundred men. The presence of a "tribune" (χιλίαρχος, *chiliarchos*, John 18:12) supports the view that a cohort is meant.[3] In addition, John 18:3 speaks

---

2. That the presence of weapons was forbidden on the Sabbath and Jewish festivals (*m. Šabb.* 6.4) has caused some to argue that Jesus's arrest could not have taken place on the night of the Passover. However, there are too many other infractions that took place at the trial of Jesus that are contrary to the idealized rules found in the Mishnah to suggest that the carrying of weapons was impossible on the day of the Passover (J. Edwards 2002: 437n54). See the introduction to 14:53–65 for a discussion of these alleged violations.

3. The reference to a Roman cohort at Jesus's arrest is often seen as being nonhistorical. But it is highly unlikely that John would have created this strong Roman involvement in the arrest of Jesus, since it conflicts with his own portrayal of a sympathetic Pontius Pilate at Jesus's trial (Bruce 1980: 9; R. Brown 1994: 1.250–51). Is it possible that in the tradition the presence of the

of a detachment of "police" (ὑπηρέτας, *hypēretas*) from the chief priests and Pharisees.[4] If the Gospels' descriptions of the "crowd" are taken seriously, this was clearly not an unorganized mob. Although seeking to avoid armed conflict if at all possible, they are strong enough to put down quickly any possible resistance that Jesus, the disciples, and other followers of Jesus might create (cf. Mark 11:15–19).

The kiss of Judas must be understood in view of the darkness of Gethsemane. Even if there were a bright moon, among the olive trees in the garden, recognizing Jesus would have been difficult. If the night were cloudy, the difficulty would have been exacerbated. Even if they knew Jesus by face, they would have difficulty in the darkness distinguishing him from the tens of thousands of pilgrims camping on the surrounding hills of Jerusalem. Furthermore, Jesus was apparently personally unknown to most of the crowd coming to seize him (R. Brown 1994: 1.251–52). Compare how in the Johannine account Jesus must identify himself to them (John 18:7–8). Judas tells the leaders of the crowd to seize[5] Jesus "securely" (ἀσφαλῶς, *asphalōs*). Although this adverb can be translated "safely" (cf. 1 Thess. 5:3), here it must mean "so that he cannot escape" (cf. Acts 16:23). **14:44–46**

Although clear in meaning, the use of the double participles "coming" (ἐλθών, *elthōn*) and "approaching" (προσελθών, *proselthōn*) in 14:45 is awkward, as the rewording by Matthew (26:49) and Luke (22:49) indicates. The term "Rabbi" may be understood as a titulary address or as a reverential greeting. Whether it was already a title in Jesus's day is debated (R. Brown 1994: 1.253n18; Donahue and Harrington 2002: 415). A kiss was a frequent form of greeting (1 Sam. 10:1; 2 Sam. 19:39; Luke 7:45; Rom. 16:16; 1 Pet. 5:14; 1 Esd. 4:47; *b. Soṭah* 13a; *b. Ḥag.* 14b; etc.). It was apparently the rabbi, however, who normally bestowed the kiss on a disciple rather than the reverse (Lachs 1987: 416). This greeting must have been normal enough, though, not to have aroused suspicion. The intensive form of the verb (κατεφίλησεν, *katephilēsen* [14:45], rather than ἐφίλησεν, *ephilēsen* [cf. 14:44]) may indicate that Judas exaggerated the kiss to show clearly whom the crowd was to seize. This is the only instance in the Gospels where such a greeting is exchanged between Jesus and the disciples. Together, the greeting and kiss strongly emphasize the despicable nature of Judas's betrayal (cf. 2 Sam. 20:9–10). Having been identified, Jesus is now seized (cf. 14:44). For "laying hands on him" (ἐπέβαλον τὰς χεῖρας αὐτῷ, *epebalon tas cheiras autō*) in a negative sense, compare Gen. 22:12;

---

tribune and part of the cohort implied for John that "the" Roman cohort was involved in the seizing of Jesus, even if the majority were in their barracks?

4. It is probable that these refer not to the Levitical temple police but to servants of the Sanhedrin who were available for police duties (Blinzler 1959: 61–70; R. Brown 1994: 1.249–50; France 2002: 593; cf. Acts 5:22, 26).

5. The word "seize" is a more accurate term for describing what happened than the term "arrest." The verb "seize" (κρατέω, *krateō*) in 14:44, 46, and 49 (cf. also 14:1) does not involve a modern-day process of arresting someone but rather a hostile kidnapping (see footnote 2 at 14:1–11).

2 Sam. 18:12; 2 Kings 11:16; 2 Chron. 23:15; Neh. 13:21 (2 Esd. 23:21 LXX); Luke 20:19; John 7:30, 44; Acts 4:3; 5:18; 12:1; and so on. For the positive use of the idiom for healing or blessing, see Mark 5:23; 6:5; 7:32; 8:25; 10:16 (cf. also 1:31; 5:41; 8:23; 9:27).

14:47-50 The pre-Markan state of the following collection of traditions is uncertain. The first tradition (14:47) involves an unnamed person in Mark: "one of those who had been standing nearby" (εἷς δέ [τις] τῶν παρεστηκότων, *eis de [tis] tōn parestēkotōn*). In the other Gospels he is more clearly defined: "one of those with Jesus" (Matt. 26:51/Luke 22:49) and "Simon Peter" (John 18:10). Elsewhere in Mark the expression "those who were standing by" is never used of Jesus's disciples (14:69, 70; 15:35, 39), and numerous scholars suggest that he was not a disciple (Gundry 1993: 860; R. Brown 1994: 1.266–67; van Iersel 1998: 438–39; Donahue and Harrington 2002: 415). Yet if we take seriously what the other Gospels say, he was a follower of Jesus. The term used for "ear" (ὠτάριον, *ōtarion*) is a diminutive and not the normal term used for "ear" (οὖς, *ous*). As a result some suggest that it may refer to an "ear lobe" (Evans 2001: 424). In two other Gospels the "ear" is described as the "right ear" (Luke 22:50; John 18:10), and "the servant of the high priest" is named "Malchus" in John 18:10. That the singular "high priest" is used in the man's description indicates that he was not simply a servant of the ruling priests, but the servant of the high priest, Caiaphas.

The term used by Mark to describe "striking" (ἔπαισεν, *epaisen*) the servant of the high priest is unusual, since this word normally refers to striking someone with the fist (Matt. 26:68; Luke 22:64). The other Synoptic Gospels use another word for "strike" (πατάσσω, *patassō*; Matt. 26:51; Luke 22:49–50), which generally is used for striking with a sword (Num. 21:24; Deut. 20:13; Josh. 19:48; 2 Sam. 15:14; 23:10; 2 Kings 19:37; Isa. 37:38; Jer. 2:30; etc.). It is unlikely that what is being referred to is a deliberate mutilation of the servant in order to prohibit him from being involved in ritual activities (cf. Lev. 21:18; Josephus, *Ant.* 14.13.10 §§365–66; contra Viviano 1989). What is involved is not a careful surgical cutting with a knife but a slashing stroke with a sword (R. Brown 1994: 1.273–74) that was probably off target.

Jesus's reference to his opponents coming after him involves a word (λῃστής, *lēstēs*) that can refer to a thief, bandit, or revolutionary. In 15:27 the two men crucified with Jesus are called λῃστάς. In John 18:40 Barabbas is called a λῃστής, and in Mark 15:7 he is described as having committed murder in an insurrection (στάσις, *stasis*). Jesus was never accused of theft, but he taught that he was bringing "the kingdom of God" (1:15),[6] which could easily be thought of as revolutionary; and since he was accused of claiming to be the "king of the Jews" (15:1–5), it is likely that λῃστής should be interpreted as "revolutionary." The great concern of the religious leadership over Jesus and the number of people sent to seize him would be highly unusual for catching a thief. For Mark's readers the term λῃστής would almost certainly have been

---

6. "Teaching" is more an activity of revolutionaries than of thieves.

understood as referring to a political revolutionary (R. Brown 1994: 1.284; Donahue and Harrington 2002: 416).

In rebuking the crowd, Jesus refers to his having been "daily" (καθ' ἡμέραν, *kath' hēmeran*) with them in the temple. This adverbial phrase can mean "day after day" or "in the daytime" (Argyle 1951). The latter is supported by Luke 21:37, and if one follows precisely the chronology of Mark's Gospel, Jesus spent only three days in the temple (11:11, 15–19; 11:27–13:1), and the first one did not involve teaching. It is highly unlikely, however, that Jesus taught on only two occasions in the temple, for the periphrasis ("was teaching" [ἤμην . . . διδάσκων, *ēmēn . . . didaskōn*]) favors a "day-after-day" teaching (cf. Luke 19:47), and this fits the chronological scheme found in the Gospel of John (Donahue and Harrington 2002: 416). The "temple" (ἱερόν, *hieron*) refers to the entire temple complex, including the Court of the Gentiles (cf. 11:11, 15 [2×], 16, 27; 12:35; 13:1, 3; also 12:41), but not the "sanctuary" (ναός, *naos*) itself (14:58; 15:29, 38). Jesus's rebuke reveals the cowardice of the crowd coming to seize him at night, for it would have been much easier to find Jesus during the daytime when he was teaching in the temple rather than in the darkness of Gethsemane. He was fully accessible to them, but because of his popularity with the people (11:18; 12:12, 37), they came at night, for fear that their seizing him during the day in the temple might result in a riot (14:2).

The expression "But [let it be] in order that the Scriptures may be fulfilled" (ἀλλ' ἵνα πληρωθῶσιν αἱ γραφαί, *all' hina plērōthōsin hai graphai*; 14:49b) emphasizes God's sovereign control over what is taking place. Compare T. Naph. 7.1, "These things must be fulfilled in their season." A verb is implied between "But" and "in order that" (Cranfield 1959: 437; Evans 2001: 426), as Matt. 26:56 indicates. Exactly what Scripture is being referred to is debated. Some suggest that it is Isa. 53:12 (Witherington 2001: 382; J. Edwards 2002: 439–40), but since Zech. 13:7 is expressly referred to in 14:27, this seems more likely (R. Brown 1994: 1.289; Evans 2001: 427; Donahue and Harrington 2002: 416).

The second part of the account (14:47–50) ends with the fulfillment of Jesus's prediction in 14:27 ("I will strike the shepherd, and the sheep will be scattered"). The emphatic "all" (πάντες, *pantes*) in 14:50 recalls not only 14:27 but 14:23, 29, and 31 as well. On the human level the frustration of the disciples and their deserting of Jesus is understandable (France 2002: 595). What could they do? Jesus did not sanction violent resistance. The armed crowd, on the other hand, did not want them as prospective martyrs and let them flee, for at this time there was no "Jesus movement" (R. Brown 1994: 1.290–91) to be concerned about, and only Jesus was important. By their seizure and elimination of Jesus, his followers would soon disappear (cf. 2 Sam. 17:1–3). Having once left (ἀφίημι, *aphiēmi*) their families to follow Jesus (1:18, 20; 10:28–29), the disciples now leave (ἀφέντες, *aphentes*) Jesus (R. Brown 1994: 1.287, 303–4). However, the readers know, both from what was said earlier in the chapter (14:28) and the gospel traditions, that this is not the end of the story. There will come a restoration (16:7), and the failures of the disciples will one day turn to faithful service even unto death.

14:51–52 The story of the "young man" (νεανίσκος, *neaniskos*) in these verses is confusing. Mark's purpose in including it is unclear.[7] There has been much discussion as to the identity of the young man. These include that he was (1) a curiosity seeker living in the area; (2) a follower of Jesus who was not one of the disciples (συνηκολούθει, *synēkolouthei*, in 14:51 and its related verbal forms are often used in Mark to describe following Jesus; note also how the crowd seeks to seize the young man); (3) John the brother of James (cf. John 18:15); (4) James the brother of Jesus; (5) Lazarus; (6) an angel (note how the angel in the tomb [16:5] is described as a "young man" [νεανίσκον]); (7) a symbolic, not historical, figure for Christian martyrs or Christians preparing for baptism; (8) a prefiguration of the risen Christ (the term σινδών [*sindōn*] or "linen garment" of the young man is used one other time in Mark, to describe Jesus's burial garment in 15:46); (9) "a dramatization . . . of the universal flight of the disciples" (Fleddermann 1979: 417); (10) an autobiographical comment by the author, John Mark. (See R. Brown 1994: 1.297–304 for a helpful summary.) The attempts to see the young man as a positive symbolic figure are unconvincing, because his fleeing naked is a sign of shame. The young man chose shame over faithfulness. The young man is clearly not an angel, for angels do not flee in fear from humans. In some way he is a follower of Jesus, and the lack of any obvious theological meaning, as indicated by its omission from Matthew and Luke, suggests that it is a historical reminiscence (Pesch 1980b: 402; Hooker 1991: 352). Although the identity of the young man cannot be known with any certainty,[8] it may be that he was known to Mark's readers (cf. 15:21).

Summary

Within the present account we see two of Jesus's three predictions concerning the disciples finding fulfillment. His prediction that one of them would betray him (14:18–21) has now been fulfilled by Judas's leading the crowd sent by the chief priests, scribes, and elders and his identifying Jesus to

7. In 1973 M. Smith (1973a; 1973b) published a presumably genuine fragment of a letter written by Clement of Alexandria, which he discovered in 1958. Supposedly written around AD 200 to a man named Theodore, it was found in a seventeenth-century edition of the works of Ignatius at the monastery of Mar Saba, located between Bethlehem and the Dead Sea. In this fragment, Clement states that he found in a MS of Mark after 10:34 a story of Jesus meeting a young man "clothed with a linen cloth over his nakedness" (the literal translation of 14:51a) who became a disciple and who was taught various mysteries by Jesus. Smith produced pictures of the MS itself, but no one else has ever seen the original MS (see R. Brown 1994: 1.296 for a translation). Whether the fragment is a forgery (see Carlson 2006) or an actual fragment of an otherwise unknown writing of Clement is debated. What is clear is that one should not build elaborate theological systems and historical reconstructions on a supposed note of Clement discovered fifteen or sixteen centuries after his death, which has been seen by only one man. It is also generally agreed now that rather than being part of a "Secret Gospel" of Mark antedating the canonical Mark, the fragment is little more than a pastiche built from materials found in the Gospel of Mark (R. Brown 1994: 1.295–97; Evans 2001: 427–28).

8. Bauckham (2006: 197–99) suggests that this may be due to a need for "protective anonymity."

them (14:44–46). Jesus's second prediction that "all" the disciples would desert him (14:27, 29, 31) is fulfilled when all flee Gethsemane after Jesus is seized (14:50). The third prediction involving Peter's denial (14:30–31) still awaits fulfillment, but this will be fulfilled that very night (14:66–72). Not only are Jesus's predictions all coming true; they also are being realized in the exact order that Jesus gave them. This indicates that Jesus is a true prophet and that he was not in the least surprised by the events taking place. He has known this from the beginning (2:20; 8:31; 9:9, 31; 10:33–34, 38, 45; 12:6–8; 14:8, 18–21, 22–25, 27, 35–42). This is furthermore not simply a human tragedy, but on the contrary the plan of God written in the Scriptures (14:49c).

The portrayal of Jesus in the scene reveals that he is master of the situation. He is confident of fulfilling the will of God (14:49c), and his royal bearing in 14:48–49 is evident. Jesus, prepared by his experience in Gethsemane, does not seek flight to safety but rebukes the crowd. Their cowardice in seeking to arrest him in the night stands in sharp contrast to his confronting them. He is a "noble figure" (Evans 2001: 430) whose behavior would have drawn admiration and respect from Mark's readers. In contrast, the disciples are seen as cowardly and full of fear. They flee, as does the young man who also followed Jesus. Things will change after the resurrection, but at the present time the disciples are not able to fulfill their promise to serve their Lord unto death (14:31). Perhaps Mark intended his readers to reflect on this and wrestle with how they themselves would respond in times of persecution (Donahue and Harrington 2002: 418–19).

Additional Notes

14:43. A few MSS add "Iscariot" (A K Θ) or "Skariot" (D).

14:43. Codices A C D N W Σ Φ read πολύς, hence a "great" crowd. Cf. Matt. 26:47.

14:44. αὐτός is lit. "he."

14:48. ἀποκριθείς is lit. "answering."

14:52. The MSS A D Θ f¹ f¹³ lat add "from them" (ἀπ᾽ αὐτῶν). This, however, seems to be a copyist's addition based on the plural verb "they seized" (κρατοῦσιν) in 14:51.

E. Jesus Is Tried by the Sanhedrin (14:53–65)

The present account closely follows the seizing of Jesus in 14:43–46, for the "and they led" (καὶ ἀπήγαγον, *kai apēgagon*) of 14:53 picks up the "and they laid hands on him . . ." (οἱ δὲ ἐπέβαλον τὰς χεῖρας αὐτῷ, *hoi de epebalon tas cheiras autō . . .*) of 14:46. Mark also prepares his readers for the following account by referring to Peter warming himself at a fire in the courtyard of the high priest (14:54), for the story of Peter's denial (14:66–72) begins with Peter in the courtyard of the high priest (14:66) warming himself (14:67).[1] The Markan account of the trial[2] consists of (1) Jesus being led to the high priest and representatives of the Sanhedrin with Peter following (14:53–54); (2) the search for witnesses against Jesus (14:55–59); (3) the high priest's direct interrogation of Jesus (14:60–61); (4) Jesus's response in which he acknowledges that he is the Messiah, the Son of God (14:62); (5) the Sanhedrin's condemnation of Jesus (14:63–64); and (6) the abuse of Jesus by the leaders of the Sanhedrin (14:65). Pryke (1978: 22, 147, 173) sees Mark's editorial work consisting of 14:53a, 57–59, 61, and 65; Donahue (1973: 65–95) sees 14:53b, 55, 59, 61b–62 as Markan; but Gnilka (1979: 276–77) sees only 14:54 (at a distance, ἀπὸ μακρόθεν, *apo makrothen*) and 14:55 (the chief priests and the whole Sanhedrin, οἱ δὲ ἀρχιερεῖς καὶ ὅλον τὸ συνέδριον, *hoi de archiereis kai holon to synedrion*) as coming from the hand of the evangelist. R. Brown (1994: 1.554) rightly points out, however, the difficulty of separating the Markan contribution from the traditional material.[3]

Additional information concerning the trial of Jesus found in the other Gospels includes Jesus being taken before Annas, a former high priest, who according to custom still bore the title "high priest" (cf. Luke 3:2; John 18:13–23) and his being sent by Pontius Pilate to Herod Antipas, the ruler of Galilee (Luke 23:6–12; cf. Acts 4:27). A possible chronology of the events surrounding the trial of Jesus involves the following: (1) Jesus is led to the home of Annas to allow time for Caiaphas to convene the Sanhedrin, where he is questioned by Annas (John 18:13–23); (2) Jesus is sent from Annas to Caiaphas (John 18:24), at whose house the Sanhedrin meets, tries,

---

1. The historicity of this account is strengthened by the reference to this unessential detail in both Mark (14:54, 67) and John (18:18; Bruce 1980: 11).

2. The question of how to define Jesus's appearance before the Sanhedrin and high priest is greatly debated. The term "trial" is used here even though what takes place is not a "trial" in our modern-day sense of the term.

3. "*Our best methods do not give us the ability to isolate confidently* [the traditional] *material in its exact wording, assigning preMarcan verses and half-verses* from the existing, thoroughly Marcan account" (his italics).

and condemns Jesus (14:53–66); (3) Peter denies Jesus (14:66–72); (4) the Sanhedrin meets early in the morning to draw up political charges against Jesus to present to Pilate (15:1); (5) Jesus is brought before Pilate for trial (15:2–5); (6) Jesus is sent by Pilate to Herod Antipas (Luke 23:6–12); (7) Jesus is sent back by Herod Antipas to Pilate, who, although seeking to avoid executing Jesus, sentences him to death (15:6–15); (8) Jesus is led away, is crucified, and dies (15:16–41); and (9) Joseph of Arimathea is granted the body of Jesus and buries him in a tomb (15:42–47).

Numerous historical questions have been raised with regard to the historicity of Jesus's trial as portrayed in the Gospels. Since the responsibility of certain Jewish leaders for Jesus's death, as portrayed in the Gospels, has been fuel for anti-Semitism over the centuries, the Gospel accounts of the trial have undergone careful and extensive investigation. That the portrayal of the trial violates many of the rules in the mishnaic tractate *Sanhedrin* (R. Brown 1994: 1.357–72; Stein 1996: 234–37) has led to numerous reconstructions of what actually took place at the trial. Yet it must be remembered that the rules found in *m. Sanh.* 4–7 were written down around AD 200 and reflect an idealization of what should have taken place in AD 30.[4] Furthermore, it is questionable whether the Sadducee-dominated Sanhedrin would have followed the idealized rules of the Pharisees found in the Mishnah (Blinzler 1961). Also, the rules of the tractate *Sanhedrin* often conflict with what Josephus says.[5] Yet even if the rules of the Mishnah were in effect in AD 30, this does not mean that they were followed in the trial of Jesus. The Gospels portray Jesus's trial as being a kind of kangaroo court, seeking not whether Jesus was guilty of a capital offense but rather to find some charge to justify putting him to death (14:55a). Finally, if one must decide between the historicity of the trial accounts in the Gospels and the mishnaic rules in effect at Jesus's trial, why choose the latter over the former? The Passion Narrative existed a century and a half before the Mishnah was written, and many eyewitnesses were still around when the account of the trial in Mark was recorded. If one argues that the Gospels were written from a Christian point of view and with a Christian bias, one can equally argue that the Mishnah was written from a Jewish point of view and with a Jewish bias. There is no need to deny the general historicity of the trial accounts in the Gospels.[6] The misappropriation of them by some people

---

4. Very few scholars would accept as authentic the quotations of Jesus found only in the early church fathers written in AD 200 or would accept as historical those events in the life of Jesus recorded only in the same church fathers.

5. Cf. how the Mishnah states that the Sanhedrin met during this period inside the temple (*m. Mid.* 5.4; *m. Sanh.* 11.2), whereas Josephus says that it met outside the temple (*J.W.* 5.4.2 §144; 6.6.3 §354; cf. also *b. Sanh.* 41a; *b. Šabb.* 15a; *b. 'Abod. Zar.* 8b).

6. Concerning the alleged anti-Semitism contained in the NT, one should read L. Johnson (1989), who points out that the criticism of Jews by Christian Jews in the NT was an internal debate that in fact was rather mild. For how intra-Jewish debate often led to violence and murder on a grand scale, cf. R. Brown 1994: 1.393–95.

seeking to justify their anti-Semitism does not mean that we must deny their use in understanding what took place, any more than the misappropriation of drugs by some people requires us to deny their use to relieve pain. That a few religious Jewish leaders in AD 30 sought Jesus's death does not deny that the vast majority of Jews were favorably inclined toward Jesus and that the Jewish people were actually the greatest obstacle for the Jewish leaders in seeking to carry out their plans to kill Jesus (14:1–2).

The historicity of the trial narrative has also been attacked by some scholars on the ground that the Jewish leadership had the right to exercise capital punishment on its citizenry at the time of Jesus, so that there would have been no need to bring Jesus to trial before Pontius Pilate (15:1–15). That Jesus was crucified by Pontius Pilate therefore indicates that it was Rome, not the Sanhedrin, that sentenced and put Jesus to death. Some therefore argue that the account of Jesus's trial before the Sanhedrin was a deliberate fiction created by the early church to switch the responsibility for Jesus's death from the Roman officials to the Jewish leadership. Support for this is seen in that the Jewish leadership was permitted to put to death any gentile who in the temple entered from the Court of the Gentiles into the inner court (Josephus, *J.W.* 6.2.4 §126; 5.5.2 §194; *Ant.* 15.11.5 §417; cf. Acts 21:27–37). Yet Josephus points out that this was a concession granted to the Jews by the Romans. That Rome granted permission for the Jews to do this in this one instance is proof that in general they did not possess this right. The Sanhedrin's putting to death James the brother of Jesus in AD 62 is also offered as evidence for the view that the Jewish leadership possessed the right to exercise capital punishment, but this example actually proves the opposite. This incident took place when a Roman governor/procurator was not present in Judea, and when the new Roman governor heard about this, he immediately removed the high priest responsible for this illegal act from the office of high priest (Josephus, *Ant.* 20.9.1 §§197–203). It seems clear from John 18:31 ("We are not permitted to put anyone to death"); *b. Šabb.* 15a; and *y. Sanh.* 1, 18a, 34; 7, 24b, 41 that in the time of Jesus the Jewish leadership did not possess the right to exercise capital punishment, except in the case of a gentile entering the inner court of the temple.

As to possible source(s) for information concerning the trial, although no apostolic eyewitness was present, information about the trial could have come from members of the Sanhedrin who appear to have been favorable to Jesus (Cranfield 1959: 439; Joseph of Arimathea is described as a member of the council, i.e., the Sanhedrin, in 15:43, and Nicodemus is described in John 3:1 as a "ruler of the Jews"), from reports of what was going on reaching those in the courtyard (Peter [14:54, 66] and possibly the apostle John [John 18:15–16]), from reports of the meeting of the Sanhedrin later recounted to others by its members, and so on. With respect to the meeting before Herod Agrippa (Luke 23:6–12), information may have come from Johanna, the wife of Herod Antipas's steward (Luke 8:3), and Manaen, a member of Herod's court (Acts 13:1). It would have been more difficult to keep hidden what took place at Jesus's trial from an interested person than to learn what took place (cf. Schubert 1984: 390–91; Bock 2000: 195–97). And the followers of Jesus were interested persons! Attempts to reconstruct the sources lying behind the account and the stages through which the narrative went (see Evans 2001: 440 for examples) are speculative, however, and of doubtful value. As to the view that the trial account was a church creation, it "is not as doctrinally coloured" as one would expect if it were a church creation (Cranfield 1959: 439). We shall seek to answer two important questions raised by the account: (1) What was false about the false witnesses' testimony in 14:58? and (2) Why was Jesus judged guilty of blasphemy for what he said in 14:62?

Exegesis and Exposition

⁵³And they led Jesus away to the high priest, and all the chief priests, and the elders, and the scribes assemble. ⁵⁴And Peter followed him at a distance ⌜all the way⌝ into the courtyard of the high priest and was sitting with the servants and warming himself at the ⌜fire⌝.

⁵⁵And the chief priests and the whole Sanhedrin were seeking testimony against Jesus in order to put him to death, and they were not finding [any]. ⁵⁶For many were giving false testimony against him, and their testimonies did not agree. ⁵⁷And certain men ⌜stood up⌝ [and] were giving false testimony against him, saying, ⁵⁸"We heard him saying, 'I will destroy this sanctuary made with hands and after three days will build another not made with hands.'" ⁵⁹And not even ⌜on this point⌝ did their testimony agree. ⁶⁰And the high priest, having stood up in their midst, asked Jesus, saying, "Are you not answering anything? ⌜What⌝ are these men testifying against you?" ⁶¹But he remained silent and was not answering anything. Again the high priest began to ask him and says to him, "Are you the Christ, the Son of the Blessed?" ⁶²And Jesus said, "⌜I am,⌝ and you will see the Son of Man sitting on the right hand of Power and coming with the clouds of heaven." ⁶³And the high priest, after tearing his garments, says, "Why do we still have need of witnesses? ⁶⁴You heard the blasphemy. ⌜What do you think?⌝" And they all condemned him as deserving to die. ⁶⁵And some began to spit on him and to cover his face and to beat him and to say to him, ⌜"Prophesy!"⌝ And the guards received him with blows.

"They led" picks up "They laid hands on him . . ." from 14:46, which in turn refers to the "crowd" sent by the chief priests, the scribes, and the elders to seize Jesus in 14:43. Mark does not give the name of the high priest in his Gospel, but from Matt. 26:3, 57, and John 18:13–18, we learn that it was Caiaphas, who ruled AD 18–36. Jesus is led to the home of Caiaphas (cf. 14:54 ["the courtyard of the high priest"] and 14:66). According to John 18:13–24, Jesus was first brought to the home of a former high priest, Annas, who was the father-in-law of Caiaphas (John 18:13), before he was taken to the home of Caiaphas.[7] Several times already we have encountered "the chief priests, the scribes, and

14:53–54

---

7. For a discussion of the location of Caiaphas's home in Jerusalem, see Evans 2001: 442.

the elders" (see 14:43) and are aware of their hostility toward Jesus and their desire to kill him (8:31; cf. 10:33; 14:1). Although this group is not synonymous with the Sanhedrin (cf. 15:1), they made up a large part of it.

To prepare the reader for Peter's denial (14:66–72), Mark comments that Peter followed Jesus (i.e., him, αὐτῷ, autō—not the crowd leading Jesus to the meeting of the Sanhedrin) into the courtyard of the high priest. "At a distance" (ἀπὸ μακρόθεν, apo makrothen) may have negative connotations with respect to Peter's following Jesus (J. Edwards 2002: 442; cf., however, Gundry 1993: 884). Nevertheless, Peter is the only disciple who follows Jesus (thus supporting his claim to greater loyalty in 14:29 and 31), and because he does so, he is in a position to deny him. By hiding, the other disciples faced no such temptation. In the courtyard Peter sits by the fire with the "servants" (ὑπηρετῶν, hypēretōn). This term can refer to the servants of the high priest or the servants of other members of the Sanhedrin who had come to the meeting. The term is used only one other time in Mark, in 14:65, where it refers to the "guards" to whom Jesus is handed over. They are probably not the same group, however, because the servants in 14:54 are in the courtyard, whereas the servants in 14:65 are inside the house, where the meeting of the Sanhedrin is taking place. In his telling of Peter's denial, Mark arranges his material in a typical Markan sandwich in which the trial (14:55–65) is sandwiched between the story of Peter's denial (14:54 and 66–72; J. Edwards 1989: 198, 211–13). In telling the story, Luke chooses to avoid switching back and forth from the account of Peter's denial and thus stays with Peter in Mark 14:54 (Luke 22:53c–54), completely recounting his denial (22:55–62) before turning to the account of Jesus's trial (22:63–71). This involves not so much a contradictory chronology but rather a different literary style in telling the story (Stein 1992a: 563–64; R. Brown 1994: 1.592).

14:55–59   The references to "all the chief priests, and the elders, and the scribes" (14:53) and "the whole Sanhedrin" (14:55) being present are probably examples of Mark's tendency to universalize (Donahue and Harrington 2002: 421). However, the attempt to see "the whole Sanhedrin" as meaning only "several members" (Evans 2001: 444) is to be rejected (cf. the "all" [πάντες, pantes] in 14:53 and 64). Even if "all" does not necessarily mean "every single one," it means "many" (cf. 1:5), rather than just "several." Gundry (1993: 896–97) argues that Mark means literally "all." According to m. Sanh. 1.6, the Sanhedrin consisted of seventy members plus the high priest, but it is uncertain whether this description can be read back to the time of Jesus. The portrayal of what takes place does not describe a legal trial. This is especially true if some of the rules in m. Sanhedrin were in effect in Jesus's day. Yet Mark's portrayal describes more than an informal hearing (contra V. Taylor 1952: 564; Evans 2001: 444). The search for witnesses (14:55), the hearing of eyewitness testimony (14:56–59, esp. 58), Jesus defending himself (14:60), the placing of Jesus under an oath (Matt. 26:63), the high priest's formal tearing of his robe (Mark 14:63), the concluding decision of the whole Sanhedrin (14:64), and so on look far more like a trial than an informal hearing (Donahue and Harrington 2002: 426–27). That it was held at night reveals the Sanhedrin's fear of Jesus and his popularity and the need to deal with the issue quickly before "the people" (14:2) became aware of what was happening and were able to react.

That the trial was not a fair trial is made clear by Mark from the beginning.[8] Mark does not describe the purpose of the Sanhedrin's meeting as seeking to determine the guilt or innocence of Jesus, for they have already decided to put him to death (14:55; cf. 14:1). Thus witnesses were sought[9] not to determine if Jesus deserved death (14:61) but rather to justify and support the predetermined decision to put Jesus to death (εἰς τὸ θανατῶσαι αὐτόν, *eis to thanatōsai auton*; an articular infinitive of purpose). Thus "while the charge was not yet decided, the verdict was!" (France 2002: 604; cf. Donahue and Harrington 2002: 427). Despite this, the testimony of the witnesses did not permit a guilty verdict, because their testimonies did not agree (14:56b, 59). Mark emphasizes the innocence of Jesus by the twofold repetition of the disagreement among the witnesses (14:56, 69). He also does this by stating that the Sanhedrin was not able to find (despite considerable effort, as the imperfect "were seeking" [ἐζήτουν, *ezētoun*] indicates) any testimony that could be used to condemn Jesus to death (14:55a). Finally, Mark emphasizes this by referring twice to the witnesses giving false testimony (ἐψευδομαρτύρουν, *epseudomartyroun*; 14:56, 57). Since it was necessary to have two witnesses agree in their testimony, no accusation of these witnesses could be accepted (Deut. 19:15).

The only specific charge of the false witnesses that Mark mentions is that "We [ἡμεῖς (*hēmeis*) is emphatic] heard him saying, 'I [this is also emphatic, as the redundant ἐγώ (*egō*) indicates] will destroy this sanctuary (ναόν, *naon*) made with hands and after three days will build another not made with hands'" (14:58). In Mark, the reader has not come across any such statement of Jesus up to this point, so the charge comes as a surprise. The nearest thing is in 13:2, where Jesus predicts the destruction of the "temple" (ἱερόν, *hieron*). However, although 13:2 could be deduced from 14:58, the reverse is not true: given 13:2, one cannot deduce 14:58. In light of John 2:19 and Mark 14:58 and 15:29 (cf. also the parallels in Matt. 26:61 and 27:40; Acts 6:14; Heb. 9:11; and Gos. Thom. 71), it appears that Jesus may very well have said something like 14:58 (E. Sanders 1985: 71–76). The sanctuary (ναός), mentioned only here and in 15:29 and 38 in Mark, refers not to the entire temple complex (ἱερόν) but to the building located in the Court of the Priests, consisting of the holy place and the holy of holies.

8. If the rules found in *m. Sanhedrin* were in effect in Jesus's day, the illegal nature of the trial is seen from several factors already mentioned. In addition, the trial was held at night, during the Passover (*m. Sanh.* 4.1), and not in the special meeting place in the temple called "the Chamber of Hewn Stone" but in the home of the high priest (*m. Sanh.* 11.2)—violations of the rules found in the Mishnah.

9. For the negative use of "seeking" (ζητέω, *zēteō*) in Mark, cf. 8:11–12; 11:18; 12:12; 14:1, 11.

The first part of the saying is reasonably clear: Jesus is saying that he himself (the "I" [ἐγώ] is emphatic) will destroy the sanctuary of the temple (R. Brown 1994: 1.439; contra Ellis 1994: 197–202). The terms "made with hands" (χειροποίητον, *cheiropoiēton*; cf. Acts 7:48; 17:24; Eph. 2:11; Heb. 9:11, 24) and "not made with hands" (ἀχειροποίητον, *acheiropoiēton*; cf. 2 Cor. 5:1; Col. 2:11) distinguish between human agency and divine agency (Donahue and Harrington 2002: 421) and may well be from the hand of Mark (Donahue 1973: 106; Ellis 1994: 199). Rebuilding "it" in three days is less clear. Some see this as a reference to the establishment of the Christian church (Juel 1977: 144–57). Others see it as referring to the construction of a future sanctuary that God himself would build. Others see it as a reference to the resurrected, glorified body of Jesus. The earlier references in the passion predictions (8:31; 9:31; 10:34) to "three days" and its association with the resurrection of Jesus argue in favor of its being a reference to the resurrected body of Jesus "not made with hands" (Hooker 1991: 359; R. Brown 1994: 1.440–44; Donahue and Harrington 2002: 421).

The question of how the statement of the witnesses in 14:58 is a "false testimony" (14:57) is less clear. There are several suggestions. One is that the witnesses were falsely testifying because they did not personally hear Jesus say this, but what they claim that Jesus said is nevertheless true. This, however, would have been too subtle for Mark's readers to have understood (R. Brown 1994: 1.445). Another suggestion is that the story is a complete fabrication of the witnesses, for Jesus never said this. Yet 15:29 and John 2:19 argue strongly against this. A more likely explanation is that the witnesses are false in thinking and suggesting that Jesus said he would personally destroy the sanctuary (i.e., the present, physical sanctuary), and that the rebuilt sanctuary (i.e., the after-three-days future sanctuary) would be similar in nature (J. Edwards 2002: 444–45; Donahue and Harrington 2002: 422). The term "another" (ἄλλον, *allon*), however, suggests that the building of the "other" sanctuary refers not to the replacement of the old physical sanctuary made with hands with another physical sanctuary made by God and therefore not made with hands, but rather to "another" kind of temple altogether, Jesus's resurrected body. This "other" sanctuary is qualitatively different in several ways: it is not made with hands, it is made in three days, and it is "another" kind of sanctuary. As a result, the witnesses of this saying not only did not agree (14:59) with each other but also were false (14:57) because they misrepresented what Jesus said. Consequently, this saying of Jesus, which was potentially dangerous, could not be used to help justify the predetermined verdict (Num. 35:30; Deut. 17:6; 19:15).

14:60–61 With the failure of the false witnesses to bring a sustainable charge against Jesus, the high priest takes a direct approach and "interrogates" (Evans 2001: 448) Jesus. Although 14:60 can be interpreted as a single question ("Have you nothing at all to answer what these men are witnessing against you?"; Donahue and Harrington 2002: 419; NEB, REB), most understand it as consisting of two questions ("Are you not answering anything [lit. 'nothing']? What are these men testifying against you?"; RSV, NRSV, NIV, TNIV, NASB, NAB). The silence of Jesus during the trial is assumed by the first question and is expressly affirmed by a twofold statement in 14:61, "But he remained silent [ἐσιώπα, *esiōpa*] and was not answering [ἀπεκρίνατο, *apekrinato*] anything [lit. 'nothing']." (Cf. also Jesus's silence before Pilate in 15:5.) Many see Jesus's silence as an allusion to Isa. 53:7, and his abuse by the guards (Mark 14:65; cf. also 15:19) as an allusion to Isa. 50:6 (Watts 2000: 362–64), but none of the Gospel writers explicitly refers here to these passages in Isaiah.

In the high priest's question, "Are *you* the Christ, the Son of the Blessed?" (σὺ εἶ ὁ χριστὸς ὁ υἱὸς τοῦ εὐλογητοῦ; *sy ei ho christos ho huios tou eulogētou?*), the "you" (σύ) is emphatic and draws attention to what Jesus himself thinks of who he is and what his mission is. "Blessed" (εὐλογητοῦ) is a circumlocution for God (Stein 1994b: 63–64) and reflects the Jewish reverence for the name of God. Although some have argued that the title "Son of the Blessed" did not exist in the time of Jesus, its authenticity is supported by the fact that Mark has no hesitation elsewhere in using the equivalent title "Son of God" (1:1; 3:11; 15:39; cf. also 1:24; 5:7; Bock 2000: 215–17). The circumlocution heightens the irony of the high priest observing theological niceties by avoiding using the sacred name for God (LORD or YHWH) while unjustly condemning Jesus to death (Donahue and Harrington 2002: 422; cf. also Hooker 1991: 360). The readers, of course, know the answer to this question. Since the opening words of the Gospel, they have known that Jesus is "the Christ, the Son of God" (1:1), and the disciples have known that he is the Christ since 8:29 (cf. also 9:41). The answer to this question is evident even to a pagan centurion (15:39). The high priest's question may have arisen from Jesus's parable of the vineyard, where he refers to himself as God's Son (12:6), for the "they" of 12:12 refers back to the "them" of 12:1, which in turn refers back to the chief priests, the scribes, and the elders of 11:27, who are present at the trial (14:53; Kingsbury 1983: 117–19).

That Jesus's disciples and followers believed that he was the Christ seems reasonably certain.[10] Throughout the Gospel, Jesus has also been described as the Son of God: in the evangelist's editorial work (1:1; 3:11), by God (1:11; 9:7), by the demons (5:7; cf. also 1:24 and 3:11), by Jesus (13:32; cf. also 12:6), and later by a pagan centurion (15:39). Whether the title "Son of God" was a synonym for "Christ" in the first century is debated. Some argue that it was not (Hooker 1991: 360), but others that it was (Evans 2001: 448–49). Several references in the Dead Sea Scrolls (4Q174 1.11; 4Q246 2.1; and 1QSa 2.11–12) seem to favor the latter position (Evans 2001: 448–49; see also Fitzmyer 1993, who is more cautious). That Jesus used this title to describe himself seems certain from 12:6 and 13:32, verses whose authenticity is all but assured by the unlikelihood that they could be creations of the early church (see the introduction to 12:1–12 and the comments on 13:32). If, as seems reason-

---

10. See R. Brown (1994: 1.473–80) for a succinct and helpful discussion of the historical question of whether Jesus was considered the Christ during his lifetime.

able, Jesus's disciples believed that he was the Christ, and since they heard him referring to himself as the Son, they would have understood these titles as "synonymous." Marcus (1989a) has provided a useful suggestion of how the title may have been used by the high priest. Rather than the title "Son of the Blessed/God" being a "non-restrictive synonym," he argues that it should be understood as in "restrictive apposition" to the title "Christ," that is, the second title qualifies the first. Thus Jesus is not being asked if he is the Son of David–Messiah but rather whether he is a quasi-divine, Son of God–Messiah (cf. 12:6 and Matt. 11:27/Luke 10:22).

14:62 The reply of Jesus to the high priest is puzzling in several ways. For one, why after all his silence does Jesus now respond to the high priest's question? Matthew helps explain this, however, for in Matt. 26:63c the question of the high priest is preceded by his having placed Jesus under an oath: "I put you under oath before the living God, tell us. . . ." This, unlike some present-day legal systems that do not require a defendant to testify against himself/herself, required a defendant to answer the question addressed to him/her. Silence would be an admission of guilt (Lev. 5:1; cf. also Prov. 29:24; Judg. 17:2; 1 Kings 22:16; *m. Šebu.* 4.13). As a result, at this point Jesus answers the question of the high priest. His answer contains two parts. The first is "I am" (ἐγώ εἰμι, *egō eimi*), and with this the "messianic secret" in Mark comes to an end. Both Matthew (26:64) and Luke (22:70) agree that Jesus's reply, while affirmative (cf. Matt. 26:64 with 26:25, where "You have said so" [σὺ εἶπας, *sy eipas*] is also used and must mean "yes"), is more reticent. In this respect Matthew's and Luke's replies are probably more authentic in wording, but all accounts record a positive reply of Jesus to the question, as the response of the Sanhedrin indicates. Note especially Matt. 26:68, where Jesus is addressed as the "Christ" because of his reply in 26:64. It is on the basis of his confession as the Christ/Messiah that Jesus is crucified as the King of the Jews (Mark 15:2–3, 12, 18–20, 26, 32). The "I am" in Mark is a simple affirmation to the high priest's question and not an allusion to the divine name (contra Stauffer 1960: 124–26).

The second part of Jesus's reply consists of two OT texts. The first (Ps. 110:1 [109:1 LXX])[11] borrows the title "Son of Man" from the second (Dan. 7:13): "You will see the Son of Man sitting on the right hand of Power." This relates to the exaltation of Christ in his resurrection (cf. Rom. 1:4; Acts 2:32–33; 5:30–31; etc.) to the right hand of "Power" (δυνάμεως, *dynameōs*), a circumlocution for God in which Jesus follows the lead of the high priest, who in his question avoided uttering the name of God by using "Blessed." The second OT text refers to the Son of Man "coming with the clouds of heaven." This is not a repetition of the first OT text but refers to the parousia (see 13:24–25, 26) of the Son of Man coming in judgment at the end of history (R. Brown

11. Psalm 110:1 is the most quoted OT passage in the NT (Matt. 22:44; 26:64; Mark 12:36; 14:62; Luke 20:42–43; 22:69; Acts 2:34–35; 5:31; Rom. 8:34; 1 Cor. 15:25; Eph. 1:20; Col. 3:1; Heb. 1:3, 13; 8:1; 10:12).

1994: 1.494–500; Evans 2001: 451–52; Donahue and Harrington 2002: 423; contra V. Taylor 1952: 568; France 2002: 612–13; cf. also Hooker 1991: 362). At that time there will take place a reversal of roles in that the Son of Man will judge those now judging him. Numerous commentators have pointed out an incongruity in the two-part answer of Jesus, for in the first part Jesus is "sitting" and in the second he is "coming." Evans (2001: 452) seeks to explain this by stating that this all takes place on God's chariot throne, where Jesus is both sitting and coming, but Mark's readers would most probably not have understood these two OT texts in this manner. Most scholars understand this as involving two different events: Jesus's resurrection and enthronement after his death, and his later parousia at the consummation of history.

In reaction to Jesus's reply in 14:62, the high priest tore his garments. This **14:63–64** should not be interpreted as an act of uncontrolled rage but rather as a formal judicial act if the rules concerning trials in *m. Sanh.* 7.5 were in effect in Jesus's day. If so, this indicates not grief (Gen. 37:29, 34; 2 Sam. 1:11–12; Job 1:20; etc.) but rather the rendering of a guilty verdict by the high priest. This would not have involved a tearing of the priestly, liturgical garments (Exod. 28:4; Lev. 16:4), which were not to be torn (Lev. 10:6), but of either his regular clothes or perhaps the inner tunics lying under the liturgical garments (R. Brown 1994: 1.517–19). The plural "garments" (χιτῶνας, *chitōnas*) is somewhat surprising, since usually only one χιτῶν (a tunic-like undergarment in contrast to a "robe" [ἱμάτιον, *himation*]) was worn, but Josephus (*Ant.* 17.5.7 §136) refers to some people wearing two such tunics. There is no allusion here to the "tearing" (ἐσχίσθη, *eschisthē*) of the temple curtain in 15:38, because a different term (διαρρήξας, *diarrēxas*) is used here (contra Hooker 1991: 357; Witherington 2001: 385).[12]

The priest then asks the rhetorical question, "Why do we still have need of witnesses?" He believes that Jesus has incriminated himself, so that there is no longer any need for witnesses. This would violate *b. Sanh.* 9b, which states, "No one can incriminate himself," but it is uncertain that such a rule was in effect four centuries earlier, in the time of Jesus, and it is also uncertain that the kangaroo court in which Jesus was tried would observe such a ruling if it conflicted with their intended purpose. On at least one other occasion, we read of an attempt by Jesus's opponents to trap him by what he said (Mark 12:13/Matt. 22:15/Luke 20:20). The implication is clear that they were seeking to use Jesus's own words to condemn him, and it was Jesus's own words that are the basis for his condemnation, according to Luke 22:71.

In Mark 14:64 we read that Jesus is condemned for "blasphemy" (βλασφημίας, *blasphēmias*), but exactly what it was in Jesus's reply that was blasphemous is unclear (see R. Brown 1994: 1.534–47; Evans 2001: 453–55; and A. Collins 2004 for helpful discussions). It is also unclear as to what constituted blasphemy in first-century Palestinian Judaism. According to *m. Sanh.* 7.5 (cf. also Philo,

---

12. The tearing of the temple curtain finds its closest analogy in 1:10, where the same term (σχιζομένους, *schizomenous*) is used.

Moses 2.38 §206), blasphemy occurred only when a person "pronounces the NAME" (i.e., the sacred name *Yahweh*), but this does not take place at Jesus's trial, as his circumlocution "Power" indicates (cf. also the high priest's "Blessed"). The claim that Jesus committed blasphemy by referring to himself as the "I am" (Exod. 3:14) is unconvincing because the parallel accounts in Matt. 26:64 and Luke 22:70 ("You have said so") are probably closer to the exact words Jesus uttered. The claim to be the Christ/Messiah was also not blasphemous in and of itself, because Bar Kokhba referred to himself as the Christ/Messiah in AD 132–135 without being accused of blasphemy (Marcus 1989a: 127–30). Jesus's claim to be the Son of Man is also unlikely to have resulted in the charge of blasphemy, for he had used this as a self-designation in over fifty separate instances (Jeremias 1967: 159–64). Was Jesus charged with blasphemy because he claimed that he would soon sit at the right hand of God and come to judge the world (A. Collins 2004: 398–400)?

It is probably not just what Jesus said in 14:62 that brought the charge of blasphemy but that this was interpreted in the larger context of what Jesus said and did in his ministry.[13] One must add the following to his statement in 14:62: his claim of the divine prerogative to forgive sins (2:5–7; cf. Luke 7:48–49; Ellis 1994: 192–94), his claim to be the Son of God (12:6), his claim to be the Son of Man of Dan. 7:13 (R. Brown 1994: 1.506–15; Stein 1994b: 135–51), his prediction that he would bring about the destruction of the temple (see 14:55–59), his claim to be Lord of the Sabbath (2:28) and being able to nullify not only the oral traditions but also aspects of the Mosaic law (7:14–23; 10:2–12; cf. also Matt. 5:21–48), and so on (R. Brown 1994: 1.523–26). It is all this along with the new claim of sitting at the right hand of God (Evans 2001: 456) and coming as the Son of Man to judge the world (and thus the Sanhedrin) that led to the charge of blasphemy.[14] And one must admit that if Jesus did not have the authority to do what he claimed above and in 14:62, the charge is correct. At the heart of this charge of blasphemy lies the question of Christology. If Jesus is the Christ, the Son of God (1:1), then what he said in 14:62 is not blasphemous; if he is not the Christ, the Son of God, then it is (Bock 2000: 30–112, esp. 110–12). At this point the Sanhedrin unanimously (πάντες, *pantes*)[15] "condemned" (κατέκριναν, *katekrinan*) Jesus as deserving

13. Although some scholars argue that it was Jesus's statement about destroying the temple (14:58) that was the basis of his being charged with blasphemy (V. Taylor 1952: 568; E. Sanders 1985: 71–76, 300–306), the charge of blasphemy against Jesus comes not after what the witnesses say in 14:58 but after what Jesus says in 14:62. In Mark, the charge against Jesus in 14:58 is referred to as coming from false witnesses (14:57). It is his claim to be the Christ, the Son of God, who would soon sit at the right hand of God and return to judge the world (and the Sanhedrin) in 14:62, that is the basis for the charge of blasphemy in 14:63–64.

14. The charge of blasphemy in Jesus's day appears to have been interpreted more broadly than in *m. Sanh.* 7.5. See A. Collins (2004: 379–401), who lists as examples CD 15.1–3; 1QS 6.27–7.2; Josephus, *J.W.* 2.8.9 §145; *Ant.* 4.8.6 §202.

15. "All" is probably hyperbolic and allows for exceptions such as Joseph of Arimathea and Nicodemus, but apart from such exceptions, Mark wants his readers to understand that the Sanhedrin was united in their condemnation of Jesus.

to die (lit. "of death"; just as he predicted in 10:33). The sentence of death, however, could not be carried out by the Sanhedrin, because they did not possess the general right to carry out capital punishment (John 18:31). As a result, they brought charges against Jesus before the one person who could, Pontius Pilate.

After the sentence is passed, "some" (τινές, *tines*) of the chief priests, elders, and scribes (this is implied from 14:53) began to "spit" on Jesus (cf. 10:34), to cover his face (περικαλύπτειν αὐτοῦ τὸ πρόσωπον, *perikalyptein autou to prosōpon*, i.e., to blindfold him), to strike him, and to challenge him to prophesy (i.e., to say who was hitting him).[16] No doubt the acknowledgment of Jesus as a prophet by the people (6:15; 8:28; cf. 6:4) and his prophecies in 14:58 and 62 lie behind this mockery. The abuse is meant not to physically harm Jesus but to shame him (cf. Num. 12:14; Deut. 25:9; Job 30:9–10). Similar abuse and mockery will occur following Jesus's condemnation by Pilate (15:16–20). After the religious leaders think that they have shamed Jesus sufficiently, they hand him over to the guards.

14:65

Summary

The christological significance of the trial account for Mark is clear. It is the climax of his portrait of Jesus (Donahue and Harrington 2002: 428). Jesus has been described as the Son of God by the evangelist in 1:1 and 3:11, by the divine voice from heaven in 1:11 and 9:7, by the demons in 5:7 (cf. also 1:24 and 3:11), by Jesus in 13:32 (cf. also 12:6), and will soon be confessed as such by a pagan centurion in 15:39. Now, here before the leaders of Israel, Jesus himself confesses that he is the Christ/Messiah, the Son of God, the Son of Man. At this point the messianic secret comes to an end. There is no longer any need to keep the "secret" from the public and the religious leaders, for his mission is about to be completed. But Mark takes care to emphasize the kind of Christ/Messiah that Jesus is. He is not the Son of David–Messiah, but the Son of God–Messiah. He makes war not with Rome but with a more important enemy, sin! He thus comes to give his life as a ransom (10:45) and to establish a new covenant by the pouring out of his life's blood (14:24). Yet Jesus is more than a righteous and noble martyr, for after three days he will be exalted and sit at his Father's right hand, awaiting the day when he will come as the Son of Man (Dan. 7:13) to judge the world.

In addition we find in the account the fulfillment of a number of Jesus's passion predictions. Some have already been fulfilled: the betrayal of Judas (14:18–21/43–46), Jesus's delivery into the hands of men (9:31/14:43–49), and the desertion of the disciples (14:27–31/32–42, 50). Some are in the process of being fulfilled: Jesus's rejection and condemnation by the chief priests,

16. For examples of games involving the blindfolding of a person, see R. Brown 1994: 1.574–75.

scribes, and elders (8:31; 10:33/14:63–64) and his suffering many things (8:31; 10:34/14:65). And some will soon be fulfilled: Peter's denial (14:29–31/66–72), Jesus's deliverance into the hands of the gentiles (10:33/15:1ff.), his being put to death (8:31; 9:31; 10:34/15:16–37), his rising from the dead after three days (8:31; 9:31; 10:34/16:1–8), and his taking his place at the right hand of God (14:62). For Mark's readers, the fulfillment of these prophecies would give them assurance that what Jesus taught (8:34–38), promised (13:11, 13), and prophesied (such as the destruction of Jerusalem [13:1–4] and the sanctuary [14:58; 15:29], and above all his return as the Son of Man [8:38; 13:24–27, 32–37; 14:62]) will also take place.

Additional Notes

14:54. ἕως ἔσω is lit. "as far as inside," i.e., "right into."

14:54. φῶς, lit. "light." Cf. Luke 22:55–56, where "fire" (πῦρ) and "light" (φῶς) are synonyms.

14:57. ἀναστάντες is lit. "standing up."

14:59. οὕτως is lit. "so."

14:60. A few witnesses (B Pᶜ W Ψ) have "because/for" (ὅτι) instead of "what" (τί).

14:62. A few later MSS read, "You have said that I am," which is an obvious conflation of Mark's "I am" and Matthew's "You have said [so]" in 26:64. Cf. also Luke's "You have said that I am" in 22:70 (Kempthorne 1976). For an opposing view, see V. Taylor (1952: 568) and Cranfield (1959: 443–44).

14:64. τί ὑμῖν φαίνεται is lit. "What does it seem to you?"

14:65. A few MSS add, "Who is it that struck you?" or "Christ, who is it that struck you?" The simple προφήτευσον is witnessed to, however, by ℵ A B C D L lat syrᵖ.

F. Jesus Is Denied by Peter (14:66–72)

At this point Mark now completes the sandwich he began in 14:54, where Peter was left in the courtyard of the high priest, warming himself by a fire. "And while Peter was below in the courtyard" (καὶ ὄντος τοῦ Πέτρου κάτω ἐν τῇ αὐλῇ, *kai ontos tou Petrou katō en tē aulē*; 14:66a) functions literarily after the trial scene (14:55–65) as a "Meanwhile back at the courtyard, Peter. . . ." The story of Peter's denial consists of three parts: (1) an introductory seam (14:66a); (2) Peter's threefold denial, which involves a dramatic progression: (a) to a woman servant, he denies that he knows Jesus (14:66b–68); (b) a continued denial of his being one of Jesus's disciples before a group of bystanders (14:69–70a); and (c) a cursing (of Jesus) and the swearing of an oath to the bystanders that he does not know "this man" (14:70b–71); and (3) Peter's recognition that he has fulfilled Jesus's prediction of a threefold denial (14:30) and his remorse (14:72). Nowhere else in the Passion Narrative do the four Gospels agree to such an extent as in the story of Peter's denial (R. Brown 1994: 1.610). There is no clear tie between the present account and what follows, for 15:1–15 will turn the readers' attention back to the fate of Jesus and his trial before Pontius Pilate. Peter will appear only one more time in Mark. After the resurrection the women at the tomb are told to tell Jesus's "disciples *and Peter*" that Jesus will meet them in Galilee (16:7). Thus Mark as we now have it concludes with an obvious allusion to Peter's forgiveness and reconciliation to Jesus, which Mark's readers already knew took place (cf. 1 Cor. 15:5).

Attempts to delineate the hand of Mark in the present account are hindered by a number of textual problems (see my translation and the additional notes). Pryke (1978: 22, 147, 174) sees 14:66a, 67a, 69–70a, 71a, and 72 as Markan; Gnilka (1979: 290–91) sees only 14:66a, 67a, and 72 as Markan. Independently of Mark, John has the same setting as Mark (the courtyard of the high priest, Caiaphas; John 18:15–16), a similar reference to Peter warming himself (John 18:18), a similar threefold denial by Peter (18:15–17, 25, 26–27), the first denial being to a female servant (18:17), a cock crowing (18:27; cf. also 13:38), and so on, suggesting that Mark's editorial work involves organizing rather than creating material (cf. Mark's sandwiching the trial narrative between Peter's denial [see 14:53–54]; however, Evans [1982: 245–59; 2001: 440–41, 463] argues against it being a Markan sandwich) and using his own style and vocabulary in writing the account (cf. the use of "began to" [ἤρξατο, *ērxato*] followed by an infinitive [14:69, 71]—see 1:45; the use of "and immediately" [καὶ εὐθύς, *kai euthys*] in 14:72—see 1:10–11; etc.). The denial of the historicity of the account (Bultmann 1968: 269) is unconvincing due to its multiple attestation in Mark and John (Fortna 1977–78: 371–83) and the difficulty of believing that anyone in the early church would create such a disparaging account of one of its most famous apostles and that the church would accept it as true and incorporate it into all of the canonical Gospels.[1] (See R. Brown [1994: 1.614–20] for a strong defense of the account's overall historicity.) The ultimate source for the account may go back to Peter himself (Nineham 1963: 399; W. Lane 1974: 541; Fortna 1977–78: 382).

Exegesis and Exposition

[66]And while Peter was below in the courtyard, one of the female servants of the high priest comes, [67]and having seen Peter warming himself [and] after looking intently at him, she says, "*You* ⌜were⌝ also with the Nazarene, Jesus." [68]But he denied [it], saying, "I neither know nor understand what you are saying." And he went outside into the entryway. ⌜And a cock crowed.⌝ [69]And the female servant, having seen him, began again to say to the bystanders, "This man is one of them." [70]And again he was denying [it]. And after a short time the bystanders again began to say to Peter, "Surely you are one of them, for you also are a Galilean." ⌜ ⌝[71]And he began to curse [Jesus] and swear [an oath], "I do not know this man about whom you are talking." [72]And immediately a cock crowed for ⌜the second time⌝. And Peter remembered the saying ⌜how⌝ Jesus said to him, "Before the cock crows ⌜two times⌝ you will deny me three times. And ⌜having rushed out⌝, he began to weep.

14:66a At this point Mark picks up the story of Peter, who is "below" in the courtyard of the high priest. Apparently, the meeting place of the Sanhedrin was on the second floor of Caiaphas's palace (see Evans 2001: 463–64). Although the story of Peter's denial in Mark is told after Jesus's trial before the Sanhedrin and before the trial in Luke, the denial of Peter probably took place during the trial.

14:66b–68 The first denial comes as a response to a statement made by one of the female servants present in the courtyard. When not on duty but on call, the servants of the high priest would have found the courtyard a natural place to gather (France 2002: 620). The term "female servant" (παιδισκῶν, *paidiskōn*) is a diminutive, but in the NT it probably just means a servant who was a woman in distinction from a man, not a young woman servant (cf. Luke 12:45; Gal. 4:22–31). Seeing Peter, she stares at him, looks him over carefully, and apparently recognizes him as a follower of Jesus, someone who was "with" (μετά, *meta*; cf. 3:14) him. Had she at one time seen Peter with Jesus (cf. John 18:26)?

1. Cf. G. Lampe 1972: 349: "The tradition that the chief apostle had repeatedly denied Christ under a much less formidable interrogation than ordinary Christians often had to face is difficult indeed to account for unless it is substantially based on the memory of something that actually happened."

Mark does not tell us how she came to this conclusion. The term "Nazarene" (Ναζαρηνοῦ, *Nazarēnou*) is also found in 1:24; 10:47; and 16:6, and it is spelled variously in the textual tradition. Here it functions as part of his name, "the Nazarene, Jesus." Because Judean Jews had a low view of Galilean Jews (John 1:46; 7:41, 52), it may be used contemptuously here (Donahue and Harrington 2002: 425; France 2002: 620).

Peter's first denial (ἠρνήσατο, *ērnēsato*) picks up Jesus's prediction of his denial (ἀπαρνέομαι, *aparneomai*) in 14:30 and 31 (cf. also 14:72) and will be used again to describe his second denial in 14:70. The two verbs (ἀρνέομαι, *arneomai*) and the compound form (ἀπαρνέομαι) are essentially synonyms (R. Brown 1994: 1.599; cf. Luke 12:9, where they are used interchangeably). The negative use of the verb can be seen in such passages as Matt. 10:33; Luke 12:9; Acts 3:13–14; 2 Tim. 2:12; 2 Pet. 2:1; 1 John 2:22–23; Jude 4; Rev. 3:8, where it involves denying Jesus. It can, however, also be used positively in the sense of denying one's own desires and following Jesus (Mark 8:34; Luke 9:23; Titus 2:12; etc.) or neutrally (Luke 8:45; John 1:20; Acts 4:16; etc.). Although Peter's reply can be interpreted as a statement ("I neither know nor understand") and a question ("What are you saying?"), it is best to understand it as a single statement ("I neither know nor understand what you are saying"). This is how Matthew (26:70) understood it. The use of "neither [οὔτε, *oute*] . . . nor [οὔτε, *oute*]" is technically incorrect, since they should not be used with synonyms, but they may catch "the repetitiveness of common speech to get across a point" (R. Brown 1994: 1.600).[2] The general meaning is clear enough (Hooker 1991: 364). Peter is denying that he is a follower of ("with") Jesus (14:67).

To escape further questions and avoid being seen by the light of the fire, Peter moves to the entryway or forecourt (προαύλιον, *proaulion*) at the entrance to the palace and away from the courtyard. The textual witnesses are divided as to whether the comment "And a cock crowed" is part of Mark or a later scribal insertion. The "least unsatisfactory conclusion" (Metzger 1994: 97) is probably to include it within brackets in the text[3] and not to place too much emphasis on it in interpreting Mark's account. Its genuineness would support the fulfillment of Jesus's prediction in 14:30, but it would be better to use 14:72 to support this.

The woman servant repeats her accusation, "This man [Peter] is one of them" **14:69–70a** (οὗτος ἐξ αὐτῶν ἐστιν, *houtos ex autōn estin*; 14:69), that is, belonging to a group known to be followers of Jesus. Her charge was probably made in the courtyard to the bystanders there, while Peter was seeking to steal away into the darkness of the forecourt (R. Brown 1994: 1.602; Donahue and Harrington 2002: 425). In contrast to Peter's first and third denials (cf. 14:68a and 71),

---

2. France (2002: 620n68) comments, "Most early Greek copyists, however, seem to have found Mark's idiom both clear and acceptable."

3. See, however, J. Wenham (1978), who argues that the original text of Mark lacked "And a cock crowed," "for the second time" (14:72), and "three times" (14:30 and 72).

Mark does not record what Peter said on this occasion but states only that he was again denying that he was "one of them." The imperfect "was denying" (ἠρνεῖτο, *erneito*) indicates the repetitiveness of his denial. Thus the second denial is more damning than the first, single denial (indicated by the aorist form of the verb [ἠρνήσατο, *ērnēsato*] in 14:68a) in intensity and scope (to the female servant and the bystanders, not just to the woman).

14:70b–71 The third denial of Peter takes place "a short time" (μετὰ μικρόν, *meta mikron*) later and is elicited by the crowd of bystanders. Mark does not indicate any change in scene, so that Peter is still envisioned in the forecourt (R. Brown 1994: 1.603) as the bystanders state, "Surely you are one of them, for you also are a Galilean" (ἀληθῶς ἐξ αὐτῶν εἶ, καὶ γὰρ Γαλιλαῖος εἶ, *alēthōs ex autōn ei, kai gar Galilaios ei*). Why they thought that Peter was from Galilee is not stated in Mark, but Matthew adds to the bystanders' statement, "for your speech/accent makes this evident" (26:73). The Aramaic spoken by Galilean Jews was apparently easily detectable (Evans 2001: 466; cf. *b. Ber.* 32a; *b. Meg.* 24b; *b. ʿErub.* 53b; cf. also Acts 2:7). In response, Peter "curses" (ἀναθεματίζειν, *anathematizein*) and "swears" (ὀμνύναι, *omnynai*). These are not synonyms but refer to two separate actions. The first involves "cursing" and can refer to calling a curse upon oneself if one is lying or will not fulfill a promise (Acts 23:12, 14, 21), but it usually functions as a transitive verb having an object, that is, cursing someone else (Merkel 1970; cf. 1 Cor. 12:3; 16:22; Gal. 1:8–9). In the present context the object is most likely Jesus (G. Lampe 1972: 354; R. Brown 1994: 1.604–5; France: 2002: 622).[4] The second verb, "swear," refers not to saying profanities or curses but to swearing an oath that what one is saying is true. What the cursing and swearing affirm is Peter's statement, "I do not know this man about whom you are talking."

14:72 The account concludes with a favorite Markan connective, "and immediately" (καὶ εὐθύς, *kai euthys*), which here should be taken at face value. Upon Peter's third denial, the cock immediately crows a second time. Thus all of Jesus's predictions concerning his betrayal by Judas (14:18–21), his desertion by the other disciples (14:27, 29), and the threefold denial by Peter (14:30) are fulfilled. The cock's crowing causes Peter to recall Jesus's prediction and to rush out and weep. The expression "a cock crowed" should be taken literally. It is not a technical term for the Roman third watch of the night (midnight to 3 a.m.) but a literal cock crowing (R. Brown 1994: 1.606). Although *m. B. Qam.* 7.7 forbade the raising of fowl in Jerusalem, *y. ʿErub.* 10.1 presupposes their existence. There is no need to deny the presence of fowl in Jerusalem or the cock crowing (see R. Brown 1994: 1.606–7). All four Gospel writers refer to it and

---

4. Cf. Pliny the Younger, *Ep.* 10.96, where people suspected of being Christians were offered three opportunities to deny that they were Christians and to curse Christ. Cf. also Mart. Pol. 9.2–3, where Polycarp is urged to "deny" (ἀρνεῖσθαι, *arneisthai*), "swear" (ὄμοσον, *omoson*), and "repent" (μετανόησον, *metanoēson*) of his being a Christian; and Justin Martyr, *1 Apol.* 31.6, where Christians were put to death by Bar Kochba during the second Jewish revolt in AD 132–135 if they did not "deny" (ἀρνέομαι) Christ and "blaspheme" (βλασφημέω).

have no difficulty assuming its historicity. Sometime in the early morning of the Passover, after the Last Supper, the cock crowed, and Peter realized that despite his earlier bravado (14:29 and 31), he had denied his Lord.

Peter's response is clear: he expresses his remorse by weeping. How to translate the participle ἐπιβαλών (epibalōn) that precedes the verb "weeping" (ἔκλαιεν, eklaien) is extremely uncertain. Some texts (D Θ latt) have "he began to" (ἤρξατο, ērxato) with the infinitive form of "weep" (κλαίειν), and its omission by both Matthew and Luke suggests difficulty with the construction.[5] R. Brown (1994: 1.609–10) lists nine different attempts to translate ἐπιβαλών. He chooses "having rushed outside" but acknowledges that this is a "very obscure phrase" (610).

Summary

Although at first glance it appears that the present account is a story about Peter and not Jesus, we should not miss the christological emphasis found in the account. (For a parallel, compare the death of John the Baptist in 6:14–29 Summary.) In the denial of Peter, we have once again the fulfillment of a prophecy by Jesus (14:30). Heaven and earth may pass away, but Jesus's words will never pass away (13:31)! We also have a sharp contrast between Peter, who quails before a female servant, and Jesus, who before the most powerful Jewish leader, the high priest, and before the "whole" Sanhedrin (14:55), fearlessly makes the good confession (1 Tim. 6:13). In light of Peter's denial, Jesus appears all the more impressive (Hooker 1991: 364; Evans 2001: 467). He serves both as Savior (10:45; 14:24) and as example. Thus believers can look to Jesus and see how he endured the cross and disregarded the shame that faced him (Heb. 12:2). The courage and resolve of Jesus indicate that his agony in Gethsemane (Mark 14:34–41) involved the unique death that he had to face, and that having watched and prayed, he was prepared to meet his death in an exemplary fashion.

On the other hand, Peter provides an example that Christians should avoid. Peter did not watch, watch, watch (13:34, 35, 37), and as a result denied, denied, cursed/swore and denied (14:68, 70, 71). Whether this account was specifically written for readers who were experiencing or had experienced persecution under Nero and denied their Lord (cf. 1 Clem. 5; Tacitus, Annals 15.44) is uncertain, but it has served as a warning for Christians throughout the centuries to watch and pray in order that they may not deny their Lord. Yet Christians can also take comfort from Peter's example. Unlike Judas's apparent indifference in Mark (France 2002: 618), Peter repented (14:72) and was restored (14:28; 16:7). His role as a leader of the church was well known to the readers of Mark; and if the Gospel was written to the church in Rome, Peter's role as a Christian leader and his

---

5. The unusual agreement between Matt. 26:75 and Luke 22:62 against Mark should be noted. Both have, "And having gone out, he wept bitterly" (ἐξελθὼν ἔξω ἔκλαυσεν πικρῶς, exelthōn exō eklausen pikrōs).

ultimate martyrdom served as an example of God's grace and forgiveness. For those who sin, even in a manner similar to Peter, all is not lost. There is the possibility of repentance and forgiveness. Yet this hope should not be viewed as an encouragement to sin; Peter would be the first to urge the importance of being a faithful witness for Christ, even if it means death. But in the greatness of God's love, denial in time of persecution is forgivable, and there can be opportunity for repentance, restoration, and service for Jesus (R. Brown 1994: 1.624–26).

Additional Notes

14:67. The verb ἦσθα is an old Attic form of the perfect tense used as an imperfect. It is found in the NT only here and in the Matthean parallel (26:69).

14:68. The MSS A C D Θ f¹ f¹³ lat read "and a cock crowed," but this is lacking in ℵ B L W. It is very difficult to choose between these two readings (Metzger 1994: 97). In any case, no theological or historical issue is at stake.

14:70. A number of MSS (A Θ f¹³) add "and your speech is like [theirs]." This is probably a later scribal insertion based on Matt. 26:73.

14:72. A few witnesses (ℵ C* L) omit "the second time" (ἐκ δευτέρου) in order to harmonize Mark with the single report of a cock crowing in Matt. 26:74; Luke 22:60; and John 18:27.

14:72. Herron (1991: 138–39) comments that "how" (ὡς) refers back not just to "what" Jesus said but "how" and "why" he said it.

14:72. The MSS ℵ C* W Δ it omit δίς to agree with Matt. 26:75 and Luke 22:61.

14:72. The interpretation of ἐπιβαλών is notoriously difficult. See the discussion of 14:72. It is not surprising that here a number of textual variants arose in an attempt to make sense of ἐπιβαλών.

G. Jesus Is Tried by Pontius Pilate (15:1–15)

The previous account involving Peter's denial (14:66–72) ends somewhat abruptly. Nothing is said as to what Peter did after he left the forecourt of the high priest, and we do not hear about him again until 16:7, where the angel tells the women at the tomb that they should tell the disciples and Peter that Jesus will meet them in Galilee. This is not surprising from the perspective of Mark, however, since his Gospel is not about Peter but about Jesus Christ, the Son of God (1:1). Thus after completing the story of Peter's denial, Mark concentrates his readers' attention on the main character of his Gospel, Jesus. There is a sense in which any subdivision of Jesus's trial before Pontius Pilate and his crucifixion (15:1–41) is arbitrary. I shall divide it into two parts: Jesus is tried by Pontius Pilate (15:1–15); and Jesus is crucified (15:16–41). The present account consists of four parts: (1) the conclusion of the Sanhedrin's meeting and their delivering Jesus over to Pontius Pilate (15:1); (2) Jesus's trial before Pontius Pilate (15:2–5); (3) the choice of Barabbas for release over Jesus (15:6–11); and (4) the condemnation of Jesus (15:12–15; cf. R. Brown 1994: 1.754–55). It must be acknowledged that there are no real literary breaks in the story between (2), (3), and (4), but for the sake of convenience, we shall deal with the material in this manner. Additional material concerning Jesus's trial before Pilate that is found in the other Gospels includes Jesus being sent by Pilate to Herod (Luke 23:6–12), Pilate's declaration of Jesus's innocence and his desire to release him (Luke 23:13–16; John 19:4–15), the dream of Pilate's wife (Matt. 27:19), and Pilate's act of washing his hands to claim his innocence in sentencing Jesus to death (Matt. 27:24–26).

The attempt to separate Mark's hand from the tradition he inherited is difficult. Pryke (1978: 22–23, 147, 174) lists the following as redactional: 15:1a, 2, 7–8, 10, 12–13a, 14b, 15c; Gnilka (1979: 297) lists only 15:1 (primarily the first half of the verse); Schmithals (1979: 2.671) lists 15:2 and 12–14; Lührmann (1987: 257) lists 15:7 and 10. The lack of agreement reveals the difficulty of distinguishing traditional material, traditional material that has been rewritten by Mark using his own vocabulary and style, and Mark's own redactional insertions. The Markan hand is seen most clearly in 15:1 (and immediately, καὶ εὐθύς, *kai euthys*—see 1:10–11; the whole Sanhedrin, ὅλον τὸν συνέδριον, *holon ton synedrion*—cf. 14:55; the double participle); 15:4, 12, 13 (again, πάλιν, *palin*—see 2:1–2); 15:5 (marvel, θαυμάζειν, *thaumazein*—see 1:21–22); 15:8 ("began to" [ἤρξατο, *ērxato*] with the infinitive—see 1:45); 15:10 (the "for" [γάρ, *gar*] explanatory clause—see 1:16–18); and so on.

Some scholars, such as Bultmann (1968: 272, 284, 306), argue that the entire Barabbas episode (15:6–14) is "obviously a legendary expansion" (cf. Crossan 1995: 111–12). We must acknowledge that there is no outside confirmation of a specific custom of releasing a prisoner at a feast or at Passover (Donahue and Harrington 2002: 432; France 2002: 629); yet there are some parallels (see 15:6–11), and all four Gospels refer to this custom (15:6–11; Matt. 27:15–21; Luke 23:18–25 [this is true even if we follow $\mathfrak{P}^{75}$ A B L and understand 23:17 as a scribal addition]; John 18:39–40). The witness of both John and the Synoptic Gospels indicates that we have two early, independent witnesses to this custom (R. Brown 1994: 1.809–10), and the inclusion of the account of Barabbas and the custom of releasing a prisoner at the feast in Matthew's and Luke's accounts indicates that the custom and story of Barabbas did not appear to them as blatantly unhistorical or radically new. If they had, they could easily have omitted it. John 18:39 suggests that the custom (not "law"!) was unique and originated with the Jews and that Rome had accepted it. If this is true, the custom would have been one granted uniquely to the Jews.[1] On the other hand, the creation of a completely fictional account of a man named Barabbas being released according to a completely fictional custom contrary to all Roman policies creates its own set of problems.

Some have also argued that the "historical Pilate" was radically different from the one found in the Gospels. Yet the overall historicity of the material in the account should be acknowledged. Pilate's portrayal is "not patently implausible" (R. Brown 1994: 1.704). His wavering character seems to fit well his backing down and reversing his decisions on several occasions in light of pressure from the Jewish people and leadership (McGing 1991: 428–35; R. Brown 1994: 1.698–705). The use of the title "King of the Jews" (15:2, 9, 12, 18, 26; cf. 15:32), which was not a favorite title of the early church (Matt. 2:2 being the only other NT use of this title outside the Gospel Passion Narrative), also supports the historical nature of the account.

Exegesis and Exposition

[1]And immediately early [in the morning], ⌜having made a plan,⌝ the chief priests with the elders and ⌜ ⌝ scribes and the whole Sanhedrin, ⌜ ⌝ having bound Jesus, led him away and handed him over to Pilate. [2]And Pilate asked him, "Are you the King of the Jews?" And he [Jesus] ⌜answered⌝ him, "You are saying so." [3]And the chief priests were accusing him of many things. [4]But Pilate again was asking him saying, "Are you not answering at all? See how many things they are accusing you of!" [5]But Jesus no longer answered anything, so that Pilate marveled.

[6]Now at the feast he was releasing to them one prisoner whom they were requesting. [7]But the man called Barabbas was in prison with the rebels who had committed murder

---

1. For some parallel examples of amnesties and releases, see R. Brown 1994: 1.815–20; Evans 2001: 479–80. We must admit, however, that we do not possess any exact analogy for the "Passover pardon" referred to in 15:6–11.

in the rebellion. ⁸And the crowd, having gone up, began to ask [that he would do] just as ⌐he was accustomed to do⌐ for them. ⁹But Pilate ⌐answered⌐ them, "Do you want [that] I should release to you the King of the Jews?" ¹⁰For he knew that the chief priests had delivered him over on account of envy. ¹¹But the chief priests stirred up the crowd in order that he should release to them Barabbas rather [than Jesus]. ¹²But Pilate again ⌐was saying⌐ to them, "What therefore do ⌐you want⌐ ⌐me to do⌐ [with] the man ⌐whom you call⌐ the King of the Jews?" ¹³But again they cried out, "Crucify him." ¹⁴But Pilate was continually saying to them, "⌐Why,⌐ what evil has he done?" But they cried out all the more, "Crucify him." ¹⁵⌐So⌐ Pilate, ⌐wishing to satisfy⌐ the crowd, released Barabbas to them and, having had Jesus scourged, delivered him over in order that he might be crucified.

"Early [in the morning]" refers to the same day in which Jesus and the dis- **15:1** ciples ate the Passover (14:17, 22). It refers in general to the early morning, not specifically to the fourth watch of the night (3–6 a.m.) in the Roman reckoning of time (R. Brown 1994: 1.628). This is how Matt. 27:1 and Luke 22:66 understand it. For Roman officials the workday often began before dawn (Sherwin-White 1965: 114), and Seneca (*De ira* 2.7.3) indicates that Roman trials began at dawn. All of 14:17–15:41 takes place between sunsets of the day that began with the eating of the Passover. The next day was the Sabbath (15:42; 16:1). "And immediately," unlike in 14:43 and 72, functions here simply as a Markan connective, with no strong temporal significance (see 1:10–11). These two temporal designations "early" (πρωΐ, *prōi*) and "immediately" (εὐθύς) describe the main verbs "led away" (ἀπήνεγκαν, *apēnenkan*) and "handed over" (παρέδωκαν, *paredōkan*), not the participles "having made" (ποιήσαντες, *poiēsantes*) and "having bound" (δήσαντες, *dēsantes*). The ex- pression "having made a plan" can also be interpreted as "having held a council." The latter could imply a second meeting or trial by the Sanhedrin, perhaps to draw up charges to present to Pilate. It is more likely, however, that the expression does not refer to a new trial or hearing taking place in the morning but alludes back to the evening trial of Jesus before the Sanhedrin in 14:53–65 (Blinzler 1959: 145–48; Matera 1982: 8–12; R. Brown 1994: 1.629–32; France 2002: 626). Thus the trial, interrupted by the story of Peter's denial (14:66–72), is now summarized and completed. The charge of "blasphemy," for which Jesus was condemned by the high priest and the Sanhedrin, would have been of no great concern to Pilate, but the political charge of claiming to be the king of the Jews would have gotten his attention. If the expression "the man you call" (ὃν λέγετε, *hon legete*; 15:12) is accepted as part of the text of Mark, the title "the King of the Jews" (ὁ βασιλεὺς τῶν Ἰουδαίων, *ho basileus tōn Ioudaiōn*) was probably the charge that the chief priests brought against Jesus before Pilate.

In this verse Mark emphasizes the role of the chief priests in bringing Jesus before Pilate (Matera 1982: 19). In 15:1 the plotters are described as "the chief priests *with* the elders and scribes." Earlier Mark described them as the "chief priests and the scribes" (10:33; 11:18; 14:1) or "the chief priests, and the scribes, and the elders" (11:27; 14:43, 53; cf. 8:31). Here the leading role of the chief priests in the trial (15:1, 3, 10, 11) and crucifixion (15:31) of Jesus is emphasized. Mark in addition stresses the role of the "whole" (ὅλον, holon) Sanhedrin. Mark 15:43 implies that Joseph of Arimathea, a member of the Sanhedrin, was not part of the Sanhedrin's desire to see Jesus killed, but the phrase "the whole Sanhedrin" here and in 14:55 does not permit one to interpret Mark to mean "a small group of the Sanhedrin membership" (contra Evans 2001: 444; see 14:55–59).

The verb "handed over" (παρέδωκαν, paredōkan) recalls the use of this same term to describe John the Baptist's being handed over to prison (1:14), the predictions of Judas's handing over/betraying Jesus (3:19; 14:10–11, 18, 21, 42, 44), and Jesus's being handed over to (sinful) men (9:31; 14:41), to the chief priests and scribes (10:33), and to the gentiles (10:33); and it will be used again when Jesus is handed over to Pilate by the chief priests (15:10), and to the soldiers for crucifixion by Pilate (15:15). Yet it also recalls that behind all this lies the divine necessity (8:31; 14:21) in which God "hands over" his Son as a ransom for many (10:45; 14:27, 36).

This is the first time that Pilate's name appears in Mark (cf. also 15:2, 4, 5, 9, 12, 14, 15, 43, 44). The name "Pilate" was his cognomen and indicates his family origin (Pilatus). "Pontius" (Luke 3:1; Acts 4:27; 1 Tim. 6:13), his nomen, indicates his tribe, but his praenomen or personal name is not given in any of the records (R. Brown 1994: 1.694). Mark makes no attempt to identify Pilate to his readers since he was probably well known in the gospel traditions (cf. 1 Tim. 6:13). Pilate was appointed by the emperor Tiberius to rule the imperial province of Judea in AD 26 and ruled there until 36. Although in the tradition he is popularly referred to as a "procurator" (cf. Josephus, *J.W.* 2.9.2 §169; Philo, *Embassy* 38 §299; Tacitus, *Annals* 15.44), this is probably anachronistic, because it was only after AD 44 that this title was attributed to Roman officials placed in charge of Judea (R. Brown 1994: 1.336–37; Evans 2001: 476–77). In Matt. 27:2, 11, 14, 15, 21, 27; 28:14 (cf. Luke 3:1) Pilate is referred to by the general term "governor" (ἡγεμών, hēgemōn). The specific title of Pilate is now known through the discovery of an inscription in Caesarea that describes him as "[Po]ntius Pilatus, [Praef]ectus Iudae" ("Pontius Pilate, Prefect of Judea"; Bond 1998: 11–12). Because of the rise in nationalistic feelings during the Passover (it celebrated Israel's deliverance from their oppressor, Egypt; the analogy of Rome's oppression and the people's desire for deliverance was always present), Pilate left his normal residence in Caesarea and resided in Jerusalem during the Passover. (Cf. Kinman [1991], who suggests that Pilate was on an official judicial tour.) His place of residence was more likely to have been the palace of Herod than the more austere Fortress of Antonia. The latter, located adjacent to the northwest corner of the temple, where it overlooked the Court of the Gentiles, was where the Roman garrison was stationed. In 15:16 Pilate's place of residence is referred to as the "palace," or πραιτώριον (praitōrion). So although tradition and popular tours of Jerusalem identify the place where Pilate stayed as the Fortress of Antonia, it is more probable that he resided at the luxurious palace of Herod when he was in Jerusalem (Benoit 1973: 167–88; R. Brown 1994: 1.705–10).

Omitting the preliminary discussion between the chief priests and Pilate, Mark   15:2–5
immediately introduces the reader to the central issue at Jesus's trial before Pilate. Pilate asks Jesus, "Are you the King of the Jews?" (σὺ εἶ ὁ βασιλεὺς τῶν Ἰουδαίων; *sy ei ho basileus tōn Ioudaiōn?*). Some see the "you" (σύ) as emphatic and containing a touch of contempt: "Are you, [such an insignificant person], the King of the Jews?" (Hooker 1991: 367; Evans 2001: 478; contra R. Brown 1994: 1.733; France 2002: 608, 627–28). However, the reply of Jesus in 15:2 uses a similar "you" (σύ) and lacks any such contempt or mockery. This indicates that finding an alleged mockery in Pilate's question is based less on the grammar of the question than on a hypothetical reconstruction of the incident. Pilate's question uses the same wording as that of the high priest in 14:61 ("Are you [σύ] the Christ, the Son of the Blessed?"), and it is best to interpret this as a straightforward question.

The title "King of the Jews" is probably a gentile's rendition of the Jewish title "King of Israel." (See examples in Evans 2001: 478.) The former is found on Pilate's lips in 15:2, 9, 12, 18 and affixed by Pilate on the cross (15:26), whereas the chief priests use "the King of Israel" in 15:32. Pilate's question may very well have come from charges the religious leaders made against Jesus (cf. Luke 23:2). Although "King of Israel/of the Jews" is never found on the lips of Jesus, his reference to his disciples sitting on his right and left hand in his glory (10:37), the salutation addressed to him on Palm Sunday hailing the coming kingdom of David (11:10) along with the application of Zech. 9:9 (Matt. 21:4) to him, his role of sitting in judgment (Matt. 25:34ff.), and so on all support the view that Jesus understood himself as a "king." Above all, it is his acknowledgment that he was the Messiah/Christ, the Son of David (i.e., the successor and superior [Mark 12:35–37] of King David), that would lead to this charge (R. Brown 1994: 1.731–32). (Cf. the use of "King of the Jews" in Matt. 2:2 to describe the Messiah/Christ of Matt. 1:1, 16, 17, 18.)

Jesus's reply, "You are saying so" (σὺ λέγεις, *sy legeis*), to Pilate is identical in all four Gospel accounts. It is the same as the reply given to the question of the high priest in Matt. 26:64 (cf. 26:25) and similar to the one given in Luke 22:70. It is not negative (contra Gundry 1993: 932–33; cf. also Pesch 1980b: 457) or "non-committal" (Hooker 1991: 367–68; cf. also J. Edwards 2002: 459) but positive, for Pilate will crucify him on this charge. Jesus's reply, however, implies that his understanding of the title is not the same as Pilate's.[2] Jesus does not see his kingship as being political in nature and involving this world (cf. John 18:36–37). At this point Mark adds that the chief priests began to accuse Jesus of "many things" (πολλά, *polla*). Although πολλά can be interpreted adverbially as "much" (Evans 2001: 478–79), it is best to interpret

---

2. Cf. V. Taylor 1952: 579: "It is an affirmation which implies that the speaker would put things differently."

it here as a direct object, "many things" (R. Brown 1994: 1.734), because it looks ahead to "how many things" (πόσα, *posa*) in 15:4. This is how Luke 23:2 understands it.

In his trial before the Sanhedrin, Jesus was silent until asked under oath (cf. Matt. 26:63) if he was the Christ, and then he answered affirmatively; in his trial before Pilate, the order is reversed. Jesus responds positively and then is silent (15:4–5). The double negatives in 15:4 (lit. "not . . . nothing" [οὐκ . . . οὐδέν, *ouk . . . ouden*]) and 15:5 (lit. "no longer . . . nothing" [οὐκέτι οὐδέν, *ouketi ouden*]) emphasize his silence. As a result of Jesus's silence, we read that Pilate "marveled" (θαυμάζειν, *thaumazein*). Later he will "marvel" over Jesus's quick death (15:44). Although some see Pilate's marveling as an allusion to Isa. 52:15 (Hooker 1991: 368; Evans 2001: 479), it is doubtful that Mark's readers would have made this connection, for Mark (and Matthew) does not mention or give any hint of this allusion. The same can be said concerning Jesus's silence in 15:4–5 being an allusion to Isa. 53:7. Mark emphasizes that even the one who ultimately condemned Jesus to death "marveled" at him. For a similar positive reaction to Jesus, compare Mark 5:20. For the general theme of the awe, wonder, and marvel that Jesus elicited, see 1:21–22.

15:6–11 "At the feast" (κατὰ ἑορτήν, *kata heortēn*) refers to the Passover (cf. 14:2, 12, 14, 16). Although a "custom" of releasing a prisoner is not directly referred to in the text, it is implied by the customary imperfect "was releasing" (ἀπέλυεν, *apelyen*; 15:6), the request of the crowd in 15:8 and 11, and the release of Barabbas in 15:15. As discussed in the introduction to this unit, many deny the historicity of this custom (Winter 1961: 91–94) because it lacks corroboration outside the Gospels. Yet if, as has been argued, this was a uniquely Jewish custom (John 18:39; cf. Matt. 27:15), the lack of mention in non-Jewish literature is not surprising. There are a number of instances of prisoners being released on holidays in the ancient world (R. Brown 1994: 1.814–20; Evans 2001: 480);[3] *m. Pesaḥ.* 8.6 and *b. Pesaḥ.* 91a speak of releasing a prisoner at the Passover. Although no explicit mention is made of the latter being a regular custom, that a ruling is given concerning this in the rabbinic literature suggests that this was not an isolated instance.

Nothing is known about Barabbas outside the Gospel accounts. The name is Aramaic and consists of בַּר (*bar*, son of) אַבָּא (*'abbā'*, the father, or a man named Abba). Attempts to see in the name an ironic pun in that the crowd chooses Barabbas over the real "Son of the Father" would almost certainly not have been picked up by Mark's Greek-speaking audience. Matthew 27:16–17 may suggest that he was called "Jesus Barabbas."[4] In Mark

---

3. Merritt (1985) suggests that the existence of such instances caused Mark to create the story of the Passover pardon. Although the lack of an exact analogy causes some scholars to deny the historicity of the pardon, the presence of various analogies causes Merritt to believe that Mark created the account in order to exonerate the Romans and to vilify the Jews.

4. This is a minority reading among the MSS (Θ f¹), but its difficulty lends support to it possibly being part of the original text of Matthew (Metzger 1994: 56).

15:7 he is described as being "in prison" (lit. "was bound") with the "rebels" (στασιαστῶν, *stasiastōn*) who committed murder in the "rebellion" (στάσει, *stasei*). Luke 23:19 (cf. Acts 3:14) states that Barabbas had committed murder in the rebellion. In the account of the crucifixion, Jesus is described as crucified between two λῃστάς (*lēstas*; Mark 15:27), and John 18:40 describes Barabbas as a λῃστής (*lēstēs*). All this has caused some to portray Barabbas as a zealot revolutionary. This, however, would be anachronistic and read the later use of the term "Zealot" in the late 60s back into Jesus's day (R. Brown 1994: 1.689–93). The use of the article in "*the* rebels" and "*the* rebellion" suggests that the incident was known to Mark's readers (R. Brown 1994: 1.796–97). (Matthew 27:16 describes Barabbas as "notorious" [ἐπίσημον, *episēmon*].) We need not envision this as a nationwide rebellion, however, and the release of Barabbas by the Roman governor suggests that those killed were not Roman soldiers. In all four Gospels, Barabbas is understood to be a real person, not a symbolic or fictional character (R. Brown 1994: 1.811–14).

The crowd "having gone up" (ἀναβάς, *anabas*) in 15:8 may suggest a literal walking uphill to get to the palace, or πραιτώριον (15:16), where Pilate was holding the trial. If so, this would support the view that Pilate was staying at the palace of Herod, located on the highest part of the western hill of the upper city (see 15:1). The request of the crowd to Pilate to keep the custom of the Passover pardon may have been seen by Pilate as an opportunity to release Jesus. This is suggested by his question concerning releasing the King of the Jews (i.e., Jesus) in 15:9, which might be seeking to elicit a positive answer (Donahue and Harrington 2002: 433). It is also suggested by the Markan explanatory comment in 15:10 that it was out of "envy" (φθόνον, *phthonon*), not zeal or jealousy, that the chief priests had delivered Jesus over to him (Hagedorn and Neyrey 1998: 38–56). The makeup of the crowd is not described, and it is unwise to identify it with the crowd of 11:18, 32; 12:12, 37; or 14:43. That the chief priests "stirred up" (ἀνέσεισαν, *aneseisan*) the crowd to have them choose Barabbas instead of Jesus indicates that the crowd was not a group of Barabbas's supporters seeking his release (contra Evans 2001: 481). There would have been no need to stir up Barabbas's supporters.

The request to release Barabbas frustrated Pilate, as the "again" (πάλιν) and **15:12–15** "was saying" (ἔλεγεν, *elegen*) indicate (contra Bond [1998: 105–19], who sees Pilate completely in charge and in control of what is taking place). Although the choice of Barabbas over Jesus was now made, the decision of what the chief priests and crowd would like to see happen to the King of the Jews is not yet clear. Their reply is appalling. "Again" they respond to Pilate, but this time, instead of asking for grace as in the case of Barabbas, they seek Jesus's condemnation and cry out, "Crucify him" (σταύρωσον αὐτόν, *staurōson auton*; 15:13). This is the first use of this verb in Mark (cf. also 15:14, 15, 20, 24, 25, 27; 16:6), although Jesus's crucifixion has been alluded to indirectly in 8:34 in the saying about taking up one's cross. Early references to the death of Jesus involve "destroy" (ἀπόλλυμι, *apollymi*), 3:6; 11:18; "kill" (ἀποκτείνω, *apokteinō*), 8:31; 9:31; 10:34; 14:1; "condemn to death" (κατακρίνω . . . θανάτῳ, *katakrinō . . . thanatō*), 10:33; 14:64; and "put to death" (θανατόω, *thanatoō*), 14:55. The pattern of three questions by Pilate to the crowd (15:9, 12, 14) and three responses of the crowd (15:11, 13, 14c) fits other such triads in Mark, such as Jesus's three prayers in Gethsemane (14:35–36, 39, 41), Peter's three denials (14:68, 70, 71), and Pilate's three questions to Jesus (15:2, 4b, 4c; R. Brown 1994: 1.825). Pilate's response (15:14) seeks the reason why the crowd wants Jesus put to death in light of his having done no "evil" (κακόν, *kakon*). Pilate's "continually saying" (ἔλεγεν, an iterative imperfect) in 15:14 reveals a sustained effort on his part to release Jesus. The response of the crowd, however, became even more vocal (περισσῶς, *perissōs*), "Crucify him." At this point Pilate, seeking to gain favor with the crowd, released Barabbas to them, had Jesus scourged, and delivered him over to the soldiers (15:16) who were to crucify him.[5] In so doing, Jesus's prediction in 10:34 is fulfilled. Scourging involved whipping with leather thongs on whose ends were tied pieces of sharp metal, bone, stone, or lead (Blinzler 1959: 222–25; Hengel 1977: 22–32). It was a preliminary part of a crucifixion (Josephus, *J.W.* 2.14.9 §§306–8; 5.11.1 §449; 7.6.4 §§200–202).

Summary

The christological emphasis of Mark in this passage is quite clear. Jesus is the King of the Jews (15:2, 9, 12, 18, 26, 32)! At the trial before the Sanhedrin, Jesus acknowledges that he is the Christ/Messiah, the Son of God (14:61–62). In the trial before Pilate, he acknowledges that he is the King of the Jews, another name for the Christ/Messiah but one even more politically dangerous. Mark wants his readers to note the similarity of these two accounts by the common elements of silence, question, and affirmation. That Jesus's answer, "You are saying so," is affirmative is clear from the fact that he is crucified under the title "The King of the Jews" (15:26), and Mark certainly does not intend his readers to assume that this title (repeated six times in the chapter) is incorrect. Furthermore, the mockery of the soldiers in 15:16–20 is based on the charge that Jesus is the King of the Jews. (Cf. also Matt. 2:2

---

5. Throughout history, numerous attempts have been made to exonerate Pilate in some way or another. He is frequently portrayed as an unfortunate man in an unfortunate political position facing an unfortunate situation, who was forced to crucify Jesus against his will. (See R. Brown 1994: 1.695–96 for various examples.) Yet it is under pressure like this that a person's true character is revealed. Even if we were to ignore all other negative evidence concerning Pilate, his role in the death of Jesus indicates that he was far more despicable than any of the religious leaders who sought Jesus's death. They acted out of "envy," to be sure, but they acted according to their convictions that Jesus had committed blasphemy and was a threat to the Jewish religion and the well-being of the nation (cf. John 11:47–50). Pilate, however, knew that Jesus had done no wrong (15:14; cf. Matt. 27:19) and deliberately chose to crucify someone he knew was innocent in order to protect his political career (cf. Herod Antipas in Mark 6:14–29). In so doing, he released a guilty criminal and sentenced an innocent Jesus to death. As a result, Pilate will be remembered in history primarily because Jesus "suffered under Pontius Pilate" (cf. 1 Tim. 6:13; Acts 4:27).

and John 18:36–37, which clearly indicate that these two evangelists understand Jesus's response as positive.) Yet Jesus's answer, while affirmative,
also makes clear that his understanding of the title "King of the Jews" is
radically different from that of Pilate. (This is made especially clear in John
18:33–37.) At this trial once again a prediction of Jesus is fulfilled. As he
predicted (Mark 10:33–34), Jesus is handed over to the gentiles (15:1), who
scourge him (15:15) and kill him (15:16–38). All takes place as he foretold.
Though innocent and knowing no sin (15:14), he gives his life as a sacrifice
for many (10:45; 14:24), so that sinners can be saved (2:17; cf. 2 Cor. 5:21).
Though innocent, he is put to death, whereas Barabbas, justly condemned
to death, goes free. Mark, however, wants his readers to remember that
behind all this lies God's hand and plan (8:31; 14:21).

In his account of Jesus's trial before Pilate, Mark also emphasizes that
Jesus was not crucified because of any crime that he had done. Pilate, who
had him crucified, clearly declares Jesus's innocence (15:14; cf. also 15:10).
Thus Jesus goes to his death not because of his being found guilty but due
to the "envy" of his enemies (15:10). In this account, Mark also emphasizes
the role of the chief priests in Jesus's death (15:1, 3, 10, 11). The reader is
already aware that they do not represent the people in this (12:12; 14:2). On
the contrary, they are acting against the people's wishes. Even the crowd
that chooses Barabbas over Jesus and yells for Jesus's crucifixion is not representative of a normal "crowd" (11:18, 32; 12:12, 37). As in later instances
in which Roman officials proclaim the innocence of Christians being tried
before them (Acts 18:14–15; 23:26–30; 25:24–27; 26:30–32), Pilate declares
Jesus's innocence. This is made even more explicit by the other Gospel
writers (Matt. 27:19, 24; Luke 23:14–16; John 19:4, 6, 12). Because of his
role in the death of Jesus, Pilate's acknowledgment of Jesus's innocence is
especially important for Mark's readers.

Additional Notes

15:1. Several MSS (D Θ it) have the verb (ἐποίησαν) instead of the participle (ποιήσαντες) and add καί before the participle δήσαντες. These appear to be later scribal attempts to improve the text (Metzger 1971: 117).

15:1. The codices ℵ D W Θ add the article τῶν before "scribes."

15:1. Several MSS add καί before δήσαντες. See first note on 15:1.

15:2. ἀποκριθεὶς ... λέγει is lit. "having answered, ... says."

15:8. ἐποίει is a customary imperfect.

15:9. ἀπεκρίθη ... λέγων is lit. "answered, ... saying."

15:12. ἀποκριθεὶς ἔλεγεν is lit. "having answered, was saying."

15:12. θέλετε is missing in ℵ B C W Δ Ψ f¹ f¹³. Fortunately the meaning is not greatly affected by its omission, but its inclusion places greater responsibility on the crowd and the Sanhedrin for the death of Jesus.

15:12. ποιήσω is lit. "I should do."

15:12. ὃν λέγετε is lacking in A D W Θ f¹ f¹³ lat.

15:14. γάρ is used here in the sense of "Why?"

15:15. "So" translates δέ here.

15:15. τὸ ἱκανὸν ποιῆσαι probably renders the Latin expression *satis facere*.

H. Jesus Is Crucified (15:16–41)

The events of 15:16–41 follow Jesus's scourging and being handed over to the soldiers for crucifixion (15:1–15). It is true that the mocking of Jesus by the soldiers (15:16–20b) could be omitted and would not be missed, for 15:20b follows 15:15 smoothly (Matera 1982: 21–24), but all four Gospels have an account of such a mocking, and in three of them it occurs after Jesus's scourging (Matt. 27:28–31a; John 19:1–15). (Luke records Jesus only being mocked by Herod Antipas and his soldiers [23:11].) Thus the mocking of Jesus had a firm place in the pre-Markan tradition of the passion. Logically, the most natural place for this tradition would be at this point in the Passion Narrative. Scholars debate whether Mark placed the tradition at this point or whether it was already there before he wrote his Gospel. The independent witness of John, however, favors its present location being part of the pre-Markan tradition (cf. R. Brown 1994: 1.872–73). The mocking is then followed by the account of the crucifixion (15:20c–39) and a concluding reference to the presence of women at the crucifixion who were followers of Jesus (15:40–41). The mention of women, along with 15:47 and the burial of Jesus (15:42–46), prepares the reader for the account of Jesus's resurrection in 16:1–8.

The present passage is organized as follows:

Jesus is mocked (15:16–20b)
   Jesus is led into the praetorium (15:16)
   Jesus is mocked (15:17–20b)
Jesus is crucified (15:20c–41)
   Jesus is led out of the praetorium to Golgotha (15:20c–22)
   Jesus is crucified (15:23–25)
   Jesus is mocked (15:26–27, 29–32)
   Jesus cries out in despair (15:33–36)
   Jesus dies (15:37–38)
   The confession of the centurion (15:39)
   The presence of women who followed Jesus is noted (15:40–41)

The historicity of Jesus's crucifixion is acknowledged by nearly everyone. Why would any Christians create such a tradition, which would be a stumbling block to Jews and folly to gentiles (1 Cor. 1:23)? However, numerous scholars reject various parts of the crucifixion account as legendary. Bultmann (1968: 272–74, 281, 284, 306) denies the historicity of the mocking of Jesus in 15:16–20a, the scriptural allusion in 15:24, the temporal designation in 15:25, the inscription on the cross in 15:26, the crucifixion of the two bandits in 15:27, the mocking in 15:29–32, much of 15:33–39, and the reference to the women in 15:40–41. All that is historical is 15:20b–24c and possibly 37. V. Taylor (1952: 584, 587) suggests that the foundational Passion Narrative consisted of 15:21–24, 26, 29–30, 34–37, and 39, to which later elements (15:16–20, 25, 27, 31–32, 33, 38, 40–41) were added. Scholars today are far less confident in their ability to perform such literary surgery on the present text. Much of the skepticism about the account is based on the passage's allusions to various OT texts, especially Ps. 22. Some maintain that these OT references caused the early church to create legendary narrative elements that were read back into the Passion Narrative. However, this misunderstands the probable relationship between the OT allusions and their narrative elements. For instance, it is probably the historical incident of the soldiers dividing the possessions of Jesus (see 15:24) that caused the early church to see this as a fulfillment of Ps. 22:18 (21:19 LXX), rather than the reverse.[1]

The extent of the Markan redaction in the passage is debated. Pryke (1978: 23, 147–48, 174–75) lists 15:16b, 18, 20c, 22b, 25–27, 29–32, 33, 34b, 36a, 39, 40a as Markan; Gnilka (1979: 306, 311–14) lists 15:16b, 19a, 20a, 23, 31 ("with the scribes, to one another"), 32c, 39, 40, 41; and Schmithals (1979: 2.677, 682–84, 692–94) lists 15:16–20, 25–26, 29b–30, 31, 32a, 33, 38–39. Such a radical assessment of the Markan redactional work is often due to the difficulty of distinguishing between the Markan retelling of the tradition in his own vocabulary and style and the addition of new Markan elements. The clearest examples of Mark's own contribution to the account are found in various explanatory comments in 15:16b, 21b, 22b, 34c–d, and 41.

Exegesis and Exposition

[16]And the soldiers led him away into the palace, that is, the praetorium, and call together the whole cohort. [17]And they clothe him in a purple robe, and having woven a thorny crown, they put [it] on him. [18]And they began to salute him, "Hail, King of the Jews!" [19]And they were continually striking his head with a reed and spitting on him, and kneeling down [in mockery] they were paying homage to him. [20]And when they had mocked him, they took off the purple robe and put his own garments on him.

And they lead him out to crucify him. [21]And they compel a certain man passing by, Simon of Cyrene, [who was] coming [in] from the country, the father of Alexander and Rufus, to take up his cross. [22]And they bring him to the place—Golgotha, which

---

1. Marcus (1992b: 175) lists the following OT allusions he finds in our account: 15:24 (Ps. 22:18), 29 (Ps. 22:7), 30–31 (Ps. 22:8), 32 (Ps. 22:6), 34 (Ps. 22:1), 36 (Ps. 69:21), and 40 (Ps. 38:11). Like most readers today, however, Mark's readers would have understood the references in the Passion Narrative as historical, especially as they heard Mark read to them for the first time. These supposed OT allusions, except for 15:24 and 34, would probably have been too vague for them to have noticed.

means "place of a skull." [23]And they were trying to give him wine mixed with myrrh, but he did not take ⌜it⌝. [24]And they crucify him and divide his garments among themselves, casting lots for them [to decide] who might take what. [25]And it was the third hour and they crucified him. [26]And the inscription of his charge read, "The King of the Jews." [27]And with him they crucify two bandits, one on the right and one on his left. ⌜28⌝

[29]And those passing by were blaspheming him, shaking their heads and saying, "Ha! [You who would be] the destroyer of the sanctuary and rebuilder [of it] in three days, [30]save yourself by coming down from the cross." [31]Likewise also the chief priest with the scribes, mocking [him] among themselves, were saying, "Others he saved; himself he cannot save! [32]Let the Christ, the King of Israel, come down now from the cross, in order that we may see and believe." And those having been crucified along with him were ridiculing him.

[33]And when it was the sixth hour, darkness came upon the whole land until the ninth hour. [34]And at the ninth hour Jesus cried out with a loud voice, "⌜Elōi, Elōi, lema⌝ sabachthani?" which means, "My God, my God, why have you forsaken me?" [35]And some of those standing by, having heard [this], were saying, "Look, he is calling Elijah." [36]But someone, having run and filled a sponge with sour wine [and] having put it on a reed, was offering [it] to him to drink saying, "Wait, let us see if Elijah comes to take him down." [37]But Jesus, having let out a loud cry, expired. [38]And the curtain of the sanctuary was split in two, from top to bottom. [39]And the centurion who had been standing opposite him, having seen that he ⌜ ⌝ expired in this manner, said, "Truly, this man was the Son of God."

[40]But there were also women observing from a distance, and among them [were] Mary Magdalene, and Mary the mother of James the younger and Joses, and Salome, [41]who when he [Jesus] was in Galilee were following him and ministering to him, and many other women who had gone up with him to Jerusalem.

After the trial before Pilate, which is envisioned as taking place "outside" (cf. John 18:28–29, 33, 38; 19:4–5), the "soldiers" (στρατιῶται, stratiōtai; these were Roman soldiers consisting mostly of auxiliaries recruited locally from the gentile population; see Webster 1969: 142–45; Schürer 1973: 1.362–63) led[2] Jesus "into" (lit. "inside") the "palace" (αὐλῆς, aulēs). Mark comments that the palace served during Pilate's stay as the "praetorium" (cf. 15:1). Normally Pilate's residence in Caesarea served as the praetorium, but when in Jerusalem, the place where Pilate, the "praetor," stayed became the praetorium (Cranfield 1959: 452; R. Brown 1994: 1.705–6). In the palace the soldiers summoned "the whole cohort" (ὅλην τὴν σπεῖραν, holēn tēn speiran). The term "cohort" comes from the Latin cohors, which refers to a tenth part of a legion, or 600 soldiers. It can be used to describe a part of the cohort, a maniple (manipulus) of 200 men, but here it is probably being used loosely (cf. "the whole Sanhedrin" in

15:16

---

2. The verb "led [away]" (ἀπήγαγον) is used here and in 14:44, 53, and in each instance it envisions a change in scene.

14:55 and 15:1) for "all the soldiers on duty at the praetorium at the time" (Donahue and Harrington 2002: 435; cf. France 2002: 637).

15:17–20b   The mocking of Jesus began with his being dressed as a "king" in a purple robe and a "crown." Matthew 27:29 mentions Jesus also being given a reed as a scepter (cf. Mark 15:19). Purple dye from Tyre was expensive and came from shellfish (R. Brown 1994: 1.865). It was a color only the wealthy could afford, was associated with royalty, and was worn by emperors and kings (1 Macc. 10:20, 62; 11:58; 14:43–44; Luke 16:19; cf. also Josephus, *Ant.* 11.6.10 §256; 17.8.3 §197). The crown is described as being woven from "thorns" (ἀκάνθινον, *akanthinon*). Understanding exactly what the crown was made of depends for the most part on whether its purpose was intended primarily for mockery or for torture (R. Brown 1994: 1.866–67). The latter is the traditional understanding and envisions a crown made from thornbush. In favor of the former is that the mockery portrayed in 15:17–19 involves not so much physical torture as humiliation. In this understanding of the crown, the "thorns" would radiate outward like rays of sunlight rather than inward (Hart 1952).

After the "royal fitting" of Jesus with a robe and crown (and in Matthew a scepter), Jesus is mocked by the soldiers (15:18–19). He is saluted (lit. "began to salute" [ἤρξαντο, *ērxanto* + infinitive; a favorite Markan construction]) as a king—"Hail, King of the Jews!"—in mock imitation of the Latin *Ave, Caesar!* (Hail, Caesar!). In addition he is struck on the head with a reed, which in Matt. 27:29 serves as a scepter (emphasizing Jesus's caricatured crown of thorns?) and spat upon (a possible allusion to Isa. 50:6). The soldiers furthermore kneel before him in mock homage to this "fake" king.[3] (Contrast the sincere kneeling of the demoniac in 5:6–7!) We possess several parallels to such mockery in the literature of Jesus's day that demonstrate the "verisimilitude" of this scene (R. Brown 1994: 1.874–77; Evans 2001: 488). The mockery of the soldiers assumes, and only makes sense when understood in light of, Jesus's condemnation as the king of the Jews in 15:2, 9, 12, 26, and 32. It is as king of the Jews that Jesus is condemned; it is as king of the Jews that he is mocked; and it is as king of the Jews that he is crucified. The scene ends with the soldiers removing the purple robe from Jesus and redressing him in his own clothes (15:20b). Nothing is mentioned concerning the crown of thorns. Victims of crucifixion were usually scourged and led out naked to be crucified (R. Brown 1994: 1.870). It may have been as a concession to Jewish sensibilities (Jub. 3.30–31; *m. Sanh.* 6.3) that the Romans allowed Jesus to wear his clothes on the route to Golgotha.

15:20c–22   After the preliminaries of Jesus's crucifixion (the scourging and mocking) were over, the soldiers led Jesus out of the palace/praetorium (cf. 15:16) for the purpose of crucifying him (15:20c). The victim of crucifixion was normally forced to carry his own cross from within the city to the place of execution

---

3. Whereas the striking and spitting describe physical abuse, it goes too far to describe them as violent actions (contra R. Brown 1994: 1.872). After having been scourged, how violent would being spit upon and being hit on the head with a reed (not a club) be (Gundry 1993: 942)?

outside the city (see Evans 2001: 499, who lists, among others, Plutarch, *De sera numinis vindicta* §9). Probably due to weakness, Jesus was not able to carry his cross all of the way. (A scourging was often enough to kill a person.) As a result a passerby, Simon of Cyrene, was pressed into service (ἀγγαρεύουσιν, *angareuousin*) and made to carry (lit. "in order that he should take up") Jesus's cross. Roman soldiers had the right to compel civilians to perform tasks for them (cf. Matt. 5:41, where the same verb is used; also Josephus, *Ant.* 13.2.3 §52). Cyrene was the capital city of the Roman province of Cyrenaica (modern Libya). Simon's two sons, Alexander and Rufus, were apparently Christians and known to Mark's readers, although not to readers of Matthew and Luke, who omit the sons' names. Whether the Rufus of 15:21 is also the Rufus of Rom. 16:13 is impossible to say.[4] The description of Simon "coming [in] from the country" suggests that this took place after Jesus was led out of the city (15:20c) and that up to this point he was able to carry his own cross. The historicity of this scene is assured not only by the references to Alexander and Rufus (could Mark have gotten away with such a fiction as his Gospel was read to its original audience?) but also by the fact that Simon is portrayed not as one who willingly took up Jesus's cross and followed him (thus he is not an example to the reader) but as one who was compelled to do so.

When a large number of victims were to be crucified, they might be crucified on a scaffold, but the cross portrayed in the present account and the other Gospels is an individual one. Three cross shapes were generally used: the *crux decussata*, in the shape of an X; the *crux commissa*, in the shape of a T; and the *crux immissa*, in the shape of a †. The last of these was probably the shape of Jesus's cross due to the reference to the inscription of Jesus's charge being placed over his head (Matt. 27:37; cf. also Luke 23:38). This was the traditional understanding of the shape of Jesus's cross in the early church (Irenaeus, *Haer.* 2.24.4; Tertullian, *Ad nationes* 1.12). The victim was forced to carry not the entire *crux immissa* but only the crossbeam or *patibulum* (Seneca, *De vita beata* 19.3) on the way to his crucifixion. The victim would carry it behind the nape of his neck, with his hands hooked over it (R. Brown 1994: 2.913). The vertical beam, or *staticulum*, was left permanently in a prominent place (like a hangman's scaffold or a guillotine in a public square) as an intended deterrent and warning to others.

The place to which Jesus was brought[5] was called, in Aramaic, גָּלְגָּלְתָּא (*gulgultā'*, Golgotha), which, as Mark explains (cf. 5:41; 15:34; also 3:17; 7:11;

---

4. It is probable that Mark's readers knew far more about Simon of Cyrene than we do. Simon is a Greek name, as are the names of his sons, Alexander and Rufus. Was he a Jew? A convert to Judaism? A local resident of Jerusalem? (See France 2002: 641.) Luke refers to a synagogue of the Cyrenians in Acts 6:9, and we read in Acts 13:1 of Lucius of Cyrene, who was a leader in the early church (cf. also Acts 11:20). The discussion of whether Simon was breaking the law by coming in from the country involves too many presuppositions: he was a Jew, this was the Passover, he was working in the fields, and so on.

5. It is uncertain if "bring" (φέρουσιν, *pherousin*) means "lead" (1:32; 7:32; 8:22; 9:17, 19, 20; 11:2, 7; cf. 4:8) or "carry" (2:3; 6:27, 28; 12:15, 16). The latter would imply that Jesus had to be

14:36), means "place of a skull."[6] This was located outside the walled city of Jerusalem in Jesus's day. John explicitly states this in 19:20, and Matt. 27:32 (going out, ἐξερχόμενοι, *exerchomenoi*) suggests this (cf. also Heb. 13:12). Places of execution were intentionally located near much-traveled roads (Mark 15:29; Matt. 27:39; cf. also Matt. 21:39; Luke 20:15), for the Romans wanted everyone to see what happened to those who broke the Roman law (Justinian, *Digest* 48.19.28.15). Later, when Herod Agrippa enlarged the city with the so-called third wall, this site was enclosed within the walled city. The present site of the Church of the Holy Sepulchre was chosen by Constantine in AD 325–335 to commemorate the place of Jesus's crucifixion and burial. In contrast to the later site called "Gordon's Calvary," which does not merit serious consideration (Barkay 1986), the Church of the Holy Sepulchre is the most likely site of Jesus's crucifixion (R. Brown 1994: 2.938–40; cf. France 2002: 642: "There are no firm grounds for disputing the traditional site"). The building of the original church by Constantine and the continued rebuilding has removed almost every indication of it having been the location of a skull-like hill that stood thirty to thirty-five feet above the surrounding quarry.

15:23–25 The reference to Jesus being offered (a tendential imperfect) "wine mixed with myrrh" before his crucifixion is often associated with the following text in the Talmud: "When one is led out to execution, he is given a goblet of wine containing a grain of frankincense, in order to benumb his senses, for it is written, *Give strong drink unto him that is ready to perish, and wine unto the bitter in soul.* And it has also been taught: The noble women in Jerusalem used to donate and bring it" (*b. Sanh.* 43a). However, the "they" who offer the wine mixture to Jesus are probably to be understood as the Roman soldiers of 15:16, who serve as the antecedent for all the following "they(s)" in 15:16b–22 (contra France 2002: 643). Sufficient wine would have a numbing effect, but it is unclear whether the presence of myrrh would have contributed anything to this. Myrrh was sometimes added to wine to enhance its taste (R. Brown 1994: 2.941; Evans 2001: 501), but its effect as a narcotic is uncertain. On the other hand, though medically the addition of myrrh may not have had any anesthetizing effect, this does not mean that people in the first century did not think that it did. It is unclear if the drink was offered by the soldiers as an act of kindness or as mockery.[7] Jesus's refusal to take it may be due to his commitment to drink the full cup that his Father had placed before him (10:38–39; 14:36). Taking a drugged drink at this point would "renege on the commitment he had made" (R. Brown 1994: 2.941–42). This seems more

---

assisted to Golgotha because of physical weakness. This would go along with the need to compel Simon of Cyrene to carry the cross (15:21). See R. Brown 1994: 2.936; France 2002: 641.

6. *Golgotha* (Aramaic), *Kranion* (Greek), and *Calvariae* (Latin) all mean "skull." "Calvary" became popular in the English-speaking world through Wycliffe's translation of the Bible into English in 1382.

7. Cf. Koskenniemi, Nisula, and Toppari (2005), who suggest that sufficient myrrh added to wine would make it too bitter to drink and thus served as a form of torture to a thirsty victim.

likely than that he wanted to keep the prophetic statement he had made that he would not drink wine until in the kingdom of God (14:25), or that the offer was a continuation of the soldiers' mockery and that Jesus would not participate in this (Evans 2001: 501).

The description of Jesus's crucifixion is extremely terse ("eloquently understated" [Senior 1984: 117]) in all four Gospels. Mark simply states, "and they crucify him" (καὶ σταυροῦσιν αὐτόν, *kai staurousin auton*; 15:24).[8] Crucifixion as a form of execution goes back at least to the seventh century BC (Hengel 1977: 22–25; G. G. O'Collins, *ABD* 1:1207). According to Herodotus (*Histories* 3.132, 159) it was associated primarily with the Medes and Persians. It became common in the western part of the Mediterranean world through Alexander the Great in the fourth century BC. In the expansion of the Roman Empire eastward, it was soon adopted as their dominant form of capital punishment for slaves and the lower classes (Hengel 1977: 51–63; O'Collins, *ABD* 1:1208). Roman citizens were exempt from this method of execution (Cicero, *Against Verres* 2.5.63, 66 §§163, 170).[9] Thus Peter, who was not a Roman citizen, was martyred by crucifixion, according to the tradition (Acts of Peter 36–40), whereas Paul, who was a Roman citizen, was martyred by being beheaded (Acts of Paul 11). Crucifixion was a form of capital punishment used even by Jews, for early in the second century BC Alexander Jannaeus crucified eight hundred Pharisees who had revolted against him (Josephus, *Ant.* 13.14.2 §380; *J.W.* 1.4.6 §97).[10] In 4 BC the Roman governor of Syria crucified two thousand Jews who had been involved in a revolt (Josephus, *Ant.* 17.10.10 §295). Also according to Josephus (*J.W.* 5.11.1 §§446–51), Titus crucified five hundred Jews a day during the siege of Jerusalem in AD 70, so that there was no longer room for crosses to be erected, nor were crosses available for all the victims. Crucifixion remained the primary form of capital punishment in the Roman Empire until AD 337, when the emperor Constantine banned it.

Although the term "crucifixion" was sometimes used to describe impalement, which would have usually caused instant death, it usually refers to affixing a person to a cross by either tying (Pliny, *Nat. Hist.* 28.11.46; Livy, *History* 1.26.6) or nailing (Philo, *Posterity* 17 §61; Lucan, *Civil War* 6.547; Plautus, *Mostellaria* 2.1 [360]; Seneca, *De vita beata* 19.3; *m. Šabb.* 6.10). The method of affixing the victim to the cross, even when it involved nailing, was not the cause of their death, since no vital organs of the body were injured. After being tied or nailed to the *patibulum* (or crossbeam), the *patibulum* and its victim were then raised by forked poles and inserted in the prepared notch in the vertical pole standing in the ground and made secure. From John 20:25 and

---

8. Cf. Matt. 27:35: "but having crucified him" (σταυρώσαντες δὲ αὐτόν, *staurōsantes de auton*); Luke 23:33: "there they crucified him" (ἐκεῖ ἐσταύρωσαν αὐτόν, *ekei estaurōsan auton*); and John 19:18: "where they crucified him" (ὅπου αὐτὸν ἐσταύρωσαν, *hopou auton estaurōsan*). In each of the four accounts, only three Greek words are used.

9. See Hengel (1977: 39–45) for a list of exceptions that prove the rule.

10. For additional examples of the use of this punishment by Jews, see R. Brown 1994: 1.533 and 541.

27 it is clear that Jesus's hands[11] were nailed to the cross (cf. Col. 2:14), and Luke 24:39 suggests that his feet were also nailed.[12] To prevent the premature death of the victim (crucifixion was intended not simply to execute but also to torture the victim to death), a *sedile*, or seat, to support the buttocks (cf. Seneca, *Ep.* 101.12, who refers to the "seat on the piercing cross"; cf. Tertullian, *Ad nationes* 1.12) and/or *suppedaneum*, or footrest, were often placed on the vertical beam. This enabled the victim to relieve the lung muscles and keep him from asphyxiating. If the victim's feet were nailed to the cross, he would relieve his lung muscles by pressing against the nails.

Death by crucifixion was slow. At times the victim would live for days. Birds and animals would often begin to feast on the victims even before they were dead. Horace (*Ep.* 1.16.46–48) describes the victims as "feeding crows on the cross." Cicero refers to crucifixion as "that cruel and disgusting penalty" and "worst extreme of the tortures inflicted upon slaves" (*Against Verres* 2.5.64, 66 §§165, 169) and says that "the very word 'cross' should be far removed not only from the person of a Roman citizen but from his thoughts, his eyes and his ears" (*Pro Rabirio* 5.16). Seneca (*Ep.* 101.14) refers to the cross as "the accursed tree," and Josephus (*J.W.* 7.6.4 §203) states that it provided "the most pitiable of deaths."[13]

The dividing of Jesus's garments by the soldiers seems to be an allusion to Ps. 22:18 (21:19 LXX; R. Brown 1994: 2.953–54) and is therefore considered by some to be nonhistorical. Yet it is referred to in all four Gospels and was apparently customary (Evans 2001: 502). It is uncertain whether "casting lots" meant that one of the soldiers brought a dice box (*pyrgos*; lit. "tower") to the crucifixion or that the soldiers played a game in which they guessed the number of outstretched fingers in another's hidden hand (R. Brown 1994: 2.955). The victims of crucifixion were normally hung naked on the cross, and the division of Jesus's clothing suggests this (Melito of Sardis, *On the Pascha* 97), but the fact that Jesus wore his garments to the place of execution (15:20) may suggest that he was permitted to wear a loincloth due to Jewish sensibilities (cf. Acts of Pilate 10.1).

Mark states that the crucifixion took place at the "third" (τρίτη, *tritē*) hour (15:25), 9 a.m. This seems to conflict with John 19:14, which states that Jesus had not yet been crucified at the "sixth" (ἕκτη, *hektē*) hour (noon). There have been numerous attempts to harmonize this apparent discrepancy (R. Brown 1994: 2.958–60). Most such attempts assume a precision in time designations that did not exist in the first century. In the NT, we have twenty-three specific temporal references. Of these, four (Matt. 20:3; Mark 15:25; Acts 2:15) refer to the "third" hour (cf. also Acts 23:23), seven (Matt. 20:5; 27:45; Mark 15:33;

---

11. "Hands" probably refers here to the wrists or forearms, since the hands would not have been able to bear the weight of the body.

12. In 1968 an ossuary was discovered in Israel containing the bones of a man who had been crucified and whose feet had been nailed independently to the sides of the vertical beam. See Fitzmyer 1978: 493–513; R. Brown 1994: 2.950–51.

13. For further reading, see Hengel 1977; R. Brown 1994: 2.945–52.

Luke 23:44; John 4:6; 19:14; Acts 10:9) to the "sixth" hour, and nine (Matt. 20:5; 27:45, 46; Mark 15:33, 34; Luke 23:44; Acts 3:1; 10:3, 30) to the "ninth" hour. Only three refer to a different hour: the "eleventh" (Matt. 20:9), the "tenth" (John 1:39), and the "seventh" (John 4:52). This raises the question of how a person might refer to an event taking place between 9 a.m. and noon. It would probably be described as either the "third" hour or the "sixth" hour (Stein 1990: 66–69). Some have suggested that John would have preferred the latter designation because of his particular reckoning of the Passover (see the introduction to 14:12–31), for at noon the Passover lambs were slain (Gundry 1993: 957; Evans 2001: 503). But could John have expected his readers to understand this? If he had to explain to them that Jews have no dealings with Samaritans (4:9), that the Jews have certain burial customs (19:40), that the word "Messiah" means "Christ" (1:41; 4:25), that "Rabbi" means "Teacher" (1:38), that "Siloam" means "Sent" (9:7), and so on, it is very unlikely that they would have known that on the sixth hour of the day before the Passover, the Passover lambs were slain, and that this coincided exactly with when Jesus was crucified. Furthermore, the sixth-hour designation in John 19:14 is associated not with the time of Jesus's crucifixion but with the verdict at his trial before Pilate. If we recognize the general preference of the third or sixth hour to designate a period between 9 a.m. and noon and the lack of precision in telling time in the first century (Miller 1983), the two different time designations do not present an insurmountable problem.

In all four Gospels, we read of an inscription (ἐπιγραφή, epigraphē; 15:26; **15:26–32** τίτλον, titlon; John 19:19) placed on the cross "over his head" (ἐπάνω τῆς κεφαλῆς αὐτοῦ, epanō tēs kephalēs autou; Matt. 27:37; cf. Luke 23:38). Although some deny the historicity of this (Bultmann 1968: 272, 284; Catchpole 1984: 328), it appears to be "historically unimpeachable" (Schneider 1984: 404; cf. R. Brown 1994: 2.968). Such inscriptions were often referred to in ancient accounts of crucifixion (Suetonius, *Caligula* 32.2; *Domitian* 10.1; Cassius Dio, *Roman Hist.* 54.3.7; Eusebius, *Eccl. Hist.* 5.1.44). The historicity of the title "King of the Jews"[14] is supported by the fact that it was not a Christian confession, is found only here with respect to Jesus's crucifixion, and is not the favorite Markan christological title (which is "Jesus Christ, the Son of God"; 1:1; 3:11; 15:39). Nevertheless, although the title was used in mockery by Jesus's opponents (15:26, 32), it is profoundly true for Mark and his readers. Jesus is the Christ, the Son of God, the King of the Jews (Kingsbury 1983: 126–29, 151–52).

Mark's reference in 15:27 to the crucifying of two "bandits" (λῃστάς, lēstas; cf. 15:6–11) with Jesus brings the preliminaries of the crucifixion to an end. Since Jesus was the most important victim, he was crucified in the center, and the others were on his right and his left. Although the "right side" and "left side" have a verbal similarity to 10:37, 40, the sharing of Jesus's reign by two

---

14. R. Brown (1994: 2.963) comments that these are "the only words pertinent to Jesus claimed to have been written during his lifetime."

disciples and the sharing of his death by two unbelievers are too radically different to establish any sort of parallel (R. Brown 1994: 2.969n84; contra Matera 1982: 62). At this point, some copyists added from Luke 22:37, "And the Scripture was fulfilled that says, 'He was reckoned with the transgressors'" (L Θ f¹ f¹³ lat). This verse (eventually numbered 28) was included in the TR by Erasmus and found its way into the Tyndale and KJV translations, but it was not part of the original Mark and should not be included.[15]

At this point, Jesus is mocked by three separate groups. Those who passed by on the road "blaspheme" (ἐβλασφήμουν, *eblasphēmoun*) him and wag their heads (15:29). The latter action may be an allusion to Ps. 22:7, but it also may simply be a common gesture of contempt (cf. Lam. 2:15). Jesus was condemned for "blasphemy" (Mark 14:64) yet is now the victim of blasphemy (Hooker 1991: 373). Their taunt "Ha! [You who would be] the destroyer of the sanctuary and rebuilder [of it] in three days" recalls the charge of the false witnesses at Jesus's trial before the Sanhedrin in 14:58. If Jesus could destroy the sanctuary and rebuild it in three days, he would possess supernatural power, and the passersby challenge him to demonstrate this power by saving himself and coming down from the cross (15:30).

The second group mocking (ἐμπαίζοντες, *empaizontes*; cf. 15:20) Jesus is made up of the chief priests with the scribes (see 15:1). They pick up the second part of the mockery of the passersby (15:30) by saying, "Others he saved; himself he cannot save" (ἄλλους ἔσωσεν, ἑαυτὸν οὐ δύναται σῶσαι, *allous esōsen, heauton ou dynatai sōsai*; 15:31). This recalls Jesus's ministry of healing ("saving": 3:4; 5:23, 28, 34; 6:56; 10:52; Donahue and Harrington 2002: 443–44; contra France 2002: 648). Like the passersby, they challenge Jesus to perform a sign (cf. 8:11) and "come down now from the cross, in order that we may see and believe" (15:32). If he would do this sign, they supposedly would believe. Mark's readers, however, know that the chief priests' and scribes' hardness of heart (3:5) would not allow them to believe and that they would attribute such a sign to Beelzebul (3:22). More important, for Jesus to save himself would be the very thing that would keep him from saving (in the ultimate sense) others, for he must pour out his life in sacrifice as a ransom for many (10:45; 14:24). The title used in 15:32 to address Jesus, "the Christ, the King of Israel," is used in mockery and is the Jewish equivalent of Pilate's "King of the Jews" (15:2, 9, 12, 18, 26). The third and final group involved in mocking Jesus is the two bandits crucified along with him (15:32b). Now "Jesus is completely alone; he has no allies, not even among those who share his fate" (Evans 2001: 506). Unlike Luke 23:39–43, Mark, Matthew, and John have no account of the repentant bandit.

15:33–36 In 15:33 Mark gives the second of the three temporal designations found in his account of the crucifixion. In the "sixth" (ἕκτης, *hektēs*) hour (lit. "when the sixth hour came") darkness comes "upon the whole land" (ἐφ' ὅλην τὴν γῆν, *eph' holēn tēn gēn*). The last term can refer to the whole earth (2:10; 9:3;

---

15. See additional note on 15:28.

13:27, 31), the shore in contrast to the Sea of Galilee (4:1; 6:47, 53), or the ground/soil (4:5, 8, 20, 26, 28, 31; 8:6; 9:20; 14:35). Here it probably refers to more than the ground/soil but less than the whole earth, or planet. Mark likely intends it to mean "the land of Judea." The symbolism of the term "darkness" is found in numerous places in the Bible. It is often associated with an act of divine judgment and may have eschatological connotations. Compare Amos 8:9: "On that day, says the Lord God, I will make the sun go down at noon, and darken the earth in broad daylight" (cf. also Deut. 28:29; Isa. 13:9–10; 24:23; Jer. 4:28; 13:16; 15:9; Ezek. 32:7–8; Joel 2:10, 31; 3:15; Zeph. 1:15; Mark 13:24–25; Acts 2:20; Rev. 6:12; etc.). For Mark, the symbolism of "darkness" does not mean that there was no physical darkness; the darkness is real, just as the judgment of Israel that it symbolizes is real. This real darkness at the crucifixion is a proleptic experience of the judgment that was coming upon Israel in AD 70. In the long list of examples given above, most are found in the poetic and metaphorical genre of prophecy, but the reference in 15:33 occurs in the genre of historical narrative. No attempt is made in Mark to explain the immediate cause of this unusual darkness. Even Luke's statement that "the sun's light failed" (23:45) is not the scientific explanation of an astronomer. Since a solar eclipse at the time of the Passover is not possible due to this being the period of the full moon, some have suggested a dust storm (sirocco), the presence of heavy dark clouds, a supernatural darkening of the sun itself, and so on. This is the first supernatural event associated with the crucifixion in Mark. The second will be the tearing of the temple veil in 15:38.

The third temporal designation, the "ninth" (ἐνάτῃ, *enatē*) hour (3 p.m.), is repeated twice (14:33b, 34a). "*Elōi, elōi, lema sabachthani?*" is the only saying of Jesus from the cross recorded by Mark (see Stein 1996: 248–52 for a brief discussion of the seven last words of Jesus). The saying is Aramaic, and Mark explains its meaning: "My God, my God, why have you forsaken me?" (cf. Aramaic also in 5:41; 7:11, 34; 11:9, 10; 14:36; 15:22). Jesus is described as crying this out "with a loud voice" (φωνῇ μεγάλῃ, *phōnē megalē*). What Mark is seeking to emphasize by this is unclear. Some suggestions are that it emphasizes Jesus's "intense physical suffering" (Donahue and Harrington 2002: 447); "the decisive character of this moment in Jesus's struggle against the power of evil" (ibid.); the strength of Jesus, the Son of God (Evans 2001: 507); or the depth of his emotion (France 2002: 652). Unfortunately, Mark does not give us any explanation. The authenticity of this saying is guaranteed by the difficulty it creates (V. Taylor 1952: 594; R. Brown 1994: 2.1051). Some understand the cry as revealing Jesus's feeling of being forsaken (V. Taylor 1952: 594; R. Brown 1994: 2.1051; Donahue and Harrington 2002: 450–51). Yet this does not take into consideration the strong Markan emphasis on the necessity of the cross (8:31; 14:21), the divine purpose of Jesus becoming a ransom for many (10:45), Jesus's sacrificial pouring out of his blood (14:24), God himself striking the Son (14:27), and so on. Furthermore, Mark's readers must have come to the reading of the Gospel with some sort of a soteriology. Would they have been familiar with some of Paul's theology, such as that found in Rom. 3:24–25; 2 Cor. 5:21; Gal. 3:13? This is quite possible, if we accept the tradition that this Gospel was written to the church in Rome. The most likely interpretation of Jesus's cry is that "the cry [is] to be understood in the light of xiv.36, II Cor. v.21, Gal. iii.13. The burden of the world's sin, his complete self-identification with sinners, involved not merely a felt, but a real, abandonment by his Father. It is in the cry of dereliction that the full horror of man's sin stands revealed" (Cranfield 1959: 458).

Yet Jesus's cry is not one of total despair, for he quotes Ps. 22:1, a lament psalm that like all lament psalms ends with a confession of confidence and/or vow or praise (Stein 1994a: 198), and he cries "*My* God, *my* God." Had not Jesus said that three days after his suffering he would be vindicated and rise (8:31; 9:31; 10:34)? Thus the present experience of suffering and abandonment by his Father would end in his being exalted to his Father's right hand (14:62; cf. Philippians, where obedience to death, "even death on a cross" [2:8], would lead to glorious exaltation [2:9–11]).

The terms Ελωι (*Elōi*; Aram. אֱלָהִי, *'ĕlāhî*; Mark 15:34) and Ηλι (*Ēlî*; Heb. אֵלִי, *'ēlî*; Matt. 27:46) sound close enough to the name "Elijah" (Heb. אֵלִיָּה, *'ēliyâ*) that some bystanders think that Jesus is calling out to the prophet to rescue him.[16] This may be an allusion to various traditions that Elijah would come to rescue the righteous (Mal. 4:5; *b. 'Abod. Zar.* 17b; *b. Ta'an.* 21a; Gen. Rab. 33.3 [on Gen. 8:1]). In response to Jesus's cry, someone runs to get a sponge, fills it with the cheap vinegary wine that the soldiers drank, places the sponge on a reed, and offers it to Jesus to drink. The use of a reed indicates that Jesus was crucified sufficiently high off the ground as to be beyond reach (Blinzler 1959: 249–50; France 2002: 655). It is unclear whether the offer of wine is to be understood as a kind gesture or an act of mockery. In favor of the latter is a possible allusion to Ps. 69:21 (68:22 LXX), but on the literary level it is questionable that Mark's readers would have been aware of this alleged allusion. Furthermore, if the "someone" was a soldier, we must remember that up to this point the soldiers have been consistently described as mocking Jesus (15:16–20a); if "someone" was one of the crowd, they have just been described as mocking Jesus (15:29–30). The offer of wine could be interpreted as an attempt to prolong Jesus's torture and keep him from dying quickly; Luke 23:36 may suggest this. In favor of it being understood as an act of kindness is Jesus's taking it (John 19:30), since Jesus was passive in all the acts of mockery done against him; and the man saying, "Wait, let us see if Elijah comes to take him down," which can be interpreted as giving opportunity for Elijah to rescue Jesus. The interpretation of it as mockery has probably the majority of supporters (Senior 1984: 124–25; Hooker 1991: 377; Donahue and

16. The crowd's thinking that Jesus was calling Elijah is a problem on the historical level. It is unclear if Jesus's audience would have made such a mistake with the Aramaic term, assuming that Jesus was speaking in his native tongue. The mistake would be more likely with the Hebrew term, assuming that Jesus was quoting from the Bible (cf. Jesus reading from the Hebrew Scriptures in Luke 4:16–20). For Mark's readers, the similarity in the Greek terms would make such confusion quite understandable (R. Brown 1994: 2.1060–63).

Harrington 2002: 448), but taking this as a kind gesture also has supporters (W. Lane 1974: 573–74; Witherington 2001: 399; J. Edwards 2002: 477).

The death of Jesus is described in stark simplicity: he gives a loud cry (a separate cry from 15:34 and not merely a death rattle) and expires (ἐξέπνευσεν, *exepneusen*). This stands in contrast to Luke 23:46 ("Father, into your hands I commend my spirit") and John 19:30 ("It is finished"). The verb "expire" is essentially a synonym for "die" (France 2002: 655–56) and carries with it no special theological freight (contra Danker [1970: 67–68], who sees Jesus's death as a result of his expulsion of the demon possessing him).[17] The views that Jesus's "expiring" (breathing out) refers to his releasing a strong wind through the Spirit that tore the temple curtain (Jackson 1987: 27–28; cf. T. Schmidt 1994: 151–52), or that "shouting out" seeks to emphasize Jesus's power (Evans 2001: 508) are unconvincing.

15:37–38

The second supernatural event associated with Jesus's crucifixion in Mark occurs at his death.[18] The veil of the sanctuary is split in two, from top to bottom. Which curtain of the sanctuary (the outer curtain separating the sanctuary from the courtyard or the one within the sanctuary before the holy of holies; Josephus, *J.W.* 5.5.4–5 §§212, 219; *Ant.* 8.3.3 §75; cf. Exod. 26:31–33, 36) is uncertain. Josephus describes the former as a magnificent tapestry eighty feet tall. In favor of this is that it is the only curtain that could have been seen by the people (W. Lane 1974: 575; J. Edwards 2002: 478). Others, due to the influence of Heb. 9:1–28 and 10:19–20, believe that it refers to the curtain leading into the holy of holies (Lightfoot 1950: 56; Gurtner 2005).[19]

Mark provides no clear interpretation of what the splitting of the curtain is meant to signify. There are two main suggestions.[20] The first sees this as an act of divine judgment on the sanctuary and the nation. Like the darkness that comes over the whole land (15:33), it symbolizes God's judgment (the curtain "is split" [a divine passive] from top to bottom) that will soon come upon the nation in AD 70 (12:9; 13:2–4, 14–22, 28–31; cf. Lives of the Prophets [Habakkuk] 12.11–12; T. Levi 10.3). It indicates that the fulfillment of Jesus's prediction in 14:58 and 15:29 has already begun, and what is represented as already fulfilled in the spiritual realm by the split curtain is proleptic of what will physically happen to the temple and sanctuary in AD 70. The second interpretation is that the term "is split" (ἐσχίσθη, *eschisthē*) recalls the only other place in Mark where this verb is used, 1:10. (The supposed analogy to 14:63 is unconvincing because it uses a different verb.) Just as at Jesus's baptism the heavens are split, revealing the unique, direct access that the Son of

17. For a discussion of various suggested physiological causes for Jesus's death, see R. Brown 1994: 2.1088–92.

18. Matthew (27:51–53) associates other supernatural events with the death of Jesus: an earthquake, the opening of tombs, and risings from the dead.

19. R. Brown (1994: 2.1109–13) considers the entire discussion of which curtain is meant as too speculative and unessential to his view that it is a sign of divine judgment upon Israel. Either curtain would do for this.

20. However, see Geddert (1989: 140–45), who lists thirty-five different interpretations.

God has with the Father, now through his sacrificial death for many (10:45; 14:24), Jesus's followers have direct access to the Father (Lightfoot 1950: 55–56; Hooker 1991: 378). This is how the writer of Hebrews understands the split curtain (6:19–20; 9:3–14, 24–28; 10:19–20). It is possible that both interpretations are implied by Mark (Chronis 1982: 107–14; cf., however, R. Brown 1994: 2.1099–1109, who argues only for the first).

15:39 "Centurion" (κεντυρίων, *kentyriōn*) is the Greek transliteration of the Latin term and refers to a Roman officer in charge of a hundred men. In the NT it occurs only in Mark 15:39, 44, and 45. In the parallel accounts (Matt. 27:54; Luke 23:47) the Greek equivalents ἑκατόνταρχος (*hekatontarchos*) and ἑκατοντάρχης (*hekatonarchēs*) of "ruler of a hundred" are used. After Jesus expires, the centurion says, "Truly, this man was the Son of God." Matthew 27:54 attributes the centurion's confession and the confession of those with him to the earthquake and "what things had taken place" (τὰ γενόμενα, *ta genomena*) described in 27:51–53, and Luke 23:47–48 attributes it to the centurion's seeing "what had taken place" (τὰ γενόμενα). In Mark, it is primarily Jesus's death itself that brings about the confession, although "in this manner" (οὕτως, *houtōs*) may allude back to the splitting of the temple curtain (R. Brown 1994: 2.1144–45; Donahue and Harrington 2002: 449). Yet how the centurion would have known this is unclear. Even the outer curtain leading into the sanctuary would not have been visible from the traditional site of the crucifixion, although it would have been possible from the Mount of Olives. Are we to assume that a report of this quickly reached the centurion and his confession took place after this? Some other suggestions for the centurion's confession are the supernatural darkness over the land (15:33), various sayings of Jesus from the cross found in the other Gospels, Jesus's loud cry at his death (15:37), Jesus's sudden death (15:44), the unknown content of Jesus's loud cry being one of praise to God or of triumph, and Jesus's peaceful death (France 2002: 659). Perhaps the best explanation may be that God granted to the centurion this insight by divine revelation (J. Edwards 2002: 481). It was "given" to him (4:11).

The confession of the centurion that Jesus is "*the* Son of God" (υἱὸς θεοῦ, *huios theou*) lacks the article in the Greek text. This and considering what a Roman soldier might have meant has led some to translate the confession as "*a* son of God" (REB, JB, footnotes in RSV and NRSV) instead of "*the* Son of God" (RSV, NAB, NASB, NJB, NIV, TNIV, NLT, ESV). In the first verse of Mark's Gospel, we also have the anarthrous use of the expression "Son of God," and in the context of Mark's Gospel it is evident that he means "the Son of God," that is, not one of the many "sons of God" but "the only Son of God." Although the term "only" (μονογενής, *monogenēs*) in John 1:14; 3:16, 18 is not used by Mark, the expressions "the Son of God/Most High God/Blessed" (1:11; 3:11; 9:7; 14:61–62; cf. also 1:24; 12:6; 13:32) all have the article "the." Grammatically, "Colwell's Rule" (Colwell 1933) indicates that the anarthrous predicate nominative is to be understood as definite (R. Brown

1994: 2.1146–50; E. Johnson 1987: 3–7, however, allows for exceptions), and the use of the article with the title throughout Mark indicates that it should be so understood here. In light of all that Mark has said in 1:1–15:38, he clearly wants his readers to understand the confession of the centurion not as saying that Jesus is "*a* son of God" but as saying "*the* beloved" (12:6) "and only Son of God" (contra Shiner 2000).

In the discussion of this passage, the particular perspective in which the "meaning" of this title is being sought is often not made clear. It is probable that the centurion's understanding of his confession was not as rich and pregnant as that of Mark and his readers. The meaning of the confession in the literary context of the Gospel (the third setting in life, or *Sitz im Leben*) and what the centurion personally meant by the confession (the first *Sitz im Leben*) are in reality two separate questions. In the first setting the words of the centurion are certainly not a taunt, for the centurion serves as a precursor of the coming acceptance of the Son of God by the gentile world. In the present setting of Mark and his readers, however, the confession carries with it the full christological meaning found elsewhere in the Gospel (Kim 1998: 238–41; contra E. Johnson 2000). The death of Jesus reveals to the gentile world that Jesus is the Christ, the Son of God. It is ironic that the Jewish leadership and onlookers mock Jesus, but a hated Roman soldier makes the greatest human confession in the entire Gospel. Some have seen an analogy between the (1) splitting of the heavens and the divine confession of Jesus's sonship in 1:11 and (2) the splitting of the temple curtain and the centurion's confession of Jesus's sonship (Ulansey 1991). But the analogy is not entirely convincing, for a true analogy would involve either (1) the crowd at Jesus's baptism responding to the splitting of the heavens and making the confession of 1:11 and the centurion responding to the splitting of the temple curtain and making the confession in 15:39, or (2) a voice coming out of the sanctuary through the split curtain confessing Jesus's sonship, just as God through the split heavens confesses Jesus's sonship at his baptism.

The Markan account of the crucifixion ends with a reference to the presence **15:40–41** of three women: Mary Magdalene, Mary the mother of James the younger and Joses, and Salome, along with unnamed women who had come up to Jerusalem (see 3:22) with Jesus. This is the first time Mark has mentioned that women followed Jesus during his ministry. The three women are described as "followers" (ἠκολούθουν, *ēkolouthoun*; cf. 1:18; 2:14, 15; 5:24; 6:1; 8:34; 9:38; 10:21, 28, 32, 52) of Jesus who "were ministering" (διηκόνουν, *diēkonoun*) to his needs. Luke 8:3 speaks of several women, Mary Magdalene being one, ministering to Jesus by the use of their (economic) resources. Their mention here prepares the reader for their role in the next two accounts, 15:43–47 and 16:1–8. The women are described as observing the crucifixion "from a distance" (ἀπὸ μακρόθεν, *apo makrothen*). There is no need to see here an allusion to Ps. 38:11 (contra Marcus 1992b: 174; J. Edwards 2002: 484), for it is doubtful that Mark expected his readers to think of this allusion as they were hearing the Gospel read to them (France 2002: 663n79). The first two women are mentioned again in 15:47 as observing the place of Jesus's burial, and all three are mentioned again in 16:1ff. as the first witnesses to the resurrection of Jesus.

Mary, from the village of Magdala located near the northwest shore of the Sea of Galilee, is also referred to in Luke 8:2 as one out of whom seven demons had been exorcised. She becomes a key witness to the resurrection in the Gospel accounts (Mark 16:1, 7; Luke 24:10; John 20:1, 11–18). There is no biblical support for the later view that she was a prostitute (Schaberg 1992). Mary, the mother of James the younger (or lesser) and Joses (cf. 6:3), is sometimes identified with Mary the mother of Jesus (cf. John 19:25–27; Bauckham 1991), but more often she is identified with Mary the mother of James the son of Alphaeus (3:18), the lesser James among the apostles. France (2002: 664) rightly raises the question of why, if she was the mother of Jesus, she is described in so clumsy a manner rather than as "Mary, the mother of Jesus." Salome appears elsewhere only in 16:1, but the parallel in Matt. 27:56 is sometimes interpreted as suggesting that she was the mother of the apostles James and John.

Summary

Within this section of the Passion Narrative, we encounter a number of Markan emphases. One involves the fulfillment of Scripture. Already we have seen the fulfillment of Jesus's predictions concerning his rejection and condemnation to death by the religious leadership (8:31; 10:33–34; 14:53–64), his betrayal to the religious leaders by one of the disciples (14:18–21, 43), his being deserted by his other disciples (14:27–31, 50), his being denied by Peter three times (14:30, 66–72), his being delivered over to the gentiles (10:33; 15:1ff.), his being mocked (10:34; 14:65; 15:16–20, 29–32), and his being scourged (10:34; 15:15). In the present account the prediction concerning his being killed (8:31; 9:31; 10:34; cf. 12:7) is fulfilled (15:15–39). Still unfulfilled is his prediction that after three days he would rise from the dead (8:31; 9:31; 10:34; 14:58; 15:29; cf. also 9:9). This will find its fulfillment in 16:1–8. In addition, Jesus's prediction about the temple's destruction (12:9; 13:1–23, 28–31; 14:57–59; 15:29), like the already now and not yet of the kingdom of God, is already now fulfilled by the divine rejection of Israel's religious leadership and worship (15:38) and awaits its consummation in the events of AD 70. "The contents of the Marcan narrative are to a great extent determined, both materially and verbally, by a desire to show fulfillment" (R. Brown 1994: 2.901). In light of this, Mark's readers should not be troubled either by the death of the Son of God or by the events occurring in Jerusalem as the Gospel is read to them. All is taking place "as it has been written" (14:21). It all lies with the will of God, and the divine necessary (δεῖ, dei; 8:31) has been in control of all that has and will take place.

Christologically, the readers of Mark have once again seen that Jesus is "the Son of God" (15:39). What God bore witness to at Jesus's baptism and transfiguration (1:11; 9:7), what Jesus has acknowledged to the Jewish leadership (14:61–62), and what demons have confessed time and time again (1:24; 3:11; 5:7) is now confessed by a Roman centurion, who represents the first of the large host of gentiles who would become followers of Jesus (13:10; 14:9). In addition, the new christological title given to Jesus in 15:2, 9, 12, 18, and 26 becomes the title for which he is crucified—the King of the Jews/Israel (15:32). Although it is used sarcastically and in mockery, it is nevertheless true. As the Christ, the Son of God, Jesus is the King of the Jews/Israel. He fulfills his first task as the King of the Jews by pouring out his life sacrificially on the cross as a ransom for many (10:45; 14:24). He will fulfill his second task as the King of the Jews when he returns at his parousia to gather his elect and to judge the world (13:24–27, 32–37; cf. 8:38). For his followers, this will involve eternal bliss; for his enemies, eternal punishment.

Additional Notes

15:23. The translation follows ℵ B Γ* Σ, which have the substantival relative pronoun ὅς instead of the ὅ found in A C L Θ Ψ f¹³. There is little difference in the meaning of the two.

15:28. Some later MSS (L Θ f¹ f¹³ lat) add, "And the Scripture was fulfilled that says, 'And he was reckoned with the transgressors.'" This, however, is clearly a later copyist's addition to the text from Luke 22:37.

15:34. Codices D and Θ read ηλι ηλι, suggesting the Heb. אֵלִי אֵלִי (ʾēlî ʾēlî) instead of the Aram. אֱלָהִי אֱלָהִי (ʾĕlāhî ʾĕlāhî). This is probably due to their following Matt. 27:46, which in turn mirrors the Heb. of Ps. 22:1 (22:2 MT). There are various spellings of the next term: λιμα (A f¹³ 33) or λαμα (B Θ D), reflecting the Heb. לָמָה (lāmâ); and λεμα (ℵ* C L Δ Ψ), reflecting the Aram. לְמָא (lĕmāʾ). See Evans 2001: 497nj.

15:39. The MSS A C W Θ f¹ f¹³ lat syr add "having cried out" (κράξας) before "expired."

I. Jesus Is Buried (15:42–47)

Most scholars acknowledge the historicity of the burial account. Even Bultmann (1968: 274) describes it as "an historical account which creates no impression of being a legend." The attempt to see it as an early church creation to fulfill Isa. 53:9 "has nothing to commend it" (Hooker 1991: 380). The reference to Jesus's burial in the early creedal formula found in 1 Cor. 15:4 and its multiple attestation in all four Gospels (Matt. 27:57–61; Luke 23:50–56; John 19:38–42) argue in favor of its historicity. The presence of women as witnesses to the burial and the resurrection adds additional historical credence to the account, for their witness was disallowed among the Jews. Thus a story created ex nihilo by the early church would have placed men rather than women as the key witnesses to Jesus's burial and resurrection. Despite this, Crossan (1995: 160–88) questions its historicity and argues that Jesus's body was probably thrown into a ditch and eaten by dogs. This did happen frequently to victims of crucifixion, but almost always in time of war (Evans 2001: 516–17; Josephus, *Ant.* 17.10.10 §295; *J.W.* 5.11.1 §450). Jewish sensibilities concerning Deut. 21:22–23[1] apparently caused Rome to allow such victims to be given decent burial. (Cf. Philo, *Flaccus* 10 §§83–84, who criticizes the Roman governor for not permitting this normal practice.)[2] Since Rome and the Jewish Sanhedrin worked together in the crucifixion of Jesus, his burial by a respected member of the Sanhedrin, not one of Jesus's known disciples, would have served Roman purposes well by ameliorating Jewish concern for not leaving the dead exposed after sunset.

With respect to the Markan editorial work in the account, Pryke (1978: 23, 148, 175) lists 15:42, 43c, and 46 as Markan. Schmithals (1979: 2.702) lists only 15:42a, and Gnilka (1979: 331) lists 15:42a, 43 ("courageously" [τολμήσας, *tolmēsas*]), and most of 44–45. The most likely candidates of Markan editorial work appear to be 15:42a (the genitive absolute that joins the present account with the preceding and the explanatory "that is, the day before the Sabbath"), 43 (the relative clause describing Joseph of Arimathea), 44 ("marveled"), and 47 (which joins this, the preceding, and the following account together). The present account consists of four

---

1. "When someone is convicted of a crime punishable by death and is executed, and you hang him on a tree, his corpse must not remain all night upon the tree; you shall bury him that same day, for anyone hung on a tree is under God's curse. You must not defile the land that the Lord your God is giving you for possession" (NRSV).

2. For examples of Jewish concern with respect to this command, cf. Tob. 1:17–18; 2:3–8; Sir. 38:16; John 19:31; 11QTemple[a] 64.7–13; Josephus, *J.W.* 3.8.5 §§377–78; 4.5.2 §317; 4.6.1 §§360–62; *Ant.* 4.8.24 §§264–65; *b. Sanh.* 46b, 47a–b; *m. Sanh.* 6.5.

parts: (1) Joseph of Arimathea's request for the body of Jesus (15:42–43); (2) Pilate's surprise at Jesus's sudden death and his inquiry concerning this to the centurion (15:44–45); (3) the burial of Jesus (15:46);[3] and (4) a reference to Mary Magdalene and Mary the mother of Joses observing the burial (15:47). The last serves as a transition between the death of Jesus (15:16–41) and his resurrection (16:1–8), just as in the early creed found in 1 Cor. 15:3ff. "he was *buried*" serves as a transition between "Christ *died* for our sins . . ." and "he *was raised* on the third day. . . ." The story of Jesus's burial concludes the Passion Narrative, which began with the plot of the Sanhedrin leaders (14:1–2) and the anointing of Jesus for burial by a faithful woman (14:3–9) and now concludes with Jesus's burial by a believing member of the Sanhedrin (15:42–46) and its careful observation by faithful women (15:47).

Exegesis and Exposition

[42]And already when evening had come, since it was the day of Preparation, that is, the day before the Sabbath, [43]Joseph of Arimathea, a respected council member, who was also himself eagerly awaiting [the coming of] the kingdom of God, ⌜courageously⌝ entered before Pilate and requested the body of Jesus. [44]But Pilate marveled ⌜that⌝ he had already died, and having called the centurion, he asked him if [Jesus] had ⌜been dead for some time⌝. [45]And having learned from the centurion [that Jesus had died], he granted the body to Joseph. [46]And having purchased a linen cloth, taking him down [from the cross], he wrapped [the body] in the linen cloth and laid him in a tomb that had been cut out of rock and rolled a stone against the door of the tomb. [47]But Mary Magdalene and Mary the mother of Joses were observing where he was laid.

15:42–43 According to Mark, the death of Jesus took place sometime after the ninth hour (3 p.m.; 15:34–37). "When evening had come" (ἤδη ὀψίας γενομένης, *ēdē opsias genomenēs*) probably means that the Passover was coming to an end and the Sabbath was approaching (Painter 1997: 209). It would begin at sunset, around 6 p.m. As a result there was little time to obtain permission from Pilate for the body of Jesus, purchase the necessary supplies for burial, and prepare the body for burial. Probably the activities of 15:43–46 took place between 4 and 6 p.m. R. Brown (1994: 2.1211–12) suggests that this would have taken "not much less than two hours." That the coming day was the Sabbath would have intensified the Jewish desire to have the victims' bodies removed from the crosses before sunset. Mark's explanation of the expression "day of Preparation" (παρασκευή, *paraskeuē*) as "the day before the Sabbath" (προσάββατον, *prosabbaton*; 15:42b) envisions an audience unfamiliar with

---

3. Although some scholars see 15:43–46 as a Markan sandwich (Donahue and Harrington 2002: 456) in which 15:44–45 is inserted between 15:43 and 46, it is probably best to reserve this expression for instances where two separate and self-standing accounts are so arranged. Mark 15:44–45 is not a self-standing account.

the Jewish calendar. (Cf. how Josephus, *Ant.* 16.6.2 §163, explains the same term to his Greek readers; see 7:3–4.)

At this point, Mark introduces his readers to a new character, Joseph of Arimathea. Arimathea probably refers to Ramathaim (1 Sam. 1:1; cf. also 1 Macc. 11:34; Josephus, *Ant.* 13.4.9 §127), which lies twenty miles northwest of Jerusalem. Joseph is described by Mark as a respected member of the Sanhedrin (εὐσχήμων βουλευτής, *euschēmōn bouleutēs*)[4] and as "awaiting" (προσδεχόμενος, *prosdechomenos*) the kingdom of God (15:43). The historicity of this man is witnessed to by his being referred to in all four Gospels. John 19:38–42 uses a different source than Mark, and both Matthew (27:57; a rich man who is a disciple of Jesus; 27:60; it was his own tomb) and Luke (23:50–51; a good and righteous man who did not consent to the Sanhedrin's plan to kill Jesus) provide additional information in their accounts that do not appear to be de novo editorial additions to Mark. We therefore possess strong multiple attestation to Joseph's historicity. There is debate over whether Mark portrays Joseph's actions as due to his being a devout Jew seeking to fulfill Deut. 21:22–23 (V. Taylor 1952: 600; Gundry 1993: 983, 985; Hooker 1991: 381; R. Brown 1994: 2.1213–19; Evans 2001: 519) or as due to his being a follower of Jesus (W. Lane 1974: 579; J. Edwards 2002: 487–88; France 2002: 665–66). In favor of the latter are the expressed statements of Matt. 27:57 and John 19:38 that Joseph was a "disciple" of Jesus and Luke's description of him as being a "good and righteous man" (23:50). Mark's statement that he was "eagerly awaiting the kingdom of God" (15:43) suggests that he should be listed among those who had responded to Jesus's pronouncement in 1:15. Furthermore, his lack of concern for the other victims crucified that day and the burial of Jesus in an expensive rock tomb that Matt. 27:60 says was Joseph's own tomb indicate that he was not motivated merely by a desire to bury the dead and protect Israel from violating God's command in Deut. 21:22–23.

15:44–45 Some see these two verses as an addition to the story (Hooker 1991: 381), for 15:46 follows 15:43 smoothly. Some even suggest that they are later additions to Mark, because both Matthew and Luke lack these verses (Bultmann 1968: 274; Evans 2001: 515–16). There is, however, no textual evidence for this in any MSS of Mark. It is best to assume that Matthew and Luke for various reasons chose to omit these verses (R. Brown 1994: 2.1220–22). This is more convincing than to assume that they were not present in the copies of Mark they used, were added later, and that all traces of the original Markan MS tradition used by the other two Gospel writers subsequently disappeared.

The surprise of Pilate at Jesus's rapid death (πάλαι, *palai*; lit. "[How] long ago [did he die?]") is natural. Crucified victims normally lived for at least a day or two. Mark emphasizes that even in his death, Jesus caused people to "marvel" (ἐθαύμασεν, *ethaumasen*; cf. 5:20; 6:6; 15:5; see 1:21–22). To confirm that Jesus had already died, Pilate called "the" centurion (probably the one in

---

4. This is clearly how Luke 23:50–51 understands the term. Cf. also Josephus, *J.W.* 2.17.1 §405, who uses the term in a similar manner.

charge of the crucifixion; 15:39), for he would be the most reliable witness as to whether Jesus had died.[5] Upon learning that Jesus was indeed dead, Pilate "granted" (ἐδωρήσατο, edōrēsato; the word implies a gracious act of favor, a gift) the "body" (πτῶμα, ptōma) of Jesus to Joseph. The use of πτῶμα here and in the death of John the Baptist (6:29), the only two occurrences of the term in Mark, may be intended to link intimately together the fates of the forerunner of Jesus and the one he proclaimed (Matera 1982: 97–99).

The hasty burial preparations of Joseph would have involved such things as purchasing a linen cloth (σινδόνα, sindona) for a shroud, removing Jesus from the cross,[6] cleaning his body, wrapping him in the shroud, and laying him inside the tomb. If, as Matt. 27:57 and John 19:38 state, Joseph was a disciple, the body of Jesus would have first been washed and the blood removed (contra R. Brown 1994: 2.1246). According to John 19:40 Jesus was buried in keeping with the Jewish tradition. This would also have included closing the eyes, trimming the hair, placing spices inside the shroud, and wrapping the body in the shroud (m. Šabb. 23.5). In the Synoptic Gospels, there is no mention of Jesus being anointed with spices for burial, but compare John 19:39–40. For Mark, however, this had already been done (14:3–9). The press of time would have limited the thoroughness of all this. The body of Jesus would then have been laid in either a "large, deep pigeon hole," a shaft about 1½ to 2 feet square and 5 to 7 feet deep, or on a stone bench (R. Brown 1994: 2.1248–49). John 20:5 and 11–12 suggest the latter (R. Smith 1967: 88). Thereupon the walk-in tomb was sealed by rolling a wheel-like stone in a trench across the entrance. In preparation for the concluding resurrection narrative, the story of Jesus's burial ends with a reference to Mary Magdalene and Mary the mother of Joses[7] carefully observing (the imperfect "were observing" [ἐθεώρουν, etheōroun] suggests this [Donahue and Harrington 2002: 455]) the proceedings. Thus they will know where Jesus was buried and how he was buried, and as a result, when they come on Easter morning, they bring spices with them to the tomb (16:1) and wonder how the stone will be removed from the entrance (16:3).

14:46–47

---

5. According to John 19:31–37 the soldiers were so certain of Jesus's death that they did not bother to break his legs (crucifragium), an act that would hasten death by adding an additional shock to the body and by making it more difficult for the victim to relieve the stress on his lungs and chest muscles by pushing against the nails. This would cause quick asphyxiation. The spear wound by one of the soldiers appears to have been an afterthought.

6. The removal of the body from the cross and the sealing of the tomb entrance by a large stone would probably have taken the efforts of several men (V. Taylor 1952: 602; France 2002: 668). (Cf. the plural verb ["they laid"] in 16:6.) It may be that the participle "taking him down" (καθελών, kathelōn) should be understood as "causative," i.e., having instructed his servants to take him down (W. Lane 1974: 580).

7. In 15:40, Mary is described as "the mother of James the younger and Joses." Here she is described in abbreviated form as "[the mother] of Joses," and in 16:1 as "[the mother] of James." Contra Matera (1982: 51), this does not imply the existence of a discrepancy in the lists found in 15:47 and 16:1. Certainly Mark did not think that the lists in these two consecutive verses contained such a discrepancy, especially since he earlier described Mary in 15:40 as the mother of both James and Joses.

Summary

The Markan message in this account almost appears as if it were written as a Christian defense against various rationalistic attacks of the nineteenth and twentieth centuries that denied the resurrection of Jesus from the dead. Many of these rationalistic attempts to portray the "resurrection" of Jesus as a resuscitation from a near-death experience, that the women went to the wrong tomb, and so on (Stein 1996: 262–70), encounter serious problems in light of the Markan description of the burial of Jesus. Twice in 15:44 Jesus's death is referred to. In 15:45 Jesus's death is confirmed by the centurion in charge of the crucifixion. Pilate confirms this in 15:45 by giving over the *corpse* to Joseph of Arimathea. Mark emphasizes that Jesus truly died (Senior 1984: 132–35; Donahue and Harrington 2002: 454). The claim that the women on Easter Sunday came to the wrong tomb is refuted if one accepts the historicity of 15:47 (see the introduction to this unit), for this claims that the women were carefully observing where Jesus was laid. By his account of Jesus's burial, Mark prepares his readers for a real resurrection three days after Jesus's death (8:31; 9:31; 10:34). This will involve not merely a resuscitation from death, such as experienced by Jairus's daughter (5:35–43), the widow of Nain's son (Luke 7:11–17), or even Lazarus (John 11:38–44), for they would all experience death again. Jesus's resurrection will be of a different order. It will be "the" eschatological event of history, for with his resurrection, death is not merely escaped for a period of time but is conquered forever.

Additional Notes

15:43. τολμήσας is an aorist participle, lit. "having dared."

15:44. After verbs expressing surprise, εἰ (if) functions like ὅτι (that). See Zerwick 1963: 404.

15:44. The unusual use of πάλαι (long ago), a hapax legomenon in Mark, has caused several copyists (B D W Θ lat) to replace it with ἤδη (already), but the more difficult πάλαι is the better reading (א A C L) and has been translated "had been dead for some time."

J. Jesus Is Raised from the Dead (16:1–8)

The present account is the last part of the Gospel of Mark that we know for certain was written by Mark. The "shorter"[1] and "longer endings"[2] of Mark are acknowledged by almost all scholars to be later additions to Mark's Gospel. The shorter ending is found essentially in four uncial MSS dating from the seventh, eighth, and ninth centuries (L Ψ 099 0112). These also include the longer ending with it. Only the Old Latin MS it[k] has the shorter ending by itself. The non-Markan origin of the shorter ending is witnessed to by its poor and late textual attestation; the fact that nine of the thirty-four words in this ending are not found elsewhere in Mark (J. Edwards 2002: 498n3); its non-Markan style; and especially by the presence of the expression "the sacred and imperishable proclamation of eternal salvation," which reflects a later date.

The longer ending has much better textual attestation (A C D K W X Δ Θ Π Ψ f[13]), but a number of these MSS have asterisks or other markings by the text indicating that the copyists thought the longer ending was spurious (Metzger 1994: 102–6). Because the longer ending was found in all the Greek MSS available to Erasmus, he included it in his Greek text of the NT, known as the Textus Receptus. The use of Erasmus's TR by the Tyndale-KJV translators resulted in their including the longer ending in the text of their translations and in their assigning it verse numbers in the

1. "And all that had been commanded them they told briefly to those around Peter. And afterward Jesus himself sent out through them, from east to west, the sacred and imperishable proclamation of eternal salvation. Amen" (NRSV).

2. [16:9]Now after he rose early on the first day of the week, he appeared first to Mary Magdalene, from whom he had cast out seven demons. [10]She went out and told those who had been with him, while they were mourning and weeping. [11]But when they heard that he was alive and had been seen by her, they would not believe it.

[12]After this he appeared in another form to two of them, as they were walking into the country. [13]And they went back and told the rest, but they did not believe them. [14]Later he appeared to the eleven themselves as they were sitting at the table; and he upbraided them for their lack of faith and stubbornness, because they had not believed those who saw him after he had risen. [15]And he said to them, "Go into all the world and proclaim the good news to the whole creation. [16]The one who believes and is baptized will be saved; but the one who does not believe will be condemned. [17]And these signs will accompany those who believe: by using my name they will cast out demons; they will speak in new tongues; [18]they will pick up snakes in their hands, and if they drink any deadly thing, it will not hurt them; they will lay their hands on the sick, and they will recover."

[19]So then the Lord Jesus, after he had spoken to them, was taken up into heaven and sat down at the right hand of God. [20]And they went out and proclaimed the good news everywhere, while the Lord worked with them and confirmed the message by the signs that accompanied it. (NRSV)

Geneva Bible and its successors. The secondary nature of the longer ending is witnessed to by a number of factors: the two oldest and best Greek MSS (ℵ and B) lack it, as does it[k]; Clement of Alexandria and Origen show no knowledge of it in their writings; Eusebius and Jerome state that the ending was not found in almost all of the Greek MSS known to them (Metzger 1994: 102–3); the vocabulary is non-Markan and contains eighteen terms not found anywhere else in Mark (J. Edwards 2002: 498n4); and the Greek style and theological content is decidedly un-Markan (contra Farmer 1974: esp. 107–9).[3] The early attestation of this ending (Epistle of the Apostles 9–10; Tatian's *Diatessaron*; Irenaeus, *Haer.* 3.10.5; possibly Justin Martyr, *1 Apol.* 45) suggests that the longer ending was composed early in the second century (Hengel 1985: 167–69n47; Kelhoffer 2000: 169–244).

If, as scholars generally agree, the "shorter" and "longer endings" of Mark are not authentic, the question still remains as to how Mark originally ended. Is Mark 16:8 the intended ending of the Gospel or has the original ending been lost? Here there is far less agreement. This question will be discussed at the end of the comment section. The present account (16:1–8) is based on traditional material available to Mark (V. Taylor 1952: 602–3), but we must make a distinction between the pre-Markan empty tomb tradition and the present Markan account of that tradition (Donahue and Harrington 2002: 459). Mark's own contribution to the tradition is seen by Pryke (1978: 23, 148, 176) in 16:2a, 4b, 7, 8c; by Schmithals (1979: 2.708) in 16:7; and by Gnilka (1978: 338) in 16:1, 2 ("very early"), 7, and 8c. Mark's contribution to the traditional material he is using is seen most clearly in 16:2 ("very early" [λίαν πρωΐ, *lian prōi*], which forms a dual temporal expression with "after the sun had risen" [ἀνατείλαντος τοῦ ἡλίου, *anateilantos tou hēliou*]), 4b (the explanatory "for" [γάρ, *gar*] clause), 7 (both 14:28 and 16:7 appear to be Markan insertions into the tradition), and 8c (the explanatory "for" [γάρ] clause). The account itself can be divided into three parts: (1) the coming of the women to the tomb to anoint the body of Jesus (16:1–4), (2) the angelic message that Jesus has been raised (16:5–7), and (3) the silence of the women due to fear (16:8).

Exegesis and Exposition

[1]And when the Sabbath was over, ⌜Mary Magdalene, and Mary the ⌜mother⌝ of James, and Salome⌝ purchased spices in order that they might go [and] anoint him. [2]And very early on the first [day] of the week, after the sun had risen, they come to the tomb. [3]And they were saying to one another, "Who will roll away the stone for us from the door of the tomb?"[4]And having looked up, they see that the stone has been rolled away, for it was very large. [5]And having entered the tomb, they saw a young man sitting on the right side clothed in a white robe, and they were utterly

---

3. Cf. esp. 16:17–18 and 20 (contrast 8:11–13). Verses 12 and 13 appear to be dependent on Luke 24:13–35.

amazed. ⁶But he says to them, "Stop being amazed. You are seeking Jesus of Nazareth, the crucified. ⌜He has risen,⌝ he is not here. See, the place where they laid him. ⁷But go, tell his disciples and Peter that he is going ahead of you ⌜into Galilee⌝. There you will see him, just as he told you." ⁸And having gone out, they fled from the tomb, for trembling and astonishment were seizing them, and they told no one anything, for they were afraid.

Mark begins the present account with a genitive absolute, "And when the Sabbath was over" (καὶ διαγενομένου τοῦ σαββάτου, *kai diagenomenou tou sabbatou*; see 1:32–34). With the end of the Sabbath (at 6 p.m. Saturday), shops would reopen and the women would be able to purchase "spices" (ἀρώματα, *arōmata*) for the purpose of anointing "him," that is, the body of Jesus (cf. T. Ab. 20.10–11). Clearly the women were not expecting Jesus's resurrection from the dead. Thus explanations of the resurrection appearances to them as due to hallucinations are unconvincing, since the emotional and psychological conditions necessary for such hallucinations were not present. Even the empty tomb did not convince Mary Magdalene that Jesus had been raised from the dead (cf. John 20:14–15). The use of spices for anointing was not to embalm the body and preserve it but to help alleviate the smell and stench of the decaying body (Donahue and Harrington 2002: 457). The women were apparently belatedly seeking to rectify what was omitted by Joseph of Arimathea at the burial (15:46 does not mention the use of spices in Jesus's hurried burial, but cf. John 19:39–40). However, "they are too late, not . . . because the body has begun to decay, but because it is no longer there" (Hooker 1991: 384).[4] The naming of the women in 16:1 is surprising, since they have been mentioned in 15:40 and in the previous verse (15:47). This suggests that Mark is using an independent tradition in 16:1–8 (Hooker 1991: 383).

The use of dual temporal designations in 16:2 is typically Markan (see 1:32–34 and 14:12; Neirynck 1988: 96). "Very early" suggests a short period before dawn (cf. 15:1; John 20:1), but Mark defines this more precisely as "after the sun had risen." No major difficulty presents itself in these two temporal expressions unless we seek to give to them a greater temporal precision than Mark intended. The discovery of the empty tomb occurs "on the first [day] of the week" (Mark 16:2; Matt. 28:1; Luke 24:1; John 20:1; cf. Acts 20:7; 1 Cor. 16:2). For fitting a resurrection "after three days" into a late Friday afternoon death and an early Sunday morning resurrection, see 8:31–32a. The approach of the woman to the tomb recalls 15:46–47. They know the location of the tomb and now reflect, perhaps for the first time, on the problem of the stone sealing the tomb, which they were not capable of removing. They (and Mark) are apparently unaware of the presence of the guard that had been placed at the tomb (Matt. 27:62–66). Mark comments that the stone was "very large"

---

4. The normal degree of decay after thirty-six hours would not have been as great as usually thought, for the Passover was during the early part of spring and not in the heat of summer, and the temperature in a rock-cut tomb would have been quite cool (France 2002: 676n22).

(μέγας σφόδρα, *megas sphodra*). His reference to the size of the stone, while explaining the women's concern in 16:3, emphasizes even more the supernatural presence of God in the account in 16:4 (Evans 2001: 535; France 2002: 678). The passive "had been rolled away" (ἀποκεκύλισται, *apokekylistai*) is a divine passive indicating that God was the ultimate cause for the stone's removal from the entrance of the tomb.[5] The majority of such stones discovered in Israel from Jesus's day are square blocks rather than circular stones. Only the wealthy could afford the circular kind of stone (Kloner 1999). Joseph of Arimathea, however, was a wealthy man (Matt. 27:57), and the verbs ἀποκυλίσει (*apokylisei*) and ἀποκεκύλισται (16:3–4) are best translated "will roll" and "had been rolled away." The reason for this miraculous act is not to allow Jesus to leave the tomb (cf. John 20:19) but to allow the women into the tomb to see that it was empty.

16:5–7   Upon entering the tomb, the women see "a young man [νεανίσκον, *neaniskon*] . . . clothed in a white robe." Although we have encountered "a young man" in 14:51–52, there is no intended relationship between the two references (France 2002: 679–80). The term is used in 14:51–52 of a young man fleeing naked from those who seize Jesus. Here the young man is described as a messenger from God. The term "young man" is used to describe angels in 2 Macc. 3:26, 33; Josephus, *Ant.* 5.8.2 §277; Hermas, *Vis.* 3.1.6; 3.4.1; and Matt. 28:2–5 clearly understands the "young man" as an angel. Mark's description of him (dressed in a "white robe" [cf. Acts 1:10; 10:30; 1 En. 62.15–16; 87.2]; sitting on the right side; and speaking as Jesus's messenger [the Greek word for "messenger" is ἄγγελος, *angelos*, or "angel"]) indicates that Mark also considered the "young man" to be an angel (Gundry 1993: 991).

The women's reaction to the theophany involves a typical combination of amazement, awe, and fright as indicated by the various terms used in 16:5–8: "utterly amazed" (ἐξεθαμβήθησαν, *exethambēthēsan*; 16:5, 6; cf. also 1:27; 10:24, 32), "trembling" (τρόμος, *tromos*; 16:8), "astonishment" (ἔκστασις, *ekstasis*; 16:8; cf. 5:42), and "fear" (ἐφοβοῦντο, *ephobounto*; 16:8; cf. 4:41; 5:15, 33; 6:50; 9:6, 32; 10:32; 11:18). These are not simply synonyms but emphasize different aspects of experiencing the presence of God in a theophany. The first three terms emphasize more the positive sense of awe, wonder, and amazement of such an experience; the last emphasizes the fear of mortal, fallen humanity experiencing the presence of God. Yet even in the experience of awe, wonder, and amazement, there is present also fear, and vice versa. Mark does not explain the exact reason for the women's amazement, but we can assume that the very large stone being rolled away, the absence of Jesus's body from the tomb, and the presence of an angelic messenger would have all contributed to this.

A word of reassurance frequently begins an angelic or theophanic address: "Stop being amazed" (cf. Gen. 15:1; Judg. 6:23; Dan. 10:12, 19; Luke 1:13, 30;

---

5. Matt. 28:2 describes the immediate cause as being the angel present at the tomb, but the ultimate cause is nevertheless God.

2:10; cf. Luke 8:50). Along with the word of assurance, the angel reveals that he knows the reason for the women coming to the tomb: "You are seeking Jesus of Nazareth" (cf. 1:24; 10:47; 14:67), "the crucified" (cf. 1 Cor. 1:23; 2:2; Gal. 3:1). Although the verb "seek" (ζητεῖτε, zēteite) appears almost exclusively in pejorative contexts in Mark, there is no reason to interpret it in terms of rebuke here (France 2002: 680; contra W. Lane 1974: 587–88; J. Edwards 2002: 494), for this would go completely against the previous words of reassurance given by the angel—"Stop being amazed" (μὴ ἐκθαμβεῖσθε, mē ekthambeisthe). In Matt. 28:5 the word of reassurance from the angel is grounded on (for, γάρ) their seeking Jesus, the crucified. Instead of finding a body to anoint, the woman are told, "He has risen [from the dead]."[6]

In his earlier passion predictions (8:31; 9:9, 31; 10:34), Mark uses the verb ἀνίστημι (anistēmi), which is active (or middle) in form and meaning, to describe Jesus's rising from the dead. Here and in 14:28 he uses the more traditional ἠγέρθη (egerthē; cf. 1 Cor. 15:4).[7] Although passive in form, ἠγέρθη is active in meaning here. This is supported by 2:12 and 6:16, where ἠγέρθη possesses an active meaning. This is clear in 2:12, where the paralytic's "rising" is in response to the command to "rise" in 2:11. It is not as clear in 6:16, but it is less likely that Herod means here and in 6:14 that God has raised John the Baptist, whom he had killed, from the dead than that he is simply stating that John had risen from the dead, for the former would be an admission that he had sinned against God. In 4:27 the passive ἐγείρηται (egeirētai) is active in meaning as are the verbs associated with it; "he would . . . scatter . . . sleep . . . rise." Compare also 13:8: "Nation will rise up" (ἐγερήσεται, egeirēsetai, a future passive in form but active in meaning); and 13:22: "False messiahs and false prophets will arise" (ἐγερθήσονται, egerthēsontai, a future passive in form but active in meaning).[8] There seems to be no distinction in Mark's use of ἐγείρω and ἀνίστημι (France 2002: 680). The angel then offers proof to the women of Jesus's resurrection: "See, the place where they laid him." Although some see this as referring back to 15:47 (Gundry 1993: 992), it is more likely that it refers to the fact that whereas the women knew the tomb in which Jesus was placed, they did not know the particular shaft or stone table (see 14:46–47) where he had been laid. Unlike John 20:6–7, the Synoptic Gospels make no mention of grave clothes being left behind in the tomb.[9]

6. "He, the one having been crucified, i.e., the historical Jesus of Nazareth, has risen." For Mark there is no distinction between the historical Jesus and the kerygmatic Christ of faith. They are one and the same!

7. Cf. the parallels to Mark 8:31 (Matt. 16:21; Luke 9:22); 9:9 (Matt. 17:9), 31 (Matt. 17:23); and 10:34 (Matt. 20:19), which all use the verb ἐγείρω (egeirō) instead of ἀνίστημι. Luke 18:33 is the lone exception.

8. Whether 14:28 (passive in form) should be interpreted as active in meaning depends on how 16:7 is interpreted, and 12:26 (passive in form) is uncertain as to whether it is active or passive in meaning.

9. For a discussion of the historicity of the empty tomb, see Craig 1985; Stein 1996: 262–70; N. Wright 2003: 686–96.

Having reassured the women concerning the resurrection, the angel now tells them to go and give a message to the disciples and Peter. Jesus's prediction of the disciples deserting him (14:27a–b) and Peter's threefold denial (14:30) have been fulfilled and so has his prediction of God smiting him, the Shepherd (14:27c). Now the angel tells the women to remind the disciples and Peter of Jesus's promise to meet them in Galilee. He is already "going ahead" (προάγει, *proagei*) of them into Galilee, and there they would meet him, just as he told them (16:7; cf. 14:28). The angelic message serves as a word of comfort and reassurance that the disciples and Peter will find forgiveness and restoration when they meet Jesus in Galilee.[10] Jesus foreknew the failures of his disciples and Peter, but he also knew that their failures were not unforgivable (3:28–30; 14:21). In Galilee they would not only experience forgiveness from the risen Christ, but their calling to be his apostles (3:14) would also be restored (contra Telford 1999: 149–50).

Although it was once popular to interpret 16:7 and 14:28 as references to the parousia (Lohmeyer 1936: 10–14; Lightfoot 1938: 55–65; Marxsen 1969: 75–95; Weeden 1971: 111–17; et al.), this view is now generally discredited (Stein 1973; Best 1983: 76–78; Lincoln 1989: 285). This is both because of the weakness of the arguments[11] and, above all, because of the arguments in favor of interpreting 16:7 and 14:28 as referring to the resurrection. The strongest of these are as follows: (1) When Mark wrote his Gospel, Peter had already died, and yet he is referred to in 16:7 as meeting the Lord in Galilee. This can refer only to a resurrection meeting and not to the parousia. (2) There existed a strong tradition that after the resurrection Jesus met with Peter privately (1 Cor. 15:5; Luke 24:34; John 21:15–19; cf. also Acts 10:41). Consequently the natural inclination of Mark's readers would have been to interpret these two passages as referring to the well-known resurrection appearance of Jesus to Peter. (3) The change in tense between the future "will go ahead of you" (προάξω, *proaxō*) in 14:28, which is said to the disciples before the resurrection, is now changed after the resurrection into a present "is going before you" (προάγει) in 16:7. If it referred to the parousia, however, one would expect a future tense in both references, since the parousia had not yet occurred. (4) Where is Jesus ever portrayed with respect to the parousia as already in Galilee awaiting his disciples? For this and other reasons, it is clear that 16:7 and 14:28 refer to a resurrection appearance of Jesus with the disciples and Peter in Galilee.[12] This conclusion has a strong bearing on whether 16:8 was

10. Cf. how in John's Gospel Peter's threefold denial (18:18, 25–27) is rectified by his threefold confession of love to the risen Christ (21:15–19).

11. E.g., the future tense, "you will see" (ὄψεσθε, *opsesthe*), it is claimed, must refer to the parousia, but a future, not-yet-realized resurrection appearance in Galilee must also use the future tense; there is no resurrection appearance of Jesus in Galilee found in Mark, but did Mark originally end his Gospel with 16:8? etc.

12. Geddert's comment (1989: 162) with respect to the many symbolic interpretations given to the term "Galilee" deserves to be repeated: "To say that Galilee is a geographical term needs to be said. Some proponents of 'symbolic' interpretations seem almost to have forgotten that."

Mark's intended ending for the Gospel. The emphasis on Jesus's meeting the disciples after the resurrection creates for the readers a clear anticipation of such a meeting.

In response to the angel's command ("Go . . ."; 16:7) the women leave the **16:8** tomb and flee. This is then explained by a typical Markan explanatory clause (see 1:16–18), "for [γάρ] trembling and astonishment were seizing them." Such a reaction is found frequently in Mark in the positive sense of denoting the awe and wonder that Jesus elicited (see 1:21–22). It is unclear if the women's reaction is to be interpreted here in the sense of holy awe (cf. how the verbal "trembling" [τρέμουσα, tremousa] is used positively in 5:33 and how "wonder" [ἐκστάσει, ekstasei] in 5:42 and its verbal form in 2:12; 5:42; 6:51 are used positively; so Pesch 1980b: 535; Dwyer 1996: 185–93) or whether it should be understood negatively as indicating fright and terror (so Lincoln 1989: 283–300; J. Edwards 2002: 496). The parallel in Matt. 28:8 ("with fear and great joy") favors the former interpretation; the context ("Stop being amazed" [Mark 16:6]; "They were afraid" [16:8]) favors the latter. The presence of wonder and awe as well as fear in theophanies suggests that these responses should not be understood as exclusive and contradictory but as inclusive and complementary. The decision as to whether Mark originally ended his Gospel with 16:8 or ended it with a reference to Jesus meeting the disciples and Peter in Galilee, which is now lost, plays a major role in such a decision. The comment "And they told no one [οὐδενί, oudeni] anything [οὐδέν, ouden; lit. 'nothing']," an emphatic double negative (cf. 15:4 and 5), can also be understood either positively or negatively (see Bode 1970: 39–42). It can mean that the women did not allow themselves to be distracted from their commission to tell the disciples the angelic message (R. Smith 1983: 42–43; Dwyer 1996: 191–92; cf. 1:44; Luke 10:4; 2 Kings 4:29),[13] or it can mean that the women failed to deliver the message. The concluding words of the verse "for they were afraid" (ἐφοβοῦντο γάρ, ephobounto gar), constitute a most unusual ending for an ancient work, but especially for a "Gospel."

The Ending of Mark

Although few scholars today argue for the authenticity of either the "shorter" or "longer ending" of Mark (see the introduction to this unit), there is continued debate over whether Mark intended to end his Gospel at 16:8. In the first half of the twentieth century, scholars were inclined to argue that 16:8 was not the intended ending of Mark (V. Taylor 1952: 609–10; France 2002: 670n1). Later in that century, a reversal of this position took place.[14] Mark was now seen as intending to end his Gospel at 16:8, and many offered explanations for why Mark chose to end his Gospel this way. Mark was seen as seeking to

---

13. Gundry (1993: 1010) suggests that the lack of an adversative "but" (δέ, de, or ἀλλά, alla) instead of an "and" (καί, kai) supports this conclusion.

14. Some of the scholars who made this view popular were Wellhausen 1909: 137; Creed 1929; Lohmeyer 1957: 358–60; and Lightfoot 1950: 80–97, 106–16.

counter an obsession with miracles by his opponents and their *theios anēr* (divine man) Christology (Crossan 1976);

force the readers "to think out for [themselves] the Gospel's challenge" (Best 1983: 132);

encourage readers to persevere despite the disobedience and failure of the disciples (Lincoln 1989: 283–300);

challenge the reader to become "the perfect disciple" and fulfill what the disciples and women failed to do (Tolbert 1989: 297–99);

have the readers "make their [own] decision" of obedience (Geddert 1989: 172);

"leave his readers to make the crucial step of faith for themselves, without presenting them with less ambiguous evidence for the resurrection" (Hooker 1991: 392);

elicit "a call for deeper commitment . . . from its hearers" (Danove 1993: 222); and so on.[15]

The main arguments put forward in favor of 16:8 being the intended ending of Mark are as follows:

1. We possess no authentic Markan material after 16:8. The shorter and longer endings of Mark are clearly inauthentic, and the best two Greek MSS of Mark (ℵ and B) end at 16:8. This is a strong argument in favor of this view.
2. There is nothing unusual with Mark ending his Gospel with a "for" (γάρ), for we find several examples of this in Greek literature (Lightfoot 1938: 11–15; Horst 1972; Cox 1993: 223–27).
3. There are convincing reasons why 16:8 serves as an appropriate ending for his Gospel (see preceding paragraph). The ending fits well the Markan motifs of astonishment and fear found throughout his Gospel (W. Lane 1974: 591–92).

The main arguments put forward in favor of 16:8 not being the intended ending of Mark (Gundry 1993: 1009–12; N. Wright 2003: 617–24; Stein 2008) are as follows:

1. Mark has emphasized the fulfillment of Jesus's prophecies throughout his Gospel. The description of his passion (8:31; 9:31; and esp. 10:33–34), the betrayal of Judas (14:18–21), the desertion of the disciples (14:27), and Peter's denial (14:29–30) have all been shown to have been precisely fulfilled. Yet if the Gospel ends at 16:8, the prophecies of Jesus's resurrection (8:31; 9:9, 31; 10:34; cf. also 14:28, 58; 15:29; 16:7) are less satisfactorily

15. See Wedderburn (1999: 135–44), Williams (1999: 26–35), and Stein (2008: 86–88) for additional attempts to explain why Mark ended his Gospel at 16:8.

fulfilled. Instead of an actual appearance of the risen Jesus, Mark concludes with the fact of the empty tomb and the angelic statement that Jesus is risen.

2. Matthew (28:8, 10), Luke (24:9–11), and John (20:1, 11–18) all record the women telling the disciples of the resurrection of Jesus. This indicates the existence of various traditions indicating that the angelic command to the women (16:7) was understood to have been carried out. It seems strange that Mark would report the angelic command to the women to tell the disciples that Jesus would meet them in Galilee, and then, despite the awareness that his readers knew of the tradition that he did, decide not to include it.

3. The existence of the shorter and longer endings of Mark show that early copyists were deeply dissatisfied with 16:8 as the final ending of Mark. Their dissatisfaction probably represents a much truer understanding of how Mark and his earliest readers felt about Mark ending at 16:8 than the existential thinking of twentieth- and twenty-first-century scholars on the subject.

4. The resurrection appearances of Jesus were such an integral part of the early church's preaching (1 Cor. 15:5–8; Acts 1:3–11, 22; 2:32; 3:15; 10:41; 13:31; the other three Gospels; etc.) that it is difficult to believe that Mark would have ended his Gospel of Jesus Christ, the Son of God, without an account of such an appearance.

5. There is no convincing reason why Mark would have wanted to end his Gospel at 16:8. The various explanations given (note the examples above) would not have convinced first-century readers of Mark. These explanations seem to arise from a twentieth-century existentialism that revels in paradox (France 2002: 671–72). It is based less on understanding Mark's own purpose in writing his Gospel than on modern literary theory.[16]

6. It is hard to imagine that a Gospel that begins with a bold, straightforward "The beginning of the gospel of Jesus Christ, the Son of God" (1:1), would end with a negative response of fear and fright by the women in 16:8. Mark's readers—and Mark clearly wrote with his first-century readers in mind—would have found this intolerable. There was no need to be coy about what Mark's readers and all Christians knew to be true:

16. This is conceded by Hooker (1991: 394), who states that even if this is not Mark's understanding, "at least the gospel's ending offers us a fine example of the value of 'reader response' criticism, since it provides us with an interpretation of the text to which author and reader together can contribute—an interpretation which corresponds with the experience of many readers of the gospel, whether or not it was in the mind of the evangelist." Cf., however, Knox (1942: 22–23): "To suppose that Mark originally intended to end his Gospel in this way implies both that he was totally indifferent to the canons of popular story-telling, and that by a pure accident he happened to hit on a conclusion which suits the technique of a highly sophisticated type of modern literature."

Jesus rose from the dead and appeared to his disciples (1 Cor. 15:4–8).[17] In light of 1:1, it is unlikely that at 16:8 the narrative "has reached its goal and been completed" (contra Petersen 1980: 152), for the Gospel of Mark is about Jesus Christ, the Son of God, not about the followers of Jesus.

7. There have been numerous attempts to discover other Greek books that end with a "for" (γάρ). That sentences can end this way (cf. John 13:13; Gen. 18:15 LXX) is evident (Cox 1993: 223–27 claims that he found over a thousand examples of this in Greek literature), and we know that paragraphs and sections can end this way (Lightfoot 1938: 11–15), but whether a book ever ended in this manner is still debated. Two examples frequently given are Plotinus, *Ennead* 5.5, and Plato, *Protagoras* 328c, but it is debated whether these are legitimate examples of a "book" ending with "for" (Horst [1972: 123–24] admits this). Regardless, even if we grant that a book can end this way, we must admit that such an ending of a book would be most unusual. Even if there were no evidence elsewhere and Mark were the only person in the history of the world to have done so, he could have ended his Gospel in this manner if he wanted to. However, the probability that he chose to end his Gospel in this most unusual manner is very low.

8. Probably the strongest argument that Mark did not originally end at 16:8 involves 14:28 and 16:7. These two verses, heavily Markan in nature, are insertions by Mark into the tradition that he inherited (Stein 1973). They refer to Jesus's meeting his disciples in Galilee "after the resurrection." That Mark inserts 16:7 immediately before 16:8 makes it extremely difficult to think that he would have placed a reference to Jesus's meeting the disciples and Peter immediately before a concluding statement that the women did not tell the disciples this angelic message. The angel furthermore points to the fulfillment of this prophecy by the comment, "just as he told you" (καθὼς εἶπεν ὑμῖν, *kathōs eipen hymin*). If Mark ended his Gospel at 16:8, this would be the only prophecy in Mark (other than those concerning the parousia) that is not fulfilled, and whereas the parousia can be fulfilled in the future, a resurrection appearance of Jesus to Peter in Galilee cannot be, for Peter is dead!

As a result of these (and other) arguments,[18] I agree with "the conjecture that the [present] text is incomplete" because I feel "compelled to do so by the document itself" (Knox 1942: 13). Since the 1990s, a number of major commentaries and works have appeared in support of the view that 16:8 was not the evangelist's intended ending (Gundry 1993; Evans 2001; Witherington

---

17. France (2002: 671–72) points out that ancient writers were more in the habit of saying as clearly as possible their intended meaning than "teasing the reader with unfulfilled promises and undelivered messages." Rhetorical subtlety does not seem to fit the first-century church.

18. See the concluding summary to this section.

2001; J. Edwards 2002; France 2002; N. Wright 2003). Does this indicate a trend? Based on existing evidence, one cannot know whether there existed a Markan ending, subsequently lost, that tells of a resurrection appearance of Jesus to the disciples in Galilee or whether for some reason (perhaps because of martyrdom or persecution) Mark was never able to write his intended ending.

Summary

To understand the Markan message contained in the present passage, it is important to ask, Who is the most important character in the account? It is clearly not the women or the angel but Jesus. As in all the preceding accounts, it is critical to remember that the Gospel of Mark is about "Jesus Christ, the Son of God" (1:1). Just as 1:2–8 is not primarily about John the Baptist but rather about Jesus Christ, the Son of God, to whom John the Baptist pointed (see 1:1–8 Summary); just as 4:35–41 is not primarily about the frightened disciples but about "Who then is this man that even the wind and the sea obey him?" that is, about Jesus Christ, the Son of God (see 4:35–41 Summary); and just as 6:45–52 is not primarily about the hard hearts of the disciples but about Jesus Christ, the Son of God, who is Lord of nature (see 6:45–52 Summary); and so on, so also 16:1–8 is not primarily about the women at the tomb but about Jesus Christ, the Son of God, who has been raised from the dead (16:6)! The purpose of the story is to "without doubt prove the reality of the resurrection of Jesus by the empty tomb" (Bultmann 1968: 287). We must therefore focus our attention on what the story tells us about Jesus. Explanations seeking to understand 16:8 as Mark's intended ending tend to ignore this and replace Mark's christological emphasis with an anthropological one focusing on the women and/or the disciples. The highpoint of 16:1–8, however, is found not in 16:8 but in the angelic message of 16:5–7, for it is not the women's actions but the angelic message that serves as the focal point for the Markan point of view. And the angelic message is clear: the crucified Jesus has risen from the dead; he is not in the tomb; the place where he was laid is empty; he is already now proceeding into Galilee, where the disciples are to meet him.

    The present account also serves as another example of how the prophecies of Jesus have been fulfilled. He predicted that he would rise from the dead (8:31; 9:9, 31; 10:34; cf. 14:58; 15:29), and this has been fulfilled. "He has risen" (16:6). The additional prediction that after his resurrection (14:28) Jesus would meet his disciples in Galilee is repeated by the angel with emphasis ("just as he told you") in 16:7. The readers are well aware that this took place, but unfortunately the account of such an appearance (found in Matt. 28:16–20 and John 21:1–23) is missing from our present form of Mark.

Additional Notes

16:1. The MSS D and it^k omit the names of the women. This is probably due to their being mentioned in the previous verse (Metzger 1994: 101).

16:1. Although the Greek construction could be translated "the sister of James," it must be translated here in light of 15:40 as "the mother of James."

16:6. The RSV, NIV, ESV, and TNIV translate the passive form as a deponent and as active, "He has risen." Cf. Zerwick 1963: 231.

16:7. Jesus's going ahead of the disciples εἰς τὴν Γαλιλαίαν is best translated "into Galilee." See comments on 14:27–28.

Works Cited

ABD   *The Anchor Bible Dictionary.* Edited by D. N. Freedman et al. 6 vols. New York: Doubleday, 1992.

Achtemeier, P. J.
1970   "Toward the Isolation of Pre-Markan Miracle Catenae." *Journal of Biblical Literature* 89:265–91.
1975   "Miracles and the Historical Jesus: A Study of Mark 9:14–29." *Catholic Biblical Quarterly* 37:471–91.
1976   "An Exposition of Mark 9:30–37." *Interpretation* 30:178–83.
1978   "'And He Followed Him'—Miracles and Discipleship in Mark 10:46–52." *Semeia* 11:115–45.

Adams, E.
2005   "The Coming of the Son of Man in Mark's Gospel." *Tyndale Bulletin* 56:39–61.

Aland, K. (ed.)
2001   *Synopsis Quattor Evangeliorum.* 15th edition. Stuttgart: Deutsche Bibelgesellschaft.

Allison, D. C., Jr.
1985   *The End of the Ages Has Come: An Early Interpretation of the Passion and Resurrection of Jesus.* Philadelphia: Fortress.
1993   *The New Moses: A Matthean Typology.* Minneapolis: Fortress.
1994   "Mark 12:28–31 and the Decalogue." Pp. 270–78 in *The Gospels and the Scriptures of Israel.* Edited by C. A. Evans and W. R. Stegner. Journal for the Study of the New Testament: Supplement Series 104. Sheffield: Sheffield Academic Press.

Ambrozic, A. M.
1972   *The Hidden Kingdom: A Redaction-Critical Study of the References to the Kingdom of God in Mark's Gospel.* Catholic Biblical Quarterly Monograph Series 2. Washington, DC: Catholic Biblical Association of America.
1975   "New Teaching with Power (MK 1:27)." Pp. 113–49 in *Word and Spirit: Essays in Honor of David Michael Stanley, S. J. on his 60th Birthday.* Edited by J. Plevnik. Willowdale, ON: Regis College Press.

Anderson, H.
1976   *The Gospel of Mark.* New Century Bible. Greenword: Attic Press.

Arens, E.
1976   *The ΗΛΘΟΝ-Sayings in the Synoptic Tradition. A Historico-Critical Investigation.* Orbis biblicus et orientalis 10. Freiburg: Universitätsverlag.

Argyle, A. W.
1951   "The Meaning of *kath' hēmeran* in Mark xiv.49." *Expository Times* 63:354.

Arnal, W. E.
2000   "The Parable of the Tenants and the Class Consciousness of the Peasantry." Pp. 135–57 in *Text and Artifact in the Religions of Mediterranean Antiquity: Essays in Honour of Peter Richardson.* Edited by S. G. Wilson and M. Desjardins. Studies in Christianity and Judaism 9. Waterloo, ON: Wilfrid Laurier University Press.

Aune, D. E.

1983 *Prophecy in Early Christianity and the Ancient Mediterranean World.* Grand Rapids: Eerdmans.

1988 "Greco-Roman Biography." Pp. 107–26 in *Greco-Roman Literature and the New Testament: Selected Forms and Genres.* Edited by D. E. Aune. Society of Biblical Literature Sources for Biblical Study 21. Atlanta: Scholars Press.

Aus, R. D.

1988 *Water into Wine and the Beheading of John the Baptist.* Brown Judaic Studies 150. Atlanta: Scholars Press.

1996 *The Wicked Tenants and Gethsemane: Isaiah in the Wicked Tenant's Vineyard, and Moses and the High Priest in Gethsemane: Judaic Traditions in Mark 12:1–9 and 14:32–42.* Atlanta: Scholars Press.

Badia, L. F.

1980 *The Qumran Baptism and John the Baptist's Baptism.* Washington, DC: University Press of America.

Bahat, D.

1995 "Jerusalem Down Under: Tunneling along Herod's Temple Mount Wall." *Biblical Archaeology Review* 21/6:30–47.

Bahr, G. J.

1970 "The Seder of Passover and the Eucharistic Words." *Novum Testamentum* 12:181–202.

Balla, P.

2005 *The Child-Parent Relationship in the New Testament and Its Environment.* Reprinted Peabody, MA: Hendrickson.

Baltensweiler, H.

1959 *Die Verklärung Jesu: Historisches Ereignis und synoptische Berichte.* Abhandlungen zur Theologie des Alten und Neuen Testaments 33. Zurich: Zwingli.

Bammel, E.

1984 "The *Titulus.*" Pp. 353–64 in *Jesus and the Politics of His Day.* Edited by E. Bammel and C. F. D. Moule. Cambridge: Cambridge University Press.

Banks, R.

1975 *Jesus and the Law in the Synoptic Tradition.* Society for New Testament Studies Monograph Series 28. Cambridge: Cambridge University Press.

Barbour, R. S.

1969 "Gethsemane in the Tradition of the Passion." *New Testament Studies* 16:231–51.

Barclay, W.

1976 *Introduction to the First Three Gospels: A Revised Edition of the First Three Gospels.* Philadelphia: Westminster.

Barkay, G.

1986 "The Garden Tomb—Was Jesus Buried Here?" *Biblical Archaeology Review* 2/2:40–57.

Barr, J.

1988 "'Abbā Isn't 'Daddy.'" *Journal of Theological Studies* 39:28–47.

Barrett, C. K.

1959 "The Background of Mark 10:45." Pp. 1–18 in *New Testament Essays: Studies in Memory of Thomas Walter Manson.* Edited by A. J. B. Higgins. Manchester: Manchester University Press.

Barton, S. C.

1994 *Discipleship and Family Ties in Mark and Matthew.* Cambridge: Cambridge University Press.

Batey, R. A.

1984 "'Is This Not the Carpenter?'" *New Testament Studies* 30:249–58.

1991 *Jesus and the Forgotten City: New Light on Sepphoris and the Urban World of Jesus.* Grand Rapids: Baker Academic.

Bauckham, R.

1991 "Salome the Sister of Jesus, Salome the Disciple of Jesus, and the Secret Gospel of Mark." *Novum Testamentum* 33:245–75.

1994a "The Brothers and Sisters of Jesus: An Epiphanian Response to John P. Meier." *Catholic Biblical Quarterly* 56:686–700.

1994b "Jesus and the Wild Animals (Mark 1:13): A Christological Image for an Ecological Age." Pp. 3–21 in *Jesus of Nazareth: Lord and Christ—Essays on the Historical Jesus and New Testament Christology.* Edited by J. B. Green and M. Turner. Grand Rapids: Eerdmans.

2006 *Jesus and the Eyewitnesses: The Gospels as Eyewitness Testimony.* Grand Rapids: Eerdmans.

Bauer, W.

1953 "The 'Colt' of Palm Sunday (Der Palmesel)." *Journal of Biblical Literature* 72:220–29.

Baumgarten, A. I.

1983 "The Name of the Pharisees." *Journal of Biblical Literature* 102:411–28.

1984 "*Korban* and the Pharisaic *Paradosis.*" *Journal of the Ancient Near Eastern Society* 16:5–17.

1987 "The Pharisaic *Paradosis.*" *Harvard Theological Review* 80:63–77.

Bayer, H. F.
1986 *Jesus' Predictions of Vindication and Resurrection: The Provenance, Meaning and Correlation of the Synoptic Predictions.* Wissenschaftliche Untersuchungen zum Neuen Testament 2/20. Tübingen: Mohr (Siebeck).

BDAG *A Greek-English Lexicon of the New Testament and Other Early Christian Literature.* By W. Bauer, F. W. Danker, W. F. Arndt, and F. W. Gingrich. 4th edition. Chicago: University of Chicago Press, 2000.

BDF *A Greek Grammar of the New Testament and Other Early Christian Literature.* By F. Blass, A. Debrunner, and R. W. Funk. Chicago: University of Chicago Press, 1961.

Beare, F. W.
1960 "The Sabbath Was Made for Man?" *Journal of Biblical Literature* 79:130–36.
1962 *The Earliest Records of Jesus.* New York: Abingdon.

Beasley-Murray, G. R.
1962 *Baptism in the New Testament.* Grand Rapids: Eerdmans.
1986 *Jesus and the Kingdom of God.* Grand Rapids: Eerdmans.
1993 *Jesus and the Last Days: The Interpretation of the Olivet Discourse.* Peabody, MA: Hendrickson.

Beavis, M. A.
1988 "Women as Models of Faith in Mark." *Biblical Theology Bulletin* 18:3–9.
1989 *Mark's Audience: The Literary and Social Setting of Mark 4.11–12.* Journal for the Study of the New Testament: Supplement Series 33. Sheffield: Sheffield Academic Press.

Beck, N. A.
1981 "Reclaiming a Biblical Text: The Mark 8:14–21 Discussion about Bread in the Boat." *Catholic Biblical Quarterly* 43:49–56.

Belo, F.
1981 *A Materialist Reading of the Gospel of Mark.* Translated by M. J. O'Connell. Maryknoll, NY: Orbis.

Benoit, P.
1973 *Jesus and the Gospel.* Vol. 1. Translated by Benet Weatherhead. New York: Seabury.

Best, E.
1965 *The Temptation and the Passion: The Markan Soteriology.* Society for New Testament Studies Monograph Series 2. Cambridge: Cambridge University Press.
1970 "Discipleship in Mark: Mark 8.22–10.52." *Scottish Journal of Theology* 23:323–37.
1975 "Mark III.20, 21, 31–35." *New Testament Studies* 22:309–19.
1976a "Mark 10:13–16: The Child as Model Recipient." Pp. 119–34 in *Biblical Studies: Essays in Honour of William Barclay.* Edited by J. R. McKay and J. F. Miller. Philadelphia: Westminster.
1976b "The Role of the Disciples in Mark." *New Testament Studies* 23:377–401.
1978 "Mark's Use of the Twelve." *Zeitschrift für die neutestamentliche Wissenschaft* 69:11–35.
1981 *Following Jesus: Discipleship in the Gospel of Mark.* Journal for the Study of the New Testament: Supplement Series 4. Sheffield: JSOT Press.
1983 *Mark: The Gospel as Story.* Studies of the New Testament and Its World. Edinburgh: T&T Clark.
1986 *Disciples and Discipleship: Studies in the Gospel of Mark.* Edinburgh: T&T Clark.

Betz, H. D.
1997 "Jesus and the Purity of the Temple (Mark 11:15–18): A Comparative Religion Approach." *Journal of Biblical Literature* 116:455–72.

Bilezikian, G. G.
1977 *The Liberated Gospel: A Comparison of the Gospel of Mark and Greek Tragedy.* Baker Biblical Monograph. Grand Rapids: Baker Academic.

Bird, M.
2003 "The Crucifixion of Jesus as the Fulfillment of Mark 9:1." *Trinity Journal* 24:23–36.

Black, C. C.
1989 *Disciples according to Mark: Markan Redaction in Current Debate.* Journal for the Study of the New Testament: Supplement Series 27. Sheffield: JSOT Press.
1994 *Mark: Images of an Apostolic Interpreter.* Columbia: University of South Carolina Press.

Black, D. A.
1988 "The Text of Mark 6.20." *New Testament Studies* 34:141–45.

Black, M.
1967 *An Aramaic Approach to the Gospels and Acts.* 3rd edition. Oxford: Clarendon.

1971   "The Christological Use of the Old Testament in the New Testament." *New Testament Studies* 18:1–14.

Blinzler, J.
1959   *The Trial of Jesus.* Translated by I. and F. McHugh. Westminster, MD: Newman.
1961   "Das Synedrium von Jerusalem und die Strafprozessordnung der Mischna." *Zeitschrift für die neutestamentliche Wissenschaft* 52:54–65.
1969   *Aus der Welt und Umwelt des Neuen Testaments: Gesammelte Aufsätze 1.* Stuttgarter biblische Beiträge. Stuttgart: Katholisches Bibelwerk.

Bock, D. L.
1994   *Luke 1:1–9:50.* Baker Exegetical Commentary on the New Testament. Grand Rapids: Baker Academic.
1996   *Luke 9:51–24:53.* Baker Exegetical Commentary on the New Testament. Grand Rapids: Baker Academic.
2000   *Blasphemy and Exaltation in Judaism: The Charge against Jesus in Mark 14:53–65.* Biblical Studies Library. Grand Rapids: Baker Academic.

Bode, E. L.
1970   *The First Easter Morning: The Gospel Accounts of the Women's Visit to the Tomb of Jesus.* Analecta biblica 45. Rome: Papal Institute.

Bond, H. K.
1998   *Pontius Pilate in History and Interpretation.* Society for New Testament Studies Monograph Series 100. Cambridge: Cambridge University Press.

Bonner, C.
1927   "Traces of Thaumaturgic Technique in the Miracles." *Harvard Theological Review* 20:171–81.

Boobyer, G. H.
1939   "Mark xii.35–37 and the Pre-Existence of Jesus in Mark." *Expository Times* 51:393–94.
1942   *St. Mark and the Transfiguration Story.* Edinburgh: T&T Clark.
1953   "The Miracles of the Loaves and the Gentiles in St. Mark's Gospel." *Scottish Journal of Theology* 6:77–87.
1961   "The Redaction of Mark IV.1–34." *New Testament Studies* 8:59–70.

Booth, R. P.
1986   *Jesus and the Laws of Purity: Tradition History and Legal History in Mark 7.* Journal for the Study of the New Testament: Supplement Series 13. Sheffield: JSOT Press.

Borg, M. J.
1984   *Conflict, Holiness & Politics in the Teachings of Jesus.* Studies in the Bible and Early Christianity 5. Lewiston, NY: Mellen.

Boring, M. E.
1991   "Mark 1:1–15 and the Beginning of the Gospel." *Semeia* 52:43–81.

Bornkamm, G.
1948   "Die Sturmstillung im Matthäusevangelium." *Wort und Dienst* 1:49–54.

Brandon, S. G. F.
1967   *Jesus and the Zealots: A Study of the Political Factor in Primitive Christianity.* New York: Scribner's.

Brewer, D. I.
1999   "Jewish Women Divorcing Their Husbands in Early Judaism: The Background to Payprus Ṣe'elim 13." *Harvard Theological Review* 92:349–57.

Bristol, L. D.
1939   "Mark's Little Apocalypse: A Hypothesis." *Expository Times* 51:301–3.

Broadhead, E. K.
1992   "Mk 1,45: The Witness of the Leper." *Zeitschrift für die neutestamentliche Wissenschaft* 83:57–65.

Brooke, G. J.
1995   "4Q500 1 and the Use of Scripture in the Parable of the Vineyard." *Dead Sea Discoveries* 2:268–94.

Brooks, J. A.
1991   *Mark.* New American Commentary 23. Nashville: Broadman.

Brower, K.
1980   "Mark 9:1: Seeing the Kingdom in Power." *Journal for the Study of the New Testament* 6:17–41.

Brown, C.
1984   *Miracles and the Critical Mind.* Grand Rapids: Eerdmans.

Brown, J. K.
2002   *The Disciples in Narrative Perspective: The Portrayal and Function of the Matthean Disciples.* Society of Biblical Literature Academia biblica 9. Atlanta: Society of Biblical Literature.

Brown, R. A.
1962   "Parable and Allegory Reconsidered." *Novum Testamentum* 5:36–45.
1966   *The Gospel according to John (i–xii).* Anchor Bible 29. Garden City, NY: Doubleday.
1970   *The Gospel according to John (xiii–xxi).* Anchor Bible 29A. Garden City, NY: Doubleday.

1994   *The Death of the Messiah: From Gethsemane to the Grave.* 2 vols. Anchor Bible Reference Library. New York: Doubleday.

1997   *An Introduction to the New Testament.* New York: Doubleday.

Bruce, F. F.

1980   "The Trial of Jesus in the Fourth Gospel." Pp. 7–20 in *Gospel Perspectives*, vol. 1: *Studies of History and Tradition in the Four Gospels.* Edited by R. T. France and D. Wenham. Sheffield: JSOT Press.

1984   "Render to Caesar." Pp. 249–63 in *Jesus and the Politics of His Day.* Edited by E. Bammel and C. F. D. Moule. Cambridge: Cambridge University Press.

Bryan, C.

1993   *A Preface to Mark: Notes on the Gospel in Its Literary and Cultural Settings.* New York: Oxford University Press.

Buchanan, G. W.

1991   "Symbolic Money-Changers in the Temple?" *New Testament Studies* 37:280–90.

Bultmann, R.

1951   *Theology of the New Testament*, vol. 1. Translated by K. Grobel. New York: Scribner's.

1968   *The History of the Synoptic Tradition.* Revised edition. Translated by J. Marsh. New York: Harper.

Bundy, W. E.

1955   *Jesus and the First Three Gospels: An Introduction to the Synoptic Tradition.* Cambridge: Harvard University Press.

Burkill, T. A.

1963   *Mysterious Revelation: An Examination of the Philosophy of Mark's Gospel.* Ithaca, NY: Cornell University Press.

1968   "Mark 3:7–12 and the Alleged Dualism in the Evangelist's Miracle Material." *Journal of Biblical Literature* 87:409–17.

Burkitt, F. C.

1906   *The Gospel History and Its Transmission.* Edinburgh: T&T Clark.

1916   "W and Θ: Studies in the Western Text of Mark." *Journal of Theological Studies* 17:139–52.

Burridge, R. A.

1992   *What Are the Gospels? A Comparison with Graeco-Roman Biography.* Society for New Testament Studies Monograph Series 70. Cambridge: Cambridge University Press.

Cahill, M.

1998   *The First Commentary on Mark: An Annotated Translation.* New York: Oxford University Press.

1999   "Not a Cornerstone! Translating Ps. 118,22 in the Jewish and Christian Scriptures." *Revue biblique* 106:345–57.

Caird, G. B.

1956   "The Transfiguration." *Expository Times* 67:291–94.

1969   "Uncomfortable Words: II. Shake Off the Dust from Your Feet (Mk 6[11])." *Expository Times* 81:40–43.

1980   *The Language and Imagery of the Bible.* Philadelphia: Westminster.

Calvin, J.

1980   *A Harmony of the Gospels Matthew, Mark, and Luke.* Translated by A. W. Morrison and T. H. L. Parker. Edited by D. W. Torrance and T. F. Torrance. 3 vols. Reprinted Grand Rapids: Eerdmans.

Campenhausen, H. von

1972   *The Formation of the Christian Bible.* Translated by J. A. Baker. Philadelphia: Fortress.

Carlson, S. C.

2006   *The Gospel Hoax: Morton Smith's Invention of Secret Mark.* Waco: Baylor University Press.

Carlston, C. E.

1961   "Transfiguration and Resurrection." *Journal of Biblical Literature* 80:233–40.

1975   *The Parables of the Triple Tradition.* Philadelphia: Fortress.

Carson, D. A.

1984   "Matthew." Vol. 8 / pp. 1–599 in *The Expositor's Bible Commentary.* Edited by F. E. Gaebelein. Grand Rapids: Zondervan.

Carson, D. A., and D. J. Moo

2005   *An Introduction to the New Testament.* 2nd edition. Grand Rapids: Zondervan.

Casey, M.

1988   "Culture and Historicity: The Plucking of the Grain (Mark 2.23–28)." *New Testament Studies* 34:1–23.

1998   *Aramaic Sources of Mark's Gospel.* Society for New Testament Studies Monograph Series 102. Cambridge: Cambridge University Press.

Catchpole, D. R.

1984   "The 'Triumphal' Entry." Pp. 319–34 in *Jesus and the Politics of His Day.* Edited by E. Bammel and C. F. D. Moule. Cambridge: Cambridge University Press.

Cave, C. H.

1979   "The Leper: Mark 1.40–45." *New Testament Studies* 25:245–50.

Charles, R. H.
1913   *The Apocrypha and Pseudepigrapha of the Old Testament*, vol. 2: *Pseudepigrapha*. Oxford: Clarendon.

Charlesworth, J. H.
1996   "Solomon and Jesus: The Son of David in Ante-Markan Traditions (Mk 10:47)." Pp. 125–51 in *Biblical and Humane: A Festschrift for John F. Priest*. Edited by L. B. Elder, D. L. Barr, and E. S. Malborn. Atlanta: Scholars Press.

Chenderlin, F.
1975   "Distributed Observance of the Passover— A Hypothesis." *Biblica* 56:369–93.

Chilton, B.
1982   "Jesus *ben David*: Reflections on the *Davidssohnfrage*." *Journal for the Study of the New Testament* 14:88–112.

Chronis, H. L.
1982   "The Torn Veil: Cultus and Christology in Mark 15:37–39." *Journal of Biblical Literature* 101:97–114.

Chwolson, D.
1908   *Das letzte Passamahl Christi und der Tag seines Todes*. 2nd edition. Amsterdam: Apa-Philo.

Cohn-Sherbok, D. M.
1979   "An Analysis of Jesus' Arguments Concerning the Plucking of Grain on the Sabbath." *Journal for the Study of the New Testament* 2:31–41.

Colani, T.
1864   *Jésus-Christ et les croyances messianiques de son temps*. 2nd edition. Strasbourg: Treuttel et Würtz.

Collins, A. Y.
1992   *The Beginning of the Gospel: Probings of Mark in Context*. Minneapolis: Fortress.
1996   "The Apocalyptic Rhetoric of Mark 13 in Historical Context." *Biblical Research* 41:5–36.
1997   "The Signification of Mark 10:45 among Gentile Christians." *Harvard Theological Review* 90:371–82.
2004   "The Charge of Blasphemy in Mark 14.64." *Journal for the Study of the New Testament* 26:379–401.

Collins, J. J.
1995   *The Scepter and the Star: The Messiahs of the Dead Sea Scrolls and Other Ancient Literature*. New York: Doubleday.

Collins, R. F.
1992   *Divorce in the New Testament*. Collegeville, MN: Liturgical Press.

2000   *Sexual Ethics and the New Testament: Behavior and Belief*. Companions to the New Testament. New York: Crossroad.

Colwell, E. C.
1933   "A Definite Rule for the Use of the Article in the Greek New Testament." *Journal of Biblical Literature* 52:12–21.

Conzelmann, H.
1953   *Die Mitte der Zeit: Studien zur Theologie des Lukas*. Tübingen: Mohr (Siebeck).

Cotter, W. J.
1986   "'For It Was Not the Season for Figs.'" *Catholic Biblical Quarterly* 48:62–66.

Countryman, L. W.
1985   "'How Many Baskets Full?' Mark 8:14–21 and the Value of Miracles in Mark." *Catholic Biblical Quarterly* 47:643–55.

Cousar, C. B.
1970   "Eschatology and Mark's Theologia Crucis." *Interpretation* 24:321–35.

Cox, S. L.
1993   *A History and Critique of Scholarship concerning the Markan Endings*. Lewiston, NY: Mellen.

Craghan, J. F.
1968   "The Gerasene Demoniac." *Catholic Biblical Quarterly* 30:522–36.

Craig, W. L.
1985   "The Historicity of the Empty Tomb of Jesus." *New Testament Studies* 31:39–67.

Cranfield, C. E. B.
1947   "The Cup Metaphor in Mark xiv.36 and Parallels." *Expository Times* 59:137–38.
1954   "St. Mark 13." *Scottish Journal of Theology* 7:284–303.
1959   *The Gospel according to Saint Mark*. Cambridge Greek Testament Commentary. Cambridge: Cambridge University Press.
1982   "Thoughts on New Testament Eschatology." *Scottish Journal of Theology* 35:497–512.
1985   *The Bible and Christian Life: A Collection of Essays*. Edinburgh: T&T Clark.

Creed, J. M.
1929   "The Conclusion of the Gospel according to Saint Mark." *Journal of Theological Studies* 31:175–80.

Crossan, J. D.
1973a   *In Parables: The Challenge of the Historical Jesus*. New York: Harper & Row.
1973b   "Mark and the Relatives of Jesus." *Novum Testamentum* 15:81–113.
1973c   "The Seed Parables of Jesus." *Journal of Biblical Literature* 92:244–66.

1976   "Empty Tomb and Absent Lord (Mark 16:1–8)." Pp. 135–52 in *The Passion in Mark: Studies on Mark 14–16.* Edited by W. H. Kelber. Philadelphia: Fortress.

1983   *In Fragments: The Aphorisms of Jesus.* San Francisco: Harper & Row.

1985   *Four Other Gospels: Shadows on the Contours of Canon.* Minneapolis: Winston.

1991   *The Historical Jesus: The Life of a Mediterranean Jewish Peasant.* San Francisco: Harper & Row.

1995   *Who Killed Jesus? Exposing the Roots of Anti-Semitism in the Gospel Story of the Death of Jesus.* San Francisco: Harper.

Crossley, J. G.

2003   "Halakah and Mark 7.4: '. . . and Beds.'" *Journal for the Study of the New Testament* 25:433–47.

2004   *The Date of Mark's Gospel: Insight from the Law in Earliest Christianity.* Journal for the Study of the New Testament: Supplement Series 266. London: T&T Clark.

2005   "The Damned Rich (Mark 10:17–31)." *Expository Times* 116:397–401.

Croy, N. C.

2001   "Where the Gospel Text Begins: A Non-Theological Interpretation of Mark 1:1." *Novum Testamentum* 43:105–27.

Culpepper, R. A.

1982   "Mark 10:50: Why Mention the Garment?" *Journal of Biblical Literature* 101:131–32.

Danby, H.

1933   *The Mishnah: Translated from the Hebrew with Introduction and Brief Explanatory Notes.* Oxford: Oxford University Press.

D'Angelo, M. R.

1992   "*Abba* and 'Father': Imperial Theology and the Jesus Traditions." *Journal of Biblical Literature* 111:611–30.

1999   "Gender and Power in the Gospel of Mark: The Daughter of Jairus and the Woman with the Flow of Blood." Pp. 83–109 in *Miracles in Jewish and Christian Antiquity: Imagining Truth.* Edited by J. C. Cavadini. Notre Dame, IN: University of Notre Dame Press.

Danker, F. W.

1963   "Mark 8 3." *Journal of Biblical Literature* 82:215–16.

1966   "The Literary Unity of Mark 14 1–25." *Journal of Biblical Literature* 85:467–72.

1970   "The Demonic Secret in Mark: A Re-examination of the Cry of Dereliction

(1534)." *Zeitschrift für die neutestamentliche Wissenschaft* 61:48–69.

Danove, P. L.

1993   *The End of Mark's Story: A Methodological Study.* Biblical Interpretation Series 3. Leiden: Brill.

Daube, D.

1956a   "Four Types of Questions." Pp. 158–69 in *The New Testament and Rabbinic Judaism.* Jordan Lectures 1952. London: Athlone.

1956b   "Public Retort and Private Explanations." Pp. 141–50 in *The New Testament and Rabbinic Judaism.* Jordan Lectures 1952. London: Athlone.

1972   "Responsibilities of Master and Disciples in the Gospels." *New Testament Studies* 19:1–15.

1990   "Critical Note—on Acts 23: Sadducees and Angels." *Journal of Biblical Literature* 109:493–97.

Davies, W. D., and D. C. Allison

1988   *A Critical and Exegetical Commentary on the Gospel according to Saint Matthew,* vol. 1: *Introduction and Commentary on Matthew I–VII.* International Critical Commentary. Edinburgh: T&T Clark.

1991   *A Critical and Exegetical Commentary on the Gospel according to Saint Matthew,* vol. 2: *Commentary on Matthew VIII–XVIII.* Edinburgh: T&T Clark.

1997   *A Critical and Exegetical Commentary on the Gospel according to Saint Matthew,* vol. 3: *Commentary on Matthew XIX–XXVIII.* Edinburgh: T&T Clark.

Deissmann, A.

1978   *Light from the Ancient East: The New Testament Illustrated by Recently Discovered Texts of the Graeco-Roman World.* Translated by L. R. M. Strachan. Reprinted Grand Rapids: Baker Academic.

Deming, W.

1990   "Mark 9.42–10.12, Matthew 5.27–32, and *b. Nid.* 13b: A First Century Discussion of Male Sexuality." *New Testament Studies* 36:130–41.

Derrett, J. D. M.

1970   *Law in the New Testament.* London: Darton, Longman & Todd.

1971   "Law in the New Testament: The Palm Sunday Colt." *Novum Testamentum* 13:241–58.

1972   "'Eating Up the Houses of Widows': Jesus' Comment on Lawyers?" *Novum Testamentum* 14:1–9.

1973   "Salted with Fire: Studies in Texts—Mark 9:42–50." *Theology* 76:364–68.

1979   "Contributions to the Study of the Gerasene Demoniac." *Journal for the Study of the New Testament* 3:2–17.

1981   "Why and How Jesus Walked on the Sea." *Novum Testamentum* 23:330–48.

2001   "'He Who Has Ears to Hear, Let Him Hear' (Mark 4:9 and Parallels)." *Downside Review* 119:255–68.

Dewey, J.
1980   *Markan Public Debate: Literary Technique, Concentric Structure, and Theology in Mark 2:1–3:6.* Society of Biblical Literature Dissertation Series 48. Chico, CA: Scholars Press.

Dibelius, M.
1934   *From Tradition to Gospel.* Translated by B. L. Woolf. London: Nicholson & Watson.

DiCicco, M.
1998   "What Can One Give in Exchange for One's Life? A Narrative-Critical Study of the Widow and Her Offering, Mark 12:41–44." *Currents in Theology and Mission* 25:441–49.

Dillon, R. J.
1995   "'As One Having Authority' (Mark 1:22): The Controversial Distinction of Jesus' Teaching." *Catholic Biblical Quarterly* 57:92–113.

Dilthey, W.
1957   *Gesammelte Schriften*, vol. 5. Göttingen: Vandenhoeck & Ruprecht.

DJG   *Dictionary of Jesus and the Gospels.* Edited by J. B. Green and S. McKnight. Downers Grove, IL: InterVarsity, 1992.

DNTB   *Dictionary of New Testament Background.* Edited by C. A. Evans and S. E. Porter. Downers Grove, IL: InterVarsity, 2000.

Dodd, C. H.
1948   *The Parables of the Kingdom.* London: Nisbet.

1955   "The Appearances of the Risen Christ: An Essay in Form-Criticism of the Gospels." Pp. 9–35 in *Studies in the Gospels: Essays in Memory of R. H. Lightfoot.* Edited by D. E. Nineham. Oxford: Blackwell.

1961   *The Parables of the Kingdom.* New York: Scribner's.

Donahue, J. R.
1971   "Tax Collectors and Sinners: An Attempt at Identification." *Catholic Biblical Quarterly* 33:39–61.

1973   *Are You the Christ? The Trial Narrative in the Gospel of Mark.* Society of Biblical Literature Dissertation Series 10. Missoula, MT: Society of Biblical Literature.

1982   "A Neglected Factor in the Theology of Mark." *Journal of Biblical Literature* 101:563–94.

Donahue, J. R., and D. J. Harrington
2002   *The Gospel of Mark.* Sacra Pagina Series 2. Collegeville, MN: Liturgical Press.

Donfried, K. P.
1980   "The Feeding Narratives and the Marcan Community: Mark 6,30–45 and 8,1–10." Pp. 95–103 in *Kirche: Festschrift für Günther Bornkamm zum 75. Geburtstag.* Edited by D. Lührmann and G. Strecker. Tübingen: Mohr (Siebeck).

Dormandy, R.
2000   "The Expulsion of the Legion: A Political Reading of Mark 5:1–20." *Expository Times* 111:335–37.

Dormeyer, D.
1974   *Die Passion Jesu als Verhaltensmodell: Literarische und theologische Analyse der Traditions- und Redaktionsgeschichte der Markuspassion.* Münster: Aschendorff.

Doughty, D. J.
1983   "The Authority of the Son of Man (Mk 2_1–3_6)." *Zeitschrift für die neutestamentliche Wissenschaft* 74:161–81.

Dowd, S. E.
1988   *Prayer, Power, and the Problem of Suffering: Mark 11:22–25 in the Context of Markan Theology.* Society of Biblical Literature Dissertation Series 105. Atlanta: Scholars Press.

2000   *Reading Mark: A Literary and Theological Commentary on the Second Gospel.* Macon, GA: Smyth & Helwys.

Dreyfus, F.
1959   "L'Argument scripturaire de Jésus en faveur de la résurrection des morts (Marc, XII, 26–27)." *Revue biblique* 66:213–24.

Drury, J.
1987   "Mark." Pp. 402–17 in *The Literary Guide to the Bible.* Edited by R. Alter and F. Kermode. Cambridge: Harvard University Press.

Dschulnigg, P.
1986   *Sprache, Redaktion und Intention des Markus-Evangeliums: Eigentümlichkeiten der Sprache des Markus-Evangeliums und ihre Bedeutung für die Redaktionskritik.* Stuttgarter biblische Beiträge 11. Stuttgart: Katholisches Bibelwerk.

Duff, P. B.
1992   "The March of the Divine Warrior and the Advent of the Greco-Roman King: Mark's Account of Jesus' Entry into Jerusalem." *Journal of Biblical Literature* 111:55–71.

Duling, D.
1975   "Solomon, Exorcism, and the Son of David." *Harvard Theological Review* 68:235–52.

Dunn, J. D. G.
1981   "The Messianic Secret in Mark." Pp. 116–31 in *The Messianic Secret*. Edited by C. Tuckett. Issues in Religion and Theology 1. Philadelphia: Fortress.

1990   *Jesus, Paul, and the Law: Studies in Mark and Galatians*. Louisville: Westminster/John Knox.

Dwyer, T.
1996   *The Motif of Wonder in the Gospel of Mark*. Journal for the Study of New Testament: Supplement Series 128. Sheffield: Sheffield Academic Press.

Dyer, K.
1998   *The Prophecy on the Mount: Mark 13 and the Gathering of the New Community*. Bern: Lang.

Eckstein, H.-J.
1996   "Markus 10,46–52 als Schlüsseltext des Markusevangeliums." *Zeitschrift für die neutestamentliche Wissenschaft* 87:33–50.

Edwards, J. R.
1989   "Markan Sandwiches: The Significance of Interpolations in Markan Narratives." *Novum Testamentum* 31:193–216.

1991   "The Baptism of Jesus according to the Gospel of Mark." *Journal of the Evangelical Theological Society* 34:43–57.

1994   "The Authority of Jesus in the Gospel of Mark." *Journal of the Evangelical Theological Society* 37:217–33.

2002   *The Gospel according to Mark*. Pillar New Testament Commentary. Grand Rapids: Eerdmans.

Edwards, R. A.
1971   *The Sign of Jonah in the Theology of the Evangelists and Q*. Studies in Biblical Theology 2/18. Naperville, IL: Allenson.

Egger, W.
1976   *Frohbotschaft und Lehre: Die Sammelberichte des Wirkens Jesu im Markusevangelium*. Frankfurter theologische Studien. Frankfurt: Josef Knecht.

Ellingworth, P.
2001   "'To Save Life or to Kill?' (Mark 3.4)." *Bible Translator* 52:245–46.

Elliott, J. K.
1974   "The Anointing of Jesus." *Expository Times* 85:105–7.

1993   *The Apocryphal New Testament: A Collection of Apocryphal Christian Literature in an English Translation*. Oxford: Clarendon.

Ellis, E. E.
1994   "Deity-Christology in Mark 14:58." Pp. 192–203 in *Jesus of Nazareth, Lord and Christ: Essays on the Historical Jesus and New Testament Christology*. Edited by J. B. Green and M. Turner. Grand Rapids: Eerdmans.

Erickson, M. J.
1984   *Christian Theology*. Vol. 2. Grand Rapids: Baker Academic.

Ernst, J.
1981   *Das Evangelium nach Markus*. Regensburger Neues Testament. Regensburg: Friedrich Pustet.

1989   *Johannes der Täufer: Interpretation—Geschichte—Wirkungsgeschichte*. Beihefte Zeitschrift für die neutestamentliche Wissenschaft 53. Berlin: de Gruyter.

Evans, C. A.
1982a   "The Function of Isaiah 6:9–10 in Mark and John." *New Testament Studies* 24:127–33.

1982b   "'Peter Warming Himself': The Problem of an Editorial 'Seam.'" *Journal of Biblical Literature* 101:245–49.

1989a   "Jesus' Action in the Temple: Cleansing or Portent of Destruction?" *Catholic Biblical Quarterly* 51:237–70.

1989b   *To See and Not Perceive: Isaiah 6:9–10 in Early Jewish and Christian Interpretation*. Journal for the Study of Old Testament: Supplement Series 64. Sheffield: JSOT Press.

1995   *Jesus and His Contemporaries: Comparative Studies*. Arbeiten zur Geschichte des antiken Judentums und des Urchristentums 25. Leiden: Brill.

2001   *Mark 8:27–16:20*. Word Biblical Commentary 34B. Nashville: Nelson.

2003   "How Septuagintal Is Isa 5:1–7 in Mark 12:1–9?" *Novum Testamentum* 45:105–10.

Eynde, S. van den
2000   "When a Teacher Becomes a Student: The Challenge of the Syrophoenician Woman." *Theology* 103:274–79.

Faierstein, M. M.

1981   "Why Do the Scribes Say That Elijah Must Come First?" *Journal of Biblical Literature* 100:75–86.

Farmer, W. R.

1974   *The Last Twelve Verses of Mark.* Cambridge: Cambridge University Press.

Fay, G.

1989   "Introduction to Incomprehension: The Literary Structure of Mark 4:1–34." *Catholic Biblical Quarterly* 52:65–81.

Feldmeier, R.

1987   *Die Krisis des Gottessohnes: Die Gethsemaneerzählung als Schlüssel der Markuspassion.* Wissenschaftliche Untersuchungen zum Neuen Testament 2/21. Tübingen: Mohr (Siebeck).

Ferguson, E.

1993   *Backgrounds of Early Christianity.* 2nd edition. Grand Rapids: Eerdmans.

Fitzmyer, J. A.

1959   "The Aramaic Qorban Inscription from Jebel Hallet Et-turi and Mark 7:11 and Matt. 15:5." *Journal of Biblical Literature* 78:60–65.

1966   *The Genesis Apocryphon of Qumran Cave 1: A Commentary.* Biblica et Orientalia 18. Rome: Pontifical Biblical Institute.

1971   *Essays on the Semitic Background of the New Testament.* London: Geoffrey Chapman.

1978   "Crucifixion in Ancient Palestine, Qumran Literature, and the New Testament." *Catholic Biblical Quarterly* 40:493–513.

1979a   "Aramaic *Kephā'* and Peter's Name in the New Testament." Pp. 121–32 in *Text and Interpretation: Studies in the New Testament Presented to Matthew Black.* Edited by E. Best and R. M. Wilson. Cambridge: Cambridge University Press.

1979b   *A Wandering Aramean: Collected Aramaic Essays.* Society of Biblical Literature Monograph Series 25. Missoula, MT: Scholars Press.

1981   *The Gospel according to Luke (I–IX): Introduction, Translation, and Notes.* Anchor Bible 28. Garden City, NY: Doubleday.

1985a   "'*Abba*' and Jesus' Relation to God." Vol. 1 / pp. 15–38 in *À cause de l'Évangile: Études sur les Synoptiques et les Actes.* Festschrift for J. Dupont. 2 vols. Lectio divina 123. Paris: Cerf.

1985b   *The Gospel according to Luke (X–XXIV): Introduction, Translation, and Notes.* Anchor Bible 28A. Garden City, NY: Doubleday.

1985c   "More about Elijah Coming First." *Journal of Biblical Literature* 104:295–96.

1987   "Aramaic Evidence Affecting the Interpretation of *Hosanna* in the New Testament." Pp. 110–18 in *Tradition and Interpretation in the New Testament: Essays in Honor of E. Earle Ellis for His 60th Birthday.* Edited by G. F. Hawthorne and O. Betz. Grand Rapids: Eerdmans.

1993   "4Q246: The 'Son of God' Document from Qumran." *Biblica* 74:153–74.

Fleddermann, H.

1979   "The Flight of a Naked Young Man (Mark 14:51–52)." *Catholic Biblical Quarterly* 41:412–18.

1981   "The Discipleship Discourse (Mark 9:33–50)." *Catholic Biblical Quarterly* 43:57–75.

1982   "A Warning about the Scribes (Mark 12:37b–40)." *Catholic Biblical Quarterly* 44:52–67.

1983   "'And He Wanted to Pass By Them' (Mark 6:48c)." *Catholic Biblical Quarterly* 45:389–95.

Ford, D.

1979   *The Abomination of Desolation in Biblical Eschatology.* Washington, DC: University Press of America.

Fortna, R. T.

1977–78   "Jesus and Peter at the High Priest's House: A Test Case for the Question of the Relation between Mark's and John's Gospels." *New Testament Studies* 24:371–83.

Fowler, R. M.

1981   *Loaves and Fishes: The Function of the Feeding Stories in the Gospel of Mark.* Society of Biblical Literature Dissertation Series 54. Chico, CA: Scholars Press.

France, R. T.

1971   *Jesus and the Old Testament: His Application of Old Testament Passages to Himself and His Mission.* Downers Grove, IL: InterVarsity.

1986   "Chronological Aspects of 'Gospel Harmony.'" *Vox Evangelica* 16:33–59.

2002   *The Gospel of Mark.* New International Greek Testament Commentary. Grand Rapids: Eerdmans.

Frei, H. W.

1974   *The Eclipse of Biblical Narrative: A Study in Eighteenth and Nineteenth Century Hermeneutics.* New Haven: Yale University Press.

Friedrich, G.
1964 "Die beiden Erzählungen von der Speisung in Mark 6,31–44; 8,1–9." *Theologische Zeitschrift* 20:10–22.

Friedrichsen, T. A.
2001 "The Parable of the Mustard Seed—Mark 4,30–32 and Q 13,18–19: A Surrejoinder for Independence." *Ephemerides theologicae lovanienses* 77:297–317.

Furnish, V. P.
1972 *The Love Command in the New Testament.* Nashville: Abingdon.
1982 "Love of Neighbor in the New Testament." *Journal of Religious Ethics* 10:327–34.

García Martínez, F.
1995 *The Dead Sea Scrolls Translated: The Qumran Texts in English.* 2nd edition. Translated by W. G. E. Watson. Grand Rapids: Eerdmans.

Gaston, L.
1970 *No Stone on Another: Studies in the Significance of the Fall of Jerusalem in the Synoptic Gospels.* Supplements to Novum Testamentum 23. Leiden: Brill.

Geddert, T. J.
1989 *Watchwords: Mark 13 in Markan Eschatology.* Journal for the Study of the New Testament: Supplement Series 26. Sheffield: JSOT Press.

Gerhardsson, B.
1967 "The Parable of the Sower and Its Interpretation." *New Testament Studies* 14:165–93.

Gibson, J.
1990 "Jesus' Refusal to Produce a 'Sign' (MK 8.11–13)." *Journal for the Study of the New Testament* 38:37–66.
1994 "Jesus' Wilderness Temptation according to Mark." *Journal for the Study of the New Testament* 53:3–34.
1996 "Another Look at Why Jesus 'Sighs Deeply': *Anastenazō* in Mark 8:12a." *Journal of Theological Studies* 47:131–40.

Gnilka, J.
1973 "Das Martyrium Johannes des Täufers (Mk 6,17–29)." Pp. 78–92 in *Orientierung an Jesus: Zur Theologie der Synoptiker.* Edited by P. Hoffmann. Freiburg: Herder.
1978 *Das Evangelium nach Markus (Mk 1–8,26).* Evangelisch-katholischer Kommentar zum Neuen Testament 2/1. Zurich: Benzinger.
1979 *Das Evangelium nach Markus (Mk 8,27–16:20).* Evangelisch-katholischer Kommentar zum Neuen Testament 2/2. Zurich: Benzinger.

Gould, E. P.
1896 *A Critical and Exegetical Commentary on the Gospel according to St. Mark.* International Critical Commentary. Edinburgh: T&T Clark.

Grant, R. M.
1946 *Second-Century Christianity: A Collection of Fragments.* London: SPCK.

Grässer, E.
1970 "Jesus in Nazareth (Mark VI.1–6a): Notes on the Redaction and Theology of St Mark." *New Testament Studies* 16:1–23.

Gray, R.
1993 *Prophetic Figures in Late Second Temple Jewish Palestine: The Evidence from Josephus.* New York: Oxford University Press.

Grayston, K.
1973/74 "The Study of Mark XIII." *Bulletin of the John Rylands University Library of Manchester* 56:371–87.

Green, J. B.
1988 *The Death of Jesus: Tradition and Interpretation in the Passion Narrative.* Wissenschaftliche Untersuchungen zum Neuen Testament 2/33. Tübingen: Mohr (Siebeck).

Grudem, W.
1994 *Systematic Theology: An Introduction to Biblical Doctrine.* Grand Rapids: Zondervan.

Grundmann, W.
1977 *Das Evangelium nach Markus.* 7th edition. Theologischer Handkommentar zum Neuen Testament. Berlin: Evangelische Verlagsanstalt.

Guelich, R.
1982 "'The Beginning of the Gospel'—Mark 1:1–15." *Biblical Research* 27:5–15.
1989 *Mark 1–8:26.* Word Biblical Commentary 34. Dallas: Word.
1991 "The Gospel Genre." Pp. 173–208 in *The Gospel and the Gospels.* Edited by P. Stuhlmacher. Grand Rapids: Eerdmans.

Gundry, R. H.
1967 *The Use of the Old Testament in St. Matthew's Gospel.* Supplements to Novum Testamentum 18. Leiden: Brill.
1993 *Mark: A Commentary on His Apology for the Cross.* Grand Rapids: Eerdmans.
1996 "ΕΥΑΓΓΕΛΙΟΝ: How Soon a Book?" *Journal of Biblical Literature* 115:321–25.

1997　　"Mark 10:29: Order in the List." *Catholic Biblical Quarterly* 59:465–75.

1999　　"No *Nu* in Line 2 of 7Q5: A Final Disidentification of 7Q5 with Mark 6:52–53." *Journal of Biblical Literature* 118:698–707.

Gurtner, D. M.

2005　　"LXX Syntax and the Identity of the NT Veil." *Novum Testamentum* 47:345–53.

Haenchen, E.

1966　　*Der Weg Jesu: Eine Erklärung des Markus-Evangeliums und der kanonischen Parallelen.* Berlin: Töpelmann.

Hagedorn, A. C., and J. H. Neyrey

1998　　"'It Was out of Envy That They Handed Jesus Over' (Mark 15:10): The Anatomy of Envy and the Gospel of Mark." *Journal for the Study of the New Testament* 69:15–56.

Hahn, F.

1969　　*The Titles of Jesus in Christology: Their History in Early Christianity.* Translated by H. Knight and G. Ogg. New York: World.

Hart, H. St. J.

1952　　"The Crown of Thorns in John 19, 2–5." *Journal of Theological Studies* 3:66–75.

1984　　"The Coin of 'Render unto Caesar . . .' (A Note on Some Aspects of Mark 12:13–17; Matt. 22:15–22; Luke 20:26)." Pp. 241–48 in *Jesus and the Politics of His Day.* Edited by E. Bammel and C. F. D. Moule. Cambridge: Cambridge University Press.

Hartman, L.

1966　　*Prophecy Interpreted: The Formation of Some Jewish Apocalyptic Texts and of the Eschatological Discourse Mark 13 Par.* Coniectanea biblica: New Testament Series 1. Translated by N. Tomkinson. Lund: Gleerup.

1997　　*"Into the Name of the Lord Jesus": Baptism in the Early Church.* Studies of the New Testament and Its World. Edinburgh: T&T Clark.

2004　　"Mk 6,3a im Lichte einiger griechischer Texte." *Zeitschrift für die neutestamentliche Wissenschaft* 95:276–79.

Hatina, T. R.

1996　　"The Focus of Mark 13:24–27: The Parousia, or the Destruction of the Temple?" *Bulletin for Biblical Research* 6:43–66.

2005　　"Who Will See 'The Kingdom of God Coming with Power' in Mark 9,1—Protagonists or Antagonists?" *Biblica* 86:20–34.

Hay, D. M.

1973　　*Glory at the Right Hand: Psalm 110 in Early Christianity.* Society of Biblical Literature Monograph Series 18. Nashville: Abingdon.

Head, P. M.

1991　　"A Textual-Critical Study of Mark 1:1: 'The Beginning of the Gospel of Jesus Christ.'" *New Testament Studies* 37:621–29.

Hedrick, C. W.

1984　　"The Role of 'Summary Statements' in the Composition of the Gospel of Mark: A Dialog with Karl Schmidt and Norman Perrin." *Novum Testamentum* 26:289–311.

Heil, J. P.

1981　　*Jesus Walking on the Sea: Meaning and Gospel Functions of Matt. 14:22–33, Mark 6:45–52, John 6:15b–21.* Analecta biblica 87. Rome: Pontifical Biblical Institute.

1990　　"Mark 14,1–52: Narrative Structure and Reader Response." *Biblica* 71:305–32.

1992　　"Reader-Response and the Narrative Context of the Parables about Growing Seed in Mark 4:1–34." *Catholic Biblical Quarterly* 54:271–86.

2000　　*The Transfiguration of Jesus: Narrative Meaning and Function of Mark 9:2–8, Matt. 17:1–8 and Luke 9:28–36.* Analecta biblica 144. Rome: Pontifical Biblical Institute.

2006　　"Jesus with the Wild Animals in Mark 1:13." *Catholic Biblical Quarterly* 68:63–78.

Hengel, M.

1969　　"Mc 7₃ πυγμῇ: Die Geschichte einer exegetischen Aporie und der Versuch ihrer Lösung." *Zeitschrift für die neutestamentliche Wissenschaft* 60:182–98.

1974　　*Property and Riches in the Early Church: Aspects of a Social History of Early Christianity.* Philadelphia: Fortress.

1977　　*Crucifixion in the Ancient World and the Folly of the Message of the Cross.* Translated by J. Bowden. Philadelphia: Fortress.

1982　　*The Charismatic Leader and His Followers.* Translated by J. C. G. Greig. Edited by J. Riches. New York: Crossroad.

1985　　*Studies in the Gospel of Mark.* Translated by J. Bowden. Philadelphia: Fortress.

1995　　*Studies in Early Christianity.* Edinburgh: T&T Clark.

2000　　*The Four Gospels and the One Gospel of Jesus Christ: An Investigation of the Collection and Origin of the Canonical*

Gospels. Translated by J. Bowden. Harrisburg, PA: Trinity Press International.

Herron, R. W., Jr.
1991   *Mark's Account of Peter's Denial of Jesus: A History of Its Interpretation.* Lanham, MD: University Press of America.

Hiers, R. H.
1968   "'Not the Season for Figs.'" *Journal of Biblical Literature* 87:394–400.

Hill, D. F.
1988   "The Walking on the Water: A Geographical or Linguistic Answer?" *Expository Times* 99:267–69.

Hoehner, H. W.
1972   *Herod Antipas.* Society for New Testament Studies Monograph Series 17. Cambridge: Cambridge University Press.
1977   *Chronological Aspects of the Life of Christ.* Grand Rapids: Zondervan.

Holladay, C. R.
1977   *Theios Aner in Hellenistic-Judaism: A Critique of the Use of This Category in New Testament Christology.* Society of Biblical Literature Dissertation Series 40. Missoula, MT: Scholars Press.

Hollenbach, B.
1983   "Lest They Should Turn and Be Forgiven: Irony." *Bible Translator* 34:312–21.

Holleran, J. W.
1973   *The Synoptic Gethsemane: A Critical Study.* Analecta Gregoriana 191. Rome: Università Gregoriana Editrice.

Holm-Nielsen, S.
1960   *Hodayot: Psalms from Qumran.* Acta theologica danica 2. Aarhus: Universitetsforlaget.

Hooker, M. D.
1959   *Jesus and the Servant: The Influence of the Servant Concept of Deutero-Isaiah in the New Testament.* London: SPCK.
1987   "'What Doest Thou Here, Elijah?' A Look at St Mark's Account of the Transfiguration." Pp. 59–70 in *The Glory of Christ in the New Testament: Studies in Christology in Memory of George Bradford Caird.* Edited by L. D. Hurst and N. T. Wright. Oxford: Clarendon.
1991   *The Gospel according to Saint Mark.* Black's New Testament Commentary. London: Black.

Horsley, R. A.
2001   *Hearing the Whole Story: The Politics of Plot in Mark's Gospel.* Louisville: Westminster/John Knox.

Horst, P. W. van der
1972   "Can a Book End with a ΓΑΡ? A Note on Mark XVI.8." *Journal of Theological Studies* 23:121–24.

Howard, J. K.
1984   "Men as Trees, Walking: Mark 8.22–26." *Scottish Journal of Theology* 37:163–70.

Hultgren, A. J.
1972   "The Formation of the Sabbath Pericope in Mark 2:23–28." *Journal of Biblical Literature* 91:38–43.
1979   *Jesus and His Adversaries: The Form and Function of the Conflict Stories in the Synoptic Tradition.* Minneapolis: Augsburg.
2000   *The Parables of Jesus: A Commentary.* Grand Rapids: Eerdmans.

Hurtado, L. W.
1983   *Mark.* New International Biblical Commentary. Peabody, MA: Hendrickson.

IDB   *Interpreter's Dictionary of the Bible.* Edited by G. A. Buttrick. 4 vols. Nashville: Abingdon, 1962.

Iersel, B. M. F. van
1962   "Die wunderbare Speisung und das Abendmahl in der synoptischen Tradition (Mk vi.35–44 par., viii.1–20 par.)." *Novum Testamentum* 7:167–94.
1964   *"Der Sohn"* in den synoptischen Jesusworten: Christusbezeichnung der Gemeinde oder Selbstbezeichnung Jesu? Supplements to Novum Testamentum 3. Leiden: Brill.
1982   "'To Galilee' and 'in Galilee' in Mark 14,28 and 16,7?" *Ephemerides theologicae lovanienses* 58:365–70.
1992   "ΚΑΙ ΗΘΕΛΕΝ ΠΑΡΕΛΘΕΙΝ ΑΥΤΟΥΣ: Another Look at Mark 6,48d." Vol. 2 / pp. 1065–76 in *The Four Gospels 1992: Festschrift Frans Neirynck.* Bibliotheca ephemeridum theologicarum lovaniensium 100. Edited by F. van Segbroek. Louvain: Leuven University Press.
1996   "The Sun, Moon, and Stars of Mark 13:24–25 in a Greco-Roman Reading." *Biblica* 77:84–92.
1998   *Mark: A Reader-Response Commentary.* Journal for the Study of the New Testament: Supplement Series 164. Translated by W. H. Bisscheroux. Sheffield: Sheffield Academic Press.

Iersel, B. M. F. van, and A. J. M. Linmans
1978   "The Storm on the Lake: Mk iv.35–41 and Mt viii.18–27 in the Light of Form Criticism, 'Redaktionsgeschichte' and Structural Analysis." Vol. 1 / pp. 17–48

in *Miscellanea Neotestamentica*. Edited by T. Baarda, A. F. J. Klijn, and W. C. van Unnik. Supplements to Novum Testamentum 47–48. 2 vols. Leiden: Brill.

Ilan, T.

1992   "'Man Born of Woman . . .' (Job 14:1): The Phenomenon of Men Bearing Metronymes at the Time of Jesus." *Novum Testamentum* 34:23–45.

Incigneri, B. J.

2003   *The Gospel to the Romans: The Setting and Rhetoric of Mark's Gospel.* Leiden: Brill.

Instone-Brewer, D.

2002   *Divorce and Remarriage in the Bible: The Social and Literary Context.* Grand Rapids: Eerdmans.

Jackson, H. M.

1987   "The Death of Jesus in Mark and the Miracle from the Cross." *New Testament Studies* 33:16–37.

Jaubert, A.

1965   *The Date of the Last Supper.* New York: Alba.

Jeremias, J.

1958   *Jesus' Promise to the Nations.* Studies in Biblical Theology 1/24. Translated by S. H. Hooke. Naperville, IL: Allenson.

1960   *Infant Baptism in the First Four Centuries.* Translated by D. Cairns. Philadelphia: Westminster.

1965   *The Central Message of the New Testament.* New York: Scribner's.

1966   *The Eucharistic Words of Jesus.* Translated by N. Perrin. Philadelphia: Fortress.

1967   "Die älteste Schicht der Menschensohn-Logien." *Zeitschrift für die neutestamentliche Wissenschaft* 58:159–72.

1969   *Jerusalem in the Time of Jesus: An Investigation into Economic and Social Conditions during the New Testament Period.* Translated by F. H. and C. H. Cave. London: SCM.

1971   *New Testament Theology: The Proclamation of Jesus.* Translated by J. Bowden. New York: Scribner's.

1972   *The Parables of Jesus.* Translated by S. H. Hooke. 2nd edition. New York: Scribner's.

Johnson, E. S.

1978   "Mark 10:46–52: Blind Bartimaeus." *Catholic Biblical Quarterly* 40:191–204.

1979   "Mark VIII.22–26: The Blind Man from Bethsaida." *New Testament Studies* 25:370–83.

1987   "Is Mark 15.39 the Key to Mark's Christology?" *Journal for the Study of the New Testament* 31:3–22.

2000   "Mark 15,39 and the So-Called Confession of the Roman Centurion." *Biblica* 81:406–13.

Johnson, L. T.

1989   "The New Testament's Anti-Jewish Slander and the Conventions of Ancient Polemic." *Journal of Biblical Literature* 108:419–41.

Juel, D.

1977   *Messiah and Temple: The Trial of Jesus in the Gospel of Mark.* Society of Biblical Literature Dissertation Series 31. Missoula, MT: Scholars Press.

Jülicher, A.

1910   *Die Gleichnisreden Jesus.* 2nd edition. 2 vols. Tübingen: Mohr (Siebeck).

Kähler, M.

1964   *The So-Called Historical Jesus and the Historic, Biblical Christ.* Translated and edited by C. E. Braaten. Philadelphia: Fortress.

Kazantzakis, N.

1960   *The Last Temptation of Christ.* Translated by P. A. Bien. New York: Bantam.

Kazmierski, C. R.

1979   *Jesus, the Son of God: A Study of the Markan Tradition and Its Redaction by the Evangelist.* Forschung zur Bibel 33. Würzburg: Echter Verlag.

Keck, L. E.

1965a   "The Introduction to Mark's Gospel." *New Testament Studies* 12:352–70.

1965b   "Mark 3:7–12 and Mark's Christology." *Journal of Biblical Literature* 84:341–58.

Kee, H. C.

1967–68   "The Terminology of Mark's Exorcism Stories." *New Testament Studies* 14:232–46.

1973   "Aretology and the Gospel." *Journal of Biblical Literature* 92:402–22.

1977   *Community of the New Age: Studies in Mark's Gospel.* Philadelphia: Fortress.

Kelber, W. H.

1972   "Mark 14₃₂–42: Gethsemane: Passion Christology and Discipleship Failure." *Zeitschrift für die neutestamentliche Wissenschaft* 63:166–87.

1974   *The Kingdom in Mark: A New Place and a New Time.* Philadelphia: Fortress.

1976a   "Conclusion: From Passion Narrative to Gospel." Pp. 153–80 in *The Passion in Mark: Studies on Mark 14–16*. Edited by W. H. Kelber. Philadelphia: Fortress.

1976b "The Hour of the Son of Man and the Temptation of the Disciples." Pp. 41–60 in *The Passion in Mark: Studies on Mark 14–16*. Edited by W. H. Kelber. Philadelphia: Fortress.

1979 *Mark's Story of Jesus*. Philadelphia: Fortress.

1983 *The Oral and the Written Gospel: The Hermeneutics of Speaking and Writing in the Synoptic Tradition, Mark, Paul, and Q*. Philadelphia: Fortress.

Kelhoffer, J. A.

2000 *Miracle and Mission: The Authentication of Missionaries and Their Message in the Longer Ending of Mark*. Wissenschaftliche Untersuchungen zum Neuen Testament 112. Tübingen: Mohr (Siebeck).

2005 *The Diet of John the Baptist: "Locusts and Wild Honey" in Synoptic and Patristic Interpretation*. Wissenschaftliche Untersuchungen zum Neuen Testament 176. Tübingen: Mohr (Siebeck).

Kempthorne, R.

1976 "The Marcan Text of Jesus' Answer to the High Priest (Mark XIV62)." *Novum Testamentum* 19:197–208.

Kertelge, K.

1970 *Die Wunder Jesu im Markusevangelium: Eine redaktionsgeschichtliche Untersuchung*. Studien zum Alten und Neuen Testament 33. Munich: Kösel.

Kilgallen, J. J.

1982 "Mk 9,1—The Conclusion of a Pericope." *Biblica* 63:81–83.

Kilpatrick, G. D.

1955 "The Gentile Mission in Mark and Mark 13⁹⁻¹¹." Pp. 145–58 in *Studies in the Gospels: Essays in Memory of R. H. Lightfoot*. Edited by D. E. Nineham. Oxford: Blackwell.

Kim, T. H.

1998 "The Anarthrous *huios theou* in Mark 15,39 and the Roman Imperial Cult." *Biblica* 79:221–41.

Kingsbury, J. D.

1981 "The 'Divine Man' as the Key to Mark's Christology—The End of an Era." *Interpretation* 35:243–57.

1983 *The Christology of Mark's Gospel*. Philadelphia: Fortress.

1990 "The Religious Authorities in the Gospel of Mark." *New Testament Studies* 36:42–65.

Kinman, B.

1991 "Pilate's Assize and the Timing of Jesus' Trial." *Tyndale Bulletin* 42:282–95.

Klauck, H.-J.

1978 *Allegorie und Allegorese in synoptischen Gleichnistexten*. Neutestamentliche Abhandlungen 13. Münster: Aschendorff.

Kline, M. G.

1975 "The Old Testament Origins of the Gospel Genre." *Westminster Theological Journal* 38:1–27.

Kloner, A.

1999 "Did a Rolling Stone Close Jesus' Tomb?" *Biblical Archaeology Review* 25/5:22–29, 76.

Kloppenborg Verbin, J. S.

2000 "Isaiah 5:1–7, the Parable of the Tenants and Vineyard Leases on Papyrus." Pp. 111–34 in *Text and Artifact in the Religions of Mediterranean Antiquity: Essays in Honour of Peter Richardson*. Studies in Christianity and Judaism 9. Edited by S. G. Wilson and M. Desjardins. Waterloo, ON: Wilfrid Laurier University Press.

2002 "Egyptian Viticultural Practices and the Citation of Isa 5:1–7 in Mark 12:1–9." *Novum Testamentum* 44:134–59.

2004 "Isa 5:1–7 LXX and Mark 12, 1, 9, Again." *Novum Testamentum* 46:12–19.

Klostermann, E.

1950 *Das Markusevangelium*. Handbuch zum Neuen Testament 3. Tübingen: Mohr (Siebeck).

Knox, W. L.

1942 "The Ending of St. Mark's Gospel." *Harvard Theological Review* 35:13–23.

Koch, D.-A.

1975 *Die Bedeutung der Wundererzählungen für die Christologie des Markusevangeliums*. Beiheft zur Zeitschrift für die neutestamentliche Wissenschaft 42. Berlin: de Gruyter.

Koenig, J.

1985 *New Testament Hospitality: Partnership with Strangers as Promise and Mission*. Overtures to Biblical Theology. Philadelphia: Fortress.

Koester, H.

1989 "From the Kerygma-Gospel to Written Gospels." *New Testament Studies* 35:361–81.

1990 *Ancient Christian Gospels: Their History and Development*. Philadelphia: Trinity Press International.

Koskenniemi, E., K. Nisula, and J. Toppari
2005   "Wine Mixed with Myrrh (Mark 15:23) and *Crucifragium* (John 19:31–32): Two Details of the Passion Narratives." *Journal for the Study of the New Testament* 27:379–91.

Kruse, H.
1954   "Die 'dialektische Negation' als semitisches Idiom." *Vetus Testamentum* 4:385–400.

Kuhn, H.-W.
1971   *Ältere Sammlungen im Markusevangelium.* Studien zur Umwelt des Neuen Testaments 8. Göttingen: Vandenhoeck & Ruprecht.

Kümmel, W. G.
1957   *Promise and Fulfillment: The Eschatological Message of Jesus.* Translated by D. M. Barton. Studies in Biblical Theology 1/23. Naperville, IL: Allenson.
1975   *Introduction to the New Testament.* Translated by H. C. Kee. Nashville: Abingdon.

Kuthirakkattel, S.
1990   *The Beginning of Jesus' Ministry according to Mark's Gospel (1,14–3,6): A Redaction Critical Study.* Analecta biblica 123. Rome: Pontifical Biblical Institute.

Lachs, S. T.
1987   *A Rabbinic Commentary on the New Testament: The Gospels of Matthew, Mark, and Luke.* Reprinted Hoboken, NJ: Ktav.

Lagrange, M.-J.
1911   *Évangile selon Saint Marc.* Études bibliques. Paris: Gabalda.

Lambrecht, J.
1967   *Die Redaktion des Markus-Apocalypse: Literarische Analyse und Strukturuntersuchung.* Analecta biblica 28. Rome: Päpstliches Bibelinstitut.
1974   "Redaction and Theology in *Mk. IV.*" Pp. 269–307 in *L'Évangile selon Marc: Tradition et rédaction.* Edited by M. Sabbe. Bibliotheca ephemeridum theologicarum lovaniensium 34. Louvain: Leuven University Press.
1992   "John the Baptist and Jesus in Mark 1:1–15: Markan Redaction of Q?" *New Testament Studies* 38:357–84.

Lampe, G. W. H.
1972   "St. Peter's Denial." *Bulletin of the John Rylands University Library of Manchester* 55:346–68.

Lampe, P.
1974   "Die markinische Deutung des Gleichnisses vom Sämann—Markus 4:10–12."

Zeitschrift für die neutestamentliche Wissenschaft 65:140–50.

Lane, A. N. S.
2004   "Did the Apostolic Church Baptise Babies? A Seismological Approach." *Tyndale Bulletin* 55:109–30.

Lane, W. L.
1974   *The Gospel according to Mark: The English Text with Introduction, Exposition and Notes.* New International Commentary on the New Testament. Grand Rapids: Eerdmans.

Lang, F. G.
1976   "*Sola Gratia* im Markusevangelium: Die Soteriologie des Markus nach 9,14–29 und 10, 17–31." Pp. 321–37 in *Rechtfertigung: Festschrift für Ernst Käsemann zum 70. Geburtstag.* Edited by J. Friedrich, W. Pöhlmann, and P. Stuhlmacher. Tübingen: Mohr (Siebeck).

Latourelle, R.
1988   *The Miracles of Jesus and the Theology of Miracles.* Translated by M. J. O'Connell. New York: Paulist Press.

Lemcio, E. E.
1979   "External Evidence for the Structure and Function of Mark iv.1–20, vii.14–23, and viii.14–21." *Journal of Theological Studies* 29:323–38.

Lewis, C. S.
1943   *Mere Christianity.* New York: Macmillan.
1975   "Fern-Seed and Elephants." Pp. 104–25 in *Fern-Seed and Elephants and Other Essays on Christianity.* Edited by W. Hooper. Glasgow: Fontana/Collins.

Lightfoot, R. H.
1934   *History and Interpretation in the Gospels.* New York: Harper.
1938   *Locality and Doctrine in the Gospels.* New York: Harper.
1950   *The Gospel Message of Mark.* Oxford: Clarendon.

Lincoln, A. T.
1989   "The Promise and the Failure: Mark 16:7, 8." *Journal of Biblical Literature* 108:283–300.

Lindars, B.
1983   *Jesus, Son of Man: A Fresh Examination of the Son of Man Sayings in the Gospels in the Light of Recent Research.* Grand Rapids: Eerdmans.

Lohmeyer, E.
1936   *Galiläa und Jerusalem.* Forschungen zur Religion und Literatur des Alten und

Neuen Testaments. Göttingen: Vandenhoeck & Ruprecht.

1957   *Das Evangelium des Markus*. Kritisch-exegetischer Kommentar über das Neue Testament. Göttingen: Vandenhoeck & Ruprecht.

Loos, H. van der

1965   *The Miracles of Jesus*. Supplements to Novum Testamentum 9. Leiden: Brill.

Lövestam, E.

1995   *Jesus and "This Generation"—A New Testament Study*. Coniectanea biblica: New Testament Series 25. Stockholm: Almqvist & Wiksell.

Lührmann, D.

1987   *Das Markusevangelium*. Handbuch zum Neuen Testament 3. Tübingen: Mohr (Siebeck).

Luz, U.

1965   "Das Geheimnismotif und die markinische Christologie." *Zeitschrift für die neutestamentliche Wissenschaft* 56:9–30.

1983   "The Secrecy Motif and the Marcan Christology." Pp. 75–96 in *The Messianic Secret*. Edited by C. Tuckett. Issues in Religion and Theology 1. Philadelphia: Fortress.

Malborn, E. S.

1985   "TH OIKIA AYTOY: Mark 2.15 in Context." *New Testament Studies* 31:282–92.

Malina, B. J.

1981   *The New Testament World: Insights from Cultural Anthropology*. Atlanta: John Knox.

Maloney, E. C.

1981   *Semitic Interference in Marcan Syntax*. Society of Biblical Literature Dissertation Series 51. Chico, CA: Scholars Press.

Maloney, F. J.

2001   "Mark 6:6b–30: Mission, the Baptist, and Failure." *Catholic Biblical Quarterly* 63:647–63.

Manson, T. W.

1937   *The Sayings of Jesus as Recorded in the Gospels according to St. Matthew and St. Luke: Arranged with Introduction and Commentary*. London: SCM.

1950–51   "The Cleansing of the Temple." *Bulletin of the John Rylands University Library of Manchester* 33:271–82.

1955   *The Teaching of Jesus: Studies of Its Form and Content*. 2nd edition. Reprinted Cambridge: Cambridge University Press.

1962   *Studies in the Gospels and Epistles*. Edited by M. Black. Philadelphia: Westminster.

Marcus, J.

1984   "Mark 4:10–12 and Marcan Epistemology." *Journal of Biblical Literature* 103:557–74.

1986a   "Entering into the Kingly Power of God." *Journal of Biblical Literature* 107:663–75.

1986b   *The Mystery of the Kingdom of God*. Society of Biblical Literature Dissertation Series 90. Atlanta: Scholars Press.

1989a   "Mark 14:61: 'Are You the Messiah-Son-of-God?'" *Novum Testamentum* 31:125–41.

1989b   "'The Time Has Been Fulfilled!' (Mark 1.15)." Pp. 49–68 in *Apocalyptic and the New Testament: Essays in Honor of J. Louis Martyn*. Edited by J. Marcus and M. L. Soards. Journal for the Study of the New Testament: Supplement Series 24. Sheffield: Sheffield Academic Press.

1992a   "The Jewish War and the *Sitz im Leben* of Mark." *Journal of Biblical Literature* 111:441–62.

1992b   *The Way of the Lord: Christological Exegesis of the Old Testament in the Gospel of Mark*. Louisville: Westminster.

1995   "Jesus' Baptismal Vision." *New Testament Studies* 43:512–21.

2000   *Mark 1–8: A New Translation with Introduction and Commentary*. Anchor Bible 27. New York: Doubleday.

Marshall, C. D.

1989   *Faith as a Theme in Mark's Narrative*. Society for New Testament Studies Monograph Series 64. Cambridge: Cambridge University Press.

Marshall, I. H.

1968   "Son of God or Servant of Yahweh? A Reconsideration of Mark I.11." *New Testament Studies* 15:326–36.

1980   *Last Supper and Lord's Supper*. Grand Rapids: Eerdmans.

Martin, T. W.

2001   "Watch during the Watches (Mark 13:35)." *Journal of Biblical Literature* 120:685–701.

Marxsen, W.

1956   *Der Evangelist Markus: Studien zur Redaktionsgeschichte des Evangeliums*. Göttingen: Vandenhoeck & Ruprecht.

1968   *Introduction to the New Testament: An Approach to Its Problems*. Translated by G. Buswell. Philadelphia: Fortress.

1969   *Mark the Evangelist: Studies on the Redaction History of the Gospel*. Translated by J. Boyce, D. Juel, and W. Poehlmann with R. A. Harrisville. Nashville: Abingdon.

Mastin, B. A.
1969   "The Date of the Triumphal Entry." *New Testament Studies* 16:76–82.

Masuda, S.
1982   "The Good News of the Miracle of the Bread: The Tradition and Its Markan Redaction." *New Testament Studies* 28:191–219.

Matera, F. J.
1982   *The Kingship of Jesus: Composition and Theology in Mark 15.* Society of Biblical Literature Dissertation Series 66. Chico, CA: Scholars Press.

1988   "The Prologue as the Interpretative Key to Mark's Gospel." *Journal for the Study of the New Testament* 34:3–20.

1989   "The Incomprehension of the Disciples and Peter's Confession (Mark 6,14–8,30)." *Biblica* 70:153–72.

Mauser, U.
1963   *Christ in the Wilderness: The Wilderness Theme in the Second Gospel and Its Basis in the Biblical Tradition.* Studies in Biblical Theology 1/39. Naperville, IL: Allenson.

May, D. M.
1993   "Mark 2.15: The Home of Jesus or Levi?" *New Testament Studies* 39:147–49.

Mayer, B.
1978   "Überlieferungs- und redaktionsgeschichtliche Überlegungen zu Mk 6, 1–6a." *Biblische Zeitschrift* 22:187–98.

Maynard, A. H.
1985   "ΤΙ ΕΜΟΙ ΚΑΙ ΣΟΙ." *New Testament Studies* 31:582–86.

McArthur, H. K.
1971   "The Parable of the Mustard Seed." *Catholic Biblical Quarterly* 33:198–210.

McCurley, F. R., Jr.
1974   "'And after Six Days' (Mark 9:2): A Semitic Literary Device." *Journal of Biblical Literature* 93:67–81.

McDonald, J. I. H.
1980   "Mark 9:33–50: Catechetics in Mark's Gospel." Pp. 171–77 in *Studia Biblica,* vol. 2: *Papers on the Gospels.* Edited by E. A. Livingstone. Journal for the Study of the New Testament: Supplement Series 2. Sheffield: JSOT Press.

McGing, B. C.
1991   "Pontius Pilate and the Sources." *Catholic Biblical Quarterly* 53:416–38.

McIver, R. K.
1994   "One Hundred-Fold Yield—Miraculous or Mundane? Matthew 13.8, 23; Mark 4:8, 20; Luke 8:8." *New Testament Studies* 40:606–8.

McKinnis, R.
1976   "An Analysis of Mark X 32–34." *Novum Testamentum* 18:81–100.

McKnight, S.
1991   *A Light among the Gentiles.* Minneapolis: Fortress.

1999   *A New Vision for Israel: The Teachings of Jesus in National Context.* Grand Rapids: Eerdmans.

Mean, R. T.
1961   "The Healing of the Paralytic—a Unit?" *Journal of Biblical Literature* 80:348–54.

Meier, J. P.
1991   *A Marginal Jew: Rethinking the Historical Jesus,* vol. 1: *The Roots of the Problem and the Person.* Anchor Bible Reference Library. New York: Doubleday.

1994   *A Marginal Jew: Rethinking the Historical Jesus,* vol. 2: *Mentor, Message, and Miracles.* Anchor Bible Reference Library. New York: Doubleday.

2000a   "The Debate on the Resurrection of the Dead: An Incident from the Ministry of the Historical Jesus?" *Journal for the Study of the New Testament* 77:3–24.

2000b   "The Historical Jesus and the Historical Herodians." *Journal of Biblical Literature* 119:740–46.

2004   "The Historical Jesus and the Plucking of the Grain on the Sabbath." *Catholic Biblical Quarterly* 66:561–81.

Merkel, H.
1970   "Peter's Curse." Pp. 66–71 in *The Trial of Jesus: Cambridge Studies in Honour of C. F. D. Moule.* Studies in Biblical Theology 2/13. Edited by E. Bammel. Naperville, IL: Allenson.

Merritt, R. L.
1985   "Jesus Barabbas and the Paschal Pardon." *Journal of Biblical Literature* 104:57–68.

Metzger, B. M.
1971   *A Textual Commentary on the Greek New Testament.* London: United Bible Societies.

1994   *A Textual Commentary on the Greek New Testament.* 2nd edition. Stuttgart: Deutsche Bibelgesellschaft.

Meye, R. P.
1968   *Jesus and the Twelve: Discipleship and Revelation in Mark's Gospel.* Grand Rapids: Eerdmans.

Meyer, B. F.
1979   *The Aims of Jesus.* London: SCM.

Milavec, A.

1990 "The Identity of 'The Son' and 'The Others': Mark's Parable of the Wicked Husbandmen Reconsidered." *Biblical Theological Bulletin* 20:30–37.

Millard, A.

1990 *Discoveries from the Time of Jesus.* Oxford: Lion.

Miller, J. V.

1983 "The Time of the Crucifixion." *Journal of the Evangelical Theological Society* 26:157–66.

Montefiore, H.

1961 "Revolt in the Desert? (Mark vi.30ff.)." *New Testament Studies* 8:135–41.

Moo, D. J.

1984 "Jesus and the Authority of the Mosaic Law." *Journal for the Study of the New Testament* 20:3–49.

Morag, S.

1972 "Ἐφφαθά (Mark vii.34): Certainly Hebrew, Not Aramaic?" *Journal of Semitic Studies* 17:198–202.

Morrice, W. G.

1972 "The Imperatival *hina*." *Bible Translator* 23:326–30.

Morris, L.

1995 *The Gospel according to John.* Revised edition. New International Commentary on the New Testament. Grand Rapids: Eerdmans.

Moule, C. F. D.

1959 *An Idiom-Book of New Testament Greek.* 2nd edition. Cambridge: Cambridge University Press.

Moulton, J. H., and W. F. Howard

1929 *A Grammar of New Testament Greek,* vol. 2: *Accidence and Word-Formation.* Edinburgh: T&T Clark.

Moulton, J. H., and N. Turner

1963 *A Grammar of New Testament Greek,* vol. 3: *Syntax.* Edinburgh: T&T Clark.

Muddiman, J.

1987 "The Glory of Jesus, Mark 10:37." Pp. 51–58 in *The Glory of Christ in the New Testament: Studies in Christology.* Edited by L. D. Hurst and N. T. Wright. Oxford: Clarendon.

Murphy-O'Connor, J.

1998 "What Really Happened at Gethsemane?" *Bible Review* 14/2:28–39.

2000 "Jesus and the Money Changers (Mark 11:15–17; John 2:13–17)." *Revue biblique* 107:42–55.

Mussies, G.

1984 "The Use of Hebrew and Aramaic in the Greek New Testament." *New Testament Studies* 30:416–32.

Myers, C.

1988 *Binding the Strong Man: A Political Reading of Mark's Story of Jesus.* Maryknoll, NY: Orbis.

NA²⁷

Novum Testamentum Graece. Edited by B. Aland, K. Aland, J. Karavidopoulos, C. M. Martini, and B. M. Metzger. 27th edition. Stuttgart: Deutsche Bibelgesellschaft, 1993.

Nardoni, E.

1981 "A Redactional Interpretation of Mark 9:1." *Catholic Biblical Quarterly* 43:365–84.

Nauck, W.

1952 "Salt as a Metaphor in Instructions for Discipleship." *Studia theologica* 6:165–78.

Neirynck, F.

1975 "Jesus and the Sabbath: Some Observations on Mark II, 27." Pp. 227–70 in *Jésus aux origines de la Christologie.* Edited by J. Dupont. Bibliotheca ephemeridum theologicarum lovaniensium 40. Louvain: Leuven University Press.

1982 "The Redactional Text of Mark." Pp. 618–36 in *Evangelica: Gospel Studies—Études d'Évangile.* Edited by F. Van Segbroeck. Bibliotheca ephemeridum theologicarum lovaniensium 60. Louvain: Leuven University Press.

1988 *Duality in Mark: Contributions to the Study of the Markan Redaction.* Revised edition. Bibliotheca ephemeridum theologicarum lovaniensium 31. Louvain: Leuven University Press.

Neusner, J.

1976 "'First Cleanse the Inside.'" *New Testament Studies* 22:486–95.

Niederwimmer, K.

1967 "Johannes Markus und die Frage nach dem Verfasser des zweiten Evangeliums." *Zeitschrift für die neutestamentliche Wissenschaft* 58:172–88.

Nineham, D. E.

1963 *The Gospel of Saint Mark.* Pelican Gospel Commentaries. Baltimore: Penguin.

Nolland, J.

2002 *Luke 1–9:20.* Word Biblical Commentary 35a. Dallas: Word.

O'Callaghan, J.

1972 "New Testament Papyri in Qumran Cave 7?" *Journal of Biblical Literature* 91/2, supplement, 1–20.

Oden, T. C., and C. A. Hall
1998   *Mark*. Ancient Christian Commentary on Scripture: New Testament 2. Downers Grove, IL: InterVarsity.

Öhler, M.
1999   "The Expectation of Elijah and the Presence of the Kingdom of God." *Journal of Biblical Literature* 118:461–76.

Olekamma, I. U.
1999   *The Healing of Blind Bartimaeus (Mk 10,46–52) in the Markan Context: Two Ways of Asking*. European University Studies Series 23. Frankfurt: Peter Lang.

Orchard, J. B.
1984   "Some Guidelines for the Interpretation of Eusebius' *Hist. Eccl*. 3:34–39." Vol. 2 / pp. 393–403 in *The New Testament Age: Essays in Honor of Bo Reicke*. Edited by W. C. Weinrich. Macon, GA: Mercer University Press.

O'Rourke, J. J.
1966   "A Note concerning the Use of ΕΙΣ and ΕΝ in Mark." *Journal of Biblical Literature* 85:349–51.

Osborne, B. A. E.
1973   "Peter: Stumbling-Block and Satan." *Novum Testamentum* 15:187–90.

Painter, J.
1997   *Mark's Gospel: Worlds in Conflict*. London: Routledge.

Parker, P.
1983   "The Posteriority of Mark." Pp. 67–142 in *New Synoptic Studies: The Cambridge Gospel Conference and Beyond*. Edited by W. R. Farmer. Macon, GA: Mercer University Press.

Parker, S. T.
1975   "The Decapolis Reviewed." *Journal of Biblical Literature* 94:437–41.

Patsch, H.
1971   "Abendmahlsterminologie ausserhalb der Einsetzungsberichte: Erwägungen zur Traditionsgeschichte der Abendmahlsworte." *Zeitschrift für die neutestamentliche Wissenschaft* 62:210–31.

Payne, P. B.
1978   "The Order of Sowing and Plowing in the Parable of the Sower." *New Testament Studies* 25:123–29.
1980a   "The Authenticity of the Parable of the Sower and Its Interpretation." Pp. 163–207 in *Gospel Perspectives,* vol. 1: *Studies of History and Tradition in the Four Gospels*. Edited by R. T. France and D. Wenham. Sheffield: JSOT Press.

1980b   "The Seeming Inconsistency of the Interpretation of the Parable of the Sower." *New Testament Studies* 26:564–68.

Peabody, D. B.
1987   *Mark as Composer*. New Gospel Studies 1. Macon, GA: Mercer University Press.

Peace, R. V.
1999   *Conversion in the New Testament: Paul and the Twelve*. Grand Rapids: Eerdmans.

Perrin, N.
1967   *Rediscovering the Teaching of Jesus*. New York: Harper & Row.

Perrin, N., and D. C. Duling
1982   *The New Testament: An Introduction*. 2nd edition. New York: Harcourt Brace Jovanovich.

Perry, J. M.
1986   "The Three Days in Synoptic Passion Predictions." *Catholic Biblical Quarterly* 48:637–54.

Pesch, R.
1968   *Naherwartungen: Tradition und Redaktion in Mark 13. Kommentare und Beiträge zum Alten und Neuen Testament*. Düsseldorf: Patmos-Verlag.
1980a   *Das Markusevangelium*, part 1: *Einleitung und Kommentar zu Kap. 1,1–8,26*. 3rd edition. Herders theologischer Kommentar zum Neuen Testament. Freiburg: Herder.
1980b   *Das Markusevangelium*, part 2: *Kommentar zu 8,27–16,20*. 2nd edition. Herders theologischer Kommentar zum Neuen Testament. Freiburg: Herder.
1996   *The Trial of Jesus Continues*. Translated by D. G. Wagner. Princeton Theological Monograph Series 4. Allison Park, PA: Pickwick.

Petersen, N. R.
1980   "When Is the End Not the End? Literary Reflections on the Ending of Mark's Narrative." *Interpretation* 34:151–66.

Pickl, J.
1946   *The Messias*. Translated by A. Green. London: Herder.

Pilgrim, W. E.
1999   *Uneasy Neighbors: Church and State in the New Testament*. Overtures to Biblical Theology. Minneapolis: Fortress.

Piper, J.
1979   *"Love Your Enemies": Jesus' Love Command in the Synoptic Gospels and in the Early Christian Paraenesis: A History of the Tradition and Interpretation of Its Uses*. Society for New Testament Studies

Monograph Series 38. Cambridge: Cambridge University Press.

Pixner, B.
1996   *With Jesus in Jerusalem*. Rosh Pina, Israel: Corazin.

Pokorny, P.
1995   "From a Puppy to the Child: Some Problems of Contemporary Biblical Exegesis Demonstrated from Mark 7:24–30/ Matt. 15:21–8." *New Testament Studies* 41:321–37.

Porter, S. E.
1992   *Idioms of the Greek New Testament*. Biblical Languages: Greek 2. Sheffield: JSOT Press.

Pryke, E. J.
1978   *Redactional Style in the Marcan Gospel: A Study of Syntax and Vocabulary as Guides to Redaction in Mark*. Society for New Testament Studies Monograph Series 33. Cambridge: Cambridge University Press.

Quesnell, Q.
1969   *The Mind of Mark: Interpretation and Method through the Exegesis of Mark 6,52*. Analecta biblica 38. Rome: Pontifical Biblical Institute.

Rabinowitz, I.
1962   "'Be Opened' = Ἐφφαθά (Mark 734): Did Jesus Speak Hebrew?" *Zeitschrift für die neutestamentliche Wissenschaft* 53:229–38.

1971   "Ἐφφαθά (Mark vii.34): Certainly Hebrew, Not Aramaic." *Journal of Semitic Studies* 16:151–56.

Räisänen, H.
1990   *The "Messianic Secret" in Mark*. Studies in the New Testament and Its World. Translated by C. Tuckett. Edinburgh: T&T Clark.

Redlich, E. B.
1939   *Form Criticism: Its Value and Limitations*. London: Duckworth.

Reiser, M.
2000   "Numismatik und Neues Testament." *Biblica* 81:457–88.

Reploh, K.-G.
1969   *Markus—Lehrer der Gemeinde: Eine redaktionsgeschichtliche Studie zu den Jüngerperikopen des Markus-Evangeliums*. Stuttgarter biblische Monographien 9. Stuttgart: Katholisches Bibelwerk.

Richardson, A.
1941   *The Miracle-Stories of the Gospels*. London: SCM.

Riesner, R.
1987   "Bethany beyond the Jordan (John 1:28): Topography, Theology and History in the Fourth Gospel." *Tyndale Bulletin* 38:29–63.

2003   "Back to the Historical Jesus through Paul and His School (The Ransom Logion—Mark 10.45; Matthew 20.28)." *Journal for the Study of the Historical Jesus* 1:171–99.

Ritmeyer, K., and L. Ritmeyer
1989   "Reconstructing Herod's Temple Mount in Jerusalem." *Biblical Archaeology Review* 15/6:23–53.

Robbins, V. K.
1973   "The Healing of Blind Bartimaeus (10:46–52) in the Marcan Theology." *Journal of Biblical Literature* 92:224–43.

Robinson, J. M.
1957   *The Problem of History in Mark*. Studies in Biblical Theology 1/21. Naperville, IL: Allenson.

Rogers, T. J.
2004   "Shaking the Dust off the Markan Mission Discourse." *Journal for the Study of the New Testament* 27:169–92.

Ross, J. M.
1987   "Another Look at Mark 8:26." *Novum Testamentum* 29:97–99.

Rudolph, D. J.
2002   "Jesus and the Food Laws: A Reassessment of Mark 7:19b." *Evangelical Quarterly* 74:291–311.

Safrai, S.
1974   *The Jewish People in the First Century*, vol. 1. Compendia rerum iudaicarum ad Novum Testamentum. Edited by S. Safrai and M. Stern. Philadelphia: Fortress.

1976   *The Jewish People in the First Century*, vol. 2. Compendia rerum iudaicarum ad Novum Testamentum. Edited by S. Safrai and M. Stern. Philadelphia: Fortress.

Saldarini, A. J.
1984   *Jesus and Passover*. New York: Paulist Press.

1988   *Pharisees, Scribes and Sadducees in Palestinian Society: A Sociological Approach*. Wilmington, DE: Glazier.

Sanders, E. P.
1969   *The Tendencies of the Synoptic Tradition*. Society for New Testament Studies Monograph Series 9. Cambridge: Cambridge University Press.

1985   *Jesus and Judaism*. Philadelphia: Fortress.

1990   *Jewish Law from Jesus to the Mishnah.* Philadelphia: Trinity.

1993   *The Historical Figure of Jesus.* London: Penguin.

Sanders, J.

1996   *The God Who Risks: A Theology of Providence.* Downers Grove, IL: InterVarsity.

Sanders, J. N.

1954   "'Those Whom Jesus Loved' (John xi.5)." *New Testament Studies* 1:29–41.

Schaberg, J.

1985   "Daniel 7, 12 and the New Testament Passion-Resurrection Predictions." *New Testament Studies* 31:208–22.

1992   "How Mary Magdalene Became a Whore." *Bible Review* 8/5:30–37, 51–52.

Schams, C.

1998   *Jewish Scribes in the Second-Temple Period.* Journal for the Study of the Old Testament: Supplement Series 291. Sheffield: Sheffield Academic Press.

Schenk, W.

1983   "Gefangenschaft und Tod des Täufers: Erwägungen zur Chronologie und ihren Konsequenzen." *New Testament Studies* 29:453–83.

Schmidt, K. L.

1919   *Der Rahmen der Geschichte Jesu: Literarkritische Untersuchungen zur ältesten Jesusüberlieferung.* Berlin: Trowitzsch.

Schmidt, T. E.

1987   *Hostility to Wealth in the Synoptic Gospels.* Journal for the Study of the New Testament: Supplement Series 15. Sheffield: JSOT Press.

1992   "Mark 10.29–30; Matthew 19.29: 'Leave House . . . and Region'?" *New Testament Studies* 38:617–20.

1994   "Cry of Dereliction or Cry of Judgment? Mark 15:34 in Context." *Bulletin for Biblical Research* 4:145–53.

Schmithals, W.

1979   *Das Evangelium nach Markus.* Ökumenischer Taschenbuchkommentar zum Neuen Testament. 2 vols. Gütersloh: Mohn.

Schnabel, E. J.

2004   *Early Christian Mission: Jesus and the Twelve.* 2 vols. Downers Grove, IL: InterVarsity.

Schneider, G.

1984   "The Political Charge against Jesus (Luke 23:2)." Pp. 403–14 in *Jesus and the Politics of His Day.* Edited by E. Bammel and C. F. D. Moule. Cambridge: Cambridge University Press.

Schnelle, U.

1998   *The History and Theology of the New Testament Writings.* Translated by M. E. Boring. Minneapolis: Fortress.

Schubert, W.

1984   "Biblical Criticism Criticised: With Reference to the Markan Report of Jesus' Examination before the Sanhedrin." Pp. 385–402 in *Jesus and the Politics of His Day.* Edited by E. Bammel and C. F. D. Moule. Cambridge: Cambridge University Press.

Schürer, E.

1973–87   *The History of the Jewish People in the Age of Jesus Christ (175 B.C.–A.D. 135).* Revised and edited by G. Vermes, F. Millar, and M. Black. 3 vols. in 4. Edinburgh: T&T Clark.

Schürmann, H.

1960   "Die vorösterliche Anfänge der Logientradition." Pp. 342–70 in *Der historische Jesus und der kerygmatische Christus: Beiträge zum Christusverständnis in Forschung und Verkündigung.* Edited by H. Ristow and K. Matthiae. Berlin: Evangelische Verlagsanstalt.

Schweitzer, A.

1910   *The Quest of the Historical Jesus: A Critical Study of Its Progress from Reimarus to Wrede.* Translated by W. Montgomery. New York: Macmillan.

Schweizer, E.

1970   *The Good News according to Mark.* Translated by D. H. Madvig. Richmond: John Knox.

Scobie, C. H. H.

1964   *John the Baptist.* London: SCM.

Scott, B. B.

1981   *Jesus, Symbol-Maker for the Kingdom.* Philadelphia: Fortress.

Seeley, D.

1993   "Jesus' Temple Act." *Catholic Biblical Quarterly* 55:263–83.

Selvidge, M. J.

1984   "Mark 5:25–34 and Leviticus 15:19–20: A Reaction to Restrictive Purity Regulations." *Journal of Biblical Literature* 103:619–23.

Senior, D.

1984   *The Passion of Jesus in the Gospel of Mark.* Wilmington, DE: Glazier.

Shae, G. S.

1974   "The Question on the Authority of Jesus." *Novum Testamentum* 16:1–29.

Shepherd, M. H., Jr.

1961   "Are Both the Synoptics and John Correct about the Date of Jesus' Death?" *Journal of Biblical Literature* 80:123–32.

Sherwin-White, A. N.

1965   "The Trial of Christ." Pp. 97–116 in *Historicity and Chronology in the New Testament*. Edited by D. E. Nineham. Theological Collections 6. London: SPCK.

Shiner, W. T.

1995   *Follow Me! Disciples in Markan Rhetoric*. Society of Biblical Literature Dissertation Series 145. Atlanta: Scholars Press.

2000   "The Ambiguous Pronouncement of the Centurion and the Shrouding of Meaning in Mark." *Journal for the Study of the New Testament* 78:3–22.

Sibinga, J. S.

1976   "Text and Literary Art in Mark 3,1–6." Pp. 357–65 in *Studies in New Testament Language and Text: Essays in Honour of George D. Kilpatrick on the Occasion of His Sixty-fifth Birthday*. Edited by J. K. Elliott. Supplements to Novum Testamentum 44. Leiden: Brill.

Smith, B. D.

1991   "The Chronology of the Last Supper." *Westminster Theological Journal* 53:29–45.

1992   "The More Original Form of the Words of Institution." *Zeitschrift für die neutestamentliche Wissenschaft* 83:166–86.

Smith, M.

1973a   *Clement of Alexandria and a Secret Gospel of Mark*. Cambridge: Harvard University Press.

1973b   *The Secret Gospel: The Discovery and Interpretation of the Secret Gospel according to Mark*. New York: Harper & Row.

Smith, R. H.

1967   "The Tomb of Jesus." *Biblical Archaeologist* 30:74–90.

1983   *Easter Gospels: The Resurrection of Jesus according to the Four Evangelists*. Minneapolis: Augsburg.

Smith, S. H.

1994   "Mark 3,1–6: Form, Redaction and Community Function." *Biblica* 75:153–74.

Snodgrass, K.

1980   "Streams of Tradition Emerging from Isaiah 40:1–5 and Their Adaptation in the New Testament." *Journal for the Study of the New Testament* 8:24–45.

1983   *The Parable of Wicked Tenants: An Inquiry into Parable Interpretation*.

Wissenschaftliche Untersuchungen zum Neuen Testament 27. Tübingen: Mohr (Siebeck).

1989   "The Gospel of Thomas: A Secondary Gospel." *The Second Century* 7:19–38.

1998   "Recent Research on the Parable of the Wicked Tenants: An Assessment." *Bulletin for Biblical Research* 8:187–216.

Soards, M. L.

1994   "Appendix IX: The Question of a Premarkan Passion Narrative." Vol. 2 / pp. 1492–1524 in *The Death of the Messiah: From Gethsemane to the Grave* by R. A. Brown. Anchor Bible Reference Library. New York: Doubleday.

Sommer, B. D.

1996   "Did Prophecy Cease? Evaluating a Reevaluation." *Journal of Biblical Literature* 115:31–47.

Sowers, S.

1970   "The Circumstances and Recollection of the Pella Flight." *Theologische Zeitschrift* 26:305–20.

Stanley, D. M.

1980   *Jesus in Gethsemane: The Early Church Reflects on the Suffering of Jesus*. New York: Paulist Press.

Stanton, G.

1995   *Gospel Truth? New Light on Jesus and the Gospels*. Valley Forge, PA: Trinity Press International.

Stauffer, E.

1960   *Jesus and His Story*. Translated by R. and C. Winston. New York: Knopf.

Stegner, W.

1967   "Wilderness and Testing in the Scrolls and in Matthew 4:1–11." *Biblical Research* 12:18–27.

1998   "Jesus' Walking on the Water: Mark 6:45–52." Pp. 212–34 in *The Gospels and the Scriptures of Israel*. Edited by C. Evans and W. Stegner. Sheffield: Sheffield Academic Press.

Stein, R. H.

1969   "What Is Redaktionsgeschichte?" *Journal of Biblical Literature* 88:45–56.

1970   "The 'Redaktionsgeschichtlich' Investigation of a Markan Seam (Mc 121f.)." *Zeitschrift für die neutestamentliche Wissenschaft* 61:70–94.

1971   "The Proper Methodology for Ascertaining a Markan Redaction History." *Novum Testamentum* 13:181–98.

1973   "A Short Note on Mark XIV.28 and XVI.7." *New Testament Studies* 20:445–52.

1976   "Is the Transfiguration (Mark 9:2–8) a Misplaced Resurrection-Account?" *Journal of Biblical Literature* 95:79–96.

1981   *An Introduction to the Parables of Jesus.* Philadelphia: Westminster.

1990   *Difficult Passages in the New Testament.* Grand Rapids: Baker Academic.

1991   *Gospels and Tradition: Studies on Redaction Criticism of the Synoptic Gospels.* Grand Rapids: Baker Academic.

1992a   *Luke.* New American Commentary 24. Nashville: Broadman.

1992b   "The Matthew-Luke Agreements against Mark: Insight from John." *Catholic Biblical Quarterly* 54:482–502.

1994a   *A Basic Guide to Interpreting the Bible: Playing by the Rules.* Grand Rapids: Baker Academic. Formerly titled: *Playing by the Rules: A Basic Guide to Interpreting the Bible.*

1994b   *The Method and Message of Jesus' Teachings.* Revised edition. Louisville: Westminster/John Knox.

1996   *Jesus the Messiah: A Survey of the Life of Jesus.* Downers Grove, IL: InterVarsity.

2000   "The Genre of the Parables." Pp. 30–50 in *The Challenge of Jesus' Parables.* Edited by R. N. Longenecker. Grand Rapids: Eerdmans.

2001   *Studying the Synoptic Gospels: Origin and Interpretation.* 2nd edition. Grand Rapids: Baker Academic.

2006   "Baptism in Luke-Acts." Pp. 35–66 in *Believer's Baptism: Sign of the New Covenant in Christ.* Edited by T. R. Schreiner and S. D. Wright. Nashville: Broadman & Holman.

2008   "The Ending of Mark." *Bulletin for Biblical Research* 18:79–98.

Steinhauser, M. G.
1986   "The Form of the Bartimaeus Narrative (Mark 10.46–52)." *New Testament Studies* 32:583–95.

1990   "The Sayings of Jesus in Mark 4:21–22, 24B–25." *Forum* 6:197–217.

Stemberger, G.
1974   "Galilee—Land of Salvation?" Pp. 409–38 in *The Gospel and the Land: Early Christianity and Jewish Territorial Doctrine.* Edited by W. D. Davies. Berkeley: University of California Press.

Sterling, G. E.
1993   "Jesus as Exorcist: An Analysis of Matthew 17:14–20; Mark 9:14–29; Luke 9:37–43a." *Catholic Biblical Quarterly* 55:467–93.

Stettler, C.
2004   "Purity of Heart in Jesus' Teachings: Mark 7:14–23 Par. as an Expression of Jesus' Basileia Ethics." *Journal of Theological Studies* 55:467–502.

Strauss, D. F.
1972   *The Life of Jesus Critically Examined.* Translated by G. Eliot. Edited by P. C. Hodgson. Philadelphia: Fortress.

Strecker, G.
1968   "The Passion- and Resurrection Predictions in Mark's Gospel (Mark 8:31; 9:31; 10:32–34)." *Interpretation* 22:421–42.

1983   "The Theory of the Messianic Secret in Mark's Gospel." Pp. 49–64 in *The Messianic Secret.* Edited by C. Tuckett. Issues in Religion and Theology 1. Philadelphia: Fortress.

Stuhlmann, R.
1972   "Beobachtungen und Überlegungen zu Markus IV. 26–29." *New Testament Studies* 19:153–62.

Such, W. A.
1999   *The Abomination of Desolation in the Gospel of Mark: Its Historical Reference in Mark 13:14 and Its Impact in the Gospel.* Lanham, MD: University Press of America.

Sutcliffe, E. F.
1954   "Effect as Purpose: A Study in Hebrew Thought Patterns." *Biblica* 35:320–27.

Swetham, J.
1987   "Some Remarks on the Meaning of ὁ δὲ ἐξελθών in Mark 1,45." *Biblica* 68:245–49.

Tagawa, K.
1966   *Miracles et Évangile: La pensée personnelle de l'évangéliste Marc.* Études d'histoire et de philosophie religieuses 62. Paris: Presses Universitaires de France.

Talbert, C. H.
1977   *What Is a Gospel? The Genre of the Canonical Gospels.* Philadelphia: Fortress.

Tannehill, R. C.
1975   *The Sword of His Mouth.* Society of Biblical Literature Semeia Supplements 1. Philadelphia: Fortress.

1977   "The Disciples in Mark: The Function of a Narrative Role." *Journal of Religion* 57:386–405.

Taylor, N. H.
1996   "Palestinian Christianity and the Caligula Crisis: Part II. The Markan Eschatological Discourse." *Journal for the Study of the New Testament* 62:13–41.

Taylor, V.
1949 *The Formation of the Gospel Tradition.* London: MacMillan.
1952 *The Gospel according to St. Mark: The Greek Text with Introduction, Notes, and Indexes.* London: MacMillan.
1954a "The Origin of the Markan Passion-Sayings." *New Testament Studies* 1:159–67.
1954b "W. Wrede's *The Messianic Secret in the Gospels: Das Messiasgeheimnis in den Evangelien.*" *Expository Times* 65:246–50.
TDNT *Theological Dictionary of the New Testament.* Edited by G. Kittel and G. Friedrich. Translated and edited by G. W. Bromiley. 10 vols. Grand Rapids: Eerdmans, 1964–76.

Telford, W. R.
1980 *The Barren Temple and the Withered Tree: A Redaction-Critical Analysis of the Cursing of the Fig-Tree Pericope in Mark's Gospel and Its Relation to the Cleansing of the Temple Tradition.* Journal for the Study of the New Testament: Supplement Series 1. Sheffield: JSOT Press.
1999 *The Theology of the Gospel of Mark.* Cambridge: Cambridge University Press.

Theissen, G.
1983 *The Miracle Stories of the Early Christian Tradition.* Translated by F. McDonagh. Philadelphia: Fortress.
1991 *The Gospels in Context: Social and Political History in the Synoptic Tradition.* Translated by L. M. Maloney. Minneapolis: Fortress.

Thiede, C. P.
1992 *The Earliest Greek Manuscript? The Qumran Payprus 7Q5 and Its Significance for New Testament Studies.* Exeter: Paternoster.

Thiering, B. E.
1970 "'Breaking of Bread' and 'Harvest' in Mark's Gospel." *Novum Testamentum* 12:1–12.

Thomas Aquinas
1874 *Catena Aurea: Commentary on the Four Gospels.* 6 vols. Oxford: James Parker.

Thrall, M. E.
1970 "Elijah and Moses in Mark's Account of the Transfiguration." *New Testament Studies* 16:305–17.

Tödt, H. E.
1965 *The Son of Man in the Synoptic Tradition.* Translated by D. M. Barton. London: SCM.

Tolbert, M. A.
1989 *Sowing the Gospel: Mark's World in Literary-Historical Perspective.* Minneapolis: Fortress.

Torrey, C. C.
1933 *The Four Gospels: A New Translation.* New York: Harper.

Trocmé, É.
1975 *The Formation of the Gospel according to Mark.* Translated by P. Gaughan. Philadelphia: Westminster.
1977 "Why Parables? A Study in Mark IV." *Bulletin of the John Rylands Library* 59:458–71.

Tuckett, C. M.
1982 "The Present Son of Man." *Journal for the Study of the New Testament* 14:58–81.
1983 *The Revival of the Griesbach Hypothesis: An Analysis and Appraisal.* Society for New Testament Studies Monograph Series 44. Cambridge: Cambridge University Press.
1988 "Mark's Concerns in the Parables Chapter (Mark 4,1–34)." *Biblica* 69:1–26.

Turner, C. H.
1924 "Marcan Usage: Notes, Critical and Exegetical, on the Second Gospel." *Journal of Theological Studies* 25:377–86.
1925 "Marcan Usage: Notes, Critical and Exegetical, on the Second Gospel." *Journal of Theological Studies* 26:225–40.
1926 "Ο ΥΙΟΣ ΜΟΥ Ο ΑΓΑΠΗΤΟΣ." *Journal of Theological Studies* 27:113–29.
1927 "Marcan Usage: Notes, Critical and Exegetical, on the Second Gospel." *Journal of Theological Studies* 28:9–30.
1928 "The Gospel according to St. Mark." Part 3 / pp. 42–124 in *A New Commentary on Holy Scripture.* Edited by C. Gore, H. L. Goudge, and A. Guillaume. London: SPCK.
1930 *The Gospel according to St. Mark.* London: MacMillan.

Turner, N.
1965 *Grammatical Insights into the New Testament.* Edinburgh: T&T Clark.

Tyson, J. B.
1961 "The Blindness of the Disciples in Mark." *Journal of Biblical Literature* 80:261–68.

Tyson, J. B., and T. R. W. Longstaff
1978 "Synoptic Abstract." In *The Computer Bible,* vol. 5. Wooster, OH: Biblical Research Associates.

UBS⁴   *The Greek New Testament*. Edited by B.
         Aland, K. Aland, J. Karavidopoulos, C. M.
         Martini, and B. M. Metzger. 4th revised
         edition. Stuttgart: Deutsche Bibelgesell-
         schaft, 1994.

Ulansey, D.
1991   "The Heavenly Veil Torn: Mark's Cosmic
         Inclusio." *Journal of Biblical Literature*
         110:123–25.

VanderKam, J. C.
1994   *The Dead Sea Scrolls Today*. Grand Rap-
         ids: Eerdmans.

Via, D. O., Jr.
1985   *The Ethics of Mark's Gospel—In the
         Middle of Time*. Philadelphia: Fortress.

Vines, M. E.
2002   *The Problem of Markan Genre: The Gos-
         pel of Mark and the Jewish Novel*. Society
         of Biblical Literature Academia biblica 3.
         Atlanta: Society of Biblical Literature.

Viviano, B. T.
1989   "The High Priest's Servant's Ear: Mark
         14:47." *Revue biblique* 96:71–80.
1990   "Rabbouni and Mark 9:5." *Revue biblique*
         97:207–18.

Von Wahlde, U. C.
1985   "Mark 9:33–50: Discipleship: The Au-
         thority That Serves." *Biblische Zeitschrift*
         29:49–67.

Wachsmann, S.
1988   "The Galilee Boat: 2,000-Year-Old Hull
         Recovered Intact." *Biblical Archaeology
         Review* 14/5:18–33.

Waetjen, H. C.
1989   *A Reordering of Power: A Sociopolitical
         Reading of Mark's Gospel*. Minneapolis:
         Fortress.

Wansbrough, H.
1972   "Mark III.21—Was Jesus out of His Mind?"
         New Testament Studies 18:233–35.

Warfield, B. B.
1950   *The Person and Work of Christ*. Edited
         by S. G. Craig. Philadelphia: Presbyterian
         & Reformed.

Watts, R. E.
1998   "Jesus' Death, Isaiah 53, and Mark 10:45:
         A Crux Revisited." Pp. 125–51 in *Jesus
         and the Suffering Servant: Isaiah 53 and
         Christian Origins*. Edited by W. H. Bellin-
         ger Jr. and W. R. Farmer. Harrisburg, PA:
         Trinity.
2000   *Isaiah's New Exodus in Mark*. 1997. Re-
         printed Grand Rapids: Baker Academic.

Webster, G.
1969   *The Roman Imperial Army of the First
         and Second Centuries AD*. New York:
         Funk & Wagnalls.

Wedderburn, A. J. M.
1999   *Beyond Resurrection*. London: SCM.

Weeden, T. J.
1971   *Mark—Traditions in Conflict*. Philadel-
         phia: Fortress.
1979   "Rediscovering the Parabolic Intent in
         the Parable of the Sower." *Journal of
         the American Academy of Religion*
         47:97–120.

Wellhausen, J.
1909   *Das Evangelium Marci übersetzt und
         erklärt*. 2nd edition. Berlin: George
         Reimer.

Wenham, D.
1974   "The Meaning of Mark III.21." *New
         Testament Studies* 21:295–300.
1984   *Gospel Perspectives*, vol. 4: *The Rediscov-
         ery of Jesus' Eschatological Discourse*.
         Sheffield: JSOT Press.

Wenham, J. W.
1978   "How Many Cock-Crows? The Problem of
         Harmonistic Text-Variants." *New Testa-
         ment Studies* 25:523–25.

Weren, W. J. C.
1998   "The Use of Isaiah 5,1–7 in the Parable
         of the Tenants (Mark 12,1–12; Matthew
         21,33–46)." *Biblica* 79:1–26.

Westerholm, S.
1978   *Jesus and Scribal Authority*. Coniectanea
         biblica: New Testament Series 10. Lund:
         Gleerup.

Wiarda, T.
2000   *Peter in the Gospels: Pattern, Personal-
         ity and Relationship*. Wissenschaftliche
         Untersuchungen zum Neuen Testament
         2/127. Tübingen: Mohr (Siebeck).

Wilcox, M.
1996   "On the Ransom-Saying in Mark 10:45c,
         Matt. 20:28c." Pp. 173–86 in *Geschichte—
         Tradition—Reflexion: Festschrift für Mar-
         tin Hengel zum 70. Geburtstag*, vol. 3:
         Frühes Christentum. Edited by H. Cancik,
         P. Schäfer, and H. Lichtenberger. Tübin-
         gen: Mohr (Siebeck).

Wilkinson, J.
1974   "Ancient Jerusalem: Its Water Supply and
         Population." *Palestine Exploration Quar-
         terly* 106:33–51.

Williams, J. F.
1994   *Other Followers of Jesus: Minor Charac-
         ters as Major Figures in Mark's Gospel*.

Journal for the Study of the New Testament: Supplement Series 102. Sheffield: JSOT Press.

1999   "Literary Approaches to the End of Mark's Gospel." *Journal of the Evangelical Theological Society* 42:21–35.

Wilson, S. G.

1995   *Related Strangers: Jews and Christians 70–170 CE.* Minneapolis: Fortress.

Winter, P.

1961   *On the Trial of Jesus.* Studia Judaica—Forschungen zur Wissenschaft des Judentums 1. Berlin: de Gruyter.

Witherington, B., III

1984   *Women in the Ministry of Jesus: A Study of Jesus' Attitudes to Women and Their Roles as Reflected in His Earthly Life.* Society for New Testament Studies Monograph Series 51. Cambridge: Cambridge University Press.

1990   *The Christology of Jesus.* Minneapolis: Fortress.

2001   *The Gospel of Mark: A Socio-Rhetorical Commentary.* Grand Rapids: Eerdmans.

Wolter, M.

2004   "'Ihr sollt aber wissen . . . .': Das Anakoluth nach ἵνα δὲ εἰδῆτε in Mk 2,10–11 parr." *Zeitschrift für die neutestamentliche Wissenschaft* 95:269–765.

Wrede, W.

1904   "Zur Heilung des Gelähmten (Mc 2,1ff.)." *Zeitschrift für die neutestamentliche Wissenschaft* 5:354–58.

1971   *The Messianic Secret.* Translated by J. C. G. Grieg. Greenwood, NC: Attic.

Wright, A. G.

1982   "The Widow's Mites: Praise or Lament—a Matter of Context." *Catholic Biblical Quarterly* 44:256–65.

Wright, N. T.

1996   *Christian Origins and the Question of God,* vol. 2: *Jesus and the Victory of God.* Minneapolis: Fortress.

1999   "In Grateful Dialogue: A Response." Pp. 244–77 in *Jesus & the Restoration of Israel: A Critical Assessment of N. T. Wright's* Jesus and the Victory of God. Edited by C. C. Newman. Downers Grove, IL: InterVarsity.

2003   *Christian Origins and the Question of God,* vol. 3: *The Resurrection of the Son of God.* Minneapolis: Fortress.

Wuellner, W. H.

1966   *The Meaning of "Fishers of Men."* New Testament Library. Philadelphia: Westminster.

Yamauchi, E.

1986   "Magic or Miracle? Diseases, Demons and Exorcisms." Pp. 89–183 in *Gospel Perspectives,* vol. 6: *The Miracles of Jesus.* Edited by D. Wenham and C. Blomberg. Sheffield: JSOT Press.

Yarbrough, R. W.

1983   "The Date of Papias: A Reassessment." *Journal of the Evangelical Theological Society* 26:181–91.

1998   "Eta Linnemann: Friend or Foe of Scholarship?" Pp. 158–84 in *The Jesus Crisis: The Inroads of Historical Criticism into Evangelical Scholarship.* Edited by R. L. Thomas and F. D. Farnwell. Grand Rapids: Kregel.

Zahn, T.

1909   *Introduction to the New Testament,* vol. 2. Translated by J. M. Trout and others. Edinburgh: T&T Clark.

Zerwick, M.

1963   *Biblical Greek: Illustrated by Examples.* Translated by J. Smith. Rome: Pontifical Biblical Institute Press.

Zerwick, M., and M. Grosvenor

1981   *A Grammatical Analysis of the Greek New Testament.* Revised edition. Rome: Pontifical Biblical Institute Press.

Ziesler, J. A.

1972   "The Removal of the Bridegroom: A Note on Mark II.18–22 and Parallels." *New Testament Studies* 19:190–94.

Index of Subjects

abomination of desolation, 11, 14, 595, 602–5
allegory, 194, 213–14, 531, 534–35
angels, 554nn6–7
Anti-Marcionite Prologue, 3, 8
apocalyptic, genre of, 582–83
audience, Markan, 9–12
authority, Jesus's. *See also* Christology
  the disciples and, 175, 296–97, 656–57, 666–67, 674–75
  exorcisms and, 21, 89–91, 189, 260–61, 451
  forgiveness and, 118–22
  from God, 528, 625–26
  healing miracles and, 21, 97–98, 122, 276, 354–55
  the Law and, 150, 157, 347, 459, 475
  nature miracles and, 22, 318–19, 326, 328
  prophecy and, 521–22, 620, 737
authorship, Markan, 1–9

biography, genre of, 20–21

Christology. *See also* cross, the; Messiah, Jesus as
  the disciples and, 175, 296–97, 656–57, 666–67, 674–75
  discipleship and, 81, 411–12, 451, 489, 693
  exorcisms and, 21, 89–91, 189, 260–61, 451
  faith and, 118, 276–77

God and, 528, 625–26
healing miracles and, 21, 97–98, 122, 276, 354–55
the kingdom and, 319, 355
the Law and, 150, 157, 347, 459, 475
Markan emphasis on, 21–23, 737
messianic secret and, 23–26, 98, 165–66, 354, 687
nature miracles and, 22, 318–19, 326, 328
prophecy and, 489–90, 521–22, 591–92, 620, 737
of the Son of God, 22–23, 61, 66, 328, 538–39, 718–19
of the Son of Man, 22, 118–22, 401–2, 409, 684–85
teaching of Jesus and, 22, 112–13, 547–48
theophany and, 61, 419–20, 616
chronology, Markan, 70–71, 631, 640–44, 646n4, 676–77, 712–13
climactic promise, 410
commentaries, goal of, 248–49
complexes, pre-Markan, 67–68, 92–93, 248
conflict stories, 67n1
cross, the. *See also* Christology
  conflict leading to, 157, 189–90, 348
  discipleship and, 32, 174–76, 407, 489, 666
  as form of execution, 711–12, 725n5

necessity of, 33–35, 401, 404, 665–66
predictions of, 141, 396–97, 477–78, 666–67
the Transfiguration and, 413–14, 419–20, 423–24
type of, 709

date of composition, Markan, 12–15
David, descent from. *See* Messiah, Jesus as
death of Jesus. *See* cross, the
desolation, abomination of. *See* abomination of desolation
disciples, the, 26–32, 169–71, 174–76, 296
discipleship
  the cross and, 32, 174–76, 407, 489, 666
  nature of, 32–33, 80–81, 406–8, 411–12
  obstacles to, 189, 451, 459–60
  the Parousia and, 608, 625
  salvation and, 474–75
  the Twelve and, 174–76, 693–94
  wealth and, 472, 579, 592
divorce, 459–60
drama, genre of, 19–20

eisegesis, 19
elect, the, 606–7
ending, Markan, 733–37
eschatology, Markan. *See also* Parousia, the
  Elijah and, 61, 425–28

Index of Authors

Index of Greek Words

Index of Scripture and Other Ancient Writings

Old Testament

New Testament

Old Testament Apocrypha

Old Testament Pseudepigrapha

New Testament Apocrypha

Rabbinic Writings

Philo

Classical Writers